Frommer's®

China

3rd Edition

*by Simon Foster, Jen Lin-Liu, Sharon Owyang,
Sherisse Pham, Beth Reiber, Lee Wing-sze,
and Christopher D. Winnan*

Here's what the critics say about Frommer's:

"Amazingly easy to use. Very portable, very complete."

—*Booklist*

"Detailed, accurate, and easy-to-read information for all price ranges."
—*Glamour Magazine*

"Hotel information is close to encyclopedic."

—*Des Moines Sunday Register*

"Frommer's Guides have a way of giving you a real feel for a place."
—*Knight Ridder Newspapers*

WILEY
Wiley Publishing, Inc.

Published by:

Wiley Publishing, Inc.

111 River St.
Hoboken, NJ 07030-5774

ISBN: 978-0-470-18184-3
Editors: Linda Barth and Myka Carroll Del Barrio
Production Editor: Eric T. Schroeder
Cartographer: Roberta Stockwell
Photo Editor: Richard Fox
Production by Wiley Indianapolis Composition Services

Front cover photo: Sunset on the Li River, Guanxi Province
Back cover photo: Bronze lion in the Forbidden City, Beijing

For information on our other products and services or to obtain technical support, please
contact our Customer Care Department within the U.S. at 800/762-2974, outside the
U.S. at 317/572-3993 or fax 317/572-4002.

Wiley also publishes its books in a variety of electronic formats. Some content that
appears in print may not be available in electronic formats.

Manufactured in the United States of America

5 4 3 2 1

Contents

(4) Beijing & Hebei   77

by Jen Lin-Liu and Sherisse Pham

(5) The Northeast   159

by Lee Wing-sze

(6) Along the Yellow River   214

by Simon Foster

(7) The Silk Routes   256

by Simon Foster

8 Eastern Central China   336

by Sherisse Pham

9 Shanghai   430

by Sharon Owyang

13 Yangzi & Beyond 693

by Lee Wing-sze

14 The Tibetan World 757

by Simon Foster

Appendix A: The Chinese Language 807

Appendix B: The Chinese Menu 843

Index 864

List of Maps

About the Authors

Simon Foster was born in London and grew up in rural Yorkshire. Family trips first kindled his wanderlust and after graduating in geography from University College London, he set off to seek what he had been studying. He started work as an adventure tour leader in the Middle East in 1997 and was then posted to India and China. Lengthy e-mails home evolved into travel writing and he has contributed to several. Simon now lives with his wife and dog in sunny southern Taiwan and leads Grasshopper Adventures' (www.grasshopperadventures.com) Taiwan and Silk Road Story photography tours. When he's not travel writing or tour leading, Simon enjoys, you guessed it, travel, whether to the Philippines or just back home to Yorkshire.

Jen Lin-Liu has worked as a freelance journalist based in China for 5years. She has written for the Associated Press, the *Chronicle of Higher Education, Newsweek,* and *The Wall Street Journal,* among other publications. Though born in Chicago, she was raised in southern California and studied at Columbia University. She is currently writing a book about how and what modern China eats. She would like to thank Wang Xin, Sherrise Pham, Hyeon-Ju Rho, and Matt Flynn for their much-needed help in traveling to far-flung places.

Sharon Owyang, born in Singapore and a graduate of Harvard University, divides her time between film and television projects in the U.S. and China, and freelance travel writing. She is the author of *Frommer's Shanghai,* 3rd Edition, and also contributed to the 1st edition of *Frommer's China.* She has also written about Shanghai, China, Vietnam, and San Diego for Insight Guides, Compact Guides, the *Los Angeles Times,* and several websites. She speaks Mandarin, Cantonese, and enough Shanghainese to be a curiosity to the locals. When she's not traveling, she pays her dues in Los Angeles, California.

Sherisse Pham graduated from the University of British Columbia and immediately hopped across the Pacific Ocean to live in Asia. She is a Beijing-based freelancer who has contributed to several Frommer's guides, including *Frommer's Vietnam, Frommer's China, Frommer's Beijing,* and *Beijing Day by Day.* She has also worked for Zagat's Survey as a shopping editor and contributed to several local and international magazines and websites. She would like to thank Karen Xiaoling Wang for her excellent work as a fact-checker and occasional translator. A big thank you also goes out to Linda Barth, her editor at Frommer's, who polished things off and fashioned it into the wonderful guide you have today.

Before she could even read, **Beth Reiber** couldn't wait to go to her grandparents' house so she could pour through their latest *National Geographic.* After living several years in Germany as a freelance travel writer for major U.S. newspapers and in Tokyo as editor of the *Far East Traveler,* she authored several Frommer's guides, including *Frommer's Japan, Frommer's Tokyo,* and *Frommer's Hong Kong.* She also contributes to *Frommer's Europe from $85 a Day, Frommer's Europe by Rail,* and *Frommer's USA,* and writes a monthly column on Japan. When not sleeping in far-flung hotels, she resides in Lawrence, Kansas, with her two sons, a dog, and a cat.

Lee Wing-sze, born and raised in Hong Kong, is a freelance writer, translator, and avid traveler. She studied English Journalism at the Hong Kong Baptist University and has worked for the city's English-language newspapers, the *South China Morning Post* and *The Standard,* and contributed to *Cosmopolitan's* Hong Kong edition. Her dream is to travel every country on the earth.

Christopher D. Winnan's love/hate relationship with the continent currently known as China has lasted more than a decade. He has lived and worked in Beijing, Shanghai, and Guangzhou, and, unable to keep his comments to himself, has written extensively in both English and Chinese, most recently for *Time Out* and *Intercontinental Press.* Last year he bought a retirement house in Thailand, but even that cannot seem to keep him away from China, and he is currently residing in Dali, Yunnan Province.

An Invitation to the Reader

In researching this book, we discovered many wonderful places—hotels, restaurants, shops, and more. We're sure you'll find others. Please tell us about them, so we can share the information with your fellow travelers in upcoming editions. If you were disappointed with a recommendation, we'd love to know that, too. Please write to:

Frommer's China, 3rd Edition
Wiley Publishing, Inc. • 111 River St. • Hoboken, NJ 07030-5774

An Additional Note

Please be advised that travel information is subject to change at any time—and this is especially true of prices. We therefore suggest that you write or call ahead for confirmation when making your travel plans. The authors, editors, and publisher cannot be held responsible for the experiences of readers while traveling. Your safety is important to us, however, so we encourage you to stay alert and be aware of your surroundings. Keep a close eye on cameras, purses, and wallets, all favorite targets of thieves and pickpockets.

Other Great Guides for Your Trip:

Frommer's Beijing
Frommer's Shanghai
Frommer's Hong Kong
Suzy Gershman's Born to Shop Hong Kong, Shanghai & Beijing

Frommer's Star Ratings, Icons & Abbreviations

Every hotel, restaurant, and attraction listing in this guide has been ranked for quality, value, service, amenities, and special features using a **star-rating system.** In country, state, and regional guides, we also rate towns and regions to help you narrow down your choices and budget your time accordingly. Hotels and restaurants are rated on a scale of zero (recommended) to three stars (exceptional). Attractions, shopping, nightlife, towns, and regions are rated according to the following scale: zero stars (recommended), one star (highly recommended), two stars (very highly recommended), and three stars (must-see).

In addition to the star-rating system, we also use **seven feature icons** that point you to the great deals, in-the-know advice, and unique experiences that separate travelers from tourists. Throughout the book, look for:

Finds	Special finds—those places only insiders know about
Fun Fact	Fun facts—details that make travelers more informed and their trips more fun
Kids	Best bets for kids and advice for the whole family
Moments	Special moments—those experiences that memories are made of
Overrated	Places or experiences not worth your time or money
Tips	Insider tips—great ways to save time and money
Value	Great values—where to get the best deals

The following **abbreviations** are used for credit cards:

AE	American Express	DISC	Discover	V	Visa
DC	Diners Club	MC	MasterCard		

Frommers.com

Now that you have the guidebook to a great trip, visit our website at **www.frommers.com** for travel information on more than 3,600 destinations. We update features regularly to give you instant access to the most current trip-planning information available. At Frommers.com, you'll find scoops on the best airfares, lodging rates, and car rental bargains. You can even book your travel online through our reliable travel booking partners. Other popular features include:

- Online updates to our most popular guidebooks
- Vacation sweepstakes and contest giveaways
- Newsletters highlighting the hottest travel trends
- Online travel message boards with featured travel discussions

What's New in China

China's international visitors have rocketed from a mere 300,000 back in 1978 to an impressive 22 million in 2006. Already pundits are predicting that in less than 6 years, the country will rank first in terms of visitors, passing the current top three of France, Spain, and the United States.

One reason for this upward surge has been China's "Golden Week" policy. Currently, China has three "Golden Week" holidays: the May Day holiday, the National Day holiday, and the Spring Festival holiday.

Three days paid vacation are given to workers, and the dates of these celebrations are carefully chosen so that workers in Chinese companies always have 7 continuous days of vacation time. These national holidays were first started by the government for China's National Day in 1999 and are primarily intended to help expand the domestic tourism market, improve the national standard of living, and allow people to make long-distance family visits. The Golden Weeks are consequently periods of greatly heightened travel activity.

Visitors should also bear in mind that, in part as a result of these Golden Weeks, the number of domestic Chinese tourists has shot from 280 million in 1990 to a whopping 1.4 billion in 2006, the majority of these being peasants from rural areas. This should give you a clear idea of how crowded many of the "must-see" spots have become. Here's more news by region.

BEIJING & HEBEI The capital's previously sparse subway system was given a boost in the fall of 2007 with the opening of **Line 5,** which runs past the east gate of the Temple of Heaven, up to Dong Dan, Dong Si, Lama Temple, and farther north to the east side of Yayun Cun (Asian Games Village). The subway system will be further improved by the summer of 2008, just in time for the Olympics, with the opening of **Lines L1, 8,** and **10. Line L1** should be particularly handy for travelers, as it connects the airport with Dong Zhi Men, an extensive bus and subway interchange point in central Beijing, and **Line 8** is especially important for Olympic goers, as it will connect passengers to Olympic Park and the Olympic Sports Center. It juts off of **Line 10,** which runs along the east and north side of Third Ring Road, with stops at China World (Guomao) and Gongti Bei Lu, near the Sanlitun Bar Street.

The old central neighborhoods of Beijing offer some wonderful new accommodations that provide comfort and character, including the **Hotel Côte Cour S.L.,** Yanyue Hutong 70 (© **010/6512-8020**), **Hotel Kapok,** Donghuamen Dajie 16 (© **010/6525-9988**), and **Gu Xiang 20,** Nanluogu Xiang 20 (© **010/6400-5566**). The Olympics has given the five-star hotel industry a boom, with the opening of hotels like **Raffles Beijing,** Dong Chang'an Jie 1 (© **800/768-9009** in the U.S., or 010/6526-3388), **Ritz-Carlton, Financial Street,** 1 Jinchengfang

Dong Jie (© **010/6601-6666**), and **Marco Polo Parkside,** Anli Lu 78 (© **010/5963-6688**). The games have also spurred existing luxury hotels like the Shangri-La Beijing to renovate and add new luxurious wings.

Beijing's newest restaurants illustrate the increasingly cosmopolitan character of the city, including the French **Jaan** in the Raffles Hotel (© 010/6526-3388), the Japanese **Haiku by Hatsune** (© 010/6508-8585, ext. 203), the Italian **Cépe** in the Ritz-Carlton, Financial Street (© 010/6601-6666), and the Cantonese **Paper** (© 010/8401-5080).

The first phase of renovations to **The Forbidden City** wraps up in 2008, but parts of the palace will remain under renovation until 2010. In the *hutong* (the traditional alley neighborhoods of Beijing) not far from Hou Hai Lake, the alley of **Nan Luogu Xiang** has blossomed into a gentrified neighborhood of cafes, bars, restaurants, and shops. It's an ideal place to see old Beijingers rubbing elbows with the hip, urban youth of China. Finally, if you really want to get a taste of the capital's youth scene, go see a show at one of the city's new live music venues, including **MAO Livehouse, The Star Live,** and the legendary **Yu Gong Yi Shan,** which just moved into the former quarters of a government official.

THE NORTHEAST   New D trains now connect **Shenyang, Changchun,** and **Harbin** to the capital city of Beijing.

As one of the cities hosting the 2008 Olympics' soccer games, **Shenyang** has been undergoing a face-lift. The city is now cleaner and less polluted. The city has also opened **Shenyang Financial Museum (Shenyang Shi Jinrong Bowuguan),** exhibiting the monetary history of the Northeast and ancient currencies found in the area. It claims to be the biggest museum of its kind in China.

The latest attraction of the Russian border town of **Manzhouli** is the **Eluosi**

Taowa Guangchang (Russian Matryoshka Dolls Plaza) erected in 2006, with over 200 nesting dolls in the plaza. It highlights the distinctive Sino-Russian culture of the town. The town's first international hotel, Shangri-La, is scheduled to open in 2008.

ALONG THE YELLOW RIVER   The long-delayed **Datong airport** finally opened in 2006 and currently has flights to Beijing, Shanghai, and Guangzhou with more connections planned for the future.

Hohhot is experiencing something a hotel building boom, with a number of international five-star operations soon to open: **Kempinski, Sheraton,** and **Shangri-La** hotels will soon top the list in Inner Mongolia.

Taiyuan's excellent new **Shanxi Museum** has finally opened its doors in an enormous building by the river that features state-of-the-art displays highlighting the province's reputation as the cradle of Chinese civilization.

THE SILK ROUTES   Xi'an's impressive history museum was undergoing extensive renovations at press time, but its collection was still open to the public and the work is expected to be completed by 2008.

Lanzhou's Provincial Museum (Sheng Bowuguan) has undergone an extensive renovation and now displays its historic collection in ultramodern format.

Dunhuang has a brand-new (tiny) train station just 6km (3¾ miles) from the town, meaning you no longer have to transfer from Liuyuan (unless you're arriving from Beijing or Shanghai).

The old town in **Kashgar,** absurdly enough, has also been handed over to a private Han company, which has set up a ticket booth at the front of certain neighborhoods, charging anyone who looks like a tourist ¥30 ($3.90/£1.90). That same company has also begun charging those who want to enter **Lake Karakul** via Karakorum Highway ¥50 ($6.50/ £3.25). Nothing seems to get done with the money, save for lining the boss's pockets, but fortunately there are ways to avoid both fees.

EASTERN CENTRAL CHINA Qingdao, a port city 890km (552 miles) southeast of Beijing, is all set to host the watersports events for the XXIX Olympiad. At press time, the city was putting the final touches on its **Olympic Sailing Center,** which includes a five-star **Inter-Continental** hotel that will serve as the athletes' village during the games. To facilitate travel to the city, brand-new express trains (train numbers starting with "D," also known as D-series trains) zip passengers to and from Beijing in a mere 5½ hours.

Several high-end hotels like **Shangri-La** and the **Hyatt** have pulled out of **Nanjing,** but that has not scared off other global hoteliers. The Accor group has opened the super swank **Sofitel Galaxy Nanjing** in the center of the city, as well as a golf resort near the **Purple Gold Mountains.** Keep an eye out for **Inter-Continental**'s ambitious downtown, six-star hotel, which is set to open in 2010.

Huang Shan is one of China's most famous and most climbed mountains. Accordingly, they've increased park entrance fees by more than 50% to ¥202 ($26/£13). Climb it now, before the next price increase!

SHANGHAI Trains to and from Hangzhou and select destinations south now operate out of the **Shanghai South Railway Station (Shanghai Nan Zhan)** in the southwestern part of town. New "D" bullet trains make the journey to Hangzhou in 1 hour and 40 minutes.

There is a new 24-hour **Shanghai Call Center** hot line (© 021/962-288) with English-speaking staff to handle almost all tourist queries. Meanwhile, Nanshi, the old Chinese city, has become incorporated into Huangpu District.

There are now **five metro lines** running with the total expected to reach 11 lines in the next decade. **Metro line 4,** tracing a circle along the Inner Ring Road and extending into Pudong should be fully operational by 2008. Several **metro stops** have been **renamed:** Henan Nan Lu has become Nanjing Dong Lu; Shimen Yi Lu has become Nanjing Xi Lu; and Dongfang Lu has become Shiji Dadao.

The venerable **Peace Hotel** has been closed for a major restoration and is expected to open in 2010 for the World Expo (hence it has been removed as a hotel listing for this edition). New luxury hotel arrivals include **Le Royal Meridien,** Nanjing Dong Lu 789 (© 021/ 3318-9999); **Radisson Hotel Shanghai New World,** Nanjing Xi Lu 88 (© 021/ 6359-9999); **Renaissance Shanghai Yuyuan Hotel,** Henan Nan Lu 159 (© 021/2321-8888); **The Regent Shanghai,** Yan'an Xi Lu 1116 (© 021/ 6115-9988); and **Hyatt on the Bund,** Huangpu Lu 199 (© 021/6393-1234). The **Pudong Shangri-La** has added a luxurious Tower Two. For the budget-minded, there are now clean and functional Chinese business motels such as the **A-Line Hotel,** and the **Jinjiang Inn** and the **Super Motel 168** chains, while those hankering for old Shanghai Chinese style can stay at the atmospheric **Old House Inn,** Huashan Lu Lane 351, no. 16 (© 021/6248-6118).

The number of dining options continues to increase, but happily many of our restaurant recommendations from the previous edition are still around and thriving. The best new arrival for this edition is the avant-garde **Jade on 36** at the Shangri-La Pudong, Fucheng Lu 33 (© 021/6882-8888).

The former Dongjiadu Fabric Market in the old Chinese city has moved a few blocks to become the **South Bund Fabric Market.** The **Xiangyang Clothing**

Market selling knockoff designer goods finally closed in July 2006. Some vendors appear to have relocated to the Qipu Lu Market in Zhabei District and the Yatai Xinyang Fashion and Gift Market at the Science and Technology Museum (Shanghai Keji Guan) stop in Pudong.

With the temporary closing of the Peace Hotel, the **Peace Hotel Old Jazz Bar Band** has moved to the Huating Hotel and Towers (© 021/6439-1000).

The new I. M. Pei–designed **Suzhou Museum** has opened in Suzhou, as has a new **Shangri-La Hotel Suzhou** (© 0512/6808-0168) and **Sofitel Suzhou** (© 0512/6801-9888).

THE SOUTHEAST   The mass industrialization and resulting levels of pollution have led us to drop a number of the more toxic coastal cities such as **Ningbo** and **Fuzhou** and replace them with cleaner, more natural destinations. These include the popular mountain retreat of **Moganshan,** the bamboo forests of **Anji**—made famous in the movie *Crouching Tiger, Hidden Dragon*—and the less well known, but no less spectacular peaks of **Yandangshan.**

HONG KONG   The **Star Ferry** has moved from its longtime location next to City Hall to the Central Ferry Piers, where ferries also depart to the Outlying Islands.

Near the Central Ferry Piers is the gorgeous **Four Seasons Hotel Hong Kong,** 8 Finance St. (© 800/819-5053 in the U.S. and Canada), which boasts the best location money can buy, next to Hong Kong Station. Unsurprisingly, its **Caprice** French restaurant (© 852/3196 8888) is one of Hong Kong's hottest dining venues, boasting great views and a dramatic setting. At the other end of the spectrum and Hong Kong Island is **Top Deck,** at the **Jumbo** (© 852/2553 3331), offering alfresco dining atop the Jumbo Kingdom floating restaurant in Aberdeen.

Peak Tower, Victoria Peak (© 852/2849 7654), has been totally renovated and now features a rooftop observation deck with 360-degree views, with free tai-chi lessons given Saturdays at 9am.

Lantau's Giant Tian Tan Buddha is now accessible via **cable car** from Tung Chung MTR subway station. Near the Buddha is the new **Ngong Ping Village** (© 852/2109 9898), with a museum devoted to the life of Siddhartha Gautama (the man who became Buddha), an animation theater, restaurants, and shops.

THE SOUTHWEST: MOUNTAINS & MINORITIES   In the last few years, **Guizhou Province** has seen almost as many new highways as the provinces on the coast. Apart from the main sights such as the caves and the falls, which are now swarming with sheeplike ganbu, the province can still be very hard to travel, and is favored mainly by Europeans with an interest in ethnography.

Most overseas tourists to Guangxi head straight for **Yangshuo,** even though old China hands are lamenting the fact that this small country town has grown far too rapidly for its own good. Despite the frantic growth and accompanying degradation, it remains one of the highlights for most visitors. For a taste of what Yangshuo and Guilin used to be like, we have added a section on the more remote area of **Bama** in northwestern Guangxi, famed for the world's highest population of healthy centenarians. Long famous for its **Foreigners' Street,** a rather tacky imitation of West Street in Yangshuo, where visiting foreigners are the main attraction for streams of gawking local tourists, **Dali** now boasts the very attractive Hong Longjing area as a pleasant alternative. The bad news is the town is growing so rapidly that it will not be long before the entire Er Hai valley is concreted over and Dali becomes a victim of its own success.

Li Jiang has become so overcrowded that we have added a number of Yunnan alternatives for those seeking more peaceful excursions. These include the charming if rather artificial town of **Shuhe,** as well as the much better value historical town of **Jianshui** and the spectacular rice terraces of nearby **Yuanyang.** Now that a regular boat service to Thailand is in operation, **Jinghong** is set to become an important gateway with the rest of Southeast Asia. In addition, we have also included the increasingly popular Vietnamese border crossing of **Pingxiang.**

The new train connection between **Nanning** and **Kunming** has opened up a great deal of eastern Yunnan. In this edition we have featured the rapeseed seas and karst terrain around **Luoping,** as this is a great place to begin exploring one of China's less traveled regions.

YANGZI & BEYOND Hongse Niandai (Red Generation) nightclub was once a highlight of any trip to **Chengdu,** with its completely red interior and roster of apolitical rock bands playing most nights. Sadly, the march of modernization has seen the red give way to the globally homogenous and the rock bands are now a thing of the past. Tragically, the name remains the same—don't be fooled.

Chongqing Municipal Museum has moved to new premises near Renmin Guangchang (People's Square). While the new facility wasn't open at the time of writing, it promises to be a much grander affair with a sexier name: the Three Gorges Museum (Sanxia Bowuguan).

Once the terminus for **Three Gorges cruises,** Wuhan has been stricken from most itineraries in favor of Yichang, a fairly uninspiring town just downstream from the Three Gorges dam. A new expressway linking Wuhan to Yichang takes about 4 hours and reduces your cruising experience by a day. But don't worry, most travelers tend to regard the stretch of the Yangzi into Wuhan as a little uninspiring.

THE TIBETAN WORLD The biggest news in the Tibetan world was the 2006 opening of the **Tibet train,** which runs from Golmud to Lhasa and now connects tourist centers across the country to the capital of the Tibetan Autonomous Region (TAR). While the train has been criticized for its environmental and social impact, the route, which takes passengers through passes over 5,000m (16,404 ft.) is one of the most stunning journeys on the planet (see "Railway on the Roof of the World," p. 782).

Following an incident at **Everest Base Camp** (and in the run-up to the Olympics), restrictions on individual foreign travelers to the TAR have tightened, meaning that you may need to be part of a group to get to Lhasa, and you'll certainly need to join one to travel along the **Friendship Highway.** See "Permit Purgatory" (p. 780) for more information.

While the TAR is undeniably worth visiting, these restrictions and greater numbers of tourists make a visit to the "other Tibet" in Qinghai, Gansu, Sichuan, and Yunnan all the more appealing. **Yushu's** airport is due for completion by 2009, which will make this distant Khampa county in Qinghai more readily accessible.

1

The Best of China

With every new edition of this book, identifying the "best of China" becomes a more and more difficult task. As this once isolated giant awakens, forces are being unleashed that impact tourism. Devastating pollution, widespread corruption, and the sheer volume of tourists have transformed many of China's best-known sights into filthy, overpriced circuses. To find the very best that China has to offer, it is sadly becoming more important to know what to avoid, rather than what to see.

Perhaps the best advice that we can give is to focus on nature. After suffering through the devastating Cultural Revolution, what little remains of the country's much-vaunted 5,000 years of culture is being lost in the rush to get rich—even small cities have become heavily polluted sweatshops. Fortunately, China still has some of the most spectacular natural scenery on the planet. Many places within the People's Republic have only recently been opened to visitors, so we have only had a few decades to unlock some of this enormous realm's secrets. While we certainly do not claim to have uncovered everything, we have been truly inspired by this huge treasure house, and have included here what we have discovered so far.

1 The Best China Experiences

- **Strolling Past the Old Russian Architecture in Harbin:** At the heart of the Russian-built city, Zhongyang Dajie's unexpected cupola-topped Art Nouveau mansions are reminders of the 1920s and 1930s, when Harbin was the liveliest stop on this leg of the Trans-Siberian Railroad. See chapter 5.

- **Exploring the Forbidden City's Forgotten Corners** (Beijing): No one fails to be impressed by the grandeur of the Forbidden City's central axis, which is all most visitors see. But the quieter maze of pavilions, gardens, courtyards, and theaters to either side have the greater charm. See p. 110.

- **Dining on Shanghai's Bund:** China's most famous waterfront street of colonial architecture, the Bund, has become the toniest address in town, with the redevelopment of a few

formerly stodgy old buildings into some of the city's finest shopping and dining establishments. These rooftop restaurants offer unsurpassed views of Shanghai, old and new. See chapter 9.

- **Cycling the City Wall in Xi'an:** The largest city walls in China have been much pierced for modern purposes and can be tackled in a modern way, too, with a breezy, traffic-light-free ride above the rooftops on rented bicycles and tandems. Behold views of remnants of vernacular architecture, clustered around small temples. See chapter 7.

- **Exploring Li Jiang's Old Town:** Built over 800 years ago and partly rebuilt after a massive 1996 earthquake, Li Jiang's old town, with its maze of cobblestone streets, gurgling streams, and original and reconstructed traditional

Naxi houses, is one of the most atmospheric places in China, hordes of tourists notwithstanding. Rise before the sun, then watch its golden rays filter through the gray winding streets, lighting up the dark wooden houses. See chapter 12.

- **Walking on the Great Wall from Jinshanling to Simatai** (Beijing): The Great Wall, winding snakelike through the mountains, was meant to be walked. This magnificent 3-hour hike follows China's greatest monument through various states of repair, from freshly restored to thoroughly crumbling, over steep peaks and gentle flats, and through patches of wilderness and rugged farmland, with over two dozen watchtowers along the way. See chapter 4.

- **Riding the Star Ferry** (Hong Kong): There's no better way to get acquainted with Hong Kong than to ride the cheapest cruise in China. The century-old green-and-white Star ferries weave between tugs, junks, and oceangoing vessels in a 5-minute harbor crossing, and thanks to the wonderful Suzy Wong novel, remain one of the territories' premier attractions. See chapter 11.

- **Exploring the karst scenery around Yangshuo:** The cruise down the now-polluted Li River between Guilin and Yangshuo may be overexposed and overpriced, but the scenery area remains captivating. Avoid the pricey taxis and motorbike rentals and explore instead in traditional Chinese style, by bicycle. Both the Yulong River and the Jin Bao are still relatively peaceful as they flick lazily through serrated hills like dragon's teeth. See chapter 12.

- **Unwinding in a Sichuan Teahouse:** One of the great pleasures of being in Sichuan is drinking tea at a neighborhood teahouse. On any given afternoon at Qingyang Gong in Chengdu,

for instance, seniors can be found playing mahjong with friends while their caged songbirds sit in nearby trees providing ambient music. As patrons eat watermelon seeds, nuts, dried squid, or beef jerky, attendants appear at regular intervals to refill their cups from copper kettles. For an afternoon of perfect relaxation, stop by and forget about sightseeing for a few hours. See chapter 13.

- **Gazing at the Sea of Terra-Cotta Warriors at the Tomb of Qin Shi Huang** (Xi'an): The first sight of the tomb, in a hangarlike building, leaves many visitors stunned and awed. This destination is at the top of almost every visitor's list, and it does not disappoint. See p. 266.

- **Strolling in Shanghai's French Concession:** The domain of the French community up until 1949 was colonial Shanghai's trendiest area, and it remains full of tree-lined boulevards, colonial mansions, and Art Deco masterpieces, now bundled up with phone lines and pole-hung washing. Some of the city's best shopping is also here. Just beyond the former concession is one of modern Shanghai's trendiest areas, the mega-development of restaurants and shops known as **Xin Tiandi.** See chapter 9.

- **Getting Lost in the lanes around Beijing's Back Lakes:** No other city in the world has anything quite like the *hutong,* narrow lanes once "as numberless as the hairs on an ox." Now rapidly vanishing, the best-preserved *hutong* are found around a pair of man-made lakes in the city center. This area is almost the last repository of Old Beijing's gritty, low-rise charm, dotted with tiny temples, hole-in-the-wall noodle shops, and quiet courtyard houses whose older residents still wear Mao suits. See the walking tour, "The Back Lakes," on p. 124.

- **Strolling the Old Neighborhoods of Kashgar:** The dusty alleys, colorful residential doorways, and mudbrick walls remain as they have been for decades. Kids with henna-dyed feet and fingernails will approach you speaking a few words of Chinese and English; men with donkey carts trudge down narrow passages; bakers arrange round large slabs of nan in coal ovens built into the ground. Spending hours watching how citizens of Kashgar live is one of the most rewarding experiences along the Silk Road. See p. 323.

- **Taking a "Peapod" Boat on Shennong Stream** (Yangzi River): Best of the Three Gorges cruise excursions, this 2-hour journey through a long, narrow canyon takes passengers to one of the famous suspended coffins of the Ba people, then returns them downstream in a fraction of the time. Along the way, howler monkeys may be spotted swinging through the trees, small waterfalls appear from the rocks, and swallows and other small birds flit about. The water in this small tributary is surprisingly clear, and the scenery and silence are thoroughly calming. See chapter 13.

2 The Best Small Towns

- **Xia He** (Gansu): This delightful monastery town nestles in a mountain valley at an elevation of 2,900m (9,500 ft.). It's divided into two sections, primarily Hui (Muslim) and Han Chinese at its eastern end, changing abruptly to Tibetan as you climb westward to the gorgeous gilded roofs of the vast Labrang Monastery. Tibetan pilgrims make you welcome on the 3km (2-mile) circuit around the monastery's perimeter. See chapter 7.

- **Manzhouli** (Inner Mongolia): A tiny town of 50,000 on the Russian border, lost in a sea of grass, Manzhouli is the East-meets-Wild-West frontier outpost David Carradine should have used as the backdrop to the TV series *Kung Fu*. It stands on the edge of the Hulun Buir, an emerald expanse of grassland shot through with radiant patches of wildflowers. See p. 210.

- **Dali** (Yunnan): This home of the Bai people, a backpacker's mecca recently gentrified for larger numbers of tourists, remains a retreat from the world. You can hike part of the impressive 19-peak Green Mountains (Cang Shan) to the west, sail on the cerulean Er Hai Lake to the east, and take a bike ride into any of the nearby Bai villages. See p. 656.

- **Dunhuang** (Gansu): Surrounded by barren deserts, this oasis town beckons with sand dunes, camel treks, and the Buddhist cave art of Mogao. Its tree-lined streets and backpacker cafes give it a laid-back feeling that is hard to find elsewhere in China. See p. 295.

- **Yangshuo** (Guangxi): While much of the central area is now tacky and overcommercialized, this small town on the Li River, nestled in a cluster of spiny pinnacles, has retained enough of its laid-back charm to be a delightful alternative to Guilin. Yangshuo is at the cutting edge of Chinese tourism and features some of its best innovations as well as some of its worst. See p. 608.

3 The Best Countryside Trips

- **Jiuzhai Gou** (Sichuan): This national park has dense forest, green meadows, rivers, rapids, ribbon lakes in various shades of blue and green, chalky shoals, and waterfalls of every kind. Of cultural interest are six Tibetan villages of the original nine from which this valley gets its name. See p. 718.

- **Chang Bai Shan** (Jilin): This long-dormant 2,600m-high (8,500-ft.) volcano is home to Tian Chi, a deep, pure, mist-enshrouded crater lake that straddles the China–North Korea border and is sacred to both Koreans and Manchurians. The northern approach to the lake, with its trail that climbs alongside the thundering Changbai Waterfall, is best in the fall. The western approach is ideal in early summer, when its vast fields of vibrant wildflowers are in full bloom. See p. 195.

- **Langmu Si** (Gansu): This Tibetan monastic center is largely unknown to Chinese tourists, and the tranquil mountain village is reminiscent of Li Jiang before it was "discovered." The town is home to two major Tibetan monasteries, housing around 1,000 monks whose chanting of the scriptures may be heard throughout the day. Ramble through narrow ravines and moraine valleys crowded with wildflowers, or take a horse trek up Flower Cap Mountain to obtain stunning views as far as the holy mountain of Amnye Machen. See p. 287.

- **Amnye Machen** (Qinghai): The route around this holy mountain, for a while believed to be the world's highest, must be clockwise—turning back is sacrilegious. So once you start on the 3-day horse trek, or the 7- to 10-day walk with the aid of a baggage-carrying yak, there's no turning back. But the scenery around the 6,282m (20,605-ft.) peak, and the company of sometimes entire villages of Tibetans, make the trek well worthwhile. See p. 775.

- **Around Li Jiang** (Yunnan): This area offers a wide variety of countryside experiences, from riding a chairlift up to the glacier park of the magnificent, snowcapped **Jade Dragon Snow Mountain,** to hiking the sheer-sided **Tiger Leaping Gorge** while the Yangzi River rages below, to being rowed in a "pig-trough" boat across the pristine **Lugu Lake**—China's answer to Lake Tahoe. See p. 675.

- **Karakul Lake** (Xinjiang): On the highway between Kashgar and Tashkurgan lie stark, jagged mountains surrounded by a pristine lake at an altitude over 4,000m (13,120 ft.). Come here for some peace and quiet and a change of scenery from the dusty Uighur towns along the Silk Road. See p. 328.

- **Wu Ling Yuan & Zhang Jia Jie** (Hunan): This scenic area is made up of three subtropical parklands, with quartzite sandstone peaks and pillars to rival Guilin's scenery. There are plentiful rare plants and insects, swarms of butterflies, a large cave with calcite deposits, and stunning views through bamboo, pine, and oak forests. See p. 753.

- **Everest Base Camp** (Tibet): Whether by 3-hour drive from the village of Pelbar, or by a 3- to 4-day trek from Tingri, the trip to the tented base camp (at 5,150m/16,890 ft.) or to rooms in Rongbuk Monastery (at 4,980m/16,330 ft.) offers unbeatable vistas of the world's toothiest snowcaps set against a startling cobalt sky. See chapter 14.

- **Hulun Buir Grasslands** (Inner Mongolia): Located just outside the remote border town of Manzhouli, the Hulun Buir's grasslands are the most pristine in China. This expanse of gentle emerald hills, perfectly punctuated with small streams and rocky outcrops, is all the more attractive for how difficult it is to reach. See chapter 5.
- **Eastern Qing Tombs** (Hebei): This rural tomb complex offers more to the visitor than the better-known Ming Tombs, but sees a fraction of the visitors. Undeniably difficult to reach, the effort is rewarded many times over by the Qianlong emperor's breathtakingly beautiful tomb chamber, **Yu Ling,** and an (unintentionally) drop-dead funny photo exhibit

of the much-maligned dowager empress Cixi. See chapter 4.
- **The Bamboo Forests of Anji** (Zhejiang): Vast oceans of bamboo, immortalized by the kung-fu acrobatics of *Crouching Tiger, Hidden Dragon,* make this is a part of the country that will appeal to the emerging generation of ecotravelers. Apart from mystical, secluded groves, the bamboo museum highlights a plant that is receiving more and more attention as we begin to recognize the importance of sustainable lifestyles. See p. 483.
- **Yandangshan** (Zhejiang): A less well known, but equally stunning collection of spectacular peaks that rival any other area in the country but as yet do not have the same stratospheric ticket prices. See p. 489.

4 The Best Mansions & Palaces

- **Wang Jia Dayuan** (Pingyao): It took a century for this vast mansion to grow to 123 courtyards and 1,118 houses; the decorative lattice screens and windows, shaped openings between rooms and courtyards, and undulating walls are exquisite examples of Ming and Qing vernacular architecture. See p. 243.
- **Potala Palace** (Lhasa): A monastery, a palace, and a prison, the Potala symbolizes the fusion of secular and religious power in Tibet in a vast, slab-sided, red-and-white agglomeration on a hilltop dominating central Lhasa. Despite the ruination of its surroundings, there's no more haunting sight within China's modern political boundaries, and nothing else that speaks so clearly of the otherness of Tibet. See p. 785.
- **The Forbidden City** (Beijing): Preeminent among the surviving complexes of ancient buildings in China, the former residence of the emperors needs far more time than most tours give it.

See "The Best China Experiences," earlier in this chapter, and p. 110.
- **Wei Huanggong** (Changchun): Also known as the Puppet Emperor's Palace and best known in the west as the setting for part of Bernardo Bertolucci's film *The Last Emperor,* this impressive palace complex, opened to visitors after an admirable full-scale restoration in 2002, was the residence of Henry Puyi, China's last emperor and subsequently puppet ruler of Japanese-controlled Manchukuo. See p. 186.
- **Wang Jia Dayuan** (Hebei): With investment from a Beijing entrepreneur, part of a traditional courtyard mansion that once housed Shanhaiguan's wealthiest burgher has been magnificently restored and is expected to expand farther south. Set in the heart of the old walled town, it also boasts a folk museum crammed with curiosities. Four of the rooms are available for overnight stays, although you'll have to be out before the next day's visitors arrive. See p. 150.

- **Qiao Jia Dayuan** (Pingyao): One of the loveliest of the several merchant family mansions of this area, this was the set for the film *Raise the Red Lantern*. With six large courtyards, 313 houses, and fine craftsmanship of lattices, lintels, carvings, wooden balustrades, and chimneys throughout, the 18th-century manse takes hours to explore. See p. 243.
- **Bishu Shanzhuang** (Chengde): The imperial summer resort and its surrounding Eight Outer Temples form another of the greatest ancient architectural complexes of China, arranged around a green valley. The temples have bizarre borrowings from a number of minority architectural traditions, and both temples and palace have 18th-century replicas of buildings of which the country is most proud. See p. 144.

5 The Best Museums

- **Hong Kong Museum of History** (Hong Kong): A life-size diorama of a Neolithic settlement, replicas of fishing boats and traditional houses, ethnic clothing, displays of colorful festivals, and whole streets of old shop frontages with their interiors removed piece by piece and rebuilt here, make this the most entertaining museum in China. See p. 576.
- **Shanxi Lishi Bowuguan** (Xi'an): If you can visit only one museum in China, this should be it. An unrivaled collection of treasures, many demonstrating Xi'an's international contacts via the Silk Routes, is more professionally displayed here than almost anywhere else in the mainland. See p. 265.
- **Sanxing Dui Bowuguan** (Chengdu): An attractive and well-laid-out museum housing items from a group of sacrificial pits, this is one of the most significant finds in 20th-century China. See p. 701.
- **Shanghai Bowuguan** (Shanghai): In terms of display and English labeling, this ultramodern museum (lights fade as you approach cabinets), loaded with stunning antiquities, is China's most modern and inviting. See p. 466.
- **Nanjing Datusha Jinianguan** (Nanjing): The deaths of over 300,000 Chinese, killed over the course of 6 weeks during the 1937 Japanese invasion of Nanjing, are commemorated here. Photographs and artifacts documenting the Japanese onslaught, the atrocities suffered, and the aftermath, are sobering, grisly, and shockingly effective. See p. 399.
- **Wang Anting Xiaoxiao Zhanlanguan** (Chengdu): Located in a narrow lane west of the main town square, this small, one-of-a-kind museum contains tens of thousands of Mao pins, Cultural Revolution memorabilia, and vintage photographs. The museum occupies the living room of its devoted proprietor. See p. 702.
- **Quanzhou Taiwan Friendship Museum** (Quanzhou): Although the Minnan design of this building is impressive, the real reason that I recommend it is to see how ridiculous (and increasingly frightening and dangerous) propaganda concerning Taiwan has become in the last few years. To paraphrase Rich Hall, in showpieces like this, China is somewhat like a beauty contestant, absolutely gorgeous until it opens its mouth. See p. 507.

6 The Best Temples

- **Kong Miao** (Qufu): One of China's greatest classical architectural complexes, this spectacular temple in Confucius's hometown is the largest and most magnificent of the hundreds of temples around the country honoring the sage. Greatly enlarged since it was originally built in 478 B.C., it has a series of gates and buildings aligned on a north-south axis and decorated with imperial flourishes like yellow-tiled roofs and dragon-entwined pillars. See p. 372.

- **Maiji Shan Shiku** (Tianshui): This haystack-shaped mountain of soft red rock, covered in brilliant green foliage, is China's prettiest cave-temple site, and the only one where statuary has been added to the cave walls rather than carved out of them. Views from the stairs and walkways lacing the cliffs are spectacular (including those straight down). See p. 276.

- **Guan Yin Dong** (Yandangshan): the Goddess of Mercy Cave consists of 10 stories of wooden timbers over 100m (328 ft.) high, and constructed deep inside a huge long vertical crevasse. Absolutely breathtaking and set in some of the most beautiful surroundings. See p. 491.

- **Zhengding** (Hebei): Neither the most spectacular nor the best known of temple groups, but within a short walking distance of each other, are some of China's oldest surviving unimproved temple buildings (one of which houses a 30m-high/90-ft. multiarmed bronze of Guanyin), and a collection of ancient pagodas so varied it's almost as if they've been set out specifically to surprise you. See p. 151.

- **Jokhang Temple** (Lhasa): The spiritual heart of Tibetan Buddhism, this temple should be visited twice: once to see the intense devotion of pilgrims circumnavigating it by prostrating themselves repeatedly across cobblestones made slippery by centuries of burning yak-butter lamps, and rubbing their foreheads against the statuary in the dim, smoky interior; and a second time in the afternoon for a closer look at the ancient images they venerate. See p. 779.

- **Temple of Heaven** (Beijing): The circular Hall of Prayer for Good Harvests, one of the finest achievements of Ming architecture, is almost as well known as a symbol of Beijing as the Tian'an Men, but the three-tiered sacrificial altar of plain stone is thought by many to be the most sublime object of beauty in China. See p. 118.

- **Sakya Monastery (Sajia Si)** (Sakya): The massive 35m (115-ft.) windowless gray walls of Lhakhang Chenmo tower above the village and fields on the southern bank of the Trum Chu. Completed in 1274, this monastery fort was largely funded by Kublai Khan, and unlike the older temples of north Sakya, it survived the Cultural Revolution. See p. 800.

- **Mogao Shiku** (Dunhuang): The biggest, best-preserved, and most significant site of Buddhist statuary and frescoes in all China, with the broadest historical range, the Mogao Caves, in their tranquil desert setting, should be your choice if you can see only one cave site. See p. 298.

- **Yonghe Gong** (Beijing): After the Qing Yongzheng emperor moved into the Forbidden City, his personal residence was converted into this temple. Several impressive incense burners are scattered throughout the golden-roofed complex, also known as the Lama Temple. A 20m-tall (60-ft.) sandalwood statue of Maitreya, the future Buddha, fills the last building. See p. 121.

- **Baoding Shan** (Dazu): Artistically among the subtlest and most sophisticated of China's Buddhist grottoes, these Song dynasty caves are situated around a horseshoe-shaped cove, at the center of which is lush forest. See p. 730.

- **Longmen Shiku (Dragon Gate Grottoes)** (Luoyang): The grottoes go well beyond just the identity of a temple, as these caves are considered one of the best sculptural treasure-troves in China. The site comprises a mind-boggling 2,300 caves and niches with more than 2,800 inscriptions and over 100,000 Buddhist statues. See p. 349.

- **Yungang Shiku** (Shanxi): These are the earliest Buddhist caves carved in China. Most were hollowed out over a 65-year period between 460 and 524. Viewed as a whole, they show a movement from Indian and central Asian artistic models to greater reliance on Chinese traditions. See p. 218.

See also Chengde's Bishu Shanzhuang and its Eight Outer Temples, in "The Best Mansions & Palaces," above.

7 The Best Markets

- **Kashgar Sunday Bazaar:** The bazaar is now split in two and not quite what it was, but the livestock part of the market, southeast of town, is still well worth visiting. Bearded Uighur men in traditional blue-and-white garb sharpen their knives and trim their sheep, small boys gorge themselves on Hami melons, and Kyrgyz in dark fur hats pick up and drop dozens of lambs to test their weight and meatiness before settling deals with vigorous and protracted handshakes. See p. 324.

- **Panjiayuan Jiuhuo Shichang** (Beijing): A vast outdoor market held on weekends, Panjiayuan teems with what is very likely the world's best selection of things Chinese: row upon row of everything from reproduction Ming furniture to the traditional clothing worn by China's many minorities to Mao memorabilia. Most of the antiques are fakes, although experts have made some surprising finds in the bedlam. See p. 135.

- **Kaifeng Tutechan Shichang** (Kaifeng): Visitors overnight in Kaifeng just so they can attend this famous and festive night market whose mainstay is the wide variety of delicious local snacks on offer, such as five-spice roasted bread, sesame soup, and spicy lamb kabob. See p. 358.

- **Khotan Sunday Market:** This is everything the Kashgar Market once was. Jewelers pore over gemstones, blacksmiths busy themselves shoeing horses and repairing farm tools, blanket makers beat cotton balls, rat-poison sellers proudly demonstrate the efficacy of their products—the sights and smells are overwhelming. Don't miss the horse-riding enclosure toward the north side of the melee, where buyers test the road-worthiness of both beast and attached cart, with frequent spectacular tumbles. See p. 331.

- **Temple Street Night Market** (Hong Kong): Prices here are outrageous compared to those at China's other markets, but the scene at this night market is very entertaining, especially the fortunetellers and street-side performers singing Chinese opera. See p. 585.

- **South Bund Fabric Market** (Shanghai): Bales and bales of fabric (silk, cotton, linen, wool, and cashmere) are sold here at ridiculously low prices. Many stalls have their own in-house tailors who can stitch you a suit, or anything else you want, at rates that are less than half what you'd pay at retail outlets. See p. 470.

- **Haizhu Square Wholesale Market** (Guangzhou): With so many markets

to choose from in a city whose very raison d'être is commerce, it is difficult to know which one to choose first. This is one of the most colorful. If it was made in China then there is a very good chance that you will find it around here somewhere. See p. 537.

8 The Best Festivals

For dates and contact information, see also the "China Calendar of Events" on p. 27.

- **Saka Dawa,** held throughout the Tibetan world, celebrates the Buddha passing away and thus attaining nirvana. It's held on the 8th to 15th days of the fourth lunar month, with religious dancing, mass chanting, and "sunning the Buddha"—the public display of giant sanctified silk portraits. See chapter 14.
- **Ice and Snow Festival** (Harbin): Not so much a festival as an extended city-wide exhibition, Harbin's Ice and Snow Festival runs from December to March every year and is without doubt the northeast's top winter attraction. The festival centers around hundreds of elaborate ice and snow sculptures, frosty reproductions of everything from Tian'an Men to Elvis. See chapter 5.
- **Sanyue Jie** (Dali): This once-religious festival celebrated by the Bai people in mid-April/early May now features 5 days and nights of considerably more secular singing, dancing, wrestling, horse racing, and large-scale trading.

This is a rare opportunity to see not only the Bai but a number of Yunnan's other ethnic minorities, gathering in one of the most beautiful and serene settings in the foothills of the Green Mountains (Cang Shan). See chapter 12.

- **Kurban Bairam** (Kashgar): Celebrations are held in Muslim communities across China, but in Kashgar they involve feats of tightrope-walking in the main square and wild dancing outside the Idkah Mosque. The 4-day festival is held 70 days after the breaking of the fast of Ramadan, on the 10th day of the 12th month (Dhul-Hijjah) in the Islamic calendar. See chapter 2.
- **Miao New Year Festival** (Xi Jiang, Langde): The Miao celebrate many festivals, but one of the biggest blowouts is the occasion of the Miao New Year, usually around December. The celebration features songs, dances, bullfights, and *lusheng* competitions, not to mention Miao women gorgeously bedecked in silver headdresses engaging in various courtship rituals. See chapter 12.

9 The Best Up-and-Coming Destinations

- **Yushu** (Qinghai): Khampa areas within the Tibet "Autonomous Regions" are closed to the individual traveler, but here these fiercely proud Tibetan warriors trade in a traditional market town beneath a stern gray-and-red monastery. See chapter 14.
- **Yanbian** (Jilin): A lush, achingly pretty hilly region perched on China's border with North Korea, parts of which have only recently been opened to tourism, Yanbian is home to the largest population of ethnic Koreans outside the peninsula itself.

Independent-minded travelers have the opportunity to explore one of the few truly bicultural societies in China. See chapter 5.

- **Pingyao** (Shanxi): Chinese tourists have discovered Pingyao, but the number of Western tourists is still relatively low at what is one of the best-preserved Ming and Qing towns in China. An intact Ming city wall surrounds clusters of elegant high-walled courtyard residences, some of which are also guesthouses. See chapter 6.
- **Bama** (Guangxi): Difficult to reach as yet, but this is what the countryside

around Guilin wants to be when it grows up. There are limited facilities, but caves and peaks that will amaze even the most experienced travelers. See chapter 12.

- **Yi Xian** (Anhui): Often visited en route to or from Huang Shan, this UNESCO World Heritage county is famous for its Ming and Qing dynasty memorial arches and residential houses. Structures with ornate brick, stone, and wood carvings are like a peek into an architectural past that is quickly being destroyed in China's booming cities.

10 The Best Local Accommodations

- **Dunhuang Shanzhuang** (Dunhuang): The finest hotel on the Silk Routes, with views of the Mingsha Shan Dunes, this imposing fortress is surrounded by stylishly renovated courtyard houses. See p. 300.
- **Lusong Yuan Binguan:** Of all Beijing's traditional courtyard-style hotels, this former imperial residence has the most character, recalling the opulence of China's "feudal" era, but with a more lived-in feel than you'll find elsewhere. See p. 97.
- **Longmen Guibin Lou** (Harbin): Built by the Russian-controlled Chinese Eastern Railroad in 1901, the Longmen has served as a hospital, the Russian embassy, and a cheap hostel for migrant workers. In the 1930s and 1940s, it was part of the illustrious Japanese-owned Yamato Hotel chain. The Chinese Railway Bureau renovated the building in 1996, preserving the original Russian woodwork and restoring much of its turn-of-the-20th-century atmosphere. Rooms are palatial and decorated with period furniture. See p. 206.
- **Seman Binguan** (Kashgar): Set on the grounds of the former Russian

consulate, this has merely two government-issued stars and poor service, but standard rooms and suites in the original and beautifully decorated consulate buildings, with their high ceilings and dramatic oil paintings, can be bargained down to low prices. This is the nearest you'll get to experiencing some "Great Game" ambience. See p. 325.

- **Deju Yuan & Tian Yuan Kui** (Pingyao): These are the top two courtyard guesthouses in a town full of ancient architecture. The Deju Yuan has rooms decorated with calligraphy and furnished with dark wooden Ming-style tables and chairs and traditional heated brick beds. The Tian Yuan Kui also offers occasional opera performances on hot summer nights when the guesthouse is full and the performers available. See p. 244.
- **Ye Baihe Binguan (Night Lily Guest House)** (Gulang Yu): One of the latest, and certainly one of the most successful conversions of early colonial architecture. A fascinating combination of Qing dynasty furniture and modern interior-design styles, although the

antique beds have been causing a ew problems for very tall foreign visitors whom they were definitely not designed for in the first place. See p. 521.

- **The Peninsula** (Hong Kong): Built in 1928 and retaining the atmosphere of its colonial past, The Peninsula has long been the grand old hotel of Hong Kong. It boasts an ornate lobby popular for people-watching, some of Hong Kong's best restaurants, and gorgeous rooms with sweeping views of Victoria Harbour. See p. 562.
- **Yangshuo Shengdi (Mountain Retreat)** (Yangshuo): Situated in one of the area's most picturesque settings,

this small but luxurious hotel is a world away from the usual trials and tribulations of traveling in China. This is the kind of place where you will want to extend your vacation indefinitely. See p. 612.

- **The Sanbao Ceramic Art Institute** (Jingde Zhen): A restored porcelain workshop complete with ancient kilns and water hammers that now functions as an artists' retreat in a superb rural location. While much of China's historical architecture is being demolished wholesale, here is a place that reveres its past and deserves our support. See p. 528.

11 The Best Buys

- **Chen Lu** (Shanxi): Seventeen small factories turn out different styles of pottery, and their showrooms have starting prices so low you'll volunteer to pay more. You can also buy original works in the houses of individual artisans. See p. 273.
- **Ba Xian An** (Xi'an): There are fakes aplenty, as everywhere else, but this bustling antiques market, fed by continuous new discoveries in the surrounding plain, is too atmospheric to miss. See p. 267.
- **Jatson School** (Lhasa): High-quality Tibetan handicrafts, including traditional Tibetan clothing, paper, incense, mandala *thangkas,* yak-hide boots, ceramic dolls, door hangings, bags, and cowboy hats, are all made on-site and sold at very fair prices. Your money goes to support Tibetan poor, orphaned, and children with disabilities. See p. 787.
- **Fake Name-Brand Clothing and Accessories:** Adequate to near-perfect imitations of items by North Face, Louis Vuitton, Prada, and just about any other expensive label you can think of can be had for a song at

several markets in China, especially at Beijing's Silk Street and Hongqiao markets, Shanghai's Xiangyang Lu market, and Shenzhen's Luo Hu Commercial City (not quite as cheaply). See chapters 4, 9, and 10.

- **Factory 798** (Beijing): We were sure that an ad hoc gathering of designers, painters, and sculptors selling avant-garde art in a former military complex wasn't something the regime would tolerate for long. We were wrong. Market rents are now charged, so don't expect to pick up a bargain, but the Dashanzi art district makes for a thoroughly enjoyable afternoon of gallery- and cafe-hopping. See p. 122.
- **Khawachen Carpet and Wool Handicraft Co. Ltd** (Lhasa): This U.S.-Tibetan factory's carpets have rich but tasteful shades woven into delightful traditional patterns. Carpets can also be made to order. You'll pay much less here than in New York or even Beijing. See p. 788.
- **Qipao:** Tailors in Beijing and Shanghai will cut a custom-fit *qipao,* the tight-fitting traditional dress better known by its Cantonese name

cheongsam, sometimes for hundreds of dollars less than in Hong Kong and the West. A quality tailored dress, lined with silk and finished with handmade buttons, typically costs between $100 and $200. Slightly less fancy versions go for as little as $50. See chapters 4 and 9.

- **Bamboo:** The ecologically minded will be impressed and amazed at the versatility of this wondrous plant. Apart from the usual carvings, look for bamboo fiber that has been made into everything from socks to bath towels and the delicious Anji Science Bamboo Beer.

- **Minority Fabrics and Costumes** (Yunnan and Guizhou): While all of the popular tourist destinations have shops selling silver Miao headdresses, those will to venture out to the lands of the more obscure ethnic minorities will be justly rewarded. A traditional Bouyi jacket from a weekly market near Luoping now holds pride of place in my own girlfriends' wardrobe, while the World Vision charity in Yuanyang supports local embroidery cooperatives that produces a range of designs from a world almost forgotten in the new millennium.

Note: Pearls, antiques, jade, jewelry in general, and objets d'art are fakes or are not worth the asking price (usually both). Unless you are an expert or are happy to have a fake, do not buy these things.

2

Planning Your Trip to China

by Christopher D. Winnan

Travel in China isn't as hard as you may think: If you can manage Paris without speaking French, you can manage Beijing without Mandarin. Tens of thousands of visitors travel in China independently each year, making their arrangements as they go, with nothing more than a guidebook and a phrase book to help them. You can certainly arrange various levels of assistance, either upon arrival or from home, but you can also travel just as freely as you would elsewhere, perhaps using agents to get your tickets, and picking up the odd day tour.

But whether you plan to travel at random, with a preplanned, prebooked route, or with a fully escorted tour, it's *vital* that you read this chapter carefully. The way you're used to traveling, even in many other developing nations, doesn't apply in China. Much of the advice on travel in China is far from wise. What's good advice in the rest of the world can be the worst advice in China, and without absorbing what's below, some of the rest of this guide may seem inscrutable.

So put down your preconceptions and read on.

1 The Regions in Brief

BEIJING, TIANJIN & HEBEI

While there's much talk of getting to the Three Gorges on the Yangzi River before the area's partial disappearance, the real urgency is to see what little is left of old Beijing, with its ancient housing and original Ming dynasty street plan. Thanks to new construction, whole city blocks can vanish at once, sometimes taking ancient, long-forgotten temples with them.

But while Beijing suffers from being communism's showpiece for the outside world and a victim of ersatz modernization, it still has far more to offer than several other Chinese cities put together, including some of China's most extravagant monuments, such as the **Forbidden City.** In addition, there's easy access to the surrounding province of **Hebei** with its sinuous sections of the **Great Wall** and vast **tomb complexes.**

THE NORTHEAST

Even if the Chinese no longer believe civilization ends at the Great Wall, most tourists still do. The frigid lands to the Northeast, once known as Tartary or Manchuria, represent one of the least-visited and most challenging regions in China, and its last great travel frontier.

Despite industrialization, the provinces of **Liaoning, Jilin,** and **Heilong Jiang,** and the northern section of **Inner Mongolia,** still claim China's largest **natural forest,** its most **pristine grasslands,** and one of its most celebrated **lakes (Tian Chi).** You'll also find architectural remnants of the last 350 years—early **Qing palaces and tombs,** incongruous **Russian cupolas,** and eerie structures left over from Japan's wartime occupation.

AROUND THE YELLOW RIVER

As covered in this book, this region comprises an area of northern China that includes **Shanxi, Ningxia,** parts of **Shaanxi,** and **Inner Mongolia,** roughly following the central loop of the Yellow River north of Xi'an. One of China's "cradles of civilization," the area is home to most of the country's oldest surviving **timber-frame buildings,** its oldest carved **Buddhist grottoes,** and **Pingyao,** one of its best-preserved **walled cities.**

THE SILK ROUTES

From the ancient former capital of **Xi'an,** famed for the modern rediscovery of the **Terra-Cotta Warriors,** trade routes ran in all directions, but most famously (because they were given a clever name in the 19th c.) west and northwest through **Gansu** and **Xinjiang,** and on through the Middle East. Under the control of Tibetan, Mongol, Indo-European, and Turkic peoples more than of Chinese, these regions are still populated with Uighurs, Tajiks, Kazakhs, Tibetans, and others, some in tiny oasis communities on the rim of the **Taklamakan Desert,** which seem completely remote from China. The Silk Routes are littered with alien monuments and tombs, and with magnificent cave-temple sights such as **Dunhuang,** which demonstrate China's import of foreign religions and aesthetics as much as the wealth generated by its exports of silk.

EASTERN CENTRAL CHINA

Eastern central China, between the Yellow River (Huang He) and the Yangzi River (Chang Jiang), is an area covering the provinces of **Henan, Shandong, Jiangsu,** and **Anhui.** Chinese culture developed and flourished with little outside influence here. **Luoyang** was the capital of nine dynasties, **Kaifeng** capital of six, and **Nanjing** capital of eight. The hometown of China's most important philosopher, Confucius, is here, as are

several of China's holiest mountains, notably **Tai Shan** and **Huang Shan,** as well as that watery equivalent of the Great Wall, the **Grand Canal.**

SHANGHAI

Shanghai is the city China boosters love to cite as representing the country as a whole, but it in fact represents nothing except itself—the country's wealthiest city, and with (if government figures are to be believed) the highest per-capita income. Look closer and you'll see many of its shiny new towers are incomplete or unoccupied. But the sweep of 19th- and early-20th-century architecture along **The Bund,** which looks as if the town halls of two dozen provincial British cities have been transported to a more exotic setting, and the maze of Art Deco masterpieces in the **French Concession** behind the Bund, make Shanghai the mainland's top East-meets-West destination, with the restaurants and a more relaxed and open-minded atmosphere to match. Nearby **Hangzhou** and **Suzhou** offer some of China's most famous scenery.

THE SOUTHEAST

South of Shanghai and the Yangzi River, the coastal provinces of **Zhejiang, Fujian,** and **Guangdong** have always been China's most outward looking. These areas, which boomed under the relatively open Tang dynasty and which were forced to reopen as "treaty ports" by the guns of the first multinationals in the 19th century, are also those most industrialized under the current "reform and opening" policy. Remembering that this is a guide for travelers rather than businesspeople, we have focused on areas of great natural beauty such as **Anji** and **Yandangshan,** rather than so called "developed" coastal cities where modern multinationals have offloaded their most substandard industrial plants and their most polluting industries. A bit inland, the impoverished pottery-producing province of **Jiangxi** shows the two-speed nature of China's growth.

HONG KONG & MACAU

Two sets of pencil-slim towers jostle for position on either side of a harbor, close as bristles on a brush. Between them, ponderous oceangoing vessels slide past puttering junks, and century-old ferries waddle and weave across their paths. The mixture of Asia's finest hotels, territory-wide duty-free shopping, incense-filled working temples, and British double-decker buses makes this city-state worth flying to Asia to see in its own right. **Macau,** a little bit of misplaced Mediterranean, is a short ferry ride away.

THE SOUTHWEST

Encompassing the provinces of **Yunnan, Guizhou, Guangxi,** and **Hainan Island,** this region is home to some of China's most spectacular mountain scenery and three of Asia's mightiest rivers, resulting in some of the most breathtaking gorges and lush river valleys in the country.

Even more appealing: This region is easily the most ethnically diverse in China. Twenty-six of China's 56 officially recognized ethnic groups can be found in the southwest, from the Mosu in **Lugu Lake** to the Dai in **Xishuangbanna,** from the Miao around **Kaili** to the Dong in **San Jiang,** each with different architecture, dress, traditions, and colorful festivals.

THE YANGZI RIVER

In addition to shared borders, the land-locked provinces of **Sichuan, Hubei,** and **Hunan** and the municipality of **Chongqing** have in common the world's third-longest river, the Chang Jiang ("Long River," aka Yangzi or Yangtze). The home of five holy Buddhist and/or Daoist mountains, this area contains some of China's most beautiful scenery, particularly in northern Sichuan and northern Hunan.

Sichuan deserves exploration using **Chengdu** as a base, and the Hunan should be explored from **Changsha.** If you're taking the **Three Gorges cruise** (available indefinitely despite what you may have heard), try to at least leave yourself a few days on either end to explore **Chongqing** and **Wuhan.** And a day trip from Chongqing to the Buddhist grottoes at **Dazu** is well worth the time.

THE TIBETAN WORLD

The Tibetan plateau is roughly the size of western Europe, with an average elevation of 4,700m (15,400 ft.). Ringed by vast mountain ranges such as the **Kunlun range** to the north and the **Himalayas,** the region offers towering scenic splendors as well as some of the richest minority culture within modern China's borders. **Lhasa,** former seat of the Dalai Lamas, is dominated physically by the vast **Potala Palace,** and emotionally by the fervor of the pilgrims to the **Jokhang Temple.** Fewer than half of the world's Tibetans now live in what is called Tibet—much Tibetan territory has now been allocated to neighboring Chinese provinces, particularly **Qinghai,** where the authorities are less watchful and the atmosphere in both monasteries and on the streets more relaxed.

2 Visitor Information & Maps

PLANNING YOUR TRIP

The mainland travel industry is, in general, a quagmire of deception, and provides no truly reliable official sources of information either within China or via its overseas operations. The branches of the China National Tourism Administration in foreign countries are called China National Tourist Offices. Nominally non-profit, they used to be little more than agents for the state-owned China International Travel Service (CITS), but they now offer links to a variety of operators. Don't expect them to be accurate about even the most basic visa or Customs regulations, or to update their websites, which sometimes give conflicting information and can't even get the names of tour operators right. **Hong Kong** and **Macau** have their own tourism agencies, which are vastly more professional. The Hong Kong Tourism Board is a source of endless quantities of free literature, maps, and helpful advice, and its website is comprehensive, accurate, and up-to-date. The Macau Government Tourism Office is the same on a smaller scale.

CHINA NATIONAL TOURIST OFFICE (www.cnto.org)

In the **United States**   New York office: 350 Fifth Ave., Suite 6413, Empire State Building, New York, NY 10118 (© **212/ 760-8218;** fax 212/760-8809; ny@cnto. gov.cn). California office: 600 W. Broadway, Suite 320, Glendale, CA 91204 (© **818/545-7507;** fax 818/545-7506; la@cnto.gov.cn).

In **Canada**   480 University Ave., Suite 806, Toronto, ON M5G 1V2 (© **416/ 599-6636;** fax 416/599-6382; www. tourismchina-ca.com).

In the **U.K.**   4 Glentworth St., London NW1 5PG (© **020/7935-9787;** fax 020/ 7487-5842; london@cnta.gov.cn).

In **Australia**   Level 19, 44 Market St., Sydney, NSW 2000 (© **02/9299-4057;** fax 02/9290-1958; sydney@cnta.gov.cn).

HONG KONG TOURISM BOARD (www.discoverhongkong.com)

In the **United States**   New York office: 115 E. 54th St., 2nd floor, New York, NY 10022-4512 (© **212/421-3382;** fax 212/ 421-8428; nycwwo@hktb.com). California office: 10940 Wilshire Blvd., Suite 2050, Los Angeles, CA 90024-3915 (© **310/208-4582;** fax 310/208-2398; jeffs@hktb.com).

In **Canada**   3rd floor, 9 Temperance St., Toronto, ON M5H 1Y6 (© **416/366-2389;** fax 416/366-1098; yyzwwo@ hktb.com).

In the **U.K.**   6 Grafton St., London W1S 4EQ (© **020/7533-7100;** fax 020/ 7533-7111; lonwwo@hktb.com).

In **Australia**   Level 4, Hong Kong House, 80 Druitt St., Sydney, NSW 2000 (© **02/9283-3083;** fax 02/9283-3383; sydwwo@hktb.com).

MACAU GOVERNMENT TOURISM OFFICE (www.macautourism.gov.mo)

In the **United States**   501 Fifth Ave., Suite 1101, New York, NY 10017 (© **646/277-0690;** fax 646/366-8170; macau@myriadmarketing.com).

In the **U.K.**   11 Blades Court, 121 Deodar Rd., London SW15 2NU (© **44/ 20-8877-4517;** fax 44/20-8874-4219; sharon@representationplus.co.uk).

In **Australia**   Level 17, Town Hall House, 456 Kent St., Sydney, NSW 2000 (© **02/9264-1488;** fax 02/9267-7717; macau@worldtradetravel.com).

In **New Zealand**   Level 5, Ballantyne House, 101 Customs St. E., P.O. Box 3779, Auckland (© **09/308-5206;** fax 09/308-5207; macau@aviationand tourism.co.nz).

FINDING MAPS

Purchasing city maps as you go is absolutely essential, even though few are bilingual. These are available at bus and railway stations and at airports for under ¥5 (65¢/30p). Get your hotel staff to circle the characters of your hotel and the main sights you plan to see, and note which is which. Now you can jump in a taxi at any point, show the driver the characters for where you want to go, and keep an eye on the route he takes. Map keys in this book have Chinese characters for the same purpose, as do "Selected Destinations by City" in appendix A. The tourist boards of **Hong Kong** and **Macau** are liberal with bilingual and trilingual free maps.

Outside of China good-quality maps are more difficult to find. One good source is International Travel Maps in Vancouver, B.C., Canada (© **604/879-3621;** www.itmb.co). Their China map has a scale of 1:4,000,000, costs around

$10, and comes highly recommended. Characters are in both English and Chinese and everything is large and clearly marked. It is very detailed, and even small towns are shown.

I also like the maps produced by Nelles Verlag (www.nelles-verlag.de), which come in a set of four (northeast, north, central, and southern China), are English only and have a scale of 1:1,500,00, each one costing around $5 to $10.

3 Entry Requirements & Customs

PASSPORTS

For information on how to get a passport, go to "Passports" in the "Fast Facts: China" section, later in this chapter—the websites listed provide downloadable passport applications as well as the current fees for processing passport applications. For an up-to-date, country-by-country listing of passport requirements around the world, go to the "Foreign Entry Requirement" Web page of the U. S. State Department at http://travel.state.gov.

VISAS

MAINLAND CHINA

All visitors to mainland China must acquire a **visa** in advance. Visas are generally not granted at the border. Visitors to mainland China must have a valid **passport** with at least 6 months' validity and two blank pages remaining. Visa applications typically take 3 to 5 working days to process, although this can be sped up to as little as 1 day if you apply in person and pay a fee. "L" (tourist) visas are valid for between 1 and 3 months. Usually 1 month is granted unless you request more, which you may or may not get according to events in China at the time. Double-entry tourist visas are also available.

You should apply to your nearest consulate. It varies, but typically your visit must *begin* within 90 days of the date of issue. Note that although postal addresses

are given below, some consulates (including all those in the U.S. and Canada) will only accept applications in person, and applications by post or courier must go through an agent, with further fees to be paid. Telephone numbers are given, but many systems are automated, and getting a human to speak to can be next to impossible; faxes and e-mail rarely get a reply, and websites are often out of date.

Applying for a visa requires completion of an application form that can be downloaded from many consular websites or acquired by mail. Temporary restrictions may be placed, sometimes for years at a time, on areas where there is unrest, and a further permit may be required. This is currently the case with Tibet where, until recently, travelers were required to form groups before entering the region, and to pay a huge price for a tour (but they were not required to actually join it on arrival). For details of Tibet permits, see chapter 14. Do not mention Tibet or Xinjiang on your visa application, or it may be turned down.

Some consulates indicate that sight of an airline ticket or itinerary is required, or that you give proof of sufficient funds, or that you must be traveling with a group, while they happily carry on business with individuals who have none of this supporting documentation. Such statements provide a face-saving excuse for refusing a visa should there be unrest or political difficulties, or should Tibet or Xinjiang appear on the application.

One passport photograph is required, as well as one for any child traveling on a parent's passport.

The visa fees quoted below by country are the current rates for *nationals of that country*, and can change at any time. U.S. citizens applying for a double-entry visa in the U.K., for instance, are charged more than British citizens. Regulations may also vary. In addition to the visa fees quoted, there may be supplementary fees for postage, and higher fees can often be paid for speedier service. Payment must always be in cash or by money order.

Once you're inside China, *single-entry tourist visas only* can usually be extended once for a maximum of 30 days at the Aliens Entry-Exit department of the Public Security Bureau (PSB) in most towns and cities. U.S. citizens pay ¥125 ($16), U.K. citizens ¥160 (£12), Canadians ¥165 (C$28), and Australians ¥100 (A$18).

Extensions within China now typically take 5 working days to process, although you may sometimes be able to cajole offices into faster service.

Consulates in the United States
Single-entry visas are $50; double-entry $75. Visit **www.china-embassy.org**, which has links to all U.S. consular sites and a downloadable application form. Applications must be delivered and collected by hand, or sent via a visa agency.

Consulates in Canada
Single-entry visas are C$50; double-entry C$75. Visit **www.chinaembassycanada. org** for an application form. Applications must be delivered and collected by hand, or sent via a visa agency.

Consulates in the United Kingdom
Single-entry visas are £30; double-entry £45. There's a supplementary charge of £20 for each package dealt with by mail.

Visit **www.chinese-embassy.org.uk** for an application.

Consulates in Australia
Single-entry visas are A$30; double-entry A$45. Add A$10 per package dealt with by mail or courier, and a prepaid return envelope.

Consulates in New Zealand
Single-entry visas are NZ$60; double-entry NZ$90. Add NZ$15 per package dealt with by mail or courier, and a pre-paid return envelope. Go to www.china consulate.org.nz for more information.

Consulates Elsewhere
A complete list of all Chinese embassies and consulates can be found at the Chinese foreign ministry's website: www. fmprc.gov.cn/eng (or various mirror sites around the world). Click on "Missions Overseas."

Buying Visas in Countries Bordering China
Note that the Chinese Consulate in Kathmandu, Nepal, will not sell visas to individual travelers wanting to enter Tibet overland, or they may stamp the visa to prohibit overland entry via the Friendship Highway. The consulate in Bishkek, Kyrgyzstan, will usually refuse visas to those not holding a fax or telex from a Chinese state-registered travel agency, or they will stamp the visa to prohibit overland entry via the Torugart Pass. Obtaining visas at the consulate in Almaty can also sometimes be difficult for nonresidents of Kazakhstan.

Buying Visas in Hong Kong
The easiest place to apply for a mainland visa is Hong Kong, where there are several China visa options. Single-entry tourist "L" visas valid for 3 months are easily obtainable, as is the (unextendable) double-entry version. Multiple-entry "F" visas are also easy to obtain via visa agents and without the letter of invitation required to obtain them at home. Single-entry visas

bought through HK agents typically cost HK$250 to HK$350 (US$25–US$30/ £12.50–£15), multiple-entry "F" visas around HK$600 (US$65/£33). Expect fees of two or three times this amount for British and American citizens. Offices located just a few minutes' walk from the main tourist areas charge less still. See chapter 11, "Hong Kong," for recommendations.

Entering the Mainland from Hong Kong & Macau

It is possible for all but British citizens to buy a permit at the Lo Wu border crossing from Hong Kong to Shenzhen, valid for 72 hours of travel in the Shenzhen Special Economic Zone *only*. According to the Guangzhou PSB, tourist visas can be purchased on arrival at Guangzhou East station by direct express railway from Hong Kong, but prices are higher than in Hong Kong and the choice of options is considerably less. It is possible to buy a 3-month "L" visa or 6-month "F" visa from

a branch of China Travel Service on the mainland side of the crossing from Macau to Zhuhai. See chapter 11 for more details.

HONG KONG VISAS

U.S., Canadian, Australian, and New Zealand citizens, and those of most other developed nations, are granted 90-day stays free on arrival. British citizens are granted 180 days. Passports should be valid for 1 month longer than the planned return date. In theory, proof of sufficient funds and an onward ticket may be demanded, but this request is almost unheard of.

MACAU VISAS

U.S., Canadian, Australian, and New Zealand citizens are granted 30-day stays free on arrival. British and most other E.U. nationals can stay up to 90 days without a visa. Passports should have at least 30 days of remaining validity upon your arrival.

4 When to Go

Weather details are given below, but a far bigger factor in your calculations should be the movement of domestic tourists who, during the longer public holidays, take to the road in the tens or even hundreds of millions, crowding all forms of transportation, booking out hotels, and turning even the quietest tourist sights into litter-strewn bedlam.

PEAK TRAVEL SEASONS

Chinese New Year (Spring Festival): Like many Chinese festivals, this one operates on the lunar calendar. Solar equivalents for the next few years are February 6, 2008; February 25, 2009; and February 13, 2010. The effects of this holiday are felt from 2 weeks before the date until 2 weeks after, when anyone who's away from home attempts to get back, including an estimated 150 million migrant workers. Although tens of thousands of extra bus

and train services are added, tickets for land transport are very difficult to get, and can command high prices on the black market (official prices also rise on some routes, and on ferries between Hong Kong and the mainland). Air tickets are usually obtainable and may even still be discounted. In the few days immediately around the new year, traffic on long-distance rail and bus services may be light, but local services may dry up altogether. Most tourist sights stay open, although some shut on the holiday itself or have limited holiday hours.

Labor Day & National Day: In a policy known as "holiday economics," the May 1 and October 1 holidays have now been expanded to 7 days each (including one weekend). These two holidays now mark the beginning and end of the domestic travel season, and mark the twin peaks of leisure travel, with the remainder of May, early June, and September also busy. Most Chinese avoid traveling in the summer except to cooler high ground or an offshore island, usually on a weekend. The exact dates of each holiday are not given out until around 2 weeks before each takes place, but it's best, if you're traveling independently, to arrive at a larger destination before the holiday starts, and move on in the middle or after the end. The disposable income to fund travel is more often found in larger cities, so these tend to become quieter, easier to get around, and less polluted. Noted tourist destinations around the country will be extremely busy, however. In **Hong Kong** and **Macau,** these are only 1- or 2-day holidays introduced in 1997 and 1999 respectively.

University Holidays: Exact term dates are rarely announced far in advance, but train tickets can be difficult to obtain as the student populace moves between home and college. Terms run for 18 weeks with 2 weeks of exams, from the beginning of September to just before Spring Festival, and from just after the Spring Festival to the end of June.

Local Difficulties: China's main international trade fair occupies the last 2 weeks of April and October, and drives up hotel prices in **Guangzhou,** where it's held, and as far away as Hong Kong. In the summer, pleasant temperatures in the **Northeast** (slightly cooler than the rest of China) draw students on summer vacation (which makes train tickets hard to acquire), as well as large Chinese tour groups; it may not be the best time for your visit. The northeast's Dalian is also overbooked during the International Fashion Festival in September (see later in this chapter). Across China, **midweek travel** is always better than weekend travel, particularly true at destinations easily tackled in a weekend, such as Wutai

Shan and Pingyao (see chapter 6, "Along the Yellow River"). Government-imposed travel restrictions in **Tibet** tend to increase around the Monlam Festival (sometime mid-Jan to mid-Feb), Saka Dawa Festival (mid-May to mid-June), and around the present Dalai Lama's birthday (July 6). The border crossing between Hong Kong and the mainland at **Lo Wu** can take a couple of hours at holiday periods.

CLIMATE

China is the third-biggest country in the world, with the second-lowest inland depression (Turpan) and some of its highest peaks (Everest and K2 are both partly in China). Its far northeast shares the same weather patterns as Siberia, and its far southwest the same subtropical climate as northern Thailand.

In the **north,** early spring and late autumn are the best times to travel, both offering warm, dry days and cool, dry evenings. During March and April winds blow away the pollution but sometimes bring sand from the Gobi and topsoil from high ground to the northeast of Beijing, increasingly desiccated by the mismanagement of water resources. The sky can at times turn a vivid yellow.

In the **south,** November to February brings a welcome drop both in temperature and in all-pervasive humidity, although in Hong Kong all public interiors and many private houses are air-conditioned year-round.

Central China has some of the country's most searing summer temperatures and bitterest winters, but it also escapes the worst of the humidity. **Tibet** has springlike days in the summer but far milder winters than most people expect, at least in Lhasa, made endurable by the dryness of the climate. The **northwest** has perhaps the greatest range of temperatures, with severe summers and winters alike, but it is also largely dry.

Average Temperature (Celsius/Fahrenheit)

	Beijing	Shanghai	Hong Kong	Xi'an	Lhasa
Jan	–3/26	4/40	16/62	0/32	–2/28
Feb	0/31	5/42	17/63	2/35	0/33
Mar	6/43	8/48	19/67	8/48	3/38
Apr	13/57	15/59	22/73	14/57	8/47
May	20/68	20/68	26/79	19/66	11/53
June	24/76	23/75	28/83	25/77	15/60
July	26/79	28/83	29/85	27/80	15/60
Aug	25/77	27/82	29/85	25/77	14/59
Sept	20/69	23/75	28/83	19/66	13/56
Oct	13/57	18/66	26/79	14/57	8/48
Nov	5/41	12/55	22/72	7/44	2/37
Dec	–1/30	6/44	18/65	1/33	–1/30

Average Precipitation (centimeters/inches)

	Beijing	Shanghai	Hong Kong	Xi'an	Lhasa
Jan	0/0.2	4/1.8	2/1.1	0/0.3	0/0.1
Feb	0/0.2	6/2.4	4/1.7	1/0.4	1/0.5
Mar	0/0.3	8/3.3	7/2.9	2/0.9	0/0.3
Apr	1/0.7	9/3.7	13/5.5	4/1.8	0/0.2
May	3/1.3	10/4.1	28/11.2	6/2.4	2/1
June	7/3.1	17/6.8	39/15.7	5/2.1	6/2.5
July	22/8.8	14/5.7	36/14.3	9/3.8	12/4.8
Aug	17/6.7	13/5.4	37/14.8	8/3.4	8/3.5
Sept	5/2.3	13/5.4	29/11.7	10/4.2	6/2.6
Oct	1/0.7	6/2.7	11/4.7	5/2.3	1/0.5
Nov	1/0.4	5/2.1	3/1.5	2/1	0/0.1
Dec	0/0.1	3/1.5	2/1	0/0.2	0/0

HOLIDAYS

Public holidays and their effects vary widely between mainland China and the two Special Administrative Regions, Hong Kong and Macau.

Mainland China

A few years ago the Chinese were finally granted a 2-day weekend. Offices close, but stores, restaurants, post offices, transportation, sights and, in some areas, banks, all operate the same services 7 days a week. Most sights, shops, and restaurants are open on public holidays, but offices and anything government-related take as much time off as they can. Although China switched to the Gregorian calendar in 1911, some public holidays (and many festivals—see below) are based on a lunar cycle, their solar dates varying from year to year. Holidays are **New Year's Day** (Jan 1), **Spring Festival** (Chinese New Year and the 2 days following it—see "Peak Travel Seasons," above, for exact dates in coming years), **Labor Day** (May 1 plus up to 4 more weekdays and a weekend), **National Day** (Oct 1 plus extra days, as with Labor Day, above).

Hong Kong

Saturday is officially a working day in Hong Kong, although many offices take the day off or only open for reduced hours. Weekend ferry sailings and other transport may vary, particularly on Sunday, when many shops are closed and opening hours for attractions may also vary. Hong Kong gets many British holidays, traditional Chinese holidays, plus modern political ones added after 1997, but in shorter forms. Banks, schools, offices, and government departments are all closed on these dates, as are many museums: **New Year's Day** (Jan 1), **Lunar New Year's Day** (for the mainland Spring Festival, but in Hong Kong the day itself plus 2 more, and an extra Fri or Mon if 1 day falls on a Sun); **Ching Ming Festival** (Apr 5), **Good Friday** (usually early Apr, plus the following Sat and **Easter Monday**), **Labor Day** (May 1), **Buddha's Birthday** (1 day in May), **Tuen Ng** (Dragon Boat Festival, 1 day in June), **Hong Kong SAR Establishment Day** (July 1), **Mid-Autumn Festival** (1 day in Sept, usually moved to the nearest Fri or Mon to make a long weekend), **National Day** (Oct 1), **Chung Yeung Festival** (1 day in Oct), **Christmas Day** and **Boxing Day** (Dec 25, and the next weekday if the 26th is a Sat or Sun).

Macau

Macau has the same holidays as Hong Kong except for SAR Establishment Day, and with similar consequences, but with the following variations: **National Day** is 2 days (Oct 1–2), **All Souls' Day** (Nov 2), **Feast of the Immaculate Conception** (Dec 8), **Macau SAR Establishment Day** (Dec 20), **Winter Solstice** (Dec 22), and **Christmas Eve** and **Christmas Day** (Dec 24–25).

CHINA CALENDAR OF EVENTS

China's festivals follow the traditional lunar calendar, and to increase confusion, some minority calendars operate according to different traditions. For conversion to solar/Gregorian calendar dates, try the websites www.est-direct.com/china/lunarcal.php or www.mandarintools.com.

The Chinese tourism industry is increasingly inventing festivals to try to boost business. Unless indicated below, be wary of any festival with the word *tourism* in its name, for instance.

For an exhaustive list of events beyond those listed here, check http://events.frommers.com, where you'll find a searchable, up-to-the-minute roster of what's happening in cities all over the world.

January

Spring Festival (Chun Jie), or Chinese New Year, is still the occasion for large lion dances and other celebrations in Hong Kong, Macau, and Chinatowns worldwide, but in mainland China it's mainly a time for returning home to feast. Fireworks are now banned in larger cities. Temple fairs have been revived in Beijing, but are mostly fairly low-key shopping opportunities. But in the countryside there's been a gradual revival of stilt-walking and masked processions. Spring Festival is on the day of the first new moon after January 21, and can be no later than February 20.

Monlam Festival is held throughout the Tibetan world (including at Xia He and Langmu Si). Monasteries are open to all, and there are religious dancing, the offering of *torma* (butter sculptures), and the "sunning of the Buddha" when a silk painting *(thangka)* is consecrated and becomes the living Buddha in the minds of believers. Typically, the festival culminates in the parading of the Maitreya Buddha through the town. Fourth to 16th days of the first lunar month (Feb 10–22, 2008; Jan 29–Feb 11, 2009). Check dates with Qinghai Mountaineering Association (© 0971/823-8922). In Tibet check with **FIT** (© 0891/634-4397; www.tibet-travel.com).

Kurban Bairam (Gu'erbang Jie), also known as the Festival of Sacrifice, is celebrated by Muslims throughout China. It marks the willingness of the prophet Abraham to sacrifice everything to God, even his son Ishmael. Celebrations in Kashgar involve feats of tightrope-walking in the main square and wild dancing outside the Idkah Mosque. The 4-day festival is held 70 days after the breaking of the fast of Ramadan, on the 10th day of the 12th month (Dhul-Hijjah) in the Islamic calendar. It falls on November 27, 2008, and annually shifts backward by 12 days.

February

The **Lantern Festival (Deng Jie)** perhaps reached its peak in the late Qing dynasty, when temples, stores, and other public places were hung with fantastically shaped and decorated lanterns, some with figures animated by ingenious mechanisms involving the flow of sand. People paraded through the streets with lightweight lanterns in the shapes of fish, sheep, and so on, and hung lanterns outside their houses, often decorated with riddles. There are some signs of the festival's revival, including at Pingyao in Shanxi Province, and at Quanzhou in Fujian. The festival always falls 15 days after Spring Festival.

March

Hong Kong Sevens Rugby Tournament, Hong Kong. Known as "The Sevens," this is one of Hong Kong's most popular and one of Asia's largest sporting events, with more than 20 teams from around the world competing for the Cup Championship. A 3-day pass costs HK$750 (US$97/£50). Contact the **Hong Kong Rugby Football Union** at © 852/2504 8311 or www.hksevens.com.hk. Fourth weekend in March.

April

Tomb-Sweeping Festival (Qingming) is still a public holiday in Hong Kong and Macau, frequently observed in Chinese communities overseas, and celebrated in more rural areas of China, as a family outing on a free day near the festival date. It's a day to honor ancestors by visiting and tidying their graves and making offerings of snacks and alcohol. April 3 to April 5 annually.

Sisters' Meal Festival (Zimeifan Jie), Taijiang, Shidong (Guizhou). Celebrated with *lusheng* (wind-instrument music) dancing and antiphonal singing, this is one of the prime occasions for young Miao men and women to socialize and find marriage partners. Elaborately dressed Miao women prepare packets of berry-stained glutinous rice to present to suitors. For exact dates, check with **CITS** Kaili (© **0855/822-2506;** www.qdncits.com). Fifteenth day of the third lunar month (usually Apr).

Water-Splashing Festival (Poshui Jie), Jinghong, Xishuangbanna. Extremely popular with Chinese tourists, the festive Dai New Year is ushered in with a large market on the first day, dragon-boat races on the second, and copious amounts of water-splashing on the third. Be prepared to get doused, but take heart because the wetter you are, the more luck you'll have. April 13 to April 15.

Luoyang Peony Festival, Luoyang. Over 300 varieties of China's best peonies, first cultivated in Luoyang 1,400 years ago, are on display at the Wangcheng Park (Wangcheng Gongyuan), which is awash in a riot of colors. April 15 to April 25.

Weifang International Kite Festival, Weifang. The kite capital of the world hosts the largest kite-flying gala in China, as hundreds of thousands of kite lovers from around the world arrive for several days of competition and demonstrations. April 19.

Hong Kong International Film Festival, Hong Kong. Over 200 films from more than 40 countries are featured at this 2-week event. Tickets cost HK$55 (US$7.15/£3.60). For more information, call ℂ **852/2734 2903** or 852/2734 9009; or visit www.hkiff. org.hk. Two weeks in April.

Sanyue Jie (Third Month Fair), Dali. This biggest festival of the Bai people had its origins over 1,000 years ago when Buddhist monks and adherents gathered to celebrate the appearance of Guanyin (the Goddess of Mercy) to the Bai. Today's festival has become more secular as the Bai and other minorities from elsewhere in Yunnan gather in the foothills of the Green Mountains (Cang Shan) for 5 days and nights of singing, dancing, wrestling, horse racing, and large-scale trading. Ask **CITS** for more information on the precise dates (ℂ **0872/219-1985**). Fifteenth day of the third lunar month (usually mid-Apr or early May).

Cheung Chau Bun Festival, Hong Kong. This weeklong affair on Cheung Chau island is thought to appease restless ghosts and spirits. Originally held to placate the unfortunate souls of those murdered by pirates, it features a street parade of lions and dragons and Chinese opera, as well as floats with children seemingly suspended in the air, held up by cleverly concealed wires. The end of the festival is heralded by three bun-covered scaffolds erected in front of the Pak Tai Temple. These buns supposedly bring good luck to those who receive them. **HKTB** organizes tours of the parade; call ℂ **852/ 2508 1234.** Usually late April or early May, but the exact date is chosen by divination.

May

Saka Dawa festival is held throughout the Tibetan world, celebrating the Buddha passing away and thus attaining nirvana. *Koras* (circuits) of holy lakes, mountains, and buildings are undertaken by the faithful. See the contact info for the Monlam Festival (Jan), above. Eighth to 15th days of the fourth lunar month (May 12–19, 2008; May 2–9, 2009).

Western Journey Festival (Xiqian Jie) marks the day in 1764 when the Qianlong emperor forced the Xibo people to move from their homeland in Manchuria to Qapqal County (southwest of Yining). Celebrations are marked by the devouring of a whole sheep cooked with coriander, preserved vegetables, and onions. Wrestling, horse riding, and archery contests evoke the Xibo's warrior ancestry. The festival is held on the 18th day of the fourth lunar month (late May to mid-June).

June

Dragon Boat Festival (Longzhou Jie), Shidong. With over 40,000 celebrants, this Miao minority festival, which bears no relation to the Han Dragon Boat Festival, commemorates the killing of a dragon whose body was divided among several Miao villages. Over the course of 3 days, dragon boat races are held in Shidong, Pingzhai, and Tanglong. For exact dates, check with **CITS** Kaili (ℂ **0855/822-2506;** www.qdncits.com). Twenty-fourth to 27th day of the fifth lunar month (usually June or early July).

Dragon Boat Races (Tuen Ng Festival), Hong Kong. Races of long, narrow boats, gaily painted and powered by oarsmen who row to the beat of drums, originated in ancient China, where legend held that Qu Yuan, an imperial adviser, drowned himself in a Hunan river to protest government corruption. His faithful followers, wishing to recover his body, supposedly raced out into the river in boats, beating their paddles on the surface of the water and throwing rice to distract water creatures from his body. There are two different races: The biggest is an international competition with 30 teams, held along the waterfront in Tsim Sha Tsui East; the following weekend, approximately 500 local Hong Kong teams compete, with races held at Stanley, Aberdeen, Chai Wan, Yau Ma Tei, Tai Po, and outlying islands. On the **mainland**, the festival is still celebrated at places connected with Qu Yuan, such as Zigui, Yichang, and Changsha. Contact **HKTB** at ℂ **852/2508 1234**. Fifth day of the fifth month (June 8, 2008; May 28, 2009) for international races.

July

Jyekundo Horse Festival, south of Yushu, Qinghai. Khampa nomads gather for a spectacular 10-day celebration involving racing, exhibitions of equestrian skill, and horse trading. Starts on July 25.

International Motorcycle Tourism Festival, Yinchuan. People from China and abroad ride/transport their motorcycles to Yinchuan. Motorcycle stunts and contests, exhibitions, and tourism activities (beware the last) make up the core activities. Visit www.ycmtf.org/english/about_us.htm for details. Held between June and August.

Lurol Festival, Tongren (Repkong). This marks the Sino-Tibetan peace treaty, signed in A.D. 822, with fertility dances and body piercing in honor of a local mountain deity, and has a pagan feel. Check with **Qinghai Mountaineering Association,** ℂ **0971/823-8922**. The 16th day of the sixth lunar month (July 18, 2008; July 8, 2009).

August

Naadam, across Inner Mongolia, including Hohhot (at the racetrack, Saima Chang, and the Hulun Buir Grasslands, outside Manzhouli). The festival features Mongolian wrestling, archery, and horse and camel racing, and occurs when the grasslands turn green. That's usually mid-August, but can be as early as July. Dates differ from place to place, and they don't

coincide with (the People's Republic of) Mongolia's Naadam festival, which is tied to their National Day and always occurs from July 11 to July 13. For exact locations and dates outside Manzhouli, call **CITS** (ℂ **0470/622-2988**).

Qingdao International Beer Festival, Qingdao. Over a million visitors descend on this seaside resort for its famous annual Bavarian bacchanal, which features everything from beer tasting and drinking contests for adults, to amusement-park rides for kids. Last 2 weeks of August (proceeding to the first Sun in Sept).

September

Formula One Racing, Shanghai. Every fall until 2010, motor-sport fans can catch Formula One drivers zooming around a state-of-the-art track in the Shanghai suburb of Anting. September to October.

International Shaolin Martial Arts Festival, Song Shan. Some patience may be necessary to negotiate the crowds of pugilists and Bruce Lee wannabes who show up to trade fists and demonstrate some truly jaw-dropping, gravity-defying martial arts skills. For details, call **CITS** (ℂ **0371/288-3442**). Second week of September.

Mid-Autumn Festival (Tuanyuan Jie) is celebrated in Hong Kong, Macau, and Chinese communities overseas, but in mainland China the last remnant of the festival is the giving and eating of *yuebing* (moon cakes), circular pies with sweet and extremely fattening fillings. Traditionally it's a time to sit and read poetry under the full moon, but pollution in many areas has made the moon largely invisible. The 15th day of the eighth lunar month (usually Sept).

International Fashion Festival, Dalian. China's most famous fashion event is the

Dalian Guoji Fuzhuang Jie. The 2-week gathering of mostly Asian garment producers offers an opening parade, a series of glamorous fashion shows held in the city's best hotels, and the sight of leggy models strutting downtown streets, making it worthwhile for nonindustry visitors, too. Mid-September.

Confucius's Birthday, Qufu. China's Great Sage is honored with parades, exhibitions, and musical and dance performances that reenact some of the rites mentioned in the *Analects (Lun Yu)*. If you wish to stay over during this time, book your hotel well in advance; decent accommodations are hard to come by then. September 28.

October

Tsongkapa's birthday is celebrated throughout the Tibetan world. The birthplace of the founder of the Geluk order of Tibetan Buddhism, **Kumbum Ta'er Si** (south of **Xining**) sees the liveliest festival. Religious dancing, mass chanting, and "sunning the Buddha" can be seen. Check with Kumbum (Ta'er Si; 🕾 **0971/223-1357**). Twentieth to 26th days of the ninth lunar month (late Oct to early Nov).

November

International Festival of Folk Songs and Folk Arts, Nanning. Many of Guangxi's minorities, including the Zhuang, the Miao, and the Dong, gather for a colorful week of ethnic song and dance performances that some have criticized as being mere "urban reenactments." A visit to a village to see the minorities in their own environment is highly recommended, but if you're short on time, this explosion of song and dance will have to suffice. Check

with **CITS** (🕾 **0851/690-1660;** fax 0851/690-1600; gzcits@china.com) for exact dates. First half of November.

Rozi Heyt (Rouzi Jie or **Kaizhai Jie)** marks the end of the monthlong Fast of Ramadan, and believers are keen for a feast. Presents are exchanged and alms are given to the poor. In Kazakh and Tajik areas this is often celebrated with a "lamb snatching" competition. A dead lamb is contested by two teams mounted on horses or yaks; the winning team succeeds in spiriting the lamb out of reach of their rivals. The festival is held for 4 days after the first sighting of the new moon in the 10th month (Shawwal) of the Islamic calendar. November 25 in 2007, moving backward by 11 days each year (Nov 1, 2008; Nov 20, 2009).

December

Miao New Year Festival, Xinjiang, Langde (Guizhou). The Miao New Year is celebrated with songs, dances, bullfights, and *lusheng* competitions. For exact dates check with **CITS** Kaili (🕾 **0855/822-2506;** www.qdncits. com). End of the 10th lunar month (usually Dec).

Ice and Snow Festival, Harbin. Every year, tens of thousands of people travel from as far south as Guangdong and brave freezing cold to see the Ha'erbin Bingxue Jie. The city's streets come alive with elaborate ice sculptures equipped with internal wires that blaze to life at night. Most impressive is the Ice and Snow Palace, a life-size frozen-water mansion with multiple levels. From late December to whenever the ice begins to melt (usually late Feb).

5 Getting There

BY PLANE

Although flying is still the most popular way to arrive, many are becoming concerned at the breakneck pace of China's civil aviation growth. China plans to spend $17.4 billion over the next 5 years to build 42 airports, expand 73 more, and move a further 11 because they are already too congested. And this kind of congestion, in addition to China's somewhat dubious air traffic control procedures, has some pundits worried about safety.

Still, Cathay Pacific Airlines, Hong Kong's main international carrier, is effortlessly superior to North American airlines in service standards, and should be the first choice for direct flights to Hong Kong where available.

Note that when you leave the country there's a **departure tax,** currently ¥100 ($13/£6.50), payable only in cash. Departure tax on domestic flights is ¥50 ($6.50/£3.25), but note that flights between the mainland and Hong Kong and Macau are treated *as international flights.* **Hong Kong's** taxes and fees are usually included in ticket prices, but **Macau's** are not. See the chapter on Hong Kong and Macau.

FROM NORTH AMERICA Among North American airlines, **Air Canada** (www.aircanada.com) flies to Beijing and Shanghai, **Northwest Airlines** (www.nwa. com) to Beijing via Tokyo, and **United Airlines** (www.ual.com) to Beijing and Shanghai.

Japan Airlines (www.jal.co.jp) flies via Tokyo to Beijing and Shanghai, but also to Dalian, Qingdao, and Xiamen. **All Nippon Airways** (www.ana.co.jp) flies to Beijing, Dalian, Qingdao, Shanghai, Shenyang, Tianjin, and Xiamen. **Korean Air** (www.koreanair.com) flies via Seoul to Beijing, Qingdao, and Shenyang; and **Asiana Airlines** (us.flyasiana.com) flies via Seoul to Beijing, Changchun, Chengdu, Chongqing, Guangzhou, Guilin, Harbin, Nanjing, Shanghai, Xi'an, and Yantai.

Hong Kong is served by Air Canada (www.aircanada.com), American Airlines (www.aa.com), Continental Airlines (www.continental.com), Delta Airlines (www.delta.com), Northwest Airlines

(www.nwa.com), US Airways (www.us airways.com), and United Airlines (www. ual.com), as well as Hong Kong's Cathay Pacific Airlines (www.cathaypacific.com). Indirect routes are offered by All Nippon Airways (www.ana.co.jp), Asiana Airlines (us.flyasiana.com), China Airlines (via Taipei; www.china-airlines.com), Eva Airways (excellent value, also via Taipei; www.evaair.com.tw), Korean Air (www. koreanair.com), and Japan Airlines (www. jal.co.jp).

FROM THE UNITED KINGDOM British Airways (www.britishairways. com) flies to Beijing and Hong Kong, and Virgin Airlines to Shanghai and Hong Kong (www.virgin-atlantic.com). Cathay Pacific (www.cathaypacific.com) also flies directly to Hong Kong. Fares with KLM Royal Dutch Airlines (www. klm.com) via Amsterdam, with Lufthansa (www.lufthansa.com) via Frankfurt, and with Finnair (www.finnair.com) via Helsinki, can often be considerably cheaper. Fares with eastern European airlines such as Tarom Romanian Air Transport (www.tarom.ru) via Bucharest, and with Aeroflot (www.aeroflot.com) via Moscow, or with Asian airlines such as Pakistan International Airlines (www. piac.com.hk) via Islamabad or Karachi, Malaysia Airlines (www.mas.com.my) via Kuala Lumpur, or Singapore Airlines (www.singaporeair.com) via Singapore, can be cheaper still. There are even more creative route possibilities via Ethiopia or the Persian Gulf States.

FROM AUSTRALIA There's not much choice to the mainland from down under, although Sydney is served by China Eastern and Air China to Beijing and Shanghai, and by Air China and China Southern to Guangzhou. Qantas (www.qantas.com.au) and Air New Zealand (www.airnewzealand.com) fly to Hong Kong, and there are possible indirect routes with Philippine Airlines (www.pal.com.ph) via Manila, and with

Garuda Indonesia (www.garuda-indonesia.com) via Jakarta. Hong Kong's Cathay Pacific (www.cathaypacific.com) flies directly from six Australian cities and Auckland.

BY ROAD

Foreign visitors are not freely permitted to drive their own vehicles into China, unless arrangements are made far in advance with a state-recognized travel agency for a specific itinerary. The agency will provide a guide who will travel in your vehicle and make sure you stick to the itinerary, or who will travel in a second vehicle with a driver. You will have to cover all the (marked-up) costs of guide, driver, and extra vehicle if needed, and of Chinese plates for your vehicle. The agency will book and overcharge you for all your hotels and as many excursions as it can. Forget it.

There are **bus services** between Sost in Pakistan and Kashgar, between Almaty in Kazakhstan and Urumqi, and between Hong Kong and Macau and various points in the mainland. The Torugart

Pass between Bishkek in Kyrgyzstan and Kashgar can be crossed if prearranged transport is waiting to collect you on the Chinese side. It's also possible to cross various borders on foot, including from Mongolia on the route from Ulaan Baatar to Beijing, from Vietnam to Yunnan and Guangxi provinces, from Laos to Yunnan, and from Macau and Hong Kong to Guangdong Province.

BY TRAIN

From Hung Hom station in Kowloon (Hong Kong), expresses run directly to Guangzhou, Beijing, and Shanghai (see www.kcrc.com for schedules and fares). From Almaty in Kazakhstan there are trains to Urumqi in Xinjiang. From Moscow there are trains via Ulaan Baatar in Mongolia to Beijing, and via a more easterly route directly to Harbin in China's northeast and down to Beijing. There are also services which start in Ulaan Baatar and run via Datong to Beijing. There is a service between Beijing and Pyongyang in North Korea.

6 Money & Costs

It's always advisable to bring money in a variety of forms on a vacation: a mix of cash, credit cards, and traveler's checks. You should also exchange enough petty cash to cover airport incidentals, tipping, and transportation to your hotel before you leave home, or withdraw money upon arrival at an airport ATM.

In many international destinations, ATMs offer the best exchange rates. Avoid exchanging money at commercial exchange bureaus and hotels, which often have the highest transaction fees.

CURRENCY
MAINLAND CHINA

For most destinations it's usually a good idea to exchange at least some money before you leave home so you can avoid the less-favorable rates you'll get at airport currency-exchange desks. **Mainland China** is

different. **Yuan,** also known as **RMB (Renminbi,** or "People's Money"), are not easily obtainable overseas, and rates are generally worse when they can be found.

There is no legal private money-changing in mainland China, and rates are fixed to be the same at all outlets nationwide on a daily basis. So change at the airport when you arrive, and then at larger branches of the Bank of China, or at desks administered by the bank in your hotel or at major department stores in larger cities. If you find a shop offering to change your money at other than a formal Bank of China exchange counter, they are doing so illegally, and you open yourself to shenanigans with rates and fake bills, which are fairly common. Even the meanest hole-in-the-wall restaurant has an ultraviolet note tester. *Do not deal with black-market money-changers.*

Hotel exchange desks will only change money for their guests, and they are open very long hours 7 days a week. **Bank hours** vary drastically from province to province, so be sure to check. See "Banks, Foreign Exchange & ATMs," in the "Fast Facts" section of each destination.

In a bid to avert a trade war with the U.S., China allowed a 2% appreciation of the yuan in 2005. It is no longer pegged solely to the U.S. dollar, but rather a basket of currencies, in an arrangement known as a "crawling peg." The U.S. dollar has recently been trading around ¥7.50, the pound sterling at ¥15.30, and the euro at ¥10.67. For this edition, we have taken ¥7.40 to the U.S. dollar as an approximate conversion. The latest rates can be found at **www.xe.com/ucc**.

There are notes for ¥100, ¥50, ¥20, ¥10, ¥5, ¥2, and ¥1, which also appears as a coin. The word *yuan* is rarely spoken, and sums are usually referred to as *kuai qian*, "pieces of money," usually shortened to just *kuai*. *San kuai* is ¥3. Notes carry Arabic numerals as well as numbers in Chinese characters, so there's no fear of confusion. The next unit down, the *jiao* (¥.10), is spoken of as the *mao*. There are notes of a smaller size for ¥.50, ¥.20, and ¥.10, as well as coins for these values. The smallest and almost worthless unit is the *fen* (both written and spoken) or cent and, unbelievably, when you change money you may be given tiny notes or lightweight coins for ¥.05, ¥.02, and ¥.01, but this is the only time you'll see them except in the bowls of beggars or donation boxes in temples. The most useful note is the ¥10 ($1.30/65p), so keep a good stock. Street stalls, convenience stores, and taxis are often not happy with ¥100 ($13/£6.50) notes.

Keep receipts when you exchange money, and you can **reconvert** excess yuan into hard currency when you leave China, although sometimes not more than half the total sum for which you can produce receipts, and sometimes these receipts must be not more than 3 months old.

HONG KONG & MACAU

In **Hong Kong** the currency is the **Hong Kong dollar** (HK$), whose notes are issued by a variety of banks, although all coins look the same. It is pegged to the U.S. dollar at around HK$7.80 to US$1. Keep foreign exchange to a minimum at the airport (use the ATMs at departures level) or at other points of entry. Do not change in hotels or banks, but with money-changers, and choose money-changers away from the main streets for a significantly better rate. Banks have limited weekend hours, but money-changers are open every day.

Macau's official currency is the **pataca** (MOP$), pegged to the Hong Kong dollar (and thus to the U.S. dollar) at a rate of MOP$103.20 to HK$100—about MOP$8 to US$1. Hong Kong dollars are accepted everywhere, including both coins and notes (even on buses), but at par. If you arrive in Macau from Hong Kong for a short stay, there's little point in changing money beforehand.

ATMs

Generally, the easiest and best way to get cash away from home is from an ATM (automated teller machine), sometimes referred to as a "cash machine," or a "cashpoint." Unfortunately, while there are many ATMs in China, many won't accept foreign cards. Check the back of your ATM card for the logos of the **Cirrus** (www.mastercard.com), **PLUS** (www.visa.com), and **Aeon** (www.american express.com), systems, and then contact the relevant company for a list of working ATM locations in China. Beijing and Shanghai are both fairly well served, and have additional Citibank and Hongkong and Shanghai Bank machines which take just about any card ever invented. But even some major tourist destinations have no ATMs that accept foreign cards, even if their screens say they do. Nevertheless, it is possible, as long as you plan ahead, to travel in China relying on ATMs—just be sure to replenish your supplies of cash long before they run out, and have a couple of hundred U.S. dollars in cash as a backup. If you do find a working ATM, keep in mind that some machines have a limit of ¥2,500 ($325/£162) per transaction, but often allow a second transaction the same day. In **Hong Kong** and **Macau** there are ATMs everywhere that are friendly to foreign cards.

Note: Many banks impose a fee every time you use a card at another bank's ATM, and that fee can be higher for international transactions (up to $5 or more) than for domestic ones. In addition, the bank from which you withdraw cash may charge its own fee. For international withdrawal fees, ask your bank.

Banks that are members of the **Global ATM Alliance** charge no transaction fees for cash withdrawals at other Alliance member ATMs; these include Bank of America, Scotiabank (Canada, Caribbean, and Mexico), Barclays (U.K. and parts of Africa), Deutsche Bank (Germany, Poland, Spain, and Italy), and BNP Paribas (France).

TRAVELER'S CHECKS

Traveler's checks are only accepted at selected branches of the Bank of China, at foreign exchange desks in hotels, at international gateways, and at some department stores in the largest cities. In the most popular destinations, checks in any hard currency and from any major company are welcome, but elsewhere, currencies of the larger economies are preferred, and hotels may direct all check-holders to the local head office of the Bank of China. U.S. dollars cash, in contrast, may be exchanged at most branches of almost any Chinese bank, so even if you plan to bring checks, having a few U.S. dollars cash (in good condition) for emergencies is a good idea. Checks attract

a marginally better exchange rate than cash, but the .75% commission makes the result slightly worse (worse still if you paid commission when buying them). Occasionally, if the signature you write in front of the teller varies from the one you made when you bought the check, it may be rejected. In **Hong Kong** and **Macau,** checks are accepted at banks and money-changers in the usual way.

CREDIT CARDS

Although Visa and MasterCard signs abound, credit cards are of limited use in China—in most cases only the Chinese versions of the cards are accepted.

Credit cards are still relatively uncommon for ordinary Chinese folk, although changes are taking places as domestic debit card companies such as Union Pay come into operation. Otherwise, an establishment will accept all of them—American Express, Diners Club, MasterCard, and Visa—or none at all. Many hotels accept foreign cards, but only the most upscale restaurants outside hotels do so, as do those high-priced souvenir shops where you are already paying well over the odds.

You can also obtain cash advances on your MasterCard, Visa, Diners Club, or Amex card from major branches of the Bank of China, with a minimum withdrawal of ¥1,200 ($156/£78) and 4% commission, plus whatever your card issuer charges—a very expensive way to withdraw cash, and for emergencies only. If you do plan to use your card while in China, it's a good idea to call your card issuer and let it know in advance.

All major credit cards are widely accepted in **Hong Kong** and **Macau.**

EMERGENCY CASH

American Express also runs an **emergency check cashing system,** which allows you to use one of your own checks or a counter check (more expensive) to draw money in the currency of your choice from selected banks. This works well in major cities but it can cause confusion in less-visited spots, and the rules on withdrawal limits vary according to the country in which your card was issued. Consult American Express for a list of participating banks before you leave home.

If you're stuck in a province where banks are closed on weekends, you can have money wired from **Western Union** (© **800/325-6000;** www.westernunion. com) to many post offices and branches of the Agricultural Bank of China across China. You must present valid ID to pick up the cash at the Western Union office. In most countries, you can pick up a money transfer even if you don't have valid identification, as long as you can answer a test question provided by the sender. This should work in Hong Kong but might cause difficulties in mainland China. Let the sender know in advance that you don't have ID.

7 Travel Insurance

The cost of travel insurance varies widely, depending on the destination, the cost and length of your trip, your age and health, and the type of trip you're taking, but expect to pay between 5% and 8% of the vacation itself. You can get estimates from various providers through **Insure-MyTrip.com.**

U.K. citizens and their families who make more than one trip abroad per year may find an annual travel insurance policy is cheaper. Check **www.moneysuper market.com**, which compares prices across a wide range of providers for single- and multitrip policies.

Most big travel agents offer their own insurance and will probably try to sell you their package when you book a holiday. Think before you sign. **Britain's Consumers' Association** recommends that you insist on seeing the policy and reading the fine print before buying travel insurance. **The Association of British Insurers** (© **020/7600-3333;** www.abi. org.uk) gives advice by phone and publishes *Holiday Insurance,* a free guide to policy provisions and prices. You might also shop around for better deals: Try **Columbus Direct** (© **0870/033- 9988;** www.columbusdirect.net).

TRIP-CANCELLATION INSURANCE

Trip-cancellation insurance will help retrieve your money if you have to back out of a trip or depart early, or if your travel supplier goes bankrupt. Trip cancellation traditionally covers such events as sickness, natural disasters, and U.S. State Department advisories. The latest news in trip-cancellation insurance is the availability of **expanded hurricane coverage** and the **"any-reason"** cancellation coverage—which costs more but covers cancellations made for any reason. You won't get back 100% of your prepaid trip cost, but you'll be refunded a substantial portion. **TravelSafe** (© **888/885-7233;** www.travelsafe.com) offers both types of coverage. Expedia also offers any-reason cancellation coverage for its air-hotel packages.

For details, contact one of the following recommended insurers: **Access America** (© 866/807-3982; www.access america.com); **Travel Guard International** (© 800/826-4919; www.travel guard.com); **Travel Insured International** (© 800/243-3174; www.travel insured.com); and **Travelex Insurance Services** (© 888/457-4602; www.travelex-insurance.com).

MEDICAL INSURANCE

For travel overseas, most U.S. health plans (including Medicare and Medicaid) do not provide coverage, and the ones that do often require you to pay for services upfront and reimburse you only after you return home.

As a safety net, you may want to buy travel medical insurance, particularly if you're traveling to a remote or high-risk area where emergency evacuation might be necessary. If you require additional medical insurance, try **MEDEX Assistance** (© 410/453-6300; www.medex assist.com) or **Travel Assistance International** (© 800/821-2828; www.travel assistance.com; for general information on services, call the company's **Worldwide Assistance Services, Inc.,** at © 800/777-8710.

Canadians should check with their provincial health plan offices or call **Health Canada** (© 866/225-0709;

www.hc-sc.gc.ca) to find out the extent of their coverage and what documentation and receipts they must take home in case they are treated overseas.

For China, purchase travel insurance with air ambulance or scheduled airline repatriation built in. Be clear on the terms and conditions—is repatriation limited to life-threatening illnesses, for instance? While there are advanced facilities staffed by foreign doctors in Beijing and Shanghai, and excellent facilities in Hong Kong, in most of China a hospital visit is to be avoided, if possible. Foreigners unfortunate enough to end up in provincial facilities do tend to get special treatment, but you are unlikely to consider it special enough. You may also face a substantial bill, and you will not be allowed to leave until you pay it *in cash*. You must claim the expense when you return home, so make sure you have adequate proof of payment.

8 Health

STAYING HEALTHY

Plan well ahead. While a trip to Hong Kong or Macau can be made with little extra protection, a trip to mainland China, depending on its duration and time spent outside larger cities, may require a few new inoculations, especially if you haven't traveled much in the less-developed world before. Some of these are expensive, some need multiple shots separated by a month or two, and some should not be given at the same time. So start work on this 3 or 4 months before your trip.

For the latest information on infectious diseases and travel risks, and particularly on the constantly changing situation with malaria, consult the **World Heath Organization** (www.who.int) and the **Centers for Disease Control** in Atlanta (www.cdc.gov). Look in particular for the latest information on SARS,

which may continue long after the media has become bored with reporting it. Note that family doctors are rarely up-to-date with vaccination requirements, so when looking for advice at home, contact a specialist travel clinic.

To begin with, your standard inoculations, typically for **polio, diphtheria,** and **tetanus,** should be up-to-date. You may also need inoculations against **typhoid fever, meningococcal meningitis, cholera, hepatitis A and B,** and **Japanese B encephalitis.** If you will be arriving in mainland China from a country with **yellow fever,** you may be asked for proof of vaccination, although border health inspections are cursory at best. See also advice on **malaria,** below. Tuberculosis is making a frightening resurgence in many parts of the country and due the explosive growth of the canine population, **rabies** is on the rise again. Less than

10% percent of dogs have been vaccinated (75% is considered the minimum standard in other parts of the world).

GENERAL AVAILABILITY OF HEALTHCARE

While the names and addresses of reliable (and very expensive) clinics with up-to-date equipment and English-speaking foreign doctors are given in this guide where available, in most cases they are not. Should you begin to feel unwell in China, your first contact should be with your hotel reception. Many major hotels have doctors on staff who will treat minor problems, and who will be aware of the best place to send foreigners for further treatment.

If you regularly take a nonprescription medication, bring a plentiful supply with you—don't rely on finding it in China. Be very cautious about what is prescribed for you. Doctors are poorly paid, and many earn kickbacks from pharmaceutical companies for prescribing expensive medicines. Antibiotics are handed out like candy, and indeed, dangerous and powerful drugs of all kinds can be bought over-the-counter at pharmacies. Misprescription is now a significant cause of death in China, including the habit of prescribing a combination of Western drugs and Chinese traditional "medicines," which react badly with each other. In general, the best policy is to stay as far away from Chinese healthcare as possible. Much of it is not good for your health. To put things in perspective, China was recently ranked 144 out of 191 countries for its healthcare services.

Contact the **International Association for Medical Assistance to Travelers (IAMAT)** (© **716/754-4883,** or 416/652-0137 in Canada; www.iamat.org) for tips on travel and health concerns in the countries you're visiting, and for lists of local, English-speaking doctors. The United States **Centers for Disease Control and Prevention** (© **800/311-3435;** www.cdc.gov) provides up-to-date information on health hazards by region or country and offers tips on food safety. **Travel Health Online** (www.tripprep.com), sponsored by a consortium of travel medicine practitioners, may also offer helpful advice on traveling abroad. You can find listings of reliable medical clinics overseas at the **International Society of Travel Medicine** (www.istm.org).

COMMON AILMENTS

The Chinese are poorly educated when it comes to health risks and personal hygiene. Spitting has worsened as smoking and pollution has increased. Even in the most prosperous cities, men and infants use the sidewalk as a public toilet. Be aware that contagious diseases including TB, rabies, and syphilis are rising steadily.

STOMACH UPSETS The greatest risk to the enjoyment of a holiday in China is one of **stomach upsets** or more serious illnesses arising from growing levels of pollution and low hygiene standards. Keep your hands frequently washed and away from your mouth. Only eat freshly cooked hot food, and fruit you can peel yourself. Avoid touching the part to be eaten once it's been peeled. Drink only boiled or bottled water. *Never* drink from the tap. Use bottled water for brushing your teeth.

RESPIRATORY ILLNESSES The second most common cause of discomfort is the upper respiratory tract infection or cold- or flulike symptoms in fact caused by **heavy pollution.** Many standard Western remedies or sources of relief (and occasionally fake versions of these) are available over-the-counter, but bring a supply of whatever you are used to.

Mosquito-born **malaria** comes in various forms, and you may need to take two different prophylactic drugs, depending upon the time you travel, whether you venture into rural areas, and which areas they are. You must begin to take these drugs 1 week *before* you enter an affected area, and *for 4 weeks after you leave it, sometimes longer.* For urban tours, prophylaxis is usually unnecessary.

OTHER RISKS   If you visit Tibet, you may be at risk from **altitude sickness,** usually marked by throbbing headache, loss of appetite, shortness of breath, and overwhelming lethargy. Other than retreating to a lower altitude, avoiding alcohol, and drinking plenty of water, many find a drug called Diamox (acetazolamide) to be effective, and used with caution. For most, one sleepless night is all you will have to endure. See box on p. 758 for more.

Standard precautions should be taken against exposure to **strong summer sun,** its brightness often dimmed by pollution but its power to burn undiminished.

The Chinese are phenomenally uneducated about **sexually transmitted diseases,** which are rife. In addition, it was recently estimated that more than 10% of the population are Hepatitis B carriers and AIDS is a growing problem. In short, you should not undertake intimate activities without protection. Condoms are widely available, including Western brands in bigger cities.

WHAT TO DO IF YOU GET SICK AWAY FROM HOME

If you have any significant health information or regular prescription, ask your doctor to write a summary of the condition in case a problem develops. If your glasses break its nice to have a photocopy of the prescription to make it easier to get replacements. Some of this is not needed for short trips so be your own judge based on length of stay, your health, and what you plan to do.

Very few health insurance plans pay for medical evacuation back to the U.S. (which can cost $10,000 and up). A number of companies offer medical evacuation services anywhere in the world. If you're ever hospitalized more than 150 miles from home, **MedjetAssist** (© **800/ 527-7478;** www.medjetassistance.com) will pick you up and fly you to the hospital of your choice virtually anywhere in the world in a medically equipped and staffed aircraft 24 hours day, 7 days a week. Annual memberships are $225 individual, $350 family; you can also purchase short-term memberships.

U.K. nationals will need a **European Health Insurance Card (EHIC)** to receive free or reduced-costs health benefits during a visit to an European Economic Area (EEA) country (European Union countries plus Iceland, Liechtenstein and Norway) or Switzerland. The European Health Insurance Card replaces the E111 form, which is no longer valid. For advice, ask at your local post office or see www.dh.gov.uk/travellers.

If you suffer from a chronic illness, consult your doctor before your departure. Pack prescription medications in your carry-on luggage, and carry them in their original containers, with pharmacy labels—otherwise, they won't make it through airport security. Carry the generic name of prescription medicines, in case a local pharmacist is unfamiliar with the brand name.

9 Staying Safe

China was long touted as one of Asia's safest destinations, but this is changing rapidly. So be cautious about theft in the same places as anywhere else in the world—crowded markets, popular tourist sights, bus and railway stations, and airports. Despite the rise in crime, the main danger of walking the ill-lit streets at night is of falling down an uncovered manhole or walking into a phone or power wire strung at neck height. Take standard precautions against pickpockets (distribute your valuables around your person, and wear a money belt inside your clothes). There's no need to be concerned about dressing down or not flashing valuables—it's automatically assumed that all foreigners are astonishingly rich anyway, even the scruffiest backpackers, and the average Chinese cannot tell a Cartier from any other shiny watch. If you are a victim of theft, make a police report (go to the same addresses given for visa extensions in each city, where you are most likely to find an English-speaking policeman). But don't necessarily expect sympathy, cooperation, or action. The main purpose is to get a theft report to give to your insurers for compensation.

Street crime increases in the period leading up to Chinese New Year as migrants from the country become more desperate to find ways to fund their journeys home. Be especially vigilant at this time of year.

Harassment of **solo female travelers** is slightly more likely if they appear to be of Chinese descent, but is very rare.

Traffic is a major hazard for the cautious and incautious alike. In Hong Kong and Macau, driving is on the left, and road signs and traffic lights are obeyed. In mainland China, driving is on the right, at least occasionally. The rules of the road are routinely overridden by one rule: "I'm bigger than you, so get out of my way," and pedestrians are at the bottom of the pecking order. Cyclists ride along the sidewalks, and cars also mount sidewalks right in front of you and park across your path as if you don't exist. Watch out for loose paving slabs caused by these selfish SUV drivers; usually they only spurt up dirty water, but twisted ankles sometimes occur, too. Cyclists go in both directions along the bike lane at the side of the road, which is also invaded by cars looking to park. The edges of the main roads also usually have cyclists going in both directions. The vehicle drivers are gladiators,

competing for any way to move into the space ahead, constantly changing lanes, and crossing each others' paths. Pedestrians are matadors pausing between lanes as cars sweep by to either side of them. In cities they tend to group together and edge out into the traffic together, causing it to swing ever farther out away from them, often into the path of oncoming vehicles, until eventually the traffic parts and flows to either side, and the process is repeated for the next lane. Whether it's more hair-raising to be in the vehicle or on the street is an open question. Driving tests are laughable, and even though China only has 2% of the world's cars, it already has 20% of all traffic-accident fatalities. The latest scourges to watch out for are rechargeable electric bicycles, which silently whiz along the sidewalk catching many pedestrians completely unawares.

Visitors should be cautious of various **scams,** especially in areas of high tourist traffic, and of Chinese who approach and speak in English: "Hello friend! Welcome to China!" or similar. Those who want to practice their English and who suggest moving to some local haunt may leave you with a bill that has two zeros more on it than it should, and there's trouble should you decline to pay. "Art students" are a pest: They approach you with a story about raising funds for a show overseas, but in fact are merely enticing you into a shop where you will be lied to extravagantly about the authenticity, uniqueness, originality, and true cost of various paintings, which you will be pressured into buying for dozens of times their actual value. The man who is foolish enough to accept an invitation from pretty girls to sing karaoke deserves all the hot water in which he will find himself, up to being forced by large, well-muscled gentlemen to visit an ATM and withdraw large sums to pay for services not actually provided.

DEALING WITH DISCRIMINATION

In mainland China, in casual encounters, non-Chinese are treated as something between a cute pet and a bull in a china shop, and sometimes with pitying condescension because they are too stupid to speak Chinese. At some sights, out-of-town Chinese tourists may ask to have their picture taken with you, which will be fun to show friends in their foreigner-free hometowns. ("Look! Here's me with the Elephant Man!") Unless you are of Chinese descent, your foreignness is constantly thrust in your face with catcalls of *"laowai"* (or *"gweillo"* in Cantonese areas), a not particularly courteous term for "foreigner." Mocking, and usually falsetto, calls of "Helloooooo" are not greetings but similar to saying "Pretty Polly!" to a parrot. Whether acknowledged or not (and all this is best just ignored), these calls are usually followed by giggles. But there's little other overt discrimination, other than persistent overcharging wherever it can possibly be arranged. Indeed, in general, foreigners get better treatment from Chinese, both officials and the general public, than the Chinese give each other, once some sort of communication is established. People with darker skin do have a harder time than whites, but those with no Mandarin will probably not notice. Hong Kong and Macau are both more tolerant, although souvenir shops and markets will overcharge wherever possible. Hong Kongers married to foreigners know to leave their spouses at home when they shop for dinner.

10 Specialized Travel Resources

TRAVELERS WITH DISABILITIES

China should not be your first choice of destination, and if it is, you should travel in a specialist group (although such tours to China are very rare) or with those who are fully familiar with giving you whatever assistance you may need.

China is difficult for those with limited mobility. The sidewalks are very uneven, and there are almost always stairs to public buildings, sights, and hotels with no alternative ramps. In theory, some major hotels in the largest cities have wheelchair-accessible rooms, but rarely are they properly executed—the door to the bathroom may be wider, or the bathroom suite lower, but not both, and other switches and controls may be out of reach. Metro stations do not have lifts, and any escalators are most usually up only.

Organizations that offer a vast range of resources and assistance to travelers with disabilitiesinclude **MossRehab** (© 800/CALL-MOSS;** www.mossresourcenet. org); the **American Foundation for the Blind** (AFB) (© 800/232-5463; www. afb.org); and **SATH** (Society for Accessible Travel & Hospitality) (© 212/447-7284; www.sath.org). **AirAmbulanceCard.com** is now partnered with SATH and allows you to preselect top-notch hospitals in case of an emergency.

Access-Able Travel Source (© 303/232-2979; www.access-able.com) offers a comprehensive database on travel agents from around the world with experience in accessible travel; destination-specific access information; and links to such resources as service animals, equipment rentals, and access guides.

Many travel agencies offer customized tours and itineraries for travelers with disabilities. Among them are **Flying Wheels Travel** (© 507/451-5005; www.flying wheelstravel.com); and **Accessible Journeys** (© 800/846-4537 or 610/521-0339; www.disabilitytravel.com).

Flying with Disability (www.flying-with-disability.org) is a comprehensive information source on airplane travel.

Avis Rent a Car (© 888/879-4273) has an "Avis Access" program that offers services for customers with special travel needs. These include specially outfitted vehicles with swivel seats, spinner knobs, and hand controls; mobility scooter rentals; and accessible bus service. Be sure to reserve well in advance.

Also check out the quarterly magazine *Emerging Horizons* (www.emerging horizons.com), available by subscription ($16.95 year U.S.; $21.95 outside the U.S.).

The "Accessible Travel" link at **Mobility-Advisor.com** (www.mobility-advisor. com) offers a variety of travel resources to disabled persons.

British travelers should contact **Holiday Care** (© 0845-124-9971 in the U.K. only; www.holidaycare.org.uk) to access a wide range of travel information and resources for the disabled and the elderly.

GAY & LESBIAN TRAVELERS

China is still in denial. Even Beijing boasts only a single gay bar of any note, but it is not permitted to describe it in print as such, and there's less still for lesbians. You don't travel to China for the gay scene any more than you'd travel to Mexico for the icebergs. Only Hong Kong and Macau are well supplied with openly gay bars and clubs. Other Asian countries have much more to offer. Even **The International Gay & Lesbian Travel Association (IGLTA; © 800/ 448-8550** or 954/776-2626; www.iglta. org) lists no gay-friendly organizations dealing with in-bound visitors to China. *Out and About* (© **800/929-2268** or 415/644-8044; www.outandabout.com), which offers gay guidebooks, has a Hong Kong title ("No other city is better equipped for the gay sport: shopping!"), but nothing for the mainland.

SENIOR TRAVEL

There are no special arrangements or discounts for seniors in China, with the exception of some familiar foreign brand-name hotels that may offer senior rates if you book in advance (although you'll usually beat those prices simply by showing up in person, if there are rooms available).

Recommended publications offering travel resources and discounts for seniors include the quarterly magazine *Travel 50 & Beyond* (www.travel50andbeyond.com) and the best-selling paperback *Unbelievably Good Deals and Great Adventures That You Absolutely Can't Get Unless You're Over 50 2005–2006, 16th Edition* (McGraw-Hill), by Joann Rattner Heilman.

FAMILY TRAVEL

China accepts children traveling on a parent's passport, although the child's photo must be submitted along with the parent's when a visa application is made.

Mainland China, however, is not the place to make your first experiment in traveling with small children, unless you are already very familiar with Third World travel or with China in particular. Your biggest challenges will be the long journeys between destinations (certainly if you travel by land), the lack of services or entertainment aimed at children, the lack of familiar foods (unless your children have been brought up with Chinese food), and hygiene.

In general, the Chinese will be fascinated by your child, especially if he or she has anything other than black hair and is not of Asian descent. Some children find Chinese strangers a little too hands-on, and may tire of forced encounters (and photo sessions) with Chinese children met on the street. But the Chinese put their children firmly first, and stand up on buses while the children sit.

Only a very few companies organize family trips to China but two of the most promising are **Pacific Delight World Tours** (www.pacificdelighttours.com) and

Rascals in Paradise (www.rascalsin paradise.com). Pacific's 15-day "Family Yangzi River Escapade" includes the Chengdu Research Base of Giant Panda Breeding, home of the Giant Panda, while San Francisco–based Rascals offers tours stretching from Beijing all the way down to Yangshuo.

To locate accommodations, restaurants, and attractions that are particularly kid-friendly, refer to the "Kids" icon throughout this guide.

Recommended family travel websites include **Family Travel Forum** (www.familytravelforum.com), a comprehensive site that offers customized trip planning; **Family Travel Network** (www.familytravelnetwork.com), an online magazine providing travel tips; **TravelWithYourKids.com** (www.travelwithyourkids.com), a comprehensive site written by parents for parents offering sound advice for long-distance and international travel with children.

11 Sustainable Tourism/Ecotourism

Each time you take a flight or drive a car CO_2 is released into the atmosphere. You can help neutralize this danger to our planet through "carbon offsetting"—paying someone to reduce your CO_2 emissions by the same amount you've added. Carbon offsets can be purchased in the U.S. from companies such as **Carbonfund.org** (www.carbonfund.org) and **TerraPass** (www.terrapass.org), and from **Climate Care** (www.climatecare.org) in the U.K.

Although one could argue that any vacation that includes an airplane flight can't be truly "green," you can go on holiday and still contribute positively to the environment. You can offset carbon emissions from your flight in other ways. Choose forward-looking companies that embrace responsible development practices, helping preserve destinations for the future by working alongside local people. An increasing number of sustainable tourism initiatives can help you plan a family trip and leave as small a "footprint" as possible on the places you visit.

Responsible Travel (www.responsibletravel.com) contains a great source of sustainable travel ideas run by a spokesperson for responsible tourism in the travel industry. **Sustainable Travel International** (www.sustainabletravelinternational.org) promotes responsible tourism practices and issues an annual Green Gear & Gift Guide.

You can find ecofriendly travel tips, statistics, and touring companies and associations—listed by destination under "Travel Choice"—at the TIES website, www.ecotourism.org. Also check out **Conservation International** (www.conservation.org)—which, with *National Geographic Traveler,* annually presents **World Legacy Awards** (www.wlaward.org) to those travel tour operators, businesses, organizations, and places that have made a significant contribution to sustainable tourism. **Ecotravel.com** is part online magazine and part ecodirectory that lets you search for touring companies in several categories (water-based, land-based, spiritually oriented, and so on).

In the U.K., **Tourism Concern** (www.tourismconcern.org.uk) works to reduce social and environmental problems connected to tourism and find ways of improving tourism so that local benefits are increased.

The **Association of British Travel Agents** (**ABTA**) (www.abtamembers.org/responsibletourism) acts as a focal point for the U.K. travel industry and is one of the leading groups spearheading responsible tourism.

The **Association of Independent Tour Operators** (**AITO**) (www.aito.co.uk) is a group of interesting specialist operators leading the field in making holidays sustainable.

Frommers.com: The Complete Travel Resource

It should go without saying, but we highly recommend **Frommers.com,** voted Best Travel Site by *PC Magazine.* We think you'll find our expert advice and tips; independent reviews of hotels, restaurants, attractions, and preferred shopping and nightlife venues; vacation giveaways; and an online booking tool indispensable before, during, and after your travels. We publish the complete contents of over 128 travel guides in our **Destinations** section covering nearly 3,600 places worldwide to help you plan your trip. Each weekday, we publish original articles reporting on **Deals and News** via our free **Frommers.com Newsletter** to help you save time and money and travel smarter. We're betting you'll find our new **Events** listings (http://events.frommers.com) an invaluable resource; it's an up-to-the-minute roster of what's happening in cities everywhere—including concerts, festivals, lectures, and more. We've also added weekly **Podcasts, interactive maps,** and hundreds of new images across the site. Check out our **Travel Talk** area featuring **Message Boards** where you can join in conversations with thousands of fellow Frommer's travelers and post your trip report once you return.

For information about the ethics of swimming with dolphins and other outdoor activities, visit the **Whale and** **Dolphin Conservation Society** (www.wdcs.org) and **Tread Lightly** (www.treadlightly.org).

12 Staying Connected

TELEPHONES

The international country code for mainland China is 86, for Hong Kong 852, and for Macau 853.

To call China, Hong Kong, or Macau:

1. Dial the international access code (011 in the U.S., 00 in the U.K.).

2. Dial the country code: 86 for China, 852 for Hong Kong, 853 for Macau.

3. For China, dial the city code, omitting the leading zero, and then the number. Hong Kong and Macau have no city codes, so after the country code, simply dial the remainder of the number.

To call within China: For calls within the same city, omit the city code, which always begins with a zero when used (010 for Beijing, 020 for Guangzhou, and so on). All hotel phones have direct dialing, and most have international dialing.

Hotels are only allowed to add a service charge of up to 15% to the cost of the call, and even long-distance rates within China are very low. To use a public telephone you'll need an IC (integrated circuit) card *(aaisei ka),* available in values from ¥20 ($2.60/£1.30). You can buy them at post offices, convenience stores, street stalls, or wherever you can make out the letters "IC" among the Chinese characters. A brief local call is typically ¥.30 (5¢/3p). Phones show you the value remaining on the card when you insert it, and count down as you talk. To call within Hong Kong: In Hong Kong, local calls made from homes, offices, shops, and other establishments are free, so don't feel shy about asking to use the phone. From hotel lobbies and public phone booths, a local call costs HK$1

(US15¢/5p) for each 5 minutes; from hotel rooms, about HK$4 to HK$5 (US50¢– US65¢/25p–30p). To call within Macau: Local calls from private phones are free, and from call boxes cost MOP$1 (10¢/ 5p).

To make international calls: From mainland China or Macau, first dial 00 and then the country code (U.S. or Canada 1, U.K. 44, Ireland 353, Australia 61, New Zealand 64). Next, dial the area or city code, omitting any leading zero, and then the number. For example, if you want to call the British Embassy in Washington, D.C., you would dial ✆ 00-1-202/588-7800. Forget taking access numbers for your local phone company with you—you can call internationally for a fraction of the cost by using an IP (Internet protocol) card, *aaipii ka*, purchased from department stores and other establishments—wherever you see the letters "IP." Instructions for use are on the back, but you simply dial the access number given, choose English from the menu, and follow the instructions to dial in the number behind a scratch-off panel. Depending on where you call, ¥50 ($6.50/£3.25) can give you an hour of talking, but you should bargain to pay less than the face value of the card—as little as ¥70 ($9/£4.50) for a ¥100 ($13/ £6.50) card from street vendors.

To use a public phone, you'll need an IC card (see above) to make the local call. In emergencies, dial 108 to negotiate a collect call, but again, in most towns you'll need help from a Mandarin speaker. From Hong Kong dial 001, 0080, or 009, depending on which of several competing phone companies you are using. Follow with the country code and continue as for calling from China or Macau.

It's much cheaper to use one of several competing phone cards, such as *Talk Talk,* which come in denominations ranging from HK$50 to HK$300 (US$6.50– US$39/£3.25–£19) and are available at HKTB information offices, convenience stores, and other places.

For directory assistance: In mainland China dial ✆ 114. No English is spoken, and only local numbers are available. If you want other cities, dial the city code followed by 114—a long-distance call. In Hong Kong dial ✆ 1081 for a local number, and 10013 for international ones. In Macau dial ✆ 181 for domestic numbers, and 101 for international ones.

For operator assistance: If in mainland China if you need operator assistance in making a call, just ask for help at your hotel. In Hong Kong dial ✆ 10010 for domestic assistance, 10013 for international assistance.

Toll-free numbers: Numbers beginning with 800 within China are toll-free, but calling a 1-800 number in the States from China is a full-tariff international call, as is calling one in Hong Kong from mainland China, or vice versa.

CELLPHONES

All Europeans, most Australians, and many North Americans use GSM (Global System for Mobiles). But while everyone else can take a regular GSM phone to China, North Americans, who operate on a different frequency, need to have a more expensive triband model.

International roaming charges can be horrendously expensive. It's far cheaper to buy a prepaid chip with a new number in China or Hong Kong (but you'll need a different chip for each destination). You may need to call your cellular operator to "unlock" your phone in order to use it with a local provider.

Renting a phone is an expensive alternative, best done from home, since such services are not widely available in China. That way you can give out your new number, and make sure the phone works. You'll usually pay $40 to $50 per week, plus air-time fees of at least $1 a minute. In the U.S., two good wireless rental companies are **InTouch USA** (© **800/ 872-7626;** www.intouchglobal.com) and **RoadPost** (© **888/290-1606** or 905/ 272-5665; www.roadpost.com).

In mainland China, **buying a phone** is the best option. Last year's now unfashionable model can be bought, with chip and ¥100 ($13/£6.50) of prepaid air time, for often around ¥800 ($100/£50), less if a Chinese model is chosen. Europeans taking their GSM phones, and North Americans with triband phones, can buy chips *(quanqiutong)* for about ¥100 ($13/£6.50). Mainland chips do not work in Hong Kong, or vice versa. Recharge cards *(shenzhouxing)* are available at post offices and the mobile-phone shops, which seem to occupy about 50% of all retail space. Call rates are very low, although those receiving calls pay part of the cost; and if the phone is taken to another province, that cost increases, making the use of ordinary phones a better deal for dialing out. In **Hong Kong** recharge cards are widely available at convenience stores and mobile-phone shops, and chips are included free with the cost of initial charge value.

Local SIM cards are readily available at any phone store in your destination city. You can use your current phone only if it is "unlocked"; that is, only if it is not programmed to work with Cingular only. If it *is* locked you can ask Cingular to unlock it; they may if you make a good case and you have had it for a year or two.

What you cannot do is keep both your Cingular number and a local China number on the same phone (phones used to be able to do this, but newer ones generally cannot, unless you can find a "dual SIM" phone). Some people solve the problem by carrying two phones; I use my Cingular and a locally purchased GSM phone with local SIM card. This really pays, because a U.S. number used in China will cost $2-plus per minute, while a local number will cost 1¢ to 5¢ depending on the local coverage area. Even calls to the U.S. from a Chinese international SIM card run only 30¢ a minute.

INTERNET/E-MAIL

Despite highly publicized clamp-downs on Internet cafes, monitoring of traffic, and blocking of websites, China remains one of the easiest countries in the world in which to get online.

WITHOUT YOUR OWN COMPUTER

Almost any hotel with a business center, right down to Chinese government–rated two-star level, offers expensive Internet access, and almost every town has a few Internet cafes *(wangba)*, with rates typically ¥2 to ¥3 (25¢–40¢/10p–20p) per hour, many open 24 hours a day. Locations of cafes are given for most cities in this guide, but they come and go very rapidly. Keep your eyes open for the *wangba* characters given in "Appendix A: The Chinese Language." In **Hong Kong** many coffee bars have a free terminal or two.

Thanks to ADSL (Asymmetric Digital Subscriber Lines) many progressive bars and guesthouses are now offering free Internet on the mainland, too. Note that many Internet bars are dark, dirty places; you will usually find that the local library is a much cleaner, often cheaper alternative.

Many media websites and those with financial information or any data whatsoever on China that disagrees with the party line are blocked from mainland China, as are some search engines.

WITH YOUR OWN COMPUTER

It's just possible that your ISP has a low-cost local access number in China, but that's unlikely. Never mind, because there's free, **anonymous dial-up access** across most of China. Look for "Dial-up is . . ." in the "Fast Facts" sections of cities in this book; you can connect by using the number we've provided, and by making the

Online Traveler's Toolbox

- **On-line Chinese Tools** (www.mandarintools.com). Dictionaries for Mac and Windows, facilities for finding yourself a Chinese name, Chinese calendars for conversion between the solar and lunar calendars (on which most Chinese festivals are based), and more.
- **Ctrip** (www.english.ctrip.com). Yet another Chinese hotel booking site, but this one has a great deal of useful travel information in English as well as a very convenient map of China interface.
- **zhongwen.com** (www.zhongwen.com). Online dictionary with look-up of English and Chinese and explanations of Chinese etymology using a system of family trees.
- **wikitravel.org** (http://wikitravel.org/en/China) is a project to create a free, complete, up-to-date, and reliable worldwide travel guide, so far with over 16,000 destination guides and other articles written and edited by Wikitravellers from around the globe, and growing all the time.
- **virtualtourist.com** (www.virtualtourist.com/travel/Asia/China/TravelGuide-China.html) An advertising-supported alternative to wikitravel, but with some 30,000 travelers tips for China alone, still a very useful resource.
- **travelchinaguide.com** (www.travelchinaguide.com) Organized by only one Chinese tour company but with an active and informative community section.
- **yunnanexplorer.com** (www.yunnanexplorer.com). A fantastically informative set of articles that is a goldmine mine for travelers to what most consider China's most beautiful province.
- **Visa ATM Locator** (www.visa.com), for locations of PLUS ATMs worldwide; or **MasterCard ATM Locator** (www.mastercard.com), for locations of Cirrus ATMs worldwide.
- **Weatherbase** (www.weatherbase.com) gives month-by-month averages for temperature and rainfall in individual cities in China. **Intellicast** (www.intellicast.com) and **Weather.com** (www.weather.com) give weather forecasts for cities around the world.
- **Universal Currency Converter** (www.xe.com/ucc). Latest exchange rates of any currency against the yuan, HK$, and MOP$.
- **Travel Warnings.** See http://travel.state.gov/travel_warnings.html, www.fco.gov.uk/travel, www.voyage.gc.ca, or www.dfat.gov.au/consular/advice.

account name and password the same as the dial-up number. Speeds vary but are usually fine for checking e-mail, although they're variable for checking mail via a Web interface. The service is paid for through a tiny increment in the low cost of a local phone call. Many hotels advertising "free Internet" simply mean that they don't charge you for calls to these numbers.

Another option in larger cities is to buy an **Internet access card** *(wangka)*. These are on sale at newspaper kiosks, phone stores, convenience stores, and department stores, and usually allow more rapid connection speeds. The back of the card (always bought for less than its face value— bargain the price well down) has instructions in English. Scratch off the panel on the back of the card, call the administration number provided, and give the card number, a contact phone number (any hotel will do), and your passport number; English is usually spoken but get hotel desk staff to assist just in case. Use the dial-up number and account number on the back of the card, and the password from behind the scratch-off panel. Online time usually costs well under ¥1 (15¢/10p) an hour. *Warning:* Many cards are only usable in the city where they are purchased.

Mainland China uses the standard U.S.-style RJ11 telephone jack also used as the port for laptops worldwide. Cables with RJ11 jacks at both ends can be picked up for around $1 (£2) in department stores and electrical shops without difficulty. In Hong Kong and Macau, however, phone connections are often to U.K. standards, although in better hotels an RJ11 socket is provided. Standard electrical voltage across China is 220v, 50Hz, which most laptops can deal with, but North American users in particular should check. For power socket information, see "Fast Facts: China," later in this chapter.

Those with on-board Ethernet can take advantage of broadband services in major hotels in China, which are sometimes free. Ethernet cables are often provided but it's best to bring your own. Details are given under each hotel listing. Occasionally Internet access is provided via the TV and a keyboard with an infrared link, but this is slow and clumsy. A growing number of hotels and guesthouses now have wireless access in public areas for those with a wireless card installed. This is especially true in popular tourist areas. Sometimes this is chargeable (five-star hotels are especially greedy in this area and demand up to ¥100/$13/£6.50 per day for wireless access). If it is important for you be online in China then try picking up an antenna so that you can access more distant but unsecured hotspots.

To find public Wi-Fi hotspots at your destination, go to **www.jiwire.com**; its Hotspot Finder holds the world's largest directory of public wireless hotspots.

Wherever you go, bring a **connection kit** of the right power and phone adapters, a spare phone cord, and a spare Ethernet network cable—or find out whether your hotel supplies them to guests.

13 Packages for the Independent Traveler

Package tours are simply a way to buy the airfare, accommodations, and other elements of your trip (such as car rentals, airport transfers, and sometimes even activities) at the same time and often at discounted prices.

One good source of package deals is the airlines themselves. Most major airlines offer air/land packages, including **American Airlines Vacations** (✆ 800/321-2121; www.aavacations.com), **Delta Vacations** (✆ 800/654-6559; www.deltavacations.com), **Continental Airlines Vacations** (✆ 800/301-3800; www.covacations.com), and **United Vacations** (✆ 888/854-3899; www.unitedvacations.com). Several big **online travel agencies**—

Expedia, Travelocity, Orbitz, Site59, and Lastminute.com—also do a brisk business in packages.

Since China reopened to foreign tourism in the early 1980s, all foreign tour operators have been required to use official state-registered travel companies as ground handlers. All arrangements in China were usually put together by one of three companies: China International Travel Service (CITS), China Travel Service (CTS), or China Youth Travel Service (CYTS). Controls are now loosening, foreign tour companies are now allowed some limited activities in China, and the range of possible Chinese partners has increased, but in effect, CITS and the like are the only companies with nationwide networks of offices, and most foreign tour companies still turn to them. They work out the schedule at the highest possible prices and send the costs to the foreign package company, which then adds its own administration charges and hands the resulting quote to you.

You could get the same price yourself by dealing with CITS (which has many offices overseas) directly. But you can get far better prices by organizing things yourself as you go along so, other than convenience, there's little benefit and a great deal of unnecessary cost to buying a package. Just about any tour operator will offer to tailor an itinerary to your needs, which means it will usually simply pass on the request to one of the state monoliths, and pass the result back to you. The benefit of dealing with a Chinese travel company directly is that you cut out the middleman, but if things go wrong, you will be unlikely to obtain any compensation whatsoever. If you book through a home tour operator, you can expect to obtain refunds and compensation if this becomes appropriate. In general, however, when organized through CITS, rail or air tickets for your next leg are reliably delivered to each hotel as you go. *Never book directly over the Web with a China-based travel service or "private" tour guide.* Many are not licensed to do business with foreigners, have not been licensed as guides, or will hugely overcharge and frequently mislead you (in the most charming way possible), and you will have no recourse at all.

If you're set on a tour, and money is no object, then start with the list of tour companies below in the next section, nearly all of which will arrange individual itineraries; or contact the **CNTO** (addresses on p. 21) to find properly registered Chinese agencies who may help you. The **Hong Kong Tourism Board** and the **Macau Government Tourism Office,** in whose territories the tourism industry is well regulated, can point you toward reputable operators and talented licensed private guides.

14 Escorted General-Interest Tours

Escorted tours are structured group tours with a group leader. The price usually includes everything from airfare to hotels, meals, tours, admission costs, and local transportation, but usually not domestic or international departure taxes.

Again, due to the distorted nature of the Chinese industry, escorted tours do not usually represent savings, but rather a significant increase in costs over what you can arrange for yourself. Foreign tour companies are now required to work with state-owned ground handlers, although some do book as much as they can directly, and some work discreetly with private operators they trust. But even as markets become freer, most deals will continue to be made with the official state operators, if only for convenience.

Tours are very attractive if you wish to see a large amount of the country very swiftly. Please read the brochures with as much skepticism as you would read a Realtor's (one man's "scenic splendor" is another's "heavily polluted"), and read the following notes carefully.

Most tour companies peddle the same list of mainstream "must-sees"—not all of which can hope to live up to the towering hype—featuring Beijing, Xi'an, Shanghai, Guilin, and the Yangzi River, with some alternative trips to Tibet, Yunnan Province, or the Silk Routes.

As with package tours, the arrangements within China itself are almost always managed by a handful of local companies, whose cupidity often induces them to lead both you and your tour company astray. Various costs, which should be included in the tour fee, can appear as extras; itineraries are altered to suit the pocket of the ground handler (local operator); and there are all sorts of shenanigans to separate the hapless tourist from extra cash at every turn, usually at whatever point the tour staff appears to be most helpful. (The driver has bottles of water for sale on the bus each day? You're paying three times the store price.)

When choosing a tour company for China, you must, of course, consider cost, what's included, the itinerary, the likely age and interests of other tour group members, the physical ability required, and the payment and cancellation policies, as you would for any other destination. But you should also investigate the following:

SHOPPING STOPS These are the bane of any tour in China, designed to line the pockets of tour guides, drivers, and sometimes the ground handling company itself. A stop at the Great Wall may be limited to only an hour so as to allow an hour at a cloisonné factory. In some cases the local government owns the shop in question and makes a regulation requiring all tours to stop there. The better foreign tour operators design their own itineraries and have instituted strict contractual controls to keep these stops to a minimum, but they are often unable to do away with them altogether, and tour guides will introduce extra stops whenever they think they can get away with it. Other companies, particularly those that do not specialize in China, just take the package from the Chinese ground handler, put it together with flights, and pass it on uncritically. At shopping stops, you should never ask or accept your tour guide's advice on what is the "right price." You are shopping at the wrong place to start with, where prices will often be 10 to 15 times higher than they should be.

Your driver gets a tip, and your guide gets 40% of sales. The "discount" card you are given marks you for yet higher initial prices and tells the seller to which guide commission is owed. So ask your tour company how many of these stops are included, and simply sit out those you cannot avoid.

GUIDES Another problem with mainland guides is that their main concern is impressing foreigners with the greatness of China. You may end up hearing an impressive array of unverifiable statistics, little stories of dubious authenticity but that will amuse you, and a detailed knowledge of the official history of a place that may bear faint resemblance to the truth. So you may be told that the Great Wall can be seen from outer space (silly), that one million people worked on building the Forbidden City (it was only 100,000 on last year's trip), and that the little old lady you've just met in a village has never seen a foreigner before (she tells every group the same thing).

Ask your tour company if it will be sending along a guide or tour manager from your home country to accompany trip members and to supplement local guides. This is worth paying more for, as it ensures a smoother trip all-around, and it helps you get more authoritative information. Otherwise, you're better off bringing background reading from home. Guides in **Hong Kong** and **Macau,** however, are often extremely knowledgeable and both objective and accurate with their histories.

TOUR COMPANIES

Between them, the following tour companies (a tiny selection of what's available) cater to just about all budgets and interests (contact them directly for specific itineraries and pricing). The companies are from the U.S., Canada, the U.K., and Australia, but many have representatives globally, and you can anyway just buy the ground portion and fly in from wherever you like.

Abercrombie & Kent (U.S.): Group size is typically 12 to 18 participants (with a maximum of 24 persons) and tour leaders include Mandarin-speaking Westerners and Chinese, and local specialist guides. Tours have a historical and cultural focus and are upmarket, using China's very best hotels and direct contact with local artists, archaeologists, and colorful personalities. In the United States (group tours and custom private tours): *(C)* 800/323-7308; fax 630/954-3324; www.abercrombiekent.com. In the U.K. (custom private tours): *(C)* 0845/0700615; fax 0845/0700608.

Academic Travel Abroad (U.S.): Groups are typically of 20 to 30 people and tour leaders are Mandarin-speaking Americans, with additional specialty study leaders. The company has been operating tours to China since 1979, and operates educational and cultural tours in China for The Smithsonian (educational, cultural) and National Geographic Expeditions (natural history, soft adventure). For more information, check the website at www.academic-travel.com, but book through individual sponsors. The Smithsonian: *(C)* 877/EDU-TOUR; fax 202/633-9250; http://smithsonianjourneys.org. National Geographic: *(C)* 888/966-8687; fax 202/342-0317; www.nationalgeographic.org/ngexpeditions.

Adventure Center (U.S.): The maximum group size is 18 (typically 12) and both foreign and local tour leaders are used. The company offers a range of trip styles from more affordable grass-roots-style trips designed for younger participants to more inclusive trips using upgraded accommodations for those wanting to combine adventure and comfort. Itineraries include walks on stretches of the Great Wall, the Eastern Qing Tombs, and Chengde. *(C)* 800/227-8747 in the U.S., or 888/456-3522 in Canada. Representatives can also be contacted in

Australia and New Zealand. See www.adventurecenter.com.

Elderhostel (U.S.): Group size ranges from 33 to 40 participants and tours are developed in cooperation with Chinese educational institutions. Excursions and activities supplement the educational theme of each course, and options include working vacations and an opportunity to teach English in Xi'an: *(C)* 877/426-8056; www.elderhostel.org.

Gecko's Adventures (Australia): Gecko's tours are aimed at a younger crowd (typically 20–40-year-olds) and tour leaders are locals with Gecko's training. Itineraries stick mainly but not entirely to the highlights, but these are more down-to-earth budget tours using smaller guesthouses, local restaurants, and public transport. Branches across Australia: *(C)* 03/9662-2700; fax 03/9662-2422; and now in the U.K. (*(C)* 01/635872300; geckosadventures.co.uk) and the U.S. too (*(C)* 800/227-8747). For representatives worldwide, see www.geckos adventures.com.

Intrepid Travel (Australia): These trips are for more adventurous travelers and are graded for physical requirements and culture shock, ranging from relaxed vacations to those requiring more strenuous effort. Itineraries are a deft mix of popular destinations and the less visited (*(C)* 1300/360-887 in Australia, or 613/9473-2626; *(C)* 613/9478-2626 or 877/448-1616 in the U.S., or 0800/917-6456 or 44(0)20/7354-6170 in the U.K.; fax 613/9419-4426; www.intrepidtravel.com).

General Tours World Traveler (U.S.): Small-group escorted tours led by a hand-picked team of English-speaking guides. Itineraries are experiential and culture-focused, and as such, shopping stops are kept to a minimum. There's a wide choice, including six different Yangzi cruises and tours covering the highlights of China plus Tibet or Japan (*(C)* 800/221-2216; www.generaltours.com).

Laurus Travel (Canada): Group sizes range from 10 to 20 people and a tour leader accompanies the tour from Canadian departure or from arrival in China. Laurus is a China-only specialist, but itineraries are mainstream (© 877/507-1177 in the U.S. and Canada, or 604/438-7718; fax 604/438-7715; www.laurustravel.com).

Pacific Delight Tours (U.S.): There are special tours for families with children and tours can be modified or extended to meet client needs. Top-range tours are accompanied by a bilingual tour manager from the West Coast onward, while others are locally hosted (© 800/221-7179; www.pacificdelighttours.com).

Peregrine Adventures (Australia): Peregrine designs its own programs and tour leaders are locals trained by the company. Trips include visits to private homes and smaller restaurants frequented by locals, and can include walks and bike rides (© 800/227-8747 in the U.S., or 03/9663-8611; fax 03/9663-8618; www.peregrineadventures.com).

R. Crusoe & Son (U.S.): Tour groups are kept small and are accompanied by a Hong Kong Chinese and are joined by local guides at each stop. Tours include extras such as a visit to an area of the Forbidden City that is usually closed to the public, private visit to the Tang dynasty murals, and a view of Xi'an's Terra-Cotta Warriors at eye level, rather than just from the viewing gallery (© 888/490-8045; www.rcrusoe.com).

Ritz Tours (U.S.): Groups range in size from 10 to 40 people; parents often bring children. Ritz's own Shanghai office organizes the selection of local ground handlers—a mixture of large and small companies, with a preference for those providing good English-speaking guides (© 800/900-2446; www.ritztours.com).

SITA World Tours (U.S. and Canada): With over 75 years of experience, SITA offers luxury, deluxe, and first class tours throughout China and the Orient, escorted by certified guides that are sensitive to the needs of the discerning traveler. SITA also guarantees its departures so there is never a concern in a tour canceling (© 800/421-5643; www.sitatours.com).

Steppes Travel (U.K.): Groups are accompanied from the U.K. by a British tour leader and tailor-made itineraries are available so that travelers can include what they want, travel when they want, choose the level of accommodations they require. The company is especially strong on the Silk Routes and Tibet (© 01285/651010; fax 01285/8858888; www.steppestravel.co.uk).

Swain Tours specializes in creating fully customized travel experiences to various destinations, including China. They're great for those seeking an off-the-beaten-path adventure (© 800/227-9246, ext. 1140; fax 610/896-9592; www.Swain Tours.com).

Tauck World Discovery (U.S.): Tauck offers 13- and 16-day itineraries in China, both featuring a 3-night Yangzi River cruise, upscale accommodations, and virtually all expenses included (four on-tour flights, 37 meals, admission to all sites and attractions, and so on) (©: 800/468-2825; www.tauck.com).

15 Special-Interest Trips

Audubon Nature Odysseys (U.S.): The Audubon Society has just started to experiment with **bird-watching tours** in China, and works through a specialist U.S. company with a Sino-American operator based in Kunming. The tour leader is a bird specialist from overseas, the tour is joined by local birding experts, and the local operator provides a bilingual guide. The itinerary is a clever combination of mainstream sightseeing and visits to out-of-the-way bird-watching areas from mountainous Yunnan Province to coastal migratory areas in Hebei (© 800/967-7425; www.audubon.org).

See MacKinnon and Phillipps's *Field Guide to the Birds of China* (Oxford) for a sample of what you might see. Birdwatchers visiting **Hong Kong** should see the Hong Kong Bird-Watching Society site at **www.hkbws.org.hk**, and First Step Nature Tours at **www.firststepnt. com.**

Bike China Adventures, Inc. (U.S.-based, with an office in China): Still one of the leaders in this field, with great organization and some of the best guides. Cycling group sizes range from one to eight participants, who have ranged in age from 18 to 86. The company is based in Chengdu and tours are accompanied by a bilingual local or foreign guide. More than 50 tours operate both around the company's Sichuan base, in neighboring provinces, and as far away as Hebei and Xinjiang, always using local hotels, guesthouses, and restaurants so there's no camping or cooking (© **800/818-1778** in the U.S.; fax 515/322-0300 in the U.S., or 01388-2266-575 in China; www.bikechina.com).

Mongol Global Tour Co. (U.S.): Custom tours are created for adventurers, gourmet food and wine-lovers, lovers of culture, and more. Their tours offer many sites and experiences not generally offered and can be designed with economy in mind. There are local guides in each city and a national guide accompanies tours of 10 or more people. For specialty groups there is often an international guide as well (© **866/225-0577** or 714/220-2579; www.mongolglobaltours.com or www.mg tourco.com).

Myths and Mountains (U.S.) is an adventure travel company that specializes in getting inside the culture of a country. Their customized trips focus on the themes of China—the culture and arts, religions and holy sites, ethnic groups and trade routes, and environment and how people have adapted to it. Tours range from the eastern coastal cities and villages all the way west and north into Tibet, Inner Mongolia, and other less-traveled areas, such as Guizhou, Yunnan and Sichuan, and Qinghai (© **800/670-6894** or 775/832-5454; fax 775/832-4454; www.mythsandmountains.com).

You might want to consider **www. wildchina.com**, one of the few online booking agencies I'd recommend for travel in China. Run by a returnee ABC (American-born Chinese) from Harvard, Wild China acts as a clearinghouse for specialized China tours. Great attention is paid to comfort and yet the destinations, such as a section of the Great Wall currently under renovation, are a little different from the usual spots. The site's collection of press articles is particularly encouraging.

16 Getting Around China

The first thing to do upon arrival at any Chinese destination is to buy a **map** for ¥5 (65¢/30p) or less. Even though few of these are bilingual, and most are inaccurate, they're essential for navigation. Your hotel staff can mark on them where you want to go, and you can show the characters to the taxi driver or bus conductor. Although building numbers are given in this book, they're useless for directions. Everyone navigates by street names and landmarks.

BY PLANE
Booking domestic flights before you arrive in China is expensive and unnecessary. The only Chinese airlines offering flights on internationally accessible ticketing systems are those that also have international routes: principally China Southern, China Eastern, and Air China. The only way to book domestic tickets before you leave home is through CITS offices (other agencies will go to CITS,

too), or through websites. In either case, you'll usually be asked to pay full fare (or more), which might be, for example, ¥1,200 ($156/£78) one-way plus perhaps a booking fee on the Beijing-to-Shanghai route. Yet you could pay ¥800 ($104/£54) or less by buying over the counter from an agent in China, depending on seasonal demand. Some ticketing websites even have full fares on their English pages and discounted fares on their Chinese-language ones. So avoid them.

Much flying in China is on a walk-in basis, especially on the most popular routes. It makes sense to book a few days ahead to get the best price, but for most of the time, on most routes, there is an oversupply of seats.

While you can buy tickets between any two destinations served by Air China at any Air China office, you'll usually get a much better price from agents in the town from which you plan to depart. Prices are always better from agents than from the airline, even if they are next door to each other, and you can and should bargain for a lower price, and shop around. No agent with an online terminal connected to the Chinese domestic aviation system charges a booking fee. Agents sitting in four- and five-star hotels will not offer you the discounts they could, however. You need to look out in the street away from your hotel. You usually *cannot* get a refund on an unused ticket from anywhere except the agent where you bought it.

BY TRAIN

The train is still the best way to travel in China for many reasons. Journeys are far more scenic and than endless highways, not to mention the growing number of road accidents. Train stations tend to be located much closer to city centers than airports, and you avoid the tedious airport waits. On sleeper services it is possible to avoid the cost of a hotel night, while still being able to spread out and

relax. Do not underestimate the advantage of being able to lie down as you travel. No matter how long the journeys are, I have never seen a fellow passenger suffer from motion sickness, an affliction that is altogether too common on buses.

Though in backwater areas, slow trains can be primitive, intercity trains are universally air-conditioned and mostly kept very clean. There are 200kmph (125-mph) trains between Shenzhen and Guangzhou, 300kmph (188-mph) trains and tilting trains using British technology under trial; the world's highest line is under construction to Lhasa; and the world's first commercial maglev (magnetic levitation) line runs from Shanghai to the Pudong airport.

SEAT CLASSES Given China's size, most intercity services are overnight (or sometimes over 2 nights), so sleeper accommodations are the most common. The best choice is **soft sleeper** *(ruan wo)*, consisting of four beds in a lockable compartment, the two upper berths slightly cheaper than the lower ones. Berths have individual reading lights and there's a volume control for the PA system. **Hard sleeper** *(yiing wo)* has couchettes, separated into groups of six by partitions, but open to the corridor. Berths are provided in columns of three and are cheaper as they get farther from the floor. The top berth has very little headroom and can be uncomfortably cramped for foreigners. The bottom berth on the other hand has the advantage of being able to stow your luggage underneath. Lights go off at about 10pm and on again at 6am. Thermoses of boiled water are in each compartment and group of berths, refilled either by the attendants or by you from a boiler at the end of each car. Compartments often have cups, but it's best to take your own or get one of the clear plastic tea flasks that many Chinese carry and are widely available in supermarkets. Bed linens are provided in both classes.

More modern trains have a mixture of Western (usually at the end of the soft sleeper carriage) and Chinese squat toilets. Washing facilities are limited, and except on the highest-quality trains, there's cold water only (and this may sometimes run out). On the very best trains there's hot water, free toothbrush and toothpaste hotel-style, and even electric hand dryers and shaver sockets. But this is rare. A tiny handful of trains have deluxe soft sleeper *(gaoji ruan wo)*, with two berths in a compartment (Kowloon-Shanghai and Kowloon-Beijing, for instance), and in the case of some trains on the Beijing-to-Shanghai run, these compartments have private bathrooms.

Almost all trains also have a **hard seat** class *(yiing zuo)*, which on many major routes is now far from hard, although not the way to spend the night. **Soft seat** *(ruan zuo)* appears on daytime expresses only, is less crowded, and is now often in two-deck form, giving excellent views.

REFRESHMENTS   Attendants push carts with soft drinks, beer, mineral water, and instant-noodle packages through all classes at regular intervals. Separate carts bring through *kuaai can* (fast food) in cardboard boxes. This is usually dreadful, and costs ¥15 ($1.95/£1). Licensed carts on platforms often sell freshly cooked local dishes, which are slightly better, and they also offer fresh fruit in season. All overnight trains have dining cars, but the food is usually overpriced and very poor in quality. It's best to bring a supply of what pleases you, bought in convenience stores, supermarkets, and bakeries.

TYPES OF TRAIN   Where possible, choose a train with a T prefix. These *tekuaai* (especially fast) trains are the expresses, and come with the highest levels of accommodations and service. Staff may be uniformed and coiffed like flight attendants, willing and helpful. K trains (*kuaaisu*—"quick speed") are more common, and nearly as good. Occasionally Y

trains (*luyou,* services for tourists) and L trains (*linshi,* temporary additional services, particularly at Spring Festival), can be found. The remaining services with no letter prefixes vary widely in quality across the country, from accommodations as good as that on K trains but at slower speeds, to doddering rolling stock on winding, out-of-the-way lines and with cockroaches and mice for company (no extra charge).

TIMETABLE   A national railway timetable can be found for sale at stations in larger cities, updated twice a year, and some regional bureaus produce their own, or smaller summaries of the most important trains. All are in Chinese only, and most are so poorly organized that they are initially incomprehensible even to most Chinese. Rail enthusiast Duncan Peattie produces an annual **English translation** of the October edition of the national timetable. At $20 for the PDF format (more for an A4), it is a very useful addition to the reference selection of independent travelers. Write **chinatt@eudoramail. com** for more information.

Timetables for a particular station are posted in its ticket office, and can be read by comparing the characters for a destination given in this book with what's on the wall.

TICKETS   Rail ticket prices are fixed by a complicated formula involving a tiny sum per kilometer, and supplements for air-conditioning, speed, and higher classes of berth (soft sleepers are typically 50% more expensive than hard sleepers). Prices, samples of which are given throughout this book, are not open to negotiation. In my experience, hard sleeper berths are quite acceptable for short overnight trips of 12 hours or so. For longer journeys of 24 hours or more, I usually spend the extra for a soft sleeper.

Ticket offices always have a separate entrance from the main railway station entrance. In a few larger cities, there are separate offices for VIPs and foreign guests, or just for booking sleepers. Payment is only in cash. In most cases bookings can be made only 4 days in advance, including the day of travel. But increasingly in larger cities, this is expanding to as many as 12 days, and the same or longer for advance telephone bookings (in Mandarin only, like almost every other telephone service in China).

Most seats on an individual train are sold at its point of departure, with only limited allocations kept for intermediate stops depending on their size and importance. Your best choice of train is always one that is setting off from where you are. If you can only obtain a hard sleeper ticket but want a soft sleeper, you can attempt to upgrade on the train. There is a desk for this purpose in the middle of the train, usually around car nos. 10 to 12.

The simplest way to book tickets is via a travel agent. The few with terminals accessing the railway system charge ¥5 (65¢/30p) commission. Most others charge around ¥20 ($2.60/£1.30), which should include delivery to your hotel. Agents within hotels often try to charge more. It's best to give agents a choice of trains and berth. You pay upfront, but the exact ticket price, printed clearly on the ticket, will depend on the train and berth obtained.

With the exception of public holidays, tickets are now rarely difficult to obtain. Ticket prices are hiked on some routes during Spring Festival.

Advance booking from overseas is possible through CITS and some other agents at large markups, and so are not advised. Contact your local China National Tourist Office to find agents (see "Visitor Information & Maps," earlier in this chapter) if you must. In **Hong Kong,** China Travel Service sells tickets for the expresses from Kowloon to Guangzhou, Beijing, and Shanghai with no commission, and tickets for a selection of trains between other Chinese cities for a reasonable markup. Never use online agents, either Hong Kong or mainland based, as they charge up to *70% more* than they should.

You'll need your ticket to get to the platform, which will only open a few minutes before or after the train's arrival (if you buy a soft sleeper ticket, you may be able to use the VIP *guii bin* waiting room, but some stations now charge to enter these facilities, regardless of the ticket you have). On the train, the attendant will swap your ticket for a token with your berth number. Shortly before arrival, she will return to reexchange it (you never miss your stop in China). Keep the ticket ready, as it will be checked again as you leave the station.

I often carry my own pillow, which makes the journey much more comfy, although sleeping pills may be the only solution for insomniacs. For those who are overweight, remember that berths are not wide, about 2 feet by 6 feet 6 inches or so and are set up for people who are generally more petite than most Americans, so a bit tight but tolerable unless you're claustrophobic.

In all the Chinese rail journeys I have made (probably in the hundreds by now) I have never had anything stolen. Take sensible precautions as you would anywhere, and keep vital items (passport/money, and so on) close to you, but there is certainly no need for paranoia.

BY BUS

China's highway system, nonexistent 20 years ago, is growing rapidly, and journey times by road between many cities have been dramatically cut to the point where on a few routes, buses are now faster than trains. Although most buses are fairly battered, in some areas they offer a remarkable level of luxury—particularly on the east coast, where there are the funds to pay for a higher quality of travel. Some buses even have on-board toilets and free bottled water.

Many bus stations now offer a variety of services. At the top end are *kongtiao* (air-conditioned) *gaosu* (high-speed, usually meaning that toll expressways are used) *haohua* (luxury) buses, on which smoking is usually forbidden and that rule is largely enforced, at least in urban areas. These tickets are usually easy to obtain at the bus station, and prices are clearly displayed and written on the ticket. There are no extra charges for baggage, which in smaller and older buses is typically piled up on the cover over the engine next to the driver. It's worth booking a day ahead to get a seat at the front, which may have more legroom and better views.

Buses usually depart punctually, pause at a checking station where the number of passengers is compared with the number of tickets sold in advance, then dither while empty seats are filled with groups waiting at the roadside who bargain for a lower fare.

The main disadvantage of this form of transportation is the other passengers. Many of the rural population are unused to travel and get sick very quickly. Although sick bags are provided, peasants still tend to puke on the floor, or down their trouser leg or lean across you so that they can vomit out of the window. Some coach companies have started handing out complimentary travel sickness pills, but rather than reassure you this will probably mean that this particular trip is going to be a long and unpleasant one.

Sleeper buses, although cheaper, should generally be avoided when an overnight train is an alternative. Usually they have three rows of two-tier berths, which are extremely narrow and do not recline fully.

Transport can vary widely in quality in rural and remoter areas, but it is usually dirty and decrepit, and may be shared with livestock.

BY CAR (TAXI)

While foreign residents of China go through the necessary paperwork, with the exception of one rental operation at Beijing's Capital Airport, self-drive for foreign visitors is not possible, and without previous experience, the no-holds-barred driving style of China is nothing you want to tackle. Renting a vehicle is nevertheless commonplace, but it comes with a driver. **Hong Kong** and **Macau** are so small that there's simply no point in renting a car and facing navigational and parking difficulties, when there are plentiful, well-regulated taxis available.

All larger mainland hotels have transport departments, but book a vehicle from a five-star Beijing hotel to take you to the Eastern Qing Tombs, for instance, and you may be asked for ¥1,200 ($156/ £78). Walk outside and flag down a taxi (not those waiting outside), and you can achieve the same thing by taxi for around ¥300 ($39/£19). Branches of CITS and other travel agencies will also be happy to arrange cars for you, but at a hugely marked-up price.

Despite the language barrier, bargaining with taxi drivers is more straightforward than you might expect. In most areas there are far more taxis than there is business, and half- and full-day hires are very welcome. To take Beijing as an example, about 67,500 taxis are cruising around empty for much of the time, the drivers typically taking in around ¥300 ($39/£19) for a 12-hour day (the drivers of cheaper taxis earn more, not less); most are glad to have a change and a day's guaranteed employment. Start flagging down cabs the day before you want to travel, and negotiate an all-in price, using characters from this book (for your destination), those written down for you by your hotel receptionist (times, pickup point, and other details), and a pen and paper (or calculator) to bargain prices. Avoid giving an exact kilometer distance, since

Ten Rules for Taking Taxis around Town

1. **Never** go with a driver who approaches you at an airport. Leave the building and head for the stand. As they are everywhere else in the world, airport taxis are the most likely to cause trouble, but drivers who approach you are usually *hei che*—illegal and meterless "black cabs."

2. Cabs waiting for business outside major tourist sights, especially those with drivers who call out to foreigners, should generally be avoided, as should cabs whose drivers ask you where you want to go even before you get in. Always flag down a passing cab, and 9 times in 10 the precautions listed here will be unnecessary.

3. If you're staying in an upmarket hotel, do not go with taxis called by the doorman or waiting in line outside. Even at some famous hotels, drivers pay kickbacks to the doormen to allow them to join the line on the forecourt. Some cabs are merely waiting because many guests, Chinese and foreign alike, will be out-of-town people who can be easily misled. Instead, just walk out of the hotel and flag down a passing cab for yourself. Take the hotel's business card to show to a taxi driver when you want to get back.

4. Better hotels give you a piece of paper with the taxi registration number on it as you board or alight, so that you can complain if something goes wrong. Often you won't know if it has, of course, and there's no guarantee that anything will happen if you complain to the hotel.

5. Look to see if the supervision card, usually with a photo of the driver and a telephone number, is prominently displayed. If it isn't, you may have problems. Choose another cab.

6. Can you clearly see the meter? If it's recessed behind the gear stick, partly hidden by the artfully folded face cloth on top, choose another cab.

7. Always make sure you see the meter reset. If you didn't actually see the flag pushed down, which shouldn't happen until you actually move off, then you may end up paying for the time the cab was in the line.

8. If you are by yourself, sit in the front seat. Have a map with you and look as if you know where you are going (even if you don't).

9. Rates per kilometer are usually clearly posted on the side of the cab. They vary widely from place to place, as well as by vehicle type. Flag-fall, not usually more than ¥10 ($1.30/65p), includes a few kilometers; then the standard kilometer rate begins. But in most towns, after a few more kilometers, the rate jumps by 50% if the driver has pushed a button on the front of the meter. This is for one-way trips out of town, and the button usually should not be pushed, but it always is. As a result, it's rarely worthwhile to have a cab wait for you and take you back.

10. Pay what's on the meter, and don't tip—the driver will insist on giving change. Always ask for a receipt. Should you leave something in a cab, there's a remarkably high success rate at getting even valuable items back if the number on the receipt is called, and the details on it provided.

if you overrun it (and with China's poor road signage and the drivers' lack of experience outside their own town centers, you're bound to get lost at least once), there will be attempts to renegotiate. For the same reason, it's best to avoid being precise to the minute about a return time, but note that especially in big cities drivers sometimes have to be back in time to hand the car to the man who will drive it through the night. Be prepared to pay road tolls, and ensure that the driver gets lunch. If you find a driver who is pleasant and helpful, take his mobile phone number and employ him on subsequent days and for any airport trips.

17 Tips on Accommodations

CHOOSING A HOTEL IN CHINA

There are two types of hotel in mainland China: the **Sino-foreign joint-venture** hotels with familiar brand-names, and **Chinese-owned and -managed** hotels. At the government-issued four- and five-star Chinese properties, they want you to think that they are at the same level as the joint-ventures; at lower levels, the accommodations can range from indescribably battered and grubby, to friendly and comfortable.

Your **first choice** at the four- or five-star level should be a familiar brand name or a property from one of the Asian luxury chains. In most cases the buildings are Chinese-owned, and the foreign part of the venture is the management company, which provides senior management and trains the staff, ensures conformity with their standards (never entirely possible), does worldwide marketing, and generally provides up to 90% of what you'd expect from the same brand at home. There are Grand Hyatts in Beijing and Shanghai. The Starwood group's St. Regis, Sheraton, and Westin brands are here, as well as Six Continents' Crowne Plaza and Holiday Inn; so are Hilton, Marriott, Ramada, Best Western, and more, although all are concentrated in China's largest cities. The Hong Kong Shangri-La group's hotels are among China's best, and they are notably successful in extracting the best from local staff. The Marco Polo and Harbour Plaza luxury brands are also in China (the Beijing Marco Polo in particular should not be overlooked). The Palace Hotel in Beijing is managed by the same company that manages the legendary Peninsula Hotel in Hong Kong (also Bangkok, New York, and other cities). Unfortunately, such large operations also have very large carbon footprints, and often put very little back into the local economies. It is therefore wise to remember that every time you open your wallet, you are voting either yes or no for the environment.

Your **second choice** should be a wholly Chinese hotel with foreigners in senior management, whose main purpose is simply to be there and make sure that things actually happen. But in this type of hotel and in the joint-venture, the general manager may be ignorant as to what's actually going on—such as the transport department using hotel vehicles for private rentals or the doormen charging taxis to be allowed to wait in the line.

Entirely **Chinese-owned and -operated** hotels at government-issued four- and five-star levels usually have one thing in common with their counterparts— they charge the same (or, at least, attempt to), but you certainly won't get value for your money. At four-star level and below, the best choice is almost always the newest—teething troubles aside, most things will work, staff will be eager to please (if not quite sure how), rooms will be spotless, and rates will be easily bargained down, since few hotels spend any money on advertising their existence. The aim is to find sweetly inept but willing service rather than the sour leftovers of the *tie faanwan* (iron rice bowl) era of guaranteed employment, for whom everything is too much effort.

A drawback for all hoteliers is that the government requires them to employ far more people than they need, and it's nearly impossible to obtain staff with any experience in hotel work. The joint-venture hotels are the training institutions for the rest of the Chinese hotel industry, which steals their local staff as soon as possible. Lower-level hotels are run on half-understood rules, with which there's half-compliance, half the time. You may stay in a three-star that has perhaps a dozen foreign guests a year, but whenever they knock on a door, housekeeping staff may announce themselves in English ("Housekeeping!") although that's the only English word they know, and 99% of their guests won't know even that. But it's written down in a manual somewhere. A hotel may have designated nonsmoking rooms, but that doesn't mean they don't have ashtrays.

Until recently throughout China, only hotels with **special licenses** were allowed to take foreign guests. This requirement has already vanished in Yunnan and Beijing, and may eventually disappear elsewhere. In theory, all hotels with such licenses have at least one English-speaker, usually of modest ability, shouted for by nervous, giggling staff as soon as you walk in.

The **Chinese star-rating system** is meaningless. Five-star ratings are awarded from Beijing authorities, but four-star and lower depend upon provincial concerns. In some areas a four-star hotel must have a pool, in others a bowling alley, and in others a tennis court. The Jacuzzi may have more rings than a sequoia, the bowling alley be permanently out of order, and the tennis court be used for barbecues (because although it's a required feature, China simply doesn't have enough tennis players), but the hotel will retain its four stars, as long as it banquets the inspectors

adequately. In general, Chinese hotels receive almost no maintenance once they open. There are "five-star" hotels in Beijing that have gone a decade without proper redecoration or refurbishment. Foreign managements force the issue with building owners, but it's rare elsewhere that standards are maintained. A new three-star will usually be better than an old four-star.

While hotel construction is growing at unprecedented rates, there are of course many downsides. According to the Xinhua News Agency, vice-minister of construction Qiu Boaxing, recent development trends can be compared to the massive destruction of cultural relics and sites that took place during The Great Leap Forward and The Cultural Revolution: "This is leading to a poor sight—many cities have a similar construction style. It is like a thousand cities having the same appearance," he said.

Outside of joint-venture hotels, don't rely on the **extras,** many of which we do not even list, and even if we do, it's no guarantee that you'll find them fit to use. Salons, massage rooms, nightclubs, and karaoke rooms are often merely bases for other kinds of illegal entertainment (for men). Fitness equipment may be broken and inadequately supervised, and pool hygiene poor, so proceed with care.

You may receive unexpected **phone calls.** If you are female, the phone may be put down without anything being said, as it may be if you are male and answer in English. But if the caller persists and is female, and you hear the word *aanmo* (massage), then what is being offered probably needs no further explanation, but a massage is only the beginning. Unplug the phone when you go to sleep.

Almost all rooms in China, however basic, have the following: a telephone whose line can usually be unplugged for use in a laptop; air-conditioning, which is either central with a wall-mounted control, or individual to the room with a remote control, and which may double as a heater; a television, usually with no English channels except CCTV 9 (to which no buttons may be tuned) and possibly an in-house movie channel using pirated DVDs or VCDs; and a thermos of boiled water or a kettle to boil your own, usually with cups (which you should wash before using) and free bags of green tea. In a cupboard somewhere there will be a quilt. Between the beds (most rooms still have twin beds) will be an array of switches, which may or may not actually control what they say they control. In the bathroom there are free soap and shampoo, and in better hotels a shower cap, and toothbrush/toothpaste package (but bring your own).

Ordinary Chinese hotels usually speak of a *biaozhun jian,* or **standard room,** which usually means a room with twin beds, occasionally with a double bed, and with a private bathroom. Often double beds have only recently been installed in a few rooms, which are now referred to as *danren jian* or single rooms. Nevertheless, two people can stay there, but the price is lower than that of a twin room. In older hotels, genuine single rooms are available, and in many hotels below four-star level there are triple rooms and quads, which can also serve as dorms shared with strangers.

Foreign **credit cards** are increasingly accepted in three-star hotels upwards, but never rely on this. Most hotels accepting foreigners have foreign exchange facilities on the premises, although some may send you elsewhere to exchange checks. Almost all require **payment in advance,** plus a deposit *(yajin),* which is refundable when you leave. Keep all receipts you are given, as you may need to show one to floor staff to get your key, and you may in fact need to hand the key back and retrieve the receipt again before you can leave. To get your deposit back, you'll need to hand over the receipt for that when you check out, and since staff occasionally forget to

enter payments in computer or ledger, you may need receipts to prevent yourself from being charged twice.

To **check in,** you'll need your passport and you'll have to complete a registration form (which will usually be in English). Always inspect the room before checking in. You'll be asked how many nights you want to stay, and you should always say just one, because if you say four, you'll be asked for the 4 nights' fee in advance (plus a deposit), and because it may turn out that the hot water isn't hot enough, the karaoke rooms are over your head, or a building site behind the hotel starts work at 8am sharp. Once you've tried 1 night, you can pay for more.

When you **check out,** the floor staff will be called to make sure you haven't stolen anything; this may not happen speedily, so allow a little extra time.

Children 12 and under stay for free in their parent's room. Hotels will add an extra bed to your room for a small charge, which you can negotiate.

SURFING FOR HOTELS

In addition to the online travel booking sites **Travelocity, Expedia, Orbitz, Priceline,** and **Hotwire,** you can book hotels through **Hotels.com; Quikbook** (www.quikbook.com); and **Travelaxe** (www.travelaxe.net).

HotelChatter.com is a daily webzine offering smart coverage and critiques of hotels worldwide. Go to **TripAdvisor.com** or **HotelShark.com** for helpful independent consumer reviews of hotels and resort properties.

It's a good idea to **get a confirmation number** and **make a printout** of any online booking transaction.

SAVING ON YOUR HOTEL ROOM

The **rack rate** is the maximum rate that a hotel charges for a room. In China these rates are nothing more than the first bid in a bargaining discussion, designed to keep the final price you will actually pay as high as possible. You'll almost never pay more than 90%, usually not more than 70%, frequently not more than 50%, and sometimes as little as 30% of this first asking price. Guidelines on discounts are given for each city. Here are some tips to lower the cost of your room:

- **Do not book ahead.** Just show up and bargain. In China this applies as much to the top-class joint-venture names as to all the others. The best price is available over the counter, as long as there's room. For most of the year, across China, there are far more rooms than customers at every level. For ordinary Chinese hotels you may well pay double by booking ahead, and there's no guarantee your reservation will be honored if the hotel fills up or if someone else arrives before you, cash in hand. E-mail is almost never replied to, and faxes get ignored. Most Chinese just show up and bargain.

- **Book online.** If you want to be absolutely certain of a particular joint-venture hotel at a busy period, look at its website for rates. Major hotel chains operating in China often have their best *published* rate on their own websites. However, these rates fluctuate constantly according to demand, and are sometimes directly linked to computerized inventory, which alters prices at frequent intervals, sometimes hourly. Prices for any time of year booked a long way ahead will always look uninviting. They'll be much cheaper nearer the time, unless some major event is taking place. Ordinary hotels, if they have a website at all, will just quote rack rates.

- **Dial any central booking number.** Contrary to popular wisdom, as the better hotels manage their rates with increasing care, the central booking number is likely to have a rate as good as or better than the rate you

can get by calling the hotel directly, and the call is usually toll-free.

- **Avoid Chinese online agencies.** Avoid booking through Chinese hotel agencies and websites specializing in Chinese hotels. The discounts they offer are precisely what you can get for yourself, and you can in fact beat them because you won't be paying their markup. Many of these have no allocations at all, and simply jump on the phone to book a room as soon as they hear from you.

IN HONG KONG & MACAU

Hong Kong in particular is well stocked with hotels that regularly make their way onto lists of the world's best. Service is second to none, and they are worth flying halfway around the world to stay in. None of what's said about mainland hotels above applies.

LANDING THE BEST ROOM

Somebody has to get the best room in the house. It might as well be you. You can start by joining the hotel's frequent-guest program, which may make you eligible for upgrades. A hotel-branded credit card usually gives its owner "silver" or "gold" status in frequent-guest programs for free. Always ask about a corner room. They're often larger and quieter, with more windows and light, and they often cost the same as standard rooms. When you make your reservation, ask if the hotel is renovating; if it is, request a room away from the construction. Ask about nonsmoking rooms and rooms with views. Be sure to request your choice of twin, queen-, or king-size beds. If you're a light sleeper, ask for a quiet room away from vending or ice machines, elevators, restaurants, bars, and discos. Ask for a room that has been recently renovated or refurbished.

If you aren't happy with your room when you arrive, ask for another one. Most lodgings will be willing to accommodate you.

18 Tips on Dining

See "Appendix B: The Chinese Menu," for hints on dining, and a city-by-city list of recommended dishes, complete with the characters to help you order them.

FAST FACTS: China

American Express Beijing: Room 2101, China World Tower, China World Trade Center; ℂ 010/6505-2639. Shanghai: Room 206, Retail Plaza, Shanghai Centre; ℂ 021/6279-8082. Guangzhou: Room 806, GITIC Plaza Hotel; ℂ 020/8331-1771. Xiamen: Room 212, Holiday Inn Crowne Plaza; ℂ 0592/212-0268. Amex offices are open Monday through Friday from 9:30am to 5:30pm. After-hours: U.S. hot line ℂ 001336/393-1111; Hong Kong hot line ℂ 00852/2885-9377. Emergency card replacement: ℂ 00852/2277-1010. Stolen checks: ℂ 010800/610-0276, toll-free.

ATM Networks See "ATMs," under "Money & Costs," earlier in this chapter.

Business Hours Offices are generally open from 9am to 6pm but are closed Saturday and Sunday. All shops, sights, restaurants, and transport systems offer the same service 7 days a week. Shops are typically open at least from 8am to 8pm. Bank opening hours vary widely (see "Currency," earlier in this chapter, and the "Fast Facts" sections for individual destinations). In **Hong Kong** most offices are open Monday through Friday from 9am to 5pm, with lunch hour from 1 to 2pm; Saturday business hours are generally 9am to 1pm. Most Hong Kong shops are open 7 days a week, from 10am to at least 7pm.

Car Rentals Rental is only possible with a Chinese driver, except in Hong Kong and Macau. See "Getting Around China," earlier in this chapter.

Cashpoints See "ATM Networks," above.

Currency See "Money & Costs" p. 33.

Customs **What You Can Bring into China**

Generally, you can bring into China anything for personal use that you plan to take away with you when you leave, with the usual exceptions of arms and drugs, or plant materials, animals, and foods from diseased areas. There are no problems with cameras or video recorders, GPS equipment, laptops, or any other standard electronic equipment. Two unusual prohibitions are "old/used garments" and "printed matter, magnetic media, films, or photographs which are deemed to be detrimental to the political, economic, cultural and moral interests of China," as the regulations put it. Large quantities of religious literature, overtly political materials, or books on Tibet might cause you difficulties (having a pile of pictures of the Dalai Lama certainly will, if discovered), but in general, small amounts of personal reading matter in non-Chinese languages do not present problems. Customs officers are for the most part easygoing, and foreign visitors are very rarely searched. Customs declaration forms have now vanished from all major points of entry, but if you are importing more than $5,000 in cash, you should declare it, or theoretically you could face difficulties at the time of departure, although once again, this would be highly unlikely.

Importing or exporting more than ¥6,000 ($780/£390) in yuan is also theoretically prohibited, but again, it's never checked. Chinese currency is anyway best obtained within China (or in Hong Kong), and is of no use once you leave.

What You Can Take Home from China

An official seal must be attached to any item created between 1795 and 1949 that is taken out of China; older items cannot be exported. But in fact you are highly unlikely to find any genuine antiques, so this is a moot point (and if the antiques dealer is genuine, then he'll know all about how to get the seal). There are no such prohibitions on exporting items from Hong Kong, which is where you can find reliable dealers with authentic pieces and a willingness to allow thermoluminescence testing to prove it.

Almost everybody is amazed at the number of cheap DVDs on sale in China. They are extremely tempting, especially compared to the ridiculous prices at home. Know that the producers of these discs are often the same gangsters who smuggle undocumented migrants in containers and sell females into sexual slavery; don't give them your money.

U.S. Citizens: For specifics on what you can bring back and the corresponding fees, download the invaluable free pamphlet *Know Before You Go* online at **www.cbp.gov.** (Click on "Travel," and then click on "Know Before You Go! Online Brochure") Or contact the **U.S. Customs & Border Protection (CBP),** 1300 Pennsylvania Ave., NW, Washington, DC 20229 (© **877/287-8667**) and request the pamphlet.

Canadian Citizens: For a clear summary of Canadian rules, write for the booklet *I Declare,* issued by the **Canada Border Services Agency** (© **800/461-9999** in Canada, or 204/983-3500; **www.cbsa-asfc.gc.ca**).

U.K. Citizens: For information, contact **HM Customs & Excise** at © **0845/010-9000** (from outside the U.K., 020/8929-0152), or consult their website at **www.hmce.gov.uk.**

Australian Citizens: A helpful brochure available from Australian consulates or Customs offices is *Know Before You Go.* For more information, call the **Australian Customs Service** at © **1300/363-263,** or log onto **www.customs.gov.au.**

New Zealand Citizens: Most questions are answered in a free pamphlet available at New Zealand consulates and Customs offices: *New Zealand Customs Guide for Travellers, Notice no. 4.* For more information, contact **New Zealand Customs,** The Customhouse, 17–21 Whitmore St., Box 2218, Wellington (© **04/473-6099** or 0800/428-786; **www.customs.govt.nz**).

Doctors & Dentists Many hotels have medical clinics with registered nurses, as well as doctors on duty at specified hours or on call 24 hours. Otherwise, your concierge or consulate can refer you to a doctor or dentist. If it's an emergency, get a Mandarin speaker to dial © **120** in mainland China, or dial © 999 in Hong Kong or Macau.

Driving Rules "I'm bigger than you, so get out of my way," sums it up. But you won't be driving anyway. When you cross a road, assume that the drivers are all out to get you. Driving is on the right. **Hong Kong** and **Macau** are far more law-abiding, and driving is on the left. See "Getting Around China" (p. 53), earlier in this chapter.

Drugstores Bring supplies of your favorite over-the-counter medicines with you, since supplies of well-known Western brands are unreliable and sometimes fake. All familiar brands are available in **Hong Kong.**

Electricity The electricity used in all parts of China is 220 volts, alternating current (AC), 50 cycles. Most devices from North America, therefore, cannot be used without a transformer. The most common outlet takes the North American two-flat-pin plug (but not the three-pin version, or those with one pin broader than the other). Nearly as common are outlets for the two-round-pin plugs common in Europe. Outlets for the three-flat-pin (two pins at an angle) used in Australia, for instance, are also frequently seen. Most hotel rooms have all three, and indeed many outlets are designed to take all three plugs. You need a uniquely Chinese adapter with three flat prongs.

Adapters are available for only ¥8 to ¥16 ($1–$2/50p–£1) in department stores; good hotels will be happy to provide adapters, however, so you needn't be concerned about bringing one. China is quite sophisticated in this area, and I found that one can easily buy a power strip that has the requisite plug to go into a Chinese wall outlet and eight universal outlets that will accept any type of plug used in the world. Just remember that power is 240V (50 Hz), so make sure anything you bring is compatible. If you have 110V devices your hotel will most likely be able to supply a voltage converter. Shaver sockets are common in bathrooms of hotels from three stars upward. In **Hong Kong** and **Macau,** the British-style three-chunky-pin plugs are standard, and these also often appear in mainland joint-venture hotels built with Hong Kong assistance. The electrical adapters you need are either those with long, fairly thin round prongs or those with shorter and fatter prongs.

Embassies & Consulates Most countries maintain embassies in Beijing and consulates in Hong Kong. Australia also has consulates in Guangzhou and Shanghai; Canada and the U.K. in Chongqing, Guangzhou, and Shanghai; New Zealand in Shanghai; and the U.S. in Chengdu, Guangzhou, Shanghai, and Shenyang.

Emergencies No one speaks English at emergency numbers in China, although your best bet will be ⓒ **110.** Find help nearer at hand. In **Hong Kong** dial ⓒ **999** for police, fire, or ambulance. In **Macau** dial ⓒ **999** for medical emergencies, ⓒ **573-333** for the police, and ⓒ **572-222** for the fire department.

Holidays See "China Calendar of Events," earlier in this chapter.

Hot Lines Hot lines and all kinds of telephone booking and information numbers are given throughout this guide. But in almost no cases whatsoever will English be spoken at the other end. Ask English-speaking staff at your hotel to find answers to your queries and to make any necessary calls on your behalf.

Internet Access Internet access through anonymous dial-up is widely available, as are Internet cafes. See "Staying Connected," earlier in this chapter.

Language English is widely spoken in Hong Kong, fairly common in Macau, and rare in the mainland, although there will be someone who speaks a little English at your hotel. Ask that person to help you with phone calls and bookings. Almost no information, booking, complaint, or emergency lines in the mainland have anyone who speaks English.

Legal Aid If you get on the wrong side of what passes for the law in China, contact your consulate immediately.

Liquor Laws With the exception of some minor local regulations, there are no liquor laws in China. Alcohol can be bought in any convenience store, supermarket, restaurant, bar, hotel, or club, 7 days a week, and may be drunk anywhere you feel like drinking it. If the shop is open 24 hours, then the alcohol is available 24 hours, too. Closing times for bars and clubs vary according to demand, but typically it's all over by 3am. In **Hong Kong**, liquor laws largely follow the U.K. model; restaurants, bars, and clubs must obtain licenses to sell alcohol for consumption on the premises, and shops must have licenses to sell it for consumption off the premises. In either case, licenses prohibit sale of alcohol to persons under 18. Licensing hours vary from area to area.

Lost & Found Be sure to alert all of your credit card companies the minute you discover your wallet has been lost or stolen. Your credit card company or insurer may require a police report number or record of the loss, although many Public Security Bureau offices (police stations) will be reluctant to do anything as energetic as lift a pen. Most credit card companies have an emergency toll-free number to call if your card is lost or stolen: In **mainland China,** Visa's emergency number is ℂ 010/800-440-0027; American Express cardholders and traveler's check holders should call ℂ 010/800-610-0277; MasterCard holders should call ℂ 010/800-110-7309; and Diners Club members should call Hong Kong at ℂ 852/2860-1800, or call the U.S. collect at ℂ 416/369-6313. From within **Hong Kong,** Visa's telephone number is ℂ 800/900 872, MasterCard's ℂ 800/966 677, Diners Club's ℂ 2860 1888, and Amex's ℂ 800/962 403. Visa also has a phone number for within **Macau:** ℂ 300-28561. Keeping a separate list of the serial numbers of your traveler's checks will speed up their replacement. Also see "Emergency Cash," under "Money & Costs," earlier in this chapter.

Mail Sending mail from China is remarkably reliable, although sending it to private addresses within China is not. Take the mail to post offices rather than using mailboxes. Some larger hotels have postal services on-site. It helps if mail sent out of the country has its country of destination written in characters, but this is not essential, although hotel staff will often help. Letters and cards written in red ink will occasionally be rejected. Overseas mail: **postcards** ¥4.20 (50¢/25p), **letters under 10 grams** ¥5.40 (70¢/35p), **letters under 20 grams** ¥6.50 (80¢/40p). EMS (**express parcels** under 500g): to the U.S.: ¥180 to ¥240 ($23–$30/ £11–£15); to Europe ¥220 to ¥280 ($28–$35/£14–£17); to Australia ¥160 to ¥210 ($20–$26/£10–£13). **Normal parcels** up to 1 kilogram (2¼ lb.): to the **U.S.** by air ¥95 to ¥159 ($12–$20/£6–£10), by sea ¥20 to ¥84 ($2.50–$14/£1.25–£7); to the **U.K.** by air ¥77 to ¥162 ($9.50–$20/£4.75–£10), by sea ¥22 to ¥108 ($11–$14/ £5.50–£7); to **Australia** by air ¥70 to ¥144 ($8.75–$18/£4.35–£9), by sea ¥15 to ¥89 ($1.90–$11/£95p–£5.50). Letters and parcels can be registered for a small extra charge. Registration forms and Customs declaration forms are in Chinese and French. The post offices of **Hong Kong** and **Macau** are entirely reliable, but both have their own stamps and rates.

Newspapers & Magazines Sino-foreign joint-venture hotels in the bigger cities have a selection of foreign newspapers and magazines available, but these are otherwise not on sale. The government distributes a propaganda sheet called *China Daily,* usually free at hotels, and there are occasional local variations. Cities with larger populations support a number of self-censoring entertainment magazines usually produced by resident foreigners and only slightly more bland when produced by Chinese aiming at the same market. Nevertheless, these do have intermittently accurate entertainment listings and restaurant reviews. A vast range of English publications is easily available in **Hong Kong** and **Macau,** as well as local newspapers such as the *South China Morning Post.*

Passports Allow plenty of time before your trip to apply for a passport; processing normally takes 3 weeks but can take longer during busy periods (especially spring). And keep in mind that if you need a passport in a hurry, you'll pay a higher processing fee.

For Residents of Australia: You can pick up an application from your local post office or any branch of Passports Australia, but you must schedule an interview at the passport office to present your application materials. Call the **Australian Passport Information Service** at ℰ **131-232,** or visit the government website at www.passports.gov.au.

For Residents of Canada: Passport applications are available at travel agencies throughout Canada or from the central **Passport Office,** Department of Foreign Affairs and International Trade, Ottawa, ON K1A 0G3 (ℰ **800/567-6868;** www.ppt.gc.ca).

For Residents of Ireland: You can apply for a 10-year passport at the **Passport Office,** Setanta Centre, Molesworth Street, Dublin 2 (ℰ **01/671-1633;** www.irlgov.ie/iveagh). Those under age 18 and over 65 must apply for a 3-year passport. You can also apply at 1A South Mall, Cork (ℰ **021/272-525**), or at most main post offices.

For Residents of New Zealand: You can pick up a passport application at any New Zealand Passports Office or download it from their website. Contact the **Passports Office** at ℰ **0800/225-050** in New Zealand, or 04/474-8100, or log on to www.passports.govt.nz.

For Residents of the United Kingdom: To pick up an application for a standard 10-year passport (5-year passport for children under 16), visit your nearest passport office, major post office, or travel agency or contact the **United Kingdom Passport Service** at ℰ **0870/521-0410** or search its website at www.ukpa.gov.uk.

For Residents of the United States: Whether you're applying in person or by mail, you can download passport applications from the U.S. State Department website at **http://travel.state.gov.** To find your regional passport office, either check the U.S. State Department website or call the **National Passport Information Center** toll-free number (ℰ **877/487-2778**) for automated information.

Police Known to foreigners as the **PSB (Public Security Bureau,** *gong'an ju*), although these represent only one of several different types of officer in mainland China, the police (*jingcha*) are quite simply best avoided. Since they are keen to avoid doing any work, you have the same interests at heart. If you must see them for some reason, then approach your hotel for assistance first, and visit the PSB offices listed in this guide as dealing with visa extensions, since these are almost the only places you are likely to find an English-speaker of sorts. In **Hong Kong** and **Macau,** however, you can usually ask policemen for directions and expect them to be generally helpful.

Radio If you own an AM/FM shortwave radio, there are many English-language broadcasts on standard FM radio in Beijing. Small (as in smaller than a mass-market paperback book) sized, battery-operated radios are commonly available in all the electronics markets in the larger cities including fully capable, digitally tuned models for about ¥120 ($15/£7.50) as well as a full range of walkie-talkie-type two-way radios, and fully functional GPS units. If you do want to hear BBC, Voice of America, or any other regularly scheduled short-wave broadcasts, I'd suggest investigating, copying, and taking along with you their broadcast schedules. The shortwave services tend to broadcast on different frequencies at different times of the day, as well as to make major changes in schedule with the changing seasons. This is because broadcast transmissions are much more susceptible to atmospheric interference, which varies with the relative position of the sun.

Restrooms Street-level public toilets in China are common, many detectable by the nose before they are seen. There's often an entrance fee of ¥.20 (5¢/5p), but not necessarily running water. In many cases you merely squat over a trough. So, use the standard Western equipment in your hotel room, in department stores and malls, and in branches of foreign fast-food chains. In Hong Kong and Macau, facilities are far more hygienic.

Safety See the sections on "Travel Insurance" and "Health," earlier in this chapter.

Smoking The government of China is the world's biggest cigarette manufacturer. China is home to 20% of the world's population but 30% of the world's cigarettes and is growing fast, especially now that young women are starting to take up the habit. About one million people a year in China die of smoking-related illnesses. In the mainland, nonsmoking tables in restaurants are almost unheard of, and nonsmoking signs are favorite places beneath which to sit and smoke. Smokers are generally sent to the spaces between the cars on trains, but they won't bother to do so if no one protests. The same is true on air-conditioned buses, where some will light up to see if they can get away with it (but usually they'll be told to put it out).

Taxes In **mainland China,** occasional bed taxes are added to hotel bills, but these are minor and usually included in the room rate. Service charges appear mostly in joint-venture hotels, and range from 10% to 15%. Many Chinese hotels list service charges in their literature, but few have the nerve to add them to room rates unless the hotel is very full. However, restaurants may add the service charge. Departure taxes must be paid in cash at the airport before flying: domestic ¥50 ($6.25/£3.10), international (including flights to Hong Kong and Macau) ¥90 ($12/£6). There are also lesser taxes for international ferry departures at some ports. In **Hong Kong,** better hotels will add a 10% service charge and a 3% government tax to your bill. Better restaurants and bars will automatically add a 10% service charge. Included in your ticket price are an airport departure tax of HK$80 (US$10/£5) for adults and children older than 12, or a marine departure tax if you depart by sea. In **Macau,** better hotels charge 10% for service as well as a 5% tax. Marine departure taxes are included in ticket prices. Airport passenger tax for flights to China are MOP$80 (US$10/£5) adults and MOP$50 (US$6.25/£3.10) children ages 2 to 12; for other destinations the tax is MOP$130 (US$16/£8) adults and MOP$80 (US$10/£5) for children. Transit passengers who continue their journey within 24 hours of arrival are exempted from passenger tax.

Time Zone The whole of China is on Beijing time—8 hours ahead of GMT (and therefore of London), 13 hours ahead of New York, 14 hours ahead of Chicago, and 16 hours ahead of Los Angeles. There's no daylight saving time (summertime), so subtract 1 hour in the summer.

Tipping In **mainland China,** as in many other countries, there is *no tipping,* despite what tour companies may tell you (although if you have a tour leader who accompanies you from home, home rules apply). Until recently, tipping was expressly forbidden, and some hotels still carry signs requesting you not to tip. Foreigners, especially those on tours, are overcharged at every turn, and it bemuses Chinese that they hand out free money in addition. Chinese never do it themselves; in fact, if a bellhop or other hotel employee hints that a tip would be welcome, he or she is likely to be fired.

In **Hong Kong** and **Macau,** even though restaurants and bars will automatically add a 10% service charge to your bill, you're still expected to leave small change for the waiter, up to a few dollars in the very best restaurants. You're also expected to tip taxi drivers, bellhops, barbers, and beauticians. For taxi drivers, simply round up your bill to the nearest HK$1 or add a HK$1 (US15¢/5p) tip. Tip people who cut your hair 5% or 10%, and give bellhops HK$10 to HK$20 (US$1.30–US$2.60/65p–£1.30), depending on the number of your bags. If you use a public restroom that has an attendant, you may be expected to leave a small gratuity—HK$2 (US25¢/10p) should be enough.

Television The propaganda machine known as the Communist Party quickly realized the potential of TV very early on, and has made sure that nearly everybody now has access to its broadcasts. No visitor should leave the PRC without sampling some of the world's most bizarre programming. In Guangdong, the Hong Kong news channels are frequently blocked, with censors on the mainland manually replacing unfavorable news items with public service broadcasts. On the mainland, there are hundreds of channels to choose from, but the best to look out for are the huge party glorification concerts where loyal masses sing hymnlike praises to the party with lyrics like "Without the Communist Party, there would be no new China."

Water Tap water in mainland China is not drinkable, and should not even be used for brushing your teeth. Use bottled water, widely available on every street, and provided for free in all the better hotels. Tap water is drinkable in Hong Kong, but bottled water tastes better.

3

Suggested Itineraries

by Christopher D. Winnan

Almost all mainstream tour companies tackle Beijing, Xi'an, Shanghai, Guilin, and the overrated Yangzi River cruise. Here are a few suggestions for trips—most of which are not too far off the main routes—you can do on your own.

China's huge size limits the number of practical ways to get around the country. While the number of cars in urban areas is exploding, private car ownership is still comparatively rare, so most people choose long-distance buses when traveling between cities. A nascent car-rental industry, poor highway conditions, substandard driving tests, and the fact that some areas are still closed to foreigners mean visitors should seek alternatives to the automobile. China's horrendous traffic accident statistics may also make visitors think twice about the safety of long distance coaches, especially sleeper buses, which can quickly become mobile torture chambers for larger western travelers.

Trains, by comparison, are cheap, reliable, and a mainstay of the middle class. China reportedly intends to increase its already vast rail network by a whopping 35% by 2020, though the downside is that trains can be very slow. For travel between provinces, **air travel** is the best choice, but along with growing environmental concerns, bear in mind that local airlines do not maintain the same level of service as the Asian flag carriers.

Tip: The most important advice I can offer is to avoid the Golden Week Holidays (first week of May and first week of Oct) and the Chinese New Year at all costs. All forms of transport are booked solid and popular destinations quickly become chaotic. Needless to say, the industry makes the most of this opportunity by hiking prices to unbelievable levels.

1 China in 1 Week: Or, China at the Speed of Light

Only a week in the Middle Kingdom is a tall order; you could spend 10 years exploring China, and still only scratch the surface. Because of the vast distances involved (both getting to China, and getting around the country), if you have just 1 week, stick to the two main centers of change, Beijing and Shanghai, and their environs.

Day ❶: Arrive in Shanghai

Arrive at the flashy new Pudong International Airport and enter China's latest and gaudiest development zone at 430kmph (267 mph) on the **maglev** (p. 431). Climb to the 88th-floor observation deck of the Jin Mao Tower ✸✸ (p. 467) to get your bearings and then cross the Huangpu River using the equally bizarre **Bund Sight-Seeing Tunnel** (p. 436). Finish the day with dinner at **Jade on 36** ✸✸✸ and an evening stroll along the Bund. See p. 458.

Suggested Itineraries

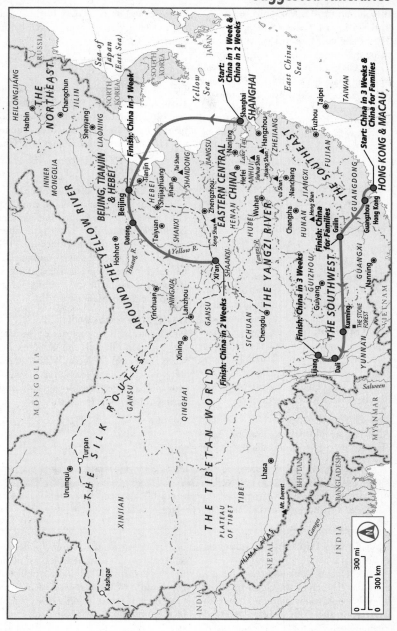

Day ❷: Shanghai Museum 𝔸𝔸𝔸 and Yu Yuan Gardens 𝔸𝔸𝔸

The **Shanghai Museum's** (p. 463) bizarre shape makes this museum China's answer to the Guggenheim; its unique architecture and many galleries deserve at least a morning's exploration. After exploring the museum, wander around **Yu Garden (Yu Yuan)** (p. 459); it makes for an interesting afternoon, especially when combined with souvenir shopping in the surrounding bazaar, and then a relaxing pot of green tea in the floating teahouse. If you have any shoe leather left, try an after-dinner stroll along one of Shanghai's main shopping arteries, **Nanjing Road** (p. 469), where very few places close before 10pm.

Day ❸: Shanghai's French Concession

The **French Concession area** (p. 433) is one of China's best preserved collections of colonial buildings, but is also full of modern surprises, such as the ambitious new **Xin Tiandi** (p. 454), a mega restaurant and retail development and a great stop for lunch. Nearby **Huaihai Zhong Lu** (p. 469) is where the fashionable spend their yuan at foreign-owned department stores and boutiques.

Day ❹: Transit Day

Allowing a full day to transfer from Shanghai to Beijing will make the process far easier and more relaxed. Once in Beijing, decompress in your hotel before exploring the city.

Day ❺: The Forbidden City & Tian'an Men 𝔸𝔸

Plan at least a morning to explore the **Forbidden City** (p. 110), Beijing's premier attraction, and an afternoon to see nearby sights like **Tian'an Men Square** (p. 116). A roast duck dinner and Chinese opera make for an excellent introductory evening to the capital.

Day ❻: Exploring the Back Lakes

Check out Frommer's walking tour that takes you among the fascinating, winding **Back Lakes** *hutong* (p. 124). In the afternoon visit the **Summer Palace** (p. 119), the grandest imperial playground in all of China. It's already a big day, but try to leave some room in the evening for an **acrobatic performance** (p. 138).

Day ❼: The Great Wall

Finish your whistle-stop tour of the Middle Kingdom literally on a high. The views from atop the Great Wall at Badaling (p. 128) are tremendous; if you're after a challenge, considering also navigating Simatai 𝔸𝔸 (p. 129).

2 China in 2 Weeks: A Fortnight Crammed with Culture

An extra week allows a visitor to head deep into the ancestral heartland of imperial China, and spend some extra time in its two largest cities.

Days ❽–❾: Extra time in Shanghai & Beijing

A week's extension allows you to spend an extra day in each of the cities. In Shanghai this would allow for a day trip to the **Master of the Nets Garden** 𝔸𝔸𝔸 in Suzhou (p. 473), or a side trip to **Anji** (p. 482) or **Moganshan** (p. 485) for those preferring nature to culture. In Beijing, an extra day touring temples would be time well spent. While most would visit the **Temple of Heaven** (p. 118), instead head over to **Lama Temple** 𝔸𝔸 (p. 121) in the morning, and follow it up with a stroll among the lakes in **Bei Hai Park** 𝔸𝔸 (p. 121).

Day ⑩: The Wild Wall

Another day means more face time with the Great Wall. **Jinshanling** 𝒜𝒜𝒜 (p. 129) is still one of the very best hikes, and shows the Wall in a very different perspective to the circus at **Badaling.**

Day ⑪: Yungang Caves & the Hanging Temple

Datong is conveniently served by train and plane, and so the **Yungang Caves** 𝒜𝒜𝒜 (p. 218) and the amazing **Hanging Temple** (p. 219) are now well within reach of Beijing.

Day ⑫: Arrival in Xi'an

Whether you decide to continue your journey by plane or by rail there is ample to see in **Xi'an** (p. 259) that will easily fill the remaining 4 days. In fact the first point of call should be China's very best museum, the **Shanxi History Museum** 𝒜𝒜𝒜 (p. 265).

Day ⑬: China's Ancient History

Marvel at the 6,000 **Terra-Cotta Warriors** at **Bingmayong** 𝒜𝒜𝒜 (p. 266) in the morning, and then if your interest in archaeology has been ignited, spend the afternoon at the **Banpo Neolithic Village** (p. 267).

Day ⑭: The Potters of Chen Lu 𝒜𝒜

After so much time at heavily populated tourist sites, a day trip to the **Potters of Chen Lu** (p. 273) makes a far less strenuous way to wind down your trip.

---

3 China in 3 Weeks: The Mountains Are High & the Emperor Is Far Away

If you are fortunate enough to have 3 weeks to spend in China, you can sufficiently explore the side of China that focuses more on its timeless, natural beauty than its somewhat more temporary, cultural splendor.

Day ①: Arrive in Hong Kong

Start the trip off with a bang by taking some time to see the bustling metropolis of Hong Kong. Whether you decide to stay at the **Peninsula** 𝒜𝒜𝒜 (p. 562) or the **YMCA** 𝒜𝒜𝒜 (p. 564), take the **Star Ferry** (p. 559) over to Central for lunch and spend the afternoon trying to absorb the 21st-century atmosphere of Asia's number-one city, as this will quickly disappear the farther you venture into mainland China. Round off the day with a visit to the **Ladies' Market** (p. 584) on Tung Choi Street or the **Temple Street Night Market** in Kowloon (p. 585).

Day ②: Hong Kong: City of Culture

Hong Kong has far too many interesting attractions to be granted only 1 day. But if museums are too stuffy for you, check in with the very well organized **Hong Kong Tourist Board** (**HKTB**; p. 557); their offerings cater to almost any taste, from harbor dinner cruises to the innovative "Meet the People" program (p. 577).

Day ③: Sampling Guangzhou

The express train to Guangzhou is fast and convenient, so an early morning start will leave you much of the day to explore both **Shamian Island** 𝒜 (p. 536) and perhaps **Huadiwan** (p. 538) later in the afternoon.

Day ④: Exploring the Commercial Heart of China

An overnight train later tonight, leaves you the day free in Guangzhou, which is a good chance to see what makes this commercial metropolis tick in and around **Haizhu Square** (p. 537); just make sure you are at the old station for the 6:30pm sleeper train to **Guilin** 𝒜 (p. 601).

Day ❺: Yangshuo ✸✸✸

An early morning arrival means that you will not have to rush down to Yangshuo, but can take your time getting to one of China's most charming small towns. Once there, spend the day wandering **Xi Jie (West Street;** p. 611), relaxing at a few of the cafes; consider Hong Kong, now a world away. Take this time to make some trip and travel arrangements for the next few days.

Day ❻: Liu Gong & Liu Sanjie

A boat trip down to **Liu Gong** (p. 614) for lunch with a gentle bike ride back through **Fuli** (p. 615) in the afternoon should leave time to see the Zhang Yimou grand waterborne epic **"Impression, Sanjie Liu"** (p. 616) in the evening.

Day ❼: The Yulong He (Jade Dragon River) ✸✸✸

Time to move out of the town, to one of the quieter accommodations such as **Yangshuo Shengdi (Mountain Retreat)** ✸✸✸ (p. 612). Here the day can be spent biking or swimming, but wherever you end up, take time to soak in the magnificent sunset.

Day ❽: China's Most Scenic Countryside

A late-morning dip followed by a hearty breakfast (p. 613) may be in order in the summer months, and this can be followed by a trip to one of the many local caves, to further escape the heat.

Day ❾: In & around Yangshuo

It is difficult to pull yourself away from scenery as spectacular as this, so why not relax here for just one more day and try your hand at Chinese cooking, tai chi, or a little calligraphy. The **Chinese Culture and Art Promotion Workshop** (p. 611) and other organizations around town can help you get started.

Day ❿: Transit from Guilin to Kunming ✸

Even though you have 3 weeks, your time is not unlimited; it might be wiser to avoid some of the more remote areas where transportation can be unreliable. For this reason, I recommend that you taxi back to Guilin airport and fly straight to Kunming.

Day ⓫: Green Lake ✸

Kunming city center might seem a little threatening after the sublime beauty of the Yulong River, so head up to the **Green Lake area** (p. 650) and spend your first day in the city acclimatizing.

Day ⓬: Stone Forest (Shi Lin) ✸✸

Spend the day at the **Stone Forest** (p. 655)—visit by organized tour or on your own by train—or, even better, at the much quieter **Black Pine Stone Forest** (p. 655), which predates the Stone Forest by about 2 million years. Take plenty of supplies in case you decide not to emerge for lunch.

Day ⓭: Discovering Dali

Night trains to **Dali** are notoriously difficult to book so grab the earliest bus possible instead and spend the rest of the day exploring the cobbled streets and streams of Dali. See p. 656.

Day ⓮: Climbing the Cang Shan

Take the cable car up to the **Cang Shan (Green Mountains;** p. 663) and follow the paths as they wind in and out of the surflike clouds.

Day ⓯: Cycling around Er Hai Lake

The view from the mountain makes **Er Hai Lake** (p. 664) irresistible; spending a day cycling along the shore or visiting some of the islands such as **Jinsuo Dao** (p. 665), filled with caves and caverns, is a must.

Day ⑯: Yunnan Markets

Organized trips are numerous, but those planning an independent visit to one of the weekly markets such as **Shaping** (p. 661) should get there early to see the local ethnic minorities descending from the surrounding mountains, either on horse or on foot, resplendent in their traditional costumes. A trip to some of the batik workshops in **Zhou Cheng** (p. 665) would round the afternoon off nicely.

Day ⑰: Transit to Li Jiang ⚑⚑

Spend the morning at a local **Dali market** (p. 661), stocking up on provisions ranging from papaya and pomegranates to chocolate chip cookies, and hop aboard the 2pm bus arriving in Li Jiang just in time to try traditional Naxi cuisine at **Naxi Fengwei Xiaochi** (p. 671).

Day ⑱: Li Jiang's Old Town ⚑⚑

A day spent exploring the attractions of the **old town** (p. 668) will hardly seem to be enough, but take advantage of some of the best tourist facilities in China. Food

lovers are especially well catered to with everything from four-cheese pizza to frog-skin fungus to tempt the appetite.

Day ⑲: Tiger Leaping Gorge ⚑

Tiger Leaping Gorge (p. 673) and the mountains surrounding it mark a suitably impressive point at which to celebrate your time in China and being winding down before your trip home.

Day ⑳: Relax in Baisha ⚑

It may be a dusty little village, but **Baisha** (p. 672) is home to some Ming and Qing dynasty temple frescoes that are well worth the visit.

Day ㉑: Transit Day

Plan on spending your last day getting back to Kunming, where you can connect to Hong Kong or maybe even Bangkok if you prefer. Take a long hard look at the magnificent 13 peaks of the Jade Dragon Snow Mountain and start planning your next trip.

4 China for Families: A 1-Week Tour

While many people will question your sanity for taking children on vacation to China (many guidebooks sternly warn against it), taking the entire tribe to China can be a uniquely rewarding experience. Here is a short venture into the south of the country to give you a taste of China.

Day ❶: Arrive in Hong Kong

Depending on how much of the day you have left once you finally touch down at **Hong Kong International Airport,** head downtown and let your kids explore all the hands-on, interactive exhibits at the **Hong Kong Science Museum,** 2 Science Museum Rd., Tsim Shat Sui East, Kowloon (✆ **852/2732 3232;** www.lcsd. gov.hk/CE/Museum/Science/eabout.htm). A jaunt aboard the **Star Ferry** (p. 559) across the harbor to Hong Kong Island is still one of the best and certainly one of the most inexpensive experiences that

that city has to offer, and it's great for a family. Once on Hong Kong Island take the world's longest escalator and continue up to **Victoria Peak** (p. 575), where a world-class selection of amusements awaits.

Day ❷: A Snapshot of Big-City Life in Guangzhou

Take advantage of the fast, reliable KCR train service and jump on an early morning **Guangzhou express** (p. 530) and arrive in plenty of time for lunch. Spend the afternoon wandering around **Zhuang**

Yuan Fang (p. 537), comparing the appearance and attitudes of Chinese youngsters with their Western counterparts. Catch an early evening sleeper to Guilin (p. 601) and see how easy it is to make friends on Chinese public transport.

Day ❸: Arrival in Paradise

Avoid the claptrap minibuses and arrange for your Yangshuo hotel to send a car to fetch you. Spend the first day acclimatizing to West Street's (Xi Jie's) (p. 611) laid-back atmosphere and great cafe food. Invest a little time in arranging a few activities for the next few days. That evening take in the local show "Impression, Sanjie Liu" (p. 616) and marvel at the magical landscape.

Day ❹: The Family That Plays Together . . .

With Yangshuo as your base, prepare to be spoiled with choices for the next few days. Activities include biking, rafting, climbing, and caving, and the list keeps growing. Wind down your busy day at Yangshuo Shengdi (Mountain Retreat) (p. 612), certainly one of the quietest accommodations in China and a well-deserved rest from the bustle of West Street.

Day ❺: More Fun in the Great Outdoors

After an early morning swim, followed by a delicious breakfast, take a leisurely bike ride out to Liu Gong Pavilion (p. 613) for lunch and then head back up stream slowly, getting up close and personal with some of the most spectacular scenery China has to offer. Spend the evening souvenir shopping in town before getting a good night's sleep.

Day ❻: Venturing Deep into the Dragon's Belly

By now, you are all probably sunburned from too much biking or hiking, so head indoors (sort of) and explore the psychedelic Silver Cave (p. 615) just south of town. If the kids enjoy their introduction to speleology, try the recommended water cave (p. 615) where they can splash about in primordial ooze to their hearts' content.

Day ❼: The Fast Track Home

While the trains are comfortable and efficient, the restrictions of having only 7 days probably means that it is wiser to fly back from Guilin to catch your connection flight home. Everybody feels the pangs of sadness as they drive away from those strange geological formations, but don't worry: They have a strange magnetic quality that will likely lure you back.

4

Beijing & Hebei

by Jen Lin-Liu and Sherisse Pham

Beijing strikes most first-time visitors as ugly. Its rivers of concrete and rows of tenements, its pollution, and its oppressive grayness are not what anyone would expect at the heart of such an otherwise vivid nation. And yet, no other city in the nation attracts more travelers.

Visitors accept Beijing's pallor because it is China's political and cultural capital, and because it offers the country's most staggering array of attractions. Best known among these are the Forbidden City, the Temple of Heaven, Tian'an Men Square, and the Great Wall—bedazzling and symbolic structures without which no trip to the country would be complete.

But grandiose emblems are not the only reason to visit Beijing. Scattered through the city's sprawl are a number of temples, museums, gardens, and other attractions that only grow in charm as they decrease in size. This principle culminates in the *hutong*, narrow lanes that twist through older sections and form an open-air museum where you can happily wander for hours without aim.

Beijing lies 120km (70 miles) west of the Bo Hai (sea), on a sandblasted plain that once separated Han Chinese–dominated territory in the south from the non-Chinese "barbarian" lands to the north. Human settlement in the area dates from the Zhou period (1066 B.C.–221 B.C.), but the first of the four capitals to occupy space here did not appear until A.D. 936, when the Mongolian-speaking Khitan built Yanjing (Capital of Swallows), southern base of power for the Liao Empire (907–1125).

The grid pattern and original walls of what is now Beijing were first laid down in the 13th century, when it was called Khanbalik ("Dadu" in Mandarin) and served as eastern capital of the Mongolian Empire, referred to in China as the Yuan dynasty (1279–1368). The city was razed, rebuilt, and renamed Beijing by Han Chinese rulers of the subsequent Ming dynasty (1368–1644), who added the Forbidden City and several other of the city's most impressive structures. Manchurian horsemen of the final Qing dynasty (1636–1912) skirted the Great Wall and established themselves in the Forbidden City in 1644. Despite their nomadic origins, Qing leaders found the Chinese system of bureaucratic rule useful in managing their new empire, a strategy mirrored in the relatively few changes they made to the city.

Some of the greatest damage to Beijing has occurred in the last 150 years. Invasions, rebellions, war with Japan, and the struggle between Communists and Nationalists in the 1930s and 1940s have altered the face of the city more than any events since the 14th century. Particularly severe was the ruin that took place in the decade after the Communist victory in 1949, when Mao, in a desire to put the stamp of his own dynasty on Beijing, leveled the city walls and the old Imperial Way and paved over both.

Present-day Beijing is a vast municipality with a population of roughly 15 million. Economic reform and preparations for the 2008 Olympics have accelerated the pace and scale of change and outfitted the city with a semblance of modernity (or at least the Chinese perception of it). Roads that once swarmed with bicycles have been taken over by automobiles. Swaths of *hutong* have been leveled to make way for office towers. And children whose parents hid tapes of Beethoven during the Cultural Revolution now have easy access to DVDs, iPods, double-tall lattes, plastic surgery, and other previously unthinkable bourgeois luxuries.

It is easy, however, to overemphasize the transformations of the past few decades in a city with so many centuries under its belt. To many observers, Beijing has hardly changed at all. The gaze of government looms as large now as it did during the Ming. Outsiders are still Philistines. People smoke in elevators, spit in the streets, fly kites, and practice tai chi *(taijiquan)* in the mornings, just as they always have. And perhaps most important, the Great Wall continues to snake along the city's northern border while the Forbidden City gleams at its center.

Beijing shares the same latitude as New York (roughly 40°N) and suffers the same weather: hot, humid summers and bitter winters. Fall, typically mid-September to mid-November, is the nicest season, with mild temperatures and relatively clear skies—by far the best time to visit. Spring brings thoroughly unpleasant sandstorms that blow down from the Mongolian steppe and coat everything in a layer of fine dust. There is little precipitation, and even less of late.

Note: Unless noted otherwise, hours listed in this chapter are the same daily.

1 Orientation

GETTING THERE & AWAY
BY PLANE

Beijing's **Capital Airport (Shoudu Jichang;** © **010/962-580** for information; domestic ticketing: © **010/6601-3336;** international ticketing: © **010/6601-6667),** is 25km (16 miles) northeast of the city center. Arrivals are on the first floor; departures are on the second. Change money at one of the handful of **exchange counters** on either floor upon arrival (open 24 hr.), as taxi drivers and shuttle buses will not accept foreign currency. There are also ATM and automatic exchange machines on both floors. Rates are the same across China, so get what you need now.

Taxis queue outside the international arrivals gate and take 30 minutes to an hour to reach the city center for ¥80 to ¥100 ($11–$13/£5.30–£6.70), plus the ¥10 ($1.35/65p) toll, depending on traffic. Bypass any drivers who approach you inside the airport, and head for the rank instead. Insist on using the meter. Air-conditioned **airport shuttle buses,** the cheapest way to get into the city, leave from in front of the domestic arrivals area. The most useful, Line 2, runs 24 hours a day and departs every 10 minutes, 7am to the last arriving flight, for ¥16 ($2.15/£1.10). Destinations include San Yuan Qiao (near the Hilton and Sheraton hotels), the Dong Zhi Men and Dong Si Shi Tiao metro stations, Beijing Railway Station, and the CAAC ticket office in Xi Dan. Lines 1 to 4 all pass through San Yuan Qiao, but only Line 2 lets off passengers at a location convenient for picking up taxis to continue to other destinations. The new Line 5 connects with the university district in the northwest, via Yayun Cun and the North Fourth Ring Road.

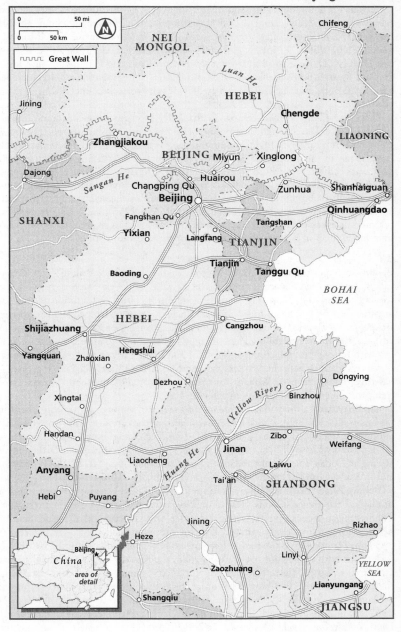

0   50 mi

0   50 km

ᒥᒪᒥᒪᒪᒥ Great Wall

Chifeng

NEI MONGOL

Luan He

HEBEI

Jining

Chengde

LIAONING

Zhangjiakou

BEIJING   Miyun   Xinglong

Dajong

Sangan He

Changping Qu   Huairou

Zunhua   Shanhaiguan

Beijing

Qinhuangdao

SHANXI

Fangshan Qu

Tangshan

Yixian

Langfang   TIANJIN

Baoding

Tianjin   Tanggu Qu

BOHAI SEA

HEBEI

Cangzhou

Shijiazhuang

Yangquan

Hengshui

Zhaoxian

Dongying

Xingtai

Dezhou

Binzhou

(Yellow River)

Handan

Zibo

Weifang

Liaocheng

Jinan

Laiwu

Anyang

Huang He

Tai'an   SHANDONG

Hebi   Puyang

Jining

Rizhao

Heze

Linyi

YELLOW SEA

China

area of detail

Běijīng

Zaozhuang

Lianyungang

Shangqiu

JIANGSU

Tickets for domestic flights (and international flights) on Chinese airlines are best purchased through a travel agent, such as **Airtrans** (next to the Jianguo Hotel; ⓒ **010/ 6595-2255**), or in one of two main ticketing halls: the Aviation Building (Minhang Dalou; ⓒ **010/6601-7755;** fax 010/6601-7585; 24 hr.) at Xi Chang'an Jie 15, just east of the Xi Dan metro station; or at the Airlines Ticketing Hall (Minhang Yingye Dating; ⓒ **010/8402-8198;** fax 010/6401-5307; 8am–8:30pm), at Dong Si Bei Dajie 394. Both ticketing halls accept credit cards and offer discounts similar to those of an agent.

Ctrip and Elong are two companies that offer excellent prices on domestic and international tickets through their online websites (www.english.ctrip.com and www. elong.net). You can book flights online and pay for tickets in cash upon delivery. You can also pay by credit card (expect a 3%–5% surcharge) after faxing through a credit card authorization form. Both companies also have English-speaking agents who can walk you through the booking process. Most hotels can arrange tickets for flights on **foreign airlines,** but they tend to levy hefty service fees. Reliable booking agents, such as **Airtrans** (next to the Jianguo Hotel; ⓒ **010/6595-2255**), are often the cheapest option, but check directly with the airlines themselves. Most major international airlines have offices in Beijing; check websites for contact information.

BY TRAIN

Beijing's two most important railway stations are the Soviet-style Beijing Zhan, southeast of Tian'an Men Square, and the newer Xi Ke Zhan (West Station), between the western Second and Third ring roads. Tickets can be purchased at both stations for any train leaving Beijing up to 4 days in advance. It is now possible to buy **round-trip tickets** *(fancheng piao)* to major destinations like Shanghai or Xi'an up to 12 days in advance, subject to availability. There are now 19 brand-new Z (direct) trains connecting with other cities, which depart at night and arrive early the following morning. Cities served are: Changchun, Changsha, Harbin, Hangzhou, Hefei, Nanjing, Shanghai (five trains), Suzhou, Wuhan (four trains), Xi'an, and Yangzhou. Tickets for Z trains may be purchased 20 days in advance.

Satellite ticket offices *(tielu shoupiao chu)* scattered throughout the city charge a negligible ¥5 (70¢/35p) service fee; convenient branches are just inside the southern entrance to Gongmei Dasha ("Artistic Mansion") at Wangfujing Dajie 200 (9am– 9pm; ⓒ **010/6523-8747**); at the *Shatan shoupiao chu* (ticket sales office) farther north at Ping'an Dadao 45, west of Jiaodaokou Nan Dajie (8am–6pm; ⓒ **010/6403-6803**); and in Sanlitun on Gongti Bei Lu (7:30am–8:30pm; ⓒ **010/6416-6001**).

Beijing Zhan (Beijing Railway Station; ⓒ **010/5182-1114**) is the easiest to reach of Beijing's two major stations, close to the city center and with its own metro station. The best place to pick up tickets is at the "ticket office for foreigners" inside the softberth waiting room on the ground floor of the main hall, in the far left corner (5:30am–11pm). This is the station for trains to Shanghai and cities in the Northeast. Tickets for both versions of the Trans-Siberian, the Russian K19 via Manchuria (Sat 10:56pm) and the Chinese K3 via Mongolia (Wed 7:40am), must be purchased from the CITS international railway ticket office inside the International Hotel (Mon–Fri 8:30am–noon and 1:30–5pm, weekends 9am–noon and 1:30–4pm; ⓒ **010/6512- 0507**) 10-minute walk north of the station on Jianguo Men Nei Dajie (metro: Dong Dan). Both trains travel to Moscow for ¥2,512 ($335/£168) soft sleeper, but only the K3 passes through Mongolia and stops in Ulaan Baatar for ¥845 ($113/£56). There is a separate train, the K23, which goes to Ulaan Baatar (Sat 7:40am). The International Hotel is also the nearest spot for picking up the **airport shuttle bus** (see above). At the **West Station (Xi Ke Zhan;** ✆ **010/5182-6253** schedule information), the best ticket outlet is not the main ticket hall but a second office inside the main building, on the second floor to the left of the elevators (signposted in English); this is also where you go to purchase tickets for the T97 express to Kowloon/Jiulong (10:06am; 27 hr.; ¥1,028/$137/£69 soft sleeper, ¥662/$88/£44 hard sleeper). The West Station is also the starting point for trains to Hanoi, but you have to buy tickets (Thurs and Sun; ¥1,163/$155/£78 soft sleeper only) at a "travel service" booth (9am–4:30pm; ✆ **010/6398-9485**) inside the Construction Bank on the east side of the station complex. The nearest airport shuttle stops at the Aviation Building in Xi Dan (see above), reachable by bus no. 52 from the station's east side. The taxi rank is on the second floor. Trains leave from here for Guangzhou, Xi'an, and other points west.

BY BUS

There is no central station in Beijing but rather a series of region-specific stations spread around the outskirts of the city. The airportlike **Lize Qiao Changtu Keyun Zhan** (✆ **010/6347-5092**), on the southwest corner of the Third Ring Road (Gongzhufen metro, then bus no. 201 to terminus) has air-conditioned services to **Taiyuan** (6:30am–11:20pm, every 20 min. 7am–5pm, less frequent after 5pm; 7 hr.; ¥130–¥171/$17–$23/£8.70–£11); **Zhengzhou** (only one bus at 5:40pm; 9 hr.; ¥190/$25/£13); and comfortable minibuses to **Shijiazhuang** (8:30am–4:50pm, every 40 min.; 3½ hr.; ¥61/$8.15/£4.10). The **Liu Li Qiao Changtu Qiche Keyun Zhan** (✆ **010/8383-1717**), southwest of the Liu Li Qiao bridge, runs luxury buses to Chengde (5:40am–6:40pm; every 20 min.; 3½ hr.; ¥60/$8/£4), Shenyang (three buses a day at 9am, 11:30am, and 9pm; 8 hr.; ¥188/$25/£13). Numerous buses from other cities arrive at the **Dongzhi Men Changtu Qiche Zhan** (✆ **010/6467-3094**), next to the Dongzhi Men metro station, but few are useful to visitors except the occasional Chengde service.

VISITOR INFORMATION

For the most current information on life in Beijing, particularly nightlife, see listings in the free English-language monthlies *Time Out* and *that's Beijing,* available in hotel lobbies and at bars in the major drinking districts (see "Beijing After Dark," p. 137). Online, *City Weekend* manages to update its website (www.cityweekend.com) regularly. The e-mail newsletter *Xianzai Beijing* (see www.xianzai.com for more information) provides a weekly list of events, plus special hotel, air ticket, and restaurant offers.

The Beijing Tourism Administration (BTA) maintains a **tourist information hot line** (some English spoken) at ✆ **010/6513-0828**. More likely to be of help are the new BTA-managed **Beijing Tourist Information Centers (Beijing Shi Luyou Zixun Fuwu Zhongxin)** located in each district and all marked with aqua-blue signs. The most competent branch is in Chaoyang District, on Gongti Bei Lu across from the City Hotel and next to the KFC (9am–5pm; ✆ **010/6417-6627;** fax 010/6417-6656; chaoyang@bta.gov.cn). Free simple maps are available at the door, and staff will sometimes make phone calls for you. Ignore their extortionist travel service.

CITY LAYOUT

Beijing is bordered to the north and west by mountains, the closest of which are occasionally visible through the haze. The city center, known to foreigners in the Qing period (1644–1911) as The Tartar City, was originally surrounded by a complex of walls and gates destroyed in 1958 to make way for the **Second Ring Road (Er Huan).** The city center is organized along a grid with major streets running to the compass points. The Third, Fourth, Fifth, and Sixth ring roads (San Huan, Si Huan, Wu Huan, and Liu Huan respectively) run concentrically ever wider out. At the center of all this is the seldom-referred-to First Ring Road (encircling Tian'an Men Sq.) and **the Forbidden City,** its own internal grid a miniature of the sprawl that surrounds it.

MAJOR STREETS
Streets in Beijing change names like high-school students change identities. Be sure to pick up a city map on arrival (see "Fast Facts: Beijing," p. 84). The best example of this is the city's main east-west artery. **Chang'an Dajie,** which runs between Tian'an Men Square and the Forbidden City, is known (east to west) as Jianguo Men Wai Dajie, Jianguo Men Nei Dajie, Dong (East) Chang'an Dajie, Xi (West) Chang'an Dajie, Fuxing Men Nei Dajie, and Fuxing Men Wai Dajie. **Ping'an Dadao,** a major avenue to the north that runs across the back of Bei Hai Park, has a similar diversity of monikers. Among important north-south streets, **Wangfujing Dajie** (2 long blocks east of the Forbidden City) is the Beijing consumer equivalent of Chicago's Magnificent Mile. **Qian Men Dajie** extends down from the southern end of Tian'an Men Square.

NEIGHBORHOODS IN BRIEF
Citywide architectural uniformity means Beijing's neighborhoods are defined more by feel than by appearance. In many cases, but not all, they correspond to districts *(qu).*

Dong Cheng District   Dong Cheng (East City) occupies the eastern half of the city center, generally defined as everything inside the Second Ring Road and north of Chang'an Dajie. This is where Tian'an Men Square, the Forbidden City, Wangfujing Dajie, Jing Shan Gongyuan, and Yonghe Gong (the Lama Temple) are located.

Xi Cheng District   The western half of the city center is home to Zhong Nan Hai, the off-limits central government compound otherwise known as the new Forbidden City, Bei Hai Gongyuan, and Bai Ta Si (White Dagoba Temple).

The Back Lakes (Shicha Hai) & Di'an Men   This area, with its sublime public lakes and well-preserved *hutong,* is where the last fading ghosts of Old (pre-1949) Beijing reside. It's popular among writers, musicians, English-language teachers, and other hipsters in the expatriate community, and their presence has helped spawn a bevy of bars and cafes (see "Beijing After Dark," later in this chapter). Several minor sights here provide excuses for a nice day of wandering (see "Walking Tour: The Back Lakes," p. 124).

Chaoyang District   A gargantuan district that encompasses almost all of eastern and northeastern Beijing outside the Second Ring Road, Chaoyang is home to the two main diplomatic areas, the Sanlitun and Chaoyang drinking districts, and the Central Business District (CBD) around the China World Trade Center. This is the richest district in Beijing, the result, according to some, of the district's good feng shui.

The South   If Chaoyang has Beijing's best feng shui, the south part of the city—composed of Chongwen, Xuanwu, and Fengtai districts—has the worst. Squalid since the city's founding, this is where you'll find the city's grittiest *hutong* and some of its best bargains on fake antiques. This is also where you'll find the Temple of Heaven (Tian Tan).

Haidian District & Yayun Cun Occupying the northwest, Haidian is the university and high-tech district, optimistically referred to in local media as "China's Silicon Valley." There is hiking in the hills in more distant parts. Yayun Cun, which will host most of the Olympic events, is home to Beijing's best new Chinese restaurants.

2 Getting Around

BY METRO The Beijing metro is the easiest and often fastest way to move around. Trains run from 5am to 11pm on two underground lines *(ditie)* and one new light-rail line *(chengtie)*. **Line 1** runs east-west past Tian'an Men and the Forbidden City. **Line 8** extends Line 1 into the eastern suburbs. **Line 2,** or the Loop Line, is a closed circle that roughly follows the path of the old Tartar City wall. The light-rail **Line 13,** connected to Line 2 at Xizhi Men (201) and Dongzhi Men (214) stations, swings far into the northern suburbs. The north-south **Line 5** addition will be completed by the time you read this. An express train linking the Dongzhi Men metro stop to the airport is scheduled to open June 30, 2008.

Paper **tickets,** purchased at booths in each station, cost ¥3 (45¢/20p) for a ride to anywhere along lines 1 and 2 (free interchange). A combined ticket *(huancheng piao)* for lines 2 and 13 costs ¥5 (60¢/35p); ¥4 (50¢/25p) for Line 8. Alternately, you can buy an electronic card that can be used for subway and bus rides. The metro card, officially known as the "Municipal Administration and Communication Card" (Shizheng Jiaotong Yikatong) can be bought for a ¥40 minimum (including ¥20 for deposit). See metro map on the inside back cover.

BY TAXI Taxis cost ¥10 ($1.35/65p) for the first 3km/2 miles, then ¥2 (25¢/15p) per kilometer. Green or yellow Hyundai Elantras are roomier and have better air-conditioning. Rates per kilometer jump by 50% after 15km (9 miles). Always insist on using the meter unless negotiating for journeys out of town, in which case be clear about the price beforehand and withhold payment until your return.

BY BUS This is how the vast majority of the city's residents move around, and riding with them is as close (literally shoulder-to-chest) as you can get to understanding the authentic Beijing. City buses and trolleys (nos. less than 124) charge a flat fare of ¥1 (15¢/5p). Longer rides on air-conditioned coaches (nos. 800–900) can cost ¥4 (55¢/25p) or more. Most buses run between 5am and 11pm (specific times are posted at the stops).

BY BICYCLE A bike is the best way to stay in touch with the city between sights, and faster than a taxi when traffic is bad, but you'll have to pay attention to the cars and other riders, both of which pose risks to the unwary. Simple bikes are available for rent at a number of hotels, usually for between ¥10 ($1.35/65p) and ¥30 ($4/£2) per day. *Warning:* Avoid the three-wheel pedicabs *(sanlunche)*—a ride almost always ends in an argument over price, and there's no such thing as a good deal.

ON FOOT Beijing is no friend of the pedestrian. The city's sights are scattered and most of its roads are broad rivers of unlovely gray with few channels for safe crossing. Use pedestrian underpasses and footbridges wherever available. *Warning:* Traffic turning right at lights does not give way to pedestrians, nor does any other traffic unless forced to do so by large groups of people bunching up to cross the road. The only parts of the city where walking is enjoyable are the few remaining *hutong* neighborhoods, where the stroll is the point. Otherwise, use a vehicle.

FAST FACTS: Beijing

American Express Emergency check-cashing is available to American Express cardholders at major branches of the Bank of China (including one in the basement of Tower 2 at the China World Trade Center) and at the CITIC Industrial Bank inside the CITIC building (Guoji Dasha) on Jianguo Men Wai Dajie, west of the Friendship Store. For a full list of check-cashing banks, and for emergency card replacement, visit the American Express office at the China World Trade Center, Beijing: room 2313-14, China World Tower 1, China World Trade Center; (℃ **010/6505-2639. After-hours:** U.S. hot line (℃ 001336/668-6809. Emergency card replacement: (℃ 00852/1220-62796. Stolen traveler's checks: (℃ 010800/ 744-0106 (toll-free).

Banks, Foreign Exchange & ATMs Larger branches of the **Bank of China** typically exchange cash and traveler's checks on weekdays only, from 9am to 4pm, occasionally with a break for lunch (11:30am–1:30pm). Most central is the branch at the bottom of Wangfujing Dajie, next to the Oriental Plaza, with forex and credit card cash advances handled at windows 5 to 11 (until 5pm). Other useful branches include those at Fucheng Men Nei Dajie 410; on Jianguo Men Wai Dajie, west of the Scitech Building; in the Lufthansa Center, next to the Kempinski Hotel; and in Tower 1 of the China World Trade Center. One other bank that offers forex is the **CITIC Industrial Bank** (see "American Express," above). Outside the airport, Bank of China **ATMs** accepting international cards include those outside the Wangfujing Dajie branch mentioned above. Others exist farther north on Wangfujing Dajie, outside the Xin (Sun) Dong'an Plaza (24 hr.); on the left just inside the Pacific Century Plaza on Gongti Bei Lu east of Sanlitun (9am–9pm); and adjacent to the Bank of China branch next to the Scitech Building (see above; also 24 hr.). The Citibank ATM east of the International Hotel and the HSBC machine at the entrance to COFCO Plaza, roughly opposite each other on Jianguo Men Nei Dajie, are useful. There are also six ATMs at the airport.

Doctors & Dentists For comprehensive care, the best choice is **Beijing United Family Hospital (Hemujia Yiyuan;** (℃ **010/6433-3960)** at Jiangtai Lu (2 blocks southeast of the Holiday Inn Lido); it is open 24 hours, staffed with foreign-trained doctors, and has a pharmacy, dental clinic, in- and outpatient care, and ambulance service. Other reputable health-service providers, both with 24-hour ambulance services, are the **International Medical Center** ((℃ **010/6465-1561**), inside the Lufthansa Center; and the **International SOS Clinic and Alarm Center** ((℃ **010/6492-9111**), in building C of the BITIC Leasing Center.

Embassies & Consulates Beijing has two main embassy areas—one surrounding Ri Tan Gongyuan north of Jianguo Men Wai Dajie, and another in Sanlitun north of Gongti Bei Lu. A third district, future home of the new U.S. Embassy, has sprouted up next to the Hilton Hotel outside the north section of the East

Third Ring Road. Embassies are typically open Monday through Friday from 9am to between 4 and 5pm, with a lunch break from noon to 1:30pm. The **U.S. Embassy** is due to move in 2008, but for now it's in Ri Tan at Xiushui Dong Jie 2 (ⓒ **010/6532-3431** or, after-hours, 010/6532-1910; fax 010/6532-4153). The **Canadian Embassy** is at Dongzhi Men Wai Dajie 19 (ⓒ **010/6532-3536;** bejing-cs@ international.gc.ca). The **British Embassy** consular section is in Ritan at Floor 21, North Tower, Kerry Centre, Guanghua Lu 1 (ⓒ **010/8529-6600,** ext. 3363; fax 010/8529-6081). The **Australian Embassy** is in Sanlitun at Dongzhi Men Wai Dajie 21 (ⓒ **010/5140-4111;** fax 010/6532-4605). The **New Zealand Embassy** is in Ri Tan at Dong Er Jie 1 (ⓒ **010/6532-2731,** ext. 220; fax 010/6532-4317).

For onward visas: the **Cambodian Embassy** (in Sanlitun at Dongzhi Men Wai Dajie 9; ⓒ **010/6532-2790**) offers 1-month visas for ¥190 ($25/£13), processed in 3 days (¥300/$40/£20 for 1 day); the **Laotian Embassy** (in Sanlitun at Dong Si Jie 11; ⓒ **010/6532-1224**) charges U.S. citizens ¥330 ($44) and Canadian citizens ¥390 (C$56) for a 30-day visa, processed in 4 days; the **Mongolian Embassy** (in Ri Tan at Xiushui Bei Jie 2; ⓒ **010/6532-1203**) charges ¥270 ($36/£18) for a 1-month visa processed in 5 days (¥495/$66/£33 for 1 day); and the **Vietnamese Embassy** (in Ri Tan at Guanghua Lu 32; ⓒ **010/6532-1155**) charges ¥350 ($47/ £23) for a single-entry 1-month visa and ¥400 ($53/£27) for a 3-month visa, both taking 4 days to process. Obtaining a visa at the **Russian Embassy** (in Sanlitun at Dongzhi Men Bei Zhong Jie 4; ⓒ **010/6532-1267 or 010/6532-1991**) is notoriously difficult; they claim you must have a "voucher" from a travel agency (*not* a hotel) in order to be granted a 1-month tourist visa (¥405/$50, 5 days to process, ¥648/$80 for 3 days service, ¥972/$120 for 1 day service; application for express service needs to be submitted before 11am and rate will be slightly higher for U.S and Australian citizens, though the embassy declines to state a definitive figure). Also, in retaliation for new U.S. immigration policies, U.S. citizens have to fill out an interrogation-style form when applying. If you have problems, contact the Beijing office of **Aeroflot** (first floor Jinglun Hotel; ⓒ **010/6500-2412**) for help.

Emergencies For medical emergencies and ambulance service 24 hours a day, call the United Family Health Center emergency number at ⓒ **010/6433-2345** or the International SOS Alarm Center (ⓒ **010/6492-9100**).

Internet Access Internet bars in Beijing are subject to numerous regulations (no one under 18, no smoking) and are restricted in number. The best bet for Internet access is any of the city's various **youth hostels;** the cost is usually ¥10 ($1.35/65p) per hour. There are two conveniently located Internet bars on the third floor of the Lao Chezhan (Old Train Station) shopping center next to Qian Men. **Qianyi Wangluo Kafeiwu** (ⓒ **010/6705-1722**) is open from 9:30am to 11pm and charges ¥20 ($2.70/£1.30) per hour in a cafe setting with a full coffee menu. A simpler, nameless place next door, open from 9am to midnight, charges ¥6 (80¢/40p) per hour. **Moko Internet Cafe (Moke Wangba;** ⓒ **010/ 6252-3712**) on Dong Si Dajie, just south of the Dong Si Mosque, is open from 8am to midnight. Rates are ¥10 ($1.35/65p) per hour downstairs, ¥4 (55¢/25p) upstairs, or free for the first hour if you spend ¥12 ($1.60/80p) in the cafe. The basement of East Gate Plaza, just south of Oriental Kenzo on Dong Zhong Jie (metro: Dongzhi Men, exit C) houses **Yuntian Wangluo** (𝄞 **010/6418-5815**) open 8am to 10pm, ¥4 (55¢/25p) per hour.

Maps & Books Maps with Chinese characters, English, and/or Pinyin can be purchased cheaply for ¥5 (60¢/35p) from vendors near major sights and in hotel lobbies and bookstores. The best selection can be found inside and immediately to the left at the **Wangfujing Bookstore** (9am–9pm) at Wangfujing Dajie 218, north of the Oriental Plaza's west entrance. English-language newspapers and magazines can be found at most five-star hotels; a newsdealer on the first floor of the **Kempinski Hotel** at Liangma Qiao Lu 50 is well stocked.

The best selection of English-language books in Beijing can be found at the clearly marked **Foreign Languages Bookstore** (Waiwen Shudian; 9am–8:30pm) at Wangfujing Dajie 235, opposite the Xin (Sun) Dong'an Plaza. Look on the left side of the first floor for China-related nonfiction, glossy *hutong* photo books, cookbooks, and the full range of Asiapac's cartoon renditions of Chinese classics. Cheap paperback versions of a huge chunk of the English canon, as well as a number of contemporary works, are sold on the third floor. A more daring collection of fiction is carried by **The Bookworm** (p. 140), which also boasts a substantial library.

Pharmacies Simple Western remedies are most likely to be found in the lobbies of international five-star hotels and at branches of **Watson's** (on the first floor of Full Link Plaza at Chaoyang Men Wai Dajie 19; 10:30am–9:30pm, and in the basement of the Oriental Plaza at the bottom of Wangfujing Dajie 1; 10am–10pm). For more specific drugs, try the pharmacies in the Beijing United Family Hospital or the International SOS Clinic (see "Doctors & Dentists," above).

Post Office There are numerous post offices across the city, including one a long block north of the Jianguo Men metro station on the east side of Jianguo Men Bei Dajie (8am–6:30pm), one inside the Landmark Tower (next to the Great Wall Sheraton), one next to the Friendship Store on Jianguo Men Wai Dajie, one on Gongti Bei Lu (opposite the Worker's Stadium), and the EMS Post Office (Beijing Youzheng Sudi Ju) at the corner of Qian Men Dong Dajie and Zhengyi Lu. There is a **FedEx** office in Oriental Plaza, room 01-05A, No. W1 Office Building. **DHL** has branches in the China World Center and COFCO Plaza, and **UPS-Sinotrans** has a useful branch in the Scitech Building at Jianguo Men Wai Dajie 22.

Visa Extensions One-time 30-day extensions of tourist visas are available at the **PSB Exit/Entry Division office** (𝄞 **010/8402-0101**) on the south side of the eastern North Third Ring Road, just east of Xiaojie Qiao (open Mon–Sat 8:30am–4:30pm). Extensions take 5 working days to process; bring your passport and two passport photos, which can be taken at the office for ¥30 ($4/£2).

Weather For daily weather forecasts, check *China Daily* or CCTV 9, China Central Television's English channel (broadcast in most hotels). There is also a weather hot line (𝄞 **121**); dial 6 after a minute or so for the report in English (¥3/40¢/20p per minute).

3 Where to Stay

No other city in mainland China offers the range of accommodations Beijing does. And with the municipal government's decision to scrap the antiquated foreigner-approved hotel system, the range has expanded even further. The high season in Beijing is not well defined, but you should generally expect lower availability and higher rates from mid-May to National Day (Oct 1) and around Chinese New Year (usually late Jan or early Feb). It is usually possible to wrangle discounts of anywhere between 10% and 50% off the rack rate even at these times, although some of the new boutique hotels located in *hutong* courtyards *(siheyuan)* will refuse to bargain except in the dead of winter.

On short visits the best option is to stay within walking distance of the Forbidden City and Tian'an Men Square, on Wangfujing Dajie or nearby. The greatest luxury and highest standards of service can be found in the Chaoyang District. For budget travelers, the obvious choice is the expanding range of comfortable but affordable hostels buried in the labyrinth of *hutong* south and west of Qian Men, with convenient metro and bus access.

NEAR THE FORBIDDEN CITY & QIAN MEN
VERY EXPENSIVE

Grand Hotel (Beijing Guibinlou Fandian)   The Grand Hotel is a separately managed 10-story 1990 addition to the west end of the Beijing Hotel complex, but with better service and a pleasant central atrium. Decently sized rooms on the west side offer good views of the Forbidden City, surpassed only by the panorama from the rooftop bar. The location is tough to beat, but your money is still better spent elsewhere.

Dong Chang'an Dajie 35, Dong Cheng Qu (at Nan Heyan). © 010/6513-7788. Fax 010/6513-0048. www.grand hotelbeijing.com.cn. 217 units. ¥3,450–¥4,600 ($460–$613/£230–£307) standard room (summer discount rate around ¥1,500–¥1,800/$200–$240/£100–£120); ¥5,175–¥5,750 ($690–$767/£345–£383) suite (summer discount rate around ¥2,600–¥4,000/$347–$533/£170–£265), plus 15% service charge, breakfast not included. AE, DC, MC, V. Metro: Wangfujing (118, exit A). **Amenities:** 4 restaurants; 2 bars; indoor pool; exercise room; Jacuzzi; sauna; concierge; tour desk; business center; shopping arcade; salon; 24-hr. room service; laundry/dry-cleaning service; executive-level rooms; currency exchange. *In room:* A/C, satellite TV, broadband Internet access, fax, minibar, hair dryer, safe.

Grand Hyatt (Beijing Dongfang Junyue) 🏃🏃 *(Kids)*   The Hyatt has an excellent location directly over the Wangfujing metro station, at the foot of the capital's most famous shopping street, and within walking distance of the Forbidden City. Rooms have the signature Grand Hyatt comfortable modernity, with convenient desktop dataports and free broadband Internet access. Well-equipped bathrooms have separate shower cubicles. Kids and adults alike will have fun with the vast un-Hyatt-like swimming pool, buried among mock-tropical decor under a ceiling of electric stars.

Dong Chang'an Jie 1, Dong Cheng Qu (within the Oriental Plaza complex). © 010/8518-1234. Fax 010/8518-0000. www.beijing.grand.hyatt.com. 782 units. ¥3,800 ($507/£253) standard room (summer discounts around ¥1,400/$187/£93), plus 15% service charge. AE, DC, MC, V. Metro: Wangfujing (118, exit A). **Amenities:** 4 restaurants; bar; cafe; indoor resort-style pool (50m/165 ft.); fitness center w/latest equipment; Jacuzzi; sauna; solarium; children's pool; airport limousine pickup; business center; shopping arcade; 24-hr. room service; massage; jogging path. *In room:* A/C, satellite TV, broadband Internet access, minibar, hair dryer, safe.

Peninsula Hotel (Wangfu Fandian) 🏃🏃🏃   The range of accommodations choices in Beijing is now so vast that no hotel can claim to be the absolute best, but if a choice had to be made, it would be the Peninsula. Many in-room features—free wireless Internet, 42-inch plasma TVs, and silent, direct-line fax machines—are simply unavailable

Beijing Accommodations, Dining & Nightlife

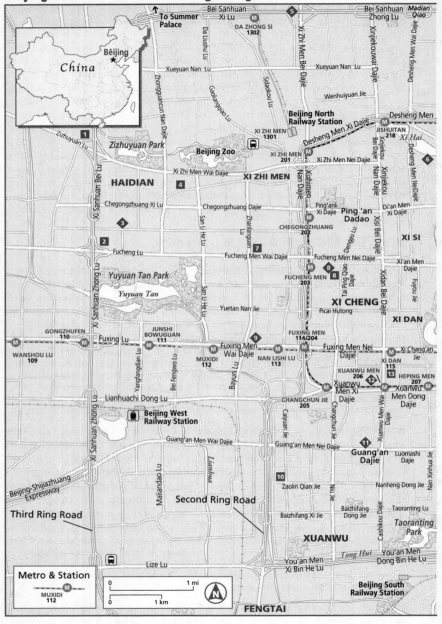

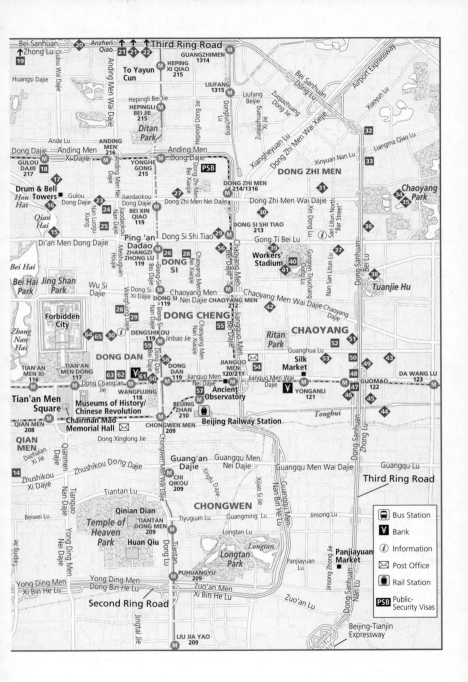

Beijing Accommodations, Dining & Nightlife Key

ACCOMMODATIONS ■

Bamboo Garden Hotel **18**
(Zhú Yuán Bīnguǎn)
竹园宾馆

Běijīng Marriott West **2**
(Běijīng Jīnyù Wànháo Jiǔdiàn)
北京金域方豪酒店

China World Hotel **48**
(Zhōngguó Dàfàndiàn)
中国大饭店

City Central Youth Hostel **57**
(Chéngshì Qīngnián Jiǔdiàn)
城市青年酒店

Crowne Plaza Běijīng **64**
(Guójì Yìyuàn Huángguān Fàndiàn)
国际艺苑皇冠饭店

Crowne Plaza Park View Wǔzhōu **21**
(Wǔzhōu Huángguān Jiàrì Jiǔdiàn)
五洲皇冠假日酒店

Far East Youth Hostel **14**
(Yuǎn Dōng Qīngnián Lǔshè)
远东青年旅社

Gōngtǐ Youth Hostel **40**
(Gōngtǐ Qīngnián Lǔshè)
工体青年旅社

Grand Hotel **63**
(Běijīng Guìbīnlóu Fàndiàn)
北京贵宾楼饭店

Grand Hyatt **61**
(Běijīng Dōngfāng Jūnyuè)
北京东方君悦大酒店

Gu Xiang 20 **24**
(Gǔ Xiàng Èr Shí)
古巷20

Hilton Běijīng **32**
(Běijīng Xīěrdùn Fàndiàn)
希尔顿饭店

Holiday Inn Central Plaza **10**
(Zhōnghuán Jiàrì Jiǔdiàn)
中环假日酒店

Hotel Cote Cour S.L. **55**

Hotel Kapok (Mùmián Huā Jiǔdiàn) **63**
木棉花酒店

International Exchange Center **7**
(Wàijiāo Xuéyuàn Guójì Jiāoliú Zhōngxīn)
外交学院国际交流中心

Kempinski Hotel **33**
(Kǎibīnsījī Fàndiàn)
凯宾斯基饭店

Kerry Centre Hotel **52**
(Běijīng Jiālǐ Zhōngxīn Fàndiàn)
北京嘉里中心饭店

Lǔsōng Yuán Bīnguǎn **25**
吕松园宾馆

The Marco Polo **13**
(Mǎgē Bóluó Jiǔdiàn)
马哥孛罗酒店

Marco Polo Parkside **19**
(Zhōngào Mǎgē Bóluó Jiǔdiàn)
中奥孛罗酒店

Park Hyatt Běijīng **47**
(Běijīng Bǎi Yuè Fàndiàn)
北京柏悦酒店

Peninsula Palace Hotel **59**
(Wángfǔ Fàndiàn)
王府饭店

Raffles Beijing **4**
(Běijīng Fàndiàn Láifóshí)
北京饭店莱佛士

Red Capital Residence **28**
东四六条9号

Ritz Carlton, Financial Street **8**
(Jīnróng Jiē Lìjiā Jiǔdiàn)
金融街丽嘉酒店

Shangri-La Běijīng Hotel **1**
(Xiānggélǐlā Fàndiàn)
香格里拉饭店

St. Regis Běijīng
(Běijīng Guójì Jùlèbù Fàndiàn) **54**
北京国际俱乐部饭店

Traders Hotel Běijīng **50**
(Guómào Fàndiàn)
国贸饭店

Zhònggōng Běijīng Shì Wěi
Bàn Jīguān Zhāodàisuǒ **26**
中国北京市委办机关招待所

elsewhere. A 4-year renovation program was completed in March 2005, and no corner of the hotel was left untouched. Service is impeccable, and helpful touches abound: Braille on all signs; a user-friendly bedside control panel that displays the outside temperature and humidity; and trilevel mood lighting. The hotel's exclusive shopping arcade is home to Jing, one of the city's best fusion restaurants.

Jinyu Hutong 8, Dong Cheng District (at intersection with Dong Dan Bei Dajie). ℭ **010/6512-8899.** Fax 010/6512-9050. www.peninsula.com. 530 units. ¥2,850 ($380/£190) standard room (discount rates around ¥1,450/$193/£97), plus 15% service charge. AE, DC, MC, V. **Amenities:** 3 restaurants; bar; indoor pool; fully equipped fitness center; sauna; concierge; tour desk; business center; forex; extensive shopping arcade; 24-hr. room service; same-day laundry/dry cleaning; nonsmoking rooms; executive-level rooms. *In room:* A/C, satellite TV/DVD, dataport, minibar, hair dryer, safe.

Raffles Beijing (Beijing Fandian Laifoshi) 𝕬𝕬   If you're looking for a slice of old-world charm, look no further than Raffles Beijing. The hotel took over management of this historic building and lovingly restored it with wood paneled floors and sparkling chandeliers. Rooms feature marble entrances and Oriental rugs, though each is decorated differently. So-called "personality suites" are named for famous historical figures; the Li Zongren (a general under Chiang Kai Shek who later became a Communist sympathizer) suite, for example, has a four-poster bed on a raised platform, Chinese bric-a-brac, and a huge bathroom with two separate entrances. Mounted black-and-white photos of old Peking adorn the walls. The huge plasma TV is a bit out of place, and cheekily encased in a early-20th-century-style gold frame. Rooms facing south look out onto Chang'an Jie, one of Beijing's main thoroughfares. Sadly, none of the rooms have balconies. Certain amenities are also inconveniently located in a separate building—you have to walk past a Japanese restaurant and a vaulted atrium to get to the pool and health club. Business travelers who don't need the historic decor might want to check out the contemporary executive suites housed in the same building as the pool and gym.

Dong Chang'an Jie 1 (1 block west of Oriental Plaza). ℭ **800/768-9009** in the U.S., or 010/6526-3388. Fax 010/8500-4380. www.beijing.raffles.com. 171 units. ¥3,800–¥4,700 ($507–$627/£253–£313) standard room (summer discounts around ¥2,000/$267/£133), plus 15% service charge. AE, DC, MC, V. **Amenities:** 3 restaurants (Chinese, French, afternoon tea); bar; indoor pool; fully equipped fitness center; saunas and steam rooms; 24-hr. concierge; tour desk; business center; 24-hr. room service; massage; babysitting; same-day laundry/dry-cleaning service. *In room:* A/C, LCD TV, fax and DVD upon request, free wireless and broadband Internet, minibar, hair dryer, safe.

EXPENSIVE

Crowne Plaza Beijing (Guoji Yiyuan Huangguan Fandian)   This hotel recently completed a massive renovation that has left it awash in sparkling white marble and public spaces with plenty of natural light. Standard double rooms are a bit on the small side, but they come with swanky new flatscreen TVs and decent-size bathrooms. The beige-and-cream decor is soothing, but the carpets don't *quite* hide the stains. The location is pretty well near perfect, and far more affordable than at The Peninsula hotel, just around the corner.

Wangfujing Dajie 48, Dong Cheng Qu (corner of Dengshikou Dajie). ℭ **010/6513-3388.** Fax 010/6513-2513. www.sixcontinentshotels.com. 395 units. ¥1,180 ($157/£79) standard room, plus 15% service charge. AE, DC, MC, V. **Amenities:** 2 restaurants; bar; tiny indoor pool; small health club; Jacuzzi, sauna, and solarium; concierge; tour desk; business center; salon; 24-hr. room service; babysitting; laundry/dry-cleaning service. *In room:* A/C, satellite TV, broadband Internet access, minibar, hair dryer, safe, iron.

Hotel Côté Cour S.L. 𝕬𝕬   This new courtyard hotel, down an unassuming alley, is the best of the bunch of a crop of new courtyard accommodations that have flooded the Beijing market. Lime-green walls, Chinese antiques, and funky tiled bathrooms make this a charming boutique experience. The outdoor garden is a great place to unwind and read if you happen to be visiting when the weather is nice; otherwise, head to the airy, art-filled lounge, where free breakfast and cappuccinos are served.

Yanyue Hutong 70. ℂ 010/6512-8020. Fax 010/6512-7295. www.hotelcotecoursl.com. 14 units. ¥1,295 ($173/£87) standard room. AE, DC, MC, V. **Amenities:** Restaurant (Chinese); bar; lounge; laundry service; same-day dry cleaning; nonsmoking floors. *In room:* A/C, satellite TV, broadband, Wi-Fi Internet, hair dryer, safe.

Red Capital Residence (Xin Hong Zi Julebu) 𝒜𝒜 Art Deco furnishings steal the show at this Cultural Revolution–themed *siheyuan*, set around a tiny central courtyard that conceals a homemade bomb shelter, now converted into a wine bar. It may be a tad museum-like, pretentious even, but if you can't resist the chance to curl up with a book in stuffed armchairs once used by Premier Zhou Enlai, then this boutique hotel is worth the price. The two Concubine's Private Courtyards, fitted with ornate Qing dynasty beds, are the most romantic rooms in the capital. Be sure to book well in advance.

Dong Si Liu Tiao 9 (walk 1 long block west from metro [Dong Si Shi Tiao; 213]; exit D], turn left into Chao Nei Bei Xiao-jie, take 4th turn on right), Dong Cheng Qu. ℂ 010/8403-5308. Fax 010/6402-7153. www.redcapitalclub.com. 5 units. ¥1,200 ($150/£75) single; ¥1,520 ($190/£95) standard room, plus 15% service charge. AE, DC, MC, V. **Amenities:** Cigar lounge; wine bar; laundry service. *In room:* A/C, satellite TV, safe.

Wangfujing Grand (Wangfujing Dajiudian) 𝒜 This is one of the better city-center hotels in this price range, with views of the Forbidden City and fresh "superior"-level rooms available for roughly the same rate as a standard room at the Crowne Plaza. Prices are the same on both sides of the hotel, so be sure to ask for a west-facing unit on one of the higher floors if you want to see the Forbidden City. Standard rooms are usually only ¥80 ($10/£5) cheaper and less recently refurbished, so go for the upgrade.

Wangfujing Dajie 57, Dong Cheng Qu (south of Chaoyang Men Nei Dajie intersection). ℂ 010/6522-1188. Fax 010/6522-3816. www.wangfujinghotel.com. 405 units. ¥2,100 ($280/£140) superior rooms (summer discounts ¥1,000/$133/£67), plus 15% service charge. AE, DC, MC, V. **Amenities:** 3 restaurants; bar; small indoor pool; exercise room; simple sauna; concierge; tour desk; business center; salon; 24-hr. room service; same-day laundry/dry-cleaning service; executive-level rooms; currency exchange. *In room:* A/C, satellite TV, broadband Internet access, minibar, hair dryer, safe.

MODERATE

Hotel Kapok (Mumian Hua Jiudian) 𝒜𝒜 Just yards away from the Forbidden City, this new boutique hotel looks like a lantern when it's lit up at night. Even trippier is the outdoor atrium with a cascading series of lights than resemble rain. Rooms come with glassed-in bathrooms and some have access to small gardens.

Donghuamen Dajie 16; see map p. 88. ℂ 010/6525-9988. Fax 010/6525-0988. www.hotelkapok.com. 89 units. ¥700–¥800 ($93–$107/£47–£53). AE, MC, V. **Amenities:** Restaurant (Western); bar; 24-hr. room service; laundry service. *In room:* A/C, satellite TV, minibar, broadband Internet, safe.

INEXPENSIVE

Far East Youth Hostel (Yuan Dong Qingnian Lushe) 𝒜 Buried deep inside one of the city's most interesting *hutong* neighborhoods, and a short walk from both the Heping Men and Qian Men metro stations, the Far East offers comfortable rooms at competitive rates. Even the hallways—partly adorned with faux brick and latticed, dark wood panels—are pleasant. The hostel maintains cheaper dorms behind a courtyard house across the street, but those in the main building are far better. The Far East is a good choice even if you usually stay at midrange places.

Finds **In the Red Lantern District**

Southwest of Qian Men, past the mercantile madness of Da Zhalan in the *hutong* that never dreamed of pedicab tour salvation, is where you'll find the **Shanxi Xiang Di'er Binguan** (🕿 010/6303-4609)—one of Beijing's most luridly compelling budget hotels. The hotel sits at the north end of Shanxi Xiang (a poorly marked and malodorous lane once at the center of the city's brothel district), and was formerly one of several houses where men of means would go to taste the pleasures of "clouds and rain" prior to 1949. Rooms are arranged on two floors around a central covered courtyard, restored to its original appearance with red columns and walls supporting colorfully painted banisters and roof beams, the latter hung with traditional lanterns. The rooms themselves are tiny and windowless, as befits their original purpose, but they now have air-conditioning, TVs, and bathrooms at a rate of ¥100 ($13/£6.70) per night. To reach the hotel, walk east from Far East Youth Hostel (see above) and turn left down the second *hutong* on the right.

Tieshu Xie Jie 113, Xuanwu Qu (follow Da Zhalan Jie west, left at fork). 🕿 010/6301-8811, ext. 3118. Fax 010/6301-8233. 110 units. ¥328 ($44/£22) standard room (often discounted to ¥200/$25/£13); ¥45 – ¥70 ($6–$9.35/£3–£4.70) dorm bed. AE, DC, MC, V. Metro: Heping Men (207), Qian Men (208). **Amenities:** Restaurant; bike rental; tour desk; coin-op laundry; self-catering kitchen; Internet access. *In room:* A/C, TV, fridge.

CHAOYANG DISTRICT
VERY EXPENSIVE

China World Hotel (Zhongguo Dafandian) 🏵🏵🏵   China World is the city's top business hotel, with an enviable location in the heart of the central business district. The attached China World shopping mall is one of the best in town, with luxury boutiques, a well-stocked supermarket and even an ice-skating rink. Standard rooms are spacious, with marble bathrooms and separate shower units, and the closets have fantastic shelving units. Get a corner room if you can—they're the same price, but bigger. For a real bargain, book yourself into a premier room, since they're the same size as an executive suite, just minus a dividing wall between the sitting area and bedroom. For wine lovers, in-house restaurant Aria was recently tapped by *Wine Spectator* as having one of the best wine lists in the world. The menu offers about 450 bottles, and sommeliers are on hand to help out with choices.

Jianguo Men Wai Dajie 1, Chaoyang Qu (at intersection with E. Third Ring Rd.). 🕿 010/6505-2266. Fax 010/6505-0828. www.shangri-la.com. 716 units. ¥3,300 ($440/£220) standard room (discount rates down to ¥1,350/$180/£90), plus 15% service charge. AE, DC, MC, V. Metro: Guomao (122, exit A). **Amenities:** 4 restaurants plus several more in attached mall; indoor pool (25m/82 ft.); golf simulator; 3 indoor tennis courts; full-service health club; separate spa w/aromatherapy; concierge; business center; shopping complex; salon; 24-hr. room service; same-day laundry/dry-cleaning service; executive-level rooms; nonsmoking rooms; currency exchange. *In room:* A/C, satellite TV, broadband Internet access, minibar, hair dryer, safe, wireless Internet access in executive rooms.

Kempinski Hotel (Kaibinsiji Fandian) 🏵   The Kempinski's plain but large and very comfortable rooms have been refurbished to a high standard. Response time to requests to the staff is the most rapid in Beijing, and its position in the Lufthansa Centre means every facility imaginable is at hand, including a wine store, airline offices and ticket agents, medical and dental clinics with Western staff, restaurants, a supermarket, a bookshop, and a department store.

Liangma Qiao Lu 50, Chaoyang Qu (east of N. Third Ring Rd., near airport expressway junction); see map p. 88. Ⓒ **010/6465-3388.** Fax 010/6465-3366. www.kempinski-beijing.com. 526 units. ¥1,850 ($247/£123) standard room (discount rates around ¥1,200/$160/£80), plus 15% service charge. AE, DC, MC, V. **Amenities:** 7 restaurants; indoor pool; outdoor tennis court; fitness center; Jacuzzi; sauna; concierge; free shuttle to airport and city center; business center; shopping complex; 24-hr. room service; same-day laundry/dry-cleaning service; executive-level rooms; 6 nonsmoking floors; currency exchange; squash courts. *In room:* A/C, satellite TV, broadband Internet access, minibar, hair dryer, safe.

Kerry Centre Hotel (Beijing Jiali Zhongxin Fandian) ★★ *(Kids)* The very hip

Kerry Centre is my top choice for a hotel in the central business district. Lounge music plays in the public spaces, and standard rooms are stylishly decorated in textured, solid colors of gold and dark green, with maroon accent pillows. My one complaint: Bathrooms are small and rather awkwardly laid out, with tubs jammed into the corner and toilets tucked behind the door. Executive floors have far roomier bathrooms and added luxuries like free broadband or Wi-Fi Internet, Bose CD players, huge plasma TVs, and DVD players. They also have the best health club in town, including a spacious gym with the latest equipment, a 35m indoor lap pool flanked by two Jacuzzis, two indoor tennis courts, and even a short outdoor jogging path. The hotel's restaurant, Horizon, is popular for its scrumptious ¥168 ($22/£11) dim sum lunch buffet for two, and its bar, Centro , is a popular gathering spot for proper cocktails and a night of people-watching.

Guanghua Lu 1, Chaoyang Qu (on west side of Kerry Centre complex, north of Guomao metro). Ⓒ **010/6561-8833.** Fax 010/6561-2626. www.shangri-la.com. 487 units. ¥3,000 ($400/£200) standard room (summer discounts around ¥1,500/$200/£100), plus 15% service charge. AE, DC, MC, V. Metro: Guomao (122, exit A). **Amenities:** 2 restaurants; bar; indoor pool; indoor basketball/tennis/badminton courts; fitness center; children's play area; concierge; tour desk; business center; shopping arcade; 24-hr. room service; same-day laundry/dry-cleaning service; executive-level rooms; 5 nonsmoking floors; currency exchange; rooftop track for running and in-line skating; sun deck. *In room:* A/C, satellite TV, broadband Internet access, minibar, hair dryer, safe.

Ritz-Carlton, Financial Street (Jinrong Jie Lijia Jiudian) ★★ Though this

hotel caters primarily to a corporate clientele, the place is decorated with such homey touches that you'll wonder if it was designed by a Chinese version of Martha Stewart. The beds are the comfiest in town, and spacious marble bathrooms feature twin sinks and televisions anchored in front of the bathtubs. The basement health club and spa are top-notch, and the luxurious swimming pool comes complete with imbedded lounge chairs that deliver water jet massages. There's even a giant-screen television along one wall. Be sure to try Cépe (p. 104), which serves Beijing's best upscale Italian fare. The only drawback is the location, which isn't particularly central, though the area is on the rise as a business district. And the hotel is attached to a chic new shopping center, home to Beijing's first Lane Crawford emporium.

1 Jinchengfang Dong Jie (next to the National Security Council bldg.); see map p. 88. Ⓒ **010/6601-6666.** Fax 010/6601-6029. www.marriott.com. 253 units. ¥1,915 ($255/£128) standard room. AE, MC, V. **Amenities:** 3 restaurants (international, Italian, Chinese); bar; indoor pool; fitness center; spa; Jacuzzi; sauna; concierge; business center; salon; room service; babysitting services; same-day laundry/dry cleaning; executive-level rooms; currency exchange. *In room:* A/C, satellite TV, Wi-Fi and broadband Internet, minibar, hair dryer, iron, safe w/built-in laptop charger, scale.

St. Regis Beijing (Beijing Guoji Julebu Fandian) ★★ When the St. Regis

reopens in late spring 2008 after an extensive 8-month renovation, it should once again be at the top of the game. No hotel in Beijing can rival the on-call personal butler service of the St. Regis, which boasts the highest staff-to-guest ratio in China. Almost unnerving attention is paid to your individual needs, down to what side of the bed you sleep on for turndown service, and what fruit you prefer in the fruit bowl.

The white marble lobby, with its towering palms and afternoon tea, is the city's most elegant, and the health club is world-class, with a spa drawing on waters a mile underground. Danieli's on the second floor is one of the city's finest Italian restaurants, and the Press Club Baris a stylish, clubby watering hole.

Jianguo Men Wai Dajie 21, Chaoyang Qu (southwest side of Ri Tan Park). ℂ 010/6460-6688. Fax 010/6460-3299. www.stregis.com/beijing. 273 units. ¥2,700 ($360/£180) standard room, plus 15% service charge. AE, DC, MC, V. Metro: Jianguo Men (120/211, exit B, 1 block away). **Amenities:** 5 restaurants; bar; indoor pool; putting green and driving area; exercise room; spa; billiards room; concierge; business center; salon; 24-hr. room service; same-day laundry/dry-cleaning service; nonsmoking rooms; cigar and wine-tasting rooms; currency exchange; 24-hr. butler service; squash courts. *In room:* A/C, satellite TV, DVD player, broadband Internet access, minibar, hair dryer, safe.

EXPENSIVE

Hilton Beijing (Beijing Xierdun Fandian) ✦   What a difference a renovation can make. Once saddled with some of the most tired guest rooms in the capital, Hilton's newly overhauled rooms now sport attractive carpets, stylish and functional glass desks, and ultracomfortable beds. The new marble bathrooms are spacious, with separate shower units and deep tubs. A sleek atrium lounge, where Chinese-inspired bird cages hang over a crescent shaped bar, was recently added. It's hip and cool, though still no match for my personal favorite hotel lounge, the Kerry Centre's Centro, which is in a better location.

Dongfang Lu 1, Dong San Huan Bei Lu, Chaoyang Qu (east side of N. Third Ring Rd., north of Xiaoyun Lu). ℂ 010/5865-5000. Fax 010/5865-5800. www.beijing.hilton.com. 377 units. ¥2,200 ($293/£147) standard room (summer discounts around ¥1,330/$177/£89), plus 15% service charge. AE, DC, MC, V. **Amenities:** 3 restaurants; bar; indoor pool; small outdoor tennis court; squash court; fitness club; Jacuzzi; sauna; bike rental; concierge; tour desk; business center; salon; 24-hr. room service; in-room massage; babysitting; same-day laundry/dry-cleaning service; 2 squash courts; valet. *In room:* A/C, satellite TV, broadband Internet access, minibar, hair dryer, safe.

Marco Polo Parkside (Zhongao Mage Boluo Jiudian) ✦✦   If you're coming to Beijing for the Olympics, the National Stadium is about a 5-minute walk away from this swank new hotel. Marble entryways lead the way to plush carpets, generous-size bathrooms with separate shower units, and chic dark-wood furniture. Even the decor is slick, with chocolate brown textured velour bed throws and subtle silkscreens. In deluxe rooms, almond-shaped bathtubs sit next to huge glass windows marking the boundary between the bedroom and the bathroom. Too scandalous? Don't worry, the press of a button sends down a curtain. Rooms facing west have a view of the National Stadium just visible beyond the neighboring high-rises. The hotel was in the midst of opening as this book went to press, so we didn't get a chance to pop into the pool, health club, or spa, which were still under construction. Staff are overeager, though still a little unsure of themselves.

Anli Lu 78 (next to Olympic Green, 1km/⅔ mile from the National Stadium); see map p. 88. ℂ 010/5963-6688. Fax 010/5963-6500. www.marcopolohotels.com/beijingparkside.html. 315 units. ¥3,000 –¥3,200 ($400–$427/£200– £213) superior/deluxe room, plus 15% service charge. AE, DC, MC, V. **Amenities:** 3 restaurants (international, Chinese, Korean); bar; indoor pool; health club; spa; concierge; business center; 24-hr. room service; laundry/dry-cleaning service; executive-level rooms; nonsmoking floors; currency exchange. *In room:* A/C, satellite TV, free broadband, minibar, hair dryer, safe.

Traders Hotel Beijing (Guomao Fandian) ✦   The greatest advantage to staying in this Shangri-La four-star hotel is access to the five-star health club facilities in the China World Hotel next door. Otherwise, Traders is a straightforward business hotel, with slightly small and plain but nicely outfitted rooms, unobtrusive service, and easy access to the metro. The only major drawback is the tiny bathrooms, but this is compensated

for by reasonably low (after-discount) room rates. The West Wing has the slightly nicer (and more expensive) rooms.

Jianguo Men Wai Dajie 1, Chaoyang Qu (behind China World Hotel); see map p. 88. ⓒ **010/6505-2277**. Fax 010/ 6505-0818. www.shangri-la.com. 560 units. ¥1,350 ($180/£90) standard room, plus 15% service charge. AE, DC, MC, V. Metro: Guomao (122). **Amenities:** 2 restaurants; bar; small exercise room; Jacuzzi; sauna; concierge; business center; shopping complex; salon; 24-hr. room service; same-day laundry/dry-cleaning service; executive-level rooms; non-smoking rooms; currency exchange. *In room:* A/C, satellite TV, broadband Internet access, minibar, hair dryer, safe.

INEXPENSIVE

Gongti Youth Hostel (Gongti Qingnian Lushe)   Located inside the Workers Stadium, in the heart of the Sanlitun bar area, this well-run YHA offers a quiet location above a three-star hotel (The Sports Inn), a view over pleasant gardens and a lake, and relatively new facilities. The fourth-floor rooms (not ideal if you have lots of luggage) are agreeably curved, and all face southeast. If you crave privacy, there are single rooms.

Gongren Tiyuchang 9 Tai, Chaoyang Qu; see map p. 88. Metro: Dong Si Shi Tiao (213, exit B), 3 long blocks east. ⓒ **010/6552-4800**. Fax 010/6552-4860. 38 units (communal bathrooms/showers). Dorm beds from ¥60 ($8/£4); ¥120 ($16/£8) single room. Discounts for YHA members. No credit cards. **Amenities:** Bike rental; travel service; self-service kitchen and laundry; Internet access; reading room. *In room:* A/C, TV, no phone.

AROUND THE BACK LAKES

MODERATE

Bamboo Garden Hotel (Zhu Yuan Binguan)   Said to be the former residence of the infamous Qing dynasty eunuch, Li Lianying, Bamboo Garden was the first major courtyard-style hotel in Beijing and is among the most beautiful. It's slightly more luxurious than the Lusong Yuan (see below), but with less character. Rooms border three different-size courtyards; each filled with rock gardens, clusters of bamboo, and covered corridors. Standard rooms in the two multistory buildings at opposite ends of the complex are decorated with Ming-style furniture and traditional lamps that cast pleasant shadows on the high ceilings.

Xiaoshi Qiao Hutong 24, Xi Cheng Qu (6th *hutong* on left walking north on Jiu Gulou Dajie, west of Drum Tower); see map p. 88. ⓒ **010/6403-2229**. Fax 010/6401-2633. 44 units. ¥580–¥680 ($77–$91/£39–£45) standard room (discounts rare). AE, DC, MC, V. **Amenities:** Restaurant; bar; concierge; travel service; business center; salon; laundry service; currency exchange. *In room:* A/C, satellite TV, fridge.

Gu Xiang 20 (Gu Xiang Er Shi) ⓐ   Opened in 2007, this intimate hotel located on a bar-lined alley in the hutongs boasts modern rooms decorated with Chinese antiques, dark wood beds, and flatscreen TVs. Rooms on the third floor are larger and some come with private balconies with views overlooking the rooftops of traditional courtyard houses nearby—it's well worth the upgrade. The English service is uneven, but everyone is friendly.

Nanluogu Xiang 20 (about 200m/656 ft. south of north entrance of Nanluogu Xiang); see map p. 88. ⓒ **010/ 6400-5566**. Fax 010/6400-3658. www.guxiang20.com. 28 units. ¥500–¥1,280 ($67–$170/£134–£340) standard room. AE, DC, MC, V. **Amenities:** Restaurant; bar; rooftop tennis court; room service; limited business center; laundry/dry-cleaning service. *In room:* A/C, satellite TV, free Wi-Fi, minibar, fridge.

Lusong Yuan Binguan ⓐⓐ   Set on the site of a Qing dynasty general's residence down a quaint *hutong* north of Ping'an Dadao is this thoroughly charming courtyard hotel. Smaller and more intimate than the Bamboo Garden, with more traditional rooms, it wins with the details—bright paneled hallway ceilings, faux rotary phones in-room, and Chinese-style wall-mounted lamps over the beds. A few rooms open directly onto quiet, semiprivate courtyards. Avoid the airless dorms in the basement.

Banchang Hutong 22, Dong Cheng Qu (walking north from Di'an Men Dong Dajie on Jiaodaokou Nan Dajie, 2nd *hutong* on left). ☏ 010/6404-0436. Fax 010/6403-0418. www.the-silk-road.com. 59 units. ¥1,100 ($147/£74) standard room (summer discounts ¥780/$104/£52, 40% discounts in winter). AE, DC, MC, V. **Amenities:** Restaurant; laundry service; limited currency exchange; Internet access. *In room:* A/C, TV.

Zhonggong Beijing Shi Wei Ban Jiguan Zhaodaisuo *(Finds)*   Normally you should give a wide berth to any venture with the words *zhonggong* (Chinese Communist Party) and *jiguan* (government organ) in the name, but this new hotel is an exception. The impressive twin-courtyard residence formerly housed Wu De, the mayor of Beijing during the Cultural Revolution, who wasn't included in the Gang of Four, but assuredly made the shortlist. Staff are surprisingly friendly, the smallish rooms are packed with amenities, and the location, in one of Beijing's best-preserved *hutong*, is hard to top.

Dong Si Liu Tiao 71, Dong Cheng Qu. ☏ 010/6401-8823, ext. 8100. Fax 010/6401-8823, ext. 8200. 16 units (13 with shower only). ¥320–¥800 ($43–$107/£21–£53) standard room (20%–30% summer discounts). No credit cards. **Amenities:** Restaurant; bike rental. *In room:* A/C, TV, fridge, safe, washing machine.

WEST SECOND RING & BEYOND
EXPENSIVE
Beijing Marriott West (Beijing Jinyu Wanhao Jiudian) *&*   This is the first full-fledged Marriott in Beijing, the second in China after the Shenyang Marriott, and both are among the country's most opulent hotels. An apartment building before the Marriott Group took over, its rooms are immense, furnished with sumptuous beds and overstuffed chairs, and 80% of them have Jacuzzi tubs. Guests also have free access to the attached Bally fitness center, but this hotel is far from the major sights.

Xi San Huan Bei Lu 98, Haidian Qu (in Jinyu Dasha, at intersection with Fucheng Lu). ☏ 010/6872-6699. Fax 010/6872-7302. www.marriotthotels.com/bjsmc. 155 units. ¥2,800 ($373/£187) standard room (summer discounts ¥1,250/$167/£83), plus 15% service charge. AE, DC, MC, V. **Amenities:** Restaurant; bar; health club w/indoor pool and tennis courts; concierge; business center; salon; 24-hr. room service; same-day laundry/dry cleaning; executive-level rooms; nonsmoking rooms; bowling center; currency exchange. *In room:* A/C, satellite TV, dataport, minibar, hair dryer, iron, safe.

Crowne Plaza Park View Wuzhou (Wuzhou Huangguan Jiari Jiudian) *(Kids)*   Far from the expatriate ghettos, the surrounding area has considerable appeal: Yayun Cun is a pedestrian-friendly residential area that boasts some of Beijing's best Chinese restaurants. Within the striking white edifice, you'll find a very North American brand of luxury, with *USA Today* delivered to your door daily; it's comfortable enough, but a bit bland. Little luxuries are lacking and service can be indifferent. It's worth upgrading to a "luxury" *(haohua)* room, as bathrooms in the "superior" *(gaoji)* rooms are a bit pokey.

Bei Si Huan Lu 4, Chaoyang Qu (northwest of Anhui Qiao on the N. Fourth Ring Rd.). ☏ 010/8498-2288. Fax 010/8499-2933. www.crowneplaza.com. 478 units. Luxury rooms ¥1,900 ($253/£127) (summer discounts ¥1,468/$196/£98), plus 15% service charge. AE, DC, MC, V. Bus: no. 803 from Anding Men metro (216, exit B). **Amenities:** 3 restaurants; bar; indoor pool; exercise room; Jacuzzi; sauna; concierge; business center; 24-hr. room service; massage; same-day laundry/dry cleaning; executive-level rooms; currency exchange. *In room:* A/C, satellite TV, broadband Internet access, minibar, hair dryer, iron, safe.

Shangri-La Beijing Hotel (Xianggelila Fandian) *&*   It doesn't look like much from the outside, but the Shangri-La is one of the finest hotels in town, especially with the new addition of the Valley Wing, a tower filled with luxurious executive rooms, which are decorated in elegantly muted earth tones and come with access to an indulgent lounge with free breakfast and afternoon cocktails and canapés. Standard rooms are a good size and comfortably furnished, if less imaginative than rooms at other Beijing

hotels in this chain. The Chi Spa, which opened in 2007, offers massages and facials in a dimmed, meditative Tibetan atmosphere. Although off by itself in the northwest, the hotel benefits from having space for a large and lush garden (featuring an outdoor bar and pond), easy access to the Summer Palaces and the Western Hills, and quick routes around Beijing via the Third and Fourth ring roads.

Zizhu Yuan Lu 29, Haidian Qu (northwest corner of Third Ring Rd.). ℂ 010/6841-2211. Fax 010/6841-8002. www.shangri-la.com. 657 units. ¥1,500 ($200/£100) standard room (summer discounts ¥1,150/$153/£177), plus 15% service charge. AE, DC, MC, V. **Amenities:** 3 restaurants; bar; indoor pool; health club w/sauna, solarium, exercise room; concierge; tour desk; business center; 24-hr. room service; same-day laundry/dry-cleaning service; executive-level rooms; nonsmoking rooms; currency exchange. *In room:* A/C, satellite TV, broadband Internet access, minibar, hair dryer, safe.

BEIJING STATION & SOUTH
EXPENSIVE

Holiday Inn Central Plaza (Zhonghuan Jiari Jiudian) ☆☆   This site was right in the middle of things during the Jin dynasty (1122–1215), but there's nothing central about the location of this stylish hotel now. However, if you're visiting Beijing to be among Chinese people, rather than to be pampered alongside tourists, I strongly recommend this hotel. Credit must be given to the local designer, who has achieved the architectural Holy Grail: minimalism without coldness. Service is equally to the point. Set in a residential area, Beijing's Muslim quarter is a short walk to the east, a lively strip of restaurants lie to the north, and it's also handy to both of Beijing's main railway stations.

Caiyuan Jie 1, Xuanwu Qu. ℂ 010/8397-0088. Fax 010/8355-6688. 322 units. ¥1,660 ($221/£111) standard room, plus 15% service charge (summer discounts ¥803/$107/£54 all-inclusive). AE, DC, MC, V. Bus: no. 395 from Changchun Jie metro (205; exit A). **Amenities:** 2 restaurants; cafe; bar; indoor pool; well-equipped exercise room; yoga room; concierge; tour desk; business center; 24-hr. room service; same-day laundry/dry cleaning; executive-level rooms; currency exchange. *In room:* A/C, satellite TV, broadband Internet access, minibar, hair dryer, safe.

The Marco Polo (Mage Boluo Jiudian) ☆ *Value*   Although not among the main clusters of foreign hotels, The Marco Polo is as close to the center of things as any of them, and is quieter and better connected than most. (The location—just south of the No. 1 Line's Xi Dan station and north of the Circle Line's Xuanwu Men station—enables guests to get in and out during the worst of rush hour.) The medium-size rooms are well-appointed, although bathrooms are somewhat cramped.

Xuanwu Men Nei Dajie 6, Xuanwu Qu (just south of Xi Dan metro stop). ℂ 010/6603-6688. Fax 010/6603-1488. www.marcopolohotels.com. 296 units. ¥2,080 ($277/£139) standard room (summer discounts up to 70%), plus 15% service charge. AE, DC, MC, V. Metro: Xi Dan (115, exit E). **Amenities:** 2 restaurants; bar; indoor pool; fitness center; concierge; tour desk; business center; salon; 24-hr. room service; laundry/dry-cleaning service; executive-level rooms; currency exchange. *In room:* A/C, satellite TV, broadband Internet access, minibar, hair dryer, safe.

MODERATE

City Central Youth Hostel (Chengshi Qingnian Jiudian) ☆☆ *Value*   Housed in the old post office building, this newly opened hostel cum hotel has an unbeatable location directly opposite Beijing railway station. The manager was inspired by a visit to the Sydney Central YHA in Australia, and has attempted to create a replica here. Standard rooms on the fifth and sixth floors are minimalist and clean, with none of the sleaze associated with other railway hotels, and at a fraction of the expense. Ask for a room on the north side, facing away from the railway station square. Dorm rooms on the fourth floor have double-glazed windows and comfortable bunk beds, but the squat toilets are a surprise for the less limber.

Airport Hotels

There are plenty of options here, all with free shuttle services. The most pleasant choice is the **Sino-Swiss Hotel** ✸ **(Guodu Dafàndian;** ☎ **010/6456-5588**; fax 010/6456-1588; www.sino-swisshotel.com), formerly a Mövenpick, with large rooms and queen-size beds for around ¥856 ($114/£57) after discount. Guests have free access to a pleasant resort-style pool complex, and regular shuttles go the airport (every 30 min. 6:15am–10:45pm) and downtown. Just south of the airport and almost within walking distance is the very basic **Air China Hotel** (Guohang Binguan; ☎ **010/6456-3440**; standard twins ¥260–¥320 ($34–$42/ £17–£21). The **Kempinski Hotel** (see earlier in this chapter), near the Third Ring Road, also has free shuttle service to the airport.

Beijing Zhan Qian Jie 1, Dong Cheng Qu. ☎ 010/6525-8066. Fax 010/6525-9066. www.centralhostel.com. ¥288 ($38/£19) standard room; from ¥60 ($8/£4) dorm beds. Discounts on dorm beds for YHA members. AE, DC, MC, V. Metro: Beijing Zhan (210, exit A). **Amenities:** Bar; billiards and movie room; bike rental; tour desk; self-service laundry and kitchen; supermarket; Internet access. *In room:* A/C, TV, broadband Internet access.

4 Where to Dine

Too many of Beijing's restaurants open and close in any given month to offer an accurate count, but it is difficult to imagine a city with more eateries per square mile, or a more exhaustive variety of Chinese cuisines. The short life span of the average restaurant in Beijing can create headaches (for guidebook writers, in particular), but the upside is a dynamic culinary environment where establishments that manage to stick around have generally earned the right to exist.

Food trends sweep through the city like tornadoes through Kansas. A few years ago it was Cultural Revolution nostalgia dishes, then fish and sweet sauces from Shanghai, and now yuppified cuisine normally served by minorities from Yunnan. Tomorrow it will be something else. See the expatriate periodicals—*Time Out* and *that's Beijing*— for notes on the latest craze.

Proper foreign food is now widely available at generally reasonable prices, so there's no reason to rely on your hotel for something non-Chinese. Foreign **fast food** and other well-known food and beverage chains, most of them American, blanket the city (that is, if you're desperately hungry and too tired to find anything else). KFC and McDonald's are ubiquitous, and a stable of Delifrance outlets (one each in Xin Dong'an Plaza and the Lufthansa Center) are convenient for breakfast. For cheap sandwiches, there are numerous Subway chains and Schlotsky's Deli (in the China World Trade Center). Among sit-down options are Pizza Hut, Sizzlers, TGI Friday's, Henry J. Beans, and the Beijing Hard Rock Cafe (check *that's Beijing* for location details).

You can buy basic **groceries** and Chinese-style **snacks** at local markets and at the *xiaomaibu* ("little-things-to-buy units") found nearly everywhere. Several fully stocked **supermarkets** and a handful of smaller grocers now carry imported wine and cheese, junk food, Newcastle Brown Ale, and just about anything else you could want, albeit at inflated prices. Supermarkets include one in the basement of the Lufthansa Center, the CRC in the basement of the China World Trade Center, and Oriental Kenzo, above Dongzhi Men metro. April Gourmet, north of Sanlitun bar street, has sliced meats, a decent cheese selection, and a full selection of familiar breakfast cereals; much the same can be found at Jenny Lou's, which has six branches in Beijing; the biggest one is near Chaoyang Park west gate. Among **delis and bakeries,** one of the best is the Kempi Deli (inside the Lufthansa Center) with good crusty-bread sandwiches.

Tour groups and those visiting expat friends tend to get trotted to restaurants with absurd prices and unappetizing food, such as those supposedly specializing in "imperial" cuisine. Fresher, better choices are set out below, but information on the showpiece eateries (Fangshan, Li Family Restaurant) can be found in the expat magazines. For restaurant locations, see the map on p. 88.

AROUND WANGFUJING DAJIE
VERY EXPENSIVE

The Courtyard (Siheyuan) ✦✦ FUSION   The Courtyard wins points for its setting in a restored courtyard-style house next to the Forbidden City, with a bright modern interior that doubles as an art gallery. Foie gras brûlée, cashew-crusted lamb chop, and black cod with tomato marmalade are longtime favorites, and the tender grilled chicken breast in lemon grass and coconut curry is superb. The wine list is the most comprehensive this side of Hong Kong, and there's an intimate cigar lounge upstairs, with views across the Forbidden City moat.

Donghua Men Lu 95 (10-min. walk, on north side of street). ⓒ 010/6526-8883. Reservations essential. Meal for 2 ¥145–¥245 ($19–$33/£9.70–£16). AE, DC, MC, V. 6–9:30pm. Metro: Tian'an Men East (117, exit B); east side of Forbidden City.

Jaan ✦ FRENCH   Here you'll find wonderful French food that pretty much sticks to tradition. Dishes are light, but filling, and resident chef Guillaume is a stickler for good ingredients—it took him 7 months to find a local vegetable supplier that was up to his standards. The menu changes every season. We highly recommend the roasted codfish with truffle macaroni cèpe emulsion. The cod seems to melt at the touch of your fork and the sauce is flavorful but not too heavy. The ambience leaves a little something to be desired—the restaurant doesn't really have a space of its own, but is separated from the main lobby by opium-bed seating—and the narrow layout makes you feel like you're in a brightly lit hallway that just happens to serve fine food.

Dong Chang'an Jie 1 (1 block west of Oriental Plaza). ⓒ 010/6526-3388. Reservations recommended. Meal for 2 ¥800–¥1,200 ($107–$160/£53–£80). AE, DC, MC, V. Noon–2pm and 6:30–10pm. Metro: Wangfujing.

⟨Value⟩ Chinese on the Cheap

Affordable Chinese food is everywhere in Beijing, and not all of the places serving it are an offense to Western hygiene standards. Adequately clean **Chinese fast-food** restaurants include Yonghe Dawang (with KFC-style sign) and Malan noodle outlets (marked with a Chicago Bulls–style graphic). A better option is the **point-to-order food courts** on the top or bottom floor of almost every large shopping center. For late-night dining, a favorite Beijing pastime, try one of the **night markets** at Donghua Men (just off Wangfujing Dajie opposite the Xin Dong'an Plaza) and on Longfu Si Jie (north of Wangfujing Dajie next to the Airlines Ticketing Hall). The famous 24-hour food street on Dongzhi Men Nei Dajie, locally known as **Ghost Street (Gui Jie),** is now much reduced, but dozens of eateries still offer hot pot, *mala longxia* (spicy crayfish), and home-style fare through the lantern-lit night.

EXPENSIVE

Made in China (Chang An Yi Hao) BEIJING   We regularly visit Made in China for its fantastic Peking Duck and its equally enthralling setting—a dining room placed in the middle of an open kitchen, illuminated by the occasional leaping flame from the stove. The Grand Hyatt's showcase restaurant offers traditional northeastern and Beijing dishes including the capital's most palatable *dou zhi* (fermented bean purée), excellent *ma doufu* (mashed soybean), and the ubiquitous *zhajiang mian* (wheat noodles with black bean mince), a dish that has spawned its own chain of restaurants. But the Peking Duck is the highlight—the presentation and flavors are impeccable. There's the odd fusion twist such as foie gras with sesame pancake, and there are excellent plain dishes such as tonghao vegetable with rice vinegar and garlic sauce. Quite unexpectedly for a Chinese restaurant, Made in China makes delicious desserts—the pear champagne and passion-fruit sorbet pack a fruity punch. Right next door you'll find the sleek **Red Moon Bar,** perfect for an aperitif.

Dong Chang'an Jie (inside Grand Hyatt); see map p. 88. ⓒ 010/8518-1234, ext. 3608. Reservations essential. Meal for 2 ¥250–¥350 ($33–$47/£17–£23). AE, DC, MC, V. 7–10:30am, 11:30am–2:30pm, and 5:30–10:30pm. Metro: Wangfujing (118, exit A).

MODERATE

Be There or Be Square (Bujian Busan) HONG KONG   This trendy Hong Kong–style cafe with cool warehouse-style decor serves all the Westernized Cantonese classics—barbecue pork with rice, black bean spareribs, beef with rice noodles, and many others—plus a selection of vaguely Western breakfast items.

Level B1 Capital Epoch Plaza at Xi Chang'an Jie 88. ⓒ 010/8391-4078. Main courses ¥20–¥50 ($3–$6.70/£1.30–£3.30). No credit cards. 9:30am–9:30pm. Metro: Xi Dan (115, exit E).

Otto's Restaurant (Richang Chacanting) ☆ HONG KONG   Otto's is authentic Hong Kong proletarian dining, down to the shouts, smoke, and indecipherable wall-mounted menu. The environment may be jarring and the staff too busy to care, but the food is tremendous, especially the range of *baozai* (clay pot) rice dishes; try the *lawei huaji baozaifan,* a mix of salty-sweet sausage and chicken. Also good, but messy, are the *suanxiang jichi* (paper-wrapped garlic chicken wings). New branches are sprouting all over town—notably a 24-hour branch just east of the north entrance to Bei Hai Park. Other locations are at Di'an Men Xi Dajie 14 (ⓒ 010/6405-8205), 2/F Shanghai Salon (ⓒ 010/6780-4350), and Hua Yuan Dong Lu 8 (ⓒ 010/8203-8155).

Dong Dan Dajie 72. ⓒ 010/6525-1783. Meal for 2 ¥60–¥80 ($8–$11/£4–£5.30). No credit cards. 10am–3am. English menu. Metro: Dong Dan (119, exit A); walk north several blocks.

CHAOYANG DISTRICT (NORTH)

VERY EXPENSIVE

Green T. House (Zi Yun Xuan) ☆ FUSION   If you're comfortable with the sentiment that "dining should be part of a lifestyle experience," you'll love this ultrachic restaurant. If you think that sounds like pretentious twaddle, try Bellagio's, right next door. The name changes from purple to green in translation; dining at Green T. is a similarly psychedelic experience. The imaginatively prepared food is light, with tea-infused flavors, but the cuisine is beside the point. The minimalist decor and attentive service attracts a fashion-conscious crowd. Another location, known as Green T. House Living, is far north of the city center at Cuigezhuang Xiang Hegezhuang Cun 318 (ⓒ 13/601137132).

Gongti Xi Lu 6 (a subtly marked door, on the east side of Bellagio's); see map p. 88. © 010/6552-8310. Reservations essential. Main courses ¥86–¥260 ($12–$35/£5.70–£17). AE, DC, MC, V. 11am–2:30pm and 6pm–midnight.

EXPENSIVE

Bellagio (Lu Gang Xiaozhen) TAIWAN   Taiwanese cuisine, characterized by sweet flavors and subtle use of ginger, is one of styles of Chinese cookery most appealing to Western palates. Don't miss the delicate *shacha niurou*, mustard greens combined perfectly with thinly sliced beef strips. *Taiwan dofu bao*, a tofu clay-pot seasoned with shallots, onion, chili, and black beans is also remarkable, as is the signature dish, *sanbei ji* (chicken reduced in rice wine, sesame oil, and soy sauce). Beijing's best pearl milk tea *(zhenzhu naicha)* comes with the tapioca balls served separately. In summer, don't miss the enormous shaved-ice desserts. Another location is at Gongti Xi Lu 6 (south of Gongti 100 bowling center; © **010/6551-3533**). Same hours and prices apply.

Xiaoyun Lu 35 (opposite Renaissance Hotel). © 010/8451-9988. Meal for 2 ¥120–¥200 ($16–$27/£8–£13). AE, DC, MC, V. 11am–4am.

Flo (Fu Lou) ✦ *Value* FRENCH   Flo occupies the front of a rather flashy building, all balustrades and staircases, with an (inaudible) nightclub at the rear. The menu is straightforward French favorites all done well: smoked salmon salad with poached egg, pan-fried rib short-loin veal with mushrooms, and the chef's specialty, hot gooseliver with apple. This place is reliable and offers good value.

Dong San Huan Bei Lu 12 (south of Great Wall Sheraton). © 010/6595-5139. Meal for 2 ¥90–¥230 ($11–$29/£5–£15); prix-fixe lunch ¥68–¥98 ($9.10–$13/£4.50–£6.50); set dinner menu ¥158 ($21/£11) available Mon–Fri. AE, DC, MC, V. 11:30am–2:30pm and 6–11pm.

Haiku by Hatsune (Yin Quan Zhi Yu) ✦✦ JAPANESE   Haiku is just as sleek, stylish, and popular as its sister restaurant, Hatsune (see below), though the menu is far more compact. The entrance to the restaurant is a long, mirrored walkway where aspiring models can work on their catwalk strut. Inside, the decor is understated and at times a little too aware of being cool and contemporary—even the sake cups are warped pieces of mini ceramic art. The sushi rolls are similar to those at Hatsune, but there's less to choose from here. Choose this restaurant over Hatsune if you're up for late-night drinks at the cool adjacent bar.

Chaoyang Gongyuan Ximen 8 hao Gongguan Nei Nance 3/F (in what looks like a parking lot across from the Goose and Duck); see map p. 88. © 010/6508-8585, ext. 203. Meal for 2 ¥200–¥250 ($27–$33/£13–£17). AE, DC, MC, V. 6:30–11:30pm.

Serve the People (Wei Renmin Fuwu) THAI   In the heart of the Sanlitun diplomatic quarter, you'll find Beijing's finest Thai food at very reasonable prices. The grilled beef salad and green chicken curry are highly recommended, and the *pad thai* (rice noodles with seafood in peanut sauce) is done to perfection.

Sanlitun Xi Wu Jie 1 (behind German embassy). © 010/8454-4580. Meal for 2 ¥150–¥200 ($20–$27/£10–£13). AE, DC, MC, V. 10:30am–10:30pm. Metro: Dongzhi Men (214/1316, exit B); walk east 4 blocks, left at Xin Dong Lu, then 1st right.

MODERATE

Annie's Cafe (Anni Yidali Canting) ✦ *Value* ITALIAN   Casual, cozy, and tremendously welcoming, Annie's is the hands-down favorite for affordable Italian fare in Beijing. Wood-fired pizzas are the most popular item, but also try the baked *gnocchi gratinate* with tomato and broccoli, or the chicken ravioli. The staff is the city's friendliest. Other locations are at Jiuxianqiao, Jiangtai Lu, Shangye Jie (© 010/6436-3735); Jianguo Lu 88 (© 010/8589-8366); and Dongsanhuan Lu 16 (© 010/6503-3871).

Chaoyang Gongyuan Xi Men (west gate of Chaoyang Park). © 010/6591-1931. Meal for 2 ¥35–¥118 ($4.70–$16/£2.30–£7.90). AE, DC, MC, V. 11am–11pm.

Beijing Dadong Kaoya Dian 🐟🐟 BEIJING   This restaurant claims to use a special method to reduce the amount of fat in its birds, although it seems unlikely that duck this flavorful could possibly be good for you. Whole ducks for ¥98 ($13/£6.50) and half-ducks for ¥49 ($6.55/£3.30) both come with a nice plain broth made from the parts you don't eat. The place is clean and classy, and has a separate nonsmoking room. Another excellent location is at 1-2/F Nanxincang International Plaza; © 010/5169-0329.

Tuanjie Hu Beikou 3 (on east side of E. Third Ring Rd., north of Tuanjie Hu Park). © 010/6582-2892. Reservations essential. Meal for 2 (including half-duck) ¥80–¥100 ($10–$13/£5.30–£6.70). AE, DC, MC, V. 11am–10pm.

INEXPENSIVE

Ding Ding Xiang *Finds* HOT POT   This Mongolian-style mutton hot pot restaurant is tremendously and justifiably popular for its signature dipping sauce *(jinpai tiaoliao)*, a flavorful sesame sauce so thick they have to dish it out with ice cream scoops. Large plates of fresh sliced lamb *(yangrou)* are surprisingly cheap; other options include beef *(niurou),* spinach *(bocai),* and sliced winter melon *(donggua pian).* Decor is plain, and the place is clean for a local restaurant. Reservations strongly recommended. Other branches (open 11am–10pm) at bldg. 31 Gan Jia Kou Xiaoqu (© 010/8837-1327); East Gate Plaza at Dong Zhong Jie 9 (© 010/6417-9289); bldg. 7 Guo Xing Jia Yuan, Shou ti Nan Lu (© 010/8835-7775); and Jian Guo Lu 87 Beijing Shin Kong Place 6/F (© 010/6530-5997).

Dong Zhi Men Wai Dong Jie 14 (opposite Donghuan Guangchang, in alley across from Guangdong Development Bank); see map p. 88. © 010/6417-2546. Reservations highly recommended. Meal for 2 ¥80–¥100 ($10–$13/£5.30–£6.70). No credit cards. 11am–midnight.

CHAOYANG DISTRICT (SOUTH)
VERY EXPENSIVE

Cépe 🐟🐟 ITALIAN   This restaurant serves the best upscale Italian fare in the city. Waitstaff wear sleek pinstripe suits and are incredibly attentive, zipping over to your table at the merest hint of a frown or inquiring look. Lorenzo, the upbeat manager, used to run Le Cirque in New York and knows his wines and dishes inside out. Seek him out if you want serious recommendations. This a place to indulge in a leisurely meal. You must order a pasta dish, as the noodles are perfectly al dente and freshly made each morning. I also highly recommend the water buffalo appetizer—it's wrapped in slices of eggplant, lightly fried, and served over a bed of fresh tomato and basil. The decor is contemporary, with an open kitchen housed behind a giant silk screen of a portebello mushroom. There are romantic, semiprivate nooks with curtains and leather chaise longues alongside the back wall. Jazz and, every now and then, an upbeat Laura Pausini song plays in the background.

Jinchengfang Dong Jie 1 (inside Ritz-Carlton Financial Street Hotel); see map p. 88. © 010/6601-6666. Dinner for 2 ¥600–¥800 ($80–$110/£40–£53). AE, MC, V. 11:30am–3pm and 6–11pm.

EXPENSIVE

Hatsune (Yinquan) ⊛ JAPANESE   Hatsune offers sushi sacrilege via Northern California, with stylish glass-and-sand decor and a list of innovative rolls long and elaborate enough to drive serious raw fish traditionalists crazy. But if you're not a purist, nearly every roll is a delight, particularly the 119 Roll—spicy-sweet with bright red tuna inside and out. Avoid the Beijing Roll, a roast duck and "special" sauce gimmick.

Guanghua Dong Lu, Heqiao Dasha C (4 blocks east of Kerry Centre, opposite Petro China bldg.). ℭ **010/6581-3939.** Meal for 2 ¥200–¥250 ($27–$33/£13–£17). Mon–Fri lunch set meals ¥65 ($8.70/£4.35); weekend lunch buffet ¥158 ($21/£11). AE, DC, MC, V. 11:30am–2pm and 5–10pm.

Horizon (Haitian Ge) *Value* CANTONESE   Horizon is one of the finest and most sumptuously decorated Cantonese restaurants in Beijing, with surprisingly reasonable prices and the city's best deal on dim sum. Shark's fin is available for those looking to impress business partners, but there are many cheaper and tastier dishes. Recommended are the stewed beef and tofu in XO sauce, a nicely presented fried mandarin fish, and battered king prawns with mustard. The weekend all-you-can-eat dim sum lunch is ¥168 ($22/£11) for two.

Inside Kerry Centre Mall, near rear entrance of Kerry Centre Hotel. ℭ **010/6561-8833,** ext. 41. Meal for 2 ¥200– ¥300 ($27–$40/£13–£20). AE, DC, MC, V. 11:30am–2:30pm and 5:30–10pm.

Huangcheng Laoma ⊛ HOT POT   This is among Beijing's largest and most agreeably decorated hot pot restaurants, and the only one that can reasonably charge such upmarket rates. Their special ingredient is "Laoma's beef," a magical meat that stays tender no matter how long you boil it. Order the split *yuanyang* pot, with both spicy broth and mild *wuyutang* (five-fish soup) in different compartments, or risk overheating your tongue.

Dabeiyao Nan Qingfengzha Hou Jie 39, south of China World Trade Center and Motorola bldg. (walk south along E. Third Ring Rd. and turn left after crossing river). ℭ **010/6779-8801.** English menu. Meal for 2 ¥180–¥200 ($24–$27/£12–£13). AE, DC, MC, V. 11am–11pm.

Le Cafe Igosso ⊛⊛ ITALIAN   A flight of stairs just north of an ugly flyover leads to one of Beijing's finest Italian restaurants. Start with an aperitif on the second-floor bar, before heading up to the small, intimate dining area, with dark wooden floors and furnishings. Service is unobtrusive, quite an achievement in such a small space. Seafood dishes are compelling, particularly the appetizers. The sea bream carpaccio marinated in seaweed has a liquid freshness, and the mustard roast duck is excellent. The crab and olive spaghetti is competently delivered, and rosemary chicken is the pick of the mains. The wine list is adventurous, with a handful available by the glass.

Dong San Huan Zhong Lu (700m/2,300 ft. south of Guomao Bridge on E. Third Ring Rd.), see map p. 88. ℭ **010/ 8771-7013.** Weekend reservations essential. Meal for 2 ¥38–¥120 ($5.10–$16/£2.50–£8). AE, DC, MC, V. 11:30am–1am. Metro: Guomao (122, exit C).

MODERATE

San Ge Guizhouren GUIZHOU   Southern China's Guizhou Province is one of the country's poorest regions, which lends a certain irony to this restaurant's hip minimalist setting and rich-artist clientele. The menu offers a stylish take on the province's Miao minority food with dishes that tend to be spicy, colorful, and slightly rough. Both tabletop hot pots—the Miao-style peppermint lamb and the cilantro-heavy dry beef—are highly recommended, as is the flavorsome but fatty *jueba chao larou* (bacon stir-fried with brake leaves) *Note:* Items listed on the menu as "vegetarian" are not.

Other branches are at bldg. 7 Jianwai SOHO (south of Guomao metro [122, exit C]; (*C*) 010/5869-0598); 2/F Ideal International Plaza on the Fourth Ring Road ((*C*) 010/8260-7670); and bldg. 8 Gongti Xi Lu ((*C*) 010/6551-8517); all daily 24 hours.

Guanghua Xi Lu 3 (walk north on Dong Da Qiao Lu from Yong'anli metro [121], turn down alley north of Mexican Wave, look for blue sign). (*C*) 010/6502-1733. Meal for 2 ¥80–¥120 ($11–$16/£5.30–£8). AE, DC, MC, V. 11am–2:30pm and 5:30–10pm.

Yunteng Binguan *(Finds)* YUNNAN   Although Yunnan is one of the poorest provinces in China, the Yunnan provincial government (which owns the restaurant) has ingredients flown in several times a week. The decor exudes less warmth than a hospital waiting room, but friendly waitstaff compensate. The signature dish, *guoqiao mixian* (crossing-the-bridge rice noodles) is worth the trip in itself, a delicious blend of ham, chicken, chrysanthemum petals, chives, tofu skin, and a tiny egg, all blended at your table with rice noodles in chicken broth. *Zhusun qiguo Ji* (mushroom and mountain herbs chicken soup) is ideal comfort food, and *zhutong paigu* (spicy stewed pork with mint), has hearty flavors.

Donghua Shi Bei Li Dong Qu 7, Chongwen Qu (follow Jianguo Men Nan Dajie south for 10 min.; on the south side of overpass). (*C*) 010/6713-6439. Meal for 2 ¥80–¥140 ($11–$19/£5.30–£9.30). AE, DC, MC, V. 11am–1:30pm and 5–10pm. Metro: Jianguo Men (exit C).

Yuxiang Renjia SICHUAN   This chain of busy restaurants has a mock-village decor and a comprehensive selection of real Sichuan dishes, slightly heavy on the oil but as flavorful as anything found outside Sichuan itself. Spicy familiars are all here and nicely done, but also try at least one of the chain's worthwhile signatures—smoked duck *(zhangcha ya)* or "stewed chicken with Grandma's sauce" *(laoganma shao ji)*. Second location at Chaoyang Men Wai Dajie 20, on fifth floor of Lianhe Dasha, behind Foreign Ministry Building just off East Second Ring Road ((*C*) 010/6588-3841; 11am–10:30pm).

Jianwai SOHO bldg. 4 (south of Guomao metro stop, exit C). (*C*) 010/5869-0653. Meal for 2 ¥80–¥120 ($11–$16/£5.30–£8). AE, DC, MC, V. 11am–3pm and 5:30–10:30pm.

BACK LAKES & DONG CHENG
EXPENSIVE

Cafe Sambal *(Finds)* MALAYSIAN   Sambal embraces and surpasses all the clichés of a chic Beijing eatery—a cozy courtyard house decorated with antique and modern furnishings, a sophisticated boss, relaxed service, and a well-balanced wine list. Try the fried four-sided bean with cashew nut sauce, the divinely creamy king prawn with yellow sauce, or the special lamb curry served in a thick, spicy coconut sauce. The signature dish, Kapitan chicken, a mildly spicy dish with a nutty aftertaste, is said to have been invented when Chinese migrants reached Penang during the Ming dynasty.

Doufu Chi Hutong 43, Xi Cheng Qu (walk south along Jiu Gu Lou Dajie, near the corner of the 5th street on left, marked by a red lantern). (*C*) 010/6400-4875. Reservations recommended. Meal for 2 ¥250–¥400 ($33–$53/£17–£27). AE, DC, MC, V. 11am–midnight. Metro: Gu Lou (exit B).

Nuage (Qing Yun Lou) *(Finds)* VIETNAMESE   Lake views from this restaurant's upstairs windows are matched only by its hallucinatory Hanoi-inspired interior, with red lanterns, reed curtains, and a long silver dragon snaking up the rear staircase. Views from the rooftop are peerless (though expensive, as you'll be charged an exorbitant 15% service fee for rooftop seating), and the food is almost as impressive: The grilled la lop leaf beef *(ye niurou juan)* is exquisite; and the *phô* (Vietnamese beef noodles in soup) has a smooth, flavorful broth.

Moments Candlelit Dinner on the Lakes

For roughly ¥400 ($54/£27) plus the cost of food, Beijing's ancient roasted meats restaurant, Kaorouji, now arranges one of the most completely enjoyable dining experiences in the city: a meal for up to eight people served aboard a narrow **canopied flat-bottom boat** 𝘢𝘢, staffed by a lone oarsman who guides the craft in a gentle arc around the man-made serenity of Qian Hai and Hou Hai. The entire trip takes roughly 2 hours. A few extra yuan buy live music and the opportunity to float candles in the lakes after darkness falls—doomed to become a cliché, but who cares? The restaurant is located next to Nuage (see above) at Qian Hai Dong Yan 14 (11am–2pm and 5–9pm; meal for 2: ¥120–¥160/$16–$21/£8–£11). To make boat arrangements, call © **010/6612-5717** or 010/6404-2554. *Note:* Boat rental prices vary from season to season, and will probably increase.

Qian Hai Dong Yan 22 (east of Yinding Bridge; northeast of Qian Hai; see map p. 88.). © **010/6401-9591**. Reservations required. Meal for 2 ¥200–¥300 ($27–$40/£13–£20). AE, DC, MC, V. 11am–2pm and 5:30–10pm.

MODERATE

Huajia Yiyuan HOME-STYLE   The chef-owner behind this popular courtyard restaurant claims to have created a new supercuisine from the best of China's regional cooking styles. Whether "Huacai" will ever spread remains to be seen, but the long menu is one of the Beijing's most impressive. The new restaurant is less raucous than the recently demolished original, but locals still crowd around tables at night to devour heaped plates of spicy crayfish *(mala longxia)* and drink green "good for health" beer. Try the *larou douya juanbing*, a mix of spicy bacon and bean sprouts rolled in pancakes roast duck–style.

Dongzhi Men Nei Dajie 235. © **010/6403-0677**. Meal for 2 ¥100–¥120 ($13–$16/£6–£8). AE, DC, MC, V. 10:30am–6:30am. Metro: Dongzhi Men (exit A).

Kejia Cai 𝘢𝘢𝘢 HAKKA   The best choice of the three restaurants whose art-rustic interiors and deft kitchens have taken a traditionally marginal cuisine and made it the center of food fashion in Beijing. Hakka cuisine is hard to define vis-à-vis other styles, but ask regular patrons of these restaurants to explain the difference and most will give a quick answer: It's better. The *yan Ju xia* (shrimp skewers served in rock salt) and *lancai sijidou* (diced green beans with ground pork) are both divine. The one dish you'll find on every table is *mizhi zhibao luyu,* "secret recipe paper-wrapped fish"—tender and nearly boneless, in a sweet sauce you'll want to drink.

East bank of Qian Hai, 50m (165 ft.) north of Bei Hai Park north entrance. © **010/6404-2259**. Meal for 2 ¥80–¥100 ($11–$13/£5–£7). AE, DC, MC, V. 11am–2pm and 5–10pm.

Kong Yiji Jiulou HUAIYANG   This extremely popular restaurant is named for the alcoholic scholar-bum protagonist of a Lu Xun short story. It's set in a traditional space pleasingly outfitted with calligraphy scrolls, traditional bookshelves, and other trappings of Chinese scholarship. Highly recommended are the *mizhi luyu,* paper-wrapped fish, and *youtiao niurou,* savory slices of beef mixed with pieces of fried dough. Fans of Lu's story will appreciate the wide selection of *huangjiu,* a sweet "yellow" rice wine aged for several years and traditionally served warm.

Desheng Men Nei Dajie (next to the octagonal Teahouse of Family Fu on the northwest bank of Hou Hai). © 010/ 6618-4917. Reservations essential. Meal for 2 ¥100–¥140 ($13–$19/£6.70–£9.30). AE, DC, MC, V. 9:30am–2pm and 5–10:30pm.

Paper (Jian) ☆ CANTONESE   This sleek new restaurant almost feels more like a nightclub than an eatery. The decor is all white and very urban minimalist. They serve contemporary Chinese food featuring plenty of seafood. Servings are small, but the eight-course set dinner menu means you get to taste a little bit of everything, from stir-fried eggplant to tiger prawns cooked in tea leaves.

Gulou Dong Dajie 138 (east of the Drum Tower); see map p. 88. © 010/8401-5080. Set menu (8-course) ¥150 ($20/£10). AE, DC, MC, V. 4–10pm.

WESTERN BEIJING & YAYUN CUN

Baihe Sushi (Lily Vegetarian Restaurant) ☆☆ VEGETARIAN   Chinese vegetarian restaurants often get bogged down torturing meaty flavors out of gluten, but at this ultraclean and friendly restaurant you'll find delectable dishes with high-quality ingredients. Start with the hearty *shanyao geng* (yam broth with mushrooms) and the slightly fruity *liangban zi lusun* (purple asparagus salad), followed by *ruyi haitai juan* (vegetarian sushi rolls) and the excellent *huangdi sun shao wanzi* (imperial bamboo shoots and vegetarian meatballs). When in season, their vegetables are sourced from an organic farm west of Beijing, so ask if they have any organic vegetables *(youji shucai)*. Monks dine for free, so you're likely to meet a few. Another branch is at Dong Zhi Men Nei Bei Xiao Jie, Cao Yuan Hutong 23 (© 010/6405-2082).

Yi He Yuan Kun Ming Hu Lu 50, 100m (328 ft.) south to the Xin Jian Gong Men (main gate of Yi He Yuan), see map p. 88. © 010/6202-5284. Meal for 2 ¥80–¥140 ($11–$19/£5.30–£9.30). V. 10am–9pm. Metro: Zhichun Lu.

Dongbei Hu ☆ NORTHEASTERN   Beijing's best Dongbei cuisine. Welcoming staff ushers you upstairs past an open kitchen with whole cuts of meat and huge jars of wine on display. Start with the refreshing cold noodle dish, *da lapi*, served in sesame and vinegar sauce. Your table will groan under the weight of the signature dish, *shouzhua yang pai* (lamb chops roasted with cumin and chili). Filling snacks, such as *sanxian laohe* (seafood and garlic-chive buns), are delicious, as is the sweet-and-sour battered eggplant *(cuipi qiezi)*.

Anhui Li Er Qu Yi Lou, Yayun Cun (300m/984 ft. east of intersection with Anli Lu). © 010/6498-5015. Meal for 2 ¥50–¥80 ($6.70–$11/£3.30–£5.30). No credit cards. 11am–10pm.

Jiuhua Shan BEIJING   Another fine roast duck eatery, this place is not quite as pleasant as the Beijing Dadong Kaoya Dian (p. 88), but it's more conveniently located for people staying on the west side of the city. Whole crispy ducks, relatively low on fat, are reasonable at ¥88 ($12/£6). Sesame buns make a nice alternative to traditional pancakes. They only roast 200 birds a day, so get there early. A new branch, with the same state-run ambience, is located inside the Worker's Stadium.

Branches at Zhengguang Lu 55 (behind the Ziyu Hotel). © 010/6848-3481. Meal for 2 (including half duck) ¥100 –¥140 ($13–$19/£6.70–£9.30). AE, DC, MC, V. 11am–2pm and 5–9pm.

Mala Youhuo ☆☆ SICHUAN   At Beijing's most popular Sichuan restaurant, service is surprisingly friendly and the mock-village decor is cheesy but fun. The signature dish, *shuizhu yu* (boiled fish with chili and numbing hot peppers), comes in three different varieties: grass carp *(caoyu)*, catfish *(nianyu)*, and blackfish *(heiyu)*. We still prefer the traditional grass carp, but blackfish makes a nice change. Adventurous diners should try *mala tianluo*, field snails stewed in chili and Sichuan pepper. Skewers are provided to extract the flesh from the sizable mollusks. Leave the innermost black part to the side, unless you want a tummy ache. A nice antidote to all the spice is a clear soup with seasonal leafy greens, *tutang shicai*. A second branch recently opened northeast of Da Zhong Si (Da Zhong Si Taiyang Yuan; C **010/8211-9966**).

Guang'an Men Nei Dajie 81, Xuanwu Qu (just south of Baoguo Si). C **010/6304-0426**. Meal for 2 ¥80–¥140 ($11–$19/£5.30–£9.30). AE, DC, MC, V. 11:30am–10:30pm. Metro: Changchun Jie (205, exit D1); walk south on Changchun Jie then turn right (west) at first major road.

Taipo Tianfu Shanzhen 👭👭 MUSHROOM HOT POT   The broth for this

mouthwatering hot pot is made by stewing a whole black-skinned chicken with 32 different kinds of mushrooms and letting the mixture reduce for hours. Already a fine meal on its own, it gets even better as you add ingredients—lamb *(yangrou)*, beef *(niurou)*, lotus root *(oupian)*, spinach *(bocai)* or, best of all, more mushrooms. Another branch is at Anhui Li Er Qu Si Hao Bei Lou 2-3/F, Yayun Cun; C **010/6496-9836**.

At south end of Erqi Juchang Lu, behind the east side of the Chang'an Shangchang (4 blocks west of the Fuxing Men metro stop). C **010/6801-9641**. Meal for 2 ¥120–¥140 ($16–$19/£8–£9.30). MC, V. 10am–11pm.

Tianjin Baijiaoyuan JIAOZI   No restaurant has managed to fill the vacuum left by

the inexplicable closing of Gold Cat, but Tianjin Baijiaoyuan comes closest. The clichéd red-and-gold interior can't match Gold Cat's old courtyard setting, but the *jiaozi* are just as delicious. The *xiesanxian shuijiao* (dumplings with shrimp, crab, and mushroom filling) and *niurou wan shuijiao* (beef ball dumplings) are treasures, best accompanied by a steaming pot of *chenpi laoya shanzhen bao* (duck, mandarin orange peel, and mushroom potage).

Xin Wenhua Jie 12A, in alley opposite The Marco Polo (see earlier in this chapter). C **010/6605-9371**. Photo menu. Meal for 2 ¥30–¥60 ($4–$8/£2–£4). No credit cards. 10am–2:30pm and 4:30–9:30pm.

Xibei Youmian Cun 👭👭 *Kids* NORTHWESTERN   Worth the trip out to Yayun

Cun in itself. Friendly staff, and bright, faux-rural decor make this the best "family restaurant" in Beijing. The signature dish is *youmian wowo* (steamed oatmeal noodles) served with mushroom *(sushijun retang)* or lamb *(yangrou retang)* broth, with coriander and chili on the side. Familiar *yangrou chuan'r* (mutton skewers with cumin) and yogurt *(suannai)* with honey make excellent side dishes, while the house salad *(Xibei da bancai)*, crammed with unusual ingredients, is a meal in itself. The one dish you must try is *zhijicao kao niupai* (lotus leaf-wrapped roast beef with mountain herbs).

Yayun Cun Anyuan 8 Lou, Chaoyang Qu (corner of Anhui Bei Li and Huizhong Bei Lu). C **010/6489-0256**. Meal for 2 ¥120–¥200 ($16–$27/£8–£13). AE, DC, MC, V. 10am–1:50pm and 5–9pm.

Xiyu Shifu 👭👭 UIGHUR   The best Uighur food this side of Turfan. The decor is

a nouveau riche fantasy of arches, Romanesque gold light fittings, and pictures of desert scenes hanging from marble walls, but it's spotless and welcoming. The *da pan ji* (diced chicken, pepper, potatoes, and thick noodles in tomato sauce) is spicy, so when they ask if you like it hot, be honest. The piping-hot *nan* (flat bread) is perfect for sopping up the delicious sauce, and the *shou zhua fan* (rice with lamb and carrot) and spicy mutton skewers with cumin and chili *(yangrou chuan)* are as tasty as anything you'll find in Kashgar.

Corner of Beichen Dong Lu and Datun Lu, opposite Olympic Park, Yayun Cun. C **010/6486-2555**. Meal for 2 ¥70–¥100 ($9.35–$13/£4.70–£6.70). AE, MC, V. 7:30am–8:30pm.

Zhang Sheng Ji Jiudian 👭 HUAIYANG   It may lack the ambience of Kong Yiji Jiu-

lou, but this branch of Hangzhou's most successful restaurant delivers more consistent

Huaiyang fare. Service is no-fuss; there's a pleasing amount of space between tables with a high ceiling and plenty of light. For starters, try the flavorsome *jiuxiang yugan* (dried fish in wine sauce). The recently added *mati niuliu* (stir-fried beef with broccoli, water chestnuts, and tofu rolls) is excellent, and nearly every table carries the signature *sungan laoya bao* (stewed duck with dried bamboo shoots and ham) which has complex, hearty flavors.

Bei San Huan, Zhejiang Dasha, Chaoyang Qu (west of Anzhen Qiao on N. Third Ring Rd.). ℂ 010/6442-0006. Meal for 2 ¥100–¥180 ($13–$24/£6.70–£12). AE, DC, MC, V. 11am–2pm and 5–9pm.

5 Exploring Beijing

No other city in China, and few other cities in the world, offers so many must-see attractions, or such a likelihood of missed opportunity. It is technically possible to see the big names—the Forbidden City, Temple of Heaven, Summer Palace, and Great Wall—in as little as 3 days, but you'll need at least a week to get any feel for the city. People spend years here and still fail to see everything they should.

Note: Most major sights now charge admission according to the season. The summer high season officially runs from April 1 to October 31 and the winter low season from November 1 to March 31.

THE FORBIDDEN CITY (GU GONG)

The universally accepted symbol for the length and grandeur of Chinese civilization is undoubtedly the Great Wall, but the Forbidden City is more immediately impressive. A 720,000-sq.-m (7.75-million-sq.-ft.) complex of red-walled buildings and pavilions topped by a sea of glazed vermilion tile, it dwarfs nearby Tian'an Men Square and is by far the largest and most intricate imperial palace in China. The palace receives more visitors than any other attraction in the country (over seven million a year according to the Chinese government), and has been praised in Western travel literature ever since the first Europeans laid eyes on it in the late 1500s. Yet despite the flood of superlatives and exaggerated statistics that inevitably go into its description, it is impervious to an excess of hype and is large and compelling enough to draw repeat visits from even the most jaded travelers. Make more time for it than you think you'll need.

ESSENTIALS

The palace, most commonly referred to in Chinese as Gu Gong (short for Palace Museum), is on the north side of Tian'an Men Square across Chang'an Dajie (ℂ **010/ 6513-2255;** www.dpm.org.cn). It is best approached on foot or via metro (Tian'an Men East, 117), as taxis are not allowed to stop in front. The palace is open from 8:30am to 5pm during summer and from 8:30am to 4:30pm in winter. Regular admission *(men piao)* in summer costs ¥60 ($8/£4), dropping to ¥40 ($5/£2.50) in winter; last tickets are sold 1 hour before the doors close. Various exhibition halls and gardens inside the palace charge an additional ¥10 ($1/50p). All-inclusive tickets *(lian piao)* have been discontinued, perhaps in an effort to increase revenues (see "The Big Makeover," below), but it's always possible these will be reinstated.

Enter through the Wu Men (Meridian Gate), a short walk north of Chang'an Dajie via Tian'an Men (see below). Ticket counters are clearly marked on either side as you approach. *Tip:* If you have a little more time, it is highly recommended that you approach the entrance at Wu Men (Meridian Gate) via Tai Miao to the east, and avoid the gauntlet of touts and souvenir stalls. **Audio tours** in several languages, including English (¥40/$5/£2.50 plus ¥500/$67/£33 deposit), are available at the gate itself,

The Big Makeover

An immense **$75-million renovation of the Forbidden City,** the largest in 90 years, will be completed in two phases (the first by 2008, the second by 2020). Work began on halls and gardens in the closed western sections of the palace in 2002, with the most effort concentrated on opening the **Wuying Dian (Hall of Valiance and Heroism)** in the southwest corner of the palace, followed by **Cining Huayuan (Garden of Love and Tranquillity)** next to the Taihe Dian. Wuying Dian, formerly the site of the imperial printing press, should be open by the time you arrive, displaying a collection of Buddhist sutras, palace records, and calligraphy. Cining Huayuan is scheduled to open in 2008. Plans also call for the construction of new temperature-controlled buildings to house and exhibit what is claimed to be a collection of **930,000 Ming and Qing imperial relics,** most now stored underground.

On the other side of the palace, within the northern section of the Ningshou Gong Huayuan, a remarkable building is undergoing restoration with assistance from the World Cultural Heritage Foundation. Qianlong commissioned the European Jesuit painters in his employ to create large-scale *trompe l'oeil* paintings, which were used both in the Forbidden City as well as in the Yuan Ming Yuan (p. 121). **Juanqin Zhai,** an elaborately constructed private opera house, houses the best remaining examples of these paintings, including a stunning image of a wisteria trellis, almost certainly painted by Italian master Castiglione. It is due to open sometime after 2008.

through the door to the right. Those looking to spend more money can hire **"English"-speaking tour guides** on the other side of the gate, for ¥200–¥350 ($27–$47/£13–£23) per person, depending on length of tour). The tour guide booth also rents **wheelchairs** and **strollers** at reasonable rates. *Note:* Only the central route through the palace is wheelchair-accessible, and steeply so.

BACKGROUND & LAYOUT

Sourcing of materials for the original palace buildings began in 1406, during the reign of the Yongle emperor, and construction was completed in 1420. Much of it was designed by a eunuch from Annam, Nguyen An. Without improvements to the Grand Canal, construction would have been impossible—timber came from as far away as Sichuan, and logs took up to 4 years to reach the capital. The Yuan palace was demolished to make way for the Forbidden City, but the lakes excavated during the Jin (1122–1215) were retained and expanded. Between 1420 and 1923, the palace was home to 24 emperors of the Ming and Qing dynasties. The last was Aisin-Gioro Puyi (see Dongbei, p. 159), who abdicated in 1912 but lived in the palace until 1924.

The Forbidden City is arranged along the compass points, with most major halls opening to the south (the direction associated with imperial rule). Farthest south and in the center is the perfectly symmetrical **outer court,** dominated by the immense ceremonial halls where the emperor conducted official business. Beyond the outer court and on both sides is the **inner court,** a series of smaller buildings and gardens that served as living quarters.

Beijing Attractions

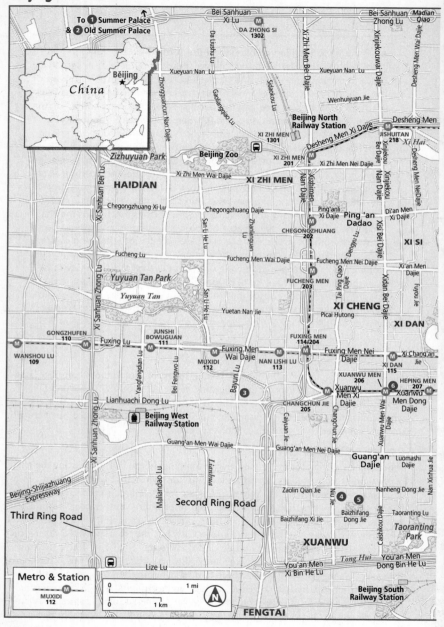

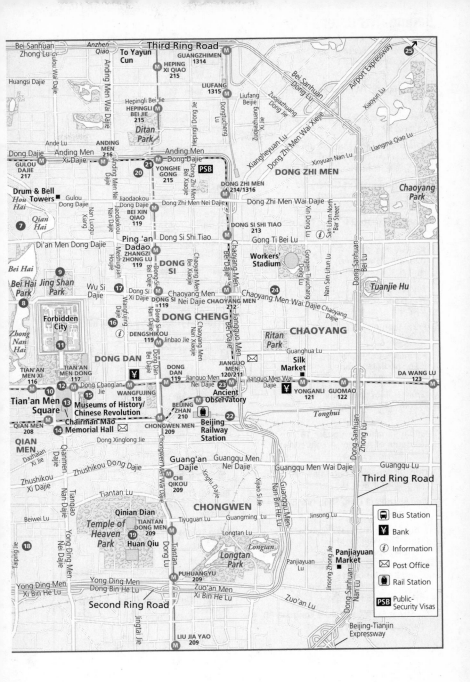

Beijing Attractions Key

Ancient Observatory 23
(Gù Guānxiàng Tái)
故观象台

Báiyún Guàn (White Cloud Temple) 3
白云观

Bei Hǎi Park (Běi Hǎi Gōngyuán) 8
北海公园

Chairman Mao's Mausoleum 13
(Mao Zhǔxi Jìniàn Guǎn)
毛主席纪念馆

China National Art Gallery 17
(Zhōngguó Měishùguǎn)
中国美术馆

Dōngyuè Miào 24
东岳庙

Factory 798 25
(Qījiǔbā Gōngchǎng)
七九八工厂

Fǎyuán Sì
(Source of Dharma Temple) 5
法原寺

Forbidden City (Gù Gōng) 11
故宫

Former Residence of Lěo Shě 16
(Lǎo Shě Jìnìanguǎn)
老舍纪念馆

Great Hall of the People 10
(Rénmín Dàhùi Táng)
人民大会堂

Gǔdài Jiànzhù Bówùguǎn 18
(Museum of Ancient Architecture)
古代建筑博物馆

Guó Zǐ Ûiàn and Kǒng Miáo 20
国子监和北京孔庙

Jǐng Shān Park (Jǐng Shān Gōngyuán) 9
景山公园

Míng Chéng Qiáng Gōngyuán 22
(Míng City Wall Park)
明城墙公园

Museums of Chinese History
and Revolution 15
(Zhōngguó Lìshǐ Gémíng Bówùguǎn)
中国历史革命博物馆

Ox Street Mosque (Niú Jiē Qīngzhēnsì) 4
牛街清真寺

Prince Gong's Mansion 7
(Gōng Wáng Fǔ)
恭王府

Qián Mén 14
前门

Summer Palace (Yíhé Yuán) 1
颐和园

South Cathedral (Nán Táng) 6
南堂

Temple of Heaven (Tiān Tán) 19
天坛

Tiān'an Mén 12
(Gate of Heavenly Peace)
天安门

Yōnghé Gōng (Lama Temple) 21
雍和宫

Yuán Míng Yuán 2
(Old Summer Palace)
圆明园

OTHER ATTRACTIONS (not on map)
Eastern Qīng Tombs
(Qīng Dōng Líng)
青东陵

Great Wall at Bādálǐng
(Bādálǐng Chángchéng)
八达岭长城

Great Wall at Mùtiányù
(Mùtiányù Chángchéng)
幕田峪长城

Great Wall at Sīmǎtái
(Sīmǎtái Chángchéng)
司马台长城

Jiétái Sì (Temple of the
Ordination Platform)
结台寺

Míng Tombs (Shísāng Líng)
十三陵

Tánzhè Sí
(Temple of the Pool and Wild Mulberry)
潭柘寺

Western Qīng Tombs (Qīng Xī Líng)
青西陵

The palace has been ransacked and parts destroyed by fire several times over the centuries, so most of the existing buildings date from the Qing rather than the Ming. Many of the roofs are trimmed in blue or green tile, which some scholars say reminded the Qing's Manchu rulers of the grasslands and fertile fields they had left behind. Only half of the complex is open to visitors (expected to increase to 70% after repairs are completed in 2020; see "The Big Makeover," above), but this still leaves plenty to see.

Tian'an Men (Gate of Heavenly Peace) 𝕱𝕱   This gate is the largest in what was once known as the Imperial City and the most emblematic of Chinese government grandeur. Above the central door, once reserved almost exclusively for the emperor, now hangs the famous **portrait of Mao,** flanked by inscriptions that read: LONG LIVE THE PEOPLE'S REPUBLIC OF CHINA (left) and LONG LIVE THE GREAT UNITY OF THE PEOPLES OF THE WORLD (right). Mao declared the founding of the People's Republic from atop the gate on October 1, 1949. There is no charge to walk through the gate, but tickets are required if you want to ascend to **the upper platform** for worthwhile views of Tian'an Men Square. The ticket office is in the second of two small red shacks, on the left after you pass through.

North of Tian'an Men Sq.; ticket office to left as you enter. Admission ¥20 ($2.70/£1.30) in summer, ¥15 ($2/£1) in winter. Summer 8am–4:30pm; winter 8:30am–4pm. Mandatory bag storage for ¥2–¥6 (30¢–80¢/15p–40p) behind and to left of ticket booth; cameras allowed.

The Outer Court   The intimidating **Wu Men (Meridian Gate),** built in 1420 and last restored in 1801, is the actual entrance to the Forbidden City. The emperor would come here to receive prisoners of war, issue proclamations, and supervise the punishment of troublesome officials. Beyond the gate, across a vast stone-paved courtyard bisected by the balustraded Jin Shui (Golden River), is the **Taihe Men (Gate of Supreme Harmony),** which marks the official beginning of the outer court.

The first of the outer courts' "Three Great Halls" (San Da Dian) is the **Taihe Dian (Hall of Supreme Harmony)** 𝕱. Located beyond the Taihe Men and across an even grander stone courtyard, it is an imposing double-roofed structure mounted atop a three-tiered marble terrace with elaborately carved balustrades. This is the largest wooden hall in China, and the most elaborate and prestigious of the palaces' throne halls; it was therefore rarely used. Emperors came here to mark the new year and winter solstice.

Immediately behind it is the **Zhonghe Dian (Hall of Perfect Harmony),** and farther on lies the **Baohe Dian (Hall of Preserving Harmony).** This last hall, supported by only a few columns, is where the highest levels of imperial examinations were held. At the rear of the hall is a carved marble slab weighing over 200 tons; 20,000 men supposedly spent 28 days dragging it to this position from a mountain roughly 50km (31 miles) away.

The Inner Court   Only the emperor, his family, his concubines, and the palace eunuchs (who numbered 1,500 at the end of the Qing dynasty) were allowed in this section, sometimes described as the truly forbidden city. It begins with the **Qianqing Men (Gate of Heavenly Purity),** directly north of the Baohe Dian, beyond which are three palaces designed to mirror the three halls of the outer court.

The first of these is the **Qianqing Gong (Palace of Heavenly Purity),** where the emperors lived until Yongzheng decided to move to another part of the city in the 1720s. Beyond are the rather boring **Jiaotai Dian (Hall of Union),** containing the throne of the empress; and the rather more interesting **Kunning Gong (Palace of**

Earthly Tranquillity), a Manchu-style bed chamber where a nervous Puyi (China's last emperor, see p. 186) was expected to spend his wedding night before he fled to more comfortable rooms elsewhere.

At the rear of the inner court is the elaborate **Yu Huayuan (Imperial Garden)** ⍟, a marvelous scattering of ancient conifers, rockeries, and pavilions said to be largely unchanged since it was built in the Ming dynasty. Puyi's famous British tutor, Reginald Fleming Johnston, lived in the **Yangxin Zhai,** the first building on the west side of the garden (now a tea shop).

From behind the mountain, you can exit the palace through the **Shenwu Men (Gate of Martial Spirit)** and continue on to Jing Shan and/or Bei Hai Park. Those with time to spare, however, should explore less-visited sections on either side of the central path.

Western Axis Most of this area is in a state of heavy disrepair, but a few buildings have been restored and are open to visitors. Most notable among these is the **Yangxin Dian (Hall of Mental Cultivation),** southwest of the Imperial Garden. The reviled Empress Dowager Cixi, who ruled China for much of the late Qing period, made decisions on behalf of her infant nephew Guangxu from behind a screen in the east room. This is also where emperors lived after Yongzheng moved out of the Qianqing Gong.

Eastern Axis ⍟ This side tends to be peaceful and quiet even when other sections are teeming. Entrance costs ¥10 ($1.35/70p) and requires purchase of essentially useless over-shoe slippers for ¥2 (30¢/15p). The most convenient ticket booth is a 5-minute walk southwest of the Qianqing Men, opposite the **Jiulong Bi (Nine Dragon Screen),** a 3.5m-high (12-ft.) wall covered in striking glazed-tile dragons depicted frolicking above a frothing sea.

The Qing dynasty Qianlong emperor (reign 1736–95) abdicated at the age of 85, and this section was built for his retirement, although he never really moved in, continuing to "mentor" his son while living in the Yangxin Dian, a practice later adopted by Empress Dowager Cixi, who also partially took up residence here in 1894. One of the highlights here is the secluded **Ningshou Gong Huayuan** ⍟⍟⍟, behind the Zhenbao Guan (Hall of Jewelry) north of the ticket booth. The Qianlong emperor composed poems and drinking from cups of wine he floated in a snake-like water-filled trough carved in the floor of the main pavilion. Qianlong's personal compendium of verse ran to a modest 50,000 poems; he was seldom short of words. East of the garden is the **Changyin Ge,** sometimes called Cixi's Theater, an elaborate three-tiered structure with trapdoors and hidden passageways to allow movement between stages. In the far northeastern corner is the **Zhenfei Jing (Well of the Pearl Concubine),** a narrow hole covered by a large circle of stone, slightly askance. The Pearl Concubine, one of the Guangxu emperor's favorites, was 25 when Cixi had her stuffed down the well as they were fleeing in the aftermath of the Boxer Rebellion. According to most accounts, Cixi was miffed at the girl's insistence that Guangxu stay and take responsibility for the imperial family's support of the Boxers.

Also worth seeing is the **Hall of Clocks (Zhongbiao Guan),** a collection of elaborate timepieces, many of them gifts to the emperors from European envoys. The exhibit costs ¥10 ($1.35/70p) and at press time was temporarily relocated in a hall to the right (east) of the Baohe Dian while the original Hall of Clocks is restored.

TIAN'AN MEN SQUARE (TIAN'AN MEN GUANGCHANG)

This is the world's largest public square, the size of 90 American football fields (40 hectares/99 acres), with standing room for 300,000. It is surrounded by the Forbidden

CLOSED
due to
accidental demolition

WEGEN BISSIGEN
EICHHÖRNCHEN GESCHLOSSEN

CERRADO
CABRAS

Κλειστό
Μετεωρίτες

POOL CLOSED
プール
も
ELECTRIC EELS
閉
鎖
中

Hotel
closed for
facelifting

FERMÉ POUR
RAISON
DE GRÈVE
DES BONNES

FECHADO!
POR CAUSA DE
ATAQUES DOS CROCODILOS

— I don't speak
sign language.

A hotel can close for all kinds of reasons.
Our Guarantee ensures that if your hotel's undergoing construction, we'll
let you know in advance. In fact, we cover your entire travel experience.
See www.travelocity.com/guarantee for details.

travelocity®
You'll never roam alone.

City to the north, the Great Hall of the People to the west, and the museums of Chinese History and Chinese Revolution to the east. In the center of the square stands the **Monument to the People's Heroes (Renmin Yingxiong Jinian Bei)**, a 37m (124-ft.) granite obelisk engraved with scenes from famous uprisings and bearing a central inscription (in Mao's handwriting): THE PEOPLE'S HEROES ARE IMMORTAL.

The area on which the obelisk stands was originally occupied by the **Imperial Way**—a central road that stretched from the Gate of Heavenly Peace south to Qian Men, the still extant main entrance to The Tartar City (see below). This road, lined on either side with imperial government ministries, was the site of the pivotal May Fourth movement (1919), in which thousands of university students gathered to protest the weakness and corruption of China's then Republican government. Mao ordered destruction of the old ministries and paved over the rubble in 1959, replacing them with the vast but largely empty **Great Hall of the People** to the west and the equally vast but unimpressive **museums** to the east, as part of a spate of construction to celebrate 10 years of Communist rule. But the site has remained a magnet for politically charged assemblies. The most famous of these was the gathering of **student prodemocracy protestors** in late spring of 1989. That movement and the government's violent suppression of it still define the square in most minds, Chinese as well as foreign. All physical traces of the crackdown disappeared after the square received a face-lift in 1999, just in time to celebrate the 50th anniversary of the founding of the People's Republic, but reminders remain in the stiff-backed soldiers and video cameras since put in place to ensure order is maintained.

There isn't much to do in the square, but early risers can line up in front of Tian'an Men at dawn to watch the **flag-raising ceremony**, a unique suffocation-in-the-throng experience on National Day (Oct 1), when what seems like the entire Chinese population arrives to jostle for the best view.

Chairman Mao's Mausoleum (Mao Zhuxi Jinian Guan)

A trip here is one of the eeriest experiences in Beijing. The decision to preserve Mao's body was made hours after his death in 1976. Panicked and inexperienced, his doctors reportedly pumped him so full of formaldehyde that his face and body swelled almost beyond recognition. They drained the corpse and managed to get it back into acceptable shape, but they also created a wax model of the Great Helmsman just in case. There's no telling which version is on display at any given time. The mausoleum itself was built in 1977, near the center of Tian'an Men Square. However much Mao may be mocked outside his tomb (earnest arguments about whether he was 70% right or 60% right are perhaps the biggest joke), he still commands a terrifying sort of respect inside it. This is not quite the kitsch experience some expect. The tour is free and fast, with no stopping or photos and no bags allowed inside.

South end of Tian'an Men Sq. Free admission. Mon–Sat 8–11:30am, sometimes also 2–4pm (usually Tues, Thurs). Bag storage across the street, directly west: ¥10 ($1.35/70p) per piece. Metro: Qian Men (208).

Qian Men

The phrase Qian Men (Front Gate) is actually a reference to two separate towers on the south side of the square which together formed the main entrance to the Tartar (or Inner) City. The southernmost Arrow Tower (Jian Lou) is no longer open to the public. You can, however, still climb the interior of the rear building (Zhengyang Men), where a photo exhibition depicts life in Beijing's pre-1949 markets, temples, and *hutong*.

Tian'an Men Sq. Admission ¥20 ($2.70/£1.30). 8:30am–4pm. Metro: Qian Men (208).

National Theatre   The controversial National Theatre, designed by Paul Andreu, is due to open west of the Great Hall of the People within the lifetime of this book. Andreu was awarded the project in 2000, and Beijingers have nicknamed it *jidanke'r* (The Eggshell). Although the project has been downsized, it still features a dazzling titanium-and-glass dome perched on a lake, and encasing three auditoriums. Patrons descend on escalators through the waters of the lake.

West of Tian'an Men Sq. and the Great Hall of the People. Metro: Qian Men (208).

THE TEMPLE OF HEAVEN (TIAN TAN)

At the same time Yongle built the Forbidden City, he also oversaw construction of this enormous park and altar to heaven to the south. Each winter solstice, the Ming and Qing emperors would lead a procession here to perform rites and make sacrifices designed to promote the next year's crops and curry favor from heaven for the general health of the empire. The park is square (symbolizing Earth) in the south and rounded (Heaven) in the north.

ESSENTIALS

Temple of Heaven Park (Tian Tan Gongyuan; ✆ **010/6702-8866**) is south of Tian'an Men Square, on the east side of Qian Men Dajie. It's open from 6am to 9pm (may close earlier in winter, depending on weather and staff decisions), but the ticket offices and major sights are only open from 8:30am to 4:30pm. All-inclusive tickets *(lian piao)* cost ¥35 ($4.70/£2.30) (¥30/$4/£2 in winter); simple park admission costs ¥15 ($2/£1). The east gate *(dong men)* is easily accessed by public transport; take the no. 39, 106, or 110 bus from just north of the Chongwen Men metro stop (209, exit B) to Fahua Si. However, the best approach is from the south gate *(nan men),* the natural starting point for a walk that culminates in the magnificent Hall of Prayer for Good Harvests.

HIGHLIGHTS

Circular Altar (Yuan Qiu)   This three-tiered marble terrace is the first major structure you'll see if you're coming from the south. It was built in 1530 and enlarged in 1749, with all of its stones and balustrades organized in multiples of nine (considered a lucky number by northern Chinese).

Imperial Vault of Heaven (Huang Qiong Yu)   Directly north of the Circular Altar, this smaller version of the Hall of Prayer was built to store ceremonial stone tablets. The vault is surrounded by the circular **Echo Wall (Huiyin Bi).** In years past, when crowds were smaller and before the railing was installed, it was possible for two people on opposite sides of the enclosure to send whispered messages to each other along the wall with remarkable clarity.

Hall of Prayer for Good Harvests (Qinian Dian) 𝄢𝄢   This circular wooden hall, with its triple-eaved cylindrical blue-tiled roof, is perhaps the most recognizable emblem of Chinese imperial architecture outside the Forbidden City. Completed in 1420, the original hall burned to the ground in 1889, but a near-perfect replica (this one) was built the following year. It stands 38m (125 ft.) high and is 29m (98 ft.) in diameter, and is constructed without a single nail. The 28 massive pillars inside, made of fir imported from Oregon, are arranged to symbolize divisions of time: The central 4 represent the seasons, the next 12 represent the months of the year, and the outer 12 represent traditional divisions of a single day. The hall's most striking feature is its ceiling, a kaleidoscope of painted brackets and gilded panels as intricate as anything in the country.

THE SUMMER PALACE (YIHE YUAN)

This expanse of elaborate Qing-style pavilions, bridges, walkways, and gardens, scattered along the shores of immense Kunming Lake, is the grandest imperial playground in China; it was constructed from 1749 to 1764. Between 1860 and 1903, it was twice leveled by foreign armies and then rebuilt. The palace is most often associated with the empress dowager Cixi, who made it her full-time residence.

ESSENTIALS

The **Summer Palace** (© 010/6288-1144) is located 12km (7 miles) northwest of the city center in Haidian. Take **bus no. 726** from just west of Wudaokou light rail station (1304, exit A); or take a 30- to 40-minute **taxi** ride for about ¥60 ($8/£4) from the center of town. A more pleasant option is to travel here by **boat** along the renovated canal system; slightly rusty "imperial yachts" leave from the Beizhan Houhu Matou (© 010/8836-3576), behind the Beijing Exhibition Center just south of the Beijing Aquarium (50-min. trip; ¥40/$5.35/£2.70 one-way; ¥70/$9.35/£4.70 round-trip; ¥100/$13/£6.70 includes round-trip travel and the entrance ticket), docking at Nan Ruyi Men in the south of the park. The gates open at 6am; no tickets are sold after 6pm in summer and 4pm in winter. Admission is ¥30 ($4/£2) for entry to the grounds or ¥60 ($8/£4) for the all-inclusive *lian piao,* reduced to ¥20 ($2.70/£1.30) and ¥50 ($6.70/£3.30) respectively in winter (Nov–Mar). The most convenient entrance is Dong Gong Men (East Gate). Go early and allow at least 4 hours for touring the major sites on your own. Overpriced **imperial-style food** in a pleasant setting is available at the Tingli Guan Restaurant, at the western end of the Long Corridor. Spots around the lake are perfect for picnics, and Kunming Lake is ideal for skating in the depths of winter.

EXPLORING THE SUMMER PALACE

This park covers roughly 290 hectares (716 acres), with **Kunming Lake** in the south and **Longevity Hill (Wanshou Shan)** in the north. The lake's northern shore boasts most of the buildings and other attractions and is the most popular area for strolls, although it is more pleasant to walk around the smaller lakes behind Longevity Hill. The hill itself has a number of temples as well as **Baoyun Ge (Precious Clouds Pavilion),** one of the few structures in the palace to escape destruction by foreign forces. There are dozens of pavilions and a number of bridges on all sides of the lake, enough to make a full day of exploration, if you so choose.

Renshou Dian (Hall of Benevolence and Longevity)   Located directly across the courtyard from the east gate entrance, Renshou Dian is the palace's main hall. This is where the empress dowager received members of the court, first from behind a screen and later from the Dragon Throne itself. North of the hall is Cixi's private theater, now a museum that contains an old Mercedes-Benz—the first car imported into China.

Long Corridor (Chang Lang) ☆   Among the more memorable attractions in Beijing, this covered wooden promenade stretches 700m (nearly half a mile) along the northern shore of Kunming Lake. Each crossbeam, ceiling, and pillar is painted with a different scene taken from Chinese history, literature, myth, and geography (roughly 10,000 in all).

Seventeen-Arch Bridge (Shiqi Kong Qiao) ☆   This 150m-long (490-ft.) marble bridge connects South Lake Island (Nan Hu Dao) to the east shore of Kunming Lake. There is a rather striking life-size bronze ox near the eastern foot of the bridge.

OTHER SIGHTS IN BEIJING
TEMPLES, MOSQUES & CHURCHES

Baiyun Guan   If the incense here smells authentic, it's because this sprawling complex, said to have been built in 739, is the most active of Beijing's Daoist temples. Chinese visitors seem intent on actual worship rather than on tourism, and the blue-frocked monks wear their hair in the rarely seen traditional manner—long and tied in a bun at the top of the head. One notable structure is the Laolu Tang, a large hall in the third courtyard built in 1228, now used for teaching and ceremonies.

On Baiyun Guan Lu, east of the intersection with Baiyun Lu (1st right north of Baiyun Qiao, directly across from Baiyun Guan bus stop), Haidian Qu. ℂ 010/6346-3531. Admission ¥10 ($1.35/70p). 8:30am–4:30pm. Bus: no. 727 from Muxidi metro (112, exit D2) to Baiyun Guan.

Dongyue Miao ✿   This Daoist temple, built in 1322 and beautifully restored a few years ago, is most famous for a series of 76 stalls ("heavenly departments") that surround its main courtyard. Garishly painted divine judges in each stall can offer relief from practically every ill—for a price. The most popular stall, not surprisingly, is the Department of Bestowing Material Happiness. English signs explain each department's function.

Chaoyang Men Wai Dajie 141, Chaoyang Qu (10-min. walk east on the north side). ℂ 010/6551-0151. Admission ¥10 ($1.35/70p); free during festivals. Tues–Sun 8am–4:30pm. Metro: Chaoyang Men (212, exit B).

Fayuan Si (Source of Dharma Temple) *Finds*   Despite guides droning on about a long and glorious history, most of Beijing's sights are relatively new, dating from within the last 600 years. This temple, constructed in 645 in what was then the southeast corner of town, retains both an air of antiquity and the feel of a genuine Buddhist monastery. Orange-robed monks, housed in the adjacent Buddhist College, go about their business in earnest. The ancient *hutong* immediately surrounding the temple are "protected" and well worth a wander.

Fayuan Si Qian Jie 7, Xuanwu Qu. Admission ¥5 (70¢/30p). Thurs–Tues 8:30–11am and 1:30–4pm. Metro: Xuanwu Men (206, exit D1).

Guo Zi Jian and Kong Miao   This classic temple-school compound, buried down a tree-shaded street east of the Lama Temple (see below), is still in use. The Kong Miao, China's second-largest Confucian Temple, is on the right, and the Guo Zi Jian (the Imperial College) is on the left, both originally built in 1306. The front courtyard of the temple contains several dozen stelae inscribed with the names of the last successful candidates in the *jinshi* (highest level) imperial examinations. The college, imperial China's highest educational institution, contains a striking glazed-tile gate with elaborately carved stone arches.

Kong Miao at Guo Zi Jian Jie 13 (walk south from station along west side of Lama Temple, turn right onto street marked with arch), Dong Cheng Qu. ℂ 010/8401-1977. Admission ¥10 ($1.35/70p). 8:30am–4:30pm. Guo Zi Jian next door: admission ¥6 (80¢/40p); 9am–5pm. Metro: Yonghe Gong/Lama Temple (215, exit C).

Ox Street Mosque (Niu Jie Qingzhensi)   This is Beijing's largest mosque and the spiritual center for the city's estimated 200,000 Muslims. Built in 996, the complex looks more Eastern than Middle Eastern, with sloping tile roofs similar to those found on Buddhist temples. Halls are noticeably free of idols, however. A small courtyard on the south side contains the tombs and original gravestones of two Arab imams who lived here in the late 13th century.

Niu Jie 88 (on east side of street), Xuanwu Qu. ℂ 010/6353-2564. Admission ¥10 ($1.35/70p) for non-Muslims. 8am–7pm. Bus: no. 61 to Libaisi from Changchun Jie metro (205, exit D1).

Yonghe Gong (Lama Temple) 𝒦𝒦   If you visit only one temple after the Temple of Heaven, this should be it. A complex of progressively larger buildings topped with ornate yellow-tiled roofs, Yonghe Gong was built in 1694 and originally belonged to the Qing prince who would become the Yongzheng emperor. As was the custom, the complex was converted to a temple after Yongzheng's move to the Forbidden City in 1744. The temple is home to several beautiful **incense burners,** including a particularly ornate one in the second courtyard that dates from 1746. The Falun Dian (Hall of the Wheel of Law), second to last of the major buildings, contains a 6m-tall (20-ft.) bronze statue of Tsongkapa (1357–1419), the first Dalai Lama and founder of the Yellow Hat sect of Tibetan Buddhism. The final of the five central halls, the Wanfu Ge (Tower of Ten Thousand Happinesses), houses the temple's prize possession—an ominous Tibetan-style **statue of Maitreya** (the future Buddha), 18m (60 ft.) tall, carved from a single piece of white sandalwood.

Yonghe Gong Dajie 12, south of the N. Second Ring Rd. (entrance on the south end of the complex). ⒞ 010/6404-3769. Admission ¥25 ($3.35/£1.70); audio tours in English additional ¥25 ($3.35/£1.70). 9am–4pm. Metro: Yonghe Gong/Lama Temple (215, exit C).

PARKS & GARDENS
Bei Hai Park (Bei Hai Gongyuan) 𝒦𝒦   This is Beijing's oldest imperial garden, roughly 800 years old, and the one city park you should not miss. Most of the park is actually a man-made lake, **Bei Hai (North Sea),** part of a series of lakes that run north along the eastern edge of the Forbidden City. The central feature is a 36m (118-ft.) Tibetan-style **White Dagoba (Bai Ta),** similar to the one at Bai Ta Si, built in 1651 to commemorate a visit by the Dalai Lama. The pagoda stands atop the artificial hill that dominates Qionghua Dao, also known as the **Jade Islet.** A hike around the island, and around the shore of Bei Hai, will take you past several beautiful pavilions and gardens. The **Round City (Tuan Cheng),** located just outside the south entrance of the park, stands on the site where Kublai Khan built his palace after establishing the Yuan dynasty (1279–1368). It contains a massive jade bowl that once belonged to him, and a 3m (10-ft.) Buddha carved out of white jade.

Wenjin Jie 1, Xi Cheng Qu (south entrance is just west of the north gate of the Forbidden City; east entrance is opposite the west entrance of Jing Shan Park). ⒞ 010/6404-0610. Admission: summer ¥10 ($1.35/70p); winter ¥5 (70¢/30p); ¥10 ($1.35/70p) extra for Yong'an Si; ¥1 (10¢/5p) extra for Tuan Cheng. 6am–9pm. Bus: no. 812 from Dong Dan metro stop (119, exit A) to Bei Hai.

Jing Shan Park (Jing Shan Gongyuan)   If you want a clear aerial view of the Forbidden City, this is where you'll find it. The park's central hill—known both as Jing Shan (Prospect Hill) and Mei Shan (Coal Hill)—was created using earth left over from the digging of the imperial moat and was the highest point in the city during the Ming dynasty. A locust tree on the east side of the hill marks the spot where the last Ming dynasty Chongzhen emperor hanged himself in 1644, just before Manchu and rebel armies overran the city.

Jing Shan Qian Jie 1 (opposite Forbidden City north gate), Dong Cheng Qu. ⒞ 010/6404-4071. Admission ¥5 (70¢/35p). Jan–Mar 6:30am–8pm; Apr–June 6am–9pm; July–Aug 6am–10pm; Sept–Oct 6am–9pm; Dec–Nov 6:30–8pm.

Yuan Ming Yuan 𝒦 *Kids*   An amalgamation of three separate imperial gardens, these ruins create a ghostly and oddly enjoyable scene, beloved as a picnic spot. Established by the Kangxi emperor in 1707, Yuan Ming Yuan is a more recent construction than the New Summer Palace to the west, but it is misleadingly called the Old Summer Palace because it was never rebuilt after troops looted and razed it during the Second

Opium War of 1860. Ironically, some of the buildings were filled with European furnishings and art. Two Jesuit priests, Italian painter Castiglione and French scientist
Benoist, were commissioned by Qianlong to design the 30-hectare (75-acre) **Xiyang
Lou (Western Mansions)** in the northeast section of the park. Inaccurate models suggest that the structures were entirely European in style, but they were curious hybrids,
featuring imperial-style vermilion walls and yellow-tiled roofs. Recently, the park has
been the center of environmental controversy: Park management decided to line the
lakes (an integral part of Beijing's water ecology) with plastic sheeting to save on water
bills and raise the water levels to allow for a duck-boat business.

Qinghua Xi Lu 28 (north of Peking University), Haidian Qu. ℂ 010/6262-8501. Admission ¥10 ($1.35/70p), ¥15
($2/£1) to enter Xiyang Lou. 7am–7pm (to 5:30pm in winter). Bus: no. 743 from east of Wudaokou metro stop (1304)
to Yuan Ming Yuan.

MORE MUSEUMS & OTHER CURIOSITIES

Ancient Observatory (Gu Guanxiang Tai) *Kids*   Most of the large bronze astro-
nomical instruments on display here—mystifying combinations of hoops, slides, and
rulers stylishly embellished with dragons and clouds—were built by the Jesuits in the
17th and 18th centuries. You can play with reproductions in the courtyard below.

Jianguo Men Dong Biaobei 2 (southwest side of Jianguo Men intersection), Dong Cheng Qu. ℂ 010/6512-8923.
Admission ¥10 ($1.35/70p). 9am–5pm. Metro: Jianguo Men (120/211, exit C).

Factory 798 (Qijiuba Gongchang) *⊛⊛*   Optimistically billed as Beijing's SoHo
district, this Soviet-designed former weapons factory is a center for local art and fashion, but its long-term survival is uncertain. Purchase a map for ¥2 (25¢/15p) on
arrival. Establishments worth your time include the **Hart Gallery**, which holds regular screenings of alternative films; **798 Space**, still covered with slogans offering praise
to Mao; **798 Photo,** immediately opposite; and **Beijing Tokyo Art Projects** (www.
tokyo-gallery.com), which boasts a formidable stable of local and international artists.
At Cafe (Aite Kafei; ℂ **010/6438-7264)** is the best of Dashanzi's middling cafes.

Jiuxian Qiao Lu 4, Chaoyang Qu (north of Dashanzi Huandao). Some galleries closed Mon. Bus: no. 813 east from
Chaoyang Men metro (212, exit A) to Wangye Fen.

Former Residence of Lao She (Lao She Jinianguan)   Lao She (1899–1966)
was one of China's greatest 20th-century writers, lauded by early Communists for his
use of satire in novels like *Teahouse* and *Rickshaw Boy* (or *Camel Xiangzi*) and perse-
cuted for the same books during the Cultural Revolution. He is said to have committed suicide but might instead have been murdered by Red Guards. The rooms contain
photos, copies of his books, and his own library (Hemingway, Dickens, Graham
Greene). Most interesting is his study, supposedly preserved the way he left it, with a
game of solitaire laid out on the bed and the calendar turned to August 24, 1966—
the day he disappeared.

Fengfu Hutong 19, Dong Cheng Qu (from Wangfujing Dajie, turn left at the Crowne Plaza along Dengshikou Xi Jie to the
2nd *hutong* on your right). ℂ 010/6514-2612. Admission ¥10 ($1.35/70p). 9am–6pm. Metro: Wangfujing (118, exit A).

Gudai Jianzhu Bowuguan (Museum of Ancient Architecture) *⊛⊛*   This exhibition, a mixture of models of China's most famous architecture and fragments of
buildings long disappeared, is housed in halls as dramatic as those on the central axis
of the Forbidden City. These were once part of the **Xian Nong Tan,** or Altar of Agriculture, now as obscure as its neighbor, Tian Tan, the Temple (properly Altar) of
Heaven, is famous. From about 1410, emperors came to this once-extensive site to

perform rituals in which they started the agricultural cycle by playing farmer and plowing the first furrows. Models of significant buildings around Beijing can help you select what to see in the capital during the remainder of your trip.

Dong Jing Lu 21, Xuanwu Qu (from bus stop, take 1st right into Nan Wei Lu and walk for 5 min., look out for an archway down a street on the left). ℂ 010/6301-7620. Admission ¥15 ($2/£1). 9am–4pm. Bus: no. 803 from just south of Qian Men (208) metro stops to Tian Qiao Shangchang.

National Museum of China (Guojia Bowuguan) ⚔ The Museum of the Chinese Revolution and the Museum of History have been united in a single building. Some effort has been made to spruce things up, and English captions have been added to a number of the displays, although they are lacking from the hilarious wax figure hall. In the past, interest centered on omissions from Chinese history; now it focuses on inclusions. Former unpersons such as Mao's ill-fated heirs apparent, Liu Shaoqi and Lin Biao, are displayed alongside their tormentors, but the Party line is scrupulously followed. Lin, the only man to outdo Zhou Enlai in his relentless obsequiousness to Mao, is still said to have plotted to seize power from the Great Helmsman. *Note:* This museum is undergoing a massive face-lift and will not reopen until sometime in 2009.

East side of Tian'an Men Sq., Dong Cheng Qu. ℂ 010/6512-8901. www.nmch.gov.cn. Admission ¥30 ($4/£2) for *tong piao*, or ¥10–¥20 ($1.35–$2.70/70p–£1.30) for each exhibit. English audio tours ¥30 ($4/£2). 9am–3:30pm. Metro: Tian'an Men East (117, exit D).

Prince Gong's Mansion (Gong Wang Fu) ⚔ This imperial residence belonged to several people, including the sixth son of the Guangxu emperor (Prince Gong), and is thought to have been the inspiration behind the lushly described mansion in Cao Xueqin's canonical 18th-century work, *Dream of the Red Chamber.* Only the garden is open to visitors, but its labyrinthine combination of rockeries and pavilions offers plenty to see.

Liuyin Jie 17 (signposted in English at top of Qian Hai Xi Dajie running north off Ping'an Dadao opposite north gate of Bei Hai Park; turn left at sign and follow alley past large parking lot. Entrance marked with huge red lanterns). ℂ 010/6618-0573. Admission ¥20 ($2.70/£1.30); ¥60 ($8/£4) including guide and opera performance. 7:30am–4:30pm.

THE HUTONG

As distinct as Beijing's palaces, temples, and parks may be, it is the *hutong* that ultimately set the city apart. Prior to the 20th century, when cars and the Communist love of grandeur made them impractical, these narrow and often winding lanes were the city's dominant passageways. Old maps of Beijing show the city to be an immense and intricate maze composed almost entirely of *hutong,* most no wider than 10m (30 ft.) and some as narrow as 50 centimeters (20 in.).

Beijing's other famous feature is the *siheyuan* (courtyard house)—traditional dwellings typically composed of four single-story rectangular buildings arranged around a central courtyard with a door at one corner (ideally facing south). Originally designed to house a single family, each one now houses up to five or six families. Until recently, as much as half of Beijing's population lived in some form of *siheyuan,* but large-scale bulldozing of the *hutong* has resulted in significant migration into modern apartment buildings. Foreign visitors charmed by the quaintness of the old houses often assume this migration is forced, and it often is. But many who move do so willingly, eager for central heating and indoor plumbing (both rare in the *hutong* neighborhoods).

The *hutong* are being leveled so rapidly that the term "fast-disappearing" is now a permanent part of their description. The best-preserved *hutong,* and the ones most likely to survive because of their popularity with tourists, are those found in the Back Lakes (Shicha Hai) and nearby Di'an Men.

The most dynamic of these hutongs can be found around the alley of Nan Luogu Xiang, a gentrifying neighborhood filled with Chinese hipsters, grungy French and Americans, and old Beijingers. Nan Luogu Xiangis the name of the north-south alley filled with a growing number of cafes, bars, restaurants, and hotels listed throughout our pages. Bar highlights include MAO Livehouse (p. 138).

Pedicab tour companies offer to bike you around this area and take you inside a couple of courtyards, but they all charge absurd rates. It's much cheaper, and far more enjoyable, to walk around on your own (see "Walking Tour: The Back Lakes," below). If you must, the **Beijing Hutong Tourist Agency** (© **010/6615-9097**) offers tours in English.

WALKING TOUR   THE BACK LAKES

Start:	Drum Tower (Gu Lou), north end of Di'an Men Wai Dajie.
Finish:	Prince Gong's Palace (Gong Wang Fu), west side of Qian Hai.
Time:	Approximately 3 hours.
Best Times:	Morning (9am) or just after lunch, no later than 1:30pm (or you risk getting locked out of Prince Gong's Palace).

There is, quite simply, no finer place to walk in Beijing. The Back Lakes area (Shicha Hai) is composed of two idyllic lakes—Qian Hai (Front Sea) and Hou Hai (Back Sea)—and the tree-shaded neighborhoods that surround them. Combined with other man-made pools to the south, these lakes were once part of a system used to transport grain by barge from the Grand Canal to the Forbidden City. Prior to 1911, this was an exclusive area, and only people with connections to the imperial family were permitted to maintain houses here (a situation that seems destined to return). A profusion of bars and cafes has sprung up around the lakes in recent years, providing ample opportunities to take breaks from your walk.

Beyond the lakes, stretching out in all directions, is the city's best-maintained network of *hutong*. Many families have lived in these lanes for generations, their insular communities a last link to Old Beijing.

Begin at Mei Lanfang Guju, corner of Deshengmen Nei Dajie:

❶ Mei Lanfang Guju

Look for the red lanterns outside this superbly preserved courtyard residence that once belonged to 1930s Peking Opera star Mei Lanfang. The pictures of the opera singer on view here illustrate the wide-ranging number of expressions used in the art form.

Turn left out of Mei Lanfang Guju and cross Deshengmen Nei Dajie. On the left, you'll walk past:

❷ Former Campus of Furen Daxue (Furen University)

The original campus of Furen University (1 Dingfu Jie), a Catholic institution founded by Chinese priests, was built in 1925. The school was shuttered and moved to Taiwan after the Communists came to power. Note the ornate facade featuring an arched doorway and the traditional sloping Chinese roof.

At the T-intersection, turn left on Liuyin Jie, and walk north. On your right is:

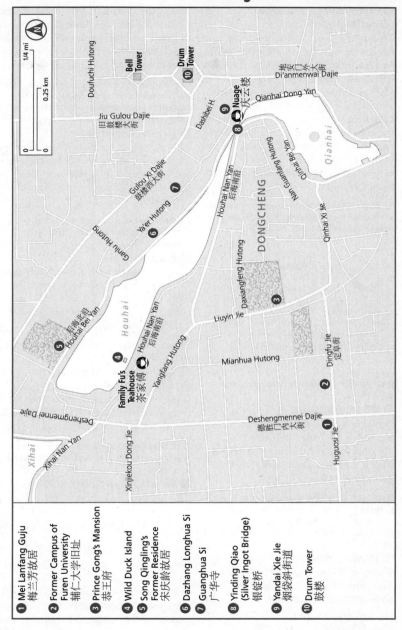

Bell Tower

Drum Tower ⑩

Doufuchi Hutong

Di'anmenwai Dajie
地安门外大街

⑨ **Nuage** 庆云楼

Qianhai Dong Yan

Jiu Gulou Dajie
旧鼓楼大街

Dashibei H.

⑧

Qianhai
Qianhai Bei Yan

Gulou Xi Dajie
鼓楼西大街

Nan Guanfang Hutong

⑦

Ya'er Hutong
⑥

Houhai Nan Yan
后海南沿

DONGCHENG

Qinhai Xi Jie

Ganlu Hutong

Daxiangfeng Hutong

Houhai Bei Yan
后海北沿

Liuyin Jie

③

Dingfu Jie
定阜街

Houhai

Houhai Nan Yan
后海南沿

⑤

Mianhua Hutong

②

④

Family Fu's Teahouse
荟家博

Yangfang Hutong

Deshengmennei Dajie
德胜门内大街

Deshengmennei Dajie

①

Huguosi Jie

Xihai Nan Yan

Xinjiekou Dong Jie

Xihai

1/4 mi

0.25 km

① Mei Lanfang Guju
梅兰芳故居

② Former Campus of
Furen University
辅仁大学旧址

③ Prince Gong's Mansion
恭王府

④ Wild Duck Island

⑤ Song Qingling's
Former Residence
宋庆龄故居

⑥ Dazhang Longhua Si

⑦ Guanghua Si
广华寺

⑧ Yinding Qiao
(Silver Ingot Bridge)
银锭桥

⑨ Yandai Xie Jie
烟袋斜街道

⑩ Drum Tower
鼓楼

❸ Prince Gong's Mansion (Gong Wang Fu)

This is the most lavish courtyard residence (Liuyin Jie 14; ✆ **010/6616-8149**; admission ¥20/$2.70/£1.30; open 8:30am–4:30pm) in the Back Lakes. The 1777 mansion was occupied by Heshen, a corrupt official who was rumored to be the Qianlong emperor's lover. Later, it became the home of Prince Gong, who negotiated on behalf of China at the end of the Second Opium War. See p. 123 for a more detailed description of Prince Gong's Mansion.

Turn right when leaving the mansion, and make a left at the T onto Yangfang Hutong. Take a right at the park and walk through it to:

TAKE A BREAK
Family Fu's Teahouse At this lakeside teahouse you can relax on Ming dynasty-era furniture while sipping longjing, a green tea from Hangzhou, one of China's famed tea-producing areas. The English-speaking owner is particularly friendly (✆ **010/6616-0725**).

Right outside the teahouse, stop and have a gawk at:

❹ Wild Duck Island

Beijing is full of loopy attractions, including this man-made steel island built in Hou hai Lake for the ducks in the area. March is a particularly busy time here as it's mating season.

Make a left out of the teahouse, and pass you'll pass Kong Yi Ji, one of Beijing's most famous restaurants on the left. Turn right at the footbridge and continue around the lake. On the left is:

❺ Former Residence of Soong Ching-ling (Song Qingling Guju)

This former imperial palace (✆ **010/6404-4205**, admission ¥20/$2.70/£1.30; open 9am–5pm, 9am–4:30pm in winter) once famously housed the wife of Sun Yat-sen, modern China's founder. This feminist hero later became a friend of

Mao's and a Communist sympathizer. China's last emperor, Henry Puyi, is said to have been born on this site. On weekends, there's a risk of being trampled by soon-to-be-wed brides in their finery.

Turn left from the residence and continue along the lake. After passing the outdoor exercise equipment (which seniors will probably be frolicking on!), look for the gate of:

❻ Dazang Longhua Si

This temple dates from 1719. Though it's now the grounds of a kindergarten, the facade—with intricate animal-shaped stone gargoyles—has been nicely preserved.

Continue along the lake and turn left at the next alley, then take a quick right on Ya'er Hutong to:

❼ Guanghua Si

Though this temple is not officially open to the public, monks have snuck us in more than once. China's last known eunuch was a caretaker of this temple for 2 decades and died here in 1996.

Retrace your steps back the lake, then turn left and continue to:

❽ Yinding Qiao (Silver Ingot Bridge)

This bridge separates Hou hai from Qianhai (Front Lake). It's usually a mess of tourists, aggressive rickshaws, and cars.

Walk away from the bridge and turn right at the sign that reads MASTER OF FOLK ARTS AND CRAFTS FINE WORK SALE:

❾ Yandai Xiejie (Tobacco Alley)

This touristy pedestrian street houses a few gems. No. 63 on the left, a folk art store, features stylish Chinese pillow covers, framed paper cuts, and cloth coasters. No. 20 on the right sells cute totes and lipstick cases made with Chinese patterns. No. 12 is the Tibetan Jewelry & Tea Bar where you can stop for a drink in the airy back room and browse their collection of Tibetan bracelets, rings, and clothing.

The end of Yandai Xie Jie brings you to Di'an-men Wai Dajie. Turning left, you will see a number of kitchen supply shops on your left, and in front of you, the looming:

⑩ Drum Tower (Gu Lou)

Drumming performances are held daily every half hour (9–11:30am and 1:30–5pm) underneath the bright yellow tile roof of the looming Drum Tower.

WINDING DOWN
Retrace your steps back to the Silver Ingot Bridge. Don't cross it, but head left down the small street. Set back from the road is **Nuage,** which delivers pricey but heavenly Vietnamese cuisine amid delightful colonial ambience (p. 106). If the weather is fine, aim for a seat on the rooftop.

TOURS

Several companies offer guided group tours of Beijing for English-speakers, but these are overpriced, often incomplete, and best thought of as an emergency measure when time is short. The most popular operators are **BTG Travel** (② 010/8563-9959; www. btgtravel.com) and **Panda Tours** (② 010/6522-2991), and both have offices scattered through the four- and five-star hotels. City-highlight tours by air-conditioned bus typically cost around ¥300 ($40/£20) per person for a half-day and around ¥500 ($67/£33) for a full day with a mediocre lunch. **China International Travel Service (CITS)** (② 010/6515-8566; www.cits.net) offers tours that are more customizable, but at a much higher fee. Instead, consider the **Chinese Culture Club** (② 010/8462-2081; www.chinesecultureclub.org), which organizes outings, lectures, and film screenings for expatriates with an interest in Chinese culture. Events are often led by prominent lecturers, discussions go well beyond the "5,000 years of history" palaver that CITS will subject you to, and they are constantly on the lookout for new attractions. A smaller operation with a similar philosophy is **Cycle China** (② 010/6424-5913; www.cyclechina.com).

6 Side Trips from Beijing

THE GREAT WALL

Even after you dispense with the myths that it is a single continuous structure and that it can be seen from space, China's best-known attraction is still a mind-boggling achievement. Referred to in Mandarin as the Wanli Changcheng (10,000-Li Long Wall) or just Changcheng for short, the Great Wall begins at Shanhaiguan on the Bo Hai (sea) (p. 148) and snakes west to a fort at Jiayu Guan in the Gobi Desert (p. 289). Its origins date from the Warring States Period (453–221 B.C.), when rival kingdoms began building defensive walls to thwart each other's armies. The king of Qin, who eventually conquered the other states to become the first emperor of a unified China, conscripted around 300,000 laborers to combine the walls into a more or less uninterrupted rampart. During the Han dynasty (206 B.C.–A.D. 220), the Wall was extended farther west, with subsequent dynasties adding their own bits and branches, which makes it difficult to pin down the Wall's precise length. It is at least 10,000km (6,200 miles) long by common estimates, but some guesses go as high as 50,000km (31,000 miles).

Most sections of the Great Wall visible north of Beijing were reconstructed by the Ming dynasty (1368–1644) in an (ultimately vain) effort to defend against attack by Manchus and Mongols from the north. The four most easily visited sections are **Badaling, Mutianyu, Juyongguan,** and the vertiginous **Simatai.**

On the Wild Wall

Sections of the Great Wall listed below are easy to reach and suitably stunning, but they represent only a part of what the Wall has to offer. People with time and an inclination to explore beyond these sections are strongly encouraged to join one of the excellent, usually multiday "Wild Wall" trips to the crumbling **"unofficial" sections of the Wall** that snake through more remote areas north of Beijing. Most weekend trips cost ¥3,600 ($450/£225) and are based at one of two **modernized farmhouses** (one better outfitted than the other). The fee includes guided hikes, 2 nights' accommodations, six meals, drinks and snacks, research and conservation contribution, and book. Details and booking information about weekend trips, day hikes, and "Extreme" treks can be found on the Wild Wall website at **www.wildwall.com**.

Badaling   The first section of the Great Wall opened to tourists, the portion at **Badaling** remains the most popular. In 1957 it was fully restored to its original Ming appearance—although the reconstruction was sloppier than subsequent efforts at Mutianyu, Jinshanling, and Simatai, where efforts were taken to preserve a sense of antiquity. Although it is one of the most dramatic sections of the Great Wall, the sheer number of visitors is overwhelming: You might not be able to see Badaling from space, but there's some chance of smelling its toilets. Set in a steep, forested mountain range, it offers tremendous views and, for those willing to travel beyond the restored sections, some worthwhile hiking. The ticket office at Badaling is open from 7am to 9pm. Admission is ¥45 ($6/£3); round-trip cable-car transportation is ¥50 ($6.70/£3.30) per person.

Badaling is roughly 70km (43 miles) northwest of Beijing. **Group tours** organized through hotel travel desks are typically combined with a trip to the Ming Tombs and cost around ¥400 ($53/£27) per person. A cheaper but still comfortable option is to take one of the air-conditioned, city-sponsored **tourist (*you*) buses** (© 010/6779-7546): *You* no. 1 leaves from the northeast side of Qian Men (every 20 min.; 6am–noon), and *you* no. 2 leaves from Dongzhi Men and the Beijing Railway Station (every 30 min.; 6:30–10am); both charge ¥50 ($6.70/£3.30), a price that includes Juyongguan (see below) and the Ming Tombs. The cheapest way to get to Badaling is on the red-and-yellow striped (air-conditioned) version of **bus no. 919** (6am–6pm; 1 hr.; ¥10/$1.35/70p), which leaves from the east side of Desheng Men. A round-trip **taxi** should cost less than ¥300 ($40/£20).

Mutianyu   The Great Wall at Badaling proved so popular that authorities restored a second section of the Wall to the east in 1986. Mutianyu is a bit rougher and slightly less crowded than Badaling, but it does have its own traffic jams in summer. As at Badaling, cable-car transportation is available. Sadly, a fence prevents you from walking onto the tempting unrestored sections. The ticket office is open 7:30am to 6:30pm. Admission is ¥40 ($4.35/£2.70) and the cable car costs ¥50 ($6.70/£3.30) round-trip.

Mutianyu is 90km (56 miles) north of Beijing, and somewhat harder to reach. Once again, most hotels can arrange **guided group tours** for around ¥250 ($33/£17). The *you* **no. 6** combines the trip to Mutianyu with visits to a temple and a lake for ¥50 ($6.70/£3.30); it leaves from the northeast side of the Xuanwu Men metro station every 30 minutes from 6:30 to 8am. A **taxi** will cost ¥350 ($47/£23).

Tip: In a quiet river valley close to Mutianyu lies Beijing's most appealing Great Wall resort, **Red Capital Ranch** ✿✿ (© **010/8401-8886**); ¥1,520–¥1,600/$190–$200/£95–£100) including breakfast, plus 15% service charge; Apr–Nov). Similar to its sister property, Red Capital Residence (p. 93), all 10 rooms are decorated with antique furnishings. Fishing, bike riding, hiking on the Wall, and even a Tibetan essential oil massage are offered. A shuttle connects with the Red Capital Residence.

Juyongguan   This is the most recently restored section of the Great Wall, and the closest to Beijing (55km/34 miles northwest, on the road to Badaling). The restoration is crisp and the sense of history rather distant. But there are fewer tour groups here, and a number of impressive Buddhist bas-relief carvings on the separate and genuinely old Yun Tai (Cloud Platform) built in 1342. The ticket office is open from 8am to dusk. Admission is ¥40 ($5.35/£2.70) in summer, ¥35 ($4.70/£2.35) in winter.

The **tourist** *(you)* and **public buses** that go to Badaling also stop here. A round-trip **taxi** ride should cost around ¥300 ($40/£20).

Simatai ✿✿   Somewhat tamed after a series of deaths led to the closing of its most dangerous stretch, Simatai nevertheless remains one of the best options for those who want more of a challenge from the Great Wall. The most harrowing portion, steep and unrestored, is on the east side of the Miyun Reservoir. Several gravel-strewn spots here require all four limbs to navigate. The endpoint is Wangjing Ta, the 12th watchtower from the bottom. Beyond this is the appropriately named **Tian Qiao (Heavenly Bridge)**, a thin, tilted ridge where the Wall narrows to only a few feet—this section is now off-limits. Despite the danger, this part of the Wall can get crowded on weekends, especially since the cable car was installed. Souvenir vendors can also be a nuisance. The round-trip hike to Tian Qiao takes roughly 3 hours at a moderate pace. The section of Simatai west of the reservoir is better restored (in the beginning at least) and connects to another section of the Great Wall, Jinshanling, in Hebei Province. The ticket office is in a small village 10 minutes' walk south of the reservoir; it's open from 8am to 7:30pm in summer (8am–dusk in winter). Admission is ¥40 ($5.35/£2.70). The cable car runs from 8am to 5pm, April to November; a round-trip ride to the No. 8 Tower costs ¥50 ($6.70/£3.35).

Simatai is 110km (68 miles) northeast of Beijing. The best no-hassle option is to go there with one of the **Youth Hostel** tours (© **010/8188-9323**). These tours typically leave Beijing's YHAs between 7am and 8am and cost ¥150 ($20/£10) for simple transportation. The *you* no. 12 travels to Simatai from northeast of the Xuanwu Men

---

A Great Hike on the Great Wall

Jinshanling ✿✿✿ (© **010/8402-4628**; ¥50/$6.25/£3.10) is one of the all-time Great Wall hikes. It's not as steep as Simatai and is more heavily restored, but with fewer visitors. The hike from here east to the Miyun Reservoir is roughly 10km (6 miles) and takes 3 to 4 hours. The middle part of the hike, as the people fall away and the Wall begins to crumble, can be truly sublime. A number of hostels provide transportation for this hike. Otherwise, you can take an air-conditioned bus from the Xi Zhi Men long-distance bus station to Miyun (every 30 min.; 6am–4pm; ¥15/$2/£1), then hire a minivan *(miandi)* to drop you off at Jinshanling and pick you up at Simatai for around ¥100 ($13/£6.70)—make sure you withhold payment until after you're picked up.

(206) metro stop (Apr to mid-Oct Sat–Sun 6:30–8:30am, every 30 min; ¥70/$9.35/
£4.70); you get about 3 hours at the site. A round-trip **taxi** ride should cost less than
¥400 ($53/£27).

Responding to the popularity of the Jinshanling-to-Simatai hike (see above), the
Simatai YHA (*C* **010/8188-9323;** standard room ¥288/$38/£19) opened in 2004.
Courtyard-style rooms are basic, but the coffee is superb, and the view of the Wall
from the patio is wonderful.

OTHER SIGHTS OUTSIDE BEIJING
THE MING TOMBS
Of the 16 emperors who ruled China during the Ming dynasty (1368–1644), 13 are
buried in this valley north of Beijing (hence the Chinese name Shisan Ling, the 13
Tombs). The Yongle emperor, who also oversaw construction of the Forbidden City,
consulted geomancers before choosing this site, considered advantageous because it is
bounded to the north by a range of protective mountains. The geography of the valley is mirrored in the tombs themselves, with each emperor buried beneath a tumulus
protected from the rear by a mountain. Only three of the Ming Tombs—**Ding Ling**,
Chang Ling, and **Zhao Ling**—have been restored, and only one (Ding Ling) has
been fully excavated. Many of the buildings mirror Ming palaces found in the city.
Because of this, the sight can be boring to people who've already had their fill of imperial architecture. However, several attractions, particularly the **Shen Dao (Spirit
Way),** make the trip worthwhile for those who have the time.

The valley is 48km (30 miles) north of Beijing, on the same road that goes to Badaling. Many **tours** to Badaling also come here, but if you want time to explore some of
the unrestored tombs (highly recommended), you'll have to make a separate trip. A
taxi hired in Beijing should cost less than ¥400 ($53/£27). The most comfortable
form of public transport is the air-conditioned **bus no. 845** from Xi Zhi Men (a 10-
min. walk south of the metro station) to Zhengfa Daxue in Changping (1½ hr.;
¥9/$1.20/60p). Then cross the street and take bus no. 314 to the Da Gong Men stop
(15 min; ¥1/15¢/5p). It is also possible to take the green-and-white *zhi* (express) version of **bus no. 919** to Zhengfa Daxue from Desheng Men (1 hr.; ¥4/55¢/25p).

Shen Dao (Spirit Way) *(★)*   The main entrance to the valley is the **Da Hong Men
(Great Red Gate),** remarkably similar to gates found in the Forbidden City, beyond
which is a pavilion housing China's largest memorial stele, and beyond that the Spirit
Way. The path, slightly curved to fool evil spirits, is lined on either side with willows
and remarkable **carved stone animals** and human figures, considered among the best
in China and far better than those found at the Qing Tombs. Not be missed.

Ticket office north of stele pavilion. Admission ¥30 ($4/£2) in summer, ¥20 ($2.70/£1.35) in winter. 8am–6pm (to
5:30pm in winter). Simple bilingual maps available here for ¥3 (40¢/20p).

Chang Ling   This tomb, home to the remains of the Yongle emperor, is the largest
and best preserved of the 13. It is essentially a Forbidden City in miniature, and perhaps disappointing if you've seen the palace already. Most striking is the **Ling'en
Dian,** an immense hall in which the interior columns and brackets have been left
unpainted, creating an eye-catching contrast with the green ceiling panels.

4km (2½ miles) due north of the Shen Dao. Admission ¥45 ($6/£3) summer, ¥30 ($4/£2) winter. 7am–4:30pm. Bus:
no. 314 or 22 to Chang Ling stop from lighted intersection just beyond north end of Spirit Way.

Ding Ling   The 4,000-sq.-m (13,000-sq.-ft.) **Underground Palace** discovered here in 1956 was the burial place of the Wanli emperor, his wife, and his favorite concubine. The "palace" is a plain marble vault, buried 27m (88 ft.) underground and divided into five large chambers. It's all a bit disappointing. The corpses have been removed, their red coffins replaced with replicas, and burial objects moved to aboveground display rooms. The original marble thrones are still here, though, now covered in a small fortune of *renminbi* notes tossed by Chinese visitors in hopes of bribing the emperor's ghost. Outside, behind the ticket office, is the respectable **Shisan Ling Bowuguan (Ming Tombs Museum).**

Admission ¥60 ($8/£4) summer, ¥40 ($5.35/£2.70) winter. 8:30am–5pm. On west side of valley; walk south from Chang Ling, take 1st right, and walk west 20 min.

EASTERN QING TOMBS 🐦🐦

The Qing Dong Ling have been open for more than 20 years but they are still little visited, despite offering considerably more to visitors than those of the Ming. Altogether, 5 emperors, 15 empresses, 136 concubines, 3 princes, and 2 princesses are buried in 15 tombs here. The first to be buried was Shunzhi—the first Qing emperor to reign from Beijing—in 1663, and the last was an imperial concubine in 1935. The tomb chambers of four imperial tombs, the **Xiao Ling** (the Shunzhi emperor), **Jing Ling** (Kangxi), **Yu Ling** (Qianlong), and **Ding Ling** (Xianfeng), are open, as well as the twin **Ding Dong Ling** tombs (the Cixi dowager empress and the Ci'an empress). Also of interest is a group site for the Qianlong emperor's concubines.

The tombs are in Zunhua County, Hebei Province, 125km (78 miles) east of Beijing. They are open from 8am to 5:30pm in summer, 9am to 4:30pm in winter. The *tong piao,* which offers access to all the tombs, costs ¥120 ($16/£8). A special Qing Dong Ling tourist bus leaves at 7:30am from northeast of the Xuanwu Men (206) metro stop and allows you about 3 hours on-site before beginning the return journey If you want to explore at your own pace, you'll have to hire a cab or take a rickety local bus to Zunhua. The local bus is found just east of the Dawang Lu (123) metro station (exit C) (6:30am–4:30pm; 3½ hr.; ¥24/$3.20/£1.60). After you get off the bus, hire a *miandi* (minivan) to take you the rest of the way for about ¥20 ($2.70/£1.30). An assortment of three-wheelers will offer their services to take you around the site, with an initial asking price of ¥10 ($1.35/70p).

The **Xiao Ling** was the first tomb on the site, and a model for others both here and at the Western Qing Tombs, although few others are so elaborate. Each tomb has an approach road or Spirit Way, which may have guardian figures. The entrance to the tomb itself is usually preceded by a large stele pavilion and marble bridges over a stream. To the right, the buildings used for preparation of sacrifices are now usually the residences of the staff, and hung with washing. Inside the gate, halls to the left and right were for enrobing and other preparations, and now house exhibitions, as usually does each **Hall of Eminent Favor,** at the rear, where ceremonies in honor of the deceased took place. Behind, if open, a doorway allows access past a stone altar to a steep ramp leading to the base of a **soul tower.** Through a passageway beneath, stairs to either side lead to a walkway encircling the mound, giving views across the countryside. If the tomb chamber is open, a ramp from beneath the soul tower leads down to a series of chambers.

The twin **Ding Dong Ling** tombs have nearly identical exteriors, but empress dowager Cixi had hers rebuilt in 1895, 14 years after empress Ci'an's death (in which she is suspected of having had a hand), using far more expensive materials. Everywhere are reminders of the Forbidden City, such as the terrace-corner spouts carved as water-loving dragons *(che)*. The interior has motifs strikingly painted in gold on dark wood, recalling the buildings where the empress spent her last years. There are walls of carved and gilded brick, and columns writhing with superbly fearsome wooden dragons. After this, the other tombs seem gaudy.

The enclosure of the **Yu Fei Yuan Qin (Garden of Rest)** contains moss-covered tumuli for 35 of the Qianlong emperor's concubines. Another is buried in a proper tomb chamber, along with an empress whom Qianlong had grown to dislike.

The **Yu Ling** has the finest tomb chamber, a series of rooms separated by solid marble doors, with walls and arched ceilings engraved with Buddha figures and more than 30,000 words of Tibetan scripture. The 3-ton doors themselves have reliefs of bodhisattvas (beings on the road to enlightenment) and the four protective kings usually found at temple entrances. This tomb is worth the trip in its own right. The **Jing Ling** is the tomb of Qianlong's grandfather, the Kangxi emperor. It's surprisingly modest given that he was possibly the greatest emperor the Chinese ever had, but that's in keeping with what is known of his character. The Spirit Way leading to the tomb has an elegant five-arch bridge; the guardian figures are placed at an unusual curve in the way, quite close to the tomb itself, and are more decorated than those at earlier tombs.

WESTERN QING TOMBS 🐦🐦

The Yongzheng emperor broke with tradition and ordered his tomb to be constructed here, away from his father (the Kangxi emperor). His son, the Qianlong emperor, decided to be buried near his grandfather and that thereafter burials should alternate between the eastern (see above) and western sites, although this was not followed consistently. The first tomb, the **Tai Ling,** was completed in 1737, 2 years after the Yongzheng reign. The last imperial interment was in 1998, when the ashes of Aisin-Gioro Henry Puyi, the last emperor, were moved to a commercial cemetery here. He and two consorts were added to four emperors, four empresses, four princes, two princesses, and 57 concubines. The site is rural, with the tombs lapped by orchards and agriculture, and with chickens, goats, and the odd rabbit to be encountered.

Chang Ling (the Jiaqing emperor's tomb), and **Chong Ling** (Guangxu) are also open, as well as **Chang Xi Ling,** with the extraordinary sonic effects of its **Huiyin Bi**—an echo wall where, as the only visitors, you'll actually be able to try out the special effects available only in theory at the Temple of Heaven.

The **Qing Xi Ling** are located 140km (87 miles) southwest of Beijing, outside Yi Xian in Hebei Province. The ticket office is open from 8am to 5pm; a *tong piao* (good for access to all the tombs) costs ¥90 ($12/£6) and is good for 2 days. There's no access by tourist bus, but that is part of the appeal for most visitors. To get there, take a bus to Yi Xian from the Lize Qiao long-distance bus station (departs every 15 min., 6:50am–5pm; 3 hr.; ¥20/$2.70/£1.30; last bus returns at 4pm). Then switch to a minivan *(miandi)* for the 15km (9-mile) ride to the tombs; the fare is around ¥20 ($2.70/£1.30). Unless you make a very early start, you may want to spend the night at the modest, Manchu-themed **Ba Jiao Lou Manzu Zhuangyuan,** just east of Tai Ling (© 0312/826-0828; ¥120/$16/£8 standard room). **Xing Gong Binguan,** near Yongfu Si on the eastern side of the tomb complex (© 0312/471-0038; standard room ¥150/$20/£10 after discount), was where Manchu rulers stayed when they came to pay their respects, and the room constructed in 1748 to house the Qianlong emperor is now rented out as two suites (¥660/$88/£44 after discount).

The **Da Bei Lou,** a pavilion containing two vast stelae, is on the curved route to the **Tai Ling.** The general plan of the major tombs follows that of the Eastern Tombs, above. In fact, the **Chang Ling,** slightly to the west, is almost identical, brick for brick, to the Tai Ling, although the rear section with soul tower and tomb mound is not open. The Jiaqing empress is buried just to the west in the **Chang Xi Ling,** on a far smaller scale, the tomb mound a brick drum. But the perfectly semicircular rear wall offers the whispering-gallery effects found at some domed European cathedrals; clapping while standing on marked stones at the center of the site produces multiple echoes, while speech is amazingly amplified. The empress can't get much peace.

Jiaqing's son, the Daoguang emperor, was meant to be buried at Qing Dong Ling, but his tomb there was flooded. The relocated **Mu Ling** appears much more modest than those of his predecessors. No stele pavilion or Spirit Way, largely unpainted, and the tomb mound is a modest brick-wall drum, but this is the most expensive tomb: wood used to construct the exquisite main hall is fragrant *nanmu*, sourced from as far away as Myanmar. The Guangxu emperor was the last to complete his reign (although his aunt, Cixi, is again suspected of shortening it), and his **Chong Ling,** which uses more modern materials than other tombs, wasn't completed until 1915, well after the last emperor's abdication.

Several other tombs are open, and more are being restored. The recently opened **Tai Ling Fei Yuan Qin** is a rather battered group of concubine tumuli, individually labeled with the years in which each concubine entered the Yongzheng emperor's service, and their grades in the complex harem hierarchy.

The ashes of **Puyi** (properly known as the Xuantong emperor) lie buried on the eastern end of the site, up a slope behind a brand-new Qing-style memorial arch *(pailou),* and behind a shoddy modern carved balustrade. Neighboring plots are available for the right price.

WESTERN TEMPLES

Buried in the hills west of Beijing, **Tanzhe Si (Temple of the Pool and Wild Mulberry)** and **Jietai Si (Temple of the Ordination Platform)** are the tranquil kinds of Chinese temples people imagine before they actually come to China. Foreign travelers seldom visit them, but the effort to come out here is worth it, if only to escape the noise and dust of the city center.

Both are easily accessible by taking **bus no. 931** from the Pingguoyuan metro station (103) at the far western end of Line 1. Take a right out of exit D and continue straight a few minutes to the bus station (be sure to take the plain red-and-beige, rather than the red-and-yellow *zhi,* version of the bus). Tanzhe Si is the last stop on this line; the trip takes 1 hour and costs ¥2.50 (35¢/15p). Basic but acceptable accommodations are available at both temples, for those who want (or need) to spend more time in quietude.

Tanzhe Si ✿✿   This peaceful complex dates from the Western Jin dynasty (265–316), well before Beijing was founded. In the main courtyard on the central axis is a pair of 30m (100-ft.) ginkgo trees, supposedly planted in the Tang dynasty (618–907), as well as several apricot trees, cypresses, peonies, and purple jade orchids. The **Guanyin Dian,** at the top of the western axis, was favored by Princess Miao Yan, a daughter of Kublai Khan; she is said to have prayed so fervently she left footprints in one of the floor stones (now stored in a box to the left).

48km (29 miles) west of Beijing. Admission ¥35 ($4.70/£2.35). 8am–5pm. Bus: no. 931. Get off at last stop and hike up stone path at end of parking lot.

Jietai Si ⍟   The **ordination platform** here, China's largest, is a three-tiered circular structure with 113 statues of the God of Ordination placed in niches around the base. It is located in the Jietai Dian, in the far-right corner of the temple. Ceremonies conducted on this platform to commemorate the ascension of a devotee to full monkhood required permission from the emperor. Other courtyards have ancient, twisted pines, as venerable as the temple itself.

13km (8 miles) east of Tanzhe Si. Admission ¥35 ($4.70/£2.35). 8am–5pm (weekends until 5:30pm). Bus: no. 931 from Tanzhe Si. The stop is marked with a huge sign pointing the way to the temple.

7 Shopping

Stores and markets in Beijing sell everything from cashmere and silk to knockoff designer-label clothing to athletic wear, antiques, traditional art, cloisonné, lacquerware, Ming furniture, Mao memorabilia, and enough miscellaneous Chinesey doodads to stuff Christmas stockings from now until eternity. Prices are reasonable (certainly lower than in the Asian-goods boutiques back home), though increasingly less so. Cheap one-time-use luggage is widely available for hauling your booty if you get carried away.

Before you rush to the ATM, however, it is important to remember that not all that is green and gleams in Beijing is jade. Indeed, the majority of it is colored glass. The same principle holds for pearls (see below), famous-brand clothing, antiques, and just about everything else. Shoppers who plan to make big purchases should educate themselves about quality and price well beforehand.

You should also be leery of any English-speaking youngsters who claim to be **art students** and offer to take you to a special exhibit of their work. This is a scam. The art, which you will be compelled to buy, almost always consists of assembly-line reproductions of famous (or not-so-famous) paintings offered at prices several dozen times higher than their actual value.

TOP SHOPPING AREAS

The grandest shopping area in Beijing is on and around **Wangfujing Dajie,** east of the Forbidden City. The street was overhauled in 1999, the south section turned into a pedestrian-only commercial avenue lined with shops, fast-food restaurants, and the city's top two malls—the Sun (Xin) Dong An Plaza and the Oriental Plaza (Dongfang Guangchang). **Dong Dan Bei Dajie,** a long block east, is a strip of clothing boutiques and CD shops popular among fashionable Beijing youth.

Other major Westernized shopping areas include the section of **Jianguo Men Wai Dajie** between the Friendship Store and the China World Trade Center, and the neighborhood outside the **Northeast Third Ring Road North,** southeast of Sanyuan Qiao around the new embassy district.

Beijing's liveliest shopping zone, the one most beloved of tourists for its atmosphere and Chinese-style goods, is the centuries-old commercial district southwest of Qian Men. **Liulichang** is an almost too-quaint collection of art, book, tea, and antiques shops lining a polished-for-tourists, Old Beijing–style *hutong* running east-west 2 blocks south of the Heping Men (207) metro station. The street is good for window-shopping strolls and small purchases—like the unavoidable **chop** (*tuzhang;* stone or jade stamp), carved with your name—but beware large purchases: Almost everything here is fake and overpriced. In a similar setting but infinitely more raucous, **Da Zhalan** (pronounced Da Shilanr in the Beijing dialect) is the affordable alternative to Wangfujing Dajie; located in a pedestrian-only *hutong* 2 blocks due south of Qian

> **(Tips) Buying Pearls**
>
> Most of the pearls on sale at Hongqiao Market are genuine, although of too low a quality to be sold in Western jewelry shops, but there are some fakes floating around. To test if the pearls you want to buy are real, try any one of the following:
>
> - Nick the surface with a sharp blade (the color should be uniform within and without)
> - Rub the pearl across your teeth (this should make a grating sound)
> - Scrape the pearl on a piece of glass (real pearls leave a mark)
> - Pass it through a flame (fake pearls turn black, real ones don't)
>
> Strange as it may feel to do these tests, vendors are generally willing to let you carry them out and might even help, albeit in bemusement. If you'd rather not bother (and most don't), just assume the worst, shop for fun, and spend modestly.

Men, it is jammed on either side with cheap clothing outlets, cheap restaurants, and cheap luggage shops.

MARKETS

Although malls and shopping centers are becoming more popular, the majority of Beijing residents still shop in markets. Whether indoors or out, these markets are inexpensive, chaotic and, for the visitor, tremendously interesting. Payment is in cash, bargaining is universal, and pickpockets are plentiful.

Hongqiao Jimao Shichang 𝒜 An outlet for cheap jewelry better known as the **Pearl Market,** Hongqiao Market is just northeast of the Temple of Heaven at Hongqiao Lu 16. The first floor smells awful (there's a seafood market in the basement), but the upper floors have cheap Western clothing, luggage, old Chinese curios, and, of course, pearls (third floor). The prices here are good and the bargaining fierce. The market is open from 8:30am to 7pm.

Panjiayuan Jiuhuo Shichang 𝒜𝒜𝒜 Eureka! Also known as the Dirt or Ghost Market, this is the Chinese shopping experience of dreams: row upon crowded row of calligraphy, jewelry, ceramics, teapots, ethnic clothing, Buddha statues, paper lanterns, Cultural Revolution memorabilia, PLA belts, little wooden boxes, Ming- and Qing-style furniture, old pipes, opium scales, and painted human skulls. There are some real antiques scattered among the junk, but you'd have to be an expert to pick them out. Locals arrive Saturday and Sunday mornings at dawn or shortly afterward (hence the "Ghost" label) to find the best stuff; vendors start to leave around 4pm. Initial prices given to foreigners are always absurdly high—Mao clocks, for instance, should cost less than ¥40 ($5/£2.70) rather than the ¥400 ($50/£27) you'll likely be asked to pay. The market is located on the south side of Panjiayuan Lu, just inside the southeast corner of the Third Ring Road.

SILK ALLEY (XIUSHUI JIE) Herded indoors in 2005, Beijing's most famous market among foreign visitors is a crowded maze of stalls with a large selection of shoes and clothing (and very little silk). Vendors formerly enjoyed so much trade they could afford to be rude, but the knockoff boot is now firmly on the shopper's foot, as Silk Alley now sees only a fraction of the business of Yaxiu (see below). Most of the original vendors are gone, unwilling (or unable) to pay the new steep rental fees. Good riddance. Under no circumstances pay more than ¥150 ($20/£10) for a North Face (North Fake, the expats call it) jacket, ¥50 ($6/£3.35) for a business shirt, or ¥100 ($13/£6.70) for a pair of jeans. Stores that sport a red flag are purported to "subscribe to higher ethics." Spot the ethical pirates. Corner of Jianguo Men Wai Dajie and Xiushui Dong Jie, above the Yong'an Li metro stop (121, exit A). It's open from 9am to 9pm.

Yaxiu Fuzhuang Shichang ⊛   Whatever you may think of their business practices, Beijing's clothing vendors are nimble: Here you'll find refugees from two outdoor markets, Yabao Lu and Sanlitun. Opened in 2002, the market occupies the old Kylin Plaza building (Qilin Dasha). The fourth floor is a fine hunting ground for souvenirs and gifts—there are kites from Weifang in Shandong, calligraphy materials, army surplus gear, tea sets, and farmer's paintings from Xi'an. The basement and the first two floors house a predictable but comprehensive collection of imitation and pilfered brand-name clothing, shoes, and luggage. The market has been "discovered" by fashion-conscious locals, and starting prices are ridiculous. The market is west of Sanlitun Jiuba Jie, at Gongti Bei Lu 58 (© **010/6415-1726**), and is open from 9:30am to 9pm.

MORE MARKETS

Similar to the Yaxiu but more fashionable and located outdoors is **Nuren Jie (Girl Street),** next to the new embassy district outside the Northeast Third Ring Road (northeast of the Lufthansa Center). **Ri Tan Shangwu Lou** (© **010/8561-9556**), at Guanghua Lu 15A (just east of the south gate of Ri Tan Park), is not as cheap as Yaxiu, but is far less nasty. From outside, it looks like an uninspiring office building, inside is shopping nirvana: More than 70 shops stocking high-quality women's clothing, footwear, and accessories. There is a smattering of shops for the chaps, too. Open 10am until 8pm.

DEPARTMENT STORES

Friendship Store (Youyi Shangchang)   This is a dinosaur from the days when foreigners used a separate kind of money and couldn't shop anywhere else. Everything's here and everything's viciously overpriced. A good source of Western periodicals, the store is open from 9am to 8:30pm. Jianguo Men Dajie 17.

Xi Dan Baihuo Shangchang   Crowded and chaotic, this is an old-school four-story department store selling everything from cosmetics to appliances, with good deals on denim and shoes. Open 9am to 8pm. East side of Xi Dan Bei Dajie (north of Xi Dan metro stop).

MALLS & SHOPPING PLAZAS

Lufthansa Center (Yansha Youyi Shangchang)   Connected to the Kempinski Hotel, this is the most comprehensive but also most expensive shopping center in northeast Beijing (open 9am–10pm), with a range of upscale specialty shops, boutiques, restaurants, and international airline ticketing offices. Liangma Qiao Lu 50 (east side of the Northeast Third Ring Rd.).

Oriental Plaza (Dongfang Guangchang)   Asia's largest shopping/office/apartment/hotel complex covers 4 city blocks of prime real estate from Wangfujing Dajie to Dong Dan Bei Dajie. The two-story arcade has hip clothing stores such as Art of Shirts and Kookai; the Wangfujing Palaeolithic Museum; and another Ole supermarket. The

Grand Hyatt (p. 87) stands above all the consumption. Summer hours are from 9am to 10:30pm; winter 9am to 10pm. Dong Chang'an Dajie. Metro: Wangfujing (118).

The Place (Shimao Tianjie)   This new behemoth, marked by a huge outdoor screen playing clips of random fashion shows, sees plenty of fashionista traffic. Spanish retailer Zara chose to set up shop here; their arrival in Beijing was highly anticipated by locals and expats alike. Makeup gurus MAC also chose The Place for their flagship store. Other retailers like French Connection, Mango, and Adidas ensure this place is virtually bargain-hunter-free. Open 10am to 10pm. Guanghua Lu Jia 9. ℂ 010/ 8595-1755.

Shin Kong Place (Xin Guang Tiandi)   Shin Kong Place sets the gold standard in Beijing luxury shopping. Opened in 2007, this indoor mall has all the labels that break the bank: Coach, Gucci, Salvatore Ferragamo, and Marc Jacobs, as well as high-end but more affordable retailers like Anya Hindmarch, Juicy Couture, Diesel, and Club Monaco. Open 10am to 10pm. Jianguo Lu 87, Chaoyang Qu. ℂ 010/6530-5888. Metro: Dawang Lu.

8 Beijing After Dark

It wasn't so long ago that the after-dark options available to foreigners in Beijing were limited to a short list of tourist-approved activities: Beijing opera, acrobatics, and wandering listlessly around the hotel in search of a drink to make sleep come faster. Now opera and acrobatics are still available, but in more interesting venues, and to them have been added a range of other worthwhile cultural events: teahouse theater, puppet shows, traditional music concerts, and even the occasional subtitled film. Beyond such edification, Beijing has China's most diverse stable of bars, clubs, discos, and cafes, cheaper and often more interesting than those of Hong Kong or Shanghai. For locations, see the map on p. 88.

PERFORMING ARTS
BEIJING OPERA

A relatively young opera form dating from only 300 years to the early Qing dynasty, Beijing Opera (Jingju) dazzles as much as it grates. Performances are loud and long, with dialogue sung on a screeching five-note scale and accompanied by a cacophony of gongs, cymbals, drums, and strings. This leaves most first-timers exhausted, but the exquisite costumes, elaborate face paint, and martial arts–inspired movements ultimately make it worthwhile. Several theaters now offer shortened programs more amenable to the foreign attention span, sometimes with English subtitles and plot summaries.

Most tourists on tours are taken to the bland, cinema-style **Liyuan Theater (Liyuan Juchang)** inside the Qian Men Hotel, where nightly performances at 7:30pm cost ¥80 to ¥480 ($11–$64/£5.35–£32). The venues below offer essentially the same performances in much better traditional settings.

Huguang Guild House (Huguang Huiguan Xilou)   This combination museum-theater was originally built in 1807. The theater is a riot of color, with a beautifully adorned traditional stage and gallery seating. It is currently Beijing's best opera venue. Nightly performances take place at 7:30pm. Hufang Lu 3, at intersection with Luomashi Dajie. ℂ 010/6351-8284. Tickets ¥150–¥580 ($20–$77). Metro: Heping Men (207, exit D1); walk south 10 min.

Zhengyici Xilou   Rumors that this 300-year-old theater had gone under are untrue, but funding problems and its position at the center of a massive urban reconstruction project have limited the number of performances. The theater is similar to the Huguang Guild House but less ostentatious, with a more local feel. Shows are held most nights at 7:30pm (call to check). This is the first choice of venue for Beijing Opera when it's open. Pray it survives. Qian Men Xi Heyan Jie 220 (walk south of the Heping Men Quanjude, take 1st left). © 010/8315-1650. Tickets ¥150–¥280 ($2–$37/£1–£19). Metro: Heping Men (207, exit C2).

ACROBATICS

China's acrobats are justifiably famous, and probably just a little bit insane. This was the only traditional Chinese art form to receive Mao's explicit approval (back flips, apparently, don't count as counterrevolution). Not culturally stimulating, it's highly recommended nonetheless.

The city's best acrobatics venue is the **Wansheng Juchang** on the north side of Bei Wei Lu, just off Qian Men Dajie (west side of the Temple of Heaven; © 010/6303-7449). The fairly famous Beijing Acrobatics Troupe performs nightly shows here at 5:30pm and 7:15pm. Tickets cost ¥100 to ¥380 ($13–$51/£6.70–£25). The acrobats of **Chaoyang Juchang** (© 010/6507-2421) at Dong San Huan Bei Lu 36 are slightly clumsier. Nightly shows at 7:15pm cost ¥120 to ¥300 ($16–$40/£8–£20).

TEAHOUSE THEATER

Snippets of Beijing opera, cross-talk (stand-up) comedy, acrobatics, traditional music, singing, and dancing flow across the stage as you sip tea and nibble snacks. If you don't have time to see these kinds of performances individually, the teahouse is a perfect solution.

Lao She Teahouse (Lao She Chaguan)   Performances change nightly at this somewhat garishly decorated teahouse but always include opera and acrobatics. It pays to buy the more expensive tickets, as rear views are obscured. Nightly shows take place at 7:50pm. Qianmen Xi Dajie 3, west of Qian Men on street's south side. © 010/6303-6830. Tickets ¥40–¥130 ($5.35–$17/£2.65–£8.50).

PUPPETS

Puppet shows *(mu'ou xi)* have been performed in China since the Han dynasty (206 B.C.–A.D. 220). Most theatrical performances, including weekend matinees, are held at the **China Puppet Art Theater (Zhongguo Mu'ou Juyuan)**, in Anhua Xili near the North Third Ring Road (© 010/6424-3698). Tickets cost ¥100 to ¥220 ($13–$29/£6.70–£15).

SMALL LIVE-MUSIC VENUES

CD Jazz Cafe (Sendi Jueshi)   After much upheaval, this amalgamation of CD Cafe and the short-lived Treelounge is the best place to see local jazz and blues acts in Beijing. If it's a special act, get there early. Open 4pm until very late. Dong San Huan, south of the Agricultural Exhibition Center (Nongzhan Guan) main gate (down small path behind trees that line sidewalk). © 010/6506-8288. Cover ¥30 ($4/£2).

MAO Livehouse   This newly opened live music venue is backed by Japanese label Bad News, home of local punk band Brain Failure. Plenty of aspiring punk rockers are loyal fans of both the band and the bar. The exterior looks like a rusty, unfinished steel warehouse. Inside, the decor is an eclectic mix of chairs and tables sandwiched between black walls. 111 Guloudajie. © 010/6402-5080.

New Get Lucky Bar (Xin Haoyun Jiuba) This odd bar is the best venue to take in one of Beijing's much-documented punk shows, often featuring the talents of Brain Failure and Hanging on the Box. If you value your eardrums, don't get too close to the speakers. In Nuren Jie area, inside Oriental Qicai World. (*C*) 010/8448-3335. Shows ¥20–¥30 ($3–$4/£1.50–£2).

Sanwei Bookstore (Sanwei Shuwu) This tiny bookshop has a teahouse upstairs that hosts intimate concerts on the weekends. On Friday it's jazz and on Saturday it's classical Chinese, usually with a minority twist. Tea and snacks, too. Performances are held at 8:30pm. Fuxing Men Nei Dajie 60, opposite the Minorities Palace (Minzu Gong). (*C*) 010/6601-3204. Tickets ¥30 ($4/£2).

The Star Live Cool musicians (Ziggy Marley, The Roots, Sonic Youth) are finally coming to Beijing, and they seem to enjoy playing at Star Live. This place is nothing like its thumping, downstairs neighbor Tango; it's small and intimate and has excellent acoustics. Ticket prices depend on the artist; expect to pay between ¥100 and ¥300 ($13–$40/£6.50–£20). 3/F,Tango, 70 Heping Xijie (50m/164 ft. north of subway station). (*C*) 010/6425-5166. www.thestarlive.com. Metro: Yongheegong.

Yu Gong Yi Shan This wonderful performance space is the best live music venue in Beijing, period. The sound isn't perfect, it can get plenty stuffy in summer, and its location in the middle of a parking lot–cum–bus depot lends it a certain seediness, but the owners have a knack for turning up the best local acts. Run by the owners of the now defunct Loup Chante, the diverse lineup—from punk to Mongolian mouth music—means you can visit night after night. It's open from 2pm to 2am. Zhangzizhong Lu, east of Lotus Lane. (*C*) 010/6415-0687. Cover varies for performances.

OTHER PERFORMING-ARTS VENUES

Beijing hosts a growing number of international music and theater events every year, and its own increasingly respectable troupes—including the Beijing Symphony Orchestra—give frequent performances. Among the most popular venues for this sort of thing is the **Beijing Concert Hall (Beijing Yinyue Ting;** (*C*) 010/6605-5812), at Bei Xinhua Jie in Liubukou (Xuanwu District). The **Poly Theater (Baoli Dasha Guoji Juyuan;** (*C*) 010/6506-5343), in the Poly Plaza complex on the East Third Ring Road (northeast exit of Dong Si Shi Tiao metro station), also hosts many large-scale performances, including the occasional revolutionary ballet. For information on other venues and the shows they're hosting, check one of the expatriate magazines (see "Visitor Information," earlier in this chapter).

BARS & CLUBS

Beijing's oldest and still most popular drinking district is **Sanlitun.** The name comes from Sanlitun Lu, a north-south strip of drinking establishments east of the Workers' Stadium between the East Second and Third ring roads that at one time contained practically all of the city's bars. Now known as North Bar Street (Sanlitun Jiuba Jie), it has been joined by other bars in the Xingfu Cun area to the west, and scattered around the stadium area. Bars here are rowdy and raunchy, and are packed to overflowing on weekends.

Popular clubs in this district include the very proud **Destination (Mudidi),** located in an alley south of the west gate of the Workers' Stadium ((*C*) 010/6416-1077 or 010/6417-7791); and **The Den (Dunhuang;** (*C*) 010/6592-6290), at the intersection of Gongti Dong Lu 4A, next to the City Hotel (Chengshi Binguan). Bars include **The**

Tree (Yinbi de Shu), with the city's best selection of Belgian beer, located west of North Bar Street, behind the eminently missable Poachers (© **010/6415-1954**); and the classy **Q Bar,** which produces the city's finest martinis, found on Nan Sanlitun Luon on the east side of the street (© **010/6595-9239**).

Similar bars surround the south and west gates of **Chaoyang Gongyuan** (park) to the east, an area the government has tried to promote as the new drinking district because it has fewer residential buildings. Worth checking out are **Souk** (© **010/6506-7309**), with excellent Middle Eastern cuisine and fruity hookas to puff on, located just behind Annie's Cafe; and the seedy **World of Suzie Wong (Suxi Huang),** the see-and-be-seen venue for nouveau riche Chinese and new expatriates. It's located just south of the west gate of Chaoyang Park (© **010/6593-6049**).

The fastest-growing spot for late-night drinking is the **Back Lakes (Shicha Hai or Hou Hai),** a previously serene spot with a few discreetly fashionable bars which now threatens to explode into a riot of hip. Neon has become a common sight, and several dance clubs are in the works, but for now this remains the finest place in the city for a quiet drink. Good bars here include supercool **Bed (Chuang Ba),** where you can enjoy an excellent caipirinha or mojito in a delightful courtyard setting, at Zhangwang Hutong 17, northwest of the Drum Tower (© **010/8400-1554**); and **Pass-by Bar (Guoke Jiuba),** which also serves passable Italian food, at Nan Luogu Xiang 108 (alley to the left/west of the Muslim restaurant on the north side of Ping'an Dadao; walk north 150m/492 ft.; © **010/8403-8004**). Finally, there is **Haidian,** the city's university district to the northwest. Bars and clubs are congregated around gates of several universities and cater to a crowd of film students, English-language majors, and aspiring writers.

Outside of the districts, one club worth checking out is **Banana (Banana),** Jianguo Men Wai Dajie 22, in front of Scitech Hotel (© **010/6528-3636**).

GAY & LESBIAN BARS

Beijing is a quiet scene for lesbians, somewhat less so for gay men. The best gay club in Beijing is **Destination (Mudidi;** © **010/6551-5138**) at Gongti Xi Lu 7, south of the Worker's Stadium west gate, where the crowd revels and the beats are right. **On/Off** (Shang Xia Xian; © **010/6415-8083**), at Xingfu Yi Cun Xi Li 5, is one of Beijing's longest standing "alternative" venues. Things have turned a tad seedy in recent times, but the crowds still flock to this venue, which now boasts a bar, a restaurant, and even an Internet cafe. For the gals, it's a slow-developing scene: Aside from Thursday nights at Destination, try the Feng Bar, just east of the south gate of the Worker's Stadium on Saturday nights.

CAFES & TEAHOUSES

Starbucks arrived at the end of the 1990s and quickly spread to all the places Beijing's wealthy and/or hip congregate, including next to the Friendship Store, in the China World Trade Center, at the Oriental Plaza and many other locations. More interesting alternatives include, **Tasty Taste (Taidi Daisi)** at Gongti Bei Men on the southwest corner of Gongti Bei Lu and Gongti Xi Lu, which delivers the finest coffee in town and a fine cheesecake to go with it (© **010/6551-1822**); or the more stylishly decorated **Cafe de Niro (Nilou Kafei)** at Sanlitun Jiuba Bei Jie Tongli Yi Ceng, just west of Sanlitun North Bar Street (and north of Aperitivo), which also has wireless Internet and reasonably priced set lunches (© **010/6416-9400**). The best spot to curl up with a book for the afternoon is **The Bookworm,** whose library of 6,000 English-language books was relocating to new premises just east of Nan Sanlitun Lu at press time

(© **010/6586-9507**). **Sculpting in Time (Diaoke Shiguang),** Beijing's original cafe/ film establishment, is now at the Beijing Institute of Technology (Weigongcun Xi Kou 7 [Ligong Daxue Nan Men]; © **010/6894-6825;** 9am–1am), just to the left of the university's south gate. The coffee shop is fast on the rise, and has a total of seven branches throughout the city. All serve adequate coffee and Western snacks, and have wireless Internet. **The Teahouse of Family Fu (Cha Jia Fu),** located at Hou Hai Nan An, next to Kong Yiji (© **010/6616-0725**), is a unique and quiet teahouse, with semiprivate rooms. It's open from 11am to midnight.

9 Chengde ★★

Hebei Province, 233km (146 miles) NE of Beijing

If you can do only one overnight side trip from Beijing, make it Chengde—the summer camp of the Qing emperors. Here, in a walled enclosure containing numerous palaces, pavilions, and pagodas as well as a vast hunting park, they escaped Beijing's blazing summer temperatures, entertained delegations from home and abroad, and practiced the mounted military skills which had originally gained them their empire. The design of the resort, built between 1703 and 1794, was shaped by its varied diplomatic functions. Some buildings are plain and undecorated to show visiting tribesmen that the emperors had not lost touch with their roots or been too softened by luxury; others were copies of some of China's most famous and elegant buildings; and some were giant edifices with hints of minority architecture, intended both to show the emperor's sympathy for the traditions of tributary and border-dwelling peoples, and to overawe their emissaries.

In 1794 Britain's Lord Macartney arrived on a mission from George III, and not finding the Qianlong emperor at home in Beijing, followed him up to Chengde. He was impressed by the resort's vast scale, and was shown around by people who anticipated modern guides' hyperbole by telling him that the gilded bronze roof tiles of the Potala Temple were of solid gold.

The Jiaqing emperor died here in 1820, as did the Xianfeng emperor in 1861, having signed the "unequal" treaties which marked the close of the Second Opium War. The place came to be viewed as unlucky, and was already decaying by the fall of the Qing in 1911. But the **Mountain Retreat for Escaping the Heat,** along with the remaining **Eight Outer Temples** around its perimeter, still form one of the greatest concentrations of ancient buildings in China. It's an 18th-century version of a "Splendid China" theme park (as seen in Florida and Shenzhen), but with oversize buildings rather than the miniatures offered there.

Ordinary Beijingren now follow imperial tradition by flocking here to escape the baking summer heat. You can hurry around the main sights by spending 1 night here, but you might want to spend 2.

ESSENTIALS

GETTING THERE   Chengde has no airport, and although it's an easy side trip from Beijing, it's not well connected to anywhere else except the Northeast. A convenient morning all-seater **train** from Beijing Zhan, the N211, departs at 7:16am, arriving in Chengde at 11:15am. It returns to Beijing as the N212, leaving Chengde at 2:40pm, arriving in Beijing at 6:38pm. Soft seat costs ¥61 ($7.60/£4.10), hard seat ¥41 ($5.10/£2.75). The railway station is just south of the city center, and bus no. 5 from outside to your right runs to several hotels and to the Mountain Resort. The ticket office (up the stairs and to the right) is open from 5am to 10:30pm with brief breaks. There are also limited services to Shenyang and (twice daily at 6:50am and 10:30pm) Shijiazhuang (one service only at 10:20pm).

The soft-seat waiting room is through a door at the far left-hand end of the main hall as you enter, while luggage storage is on the right-hand side. On the train both to and from Beijing, enterprising staff sell tea for ¥3 (40¢/20p), instant coffee for ¥5 (65¢/35p), maps, and hotel reservations (do *not* book with them). About 1¼ hours after you leave Beijing, you'll see a crumbling stretch of the Great Wall.

At least until construction of a new road/rail interchange station at Dongzhi Men is complete, **bus** departures for Chengde from Beijing are more frequent from Liu Li Qiao Changtu Qiche Keyun Zhan (© 010/8383-1717 or 010/8383-1720, southwest of the Liu Li Qiao bridge). The 233km (144-mile) trip costs ¥60 ($8/£4) for an Iveco or similar, with departures about every 20 minutes from 5:40am to 6:40pm. The current journey takes about 3½ hours, but a new highway (due for completion by the time you read this) should cut journey times to around 2½ hours, while increasing prices. At the moment it's possible to alight and see the Great Wall at Jinshanling en route, and subsequently flag down a passing bus to finish the trip. Express buses from Beijing run to and from the forecourt of Chengde railway station. Escape the pestering of touts by dodging into a branch of the Sichuan restaurant Dongpo Fanzhuang, opposite and to the left (south) where you alight, and if you're ready for a quick lunch, have it here. The main long-distance bus station has been demolished to make way for an extension of the Sheng Hua Dajiudian, and most buses now depart from the **Qiche Dong Zhan** (© 0314/212-3588), a ¥20 ($2.70/£1.30) taxi ride south, or take bus no. 118, which passes Yingzi Dajie and the Mountain Resort. The ticket office is open from 5:30am to 5pm. There are two services to Shijiazhuang (11am and 2pm; 8 hr.; ¥121/$16/£8.10), with seven buses connecting with Qinhuangdao (6:30am, 7:30am, 8:05am, 8:30am, 10am, 1pm, and 5pm; 6 hr.; ¥81/$11/£5.40). Buses to Beijing run every 20 minutes, but it's easier to flag an Iveco from outside the railway station.

GETTING AROUND   **Taxi** meters are generally not used. The fare is ¥5 (65¢/35p) in town, or ¥10 ($1.35/70p) to the outer temples. If the meter is started, ¥5 (65¢/35p) flagfall includes 1km; then ¥1.40 (20¢/10p) per kilometer, jumping 50% after 8km (5 miles). **Buses** usually charge ¥1 (15¢/5p).

VISITOR INFORMATION   For tourist complaints, call © 0341/202-4549.

FAST FACTS

Banks, Foreign Exchange & ATMs   The main foreign exchange branch of the **Bank of China** (open 8am–5:30pm; to 6pm in summer) is at the junction of Dong Dajie and Lizheng Men Dajie. Another convenient branch is at Lizheng Men Dajie 19, just east of the Mountain Villa Hotel. Both have ATMs that accept foreign cards, as does a branch on the corner of Nan Yingzi Dajie and Xinhua Lu.

Internet Access   Internet cafes are few and mostly far from the usual visitor areas. Follow Nan Yingzi Dajie south until you cross the railway line, turn right into Shanxi Ying to find a cluster of Internet bars (open 8am–midnight) on the first corner, which charge ¥1.50 (20¢/10p) per hour.

Post Office   The post office is on Yingzi Dajie at its junction with Dong Dajie. It's open from 8am to 5:30pm (to 5pm in winter).

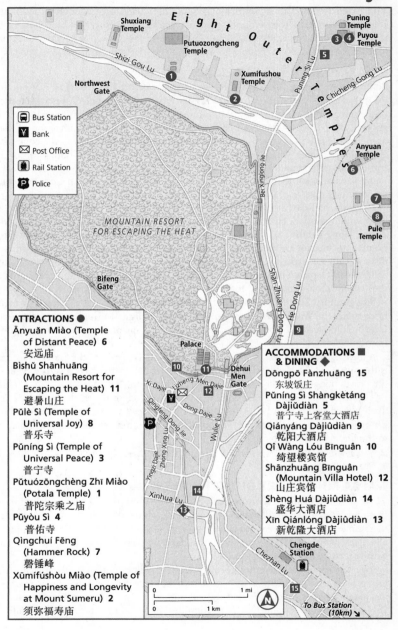

Shuxiang Temple

Eight Outer Temples

Puning Temple

Putuozongcheng Temple

Puyou Temple

Shizi Gou Lu

3 **4**

5

Puning Si Lu

Chicheng Gong Lu

Northwest Gate

Xumifushou Temple

1

2

Bei Xinglong Jie

Anyuan Temple

6

🚌 Bus Station

¥ Bank

✉ Post Office

🚉 Rail Station

🅿 Police

7

8

Pule Temple

MOUNTAIN RESORT FOR ESCAPING THE HEAT

Shan Zhuang Dong Lu

He Dong Lu

Bifeng Gate

9

ATTRACTIONS ●

Ānyuǎn Miào (Temple of Distant Peace) **6**
安远庙

Bìshǔ Shānhuāng (Mountain Resort for Escaping the Heat) **11**
避暑山庄

Pǔlè Sì (Temple of Universal Joy) **8**
普乐寺

Pǔníng Sì (Temple of Universal Peace) **3**
普宁寺

Pǔtuózōngchèng Zhī Miào (Potala Temple) **1**
普陀宗乘之庙

Pǔyòu Sì **4**
普佑寺

Qìngchuí Fēng (Hammer Rock) **7**
磬锤峰

Xūmífúshòu Miào (Temple of Happiness and Longevity at Mount Sumeru) **2**
须弥福寿庙

Palace

10 **11**

Dehui Men Gate

Xi-Dajie

Lizheng Men Dajie

12

Qingfeng Dong Jie

Dong Dajie

¥

✉

🅿

Yingzi Dajie

Zhong Xing Lu

Wulie Lu

Xinhua Lu

14

13

ACCOMMODATIONS ■ & DINING ◆

Dōngpō Fànzhuāng **15**
东坡饭庄

Pǔníng Sì Shàngkètáng Dàjiǔdiàn **5**
普宁寺上客堂大酒店

Qiányáng Dàjiǔdiàn **9**
乾阳大酒店

Qǐ Wàng Lóu Bīnguǎn **10**
绮望楼宾馆

Shānzhuāng Bīnguǎn (Mountain Villa Hotel) **12**
山庄宾馆

Shèng Huá Dàjiǔdiàn **14**
盛华大酒店

Xīn Qiánlóng Dàjiǔdiàn **13**
新乾隆大酒店

Chengde Station

Chezhan Lu

15

0 ___ 1 mi
0 ___ 1 km

N

To Bus Station (10km) ↘

Visa Extensions   Walking south along Nan Yingzi Dajie, turn right after the Xinhua Bookstore into Xiao Tong Gou Jie, then take the first left. Next to a branch of CITS you'll find a sign that reads ALIENS EXIT-ENTRY DEPARTMENT. Open Monday to Friday 8:30am to noon; 2:30 to 5:30pm in summer (1:30–5:30pm in winter).

RELAXING WITH THE EMPERORS

Bishu Shanzhuang (Mountain Resort for Escaping the Heat) ⟨ℛ   While the "Winter Palace," as Beijing's Forbidden City was sometimes called, was the creation of the indigenous Ming dynasty, the summer palace at Chengde was entirely the creation of the Manchu Qing, and lay beyond the Great Wall in the direction of their homelands. Here the emperor and the Manchu nobility would play at the equestrian and military talents, which had won them China in the first place, both with formal contests in archery and with hunting in the well-stocked park. The lakes and their many pavilions, stuffed with treasures, provided the emperor and his consorts with more refined diversions.

There's a half-day of wandering here, although many of the buildings shown as lying within the park have long since vanished. The most important remaining is the **Zheng Gong (Main Palace).** The message here is one of simplicity and frugality (the beams and columns are very plain, although actually made of hardwoods brought long distances at great expense), with a pleasing elegance in great contrast to the usual Qing gaudiness. The palace now serves as a museum, displaying ancient military equipment in the front rooms and period furnishings and antiquities at the rear.

Straight north, up the west side of lakes dotted with pavilions and crossed by many bridges, lies the **Wenjin Ge (Pavilion of Literary Delight),** a ripple-roofed southern-style building reached through a rockery, which is a copy of a famous library building from Ningbo.

A little farther northeast, the handsome **Liu He Ta (Pagoda of the Six Harmonies)** is the most striking building in the park. Its nine brick stories have green- or yellow-tiled eaves hung with bells and topped by a golden knob.

The pagoda is near the east entrance of the park, close to which the retired and unemployed can be found enjoying a game of croquet. If you've already examined the gaudy pavilions around the lakes, it's possible to leave this way to walk or catch a bus to the Eight Outer Temples.

Main entrance (Zheng Men) in Lizheng Men Dajie. ⓒ 0314/207-6089. Admission ¥90 ($12/£6), ¥60 ($8/£4) in winter. 6am–8pm (to 6pm in winter).

WAI BA MIAO (EIGHT OUTER TEMPLES) ⟨ℛ⟩⟨ℛ⟩

There were originally 12 temples, built between 1713 and 1780, and not all of those that remain are open to the public. Summer hours are May 1 to October 15; outside these times, some lesser temples may be shut. Several temples have features unique to Chengde. Most are extremely grand and suitably impressive (their purpose, after all), with successive halls on rising ground.

Tip: Puning Si and the other northern temples are on morning itineraries for tour groups, followed by Pule Si and the eastern temples in the afternoon. If you're traveling independently, work the other way around. You can also buy a *tao piao* for ¥80 ($11/£5.35), which includes entry to Xumifushou Miao, the Potala Temple, Pule Si, and Anyuan Miao.

Bus no. 118, from Yingzi Dajie or the Mountain Resort main entrance, will take you to the northern group of temples.

Xumifushou Miao (Temple of Happiness and Longevity at Mount Sumeru)

Partly inspired by Tashilhunpo in Tibet (p. 794), this temple was constructed to make the Panchen Lama, number two in the Tibetan religious hierarchy, feel at home during a visit in 1780.

Shizi Gou Lu. © 0314/216-2972. Admission: summer ¥30 ($4/£2), winter ¥20 ($2.70/£1.30). 8am–6pm (8:30am–4:30pm in winter). Bus: no. 118 to Xumifushou Zhi Miao.

Putuozongcheng Zhi Miao (Potala Temple)

Five minutes' walk west, the Potala Temple, its tapering windows and slab-sided walls obviously influenced by Tibet, is in no way "a copy of the Potala Temple in Lhasa" (p. 785), as local guides like to say. Many windows are blind, and several outbuildings are solid, just intended to add to the massy splendor of the whole. Items on display in the surrounding galleries include two nine-story sandalwood pagodas climbing through holes cut in the floors, young girls' skulls fused with silver and once used as drinking vessels, and anatomically detailed esoteric statuary of sexual acts.

Shizi Gou Lu. © 0314/216-3072. Admission: summer ¥40 ($5.35/£2.70), winter ¥30 ($4/£2). 8am–6pm (8:30am–5pm in winter). Bus: no. 118 to Putuozongcheng Zhi Miao.

Puning Si (Temple of Universal Peace)

The main Hall of Mahayana is impressive—story upon story of red walls and yellow roofs, topped with a gold knob surrounded by four mini-pagoda-like points. More impressive still is its contents, a giant copper-colored wooden Guanyin figure more than 22m (73 ft.) high, the largest of its kind in the world. It's possible to climb three levels of interior galleries to look the figure in the eye, as she sits in dusty gloom. While other sights in Chengde are managed by the sleepy local tourism bureau, this temple is run by an entrepreneurial group of monks: The temple now sports a hotel (see below) and a tacky but entertaining re-creation of a Qing market, and offers an evening show promising blessings and exorcisms by "real Tibetan lamas."

Off Puning Si Lu. © 0314/205-8203. Admission ¥50 ($6.70/£3.30), ¥10 ($1.35/65p) to climb the Hall of Mahayana. 8am–5:30pm (8:30am–4:30pm in winter). Bus: no. 6 or 118 to Puning Si.

Puyou Si

Next door to Puning Si, this temple was closed for renovations when I last visited. The point of entering is to see the remainder of a collection of statues of the 500 arhats (the first followers of the Sakyamuni Buddha). Many of these were destroyed in 1937 during the Japanese occupation, but the remainder have a lively jollity, and are hung with scarves placed by respectful devotees.

© 0314/216-0935. Admission ¥20 ($2.70/£1.30). 8am–5:30pm (8:30am–4:30pm in winter).

Pule Si (Temple of Universal Joy)

Tibetan advisors were employed in the design of this temple, built to receive annual tributary visits from defeated Mongol tribes. But the most striking element is the copy at the rear of the circular Hall of Prayer for Good Harvests from the Temple of Heaven. Shady benches around the quiet courtyards make perfect picnic stops.

Off Hedong Lu. © 0314/205-7557. Admission: summer ¥30 ($4/£2), winter ¥20 ($2.70/£1.30). 8am–6pm (to 5pm in winter). Bus: no. 10 from Wulie Lu to terminus. Taxi: a short ride from Puning Si.

Qingchui Feng (Hammer Rock)

Bus no. 10's terminus is actually the cableway to Hammer Rock. The characters specifically mean a kind of hammer for striking a Buddhist musical instrument, but the shape of this clublike column will inevitably remind all who see it of something completely different. It reminds the Chinese of that, too—they're just being polite. Pleasant strolls across the hills and sweeping views of the valley await those who ascend.

© **0314/205-7135.** Admission ¥25 ($3.35/£1.70). 24 hr. Cable car ¥27 ($3.60/£1.80) one-way; ¥42 ($5.60/£2.80) round-trip. Runs Apr 1–Oct 30, 7:30am–5:30pm.

Anyuan Miao (Temple of Distant Peace)   Built in 1764, this is another example of architectural diplomacy, built in imitation of a temple (now long-vanished) in Yining on China's remote western borders (p. 332) to please Mongol tribes that were resettled around Chengde. You'll almost certainly be the only visitor.

© **0314/205-7809.** Admission ¥15 ($2/£1). Summer only: 8am–5pm. A 15-min. walk north of Pule Si.

SHOPPING

A lively **market** takes over the upper part of Yingzi Dajie at night, interesting for its color rather than for what's on sale. The street also has several department stores with ground-floor supermarkets. Toward the post office there's a couple of bakeries where you can pick up snacks for the onward journey.

WHERE TO STAY

From the first week of May to the first week of October the town is busy, weekends particularly so, but only during the weeklong national holidays should it be difficult to find a room. Otherwise, the town has an excess of accommodations and, even in peak season, all hotels will have 20% discounts, rising to as much as 70% in the off season for the gently persuasive bargainer who just shows up. A 50% discount is taken for granted; you work down from there.

EXPENSIVE

Puning Si Shangketang Dajiudian ★★ *Finds*   Run by the market-savvy monks of Puning Si, this newly opened hotel offers cozy accommodations within the west wing of the temple. Rooms are tastefully decorated with dark wood furniture and handmade paper lamps and are set around eight tranquil courtyards, which boast rock gardens and ponds. Buddhist touches are in evidence: There's a large (if overpriced) vegetarian selection in the main restaurant, the proscription against soft beds is enforced, and there's little chance of sleeping in—the temple bells peal at 7:30am.

Puning Si. © **0314/205-8888.** 100 units. ¥580 ($77/£39) standard room. 50% summer discounts offered. No credit cards. **Amenities:** 2 restaurants; indoor pool; exercise room; large game room; tour desk; business center; next-day laundry. *In room:* A/C, TV, fridge, safe.

Sheng Hua Dajiudian   Opened in 2003, the four-star Sheng Hua is Chengde's best hotel in terms of furnishings. Rooms are spacious; luxury twin (standard) rooms even come equipped with their own computer. Bathrooms are well outfitted and come with elaborate massage-jet showers. A new wing, located on the site of the old bus station, opened in 2006. It houses a pool and fitness center. Staff is helpful with inquiries, and speaks English and French.

Wulie Lu 22. © **0314/227-1188.** Fax 0314/227-1112. 114 units. ¥700–¥980 ($93–$131/£47–£65) standard room; ¥1,500–¥5,800 ($200–$773/£100–£387) suite. 30%–40% summer discounts offered. AE, MC, V. **Amenities:** 2 restaurants; teahouse; business center (Internet access ¥35/$4.70/£2.35 per hour); forex; next-day laundry/dry cleaning. *In room:* A/C, TV, broadband Internet access, fridge, hair dryer, safe.

MODERATE

Qi Wang Lou Binguan ★   Once good enough for the Qianlong emperor, it's now good enough for party luminaries, though it's less expensive than this would suggest.

Peacocks roam the gardens of this courtyard-style hotel, doubtless more relaxed than they were during Qianlong's time. Standard hotel interiors have been recently renovated, and there are yet higher standards in a new building, opened in 2004. Inexpensive bike rental is offered, an excellent way to explore the town. Avoid the diabolical Western breakfast.

Bi Feng Men Dong Lu 1 (a narrow street running up the west side of the park). (✆ 0314/202-4385. Fax 0314/ 202-1904. 84 units. ¥500–¥800 ($67–$107/£33–£53) standard room; from ¥400 ($53/£27) 3-bed basement room in new building; ¥1,000–¥6,000 ($133–$800/£67–£400) suite. Typical 50% discount off season. AE, MC, V. Bus: no. 5 from railway station to Bishu Shanzhuang. **Amenities:** Restaurant; bar; teahouse; bike rental ¥50 ($6.70/£3.35) per day. In room: A/C, TV.

Shanzhuang Binguan (Mountain Villa Hotel)   Once the only hotel in town, this six-building monster directly opposite the Mountain Resort underwent a full renovation, which was completed in 2005. Happily, the hotel maintained a variety of simpler, cheaper rooms with common bathrooms for budget travelers. Usually these longer-standing hotels should be your last choice, but here a real effort has been made to stay in competition with the newer hotels.

Xiao Nan Men Jie 11 (opposite main entrance to Mountain Resort). (✆ 0314/209-1188. Fax 0314/203-4143. mvhotel@ cs-user.he.cninfo.net. 370 units. ¥270 ($36/£18) triple, ¥280 ($37/£19) single, both with common bathroom; ¥580– ¥680 ($77–$91/£39–£45) standard room; ¥880–¥2,000 ($117–$267/£59–£133) suite. AE, DC, MC, V. Bus: no. 5 from railway station to Bishu Shanzhuang. **Amenities:** 2 restaurants; fitness room; tour desk; bike rental ¥60 ($8/£4) per day; business center (Internet access ¥10/$1.35/70p per hour); forex. In room: A/C, TV, broadband Internet access on request, hair dryer, safe.

WHERE TO DINE

The **night market** on Yingzi Dajie runs through the heart of town. Stalls sell kabobs for ¥1 (15¢/5p) and a wide assortment of other Chinese fast food, eaten at tables behind each stall.

As befits a former hunting ground, Chengde's specialty is game. The town is almost like a remote outpost of Guangdong, of whose residents other Chinese say, "They eat anything with legs except a table, and anything with wings except an airplane." Donkey, dog, and scorpion are on menus. But so are deer, *shan ji* ("mountain chicken"— pheasant), and wild boar—often as unfamiliar ingredients cooked in familiar styles. Stir-frying makes venison tough, but wild boar softens up nicely while retaining its gamey flavor.

The best restaurants are in larger hotels such as the **Qianyang Dajiudian.** Try *lurou chao zhenmo* (venison stir-fried with hazel mushrooms) and *quechao shanji pian* ("Sparrow's nest" pheasant slices). The **Xin Qianlong Dajiudian,** just south of the Sheng Hua Dajiudian on Xinhua Lu (✆ 0314/207-2222), open from 11am to 9pm, has attentive service, good portions, and a picture menu. Plump dumplings stuffed with donkey meat and onions are called *lurou dacong shuijiao*; 200 grams or four *liang* (*si liang*) should be enough per person. *Cong shao yezhurou* (wild boar cooked with onions) and *zhenmo shanji ding* (nuggets of pheasant with local mushrooms) are both good. As long as you don't venture into scorpion or roe deer backbone marrow, a meal costs around ¥80 ($11/£5.35) for two. There's an older branch at Zhong Xing Lu 2. **Dongpo Fanzhuang** offers authentic Sichuan cuisine, and now runs four outlets, all staffed with natives of Chengdu. Convenient branches are located opposite the railway station and at Xiao Nan Men (✆ 0314/210-6315), a 5-minute walk east from the main entrance to the Mountain Resort. Open 9am to 10pm, no English menu, but the duty manager will do his best to translate for you.

10 Shanhaiguan ⍟

Hebei Province, on the Bo Hai coast, 439km (274 miles) E of Beijing

Eventually the Great Wall gives up its mad zigzagging from high point to high point and plunges spectacularly down a mountainside to run across a small plain and into the sea. On its way it briefly doubles as the eastern city wall of the garrison town of Shanhaiguan (Pass Between Mountains and Sea), built during the Ming dynasty to prevent the easy passage of mounted invaders from the Northeast.

The Wall was never an effective defense mechanism, and Shanhaiguan became irrelevant after 1644 when, following the overthrow of the Ming dynasty by peasant rebellions, the dismayed defenders here allowed Qing forces through. Once the enemy was within the gates, the Wall became pointless, lying as it did within Qing territory, and it was allowed to fall into ruin until the imperatives of tourism rebuilt parts of it.

Each year large quantities of material are still carted away for incorporation in domestic buildings, and local governments breach the Wall when it suits them. At Shanhaiguan a local vegetable wholesaler was made to rebuild a section of the Wall when he pulled it down to expand his warehouse. The local government then plowed a new expressway straight through it and permitted the display of advertising on its side, to ". . . rejuvenate the national industry that will face increased competition after China's entry into the World Trade Organization," according to *China Daily*.

Entrance prices to attractions in Shanhaiguan are in constant flux, and off season may be as low as half the high-season rates quoted here, although that fact isn't often posted. Whatever the season, always ask for a discount.

ESSENTIALS

GETTING THERE   Qinhuangdao **airport** is just outside town to the south, reached by taxi, with infrequent flights from Taiyuan, Harbin, Changchun, Dalian, and Shanghai. **Train** services from major cities in the Northeast pass through Shanhaiguan on their way to many southern destinations, but **Qinhuangdao** is better served from Beijing—take the T509 at 7:30am, arriving in Qinhuangdao at 10:28am. This is an all soft-seat train that marks the return of class designations to Chinese trains—imagine the embalmed Mao a-spin. *Yi deng* (first class) is ¥97 ($13/£6.50). Outside the Qinhuangdao railway station, cross the road and turn left to find bus no. 33. It reaches Shanhaiguan in about 30 minutes, for a fare of ¥2 (25¢/15p). The bus drops you at the south gate of the old city walls (Nan Men). Trains directly to Shanhaiguan from Beijing tend to be slower or ill-timed, although the T11 departing at 1:20pm and arriving at 4:26pm is a possibility. Shanhaiguan's new railway station (© **0335/794-2242**) is a few minutes' walk southeast of the south gate. The T12 returns to Beijing at 1:37pm, arriving at 6:17pm, and the speedier T94, which departs at 7:10pm, arrives at 9:54pm. Tickets are set aside for both trains, but unless you're fortunate, you'll probably have to buy a seatless ticket and upgrade on the train. It's safer to return to Qinhuangdao, where the T510 at 1:37pm reaches Beijing Station at 4:42pm.

For **bus** services it's again better to return to Qinhuangdao, with twice-daily connections to Beijing's Xi Zhi Men bus station and others to Beijing Railway Station, for ¥60 ($7.50/£4). Bus no. 33 to Qinhuangdao Railway Station runs every 2 to 5 minutes from 6:20am to 7pm.

GETTING AROUND   **Buses** have conductors and cost ¥1 (15¢/5p). A **tourist shuttle service** runs from Nan Men (South Gate) to the Tianxia Diyi Guan and Jiao

Shan at 8:30am, 11am, and 3:30pm, summer only. Most **taxis** have a flagfall of ¥8 ($1.05/55p), which includes 2km (1¼ miles), then charge ¥1.20 (15¢/5p) per kilometer up to 8km (5 miles), then ¥1.80 (25¢/10p) per kilometer thereafter. Use one taxi to see all the sights. Insist that the "one-way" button is not pushed, and then this should be about 32km (20 miles), and cost less than ¥50 ($6.70/£3.35), including waiting time. There's also an assortment of meterless rickety three-wheelers with extravagant ideas about the depth of foreigners' pockets. A better choice is to rent a **bicycle** from one of the cluster of stores on Nan Dajie.

FAST FACTS

Banks, Foreign Exchange & ATMs   The main **Bank of China** (8:30am–5pm) is just inside the city wall's southeast corner at Diyi Guan Lu 60. There is no ATM.

Internet Access   The **Lingshi Wangba,** between the post office and the Friendly Cooperate Hotel, charges ¥2 (25¢/10p) per hour.

Post Office   The post office is on Nan Guan Dajie, right next to the Friendly Cooperate Hotel. Hours are from 8am to 6pm.

INSPECTING CHINA'S DEFENSES

Tianxia Diyi Guan   The "First Pass Under Heaven" is the east gate of the city's walls and a gate through the Great Wall itself, originally defended by towers overlooking a large walled enclosure, most of which still stands. The only entrance was from the south, and would have required a sharp left turn to reach the main gate while coming under attack from all sides. To the north and south the Wall is heavily restored, the odd reconstructed tower holding either a small exhibition or a shop. It was once possible to walk north to Jiao Shan; the way is now barred by a metal door.

⊙ 0335/505-1106. Admission ¥40 ($5.35/£2.70). 7am–6pm (to 5:30pm in winter). From the south gate, walk north up Nan Dajie and turn right at Dong Dajie, or walk west outside the walls and turn left up Diyi Guan Lu inside the east wall—also the route any taxi will take. Alternatively, enter the south gate and simply zigzag through the back streets—worthwhile in itself, because there's no way through the walls once you're inside; you can't get lost.

Jiao Shan ⊛   The rebuilt Wall plunges spectacularly down the mountainside, so your climb up it is consequently steep. There are handrails to assist you, and ladders up the sides of watchtowers, or the alternative of a chairlift for ¥15 ($1.90/£1) one-way, ¥20 ($2.50/£1.30) round-trip. The towers are certainly worth scaling for the views of the Wall wriggling down the hillside and running away to the sea. Higher up, the Wall becomes more attractively decayed but still safely passable, and those with the stamina (and a picnic) can travel some distance.

⊙ 0335/505-6380. Admission ¥15 ($2/£1). Open 24 hr. 3km (2 miles) north of Shanhaiguan, and best reached by taxi.

Lao Long Tou   A few years ago the "Old Dragon's Head" was just rubble, with the odd stone sticking out of the sea. The Great Wall's final kilometer was re-created in 1992, and it runs past a brand-new "old barracks area" (with shops) and a final tower before it expires in the sea. Stand at the Wall's end, look back, try to see beyond the tawdry desperation for the tourist dollar, and view the Wall as the beginning of a vast drama, ending thousands of kilometers away in Gansu Province. It's the culmination of a Ming dynasty arms race, the "Star Wars" project of its time, which nearly sank the national economy and which turned out to be pointless since scruffy little men on ponies armed with bows and arrows, the "terrorists" of their day, regularly got through it.

Stairs to the right lead down to a beach where Chinese, most of whom live a very long way from the sea, paddle in search of pebbles and shells. Beyond lies a small temple to the Sea God, rebuilt in 1989, an excellent vantage point for photography of the "Old Dragon's Head" itself.

C 0335/515-2996. Admission ¥50 ($6.70/£3.35). 7:30am–6pm (5:30pm in winter). Bus: no. 13 south down Nan Hai Xi Lu (everyone knows where you want to get off, at a point where the road forks); or bus no. 23 (which terminates here).

Mengjiangnu Miao   This temple, a reminder of the Great Wall's human cost, is linked to a myth that crops up repeatedly around China, where compulsory labor on vast civil engineering projects led to the deaths of tens of thousands: Husband goes off to imperial construction project, and nothing more is heard. Eventually wife goes to look for husband, discovers that he has died during his labors, and the Wall crumbles under the weight of her tears to reveal his bones. She subsequently chooses suicide in preference to becoming an imperial concubine.

Such was the fate of the probably mythical Mengjiangnu. Her temple is on a look-out point up a steep flight of stairs, called "Looking for Husband Rock," and consists of some remarkably battered halls and oddly shaped rocks, labeled opportunistically as her bed, dressing table, and so on.

C 0335/505-3159. Admission ¥25 ($3.35/£1.70). 7am–7pm (to 6pm in winter). 8km (5 miles) east of town.

Wang Jia Dayuan 𝕬𝕬   This small but fascinating folk museum provides a clue as to what the Cultural Relics Bureau could achieve if it were properly funded and had some marketing savvy. With investment from a Beijing entrepreneur, part of a court-yard mansion that once housed Shanhaiguan's wealthiest burgher has been sensitively renovated and is slated to expand farther south. Exhibits are crammed with curiosities: a mustache comb, a portable barber's chair, sepia pictures of the former residents, and an impressive collection of shadow puppets and ceramics. Four of the rooms are available for overnight stays for ¥298 to ¥398 ($37–$50/£20–£27), with meals included.

Dong San Tiao 29. *C* 0335/506-7700. www.wjdy.com.cn. Admission ¥30 ($4/£2). Includes English-speaking guide. Open daylight hours. From Nan Men, walk north up Nan Dajie, take the 5th turn on the right.

WHERE TO STAY

A single night in Shanhaiguan is enough. Few hotels take foreigners, and most are fairly modest. The town's coastal position makes May to August its busiest months, with visitors from Beijing escaping the city heat. There are one or two resort hotels which are rather far-flung, inconvenient, overpriced, and of two minds about taking foreigners. The **Jiguan Zhaodaisuo,** Dong Si Tiao Hutong 17 (make a right turn about 4 blocks north of the south gate; *C* **0335/505-1938;** fax 0335/505-1490), is an acceptable choice, plus it provides a rare chance to stay in something approaching traditional Chinese housing, an old courtyard residence in the Shanhaiguan back streets that's been refurbished. Opened as a hotel in 2002, its rooms (¥120/$16/£8 standard room; no credit cards), which open on to courtyards are bright, cheerful, and simply furnished.

WHERE TO DINE

Close to the Jiguan Zhaodaisuo on Nan Dajie is the friendly **Si Tiao Baoziguan,** which boasts an English-speaking staff member. Smock-clad ladies roll the dumplings in an open kitchen while locals queue out the door for dumpling heaven. Perfect for an early start, they're open 6am to 6:30pm. Shanhaiguan's locals wistfully recall a time when they dined on unfarmed fish, but despite the depletion in fish stocks, Shanhaiguan is still renowned for its seafood.

11 Shijiazhuang

Hebei Province, 269km (168 miles) SW of Beijing

Hebei's nondescript capital is one of the few places in China where the intention to rebuild everything from scratch in only 20 years is actually improving the city. Down-at-the-heel Shijiazhuang is an accident arising from the crossing of major north-south and east-west railway lines—here X really does mark the spot. It's grown from village to provincial capital in 100 years.

Even that status is a hand-me-down from Tianjin, after the metropolis gained the right to report directly to Beijing rather than through the provincial government. As a result there's little of glamour here. But the city has a decent infrastructure for visitors and provides a base for exploring marvelous sights in the surrounding countryside, including **Zhengding** ♠♠, about 15km (10 miles) northeast. It was an important town for centuries before anyone had heard of Shijiazhuang. Today it is still home to **Longxing Si** ♠♠, one of the oldest, most atmospheric, and (luckily) least "restored" Chinese temples. Zhengding is also home to a number of pagodas so different from each other it's hard to believe they were produced by the same culture. **Zhao Xian,** 42km (26 miles) southeast, has an important example of religious revival in the large Zen (Chan) Buddhist temple, the **Bailin Si.** It also has the elegant **Zhaozhou Qiao** ♠—the first bridge of its kind in the world. Roughly 80km (50 miles) southwest, **Cangyan Shan** has the bridge-top temple featured in the closing scenes of *Crouching Tiger, Hidden Dragon.* **Note:** Please turn to appendix A for Chinese translation of key locations in this section.

ESSENTIALS

GETTING THERE The **airport** is 33km (20 miles) to the northeast. A shuttle bus for ¥20 ($2.70/£1.35) meets flights and runs to the CAAC ticket office at Zhongshan Dong Lu 471, on the east side of town at the terminus of bus no. 5 to the center. **CAAC** (open 8am–8pm) has a 24-hour flight-booking line (© **0311/8505-4084**). Buy in town from agents such as the **Hebei Oversea Tour Aviation Ticket Center** (Hebei Haiwai Luyou Hangkong Piaowu Zhongxin), inside the Tiedao Dasha, Zhongshan Dong Lu 97 (© **0311/8607-7777;** open 8am–9pm) on the corner of Ping'an Bei Dajie. They also have a branch inside the Hebei Century Hotel (open 9am–9pm). There are air connections to most provincial capitals, including daily flights to and from Beijing, Hohhot, Shanghai, and Xi'an.

Since Shijiazhuang's prosperity, such as it is, originates with its railway connections, it's right that the **railway station** is in the center of town. Getting there from **Beijing West** couldn't be easier, with six daily express trains taking 2 hours and 40 minutes; tickets (¥60/$8/£4 soft seat) can be bought outside waiting room 3 or on the train itself. These are all-seat double-decker trains with snack service. Taking the T511 from Beijing at 7:30am and returning by the T514 at 5:58pm can make Shijiazhuang a possible day trip. Shijiazhuang is also a stop on the T97/98 run between Beijing West and Kowloon (¥965/$129/£64 soft sleeper; ¥705/$94/£47 hard sleeper), arriving at 3:18pm from Kowloon and leaving at 12:47pm headed south. You will need your passport to book this ticket. Most south- and southwest-bound trains from Beijing stop at Shijiazhuang, offering connections to Taiyuan, Xi'an, and points as far flung as Urumqi. **Rail tickets** can be booked by telephone (© **0311/8699-5426;**

8am–6:30pm) for a ¥10 ($1.35/70p) commission. The railway station has been renovated, and boasts 17 windows from which tickets can be purchased. Window 1 is for soft-seat tickets only, windows 8 through 19 are normal ticket windows, and 20 through 24 are for 10-day advance purchases. There's even a screen displaying the availability of tickets.

Shijiazhuang is littered with **bus stations.** The most important of them, **Changtu Keyun Zhan,** is a 5-minute walk south of the railway station on Zhan Qian Lu. Destinations served include Ji'nan (241km/149 miles; ¥90/$12/£6), Tai'an (281km/174 miles; ¥80/$11/£5.35), Zhengzhou (437km/271 miles; ¥110/$15/£7.35), and Qinhuangdao (480km/298 miles; ¥140/$19/£9.35). There are frequent connections to several Beijing bus stations, including Lize Qiao (7am–5:30pm) and Lianhua Chi (6:30am–4pm; 3½ hr.). But the real competition with the rail link to Beijing is just to the right at the **Keyun Zong Zhan,** where the Alsa company runs luxury coaches to Beijing Liu Li Qiao (roughly every 25 min. 6am–7pm; returning 12:30–7:30pm; ¥70/$9.35/£4.70). In addition, twice-daily super luxury buses have large, airline-style tiltable seats, only three across the bus (¥90/$12/£6), departing at 8:10 and 9:25am, returning at 3:10pm and 4:40pm. For service from Beijing call © **010/6386-1263;** from Shijiazhuang call © **0311/8702-5775.** They also run two morning services to Ji'nan and Zhengzhou, with afternoon returns.

GETTING AROUND   Taxis are mostly Jettas and Fukang, and cost ¥1.40 (20¢/ 10p) per kilometer. Xiali cost ¥1.20 (15¢/5p) per kilometer. Flagfall of ¥5 (65¢/35p) includes 2km. Add 50% after 6km (3¾ miles), and 20% from 11pm to 5am.

VISITOR INFORMATION   CITS, at Donggang Lu 26, quotes imaginative prices for cars and guides. However, it does have some good English-speakers, so if you're desperate, call them at © **0311/8581-5102.**

FAST FACTS

Banks, Foreign Exchange & ATMs   There's a handy branch of the **Bank of China** on the north side of the Dongfang Dasha, Zhongshan Xi Lu 97, close to the railway station. Hours are Monday through Friday from 8:30am to noon and 2:30 to 5pm. Forex is available at counters 4 to 7. Another useful branch lies near a KFC just west of the World Trade Plaza on Zhongshan Dong Lu (same hours). Both branches have ATMs that accept foreign cards.

Internet Access   Dial-up is © **163** or 169.

Post Office   The post office near the railway station (corner of Gongli Jie and Zhongshan Xi Lu) is open from 8:30am to 6pm. There's a more centrally located post office in Jianshe Nan Dajie; its hours are 8:30am to 6:30pm.

Visa Extensions   The city **PSB** is 1 block north of Zhongshan Xi Lu, and 2 blocks east of Zhonghua Bei Dajie, at Liming Jie 8. The visa office has a separate entrance on the east side of the building. Walk up Qingnian Jie on the west side of the Huabei Shangcheng (department store), across the next junction, and the office is on your left (© **0311/8686-2500**). Hours are Monday to Friday from 8:30am to noon and 1:30 to 5:30pm.

WALKING TOUR ▐ THE PAGODAS OF ZHENGDING ⨂⨂

Getting There:	Take minibus no. 201 from the enclosure between Zhan Qian Jie and the railway station; it drops you at Zhengding bus station for ¥3 (40¢/20p). Ignore *sanlunche* (three-wheeler) drivers and take minibus no. 1 from the same spot to its terminus outside Longxing Si (¥1/15¢/5p). A *sanlunche* will cost you ¥5 (65¢/35p). A harder-to-find alternative is a tourist service that runs every 15 minutes from near the no. 50 bus stop farther south on the road running directly in front of the station, just north of the bus station, to outside Kaiyuan Si; the fare is ¥3 (40¢/20p). It is possible to stay at the (nominally) four-star Golden Star Holiday Hotel (ℂ 0311/825-8888), just north of Longxing Si, at Xingrong Lu 68.
Start:	Longxing Si.
Finish:	Changle Men.
Time:	At least half a day.
Best Times:	Weekdays between 8am and 4pm.

In once-important, long-irrelevant Zhengding, only a little exertion brings a lot of pleasure, including sights like some of the oldest surviving wooden buildings in China, a vast 27m (90-ft.) 10th-century bronze statue of Guanyin, four very different pagodas, and a fragment of city wall.

Bus no. 1 terminates at the main entrance. We recommend that you purchase an all-inclusive ticket *(taopiao)* for ¥60 ($7.50/£4), which covers all the sights described here, except for the Linji Si, which is managed by the Religious Affairs Bureau. The ticket includes entrance to a Confucian Temple of minor interest, containing a rather gruesome exhibition on the Japanese occupation.

❶ Longxing Si

Open 8am to 5:30pm; ¥40 ($5.35/£2.70), the Longxing Si dates its foundation from the Sui dynasty (581–618), and has three particularly unusual and interesting halls. The **Moni Dian (Manichean Hall),** built around 1052, rebuilt in 1563, and restored with tact from 1977 to 1980, is almost square in plan, with gabled porches on all four sides. Inside, five gilded figures are approached across a dark uneven floor past vast columns, some of which have a slight lean; the walls carry faint traces of early frescoes, miraculously unretouched. Through a gate beyond, a small altar building houses a two-faced, four-armed and rather delicately executed figure from 1493, hung with scarves of honor. To the right the Pavilion of Kindness contains a 7.4m (24-ft.)

Maitreya carved from a single piece of wood. To the left, the two-story **Zhuanlun Cang Dian (Turning Wheel Storage Hall)** of the Northern Song (960–1127) seems to have three stories due to an external gallery with "waist eaves." The ground floor is dominated by a 7m-high (23-ft.) octagonal revolving bookcase, as complex in its design as a miniature temple. The climax is the **Pavilion of Great Benevolence,** also Northern Song, a vast hall seven bays wide containing a massive 27m (90-ft.) bronze Guanyin with a "thousand arms" whose angularity gives her a rather crustacean look. The figure was cast upon the instructions of the first Northern Song emperor in about 971. You can climb several dusty floors to look her in the eye. The rearmost Ming-era hall was brought to the site from another temple in 1959, and contains a remarkable three-layered statue of 12 figures seated on lotus thrones. One side hall contains a bizarre exhibition (¥5/65¢/35p) that includes what is claimed to be a 2,100-year-old Han dynasty jade burial suit, reconstructed from hundreds of small jade plates and held together with cloth-covered gold wire. If it's the genuine article, it's priceless, but the presence in the exhibition of a pickled turtle, a dilapidated butterfly collection, and other bric-a-brac suggests otherwise. Continue through to **Kunlu Dian (Hall of Vairocana),** an exquisitely carved effigy of four bodhisattvas, dating from the late Ming.

Leaving the temple, note the rough map near the ticket office to the right. Turn right (west) from the temple and walk for 10 minutes.

❷ Tianning Si

If you are here in the spring, the *wutong* (Chinese parasol) trees you'll see will have spectacular cascades of pink blossoms. The **Lingxiao Ta** (pagoda), all that remains of the temple, is clearly visible to your right. Open 8am to 5:30pm; ¥10 ($1.35/70p), the Song dynasty nine-story octagonal brick structure, at 41m (134 ft.), is the tallest of the town's remaining pagodas. To climb it, enter from the far (north) side. If you are lucky the attendant will hand you a flashlight, but if not, the climb to the second, third, and fourth floors is through narrow passages within the brick walls, with short periods of pitch-darkness to start with. Keep your head *down*. The remainder of the climb to the ninth floor is by wooden staircases in the interior. A central set of trunks bound with hoops of iron, which radiate support beams, sit on fat brackets.

From the top, looking southwest, you can see the squat, square form of your next destination.

Return to the main road and turn right. After less than 5 minutes, Lishi Wenhua Jie "Historical and Cultural Street" is on the left at a bizarre statue-cum-roundabout. Turn left. There's a supermarket with snacks on the corner, and the street has a number of modest restaurants, which are less modest than anything else in the town. Kaiyuan Si is a short distance down to the right.

❸ Kaiyuan Si

Two minor buildings stand here, including a heavily renovated late-Tang bell tower, which can be climbed for a closer view of a 2.9m (9½-ft.) bronze bell. Open 8am to 5pm; ¥15 ($2/£1).

The nine-story **Xumi Ta** will seem familiar to those who've visited Xi'an—a tapering, brick, four-sided building, with a projecting ridge between each floor and a plainness that makes the Lingxiao Ta look fussy. There are local claims that it dates from 636, but as Xi'an's Great Goose (p. 265) is supposedly based on information brought back to China by the peripatetic monk Xuanzang, and its construction didn't start until 16 years later, one story is wrong (although Xuanzang is said to have been in the area—see Bailin Si, below). But the stately Xumi Ta certainly looks its age—quite a few of the bricks have fallen out, providing handy niches for nesting sparrows, and it's fenced off. Around the base are eight tubby martial figures, simply carved but full of life. If you do go in, note the carvings of dragons and flowers. The interior floors are missing, and the main floor is slippery with guano, but there's an impressive view up the resulting vertical tunnel.

One area of the temple's ruined remains has been labeled STONE INSCRIPTION GARDEN and contains forlorn rows of chipped statuary and chunks of stelae probably smashed in the Cultural Revolution, along with the cracked remains of the largest *bixi* you'll ever see, its claws 6 inches long. Often mistakenly described as turtles, *bixi* are in fact a primitive kind of dragon (not only with claws, but teeth). This one was accidentally discovered in June 2000 during construction work, as illustrated by photographs in the entrance hall as you leave.

Outside, turn right. You'll see a few street vendors selling birds, flowers, plants, and fish, and almost immediately on the left the entrance to the ancestral hall of the Liang family.

❹ Liangshi Zongci

This hall is a single unit five bays wide in brown wood, containing a small exhibition (pictures, family tree) of the Liang family. Open 8am to 5pm (closed at lunchtime); ¥5 (65¢/35p).

Outside, turn left. Along the length of this street are antiques and memorabilia shops (with lower prices than most because they are aimed at domestic tourists) selling everything from Buddhist bits and pieces to Mao memorabilia. Still, expect most objects to be fake, and pay only a small fraction of initial asking prices. There are also places to buy ice cream, and assorted restaurants offering *jiaozi* and Beijing duck. Keep looking on the left for a large sign with a picture of pagoda, and turn left there.

⑤ Linji Si

Open 7:30am to 5pm; ¥15 ($2/£1), this temple claims to have been founded by the Eastern Wei dynasty (534–49). Its **Chengling Ta** was built to house the remains of the founder of a Zen Buddhist (Chan) sect still popular in Japan, who died late in the Tang dynasty in 867. The slender, octagonal brick pagoda is in a highly ornamental style; an elongated lower floor sits on a brick plinth carved with lotus petals. Eight further tiny stories, each with decorative brick brackets and eave figures, are topped by an umbrella spire. Roughly 30m (98 ft.) high, the pagoda was restored in 2001 and cannot be climbed. A handful of monks are in residence.

Turn right out of the temple and left at the main street. The Guanghui Si is a well-signposted left turn a few minutes farther along.

⑥ Guanghui Si

This temple's bizarre **Hua Ta,** dating from around 1200, is obviously a direct descendant of Indian stupas, consisting of a central brick pavilion topped with a stone spire covered with intricate statuary of elephants, other animals, and figures—some headless, some faceless, and some intact—finished with a brick point on top. The central pavilion is supported by four smaller, rebuilt pavilions. A climb up two floors to a platform (again, watch your head) gives views of the earthen core of the old city wall, the fields still inside it, and a modern mosque. Open 8am to 5:30pm; ¥10 ($1.35/70p).

Again return to the main road and turn left. The south gate of the city wall is straight ahead; the entrance is to the right.

⑦ Changle Men

As is usual with city walls, the brick has been taken away to use in domestic construction—all except for those structurally necessary to maintain the gates, unless the wall is breached elsewhere (or removed, earthworks and all). Here the gate and its tower have been rebuilt. Open 8am to 5:30pm; admission is ¥10 ($1.35/70p).

To return to Zhengding, flag down the yellow bus no. 2, which returns in the direction you have walked to the long-distance bus station.

BAILIN SI & ZHAOZHOU QIAO ☀

Bailin Si   The Cultural Revolution was so thorough here that only the Jin dynasty (1115–1234) pagoda was left standing. The extensive complex has been reconstructed over the last few years entirely with donations from the faithful, and includes one of the largest "10,000 Buddha" halls in the world.

The temple saw the foundation of a sect of Zen (Chan) Buddhism, and its beginnings date from 220 during the Eastern Han dynasty. Xuanzang is said to have studied here before his trip to India in search of authoritative texts. The temple is entered through a small grove of cypresses (for which it is named), and has a calm bustle of activity from shaven-headed monks in orange and brown robes. One or two English-speakers tend to seek out foreign visitors and are happy to answer queries, show you around, and explain Zen principles and the *Shenghuo* (life) variant introduced by Venerable Master Jinghui, the driving force behind the temple's change from weeds and rubble into an impressive complex. Then-President Jiang Zemin visited in 2001. Perhaps the rumors are true and he is a closet Buddhist.

Free admission. 8am–4pm. In Shijiazhuang, take bus no. 26, 30, or 35 from the train station to Nan Jiao Keyun Zong Zhan and catch a bus to Zhao Xian (30–45 min.; ¥9/$1.20/£60), tell the driver that you wish to get off at Bailin Si, and they will drop you off at the gate. If you can't make yourself understood, jump off at a traffic island with a mini-pagoda in the middle. The road to the left, Shi Ta Lu, takes you to Bailin Si in 10 min. on foot. Alternatively, if you head straight on down Shi Qiao Dajie (Stone Bridge St.), you'll pass the earthen core and one or two watchtowers of the city wall, and get to a major junction straight over which is Zhaozhou Qiao, about a 30-min. walk. Or take a *sanlunche* (¥3/40¢/20p) or minivan (¥5/65¢/35p).

Zhaozhou Qiao 😊   Also known as Anji Qiao (Safe Crossing Bridge) and Da Shi Qiao (Big Stone Bridge), this is often labeled the oldest surviving bridge in China. There are probably older bridges, but this one was constructed between 595 and 605, and unlike China's wooden structures it is largely original in its current form. A mecca for architects and civil engineers as well as historians, it was the first bridge in the world to use a segment of an arc rather than a complete semicircle for its arch, giving a far more shallow curve to the road deck and thus making crossings for carts and horses much easier. This was a major design breakthrough, but it would be 800 years before a similar approach would be tried in Europe, and nearly 1,300 years before Europe tried using the spandrel—piercing the buttresses at either end of the bridge so as to reduce pressure on the foundations and allow floodwaters to pass without sweeping the bridge away.

The parallel stone ribbons that form the main arch are surprisingly flexible and things of beauty in themselves. Until recently the bridge was still in use, but traffic is now diverted, and some of the damaged carvings on the superstructure, including scowling mythical beasts called *taotie,* have been replaced.

Sadly, the bridge's conversion to a tourist sight has brought pedalos (pedal boats) that wallow in the murky, tadpole-filled waters beneath, as well as construction of a hideous parallel concrete pedestrian bridge, mainly to obscure views from the new road bridge and thus increase receipts. But don't let this stop you from viewing China's most significant contribution to architectural method.

See directions for Bailin Si, above. The ticket booth is to the right of the main entrance. Admission ¥35 ($4.70/£2.35). 7:30am–7pm (to 5:30pm in winter). © 0311/8490-2618. To find buses to Shijiazhuang, return to the traffic island by foot or taxi, and continue to the next T-junction. (If you turn left and walk for a few minutes, on your right you'll find another, smaller bridge constructed in the same style, with no entrance fee at all.)

CANGYAN SHAN

This wooded mountain is part of the Taihang range, about 80km (50 miles) southwest of Shijiazhuang; its summit is at 1,044m (3,424 ft.). The main point of visiting is a staircase of more than 300 steps leading up a cleft and beneath two parallel bridges, each topped by a temple, originally Sui dynasty (518–618). The setting is as spectacular as it looks in the closing scene of the film *Crouching Tiger, Hidden Dragon* (although the final jump is reportedly from Huang Shan), and the location, especially from the stairs below and on a misty day, makes for some spectacular photography. The paths which lace the mountainside do not lead to any other equally spectacular sights, and some have crumbled away. Take a picnic. The 2-hour minibus trip begins rather early in the morning.

Admission ¥50 ($6.70/£3.35). © 0311/8232-4128. Bus: to Cangyan Shan from the Xiwang Changtu Keyun Chezhan (take bus no. 9 from the rail station to the terminus) in Xinhua Lu. It departs at 7am and returns late afternoon. Return fare is ¥26 ($3.50/£1.75).

WHERE TO STAY

EXPENSIVE

Hebei Century Hotel (Hebei Shiji Dafandian)   This Chinese five-star, 29-floor glass cylinder tower opened in 2000 with a cavernous lobby and good-size rooms, if typically tiny bathrooms. The guest rooms have the standard neoclassical cabinetry of international five-stars, but someone involved in the design has been a bit more adventurous with color than is common to Chinese-run hotels, and service is a notch above average, too.

Zhongshan Xi Lu 145 (just west of the city PSB, corner of Zhonghua Bei Dajie). ℭ **0311/8703-6699.** Fax 0311/ 8703-8866. www.hebei-centuryhotel.com. 439 units. ¥610–¥750 ($81–$100/£41–£50) standard room; ¥1,100– ¥6,000 ($147–$800/£73–£400) suite. 30%–50% discounts easily obtained. AE, DC, MC, V. Bus: no. 1 west along Zhongshan Xi Lu. **Amenities:** 4 restaurants (Western, Korean, 2 Chinese); nightclub; indoor swimming pool; tennis; fitness room; sauna; billiards; children's play area; tour desk; business center. *In room:* A/C, satellite TV, computer (executive floors), broadband Internet access, minibar, hair dryer, safe.

World Trade Plaza Hotel (Shimao Guangchang Jiudian) ✵   This former Crowne Plaza was recently the victim of a buy-out by its Chinese partner. For the moment, this centrally located five-star hotel is the first choice for foreign visitors, but parts of the operation are already veering out of control, particularly the enthusiastic "massage" service, which occasionally solicits from door to door. North-facing rooms are quieter, and the larger "executive rooms" *(shangwu jian),* which are appealingly arranged with a glass divider between the resting and the work area, are excellent value. The second-floor restaurant offers the finest Western cuisine in town.

Zhongshan Dong Lu 303 (opposite Sheng Bowuguan/Provincial Museum). ℭ **0311/8667-8888.** Fax 0311/8667-1694. www.wtphotels.com. 238 units. ¥940 ($125/£63) standard room; from ¥1,820 ($243/£121) suite; plus 15% service charge. Best rates often 50% less. AE, DC, MC, V. **Amenities:** 3 restaurants (Western, 2 Chinese); cafe; fitness room w/access to off-site facilities; Jacuzzi; sauna; limousine service; railway station shuttle; business center with translation services; forex; laundry/dry cleaning. *In room:* A/C, satellite TV, dataport, minibar, safe, iron.

MODERATE

Huiwen Jiudian   The 26-floor Huiwen, which upgraded from three stars to four stars following renovations in 2003 (though it must have been quite a banquet for the hotel inspectors), is the best choice of a clutch of hotels conveniently opposite the railway station, and less than 10 minutes' walk north of the long-distance bus station. The hotel is adequately clean and well run, but it needs at least one more elevator, and lighting in the bathrooms is poor. Public transport to most out-of-town sites leaves from stops nearby.

Zhan Qian Jie 6 (opposite railway station exit—look for Xinhua Bookstore sign). ℭ **0311/8787-9988.** Fax 0311/8786-5500. 180 units. ¥268–¥348 ($36–$46/£18–£23) standard room; ¥490 ($65/£33) suite. Discounts around 20%. No credit cards. **Amenities:** 3 restaurants; teahouse; nightclub; fitness room; bowling; pool table; business center. *In room:* A/C, TV, broadband Internet access, hair dryer.

WHERE TO DINE

The usual fast-food culprits are here: KFC is opposite the Yanchun Garden Hotel, Zhongshan Dong Lu 195, and just west of the World Trade Plaza on Zhongshan Dong Lu, along with a McDonald's. Extensive Western menus are available at both hotels; you can also find a branch of the excellent Shanghai restaurant, **Soup Best Shen,** at the Yanchun Garden. There's budget eating opposite the station, including two branches of **California Beef Noodle King (Meiguo Jiazhou Niurou Mian Dawang),** and a branch of the **Malan** noodle chain next to Quanjude (see below). At any of these you can fill yourself for ¥5 (65¢/35p). The vast Renren Le Supermarket is located underneath the Mao park, just east of the Yanchun Garden Hotel. The Great Helmsman transformed into the Great Spruiker. Another supermarket for travel snacks, open from 9am to 7:30pm, is located at Zhongshan Xi Lu 83, just west of the station. Shijiazhuang is best at offering Beijing specialties in quieter environments and for lower prices.

Quanjude ✦ BEIJING   The national capital's best-known supplier of its signature roast duck dish provides a better atmosphere, better service, and lower prices at this provincial branch than it does at home. The grand two-story building with a sweeping central staircase bustles pleasantly. The ovens are visible at the rear and use the traditional fruitwood method for baking the duck, which is as moist and succulent as it should be. The downstairs area also offers Shandong dishes, which you select from illuminated shelves. Upstairs has full waitress service. If you are by yourself, a half duck *(ban zhi)* is only ¥49 ($6.55/£3.30) There's another branch on the south side of Heping Xi Lu just west of Ping'an Jie.

Jianshe Nan Dajie 7, just south of the Yanchun Garden Hotel. © 0311/8621-1566. Duck sets (with pancakes, condiments, and soup) ¥98—¥138 ($13–$18/£6.55–£9.20). No credit cards. 11am–2pm and 5–9pm.

Shao'erzai CHAOZHOU   This branch of the roast goose specialist offers Chaozhou cuisine's most famous dish, very popular throughout Guangdong and Hong Kong. The large and busy restaurant is set back from the main road in a courtyard, but it's easily spotted by the big roast goose sign.

Zhongshan Dong Lu 189, just west of the Yanchun Garden Hotel. © 0311/8609-6666, ext. 8888. Meal for 2 ¥100 ($13/£6.70). No credit cards. 10:30am–2pm and 5:30–8:45pm.

The Northeast

by Lee Wing-sze

Even if the Chinese no longer believe civilization ends at the Great Wall, most tourists still do. The frigid lands to the northeast, once known as Tartary or Manchuria and now referred to simply as Dongbei (the Northeast), represent one of the least visited and most challenging regions in China and its last great travel frontier.

Dongbei was the birthplace of China's final dynasty, the Manchu-ruled Qing (1636–1912). It was declared off-limits to Han Chinese from 1644, when the first Qing emperor took up residence in the Forbidden City, until the dynasty began to lose power in the late 19th century. The ban preserved Dongbei's image as a mysterious and menacing place separate from China proper. "The Chinese talk of Tartary as a country half as big as the rest of the world besides," Lord Macartney, George III's emissary to the court of the Qing Qianlong emperor, wrote in the early 18th century. "But their conceptions of its limits are very dark and confused. There is a wide difference between pretension and possession."

Japan and Russia waged a series of battles for control of Dongbei in the first half of the 20th century; the Chinese finally took genuine possession of the region at the end of World War II. Using Japanese- and Russian-built railroads, China's new Communist leaders made it the center of their efforts to bring the country into the industrial age.

The name "Dongbei" now conjures images not of wild invaders on horseback, but of ruddy-faced factory workers famous for their friendliness. Despite industrialization, Dongbei still claims China's largest natural forest, its most pristine grasslands, and one of its most celebrated lakes (Tian Chi). What makes the region unique, however, are the architectural remnants of the last 350 years—early Qing palaces and tombs, incongruous Russian cupolas, and eerie structures left over from Japan's wartime occupation.

The region is undergoing a tourism makeover in an attempt to replace income lost in a recent spate of state-owned factory closures. It is still frankly a difficult place to visit, with overpriced hotels, industrial malaise, and a paucity of English-speakers. Yet the difficulty offers its own reward: the chance to travel in a place largely free of the exploitation and cultural hyperbole common to tourism in more accommodating parts of China.

Note: Unless noted otherwise, hours listed in this chapter are the same daily.

1 Shenyang

Liaoning Province, 868km (538 miles) NE of Beijing, 544km (337 miles) SW of Harbin

Shenyang is the largest city in Dongbei and on its way to being a lovely gateway as one of the four hosting cities for the 2008 Olympics soccer matches. The city—formerly a sprawling chaos of dirt and noise, where historical buildings stood bathed in the neon of new consumerism—has benefited from efforts to reduce pollution and boost citizens' English fluency. It was the birthplace of the Qing dynasty in the 15th century and is now the capital of Liaoning, Dongbei's southernmost and wealthiest province. Many travelers spend only enough time here to switch trains, but it is worthwhile to linger in the city, which is home to several of Dongbei's most fascinating historical attractions.

Shenyang has existed under various names since the Tang dynasty (618–907) and has been the region's most strategically important city since 1625, when Jurchen founders of the Qing dynasty (1626–1912) made it their capital (Shenjing). The Qing's leaders stayed here for 19 years, perfecting a system of government modeled on the Chinese and plotting an attack on the weakened Ming from inside their palace, which still stands in the city center. With the decline of the Qing at the start of the 20th century, the city (renamed Fengtian) fell under the influence of legendary warlord Zhang Zuolin. Zhang ruled Manchuria from his downtown residence courtyard complex just south of the Qing palace, until his assassination by Japanese soldiers in 1928. The city drifted without obvious leadership until the fall of 1931, when Japan's Kwantung Army used the "discovery" of a small hole blasted in their railway line north of the city (known to them as Mukden) as a pretense to invade. The attack, referred to in China as the September 18th (or Mukden) Incident and immortalized in a museum in the north part of the city, eventually led to the establishment of Manchukuo (Mandarin: *Manzhou Guo*), the puppet state Japan used to mask its territorial ambitions during World War II.

The mayor who transformed Dalian (p. 174) into the shimmering pride of northern China, now the governor of Liaoning Province, has vowed to work his magic on the capital. Shenyang has never been pretty, but perhaps it doesn't need to be. "[Mukden] is ancient and dusty, with nothing especially attractive," one visiting Catholic missionary wrote in 1919. "I found it very interesting." The same holds true today.

ESSENTIALS

GETTING THERE Flights connect Shenyang's **Taoxian International Airport (Taoxian Guoji Jichang)** with every major Chinese city, including Beijing (12 flights daily), Shanghai (16 flights daily), Guangzhou (five flights daily), Shenzhen (six flights daily); there are also connections to New York, California, Seoul, and Tokyo. Flights can be booked at the **China Northern Airlines** ticket office (**Zhongguo Beifang Hangkong Shoupiao Chu;** ⓒ **024/2383-4089**), located at Zhonghua Lu 117, north of Shiyi (11) Wei Lu. The office is open from 8am to 5pm. The airport is 30km (19 miles) south of downtown. An **airport shuttle** runs from the ticket office every half-hour (¥10/$1.30/65p; 45 min.). **Taxis** at the ticket office offer to take groups for ¥15 to ¥20 ($1.95–$2.60/£1–£1.30) per person; other taxis charge ¥60 ($7.80/£3.90), including the ¥10 ($1.30/65p) road toll. Cash and traveler's checks can be exchanged at a kiosk near the international arrivals area.

Shenyang has two main **railway stations:** the Russian-built **Shenyang Zhan (Shenyang Railway Station)** on the western edge of downtown, and the modern **Shenyang Bei Zhan (Shenyang North Station),** north of Shifu Guangchang. Trains to Beijing (4 hr.; ¥218/$28/£14), Dalian (3½ hr.; ¥55/$7.15/£3.60), Changchun (2 hr. 11 min.; ¥93/$12/£6.05), and Dandong (3½ hr.; ¥24/$3.10/£1.55) stop at both railway stations. Trains to Shanghai (28 hr.; ¥430/$56/£28) and Harbin (4 hr.; ¥203/$26/£13) leave only from Shenyang Bei.

Shenyang's main **long-distance bus station, Qiche Kuaisu Keyun Zhan** (ticket office open 6am–6pm; © 024/2251-1223), is on Huigong Jie behind the Times Plaza Hotel. **Luxury coaches,** the best way to travel by bus, go to Harbin (6½ hr.; ¥138/$18/£9); Changchun (3⅓ hr.; ¥82/$11/£5.30), Dalian (4 hr.; ¥107/$14/£7), and Dandong (3 hr.; ¥66/$8.60/£4.30).

GETTING AROUND   The two areas in Shenyang where it is feasible to walk are the old city center, a 5-sq.-km (2-sq.-mile) area surrounding the Imperial Palace (Gu Gong), and the shopping district east of Shenyang Zhan. Most sights, however, are scattered in the sprawl outside these areas. **Taxis** charge ¥8 ($1.05/50p) for the first 3km (2 miles), then ¥1 (15¢/10p) for every 550m (⅓ mile). **Buses** charge ¥1 to ¥2 (15¢–25¢/10p–15p) and congregate at the two railway stations. Bus no. 203 travels from Shenyang Zhan via Shifu Guangchang to Shenyang Bei Zhan; a circle-line *(huan)* bus goes from Shenyang Zhan past Taiyuan Jie to Zhong Jie (see "Shopping," later in this chapter) and the Gu Gong. Maps can be bought at Shenyang Bei Zhan.

FAST FACTS

Banks, Foreign Exchange & ATMs   The main branch of **Bank of China** is at Shifu Lu 253, west of the Shifu Guangchang (open Mon–Fri 8am–noon and 1–4pm; ✆ 024/2285-7569). Traveler's checks and cash can be exchanged at window 28 on the second floor; credit card transactions are handled on the third floor. There are no international ATMs anywhere in town.

Consulates   All consulates are located in a single, heavily fortified compound at the intersection of Shisi (14) Wei Lu and Bei San Jing Jie. The **United States Consulate** (open Mon–Wed and Fri 1:30–4:30pm; ✆ 024/2322-1198) is closest to the corner at Shisi Wei Lu 52. The **Japanese Consulate** (open Mon–Fri 8:30am–noon and 1:30–5:15pm; ✆ 024/2322-7490) is next door. The surly staff at the **Russian Consulate** (Mon–Fri 9:30am–noon and 3–4pm; ✆ 024/2322-3927), in the rear of the compound, don't speak English, and will almost never grant you a tourist visa; arrive early if you want to try your luck.

Internet Access   The 24-hour Internet cafe **Tietong Xinganxian Wangba** (¥4/50¢/ 25p per hour) is 2 blocks east of the railway station on Zhonghua Lu. Dial-up is ✆ 165.

Post Office   The main post office is at the corner of Zhongshan Lu and Taiyuan Bei Jie (open May–Sept 8am–5:30pm; Oct–Apr 8am–5pm).

Visa Extensions   Visa extensions are available at the **PSB** Exit/Entry office (✆ 024/ 2310-5937) in the old Bank of Communications building (third floor, northeast entrance), at the intersection of Bei San Jing Jie and Shiyi Wei Lu (open Mon–Fri 8:30–11am and 1–4pm). Visas take 1 week to process, and require a hotel registration card and proof of at least ¥20,000 ($2,600/£1,300) in a bank account.

EXPLORING SHENYANG

The one attraction within walking distance of the downtown hotels is **Zhongshan Guangchang (Sun Yat-sen Square),** 4 blocks northeast of Shenyang Zhan on Zhongshan Lu. It's notable for its striking **statue of Mao,** which stands proudly surrounded by a teeming mass of soldiers, peasants, and workers all bearing weapons of the revolution (guns, sledgehammers, Mao's little red book) and staring grim-faced at the banks and hotels that now surround the square.

Bei Ling 🌟🌟   This august tomb at the center of an Eastern Eden of ponds, pavilions, twisting paths, and 300-year-old pines contains the remains of Qing dynasty founder Huang (the Manchurian Tai Zong emperor, Abahai). The eighth son of Nurhaci, the Jurchen chieftain who unified Manchuria in the early 17th century, Huang Taiji rose to power shortly after his father's death, proclaimed the founding of the Qing dynasty in 1636, then conquered Korea.

Construction of the tomb (also known as Zhao Ling) began in 1643, the year Huang Taiji died, and took 8 years to complete. A central path leads visitors through the front gate, past a stone army of guardian animals and into Long'en Dian, a large hall housing the emperor's memorial tablet. Climbing up onto the encircling wall at the northern end will put you at eye level with the tomb itself, a simple dirt hill topped by a lonely tree. Huang Taiji's body lies somewhere beneath. The tomb lies at the northern end of Bei Ling Park, former imperial cemetery turned public space.

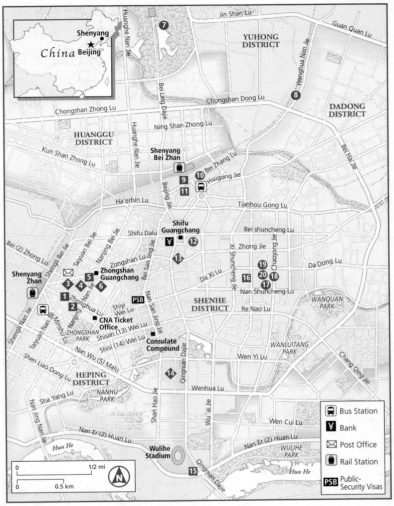

China
Beijing
Shenyang

Jin Shan Lu
Guan Quan Lu
YUHONG DISTRICT
Huanghe Nan Lu
Wanghua Nan Jie
Chongshan Dong Lu
DADONG DISTRICT
Chongshan Zhong Lu
Ning Shan Zhong Lu
HUANGGU DISTRICT
Kun Shan Zhong Lu
Huanghe Nan Lu
Bei Ling Dajie
Beijing Jie
Shenyang Bei Zhan
Bei Zhang Lu
Huigong Jie
Bei Hai Jie
Ha'erbin Lu
Tianhou Gong Lu
Shifu Guangchang
Bei shuncheng Lu
Shifu Dalu
Shenheng Jie
Zhong Jie
Da Dong Lu
Bei (2) Zhong Lu
Taiyuan Bei Jie
Nanjing Bei Jie
Zongshan Lu
Zhongshan Guangchang
Da Xi Lu
Chaoyang Jie
WANQUAN PARK
Shenyang Zhan
Zhonghua Lu
Nan San Jing Jie
Nan Shuncheng Lu
SHENHE DISTRICT
Re Nao Lu
Shengli Nan Lu
Taiyuan Nan Jie
Minzhu Lu
PSB
CNA Ticket Office
Shiyi Wei Lu
Shisan (13) Wei Lu
WANLIUTANG PARK
ZHONGSHAN PARK
Shisi (14) Wei Lu
Consulate Compound
Wen Yi Lu
Shen Liao Dong Lu
Nan Wu (5) Malu
Qingnian Dajie
HEPING DISTRICT
NANHU PARK
Wenhua Lu
Chang Qing Jie
Sha Yang Lu
Shan Hao Jie
Nan Jing Nan Jie
Wu'ai Jie
Wen Cui Lu
Nan Er (2) Huan Lu
Hun He
Wulihe Stadium
Qingnian Dajie
WULIHE PARK
Nan Er (2) Huan Lu
Hun He

0   1/2 mi
0   0.5 km
N

Bus Station
Bank
Post Office
Rail Station
Public-Security Visas

Taishan Lu 12, at northern end of Bei Ling Dajie. ℂ 024/8689-6294. Admission ¥30 ($3.90/£1.95) 7am–6pm plus ¥6 (80¢/40p) for Bei Ling Park entrance. Bus: no. 217 from Shenyang Bei Zhan; get off at Bei Ling Gong Yuan Zhan. Taxi: 20 min. from downtown (¥15/$1.95/£1).

Gu Gong (Imperial Palace) ✦ For those who have visited its predecessor in Beijing, the first and most obvious difference will be size. Shenyang's humble imperial abode covers roughly 60,000 sq. m (645,835 sq. ft.), less than a 10th the area of the Forbidden City. This means you don't have to run a tourist marathon to see all the offerings, nor do you need to devote an entire day to exploration.

The palace is largely modeled after Beijing's Gu Gong, but architecturally blends intricate Mongolian- and Tibetan-influenced carvings favored by the early Qing.

Shenyang Key

Minorities & the Manchu Myth

Manchurians, one of China's more numerous ethnic minorities with a population of 11 million, did not actually exist until a dozen years before they conquered China. Originally a loose alliance of nomadic tribes, they became Manchus (the exact meaning is unknown but the name was probably taken from a Buddhist term meaning "great good fortune"), after Qing founder Huang Taiji invented the label to unify his people and distance them from their barbarian roots. But it was Nurhaci, Huang Taiji's father, who paved the way for the Manchu conquest of Ming China. Nurhaci was bent on instilling loyalty and demanded men who surrendered to him to imitate the Manchu tradition of shaving the front of the forehead and braiding hair in the back into a long "queue," a law that was also enforced during the reign of Huang Taiji. By 1645, any man who did not comply faced execution. The Chinese were humiliated by the order at the time, but the queue has recently been reclaimed as Chinese cultural history, and makes frequent appearances on dozens of widely popular Chinese period soap operas.

Manchu culture borrowed heavily from a number of ethnic groups, especially in architecture (see Gu Gong, below), but many of their customs disappeared after they established the Qing and adopted Chinese habits—a phenomenon Chinese historians still note with pride. Some aspects of Manchu culture have survived, however. Most notable among these are *kang*, heated brick beds still found in some Dongbei homes, and *qipao* (traditional fitted dresses), made famous in 1930s Shanghai.

Dongbei is technically home to more than a dozen other ethnic groups, including Mongolians, Russians, and Koreans. But the majority of them were, at one time or another, considered Manchurian. Victims of successive assimilation, most are now practically indistinguishable from Han Chinese. A few distinct minority cultures have managed to survive, if only barely, in the more remote corners of the Northeast. These include a few nomadic **Oroqen** hunters and reindeer-herding **Ewenkis** in the Greater Xing'an Mountains (on the border between Inner Mongolia and Heilongjiang Province), and the **Hezhe,** the majority of whom live in northeastern Heilongjiang Province. Numbering fewer than 5,000, Hezhe are famous for their fish-skin clothing, a typical suit of which costs between ¥5,000 and ¥6,000 ($650–$780/£325–£390) and uses roughly 250 kilograms (550 lb.) of pike, carp, or salmon.

Unfortunately, many of the exhibitions are poorly cared for, such as Zhong Zheng Dian, where emperor Abahai once attended to political affairs. Viewed from afar, the carved oak throne and emperor-yellow cushion have faded under a thick layer of dust into dull wood and a sickly pale color.

On the northeastern side is the oldest and most impressive structure in the Gu Gong: **Da Zheng Hall (Da Zheng Dian)** and the surrounding **Pavilion of Ten Kings (Shi Wang Ting).** The original gate housed to the east of the main entrance is now closed to the public, so visitors will stumble upon this homage to the

Manchurian army either from a small door on the west, or from the back. The two pavilions closest to the hall display the offices of the left and right wings, while the remaining eight pavilions display various Qing weaponry and replicas of the armor and the colorful banners (two each of yellow, red, blue, and white) of the eight divisions of the Manchu army. Da Zheng Hall is where Dorgon, Huang Taiji's younger brother and regent to his successor Shunzhi (the first Qing emperor to rule from Beijing), is said to have given the orders to invade China.

Shenyang Lu 771. (C) 024/2484-4192. Admission ¥50 ($6.50/£3.25). English guidebook with plenty of grammatical mistakes ¥25 ($3.25/£1.65). 8:30am–6pm. Bus: no. 213 from Bei Ling Park Zhan to Gu Gong stop; walk east along Chaoyang Lu.

Liaoning Provincial Museum (Liaoning Sheng Bowuguan) ⭐ *Kids*   Don't let the giant brontosaurus guarding the entrance wagging its tail and giving a mechanical roar every few seconds deter you; this museum, opened in late 2004, houses an impressive collection of pieces mostly from the Qing dynasty. The large, circular layout gives the museum a comfortable, open feel, while the vaulted ceilings absorb the sounds of chattering tour groups. Notable exhibits include the Zhongguo Gudai Shibei Zhi Zhan, classical **Chinese stone tablets** tracing calligraphy from the Han dynasty, and the Gudai Huobi Zhan, or the **Chinese Money exhibition,** which displays everything from rudimentary seashell beads to ancient gold ingots from which the auspicious Chinese delicacy *jiaozi* (steamed dumplings) get their shape. On the third floor, the curators have imported leftover Jurassic Park props. This exhibit appears to be purely for entertainment and does not suggest that dinosaurs ever existed here.

Fu Da Lu 363, at Shifu Guangchang. (C) 024/2274-1193. Admission ¥20 ($2.60/£1.30). Audio tours in English and Chinese (available at coat check) ¥10 ($1.30/65p) plus ¥100 ($13/£6.50) and ID deposit. 9am–4pm.

9.18 Museum (Jiuyiba Bowuguan)   This revamped museum in northern Shenyang offers a decidedly biased view of the Mukden Incident (1931) in which Japan staged an attack on its own South Manchurian railway line at Liutiao Hu as a pretense to invade the Northeast. Four large characters displayed under a clock frozen at 10:20 read *"Wu wang guo chi"*—"Never forget the national disgrace." The museum strives to offer a variety of unorthodox presentations. One exhibition, documenting the Rise of the Anti-Japanese Army of Resistance (coincidentally supported by the CPC, and in direct disobedience of Koumintang orders of nonresistance) replicates a guerrilla warfare conference using full-size wax figures meeting in a large fake forest. Nearby are miniature clay figurines behind glass casing, with stunted comical bodies and expressions, celebrating the army's successes. Oil paintings and blown-up photos adorn the walls. The mixing and matching of presentation styles makes for muddled exhibitions. Other displays touch on the Unit 731 biological weapons experiments (see "Harbin," p. 199) and the Nanjing Massacre (p. 399).

Wanghua Jie 46 (at Chongshan Lu, southeast of Bei Ling). (C) 024/8832-0918. Admission ¥28 ($3.65/£1.80). 8am–5:30pm. Bus: no. 253 from Da Xi Men (west of Gu Gong).

Shenyang Financial Museum (Shenyang Shi Jinrong Bowuguan)   Opened in late 2006, this museum is now the biggest of its kind in China. The European-style architecture, listed in the National Important Relics Protective Institutions in 1996, is the former site of the Frontier Bank established in the 1930s. The ground floor, decorated in the style of the original Frontier Bank lobby, is filled with over 80 vivid full-size wax figures demonstrating how the bank worked before computers dominated

our lives. At press time, the museum had opened seven rooms, displaying the financial history of the Northeast, ancient Chinese currency discovered in the area, and 1940s money featuring portraits of Dr. Sun and Mao, as well as other early foreign paper money. However, the descriptions are mostly in Chinese, with little and simple English. More rooms are expected to open by the time you read this.

On Chaoyang Lu, east of Zhang Residence (below). Admission ¥30 ($3.90/£1.95). English audio guide ¥20 ($2.60/£1.30) plus ¥200 ($26/£13) and ID deposit. 8:30am–5:30pm.

Zhang Residence (Zhang Xueliang Jiuju Chenlieguan) This resurrected courtyard house south of the Gu Gong, originally known as Shuai Fu (the Commander's Palace), was the home of warlord Zhang Zuolin and his celebrated son, Marshal Zhang Xueliang. The residence provides a glimpse into the almost-imperial world inhabited by the powerful warlords who ruled parts of China after the Qing dynasty collapsed. A study in the Xiaoqing Lou, a small European-styled house next to the main courtyard complex, is where Zhang Zuolin died after Japanese assassins exploded a bomb under his private train in 1928.

Corner of Chaoyang Lu and Nan Shuncheng Lu. ✆ 024/2484-2454. Admission ¥50 ($6.50/£3.25). 8:30am–5:30pm. Walk west from Gu Gong; take a left on Zhengyang Jie.

OUTSIDE SHENYANG

Qian Shan ✪ Once a quiet mountain retreat, Qian Shan, one of Dongbei's most accessible getaways, is slowly being taken over by tourists scrambling over the Song dynasty temples and zipping through the park on electric shuttle buses that charge ¥10 ($13/£6.50) a ride. Getting off the main road, which twists through the national park, leads to a more serene and pleasant experience. Climbing is not highly favored by the teeming hordes of visitors, so it's quite easy to escape to a pleasant hike off the well-worn paths leading to sites and temples, though you have to climb quite a distance to get away from the karaoke bar speakers blasting on the northeastern slope.

The Bei Bu (Northern Ravine), with signs in English, can be seen in 1 day. Xianren Tai (Peak of the Immortals), site of the legendary Da'an Temple, requires an overnight trip. There are several affordable hotels in the area. Modest rooms are available in some of the Buddhist temples if you ask nicely.

17km (11 miles) south of An Shan. Admission at main gate ¥50 ($6.50/£3.25), temples ¥5–¥20 (65¢–$2.60/35p–£1.30). Open 24 hr. Bus: Catch large air-conditioned bus to An Shan (every 15 min; 2 hr., ¥22/$2.85/£1.40, plus ¥1/15¢/10p mandatory insurance) near Wenhua Gong, 3 blocks southeast of Shenyang Zhan on Minzhu Lu; then take minibus from Jian Guo Nan Lu (40 min.; ¥2/25¢/15p) to Qian Shan. Last bus back to Shenyang leaves An Shan at 7pm.

WHERE TO STAY

High season in Shenyang runs from March to mid-October. Hotels become especially crowded with conventions in early September. Room rates are high, even with the customary 15% discount, but some high-end hotels offer good deals in summer. More budget options are now available. The most convenient choice, the **Peace Hotel (Heping Binguan,** Zhongshan Lu 97; ✆ 024/2349-8888), located in a massive brick building painted red and white north of the Shenyang Zhan, has a large variety of simple but old rooms. A standard room costs ¥200 ($26/£13) and a triple costs ¥260 ($34/£17). **Home Inn (Rujia,** Zhengyang Jie 196; ✆ 024/2486-1999; www.home inns.com) is just 10-minute walk from Gugong and offers clean and cozy rooms. Its proximity to a number of attractions and the Zhong Jie business area makes it a good budget pick. A standard room costs ¥199 ($26/£13).

VERY EXPENSIVE

Shenyang Marriott (Shenyang Huangchao Wanhao Jiudian)   This ostentatious hotel—the only full-fledged Marriott in China until the chain opened a second branch in Beijing in 2002—is no longer under the management of the Marriott. The property is luxurious, but its blinding exterior and the gold-and-crystal garishness of its lobby can leave you craving subtlety. Guest rooms mirror the rest of the hotel, with plush beds and beautiful redwood furniture. Small bathrooms have generous marble fittings.

Qingnian Dajie 386. © **024/2388-3456.** Fax 024/2388-0677. 435 units. ¥699–¥758 ($91–$99/£45–£49) standard room. 15% service charge. Rates include breakfast. AE, DC, MC, V. **Amenities:** 3 restaurants; deli; bar; cigar room; small indoor pool; nice exercise room; concierge; business center; salon; 24-hr. room service; same-day laundry/dry cleaning; nonsmoking rooms; executive-level rooms. *In room:* A/C, satellite TV, dataport, minibar, fridge, hair dryer, safe.

Sheraton Lido (Lidu Xilaideng Fandian) ☞   This is the best five-star in Shenyang. Decorated throughout with fine, original artwork, it offers the city's largest and classiest rooms—a stark contrast in style to the neighboring Marriott's rooms. Standard guest rooms have large bathrooms with separate bathtub and shower. The fourth floor has an indoor climbing wall.

Qingnian Dajie 386 (south of Wulihe Stadium). © **024/2318-8888.** Fax 024/2318-8000. www.sheraton.com/shenyang. 590 units. ¥733–¥933 ($95–$121/£48–£61) standard room. 15% service charge. Rates include breakfast. AE, DC, MC, V. **Amenities:** 3 restaurants; deli; bar; indoor pool; golf simulator; health club and spa; concierge; business center; forex; salon; 24-hr. room service; same-day laundry/dry cleaning service; nonsmoking floors; executive-level rooms. *In room:* A/C, satellite TV, dataport, broadband Internet access, minibar, fridge, hair dryer, iron, safe.

Traders Hotel (Shangmao Fandian) ☞   Its convenient location, in the midst of the Taiyuan Jie shopping district and within walking distance of Shenyang Zhan, is the number-one advantage of this Shangri-La-managed four-star hotel. Service is stellar, standard rooms are spacious with a subtle Oriental touch, and the bathrooms are virtually spotless. Wireless Internet connection is available on the 21st floor.

Zhonghua Lu 68 (at Taiyuan Jie). © **024/2341-2288.** Fax 024/2341-1988. www.shangri-la.com. 588 units. ¥540–¥620 ($70–$81/£35–£40) standard room. 15% service charge. Rates include breakfast for 1. AE, DC, MC, V. **Amenities:** 2 restaurants; deli; bar; small exercise room; Jacuzzi; sauna; concierge; business center; forex; large shopping center; salon; 24-hr. room service; same-day laundry/dry cleaning service; nonsmoking rooms; executive-level rooms. *In room:* A/C, satellite TV, broadband Internet access, minibar, fridge, hair dryer, safe.

EXPENSIVE

Gloria Plaza Shenyang (Shenyang Kailai Dajiudian) *Value*   The Gloria Plaza was the first international hotel to open in the Shenyang Bei Zhan area and is still a reliable luxury standby. Well-maintained guest rooms are unremarkably decorated but comfortable and have small but clean bathrooms.

Yinbin Jie 32 (at Bei Zhan Lu). © **024/2252-8855.** Fax 024/2252-8533. www.gphshenyang.com. 383 units. ¥458 ($60/£30) standard room. 15% service charge. AE, DC, MC, V. **Amenities:** 2 restaurants; bar; health club and spa; concierge; business center; salon; limited room service; laundry service; dry cleaning. *In room:* A/C, satellite TV, broadband Internet access, minibar, fridge.

New World Courtyard (Xin Shijie Wanyi Jiudian)   The New World Courtyard, Shenyang's first international joint-venture hotel, is the only real downtown luxury alternative to Traders. Little has been done to update facilities since its opening in 1994, but rooms are spacious and comfortable enough, and service is courteous.

Nanjing Nan Jie 2 (at Zhongshan Lu). © **024/2386-9888.** Fax 024/2386-0018. 263 units. ¥318 ($41/£21) standard room. 15% service charge. DC, MC, V. **Amenities:** 3 restaurants; exercise room (w/rusty equipment); sauna;

concierge; business center; forex; salon; limited room service; in-room massage; laundry service; dry cleaning. *In room:* A/C, satellite TV, minibar, fridge.

Times Plaza (Shidai Guangchang Jiudian)   Located just opposite Shenyang Bei Zhan, the well-situated Times Plaza is another good four-star selection in the area. Though guest rooms are fairly standard, if large, the beds are comfy and the bathrooms are clean, with shower and tub.

Beizhan Lu 99, Shenhe (opposite to Beizhan Railway Station). © 024/2253-2828. Fax 024/2253-0588. 274 units. ¥399 ($52/£26). AE, DC, MC, V. **Amenities:** Restaurant; deli; bar; exercise room; salon; concierge; business center; forex; limited room service; massage; laundry service; dry cleaning. *In room:* A/C, satellite TV, minibar, fridge, safe.

MODERATE

Liaoning Hotel (Liaoning Binguan) 🦋 *(Finds*   Originally part of the illustrious Japanese-run Yamato chain, the Liaoning is one of a very few truly charming hotels in the Northeast. The building (constructed in 1927) underwent an admirable $3.75-million restoration in 2001, giving new life to the original marble staircase with its well-worn brass handrails and intimate green-and-white tile lobby. Guest rooms are high-ceilinged and simply furnished; bathrooms are small but pleasant. The Liaoning's central location on Zhongshan Guangchang adds to the charm.

Zhongshan Lu 97, south of Zhongshan Guangchang. © 024/2383-9166. Fax 024/2383-9103. 79 units. ¥260–¥350 ($34–$46/£17–£23) standard room. No credit cards. **Amenities:** 2 restaurants; outdoor tennis court; exercise room; sauna; beautiful game room (chess and card tables); business center; laundry. *In room:* A/C, TV, dataport, fridge, hair dryer, safe.

INEXPENSIVE

Shenyang Post Hotel (Shenyang Youzheng Dasha)   The hallways in this government-run three-star are typically depressing, but its newly renovated rooms are surprisingly comfortable and clean. Prices are far lower than they should be. The hotel is also conveniently located next to Shenyang Bei Zhan.

Bei Zhan Lu 78. © 024/2259-3333. Fax 024/2252-2369. 214 units. ¥228–¥268 ($30–$35/£15–£17) standard room. No credit cards. **Amenities:** Restaurant; business center; laundry. *In room:* A/C, satellite TV, hair dryer.

Top Star (Qidouxing Shangwu Luguan) *(Value*   Here the rooms are spacious and clean, with a stylish minimalist design. Some of the single and double-bed rooms have a transparent shower cubicle placed separately in the room, adding a playful touch.

Shenyang Lu, Donghuanan Xiang 7. © 024/2410-7777. www.topstarhotel.com. 201 units. ¥188–¥267 ($24–$35/£12–£17) standard room. No credit cards. **Amenities:** Restaurant; deli; self-service laundry; nonsmoking rooms; reading and video playing center. *In room:* Cable TV, broadband Internet access, hair dryer.

WHERE TO DINE

Shenyang boasts a fair selection of Japanese restaurants. The classiest is **Mikado,** in the Shenyang Marriott (see above), with a specialization in teppanyaki and fine sushi served in private tatami-mat rooms. Cheaper and more convenient is the **Qianyi Lamian Dian** (Tianjin Bei Jie, north of the Dongbei Cinema; © 024/2341-9941), open from 10am to 10pm. The small but lively Japanese noodle shop (with a picture menu) is located just southeast of the Shangri-La. You'll find **KFC, McDonald's, Pizza Hut,** and **Häagen-Dazs Cafe** on Zhonghua Jie, south of Shenyang Zhan, and a pair of **McDonald's** on Taiyuan Jie and Zhong Jie; Zhong Jie also has a **Pizza Hut.** For groceries, go to **Wal-Mart** on Zhonghua Jie, near Shengyang Zhan, or the **Carrefour** near Shenyang Bei Zhan.

Ma Family Shaomai (Ma Jia Shaomai Guan) ✿ CHINESE/MUSLIM   Great-great-great-grandpa Ma is rumored to have first sold these award-winning *shaomai* (steamed open-top dumplings) from a street-side wheelbarrow in 1796. Prices on the menu are for a plate of 10 dumplings—eight dumplings for one hungry person is more than enough. The most delicious offering here is the *chuantong* (traditional) *shaomai*, with beef and ginger. *Yu cui* (jade green) *shaomai*, with egg and spring onion is excellent vegetarian fare.

Taiyuan Jie 12, Heping. ✆ **024/8383-1555.** Meal for 2 ¥25–¥50 ($3.25–$6.50/£1.65–£3.25). No credit cards. 10am–9pm.

Xinglongxuan Jiaozi Guan ✿ JIAOZI   Unmistakable with its bright red facade, this restaurant is cheaper and livelier than the "tourist-approved" Laobian Jiaozi Guan, and its *jiaozi* are just as delicious. Try the *bianxian sanxian* (egg, shrimp, and chives stir-fried before wrapping) or the standard *zhurou baicai* (pork and cabbage).

Zhongshan Lu 258, at Yi Jing Jie (1 block east of Golden Hotel). ✆ **024/2270-0209.** Meal for 2 ¥15–¥40 ($1.95–$5.20/£1–£2.60). No credit cards. 9am–10pm.

SHENYANG AFTER DARK

Shenyang goes to bed at around 10pm on most Saturdays, but late nights can still be had. **Mulligan's,** an Irish pub inside the Holiday Inn Hotel, at Nanjing Bei Jie 206 (✆ **024/2334-1888**), with its wide selection of international beers and a tolerable level of kitsch, is a not bad choice. If you order a bottle of whiskey but can't finish it, the bar will hang a name tag on it and throw it in a glass display case near the door, where it will wait until the next night of debauchery. **Babyface Club,** Shisan (13) Wei Lu 5, Heping District (✆ **024/2324-8888**), and **Bacchus Bar,** Nan Sanjing 37, Heping (✆ **024/2270-2529**), are popular among locals.

2 Dandong

280km (173 miles) S of Shenyang, 370km (229 miles) NE of Dalian

Visitors come to **Dandong** for one reason: to see North Korea. Situated on a bend in the Yalu Jiang (Green Duck River) and connected by rail bridge to the North Korean town of Sinuiju, the city has built a robust economy around the geographical voyeurs who rush to the border every summer. For all its wealth, Dandong remains a Chinese city, with crowded tenement buildings and a new riverside development area already stained by pollution, but it gleams in comparison with its neighbor.

ESSENTIALS

GETTING THERE **Flights** leave the airport (Dandong Jichang), 13km (8 miles) west of town, for Shanghai (Tues and Sat) and Shenzhen (Tues and Sat). Purchase tickets at the **CAAC ticket office (Minhang Shoupiao Chu;** ✆ **0415/221-7999;** open Mon–Sat 8–11:30am and 1–4:30pm) at Jinshan Dajie 50 (intersection with San Wei Lu). The **airport shuttle** (30 min.; ¥5/65¢/35p) leaves from the CAAC office 2 hours before each flight. By **taxi,** it's a 20-minute ride for ¥40 ($5.20/£2.60).

Dandong's **railway station** is on Shi (10) Wei Lu, on the western edge of town. Trains go to Beijing (6:31pm; 14 hr.; ¥263/$34/£17), Shenyang (three daily; 3½ hr.; ¥24/$3.10/£1.55), Dalian (8:36pm; 11 hr.; ¥110/$14/£7.15), and Changchun (6:47am; 9¾ hr.; ¥89/$12/£5.80). **International trains** go to Pyongyang (¥180/$23/£12) and Moscow (¥3,000/$390/£195); tickets for these are available in the **CITS** foreign office (✆ **0415/213-2237;** open Mon–Fri 8:30–11am and 1:30–5pm). The office is located

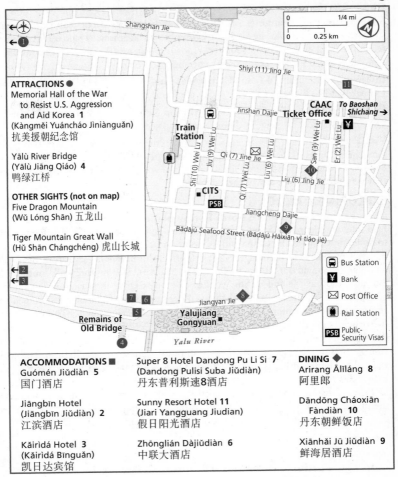

ATTRACTIONS ●
Memorial Hall of the War
   to Resist U.S. Aggression
   and Aid Korea **1**
(Kàngmĕi Yuáncháo Jìniànguăn)
抗美援朝纪念馆

Yālù River Bridge
(Yālù Jiāng Qiáo) **4**
鸭绿江桥

OTHER SIGHTS (not on map)
Five Dragon Mountain
(Wŭ Lóng Shān) 五龙山

Tiger Mountain Great Wall
(Hŭ Shān Chángchéng) 虎山长城

Shangshan Jie

Shiyi (11) Jing Jie

Jinshan Dajie

CAAC
Ticket Office

To Baoshan
Shichang →

Train
Station

Qi (7) Jine Jie

Liu (6) Jing Jie

CITS

PSB

Jiangcheng Dajie

Bādàjú Seafood Street (Bādàjú Hǎixiān yī tiáo jiē)

Shi (10) Wei Lu
Jiu (9) Wei Lu
Ba (8) Wei Lu
Qi (7) Wei Lu
Wu (5) Wei Lu
Liu (6) Wei Lu
San (3) Wei Lu
Er (2) Wei Lu

Jiangyan Jie

Yalujiang
Gongyuan

Remains of
Old Bridge

Yalu River

🚌 Bus Station
¥ Bank
✉ Post Office
🏢 Rail Station
PSB Public-
Security Visas

ACCOMMODATIONS ■
Guómén Jiŭdiàn **5**
国门酒店

Jiāngbīn Hotel
(Jiāngbīn Jiŭdiàn) **2**
江滨酒店

Kăirìdá Hotel **3**
(Kăirìdá Bīnguăn)
凯日达宾馆

Super 8 Hotel Dandong Pu Li Si **7**
(Dandong Pulisi Suba Jiŭdiàn)
丹东普利斯速8酒店

Sunny Resort Hotel **11**
(Jiari Yangguang Jiudian)
假日阳光酒店

Zhōnglián Dàjiŭdiàn **6**
中联大酒店

DINING ◆
Arirang Ālǐláng **8**
阿里郎

Dāndōng Cháoxiān
   Fàndiàn **10**
丹东朝鲜饭店

Xiānhǎi Jū Jiŭdiàn **9**
鲜海居酒店

in the double-spired Shuangxing Dasha across from the station (see "Border Crossing: North Korea & Russia," below).

The **long-distance bus station** (© 0415/213-4571) is across the street from the railway station, at the corner of Shi Wei Lu and Gong'an Jie, with coaches to Shenyang (2½ hr.; ¥64/$8.30/£4.15) and Tonghua (¥52/$6.75/£3.40), and **Dalian express buses (Dalian Kuai Ke)** (7:35am, 8:30am, 12:30pm, and 1:50pm; 4 hr.; ¥85/$11/£5.50).

VISITOR INFORMATION   For tourist complaints, call © 0415/314-7937.

GETTING AROUND   Most of Dandong lies north of a V formed by the Yalu Jiang and the train tracks. Shi Wei Lu follows the tracks to the Yalu Jiang Gongyuan, facing North Korea. **Taxis** are ¥6 (80¢/40p) in town.

FAST FACTS

Banks, Foreign Exchange & ATMs Cash and traveler's checks can be exchanged from 8am to 4pm inside the **Bank of China** branch at Jinshan Dajie 60 (at its intersection with Er Wei Lu; open Mon–Fri 7:30–11:30am and 1–5pm). A 24-hour international ATM is located at the bank's entrance.

Internet Access The 24-hour **Wuxian Wangyuan** is on Shiyi (11) Jing Jie, north of Liu (6) Wei Lu. It charges ¥2 (25¢/15p) per hour. Dial-up is ⓒ **96163.**

Post Office The main post office, open from 8am to 5:30pm, is on the corner of Qi (7) Wei Lu and Qi Jing Jie. Phone cards are sold inside.

Visa Extensions For visa extensions, go to room 112 of the main **PSB** office at Jiangcheng Dajie 15, behind Shuangxing Dasha (ⓒ **0415/210-3393;** open Mon–Fri 8am–noon and 1:30–5:30pm). You'll have to show a hotel registration card and proof that you have $100 per day of the extension.

EXPLORING DANDONG

There isn't much to see at the **North Korean border,** but the contrast between lively Dandong and depressed Sinuiju does provide a vivid illustration of the different paths to development taken by China and its Communist ally. There are two ways to see the border—by boat and by bridge. Most visitors do both. **Boats** leave from inside the Yalu Jiang Gongyuan (6:30am–5:30pm; ¥1/15¢/10p), a 10-minute walk south of the railway station at the end of Shi Wei Lu. The boats range in size, from large, tacky Chinese-roofed floats to small speedboats. Prices are highly negotiable, but in general, you should not pay more than ¥10 ($1.30/65p) per person, and chartering a small speed boat should cost no more than ¥30 ($3.90/£1.95). Drivers will hand you a flimsy life jacket, then whip you around to within 3m (10 ft.) of Sinuiju so you can take pictures of the rusting cargo boats, a shipyard, and waving children. A few blocks west, along Jiangyan Jie, is the **Yalu Jiang Qiao** ⓡ (ⓒ **0415/312-4767;** 6am–6pm; ¥20/$2.60/£1.30), a unique horizontal rotation bridge bombed by the United States in 1950. Korea dismantled its half shortly after the Korean War armistice, rendering the bridge useless. You can wander out to the still-mangled end of the Chinese section, where someone has installed a pair of bomb casings as a reminder.

Tips Border Crossing: North Korea & Russia

At press time, United States citizens were not allowed to travel from Dandong to North Korea. CITS in Dandong can arrange tours for other nationalities, but independent Beijing-based operations like foreign-run Koryo Tours (www.koryogroup.com) can also pick you up in Dandong, charge roughly the same rates, and have more experience with foreigners. The paperwork takes 2 weeks to process.

Crossing the border from Dongbei into **Russia,** either on the Trans-Siberian train or at one of the border posts in Heilong Jiang and Inner Mongolia, is easier but also requires a visa. Tourist visas can usually only be arranged at the Russian Embassy in Beijing. Keep in mind you'll have to arrange for a Chinese **double-entry visa** if you plan to come back to China from either country.

You might guess what kind of perspective a museum clunkily named the **Memorial Hall of the War to Resist U.S. Aggression and Aid Korea (Kangmei Yuanchao Jinianguan;** open 8am–5pm; ¥30/$3.90/£1.95) might have. Nevertheless, it offers an interesting Communist revisionist's look at the Korean War with black-and-white photos, surprisingly clear English translations, and patriotic music piped in. The museum requires some effort to reach—not just because it's located on a hill on the north side of Shangshan Jie, in the northwest part of town, but because the stairs to the memorial are quite a climb. The museum is to the right of the memorial, and behind the museum are some rusty rail cars, tanks, and fighter planes used during the war. Take bus no. 21 from the railway station, get off at the Tiyuguan, and walk northwest.

OUTSIDE DANDONG

Five Dragon Mountain (Wu Long Shan) The 20-minute drive from downtown Dandong puts you in an idyllic setting with plenty of hikes and a temple housing 20 monks. Ignore the tacky faux-Japanese "villas" at the front of the park, and concentrate on the nature within. It's particularly nice in the autumn when the leaves change colors.

Admission ¥36 ($4.70/£2.35). Open 24 hr. Round-trip taxi from center of town ¥80 ($10/£5.20).

Tiger Mountain Great Wall (Hu Shan Changcheng) 𝒢★ Tiger Mountain, a short, steep, and impeccably restored section of the Great Wall located 30km (19 miles) northeast of Dandong, forms part of China's border with North Korea. A brief hike along the Wall provides beautiful views of surrounding cornfields, and the return path takes you right up against the small stream that separates Chinese and North Korean territory. South Chinese sometimes wander onto stones set in the stream just behind the Wall to trade goods and information with North Korean soldiers and farmers. *Warning:* Cross over on the stones yourself and you risk arrest.

ⓒ 0415/557-8511. Admission ¥40 ($5.20/£2.60). Museum ¥10 ($1.30/65p). Open 24 hr. Tourist bus (40 min.; ¥11/$1.45/70p round-trip) leaves from left side of long-distance bus station at 8:10am and 1pm, returns from mountain 10:30am and 3:20pm.

WHERE TO STAY

A recent boom in hotels in Dandong means that travelers have a lot more choices and bargaining power. The **Jiangbin Hotel** 𝒢★ (Yanjiang Kaifaqu Fangba 5 Hao Lou; ⓒ **0415/315-3748;** fax 0415/314-2835; Visa accepted) is one of the best values in town, with stylish, modern rooms—complete with computer and free Internet access—facing the river (¥300–¥600/$39–$78/£20–£39; 40% discount available). **Sunny Resort Hotel** 𝒢★ (Xian Qian Jie 1, Yuanbaoqu; ⓒ **0415/288-3333;** fax 0415/288-7999; www.jryghotel.com) is the city's newest four-star hotel. The rooms and bathroom are clean and modern, with a soothing ambience (¥338–¥368/$44–$48/£22–£24; 15% service charge; Amex, Diners Club, MasterCard, Visa accepted).

Another four-star hotel is the **Zhonglian Dajiudian** 𝒢★ (Shangmao Luyou Qu A Qu 1; ⓒ **0415/317-0666;** fax 0415/317-0888; www.zlhotel.com.cn), located opposite the Yalu Jiang Qiao. The hotel offers a nice Western food buffet, a bowling center, and surprisingly large rooms with generously sized beds and impeccable bathrooms (¥489–¥658/$64–$86/£32–£43; Amex, Diners Club, MasterCard, Visa accepted). The hotel cafe looks onto North Korea; come with a pair of binoculars that you can use to gaze at North Korea from rooms overlooking the river. Next to it is a budget hotel, **Super 8 Hotel Dandong Pu Li Si** (Binjiang Zhong Lu 64-2; ⓒ **0415/ 2312-2222;** www.super8.com.cn; ¥138–¥228/$18–$30/£9–£15; Amex, Diners Club,

MasterCard, Visa accepted). Opened in 2007, the hotel has guest rooms that are spacious but lack character; the shower-only bathrooms are kept clean. Some rooms overlook the Yalu Jiang Qiao.

WHERE TO DINE

Downtown Dandong is full of small, nondescript home-style restaurants and *jiaozi* houses, and the river promenade has a number of upscale Japanese and Korean eateries. The **Dandong Chaoxian Fandian** ⚔ (✆ **0415/313-9919;** open 10am–9pm), northeast of the railway station at Qi Jing Jie 37, serves the best Korean cold noodles *(lengmian)* in town for a mere ¥3.50 (45¢/25p). Along the strip of Korean eateries that line the river, locals consider **Arirang (Alilang)** (✆ **0415/212-2333;** 9am–9:30pm) a pretty good choice. The nice Korean setting with comfortable booths and private rooms is a nice place to relax after boating. Try the *shiguo Banfan* (stone pot rice), known as *bibimbop* in Korean, the *huoguo* (hot pot), or the *shengban niurou* (raw beef). If you're really feeling adventurous, you might consider the *xiangla gourou* (spicy dog). The best place to try the local seafood, which area residents rave about, is at **Xianha iJu Jiudian** (Badaju Haixian Yitiao jie; ✆ **0415/216-5763;** 9am–midnight). It offers a simple, clean interior and a back room full of tanks of live seafood that you can wander through.

3 Dalian ⭐⭐ & Lushun

397km (246 miles) S of Shenyang

Dalian is the supermodel of Chinese cities. Thoroughly modern, sartorially savvy, and unabashedly narcissistic, it is also the largest and busiest port in northern China. Dalian's straightforward beauty can be refreshing in a region where most towns are of the interesting-but-homely type, and indeed, there are few more enjoyable activities after a week in the Dongbei gloom than a sunlit stroll along the city's supremely walkable streets. The mere fact that the city has a definable downtown, unlike other cities in China, is to be lauded.

Like Shanghai and Hong Kong, the cities to which it is most often compared, Dalian isn't really Chinese. Located just north of the Lushun naval base at the tip of the Liaodong Peninsula, it was conceived by Russia's czarist government as an ice-free alternative to Vladivostok. Construction of the port, originally called Dalny, got off to a quick start after Russia secured a lease on the peninsula in 1898; however, it lost the city and Lushun to Japan in the Russo-Japanese War (1904–05). Dalian (in Japanese: *Dairen*) soon grew into the pleasantly sophisticated port Russia had imagined.

Communist-era industrial development swamped Dalian in thick clouds of factory smoke, but it was miraculously resurrected in the mid-1990s by Mayor Bo Xilai, who tried to model the new Dalian on cities he had seen in Europe. This led him to introduce several revolutionary measures—including a hefty fine for public spitting—that have become a model for urban renewal projects throughout China. Today, Dalian is considered a vision of China's future both by optimists, who laud its beauty and modernity, and by more cynical observers, who point wryly to the same silver skyscrapers and note how many are empty. Striking as the modern buildings are, it is the old colonial architecture, remnants of Japanese and Russian rule contrasting pleasantly with the newness around them, that is the city's most interesting attraction.

Fashion designers and consumers from China, Japan, Korea, and Hong Kong descend on Dalian in mid-September for the 2-week **Dalian International Fashion**

Dalian

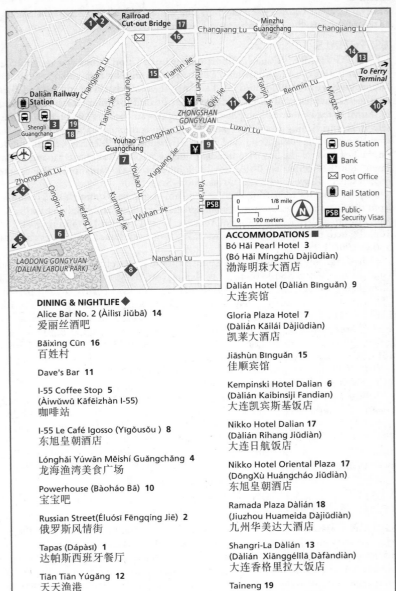

Railroad Cut-out Bridge 17

Changjiang Lu

Minzhu Guangchang

Changjiang Lu

Tianjin Jie

Minshen Jie

Qiyi Jie

Renmin Lu

Mingze Jie

To Ferry Terminal

Youhao Lu

Tianjin Jie

Youhao Lu

ZHONGSHAN GONGYUAN

Luxun Lu

Dalián Railway Station

Shengli Guangchang

Youhao Zhongshan Lu Guangchang

Zhongshan Lu

Yuguang Jie

Kunming Lu

Wuhan Jie

Yan'an Lu

Qingni Jie

Jiefang Lu

Nanshan Lu

LAODONG GONGYUAN (DALIAN LABOUR PARK)

🚌 Bus Station
¥ Bank
✉ Post Office
🚉 Rail Station
PSB Public-Security Visas

0   1/8 mile
0   100 meters

ACCOMMODATIONS ■

Bó Hǎi Pearl Hotel **3**
(Bó Hǎi Míngzhū Dàjiǔdiàn)
渤海明珠大酒店

Dàlián Hotel (Dàlián Bīnguǎn) **9**
大连宾馆

Gloria Plaza Hotel **7**
(Dàlián Kǎilái Dàjiǔdiàn)
凯莱大酒店

Jiāshùn Bīnguǎn **15**
佳顺宾馆

Kempinski Hotel Dalian **6**
(Dàlián Kaibinsiji Fandian)
大连凯宾斯基饭店

Nikko Hotel Dalian **17**
(Dàlián Rihang Jiǔdiàn)
大连日航饭店

Nikko Hotel Oriental Plaza **17**
(DōngXù Huángcháo Jiǔdiàn)
东旭皇朝酒店

Ramada Plaza Dàlián **18**
(Jiuzhou Huameida Dàjiǔdiàn)
九州华美达大酒店

Shangri-La Dàlián **13**
(Dàlián Xiānggélǐlā Dàfàndiàn)
大连香格里拉大饭店

Taineng **19**
(Taineng Shaokao Dian)
太能烧烤店

DINING & NIGHTLIFE ◆

Alice Bar No. 2 (Àilìsī Jiǔbā) **14**
爱丽丝酒吧

Bǎixìng Cūn **16**
百姓村

Dave's Bar **11**

I-55 Coffee Stop **5**
(Àiwǔwǔ Kāfēizhàn I-55)
咖啡站

I-55 Le Café Igosso (Yīgǒusǒu) **8**
东旭皇朝酒店

Lónghǎi Yúwān Měishí Guǎngchǎng **4**
龙海渔湾美食广场

Powerhouse (Bàohǎo Bā) **10**
宝宝吧

Russian Street(Éluósī Fēngqíng Jiē) **2**
俄罗斯风情街

Tapas (Dápàsī) **1**
达帕斯西班牙餐厅

Tiān Tiān Yúgǎng **12**
天天渔港

Festival (Dalian Guoji Fuzhuang Jie). The festival isn't as important or glamorous as the city claims, but it's worth seeing if you're in the area.

ESSENTIALS

GETTING THERE   Dalian's **airport (Zhoushuizi Guoji Jichang)** is roughly 5km (3 miles) northeast of downtown on Yingke Lu (20 min. by taxi; ¥30/$3.90/£1.95), airport buses cost ¥10 ($1.30/65p). Exchange traveler's checks on the second floor, next to the international check-in desk (no credit cards). **China Northern Airlines,** in the Minhang Dasha at Zhongshan Lu 143 (open 6am–6pm; ℂ **0411/8280-2886**), sells tickets to Beijing (11 flights daily), Shanghai (seven flights daily), Guangzhou (five flights daily), Hong Kong, and Seoul. **All Nippon Airlines** has a ticket counter on the first floor of the Sen Mao building (intersection of Zhongshan Lu and Wuhui Lu; ℂ **800/810-5551;** fax 0411/369-2508; open Mon–Fri 9am–5pm). The counter sells tickets to Tokyo (daily) and Osaka (Mon–Sat).

    Airport shuttles (departing every 2 hr.; 8am–4:40pm; 20 min.; ¥10/$1.30/65p) from the Furama Hotel (next to the Shangri-La, see below) and Minhang Dasha. Or take **bus** no. 701 from the corner of Yuguang Jie and Youhao Lu (45 min.; ¥1/15¢/ 10p). By **taxi,** the trip between the airport and downtown takes 20 minutes and costs ¥30 ($3.90/£1.95).

    Dalian's **railway station (Dalian Zhan)** is in the center of town, opposite Shengli Guangchang (Victory Sq.). Trains go to Beijing (two daily; 11½ hr.; ¥257/$33/£17), Shanghai (1:08pm; 22½ hr.; ¥446/$58/£29), Shenyang (five daily; 3½ hr.; ¥55/$7.15/£3.60), Harbin (9:54pm; 9 hr.; ¥231/$30/£15), Dandong (8:46am; 10½ hr.; ¥110/$14/£7.15), and Lushun (6:55am; 1¾ hr.; ¥10/$1.30/65p). Most **long-distance buses** congregate around Shengli Guangchang (ℂ **0411/8362-8681**). Express air-conditioned coaches to Dandong (eight daily; 4 hr.; ¥85/$11/£5.50) and Lushun (¥11/$1.45/70p) leave from the square's west side; buses to Harbin (one daily; 13 hr.; ¥210/$27/£14) and Changchun (two daily; 8 hr.; ¥156/$20/£10) and to Shenyang (10 daily; 4 hr.; ¥107/$14/£6.95) leave from the east side.

    Ferries leave from the Dalian Keyun Zhan (ℂ **0411/8263-6061** or 0411/8262-5349), on Gangwan Jie (east end of Renmin Lu), for Yantai (2pm; 3 hr.; ¥230/$30/ £15), Tianjin (even days 8pm; 12 hr.; ¥130–¥720/$17–$94/£8.45–£47), and Incheon (Renchuan) in South Korea (Mon, Wed and Fri 2:30pm; ¥1,010/$131/£66). The ticket office is open from 4am to 10pm; Yantai express tickets are also sold at booths near Shengli Guangchang. Take bus no. 801 (15 min.; ¥1/15¢/65p) from Youhao Guangchang. The 10-minute taxi ride costs ¥10 ($1.30/65p).

VISITOR INFORMATION   The **Tourism Bureau** has an information line (ℂ **0411/96181**) and a complaint line (ℂ **0411/8433-9970**).

GETTING AROUND   Downtown Dalian is arranged around a series of traffic circles. The two most important are **Youhao Guangchang (Friendship Square),** dominated by a glass globe in the center, and **Zhongshan Guangchang,** the city's transportation center. Ten roads radiate from Zhongshan Guangchang, including Renmin Dajie, a major avenue that runs east to the wharf, and Zhongshan Lu, which runs west past the railway station to the city's far southwestern corner. **Taxis** charge ¥8 ($1.05/50p) for the first 3km (2 miles), then ¥2 (25¢/15p) per kilometer; it's 30% extra from 10pm to 5am. Regular **buses** (without air-conditioning) cost ¥1 (15¢/10p), air-conditioned and minibuses cost ¥2 (25¢/15p); pay as you get on. Bus no. 801 runs the length of Zhongshan Lu and Renmin Dajie. A **tour bus** takes visitors around the city from the south side of Dalian Railway Station South Square to Zhongshan Guang-chang (every 30 min.; 1½ hr.; ¥10/$1.30/65p). Real Japanese-built **trolleys** go from Erqi Guangchang in the east to Xinghai Gongyuan in the southwest.

FAST FACTS

Banks, Foreign Exchange & ATMs   The main **Bank of China** branch is in a large tower on the corner of Yan'an Lu and Baiyu Jie, behind the Dalian Hotel on Zhong-shan Guangchang (open Mon–Fri 8:30am–4:30pm). Traveler's checks and cash can be exchanged at window 32, and credit cards are handled at window 11 (both on the sec-ond floor). There are international ATMs next to the old Bank of China on Zhong-shan Guangchang and inside the Nikko's shopping arcade.

Internet Access   **Buye Cheng Wangyuan** (24 hr.; ¥3/40¢/20p per hour) is the most central Internet bar, located underground on the northwest corner of Shengli Guangchang. Dial-up is 🕾 **165** or 169.

Post Office   The central post office is located several blocks north of Zhongshan Guangchang, on the corner of Shanghai Lu and Changjiang Lu (open May–Sept 8am–7pm; Oct–Apr 8am–6pm).

Visa Extensions   Visa extensions are easy to obtain; you need only a passport and hotel registration to obtain one. Go to the **PSB** Exit/Entry Office on the corner of Yan'an Lu and Wuhan Jie (second floor; 🕾 **0411/8280-2722;** open Mon–Fri 8–11:30am and 1–5pm). Extensions take 5 days to process.

EXPLORING DALIAN

Dalian's most impressive buildings surround **Zhongshan Guangchang.** Highlights are the late Renaissance–style white-brick and green-domed Bank of China (built in 1909) on the north side of the square, and the Dalian Hotel (see "Where to Stay," below) directly opposite. The city recently made an effort to recapture some of its Russian history with **Eluosi Fengqing Jie (Russian Street),** a collection of mostly new Russian-style structures north of the railway cutout, above Shanghai Lu. The large, dilapidated yellow-brick building at the end of the street was the municipal gov-ernment office when Russia still controlled the city. A stroll around the neighborhood surrounding **Nanshan Riben Fengqing Jie** will give you a glimpse of old Japanese housing, though the street itself is full of suspiciously modern homes. For a less pretty but still interesting taste of modern Chinese architecture, head to **Renmin Guangchang** (1km/½ mile east of the railway station on Zhongshan Lu; bus: nos. 801 and 701). This large square, surrounded on three sides by ominous government build-ings, is pleasant at night when lights illuminate the fountain.

The Beaches & Binhai Lu *(Kids*   Dalian's seaside location is the major draw for Chi-nese tourists. Most of its beaches are pebbly and polluted, but the simple presence of the ocean and its attendant sea air provide respite from the rigors of travel. Binhai Lu meanders next to the coastline and gives breathtaking views of the sea. Start your jour-ney by taking a taxi or bus no. 203 to Donghai Gongyuan (entrance fee ¥10/$1.30/ 65p), located about 5km (3 miles) east of downtown. In a nearby plaza at the north gate of the park, locals enjoy watching the sun rise. Continue on, by taxi, to **Bangchui Dao.** It was once the exclusive playground of Communist Party higher-ups and is now a pristine, hedge-lined country club only accessible by car (15 min.; ¥20/$2.60/ £1.30). The city's nicest beach is a 30-minute walk past the gate (¥20/$2.60/£1.30). Just west of Bangchui Dao is **Laohu Tan (Tiger Beach),** a popular beach that also features Dalian's best aquatic theme park, **Laohu Tan Haiyang Gongyuan** (see below). A few kilometers west is the relatively clean **Fu Jia Zhuang Beach** (¥5/65¢/ 35p). This is where the city's serious swimmers gather for a brisk dip before work. Take bus no. 5 (25 min.) from Qingniwa Qiao (north of Shengli Guangchang). **Xinghai Gongyuan**, 5km (3 miles) southwest of downtown, was originally a Japanese resort and is now Dalian's most accessible but crowded beach. Nearby is **Sun Asia Ocean World (Shengya Haiyang Shijie;** see below).

Jinshi Tan (Gold Pebble Beach) ★ *Moments*   With a little effort you can enjoy a clean beach without loudspeakers, tour groups, or other tackiness that infects the city shores. Hop on the light rail (*qinggui*) at the Dalian Zhan railway station and take it to the last stop, Jinshi Tan; the ride takes about an hour and passes by suburbs and factories along the coast. Taxis are sparse, so once you arrive, take a private car (¥5/65¢/35p) or a horse-drawn carriage (¥10/$1.30/65p) to the area's best strip of beach, **Huangjin Hai'an.** It's a good swimming spot and the fine-pebble beaches are nearly empty except during the high season (Aug–Sept). About 100m (328 ft.) north of the station is the **Dalian Wax Museum (Laxiang Bowuguan;** © **0411/8790-2006;** open 8am–5pm), where for ¥30 ($3.90/£1.95) you can stroll past replicas of Jackie Chan, Sun Yat-sen, Adolf Hitler, Zhang Ziyi, and Kate Winslet—direct from the set of *Titantic,* with piped-in Celine Dion music.

Laohu Tan Haiyang Gongyuan (Tiger Beach Ocean Park)   Tacky cartoonish signboards, dancing clowns, and cheesy shows with dolphins abound, but the locals love it. It's worth a look for its aquarium, its display of polar animals, and a wild bird park, called the niaoyulin. Avoid the "4-dimension pleasure theater" at all costs.

Binhai Lu 9. © **0411/8239-9398.** Admission ¥15 ($1.95/£1). 7:30am–5:40pm. Bus: no. 2, 4, 403, 404, 30, 521, or 524.

Lushun   Known to war historians as Port Arthur, Lushun has been the most important, and most sensitive, naval base in northern China for roughly 100 years. Little used during the Qing dynasty, it became a formidable installation under Russia, was captured and expanded by Japan after the Russo-Japanese War, and was finally returned to Chinese control after World War II. *Warning:* Most of the area is a military zone and officially off-limits to the public; do not cross the railroad tracks, which mark off the restricted area. For more information, contact the PSB (© **0411/8661-3411**).

Only two historical sights fall north of Lushun Bei Lu, both of which will appeal primarily to military history buffs. The express air-conditioned coaches to Lushun (1½ hr.; ¥11/$1.45/70p) leave from the square's west side every hour. To reach there by taxi, it costs ¥250–¥300 ($33–$39/£16–£20) round-trip. Some travel agencies, and even the Dalian Tourism Bureau, will claim that you can see other sights, but the *only* believable authority here is the PSB (see "Fast Facts," earlier in this chapter).

The **Shuishi Ying** (© **0411/8623-3509;** ¥40/$5.20/£2.60; open 7:30am–5pm), in the village of Shuishi, is where commanders of the Japanese and Russian armies met to discuss and sign Russia's surrender of Lushun in 1905. The tiny house, chosen because it was the only major structure still standing after both sides bombed the town, contains the original table on which the agreement was signed.

The **203-Meter Mountain (Erlingsan Gaodi)** ★ was Russia's rear defense base during the Russo-Japanese War and the site of one of the war's most pivotal battles. Between 10,000 and 17,000 Japanese soldiers, including the Japanese commander's son, died taking the mountain. A few of the trenches where they fought have been preserved, served by trails near the summit. An exhibition room halfway up the hill contains several Qing-era photos of the port and a few rusted swords and bullets used in the battle. Most striking is a large, bullet-shaped monument on the summit, erected by the Japanese and defaced by Russian tourists. You can look down into the port itself from here. The site is open 24 hours; admission is ¥30 ($3.90/£1.95); for information, call © **0411/8639-8277.**

Shengya Haiyang Shijie (Sun Asia Ocean World)   Ocean World does not compare with its rival, Tiger Beach Ocean Park, but the addition of a polar aquarium and the world's longest underwater aquarium tunnel (116m/380 ft.) may make it a worthwhile stop. Call ahead for free English-speaking guides, who will explain which of the animals in the tanks are edible. Take bus no. 801 from Qingniwa Qiao (30 min.).

Just east of Xinghai Park. © **0411/8458-1113.** www.sunasia.com. Admission (to Ocean World only) ¥100 ($13/ £6.50) adults, ¥50 ($6.50/£3.25) children. Combo tickets to both Ocean and Polar World ¥150 ($20/£9.75) adults, ¥75 ($9.75/£4.90) children. Summer 8:30am–5:30pm; winter 9am–4pm. Bus: no. 22, 23, 202, 709, 711, 801, K901, 502, 523, or 531.

SHOPPING

Dalian is a petite female shopper's paradise, with a range of Japanese, Korean, and western fashions. **Qingniwa Jie,** south of Shengli Guangchang (open 9am–9pm), is a materialistic mecca of malls, hotels, fast-food outlets, boutiques, and elaborate window displays unlike anything in China outside Shanghai. The prices are very reasonable and the spectacle of so many well-dressed Chinese people in one place is a strange, pleasant shock. If the labyrinth of underground shops, called the **Dixia Shangchang,** is too overwhelming, try the Japanese department stores Itokin (Yidujin). **Russian Street (Eluosi Fengqing Jie)** lacks any real Russian people, but is full of stalls with the country's goods, including chocolates, whiskey flasks, vodka, and dolls.

WHERE TO STAY

Dalian has the Northeast's largest selection of luxury hotels. Rooms are both hard to find and absurdly expensive during the September Fashion Festival, but discounts otherwise typically reach 50%.

VERY EXPENSIVE

Kempinski Hotel Dalian (Dalian Kaibinsiji Fandian) ⍟   Opened in 2005 by a German hotelier group and located just a street across the commercial and shopping center, the Kempinski Dalian has become one of the best choices in the city. The guest rooms, overlooking the picturesque Labor Park, are spacious, with stylish European furniture and plush beds. Bathrooms are nice with separate shower and tub.

Jiefang Lu 92 (on the east of Labor Park). © **0411/8259-8888.** Fax 0411/8259-6666. www.kempinski-dalian.com. 454 units. From ¥892 ($116/£58) standard room. 15% service charge. Rates include breakfast. AE, DC, MC, V. Amenities: 4 restaurants; deli; bar; indoor pool; health center and spa; salon; concierge; business center; same-day laundry/dry cleaning service; executive-level rooms. In room: A/C, flatscreen TV, satellite TV, broadband Internet access, minibar, fridge, hair dryer, safe.

Nikko Hotel Dalian (Dalian Rihang Jiudian) ⍟   Formerly the Hilton, the hotel changed to Japanese management in 2005 and has undergone a renovation. Guest rooms are tastefully modern, decorated in solid colors with lots of glass. Bathrooms are somewhat cramped, with separate tub and shower. Units at the top of the tower sway a bit in the wind, and traffic noise can be problematic, but the views are spectacular. Close to Zhongshan Guangchang.

Changjiang Lu 123 (at Minsheng Jie). © **0411/8252-9999.** Fax 0411/8252-9900. www.nikkodalian.com.cn. 372 units. ¥720–¥960 ($94–$125/£47–£62) standard room; ¥1,100–¥1,380 ($143–$179/£72–£90) suite. 15% service charge. AE, DC, MC, V. **Amenities:** 3 restaurants; deli; bar; indoor pool; outdoor tennis court; luxurious health club and spa; concierge; business center; forex; small shopping center; salon; 24-hr. room service; same-day laundry/dry cleaning service; nonsmoking rooms; executive-level rooms. *In room:* A/C, satellite TV, dataport, broadband Internet access, minibar, fridge, hair dryer, safe.

Shangri-La Dalian (Dalian Xianggelila Dafandian) 🏮🏮   With the recent
turnover in management and ownership of other hotels, Shangri-La's Northeast flagship seems to be the most reliable option. Standard rooms are incredibly spacious, tasteful, and comfortable. Bathrooms, the nicest in town, have separate shower and tub. Service is impeccable. The central courtyard garden is a pleasant place to rest your feet after a walk on Binhai Lu.

Renmin Lu 66. ⓒ **0411/8252-5000.** Fax 0411/8252-5050. www.shangri-la.com. 563 units. ¥1,000–¥1,500 ($130–$195/£65–£97) standard room. 15% service charge. AE, DC, MC, V. **Amenities:** 3 restaurants; deli; bar; cigar room; indoor 25m (82-ft.) pool; indoor/outdoor tennis courts; health club and spa; concierge; business center; forex; salon; 24-hr. room service; same-day laundry/dry cleaning service; nonsmoking rooms; executive-level rooms. *In room:* A/C, satellite TV, broadband Internet access, minibar, fridge, hair dryer, iron, safe.

EXPENSIVE
Bo Hai Pearl Hotel (Bo Hai Mingzhu Dajiudian)   This Chinese-run four-star is
typically tacky (note the frightening harpy statues at the door), but the hotel's location directly east of the railway station is as convenient as it gets in Dalian. Standard rooms are small with undersize bathrooms. Facilities and staff are slightly above par.

Shengli Guangchang 8. ⓒ **0411/8882-8333.** Fax 0411/8881-8158. 366 units. ¥388–¥488 ($50–$63/£25–£32) standard room. AE, DC, MC, V. **Amenities:** 2 restaurants; bar; small indoor pool; gym; sauna; salon; concierge; business center; forex; limited room service; laundry. *In room:* A/C, satellite TV, minibar, fridge, hair dryer.

Ramada Plaza Dalian (Jiuzhou Huameida Dajiudian)   The hotel is well located
near the railway station and popular among Japanese travelers. The recently renovated rooms are spacious and stylish, with large beds and flatscreen TVs. The bathrooms are clean, but are somewhat incommodious.

Shengli Guangchang 18. ⓒ **0411/8280-8888.** Fax 0411/8280-9704. www.ramada.com. 366 units. ¥550–¥800 ($72–$104/£36–£52) standard room. AE, DC, MC, V. **Amenities:** 2 restaurants; bar; indoor pool; gym; sauna; concierge; business center; limited room service; laundry; nonsmoking rooms. *In room:* A/C, satellite TV, broadband Internet access, minibar, fridge, hair dryer, safe.

MODERATE
Dalian Hotel (Dalian Binguan) 🏮   The Dalian, built in 1909 on the south side of
Zhongshan Guangchang, was described in a 1920s guidebook as "one of the finest hotels in the Far East." Originally a part of the Japanese-owned Yamato Hotel chain, it was restored to a semblance of its former appearance in 1997 but still lacks the charm of its counterparts in other northeastern cities. Guest rooms are large with small beds but clean, sizable bathrooms. Furnishings fail to match the grandeur of the building itself, but no other hotel in Dalian can claim as much history.

Zhongshan Guangchang 4. ⓒ **0411/8263-3111,** ext. 1101. Fax 0411/8263-4363. www.dl-hotel.com. 86 units. ¥498 ($65/£32) standard room. AE, MC, V. **Amenities:** 3 restaurants; business center; forex; laundry. *In room:* A/C, satellite TV, fridge, hair dryer.

Gloria Plaza Hotel (Dalian Kailai Dajiudian)   After an upgrade, the Gloria Plaza
is now a more pleasant place to stay. Guest rooms and bathrooms are now bigger in size, everything is clean, and the staff is friendly. There is a new lady floor decorated with a feminine touch, catering for women traveling alone. Cheaper units on lower floors receive little natural light.

Yide Jie 5 (at Youhao Guangchang). ℂ **0411/8280-8855**. Fax 0411/8280-8533. www.gphdalian.com. 211 units. ¥407–¥781 ($53–$102/£26–£51) standard room. 10% service charge. AE, DC, MC, V. **Amenities:** 2 restaurants; bar; business center; forex; laundry; 24-hr. room service; women's floor; executive rooms. *In room:* A/C, satellite TV, broadband Internet access, fridge, minibar, safe.

INEXPENSIVE

Jiashun Binguan   This amiable guesthouse, sandwiched between a McDonald's and a KFC on Shanghai Lu, offers small and simple but clean standard rooms with acceptable bathrooms. Discounts are generous.

Shanghai Lu 61 (opposite Paris Shopping Center). ℂ **0411/8280-7885**. Fax 0411/8269-1463. 64 units. ¥260 ($33/ £17) standard room. No credit cards. **Amenities:** Restaurant. *In room:* A/C, TV.

WHERE TO DINE

Dalian's specialty is seafood, but the city is surprisingly cosmopolitan in its international restaurant choices. For excellent **dim sum** head to the Shangri-La Hotel's Shang Palace (Renmin Lu 66; ℂ **0411/8252-5000**). A number of **fast-food outlets**—McDonald's, KFC, Pizza Hut—can also be found at Shengli Guangchang and on Qingniwa Jie. The underground market has a large **food court** with several point-to-choose Chinese stalls. Youhao Guangchang boasts a couple of **burger and pizza restaurants.**

Baixing Cun ⊕ HOME-STYLE   This is a delightful, if somewhat stiff, outgrowth of the yuppie countryside trend in Chinese dining. Servers' peasant uniforms are a bit too perfectly pressed, but the glass-topped wood tables and beautiful glazed dishes make for a pleasant setting. The restaurant specializes in clay pot soups, like the light and flavorful *xianggu guishi wei tuji* (chicken and mushrooms). Order *yumimian bing* (corn cakes) to dip in the soup or to sop up sauce left over from one of many well-prepared home-style dishes.

Changjiang Lu 128. ℂ **0411/8258-0228**. Meal for 2 ¥60–¥100 ($8–$12/£4–£6). No credit cards. 10am–10pm.

I-55 Coffee Stop (Aiwuwu Kafeizhan I-55) ⊕ AMERICAN   Owned by an American expatriate who made sure to include all the details—chalkboard menus and corner couches, world music soundtrack, a Scrabble set propped on a shelf—I-55 is a good place to get an American craving satiated. The cafe roasts its beans on-site and serves a good cup of coffee. The Philly cheesesteak is probably the best you'll get in China, with freshly baked bread, lots of flavorful beef, cheese, and mayo. It also offers good desserts and a weekend breakfast buffet for ¥55 ($6.70/£3.35). The staff speaks English. Relax with a book on the peaceful outdoor patio.

Gaoerji Lu 67 (at Jinian Jie, 2 blocks north of Renmin Guangchang). ℂ **0411/8369-5755**. Coffee drinks ¥20–¥30 ($2–$4/£1–£2); breakfast/lunch ¥33 ($4/£2). No credit cards. 9am–midnight. Bus: no. 701, 801, or 401.

Le Cafe Igosso (Yigousou) ITALIAN/FRENCH   This Japanese-run bistro, with its dark wood-paneled walls and fine white tablecloths, is as close as you'll get to authentic European dining in the Northeast. Music is subtle, service is silent and attentive, and the wine list is extensive. The English-language menu is mostly Italian, with a few French (foie gras) and Japanese (marinated octopus) selections. The beef carpaccio, drizzled with cream and generously garnished with capers and green onions, is rich but enjoyable. Fresh pasta and risotto dishes are small and simple. Desserts (posted next to the open kitchen) change daily.

Nanshan Lu 45 (at Kunming Jie, east of Laodong Gongyuan). ℂ **0411/8265-6453**. Main courses ¥40–¥80 ($5–$10/£2.50–£5). AE, MC, V. Mon–Sat 11am–2am; Sun 11am–11pm.

Fun Fact Dumplings & Dog Meat

Generally speaking, food is not one of Dongbei's finer attractions, but there is at least one aspect of Dongbei cuisine that will appeal to epicures: the delectable meat- and vegetable-filled ravioli-like dumplings known as *jiaozi*. Cheap and satisfying, *jiaozi* are popular all over China but are nowhere as divine as in the Northeast. Cooked in one of three ways—boiled *(shuijiao)*, steamed *(zhengjiao)*, or pan-fried *(jianjiao)*—they are most commonly filled with a mix of pork and cabbage *(zhurou baicai)* and served with a soy-and-vinegar dipping sauce, to which you add your own chopped garlic, chili oil, and mustard. Alternatives are endless. Absolutely not to be missed.

Probably more well known but significantly less appetizing is **dog *(gourou)***, Dongbei's other signature food. A Korean import shunned by Manchurians but valued among Chinese for its warming properties, it is a winter item most commonly eaten in hot pot. Dog meat turns greenish when boiled; trying it, according to one traveling companion of mine, is "like eating a piece of beef then licking a filing cabinet."

Longhai Yuwan Meishi Guangchang ★ (Finds) SEAFOOD   Yes, it's a gaudy sight, with its faux-marble staircase, but the dishes here will make up for it. Recommended by a local food writer, this recent addition to the Dalian restaurant scene is located near Xinghai Guangchang. Try the salt-dried yellow fish *(yancheng huanghuayu)*, spinach with mussels *(buocai ban maoxian)*, pig stomach cabbage soup *(nongtang zhudu wawacai)*, and fish dumplings *(bayu shuijiao)*. Be prepared for plenty of raw garlic. Each table is set in a private room with a flatscreen television.

Tongtai Lu 21. ⓒ **0411/8368-5555.** Meal for 2 ¥150–¥400 ($18–$50/£9–£25). MC, V. 11am–10pm.

Taineng ★ (Value) KOREAN   This always-packed joint offers authentic and good-value Korean dishes. Try the stone pot rice *(shiguo banfan):* It's tasty and not too spicy, with loads of different toppings. The restaurant also makes delicious spicy tofu soup *(doufu tang)* and Korean cold noodles.

Shengli Guangchang 18 (G/F of Ramada Hotel). ⓒ **0411/8263-3676.** Meal for 2 ¥50–¥150 ($10–$50/£5–£25). DC, MC, V. 11am–10pm.

Tapas (Dapasi) ★ SPANISH   On the edge of Russian Street, this two-level restaurant feels more like a hacienda in Galicia than a restaurant in Dalian. The wine list features wines from Spain, and the menu offers an exhaustive list of tapas good for a snack or a whole meal. Try the gratin mushroom tart, the pancetta with garlic, and the baked peppers on toast. Staff can speak English.

Tuanjie Jie 19 (near Russian St.). ⓒ **0411/8254-0996.** Tapas ¥8–¥30 ($1–$3.60/50p–£1.80); meal for 2 ¥70–¥100 ($8.50–$12/£4.25–£6). AE, MC, V. 11:30am–10:30pm.

DALIAN AFTER DARK

The majority of nightspots in Dalian are neon karaoke dives that cater to naughty Japanese businessmen, but there are a few pleasant exceptions. Resident foreigners favor the subterranean Makewei, known to English-speakers as **Dave's Bar** (south end of Qiyi Jie; ⓒ **0411/8282-2345;** open from 1pm until late), a UN of watering holes just northeast of Zhongshan Guangchang. Americans, Russians, Europeans, Asians, and Africans mix and flirt at Dave's without prejudice over bottles of Tsingtao beer. **Powerhouse (Baohao Ba),** Wuwu Lu 6 in the Zhongshan District (© **0411/8272-7971;** open 5pm–1:30am) has live Chinese rock-'n-roll music and is popular among locals. Just behind the Shangri-La Hotel, **Alice Bar No. 2** (Zhifu Jie 8; © **0411/8256-1313;** open 6pm–daylight)—*not* to be confused with Alice's seedier No. 1 bar, just east of the Shangri-La—has a Filipino band nightly and draws the area's expats until the wee hours. **I-55** (see "Where to Dine," above) is open until midnight.

4 Changchun

Jilin Province, 302km (187 miles) NE of Shenyang, 250km (155 miles) SW of Harbin

Changchun is remote enough to feel authentic, is friendly and modern enough to be comfortable, and has just enough pop-history background to make it interesting. Between 1932 and 1945, it was the capital of Japanese-controlled Manchukuo (Manzhou Guo) and home to puppet ruler Henry Puyi, the bespectacled final Qing emperor best known to Westerners as the subject of Bernardo Bertolucci's lush biopic *The Last Emperor.* The city provided a base for Japan's brutal World War II colonization campaign and was slated to sit at the center of a postwar empire that never materialized.

Changchun, now the capital of Jilin Province, has gained fame in the modern era as the Detroit of China, producing first Red Flag cars for Communist Party cadres and later Volkswagens for China's new middle class. Recent economic hardships have sent the city in search of tourism dollars and prompted admirable restorations of several Manchukuo-era buildings. But the city's greatest attraction is still its people, as unpretentious, warm-hearted, and quick-witted as any in the country.

The rest of Jilin Province mirrors Changchun in many ways. Less convenient than Liaoning to the south and lacking the "extreme travel" cachet of Heilong Jiang and Inner Mongolia to the north and west, it quietly offers several of Dongbei's most enjoyable attractions. **Chang Bai Shan** (p. 195), a dramatic mountain straddling the China–North Korea border, is the most famous. Just as compelling is the seldom-visited **Yanbian Korean Autonomous Prefecture** (p. 192) to the north.

ESSENTIALS

GETTING THERE   Changchun's **Longjia Airport**, opened in 2005, is 31km (19 miles) northeast of town. Flights connect it to major cities including Beijing, Shanghai, Guangzhou, Dalian, Hong Kong, Seoul, and Tokyo. The **China Eastern Airlines** ticket office (**Zhonguo Beifang Hangkong Shoupiao Chu;** © **0431/272-5001** and 0431/272-5026; open 8am–4:40pm) is at Xinfa Lu 32, through the second door on the building's west side. Airport buses from Menghan Binguang and Changchun Zhan go to the airport every hour; it takes 20 minutes and costs ¥20 ($2.60/£1.30). By taxi, fares cost ¥60 to ¥70 ($7.80–$9.10/£3.90–£4.55).

Express **trains** connect to Beijing (two daily; 6 hr.; ¥298–¥311/$39–$40/£19–£20), Harbin (two daily; 1½ hr.; ¥76/$9.90/£4.95), Shenyang (10 daily; 2 hr. 11 min.; ¥93/$12/£6.05), Jilin City (10 daily; 1½ hr.; ¥16/$2.10/£1.05), Shanghai (12:55pm; 29 hr.; ¥458/$60/£30), and Dalian (6:18am; 7½ hr.; ¥175/$23/£11). The railway station (Changchun Zhan) is north of downtown, at the top of Renmin Dajie.

Air-conditioned **buses** to Harbin (all day; 3½ hr.; ¥76/$9.90/£4.95) and Shenyang (all day; 3½ hr.; ¥82/$11/£5.30) leave from a white building at Renmin Dajie 6 (behind the Chunyi Binguan). Regular buses to Jilin City (2 hr.; ¥24/$2/£1) leave

Changchun

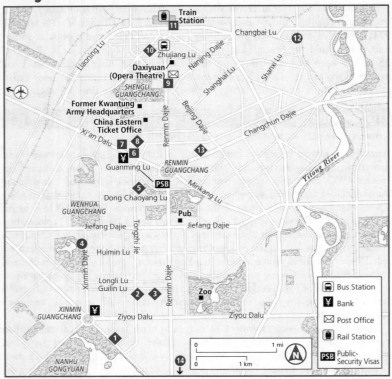

every few minutes from the north side of the building. Private **cars** leave from the railway station parking lot for cities east; prices are negotiable (¥200/$26/£13 to Yanji is reasonable).

GETTING AROUND   Jetta **taxis** charge ¥5 (65¢/35p) for the first 2.5km (1½ miles), then ¥1.30 (20¢/10p) per kilometer. **Buses** (¥1–¥2/15¢–25¢/10p–15p) are pay-as-you-board. Bus no. 6 runs from the railway station through the middle of town on Renmin Dajie; bus nos. 62 and 362 both wind from the railway station to Renmin Guangchang and pass Xinmin Guangchang, with stop announcements in English.

FAST FACTS

Banks, Foreign Exchange & ATMs   The most convenient **Bank of China** branch is on Tongzhi Jie, south of the Xi'an Dalu intersection (open Mon–Fri 8:30am–4:30pm; Sat–Sun 9am–4pm). Traveler's checks and credit card transactions are handled on the second floor (*not* available 11:30am–1pm), and there's an ATM on the first floor. Another ATM across the street from the Shangri-La hotel dispenses up to ¥2,500 ($300/£150).

Internet Access   Several Internet bars can easily be found near the train station. Most open from 8am to midnight and charge ¥2 (25¢/15p) to ¥4 (50¢/£25) per hour.

ACCOMMODATIONS ■

Chángchūn Maxcourt Hotel **7**
(Chángchūn Jílóngpō Dàjiǔdiàn)
长春吉隆坡大酒店

Chūnyí Bīnguǎn **11**
春谊宾馆

Paradise Hotel **9**
(Yuèfǔ Dàjiǔdiàn)
乐府大酒店

Shangri-La Chángchūn **6**
(Chángchūn Xiānggélǐlā Dàfàndiàn)
长春香格里拉大饭店

ATTRACTIONS ●

Changchun World Sculpture Park **14**
(Changchun Shijie Diaosu Gongyuan)
长春世界雕塑公园

Wěi Huánggōng **12**
(Puppet Emperor's Palace)
伪皇宫

Wěi Mǎnzhōu Guó Guówùyuàn **4**
(Manchukuo State Council)
伪满洲国博物馆

DINING ◆

Amigo Bar **13**

Bar Street (Jiuba Jie) **3**
酒吧街

Dàqīnghuā Jiǎozi **10**
大清花饺子

French Bakery (Hóng Mòfáng) **2, 8**
红磨坊

Lao Ma Shuo Gan Mian **1**
老妈手擀面

Xiàngyáng Tún **5**
向阳屯

Into Internet Bar, which is located at the intersection of Tongzi Jie and Guilin Lu, can hold up to 1,000 people. Dial-up is ✆ **169.**

Post Office   The most convenient post office (Kuancheng Youdianju; May–Sept 8:30am–5:30pm; Oct–Apr 8:30am–5pm) is in an old green building south of the long-distance bus station on Renmin Dajie.

Visa Extensions   Visa extensions are easy to obtain (passport and hotel registration only) at the imposing **PSB Exit/Entry office** on Guangming Lu (✆ **0431/209-8305;** open Mon–Fri 8:30–11:30am and 1:30–5pm), behind PSB headquarters on the southwest side of Renmin Guangchang.

EXPLORING CHANGCHUN

Changchun's chief attraction is the ghost of Japanese occupation, which still lingers in the more than two dozen ministry buildings left scattered throughout the city. The **former Kwantung Army headquarters** is an impeccably preserved Japanese-style castle on Xinfa Lu (now occupied by the Communist Party) near the China Northern Airlines ticket office. Guards might let you roam around the grounds if you promise not to take pictures. There are also a number of buildings lining Xinmin Lu south of the **Wenhua Guangchang (Culture Square),** site of a never-completed imperial Japanese palace and now home to the main building of Jilin University. The grim building southeast of the square, fronted by a statue of infamous Canadian doctor Norman Bethune, is the former site of the **Wei Manzhou Guo Guowuyuan (Manchukuo State Council).** A bizarre English-language tour here (8:30am–6pm; ¥20/$2.60/£1.30) includes a ride in a 70-year-old solid brass Otis elevator once used by Henry Puyi (see Wei Huanggong, below). Bilingual maps are available (¥5/65¢/ 35p) at the Wei Huanggong.

Changchun World Sculpture Park (Changchun Shijie Diaosu Gongyuan) 🐾

Over 390 sculptures by artists from 172 countries such as China, Russia, Africa, and Korea are exhibited inside this park, which is located in the south of the city. The 92-hectare (227 acre)park, opened in 2003, is vast; artworks are placed along the two long main roads as well as surrounding the lake in the center of the park. The art gallery at the right side of the entrance features different exhibitions from time to time. Though not every piece of the artwork is exceptional, some of them are pretty impressive. Outstanding pieces include Russian artist Pavel Shaposhnik's *Golden Dream,* a cast bronze sculpture featuring a man falling asleep on a bench, placed near the exit of the art gallery; and mainland artist Chen Tao's *Dressing Girl,* outside the art gallery.

Renmin Dajie 9518. ⓒ 0431/8537-9001. Admission (park and art gallery) ¥30 ($3.90/£1.95). Park 7am–6pm; gallery 9am–4pm. Bus: no. 112, 240, or 270.

Wei Huanggong 🐾★★   "The Puppet Emperor's Palace" is where Aisin-Gioro "Henry" Puyi, China's last emperor, spent 13 years as an impotent sovereign under Japanese control. This complex of imperial-style buildings, formerly criticized by travelers as shabby and boring, recently underwent a multimillion-dollar makeover and is now among the Northeast's premier historical attractions.

Installed as emperor of China in Beijing in 1908, at the age of 3, Puyi was deposed by Republican forces in 1912 (at a time when he was still breastfeeding) and eventually fell into the hands of the Japanese. In 1932, eager to use Puyi's Manchurian face as a screen for its war efforts in the Northeast, Japan convinced him to move to Changchun and made him president (later emperor) of Manchukuo. He lived a futile life here, taking orders from the Japanese army and subsisting on Qing restoration fantasies, until he was captured by the Soviets in 1945. He spent 14 years in prison, was "rehabilitated," and worked as a gardener until his death in 1967.

The palace was damaged when Soviet troops occupied Changchun, so much of the furniture and trappings on display here are replicas. Otherwise, the restoration is meticulous. Most impressive is the Tongde Dian (originally the Jilin Salt Tax Collection Office, and therefore sometimes referred to as the Salt Palace because it was built using money from Japan's salt-mining operations), a building Puyi supposedly never used for fear the Japanese had bugged the rooms. The main hall is recognizable as the setting for a dance party scene in *The Last Emperor,* although it was never actually used for that purpose.

Guangfu Bei Lu 5. ⓒ 0431/8286-6611. Admission ¥80 ($10/£5.20). May–Sept 8:30am–4:20pm; Oct–Apr 8:30am–3:40pm. English audio guide ¥20 ($2.60/£1.30). Bus: no. 18 (2 stops from the railway station; walk east on Guangfu Lu) or no. 264 (from the Wenhua Guangchang).

SHOPPING

Changchun is one of China's top producers of ginseng, available in any one of the city's ubiquitous pharmacies. For more conventional shopping, try the upscale **Chongqing Lu** or **Guilin Lu** (east of the Tongzhi Jie intersection), a hip and haphazard street lined with Korean clothing shops and stuffed-animal stores. The **underground market** in front of the railway station was once part of an underground bomb shelter connected by tunnels to the Manchukuo ministries.

WHERE TO STAY

Rooms are scarce in late summer, when the city hosts a series of conferences and industry fairs, but discounts of up to 30% are common at other times of the year. Budget hotels generally do not accept foreigners.

EXPENSIVE

Shangri-La Changchun (Changchun Xianggelila Dafandian) ★★ The Shangri-La is Changchun's oldest five-star property and still the only hotel in town that provides luxury with class. Standard rooms are spacious, with large beds and generously sized bathrooms, and the hotel's staff is head-and-shoulders above any other in the city. The Shangri-La is centrally located at the edge of the city's most upscale shopping district, a short walk from Renmin Guangchang.

Xi'an Dalu 569. ℂ **0431/8898-1818.** Fax 0431/8898-1919. www.shangri-la.com. 458 units. ¥980 – ¥1,400 ($127–$182/£64–£91) standard room. 15% service charge. AE, DC, MC, V. **Amenities:** 2 restaurants; deli; bar; bakery; outdoor beer garden and evening barbecue in summer; bar; small indoor pool; outdoor tennis court; health center and spa; concierge; business center; forex; salon; 24-hr. room service; same-day laundry/dry cleaning; executive-level rooms. In room: A/C, satellite TV, broadband Internet access, minibar, fridge, hair dryer, iron, safe.

MODERATE

Changchun Maxcourt Hotel (Changchun Jilongpo Dajiudian) This Malaysian-run four-star is the best deal in town. Bathrooms are small, but guest rooms themselves are some of the most comfortable in the city—especially those on the newly renovated 19th and 20th floors—and service is decent.

Xi'an Dalu 823. ℂ **0431/8896-2688.** Fax 0431/8898-6288. www.maxcourt.com. 228 units. ¥800 ($104/£52) standard room. Over 40% discount. 15% service charge. Rate includes breakfast. AE, DC, MC, V. **Amenities:** 4 restaurants; bar; small indoor pool; health club; full-service spa; game room w/bowling alley; business center w/Internet access; forex; 24-hr. room service; same-day laundry/dry cleaning. In room: A/C, satellite TV w/pay movies, dataport, minibar, fridge, hair dryer, safe.

INEXPENSIVE

Chunyi Binguan The Chunyi, built in 1909, is the least impressive of the former Yamato Hotels, and is attractive now only for its convenient location just across the street from the railway station. The original gate is still here, but the exterior is crumbling and the interior retains only a whisper of history. Rooms are worn and bathrooms are small.

Renmin Dajie 80 (southeast of railway station). ℂ **0431/8209-6888.** Fax 0431/8896-0171. 280 units. ¥249–¥288 ($32–$37/£16–£19) standard room. Rates include breakfast. AE, DC, MC, V. **Amenities:** Restaurant; bar; business center; massage; forex; limited room service; laundry. In room: A/C, TV.

Paradise Hotel (Yuefu Dajiudian) ★ An institution among travelers in Changchun since it opened in 1994, the Paradise is one of a handful of state-run three-stars in China that have a firm grasp on the concepts of service and maintenance. Newly renovated doubles, equipped with a queen-size bed, are cramped. Standard rooms are larger but older. Both are nicely appointed with lacquer furniture, large TVs, and small but very clean bathrooms. Some of the staff speak English. The place fills up in summer, so call ahead.

Renmin Dajie 1078 (south of the Agricultural Bank of China building). ℂ **0431/8209-0999.** Fax 0431/8271-5709. www.yuefuhotel.com. 200 units. ¥258 – ¥398 ($34–$52/£17–£26) standard room. AE, DC, MC, V. **Amenities:** 4 restaurants; bar; gym; business center; laundry. In room: A/C, satellite TV, dataport.

WHERE TO DINE

A number of restaurants in Changchun serve reasonable regional cuisine. Otherwise, The **Coffee Garden** of Shangri-La has satisfying Western dishes. **KFC** and **McDonald's** branches are plentiful throughout the city. There are also a **Pizza Hut** on the right side of the square in front of the railway station and **Subway** on Longli Lu, near Tongzhi Lu.

French Bakery (Hong Mofang) WESTERN   Now with two locations, this dark and low-ceilinged cafe with French movie posters pasted to its fake brick walls has long been a haven for Changchun's foreign residents. A very clean kitchen produces simple sandwiches, omelets, pizza, and near-authentic pastries. Coffee drinks are genuine. Olive oil, Tabasco sauce, Heinz barbecue sauce, and ground coffee are for sale on a small shelf near the door. Another location is at Chongzhi Hutong 137 (walk 1 block north of the Shangri-La Hotel on Chongqing Lu, then make a left at the Charter Shopping Center; © **0431/8898-1958;** 9:30am–midnight).

Guilin Lu 745 (east of Tongzhi Jie intersection). © **0431/8562-3994.** Meal for 2 ¥20–¥30 ($2.60–$3.90/£1.30–£1.95); coffee ¥10–¥15 ($1.30–$1.95/70p–£1). No credit cards. 8am–10:30pm.

Lao Ma Shuo Gan Mian 🌟 *(Value* SICHUAN   This successful chain has a handful of branches in Changchun. Its original shop at Changqing Road, with home-style decor, is the busiest one; it's hard to find a table during peak hours. The food is generally tasty. The Sichuan dishes—such as mouthwatering chicken *(kou shui ji),* served with a special hot-and-sour sauce, crushed peanuts, and green onion—leave me wanting more after finishing one dish. The noodles are also good, but most of them are served in red spicy broth.

Changqing Lu 46 (near Gongnong Dalu intersection). © **0431/8563-0696.** Meal for 2 ¥40–¥60 ($5.20–$7.80/£2.60–£3.90). No credit cards. 9am–10pm.

Xiangyang Tun 🌟🌟🌟 HOME-STYLE   This delightful countryside eatery, with a statue of Mao out front and calligraphy-covered walls in the main dining room, is the favorite for home-style fare. Try the *jiaji dun zhenmo*—tender pieces of chicken stewed with mushrooms in a dark savory sauce—and the *da paigu* (big ribs), a melt-in-your-mouth house specialty with meat that literally falls off the bone.

Dong Chaoyang Lu 433 (east of Tongzhi Jie intersection). © **0431/898-2876.** Meal for 2 ¥30–¥60 ($3.90–$7.80/£1.95–£3.90). No credit cards. 10:30am–11pm.

CHANGCHUN AFTER DARK

Changchun is the birthplace of *errenzhuan,* a mix of stand-up comedy and opera that is thoroughly vulgar and, for those who can understand Mandarin, very entertaining. Real fans head to the raucous, smoke-filled **Heping Daxiyuan,** a block north of the post office on Renmin Dajie (© **0431/893-4304**), where tawdry performances get audiences roaring with laughter and keep them that way most of the night. Nightly shows at 7:40pm cost ¥10 to ¥50 ($1.30–$6.50/65p–£3.25). The Longli Lu, near Guilin Lu and Remin Jie, is the "Bar Area," with a number of local bars to choose. Two popular disco clubs, **Mayflower (Wuyuehua Jiuba;** © **0431/893-322),** tucked underground on the south side of the Wenhua Huodong Zhongxin on Renmin Dajie, and **SOS Storm (Qian Ren SOS Storm;** © **0431/8564-6060)** on Fujin Lu 9, which organized the first international music festival in Changchun in late 2006, are popular with foreigners and stay open late.

5 Jilin City

Jilin Province, 128km (79 miles) E of Changchun

Jilin, one of the oldest settlements in the province and a legendary shipbuilding center during the Qing dynasty, is famous now for its delicate winter scenery. The city's original name was *Jilin Wula* (Manchurian for "along the river"), because it straddles a bend in the Songhua Jiang (Sungari River). It was hit hard in World War II and, despite one of the country's more impressive urban renewal plans, it will probably never recover its old prestige. Most visitors now use it as a staging point for trips to the Chang Bai Shan Nature Preserve (p. 195).

ESSENTIALS

GETTING THERE   Trains travel from Jilin to Changchun (10 daily; 1½ hr.; ¥16/$2.10/£1.05), Yanji (six daily; 9 hr.; ¥66/$8.60/£4.30), Shenyang (six daily; 5–5½ hr.; ¥118/$15/£7.70), Harbin (5½ hr.; ¥35/$4.55/£2.30) and Beijing (9:47pm; 12 hr.; ¥263/$34/£17). The **railway station (Jilin Zhan)** is north of the river, at the intersection of Zhongkang Lu and Chongqing Jie; the ticket office is open from 5am to 1:30am. The main **long-distance bus station (Gonglu Keyun Zong Zhan or Chalu Xiang)** is at Zhongkang Lu 13, west of the railway station; buses leave from here for Tonghua (all day; ¥18/$2.35/£1.20), Harbin (6½ hr.; ¥138/$18/£9), and Yanji (8am; 6 hr.; ¥84/$11/£5.45). **Express buses** to Changchun (every 30 min., 6am–6pm; 2 hr.; ¥33/$4.30/£2.15) depart from the Linjiang Men Keyun Zhan on Xi'an Lu, a block west of Linjiang Guangchang. **Flights** to Beijing (Wed and Sat) and Shanghai (Wed and Sun) leave from the Gudianzi Jichang, 30km (19 miles) west of the city. The **CAAC ticket office (Minhang Shoupiao Chu;** ✆ **0432/245-4260; open 8am–5pm)** is behind the Dongguan Hotel at Chongqing Lu 1. An **airport shuttle** leaves from here at 11:30am and costs ¥10 ($1.30/65p). A **taxi** to the airport costs ¥40 ($5.20/£2.60).

VISITOR INFORMATION   For tourist complaints, call ✆ **0432/245-7524.**

GETTING AROUND   Jilin Dajie, the main thoroughfare, runs north-south through the middle of town. Most **buses** (¥1/15¢/10p) stop at the railway station; bus no. 32 leaves from the railway station and travels along Jilin Dajie. **Taxis** charge ¥5 (65¢/35p) for the first 2km (1¼ miles) and ¥1.80 (25¢/£15) per kilometer after that.

FAST FACTS

Banks, Foreign Exchange & ATMs   The main **Bank of China** branch is inconveniently located on Shenchun Jie, at the east end of the Linjiang Qiao (Linjiang Bridge). It's open May through September from 8:30am to 4:30pm and October through April from 8:30am to 4pm. Windows on the left handle traveler's checks and credit card transactions (*not* available 11:30am–1pm). There's an international ATM just inside the door.

Internet Access   There are several **24-hour Internet bars** charging ¥2 to ¥4 (25¢–50¢/15p–25p) per hour on Chaoyang Jie. Dial-up is ✆ **16300.**

Post Office   The main post office is on Jilin Dajie (open 8:30am–4:30pm), north of the Jilin Bridge.

EXPLORING JILIN

Jilin is host to a scene of unearthly beauty in winter, when steam rises from the Songhua River and condenses on nearby trees. The phenomenon, dubbed *wusong* (ice-rimmed trees) ✿ in Mandarin, is a byproduct of the nearby Fengman Hydro-electric Dam, which feeds warm water into the Songhua and keeps it from freezing despite air temperatures of −22°F (−30°C). To see this, get up early and walk along any section of the pleasant riverside promenade that follows Songhua Jiang Lu, or you can take the touring cart (¥2 single trip; ¥4 round-trip) on Jiangbin Xi Lu, outside the Shijie Guangchang, to enjoy the beautiful river. Also beautiful is an old **Catholic Church (Tianzhu Jiaotang),** built in 1917 and restored in 1980, opposite the promenade on the west side of Jiangcheng Guangchang; it isn't open to tourists, but you might convince someone in the attached hospice to let you in for a look.

IN TOWN
Wen Miao   This decrepit, charming Confucian temple is notable for its exhibition on the Qing dynasty imperial examination system, inside the first hall on the right. A mural at the entrance to the exhibit depicts a mountain of men stepping on each other in an effort to climb the Confucian hierarchy. Inside are reproductions of "cheat sheets"—pieces of clothing covered in thousands of near-microscopic characters found on Qing-era candidates in Beijing.

Nanchang Lu. Admission ¥15 ($1.95/£1). 8:30am–4pm (May 1–Oct 1 until 5pm); closed holidays. Bus: no. 103 to Jiangcheng Guangchang, then walk east 2 blocks on Jiangwan Lu and turn left at the Jiangcheng Hotel.

Yunshi Bowuguan (Meteorite Museum) _Kids_   On March 8, 1976, one of the largest meteorite showers in recorded history fell on a 500-sq.-km (195-sq.-mile) area around Jilin, pelting the city with 4,000 kilograms (4.4 tons) of rock and giving it a reason to open this museum. The facility has recently been renovated but has very few English captions. The main reason to come here is the world's largest stony meteorite (1,774kg/3,921 lb.), which hovers dressed in a blue velvet skirt in the middle of the hall. Records show that the meteorite's impact registered 1.7 on the Richter scale. Visitors are allowed to touch a smaller meteorite in the adjacent room.

Jilin Dajie 100. ℂ 0432/466-1214. Admission ¥40 ($5.20/£2.60) adults, ¥15 ($1.95/£1) children. 8:30am–4:30pm. Bus: no. 32 to Jiang Nan Gongyuan, then walk south past a large statue of Mao.

WHERE TO STAY
Jilin's hotels are busy year-round but only fill up during major Chinese holidays. Discounts range from 15% to 25% in summer.

EXPENSIVE
Century Hotel (Shiji Dafandian)   An exaggerated statue of Cretheus on Argus at the entrance is the first of many ancient Greek and Roman flourishes installed throughout this odd hotel. Nominally managed by Swiss-Belhotel but dominated by its Chinese owner, the Century feels grossly out of place in Jilin. Still, it is the city's nicest hotel, and close to the sights. Rooms are spacious and opulent, with fluffy beds, pale walls, and dark wood furniture.

Jilin Dajie 77 (at Yishan Lu). ℂ 0432/216-8888. Fax 0432/216-8777. www.centuryhotel.com.cn. 268 units. ¥800 ($104/£52) standard room including breakfast. 10% service charge. AE, DC, MC, V. **Amenities:** 4 restaurants; bar; nightclub; small indoor pool; tennis and squash court; health club and spa; business center; forex; limited room service; dry laundry/cleaning. *In room:* A/C, satellite TV, broadband Internet access, minibar, fridge, hair dryer, safe.

Crystal Hotel (Wusong Binguan) ✿   Once the only luxury hotel in Jilin, this four-star still offers the city's best combination of comfort and service. Perched several kilometers northeast of the railway station on the east bank of the Songhua Jiang, it is far from most sights in the city but provides good views of the ice-rimmed trees in

Jilin City

DINING◆

Lìyǎdé Shífǔ **6**
利雅得食府

Outdoor street stalls **7**
(dà páidǎng)
大排挡

Zhōnghuá Míng Shífǔ **5**
中华名食府

ATTRACTIONS●

Wén Miào **4**
文庙

Yǔnshí Bówùguǎn **2**
(Meteorite Museum)
陨石博物馆

ACCOMMODATIONS■

Century Hotel (Shìjì Dàfàndiàn) **1**
世纪大饭店

Crystal Hotel
(Wùsōng Bīnguǎn) **10**
武松宾馆

Dōngguān Bīnguǎn **3**
东关宾馆

Empire Garden Hotel **11**
(Wangjia Huayuan Jiudian)
皇家花园酒店

International Hotel **9**
(Guójì Dàfàndiàn)
国际大饭店

Lǚyóu Bīnguǎn **8**
(Tourism Hotel)
旅游宾馆

Star Garden Fashion Business Hotel **12**
(Xingyuan Shishang Shangwu Jiudian)
星苑时尚商务酒店

Legend:

- Bus Station
- ¥ Bank
- ⊠ Post Office
- Rail Station
- † Church

China — Jilin — Beijing

Wild China: Yanbian

Koreans first fled across the border to Yanbian, a seldom-visited area of greener-than-green hills and fertile fields nestled in the northeastern corner of Jilin Province, after the first of several severe famines struck the Korean peninsula in 1869.

Subsequent diasporas in the 20th century, the result of continued food shortages and a pair of brutal Japanese occupations, turned the area into what many now call the Third Korea. Now officially called the Yanbian Chaoxian (Korean) Autonomous Prefecture, it is home to the largest population of ethnic Koreans outside the peninsula itself.

Many parts of Yanbian have only recently been opened to tourists, and even those areas that have been open for years see few Westerners. Facilities are minimal and English almost nonexistent. But people adventurous enough to travel here can enjoy one of Dongbei's most peacefully stunning landscapes—a sublime combination of Scotland and Japan—and interact with one of China's only truly bicultural societies.

The capital of Yanbian is **Yanji,** a rapidly developing city where all of the street signs, and most of the residents, are bilingual. Bland and somewhat rigid, its chief value is as a base for journeys to the surrounding countryside, Chang Bai Shan, and the North Korean border.

A late-afternoon bus ride through the **Yanbian countryside** ★★★, as sunlight glitters on fields of rice and warms the upturned roofs of Korean huts, is one of the most exquisite experiences available in the Northeast. The best excuse to take such a ride is **Fangchuan,** a tiny town at the end of a needle-thin strip of Chinese territory between North Korea and Russia, and China's preeminent border-viewing spot. A view from the tower here (¥20/$2.60/£1.30) provides vistas of Russia, North Korea and, on a clear day, the northern edge of Japan. You have two choices as to how to get there: public transportation or taxi. A **taxi** will save you a lot of hassle; a round-trip ride from Yanji to Fangchuan costs ¥400 ($52/£26). You can have the driver wait for you while you sightsee. Have the driver wait outside the ticketing area or pay an additional ¥10 ($1.30/65p) to take the car all the way to the tower. Otherwise, from the Yanji railway station, catch the 6am bus to Hunchun (1½ hr.; ¥25/$3.25/£1.65). Once you arrive in Hunchun, take a (¥2/25¢/15p pedicab ride to the Hunchun's Zonghe Shichang, where you can take a minibus (¥10/$1.30/65p one-way) to the border's edge. It will drop you off about 3km (2 miles) from the viewing tower in Fangchuan, but you can bribe them a few extra dollars to take you farther. Be certain to ask about the availability of return buses to Hunchun, as schedules are virtually nonexistent and service is largely determined by whether or not there are enough passengers to fill a bus.

Warning: North Koreans continue to flow into Yanbian, but without official permission. Though identity checks aren't as strict as they used to be, it is always a good idea to carry your passport with you at all times.

GETTING THERE   Trains connect Yanji to Beijing (12:29pm; 23 hr.; ¥363/$47/£24), Changchun (four daily; 9½ hr.; ¥93/$12/£6.05), and Shenyang (3:19pm; 15 hr.; ¥131/$17/£8.50). The **railway station (Yanji Zhan)** is to the south, at the end of Zhan Qian Jie; the ticket office is open from 4:30am to 10:30pm. **Buses** to Chang Bai Shan (p. 195) and towns in the countryside leave from the Dongbeiya Keyun Zhan (on Chang Bai Lu, northeast of railway station); the ticket office is open from 5am to 4:30pm. Buses also leave from the railway station parking lot. **Flights** to Beijing (two to three daily; ¥1,130/$147/£73), Shenyang (one daily; ¥740/$96/£48), Shanghai (Mon and Fri; ¥1,760/$229/£114), and Seoul (one daily, except Tues; ¥2,510/$326/£163) depart from a small airport 6km (3¾ miles) west of the railway station; a taxi ride there costs ¥10 ($1.30/65p). Taxis do not use meters; rides are either ¥5 (65¢/35p) or ¥10 ($1.30/65p), depending on distance. Negotiate the price before you get in. Purchase flight tickets at the **CAAC ticket office** (© 0433/291-5555; open 8am–9pm) inside the Xiangyu Dajiudian above the Yanxin Bridge, north of the railway station.

WHERE TO STAY & DINE   Yanji's most convenient hotel is the **Dazhou Hotel** (Tie Bei Lu 439; © 0433/619-5555; fax 0433/619-5999), across the railway station. The four-star hotel opened in late 2005, has clean and spacious units (¥320–¥420/$42–$55/£21–£27) standard room), with competent service. The joint-venture **Yanbian International Hotel (Yanbian Dayu Fandian)** 𝕒, Youyi Lu 118, Juzi Jie intersection (© 0433/250-9999; fax 0433/250-6999), is Yanji's largest and most luxurious hotel, overlooking the Bu'er Hatong River. The small but tasteful rooms cost ¥480 ($62/£31) and come with breakfast. Yanji's food specialty is the authentic Korean cuisine. A favorite dish is *lengmian* (cold noodles), semitranslucent wheat noodles served in a cold broth with various toppings such as pickled cabbage, beef, pine nuts, and Korean chili paste garnished with an apple slice. Both **Jindalai Fandian** 𝕒 (Hailan Lu 42, at Xinhua Jie; © 0433/252-8590) and **Mozhate Kuaicandian** 𝕒 (Hailan Lu 29; © 0433/253-8198) serve great and good-value Korean food and the best *lengmian* in town. The former offers less of a third-grade cafeteria ambience, while the latter has a more comfortable setting and serves tasty tofu hot soup *(doufutang)* and grilled fish. Both restaurants are open from 10am to 10pm.

winter. Decent-size rooms are nicer than the hotel's worn exterior would suggest. Corner rooms are larger and offer the best river views. Bathrooms are clean. Spacious standard rooms on floors 1 through 3 of satellite building C are a good value at about 20% less than comparable rooms in the main building.

Longtan Dajie 29 (south of Longtan Bridge). ℂ **0432/398-6200.** Fax 0432/398-6501. www.crystal-hotel.com.cn. 152 units. ¥312 ($41/£20) standard room in bldg. C; ¥440 ($57/£29) standard room in main building. AE, DC, MC, V. 15% service charge. Rates include breakfast for 2. **Amenities:** 2 restaurants; bar; small exercise room; nice spa w/river view; bowling alley; business center; limited room service; laundry. *In room:* A/C, satellite TV, fridge, hair dryer (upon request).

Empire Garden Hotel (Wangjia Huayuan Jiudian) ♔
Formerly the Yideyuan Hotel, the Empire Garden Hotel was renamed in 2004 and became the only five-star hotel in Jilin. Situated in the east of the railway station, the hotel is far from the city's attractions, but provides good service and comfy rooms. The lobby has a nice and big garden with loads of greenery and wooden furniture.

Liaoning Lu 10, Jiefang Dadao Bei Duan (east of railway station). ℂ **0432/216-9090.** Fax 0432/216-9000. www. eghotel.com. 308 units. ¥400–¥440 ($52–$57/£26–£29) standard room. AE, DC, MC, V. **Amenities:** 3 restaurants; nightclub; indoor pool; indoor tennis court; exercise room and spa; 24-hr. room service; laundry. *In room:* A/C, satellite TV, broadband Internet access, minibar, fridge, safe.

MODERATE

Dongguan Binguan
Built in 1957 just north of the Jilin Bridge, the Dongguan is a relic, but a convenient one, with a great location and two travel agencies (including a CITS branch) on-site. The main building, a white behemoth with a traditional green tile roof, underwent minor renovations in 2002 and offers worn but clean standard rooms with small bathrooms. Similar rooms on the first floor of the rear building are heavily discounted. The nicest standard rooms are in the new building. Rooms on the south side of the main building and west side of the new building offer views of the river.

Jiangwan Lu 2. ℂ **0432/216-0188** or 0432/216-0118. 157 units. ¥200 ($29/£14) standard room; ¥260 ($34/£17) in new building. AE, DC, MC, V. No credit cards. Rates include breakfast. **Amenities:** Restaurant; bathing center; salon; massage; small business center. *In room:* A/C, satellite TV.

International Hotel (Guoji Dafandian)
This three-star no longer gleams the way it used to, but it's the best-equipped hotel in the railway-station area. Well-maintained standard rooms are the most expensive; the cheapest rooms, on the seventh and eighth floors, are worn with hard beds.

Zhongxiling Jie 20 (southwest of railway station). ℂ **0432/612-9818.** Fax 0432/255-3788. 191 units. ¥148–¥480 ($19–$62/£9.60–£31) standard room. AE, DC, MC, V. **Amenities:** 3 restaurants; pool; exercise room; bowling alley; laundry. *In room:* A/C, TV.

INEXPENSIVE

Star Garden Fashion Business Hotel (Xingyuan Shishang Shangwu Jiudian) (Value)
Opened in 2007, this new business hotel offers spacious and comfortable rooms and is a good value. However, there is no elevator in the five-story hotel. Rooms are painted in warm yellow and filled with youthful decoration; the shower-only bathrooms are clean. The large duplex rooms on the fifth floor are the nicest.

Xinchang Jie, Donghong Lu 18 (opposite to Gonganxiaqu Yiqu). ℂ **0432/252-8333** or 0432/252-7444. www.star garden.com.cn. 75 units. ¥98–¥198 ($13–$26/£6.40–£13) standard room. No credit cards. **Amenities:** Restaurant; business center. *In room:* A/C, satellite TV, broadband Internet access.

WHERE TO DINE

A **KFC** and a **McDonald's** are inside the Fu-Mart at the intersection of Jiefang Lu and Hunchun Lu; the Fu-Mart also has a **supermarket.** The Century Hotel's Western restaurant serves decent pizza and salads and offers occasional buffet promotions for about ¥60 ($7.50/£3.75) per person. There are several **Korean cold-noodle** restaurants around the railway station (see box, "Wild China: Yanbian," p. 192). For a more adventurous and truly local dining experience, try the block of **outdoor street stalls** *(da paidang)* at the night market on Hunchun Lu ⚑, just north of Jiefang Zhong Lu. You can choose from hot pot, seafood, or *guotie,* meat and vegetables you cook yourself at the table in an iron pan. It's open nightly May through October, from 5pm until late.

Liyade Shifu ⚑ MUSLIM   By far the most upmarket Muslim restaurant in the city, Liyade lacks the gritty appeal of Jilin's other Hui minority eateries but still manages to serve some fine mutton dishes. Portions are small but well presented. Don't miss the *shousi yangrou,* tender bits of torn lamb served with soy-and-garlic dipping sauce.

Jiefang Zhong Lu 56 (west of Jilin Dajie). ✆ 0432/208-1010. Meal for 2 ¥70–¥120 ($9.10–$16/£4.55–£7.80). No credit cards. 10am–10pm.

Zhonghua Ming Shifu DONGBEI   This unpretentious local favorite serves up regional cuisine at reasonable prices. The house specialty is *zhen bu tong tanrou,* pieces of fatty pork braised in a homemade beer-based sauce until melt-in-your mouth tender. Also try the *da ban shuilapi,* a huge plate of mung-bean flour noodles served cold with cilantro, peanuts, bits of pork, and julienned cucumbers, all mixed together with a spicy sesame sauce.

Jiefang Dalu just west of Tianjin Jie, on the south side of the street. ✆ 0432/243-8333. Meal for 2 ¥50–¥70 ($6.50–$9.10/£3.25–£4.55). No credit cards. 10:30am–9pm.

6 Chang Bai Shan ⚑

Jilin Province, 565km (350 miles) E of Jilin City

Chang Bai Shan (Long White Mountain) is the mythical source of Manchurian and Korean culture, the center of the 200,000-hectare (494,000-acre) **Chang Bai Shan Nature Preserve,** the tallest peak in Dongbei, and the region's most impressive attraction. The main reason to visit is **Tian Chi (Heavenly Lake)** ⚑, a pristine, 2-million-year-old fog-enshrouded lake set deep in the crater at the top of the mountain. Roughly 13km (8 miles) in circumference, it straddles the Chinese–North Korean border and is the source of the Songhua River. Below the lake, the mountain is home to a truly impressive range of flora—over 80 tree and 300 medicinal plant species, including ginseng, Korean pine, and the rare Chang Bai larch.

The mountain was considered forbidden territory throughout most of the Qing dynasty, and Han Chinese who wandered into the area, usually in search of ginseng, were sometimes beaten to death with sticks. Extreme as it sounds, visitors today might find themselves wishing for a similar policy to protect the mountain from new hordes of trash-shedding Chinese and South Korean tourists. The mountain's UNESCO World Natural Reserve status has done little to this end and, moreover, seems to be the justification for supplementary admission fees, capitalizing on every single scenic spot on the mountain. By the time you get there, it is more than likely that there will be additional fees to enter spots that were previously included in the general admission price.

Snow makes routes impassable from early October to late May, and even in summer the weather is maddeningly unpredictable (bring a raincoat). The best time to visit is early September, when the weather clears somewhat and the lake is most likely to be visible. Unfortunately, September is also when an army of South Koreans flood the area, taking up hotel rooms as far west as Jilin City and driving up prices.

THE NORTHERN APPROACH

One of only two routes open to foreigners (the others enter or venture too close to North Korea), this is the most convenient and scenic way to tackle the mountain. It is possible to see Tian Chi and return to Erdao Bai He (see below) in a single day using this approach, but it's worthwhile to spend at least 2 days here.

ESSENTIALS

GETTING THERE   The route begins at **Erdao Bai He** (Bai He for short), a small town 25km (16 miles) north of the mountain, named for a river that flows down from Tian Chi. The best way to reach Bai He from the north or west is through Yanji (see "Wild China: Yanbian," above); during peak season, which starts around mid-June, a **tourist express** leaves Yanji's long-distance bus station at 5:30am and goes directly to the mountain gate. The 3-hour trip costs ¥55 ($7.15/£3.60) one-way; ¥110 ($14/£7.15) same-day round-trip including lunch. Or you can catch one of several Bai He–bound buses (191km/118 miles; 4 hr.; ¥32/$4.15/£2.10) that leave from the Yanji railway station. From the south, the easiest approach is by **train** via Tonghua (two daily; 5½ hr.; ¥103/$13/£6.70), Jilin (one daily; 16 hr. 40 min.; ¥125/$16/£8.15) or Shenyang (one daily; 13½ hr.; ¥103/$13/£6.70).

Buses (¥40/$5.20/£2.60) and **private cars** (¥80–¥100/$10–$13/£5.20–£6.50) gather every morning at the Bai He railway station, at the north end of town, for trips to the *daozhankou* (vehicle switching station), 17km (11 miles) up the mountain from the main gate. **Admission** at the main gate costs ¥100 ($13/£6.50) for adults and ¥50 ($6.50/£3.25) for students and children.

TOURS   Many travel agents in Jilin offer a 3-day Chang Bai Shan tour for ¥500–¥650 ($65–$85/£33–£42). The tours are certainly reasonably priced but they don't leave much time to enjoy anything but the lake. In Yanji, **CITS** (Jixi Jie 4, south of the intersection with Xin Gongyuan Lu; ⓒ 0433/272-0022) offers a 1-day tour for ¥300 ($39/£20), which includes lunch and all fees for the mountain during weekends. *Note:* It's extremely difficult to beat the CITS price if you are a solo traveler and want to return to Yanji the same day.

SEEING THE LAKE

SUVs (30 min.; ¥80/$10/£5.20 per person) travel from the *daozhankou* to a parking lot in front of the hot springs just below Tian Chi. Admission costs ¥100 ($13/£6.50), and for an additional ¥45 ($5.85/£2.95) a tour bus will take you around the park to see Tian Chi and the hot springs. From the parking lot you will have to climb an incredible number of paved stairs (¥25/$3.25/£1.65) to view the lake. More enjoyable is the 2-hour hike, which follows a smaller road up a narrow valley, crosses a bridge, then climbs past the 68m (223-ft.) **Changbai Shan waterfall** to the north shore *(bei po)* of the lake. Rock slides sometimes block the trail, in which case you may be able to seek out a freelance guide (¥100/$13/£6.50 per person) to show you an alternate route. Go early in the morning to avoid the crowds. Once you arrive, search out Mr. Song, an ex-reporter and photographer who lives by the lake and likes to tell tales of the mythical **Tian Chi monster** *(guaiwu)* over harsh glasses of Chinese moonshine.

OTHER SIGHTS

Chang Bai Shan is home to a number of volcanic **hot springs,** the largest of which seeps steaming out of the rock south of the waterfall. Water from the springs commonly reaches 180°F (80°C); vendors sell eggs boiled in the springs (¥10/$1.30/65p for four). The **Wenquan Yu,** in a small white building that's a 10-minute walk below the waterfall (on the left side as you descend), charges ¥80 ($5.20/£10) for a pleasant soak in its hot-spring baths. Also on the mountain, 4km (2½ miles) below the *daozhankou,* is the truly magical **Dixia Senlin (Underground Forest)** ☆ (includes the Heavenly Pool (Xiao Tian Chi), a lush forest that becomes progressively more alien as it descends, with the Erdao Bai He 60m (200 ft.) below the mountain stratum (bring bug spray). In Bai He itself, between the railway station and the rest of town, is **Meiren Song Senlin (Sylvan Pine Forest;** 6am–6pm; ¥8/$1.05/50p), with a stunning forestry of sylvan pines *(meiren song),* a rare species that grow only on the northern slope of Chang Bai Shan between 650m and 1,600m (2,100–5,200 ft.).

WHERE TO STAY & DINE

Rooms in most hotels are outfitted with **kang**—heated brick platform beds, favored by Koreans and Manchus, either raised or sunk into the floor and covered with quilts. A group of families have set up small guesthouses next to the railway station in Bai He, where it is possible to sleep on a *kang* and enjoy home cooking for as little as ¥50 ($6.50/£3.25).

If you prefer a mattress, Bai He's largest and nicest hotel is the **Xinda Binguan** (© 0433/572-0111; fax 0433/572-0555; 116 units), on the east side of Baishan Dajie just south of the Meiren Song Senlin. Simple but spacious and clean rooms with slightly dirty bathrooms cost ¥380 ($49/£25). The **Fubai Binguan** (© 0433/571-8372; www.cbstianchi.com/fb-about.asp; 68 units), inside the Bai He Forestry Bureau complex south of the railway station, has clean guest rooms with small but tidy bathrooms for ¥220 to ¥220 ($26–$29/£13–£14), as well as beds for ¥50 ($6.50/£3.25).

If you plan to spend more than a day at Chang Bai Shan, it makes sense to pay the extra money and stay on the mountain. The **Athlete's Village,** at the *daozhankou* **(Yundongyuan Cun;** © 0433/574-6008; fax 0433/574-6055; 59 units), offers basic but comfortable rooms with TVs and small, clean bathrooms in a ski-lodge setting for ¥560 ($73/£36). A 15-minute walk up the road, in a large, traditional Korean-style building, is the **Chang Bai Shan International Hotel (Chang Bai Shan Guoji Binguan;** © 0433/574-6004; fax 0433/574-6002; 42 units), which offers relatively luxurious standard rooms with plush beds and clean marble bathrooms (¥700/$91/£46; Amex, Diners Club, MasterCard, Visa accepted). Next door, the impeccable **Chang Bai Shan Daewoo (Chang Bai Shan Dayu Fandian)** ☆☆ (© 0433/574-6011; fax 0433/574-6012; 59 units) offers a choice of bed or water-heated *kang* (¥960/$125/£62; Amex, Diners Club, MasterCard, Visa accepted).

All of the hotels mentioned above serve overpriced but adequate food. Restaurants in town are mostly dives, but they are significantly cheaper and serve comparable fare. The best meal (also the most expensive) can be found at the Chang Bai Shan Daewoo.

THE WESTERN APPROACH

Still in the process of being developed, this route lacks the grandeur of the northern approach but compensates with a more subtle beauty. The starting point is the dusty village of Songjiang He, 40km (25 miles) west of Chang Bai Shan, connected by a newly paved road to a saddle of rock overlooking Tian Chi on the border with North

> **Tips   Hiking West to North**
>
> Development of the western approach has made it possible to hike around Tian Chi and see both sides of the lake in 2 days, provided you have a tent, warm clothes, and plenty of food and water. The **hike from the west shore** along the ridge past Baiyun Feng to the waterfall on the north shore takes roughly 6 hours. Once you reach the waterfall, you can hike down to the hot spring, camp, and catch a ride to Bai He the next morning. Buses back to Songjiang He (3 hr.; ¥13/$1.70/85p) leave from the long-distance bus station on Baishan Dajie at 2pm.
>
> **Warning:** The path is rocky and the weather unpredictable—for experienced hikers only.

Korea. The chief attraction here is the plant life, which changes gradually from ghostly forests of birch at the lower elevations to vivid fields of wildflowers and grassy tundra just below the lake. The flowers are at their most vibrant in early June.

ESSENTIALS

GETTING THERE   The best way to get to Songjiang He is by bus from Changchun (5:30am; 9 hr.; ¥42/$5/£2.50) or Jilin (1pm; 14 hr.; ¥116/$15/£7.50); or by train from Tonghua (6:05am; 7½ hr.; ¥35/$4.55/£2.30). The long-distance bus station, in a blue speckled building with a red-tile roof, is a 20-minute walk south of the railway station on Zhan Qian Jie, the city's main thoroughfare.

TOURS   The **Songjiang He Forestry Company** (✆ 0439/631-8461), with a travel office inside the Songjiang He Binguan (see "Where to Stay & Dine," below), is the only organization officially allowed to run tours of the western slope. The 2-day tour costs ¥440 ($57/£29) and includes admission and lunch, but no English is spoken. If you can speak Mandarin, it's much cheaper to hire a private car; drivers will approach you at the railway station. A reasonable price range is ¥150 to ¥250 ($20–$33/£9.75–£16).

EXPLORING THE MOUNTAIN

The **Xi Po Shan Men (West Slope Mountain Gate),** located 44km (27 miles) west of Tian Chi, is open from 6:30am to 4:30pm; admission is ¥100 ($13/£6.50). The drive from the gate runs past birch forests and fields of wildflowers, ending at a steep set of stairs that leads to Tian Chi and the No. 5 border stone, which marks the beginning of North Korea. Birds and Chinese tourists cross the border at will, but soldiers stationed by the stone keep foreigners from doing the same. There is a 3-hour round-trip hike from here to Baiyun Feng, the highest point (2,691m/8,826 ft.); it's the second peak to the left as you face the lake.

None of the other sights in the area are particularly impressive or worth the extra money your driver will demand.

WHERE TO STAY & DINE

The only proper hotel in Songjiang He is the dark **Songjiang He Binguan** (✆ 0439/631-3601;** fax 0439/631-8820; 90 units) on Gongyi Dajie, across from the Senlin Huodong Zhongxin. Partially refurbished rooms with acceptable bathrooms cost ¥240 ($31/£16), but this can be bargained below ¥200 ($26/£13) even in the high season. The hotel serves mediocre food, but independent restaurants aren't much better.

7 Harbin

Heilong Jiang Province, 1,421km (881 miles) NE of Beijing, 553km (342 miles) NE of Shenyang

Harbin (Ha'erbin), originally a Russian-built railway outpost carved out of the wilderness on the banks of the Songhua Jiang (Sungari River), is the northernmost major city in China and capital of Heilong Jiang Province. Named for the Black Dragon River that separates Dongbei from Siberia, Heilong Jiang represents China's northern limits. It is the country's coldest province, with winter temperatures that hover, on average, around –15°F (–26°C). Like many border regions, it is an amalgamation of clashing extremes, home to one of China's roughest mountain ranges (the Greater Hinggan or Da Xing'an Ling), some of its most fertile soil, its largest oil and coal fields, its most pristine wilderness, and most of its few remaining nomad groups.

Harbin itself suffers from a similar internal antagonism, one that ultimately makes it the most compelling destination in Dongbei. The city was founded in 1897 as a camp for Russian engineers surveying construction of the eastern leg of the Trans-Siberian railroad (called the China Eastern Railroad, or CER). Demand for labor and the city's laissez-faire atmosphere quickly attracted a diverse population of outcasts from Latvia, the Ukraine, and Poland, as well as Manchuria. It was, at its height, one of the most bizarrely cosmopolitan cities in Asia—cold, dirty, rife with speculation and venereal disease, architecturally vibrant, and a model for ethnic and religious tolerance. The town fell under Japanese control during World War II and was finally recaptured in 1946.

Most original foreign residents fled at the end of World War II. The city has begun to recover some of its former face, however, as trainloads of Russian merchants and prostitutes flood back to take advantage of China's new economic momentum. Harbin attracts visitors year-round, especially in winter, when it hosts the famous **Ice and Snow Festival (Bingxue Jie)** ☆. The summer's mild temperatures allow for leisurely strolls past the truly stunning clusters of Russian buildings, with their lonely cupolas and embellished pediments, that still brighten older parts of town.

The Ice and Snow Festival has successfully turned the city's worst feature—villainous winter cold—into its greatest asset. The winter, despite the frostbite-inducing weather, is the best time to come as it's the town's most festive time of year. The festival now covers most of the city and features some truly outstanding ice and snow sculptures. Past highlights have included translucent reproductions of the Great Wall and Beijing's Gate of Heavenly Peace (Tian'an Men), life-size pagodas, structurally sound multilevel houses, and a massive statue of Elvis—all equipped with internal lights.

It's easy to underestimate the cold (temperatures often drop below –22°F/–30°C), so bring more warm clothing than you think you'll need. Wearing five layers of sweaters and a down coat might sound ridiculous until you get there. Admission can be expensive, but there are increasing numbers of free displays on Zhongyang Dajie and other major streets. Major venues include **Zhaolin Gonyuan** on Shangzhi Jie for ice sculpture; **Taiyang Dao Gongyuan (Sun Island Park),** across the river for snow sculptures; and the **Ice and Snow Palace (Bingxue Gong),** a collection of buildings constructed entirely of ice and snow on the banks of the Songhua Jiang. Admission to each venue is ¥150 ($20/£9.75) for adult and ¥75 ($9.75/£4.90) for children and students.

ESSENTIALS

GETTING THERE   Flights connect Harbin with Beijing, Shanghai, Dalian, and Guangzhou; international routes include Hong Kong (daily), Seoul (daily), and

Niigata (Mon, Wed, Fri, and Sun). The **Taiping International Airport (Taiping Guoji Jichang)** is 30km (19 miles) south of central Harbin. An ICBC booth next to the international departures area on the second floor exchanges traveler's checks and cash. The **CAAC ticket office (Minhang Shoupiao Chu; ℂ 0451/8265-1188;** fax 0451/8231-9343; domestic 6am–9pm, international 8am–4pm) is in a large white tiled building with a red roof, 4km (2½ miles) south of the railway station at Zhongshan Lu 99. An **airport shuttle** (50 min.; ¥20/$2.60/£1.30) leaves the CAAC office every 30 minutes from 6am to 6pm. **Taxis** to the airport from downtown (¥100/$13/£6.50), including ¥20 ($2.60/£1.30) toll, take between 40 minutes and an hour, depending on traffic. Leave early either way.

Harbin's **main railway station (Ha'erbin Zhan)** is on Tielu Jie, between Nangang and Daoli districts. Trains depart from here for Beijing (3:48pm; 8 hr.; ¥386/$50/£25), Dalian (9:04pm; 9 hr.; ¥231/$30/£15), Shenyang (six daily; 4½–5 hr.; ¥76/$9.90/£4.95 hard seat; ¥139/$18/£9 hard sleeper), Qiqihar (10 daily; 2½ hr.; ¥44/$5.70/£2.85), and Manzhouli (7:58pm; 14 hr.; ¥176/$23/£11). The ticket sales office is on the right side of the station (ℂ 0451/8690-2828); tickets can be bought 5 days in advance. For tickets to Khabarovsk and Vladivostok, visit the **Harbin Railway International Travel Service (Ha'erbin Tiedao Guoji Luxingshe; ℂ 0451/8642-7735;** open Mon–Fri 8am–5pm) on the seventh floor of the Kunlun Hotel, west of the main station. **CITS** (Xidazhi Jie 13, west of Hongbo Guangchang; ℂ 0451/5366-1167; 8:30am–5:30pm) and the **Heilong Jiang Overseas Tourist Company (Heilong Jiang Haiwai Luyou Gongsi;** 11th floor of Hushi Dasha, on west side of railway station; ℂ 0451/5363-4000; fax 0451/5362-1088) sell tickets for the **Trans-Siberian Railroad** (2 weeks to process).

The central **long-distance bus station (Changtu Keyun Zhan)** is across from the railway station, a building next to the Bei Bei Hotel. Luxury air-conditioned buses go to Qiqihar (4 hr.; ¥50–¥55/$6.45–$7.15/£3.20–£3.60) and Wu Da Lianchi (9am and 11:30am; 5½ hr.; ¥55–¥69/$7.15–$9/£3.60–£4.50), and Changchun (3½ hr.; ¥76/$9.90/£4.95). Regular buses go to Yanji (3:30pm; 9 hr.; ¥112/$15/£7.30) and Dalian (4:40pm; 13 hr.; ¥210/$27/£14). The ticket sales office is open from 5:30am to 6pm (luxury tickets at windows 7–11).

GETTING AROUND   Nearly everything of interest falls into one of two old districts—Daoli and Nangang—divided by the train tracks that run past the main station. The Songhua Jiang (Sungari River) forms the city's northern border and divides it from Taiyang Dao, a new island development area that seeks to imitate Pudong in Shanghai.

Taxis cost ¥8 ($1.05/50p) for first 3km/2 miles, then ¥1.90 (25¢/15p) per kilometer. A number of useful **buses** (¥1–¥2/15¢–25¢/10p–15p) stop at the railway station; **bus no. 13** goes from the station through the heart of Daoli.

FAST FACTS

Banks, Foreign Exchange & ATMs   The main **Bank of China** branch (open Mon–Fri 8:30am–4:30pm) is at Hongjun Jie 20, 1 block north of Hongbo Guangchang. Credit cards and traveler's checks are handled at window 2 on the second floor (*not* available 11:30am–1pm). There is an international ATM on the premises. A second branch at Xi Shi (10) Daojie 29 (east of Zhongyang Dajie) exchanges traveler's checks and cash (Mon–Fri 8:30am–4:30pm).

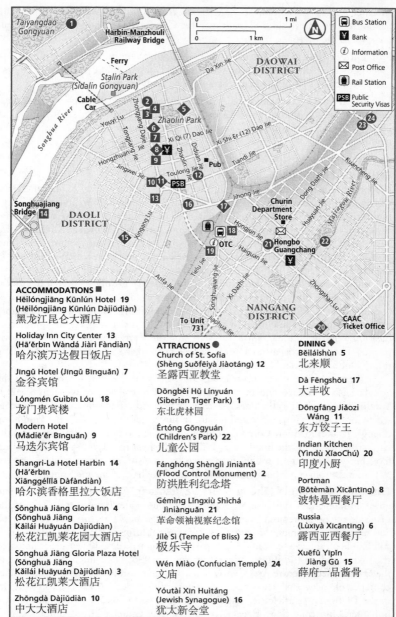

Taiyangdao Gongyuan **1**

Harbin-Manzhouli Railway Bridge

Ferry

Stalin Park (Sidalin Gongyuan)

Cable Car

Songhua River

DAOWAI DISTRICT

Da Xin Jie

Zhaolin Park

Xi Qi (7) Dao Jie

Xi Shi Er (12) Dao Jie

Pub

Tiandi Jie

Songhuajiang Bridge 14

DAOLI DISTRICT

Jihong Jie

Churin Department Store

Hongbo Guangchang

Kuancheng Jie

OTC

NANGANG DISTRICT

To Unit 731

Zhongshan Lu

CAAC Ticket Office

🚌	Bus Station
¥	Bank
ⓘ	Information
✉	Post Office
🚇	Rail Station
PSB	Public Security Visas

0 — 1 mi
0 — 1 km

ACCOMMODATIONS ■
Hēilóngjiāng Kūnlún Hotel **19**
(Hēilóngjiāng Kūnlún Dàjiǔdiàn)
黑龙江昆仑大酒店

Holiday Inn City Center **13**
(Hā'ěrbīn Wàndá Jiàrì Fàndiàn)
哈尔滨万达假日饭店

Jīngǔ Hotel (Jīngǔ Bīnguǎn) **7**
金谷宾馆

Lóngmén Guìbīn Lóu **18**
龙门贵宾楼

Modern Hotel
(Mǎdié'ěr Bīnguǎn) **9**
马迭尔宾馆

Shangri-La Hotel Harbin **14**
(Hā'ěrbīn
Xiānggélǐlā Dàfàndiàn)
哈尔滨香格里拉大饭店

Sōnghuā Jiāng Gloria Inn **4**
(Sōnghuā Jiāng
Kǎilái Huāyuán Dàjiǔdiàn)
松花江凯莱花园大酒店

Sōnghuā Jiāng Gloria Plaza Hotel
(Sōnghuā Jiāng
Kǎilái Huāyuán Dàjiǔdiàn) **3**
松花江凯莱大酒店

Zhōngdà Dàjiǔdiàn **10**
中大大酒店

ATTRACTIONS ●
Church of St. Sofia
(Shèng Suǒfēiyà Jiàotáng) **12**
圣露西亚教堂

Dōngběi Hǔ Línyuán
(Siberian Tiger Park) **1**
东北虎林园

Értóng Gōngyuán
(Children's Park) **22**
儿童公园

Fánghóng Shènglì Jìniàntǎ
(Flood Control Monument) **2**
防洪胜利纪念塔

Gémìng Lǐngxiù Shìchá
Jìniànguǎn **21**
革命领袖视察纪念馆

Jílè Sì (Temple of Bliss) **23**
极乐寺

Wén Miào (Confucian Temple) **24**
文庙

Yóutài Xīn Huìtáng
(Jewish Synagogue) **16**
犹太新会堂

DINING ◆
Běiláishùn **5**
北来顺

Dà Fēngshōu **17**
大丰收

Dōngfāng Jiǎozi
Wáng **11**
东方饺子王

Indian Kitchen
(Yìndù XiǎoChú) **20**
印度小厨

Portman
(Bōtèmàn Xīcāntīng) **8**
波特曼西餐厅

Russia
(Lùxīyà Xīcāntīng) **6**
露西亚西餐厅

Xuēfǔ Yīpǐn
Jiàng Gǔ **15**
薛府一品酱骨

Internet Access   Go online at the 24-hour **Yidu Kongjian Wangba** (¥3/40¢/20p per hour) on the north side of Hongzhuan Jie, a block west of Zhongyang Dajie. Dial-up is ℭ **16900** or 165.

Post Office   The main post office (**Nangang Youzhengju;** open May–Oct 8am–7pm, Nov–Apr 8am–6:30pm) is on the corner of Dong Dazhi Jie and Fendou Lu, several blocks east of Hongbo Guangchang. Phone cards are sold inside.

Visa Extensions   Visa extensions are available inside the **PSB** Exit/Entry Administration Office (ℭ **0451/8466-1435;** Mon–Fri 8–11:40am and 1:30–4:40pm) at Duan Jie 26, near the bottom of Zhongyang Dajie. Passport and hotel registration are required.

EXPLORING HARBIN
ZHOGNYANG DAJIE ⚑⚑

A cobbled, tree-lined street located in the heart of Daoli District, Zhongyang Dajie was once the buzzing heart of social and commercial life in Harbin, home to the city's most exclusive hotels and shops. "From 3am until nightfall, it was alive with throngs of people," a Japanese visitor wrote of the avenue, originally known as Kitaiskia (Chinese) Street, in 1926. "The Russian women with their gaudy early summer hats and clothing together with their white shoes formed a spectacle to be seen nowhere else in the Far East save Shanghai." The scene today is much the same, but with Russian faces few and far between. Particularly vibrant is the **pedestrian-only section** at the southern end, where Chinese women in absurd fur coats window-shop a new generation of boutiques set up in the old Russian buildings, beautifully restored with explanatory plaques in English. The old-world charm, however, has not stopped the commercial invasion of fast-food restaurants, Wal-Mart, and the Warner Brothers–branded movie theater. The luxury department store Lane Crawford has opened a branch, selling pricey Dunhill, St. John, and Mont Blanc items.

At the top of the street, constructed along a large embankment erected after the Songhua River flooded and buried Harbin under several feet of water in 1932, is **Sidalin Gongyuan (Stalin Park),** a recently repaved stretch of trees and benches where locals gather to exercise and gossip. In the center of the park is the **Fanghong Shengli Jinianta (Flood Control Monument).** The monument commemorates the city's struggle against the floods of 1957, when the river rose 1.2m (4 ft.) above street level but was kept from spilling into town by an army of soldiers and volunteers. Water levels from other big floods are marked at the base of the monument.

Church of St. Sophia (Sheng Suofeiya Jiaotang) ⚑⚑
The brick spires and green dome of the Church of St. Sophia rising out of the chaos east of Zhongyang Dajie are the divine reminders of a more inspired age in architecture. Erected in 1907 and rebuilt several times, the church took its current form in 1932. The handiwork is still visible on the vaulted ceilings and painted chambers, despite near-destruction by the Red Guards in the 1960s and a restoration in 1996. The church is now home to the **Harbin Architecture Arts Center.** An exhibition inside contains photos of other churches, old newspaper clippings, and an interesting scale model of Nangang District in the 1920s. The rear cloister, used for storage prior to 2002, now contains a small but interesting collection of religious objects. The church's incongruous beauty is enhanced by dozens of white pigeons (kept in place with the promise of free food from feeders in the surrounding square). Pocket-size guides to old Harbin, with color photos and bilingual introductions to several buildings, are sold inside.

> ### *Fun Fact*   Zion That Wasn't
>
> Unlikely as it sounds, Jews fled to Harbin in such numbers in the early 1900s (the population reached 25,000 at its height) that Manchuria ranked just below Morocco and Palestine on early-20th-century lists of potential sites for a Jewish homeland. Fleeing official discrimination and a revival of pogroms in czarist Russia, they were instrumental in Harbin's development but fled en masse for the real Zion shortly after World War II. The only obvious Jewish structures still remaining in the city are the **Modern Hotel** (see "Where to Stay," below); and a **music and Torah school** at Tongjiang Jie 86 (a block west of Zhongyang Dajie), a ragged structure built in 1919 with Star of David window frames that now houses the No. 2 Korean Middle School (Chaoxian Er Zhong).

Intersection of Toulong Jie and Zhaolin Jie. Admission ¥15 ($1.95/£1). 8:30am–5pm. *©* **0451/8468-6904.** Bus: no. 103 from the railway station to Hayibai, then walk 2 blocks east on Toulong Jie.

Dongbei Hu Linyuan (Siberian Tiger Park) *Overrated*   The Siberian Tiger Park is more like an impoverished prison for the tigers—with rusty fences and dilapidated watchtowers—but it may be worth a visit to see the rare felines. Your entrance fee gets you a seat on a typical Chinese minibus that rolls onto the fenced-in .4-sq.-km (.2 sq.-mile) premises on a dirt road. The bus gets close enough for you to snap good photos and ogle the tigers' paws that are as large as human heads. The park, created in 1986, increased its tiger population from the original 8 to nearly 300, but the facility is more tourist attraction than breeding center. For your sadistic pleasure you may order a meal for the tigers, served via a caged jeep; on the feeding menu are a live bird (¥40/$5.20/£2.60), a live duck (¥100/$13/£6.50), and a live cow (¥1,500/$195/£98). Sadly, some of the tigers are confined to tiny cages, pacing about in their mini insane asylums; others seems to be in a semipermanent state of slumber.

10km (6 miles) north of the city center. www.dongbeihu.net.cn. Admission (including tour) ¥50 ($6.50/£3.25) adults, ¥25 ($3.25/£1.65) children. May–Sept 8am–6pm; Oct–Apr 8:30am–4pm. Last tour 30 min. before closing. Bus: no. 85 from south end of Gonglu Daqiao (40 min). Cable car: from Sidalin Gongyuan to Taiyang Dao Gongyuan (¥30/$3.90/£1.95), then minibus to park entrance (20 min.; ¥30/$3.90/£1.95).

Ertong Gongyuan (Children's Park) *Kids*   Built in 1925, this park is famous for its Children's Railroad (Ertong Tielu), a working pint-size replica of the real thing. The train (¥5/65¢/30p), complete with small hard-seat benches, travels a 2km (1¼-mile) circle from "Beijing Station" (Beijing Zhan) behind the main entrance to "Harbin Station" (Ha'erbin Zhan) at the opposite end of the park and back again.

Fendou Lu 295. *©* **0451/5363-8415.** Admission ¥2 (25¢/15p) adults, ¥1 (15¢/10p) children. May–Sept 4:30am–10pm; Oct–Apr 6:30am–6pm. Bus: no. 8 from top of Zhongyang Dajie. Or walk 4 blocks southeast from the main post office.

Geming Lingxiu Shicha Jinianguan   This elegant mansion, built in 1919 by a Polish merchant and opened as a museum in 2002 after a 3-year restoration effort, was where China's top Communist leaders stayed during official inspections of Heilong Jiang. Sumptuously designed rooms on the first floor contain several mementos, including a bathrobe once used by Zhou Enlai. An impressive spiral staircase leads up to the room where Mao slept, still with the original bed.

Yiyuan Jie (off Hongjun Jie). *©* **0451/5364-2522.** Admission ¥6 (75¢/40p). 9am–4pm. Located behind Sinoway Hotel; it's the 2nd old mansion on the left.

Jile Si (Temple of Bliss)   Jile Si is the largest active Buddhist temple in Heilong Jiang Province, a beautiful complex welcoming tourists but not made for them. Most impressive are the halls on either side of the main pavilion in the northeastern half, each filled with 500 individually carved arhats *(luohan)*, or Buddhist saints. The hall on the right is devoted to Manchu namesake Wenshu Pusa (Sanskrit: *Manjusri*), the tiger-riding Bodhisattva of Wisdom (see "Minorities & the Manchu Myth," p. 165). There's a smaller temple next door called Puzhao Si that is open on the 1st and 15th day of each Chinese lunar month.

Dong Dazhi Jie 9. Admission ¥10 ($1.30/65p). May–Sept 8am–4:30pm; Oct–Apr 8am–4pm. Bus: no. 104/14 from Hongbo Guangchang to Youleyuan; walk northeast on Xuanpu Jie, then take a left on Dong Dazhi Jie.

Unit 731 Museum (Qinhua Rijun Diqisanyao Budui Jiuzhi) 🏵️🏵️   What happened here is little known in the Western world, which makes this museum a very worthwhile visit despite being located in Harbin's inconvenient suburbs. Between 1939 and 1945, members of Japan's Unit 731 killed roughly 3,000 Chinese, Russian, Mongolian, and North Korean prisoners of war in a series of nauseating experiments designed to perfect their biological weapons program. Japanese soldiers blew up most of the 6-sq.-km (2-sq.-mile) facility at the end of the war, and the unit's existence was kept covered up for decades with the help of the United States government, rumored to have purchased the research with a promise of immunity for participating doctors. A documentary about 731 released in the 1990s prompted Harbin to renovate the facility and add English signs in 2001. Ironically, the museum now stands in an area of town where many of China's pharmaceutical companies are located.

What's best about the museum is that it lets the images and details tell the story, rather than resorting to the heavy-handed propaganda that plagues other Chinese war memorials like the Nanjing Massacre Site. An exhibition in the main office building contains a series of grim but nicely presented displays on the experiments, in which victims (called *maruta,* Japanese for "log") were frozen, burned, injected with hemorrhagic fever virus, exposed to plague and cholera, and sometimes dissected alive. Most chilling is the medical instruments display (room 9), with its test tubes, needles, saws, and coat rack vivisection hooks (used to "hang human viscera," aka organs). The smokestacks of a large incinerator, where dead *maruta* were burned, still stand on the edge of a weed-strewn field in back.

Once you tour the museum, a guide can take you to the museum's backyard to see where the original germ factory stood (now a pit with overgrown weeds), the remnants of a power-generating facility for the factory, and a series of sheds where the Japanese once bred disease-carrying rats for the experiments.

Xinjiang Dajie 25 (west of the train tracks), Pingfang Qu. © **0451/8680-1556**. Admission ¥20 ($2.60/£1.30). 8–11:30am and 1–4pm. Bus: no. 338 or 343 from Kunlun Hotel (20km/12 miles; 45 min.; ¥2.50/35¢/15p) to Xinjiang Dajie;10-min. walk from the stop.

Wen Miao (Confucian Temple)   If you're looking for a brief respite from grimy urban life and a more solemn place than Jile Si, visit this wooden temple, one of the largest Confucian temples in China. Built in 1926, Wen Miao, with its 20m-high (66-ft.) ceilings, is now part of Harbin Engineering College campus. At the time of writing, the buildings adjacent to the main palace that make up the temple's main courtyard were being converted into the Nationalities Museum of Heilong Jiang Province. Students painting still lifes in the courtyard and the temple's huge pine trees give it an air of tranquillity.

Wenmiao Jie 9. Admission ¥15 ($1.95/£1). 8:30am–4pm. Walk from Jile Si across the street to the Harbin Engineering College, then walk inside about 5 min.

Youtai Xin Huitang (Jewish Synagogue) ⚑   Once the center of Harbin's vibrant Jewish community that numbered around 20,000 during the early 20th century, this three-story temple underwent an extensive renovation and reopened to the public in 2005. Today, with few Jews remaining in the city, government officials turned the synagogue into a contemporary art museum featuring Jewish and Russian artists.

162 Jing Wei Jie, Dao Li District. ℭ 0451/8763-0882. Admission ¥10 ($1.30/65p). 9am–5pm. Bus: no. 2.

WHERE TO STAY

If you want to visit Harbin during the Ice and Snow Festival—December to early March, when thousands flood the city—try to book a room at least 2 weeks to a month in advance. Some hotels offer minor discounts during the festival. Discounts at other times range from 30% to 50%.

EXPENSIVE

Shangri-La Hotel Harbin (Ha'erbin Xianggelila Dafandian) ⚑⚑   The Shangri-La is the finest hotel in central Harbin, and the only five-star in Daoli District. Rooms, most of which have recently undergone extensive renovations, are comfortable and tasteful. Service is fantastic. The only drawback is that the hotel is not within walking distance of Harbin's fabled architecture, but its location on the river (across from the Ice and Snow Palace) becomes ideal in winter.

Youyi Lu 555 (east of Songhua Jiang Gonglu Bridge), Daoli District. ℭ 0451/8485-8888. Fax 0451/8462-1777. www.shangri-la.com. 342 units. ¥1,450 ($189/£94) standard room. 15% service charge. Rate includes breakfast for 1. AE, DC, MC, V. Amenities: 2 restaurants; bar; indoor pool; outdoor tennis courts; health club and spa; concierge; business center; forex; salon; 24-hr. room service; same-day laundry/dry cleaning; nonsmoking rooms; executive-level rooms. In room: A/C, satellite TV, broadband Internet access, minibar, fridge, hair dryer, safe.

Songhua Jiang Gloria Plaza Hotel (Songhua Jiang Kailai Huayuan Dajiudian)   This relatively new hotel is a welcome addition to Harbin's travel scene, with clean rooms and an unmatched location right next to the Flood Control Monument. With just 83 rooms few tour groups stay here, making management more attuned to the independent traveler. The suites on the top floor share a common private balcony overlooking the river. (Don't confuse this hotel with the Gloria Inn, a midprice hotel listed below.)

Er Daojie 259, Daoli District. ℭ 0451/8677-0000. Fax 0451/8677-0088. www.gpharbin.com. 83 units. ¥880–¥980 ($114–$127/£57–£64) standard room; ¥1,880 – ¥2,880 ($244–$374/£122–£187) suite. 15% service charge. 30%–50% discounts. AE, DC, MC, V. Amenities: 2 restaurants; bar; business center; ticketing and tour arrangements; 24-hr. room service; forex; same-day laundry/dry cleaning. In room: A/C, TV, broadband Internet access.

MODERATE

Holiday Inn City Center (Ha'erbin Wanda Jiari Fandian)   The Holiday Inn, Harbin's finest hotel 5 years ago, now feels more like a midrange Chinese hotel than a respectable joint-venture. But its convenient location at the bottom of Zhongyang Dajie, solid service, and one of the best Western restaurants in Harbin still make it an attractive option. Rooms are large, clean, and comfortable but somewhat worn and outdated.

Jing Wei Jie 90, Daoli District. ℭ 0451/8422-6666. Fax 0452/8422-1663. www.holidayinn.com. 148 units. ¥558 ($73/£36) standard room. 15% service charge. Rates include breakfast. AE, DC, MC, V. Amenities: 2 restaurants; bar; basic health club; sauna; business center; forex; room service; laundry/dry cleaning; executive-level rooms. In room: A/C, satellite TV, broadband Internet access, minibar, fridge, hair dryer, safe.

Jingu Hotel (Jingu Binguan) _Value_   While this hotel might belong in the "moderate" category, the management is so generous with its discount that it is a good choice for the budget traveler. The beds are slightly hard, but the bathrooms are sparkling clean. Located on Zhongyang Dajie, the location puts you in the heart of the pedestrian walk. Some English is spoken by the staff.

Zhongyang Dajie 185, Daoli District. ℂ 0451/8469-8700. Fax 0451/8469-8458. www.jinguhotel.com.cn. 213 units. ¥588 ($76/£38) standard room. 20% discounts. 10% service charge. AE, DC, MC, V. **Amenities:** 2 restaurants; bar; sauna; salon; business center; limited room service; ticketing center; bank; forex; bowling. _In room:_ A/C, satellite TV, broadband Internet access, minibar, safe.

Modern Hotel (Madie'er Binguan) _✦_   The most glamorous hotel in Harbin during the city's heyday, the three-story Art Nouveau hotel, built in 1906, fell on hard times in the early Communist era. While it's improved significantly since, say, the Cultural Revolution, the rooms don't measure up to the history of the place. Still, the location smack in the middle of Zhongyang Dajie and the fair prices make it a very good choice. Standard rooms are rather lackluster and devoid of character; bathrooms are small but very clean.

Zhongyang Dajie 89 (at Xiba Daojie, entrance in back), Daoli District. ℂ 0451/8488-4444. Fax 0451/8461-4997. www.modern.com.cn. 160 units. ¥980 ($127/£64) standard room. 50% discounts. Rates include breakfast. AE, DC, MC, V. **Amenities:** 2 restaurants; bar; indoor pool and health club (in neighboring building); business center; forex; laundry. _In room:_ A/C, satellite TV, broadband Internet access, minibar, fridge.

INEXPENSIVE

Longmen Guibin Lou _✦✦✦ Finds_   Built in 1907, this inexplicably ignored yellow-and-white Russian building behind the nondescript Longmen Hotel is the most beautifully restored of the old Yamato Hotels. Rooms are spacious and nicely appointed with period furniture. History buffs with money to spare can stay in the suite, outfitted with a beautiful bed from the 1930s, where Zhang Xueliang (see "Shenyang," p. 159) held court when in Harbin. Dining rooms on the first floor still display the original Russian woodwork and contain several turn-of-the-20th-century relics, including an old wooden icebox and a still-functioning phonograph.

Hongjun Jie 85 (at Jianzhu Jie, opposite the railway station), Nangang District. ℂ 0451/8679-1888. Fax 0451/8363-9700. 235 units. ¥480 ($62/£31) standard room. 50% discount. MC, V. **Amenities:** 4 restaurants; bar; new spa; billiards room; business center; forex; salon; limited room service; laundry/dry cleaning. _In room:_ A/C, TV, minibar, fridge.

Songhua Jiang Gloria Inn (Songhua Jiang Kailai Shangwu Jiudian)   The Songhua Jiang Gloria prospers almost entirely from its location just south of the Flood Control Monument. The hotel, inside a large European-style building, underwent partial renovation in 2001. Rooms are midsize with the green carpets and multilevel ceilings typical of Gloria hotels—worn but still livable. Bathrooms are small and tidy.

Zhongyang Dajie 257, Daoli District. ℂ 0451/8463-8855. Fax 0451/8463-8533. www.giharbin.com. 294 units. ¥450–¥550 ($59–$72/£29–£36) standard room. 15% service charge. 20%–30% discounts. AE, DC, MC, V. **Amenities:** 2 restaurants; business center; 24-hr. room service; ticketing and tour arrangements; forex; same-day laundry/dry cleaning; complimentary scheduled airport shuttle. _In room:_ A/C, satellite TV, minibar, fridge.

WHERE TO DINE

The basement of the Zhongyang Shangcheng, at Zhongyang Dajie 100, has a **food court** with point-to-choose Chinese food and a well-stocked **supermarket.** Zhongyang Dajie is also home to two **McDonald's** and two **KFC** branches. For quick and convenient local food from 9am to 9pm, try the *shaguo shizitou* (smoky tofu, carrots, and a large meatball in savory broth) and pancakes *(bing)* at **Lao Shanghai** (ⓒ 0451/ 8262-6335), located above a bakery at the corner of Zhongyang Dajie and Da'an Jie.

Beilaishun MUSLIM This long-lived Muslim restaurant, named after the legendary Donglaishun in Beijing, is often packed in winter, when believers and atheists alike quiet their shivers over the steam from brass hot pots *(huoguo)*. Thin-sliced mutton is the main hot pot ingredient, but it's big on the menu, too: Try the *pa yangrou tiao*—tender, baconlike strips of lamb braised in a simple soy-and-garlic sauce.

Youyi Lu 51 (next to Children's Hospital). ⓒ 0451/8461-3530. Meal for 2 ¥40–¥100 ($5.20–$13/£2.60–£6.50). No credit cards. 11am–9pm.

Da Fengshou 🌟🌟 *(Finds)* DONGBEI Everything about this immensely popular place is authentic Dongbei: Diners sit on benches and drink beer out of bowls, waitresses unceremoniously dump handfuls of sunflower seeds on the table as appetizers, and the dishes are immense. Avoid the pig-face set dinner and go instead for *jiachang tudouni*, a Chinese take on garlic mashed potatoes. The entrance is marked by a huge neon sign and a long, lantern-lit pathway.

Yimian Jie 283 (north of traffic circle next to railway bridge). ⓒ 0451/5364-6824. Meal for 2 ¥30–¥60 ($3.90–$7.80/£1.95–£3.90). No credit cards. 9am–9pm.

Dongfang Jiaozi Wang 🌟🌟 JIAOZI So popular it inspired a region-wide chain, this original branch is classier than other members of the "Eastern Dumpling King" family and serves some of the best *jiaozi* in China. Order a cold dish and a plate of *sanxian* (shrimp, pork, and Chinese chive) or *songren yumi* (corn and pine nut) *shuijiao*, then wander over to the glass-enclosed kitchen to marvel as the restaurant's army of chefs wrap and boil the dumplings with inconceivable speed.

Zhongyang Dajie 39. ⓒ 0451/8465-3920. Meal for 2 ¥15–¥30 ($1.95–$3.90/£1–£1.95). No credit cards. 10:30am–9:30pm.

Indian Kitchen (Yindu Xiao Chu) INDIAN Indian food in northeastern China? It may sounds weird, but this popular Indian-owned chain in China pulls off a decent garlic nan, cashew pilau, and butter paneer. Located on Indian Street (see "Shopping," below), the restaurant is a good choice for vegetarians and meat-eaters alike. The food tends to be more sweet than spicy, but you are free to ask one of the three Indian chefs in the glass-encased kitchen to kick up the heat.

Yindu Jie 154, Nangang District. ⓒ 0451/8263-8888. English menu. Meal for 2 ¥20–¥60 ($2.60–$7.80/£1.30–£3.90). No credit cards. 10am–2am.

Portman (Boteman Xicanting) WESTERN A ritzy place for a meal—you can't miss the white grand piano and giant fireplace surrounded by glass in the center of the four-story restaurant—the Portman serves standard Western food in Harbin, with decent service. The cabbage rolls with cream sauce are juicy and the Russian red soup is hearty with spice. At all costs avoid the mashed potatoes, which have a sweetness to them that should be illegal. If you must have some starchy tubers, go for the potato salad, which is perplexingly like mashed potatoes, but served cold. A wide range of chicken, fish, and steak dishes is also available. Live-music performances run every night from 6 to 10pm, but are not very impressive.

Xiqi Daojie 63, just off Zhongyang Dajie. ⓒ 0451/8468-6888. English menu. Meal for 2 ¥80–¥140 ($10–$18/ £5.20–£9.10). No credit cards. 11am–2am.

Russia (Luxiya Xicanting) ⚔ RUSSIAN/COFFEE   This small cafe decorated with heirlooms left behind by a Russian family is a rare reminder of China's treaty port days, when expatriates would suffer the chaos of prewar China by day and retreat at night to the softly lit, lace-covered comfort of their homes to drink coffee and write fantastic letters to the people they'd left behind. The cafe, nestled inside the cracked-wall room of an old Russian building near the top of Zhongyang Dajie, serves a small selection of Western dishes. The hearty red vegetable soup is satisfying; however, their signature dish, "pot beef," a steaming stew of beef, carrot, and tomato, is not particularly outstanding. The best is just spend the day here with a few cups of coffee and a book.

Xitou Daojie 57. ℂ 0451/8456-3207. English menu. Meal for 2 ¥60–¥100 ($7.80–$13/£3.90–£6.50). No credit cards. 9am–midnight.

Xuefu Yipin Jiang Gu ⚔ DONGBEI   This loud establishment is a favorite among locals. Though there are no English-speakers here, the simplicity of ordering is a huge bonus: simply go to the display section in the back and point to what you want. The advertised specialty is the pork ribs *(jiang gu)*. If you're adventurous, you can get the *gubang* (pork legs); locals enjoy sucking the marrow out of the bones. Every table setting comes with a pair of plastic gloves that diners don to pick up the giant drumsticks. Also try the tasty four-mushroom soup (Yipin Juntang), the pumpkin fries, and the fried crepes with vegetables and egg (Danhuang Junangua).

Tongda Jie 329, Daoli District. ℂ 0451/8762-1288. Main courses ¥15–¥50 ($1.95–$6.50/£1–£3.25). No credit cards. 11am–9pm.

SHOPPING

Aside from **Zhongyang Dajie,** the biggest commercial street is **Guogeli Jie,** where the government has recently organized several streets around themes. There is a street for children (clothing and toys), women (clothing), and, bizarrely, Indians. The Indian street features some saris, but little else from the Indian subcontinent is evident here. The **Churin Department Store (Qiulin Baihuo),** located in an immense green baroque-style building on the north side of Dong Dazhi Jie (opposite the main post office), was once one of the largest department stores in East Asia. The first floor is where you'll find Harbin's best *dalieba*—heavy circular loaves of crusty bread—and Russian-style red sausage *(hongchang),* which you can take for a picnic in the nearby Children's Park. A few blocks west, at the intersection of Dong Dazhi Jie and Hongjun Jie, is the **Hongbo Shichang,** one of the largest underground markets in the Northeast. The market is set up inside an old air-raid shelter, located underneath the former site of the St. Nicholas Church (destroyed by Red Guards in the 1960s), and offers everything from fur hats to black-market video games.

HARBIN AFTER DARK

The Popov distillery left town long ago, but foreign residents still imbibe plenty of vodka at **Blue Kiss (Bulusi Jiuba;** ℂ 0451/8468-4277). The drinks-and-dance venue at Diduan Jie 100, near Toulong Jie, is open from 1pm to very late; go late on a weekend night for the must-see variety show, a mix of high-kick quasi-striptease numbers that leaves even regular visitors shaking their heads in slack-jawed wonder. A less raunchy choice, **Portman** (see "Where to Dine," above) is open late and serves passable pitchers of dark draft beer. **St. Petersburg** on Guogeli Jie offers an environment similar to an American chain restaurant (Guangmang Jie 140; ℂ 0451/8260-3737). Wherever you end up, do try the refreshing and light Harbin Beer, known as Hapi by the locals, which is China's oldest brew.

8 Wu Da Lianchi

Heiilong Jiang Province, 340km (210 miles) NW of Harbin

Wu Da Lianchi (Five Linked Lakes) is an utterly strange health retreat wedged between the Greater and Lesser Hinggan (Xing'an) mountains, several hundred miles north of Harbin. The area is named for a series of connected lakes, formed 260 years ago by lava flows from the two youngest of 14 local volcanoes. Wu Da Lianchi is celebrated among Chinese for its pungent natural springs, water from which is rumored to cure everything from gastritis to chronic cardiocerebral angiopathy. The springs are disgusting, but the area's physical oddity is fascinating. Avoid the summer miracle-cure crowd if at all possible.

ESSENTIALS

Air-conditioned **coaches** (5½ hr.; ¥55–¥69/$7.15–$9/£3.60–£4.50; ¥90/$12/£5.85 for luxury bus) leave the **Harbin long-distance bus station** (© 0451/8283-0117) at 9am and 11:30am stop at the Worker's Sanatorium (see "Where to Stay," below). Return buses leave from the same spot at 6am, and at 1:30pm during the high season (June–Aug). Brochures with Chinese maps are sold in the Worker's Sanatorium (see below).

EXPLORING WU DA LIANCHI

Wu Da Lianchi's most impressive sight is not the lakes but the lava fields, collectively dubbed **Shi Hai (Sea of Stone),** which spread out for miles around the area's two largest volcanoes and look vaguely like charred marshmallow. At the center of this is **Laohei Shan** ✿ (also known as Heilong Shan, or Black Dragon Mountain), tallest of the Wu Da Lianchi volcanoes. An hour-long circumnavigation of the crater's edge, with its twisted birch trees and lichen-covered desolation, provides panoramic views. The **Bing Dong** (8am–4pm; ¥30/$3.90/£1.95), 7km (4⅓ miles) east of the Worker's Sanatorium, is a system of sub-freezing caves that contains an exhibition of colorful but underwhelming ice lanterns. Aviod going to **Nanquan**; it charges ¥20 ($2.60/ £1.30) for drinking the "natural spring water," which has an unpleasant rusty taste.

Private **minivans** are the only way to see most sights in Wu Da Lianchi. Drivers gather near **a large bilingual map** of the area opposite the entrance to Nan Quan (South Spring), a 30-minute walk east of the Worker's Sanatorium. Negotiations for a full tour of the area (25km/16 miles) usually start at around ¥150 ($20/£9.75) a car or ¥50 ($6.50/£3.25) per person. **Entrance tickets cost** ¥60 ($7.80/£3.90) including access to the volcano and lava fields.

WHERE TO STAY

Wu Da Lianchi swims with sanatoriums and guesthouses, all offering the same basic accommodations. The most convenient and popular option is the **Wu Da Lianchi Worker's Sanatorium (Gongren Liaoyangyuan;** © **0456/722-1569;** fax 0456/ 722-1814; www.wdgl.com.cn; 350 units), a large complex just east of the central traffic circle. Standard rooms in the main building (¥210/$27/£14) are dark but clean with passable bathrooms. Suites with air-conditioning and 24-hour hot water (¥580– ¥880/$75–$114/£38–£57) are in a separate building. Twenty percent discounts are available. At least one building is kept open all year. Each has its own restaurant, although neither serves particularly great food.

9 Manzhouli

Inner Mongolia, 981km (608 miles) NW of Harbin

A tiny frontier town of 50,000 lost in a sea of grass in the northeast corner of Inner Mongolia, Manzhouli is the East-meets-Wild-West frontier outpost David Carradine should have used as the backdrop to *Kung Fu.* Born almost overnight in the early 1900s, it was once the primary channel for trade between China and Russia. Russians can be seen everywhere in the streets. Most of the signs are written in Chinese, Russian, and Mongolian and many businessmen speak fluent Russian. A new wave of Russian traders has revitalized the city, effecting a return to the rough-and-tumble days of its founding. It is the most convenient base for trips into the gorgeous **Hulun Buir,** home to China's most pristine grasslands.

ESSENTIALS

GETTING THERE   The **Manzhouli Airport** (Manzhouli XiJiao JiChang) is located 9km (6 miles) southwest of the town. Purchase tickets for flights to Beijing (daily), Harbin (daily), Changchun (Wed and Sun) and Hohhot (daily) at the CITS at the International Hotel ticket office (© **0470/622-8319;** 8:30–11:30am and 2–5pm). There is no airport shuttle to Manzhouli airport, but a taxi ride takes 20 minutes and costs ¥40 ($5.20/£2.60).

Trains connect Manzhouli to Beijing (11:56pm; 30 hr., ¥292/$38/£19), Harbin (6:30pm; 14 hr.; ¥231/$30/£15), Qiqihar (7:10pm; 11 hr.; ¥164/$21/£11), and Hailar (six daily; 3 hr.; ¥27/$3.50/£1.75). The Trans-Siberian train comes through twice a week, usually Friday and Sunday morning, with stops in Irkutsk and Moscow; book tickets through CITS. The **railway station** (© **0470/225-2261**) is opposite downtown, south of the tracks; ticket office is open from 5am to 10pm. Purchase tickets for the Trans-Siberian at the business center inside the International Hotel. (*Note:* You must have arranged a Russian tourist visa in Beijing if you want to board the train.)

The **long-distance bus station (Guoji Keyun Zhan)** is north of the tracks on Yi Daojie, a 5-minute walk west of the railway footbridge. Iveco buses depart from here for Hailar (3 hr.; ¥32/$4.15/£2.10) every 30 minutes from 7:30am to 5:30pm.

GETTING AROUND   Most of Manzhouli is located north of the train tracks (behind the railway station) and is easily navigated on foot. **Taxis** charge ¥7 (90¢/45p) anywhere in town, ¥10 ($1.30/65p) between the railway station and the center; beyond 10km (6¼ miles), add an extra ¥10 ($1.30/65p). Several bus routes, costing ¥1 (15¢/10p), go around the town.

FAST FACTS

Banks, Foreign Exchange & ATMs   The **Bank of China** (open Mon–Fri 8am–noon and 2–6pm) is at San Daojie 38. Cash and traveler's checks are exchanged in the main hall on the right; credit card transactions (MasterCard, Visa only) take place inside a separate entrance on the left.

Internet Access   There is a row of 24-hour basement-level **Internet bars** on Er Daojie, near the International Hotel, and one of them is called Meng Gongchang (© **1394/700-8393**); they charge ¥2 (25¢/15p) per hour of access. Dial-up is © **16900** or 16901.

Post Office   The post office (open Mon–Fri 8:30am–5:30pm; Sat–Sun 9am–4pm) is located at the corner of San Daojie and Haiguan Lu.

IN & AROUND MANZHOULI

A few Russian wood houses still stand in the center of Manzhouli, and the free flow of cash and vodka lends a certain exhilaration to the place, but most points of interest lie elsewhere. The closest attraction, only 10km (6 miles) west of town, is the old **Sino-Russian border crossing (Guo Men;** 🕿 **0470/629-1562;** 8am–5pm; admission ¥20/$2.60/£1.30). If you want your taxi to drive onto the premises, they'll charge you an extra ¥5 (65¢/35p). Nothing much happens here anymore, as most Russians enter China through a new border crossing farther north, but you can still watch trains pass across the border between China and Russia. There is a small exhibition that tells the history of the area inside the building. Access is by taxi only (20 min.; ¥40/$5.20/£2.60 round-trip). A **trade market (Zhonge Hushi Maoyi Qu),** is located in a pink Russian-style building beside Guo Men; it opens in the morning, and all kinds of products, from food to furs can be bought there, including fake ones. On the way to the Sino-Russian border crossing, you will see the new **Eluosi Taowa Guangchang (Russian Matryoshka Dolls Plaza) on the right-hand side.** Opened in 2006, the plaza has a giant Russian Matryoshka doll towering 30m (90 ft) and over 200 colorful nesting dolls representing different countries. There are also several fairy-tale-like Russian-style structures built around the plaza to give the place an exotic ambience. A light and fountain show is staged at the plaza at 9pm every night.

Dalai Hu 🕿   Also known as Hulun Hu (*Hulun Nur* in Mongolian), this immense lake emerges seamlessly out of the landscape 36km (22 miles) south of Manzhouli—a liquid equivalent to the grasslands that surround it. Dalai Hu is China's fifth-largest lake (2,399 sq. km./936 sq. miles) and a popular feeding ground for rare bird species. A small resort on the north shore offers boating, swimming, and fishing. In pleasant weather vendors sell barbecued fish and shrimp skewers fresh from the lake for ¥2 to ¥3 (25¢–40¢/15p–20p). The lake is also open in the winter, but is much less interesting without boat access.

The only way to get to the lake from Manzhouli is by taxi (1 hr.; ¥100–¥150/$13–20/£6.50–9.75 round-trip). Admission at the main gate, just north of the resort, costs ¥7 (90¢/45p) for each person including the driver plus another ¥10 ($1.30/65p) for taxi entrance. A boat ride on the lake costs ¥20 ($2.60/£1.30) and a motorboat ride costs ¥10 ($1.30/65p) for 10 minutes.

Hulun Buir Grasslands (Hulunbei'er Caoyuan) 🕿🕿🕿   No other grasslands in Inner Mongolia can match the Hulun Buir, an emerald expanse shot through with radiant patches of wildflowers that spreads over the hills outside Manzhouli. The grass here is twice as long as anything found outside Hohhot, and people are scarce. Nothing this beautiful lasts long, though: The season for seeing the grasslands at their most vibrant runs only from late June to mid-August.

The only organization in Manzhouli officially allowed to arrange tours of the grasslands is **CITS** (inside the International Hotel; 🕿 **0470/622-4241;** fax 0470/622-4540; open 8:30am–5pm). They offer different types of tours around the grasslands. Three-day tours (¥700/$91/£46 per person) include accommodations in a yurt, horse riding, a mutton banquet, and a visit to Dalai Hu (see above); 2- and 5-day tours are also available. Other attractions around Manzhouli, such as Golden Shore (Jin Hai'an) and the Birds' Kingdom (Wulan Pao), may be added to your tour. If you speak Mandarin and don't mind modest facilities, a better option is to negotiate a stay with one of the local families that approach visitors at the railway station. If you decide to do this, be clear about the details and withhold final payment until your stay is over. Visit www.mzlcits.com for more information.

The Hulun Buir is the backdrop to one of China's most authentic **Naadam** festivals (see also "Hohhot," p. 221), held every summer, usually between mid-July and mid-August. Call CITS for details about the date and location.

Zhalainuo'er   The turn-of-the-20th-century Russian-built open coal mine *(meikuang)* is a hideous scar on an otherwise pristine landscape, but few other places in Asia can offer what it does: the chance to see 22 steam trains from the 1920s and 1930s in still-chugging order. CITS (see Hulun Buir Grasslands, above) offers multi-day tours which include a ride on one of the working engines; the price depends on which attractions you choose. It is possible, however, to visit on your own. The mine is 18km (11 miles) south of Manzhouli, and admission is free. The best time to visit is between October and March, when the steam is most dramatic. A bus to Zhalainuo'er (30 min.; ¥3/40¢/20p) leaves from the intersection of Si Daojie and Xinhua Lu in Manzholi and drops you in the center of town. From there, hire a taxi to tour the mine for ¥40 to ¥60 ($5.20–$7.80/£2.60–£3.90). The easier but pricier option is to simply hire a taxi in Manzhouli for ¥70 to ¥100 ($9.10–$13/£4.55–£6.50).

WHERE TO STAY

All of Manzhouli's hotels are located north of the train tracks. Most offer discounts of 20% or more outside July and August.

Friendship Hotel (Manzhouli Youyi Binguan)   The formerly unremarkable Friendship Hotel now offers nice rooms, with good service and easy access to the railway station. Renovated in 2006, the standard rooms are spacious, clean, and bright, with large beds and sparkling-clean bathrooms. The hotel isn't as lively as some of its competitors, but this could change as word spreads.

Yi Daojie 26 (between Xinhua Lu and Haiguan Lu). (C) **0470/624-8888.** Fax 0470/622-3828. 92 units. ¥420–¥440 ($55–$57/£27–£29) standard room; ¥880 ($114/£57) suite. Rates include breakfast. No credit cards. **Amenities:** 2 restaurants; bar; small indoor pool; business center; forex; laundry. *In room:* A/C, TV, fridge.

Home 1 Hotel (Jiayi Jiudian)   Opened in mid-2007, this modern and small hotel is located in the city center. There are no extra amenities in the six-story hotel, but service is satisfying. The rooms are small but comfy and clean, with flatscreen TVs, stylish lamps, and minimal design. Bathrooms are cramped, with showers only. A big pane of glass is used to separate the bathroom and bedroom.

Xinghua Lu 8. (C) **0470/623-1888.** Fax 0470/623-9222. 72 units. ¥480 ($62/£31) standard room. No credit cards. *In room:* Satellite TV.

Jiangnan Dajiudian   Opened in 2005, this modern hotel is located in the city center and caters to Russian traders, but all are welcome. It's one of the cleanest and newest hotels in town. The rooms are quite spacious but the bathrooms are small with showers only.

Haiguan Lu 8. (C) **0470/624-7888.** Fax 0470/624-7990. 145 units. ¥280 ($36/£18) single room; ¥480 ($62/£31) standard room; ¥880 ($114/£57) suite. No credit cards. **Amenities:** 2 restaurants; indoor pool; gym; sauna; massage; salon; business center. *In room:* TV.

WHERE TO DINE

The local specialty is *shuan yangrou,* a form of mutton hot pot that uses plain boiling water instead of broth. The best is found at **Mengxiangyuan Huoguo** (Ⓒ **0470/ 622-0989;** open 10am–5am; meal for two ¥30–¥50/$3.90–$6.50/£1.95–£3.25), an unassuming restaurant on Wu Daojie. They're famous for their fresh lamb but do offer a vegetarian option *(qingshui guodi).*

The city's busiest Russian restaurants are **Xinmanyuan Xicanting,** San Daojie 38 (Ⓒ **0470/622-2008;** open 7am–1am; meal for two ¥30–¥50/$3.90–$6.50/£1.95– £3.25), and **Beijiaerhu Xicanting,** Zhongsu Jie 23 (Ⓒ **0470/623-4689;** open 7am until late; meal for two ¥30–¥60/$3.90–$7.80/£1.95–£3.90), a strange and raucous eatery-cum-nightclub located behind the International Hotel (look for the white-and-green awning). Best are the bowls of hearty *suba tang* (beef, potato, and carrot in creamy tomato broth). **Delifrance** (**Damofang;** Ⓒ **0470/629-8765;** open 7am– 10pm; ¥12–¥18/$1.55–$2.35/80p–£1.15), directly across from the International Hotel on San Daojie, serves horrible coffee but has a large variety of satisfying rice plates. The best plates are rice with beef and black pepper and the *sanxian fan,* or rice with three flavors.

There is a **KFC** at Beifang Shichang, on Wu Daojie.

For a lunch or dinner in the middle of the grasslands, head to **Dongfang Han** holiday restaurant. Located 20 minutes south of downtown, a taxi ride will cost ¥40 ($5.20/£2.60). You can order a whole lamb and eat in a yurt, a traditional Mongolian felt tent. Other activities include horseback riding and Mongolian dancing.

6

Along the Yellow River

by Simon Foster

The six cities and one mountain village featured in this chapter cover an area of northern China that includes parts of Shanxi, Shaanxi, Inner Mongolia, and Ningxia, roughly following the central loop of the Yellow River, north of Xi'an.

This arid portion of China contains desert, grassland, and, most conspicuously, loess plateau made of the powdery yellow soil that gave the Yellow River and the legendary Yellow Emperor their names. (For an object lesson in what makes the river yellow, wash your T-shirt in the sink after a day of touring the loess cliffs of Yan'an.) This powder of sand and silt has for millennia been deposited over this part of north and northwest China by winds blowing across the Gobi Desert.

Rich in history, the area lays claim to most of China's oldest surviving timber-frame buildings, its oldest carved Buddhist grottoes, and the mausoleums of nine Xi Xia (1038–1227) emperors. The area around Taiyuan in Shanxi Province is recognized as one of China's "cradles of civilization," and it was here that the mythical sage kings Yao, Shun, and Yu are said to have performed their miracles.

From Beijing, Datong is the logical gateway. Going south, a 10-day itinerary might include Datong; the sacred Buddhist mountain, Wutai Shan; the Shanxi capital of Taiyuan; and Pingyao, one of China's best-preserved walled cities. For the grasslands of Inner Mongolia and the relics and monuments of the tribes from beyond the Great Wall, go west from Datong—first to Hohhot, and then to Yinchuan, the provincial capital of Ningxia. There is enough to see for a 3- or 4-day stay in each city. The revolutionary sites and cave dwellings of Yaan'an could be added as the last stop on either itinerary or as the steppingstone between the two.

Piercing winds and icy air currents from the north keep most travelers away from this region from late November to mid-March. Moving south, summer temperatures can be scorching, but evenings are generally comfortable.

Note: Unless noted otherwise, hours listed in this chapter are the same every day.

1 Datong

Shanxi Province, 379km (236 miles) W of Beijing, 284km (176 miles) SE of Hohhot, 350km (217 miles) N of Taiyuan

In 398, Datong (then Ping Cheng) became the capital of the Xianbei tribes' first Chinese-style state—as opposed to a tribal confederation—under the Northern Wei dynasty. Modeled after the Han Chinese capital of Chaang'an (Xi'an), Datong remained their political center for the next hundred years, and it was during this period that most of the Yungang Buddhist Caves were carved out. Four hundred years after the Wei moved their capital south to Luoyaang in a step toward Sinicization, the Khitan (or Qidan) established their Liaao dynasty (907–1125) capital in Datong. Two

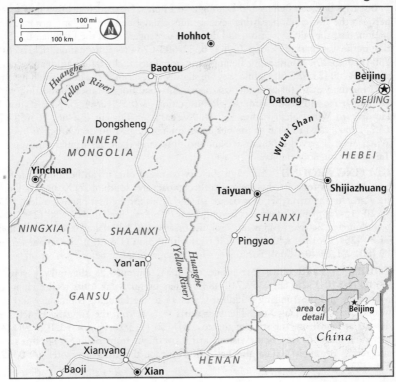

buildings from that era survive at Huaayan Monastery, which with the Yungang Caves and the spectacular Hanging Temple give ample reasons to visit.

Modern Datong is an industrial center with an abundance of coal that is both a blessing and a curse. Without it, Datong's economy would collapse; with it, skies are rarely clear and lung disease is common. In 2001, the city began implementing pollution-control measures; while some industries have been closed, the air is still thick in Datong.

It's possible to visit Datong as a long day trip from Beijing (see "Tours," below), but to see all the sights, 2 days are needed.

ESSENTIALS

GETTING THERE Datong's **airport** finally opened in 2006 and offers flights to Beijing (Mon, Wed, Fri, and Sun), Shanghai (Tues and Thurs) and Guangzhou (Mon and Fri). The airport is 15km (9 miles) east of the city and can be reached by buses from outside the Wuzhou Dajiudian on Binxi Lu (¥10/$1.30/£65p) or taxi (¥35/$4.55/£2.30).

There are plenty of **trains** between Beijing Xi Zhan and Datong, which take around 6 hours. Trains from Taiyuan take a similar length of time, although the N266, which leaves at 8:19am, is a little faster. Heading west, the Beijing-Baotou line has plenty of services, connecting Datong with Hohhot in around 4 hours.

Bus trips between Beijing and Datong take 4 hours. Large, deluxe buses now travel between the two cities, departing several times a day from the old long-distance bus station, near the railway station, and dropping passengers off at the Liuliqiao Bus Station in the west part of Beijing. Call ℂ **0352/603-6784** for information; tickets costs ¥80 ($10/£5.20). Minivans for Beijing leave from outside the train station and charge around ¥100 ($13/£6.50); while they are slightly quicker than the buses you'll have to wait for the van to fill up with passengers. Air-conditioned buses connecting with Hohhot arrive and depart from the old bus station (¥70/$9.10/£4.55; 3 hr. 40 min.). Heading to Wutai Shan (4 hr.; ¥62/$8.05/£4.05) or Taiyuan (3½ hr.; ¥65/$8.45/£4.25) you'll need to head to the bus depot on Yantong Xi Lu near Xingjian Bei Lu. Wutai Shan is served by buses at 8am and 4pm, and there are regular minivans to Taiyuan throughout the day.

GETTING AROUND   Although the city is spread out, it can be toured on foot because the few tourist sights are in a fairly compact area south of Da Xi and Da Dong Jie. Rates for the two types of **taxis** are ¥6 (80¢/40p) for the first 3km (2 miles), then ¥1.20 (15¢/10p) per kilometer. Beyond 8km (5 miles), the fare is ¥1.80 (25¢/10p) per kilometer. Between 10pm and 7am, the first 3km (2 miles) are ¥6 (80¢/40p), then ¥1.80 (25¢/10p) per kilometer. Most trips within 3km (1.8 m) in the city are ¥6 to ¥9 (80¢–$1.20/40p–60p). For longer trips, negotiate a price before you set off.

TOURS   A **CITS** office just inside the main entrance to the railway station (ℂ **0352/510-1326;** fax 0352/712-4882) offers useful 1-day tours to the Hanging Monastery and the Yungang Buddhist Caves, or to the Hanging Monastery and the wooden pagoda in Ying Xian. The tour starts at 9am from the Yungang Hotel, and departs at 9am from the station; the cost is ¥100 ($13/£6.50), or ¥220 ($29/£14) including entrance fees. Some visitors arrive overnight from Beijing, take this tour, and return overnight. CITS also has offices outside the Yungang Hotel (ℂ **0352/ 510-2777**).

FAST FACTS

Banks, Foreign Exchange & ATMs   The main **Bank of China** (Yingbin Lu near Hongqi Nan Jie; Mon–Fri 8am–noon and 2:30–6:30pm) has full-service foreign exchange and an ATM that accepts international cards.

Internet Access   Internet cafes can be found throughout the city; a convenient *wangba* is directly opposite the railway station. Dial-up is ℂ **169.**

Post Office   The main post office is on Hongqi Square (8am–6:30pm).

Visa Extensions   The **PSB (Gonganju;** open Mon–Fri 8am–noon and 3–6:30pm) is on Xinjian Bei Lu. Visas can be extended while you wait.

AROUND TOWN

If you have time after a visit to Huayan Si, Datong's **Jiulong Bi (Nine Dragon Wall;** Da Dong Jie, east of Da Nan Jie; ¥10/$1.60/65p; open May–Sept 7:30am–7:30pm, Oct–Apr 8am–6pm; bus: no. 4) is a fine example of a spirit screen, designed to fend off ghosts and evil spirits that can only move in straight lines. The brightly colored glazed wall with nine writhing dragons was built in 1392 in front of a prince's mansion, long ago razed by fire. The much-restored **Shanhua Si,** west of Nan Men Jie, last rebuilt in 1445, is also a pleasant escape from Datong's dusty streets. Most impressive are the beautiful timber doors of the **Hall of Three Sages (San Sheng Dian;** ¥20/ $2.60/£1.30; open 8am–6pm).

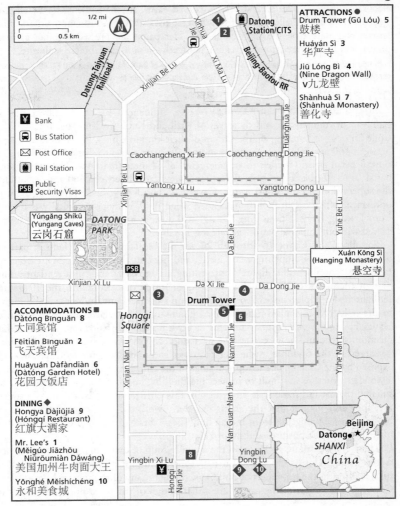

ATTRACTIONS ●
Drum Tower (Gǔ Lóu) **5**
鼓楼

Huáyán Sì **3**
华严寺

Jiǔ Lóng Bì **4**
(Nine Dragon Wall)
∨九龙壁

Shànhuà Sì **7**
(Shànhuà Monastery)
善化寺

Map Legend

¥ Bank

🚌 Bus Station

✉ Post Office

📷 Rail Station

PSB Public
Security Visas

Yúngǎng Shíkū
(Yungang Caves)
云岗石窟

DATONG
PARK

Xuán Kōng Sì
(Hanging Monastery)
悬空寺

Drum Tower

Honggi
Square

ACCOMMODATIONS ■
Dàtóng Bīnguǎn **8**
大同宾馆

Fēitiān Bīnguǎn **2**
飞天宾馆

Huāyuán Dàfàndiàn **6**
(Dàtóng Garden Hotel)
花园大饭店

DINING ◆
Hongya Dàjiǔjiā **9**
(Hóngqí Restaurant)
红旗大酒家

Mr. Lee's **1**
(Měiguó Jiāzhōu
Niúròumiàn Dàwáng)
美国加州牛肉面大王

Yǒnghé Měishíchéng **10**
永和美食城

Beijing
Datong● ★
SHANXI
China

Huayan Si ⚑ This monastery has separate upper and lower temples that share a lane. The upper temple's massive main hall, the **Daxiong Bao Dian** of 1140, is one of China's few surviving 12th-century buildings. Inside are the lined-up Buddhas of the Five Directions (including the center), seated on elaborately decorated lotus thrones and set off by small standing attendants.

Most significant of all the halls in the two temples is the **Bojia Jiaozang Dian** of 1038, a very rare example of a Liao dynasty building. Inside, Buddhist sutras (scriptures) are stored in one of the finest and best-preserved examples of the miniature timber buildings favored by the period's architects for housing sutras. Named the **Celestial Palace Pavilion (Tiangong Louge),** the sutra cabinet is an exquisite dollhouse with elaborate bracketing, an arched bridge, curved eaves, and balconies. The 31 elegant stucco statues in the hall also date from the Liao dynasty. One of the most prized is the female bodhisattva on the right-hand side. Her palms are pressed together as if in prayer, and her lips are parted, revealing her teeth—a rarity in Chinese sculpture.

Both Upper and Lower temples are down a lane off the south side of Da Xi Jie. Admission ¥20 ($2.60/£1.30) each temple. May–Sept 8am–6pm; Oct–Apr 8:30am–5:30pm. Bus: no. 4 from railway station.

OUT OF TOWN

Yungang Shiku (Yungang Caves) ★★★   Influenced by the Buddhist site of Bamiyan in Afghanistan and the caves of Kizil and Kuqa (in Xinjiang, p. 317), the stone carvings of Yungang are the earliest of their kind in China. Hewn in three stages between 460 and 524, they show the movement from a heavy reliance on Indian and central Asian artistic models to an emergence of Chinese traditions. The caves numbered 16 to 20 (the "Five Caves of Tan Yao") were carved between 460 and 465 under the supervision of a Buddhist monk. Caves 1, 2, and 5 to 13 were carved in the second stage, which began in 470 and ended when the Wei dynasty capital was moved from Datong (at that time Ping Cheng) to Luoyang in 494. The remaining caves, carved without imperial patronage, are less notable.

For sheer size, **Caves 16 through 20** are the most impressive. Made in part to honor the reigning emperor, Wen Cheng, and his four predecessors, each cave contains one central Buddha figure (representing an emperor) and his attendants. The best of them, **Cave 18,** contains the colossal image of Sakyamuni, the 10 *arhats* (enlightened disciples) associated with him, and two attendant Buddhas. The Buddha to the right of Sakyamuni has a webbed hand—one of the 32 marks of a superior being. His robe was originally red, his face white, and his hair black. Traces of his green mustache and beard can still be seen, and echo the art of Iran.

Largest of the Buddhas in the Tan Yao caves is the sitting figure in **Cave 20,** now exposed by the collapse of the top and sides of the cliff. Holes for beams indicate that a wooden structure was built to protect the Buddha, but that, too, is long gone. The squared figures and static style are typical of this early period of Northern Wei statuary; they also suggest that the artists may have worked from sketches or drawings brought back by pilgrims from Indian holy sites. Notice in the later carvings the fluidity of line in the postures and draped clothing.

There is much more going on in the second group of caves, many of which depict stories from Buddhist scriptures. **Cave 1** is interesting for its Chinese-style architectural features in the bas-reliefs of buildings, though many of the images have eroded. **Cave 3** is the largest of the caves. The fuller bodies of the three Buddhist images it contains suggest it was carved as late as the Sui or the Tang dynasties. **Caves 5 and 6** were both carved before 494, but the four-story wooden facade dates from 1651. **Cave 5** houses the largest carving at Yungang—a stunning Sakyamuni in meditation. In **Cave 6** look for the two Buddhas, Sakyamuni and Prabhutaratna, facing each other. This customary pairing alludes to an episode from the Teaching of the Lotus Sutra. In this episode, a stupa (shrine) containing the relics of the Prabhutaratna Buddha appears in the sky. Surrounded by Buddhas and bodhisattvas, Sakyamuni rises to the stupa and unlocks it with his finger. Out comes the extinct Prabhutaratna, who praises and congratulates him. Other episodes from the life of Sakyamuni decorate the walls. On the entrance arch of **Cave 8** are contented images of Shiva and Vishnu (two of several Hindu divinities who found their way into Buddhism). The discs they hold represent the sun and the moon. Some sources identify the small bird on Vishnu's chest, and the larger one on which his feet rest, as the mythical *garuda*—the vehicle (and disciple) of Vishnu; others, less convincingly, call them phoenixes, a Chinese motif. Traces of ancient Greece appear in the classical bow with inward curve at its center. (As in this relief, the bow is commonly held in the left "wisdom" hand. Presumably the missing right "method" hand held an arrow.) A seated Maitreya Buddha (Future Buddha) dominates **Cave 13.** Most delightful about this statue is the figurine of a four-armed attendant who stands on the Buddha's thigh while supporting its huge raised arm—the artists' solution to a crack in the stone. Allow yourself at least 2 hours to see the main caves.

16km (10 miles) west of Datong. Admission ¥60 ($7.80/£3.90). 8:30am–5:30pm. Bus: no. 3-2 (¥2.50/35¢/15p) from railway station; last bus returns at 7pm. A taxi should charge ¥30 ($3.90/£1.95) one-way, or ¥80 ($10/£5.20) round-trip, including waiting time.

Xuankong Si (Hanging Temple)   This temple, clinging to the side of a cliff, is composed of some 40 connected halls that appear to be supported by toothpicks. Looking more like a wooden model than anything weight-bearing, it is actually supported by sturdy timbers that extend deep into the mountain. Founded in the Northern Wei dynasty (386–534), the temple contains Buddhist, Daoist, and Confucian chambers, along with a chamber, the Sanjiao Dian (Three Teachings Hall), that combines all three. Sakyamuni is in the center with Confucius to his right and Laozi to his left. While the temple is marvelous, be prepared for the particularly unattractive surroundings—a huge parking lot and, beyond that, a dam and reservoir.

62km (39 miles) south of Datong. Admission ¥60 ($7.80/£3.90). Summer 8am–6pm; winter 8am–6:30pm. Minibuses to Hunyuan (near the monastery) leave from the station opposite the railway station when they fill up. Price isn't fixed, so bargain; expect to pay ¥8–¥12 ($1.05–$1.55/50p–80p). From Hunyuan, it's another 6km (4 miles) to the monastery by minibus (about ¥5/65¢/35p) or taxi (about ¥9/$1.15/60p).

Ying Xian Mu Ta (Ying Xian Wooden Pagoda) ☞   Built in 1056 during the Liao dynasty, this impressive building is China's oldest surviving wooden pagoda. From the outside, it appears to have only five stories, though it actually has nine; and its complex system of supports includes 54 kinds of brackets. Frescoes on the ground floor and a gilded statue of Sakyamuni date from the Liao dynasty. During a 1974 renovation, engraved sutras and documents related to the construction of the pagoda were discovered inside one of the statues of Buddha. Unfortunately, visitors are now only allowed to climb to the second level of this delicate structure.

For those on their way from Datong to Wutai Shan, it's possible to visit the Hanging Temple and Wooden Pagoda in a day, then spend the night in Ying Xian and leave the next morning for Wutai Shan. East of the pagoda, the friendly, affordable **Lihua Chun Binguan,** Yinghun Lu (eastern extension of Xinjian Dong Lu; ℰ **0349/502-9593**), is the best hotel in Ying Xian, and its restaurant serves good Cantonese and local dishes. Standard rooms go for ¥88 to ¥108 ($11–$14/£5.70–£7). The hotel can arrange for north- or southbound hotel pickup. The minibus to Wutai Shan charges ¥35 ($4.55/£2.30) for the 2-hour trip.

76km (47 miles) south of Datong. Admission ¥60 ($7.80/£3.90). Winter 7:30am–7pm; summer 8am–6:30pm. Minibuses to Ying Xian leave from the station opposite the railway station (¥10–¥15/$1.30–$1.95/65p–£1; 2 hr.) and drop passengers near the Wooden Pagoda. Minibuses also leave from Hunyuan (¥10/$1.30/65p for the 1½-hr. drive).

Jing Xia You (Coal Mine Tour)   One of Datong's latest travel fads is a visit to a local coal mine. You get to suit up in a real coal miner's outfit complete with boots and light-equipped helmet and spend 2 hours underground, albeit at a distance more comfortable than the coal miners are used to. A miner's elevator will take you down into the mine, and then you'll board a small train to reach a point where miners are digging. You may also have lunch with the coal miners in their cafeteria. Tours can be arranged by CITS. To reserve a place call 1 day in advance; a minimum of 10 are required for the tour to run.

30 min. outside Datong. Call CITS for reservations ((℃) 0352/510-2777). Tour price ¥150/$20/£9.75.

WHERE TO STAY

CITS agents are likely to meet you coming out of the Datong railway station. They can book a hotel for you on the spot, but you'll get a better discount by shopping around and doing the negotiating yourself. A few years ago, visitors to Datong had limited choices when looking for a hotel. However, in recent years a number of comfortable and reasonably priced hotels have opened offering a wide variety of choices, although budget options are limited to those by the train station. Try the **Feitian Binguan** (℃ **0352/281-5117**), where passable twins can be haggled to ¥120 ($16/£7.80).

Datong Bingun   With its manicured gardens, park-size lawn with gazebo, and manor-house facade, this is one of the more pleasant of Datong's hotels. Service is excellent, rooms are clean and comfortable, bathrooms are a decent size, and the price is reasonable. Some of the standard rooms have small balconies, which are worth requesting. Rooms facing the street overlook the front lawn and the adjacent "musical fountain."

Yingbin Xi Lu 37. (℃) **0352/586-8666**. Fax 0352/586-8200. www.datonghotel.com 221 units. ¥500–¥580 ($65–$75/ £33–£38) standard room. Some rates include breakfast. 30% discount available. 15% service charge. AE, DC, MC, V. Bus: no. 1 or 5. **Amenities:** Restaurant; bar; ticketing; business center; limited forex; limited room service; laundry/dry cleaning. *In room:* A/C, TV w/video on demand, minibar, fridge, hair dryer.

Huayuan Dafandian   The Datong Garden Hotel, one of the city's newest hotels, is clean and well priced, and the service is friendly—a big improvement over the old state-run hotels that once monopolized the travel business in Datong. The guest rooms in this four-star hotel are well sized and furnished with Ming and Qing dynasty-style pear-wood furniture. It's also conveniently located in the center of Datong, near the Drum Tower and restaurants and shopping centers.

Da Nan Jie 59. (℃) **0352/586-5825**. Fax 0352/586-5824. 108 units. ¥820 ($107/£53) standard room; ¥880 ($114/ £57) deluxe standard. Rates include breakfast. Up to 40% discount available. 15% service charge. AE, MC, V. **Ameni-ties:** Western and Chinese restaurants; bar; ticketing; business center; forex; limited room service; laundry/dry cleaning. *In room:* A/C, TV, broadband Internet access, minibar, fridge, hair dryer.

WHERE TO DINE

There are plenty of dining options along Yingbin Xi Lu, including the low-key **Hongya Restaurant,** which serves good Cantonese, and the ultra-sleek three-story **Yonghe Meishicheng,** across from the Yungang Hotel and offering Shanxi, Sichuan, and Cantonese dishes. The Chinese restaurant on the first floor of the **Yungang Hotel** serves delicious *jiaozi* (12 per serving) for ¥2.50 (35¢/15p). For vegetarian *jiaozi,* order a half-hour ahead. They also offer a wide variety of regional dishes. The train station is also surrounded by a host of cheap eateries serving cut beef noodles, and there's a branch of **Mr. Lee's noodles (Meiguo Jiazhou Niuroumian Dawang)** across from the Feitian Binguan.

For a Western breakfast, try the Datong hotel. There's a **KFC** at the main square, Hongqi Guangchang, and many other branches are scattered around the city.

2 Hohhot ✿

Inner Mongolia, 410km (255 miles) W of Beijing

By Chinese standards, Hohhot, the capital of Inner Mongolia Autonomous Region, has a short history. In 1557, when the Mongolian prince, Altan Khan, ordered the construction of a large Tibetan-Buddhist complex, he had his own agenda. (In a historical twist, his workforce was made up of captured Han Chinese artisans and Han peasants forced into labor.) Completion of such a complex would legitimize his rule over the southern Mongolian tribes and secure the recognition of the Ming Empire. By 1579, Da Zhao Temple, which still survives, was completed, and by 1590 the town of Hohhot (in Mandarin Huhehaote, or simply Hu Shi) had sprung up around it.

From the beginning, the city was both Mongolian and Han Chinese, and though the ratio has fluctuated wildly over 4 centuries, the population has always been culturally mixed. In the 19th century, the Hui (Chinese Muslims) became the third-largest ethnic group in the city. Population claims are rarely reliable when they're about China, but it's said that currently for every Mongolian in Hohhot, there are 12 Han Chinese.

Hohhot is a pleasant city with some good hotels, excellent restaurants, modern stores, and worthwhile sights.

ESSENTIALS

GETTING THERE   The **airport** is 16km (10 miles) east of town. A taxi into town costs about ¥25 to ¥30 ($3.10–$3.75/£1.55–£1.85). Locals negotiate the price in advance and don't use the meter. The CAC (Zhongguo Minhang) shuttle (¥5/65¢/35p) meets flights and is also an option. It leaves from CAC's main ticket office on Xilin Guole Lu just south of Wulanqiate Xi Jie 1½ hours before every flight. There are direct flights from many major cities in China, including Beijing, Shanghai, Chengdu, and Guangzhou. **Mongolian Airlines (MIAT; ⓒ 0471/430-2026)** shares offices with the Mongolian Consulate (Menggu Lingshiguan) and offers flights to Ulan Batar.

The **railway station** is in the north part of town. Of the many trains linking Hohhot with Beijing, the K90 (10 hr.) at 9:23pm is the most convenient. Datong is also on this line. Another useful service is the K43 link with Lanzhou (17 hr.). Yinchuan (8 hr.) and Zhongwei (11 hr.) are two of the stops on this line. Tickets can be bought in advance at all windows, but sleepers are often in short supply. Try agents in hotels for these.

The **Long-Distance Bus Station** is west of the railway station. There are hourly buses to Beijing (6 hr.; ¥130/$17/£8.45) and Datong (4 hr.; ¥45/$5.85/£2.95). Yinchuan is served by one sleeper bus daily at 6pm (10 hr.; ¥145/$19/£9.45). To get to the grasslands, Xilamuren is served by hourly buses (2 hr.; ¥20 ($2.60/£1.30) from 7:50am.

GETTING AROUND   **Bus** fare is ¥1 (15¢/5p); **minibus** fare is ¥1.50 (20¢/10p). The **taxi** rate for the first 2km (1¼ miles) is ¥6 (80¢/40p); after that, it's ¥1 (15¢/5p) per kilometer.

TOURS   The **CITS** office is located on the third floor, Yishuting NanJie 95 (ⓒ 0471/628-3861). It can arrange expensive tours to the grasslands with an English-speaking guide (from ¥350/$46/£23). Most hotels have desks offering cheaper, non-English tours. Shop around and bargain.

FESTIVALS & SPECIAL EVENTS Da Zhao has more than a dozen temple festivals. Among the best are **Songjing Da Fahui** (8th–15th days of the first and sixth lunar months), 8 days of prayer and chanting sutras; **Songbalin** (14th day of the first and sixth lunar months), a morning spent exorcising demons—chanting, performing ritual dance, burning of demon effigy; **Liang Dafo** (15th day of the first and sixth lunar months), which begins with the Sunning of the Maitreya *thangka* (a giant image of the Future Buddha hung in the courtyard to air and be admired), and is followed by prayer, chanting, ceremonial dance and music, circumambulation, and alms-giving; and **Mani Hui** (14th–17th day of the eighth lunar month), Da Zhao's most solemn festival of the year, 3 days and nights of continuous prayer for good fortune (at the end, visitors who give alms are rewarded with a packet of "sacred medicine," said to cure all manner of illness and disease).

The traditional sports festival, **Nadam,** which features wrestling, horse and camel racing, and archery, occurs when and if the grasslands turn green. That's usually mid-August, but it can be as early as July. Last-minute cancellations aren't uncommon. Note that the dates don't coincide with (the People's Republic of) Mongolia's Nadam festival, which is tied to their National Day and always occurs from July 11 to July 13.

FAST FACTS

Banks, Foreign Exchange & ATMs Two branches of **Bank of China** that have full-service foreign-exchange counters and 24-hour ATM access are at Xincheng Dong Jie 88 (2 blocks east of the Xincheng Dong/Xi Jie and Xincheng Bei/Nan Jie intersection); and on the south side of Xinhua Dajie between Xilinguole Bei Lu and Yingbin Bei Lu. Hours are 8am to noon and 2:30 to 5:30pm. There's also an ATM in the lobby of the Guohang Dasha hotel.

Consulates The **Mongolian Consulate** (ⓒ **0471/4303-3254**) issues 30-day tourist visas at Xincheng District, Wulan Xiaoqu, No. 5. Service is available Monday, Tuesday, and Thursday from 8:30am to 12:30pm. Two photographs are required. The next-day fee is ¥495 ($62/£32); regular processing can take a week and costs ¥270 ($35/£18). Take bus no. 2 or 16.

Internet Access There's a no-name Internet cafe opposite the station, next to a small Bank of China. It's open 8am to 3:30am and charges ¥2 (25¢/15p) per hour. Dial-up is **169.**

Post Office The main branch of the post office is on Zhongshan Dong Lu (open 8am–6:30pm summer, until 6pm winter).

Visa Extensions The visa office (Mon–Fri 8am–noon and 2:30–5:30pm) is on the left beyond the guards at the **PSB office** (**Gonganju;** ⓒ **0471/669-0018**) at Zhongshan Xi Lu 42, almost opposite the big pink Minzu Shangchang.

WALKING TOUR	HOHHOT: TEMPLE TO TEMPLE

Getting There:	Starting from the railway station, walk west on Chezhan Xi Jie to Tongdao Jie. Take bus no. 6 going south, and get off at the stop called Xiao Shizi.
Start:	Xiao Shizi bus stop.
Finish:	Zhongshan Jie.
Time:	Half a day.
Best Times:	8am to 4pm any day.

Hohhot

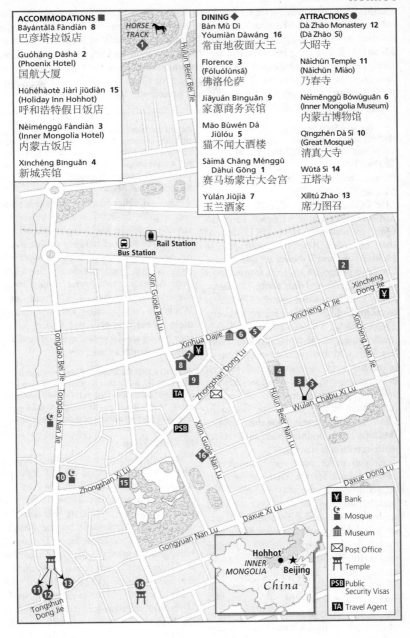

ACCOMMODATIONS ■

Bāyántǎlā Fàndiàn **8**
巴彦塔拉饭店

Guóháng Dàshà **2**
(Phoenix Hotel)
国航大厦

Hūhéhàotè Jiàrì jiǔdiàn **15**
(Holiday Inn Hohhot)
呼和浩特假日饭店

Nèiménggǔ Fàndiàn **3**
(Inner Mongolia Hotel)
内蒙古饭店

Xīnchéng Bīnguǎn **4**
新城宾馆

DINING ◆

Bàn Mǔ Dì
Yóumiàn Dàwáng **16**
常亩地莜面大王

Florence **3**
(Fóluólúnsā)
佛洛伦萨

Jiāyuán Bīnguǎn **9**
家源商务宾馆

Māo Bùwén Dà
Jiǔlóu **5**
猫不闻大酒楼

Sàimǎ Chǎng Ménggǔ
Dàhuì Gōng **1**
赛马场蒙古大会宫

Yùlán Jiǔjiā **7**
玉兰酒家

ATTRACTIONS ●

Dà Zhāo Monastery **12**
(Dà Zhāo Sì)
大昭寺

Nǎichūn Temple **11**
(Nǎichūn Miào)
乃春寺

Nèiménggǔ Bówùguǎn **6**
(Inner Mongolia Museum)
内蒙古博物馆

Qīngzhēn Dà Sì **10**
(Great Mosque)
清真大寺

Wǔtǎ Sì **14**
五塔寺

Xílìtú Zhāo **13**
席力图召

HORSE TRACK 1

Rail Station
Bus Station

Xilin Guole Bei Lu

Hulun Beier Bei Jie

Tongdao Bei Jie

Tongdao Nan Jie

Xinhua Dajie

Zhongshan Dong Lu

Xincheng Xi Jie

Xincheng Dong Jie

Xincheng Nan Jie

Hulun Beier Nan Lu

Wulan Chabu Xi Lu

Daxue Dong Lu

Xilin Guole Nan Lu

Zhongshan Xi Lu

Daxue Xi Lu

Gongyuan Nan Lu

Tongshun Dong Jie

¥ Bank
✡ Mosque
🏛 Museum
✉ Post Office
⛩ Temple
PSB Public
Security Visas
TA Travel Agent

Hohhot
INNER MONGOLIA
★ Beijing
China

Hohhot's most renowned temples, **Da Zhao, Xilitu Zhao,** and **Wuta Si,** are in the oldest parts of town—the Yuquan District in the southwest corner of the city. Just to the north is the **Muslim Quarter (Huimin Qu)** with Hohhot's **Qingzhen Da Si (Great Mosque).** Before long, every trace of the flat-topped mud-and-brick houses and storefronts that used to dominate this area will be gone; for a glimpse of the past, go now. By setting out an hour earlier, it's possible to add the Great Mosque to your walk. Better still, devote a full day to the four sites and explore the Muslim Quarter, too.

From the Xiao Shizi bus stop, walk about 50m (160 ft.) west on the small street called Tongshun Dong Jie. The temple is on the right.

❶ Da Zhao

It's said that at one time this 6th-century temple (Apr–Sept 8am–7:30pm, Oct–Mar 8:30am–5:30pm; ¥20/$2.60/£1.30) had over 400 lamas in residence. Later, the Qing government (1644–1911) decreed that no more than 80 could live in Hohhot's earliest Tibetan temple. Today Da Zhao houses 16 students from all over Inner Mongolia and only about 50 monks, but it is still an active center of Buddhist worship. Unlike Beijing's famed lamasery, Yonghe Gong, Da Zhao looks and feels much more like the monasteries of Tibet, but with Chinese characteristics. Instead of offerings of tsampa (roasted barley), devotees leave mounds of uncooked rice; and the pervading smell is of incense rather than rancid yak butter. But as in Lhasa, worshipers here drape their favorite Buddhas and bodhisattvas with shiny white ceremonial scarves.

As you make your way through the complex, look for Da Zhao's three most prized holdings: the 400-year-old Silver Buddha; in front of it, a pair of vivid golden dragons coiled around two floor-to-ceiling pillars; and exquisite Ming wall murals (in their original paint) depicting stories from Buddhist lore. Go all the way to the back of the complex to find a library full of antique sutras wrapped in orange and yellow cloth. Peek into the less-visited side chambers, too, where you're likely to find a lone lama chanting and playing Tibetan cymbals or a devotee kowtowing in the half-dark.

As you come out of the Da Zhao temple from the main entrance, turn right, go around the corner, and walk along the west wall for 60m (200 ft.). A lama temple that was once part of the Da Zhao temple complex is on your left.

❷ Nai Chun Miao

There's no ticket kiosk because this temple, restored in 2004, is rarely visited by anyone outside the neighborhood. A painting of a sinner hanging upside down by his ankles, blood dripping over his face, adorns both panels of the main door. According to a young monk outside the temple, the hall is 300 years old. While the door paintings are considerably more recent, the wall and ceiling paintings inside are darkened with age and are certainly worth a look.

Walk back past Da Zhao, and continue about 90m (300 ft.) to Da Nan Jie. Cross over, turn left, and walk about 30m (100 ft.). This will take only about 10 minutes if you don't stop to take pictures and peer into shops and side alleys along the way.

❸ Xilitu Zhao

The temple (Apr–Sept 8am–7:30pm, Oct–Mar 8:30am–6pm; ¥10/$1.30/65p) is visible down the first lane, Da Nan Jie, though you wouldn't know it by the plaque above the front gate that uses the name given this temple by the Kangxi emperor in 1696: Shou Si, or Temple of Extended Longevity. Like Da Zhao, this Buddhist temple was constructed during the Wanli reign (1572–1620) of the Ming dynasty and remains active, with 16 monks in residence. Razed by fire in the 19th century, it was rebuilt only to be damaged during the Cultural Revolution (1966–76). Its latest humiliation is the transformation of its front buildings into souvenir shops. However, a short distance into the complex, it starts feeling more like a temple than a tourist spot.

One highlight is the Buddhist ornaments crowning the central hall. In front is the Wheel of Dharma flanked by two deer, representing the Buddha's first turning of the dharma wheel in the Deer Park. Behind the wheel are two victory banners and a jeweled trident symbolizing the Three Buddhas (past, present, and future) and the Three Jewels (the Buddha, the doctrine, and the monastic community; or body, speech, and mind). Inside the main building is a typical Tibetan prayer hall with cylindrical banners that hang from the ceiling, a white elephant (identified with the Buddha), and sutras lining the walls. On the first day of each lunar month, from 9am to noon, the monks can be heard (and viewed) chanting sutras in the main hall.

The walk from Xilitu Zhao to Wuta Si threads through another traditional neighborhood where everyone knows each other and "real Chinese life" abounds. Exiting Xilitu Zhao, turn left (eastward) down Xingsheng Street and continue walking until you reach a small playground. (En route, you'll pass old brick single-level storefronts on both sides and a toilet on the left.) Pass the playground and turn right, walking along the far side of the playground, which in summer is lined with billiards tables. Continue past a small outdoor market on the right and a narrow lane on your left. At the second narrow lane, Xiao Zhao Xiang, turn left. Ahead, on the right, a new two-story gray building with a traditional Chinese roof takes the place of the mud-and-brick buildings. You'll see the five spires of Wuta Si straight ahead, on Wuta Si Hou Jie.

➍ Wuta Si

This rare Indian-style five-pagoda Buddhist temple (Apr–Sept 8am–6:30pm, Oct–Mar 8am–6pm; ¥35/$4.55/£2.30) is one of only six *jingang baozuo* (diamond throne pagodas) in China. Built between 1727 and 1732, it was quite likely modeled after Beijing's Wuta Si, constructed 300 years earlier. Like that one, Hohhot's Wuta Si is the only remaining structure of a much larger temple complex that fell into disrepair. Notable features are the 1,561 stone-carved images of Buddha that cover the middle and top portions of the temple; the graceful bas-relief images of bodhisattvas, bodhi trees, and sacred creatures gracing the base of the temple; and the astronomical map on the back wall purported to be the only one of its vintage written in Mongolian script. Carved in stone, it depicts the 24 seasonal periods of the lunar year, 28 planets, some 270 constellations, over 1,550 stars, and the 12 astrological divisions. Climb to the top of the temple for a view of the changing neighborhood.

To get back to Zhongshan Jie from Wuta Si, as you leave from the main gate, turn right (eastward) and walk about 100m (330 ft.) to the main street, Gongyuan Xi Lu. Across the street catch bus no. 26, which will take you to Zhongshan Road. The bus turns right and follows Zhongshan a block beyond the Neimenggu Bowuguan (Inner Mongolian Museum), where it turns left (north) onto Hulunbeier Lu.

IN & AROUND HOHHOT

Neimenggu Bowuguan (Inner Mongolia Museum) ✯✯ *Kids* Hohhot's museum is home to a rare and magnificent collection of cultural relics left behind by nomadic clans from the north. As befits a collection this important, the displays are adequately lit and include Chinese and English introductions and explanations (though in the case of the minority exhibit their main purpose is to propagandize). The first floor's north wing is devoted to minority costumes, musical instruments, and fishing and hunting implements, but the main attraction is the south wing, which houses skeletal fossils of a broad range of prehistoric behemoths. On the second floor, a fine collection of ruins and relics from the Stone Age forward reflects the artistic refinement and creative abilities of the various northern cultures. Not to be missed are the graceful gold Xianbei belt buckles, to which a 4th-century poet compared a maiden's "exquisite neck." Also of note are sets of pottery figures from a nearby Northern Wei tomb. Among them is a pair of troll-faced pottery tomb-guardians, and eight pottery figurines of a musical troupe and a dancer who look more like a mime troupe, their wooden instruments having long ago disintegrated. After seeing this collection, you may never think of ancient Mongols, Huns, or Tartars in terms of "hordes" again.

Xinhua Dajie 2. Admission ¥10 ($1.30/65p). Apr–Sept 9am–5pm (last ticket 4pm); Oct–Mar 10am–4:30pm (last ticket 3:30pm). Bus: no. 4 on Xincheng Xi Jie; no. 19 on Zhongshan Lu.

Qingzhen Da Si (Great Mosque)   As beautiful as this 360-year-old mosque is, it has yet to become a standard tourist sight. Typically, a few seniors are chatting and passing time in the courtyard. The buildings include the prayer hall with a beautiful ceiling painted with pink flowers; the teaching hall; and a 15m-tall (49-ft.) wooden pavilion (a Chinese version of the minaret), which, with permission, can sometimes be climbed. (*Note:* A sign in Chinese at the mosque's entrance requests no shorts, short skirts, smoking, or loud talking.) The back exit leads through a small street lined with food stalls on one side and tables and chairs on the other. Here you'll find Muslim snacks such as noodles and kabobs. To get back to Tongdao Jie, walk the full length of the lane.

Tongdao Jie (near Zhongshan Xi Lu intersection). Free admission. 10am–4pm. Bus: no. 3, 19, or 21 to Tongdao Jie and Zhongshan Xi Lu intersection.

THREE WAYS TO THE GRASSLANDS

BY BUS   Hourly buses head for Xilamuren Da Caoyuan from the bus station. For a day trip, take the 7:50am bus and return on the last bus around 3pm (check on the exact time before leaving). The drive takes about 2½ hours—much of it through the scrub, wild grass, and cultivated forests that carpet the Da Qing Mountain range. About 65km (40 miles) out of Hohhot, the bus makes a 10-minute stop in the small town of Wuchuan. Before leaving Wuchuan, let the driver know you wish to get off at **Luyou Dujiacun (Traveler's Holiday Village),** which is about 30km (19 miles) from Wuchuan. A set of tourist *ger* (the Mongolian word for the circular felt tents known in central Asia as yurts) are visible across the street about 300m (1,000 ft.) away. Mr. Bao, who operates these with his wife, has horses, and though he's not inclined to let you ride off on your own, he and his yellow dog are affable riding companions. (When the mood strikes, he breaks into song—anything from Mongolian folk to "The East Is Red"). With an hour, he can take you to a famous *oboo* (stone memorial) in the area. More time allows you to ride deeper into the grasslands and visit a herdsman's family living in a real *ger* rather than one for tourists. The going rate is ¥25 ($3.25/£1.65) per hour, though the first asking price will probably be double that. The Bao family can also prepare a delicious Mongolian lunch (even vegetarian, if requested), which will include Mongolian milk tea and the homemade snacks that go with it. You may get *shouba rou* (hand-held meat)—mutton on the bone, eaten with the hands. The return bus passes the spot by the roadside where you were dropped off in the morning.

BY TAXI   If you balk at taking a crowded, smoke-filled rattletrap with no air-conditioning, opt for a private taxi. Drivers are at the ready at the bus and railway stations. Prices can vary drastically, so ask around and compare. (This will amount to you and the driver pushing a calculator back and forth at each other.) Round-trip fare should

---

Moments **Skulls for Sale**

It's not unusual on warm summer evenings to see someone peddling cow or sheep skulls on the city squares. Their buyers are probably opening a new business soon. A traditional belief is that after you eat a cow or sheep, its spirit is still alive. If you display the skull in a prominent place, the living spirit will attract other cows or sheep your way. The skull continues to be a symbol of good luck and a promise that business will thrive. The first asking price for a cow skull is ¥280 ($36/£18), for a sheep skull, ¥160 ($21/£10).

---

be around ¥200 to ¥250 ($26–$33/£13–£16), but you'll want to be certain the driver is taking you to a set of *ger* where you'll be able to ride horses and get a Mongolian meal.

TOURS   One-day tours to Xilamuren Da Caoyuan start at ¥280 ($36/£18) per person for a group of two to five. The tour includes a visit to a herding family, performance of Mongolian song and dance, and a wrestling demonstration. Unless you speak Mandarin, **CITS** is the most reliable way to go, though not the most adventurous. The office is third floor at Yishuting NanJie 95 (© **0471/628-3861**).

SHOPPING

The **Minzu Shangchang (Mongolian Minority Department Store)**—one of the biggest stores in Hohhot—is a one-stop shopping opportunity on Zhongshan Xi Lu at the Gongyuan Jie intersection. On the first floor are a **bakery** and a large, well-stocked **supermarket** that's worth a visit if you're shopping for food, travel snacks, or alcohol. The second floor has Mongolian handicrafts, traditional costumes, swords, teapots, jewelry, and more. For travel snacks, you could also visit **Parkson** supermarket, which has just about anything you could want. Be prepared to check your backpack or let it be sealed in shrink-wrap so you can keep it with you. Store hours are from 9am to 8pm. It's located at Zhongshan Xi Lu 212 at Tongdao Nan Jie.

WHERE TO STAY

Hohhot's hotel scene is developing quickly, and by the time you read this there should be three new international five-star affairs in the city: the Kempinski, a Shangri-La, and a Sheraton. The Shangri-La will enjoy a prime location on Xilin Guole Nan Lu and looks set to provide the usual service and amenities you'd expect. At the other end of the scale, there are plenty of cheapies near the train station where you can get a passable room with en-suite for around ¥80 ($10/£5).

EXPENSIVE

Guohang Dasha (Phoenix Hotel)   Completed in 2001 and owned by Air China, this four-star hotel equals or surpasses a good number of China's so-called five-star hotels. From the moment you step into the lobby, you know you're in an international hotel. Many of the staff have been trained in Shanghai and are competent and eager to please. Standard rooms are spacious with large twin beds and bathroom facilities are high in quality. The rooms have blond wood desktops and crisp white down comforters; they are light, airy, and well maintained.

Xincheng Bei Jie (north of Xincheng Bei/Nan Jie and Xincheng Xi/Dong Jie junction). © **0471/660-8888**. Fax 0471/628-0959. www.ni-phoenix.com.cn. 280 units. ¥898–¥958 ($117–$125/£58–£62) standard room; from ¥1,598

($208/£104) suite. Rates include breakfast or use of sauna/swimming pool. Usual discount 25% with breakfast; 35% without breakfast. Bus: no. 2 from the railway station. AE, DC, MC, V. **Amenities:** 5 restaurants; bar; large indoor pool; outdoor tennis court; health club and sauna; complimentary airport transfer; very helpful business center; ATM; forex; 24-hr. room service; laundry/dry cleaning. *In room:* A/C, satellite TV w/pay movies, dataport, minibar, fridge, hair dryer, safe.

Huhehaote Jiari jiudian (Holiday Inn Hohhot) 🟊

The city's first four-star hotel is within walking distance of Hohhot's shopping and commercial areas. All rooms are spacious and very comfortable, but the rooms on the executive sixth and seventh floors are particularly good and include a free nightly snack buffet in the executive lounge. The deluxe studios are also a good option and feature large bathrooms with sauna. As one of the few hotels in town with international management, this is currently the safest bet in town, although competition is heating up. There is an Italian restaurant, Buon Appetito; a Western restaurant serving Western and Asian dishes; and a Chinese restaurant serving Cantonese, Sichuan, and Hunan specialties.

Zhongshan Xi Lu. ✆ 0471/635-1888. Fax 0471/635-0888. 198 units. www.holidayinn-hohhot.com. ¥900 ($117/£59) standard room; ¥1,100 ($143/£72) executive club room; ¥1,400 ($182/£91) deluxe studio; ¥1,700 ($221/£111) executive suite. Rates include breakfast. AE, DC, MC, V. **Amenities:** 3 restaurants; business center; health center w/sauna and whirlpool; laundry/dry cleaning service; coin-op washer/dryer; ATM. *In room:* A/C, satellite TV, high-speed Internet, hair dryer.

Neimenggu Fandian (Inner Mongolia Hotel) 🟊

The Neimenggu was entirely rebuilt to five-star standards in 2001. In addition to having all the trappings of an international hotel (including a sweeping lobby staircase), it has the best non-Chinese cuisine in the province, served in three of Hohhot's handsomest restaurants. Guest rooms and bathrooms are spacious and attractive, service is excellent, and the decor in the hotel's lounges, bars, and tearooms is elegant. Located around the corner from the Xincheng Hotel, it hasn't the gorgeous grounds of its competitor, nor the warmth, but there is a public park right across the street. Get the best of both five-star worlds by staying at the Xincheng and dining here.

Wulanchabu Xi Lu (east of Hulunbeier Nan Lu). ✆ 0471/693-8888. Fax 0471/695-2288. www.nmghotel.com. 345 units. ¥800–¥960 ($104–$125/£52–£62) standard room; from ¥1,600 ($208/£104) suite. AE, MC, V. Bus: no. 37 from the railway station to Wulan Chabu Xi Lu; from there, walk east. **Amenities:** 4 restaurants; bar; large indoor pool; health club; Jacuzzi; sauna; business center; forex; 24-hr. room service; laundry/dry cleaning. *In room:* A/C, satellite TV w/pay movies, dataport, minibar, fridge, hair dryer, safe.

Xincheng Binguan 🟊🟊 (Kids)

The grounds of this hotel and garden complex in the heart of the city cover 119,000 sq. m (1,280,904 sq. ft.) and include a lake, a park, a large sports complex, and a set of *ger* tents. Originally built in 1958, the Xincheng underwent a 2001 renovation that produced Hohhot's first five-star hotel. This is the place to take a break from traveling. If you have kids, send them off to swim, bowl, or play video games while you treat yourself to a massage in what the expats say is the best spa in town. If you opt for a deluxe standard, ask for a room with a front view (overlooking gardens, a fountain and, in the distance, a bustling avenue) in the renovated building A.

Hulunbeier Nan Lu 40. ✆ 0471/666-0888. Fax 0471/666-0090. www.xincheng-hotel.com.cn. 300 units in buildings A and B; 5 villas with luxury rooms. From ¥680 ($88/£44) standard room; from ¥1,680 ($218/£109) suite. AE, DC, MC, V. Bus: no. 37 from railway station. **Amenities:** 12 restaurants; bar; large pool; indoor tennis courts; squash court; health club; sauna; bike rental; bowling alley; billiards; video arcade; business center; forex; limited room service; massage; laundry/dry cleaning. *In room:* A/C, satellite TV, dataport, minibar, fridge, hair dryer, safe.

MODERATE

Bayantala Fandian *(Value* Renovated in 2002, the VIP Building in this clean, appealing hotel near Xinhua Guangchang offers the usual twin beds and small bathrooms, but everything is spotless and well maintained. The VIP Building boasts a branch of Beijing's most famous Peking Duck restaurant, Quanjude. Though the "Main Building" is less charming, it, too, is clean, and offers standard twins, economy rooms and dorm beds for in a setting a notch above the usual dorm standard.

Xilinguole Bei Lu 42 (between Xinhua Dajie and Zhongshan Xi Lu). ℂ 0471/696-3344. Fax 0471/696-7390. 173 units with bathroom in VIP Building; 244 economy units (some with shower only, some with common bathroom) in Main Building. ¥380 ($49/£25) standard room in VIP Building (off season as low as ¥200/$26/£13); ¥560 ($73/£36) suite. Rates in VIP Building include breakfast. ¥280 ($36/£18) standard room in Main Building; ¥70 ($9.10/£4.55) economy room in Main Building. ¥30 ($3.90/£1.95) dorm bed in Main Building. No credit cards. Bus: no. 34 or 35 from the railway station. **Amenities:** 8 restaurants; small business center; laundry/dry cleaning. *In room:* A/C, TV.

INEXPENSIVE

Jiayuan Binguan *(Value* One of a new breed of budget business hotels sweeping the nation, the Jiayuan offers small, clean, and modern rooms decked out with cheap, functional furniture that looks good now but may suffer a few years down the line. While the hotel's location in a factory courtyard is a little bizarre, it lies in the heart of modern downtown Hohhot, and all of the well-priced rooms have Internet access.

Xilinguole Bei Lu (look for the sign above an archway just south of the Bayantala Fandian). ℂ **0471/626-2228.** 80 units. ¥139–¥199 ($18–$26/£9.05–£13). No credit cards. **Amenities:** Restaurant; small business center. *In room:* A/C, TV, broadband Internet access, minibar.

WHERE TO DINE

There are **McDonald's** and **KFC**s popping up all over Hohhot, particularly along Zhongshan Xi Lu, where you'll also find a **Pizza Hut.** But Hohhot's varied and satisfying Mongolian cuisine—a big change from the mainstream Chinese diet—should get priority. In addition to the restaurants listed below, there's plenty of good street eats to be enjoyed; tables are set up along Xilinguole Bei Lu near the junction with Zhongshan Lu on a summer's evening and sell beer and tasty kabobs.

Ban Mu Di Youmian Dawang ✮✮✮ *(Value* MONGOLIAN Eating in this lively restaurant specializing in pastas and pancakes made of husked wheat will put you in a good mood. The decor is a mix of Mongolian *ger* and prettified farmhouse. The walls are brightly decorated with floral and folk designs. The waitresses, dressed in equally bright colors and busy patterns, are friendly and efficient. Best of all, the food is inexpensive and exceptionally tasty. Try house specialties like *wowo,* husked wheat pasta shaped by curling the dough around the little finger then pressed together in a bamboo steamer, forming what looks like honeycomb made of pasta. *Dundun*—husked-wheat pancakes filled with carrots, potato, and cabbage—are rolled up and sliced like Mediterranean levant sandwiches. Also try *wo bing,* or corncakes, which diners dunk like doughnuts into a soup of vinegar, sesame oil, and soybeans.

Xilin Guole Lu (just north of the Shangri-La). ℂ 0471/691-0168. Reservations recommended. Meal for 2 under ¥40 ($5.20/£2.60). No credit cards. 11:30am–2pm and 6–9:30pm.

Florence (Foluolunsa) ✮ *(Value* ITALIAN/AMERICAN This attractive restaurant serves authentic pasta, pizza, and baked lasagna. The chef has worked in several international hotels—most recently in Xi'an's Sheraton—which may be how poached salmon, lobster Newburg, and T-bone steak ended up on an Italian menu (not to mention the burger, fries, and club sandwich). Though neither the selection nor the dishes themselves demonstrate creativity, this is the best place to satisfy a craving for Western food. You can also drop in for tiramisu and espresso or order takeout. A violin soloist serenades diners nightly, and dinner is by candlelight, but dress is as casual or as formal as you like.

In the Neimenggu Fandian, Wulanchabu Xi Lu (east of Hulunbeier Nan Lu). © 0471/693-8888. English menu. Pasta, pizza, and sandwiches ¥32–¥48 ($4.15–$6.25/£2.10–£3.10); steaks, seafood ¥78–¥128 ($10–$17/£5.05–£8.30). Buffet lunch ¥88 ($11/£5.70), buffet dinner ¥98 ($13/£6.35). AE, DC, MC, V. Noon–2pm and 6–9pm.

Mao Buwen Da Jiulou ⭐ HOME-STYLE/JIAOZI   In addition to local specialties and 80 kinds of *jiaozi* (¥16–¥20/$2.10–$2.60/£1.05–£1.30 for 40), the menu includes Cantonese, Sichuan, and Shandong specialties. The best time to come is between 8pm and 2am, when you'll find the place packed with locals enjoying a late supper of cold dishes and beer topped off by a plate of *la mian* (you can watch the chef stretch and swing the dough as it is transformed into noodles before your eyes). Highly recommended dishes are *suancai rou chao fen* (wheat noodles mixed with shredded pork, green pepper, cabbage, and spices); *su hezi* (fried vegetable pie stuffed with chives, crumbled scrambled egg, carrots, and tree ear fungus); the refreshingly light *shenxian baicai tang* (immortals' cabbage soup), which includes cabbage, shrimp, mushrooms, and carrots; and *tese kao runiu* (barbecued marinated veal). Before barbecuing, the veal is soaked for a day in a marinade containing over two dozen herbs and spices, the sum of which are said to balance *yin* and *yang*.

Hulunbeier Bei Kou 91 (at Zhongshan Dong Lu intersection). © 0471/629-6558. Meal for 2 ¥20 ($2.60/£1.30) and up. No credit cards. 10am–2am.

Yulan Jiujia ⭐⭐ Finds MONGOLIAN   There's no better place to be introduced to Mongolian cooking than this clean, friendly, family-operated restaurant named after its female proprietor, Chen Yulan. Though no one speaks English, the staff will bring out ingredients from the kitchen to show you what goes into any particular dish.

Their best Mongolian specialties include various types of *guozai*. This stew comes to the table in a pot with flame underneath. Unlike hot pot, the ingredients are already cooked when the dish is set in front of you. Just stir it a bit and remind your waiter to put the flame out when it gets too hot. A Mongolian favorite is *guozai suancai* (pickled vegetables and sheep organ *[yang zasui]* stew) made of mutton, sheep heart, lung, liver, intestines, cilantro, hot pepper, green vegetable, and spices. A Mongolian friend says Yulan's version of this is exactly right. If you're not inclined to eat internal organs, the dish is also made with the same vegetables and spices combined with mutton *(yangrou)*, beef *(niurou)*, or chicken *(jirou)*.

Chao mian are Mongolian-style fried wheat noodles that can be ordered with or without meat and include cilantro, sesame seeds, and garlic. *Naicha,* the milk tea of Hohhot—made with cow's milk—is absent the pungent mutton taste associated with milk tea of the outer steppe. Here, the tea is usually served salted with a dish of sugar on the side. Snacks such as *guotiao* (sticks of crisp fried dough) and pats of *naipizi* ("milk skin" which, in taste and texture, falls between cream and fresh butter) are eaten on their own or tossed into the tea along with *chao fen,* processed millet that looks like tiny yellow beads. *Liangfen* are thick translucent grain noodles served cold in a thin broth made of vinegar, soy sauce, sesame seeds, and hot pepper. If the slimy texture of the noodles isn't an obstacle, you'll find this a delicious dish. In addition to Mongolian specialties, the chef makes a variety of noodle dishes, vegetable and meat dumplings, and delicious *jiachang cai* (Chinese home-style fare).

Just down the alleyway that runs along the north side of the Bayantala Hotel on Xilinguole Bei Lu. It's the 1st restaurant on your right. ✆ **0696/3344-6101**. Meal for 2 ¥20 – ¥40 ($2.60–$5.20/£1.30–£2.60). No credit cards. 10am–10pm (to 9pm in winter).

HOHHOT AFTER DARK
Saima Chang Menggu Dahui Gong
A performance stage and over 100 *ger* (or yurts) have been erected on the large open field next to Hohhot's horse-racing track. They comprise one big restaurant specializing in Mongolian fare—from noodles to an entire barbecued goat. Even if you're not interested in eating, the time to come is between 6:30 and 9pm, when Mongolian folk musicians and dancers perform on the outdoor stage free of charge. On hot summer nights, Mongolians and Han alike bring their families for an inexpensive evening out. The combination of *ger,* outdoor music, and a crowd lends a county-fair atmosphere.

Saima Chang (Hohhot's horse-racing track). No credit cards. Restaurant: 9am–2:30pm and 5–10pm. Performance: 6:30–9pm. Performance canceled in snow or heavy rain. Bus: no. 13 north along Hulunbeier Lu to the racetrack.

3 Yinchuan (★)

Ningxia Province, 1,369km (845 miles) W of Beijing, 723km (450 miles) NW of Xi'an

Compared to the other major cities in this chapter—particularly the dirty duo of Datong and Taiyuan—Yinchuan is a breath of fresh air. Capital of the Ningxia Hui Autonomous Region, it has a population under a million, its tree-lined streets still have relatively few automobiles, and it is rumored (read: reported by the *People's Daily*) to be the quietest city in China. It has also escaped the extreme poverty associated with this province by having the good fortune to be hydrated by the Yellow River and an irrigation system first built during the Han dynasty. Nearly a third of the region's population is Hui (Chinese Muslims), and a significant percentage live in the capital, adding a cultural diversity less apparent in other Chinese capitals. This is an easy town to settle down in for a few days. Hotel rates aren't exorbitant, the food is good, and most of the sights are within walking distance or easy to get to by bus or taxi.

The best time to visit is between May and October. Though summer temperatures can soar, the dry climate makes even the hottest days bearable. ***Note:*** Yinchuan holds its annual Motorcycle Tourism Festival for a week sometime between June and September (check with CITS for exact dates). The emphasis is on tourism, so unless you're prepared for throngs of unregenerate cap-wearing tourists and dancers in go-go boots performing the "songs and dances of the Western Xia," it may be a good time to stay away.

ESSENTIALS
GETTING THERE   There are direct **flights** from most major cities, including Beijing, Shanghai, Chengdu, Guangzhou, Taiyuan, and Xi'an. Discounts are usually available. The **CAC** office (✆ **0951/691-3456**) is located in the Minhang Hotel (Minhang Dasha) at the intersection of Nanhuan Dong Lu and Bei Jie, south of Nan Men. A bus costing ¥15 ($1.95/£1) to **Hedong Airport** leaves the hotel 95 minutes before flights for the 25-minute trip. Buses meet every flight. A taxi into town costs about ¥50 ($6.50/£3.25).

The **railway station** is in the new part of town, but there's a booking and ticket office in the old town on Xinhua Dong Jie. Major connections are with Beijing (K177/K178; 19 hr.) and Xi'an (2585/6 and 2587/8; 15 hr.). Trains connecting Hohhot and Lanzhou stop in Yinchuan (2635; 9 hr.).

The (Nearly) Lost Dynasty of the Xi Xia

After Genghis Khan died in 1227 near the Xi Xia (Western Xia) capital of Zhongxing Fu (present-day Yinchuan), his corpse was carried in an ox-drawn chariot—the centerpiece of a grand procession that led back to the Mongolian steppe. En route, any person or beast in the procession's path was slaughtered—in offering to the Khan's spirit and to keep news of his death from spreading. As dour as it must have been, the escorting soldiers might have smiled to themselves in the knowledge they were returning home victorious—having once and for all defeated the Xi Xia (Western Xia) dynasty (1038–1227), which had lasted almost 200 years.

Today the Xi Xia is somewhat of a mystery. It was never recognized as a legitimate dynasty by the Chinese, so there is no official history of the empire or its people, the Tangut; and Xi Xia documents—written in a system fashioned after but different from Chinese—have been difficult to decipher. It's known that the ancient Tangut nomads came from what is now Sichuan, Qinghai, and Tibet. By the Tang dynasty (618–907), they had a leader and were one of the major players (along with the Khitan and Jurchen) in the ongoing struggle for territory. By the early 11th century they had defeated the Song imperial army, declared an independent empire, and extracted an annual tribute of tea, cloth, silk, and silver from the Song empire. Almost a century later, the Xia's alliance with the Jin (the Jurchen state) ignited the wrath of Genghis Khan, who personally led his troops south to destroy the "Great Xia," as they called themselves. At its height, the Xi Xia empire controlled much of what is now Qinghai, Gansu, Ningxia, and Inner Mongolia. This obscure Buddhist state left behind imperial mausoleums, religious monuments, its own written language, and cultural relics that reveal a passion for Buddhist art, fine pottery, sculpture, and exquisite gold and silver artifacts. Much of what remains can be seen in and around Yinchuan.

The **long-distance bus station (qichezhan)** is in the southeast corner of the old city on Shengli Bei Jie. Xi'an (720km/447 miles; 8 hr.; ¥138/$18/£8.95) is served by express buses at 7:30am, 8:30am, 9:30am, and 4:30pm, 5:30pm, and 6:30pm. Four buses connect with Taiyuan (763km/474 miles; ¥122/$16/£7.85); three express buses connect with Yan'an (449km/279 miles; 5 hr.; ¥108/$14/£7); and with Lanzhou (514km/320 miles; 5 hr.; ¥96/$13/£6.25). Tickets can be bought up to 4 days in advance at the bus station.

GETTING AROUND   Yinchuan has a new town (as of the 1960s) and an old town. The railway station is in the new town, but everything else the traveler would need or want is in the much more charming old town 10km (6 miles) to the east. **Taxis** wait in the parking lot at the railway station to transport passengers to the old (around ¥20/$2.60/£1.30). **Minibus** no. 1 goes from the railway station to the Nan Men Qichezhan (South Gate Bus Station) via Jiefang Jie, which runs east to west through the center of the old town; the fare is ¥3 (40¢/20p). **Bus** no. 11 from the

Yinchuan

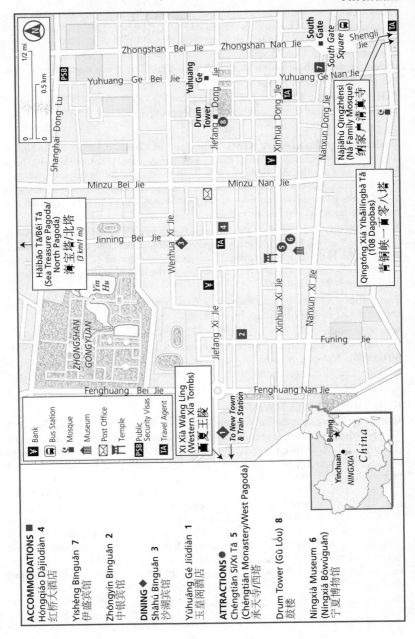

1/2 mi
0.5 km

Shanghai Dong Lu

Zhongshan Bei Jie   Zhongshan Nan Jie

South Gate

South Gate Square

Shengli Jie

PSB

Yuhuang Ge Bei Jie

Yuhuang Ge

Yuhuang Ge Nan Jie

Najiāhù Qingzhēnsì
(Nà Family Mosque)
纳家户清真寺

Drum Tower

Jiefang Dong Jie

Xinhua Dong Jie

Nanxun Dong Jie

Minzu Bei Jie   Minzu Nan Jie

Hǎibǎo Tǎ/Běi Tǎ
(Sea Treasure Pagoda/
North Pagoda)
海宝塔/北塔
(3 km/1 mi)

Jinning Bei Jie

Wenhua Xi Jie

Qīngtóng Xiá Yìbǎilíngbā Tǎ
(T08 Dagobas)
青铜峡一百零八塔

Yin Hu

ZHONGSHAN GŌNGYUÁN

Jiefang Xi Jie

Xinhua Xi Jie

Nanxun Xi Jie

Funing   Jie

Fenghuang Bei Jie   Fenghuang Nan Jie

Xī Xià Wáng Líng
(Western Xià Tombs)
西夏王陵

To New Town
& Train Station

Beijing ★

China

Yinchuan ●
NINGXIA

¥ Bank
🚍 Bus Station
☪ Mosque
🏛 Museum
✉ Post Office
⛩ Temple
PSB Public Security Visas
TA Travel Agent

railway station follows the same route, but turns north instead of south at the end of Jiefang Dong Jie. Bus fare within the old city is ¥1 (15¢/5p). Taxi rates are ¥5 (65¢/ 35p) for the first 3km (2 miles), then between ¥1 and ¥1.40 (15¢–20¢/5p–10p) per kilometer. Beyond 8km (5 miles), the rate is ¥1.50 (20¢/10p) per kilometer. Fares within the old town will rarely exceed ¥6 (80¢/40p). *Tip:* When negotiating trips to out-of-town sites, local residents calculate ¥1 (15¢/5p) per kilometer.

TOURS   Ningxia **CITS,** at Beijing Dong Lu 375 (© **0951/671-9792**), arranges pricey tours to nearby sites, Zhongwei, and Shapotou.

FAST FACTS

Banks, Foreign Exchange & ATMs   The **Bank of China,** at Jiefang Xi Jie 80, has a 24-hour ATM. Change traveler's checks and foreign currency at window 10. Bank hours are Monday through Friday from 8:30am to 6:30pm during summer and until 6pm in winter. Banks are open from 9am to 5pm on weekends. For cash advances on credit cards, go to the second floor of the branch at Xinhua Dong Jie 5, which also has a 24-hour ATM and foreign exchange.

Internet Access   Just south of the Yuhuang Ge, there's a true Internet bar *(wangba)* at Yuhuang Ge Nan Jie 53. Cocktails are served up front; the computers are in a small room at the back. The bar is open 24 hours and charges ¥2 (25¢/15p) per hour. There's also a comfortable Internet cafe opposite the Zhongyin Binguan on Funing Jie. Dial-up is © **163** or 169.

Post Office   The main post office (open 8am–6pm) is on the northwest corner of the Jiefang Xi Jie and Minzu Bei Jie intersection.

Visa Extensions   The Exit-Entry Office of the **PSB** is in the northeast quadrant of the old town at Yuhuang Ge Bei Jie 105, entered from Shanghai Dong Lu (© **0951/ 501-5976**). It's open Monday through Friday from 8:30am to noon and 2:30 to 6:30pm. The official processing time is 3 to 5 days, but it's usually done overnight. Take bus no. 4 from Wenhua Jie.

IN & AROUND THE TOWN

Chengtian Si and Ningxia Bowuguan (Chengtian Temple and Ningxia Museum)

The museum is set in the tranquil grounds of Chengtian Temple, which also goes by the name of its Xi Ta (West Pagoda). First erected in 1050, the pagoda did not survive Yinchuan's devastating 1739 earthquake. The existing pagoda dates from 1820, and visitors are allowed to climb the 11-story building.

The museum collection is divided into four parts, distributed among three build-ings. The first two sections share a building and are devoted to the history, language, and relics of the Western Xia dynasty. Of all the sites in and around Yinchuan, these two rooms have the most helpful English explanations. The advantage to making this your first stop is a better understanding of the culture that is most connected with the out-of-town tombs and pagodas. The second building houses relics of the Commu-nist revolution and has no English labeling. A third hall focuses on the Hui (Muslim) "nationality," and has only an English introduction.

Jinning Jie 6. Admission to museum and pagoda ¥22 ($2.85/£1.45). 8am–6pm. Bus: no. 2.

Haibao Ta/Bei Ta (Sea Treasure Pagoda/North Pagoda)   In a province that has more than its share of stately pagodas, Haibao Ta is one of the loveliest. Originally built in the 5th century, it was toppled by the 1739 earthquake and rebuilt in the

original style some 30 years later. Restored since then, it has retained its distinctive cross-shaped ground plan that adds depth and complexity to the four-sided tower. Its rare peach-shaped steeple of glazed green tiles is one of only two—the other crowns Chengtian Temple's West Pagoda.

3km (1¾ miles) north of town along Jinning Bei Jie. Admission ¥20 ($2.60/£1.30). Summer 8am–6pm; winter 9am–5pm. No public bus. Taxi from town center ¥5 (65¢/35p).

Najiahu Qingzhensi (Na Family Mosque) A good time to visit this 490-year-old wooden mosque is morning, as the town begins to stir. From the three-storied entrance gate, you can look east over the flat-topped brick houses and into small yards and alleys. The population of greater Yongning (which is a half-hour drive south of Yinchuan) is about 80% Hui, while this old village that immediately surrounds the mosque is 100% Hui—that being one of the requisites of residing in this well-preserved section of town. To this day a majority of residents are part of the Na family after which the mosque was named. According to the septuagenarian caretaker, the mosque escaped the destruction of the Cultural Revolution because the tightly knit community kept constant watch over it and refused entrance to the Red Guards. These days, visitors are invited into the pretty and peaceful courtyard. If you come alone or with only a few people, the caretaker may also let you into the prayer hall.

23km (14 miles) from Yinchuan in the town of Yongning, at Guo Dao 109. Admission ¥10 ($1.30/65p). 6am–noon and 1:30–4pm. Bus: green no. 9 opposite Nan Men to Yongning; you'll be dropped at the Xinzhaizi Lukou (Xinzhaizi intersection). Walk west about 300m (1,000 ft.). You'll cross a small timber bridge. Look for the mosque on your left. Taxis charge around ¥60–¥80 ($7.80–$10/£3.90–£5.20) for the round-trip, including waiting time.

Qingtong Xia Yibailingba Ta (108 Dagobas) Little is known about the 108 dagobas that stand like bowling pins on the side of the Qingtong Gorge, near the Yellow River. In the Ming dynasty they were referred to as the "ancient pagodas" (*gu ta*) and their origin was already a mystery. Today scholars associate them with the Western Xia dynasty because other relics and remains from the Xia culture have been unearthed in the vicinity. Their shape—like a Buddhist alms bowl—is similar to that of the classic Tibetan stupa, supporting the accepted belief that Tibetan Buddhism thrived in this area during the Western Xia and Yuan dynasties. Extensive repairs were made to them in 1987, but the dagobas are unusual and worth the visit. On the way, consider stopping at the Najiahu Qingzhensi (see above).

82km (51 miles) south of Yinchuan, near Qingtong Xia Zhen. Admission ¥30 ($3.90/£1.95). 7:30am–7pm. Bus: no. 153 to Qingtong Xia Zhen (not to be confused with Qingtong Xia Shi, where the bus may stop on the way). Minibuses wait at the drop-off point. The asking price will be higher if the minibus isn't full. Hard bargaining might get it down to ¥20 ($2.60/£1.30). If the minibus is full, it should be considerably less. To walk from the drop-off junction, take the road to the right. Turn left at the hydroelectric plant; then continue toward the right until you reach the dam. (Signs in English point the way.) Cross the Yellow River by ferry (¥15/$1.95/£1 round-trip), then hike up and over. Follow the trail to the dagobas. A taxi from Yinchuan and back, including road toll and parking, should be around ¥200 ($26/£13) and take 90 min. one-way.

Xi Xia Wang Ling (Western Xia Tombs) As the tourism bureau develops this spot, it is fast acquiring a theme-park aura. But if you can forgive the modern "Spirit Way" (fashioned after the path to the Ming tombs), skip the cheesy reenactment scenes of Xia life in the "Art Hall," and ignore promoters' claims that these are "China's Pyramids," you'll be able to appreciate this intriguing site. The tombs of nine Xia kings are spread across a 5×11km (3×7-mile) area at the foot of the Helan Mountains. In the fashion of Tang imperial tombs, each of these was originally surrounded by a 1-hectare (2½-acre) mausoleum composed of eight different types of traditional buildings. While only ruins survive, all but one of the nine imperial tombs remain intact. Dotting the landscape, the eerie, mud-encased pyramids resemble giant termite mounds. A two-story museum contains most of the relics, such as compelling stone plinths carved to look like potbellied gnomes on their knees, eyes and foreheads bulging as if from the weight they bear.

38km (24 miles) west of Yinchuan on eastern slopes of Helan Mountains. Admission ¥40 ($5.20/£2.60). Public buses leave from Nan Men. Taxi round-trip: negotiate for ¥100–¥150 ($13–$20/£6.50–£9.75).

SHOPPING

The largest supermarket in town is the **Hualian Chaoshi** (9am–10pm) under Nan Men Square opposite the bus station.

WHERE TO STAY

Hongqiao Dajiudian   This is the closest Yinchuan gets to a four-star hotel. Rooms are well maintained and carpets are clean (if a little worn) while midsize bathrooms have combo tub/showers. The hotel isn't in the heart of the tourist area, but it's only a few blocks west of Gu Lou (the Drum Tower), which is the center of town. It's popular, and is especially busy on weekends.

Jiefang Xi Jie. ✆ **0951/691-8888.** Fax 0951/691-8788. 231 units. ¥339 ($44/£22) standard room; from ¥680 ($88/£44) suite. 10% discount often available. AE, DC, MC, V. Bus: no. 1 or 11 from railway station. **Amenities:** 2 restaurants; bar; fitness center; ticketing; business center; forex; limited room service; laundry/dry cleaning. *In room:* A/C, satellite TV, Internet access, minibar, fridge, hair dryer, safe.

Yisheng Binguan   This budget hotel north of Nan Guan Mosque is modest, exceptionally clean, and one of the few inexpensive guesthouses in Yinchuan that isn't dismal. Guest rooms are bright and airy, although those which front the street are a little noisy. Each room has a private bathroom and shower without a separate cubicle. The hotel's location—within walking distance of Nan Men, the bus station, and the Nan Guan Mosque—makes it prime for sightseeing.

Nanxun Dong Jie 67 (northeast corner of Nanxun Dong and Yuhuang Ge Nan Jie intersection). ✆ **0951/604-1888.** 12 units. ¥118–¥128 ($15–$17/£7.65–£8.30) standard room. 20% discount sometimes available. No credit cards. Bus: no. 2 or 17. **Amenities:** Teahouse. *In room:* TV.

Zhongyin Binguan   Opened in 1997 and recently renovated, this hotel is located on a pleasant leafy street. It has clean, bland, airy rooms and offers good value.

Funing Jie 27. ✆ **0951/501-1918.** Fax 0951/504-7545. 39 units. ¥268–¥288 ($35–$37/£17–£19) standard room; ¥580–¥880 ($75–$114/£38–£57) suite. Nondiscounted rates include breakfast. Up to 40% discount available. AE, DC, MC, V. Bus: no. 1 or 11 from railway station to Funing Jie, then walk 2 min. south. **Amenities:** Restaurant; bowling alley; ticketing; business center; limited room service. *In room:* A/C, TV, minibar, fridge, safe.

WHERE TO DINE

Shahu Binguan 🍴 *Value* CHINESE FAST FOOD   By 7am customers are lined up at this restaurant's outdoor stand to buy *baozi* (stuffed steamed buns) for takeout. Generous portions of good, inexpensive food have turned this restaurant into the most popular breakfast spot in Yinchuan. According to one taxi driver, a ¥3 (40¢/20p) *baozi* at Shahu is one and a half times the size of a ¥3-*baozi* anywhere else. For very little money you can sample lots of local specialties; choose from among noodle dishes, savory pancakes, eight-treasure soups *(babao zhou)*—of which there are many kinds—and every sort of *baozi, jiaozi,* and *hezi* (steamed buns, Chinese ravioli, fried meat or vegetable pies). A sample breakfast costing just ¥8 ($1.05/50p) includes a bowl of noodles, three vegetarian *baozi,* two fried *jiaozi,* and two crepes stuffed with chives, egg, and cilantro. And there are many more choices for meat eaters and vegetarians alike. Customers pay food servers with coupons purchased in advance from the cashier. Unspent coupons can also be redeemed there.

Wenhua Xi Jie 22 (on the ground floor of the Shahu Hotel). (**C**) **0951/506-9128**. Meal for 2 ¥16 ($2.10/£1). No credit cards. 6:30am–2pm and 5–10pm. Bus: no. 4 or 18.

Yuhuang Ge Jiudian 🐦🐦 HOME-STYLE   This family-operated restaurant at the west end of town is out-of-the-way but worth the trip. The decor is simple and characteristic of this style of restaurant—fluorescent lights and neat rows of tables for four—but what it lacks in ambience it makes up for in great food. Try the *guantang baozi.* These unleavened *baozi* served in a bamboo steamer are a Xi'an specialty. The choice of stuffing includes beef *(niurou),* mutton *(yangrou),* or vegetable *(suxian).* Their version of *tudou si* (shredded potatoes with slivers of green and red pepper) is also delicious, as is sweet *babao zhou* (eight-treasure soup), made with sesame seeds, peanuts, rice, lotus seeds, and *gouqi* (sometimes translated "wolfberry"), the ubiquitous dried fruit from this area that resembles a red raisin and is considered good for the health by Chinese.

Jiefang Xi Jie 158 (not to be confused with Yuhuang Ge Hotel in the east of town). (**C**) **0951/505-4758**. Meal for 2 ¥20–¥50 ($2.60–$6.50/£1.30–£3.25). No credit cards. 10am–10pm.

4 Yan'an

Shanxi Province, 371km (230 miles) N of Xi'an

For 10 years between 1937 and 1947, the dusty, desolate town of Yan'an in Shaanxi Province (spelled with two a's to distinguish it from its neighbor, Shanxi) was the site from which the Chinese Communist Party consolidated power and spread revolution. It was here that Mao seized leadership of the party and formulated the theories that came to be known as "Mao Zedong Thought." As the Japanese took control of the eastern part of the country, intellectuals from all over China moved to impoverished Yan'an, eager to make their contribution and share in the collective experiment. Among them were the writer Ding Ling (who was chastised by Mao for her essay on International Women's Day—"Thoughts on March 8"—which pointed out gender inequities in Yan'an) and the Shanghai starlet Jiang Qing, who became Mao's third wife and, later, a key player in the Cultural Revolution. This part of northern Shanxi was also the location of Chen Kaige's affecting 1984 film *Yellow Earth,* about the impact on villagers of a young Communist soldier who goes into the countryside to collect folk songs.

Like Mao's birthplace of Shao Shan, Yan'an was a place of pilgrimage during the 1960s, and today is a major point for Chinese making Red Tours, or visiting revolutionary sites, but quite what The Great Helmsman would make of the town's somewhat sleazy feel after dark is an interesting question! Nevertheless, the appeal of this part of Shanxi is its very austerity—the cave dwellings, the dry terraced hills, and the yellow loess that covers it all. The "revolutionary sites" that have become such a part of the founding myth of the PRC will also draw anyone with an interest in modern Chinese history, but, coming from Xi'an or Beijing, Yan'an feels refreshingly undiscovered by foreign travelers. *Note:* Please turn to appendix A for Chinese translations of key locations.

ESSENTIALS

GETTING THERE   Yan'an Airport is 10km (6 miles) northeast of town. Taxis cost ¥20 ($2.60/£1.30) to the center of town. Yan'an is connected by air with Beijing and Xi'an (daily).

The Yan'an **railway station** is at the south end of town. Trains to Xi'an take as little as 5 hours; the K558 (11:56am) is convenient. The T45 at 3:34pm takes around 15 hours to reach Beijing. You can buy tickets at the station, but it's easiest to proceed through the train ticket booking office in town, next to the Yan'an Tourist Hotel (Yan'an Luyou Dasha) on Zhongxin Jie.

Buses arrive and depart from the **bus station** opposite the railway station, although some services leave from the **Dongguan Jie qichezhan (bus station).** From Pingyao or Taiyuan, it's easiest to go to Xi'an first, then transfer to bus or train for Yan'an. Buses connecting Xi'an and Yan'an leave throughout the day for the 4-hour journey costing ¥76 ($9.90/£4.95). Overnight buses connect Yan'an to Luoyang and Yinchuan from the Dongguan Jie qichezhan.

GETTING AROUND   Shaped like a Y, the city of Yan'an traces the Yan River as it forks to the east and west. The town is small by Chinese standards and easy to navigate on foot, since its commercial district is concentrated in a few blocks around Zhongxin Jie (Central St.) and Da Qiao Jie (Big Bridge St.). City **bus** rides cost ¥1 (15¢/5p). Rates for **taxis** are ¥5 (65¢/35p) for the first 3km (2 miles), then ¥1.20 (15¢/10p) per additional kilometer. Between 10pm and 7am, the first 3km (2 miles) are ¥5.90 (75¢/40p). Most destinations within the city are under ¥10 ($1.30/65p).

TOURS   CITS (© 0911/212-3320) is a short distance down the alley next to the Yan'an Binguan. The office is on the second floor of the brick compound to your right. Hours are Monday through Friday from 8am to noon and 2 to 6pm, but the office is occasionally empty even then.

FAST FACTS

Banks, Foreign Exchange & ATMs   The **Bank of China,** at Zhongxin Jie and Bei Guan Jie, changes cash and has an international ATM. There's another convenient branch offering the same services next to the Yinhai Guoji Dajiudian. Both branches are open Monday through Friday from 9am to 5:30pm, and 9am to 4pm on weekends.

Internet Access   There's a handy 24-hour Internet cafe above the post office (the stairway is in between the post office itself and the China Postal Savings next door). Another useful 24-hour Internet room is located next to the bus station. Both places charge ¥3 (40¢/20p) per hour. Dial-up is © 163.

Post Office   The post office is on Zhongxin Jie, south of Yan'an Binguan. It's open 8am to 6pm.

IN & AROUND TOWN

Between 1936 and 1947 the Communists had four different bases in Yan'an, each of which comprised cave homes common to the area. Each site is actually very similar, featuring homes cut out of the side of the loess hills, and with a spartan air about them. The rooms are simple, with only basic comforts, such as a desk, chair, and *kang,* the coal-heated brick platform beds. Shops at each of the sites sell a variety of revolutionary kitsch. You can take public bus nos. 1, 7, 8, and 13 to visit these sites. A taxi can be hired to visit all four for about ¥100 ($13/£6.50).

Bao Ta (Bao Pagoda)   Built in the Song dynasty and renovated in the 1950s, the 44m (144-ft.) Bao Pagoda, which can be seen from anywhere in the city, is a national symbol of China. The structure is located on a hill on the southeast side of the Yan River and offers excellent views of the city and nearby countryside.

Bao Pagoda, seen from anywhere in the city, can be reached on foot from the downtown area within just a few minutes. Admission ¥41 ($5.35/£2.65). 8am–6pm (to 5:30pm in winter).

Fenghuang Shan (Phoenix Hill)   During the months after the Long March when the Communist Party first arrived in Yan'an, it chose this site for its headquarters. Of greatest interest are the cave dwellings of Mao Zedong, Zhou Enlai, and Zhu De, who lived here between 1937 and 1938. Brick floors, simple wooden furniture, and graceful window lattices give these austere rooms a cozy quality. On display are intriguing photographs from the Yan'an years, Lenin's funeral, and the raised *kang*.

Entrance on Zhongxin Jie, a few hundred yards south of the Yan'an Hotel, before the post office. Admission ¥9 ($1.15/60p). 8am–6pm (to 5:30pm in winter).

Geming Jinianguan (Revolutionary Memorial Hall/Museum)   While Mao lies under glass in Beijing, the trusty white steed that transported him through northern Shanxi in 1947 stands stuffed behind glass at this museum. According to the sign on the window, the horse, who was then living in the Beijing Zoo, one day turned in the direction of Zhong Nan Hai (where Mao was living at the time), neighed loudly, and went on to join Marx. Unfortunately, there is no English signage, so without a familiarity with the players, the photographs on display have little meaning. The museum houses an interesting collection of old weapons, many of them handmade and crude, personal effects, and military gear. Unless you have a deep knowledge of Communist Party history, the museum—established in 1950 as "a classroom for advancing patriotism, revolutionary tradition, and the Yan'an spirit"—shouldn't take more than a half-hour of your time.

Northwest of the city center along Zaoyuan Lu. Admission ¥21 ($2.75/£1.35). 8am–6pm (to 5:30pm in winter).

Wangjiaping Geming Jiuzhi (Former Revolutionary Headquarters at Wangjiaping)   A 5-minute walk south of Geming Jinianguan is the site of the general office of the Eighth Route Army and headquarters of the CCP Central Military Commission from 1937 to 1947. Mao, Zhu De, Zhou Enlai, and other top brass also lived here at various times. In March 1947, as the Guomindang (KMT) army moved into northern Shanxi, the CCP abandoned Yan'an, and during the following 13 months of Nationalist government occupation, the Wangjiaping buildings were destroyed. Some years later, after the end of the civil war, they were restored according to the original layout and design. The simple mud dwellings and halls, with their low-pitched rooflines and arched doorways and windows that mimic the surrounding hills, are worthy of Frank Lloyd Wright in the way they blend with the natural environment. The site is similar to Fenghuang Shan (above), but on a much larger scale. If you don't have time for both, this is the one to see.

Situated on Zaoyuan Lu. Admission ¥11 ($1.45/70p). 8am–6pm (to 5:30pm in winter).

Yangjialing Jiuzhi (Yangjialing Revolutionary Headquarters)   The Communist pantheon of Mao, Zhu De, Zhou Enlai, and Liu Shaoqi all lived here at one time or another, but this was also the site of the famous Yan'an Forum on Literature and Art in May 1942. The forum, in which Mao argued that art and literature should serve the people, was to have a profound impact on the arts in China in the following decades. Visitors to Mao's room toss cigarettes onto the former leader's bed as a sign of respect.

Northwest of the Revolutionary Memorial Hall. Admission ¥16 ($2.10/£1.05). 8am–6pm (to 5:30pm in winter).

WHERE TO STAY

Yan'an has a reasonable choice of hotels, an expanding number of which are open to foreigners. If you're after something cheaper than those listed below, there are a few options near the train and bus stations, and the **Jinrong Binguan** (© **0911/288-5001**) on Er Dao Jie has passable twins for ¥160 ($21/£10).

Yan'an Binguan   Dignitaries such as Ho Chi Minh, Lee Kuan Yew, Zhou Enlai, and Jiang Zemin have stayed at this Soviet-style hotel, but until an upgrade in 2000, it had only three stars. While the rooms are now looking a little worn, and there's no hot water from the sink faucets in the spacious bathrooms, service has definitely moved up a gear. Gone are the days of old, when guests were subjected to suspicious glances from front-desk staff; instead reception is friendly and helpful, and the hotel even managed to win a provincial tourism award in 2005.

Zhongxin Jie 56. © 0911/211-3122. Fax 0911/211-4297. 193 units. ¥480–¥580 ($62–$75/£31–£38) standard room; ¥1,160–¥2,880 ($151–$374/£75–£187) suite. Most rates include breakfast. 30% discount available. 10% service charge. No credit cards. Bus: no. 3, or no. 12 from railway station. **Amenities:** 2 restaurants; indoor pool; ticketing; business center; limited room service; laundry/dry cleaning. *In room:* A/C, TV, Internet access, fridge.

Yasheng Dajiudian   A welcoming, efficient staff and bustling lobby make this three-star hotel instantly seem inviting. However, hallways are dim and rather cavernous, and the smallish guest rooms look a little past their best, particularly the carpets and bathrooms. However, the location is great and the hotel is surrounded by restaurants and bustling food stalls.

Er Dao Jie, Zhong Duan. © 0911/213-8336. Fax 0911/213-8063. 189 units. ¥328 ($43/£21) standard room. No credit cards. **Amenities:** 2 restaurants; ticketing; business center; limited room service; laundry/dry cleaning. *In room:* A/C, TV.

Yinhai Guoji Dajiudian (Silver Seas International Hotel)   The city's newest and most fashionable hotel is conveniently located in the center of the city. The staff is professional, and unlike the other hotels in Yan'an, the rooms of this four-star property are bright, modern-looking, and spacious.

Da Qiao Jie. © 0911/213-9999. Fax 0911/213-9666. 189 units. ¥688–¥738 ($89–$96/£45–£48) superior and deluxe rooms. No credit cards. **Amenities:** 2 restaurants; pool; health club; ticketing; business center; 24-hr. room service; laundry/dry cleaning. In room: A/C, TV, Internet access, fridge.

WHERE TO DINE

One of the best areas to find good, inexpensive dishes is along Er Dao Jie in the vicinity and north of Yasheng Hotel. In warm weather this is a popular stretch for evening strolls. Along nearby Da Qiao Jie, you'll also find outdoor stalls and small restaurants selling *jiaozi* (Chinese ravioli), meat kabobs for a paltry 4 mao (less than a penny), *yangrou pao mo* (mutton soup), and pasta, including *daoxiao mian*—knife-pared noodles—made by paring slices off a block of pasta dough into a large pot of boiling water. Supposedly, in earlier days, the chef placed a clump of dough atop his cotton skullcap and, with a knife in each hand, whittled away above his head—pasta strips flying—until all the dough was in the pot.

Wuqi Dajiudian ☆☆ SHANXI   Despite its simple, somewhat dingy (but clean) appearance, this is probably the best restaurant in the city. Locals crowd the place every evening, chatting noisily as they toast each other between mouthfuls of tasty Shanxi specialties. The drink of choice is *mijiu*, an alcoholic beverage made from millet; this local version, served heated from a small kettle, is a bit cloudy and sweet, and it goes well with the local cuisine. Among the tasty offerings are *huangmomo* (sweet steamed millet cake), *youmomo* (fried doughnut made of millet), *kucai tudou* (mashed potatoes with wild vegetables), *qiaomian hele* (pressed buckwheat noodles with a vinaigrette dressing), and *yougao* (a pan-fried sticky rice cake).

Beiguan Jie, opposite Yanan Middle School. (ⓒ) 0911/213-9720. Meal for 2 ¥25–¥40 ($3.25–$5.20/£1.65–£2.60). No credit cards. Breakfast 7–9am; lunch 10am–2pm; dinner 4:30–9:30pm.

5 Pingyao ⟨★⟩

Shanxi Province, 616km (383 miles) SW of Beijing, 100km (62 miles) S of Taiyuan, 540km (335 miles) NE of Xi'an

The great majority of Chinese cities have histories extending back hundreds and often thousands of years, but few have anything outside of a museum to show for it. The central Shanxi city of Pingyao is an exception. This 2,700-year-old city had its heyday during the late Ming and Qing dynasties, and the walled city that survives today was largely built then, though a few Yuan dynasty structures also survive. Chinese and overseas travelers come to this area to see some of the best-preserved traditional architecture in China: gray-brick courtyard homes *(siheyuan)*, extravagant family mansions (one of which was the set for Zhang Yimou's *Raise the Red Lantern*), a Ming city wall, Daoist and Buddhist temples, and China's earliest commercial banks. Visitors also get to stay in restored courtyards, sleep on a *kang* (heated brick bed), and eat wonderful Shanxi cuisine, which for some reason has yet to catch on in the West.

But Pingyao isn't all quaintness and old-world charm. Like any place in China dependent on tourism, it has an overabundance of vehicles of every kind, fake antiques, touts, and, well, tourists. Visitors on foot will have to avoid the speedy electric buggies which cart Chinese tourists around and as more residents of the old city are moved to modern apartments with modern plumbing, this World Heritage city faces the threat of becoming an over-precious imitation of itself. However, for now, Pingyao still has the vitality of a thriving town behind the veneer of an ancient one. *Note:* Turn to appendix A for Chinese translations of key locations.

ESSENTIALS

GETTING THERE   Overnight **trains** from Beijing save you a night's hotel stay and arrive in Pingyao in the morning. The 1163, which leaves Beijing at 7:03pm, is the most convenient train. Coming from Xi'an there are several trains during the day, or the 2536, which leaves at 8:08pm arrives in Pingyao early the following morning. Moving on to Beijing, the K604 leaves at 7:11pm and arrives the following morning. To Xi'an, the 2535 departs at 8:02pm. Pingyao has a tiny sleeper allocation, so if you want a berth you'll have to pay the price of a ticket from Taiyuan and will be given a photocopy of the ticket which you can exchange onboard. Most hotels can arrange this service for ¥40 to ¥50 ($5.20–$6.50/£2.50–£3.25).

Luxury **buses** from Beijing's Lize Qiao Long-Distance Bus Station leave every 20 minutes for Taiyuan (7 hr.; ¥140/$18/£9.10), where you'll need to transfer to a Pingyao service (2 hr.; ¥27/$3.50/£1.75).

GETTING AROUND   Trains and buses arrive at the Pingyao **railway station** in the "modern" city that is west of the ancient wall. The 7-minute ride by **bicycle rickshaw** to the old city is ¥2 to ¥10 (25¢–$1.30/15p–65p), depending on your negotiating skills. Taxis aren't allowed into the narrow streets of old Pingyao, so walk a short stretch or take a bicycle rickshaw. The better courtyard hotels will arrange free pickup with a taxi for people arriving on the morning train. Most of the courtyard hotels are in the vicinity of the Shi Lou (Market Building)—the tallest building in sight—at the center of the ancient town, on Nan Dajie (also called Ming Qing Jie).

The old town has only four main streets and a number of small lanes, so most places are within walking or biking distance. A ride on a motorcycle or bicycle rickshaw to places within the wall costs only a few yuan. A bicycle rickshaw that can accommodate two people can be hired for ¥40 ($5.20/£2.60) for a whole day. Several of the courtyard hotels rent bicycles for around ¥10 ($1.30/65p) per day. There's also **bike rental** at Xi Dajie 50 (near Bei Dajie). If you want to join the hordes you can also take a seat on one of the numerous electric buggies that circuit the main sites for ¥10 ($1.30/65p).

TOURS   Most of the courtyard hotels can arrange cars and buy bus and train tickets for a small fee.

FAST FACTS

Banks, Foreign Exchange & ATMs   None available, but many of the hotels will exchange major foreign currencies, including U.S. dollars, euros, and yen.

Internet Access   Internet cafes can be found throughout the old town, and in the dining and lobby areas of many courtyard hotels. They charge ¥6 (80¢/40p) per hour. Dial-up is ℂ 169.

Post Office   The old town's post office is at Xi Dajie 1 and is open from 8am to 6pm.

EXPLORING THE TOWN

The ancient town within the 6km-long (4-mile) city wall is ideal for walking. Take your map, head in any direction, and you're bound to find traditional architectural and cultural gems. Indeed, the town's charm is most alive away from the tourist crowds at the main sights. On the way, you'll get to see how some of the 30,000 current residents of Pingyao live. While in the past tickets had to be purchased separately for each site, visitors must now buy a 2-day pass for ¥120 ($16/£7.80) that allows entrance to the town's 20 most popular sites. These sites are open from 8am to 6pm in the summer. A few lesser-known sites in town still require a separate ticket.

A good first stop is the three-story **Shi Lou (Market Building)** that marks the city center and affords the best view of the old town. The well-preserved Ming dynasty **ancient city wall** *(gu chengqiang),* made of rammed earth and bricks, also affords views of the old city and outlying areas. It takes about an hour to walk the circumference of the wall. Near the center of town, **Ri Sheng Chang** and **Bai Chuan Tong**— headquarters of two of 19th-century China's leading money exchanges—are reminders that this remote town was once the financial center of the Qing government. Both compounds have been transformed into museums that look much more like elegant courtyard residences than banks. Restored and rebuilt, Ri Sheng Chang (Xi Dajie 38) is an engaging museum consisting of three courtyards and almost two dozen halls and rooms. Bai Chuan Tong (Nan Dajie 109) is now a furniture museum consisting of bedrooms, parlors, a kitchen, and a room for taking snuff (and probably opium)—all furnished and decorated in Ming and Qing styles.

A few blocks southeast of the Market Building on Chenghuang Miao Jie are three Daoist temples in one, the **Chenghuang Miao, Caishen Miao,** and **Zaojun Miao,** honoring the City God, the God of Wealth, and the Kitchen God. The separate but connected buildings are meant to imitate the arrangement of the government seat and its offices. Start at the Temple of the City God. At the back, where scriptures would normally be, the walls have *trompe l'oeil* murals of bookshelves filled with books and scrolls. Turn right (east) to get to the Kitchen God Temple. To get to the less obvious Temple of the God of Wealth, go to the back of the first temple and take the door to the left (west). This Ming dynasty complex burned down twice and was last rebuilt in 1864. Follow Chenghuang Miao Jie west (where it becomes Zhengfu Jie) to visit the **Xianya Shu** (or Yamen). This was the administrative office that meted out justice, such as it was, during the Ming and Qing dynasties. On the east side, there was a summoning drum *(dengwen gu)*. When someone had a complaint, they beat the drum to call for the Yamen chief, who would then hear the case and make his judgment. You may catch performers in rehearsal for operas and reenactments of trials that are performed here at select times throughout the week. A fine example of a wealthy urban residence, the former home of pioneering banker Lei Lutai, **Lei Lutai Guju,** Shuyuan Jie, is also worth a visit for its four rows of connecting courtyards, each in a different style. In the front courtyard, a "certified fortuneteller" reads hands, faces, and astrological charts—alas, only in Chinese.

A Buddhist temple (open 8am–6pm; ¥20/$2.60/£1.30) within biking or driving distance of Pingyao is **Zhenguo Si,** 12km (7½ miles) northeast of the old town. Its **Wanfo Dian (Palace of Ten Thousand Buddhas),** from the Tang dynasty, is another of China's oldest timber-frame buildings. Inside, its impressive statuary dates to the Five Dynasties (907–60). One of the pleasures of this less-visited temple is its tranquil atmosphere, due in part to an absence of touts and souvenir stalls.

OUT OF TOWN

Qiao Jia Dayuan 🐸🐸   This is the best-known of Shanxi's merchant-family mansions *(dayuan,* or "grand courtyards"), and where Zhang Yimou's *Raise the Red Lantern* was filmed. Almost midway between Taiyuan and Pingyao, it is easily reached from either city. Containing six large courtyards and 313 houses, the compound was constructed in 1755 by Qiao Guifa, the first member of the family to strike it rich selling tea and bean curd in Baotou, beyond the Great Wall. Returning to his hometown, he built his dream home, to which successive generations added until it reached its present size. Give yourself at least 2 hours.

Admission ¥40 ($5.20/£2.60). 8am–7:30pm (to 6pm in winter). Avoid weekends. Buses between Pingyao and Taiyuan will drop you off. Follow signs to Qiao Family Courtyard (10-min. walk). Round-trip taxi 40 min. from Pingyao, 45 min. from midtown Taiyuan, is ¥150–¥200 ($20–$26/£9.75–£13).

Shuanglin Si 🐸   This Buddhist temple is 6km (4 miles) southwest of Pingyao and easily reached by bicycle, motor-rickshaw (¥20–¥30/$2.60–$3.90/£1.30–£1.95 round-trip), or taxi ¥50 ($6.50/£3.25). Built in the 6th century, the complex underwent large-scale renovations during the Ming dynasty. It is most famous for the 2,000-plus painted statues distributed among 10 halls in three connected courtyards. Highlights include the arhats in **Tianwang Dian.** Princely and dignified, they are a refreshing change from the usual gilded, grotesque variety. Statues of worshipers depict commoners in everyday dress looking humble and devout and nothing like the serene, finely clad bodhisattvas nearby. In the **Pusa Dian (Bodhisattva Palace),** which contains a thousand-armed Guanyin, look up at the ceiling where the green, three-clawed, round-bellied figure of a guard keeps watch.

Qiaotou Cun. Admission ¥25 ($3.25/£1.65). 8am–6pm (8:30am–5pm winter).

Wang Family Courtyard (Wang Jia Dayuan) 🐸🐸   Sixty kilometers (37 miles) south of Pingyao, this *dayuan* dwarfs the Qiao family's mansion. First constructed in the mid–17th century, its expansion continued for over a century. Walking through the 123 courtyards and 1,118 houses takes around 3 hours, but the time is well spent. The decorative lattice screens and windows, shaped openings between rooms and courtyards, and undulating partition walls are exquisite examples of Ming and Qing vernacular architecture. Rarely are so many classic styles found all in one place. Also of note and well worth looking for are the cave dwellings at the compound's periphery.

Admission ¥66 ($8.60/£4.30). 8am–7:30pm (to 6pm in winter). Buses connect Taiyuan and Pingyao to the town nearest Wang Jia Dayuan, Lingshi Cheng. Buses between Lingshi Cheng and Wang Jia Dayuan leave every 10 min. and cost ¥1 (15¢/5p). Round-trip taxi from Pingyao is ¥200 ($26/£13).

Yi Yuan (Grace Vineyard) ★★ *Finds*   This Hong Kong–Chinese joint venture winery, which is run by a French wine master, produces probably the best wine in China—but it's exported to Europe. This countryside winery, about 90 minutes from Pingyao on the road to Taiyuan, is a pleasant place to visit. You can sample some of the excellent wine, examine the state-of-the-art production facilities, and walk through the vineyard and adjoining fruit orchards.

Free admission. Round-trip private taxi (¥300/$39/£20) can be arranged through the Tian Yuan Kui hotel listed below.

WHERE TO STAY

There are now many courtyard hotels within the old town, and more opening every day. Prices vary and bargaining is expected. Standard and deluxe rooms are decorated in Qing style and have large *kang* heated brick beds and small modern bathrooms. Budget rooms have conventional beds and less traditional ornamentation. Some of the better guesthouses now accept foreign credit cards as well as exchanging major foreign currencies. Most, including the two guesthouses recommended here, have bike rentals for around ¥10 ($1.30/65p) per day.

Deju Yuan ★★   A gracious host, excellent cooking, and attention to decor make this—along with Tian Yuan Kui (below)—one of the top two courtyard guesthouses in town. Attractive standard rooms come with large *kang* beds. A three-room suite has two bedrooms connected by a living room and is ideal for families. Bathrooms are slightly bigger than those elsewhere in town.

Xi Dajie 43. © 0354/568-5266. Fax 0354/568-5366. www.pydjy.com. 19 units. ¥158–¥368 ($21–$48/£10–£24) small to large standard rooms; ¥488 ($63/£32) suite. 20% discount Nov–Mar. V. **Amenities:** Restaurant; ticketing; free transport from railway station; laundry. *In room:* A/C, TV.

Tian Yuan Kui ★★   Like Deju Yuan, this appealing courtyard guesthouse, which opened in 2000, gets a mix of Chinese, European, and North American guests. Aware of growing competition, its savvy proprietors have continually renovated and added services and facilities to keep ahead of the pack. In 2003 the guesthouse added Internet access in the cafe. Rooms come in a variety of shapes and sizes, and prices vary accordingly; check out a few before you choose. In summer Shanxi opera performances (*Jin ju*) can be arranged for ¥300 to ¥500 ($39–$65/£20–£33).

Nan Dajie (Ming Qing Jie) 73. © 0354/568-0069. Fax 0354/568-3052. www.pytyk.com. 25 units. ¥100–¥400 ($13–$52/£6.50–£26) standard room. No credit cards. **Amenities:** Restaurant; ticketing; free transport from railway station; laundry/dry cleaning; Internet access. *In room:* A/C, TV.

WHERE TO DINE

Most Pingyao restaurants specialize in Shanxi and local cuisine, which emphasize wheat pastas, meat pies, Pingyao beef (similar to corned beef in color and taste), and fried cakes and breads. Two of the best restaurants in town are in the recommended **Deju Yuan** and **Tian Yuan Kui** guesthouses. Dinner for two costs ¥30 to ¥50

($3.90–$6.50/£1.95–£3.25). Nearly every restaurant in town serves a version of *lao-lao youmian* (sometimes called *wowo*). These small rings of husked-oat pasta are served pressed together in a bamboo steamer. The sauce that accompanies the dish varies from place to place, but Deju Yuan serves one of the best. The pasta is so substantial that it almost tastes like cornmeal, while the tomato-based sauce—flavorful and slightly hot—is reminiscent of a light tamale sauce. *Xiangsu ji* (crispy aromatic chicken) is also highly recommended, as is the lightly sweet *youzha gao* (crispy puff with date and red bean paste). Try corned beef with potatoes *(tudou shao niurou)* at Tian Yuan Kui; or try any of their numerous noodle dishes, made from husked oat, yellow bean, or sorghum flour. Most famous is the pasta shaped like little cats' ears *(mao erduo)*. Both restaurants also serve excellent Western breakfasts, including delicious omelets and fruit crepes. For a drink or dessert, try the **Sakura Cafe**, located on the corner of Xi Dajie and Nan Dajie; it has other branches throughout China, and even one in Laos.

In the lanes, look for the **mobile stand** selling "beggar's" chicken *(jiaohua ji)*. The chicken is wrapped in two layers of paper, then packed in loess mud ("yellow earth") and cooked over an open fire for 2 hours.

PINGYAO AFTER DARK

As well as the growing collection of bars along Xi Dajie, Pingyao now has a "cultural show," the **Wild Jujubes Dance Drama,** which is held at the Yunjicheng Performance Center. Like Liu Sanjie in Yangshuo, the show tells a local love story (coined "the Chinese Romeo and Juliet") in truly dramatic fashion, complete with a huge cast and state-of-the-art lighting. It's not everyone's cup of tea, especially as seats cost ¥288 to ¥388 ($37–$50/£19–£25). Tickets can be arranged through most guesthouses or by calling ✆ **0354/568-9280.**

6 Taiyuan

Shanxi Province, 500km (310 miles) SW of Beijing, 651km (405 miles) NE of Xi'an

During the 77 years of disunion that followed the collapse of the Tang dynasty, northern China was up for grabs by the various kingdoms that came to be known as the Five Dynasties (907–60). Each laid claim to Taiyuan (then called Jinyang) until the first emperor of the Song dynasty (960–1279) stepped in and annihilated the city, going so far as to divert the Fen River so that it would wash away any evidence that Jinyang ever existed. Modern Taiyuan—the capital of Shanxi Province—is located on the site of the rebuilt city.

Today things are more tranquil, but not necessarily better for your health. A 1999 report found this sooty industrial city to be the most polluted in the country and city officials, shamed into action, began to take strides toward cleanup. At press time, the main road, Yingze Dajie, was being widened, disrupting traffic and making much of the city resemble a building site. The new Shanxi Museum is definitely worth a visit and by the time you get here the roadwork should be finished, but still you may want to limit your stay in this environmentally challenged city to a day or two at most.

ESSENTIALS

GETTING THERE   Wusu Airport is 15km (9 miles) southeast of town. Useful connections include flights from Hong Kong (two flights weekly), Beijing (several flights daily), Shanghai (one or two flights daily), and Xi'an (four flights daily). **China**

Eastern Airlines runs an airport shuttle bus from its office at Yingze Dajie 158, 2 hours before flights; shuttle fare is ¥10 ($1.30/65p).

The main **railway station** is on the east side of town at the start of Yingze Dajie. There are plenty of connections with Beijing; the K604 leaves at 8:46pm and arrives in the capital at 6:39am the following morning. The fastest train to Datong is the N266, which leaves at 8:19am and takes a little over 5 hours. Pingyao is served by several daily trains on the Taiyuan-Yuncheng route (2 hr.). Of the services to Xi'an, the 2535 is the most convenient, although it's a slow train, leaving at 6:12pm and arriving at 7:45am.

Most long-distance buses connect with Taiyuan's **Main Bus Station (Qichezhan)** west of the railway station, but Wutai Shan (4 hr.; ¥57/$7.40/£3.70), is served from the shiny new easterly Dong Kezhan, while Pingyao (2 hr.; ¥27/$3.50/£1.75) buses leave from the Jian Nan station. Luxury buses link Taiyuan's Main Bus Station with Beijing's Lize Qiao Bus Station (7 hr.; ¥140/$18/£9.10) and Datong (4 hr.; ¥68/$8.85/£4.40).

GETTING AROUND   City **bus** fare is ¥1 (15¢/10p); with air-conditioning, the fare is ¥2 (25¢/15p). The most common **taxi** is the Fukang. The fare for the first 3km (2½ miles) is ¥8 ($1.05/50p); after that it's ¥1.10 (15¢/10p) per kilometer. Beyond 10km (6¼ miles), it's ¥1.60 (20¢/10p) per kilometer.

TOURS   A helpful branch of **CITS** is at Pingyang Lu 38 (© 0351/882-2777).

FAST FACTS

Banks, Foreign Exchange & ATMs   The **Bank of China** (open Mon–Fri 8am–5:30pm) at Yingze Dajie 288 has an ATM and full foreign-exchange facilities.

Internet Access   There's a small 24-hour *wangba* at Shangma Jie 54, on the way to Chongshan Si. It charges ¥2 (25¢/15p) per hour. The **Xinyi Wangba,** with the same hours and rates, is just around the corner at Shangma Jie 20. Enter through a courtyard with grapevines. Internet dial-up is © 169.

Post Office   The main post office (Mon–Fri 8am–7:30pm) is opposite the railway station.

Visa Extensions   The **PSB** is at Houjia Xiang 9 (© 0351/461-2787; open Mon–Fri 8:15–11:45am and 2:45–5:45pm).

EXPLORING TAIYUAN

The new provincial museum (see below) has superceded the collections to be found at the Daoist temple Chunyang Gong and the former Confucian temple Wen Miao; nevertheless, both are still worth visiting for the tranquil escape from the mean streets of Taiyuan. **Chunyang Gong** (Qifeng Jie 1, around the block from KFC) is dedicated to Lu Dongbin, the Tang dynasty poet, calligrapher, and wine connoisseur who, by the time of the Song dynasty, was worshiped as one of the Eight Immortals of Daoism. He's usually depicted as an impassive scholar with two long wisps of mustache and a thin pointed beard, holding a double-edged sword given to him by a dragon. The main hall is the **Lu Zu Dian,** which is dedicated to him. The temple is open from 9am to 5:30pm; admission is ¥10 ($1.30/65p). The grounds of the **Confucian Temple (Wen Miao)** on Shangguan Xiang have gardens and covered walkways, making this a pleasant place to amble, and there's also a handicrafts collection (from the Ming and Qing dynasties) including paper cuttings, traditional dress, jewelry, and jade work. Hours are from 9am to 5pm. Admission is ¥5 (65¢/35p).

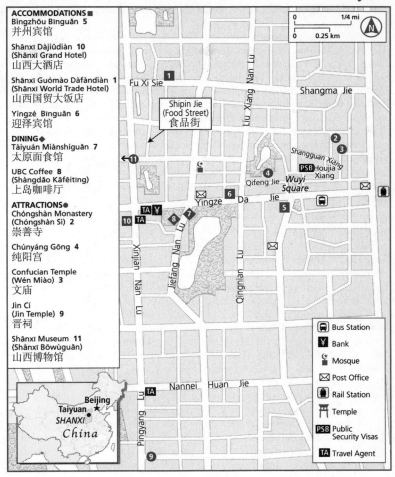

Taiyuan

ACCOMMODATIONS ■

Bìngzhōu Bīnguǎn **5**
并州宾馆

Shānxī Dàjiǔdiàn **10**
(Shānxī Grand Hotel)
山西大酒店

Shānxī Guómào Dàfàndiàn **1**
(Shānxī World Trade Hotel)
山西国贸大饭店

Yíngzé Bīnguǎn **6**
迎泽宾馆

DINING ◆

Tàiyuán Miànshíguǎn **7**
太原面食馆

UBC Coffee **8**
(Shàngdǎo Kāfēitīng)
上岛咖啡厅

ATTRACTIONS ●

Chóngshàn Monastery
(Chóngshàn Sì) **2**
崇善寺

Chúnyáng Gōng **4**
纯阳宫

Confucian Temple
(Wén Miào) **3**
文庙

Jìn Cí
(Jin Temple) **9**
晋祠

Shānxī Museum **11**
(Shānxī Bówùguǎn)
山西博物馆

Bus Station
Bank
Mosque
Post Office
Rail Station
Temple
PSB Public Security Visas
TA Travel Agent

Fu Xi Sie
Shipin Jie (Food Street) 食品街
Shangma Jie
Liu Xiang Nan Lu
Shangguan Xiang
PSB Houjia Xiang
Qifeng Jie
Wuyi Square
Yingze Da Jie
Xinjian Nan Lu
Jiefang Nan Lu
Qingnian Lu
Nannei Huan Jie
Pingyang Lu

Beijing
Taiyuan ★
SHANXI
China

Shanxi Museum (Shanxi Bowuguan) ★★ The imposing new Shanxi Museum opened west of the Fen River in September 2005 and proudly reinforces the province's status as the cradle of Chinese civilization. The first floor has some interesting photographs of the various excavated sites around the province, while the second floor details Shanxi's history from earliest times through to the Jin dynasty. Along with the seemingly obligatory ridiculous caveman models, sections on Neolithic and Paleolithic history have some genuine finds such as arrowheads, flints, and teeth. Excavations at Taosi walled town have helped further convince historians that the town was the legendary capital of Yao, and there are jade and lacquer items from the site on display. The best displays on this floor, though, are the articles discovered in Minister Zhao's tomb, which include enormous bronze cauldrons, bells, stone chimes, and a life-size chariot. The wealth of treasures found in this tomb and the 10,000 articles retrieved from the Marquis of Jin's tombs are indicative of the rising power of the Jin at that time.

The third floor is another winner and offers an exquisite collection of Buddhist statuary and stelae from around the province. The statues are tastefully set into alcoves in the mock-adobe walls, and the lighting is subtle yet clearly defines the fine craftsmanship of the stone carving. The fourth floor holds a series of collections including the standard coins and currency, and calligraphy and painting, along with some beautiful Buddhist frescoes and fine jade pieces. There's also a display of Shanxi architectural splendor, which includes some beautifully detailed roof ornaments and models of some of the province's most famous buildings. However, it seems that the powers that be ran out of time, energy, or translators: While floors two and three have detailed English captions, the fourth floor has only the most cursory of introductions in English. English audio guides are planned for the future. Allow a couple of hours for a visit.

Binhe Xi Lu. 🕐 0351/878-9222. Admission ¥20 ($2.60/£1.30). 9am–5pm (closed the 15th and 30th of every month). Taxi from the center of town costs ¥10–¥12 ($1.30–$1.55/65p–80p).

OUT OF TOWN

Jin Ci (Jin Temple) 🐾🐾   The site of Jin Ci is a large park with gardens and a lake, as well as pavilions, halls, and temples from various dynasties, beginning with the Song (960–1279). It isn't known when the original temple was built, but the earliest written reference to Jin Ci is from the 6th century. As you stroll the grounds, the one building that must not be overlooked is **Shengmu Dian (Hall of the Holy Mother).** Located at the back of the park, it is recognizable by its double-eaved roof and its extraordinary writhing dragons, each carved out of wood and coiled around one of the building's eight front columns. First completed in 1032, the hall was restored several times—most recently in the Ming dynasty—but without ever altering the original architectural style and design. Today, along with a handful of other Shanxi buildings, it is one of the earliest surviving wooden halls in China.

The contents of the hall are equally impressive. Inside is a statue of the honored matriarch—the mother of the founder of Jin—surrounded by a retinue of life-size handmaidens, actresses, and eunuchs. Dating from the Song, these gorgeous painted clay figures reveal much about court customs and dress. Sitting in lotus position, the Holy Mother is the picture of composure. Standing third in attendance on her right is a eunuch with one ear bigger than the other and one eye crossed—from listening intently to his mistress while never daring to look at her directly. Some of the actresses are dressed as male characters, evident from their stances—toes pointed outwards—and flat-topped headdresses.

Directly opposite the Hall of the Holy Mother, across the **Flying Bridge Over the Fish Pond (Yuzhao Feiliang),** is the **Xian Dian (Hall of Offerings),** where offerings were made to the Holy Mother, believed to have magic powers. Built in 1168 and rebuilt 400 years later, the hall was last restored in 1955.

Admission ¥40 ($5.20/£2.60). Summer 8am–6:30pm; winter 8:30am–5:30pm. Bus: no. 804 (¥2/25¢/15p) from railway station or on Xinjian Nan Lu, just south of Yingze intersection in front of the Industrial and Commercial Bank. On arrival, motorcycle-taxi drivers may try to convince you that the distance to the temple is too far to walk; in fact, it's a short (10-min.) walk through the park. Cross the parking lot and go through a small film-and-map store to the park entrance on the other side.

WHERE TO STAY

Most of Taiyuan's accommodations options lie along or near Yingze Dajie Yingze Dajie. While there are plenty of upscale and midrange options, budget choices are more limited. If you don't want to spend too much, the cheaper rooms at the Yingze are an option, but the best choice is the recently renovated rooms in the West Wing of the **Bingzhou Binguan** (② 0351/822-6139). The hotel is on the southwest corner of Wuyi Square; rooms cost around ¥200 ($26/£13).

Shanxi Dajiudian (Shanxi Grand Hotel) Plush sofas, high-ceilinged guest rooms, quality bathrooms, and business suites featuring computers with Internet access make this four-star hotel a good choice, although the rooms at the Yingze Binguan are larger.

Xinjian Nan Lu 5. ② 0351/882-9999. Fax 0351/404-3525. 166 units. ¥680 ($88/£44) standard room; from ¥1,580 ($205/£103) suite. Most rates include breakfast. 10% discount available. 15% service charge. AE, DC, MC, V. Bus: no. 1 from railway station. **Amenities:** 2 restaurants; bar; indoor pool; health club; sauna; in-room massage; ticketing; airport shuttle; business center; forex; ATM in lobby; limited room service; laundry/dry cleaning. *In room:* A/C, satellite TV, dataport, minibar, fridge, hair dryer, safe.

Shanxi Guomao Dafandian (Shanxi World Trade Hotel) This is Taiyuan's first five-star hotel, and while the lobby is grand, and the rooms quite spacious and comfortable, the service is still a bit rough around the edges for an expensive hotel. That said, this is the most comfortable and modern hotel in the city, with facilities and amenities that can be found in most five-star international hotels.

FuXi Jie. ② 0351/868-8888. Fax 0351/868-9888. www.sxwtc.com. 398 units. ¥810 ($105/£53) standard room; ¥1,290 ($168/£84) deluxe. Discount available. AE, DC, MC, V. **Amenities:** 4 restaurants; bar; indoor pool; fitness center; sauna; ticketing; business center; forex; limited room service; laundry/dry cleaning. *In room:* A/C, satellite TV, dataport (select floors), minibar, fridge, hair dryer, safe.

Yingze Binguan ⊛ This pleasant hotel has a recently renovated four-star (west) and an older two-star (east) wing, and is conveniently located less than 3km (2 miles) south of the railway station. Management and staff go out of their way to meet guests' needs, and the business center's post office is convenient and reliable. Guest rooms in the east wing are the standard issue (two beds, two chairs, and coffee table) but are clean and well maintained, although the bathrooms are a little shabby. The west wing offers decidedly more luxury and features spacious, thick carpeted rooms, some of which have computers.

Yingze Dajie 189. ② 0351/882-8888. Fax 0351/882-6688. book@shanxiyingzehotel.com. 457 units. West wing ¥1,180 ($153/£77) standard room; from ¥2,200 ($286/£143) suite. East wing ¥190 ($25/£12) standard room. Up to 40% discount available in west wing. AE, DC, MC, V. Bus: no. 1 or 6 from railway station. **Amenities:** 3 restaurants; bar; fitness center; sauna; ticketing; business center; forex; room service; laundry/dry cleaning. *In room:* A/C, satellite TV, broadband Internet access, minibar, fridge, hair dryer, safe.

WHERE TO DINE

Shanxi cuisine is famous for its buckwheat, sorghum, bean, and potato-flour pastas—all currently enjoying increased popularity in China—as well as for its vinegar *(cu)*. A favorite dish that employs potato-flour noodles, vinegar, soy sauce, and spring onion is *liangfen*. Served cold, the dish is particularly refreshing on muggy summer evenings. Like Italian pastas, *cuojianer* (twisted points), *mao erduo* (cats' ears), and a variety of others are named for their shapes. Two winter specialties are Shanxi beef or lamb hot pot *(huoguo)* and—for breakfast—mutton soup *(tounao)*. Made with fatty mutton, yam, lotus, and herbs (to mask the gamy taste), it goes well with the flatbread called *xiaobing* and fortifies you against the winter cold.

The best place to get these local specialties is at the Shipin Jie **night market,** parallel and west of Jiefang Lu, which is lined with some small stands and a number of restaurants serving local specialties and various other Chinese cuisines.

For fast food, **McDonald's** is on the southeast corner of Wuyi Square; it's open from 7am to midnight. **KFC** is on the corner of Liuxiang Nan Lu and Yingze Dajie and elsewhere around the city. For a decent cup of coffee and passable pizza, sandwiches, steak, and spaghetti, there's a branch of **UBC Coffee (Shangdao Kafeiting)** on Jiefang Lu, just south of Yingze Dajie. For snacks and supplies, the **Meet All supermarket** on the northeast corner of Wuyi Square has a good range of products.

Taiyuan Mianshiguan 🍴 (*Value* SHANXI   This excellent restaurant serves typical Shanxi dishes. Try *guoyou rou* (pork "passed through oil"), *mao erduo* (cats' ears), actually small triangles of dough served in a soup or fried with meat and vegetables, *liangfen,* a cold potato-flour noodle dressed in vinegar and soy sauce, and other local dishes. The restaurant, which has two large levels, is bright and very clean, and is popular with businesspeople and upper-middle-class Chinese.

Jiefang Lu 17. (*C*) **0351/404-1881.** Meal for 2 ¥25–¥40 ($3.30–$5.20/£1.65–£2.60). No credit cards. 11am–3pm and 5:30–9:30pm.

7 Wutai Shan ⟨★⟩

Shanxi Province, 327km (203 miles) SW of Beijing, 210km (130 miles) S of Datong, 238km (148 miles) N of Taiyuan

The mountain known as Wutai or "Five Platforms" is actually a cluster of mountains, which long ago collectively became the northernmost sacred peak of Buddhism. Situated roughly halfway between Datong and Taiyuan, Wutai Shan is, in Buddhist lore, the earthly residence of the great bodhisattva Manjusri. Often depicted astride a lion, he is said to embody the perfection of wisdom. To this day, though tourists far outnumber them, pilgrims come entreating Manjusri to reveal himself again. The peaks of Wutai Shan have an average height of 2,000m (6,561 ft.) above sea level, and from northeast to southwest they stretch 120km (75 miles). Cradled at their center is the small town of Taihuai Zhen, with an elevation of 1,680m (5,500 ft.). Part tourist slum, part sacred site, the town is a combination of souvenir shops, restaurants, temples, and shrines. Summer is the best time to visit—when Wutai Shan offers an escape from the heat and humidity of lower climes. In July and August, the average temperature is only about 50°F (10°C), with warm days and cool nights. Even at this most temperate time of year, the mountain itself is rarely overcrowded during the week. Weekends are another story, and national holidays should be avoided at all costs. Winters are severely cold, with temperatures dipping as low as –40°F (–40°C). Even in June, snow is not unheard of.

One of the liveliest of Wutai's temple festivals is held on the 14th and 15th days of the sixth lunar month, when demons are exorcised and the Diamond Sutra is honored in a ritual dance. All who join the parade from Pusa Ding to Luohan Temple are promised blessings. ***Note:*** Turn to appendix A for Chinese translations of key locations.

ESSENTIALS

GETTING THERE   Most visitors arrive by bus from Taiyuan to the south or Datong to the north. Wutai Shan has no airport. The Wutai Shan **railway station** is in Shahe, 48km (30 miles) and an hour-plus drive from Taihuai. There are daily fast trains to and from Beijing and Taiyuan (4 hr.) on the Beijing-Taiyuan line (K702/701). **Buses** between Shahe Railway Station and Taihuai Zhongxin Tingche Station leave regularly throughout the day for ¥20 ($2.60/£1.30). A **taxi** between Shahe and Taihuai is around ¥150 ($20/£9.75). Allow 2 hours if you're catching a train in Shahe. There are daily buses connecting Taihuai with Taiyuan (4 hr.; ¥57/ $7.40/£3.70), Datong (5 hr.; ¥60/$7.80/£3.90), and Beijing (6 hr.; ¥131/$17/£8.50). Buses drive into Taihuai and will drop you at your hotel if you know where you're staying. The bus station is in the south of town. The ticket office opens at 5:30am. Buses to Datong leave from various small hotels on the main street beginning around 6am. If you'd rather not have to wave one down, ask your hotel or a CITS branch to arrange hotel pickup (no service fee). In summer only, a direct bus to Hohhot leaves daily at 7am from Yingfang Street (8 hr.; ¥85/$11/£5.55).

Admission to the Wutai Shan area is ¥90 ($12/£5.85). All vehicles are stopped at the gate while an attendant collects money and passengers grumble about government corruption and the latest price hike.

GETTING AROUND   The town of Taihuai runs along the valley nestled between the peaks of Wutai Shan and is small enough to cover on foot in under an hour. The main street (Taihuai Jie/Yingfang Jie) runs north-south along the Qingshui River. Minivans trawl the stretch from town to the area in the south where the best hotels are, picking up passengers for a few yuan. The mountains rise to the immediate east, while two small streets running west off the main street lead to Taihuai's temple area. Although the streets have names, nobody uses them; even maps dispense with them. Directions to anyplace begin with the name of the nearest temple, many of which can be reached on foot. East of the village a cable car goes up to **Dailou Peak** (¥35/$4.55/ £2.30 one-way; ¥65/$8.45/£4.25 round-trip). Alternatively you can walk there in under an hour, or ride a horse for ¥30 ($3.90/£1.95); ¥55 ($7.15/£3.60) round-trip.

TOURS   Tour buses and taxis go to the mountain temples from the **Wutai Shan Tour Taxi Ticket Office (Wutai Shan Luyou Che Chuzu)** on Yingfang Street (across from the White Pagoda and the parking lot/night market). Buses carry 15 passengers and don't set out until they're full. They charge ¥10 ($1.30/65p) per person per temple. Taxis can take up to four passengers and charge ¥200 ($26/£13) for a 6-hour tour visiting 10 temples. **CITS** has a number of generally unhelpful branch offices in Taihuai. The main office is at Ming Qing Jie 18 (© **0352/510-2265;** open 7:30am– 8pm). They don't have their own vehicles, but they will arrange a car, driver, and English-speaking guide for a full-day tour to the outlying temples for about ¥400 ($52/£26) for up to three people.

FAST FACTS

Banks, Foreign Exchange & ATMs   The **Bank of China** (open 8am–noon and 2:30–6:30pm; winter 8:30am–6pm), Yingfang Jie, only exchanges U.S. dollars; no traveler's checks. Restaurants will sometimes change foreign currency, but it's best to arrive with enough yuan for the duration of your stay.

Internet Access   Feiyu Diannao (8am–midnight; ¥4/50¢/25p per hour) is on the main street as you head south, just before the turnoff to the Friendship Hotel. Look for the ENGLISH INTERNET sign. There are several other Internet cafes in the area around the main street.

Post Office   The post office (8am–8pm; winter 8am–6pm) is on Yingfang Jie after it rounds the corner from the main street, half hidden by souvenir stalls. The entrance is up a staircase behind the stalls.

AROUND THE MOUNTAINS

One of the delights of Taihuai Village is the variety of people it attracts. Nuns, monks, and lamas from different orders and from all over China, Japan, Nepal, and Thailand come to Wutai Shan in the summer—some to climb the five terraces, others to simply take part in the many temple activities. The mountain also has a special religious significance for Tibetan Buddhists and so attracts Tibetan monks, nuns, and laypeople from all over China. Ask around and you will usually learn of some mass gathering in one or another of the temples. Alms meals *(dazhai)* for the nuns and monks (paid for by wealthy patrons to amass good karma) take place frequently all summer. Observers are welcome as long as you're quiet and very discreet with cameras.

TEMPLES IN TAIHUAI

There are close to a dozen temples in the small town of Taihuai Zhen. West of town, next to the bell tower, **Xiantong Si** is the largest and one of the oldest of the temples at Wutai Shan. It was first built in A.D. 68; the surviving halls date from the Ming and Qing dynasties. Climb the belfry for a commanding view of the town and mountains. Also be sure to visit the **Tong Dian (Bronze Hall),** which is lined with thousands of miniature statues said to symbolize the myriad bodhisattvas to whom Manjusri read the Buddhist scriptures while he lived on Wutai Shan. The bronze roof and outside structures are remarkable for their flawless imitation of timber construction and wood design.

A 5-minute walk south of Xiantong Si is **Tayuan Si,** easily recognized by its tall white pagoda which dominates Taihuai's skyline and has become the symbol of Wutai Shan. A smaller pagoda is said to contain strands of Manjusri's hair. Equally famed is the two-story **Sutra Library** in Tayuan Si. At its center is a revolving wooden bookcase that dates from the Ming dynasty. Now empty and unable to turn, it once held more than 20,000 volumes of Buddhist scriptures, written in Chinese, Mongolian, and Tibetan.

Admission to temples ¥3–¥6 (40¢–80¢/20p–40p). 7am–6pm or later.

MOUNTAIN TEMPLES

The temples on the mountains are generally of less note than those in town, but two of the most famous are **Nan Shan Si** and **Longquan Si.** The former is 2km (1¼ miles) south of Taihuai Zhen. Longquan Temple is another 2km (1¼ miles) in the same direction, so they are easily visited together and, within a few hours, can be done on foot. Like several of Wutai's temples, they claim 108 stairs leading to the entrance gate. Though none of them seem to have exactly that number, the point is that the steps represent the 108 worries (or delusions) of mankind. With each step a worry is cast off, so that by the time visitors reach the gate, you are cleansed with sweat and worry-free. A variation on the theme equates the silent and earnest counting of each stone stair with the meditative chanting of the Buddhist rosary (of 108 beads). With every step, the pilgrim has a chance to reach a pure land, free of temptations and defilements.

Founded in the Later Liang dynasty (907–23) and rebuilt in 1937 on seven terraced levels, Nan Shan Si is one of Wutai Shan's largest temples. Visitors come to see its 18 superb clay arhats (enlightened disciples) in the **Hall of the Great Buddha (Dafo Dian)**—the sleeping arhat is considered the best for its lifelike posture and craftsmanship. In the same hall, to the right of the large gilded Sakyamuni, look for the white marble statue of Avalokitesvara (Guanyin) holding a plump baby boy on her knee. Worshipers bring offerings to her in hopes of male offspring.

Located at the foot of Wutai Shan's central peak, Longquan Si or Dragon Spring Temple has three courtyards connected to one another by moon-shaped gates. The main halls can be found in the east courtyard. At the front, the **Hall of Celestial Kings (Tian Wang Dian)** houses, among others, the Buddha With a Cloth Sack (Budai Fo). This rotund Buddha with an exposed potbelly was a Tang dynasty monk who—with his walking stick and sack of worldly belongings—roamed from place to place carefree and begging. He had in his favor the gift of predicting the future and forecasting the weather, and was believed to be an incarnation of Maitreya, the Future Buddha. A purely Chinese creation, he only appears in temples built after the Ming dynasty (1368–1644). The stupa in the central courtyard contains the remains of Puji, the abbot of Nan Shan Temple who died in 1917 believing he, too, was an incarnation of Maitreya. The four images on the sides of the stupa are of Puji/Maitreya at different ages.

TEMPLES BELOW

Two of only three Tang dynasty (618–907) wooden buildings still standing in China—**Nanchan Si** and **Foguang Si**—are located between Wutai Shan and Taiyuan. With 120km (75 miles) separating them, visiting both in 1 day is best done en route from one town to the other rather than as a day trip from either point. Since both are also well off the main road, they aren't on the regular bus route. A taxi between Taiyuan and Taihuai Village that includes stops at both temples costs around ¥400 ($52/£26). A day trip from Taihuai Village to both temples and back costs ¥200 to ¥300 ($26–$39/£13–£20). Allow 6 to 7 hours for the round-trip. Buses to Taiyuan pass the turnoffs to these temples, and those with light luggage can hop off and negotiate with waiting taxis for each side trip.

Nanchan Si (Temple of Southern Meditation) ⍟

About 177km (110 miles) south of Wutai Shan, turning west off the main road to Taiyuan, a dusty loess road leads to this tranquil ancient temple. It's said that this temple escaped the great Tang persecution of Buddhism in 845 because it was so far from the assemblage of temples on Wutai Shan. Today, its small, perfectly proportioned main hall, **Dafo Dian (Hall of the Great Buddha),** is reason enough to make the trip. Built in 782, the wooden-frame building has been much restored, but—unlike the other halls in this complex, which are distinctly of Ming and Qing design—it has retained its original proportions and graceful Tang design. Features to notice are its gently sloping roof, markedly different from the steep gabled roofs of the previous Northern Wei and Sui dynasties. Along the main roof ridge, the pre-Ming ornaments that curl toward each other are called *chiwei,* meaning "owl tails." The word refers to a mythical sea monster—one of the sons of the dragon—believed to protect against fire. Inside the hall are 17 Tang dynasty painted clay statues stationed around the large figure of Sakyamuni. The large statue in the far left corner is Manjusri riding a lion.

Foguang Si (Temple of Buddha's Light) ⍟

The temple is 35km (22 miles) south of Taihuai Village. First built during the Northern Wei dynasty when Buddhism was the official religion, it had greatly expanded by the time it fell victim to the Tang anti-Buddhist campaign of 845. After its total destruction, it was rebuilt 12 years later with the help of a female benefactor named Ning Gongyu. The one hall associated with her, **Dong Dadian (Eastern Great Hall),** survives today. Like the Nanchan's Hall of the Great Buddha, it is the only Tang-style building amid a cluster of mostly Ming and Qing dynasty halls.

To get to the Eastern Great Hall, follow the cobblestone path through the first courtyard. This leads through a deep archway similar to a city-wall gate, followed by a steep stone staircase. The statues, calligraphy, and wall paintings within are from the Tang (618–907) and Song (960–1279) dynasties, while the 296 arhats (enlightened disciples) on either side—remainder of the original 500—date to the Ming. Note the more elaborate bracketing, double roofs, and ridge ornaments of this hall compared with the simple elegance of Nanchan Si.

SHOPPING

All manner of Buddhist art, clothing, and accouterments are sold in several small shops on and off the main street. Paintings on fabric *(tiaofu)* and religious scrolls sell for around ¥25 ($3.25/£1.65), while the biggest prayer beads you'll ever see cost a mere ¥20 ($2.60/£1.30).

WHERE TO STAY

Wutai Shan's best accommodation lies east of the river along Ming Qing Jie and farther south. There are a numerous small, very inexpensive hotels in the center of Taihuai Zhen, but cleanliness is a problem, so they're only for people traveling on a very tight budget. You'll be approached by hotel touts if you get off the long-distance bus in this part of town.

If you want to stay close to the restaurants and shops in town, try the **Chaoyang Binguan** (C 0350/654-5945), just below Xiantong Si, where you'll find passable rooms on the second floor for ¥100 to ¥120 ($13–$16/£6.50–£7.80). Alternatively, the **Jinjie Shanzhuang,** east of the river in the north of town, offers slightly better accommodations for ¥150 to ¥200 ($20–$26/£9.75–£13). High season is May through October, but even then hefty discounts are possible Monday through Thursday.

Qixiange Binguan ∕ε   Off the main road and next to the mountain, Qixiange has the best setting and is especially quiet and relaxing, though slightly far from town. The nicest rooms are in the Yedou 3 building, but the best views are in the Jinxiu building opposite, which is next to the mountain. Slightly smaller, the rooms are still comfortable, and they face a small mountain road favored by cycling teams for their daily workouts.

Off the main street, about 5km (3 miles) south of town. Look on the left for a small bridge that spans a stream. After crossing the bridge, continue for about 200m (650 ft.); hotel is on the left. C 0350/654-3475. Fax 0350/654-2183. 93 units. ¥380 ($49/£25) standard room; ¥898 ($117/£58) suite. Some rates include breakfast. 10%–20% discount available. No credit cards. **Amenities:** Restaurant; bar; gym; ticketing; business center; limited room service; laundry/dry cleaning. *In room:* TV, hair dryer.

Yinhai Shanzhuang   Built in the Qing style, this four-story complex, with its gray buildings, red trim, and bright green and gold roofs with upturned eaves, looks almost like another mountain temple. Mostly catering to tour groups, the hotel is a bit dark, but is probably the best hotel in Wutai Shan. For the best view, request a room facing south and the Nanchan Si, which is just a 20-minute walk away.

Xiao Nanpo Cun, on the main street, 3km (2 miles) south of town, opposite Nanchan Si. C 0350/654-3676. Fax 0350/654-2949. 80 units. ¥670 ($87/£44) standard room; ¥1,280 ($166/£83) suite. 30% discount sometimes available. No credit cards. **Amenities:** 2 restaurants; bar; ticketing; limited room service. *In room:* TV, hair dryer.

WHERE TO DINE

Wutaai Shan's main strip is lined by identical restaurants that mostly offer the same variety of bland Chinese staple dishes, so it's worth trying one of the decent vegetarian restaurants in town. For a change, **Xiaochen Hotpot (Xiaochen Huoguo),** just east off the northern part of Yingfang Jie, serves tasty and inexpensive *yuanyang huoguo* (yinyang hot pot).

Furen Ju Jiulou ♠ SHANXI   Serving everything from dog, deer, and donkey to delicious sesame paste with transparent green-pea noodles *(maajiang fenpi),* this clean, pleasant restaurant specializes in local dishes such as *da dun gutou* (seared pork ribs), *jiang men xiao tudou* (stewed baby potato with sesame paste), and *shao taaimo* (simmered wild mushrooms). A sandwich board with some English and photographs of many of the dishes takes the anxiety out of ordering.

Yingfang Jie (on the main street in the north part of town; just south of Guanghua Temple). ✆ 0350/654-5646. Meal for 2 ¥30–¥50 ($3.90–$6.50/£1.95–£3.25). No credit cards. 6am–11pm.

Jingxin Zhai ♠♠ VEGETARIAN   This restaurant has a worn look to it, but serves excellent vegetarian food. Try some of the following dishes as you listen to soft Buddhist chants being played over and over again: *iqi yaangyaang* (spicy mock chicken cubes fried with dried red peppers*)*, *luohan zhai* (traditional mixed vegetables fried with bean-starch noodles), *huakai xianfo* (mock ham on a bed of braised tofu), and *supaai* (deep-fried "meat" smothered with succulent brown sauce).

Just off the main street in the north part of town. ✆ 0350/654-5036. Meal for 2 ¥60–¥200 ($7.80–$26/£3.90–£13). No credit cards. 9am–2pm and 5–9pm.

Yizhan Mingdeng Quaansu Zhai ♠♠ VEGETARIAN   This pleasant restaurant serves delicious, reasonably priced vegetarian dishes that make it popular with local and visiting monks, nuns, and laypeople. Some of the excellent dishes here include *baaiguo naangua bao* (stewed gingko nut with pumpkin), *lancai roumo sijidou* (olive leaf fried with string beans), *huakai xianfo* (braised tofu in aromatic broth), *jinshang tianhua* ("shredded pork" with yuxiang flavor), and *tieban heijiao niupaai* (grilled "steak" with black-pepper sauce).

On the main street in the north part of town, just south of the taxi rental office. ✆ 0350/654-5674. Meal for 2 ¥40–¥80 ($5.20–$10/£2.60–£5.20). No credit cards. 7:30am–10:30pm.

The Silk Routes

by Simon Foster

China was first known in the West as Seres, the land of silk or serica. The Romans were entranced by this strong but delicate thread, and believed it was combed from trees. But it was also viewed as a decadent, effeminate luxury—for the appetite of Rome's better classes for silk was rarely sated, and without a luxury (other than glass) to export in return, silk imports emptied Rome's coffers. As a result, in A.D. 14 the Roman Senate forbade the wearing of silk by men, and Caligula, who was fond of diaphanous silk garments, was disparagingly referred to as Sericatus.

In Tang China, silk was the most important form of legal tender; taxes, fines, and officials' wages were all measured in bales of silk. Silk was used to buy off raiding armies of Uighurs and Tibetans and (it was hoped) make them a bit less barbaric.

The term "Silk Road," coined in the 19th century by German geographer Ferdinand von Richthofen, is both an evocative and misleading appellation. The trade routes that connected China and the West from the 1st century B.C. until the 10th century A.D. carried a whole inventory of luxuries and necessities beyond silk, from gold and jade to wool and rhubarb. Nor was the road traveled from end to end. Chinese merchants rarely went beyond the edges of the **Taklamakan Desert** before turning the goods over to Sogdian or Parthian caravans, who were left to face the forbidding

mountain passes of the Pamirs. Only devoted missionaries went farther, like the legendary monk Xuanzang, who spent 15 years traveling across India and central Asia in search of Buddhist sutras.

Silk was just one of many goods transported over these vast distances. Apricots, peaches, and pears reached the West, while China gained the fig tree and the grapevine. China imported spices, woolen fabrics, horses for military campaigns, and foreign novelties such as musical instruments, coral, colored glass, and jewels, which fascinated the courts. Traders also brought foreign ideas, and were soon followed by missionaries of many faiths. Nestorian Christianity, Zoroastrianism, Manichaeism, and, most significantly, Buddhism, were welcomed by a confident and cosmopolitan civilization. Doctrines and art spread eastward, leaving spectacular monuments in the cave temples of **Dunhuang, Mai Shan,** and **Kizil.**

The Silk Road wasn't one road at all, but a series of routes emanating from the capital of Chang'an. From Chang'an, camel trains would follow the Wei River west before branching into several different routes.

The southern route passed through **Dunhuang, Miran,** and **Khotan,** in the shadow of the mighty **Kunlun Shan,** whose meltwater streams fed thriving Buddhist communities. Intrepid travelers today, tolerant of bare-bones transportation and accommodations, can still

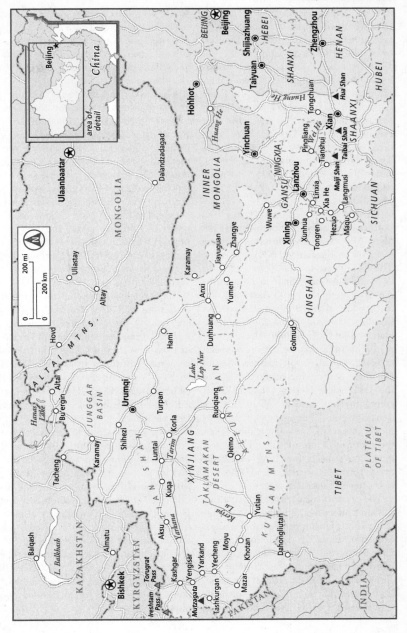

traverse the route, which will lead to bustling towns such as Khotan with ancient markets and traditions undisturbed by either tourism or modernization.

The middle route was initially (1st c. B.C.– 4th c. A.D.) popular, allowing merchants to float on barges down the Tarim River from the garrison town of Loulan to Korla and **Kuqa.** But when the river changed course, and Lop Nor Lake "wandered off," this route was abandoned. Thanks to more recent nuclear testing, which finally ended in 1996, this route will likely remain closed for the half-life of plutonium.

The northern routes, skirting the northern and southern foothills of **Tian Shan (the Heavenly Mountains),** were menaced by Kazakh and Kyrgyz bandits. The bandits are less of a problem these days, and most travelers follow the northern route along the He Xi corridor to the mighty fort of **Jiayu Guan,** the peerless Buddhist caves of Dunhuang, and the grape trellises of **Turpan.** Beyond, the road leads to fascinating oasis towns such as Kuqa, and the great market town of **Kashgar,** skirting the northern edge of the Taklamakan Desert. (Taklamakan is commonly translated as "go in and you don't come out," but in ancient Uighur it means "vineyard," evoking a time when the region was more fertile.) The desert dunes have been marching south for many years, threatening the oasis towns of the ancient southern route.

The present character of the Silk Road is Islamic rather than Buddhist. An exodus of the Turkic Uighur peoples from western Mongolia displaced the Indo-European inhabitants, the Tang dynasty fell, and Islam gradually spread east through the Tarim Basin. With the rise of sea trade, land routes fell into disuse. Settlements and temples (which also functioned as banks) were abandoned to the desert. They remained undisturbed until the turn of the 20th century, when archaeologists from Britain, France, Germany, Russia, Japan, and (later) America came searching for lost Buddhist kingdoms.

The adventurers saw the Han Chinese as fellow colonizers, keeping the Turkic Uighurs in their place. British diplomat Eric Teichman believed "the Turkis are a patient, contented and submissive people, made to be ruled by others." Xinjiang means "new territories," rather a giveaway in itself, but many Han guides will try to persuade you that this region has always belonged to China. Most Uighurs would prefer to rule themselves, and they still practice a form of Islam that is both tolerant and catholic, recalling a time when towns such as Kashgar were centers of Islamic learning.

Turkic Uighurs make up the majority of the population in Xinjiang, but they are gradually being displaced by a wave of migrants from the east. After an absence of over a millennium, Han Chinese are reasserting control over the Silk Routes with a ruthlessness that the Wudi emperor (reigned 141–87 B.C.)—the first ruler to control the Silk Routes—would have envied.

Travel along the Silk Routes has always been arduous, temperatures are extreme, the distances involved are considerable, and it's very dusty. Peak season is early May and mid-July to mid-October. Outside of Xi'an, Lanzhou, Dunhuang, and Urumqi, expect little in the way of luxurious lodgings. The more adventurous should seek out the Uighur trading centers of Kashgar, Khotan, and Kuqa, or the Tibetan monastic settlements of **Xia He** and **Langmu Si.** *Note:* Unless otherwise noted, hours listed for attractions and restaurants are daily.

1 Xi'an

Shanxi Province, 1,200km (744 miles) SW of Beijing

Surrounded by rich loess farmland, Xi'an (Western Peace), the present capital of Shanxi Province, was home to the ruling houses of the Qin, Han, Sui, and Tang dynasties, when it was known as Chang'an (Eternal Peace). The city reached a peak during the Tang dynasty (618–907), when it was the military and trading base for China's shaky control of the Silk Routes. During the Xuanzong reign of the Tang (712–55), Chang'an boasted two million taxable inhabitants and was the largest, most cosmopolitan settlement in the world.

The scale of the metropolis is readily imagined—what are now referred to as the city walls were rebuilt during the Ming dynasty (1644–1911) on the remains of Tang palace walls. The Tang city walls extended 8km (5 miles) north-south and almost 10km (6 miles) east-west, and the south gate opened onto a tree-lined avenue 150m (500 ft.) wide, down which foreign emissaries would once approach the metropolis. The Tang era was a high point for advocates of "foreign religions" as Manicheans, Nestorians, and Buddhists flocked to the capital. Buddhism in particular enjoyed royal patronage.

Surviving monuments open a window onto the imperial power and cosmopolitan style of the old capital. The short-lived totalitarian state of Qin Shi Huangdi is reflected in the awe-inspiring massed terra-cotta armies of the **Qin Bingmayong Bowuguan.** The influence of Buddhism is clear from the majestic spire of the **Da Yan Ta (Great Goose Pagoda),** constructed under the supervision of Xuanzang (d. 664), who returned to China in 645 after 15 years of travel across India and central Asia. Evidence of the flourishing trade along the Silk Routes may be found in the **Shanxi History Museum** and **Famen Si.**

Today, in spite of pollution, searing summer heat, and freezing winters, Xi'an is a joy to visit. The central city is pleasantly compact and its grid layout within the city walls makes it easy to navigate. There is enough to see in and around Xi'an to keep even the most energetic visitor busy for a week or two. It's the most-visited town on the Silk Routes, which brings the usual annoyances. Nevertheless, locals are easygoing and disparaging of their ancient capital, shaking their heads in regret that their ancestors "fell behind" their richer cousins in Beijing. However, the armies of Chinese tourists and foreign visitors, along with the legion of upscale new malls full of well-dressed shoppers let you know Xi'an's not that far behind.

ESSENTIALS

GETTING THERE Numerous direct **flights** connect Xianyang Airport with all major cities in China, including Beijing, Shanghai, Chongqing, Chengdu, Kunming, Urumqi, Lhasa, and Hong Kong. The **CAAC office,** located at Dongmen Wai, Shimao Dasha (✆ **029/8248-1111**), will deliver airline tickets free of charge. You can also book tickets through the ticketing agency on the ground floor of the Melody Hotel on Xi Dajie (✆ **029/8728-2615**). **Airport shuttle buses** (¥25/$3.25/£1.65) depart from the CAAC office and from outside the Melody Hotel on the hour from 6am to 7pm; aim to leave at least 2 hours before your flight. A **taxi** from the airport into town costs about ¥150 to ¥180 ($20–$23/£9.75–£12) dependent on the time of day.

The **railway station** is located outside the northeast side of the city wall, 20 minutes by double-decker bus no. 603 from the main hotel area. The station is open 24 hours, and window 4 should have an English-speaker. Ticket refunds can be obtained

Xi'an

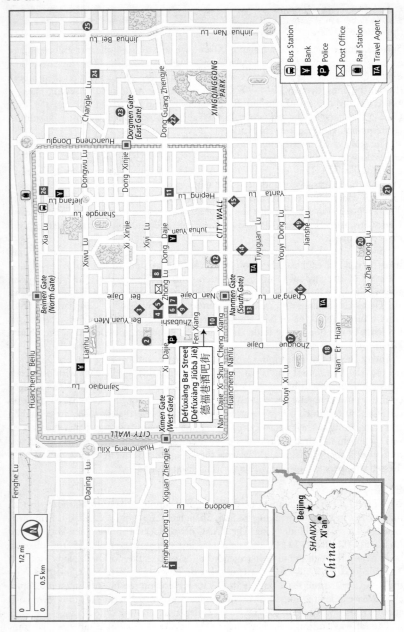

Legend:
- Bus Station
- ¥ Bank
- P Police
- Post Office
- Rail Station
- TA Travel Agent

Jinhua Bei Lu

Jinhua Nan Lu

Changle Lu

Dong Guang Zhengjie

XINGQINGGONG PARK

Dorgmen Gate (East Gate)

Dong Guang Zhengjie

Huancheng Donglu

Dong Xinjie

Dongwu Lu

Heping Lu

Yanta Lu

Shangde Lu

Xi Xinjie

Juhua Yuan

CITY WALL

Tiyuguan Lu

Youyi Dong Lu

Jianshe Lu

Xiyi Lu

Dong Dajie

Xia Zhai Dong Lu

Xia Lu

Xiwu Lu

Beimen Gate (North Gate)

Bei Dajie

Zhong Lu

Nan Dajie

Nanmen Gate (South Gate)

Chang'an Lu

Bei Yuan Men

Zhubashi

Fen Xiang

Lianhu Lu

Huancheng Beilu

Sanqiao Lu

Nan Dajie Xi Shun Cheng Xiang

Huancheng Nanlu

Zhouque Dajie

Nan Er Huan

Ximen Gate (West Gate)

Défuxiàng Bar Street (Défuxiàng Jiǔbā Jiē)
德福巷酒吧街

Youyi Xi Lu

Huancheng Xilu

CITY WALL

Fenghe Lu

Daqing Lu

Xiguan Zhengjie

Laodong Lu

Fenghao Dong Lu

1/2 mi

0.5 km

Beijing

SHANXI

Xi'an

China

ACCOMMODATIONS ■

Bell and Drum Hotel 4
(Zhōnggǔlóu Dàjiǔdiàn)
钟鼓楼大酒店

Bell Tower Hotel 7
(Zhōnglóu Fàndiàn)
钟楼饭店

Howard Johnson Ginwa Plaza Hotel 13
(Jīnhuā Háoshēng Guójì Dàjiǔdiàn)
金花豪生国际大酒店

Hyatt Regency Xī'ān
(Kǎiyuè Fàndiàn) 11
凯悦饭店

Jiěfàng Fàndiàn 26
解放饭店

Melody Hotel 6
(Měilún Jiǔdiàn)
美伦酒店

Shangri-La Golden Flower 24
(Jīnhuā Fàndiàn)
金花饭店

Sheraton Xī'ān
(Xǐláidēng Dàjiǔdiàn) 1
喜来登大酒店

Wǔyī Fàndiàn 8
(May First Hotel)
五一饭店

Xī'ān Shūyuàn Qīngnián Lǚshè 10
(Xī'ān Shūyuàn Youth Hostel)
西安书院青年旅社

ATTRACTIONS ●

Bànpō Bówùguǎn 25
(Bànpō Neolithic Village)
半坡博物馆

Bā Xiān Ān 23
(Temple of the Eight Immortals)
八仙庵

Běilín Bówùguǎn 12
(Forest of Stelae)
碑林博物馆

Dà Qīngzhēnsì 2
(Great Mosque)
大清真寺

Dà Yàn Tǎ 21
(Great Goose Pagoda)
大雁塔

Shǎnxī Lìshǐ Bówùguǎn 20
(Shǎnxī History Museum)
陕西历史博物馆

Small Goose Pagoda 17
(Xiǎo Yàn Tǎ)
小雁塔

Xī'ān Gǔwán Chéng 18
西安古玩城

DINING ◆

Dé Fā Chāng 5
德发昌

Fánjì Làzhī Ròudiàn 9
樊记腊汁肉店

Highfly Pizza 15
(Gāofēi Bǐsà)
高飞比萨

Jiǎsān Guàntāng Bāozi 3
贾三灌汤包子

Lǎ Sūn Jiā 22
老孙家

Shǎnxī Grand Opera House 14
(Shǎnxī Gēwǔ Dà Xìyuàn)
陕西歌舞大戏院

Táng Dynasty 16
(Táng Yuè Gōng)
唐乐宫

Wénháo Záliáng Shífǔ Lǎo Diàn 19
文豪杂粮食府老店

⟨Tips⟩ Alternate Ways to Book Rail Tickets

The station can get crowded, so either book tickets through your hotel, which will charge around ¥50 ($6.50/£3.25) and ¥80 ($10.40/£5.20) to book a ticket, or visit a branch of the **Industrial and Commercial Bank of China (Gongshang Yinhang),** which levies a reasonable ¥5 (65¢/35p) service charge. The closest branch to the railway station is 1.6km (1 mile) south of the station at Wulukou Gonghang, Jiefang Lu 288; tickets are sold between 8:30am and 5pm on weekdays and from 9:30am to 3pm on weekends. There's a convenient **central branch** at Nan Dajie 50 (© **029/8726-3725**), which operates the same hours.

---

from window 2. The fastest trains to Beijing are the Z20 (11 hr.) at 8:16pm, the T42 (12 hr.) at 6:48pm, and the T232 (12 hr.) at 6:10pm. Other useful trains are the T115 to Shanghai (16½ hr.) at 9:13pm; the K84 to Guangzhou (27 hr.) at 8:33am; the K119 to Lanzhou (10 hr.) at 10:26pm; the K165 at 10:18pm, which passes through Chengdu (16 hr.) and terminates in Kunming (36 hr.); the T54 to Zhengzhou (6 hr.) at 11:32pm; the T69 to Urumqi (27 hr.) at 7:09am; and the K544 to Chongqing (14 hr.) at 7:22pm.

The **bus station (Xi'an Qiche Zhan;** © **029/8742-7420)** is directly opposite the railway station. Regular buses connect with Hua Shan (2 hr.; ¥22 ($2.85/£1.45), Zhengzhou (573km/355 miles; 6 hr.; ¥133/$17/£8.65), Luoyang (425km/264 miles; 4 hr.; ¥61/$7.95/£3.95), Taiyuan (685km/425 miles; 8 hr.; ¥112/$15/£7.30), Tianshui (380km/236 miles; 6 hr.; ¥76/$9.90/£4.95), Tongchuan (100km/62 miles; 1½ hr.; ¥23/$2.95/£1.45), and Yan'an (402km/249 miles; 4 hr.; ¥71/$9.25/£4.60). Afternoon sleeper buses connect with Yinchuan (720km/446 miles; 12 hr.; ¥130/$17/£8.45).

CITY LAYOUT   The center of town is generally denoted by the massive Ming **Bell Tower (Zhong Lou),** which marks the crossroads between the main north-south and east-west roads—which connect with the four main city gates. The main arteries are **Bei, Nan, Dong,** and **Xi Dajie** (North, South, East, and West aves.). Most of the main hotels, and many of the main sights and restaurants, are along these roads.

GETTING AROUND   Regular **buses** cost ¥1 (15¢/5p), while K buses, which are air-conditioned, charge ¥2 (25¢/15p). Most **taxis** are green Santana sedans that charge ¥6 (80¢/40p) for the first 3km (2 miles), then ¥1.40 (20¢/10p) per additional kilometer; add ¥1 (15¢/5p) if you're traveling between the hours of 10pm and 5am. You'll encounter few problems with drivers overcharging or failing to start the meter, but they will round the fare up or down to whole yuan, so don't sit around waiting for change.

Xi'an is flat and thus seems suitable for **biking,** but the streets are congested, and traffic rules are often ignored by motorists. Aside from a ride along the top of the city walls, cycling in Xi'an is only recommended for the experienced urban cyclist.

TOURS   Many travel agencies and hotels offer 1-day tours of the sights around Xi'an. The most popular tour follows the **Eastern Route (Dong Xian),** which usually includes the **Terra-Cotta Warriors (Qin Bingmayong Bowuguan), Huaqing Chi (Huaqing Pools),** and **Banpo Bowuguan.** The less-traveled **Western Route (Xi Xian)** should include Famen Si, Qian Ling (Tang dynasty tombs), and perhaps Mao Ling (Han dynasty tombs) and Xianyang Bowuguan (Xianyang Museum); in this book, we'll focus on the Eastern Route.

CITS, at Chang'an Bei Lu 48 (© **029/8526-2066;** fax 029/8526-7487; www.cits xa.com), offers some of the most reasonably priced tours in town, charging ¥600 ($78/£39) for the Western Route, and ¥350 ($46/£23) for the Eastern Route daily. They have plenty of branches around the city including one on the second floor of the Bell Tower Hotel (© **029/8760-0227**). Another option on the second floor of the Bell Tower Hotel is the **Golden Bridge Travel Service** (© **029/8725-7975**), which charges ¥350 ($46/£23) for the Eastern Route and ¥500 ($65/£33) for the Western Route. Most hotels offer their own tours, and hostels offer cheaper versions of the same.

FAST FACTS

Banks, Foreign Exchange & ATMs   The most effective **Bank of China** is the city branch at Jiefang Lu 157 (© **029/8762-0755;** open 9am–6pm Mon–Fri, 9am–4pm weekends). It's about 400m (¼ mile) south of the railway station, on the west side of Jiefang Lu, next to the Silk Road Hotel. The provincial branch is located in the center of town, on the corner of Juhua Yuan at Dong Dajie 306 (© **029/8726-7644;** same hours). Counter 12 is for foreign exchange and windows 17 and 18 can give advances on credit cards. Several ATMs are accessible 24 hours and accept foreign credit cards. There's also a branch, with an ATM, just 180m (590 ft.) south of the Bell Tower at Nan Dajie 29 (© **029/8728-1287;** same hours).

Internet Access   In the railway area, there are many Internet cafes on Shangde Lu. A reasonable choice is the 24-hour **Wangshi Ru Feng Internet Cafe** (on the east side of the road, just south of the intersection with Xi Ba Lu), which charges the standard rate of ¥3 (40¢/20p) per hour. Branches of Starbucks (in the Drum Tower Square, another on Dong Dajie) provide free wireless Internet access for customers with note-book computers. Dial-up is © **169.**

Post Office   The **main branch** is at the northwest corner of the Bell Tower at Bei Dajie 1, open 8am to 8pm.

Visa Extensions   Extensions can be obtained from the PSB, located 2 blocks west of the Bell Tower on the south side of the road at Xi Dajie 138 (© **029/9727-5934;** open Mon–Fri 8:30am–noon and 3–6pm); they take 3 days to process.

EXPLORING XI'AN

Xi'an has a bewildering array of sights that often confound the visitor with little time to spare. The Terra-Cotta Warriors are a must, as is the Shanxi History Museum, but make sure you also leave time for a walk or bike ride along the city walls, a dumpling banquet, and an alfresco meal of kabobs in the Muslim markets after visiting the Great Mosque.

Ba Xian An (Temple of the Eight Immortals) ☆ *(Finds)*   Tucked away in a narrow alley the tour buses can't reach is the most charming temple in Xi'an. As with the Great Mosque, the walk into it is half the adventure, with a flea market out front in some of the temple's old buildings. This becomes a huge antiques market on Wednesday and Sunday mornings (see "Shopping," below). Inside the temple, monks, their hair tied up in traditional Daoist fashion, play chess and are always keen for a chat. The folk legend of the **Eight Immortals (Ba Xian)** is said to have originated here during the late Tang dynasty. The temple was expanded during the Qing dynasty and was a favorite haunt of the Cixi dowager empress during the time she spent in Xi'an after her escape from Beijing following the Boxer Rebellion. As you look at the temple murals, note the influence of Confucianism on its supposed alter-ego, Daoism: The eight Immortals have a strict hierarchy, with Lu Dongbin in front on his tiger, the rotund Tieguai Li waddling along with his crook to his side, and the one woman, He Xiangu, near the back, carrying a lotus flower.

Wu Dao Shizi Dongjie (from An Ren Fang, continue east 135m/450 ft. before heading south down the 1st alley on your right; turn right when the road meets a T-junction. Immediately take a left and continue south to the back of the temple, following the incense vendors). Free admission. 7:30am–6pm. Bus: no. 13 or 42 from the station, or bus no. 4 or 11 from the Bell Tower to An Ren Fang.

Beilin Bowuguan (Forest of Stelae) ⋒ Formerly the Shanxi Provincial Museum, the Forest of Stelae is situated in a former Confucian temple (ca. 1087) that the literature describes as "unsophisticated and elegant." Originally forming the basis of a Tang university, many of the stelae have traveled a long way to get here; they were floated downriver on rafts to Luoyang during the Song dynasty before returning here in 1087. Stelae are often borne on bixi, legendary turtlelike creatures descended from the Dragon King *(longwang)* that were renowned for their incredible strength and endurance. As there is little English signage, the stelae can be a little hard to appreciate for non-Chinese-speakers, but the serene atmosphere of the courtyards and their contorted time-old trees require no translation.

In the main courtyard, the first major stele was composed by the Xuanzong emperor in 745; the exposition on filial piety predated the influential "three character classic" *(san zi jing)*. Room 1 houses the Confucian classics, including The Analects, The Spring and Autumn Annals. Candidates for official examinations would pore over rubbings taken from these stelae and would be expected to know the classics by heart—an educational style that unfortunately still holds sway in China. Immediately to your left in room 2 is the Nestorian Stele. Nestorian Christians were drummed out of the Church for maintaining that Jesus was both human and divine and that Mary was the mother of "the man Jesus," and not the mother of God. The stele records the visit of a Nestorian priest to Chang'an and the founding of a Nestorian chapel, providing evidence of a Nestorian presence in China as early as A.D. 635. The influence of other faiths is clear—the Maltese cross is set amid Daoist clouds, supported by a Buddhist lotus flower. Rooms 2 and 3 also house the work of master calligraphers, such as Wang Xizhi, whose writings are still used as models by calligraphy students. Room 4 has pictorial stelae, including a famous image of Confucius. Here you will encounter a demonstration of "rubbing," whereby moistened paper is hammered onto the inked stones, color is tapped on using a wooden disk wrapped in a cloth, and the impression is dried before being gobbled up by Japanese tour groups. It isn't a gentle process, and it's easy to see why many stelae are almost unreadable. Double back to your left to enter rooms 5 to 7, as well as a gallery of stone sculpture containing an exquisite statue of a bodhisattva that shows Indian and Grecian influences.

Wenyi Bei Lu 18. ⓒ **029/8725-8448**. Admission ¥45 ($5.85/£2.95). Summer 8am–7pm; winter 8am–5:30pm. Bus: no. 14, 402, or 239.

Da Qingzhensi (Great Mosque) ⋒ Founded during the height of the Tang dynasty in 742, this is one of the most tranquil places in town and the center of a sizable Muslim community, residents in Xi'an for over 1,200 years. As with Baxian An, half the adventure is getting there, as you veer left just north of the Drum Tower. The covered alleyway, Huajue Xiang, has good-humored vendors selling all manner of weird merchandise (see "Shopping," below) and it may take you a few attempts to find the mosque. The courtyards are spacious and have a gardenlike feel, with a wonderful fusion of Arabian and Chinese architectural styles. To the right of the entrance is a hall filled with exquisite Ming furniture. The central courtyard has a triple-eaved octagonal "minaret" from which worshipers were traditionally called to prayer, although it is far more akin to a Chinese pagoda. The prayer hall is normally closed to non-Muslims. As this is an active mosque, be circumspect in taking photographs. Avoid visiting on Friday, when access to the mosque is restricted. Be sure to bring mosquito spray in the summer.

Huajue Xiang 30. ⓒ 029/8727-2541. Admission ¥12 ($1.55/80p). Apr–Oct 8am–7pm; Nov–Mar 8am–5pm. Bus: no. 221, 29, 6, or 618.

Da Yan Ta (Great Goose Pagoda) & Da Ci'en Si (Temple of Great Goodwill) ⭐

This is the best-known temple in Xi'an, and worth a visit if, like many in the U.K. and Australia, you were entranced by the TV version of "Monkey" as a child. The scripture-collecting journey of Xuanzang (596–664) to India, on which the show was based, lasted 15 years, and was immortalized and lampooned in Wu Cheng'en's novel *Journey to the West (Xi You Ji)*. But the journey was not the end of Xuanzang's travails. Upon his return, he requested the construction of a pagoda to house the scriptures; his request was accommodated inside a temple built from 647 to 652 by Prince Li Zhi in honor of his mother, Empress Wen De. Construction of the pagoda commenced in 652, in a style similar to those seen by Xuanzang in India—hence the simple, tapering structure. Xuanzang is credited with translating 75 texts into over 1,000 volumes, an amazing feat since the originals contained a host of specialized terms with no Chinese equivalents.

Halls at the back of the temple contain murals depicting Xuanzang's journey—in many pictures, he is shown holding a fly whisk, intended to send evil spirits into flight. To the left and right of the pagoda's south entrance are prefaces to the texts written by Taizong and Gaozong. Above the east and west doors are barely visible Tang carvings of the Buddha. The temple's perimeter has recently undergone redevelopment and the result is as good as Chinese urban planning gets. To the north of the pagoda is the north plaza *(bei guangcang)*, which boasts a large pool of fountains, benches, and retail shops lining the mall. A water fountain and light show kicks off nightly at 8pm.

Admission ¥25 ($3.25/£1.65). 8am–6pm. Bus: no. 610 (from the station).

Shanxi Lishi Bowuguan (Shanxi History Museum) ⭐⭐⭐

If you visit one museum in China, make it this one, for its unrivaled collection of treasures. The museum was being renovated at press time and its manifold riches should be displayed even more alluringly by the time you visit. As you enter, start with the hall on the left, pull on a jacket to brave the fierce air-conditioning, and ignore the man who tries to drag you to his display of "original art." Items are displayed chronologically, starting with the Shang dynasty (ca. 17th c.–11th c. B.C.) and the Zhou dynasty (ca. 11th c.– 221 B.C.) on the ground floor, including items that speak to eating, drinking, and merriment in the Western Zhou (ca. 11th c.–771 B.C.).

Things take a martial turn as you enter the Qin dynasty (221–206 B.C.): Aside from the bronze swords and rusting iron weapons (which gave the Qin a decisive military edge), a striking exhibit is a **tiger-shaped tally** covered in characters *(duhu fu)* which gave its owner, one General Du, imperial authorization to mobilize over 50 soldiers at will. As you move on to the Tang dynasty (618–907), the influence of Buddhist art from the Silk Routes becomes apparent—carvings are more sophisticated, and bright colors are introduced. Perhaps the most startling exhibits are the frescoes *(bihua)* relocated from the Tang tumuli around Xi'an. A depiction of **ladies-in-waiting** (*gongnu tu*) 🟊🟊 shows nine women carrying the tools of their trade—candelabras, fans, cloth bundles, powder boxes, even fly swatters. Two of them are dressed in male clothing. Another fresco (*ma qiu tu*) shows noblemen enjoying the newly imported game of polo. **Ceramic tomb guardians** point to a lively trade with the outside world—there's a trader from Africa and a fanciful depiction of a man on horseback battling a leopard. You can easily spend 3 or 4 hours here.

Xiao Zhai Dong Lu 91. ⓒ 029/8525-4727. Admission ¥50 ($6.50/£3.25) Mar–Nov; ¥35 ($4.55/£2.30) Dec–Feb. Mar–Nov 8:30am–5:30pm; Dec–Feb 9am–5pm. Bus: no. 5 (from the station) or 610 (from just north of the Bell Tower to Lishi Bowuguan).

Xi'an Chengqiang (City Wall) 🟊
The largest and best-preserved city wall in China is definitely worth a visit. The pieces of the wall have recently been reconnected so that you can do the 14km (8¾-mile) loop around it by foot, bicycle, or a golf cart. The walls were built during the early Ming dynasty, on the remains of Tang palace walls. The original city walls were much farther out, well past Da Yan Ta. The surrounding moat is currently being cleaned up in phases, and should be completed by the Olympics in 2008. The South Gate (Nan Men) is the best place to start your exploration. Individual (¥20/$2.60/£1.30) and tandem bicycles (¥30/$3.90/£1.95) may be rented by the hour from here, or just east of Heping Men. A ride on a golf cart around the wall costs (¥50/$6.50/£3.25). To do the entire loop takes 3 to 4 hours by foot, 2 to 3 hours by bicycle, and 1 hour by cart. The wall provides little protection from sun or wind, so dress accordingly.

Admission ¥40 ($5.20/£2.60). Apr–Oct 8am–9:30pm; Nov–Mar 8am–6pm.

AROUND XI'AN
EASTERN ROUTE (DONG XIAN)
Of the two common tours from Xi'an, the Eastern Route is shorter, less expensive, and more popular than the Western Route. There is enough to keep you interested for a whole day, but organized tours of the Eastern Route include "shopping" and sights of dubious merit. While tours are convenient if you have the time, you can do without one. If you are short on time, simply visit Bingmayong as a half-day trip.

Bingmayong (Terra-Cotta Warriors) 🟊🟊🟊
This is the reason most visitors come to Xi'an, and unlike many big sights in China, it does not disappoint. Amazingly, the warriors are just one piece of Qin Shi Huang's attempt to reconstruct his empire for the afterlife. The tomb to the west is supposedly booby-trapped and is still to be fully excavated, but it is said to include a full reconstruction of the ancient capital, complete with rivers and lakes of mercury. According to historian Sima Qian, over 700,000 workers were drafted for the project, and those involved in the construction of the tomb were rewarded with graves beside their emperor. Tourism officials pray that the warriors are "just the tip of the iceberg," but it is just as likely that the tomb was plundered during the Tang or Song dynasties. *Tip:* To fully appreciate the majesty of the warriors, try to get to the site as early as possible and race to Pit 1; if you get here ahead of the crowds, you should manage a few minutes of solitude with the one of the world's greatest historical finds.

It's hard not to get a shiver down your spine as you survey the unromantically named **Pit 1** 🟊🟊🟊, with four columns of warriors in each of the 11 passageways; there are over 1,000 infantry in battle formation, stretching back 182m (600 ft.). Originally painted in bright colors, they were constructed from interchangeable parts sealed together by clay. Because the heads were hand-molded, no two appear the same. Qin Shi Huang's army was drawn from all over his vast empire, and this ethnic diversity is reflected in the variety of hairstyles, headdresses, and facial expressions. Even on the mass-produced bodies, the level of detail is striking, down to the layering of armor and the studs on archers' shoes that prevented them from slipping. The average height of the warriors is 1.8m (5 ft. 11 in.); senior officers are taller. Most of the 1,400 soldiers in **Pit 2** are less intact than those in Pit 1, although the statues show greater diversity of posture. The highlights here are encased in glass cabinets around the edge of the pit; look for the 2m (6½-ft.) general. **Pit 3** is much smaller and houses the headquarters, with 68 senior officers.

A **small hall** just to the right of Pit 1 contains a display of two magnificent bronze chariots, reconstructed from nearly 3,500 pieces excavated from a pit to the west of the tomb.

The tour bus will drop you off in a parking lot; you can either walk the 1km (⅔ mile) to the museum's entrance or take a trolley for ¥15 ($1.95/£1) round-trip ticket. An English-speaking guide (¥100/$13/£6.50) can be arranged on the spot at the tour guide center *(daoyou fuwu zhan)* located near a red umbrella to the right of the entrance.

ⓒ 029/8391-1961. Admission: Main exhibits Mar–Nov ¥90 ($12/£5.85); Dec–Feb ¥65 ($8.45/£4.25). 8am–5pm. Bus: no. 306 (leaves from the front of the railway station, on the east side). Take the large A/C bus (¥5/65¢/35p) rather than the minibuses that leave when full. Round-trip taxi from the city costs ¥200–¥300 ($26–$39/£13–£20).

Banpo Bowuguan (Banpo Neolithic Village)   If you're interested in archaeology, this is an essential visit. Otherwise, you can give it a miss. Given the amount of material unearthed here since its discovery in 1953 (tools, pottery, burial jars, and so on), it's amazing that only one-fifth of the site has been excavated (mostly due to the cost of preserving what has been discovered). The village, traced from the Yangshao culture, was occupied from about 5000 to 4000 B.C.

Banpo Bowuguan (from the Banpo Bowuguan bus stop, walk back toward town and turn left at the 1st cross street). Admission ¥30 ($3.90/£1.95). 8:30am–5pm. Bus: no. 11 (from just north of the Bell Tower) or no. 105 (from the station). Continuing on to Huaqing Pools and Bingmayong is tricky, but possible. Take bus no. 105 back toward town as far as Wanshou Lu. Catch bus no. 512 north far as Wang Jia Fen (3 stops) and then catch bus no. 306 east.

SHOPPING

Ba Xian An   The outdoor antiques market on Wednesday and Sunday mornings is the most atmospheric in town. Despite a sign warning that antiques must be declared with Customs before you leave China, there's no guarantee that what you buy is a genuine antique. But there is a buzz to the place, and you can find some wonderful Cultural Revolution kitsch, ceramics, bronze Buddhas, and Qing coins. See the Ba Xian An review in "Exploring Xi'an," above, for directions.

Gu Wenhua Jie   This enjoyable street for browsing is east of Nan Men, on the way to Beilin Bowuguan. Shops sell huge paint brushes, rubbings, paintings, and musical instruments, and you can watch artists at work in this faithfully restored street.

Huajue Xiang   The most enjoyable place to shop for souvenirs is the covered alleyway that leads to **Da Qingzhensi.** Shopping here is a blood sport, and you are the game, but the vendors are friendly. Interesting finds include feng shui compasses, Mao lighters, Tibetan prayer wheels, Little Red Books in French, and gnarled walking sticks.

Xi'an Guwan Cheng   With peasants finding that their fields are full of valuable antiques stored in the graves of their prosperous ancestors, digging is going on at a furious pace in the countryside surrounding Xi'an. Factories producing excellent copies are also very busy. If you're after a genuine antique, you have some chance of finding one here. There are fakes aplenty, but this market is geared to locals, so asking prices are not as absurd as elsewhere. There are bronzes of all kinds, heroic comic books from the Cultural Revolution, and weird *Kama Sutra*–inspired woodcarvings. Be wary when purchasing bronzes, which tended to be melted down and reused over the ages (unless they were buried). Your best bets are ceramics and pottery. Open April through October from 9:30am to 6pm, and November through March from 10am to 6pm.

Zhu Que Dajie Zhong Duan 2. Bus no. 6 from south of Bell Tower to Xi'an Guwan Cheng.

WHERE TO STAY

Xi'an has an ever-increasing array of accommodations options to choose from. Hostels are popping up all over the city and, at the other end of the scale, the Shangri-La has a new venture planned in the western outskirts. The Accor group recently opened a prestige development containing a Sofitel, Mercure, and Grand Mercure within the city walls. However, its location a little too far from the sights, and the hodgepodge of styles and poor service have thus far proven to be stumbling blocks. All hotels listed below will offer some discount, and reductions of as much as 50% off the rack rates can be achieved with bargaining.

The locals don't go anywhere near the railway station unless they are catching a train as it's not a particularly safe area, and if you have any time on your hands, it's best to follow their example. If you must, try the **Jiefang Fandian,** Jiefang Lu 181 (© **029/8769-8888;** fax 029/8769-8666; ¥280–¥380/$36–$49/£18–£25 standard room, ¥480/$62/£31 suite), directly across from the railway station on the left; it has a restaurant and negotiable rates. The major attractions and restaurants are clustered around the southern and central parts of town, which are safer places to find lodgings.

VERY EXPENSIVE

Hyatt Regency Xi'an (Kaiyue Fandian)   If you're used to the luxuries of the Hyatt brand, you might be a little disappointed here. Nevertheless it still remains the five-star hotel with the best location, and 2004 renovations have yet to show their age. If you stay here, try to upgrade to the executive rooms, which include free entrance to a quiet ninth-floor lounge with wireless Internet connection.

Dong Dajie 158. © **029/8769-1234.** Fax 029/8769-6799. www.xian.regency.hyatt.com. 315 units. ¥1,400 ($182/£91) standard room; from ¥2,400 ($312/£156) suite. 15% service charge. 20%–40% discounts. AE, DC, MC, V. Bus: no. 611 from the station to Dachashi; continue south for 54m/180 ft. and cross to the street's southeast side. **Amenities:** 2 restaurants; bar; cafe; tennis courts; health club and spa; bike rental; concierge; airport shuttle; business center; 24-hr. forex; salon; 24-hr. room service; in-room massage; same-day laundry/dry cleaning; executive-level rooms; wireless access in atrium and in 9th-floor executive lounge. *In room:* A/C, TV, broadband Internet access (¥80/$10/£5.20 per day), minibar, fridge, iron, safe.

Shangri-La Golden Flower (Jinhua Fandian) ✿✿   Of Xi'an's several five-star hotels, the Golden Flower boasts the best rooms: spacious, with huge comfy beds, and well-appointed with nice bathroom and lighting fixtures. Service is solid here. Located outside the city wall, the hotel is inconvenient for walking around, but a 15-minute taxi ride will get you to the center of town. Stay here if you're in town just to see the Terra-Cotta Warriors, as it is closer to the expressway leading to the treasures than other luxury hotels.

Changle Xi Lu 8 (3km/2 miles east of city wall). © **029/8323-2981.** Fax 029/8323-5477. www.shangri-la.com. 416 units. ¥1,198 ($156/£78) standard room; from ¥2,328 ($303/£151) suite. Up to 40% discounts. 15% service charge.

AE, DC, MC, V. Bus: no. 105 (from the station) or 11 (from east of Bell Tower). **Amenities:** 2 restaurants; bar; cafe; large indoor swimming pool; health club and spa; concierge; tour desk; 24-hr. business center; 24-hr. forex; salon; 24-hr. room service; in-room massage; same-day laundry/dry cleaning; executive-level rooms. *In room:* A/C, satellite TV, broadband Internet access, minibar, fridge, iron, safe.

Sheraton Xi'an (Xilaideng Dajiudian) 🌴🌴 Located over 1.6km (1 mile) west of the city walls, the Sheraton has improved remarkably in recent years, and service is the best in Xi'an. Renovations are ongoing. Rooms are modern and well-appointed, with sturdy beds and plush carpets. After a day braving the grimy air of Xi'an, you can seek refuge in the immaculate bathrooms. The Gate West Restaurant offers tasty Western fare.

Fenghao Dong Lu 262. 🄲 **029/8426-1888.** Fax 029/426-2188. www.sheraton.com/xian. 338 units. ¥1,359 ($177/£88) standard room; from ¥2,942 ($382/£191) suite. Up to 40% discount. 15% service charge. AE, DC, MC, V. Bus: no. 611 from the station and west of the Bell Tower to Fenghao Dong Lu. **Amenities:** 3 restaurants; cafe; bar; large indoor swimming pool; health club; spa; game room; concierge; tour desk; airport shuttle; 24-hr. business center; 24-hr. forex; salon; 24-hr. room service; in-room massage; same-day laundry/dry cleaning; executive-level rooms. *In room:* A/C, satellite TV, broadband Internet access (¥50/$6.50/£3.25 per day), minibar, fridge, hair dryer, iron, safe.

EXPENSIVE
Bell Tower Hotel (Zhonglou Fandian) This is a solid choice one notch down in price from the international hotels with a fantastic location. Rooms are spacious and bathrooms are modern and clean. The lunch buffet on the second floor is still the best all-you-can-eat value in town. In the hotel are branches of both CITS and Golden Bridge Travel. Service seems to be surprisingly competent for a state-run hotel.

Nan Dajie 110 (southwest corner of Bell Tower). 🄲 **029/8760-0000.** Fax 029/8721-8767. 300 units. ¥850–¥900 ($111–$117/£55–£59) standard room; from ¥1,280 ($166/£83) suite. 15% service charge. 40% discount. AE, DC, MC, V. Bus: no. 603 from the station. **Amenities:** 3 restaurants; cafe; health club; concierge; tour desk; business center; 24-hr. forex; shopping arcade; next-day laundry/dry cleaning. *In room:* A/C, TV, broadband Internet access, minibar, fridge, hair dryer.

Howard Johnson Ginwa Plaza Hotel (Jinhua Haosheng Guoji Dajiudian) 🌴 While the brand name may conjure memories of cheap motels and roadside diners in the U.S., Howard Johnson's has arrived in Xi'an in style. Located right outside the southern city wall, this is one of the best-run new hotels on the market. The lobby is Miami-style tacky, but the rooms are tastefully done, and bathroom fixtures are modern. Some rooms have great views of the wall—try to book one of these. The hotel is well equipped to deal with English-speaking travelers, with at least one overseas employee on staff at all times. Wi-Fi connections are available at all the restaurants, the lobby, club floor lounge, and banquet rooms.

Huangcheng Nan Jie 18. 🄲 **029/8842-1111.** Fax 029/8206-8888. 324 units. ¥788 ($102/£51) standard room. 15% service charge. AE, DC, MC, V. **Amenities:** 3 restaurants; lobby lounge; concierge; business center; gift shop; 5 non-smoking floors. *In room:* A/C, satellite TV, minibar, hair dryer, safe.

MODERATE
Bell and Drum Hotel (Zhonggulou Dajiudian) 🌴 A great location, clean, pleasant and decent-size rooms, and friendly management all combine to make the Bell and Drum one of the best deals in the city. This fact doesn't go unnoticed by budget tour operators, though, and the hotel is often full of foreign groups. Some rooms on the seventh floor enjoy views of the Bell Tower, but make sure you avoid rooms ending in 18 as they have an obstructive pillar in the middle of the room.

She Hui Lu 1. 🄲 **029/8812-8340.** 110 units. ¥230 ($30/£15) standard room; ¥510 ($66/£33) suite. AE, DC, MC, V. Bus no. 603 from railway station. **Amenities:** Restaurant; exercise room; tour desk; forex; business center; laundry service/dry cleaning. *In room:* A/C, TV.

Melody Hotel (Meilun Jiudian)   Its location and price make the Melody a good midrange choice. Although showing signs of wear, rooms are clean and bright, and it's worth paying a little extra for a view of the Drum Tower, which is directly opposite. The Melody opened in 2001 and is an entirely private venture. If you've ever wanted to try the full-body shower featured in the movie *Shower (Xizao)*, this is the place.

Xi Dajie 86 (opposite the Drum Tower). © **029/8728-8888**. Fax 029/8727-3601. 136 units (shower only). ¥498 ($65/£32) standard room; ¥888 ($115/£58) suite. AE, DC, MC, V. **Amenities:** Restaurant; bar; concierge; same-day laundry service/dry cleaning. *In room:* A/C, TV, broadband Internet connection (¥20/$2.60/£1.30 per day), minibar, fridge, hair dryer.

Wuyi Fandian (May First Hotel)   Stung by exclusion from various travel guides, the first hotel in town to accept foreigners has renovated most of its rooms in the last few years. Avoid the cheapest, windowless standard rooms. May First requires that their staff take classes in English and politeness, which is more than can be said for some five-star hotels in town. Lugging your bags up the stairs to reception is inconvenient, but with a bustling food court downstairs and elevators that only take four people, a stay here is reminiscent of Hong Kong in the 1970s.

Dong Dajie 351 (225m/750 ft. east of Bell Tower, on north side). © **029/8768-1098**. Fax 029/8721-3824. www.may-first.com. 138 units. ¥208–¥338 ($27–$44/£14–£22) standard room. No credit cards. **Amenities:** Restaurant; food court; tour desk; same-day laundry/dry cleaning. *In room:* A/C, TV.

INEXPENSIVE

Xi'an Shuyuan Qingnian Lushe (Xi'an Shuyuan Youth Hostel) ✰✰ *Finds*   Youth hostels are taking over the budget accommodations niche in China, and this one is the best option in town. A magnificent restored courtyard residence, it formerly housed the Xianyang County government. The hostel was recently extensively renovated and its clean, simple standard twins offer good modern bathrooms. You also get English-speaking staff, an excellent location, impartial and useful information, free Internet access, and that rare commodity in China—ambience.

Nan Dajie Xi Shun Cheng Xiang 2A (27m/90 ft. west of the South Gate, just inside the city wall). © **029/8728-7721**. Fax 029/8728-7720. www.hostelxian.com. 45 units (shower only). ¥160 ($21/£10) standard room; from ¥30–¥50 ($3.90–$6.50/£1.95–£3.25) dorm. No credit cards. Bus: no. 603 from the railway station to Nan Men. **Amenities:** Cafe; bike rental; concierge; tour desk; railway station courtesy car; laundry and kitchen facilities; Internet access. *In room:* A/C, TV, no phone.

WHERE TO DINE

Xi'an has a good variety of eateries, with some fine dumpling houses, atmospheric restaurants with outdoor seating along Bei Yuan. If you feel the need for some Western intake, there's an overload of **McDonald's, KFCs,** and **Starbucks,** all of which can be found around the Bell Tower central intersection.

De Fa Chang ✰✰ *Kids* DUMPLINGS   Dumplings are raised to a high art form at this lively restaurant located next to the Bell Tower Square. The canteen downstairs is always bustling and serves a variety of dumplings and side dishes that are wheeled around on carts. Upstairs De Fa Chang is a little more refined, but the 18-course dumpling meal is a steal at ¥60 ($7.80/£3.90). Tasty *xiaochi,* or little eats, resembling flying saucers, mouse heads, and walnuts will also come in a steady stream to your table.

Zhonglou Guangchang. © **029/8721-4060**. Meal for 2 ¥40–¥160 ($5.20–$21/£2.60–£10). No credit cards. 8:30am–9pm.

Fanji Lazhi Roudian SHANXI   This is the most famous vendor of Shanxi's most widely consumed snack—*rou jia mo,* finely chopped pork pressed between two halves of a solid steamed bun. Xi'an's answer to the hamburger makes a perfect snack on the run, but you can almost feel your arteries clogging up as you wolf it down. Ask for the good-quality *(youzhi)* bun (¥4/50¢/25p).

Zhubashi Jie 46 (from Gu Lou, the shop is opposite, 45m/150 ft. south of Xi Dajie on the road's east side). Meal for 2 less than ¥20 ($2.60/£1.30). No credit cards. 8am–10pm. Bus: no. 611 from the station to Gu Lou.

Highfly Pizza (Gaofei Bisa) WESTERN   Outside of the five-star hotels and the inevitable KFCs, Xi'an offers little in the way of Western food. It's a relief to find pizza (the four-cheese and pepperoni pizzas are superb), real oven-baked penne, tuna sandwiches, chocolate brownies, even Texas stew. There are vegetarian options, the kitchen is spotless, and the entire restaurant is nonsmoking.

Heping Men Wai Shengli Fandian. ℂ **029/8785-5333.** Meal for 2 ¥80–¥100 ($10–$13/£5.20–£6.50). No credit cards. 9am–10:30pm. Bus: no. 5 (from station) or no. 601 (from north of Bell Tower to Heping Men).

Jiasan Guantang Baozi ⊀ MUSLIM   Still the most famous of the Jia Brothers' restaurants, you'll know you're there when you see the monstrous blue arch over the entrance and a wall festooned with photographs of Xi'an notables—TV hosts, writers, and musicians. The specialty dish is *guantang baozi,* with a choice of beef, lamb, or "three flavors"—lamb, mushroom, and prawn. The dumplings have piping-hot soup inside, so let them cool before testing your chopstick skills. This dish is best washed down with *ba bao tian xifan,* a sweet rice porridge filled with peanuts, sultanas, hawthorn, and medlar berries.

Bei Yuan Men 93 (135m/450 ft. north of Drum Tower, on the east side). ℂ **029/8725-7507.** Meal for 2 less than ¥30 ($3.90/£1.95). No credit cards. 8am–10pm.

Lao Sun Jia ⊀ SHANXI   The original restaurant, opened in 1898, is still the best place to sample Xi'an's most celebrated dish, *yangrou paomo.* There are now three branches, two of them on Dong Dajie. The branch with the best reputation at the moment is located inside a large hotel. On the first floor, you can dine with the masses—not recommended unless you want to be the main attraction. The second floor is a point-to-choose *xiaochi* (snack) restaurant.

Recommended dishes include the lamb dumplings *(suan tang shuijiao)* and a local favorite, *fenzheng yangrou,* two steamed buns perched delicately to the side of a pile of mince and flour. Order *yangrou paomo* on the third floor. You will face an empty bowl and two steamed buns, as well as plates of chili, coriander, and cloves of garlic that have been marinated in vinegar and sugar for several months. Tear the buns into tiny pieces and pop them into the empty bowl. When you've finished, your bowl will be taken away and refilled with broth and noodles. Stir in the coriander and chili, and when your palate gets greasy, nibble a clove of garlic and encourage your friends to do likewise. If the star dish doesn't fill you up, the stewed oxtail *(hongshao niuwei)* and bok choy with mushrooms *(bilu za shuang gu)* are recommended. Don't bother with the fourth floor, unless you are entertaining a government official looking for a bribe.

Dong Guan Zheng Jie 78 (from Dong Men, cross the road, walk 27m/90 ft. north, turn right, and walk 45m/150 ft. east). ℂ **029/8221-2935.** Reservations recommended on weekends (3rd floor). ¥60 ($7.80/£3.90) on 2nd floor, ¥200 ($26/£13) on 3rd floor. No credit cards. 11am–9pm. Bus: no. 45 from just east of Bell Tower to Dong Men.

Wenhao Zaliang Shifu Lao Dian SHANXI   This is one of the more affordable and healthy theater/banquet restaurants in Xi'an. You won't leave with a grumbling

Chinese Shadows

Piying was the staple entertainment of rural Shanxi before karaoke. Puppets are carved from leather and dyed dazzling colors—many date from the Qing dynasty (1644–1911). There are over 600 different plays, ranging from legends to love stories to kung-fu epics. Unlike opera, this is loud, irreverent entertainment for the masses. This art will probably die out in Shanxi; its main exponent is a septuagenarian, and his only student is a few years younger. It takes 10 years to learn the craft, and for most, driving a taxi is a more appealing option. For now, the puppet troupe (Shanxi Hu Xian Piying Yishutuan) also performs at Dongfang Dajiudian.

stomach after you polish off up to eight appetizers, eight main courses, and 20 snacks *(xiao chi).* There are three different banquets available, and if you book in advance, you may be able to get a table close to the shadow puppet show (see "Chinese Shadows," above), which is held every night on the third floor. Worth looking out for are a delicious steamed corn bun *(wotou)* and a nutty sweet-potato pancake *(shan nan xiangyu bing).*

Jianshe Lu 2. (From Lu Jia Cun, walk south 54m/180 ft. and turn right into Jianshe Lu. The restaurant is 225m/750 ft. ahead, on the north side.) ℂ 029/8553-5555. Reservations recommended. Meal for 2 ¥120 – ¥200 ($16–$26/£7.80–£13). No credit cards. 9:30am–11pm. Bus: no. 606 (from just north of Bell Tower) or no. 5 (from the railway station to Lu Jia Cun).

XI'AN AFTER DARK

As well as the cultural entertainment options listed below, Xi'an also has a fairly lively nightlife scene; the best place to sample this is **Defuxiang Bar Street (Defuxiang Jiuba Jie),** northwest of Nan Men, where there are plenty of different bars to choose from.

THE PERFORMING ARTS

Two companies perform Tang-style banquets and musicals to entertain visitors. The competition for the group-tour dollar is fierce.

Shanxi Grand Opera House (Shanxi Gewu Da Xiyuan)   While it can't compete with Tang Yue Gong (see below) as a spectacle, this opera company has a more authentic feel, with revolutionary credentials tracing its origins to the Northwest Culture Work Group in Yan'an. If you opt for the dinner, you'll gorge on dumplings with 20 different fillings. Be sure to book in advance. Voice-overs are in Chinese and English. Dinner starts at 7:20pm and the show starts at 8:45pm. Wen Yi Lu 165. ℂ 029/8785-6012. Reservations required. Dinner and show ¥278 ($36/£18); show only ¥198 ($26/£13). AE, DC, MC, V. Bus: no. 14 from the station, or no. 208 from south of the Bell Tower to Diao Jia Cun.

Tang Dynasty (Tang Yue Gong)   Run by a Hong Kong entrepreneur, this show delivers all your fantasies of Asia at once: lavish costumes modeled on the Mogao cave paintings, a six-course banquet (watch out for the rice wine), hammy acting, and some amazing music and dance. Gao Ming's performance of the Spring Oriole's Song on a vertical bamboo flute, the *pai xiao,* is almost worth the money in itself. If you can get past the slickness and the feeling that it's just for foreigners (the voice-overs are all in English), the show makes a spectacular night out. Dinner starts at 7pm; the show begins at 8:30pm. Chang'an Lu 75. © 029/8782-2222. Fax 029/8526-1619. www.xiantangdynasty. com. Reservations required. Dinner and show ¥410 ($55/£27); show and cocktail ¥200 ($26/£13). AE, DC, MC, V. Bus: no. 603 from station or north of Bell Tower to Cao Chang Po.

A SIDE TRIP FROM XI'AN: THE POTTERS OF CHEN LU 𝒜𝒜

This tiny group of villages in undulating terrain north of Xi'an has been turning out exquisite pottery since the Tang dynasty, and is free of the hype that surrounds Jingde Zhen (p. 524). Locals joke that Chen Lu "eats pottery," and while this may be fiction, walls are made of ceramic urns rather than bricks. Elegant cups that would fetch tidy sums in Xi'an lie by the side of the road. No fewer than 17 small factories turn out different styles of pottery, ranging from the sleek black *heiyou* to the rusty shades of *tiexiu hua* and the blues and whites of *qing hua*. It's an old-fashioned town: People call each other "comrade" *(tongzhi)* without the overtone of homosexuality that it now usually bears in urban China, wear Lei Feng hats with thick tops and earflaps without irony, and offer cigarettes on reflex when they meet a stranger.

If you visit on a day trip, it's doubtful you'll have time to explore all the factories and shops. The best bargains are found in the factory showrooms, where the starting prices will have you offering more money, but you're more likely to come across original works in the houses of individual artisans. The main factory, **Chen Lu Taoci Chang** (© 0919/748-3343), has an exhibition of antique ceramics, including Tang dynasty moxibustion cups, hat canisters from the Yuan dynasty, and ceramic pillows—still used by villagers today! Visit the exhibition before going on a spending spree, as staff can advise you on which factories make which kinds of pottery. Exquisite bowls in *qing hua* style cost as little as ¥10 ($1.30/65p), while original works are considerably more expensive. Individual artisans are proud to display their wares and may hail you in the street. **Xu Kuaile** (© 0919/748-2235) is a well-known local artisan.

The guesthouse at Chen Lu isn't someplace you'd willingly reside and given the town's proximity to Xi'an there's no need to stay. But in this relaxed town, you won't be short on offers to stay and dine with the villagers, whose houses often have domed roofs in the manner of pottery kilns. Before you agree, check what sort of headrest your host has in mind. Ceramic pillows take some getting used to.

Chen Lu is a 1½-hour drive from Xi'an, but most tour agencies will look blank when you mention it. A taxi should cost no more than ¥300 ($39/£20) for the round-trip. Air-conditioned buses depart for Tongchuan (100km/62 miles; 1½ hr.; ¥23/$2.95/£1.45) from the main bus station every 15 minutes from 6:30am to 9pm. In Tongchuan, continue north to the first roundabout for 630m (2,066 ft.), or catch bus no. 8 to the roundabout at Yigu Liangzhan. From south of the roundabout, white minivans leave when full for Chen Lu (18km/11 miles; 40 min.; ¥3/40¢/20p).

2 Hua Shan

Shanxi Province, 120km (74 miles) E of Xi'an

The first king of Shang made a sacrifice on Hua Shan in 1766 B.C., and Han Wudi (reigned 141–87 B.C.) declared it the Sacred Mountain of the West. The mountain's present popularity with Chinese tourists was aided by Jin Yong's martial-arts novel *Hua Shan Lun Jian*, which is filled with heroic swordsmen, mythical beasts, and beautiful maidens. Add a popular soap opera set against the granite bluffs, precariously perched pine trees, and Daoist temples dangling from precipitous peaks, and Hua Shan's popularity with the locals was guaranteed. Hua Shan sees few foreign visitors, which is a shame, because the climb is a more pleasant experience here than at many of the other four Daoist holy mountains in China (where you can be pestered off the mountain by local tourists who see you as part of the entertainment). The scenery is spectacular, the Daoist monks are friendly, and the air is clear enough to make the sunrise worth seeing. The best times to visit are midautumn, when the trees are a magical, colorful jumble, or spring, when the wildflowers bloom. Winter is picturesque but bitterly cold.

ESSENTIALS

GETTING THERE   Hua Shan can be visited as a 1- or 2-day trip from Xi'an. Regular **buses** leave from the main bus station from 7am (2 hr.; ¥22/$2.85/£1.45). Ignore touts who try to drag you away to their minibuses. If you are walking up, ask the conductor to drop you at Hua Shan Kou, a village at the base of the mountain, or say that you are walking the *lao lu* (old road). To reach the cable car, stay on the bus to the park entrance and connect with another bus (¥10/$1.30/65p) that takes a further 25 minutes. Entry to Hua Shan is ¥70 ($9.10/£4.55). The last bus returns to Xi'an from the cable car stop at 4pm, and minibuses run until 7pm.

Connect by **rail** via Hua Shan railway station. There is a minibus every half-hour to Hua Shan Kou (20 min.; ¥3/40¢/20p); or hail a red minivan that will take you there for the same price. Trains back to Xi'an (2 hr.) cost between ¥10 ($1.30/65p) and ¥20 ($2.60/£1.30) and depart every hour or so.

VISITOR INFORMATION   The **Hua Shan Tourist Bureau** (© **0913/436-6650;** fax 0913/436-3578) is inside the Hua Shan Financial Hotel.

EXPLORING THE AREA

Consider the cable car, particularly if you only have 1 day in your schedule. The mountain is a tough 2,000m (6,600-ft.) climb, especially if you don't have a head for heights. If you have 2 or more days, walk up and stay at one of the guesthouses on the mountain. You will enjoy a feeling of smugness when you meet the masses piling out of the cable cars at **North Peak** (**Bei Feng;** 1,613m/5,295 ft.). By staying on the mountain, you can see the sunrise and the sunset, and enjoy the mountains when the light is soft.

Chinese guidebooks recommend climbing up at night with a flashlight to see the sunrise (presumably skipping the entrance fee). The locals say, "You don't fear what you can't see" (*"Bu jian bu pa"*). This is not sensible. The cable car (¥110/$14/£7.15 round-trip; ¥60/$7.80/£3.90 one-way) reaches Bei Feng in 10 minutes, about 4 hours quicker than you would on foot. If you want to save your knees and leave yourself more time on the mountain, take the cable car down.

On the old road, it's 8km (5 miles) to Bei Feng, all uphill. You can take a taxi for ¥20 ($2.60/£1.30). The last mile to North Peak is steep, narrow, and slippery, particularly through **Heaven's Well** (**Tian Jing**).

Chinese tour groups, bedecked in yellow hats and white gloves, will gape at you, and souvenirs, bottles of water, and cucumbers will be waved in your face, but there is an enjoyable spirit of camaraderie among the hikers. And at least one of the souvenirs is worth purchasing. Chinese visitors have their name engraved on a brass padlock (¥2/25¢/15p) wishing good health for the family (or a long and happy relationship for young couples) and attach it to one of the many chain railings.

WHERE TO STAY & DINE

Outside of early May and mid-October, there is a surplus of accommodations on Hua Shan, so discounts of 30% to 50% are easily obtained. Dining on the mountain is basic and overpriced; take as much food as you can carry.

If you arrive at Hua Shan late at night, there are a couple of passable hotels in **Hua Shan Kou,** and unlike the lodgings on Hua Shan itself, they have showers. The dark, midsize rooms of the **Hua Shan Jinrong Binguan (Hua Shan Financial Hotel),** Yu Quan Lu Zhong Duan (© **0913/436-3119;** fax 0913/436-3124; ¥320/$42/£21 twin, from ¥588/$76/£38 suite), are overpriced, and service isn't exactly effusive. The best rooms are in building 4, which was renovated in 2001. The Hua Shan Tourist Bureau and a restaurant are located here. The **Xi Yue Binguan,** Yu Quan Lu Zhong Duan (© **0913/436-8298;** ¥198/$26/£13 twin), easily spotted because of its traditional sloping tiled roof, is friendlier and a better value than the Financial. It was renovated in 2002 but the money ran out, leaving the corridors dark and dank.

On the mountain, facilities are basic, there are no bathrooms or showers, and pit toilets are common. Problems with wastewater treatment may lead to the closure of many hotels, so call ahead to check if your intended lodgings are still there. The **Bei Feng Fandian,** Hua Shan Fengjing Qu Bei Feng (© **0913/430-0062;** ¥300/$39/£20 twin without bathroom), is a 5-minute walk from the cable car—perfect for the lazy and the late. Both the sunset and the sunrise can be enjoyed from the North Peak. The hotel offers a competent staff, clean rooms, a restaurant, and magnificent views.

3 Tianshui

Gansu Province, 385km (239 miles) W of Xi'an, 294km (182 miles) SE of Lanzhou

Tianshui is divided into two parts—the main town of **Qin Cheng,** and the smaller township of **Beidao Qu,** 15km (9 miles) down the Wei river valley to the west. Both townships are unexceptional; the main reason to visit is a clamber around the stunning Buddhist caves of Maiji Shan, a 1-hour bus ride from Beidao Qu. *Note:* Please turn to appendix A for Chinese translations of key locations.

ESSENTIALS

GETTING THERE The **railway station** is in the north of Beidao Qu, with many trains from Lanzhou (4 hr.) and farther west, and from Xi'an (4 hr.) and farther east. Tianshui's allocation of tickets is limited, so you may need to proceed through CITS in Qin Cheng. Heading west for Lanzhou are the T75 (10:13am), T113 (8:34am), and T117 (11:03pm). To Xining, the speediest choice is the T151 (8 hr.; 6:29am). To Chongqing, the only direct train is the K554 (19 hr.; 2:28pm). Pray for an upgrade. To Xi'an, take the T152 (6:47pm) or the T115 (4:46pm) that continues to Shanghai. Beijing trains (17 hr.) include the T70 (8:46pm), T152 (6:47pm), and T76 (11:17pm).

Connecting with Xi'an (380km/236 miles; 6 hr.), the **bus** is your best option. From the **Beidao Qu long-distance bus station** on Jiaotong Lu there are buses for Xi'an (¥70/$9.10/£4.55) from 7am to 8pm. Buses depart half-hourly for Lanzhou (¥60/$7.80/£3.90).

The main bus station in Qin Cheng is 3 blocks east and 2 blocks north of the main square at Shandong Lu 31 (© **0938/821-4028**). Hourly buses depart for Xi'an (7am–4:30pm.; ¥70/$9.10/£4.55); half-hourly buses head to Lanzhou (8am–5pm; 381km/236 miles; 4 hr.; ¥57/$7.40/£3.70); two services daily run to Linxia (4 hr.;

¥47/$6.10/£3.05) and there are buses at 6am and 5pm for Yinchuan (610km/378 miles; 15 hr.; ¥80/$10/£5.20).

GETTING AROUND Bus no. 6 from the railway station connects Qin Cheng with Beidao Qu (15km/9¼ miles; 30 min.; ¥2/25¢/15p). The first bus is at 6:20am; the last bus departs at 11:30pm. Taxis in both areas cost ¥5 (65¢/35p), white mini-vans ¥3 (40¢/20p).

TOURS & GUIDES CITS at 2 Wulong Lu (© 0938/273-3710; fax 0938/272-1948; www.tianshuitour.com) is useful if you are looking for an English-speaking guide (¥150/$20/£9.75 per day), but don't expect obligation-free advice. They are open from 8:30am to 6pm.

FAST FACTS

Banks, Foreign Exchange & ATMs The main **Bank of China** is located at Jianshe Lu 8 (© 0938/821-3515) in Qin Cheng, 800m (2,624 ft.) east of the northeast corner of the main square on the north side of the road. The building has massive bronze lions out front. It's open from 8:30am to noon and 2:30 to 6pm on weekdays.

Internet Access An **Internet bar** on the second floor of Gonghui Dasha charges ¥2 (25¢/15p) per hour. Dial-up is © 169.

Post Office The main post office is located on the northwest corner of the main square in Qin Cheng.

SEEING THE SIGHTS

Maiji Shan Shiku 𝄐𝄐 These are some of the most remarkable Buddhist caves in China, demonstrating a fine range of statuary styles amid spectacular scenery. Located 30km (19 miles) southeast of Tianshui, the haystack-shaped mountain is home to 194 extant caves, most on the western side of the mountain. The first caves were carved out during the Later Qin (384–417), a non-Han dynasty established during the Sixteen Kingdoms Period. Unlike other Buddhist caves, these saw little construction during the Tang dynasty, due to a series of earthquakes. The most serious occurred in 734, when the middle part of the grottoes collapsed. Significant statuary dates from the Northern Wei, Northern Zhou, and Sui dynasties.

Unlike other sites, the statuary here was not carved from the crumbling red rock, but added to it. **Grotto 18** explains the method of construction: A wooden superstructure is hauled up the mountain, bored into the soft cliffs, and coated with clay. Striking grottoes include **no. 191,** which houses a menacing winged figure with bulging eyes as its centerpiece; **no. 13,** with a huge Buddha and two attendant bodhisattvas dating from either the Northern Zhou dynasty or the Sui dynasty; and **no. 5,** with a sensuous bodhisattva dating from the Tang dynasty. As you scramble up the ladders that connect the caves, the charming scenery complements the statuary.

Many of the most interesting caves are off-limits without payment of between ¥300 ($39/£20) and ¥600 ($78/£39) per group. If you have either the money or many likeminded friends, cave **no. 133** (¥600 ($78/£39) from the Northern Wei (which is actually a tomb) is recognized as Maiji Shan's best. It contains 18 carved granite stones that depict the life of the Buddha. A sublime statue stands to the right, depicting one of Buddha's disciples, Bhiksu, smiling enigmatically as he listens to the master. When (now ex-) Prime Minister Zhu Rongji visited in 2001, he was depressed by the poverty he saw on his tour of Gansu. After staring at this statue, his good humor returned.

Buses for Maiji Shan (1–1½ hr.) leave Beidao Qu railway station from 7am, with the last bus leaving the mountain at 6pm. The bus will stop at a ticket office, where you pay ¥80 ($10/£5.20) to enter the "scenic area." Collect a map of the area, which is included in the price but is not offered without prompting. The bus stops farther up the mountain; the 10-minute walk to the ticket office takes you through souvenir stalls and excited locals letting off firecrackers. There are no English-speaking guides on-site, so unless you are fluent in Mandarin, there is no need to pay for a guide if you arrange one in advance through CITS. Take a picnic, and leave time to explore the surrounding mountains and the botanical gardens.

© 0938/223-1031. Admission: Scenic area ¥80 ($10/£5.20) entrance to the caves, ¥50 ($6.50/£3.25) for a guide; entrance to "special caves" ¥300–¥600 ($39–$78/£20–£39). 9am–6pm. Minibus from railway station ¥10 ($1.30/65p).

WHERE TO STAY

Unless you have an early bus to catch from the main bus station in Qin Cheng, stay in Beidao Qu, which is handier for both the railway station and Maiji Shan. Discounts of 20% are easily obtained at all establishments. Going against the trend elsewhere, the best hotels in Beidao Qu are near the railway station and the best among them is the two-star **Maiji Dajiudian**, Tianshui Huoche Zhan Guangchang Xi Ce (© **0938/492-0000**; ¥204/$27/£13 twin). The hotel has bright, clean rooms (the best are on the sixth floor, facing away from the railway station), an efficient staff, and a restaurant. If you decide to stay in Qin Qheng, the two-star **Tianshui Dajiudian,** Dazong Lu Nan Kou 1 (© **0938/828-9999;** fax 0938/821-1301; ¥146–¥172/ $19–$22/£9.50–£11 twin) is the best choice for facilities and location. But if you want to spent the night at Maiji Shan, **Zhiwuyuan Zhaodaisuo** (© **0938/223-1029;** ¥100/$13/£6.50 twin in old wing, ¥280–¥360/$36–$47/£18–£23 cabin) is a real find. The setting is the botanical gardens behind the mountain, amid imposing oak and birch forests, and the cabins are good value—you can pay by the bed. By car, take a road to the left 720m (2,362 ft.) past the scenic area ticket office and continue uphill for 3km (2 miles), or walk 15 minutes past the Maiji Shan caves.

WHERE TO DINE

Beidao Qu may not be a culinary paradise, but it sports honest eateries serving generous portions for around ¥10 ($1.30/65p) per person. Elbow past the locals to find a seat in **Niu Dawan,** a halal (the Muslim equivalent of kosher) restaurant north of the bus station on Er Ma Lu. There's one dish to order—*niurou mian* (beef noodles), and two choices to make—thick *(kuan)* or thin *(xi)* noodles, and whether to add more beef *(jia rou)*.

A friendly establishment just west of the Gonghui Dasha, the **Tian Xi Xiaochidian** is run by three retired sisters and serves generous portions for around ¥10 ($1.30/65p) per person. Filling *chao mian* (stir-fried noodles) or a stone bowl of bubbling *shaguo jikuai* (chicken clay pot) are perfect after a hike in the mountains.

4 Lanzhou

Gansu Province, 665km (412 miles) W of Xi'an, 514km (319 miles) SW of Yinchuan

This was once the point where the Silk Routes crossed the Yellow River; however, whatever charms the old town possessed were buried long ago. In 1998, **Lanzhou** won the title of the planet's most polluted city by a considerable margin (Chinese towns filled 7 of the top 10 places). This dubious distinction led to humorous attempts to rectify the problem—one entrepreneur got backing for a scheme to knock a hole in the surrounding mountains to "open the window" on Lanzhou's smog. Alas, after 18m (60 ft.) of leveling, and much talk of villas and technology parks, this grand dream of moving the mountain ended when planners discovered that Lanzhou was hemmed in, not by one mountain, but by 24km (15 miles) of mountains. Plans to convert the city's largest polluter—a coal-fired power station—to natural gas also fell through when the German partner found that the numbers didn't add up. In spite of further token attempts to clean up (including civil servants having to walk to work on particularly bad days) the city remains in the world's top 10 most polluted cities.

Lanzhou offers a glimpse of what lies farther northwest, but there are few reasons to linger. The museum is worth a look, and the town is a comfortable base for trips south to Bingling Si, Xiahe, and Langmusi. But your first action should be to book a ticket out of town.

ESSENTIALS

GETTING THERE   The airport is 75km (47 miles) to the north. **China Eastern Airlines** (© 0931/882-1964; fax 0931/882-8174; open 8am–9pm) has its main office opposite the JJ Sun Hotel. They can book tickets on any Chinese airline. Buses for the airport (1 hr.; ¥30/$3.90/£1.95) leave 2 hours before each flight.

Queues at the new **railway station** (© 0931/492-2222) in the south of town can range from very short to very long. It's worth a shot to go directly here if you are hoping to head out of town quickly. Sleeper tickets may also be purchased through your hotel or from the largest ticket outlet in the Railway Bureau (Tieluju) at Hezheng Lu 156, on the first floor of the Jinlun Dasha. Take bus no. 34 from the station to Tieluju.

Trains originating in Lanzhou connect with Beijing (T76: 7:22pm, 20 hr.; K44: 4:03pm, 27 hr.), Shanghai (T118: 12:47am, 25 hr.), Urumqi (T295: 4:01pm, 24 hr.), Xi'an (K120: 9:58pm, 10 hr.), Guangzhou (K228: 11:22pm, 36 hr.), Chengdu (K348: 4:27pm, 22 hr.), Pingliang (N906: 7:32pm, 12 hr.), Jiayuguan (N851: 8:50pm, 11 hr.), Xining (T207: 7:42am, 3 hr.; T209: 4:18pm), and Golmud (T27: 4:11pm, 15 hr.). The speediest connection with Yinchuan is the K916 at 10:21pm (9 hr.).

Most regional services depart from the hectic **South Bus Station (Nan Zhan)** in the far southwest of town (© 0931/291-4066), a ¥10 ($2.60/£1.30) taxi ride from the center. Be prepared for some aggressive touts selling the Xia He services; if you arrive with a long wait for a direct service, head to Linxia (or Hezuo) and change there—don't believe a word the touts tell you about the availability of onward buses. Buses connect with Hezuo (258km/160 miles; 5 hr.; ¥44/$5.70/£2.85) every half-hour from 7am to 4pm; with Linxia (149km/92 miles; 4 hr.; ¥27/$3.50/£1.75) every 20 minutes from 7am to 6pm; and with Xining at 10am, 11am, and noon (there are more Xining services from the long-distance station). There are three direct buses to Xia He (256km/159 miles; 4 hr.) at 6:30am, 8:30am, and 2pm (¥44/$5.70/£2.85). The **West Bus Station** at Xijin Dong Lu 486 (© 0931/291-9537) has direct buses to Liujia Xia (2 hr.; ¥12/$1.55/80p) that run regularly between 7:20am and 6pm.

The **long-distance bus station** at Pingliang Lu 133 (© 0931/456-2222) is just northwest of the railway station. Buses connect with Xining (3 hr.; ¥53/$6.90/£3.45) every 45 minutes between 7:30am and 7:30pm. There is one sleeper bus to Xi'an every evening at 8:30pm (10 hr.; ¥120/$16/£7.80).

GETTING AROUND   Green Santanas charge ¥7 (90¢/45p) for the first 3km (2 miles), then ¥1.40 (20¢/10p) per kilometer; add a night surcharge (¥1.60/20¢/10p) from 10pm to 5am. Buses start at ¥1 (15¢/5p), which is paid on boarding at the front

Lanzhou

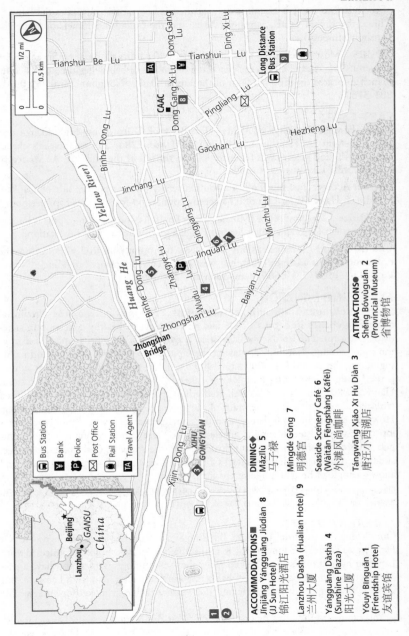

Bus Station
Bank
Police
Post Office
Rail Station
Travel Agent

Tianshui Be Lu

Dong Gang Xi Lu
Dong Gang Lu

Tianshui
Ding Xi Lu

Long Distance Bus Station

CAAC
Dong Gang Xi Lu

Pingliang Lu

Hezheng Lu

Binhe Dong Lu

Gaoshan Lu

Jinchang Lu

Qingyang Lu

Minzhu Lu

Jinquan Lu

Huang He

Zhangye Lu

Baiyan Lu

Binhe Dong Lu

Wudu

Zhongshan Lu

Zhongshan Bridge

(Yellow River)

Xijin Dong Lu

XIHU GONGYUAN

Beijing
GANSU
China
Lanzhou

ATTRACTIONS●
Shěng Bówùguǎn 2
(Provincial Museum)
省博物馆

DINING◆
Mǎzǐlù 5
马子禄

Mingdé Gōng 7
明德宫

Seaside Scenery Café 6
(Wàitān Fēngshàng Kāfēi)
外滩风尚咖啡

Tángwāng Xiǎo Xī Hú Diàn 3
唐汪小西湖店

ACCOMMODATIONS■
Jǐnjiāng Yángguāng Jiǔdiàn 8
(JJ Sun Hotel)
锦江阳光酒店

Lanzhou Dasha (Hualian Hotel) 9
兰州大厦

Yángguāng Dàshà 4
(Sunshine Plaza)
阳光大厦

Yǒuyì Bīnguǎn 1
(Friendship Hotel)
友谊宾馆

279

of the bus. Bus no. 1 is useful; it starts at the railway station and passes the Bank of China, the JJ Sun Hotel, Sunshine Plaza, and the Friendship Hotel (opposite the Lanzhou Museum).

TOURS Most **hotels** have tour desks which offer tours to Bingling Si. There are numerous branches of **CITS,** each accusing the others of being illegitimate. A helpful branch is located on the 11th floor of the Luyou Dasha, Nongmin Xiang (© **0931/ 881-3133**).

FAST FACTS

Banks, Foreign Exchange & ATMs The **Bank of China** (Mon–Fri 8:30am–noon and 2:30–6pm) at Tianshui Lu 589 (© **0931/841-7284**) accepts traveler's checks (counter 48) and credit cards (counter 47). To the left of the building, ATMs accept foreign cards. Take bus no. 1 to Panshi Lu.

Internet Access Just south of Lanzhou University on the opposite side of Tianshui Nan Lu, **E Hang Wang Lou** offers a speedy connection for ¥2 (25¢/15p) per hour.

Post Office The post office (Minzhu Dong Lu 104; Mon–Fri 8am–7pm) is located on the corner of Minzhu Dong Lu and Pingliang Lu near the East Bus Station.

Visa Extensions Visa extensions are processed promptly up to 2 weeks before the expiration date at a helpful **PSB,** just west of the city government building at Wudu Lu 310 (© **0931/871-8606;** 8am–noon and 2:30–6pm).

EXPLORING LANZHOU

Sheng Bowuguan (Provincial Museum) The newly renovated Provincial Museum reopened its doors in 2006 and now displays its healthy collection in state-of-the-art form. The late Neolithic pottery is particularly impressive, most of it from the region around Tianshui, displaying the rapid progress in both pottery and painting during this period (ca. 3000 B.C.–1900 B.C.). The museum's most famous exhibit is the **Flying Horse (Tong Ben Ma)** ✪, taken in 1969 from the tomb of an Eastern Han (25–220) general near Wuwei. Staff admit that the bronze horse on display is a replica; the real article is in the vaults of the museum, and another copy is in Beijing. However, the original was damaged in the copying process, and the mold was either lost or destroyed, so this copy is priceless. Other items from the tomb include bamboo strips containing meticulous instructions on the etiquette of drinking, marriage, and death. Call in advance or contact CITS to arrange an English-speaking guide, and allow a couple of hours for a leisurely visit.

Directly opposite the Friendship Hotel (Youyi Binguan). © **0931/234-6306**. Admission ¥35 ($4.55/£2.30); English-speaking guide ¥100 ($13/£6.50). 9am–5pm. Bus: no. 1 to Youyi Binguan.

A NEARBY GROTTO

Once a long day trip from Lanzhou, Bingling Si may now be visited on the way to Xia He. The town nearest Bingling Si is Liujia Xia, which was recently connected with Lanzhou by an expressway. The trip takes about 90 minutes. Unless you have a passion for cave temples, this one's probably not worth the long haul from Lanzhou, but if you're heading south to Xia He and the weather is fine, it makes for an agreeable outing.

You can get to the caves by bus from the West Bus Station at Xijin Dong Lu 486, or more simply arrange a private car through CITS (¥400/$52/£26). However you get here, on arrival at Liujia Xia, you'll be bundled off to the ticket office, where you purchase an entry ticket for the San Xia Dam (¥30/$3.90/£1.95)—formerly China's largest and single reason that the Yellow River ends well short of the sea—and a boat ticket. The public ferry costs ¥30 ($3.90/£1.95), though the staff will deny its existence. It's better to take the fast boats instead, as they get you to the caves 2 hours faster. A round-trip ticket is ¥80 ($10/£5.20). Those continuing to Linxia (25km/16 miles; 40 min.; ¥5/65¢/35p; last minibus 6pm) and then to Xia He (107km/66 miles; 2½ hr.; ¥9/$1.15/60p) should ask to be dropped at Lianhua Tai on the way back. (If you've got your private boat, you can ask that they take you here.) The last bus back to Lanzhou (¥10/$1.30/65p) leaves at 6:30pm. If you stay in Liujia Xia, the best lodgings are the Huang He Binguan and the cheaper Liu Dian Binguan.

There's a mock-fort hotel to the left (west) of the grottoes. Head straight for the caves, as most boats only wait for an hour. Two-thirds of the caves were carved in the Tang dynasty, but examples range from the Northern Wei (368–534) to the Ming dynasties. Pay ¥80 ($10/£5.20) at the ticket office and turn right; follow a narrow pathway around. A 27m (90-ft.) Maitreya (Buddha of the Future) with prominent nipples—a decidedly non-Han Chinese touch—dominates the valley. Higher up the cliff face is **Cave 169** ✹ (¥300/$39/£20 extra!), one of the most ancient in China, showing Indian influences. Unlike most cave temples, the upper caves are natural. Unfortunately, 200 lower caves were flooded when the dam was completed.

WHERE TO STAY

Lanzhou may be a dump, but it has new hotels with comfortable beds where 30%-to-50% discounts are often negotiable. However, for those on a tight budget, options are few with many likely looking establishments not open to foreigners.

Jinjiang Yangguang Jiudian (JJ Sun Hotel)   A quick taxi ride from the railway station, this Hong Kong–managed hotel is a good option. The beds are a bit hard for a four-star, but the staff is professional, guest rooms are spotless, and bathrooms are immaculate. It's worth asking for a south-facing room on a high floor as there are good views over the city to the mountain to be enjoyed (if Lanzhou's notorious pollution allows).

Donggang Xi Lu 589. ✆ **0931/880-5511.** Fax 0931/885-4700. www.jjsunhotel.com. 236 units. ¥800 ($104/£52) standard room; from ¥1,500 ($195/£98) suite. Discounts of 20%. Rates include full breakfast. 15% service charge. AE, DC, MC, V. **Amenities:** 2 restaurants; cafe; concierge; business center; 24-hr. forex; same-day laundry/dry cleaning. *In room:* A/C, TV, broadband Internet access (¥30/$3.90/£1.95 per day), minibar, fridge, hair dryer, safe.

Lanzhou Dasha (Hualian Hotel Group)   Directly opposite the train station, this budget favorite isn't too bad given the price, and is very convenient if you want to minimize your time in Lanzhou. There is a wide range of rooms from ultra-cheap common rooms without bathrooms, to better standard twins.

Tianshui Nan Lu. ✆ **0931/499-2101.** 394 units. ¥98–¥188 ($13–$24/£6.35–£12) standard room; ¥58 ($7.55/£3.75) common room. No credit cards. **Amenities:** 2 restaurants; business center; tour desk. *In room:* TV.

Yangguang Dasha (Sunshine Plaza) ✹✹ *Value Kids*   Easily the best hotel in town, the Sunshine Plaza has great service and comfortable rooms. The standard rooms have plush beds and thick carpets but it's worth spending the extra ¥100 ($13/£6.50) on the deluxe versions that have raised sitting areas and are more spacious. The game room is inspired; you can practice your golf swing, grand-prix driving, skiing, dancing, and even shuffleboard, a spectator sport in China. Facilities for travelers with disabilities are available.

Qinyang Lu 408. ✆ **0931/460-8888.** Fax 0931/460-8889. www.sunshineplaza.com.cn. 223 units (shower only). ¥1,080–¥1,180 ($140–$153/£70–£77) standard room; from ¥1,580 ($205/£103) suite. Discounts of 30%. Rates include breakfast. 15% service charge. AE, DC, MC, V. **Amenities:** 2 restaurants; nightclub; huge game room; concierge; courtesy car; business center; executive business services; 24-hr. forex (no traveler's checks); 24-hr. room service; same-day laundry/dry cleaning. *In room:* A/C, satellite TV, broadband Internet access, minibar, fridge, hair dryer, safe.

Youyi Binguan (Friendship Hotel)   While it won't win any awards, the long-established Friendship has good facilities and pleasant enough rooms, and its location directly opposite Lanzhou's only real "sight"—the museum—makes it a convenient option. There are several wings to this monster of a hotel; the west wing has light, bright, and quiet rooms, with carpets that are only mildly worn and good bathrooms. The hotel is popular with tour groups.

Xiji1n Xi Lu 16. (C) **0931/268-9169.** Fax 0931/233-0304. 597 units. ¥280 ($36/£18) standard room; ¥730 ($95/£47) suite. Discounts of 20%. AE, DC, MC, V. **Amenities:** Several restaurants; tennis court; health center; business center; tour desk; forex; laundry/dry cleaning. *In room:* A/C, TV.

WHERE TO DINE

Those craving junk food will find a **KFC** on the northeast corner of Zhongshan Lu and Zhangye Lu, as well as a **Dicos** at the train station end of Pingliang Lu. **Seaside Scenery Cafe (Waitan Fengshang Kafei)** at Nanguan Shizi Shiyou Dasha 1 Lou (**(C) 0931/844-8396**), serves eminently drinkable coffee—but be sure to specify hot *(re),* iced *(bing),* or by the pot *(hu).* The menu offers steaks, spaghetti, and Japanese set meals.

Mazilu ⭐⭐ *(Value* GANSU   Be prepared to have one of the best noodle experiences of your life. The drafty, warehouse-style restaurant, open for breakfast and lunch, doesn't have much atmosphere, but no one's here for the decor—it's all about the beef noodles, which is the only thing you can get here. Lanzhou *niurou lamian* has migrated to all parts of the country by way of little street-side noodle shops, but this is the real deal, and known by locals as the best place to sample the dish. Pay your ¥3.50 (45¢/25p) to the cashier, who will give you a ticket to collect your bowl at the back of the restaurant. The tender, thin noodles are boiled in a huge vat of beef broth, then chili and sesame sauce and bits of beef are tossed in at the last minute.

Dazhong Xiang. No phone. Meal for 2 ¥7 (90¢/45p). No credit cards. 6:30am–2:30pm.

Mingde Gong ⭐ GANSU   The Mingde Gong, a four-story palace that gets progressively more luxurious as you ascend (culminating in dark wood-paneled rooms, gold-plated cutlery, and some of the biggest karaoke TVs you'll ever see), is the flag-bearer for Gansu cuisine—"long cai." While the boss is a Hui entrepreneur, the chefs hail from Beijing and Guangzhou. Signature dishes include *menggu yangpai* (Mongolian lamb), the huge and spicy *kao yangtui* (roast leg of lamb with walnuts), a deep-fried lamb and green-pepper pancake *(bobing yangrou),* and the sweet vegetarian dish, *xishi jinju baihe.*

Jiuquan Lu 191. (C) **0931/466-8588.** Meal for 2 ¥90–¥170 ($12–$22/£5.85–£11). No credit cards. 10:30am–10pm.

Tangwang Xiao Xi Hu Dian GANSU   Regional specialties are scarce, but locals are proud of *shouzhua rou* (grabbed meat): hunks of beef dunked in salt and pepper and chased by a clove of raw garlic (optional!). Ask for a lean portion *(shou fen),* unless you want to guzzle on huge lumps of lard. The *xilie niurou mian* (beef noodles) are also first-rate. Lanzhou's liveliest night market, Xiao Xihu Yeshi, is directly across the road.

(C) **0931/260-2398.** Meal for 2 less than ¥40 ($5.20/£2.60). No credit cards. Open 24 hr. Bus: no. 1 to Xiao Xi Hu.

5 Linxia

Gansu Province, 149km (92 miles) SW of Lanzhou, 107km (66 miles) NE of Xiahe

"All writers agree on the commercial ability and energy of the T'ung-kan [Hui], as well as on their surliness, ill manners and hostile suspicion of strangers. . . ." This judgment by American journalist Owen Lattimore seems harsh until you visit Linxia, a predominantly Hui town (with a smattering of Bao'an and the Altaic Dongxiang minorities). Those wishing to stay in a traditional, non-Uighur Islamic town should visit Xunhua in eastern Qinghai. However, if you arrive late an overnight stay in Linxia may be unavoidable.

GETTING AWAY The **West Bus Station (Xi Zhan; ℂ 0930/621-2177)** has buses every half-hour for Lanzhou (149km/92 miles; 3 hr.; ¥29/$3.75/£1.90) from 7am to 3pm; Hezuo (106km/66 miles; 2 hr.; ¥19/$2.45/£1.25) every half-hour from 6:30am; Xining (269km/167 miles; 4 hr.; ¥44/$5.70/£2.85) at 6am; Xunhua (115km/71 miles; 2½ hr.; ¥19/$2.45/£1.25) and Tongren (183km/113 miles; 5 hr.; ¥34/$4.40/£2.20) at 6:30am. If you're heading to Xia He (107km/66 miles; 2½ hr.; ¥14/$1.80/90p), you'll have to brave the pickpockets at the **South Bus Station (Nan Zhan; ℂ 0930/621-2767)**; there are buses every half-hour from 7am to 4:30pm.

WHERE TO STAY

As long as you get here by midafternoon, there's really no need to stay in Linxia, but if you find yourself stuck here, the **Linxia Fandian** at Hongyuan Lu 9 (ℂ **0930/623-0080;** fax 0930/621-4412) is a reasonable option with twin rooms in the old wing for ¥180 ($23/£12), and better rooms in the new wing (¥253/$33/£16). Head east from Xi Zhan along Minzhu Xi Lu, then turn down the first street on your right (south).

6 Hezuo

Gansu Province, 258km (160 miles) SW of Lanzhou, 72km (45 miles) SE of Xiahe

Aside from a substantial Tibetan population, the capital of Gan Nan (Southern Gansu) Prefecture is much like any other Han town of recent construction. However, as a transit point, it is infinitely preferable to Linxia.

ESSENTIALS

GETTING THERE Hezuo has two bus stations. Most buses from Lanzhou arrive at the Central Bus Station, which is far more convenient than the new South Bus Station, in the far south of town. The **Central Bus Station, Hezuo Qichezhan (ℂ 0941/821-2422)** has buses for Linxia (106km/66 miles; 2 hr.; ¥13/$1.65/80p) every 20 minutes from 6am to 5:40pm and Xia He (72km/45 miles; 1½ hr.; ¥12/$1.55/80p) every 30 minutes between 6:30am and 5:50pm. Buses depart for Lanzhou (258km/160 miles; 5 hr.; ¥44/$5.65/£2.85) at 8am and 9am. Buses for Langmu Si (173km/107 miles; 5 hr.; ¥28/$3.65/£1.80) depart at 7am, 10:20am, and 12:20pm. There is a bus for Xining at 6:30am (331km/205 miles; 5 hr.; ¥51/$6.65/£3.30). The **South Bus Station (Qiche Nan Zhan; ℂ 0941/821-3039)** has buses for Ruo'ergai (7 hr.; ¥46/$6/£3) in northern Sichuan at 7:30am and 10:30am; the latter continues on to Aba (583km/361 miles; ¥82/$11/£5.35) the following day.

FAST FACTS

Visa Extensions The Hezuo PSB office is on Renmin Lu, near the large square (ℂ **0941/821-3953**).

EXPLORING HEZUO

Milarepa Tower *ⓡ*   Part of the Hezuo Monastery, this nine-story tower was built in 1678, but was burned down during the Cultural Revolution. In the late 1980s, government officials allowed the tower's rebuilding, which was completed in 1994. It's worth a rickety climb up the nine floors not only for the artifacts but also for the decent view of the city from the top. A nice monk named Chinpa who oversees the grounds may invite you in his office for tsampa and tea if you speak a bit of Chinese or Tibetan.

At the north end of Renmin Lu. Admission ¥20 ($2.60/£1.30); if you look Chinese, they'll let you in half price. Open daylight hours.

WHERE TO STAY

Jiaotong Binguan   The Traffic Hotel is hardly the Hilton, but it's cheap, central and only a couple of minutes walk from the bus station. The standard twins are bright and clean, but the beds are hard and the bathrooms could do with a refit. Hot water is available 8pm to midnight.

Turn right out of the Central Bus Station and continue for 100m; the hotel is on your right. ℂ 0941/822-1300. 34 units. ¥80 ($10/£5.20) standard room. No credit cards In room: TV.

Xiangbala Dajiudian   One of Hezuo's newer establishments, this is the most comfortable hotel in town. Aside from the annoying instrumental music piped in through speakers in the lobby and the hallways (during working hours), there's nothing offending about this three-star place. Rooms are clean and bathrooms have been well scrubbed. The first floor features a Tibetan-style bar that features a nightly dancing and singing performance.

Renmin Jie 53. ℂ 0941/821-3222. Fax 0941/821-8899. 90 units. ¥280 ($36/£18) standard room; ¥880 ($114/£57) suite. Discounts of 30%. No credit cards. **Amenities:** 3 restaurants; business center. In room: TV.

WHERE TO DINE

There's a market with an interesting mix of street stalls and small restaurants selling dumplings, Muslim food, and noodles not far from the bus station on the corner of Renmin Lu and Dong Er Lu. Once you've sated your hunger, you can stroll around the market, which features everything from live birds to athletic shoes.

7 Xia He (Labrang) *ⓡⓡⓡ*

Gansu Province, 256km (159 miles) SW of Lanzhou, 72km (45 miles) W of Hezuo

The delightful monastery town of **Xia He** is nestled north of the banks of the **Da Xia He (Sang Qu)** at an elevation of 2,900m (9,500 ft.). Not surprisingly, it gets very cold in winter, dipping to −4°F (−20°C); even in August, the average temperature is a cool 59°F (15°C). The town is divided into two sections. Primarily Hui and Han at its ever-expanding eastern end, it changes abruptly to Tibetan as you approach the monastery in the west. *Note:* Please turn to appendix A for Chinese translations of key locations.

ESSENTIALS

GETTING THERE   Buses (ℂ 0941/712-1462) connect with Hezuo (72km/45 miles; 1½ hr.; ¥12/$1.60/80p) every 30 minutes from 6:10am to 6:10pm; Linxia (107km/66 miles; 2½ hr.; ¥19/$2.45/£1.25) every 30 minutes from 6am to 5:30pm;

Lanzhou (256km/159 miles; 5 hr.; ¥44/$5.70/£2.85) at 6:30am, 7:30am, and 2:30pm; Tongren (107km/66 miles; 4 hr.; ¥21/$2.75/£1.35) at 7:30am; and Amchog (72km/ 45 miles, 2 hr.; ¥19/$2.45/£1.25) at 11:30am. The Tongren service connects with a Xining bus.

If there's a group of you, **minivans** to Langmu Si (5 hr.; ¥700/$91/£46) can be arranged through the Overseas Tibetan Hotel, Tara Guesthouse or at the bus station. *Warning:* If you're taking the rough but scenic route southeast via Amchog, hire a Tibetan driver and bring cigarettes; banditry, in the form of determined children with large rocks, or nomads on horseback, is common.

GETTING AROUND   **Bicycles** can be rented from most guesthouses for ¥15–¥20 ($1.95–$2.60/£1–£1.30) per day. **Shared taxis** or **motorcycle carts** should take you anywhere in town for ¥1 (15¢/5p), but they'll try for more.

TOURS & GUIDES   Tsewong of Tsewong's Cafe is a good resource for travel information and can put you in touch with local drivers and tour guides.

FAST FACTS
Banks   Forex services are unavailable in Xia He.

Internet Access   Internet access can be found at many of the guesthouses and cafes including Tsewong's Cafe and the Overseas Tibetan Hotel. The charge is ¥4 to ¥5 (50¢–65¢/25p–35p) per hour.

Post Office   The post office (open 8am–6pm) a few hundred meters west of the bus station on the south side of the road.

Visa Extensions   You used to be able to previously get them done here, but now it's only possible in at the Hezuo PSB office (p. 283).

EXPLORING XIA HE
A 3km (2-mile) clockwise perambulation (kora) of the monastery is an excellent way to begin the day. You may find yourself befriended by delightful elderly pilgrims or by young monks keen to practice their English. If your schedule allows, time your visit to coincide with the **Monlam Festival,** held on the 4th to 16th days of the first lunar month (Feb–Mar). The monastery is open to all during the festival, and on the 13th day you can watch the "sunning of the Buddha." An enormous *thangka* (silk painting) is spread across a **Thangka Wall** on the south bank of the Sangchu. When sanctified, it effectively becomes the Buddha in the minds of believers. The following days feature religious dancing and the offering of *torma* (butter sculptures).

A hike up into the hills gives you a magnificent view of the monastery. Just west of it is a small, friendly nunnery.

Labuleng Si (Labrang Monastery) ✸✸   As any monk you come across will tell you, Labrang Monastery, founded in 1709, is one of the six largest monasteries of the Geluk order, and the largest monastery in Amdo. Unlike most large religious institutions, it escaped desecration during the Cultural Revolution, although the number of monks and nuns was reduced from over 4,000 to the present number of just over 1,000. The head lama ranks behind only the Dalai Lama and the Panchen Lama, and with the passing away of the sixth incarnate lama (whose stupa rises in the south of the complex), the monastery is in transition. There are colleges for esoteric and exoteric Buddhism, astronomy, mathematics, geography, and medicine. Amdo monks see themselves as the true holders of the faith—looking down on the Khampas and central

Tibetans as soldiers and politicians respectively—and the monks take pride in the appearance of their monastery. Stunning *thangkhas* adorn the walls, and many beams and finials are inscribed with sacred and protective script.

The most striking building is the **Assembly Hall** 𝔊, with its golden roof. This is a recent addition, as the original burned down in 1985. The **museum** and a display of frozen **butter sculptures**—including memorable sculptures of Jiang Zemin and his cronies—are also worth seeking out. Just to the right of the main entrance is the School of Buddhist Studies, where monks are often keen to practice their English. There is no charge for wandering at will through the various buildings, but to get a better understanding of the monastery, taking one of the two daily English-speaking tours is advised. There's an entry fee of ¥10 ($1.30/65p) to visit the golden **Gongtang Pagoda**, reached from the south kora, which is thoroughly worthwhile as from the top you'll get fine views over the monastery.

Free admission; ¥40 ($5.20/£2.60) for twice-daily English tour (10:15am and 3:15pm) from the front gate. Closed Nov–Feb.

AROUND XIA HE

About 13km (8 miles) up the Da Xia He are the grasslands of Sangke (entry ¥5/65¢/35p), an ideal place for horse riding (¥20/$2.60/£1.30 per hour). The grass-lands are most spectacular in July and August, when the canola is flowering. Minivans wait outside the Tara Guesthouse and should charge about ¥40 ($5.20/£2.60) round-trip; or you can ride out by bike in an hour or so. (Bikes may be rented from Tara Guesthouse for ¥15/$1.95/£1 per day.) Some of the recent tourist developments—there are 18 "holiday villages" in the grasslands—are so appalling they are attractions in their own right. More spectacular grasslands are reached by turning left onto a sea-sonal road 12km (7½ miles) beyond town; continue southeast up the Xia He valley and over a pass toward the monastery town of **Amchog (A'muquhu).** Vast grasslands populated by marmots, vultures, and real nomads are your reward. You can arrange camping trips out to these grasslands through Tsewong's Cafe and the Overseas Tibetan Hotel for ¥100 to ¥150 ($13–$20/£6.50–£9.75) per person.

WHERE TO STAY

Xia He has a reasonable selection of places to stay, but note that most hotels only have hot water for a limited number of hours in the morning and then again in the evening.

Labuleng Binguan (Labrang Hotel)   Situated far west of town beyond the monastery, the Labrang was once Xia He's premier hotel. These days, in spite of its lovely, tranquil setting, it feels a forlorn place, although recent renovations have improved things a little. The south building *(nan lou)* is an unimaginative construc-tion with clean, overpriced rooms, while the Tibetan villas to the north of the com-plex feature enormous bathrooms, thick rugs, and obscene brown padded walls.

Laizhou Cun 70, 747100. ℂ **0941/712-1849.** Fax 0941/712-1328. 98 units (36 with shower only). ¥180–¥280 ($23–$36/£12]–£18) standard room; ¥580 ($75/£38) suite. No credit cards. **Amenities:** Restaurant; bar. *In room:* TV.

Overseas Tibetan Hotel (Huaqiao Fandian) 𝔊   The manager, Losang, is a Nepalese Tibetan who earned an MBA in the U.S. and does his best to instill a service ethic into his often lethargic staff. Once a dreary concrete monolith, this hotel has been greatly improved by successive additions to the second and third floors. The hotel offers a range of accommodations. The midsize rooms with twin beds on the third floor were added in

2001 and are the best in town, with tasteful Tibetan decorations and well-appointed bathrooms. On the second floor cheaper kang rooms are also decent, but the first-floor dormitory rooms suffer from damp.

Renmin Xi Jie 77, 747100. (℃) 0941/712-2642. Fax 0941/712-1872. othotel@public.lz.gs.cn. 35 units. ¥140–¥200 ($18–$26/£9.10–£13) standard room; ¥20 ($2.60/£1.30) dorm bed. No credit cards. **Amenities:** Restaurant; bike rental (¥20/$2.60/£1.30 per day); next-day laundry; Internet access. *In room:* TV, no phone.

Tara Guesthouse (Zhuoma Lushe) *Overrated*   If any hostel deserves the dreaded "backpacker mecca" title, this establishment does. Tara wrote to complain about the review we gave her establishment in our first edition, but two visits later, things are little better. Although popular with foreign travelers and boasting a prime location, the dormitories and many of the cozy-looking kang rooms are dank; the modernized shared bathrooms are a big improvement. The staff is friendly, but their English is limited.

Yage Tang 268, 747100. (℃) 0/138-9391-6260. t-dolma@yahoo.com. 19 units (shared bathroom). ¥20 ($2.60/£1.30) dorm bed; ¥50–¥70 ($6.50–$9.10/£3.25–£4.55) standard. No credit cards. **Amenities:** Bike rental (¥15/$1.95/£1 per day). *In room:* TV, no phone.

WHERE TO DINE

Everest Cafe WESTERN/CHINESE   Attached to the Overseas Tibetan Guesthouse, the restaurant is conveniently located for you to grab breakfast in the mornings before you start your pilgrimage around the monastery. The also offer a range of sandwiches, milkshakes, and *lassis*. The Chinese food is reminiscent of what you'd find at a Chinese restaurant in America.

Renmin Xi Jie 77. (℃) 0941/712-2642. Meal for 2 ¥30–¥50 ($3.90–$6.60/£1.95–£3.25). No credit cards. 6:30am–11pm.

Tsewong's Cafe *⋆* WESTERN/CHINESE   Opened by a former employee of the Overseas Tibetan Guesthouse, this cafe serves better than average Western food in a clean environment. The "real pizza by oven" is recommended—the crust is nice and cheesy and the sauce consists of fresh tomatoes. The burritos come a close second and the Chinese dumplings and the chocolate pancakes with Nutella are also popular. By the time you get here, the cafe should be brewing the best coffee in town. Tsewong is also a great resource for information about day trips around Xia He.

Renmin Xi Jie, located on the same side of street as the Overseas Tibetan Hotel, about 100m (328 ft.) in the opposite direction of the monastery on the 2nd floor. (℃) 0/1389-397-9763. www.tsewongs-cafe-xiahe.de. Meal for 2 ¥30–¥80 ($3.90–$10/£1.95–£5.20). No credit cards. 7am–10pm.

8 Langmu Si (Taktsang Lhamo) *⋆⋆*

Gansu Province, 431km (267m) S of Lanzhou, 91km (56m) NW of Ruo'ergai

Perched on the border of Sichuan and Gansu, this Tibetan monastic center is slowly becoming known to Chinese tourists, but still lacks the commercial feel of Xia He. The tranquil mountain village is reminiscent of Lijiang before it was "discovered." It is hoped Langmu Si can escape UNESCO listing for a few more years.

ESSENTIALS

GETTING THERE   Daily **buses** connect with Hezuo (173km/107 miles; 3 hr.; ¥28/$3.65/£1.80) at 6.30, 7:30am and noon. To the south, a bus connects with Ruo'ergai (91km/56 miles; 2 hr.; ¥20/$2.60/£1.30) at 7am. Plans for a daily Songpan bus have yet to materialize; a minibus to Songpan may be arranged through the Overseas Tibetan Hotel(¥800/$104/£52 for a 6-seat bus).

EXPLORING LANGMU SI

The town is home to two major Geluk monasteries, **Sertri Gompa** (¥16/$2.10/£1.05 admission) and **Kirti Gompa** (¥15/$1.95/£1 admission), situated in Gansu and Sichuan respectively. Both were razed during the Cultural Revolution and rebuilt during the early 1980s. Together, they house about 1,000 monks. True to the factional traditions of Tibetan Buddhism, they refer to each other as "that place in the other province." While the buildings are of recent construction, both are lively centers of worship, and the sound of monks chanting the scriptures may be heard throughout the day. A magnificent view of the surrounding countryside may be had from Sertri Gompa.

There are some delightful rambles around Langmu Si. If you head southwest beyond Kirti Gompa, a succession of narrow ravines and moraine valleys crowded with wildflowers, birds, and bubbling springs show the way to an abrupt pass. Continuing over the pass, you eventually connect with the Langmu Si–Maqu road, but this is a strenuous tramp through wild nomad country and should only be attempted by well-equipped parties. Another stiff hike is to the top of the distinctively shaped **Hua Gai Shan (Flower Cap Mountain)** ☀☀; this is best done as a horse trek (¥120/$16/£7.80 per day), camping overnight on the peak. Traditionally, only men are allowed to sleep on the mountain, but this taboo is relaxed for foreigners. On a clear morning, you can see the holy mountain of Amnye Machen in Qinghai. On the 15th day of the 6th month of the lunar calendar, a magnificent **"sunning of the Buddha" festival** takes place on a broad plateau just below the peak, the consecration of the *thangka* heralded by lamas trumpeting from the summit. A nearby hot spring is also a popular destination for horse treks.

Langmu Si is a popular spot to attend a **sky burial** or *chadur* (¥16/$2.10/£1.05 admission to Sertri Gompa). To reach the spot, head past the gate of Sertri Gompa and veer toward the left, walking about 1km (⅔ mile). In this arid, treeless land, an alternative to cremation or burial had to be found for the people of the Tibetan plateau. The remains of the deceased (whose soul is thought to have already left the body) are dismembered and offered to huge vultures. Nothing is wasted; even the bones are ground up by attendants. If attending the funeral of a stranger doesn't put you off, be aware that Langmu Si is a small town, so you may have to wait a few days for someone to die. This is not a tourist show and you should keep a respectful distance. A large breakfast beforehand is not advised.

WHERE TO STAY

Langmu Si has a reasonable collection of hotels, although rooms with bathrooms are few and far between, and wherever you stay hot water will only be available for a limited period in the evening.

Langmu Si Dajiudian ☀ This grand new edifice looks a little out of place in ramshackle Langmu Si, but it's by far the most comfortable offering in town. The rooms are clean, modern and tasteful and are decked out with pine furniture. The suites are plushly carpeted, and the rooms at the front of the hotel enjoy good views over Kirtri Gompa. Rooms are a little overpriced at high-season rack rate, but outside of the May and October Golden Weeks, you should be able to negotiate a good deal. Not to be confused with the Langmu Si Binguan, opposite the bus stop, which is a far cheaper (but still perfectly acceptable) option.

Langmu Si (opposite the Kirtri Gompa ticket office and the mosque). ℂ 0941/667-1555. 55 units. ¥300 ($39/£20) standard room; ¥1,388 ($180/£90). Discount of 50%. No credit cards. *In room:* TV.

Nomad's Youth Hostel (Lupeng Qingnian Luguan) ⭐ Opened by an avid Chinese backpacker from Henan province, this second-floor guesthouse has great service, wood floors, and a row of airy communal rooms with dorm beds. Try to snag the one private room here by calling in advance. When the hostel is full, Tibetan dance performances are held in the grounds behind the hostel, which inevitably turn into a late-night drinking fest. The owner, Mr. Zhang, is an encyclopedia of travel information and can help arrange treks around the area. There is usually an English-speaking staff member around.

Langmu Si (halfway to Sertri Gompa from the bus stop). ℂ 0941/667-0004. Fax 0941/667-1460. lphy717@163.com. 20 dorm beds, 1 standard room. ¥15 ($1.95/£1) dorm bed; ¥40 ($5.20/£2.60) standard room. No credit cards. In room: No phone.

Sana Hotel (Sana Binguan) The plentiful standard rooms don't come with private bathrooms but offer a nice view of the temple from their windows and the sound of a running river creek will lull you to sleep. The Muslim owner Yang Jincai is a jolly fellow who will encourage you to soak in the hot springs.

Langmu Si (a little beyond Nomad's toward Sertri Gompa). ℂ 0941/667-1062. 30 units. ¥15 ($1.95/£1) dorm bed; ¥30 ($3.90/£1.95) standard room. No credit cards. In room: No phone.

WHERE TO DINE

Ali's Cafe ⭐⭐ (ℂ 0941/667-1090), just before the turn to Sertri Gompa, offers a homey ambience, cheap prices, and an affable owner, Ali—a great place to relax after a hike. Hearty backpacker fare is offered by **Leisha's Cafe** (ℂ 0941/667-1179), near the bus stop. Fans of "competitive eating" should inquire about the Yak Burger Challenge. Another cafe worthy of note is **Shanghai Times (Shanghai Shiguang;** ℂ 0941/667-1508 or 0/1389-398-9290), which offers freshly ground coffee with one refill for ¥10 ($1.30/65p) and a decent spaghetti Bolognese. Shanghai Times is on the second floor of the building opposite the bus stop.

9 Jiayu Guan

765km (474m) NW of Lanzhou, 383km (237m) E of Dunhuang

At the northwest end of the narrow **He Xi corridor** lies a fort that marks the western extremity of the Ming Great Wall. During the Ming dynasty, **Jiayu Guan** was regarded as the end of the Chinese world, beyond which lay the strange lands and peoples of the western lands. Just as transportation to Australia struck fear into Britons, exile ranked just behind decapitation and death by strangulation in the Qing penal code. Many common criminals passed through the gates of Jiayu Guan, but so did victims of court intrigues, such as commissioner Lin Zexu (1785–1850), who tried to suppress the opium trade in Guangzhou (Canton) but found himself banished to Yining. The only people regarded as less fortunate were those who built the Ming Wall. Its construction was estimated to have claimed eight million lives—one life for every yard. Jiayu Guan today is a quiet and semiprosperous steel town. It's worthwhile to spend a day here to visit the fort.

ESSENTIALS

GETTING THERE The **airport** is 15km (9 miles) northeast of downtown. A taxi there costs ¥25 ($3.25/£1.65), or you can take a shuttle bus for ¥9 ($1.15/60p) from the CAAC office at Xinhua Zhong Lu 4–3 (ℂ 0937/628-8777; open 8:30am–5:30pm), about 90m (300 ft.) south of the main roundabout. Because all flights leave at 6pm, the airport shuttle departs from outside the CAAC office at 4:30pm. Jiayu Guan has daily connections with Lanzhou and Xi'an.

The **railway station** (© 0937/597-2512) is 4km (2½ miles) southeast of the center of town. A taxi from the station should cost ¥10 ($1.30/65p). Heading west, your chances of obtaining a sleeper ticket are slim. Proceed through your hotel travel agent (around ¥30/$3.90/£1.95 commission), or buy a hard-seat ticket and try to upgrade. Heading east, things are a little easier; the N852 is a good option to Lanzhou (8:40pm; 10 hr.).

The **bus station** is on the southeast corner of Shengli Zhong Lu and Xin Xi Lu. Daily buses connect with Dunhuang at 9am, 10:30am, and 2:30pm (383km/237 miles; 5 hr.; ¥70/$9.10/£4.55). Sleeper buses for Lanzhou (765km/474 miles; 13 hr.; ¥150/$20/£9.75) leave at 2:30pm, 4:30pm, and 6:30pm. Bus insurance was once mandatory for those traveling east, although this ruling seems to have been relaxed and I wasn't asked for it once, nor did I meet any foreigners who were. Nevertheless, as the kind lady at China Life explained to me, "If you meet an accident you will be very happy [to have bus insurance]," which costs ¥40 ($5.20/£2.60) and will cover you to the tune of ¥240,000 ($31,200/£15,600). **China Life (Zhongguo Renshou Baoxian Gongsi** can be found just south of the Bank of China, at Xinhua Zhong Lu 36 (© 0937/626-1434). It's open weekdays from 8:30am to 12:30pm and 2:30 to 6:30pm, weekends from 10am to 4pm.

GETTING AROUND   Santana **taxis** cost ¥7 (90¢/45p) for the first 3km (2 miles), ¥1.40 (20¢/10p) per kilometer thereafter, with a night surcharge of ¥1.40 (20¢/10p) from 10pm to 5am. *Xiali* taxis charge ¥6 (80¢/40p) for the first 3km (2 miles), and ¥1.20 (15¢/10p) per kilometer thereafter. **Bus** nos. 1 and 2 run from the railway station; both cost ¥1 (15¢/10p). With wide, tree-lined bicycle lanes, **bikes** are the best way to get around. The standard rate is ¥2 (25¢/15p) per hour, or ¥10 ($1.30/65p) per day.

TOURS   **Jiayu Guan International Tours** is run by the friendly Qin Jian. His office is on the second floor of Shengli Bei Lu 2 (© 0937/622-2586; fax 0937/622-6931; www.westtour.cc). Hours are from 8:30am to 12:30pm and 2:30 to 6:30pm. Rates for train tickets and tours are reasonable.

FAST FACTS

Banks, Foreign Exchange & ATMs   You can change traveler's checks at the **Bank of China** (open weekdays 9am–5:30pm, weekends 9:30am–4:30pm) at Xinhua Zhong Lu 42, and there's an ATM which accepts foreign cards.

Internet Access   The best Internet cafe is **Jin Changcheng Wangba,** located on the second floor of the Wenhua Huodong Zhongxin, just south of the night market. Dial-up is © 169.

Post Office   The main post office (© 0937/632-4185; open 8:30am–7pm) is on the southeast corner of the main roundabout at Xinhua Zhong Lu 1.

Visa Extensions   The **PSB** is on Yingbin Zhong Lu (© 0937/631-6927, ext. 3016), but if you ask your hotel, a PSB officer will come to you.

EXPLORING JIAYU GUAN

Jiayu Guan Chenglou (Jiayu Guan Fort) 🌟🌟   The Ming dynasty's rebuilt section of the Great Wall is still most people's image of China, and this final outpost, surrounded by desert and backed by snowcapped mountains, is the best-preserved and

Jiayu Guan

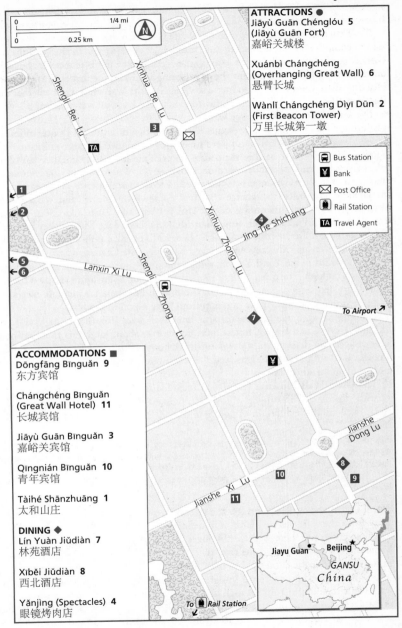

0 · 1/4 mi
0 · 0.25 km

N

🚌 Bus Station
¥ Bank
✉ Post Office
🚆 Rail Station
TA Travel Agent

Xinhua Bei Lu

Shengli Bei Lu

TA

3

1

2

5

6

Lanxin Xi Lu

Shengli Zhong Lu

Xinhua Zhong Lu

Jing Tie Shichang

4

7

To Airport ↗

¥

Jianshe Dong Lu

Jianshe Xi Lu

8

9

10

11

Jiayu Guan ● Beijing ★
GANSU
China

To 🚆 Rail Station

most spectacular of the lot. First built in 1372, then expanded and reinforced in 1539, it was the final project of the Ming rebuilding. Entering from the east, you first come to the **Wenchang Pavilion,** restored in the late Qing dynasty, where intellectuals were said to compose poems, lamenting their rotten luck in being sent to live with the barbarians beyond the Wall. Before leaving, they could enjoy performances at the open-air theater opposite. After passing through **Guanghua Men,** the first of the three main 17m (56-ft.) towers, they would hurl a stone against the Wall to find out whether they would ever return to civilization. If the stone bounced back, all was well, but if it slithered quietly down the Wall, hope was lost.

Another legend associated with the Wall shows that obsession with quantification started long before 1949. The project's supervisor demanded an exact estimate of the number of bricks to be used in the construction of the fort; if the number was off by one brick, the death penalty awaited one Engineer Yi. When the fort was completed, Yi found that there was one brick left over. Faced with evidence of his failure, Yi declared it "the brick to balance the fort" *(ding cheng zhuan)* and walked away unscathed. The brick sits on the side of **Hui Ji Men,** and locals joke about tripping on it. The second main tower, **Rou Yuan Men,** represents the Ming policy of peaceful coexistence with the ethnic minorities beyond the Wall, a policy that ended in the Qing dynasty, when Xinjiang was dragged back into the Chinese empire. Inside the main courtyard is the **Youji Yamen,** where the unfortunate generals were stationed with their families. The building is unremarkable but for an **antiques shop** on the east side. Most items are copies, and all are overpriced, but there are genuine pieces left over from the relocation of the museum from Jiayu Guan to the fort.

Continuing west, you face the massive outer Wall, over 10m (33 ft.) high, and pass through **Jiayu Guan Gate.** Chinese tour groups joke about forgetting their passport, ride camels, and dress up in funny minority costumes, but in the past it was no joke. Locals called it the Gate of Sighs, and the walls were scrawled with hastily composed poems by unfortunate exiles.

The **Great Wall Museum** (admission included in the price of the ticket; located near the fort's exit; 8:30am–8pm July–Oct, 8:30am–7pm Nov–June) is worth a visit for its well-curated exhibition of photos and models of various spots along the Great Wall.

Admission ¥61 ($7.95/£3.95), including entry to the Changcheng Bowuguan (Great Wall Museum). July–Oct 8:30am–7:30pm; Nov–June 8:30am–5:30pm. (Times listed are hours of ticket booth; the fort closes a half-hour after the last ticket sold.) Take a taxi (¥12/$1.55/80p), ride a bike, or walk the 5km (3 miles) from town. Turn right about 1km (½ mile) after the railway bridge, follow a line of concrete camels, and eventually turn left at a signposted fork in the road.

Wanli Changcheng Diyi Dun (First Beacon Tower)

Seven kilometers (4⅓ miles) away from the Fort lies this fairly untouched crumbling bit of the Great Wall and watchtower. A visit here is preferable over a visit to the Overhanging Great Wall because it feels less fake, and the river that runs through a steep gorge near the tower makes for a dramatic sunset photo op. On the way you'll notice that, true to form, history hasn't stood in the way of "progress" and an expressway runs directly under the wall, while the rail line runs through it! At the gorge visitor center you can strap on a body harness and be pitched out over the gorge via a cable (¥31/$4.05/£2), but remember that in the event of an accident, you're unlikely to sue and win in China. It's also worth visiting the mock-up Chinese military encampment 1km (½ mile) back toward the ticket office. There are stone yurts, catapults, cannons and the opportunity

Gliding Heaven

Gliding above Jiayu Guan Fort, the Overhanging Great Wall and the surrounding snowcapped peaks provide an unforgettable experience. Start at the **Jiayu Guan Gliding Base (Huaxiang Jidi; © 0937/638-1070)**, located inside the old airport, 25km (16 miles) northeast of town. The gliding season is from mid-June to September, when the warm ascending airflow of the Jiayu Guan basin can lift gliders nearly 6km (4 miles) up. If you don't have a gliding license, training courses are available, but you'll need a very good translator. Basic and overpriced accommodations are available at the base. Whatever your arrangements, make them at least a month in advance, and be sure to get them in writing. It may be best to proceed through CITS.

to try your hand at some archery (¥1/15¢/5p per arrow). But best of all there's a rickety suspension bridge across the gorge that gives stunning views in both directions. Make sure your taxi waits for you, as it's difficult to arrange a car back to town.

Admission ¥21 ($2.75/£1.35). 8am–6pm. Take a taxi, round-trip for ¥20 ($2.60/£1.30).

Xincheng Wei Jin Mu (Wei-Jin Tombs)   Twenty kilometers (12 miles) northeast of Jiayu Guan, this is sometimes misleadingly called the Dixia Hualang (Underground Art Gallery). There are thousands of tombs in this area dating from the Wei (220–65 B.C.) and Jin (A.D. 265–420), but only one is open to the public. You will see the tomb of a sixth-rank official, the lowest rank in the imperial pecking order. The valuables were plundered soon after the tomb was sealed, probably by the builder, judging from the accuracy of the thief's tunnel. Compared with Buddhist art, the murals in the tomb are crude cartoons. Detailed instructions on slaughtering pigs, goats, and cows leave no doubt as to what the owner was hoping for in the next world. There is evidence that sericulture had already spread to this part of the empire, that barbecues were enjoyed before Australia was colonized, and that officials were plumper than their servants. Murals detail the official's trip to the capital in Luoyang, doubtless the highlight of his career. The remaining contents of the tomb are on display in an **exhibition center,** and include black stone pigs found in the hands and the mouth of the official's corpse. He liked his pork.

Admission ¥41 ($5.35/£2.65); guide fee ¥50–¥100 ($6.50–$13/£3.25–£6.50), depending on depth of explanation. 8:30am–8:30pm.

Xuanbi Changcheng (Overhanging Great Wall) *Overrated*   Built in 1539, this is supposedly as far as northwest as the Wall goes, but that's a myth. (There are sites farther west near Dunhuang.) This is part of the government's effort to capitalize on tourism by creating as many useless sites as possible in an effort to boost tourism revenues. Farmers were putting the masonry to better use before this section of the Wall was restored in 1988. It's a sweaty 20-minute climb into the desolate **Hei Shan (Black Mountains)** as the Wall rises at a 45-degree angle for 500m (1,640 ft.). Chinese tourists arrange stones into the equivalent of "John loves Mary." Farms in the village below are a small finger of green in an immense desert. This section is 8km (5 miles) north of the fort, and can be reached by taxi or bike. Take plenty of water.

Admission ¥21 ($2.75/£1.35). Apr–Oct 8:30am–8:30pm; Nov–Mar 8:30am–6pm.

SHOPPING

Much of the stock in the Baihuo Dalou, on the northeast side of the main round-about, looks like it hasn't moved since the Cultural Revolution. This is a chance to pick up Seagull cameras, mahjong tiles, and chess sets at 1960s prices. For a supermarket try the Xinhua Chaoshi, near the Xibei Jiudian on Xinhua Nan Lu.

WHERE TO STAY

Jiayu Guan suffers from a glut of mediocre three-star options. Outside the busy season in early May and mid-July to October, occupancy rates run as low as 20%, so discounts of at least 40% can be obtained. During the busy season, a 20% discount should be given.

EXPENSIVE

Changcheng Binguan (Great Wall Hotel) A favorite with tour groups since 1987, this sprawling, comfortable three-star hotel, whose exterior is a tacky replica of the Jiayuguan Fort outlined in white Christmas lights at night, is probably the most used to dealing with foreign tourists. The hotel is set in pleasant grounds and service in the hotel is friendly, but they won't offer much of a discount in the high season. The difference in quality between the standard rooms and the deluxe versions isn't worth the extra outlay.

Jianshe Lu 6 (from Sifaju walk back 50m/164 ft. and the hotel is on your right). ⓒ 0937/622-5200. Fax 0937/622-6016. 156 units. ¥560–¥760 ($73–$99/£36–£49) standard room; from ¥980 ($127/£64) suite. Discounts of 50%. AE, DC, MC, V. Bus: no. 2 to Sifaju. **Amenities:** Restaurant; swimming pool; exercise room; bike rental; concierge; tour desk; business center; 24-hr. forex; same-day laundry/dry cleaning. *In room:* A/C, TV, fridge.

Jiayu Guan Binguan ✶ Right in the center of town, this four-star hotel has been giving birth to new wings since 1983, most recently the west wing. The rooms are the cleanest and most comfortable in town, and service is very professional. This is where government officials stay when they come to Jiayu Guan.

Xinhua Bei Lu 1. ⓒ **0937/620-1588.** Fax 0937/622-7174. 180 units. ¥668–¥780 ($87–$101/£43–£51) standard room; from ¥1,080–¥1,280 ($140–$160/£70–£83) suite. Discounts of 40%–50%. AE, DC, MC, V. Bus: no. 1 to Youdian Dalou. **Amenities:** 2 restaurants; game room; concierge; tour desk; business center; 24-hr. forex; same-day laundry; next-day dry cleaning. *In room:* A/C, TV, fridge, hair dryer.

MODERATE/INEXPENSIVE

Dongfang Binguan (Value) This new hotel out toward the train station offers decent rooms at a good price. However, beds can be a bit hard and bathrooms are slightly cramped. Service is friendly, though little English is spoken.

Yingbin Lu, Shanchun Zonghe Lou. ⓒ 0937/630-1866. Fax 0937/630-1027. 70 units (shower only). ¥320 ($42/£21) standard room; ¥480–¥680 ($62–$88/£31–£44) suite. Discounts of 50%. No credit cards. **Amenities:** Restaurant; business center. *In room:* A/C, TV, hair dryer.

Taihe Shanzhuang ✶ (Value) Located within the grounds of the Jiayu Guan Fort, this replica of a Qing dynasty courtyard house allows you to spend more time at Jiayu Guan's main attraction and to view the fort at sunrise and sunset, when the earthen ramparts are highly photogenic. The standard rooms are small and shabby, so it's worth the extra outlay to take a suite. Beds are hard and bathrooms are slightly grimy but the atmosphere is unbeatable. The restaurant fare is decent. Combined with the magnificent fort, this guesthouse makes for the pretty good "real China" experience.

Jiayu Guan Guancheng (150m/492 ft. past the back entrance to the fort). ⓒ 0937/639-6622. 18 units (shower only). ¥120–¥160 ($16–$21/£7.80–£10) standard room; ¥360 ($47/£23) suite. No credit cards. **Amenities:** Restaurant. *In room:* A/C, TV.

WHERE TO DINE

Jiayu Guan is a prosperous steel town, so the restaurants—unlike the hotels—do well year-round. The main outdoor food markets are Fuqiang Shichang and Jingtie Shichang. The night market on the north side of Jingtie Shichang is the liveliest in town. Sheep carcasses dangle, beer flows, and vendors make fun of their regular customers. No one knows the name of the night market's greatest showman, who is simply called **Yanjing (Spectacles)**. His shop is easy to spot, under a sign with a caricature of a man with huge glasses and a smock. The caricature is on the mark and Spectacles will serve you tasty Uigher lamb skewers *(yangrou chuan)* or mini–lamb chops *(yangpai)* by the handful *(ba)*—about 20 in each serving, give or take a couple. But make sure you know what you're eating.

Lin Yuan Jiudian ✦✦ CANTONESE   With a Cantonese chef poached from one of Xi'an's top restaurants, this is where the locals go for a treat. The *fugui niurou* is akin to roast beef on sesame toast, while *xiqinbaihe chao xian you* (fresh squid on a bed of celery, field mushrooms, and lotus) is a Cantonese favorite.

Xinhua Zhong Lu 34 (2nd floor of the Lin Yuan Hotel). ✆ 0937/620-3777. Meal for 2 ¥80–¥120 ($10–$16/£5.20–£7.80). No credit cards. 9:30am–10pm. Bus: no. 1 to Baoxian Gongsi.

Xibei Jiudian ✦ *Value* GANSU/UIGHUR   The helpful staff and picture menu makes it easy to choose dishes, but the delicious *kao yangpai* (grilled rack of lamb), is the one to try. Dipped in a salt-and-pepper concoction, the lamb is grilled so that the meat is tender and the outer layer crisp. One large order of lamb *(yangrou)* and a couple of local beers *(pijiu)* makes a fantastic meal for two.

Xinhua Nan Lu. ✆ 0937/623-3208. Meal for 2 ¥80 ($10/£5.20). No credit cards. 9am–10pm. Bus: no.1.

10 Dunhuang

Gansu Province, 383km (237 miles) W of Jiayu Guan, 524km (325 miles) NE of Golmud

Dunhuang's name (blazing beacon) derives from its function as a Han Chinese garrison town, but the Tang name of Sha Zhou (sand district) describes it better, hemmed in by sand dunes and bleak, pebbly desert. The middle and southern Silk Routes set off from Dunhuang, passing through the remote garrison town of **Loulan** (abandoned when Lop Nor Lake "wandered off" in the 4th c.) and through the **Lop Desert.**

A large number of the early residents of Dunhuang were not Han, and the town came under the sway of the Tibetans, the Uighurs, and the Xi Xia, only really becoming a Han town after the colonization of the western regions was initiated during the Qing dynasty. The town is dependent on tourism, and despite efforts to develop other sites, it is the peerless **Mogao cave-temple complex** that makes Dunhuang the essential stop on the Silk Routes.

ESSENTIALS

GETTING THERE   The **airport** is 13km (8 miles) east of Dunhuang, just past the turnoff to the Mogao caves. Public buses (¥5/65¢/30p) connect with flights, or you can try your luck bargaining with taxi drivers without meters, who should charge no more than ¥30 ($3.90/£1.95) to the center of town. The most useful office of **CAAC** (8am–8pm) is by the Dunhuang Binguan at 12 Yangguan Dong Lu (✆ 0937/882-2389). They will deliver tickets to your hotel, so there is no need to book tickets through hotel travel agencies, who will charge up to ¥70 ($9.10/£4.55) for making a local call. Daily flights connect with Lanzhou (¥1,160/$151/£75),

Urumqi (¥840/$109/£55), Xi'an (¥1,810/$235/£118), and Beijing (¥2,010/$261/£131). There are fewer flights in winter.

Dunhuang's tiny new **railway station** is 6 miles out of town (¥15/$1.95/£1 by taxi or ¥3/40¢/20p by local bus), and has services to Turpan and Urumqi (T216 at 8:16pm), Jiayu Guan (7528 at 4:10pm), Lanzhou (858 at 7:25pm), and even Xi'an (K592 at 9:30am). Coming to or from Beijing or Shanghai you'll still have to come via the old railhead 130km (81 miles; 2–3 hr.) away at Liuyuan. From Liuyuan station, you will have no trouble finding minibus drivers, who ask ¥30 ($3.90/£1.95) for the ¥15 ($1.95/£1) trip to Dunhuang. Taxis will make the trip in either direction for ¥100 to ¥120 ($13–$16/£6.50–£7.80) or ¥30 ($3.90/£1.95) per person if you share. If you are the last tourist around after a train pulls away, you can bargain hard as the station suffers from a glut of drivers. Buses for Liuyuan railway station leave Dunhuang's long-distance bus station at 7:30am, 9:30am, 11am, noon, 2pm, 4pm, 6pm, and 7:30pm (¥20/$2.60/£1.30). You can buy train tickets at either rail station, from the ticket office (8am–noon and 2–4pm) next to the bank on Yangguan Zhong Lu, through your hotel or a travel agent.

The **bus station** is on Ming Shan Lu (© 0937/882-2174), diagonally opposite the Feitian Binguan. Daily buses connect with Jiayu Guan (383km/237 miles; 6 hr.) hourly from 8am, but it's worth taking the quicker and more comfortable fast services at 8:30am and 2:30pm (5 hr.; ¥66/$8.60/£4.30); with Lanzhou at 10:30am and 7:30pm (1,148km; 16 hr.; sleeper bus; ¥227/$30/£15 lower berth, ¥214/$28/£14 upper berth); with Golmud at 9am (524km/325 miles; 10 hr.; ¥99/$13/£6.40 lower berth, ¥89/$12/£5.75 upper berth); and with Xining at 11am (1,067km/662 miles; 19 hr.; ¥182/$24/£12).

GETTING AROUND   **Taxis** fill Dunhuang's narrow streets; most are gypsy cabs. The rate should be ¥5 (65¢/30p) for a short ride; ¥10 ($1.30/65p) for a longer one. Get around on foot, or hire a **bike** for ¥1 (15¢/5p) per hour. There are also a few **bus** routes, of which no. 3 running to the Singing Sand Mountains, the unnumbered airport (¥5/65¢/35p), and train station (¥3/40¢/20p) routes are the most useful. There is also a new bus service (again unnumbered) that runs from the Dunhuang Fandian near Charley Johng's cafe to the Mogao Caves for ¥8/$1.05/50p.

TOURS   **CITS** is inside the compound of the Dunhuang Guoji Dajiudian at Ming Shan Lu 32 (© 0937/882-2474; fax 0937/882-2173; www.dhcits.com; open 8am–noon and 3–6pm), on the right as you enter.

FAST FACTS
Banks, Foreign Exchange & ATMs   You can change traveler's checks at the **Bank of China** (8:30am–5:30pm) at Yangguan Zhong Lu 13.

Internet Access   Most of the backpacker cafes on Ming Shan Lu offer Internet access, often giving 30 minutes free use if you eat there.

Post Office   The main post office (open 8:30am–7pm) is on the northwest corner of the junction of Yangguan Lu and Sha Zhou Lu.

EXPLORING DUNHUANG
Mingsha Shan & Yueya Quan (Singing Sand Mountains & Crescent Moon Spring) ⋒   When Aurel Stein settled down by the spring to churn out his memoirs, he opined, "It lay hidden away amidst high sands beyond the southern edge of the oasis and about three miles from the town. For the desert wanderer there could be no

Dunhuang

ACCOMMODATIONS ■

Dūnhuáng Dàshà **8**
(Dūnhuáng Building)
敦煌大厦

Dūnhuáng Guójì Dàjiǔdiàn **9**
(Dūnhuáng International Hotel)
敦煌口际大酒店

Dūnhuáng Shānzhuāng **11**
(The Silk Road Dūnhuáng Hotel)
敦煌山庄

Fēitiān Bīnguǎn **7**
飞天宾馆

Jīnyè Bīnguǎn **10**
(Golden Leaf Hotel)
金叶宾馆

DINING ◆
Charley Jhong's Café **5**

Dá Jì Lǘròu **2**
Huángmiàn Guǎn
达记驴肉黄面馆

John's Information Café **6**
(Yuēhàn Cāntīng)
约翰餐厅

Night Market (Yèshì) **3**
夜市

ATTRACTIONS ●
Míngshā Shān **12**
(Singing Sand Dunes)
鸣沙山

Mògāo Shíkū **4**
(Mògāo Caves)
莫高石窟

Xī Qiān Fó Dòng **1**
(Western Thousand
Buddha Caves)
西千佛洞

To Airport ✈→
(13 km)

Yanguan Zhong Lu

Yanguan Dong Lu

Shichang Xiang

Xinjian Lu

Huancheng Nan Lu

Dunyue Lu

Shazhou Bei Lu

Shazhou Nan Lu

Mingshan Lu

Henshui Lu

Xiyu Jie

✈ Airport
¥ Bank
P Police
⊠ Post Office
TA Travel Agent

0   1/8 mile
0   100 meters

N

297

more appropriate place of rest, I thought, than this delightful little pilgrimage place enclosed all around by sand-ridges rising to over 75 meters in height. There was a limpid little lake, of crescent shape and about a quarter of a mile long, which has given the locality its name and its sanctity."

Stein's peaceful temple was razed during the Cultural Revolution and is now a souvenir shop. The limpid "lake" is a fenced-off muddy pond reduced to half the original size, a result of the ongoing exploitation of underground water. The pilgrimage is marked by a gauntlet of stalls selling stuffed toy camels, batik, and glow-in-the-dark cups, culminating in a ticket office charging ¥80 ($10/£5.20) to see a naturally formed attraction. Inside the entrance there are camels (¥30/$3.90/£1.95) or carts (¥10/$1.30/65p) to take you to the lake, and toboggans (¥10/$1.30/65p) to take you down the sand dunes, which make for a fun, if sandy experience. If you've never seen desert dunes, it's worth the effort, especially just before sunrise or sunset, when the delicate contours and colors of the dunes are beguiling. The best way to avoid the crowds is to hike up the wooden stairs near the toboggan for ¥10 ($1.30/65p) and then find your own way down, following a ridge.

Admission ¥80 ($10/£5.20). 7am–10pm. Taxi ¥10 ($1.30/65p) or minibus no. 3.

Mogao Shiku (Mogao Caves) ⚘⚘⚘   Here is the biggest, best-preserved, and most significant site of Buddhist statuary and frescoes in all of China—and the best-curated site, too. A guide is compulsory, as is leaving your bag and camera (no charge) at the gate. Generally the guides, who all have bachelor's degrees, are excellent, sometimes going well beyond the script. Tours, which depart every few minutes and are limited to about 20 people, usually take 2 hours and cover 10 of the 30 caves that are open to the public; Caves 16, 17, 96, 130, and 148 are included on all tours. It is worth spending the entire day at Mogao Shiku, even though this means that you have to pay for admission twice. Tours in the afternoon are less crowded, and you may get a guide to yourself. Or come right as the caves open in the morning, before the tour groups arrive. Although guides have powerful flashlights, it's worth bringing your own to see the murals in some of the darker caves.

Before you reach the grottoes you'll see the **Dunhuang Exhibition Centre** ⚘, which includes a copy of the one of the earliest grottoes, **Cave 275,** dating from the short-lived 5th-century Northern Liang dynasty, including a *Jataka* (moral story) from one of the historical Buddha's previous lives. He is depicted as a Kushan king, allowing an attendant to cut the flesh from his leg as ransom for a dove that sits in his palm. *Jataka* were popular in the early caves, gradually being displaced by stories from the Mahayanist sutras in later caves as the influence of the "Pure Land Sect" of Chinese Buddhism grew. The subject matter of these *Jataka* was frequently gory. **Cave 285,** for example, tells the tale of 500 rebels who fought against the corrupt King Prasenajit and had their eyes gouged out and were banished to the wilderness before the gods took pity on them and allowed them to be tonsured as monks, their sight restored by the Buddha. Upstairs is a somewhat out-of-place exhibition of Tibetan bronze statues, both complete and beheaded, that were rescued from Red Guards by the canny curator.

All together, there are 492 caves, of which you will see less than a mere 10 on the 2-hour tour. Your first stop on the tour will be **Cave 17** (the Library Cave). The cave was sealed off sometime after 998 (the year of the last dated manuscript), perhaps out of fear of the spread of Islam—the Buddhist kingdom of Khotan was captured and sacked in 1006. In 1900, the cave was rediscovered by Wang Daoshi (Abbot Wang), the self-appointed guardian of the caves. First among the villains was archaeologist

Aurel Stein, a Hungarian who obtained British citizenship (and later a knighthood), and who arrived during the winter of 1907. The Chinese commentary is only slightly more damning than the English translation, accusing Stein of "purchasing by deceit" over 7,000 complete manuscripts and silk paintings from the "ignorant" Abbott Wang for a paltry £130. Next came young French Sinologist Paul Pelliot, whose mastery of Chinese gave him a selectivity his predecessor lacked—Stein returned to London with over 1,000 copies of the Lotus Sutra. Pelliot obtained thousands of documents for even less—only £90! The Chinese save their greatest condemnation for Langdon Warner, who removed 12 murals **(Cave 323)** and a statue **(Cave 328).** Warner justified his theft as a way of avoiding the "renovations" funded by Abbot Wang. A map illustrates how the contents are spread around the world.

Curators, fearing that increased tourist activity is damaging the coloration of the frescoes, are closing some caves to the public. Some caves, considered of particular interest and import (such as Caves 275 and 285, detailed above), can be visited for an additional fee of ¥200 ($26/£13) per cave. The caves depicting acts of love-making, much touted in other guidebooks, are generally off-limits. Remarkable early caves (usually open) include **Cave 259,** commissioned during the Northern Wei (A.D. 386–535); and **Cave 428,** where an early incarnation of the historical Buddha sacrifices himself to feed a tigress and her cubs. It's also worth asking to see **Cave 249,** which dates from the Western Wei; the cave's small size allows in enough daylight to see the exquisite lapis lazuli artwork on the ceiling. Later caves, such as **Cave 96,** which houses a 36m (116-ft.) Buddha, and **Cave 148,** which contains a serene 17m (56-ft.) Sleeping Buddha, indicate that artisans from the Tang court found their way to Mogao. Some lower caves were affected by floodwaters from the Daquan River, and sunlight has caused lead-based pigments to turn black, but the overall state of preservation is incredible. Caves are grouped roughly by period, and it is intriguing to view the steady transformation of facial features from Greco-Indian to plumper, more feminine Chinese features.

Admission ¥180 ($23/£12), includes English-speaking guide. 8:30am–5pm (ticket booth hours; the caves close at 6pm). To make the 30-min. journey to the caves, buses leave every 30 min. (from 7:30am, last bus returns at 6pm; ¥8/$1.05/50p each way) from the Dunhuang Fandian, and minibuses leave from Charley Jhong's Cafe at 8:30am and return at 12:30pm (¥20/$2.60/£1.30 round-trip). Taxis, highly recommended, cost ¥80–¥100 ($10/£5.20) for the round-trip.

Xi Qian Fo Dong (Western Thousand Buddha Caves)

The missionary Mildred Cable described the scene: "At the edge of the cliff was a rough opening, and from it a very precipitous path led down to a narrow ledge from which the new caves opened . . . they were comparable to the better known Thousand Buddha Grottoes . . . the figures were free and stately, with flowing lines and elegant draperies, and the frescoes showed the same clear warm tints."

Located 35km (22 miles) southwest of town, the valley is easily accessed as a halfday trip, but it's still a scramble down to the caves. They were largely built by locals from the nearby village of Nan Hu, and have several *Jataka* stories not covered by the Mogao caves. Most of the statuary (with the exception of Caves 5 and 16) was repainted to poor effect during the Qing dynasty. The most spectacular murals are located in **Cave 15** ☞, which is not open to the casual visitor without payment of an additional fee. The stunning blues and muscular bodhisattvas of the Northern Wei **(Cave 5)** and Northern Zhou **(Cave 6)** are in real contrast to the plump, feminine bodhisattvas of the Middle Tang **(Cave 15).** To reach the site, a taxi may be hired for

¥60 ($7.80/£3.90); or take any bus heading west from Dunhuang for ¥5 (65¢/35p).
From the road, it's a 15-minute walk south to the cliff face, with a set of stairs to the
left leading down to the ticket office.

Admission ¥30 ($3.90/£1.95). 8am–6pm. No English tour guide. Taxis make the trip from Dunhuang for ¥60 ($7.80/£3.90) round-trip.

A SIDE TRIP TO HAN DYNASTY RUINS ✦

If you're a history buff who is tired of seeing fake renditions of the Great Wall, this 92km
(57-mile) journey into the desert to visit these desolate Han dynasty ruins is a worthwhile day trip. The ruins comprise three separate locations: **Yumen Guan (Jade Gate),**
an ancient watchtower made of mud, straw, and stone, and the lesser-known **He
Cangcheng** and **Han Changcheng.** On the way to these ruins you'll pass another historic site called Yangguan (Sun Gate). Yumen Guan and Yang Guan were the traditional
border crossings that marked the beginning of the territory ruled by the Han dynasty.
Today, however, Yang Guan is a tacky site geared toward Chinese tour groups; it features
an unspectacular watchtower surrounded by a fake village, and a terribly curated
museum. Skip this and continue to the Yumen Guan ticket counter, which appears in
the middle of the desert, along a long stretch of road. Pay here (¥30/$3.90/£1.95) and
drive for another 30km (19 miles) to reach Yumenguan. The highlight of the three is
Han Changcheng ✦✦, which translates at River Warehouse Town. It's 13km (21 miles)
east of Yumen Guan on a dirt road and is a rather crumbling building that was used as
a storage unit. Five kilometers (8 miles) to the east of Yumen Guan is Han Changcheng,
which features one watchtower and a remnant of the Great Wall that's several hundred
yards long. Few tour groups, if any, make it out here. Plan for a trip that takes roughly
7 hours. A round-trip taxi ride costs ¥350 ($46/£23).

WHERE TO STAY

Dunhuang has a surplus of accommodations. During the peak season, hotels offer
20% discounts; during the low season, discounts of up to 60% are readily negotiated.
In spite of what you may be told, most of the budget accommodations (including the
Feitian Binguan) only have hot water for a limited number of hours in the evening; if
you're told the hotel has 24-hour hot water, ask for a demonstration!

VERY EXPENSIVE

Dunhuang Shanzhuang (The Silk Road Dunhuang Hotel) ✦✦   This four-star
Hong Kong venture is the finest hotel on the Silk Routes, and one of the most unique
hotels in the country. It lies 4km (2½ miles) south of town, just before the Ming Shan
Dunes, which loom in the background. Designed by a Chinese-American architect,
the gigantic, airy lobby gives you a sense of calm that rarely exists in China. The main
building mimics the look of the Mogao Caves, and the high-ceilinged rooms feature
finely crafted wooden furnishings and cool stone floors that mesh perfectly with the
desert surroundings. Bathrooms, which feature showers lined with black stone, are
fantastic. Bill Gates was duly impressed with the villas, which feature a mixture of
Tang and Han architectural styles. An aptly named "student building" with beds for
¥80 ($10/£5) also houses the staff, while next door the new "professional quarters"
offer simpler rooms set around an empty courtyard and lower prices, but full use of
the hotel's facilities. Service is top-notch. The **rooftop patio** ✦ is a must for a sunset
and beautiful views of the dunes—it's open to the public in the evenings. If you ask
management, breakfast can be served on the patio for hotel guests. Dinner at the
restaurant adjoining the hotel is decent, featuring spicy Chinese dishes, and there's a

nightly dance performance in season (May–Oct) that begins at 9:30pm (¥96/$13/£6.25). The hotel features a very professional massage center, as opposed to the dodgy kind on offer at many Chinese hotels.

Dunyue Lu. © **0937/888-2088**. Fax 0937/888-3245. www.dunhuangresort.com. 246 units, 21 villas. ¥800 ($100/£52) standard room; from ¥2,000 ($250/£130) suite; from ¥2,000 ($250/£130) villa room; professional room ¥330 ($43/£21). AE, DC, MC, V. **Amenities:** 2 restaurants; cafe; bar; sauna; bike rental; concierge; tour desk; evening shuttle bus to town; 24-hr. business center; 24-hr. forex; salon; 24-hr. room service; massage; same-day laundry/dry cleaning. *In room:* A/C, limited satellite TV, broadband Internet access (in some), fridge, hair dryer.

EXPENSIVE

Dunhuang Guoji Dajiudian (Dunhuang International Hotel) *Value* While

its bathroom-tile exterior surely won't win any awards, the rooms here are some of the best in town for the price. The rooms are decorated in simple tones and feature modern headboards and comfy beds, but service is hit-or-miss. You can save ¥100 ($13/£6.50) by choosing a standard room over an executive room, the only difference being that the executive rooms feature slightly more modern bathrooms. The Korean restaurant on the premises serves tasty barbecued beef.

Mingshan Lu 28. © **0937/882-8638**. Fax 0937/882-1821. dhgjdid@public.lz.gs.cn. 156 units. ¥588 ($76/£38) standard room; ¥998–¥1,288 ($129–$168/£65–£84) suite. AE, DC, MC, V. Rates include full breakfast. **Amenities:** 3 restaurants; cafe; bar; concierge; tour desk; business center; 24-hr. forex; 24-hr. room service; massage; same-day laundry/dry cleaning; karaoke. *In room:* A/C, TV, broadband Internet access, minibar, fridge, safe.

MODERATE

Dunhuang Dasha (Dunhuang Building) This unglamorous three-star hotel is

owned by the Tax Department, so there is no danger of it running short of money for renovations, which are continuous. Rooms are clean and bright, and the hotel's location—in a quiet area south of the center of town—is a definite advantage.

Sha Zhou Nan Lu 15. © **0937/882-5006**. 101 units. ¥480 ($62/£31) standard room; ¥880 ($114/£57) suite. 20% discount. No credit cards. **Amenities:** Restaurant; bar; concierge; business center; same-day laundry/dry cleaning. *In room:* A/C, TV, fridge.

Jinye Binguan (Golden Leaf Hotel) Located 1.6km (1 mile) south of the center

of town, this is a decent three-star choice. An orchard provides grapes, apricots, and peaches for the hotel restaurant. All of the rooms are in good condition, but it's worth asking for a room overlooking the orchard, as rooms facing the main road are noisy. "Golden leaf" is a reference to tobacco: The hotel is owned by the Gansu Tobacco Company.

Ming Shan Lu 37. © **0937/885-3338**. Fax 0937/885-1248. 93 units. ¥422 ($55/£27) standard room; ¥680–¥880 ($88–$114/£44–£57) suite. Rates include full breakfast. 20% discount. No credit cards. **Amenities:** Restaurant; bar; large exercise room; game room; concierge; tour desk; business center; same-day laundry/dry cleaning. *In room:* A/C, TV, fridge.

INEXPENSIVE

Feitian Binguan (Feitian Hotel) Among the hotels at the bottom of the market,

this is probably the safest bet and the friendly staff are used to accommodating foreign backpackers. There are bright, pleasant standard rooms with vast bathrooms, as well as basic triples that can be shared as dorms but you'll have to use the scrappy shared bathrooms. Whichever kind of room you take, there's only hot water between 7pm and midnight. Book ahead during the busy season as rooms fill up quickly. If the hotel is full there are plenty of other cheap but acceptable options nearby; try the Five Rings over the road. The Feitian is conveniently located across the street from the long-distance bus station and near the ever-growing Western-cafe ghetto on Ming Shan Lu. A branch of John's Information Cafe is also on-site.

Ming Shan Lu 22. ✆ 0937/882-2337. 55 units. ¥40 ($5.20/£2.60) dorm bed in a triple room; ¥388 ($50/£25) standard room. Discounts of up to 70% on standard room. No credit cards. Amenities: 2 restaurants; business center; travel agent; same-day laundry. In room: A/C, TV, broadband Internet access (in some).

WHERE TO DINE

Clustered around the Feitian Hotel are small restaurants with English menus, offering "Western" food and overpriced Chinese fare. Favorites are **Shirley's, Charley Johng's Cafe,** and **John's Information Cafe,** all located on Ming Shan Lu. Charley's has the best service. A favorite local drink served at many restaurants, including John's, is the delicious *xingpishui* (dried apricot juice), which is generally home-brewed by soaking the apricots in water, then adding sugar for a tart and sweet combination. If you want to experience a meal in a traditional-style courtyard house, Charley Johng can take you out to his (basic) guesthouse, set amid apricot orchards just yards from the dunes—ask at the cafe.

Da Ji Lurou Huangmian Guan *(Finds)* GANSU   Surprisingly, the specialty dish of Dunhuang is *lurou huangmian* (donkey meat yellow noodles). More surprisingly, it's delicious. It is claimed that the method of making the noodles is revealed in Cave 265, but the cave isn't open to the public and the owners of this noodle shop aren't talking. The noodles are cooked with tomato, tofu, mushrooms, and plenty of garlic—a small plate *(xiaopan)* is more than sufficient. To accompany the main dish, order some donkey meat *(lurou)*. Half a *jin (ban jin),* which is half a kilo, is enough for two. The meat is lean and tastes a little like roast beef. You'll be served a bowl of finely chopped garlic, to which you should add chili sauce and vinegar to taste, before dipping the meat in it. If you want to meet some locals, this market street is a better choice than the tacky main night market *(yeshi).* An after-dinner stroll through the charming narrow lanes provides a rewarding glimpse of the old town.

Da Shichang (just south of the gate that marks the entrance of the market from Yangguan Zhong Lu). ✆ 0937/383-7228. ¥10 ($1.30/65p) per person. No credit cards. 10:30am–10:30pm.

11 Turpan (Tulufan) ★/★

Xinjiang Province, 187km (116 miles) SE of Urumqi

Early European visitors were preoccupied with the overwhelming heat of this delightful oasis town. Set in the **Turpan Depression,** 154m (505 ft.) below sea level at its lowest point at **Lake Ayd Inkol (Aiding Hu),** the town experiences midday temperatures hovering above 113°F (45°C) during the summer months. The American journalist Lattimore found some relief: "Over the central streets, which are at once passageways and market-places, are trellises, covered with mats, gourd-vines, and the branches of willows and poplars. In the checkered shade the people step softly, loose-robed and barefooted or slipper-shod; as they chatter in Turki, guttural but soft, the eyes of women flash under stenciled eyebrows and the teeth of men flash from black beards . . ."

The green fields that surround Turpan are sustained by the *karez* irrigation system, thought to have been introduced in Persia 2 millennia ago. A web of 1,610km (1,000 miles) of covered water channels brings water from the mountains to the north and west of Turpan. Keeping the *karez* clear requires considerable effort, and locals are proud of this ongoing engineering achievement. Turpan is surrounded by significant

Turpan

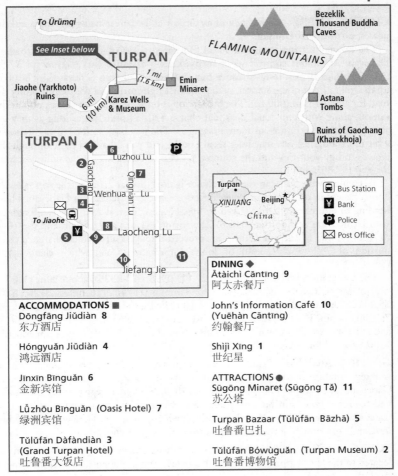

See Inset below

To Ürümqi

TURPAN

FLAMING MOUNTAINS

Bezeklik
Thousand Buddha
Caves

1 mi
(1.6 km)

Emin
Minaret

Jiaohe (Yarkhoto)
Ruins

6 mi
(10 km)

Karez Wells
& Museum

Astana
Tombs

Ruins of Gaochang
(Kharakhoja)

TURPAN

Luzhou Lu

Gaochang Lu

Qingnian Lu

Wenhua Lu

To Jiaohe

Laocheng Lu

Jiefang Jie

Turpan

XINJIANG   Beijing ★

China

🚍 Bus Station
¥ Bank
🅿 Police
✉ Post Office

DINING ◆
Ātàichì Cāntīng **9**
阿太赤餐厅

John's Information Café **10**
(Yuēhàn Cāntīng)
约翰餐厅

Shìjì Xīng **1**
世纪星

ATTRACTIONS ●
Sūgōng Minaret (Sūgōng Tǎ) **11**
苏公塔

Turpan Bazaar (Tǔlǔfān Bāzhā) **5**
吐鲁番巴扎

Tǔlǔfān Bówùguǎn (Turpan Museum) **2**
吐鲁番博物馆

ACCOMMODATIONS ■
Dōngfāng Jiǔdiàn **8**
东方酒店

Hóngyuǎn Jiǔdiàn **4**
鸿远酒店

Jīnxīn Bīnguǎn **6**
金新宾馆

Lǜzhōu Bīnguǎn (Oasis Hotel) **7**
绿洲宾馆

Tǔlǔfān Dàfàndiàn **3**
(Grand Turpan Hotel)
吐鲁番大饭店

ancient sites, all readily accessed by car or minibus. Often an independent kingdom, it has maintained a strong sense of local identity, and observes a relaxed and tolerant version of Islam.

The annual grape festival, which runs in late August for about a week, brings fruit vendors, winemakers, and loads of tourists from around China. It's a fun time to visit—as the city becomes a lively, teeming mass of humanity, you can sample unlimited grapes on the trellis-lined streets or Turpan and witness a fantastic fireworks display on the night before the festival officially kicks off.

Warning: In contrast to its torpid, laid-back feel, Turpan has an unfortunate, but deserved reputation as a town in which you should be wary of your belongings; petty theft and pickpocketing (usually while you are being distracted) are rife. Leave your valuables in the hotel safe and be very aware of your personal space.

ESSENTIALS

GETTING THERE   As yet, talk of an airport at Turpan remains just that, and the nearest **airport** is at Urumqi.

The **railway station** is located 54km (33 miles) north of Turpan in drab town of Daheyan. Minibuses connect with **Turpan's long-distance bus station** for ¥7.50 ($1/50p). The Turpan **long-distance bus station** in Daheyan is reached by heading up the hill in front of the station, taking the first right turn, and continuing along the road for about 180m (600 ft.). The bus station is on your left. Some buses wait at the station, along with individual taxis that charge ¥10 ($1.30/65p), as long as they are able to fill a car with three or more passengers. The way back to the railway station is a bit more arduous; bus schedules seem erratic, and you'll have to fight through the crowds to buy your ticket at the counter. It's best to take a taxi to the railway station for ¥60 ($7.80/£3.90).

To connect with Kashgar, the best choice is the N887 at 2:10pm; the trip takes 21 hours. Except in peak season, sleeper tickets are readily purchased in Daheyan. Those heading to Urumqi are better served by bus. Heading east, sleeper tickets are tighter; your chances are best on the 1046 to Zhengzhou (41 hr.) at 11:50pm and the 1044 to Xi'an (40 hr.) at 1:47am. Otherwise, proceed through CITS which charges a commission of ¥40 ($5.20/£2.60) or John's Information Cafe, which charges ¥50 ($6.50/£3.25).

The **bus station** is at Lao Cheng Lu 27 (© **0995/852-2325**), about 90m (300 ft.) west of the central roundabout. Buses for Urumqi (187km/116 miles; 2½ hr.; ¥40/ $5.20/£2.60; taxi [Santana] ¥65/$8.25/£4.10 per person) leave every 20 minutes from 7:30am to 8pm. There are daily buses for Kuqa (638km/396 miles; 8 hr.; ¥120/$16/£8) and a sleeper bus for Kashgar (1,385km/859 miles; 24 hr.; ¥210/$27/£14 upper berth, ¥200/$26/£13 lower berth). Both depart at 1pm.

GETTING AROUND   Turpan is a small town, and nearly everything is within walking distance of the center, marked by the intersection of Lao Cheng Lu and Gaochang Lu. Taxis within the city cost ¥5 (65¢/30p). Most sights are outside town and require a **taxi, minibus,** or **bike,** which can be hired from John's Information Cafe. Your presence is noted by local drivers when you arrive. They will politely but insistently offer tours of the eight sights *(bage difang)*. Decline.

TOURS   CITS (© **0995/818-2318;** turpancits@sina.com; open 8am–9pm) is located to the left-of-front gate of the Oasis Hotel (on the opposite side from Qingnian Lu).

FAST FACTS

Banks & Foreign Exchange   You can change traveler's checks and draw money on your credit card from counters 3 to 5 at the **Bank of China,** just west of the main roundabout, at Lao Cheng Lu 18. It also has an ATM and is open 9:30am to 1pm and 4:30 to 7:30pm.

Internet Access   There's Internet access at John's Information Cafe in the Turpan Hotel on Qingnian Lu. Dial-up is © **165.**

Post Office   The main post office (open 9am–7:30pm summer; 9:30am–7pm winter) is west of the bus station.

Visa Extensions   The **PSB office** (Mon–Fri 9:30am–1pm and 4:30–7:30pm) on Luzhou Dong Lu (© **0995/856-4409**) takes an hour or so to process extensions.

SEEING THE SIGHTS

Tulufan Bowuguan   Although the space-age exterior and lobby belie the sloppily curated interior, this is worth an hour of pottering, especially in the midday heat. Many of the exhibits are from the **Astana graves,** and attest to the preservation qualities of Turpan's arid climate. You'll see dumplings, cakes, and sultanas, all at least 13 centuries past their best. Other grave goods include a rooster-shaped pillow to ensure its owner didn't sleep through the afterlife, and the naturally mummified bodies of some of the inhabitants. The macabre nature of the exhibit attracted experts from the **Beijing Natural History Museum,** who have added a reproduction of a Gaochang army general and his wife. The final exhibition hall features the skeleton of a 9m-long (30-ft.) herbivorous dinosaur, *Paraceratherium Tienshanensis,* and *various Jurassic Park*–inspired replicas.

Gaochang Lu 26. Admission ¥20 ($2.60/£1.30). 9:30am–7:30pm.

AROUND TURPAN

The "eight sights" around Turpan can easily be visited in 1 day. These are the ancient city of **Gaochang,** the **Astana tombs,** the **Bezeklik Caves,** the **Flaming Mountains** (made famous by Ang Lee's *Crouching Tiger, Hidden Dragon*), **Putao Gou (Grape Valley), Sugong Minaret (Sugong Ta),** the *karez* irrigation channels, and the ancient city of **Jiaohe.** Private minibus drivers charge around ¥50 to ¥60 ($6.50–$7.80/£3.25–£3.90) per person for the tour. The air-conditioned CITS minibus (which runs July–Oct) is worth considering, as it includes an English-speaking guide and costs ¥60 ($7.80/£3.90) per person in summer or ¥80 ($10/£5.20) in winter. Hiring a taxi allows you to be selective, and prices can be as low as ¥150 ($20/£9.75) for a Santana in the off season, rising to a CITS high of ¥350 ($46/£23).

Several of the eight sights are not worthwhile. The ticket seller at Astana tells you to "save your money for the museum." The road to Gaochang passes the Flaming Mountains, and Bezeklik is in them, so don't stop at the designated site unless you want to spend ¥40 ($5.20/£2.60) to accompany hordes of tour groups having camel rides or their photo taken next to a giant tacky thermometer. There's a no-stopping zone for a kilometer along the road past the site, but if you get your driver to pull up anywhere after this you'll have an empty desert vista before you and not a megaphone in sight. The *karez* wells are unimpressive, and there are grape vines in Turpan, so there's no need to pay ¥20 ($2.60/£1.30) for an overpriced meal at Grape Valley. Organize a half-day tour including Gaochang, Bezeklik, Sugong Minaret, and Jiaohe, or take a 1-day tour with a visit to Tuyoq in the morning. Sugong Minaret and Jiaohe can also be reached by bike.

Bozikelike Qian Fo Dong (Bezeklik Thousand Buddha Caves)   The setting of Bezeklik Caves, in a ravine deep in the Flaming Mountains, is more spectacular than the contents of the caves. Bezeklik was stripped by several German expeditions—led by Albert Grunwedel and his nominal understudy, Albert von Le Coq—and relocated to the Museum fur Indische Kunst in Berlin. Grunwedel was reluctant to remove Buddhist antiquities, but Le Coq deemed it essential for their preservation, sparing them from Muslim iconoclasts and practical-minded farmers who would scrape off paintings for use as fertilizer. Nearly all the large wall paintings were destroyed during Allied bombing raids on Berlin in 1943 and 1945. What little is left in the few caves that are open, particularly in no. 39, hints at a distinctly Indo-Persian style. The new *Journey to the West* statue outside is rather special. About 1.6km (1 mile) back down the road, there's a collection of new statues, including a Laughing Buddha, which aren't worth paying the ¥20 ($2.60/£1.30) to look around, but the picturesque vineyard set at the verdant valley bottom (included in the same ticket) is worth a wander down to, even if you don't enter the site.

Admission ¥20 ($2.60/£1.30). Summer 9am–8pm; winter 9am–7pm.

Gaochang (Karakhoja)   Located 45km (28 miles) southeast of Turpan, Gaochang was founded during the Han dynasty as a garrison town to supply troops engaged in the conquest of the "Western Regions." Gaochang rose to prominence, becoming the capital of the region and maintaining its influence even when it passed from Chinese hands. Xuanzang visited in A.D. 630, and the king of Gaochang was so impressed by his preaching that he took the young monk captive. Xuanzang went on a hunger strike and was released with a promise to return. He wriggled out of his pledge, returning to China by the southern Silk Route. In any event, the king was dead before he returned, as Turpan returned to Chinese control.

During the Tang dynasty, Gaochang was a thriving artistic and spiritual center for Buddhism and Manichaeism, and most relics recovered by Albert von Le Coq, Stein, and Chinese archaeologists date from this period. There is a **Manichean shrine** northeast of the city walls, but the contents of its library were thrown into a river 5 years before Le Coq arrived. The man feared "the unholy nature of the writings and . . . that the Chinese might use the discovery as a pretext for fresh extortions."

Gaochang is a significant site, but aside from the city walls and the restored **Buddhist temple,** the weathered mud-brick buildings are hard to discern. A donkey-cart ride to the Buddhist temple costs ¥5 (65¢/35p) each way.

Admission ¥40 ($5.20/£2.60). 8:30am–7:30pm.

Jiaohe (Yarkhoto) ✦   Ten kilometers (6¼ miles) west of Turpan, these ruins are better preserved and enjoy a more spectacular location than Gaochang, though they are historically less significant. If you have time for only one set of ruins, come here—it's closer and more dramatic. Originally a Han garrison town, it has no city walls, as the site (which means "meeting of the rivers") is bounded by steep ravines. A clear central avenue runs east-west through the town, with residential, religious, and governmental areas delineated. The reason for the demise of the settlement during the Yuan dynasty is unclear, but the depth of the numerous wells suggests the water supply may have run out. Sunset is the best time to go; not only for photos, but to avoid most of the tour groups. Walk in a clockwise direction to further avoid the remaining tour groups, which always seem to make their pilgrimages in a counterclockwise circle. Jiaohe can be reached by taxi for ¥30 to ¥40 ($3.90–$5.20/£1.95–£2.60) round-trip; make sure your driver waits for you as there aren't many spare drivers in the parking lot.

Admission ¥40 ($5.20/£2.60). 8:30am–7:30pm.

Sugong Ta or Emin Ta (Sugong Minaret)   The mosque was built in 1778 by Prince Suleiman in honor of his father, Prince Emin, one of the few rulers of Turpan to have made the pilgrimage to Mecca. One of the first Western visitors was Francis Younghusband, who was less than overawed: "Some 3 miles from Turfan we passed a mosque with a curious tower, which looked as much like a very fat factory chimney as anything else. It was about 80 feet high, circular, and built of mud bricks, and it was ornamented by placing the bricks at different angles, forming patterns." On a deep blue-sky day, the mosque's graceful combination of adobe curves and angles are beautifully softened by the surrounding grapevines and it's hard not to be drawn to the "chimney," which is actually 40m (132 ft.) tall. The style is neither Han nor Hui, but similar to those found farther west on the Silk Routes. The mosque is not the oldest in Turpan, but it's the best preserved. It's open for worship at 2:30pm on Friday, when entry for non-Muslims is restricted.

Admission ¥30 ($3.90/£1.95). 8am–7:30pm. Bus: no. 6 to the terminus; continue east for 10 min.

TUYOQ: A UIGHUR STRONGHOLD *

Less than 20km (12 miles) beyond Gaochang, the idyllic Uighur village of Tuyoq is a fine day trip, and can be included in a tour. A leisurely day trip to Tuyoq, stopping at Gaochang on the way back, can be arranged with individual taxis for ¥250 ($33/£16). Direct buses to Tuyoq (¥7.50/$1/50p) leave Turpan at noon, 2pm, and 4pm. Buses to **Lukeqin** (¥9.50/$1.25/60p) pass Tuyoq, and leave from 10am; the last bus back to Turpan leaves Lukeqin at around 5pm, passing Tuyoq about 20 minutes later. Bus station staff, in the pay of taxi drivers, will do everything they can to persuade you that the bus goes nowhere near Tuyoq. If you catch the Lukeqin bus, you will be dropped at the south end of the sprawling settlement, leaving a hot but fascinating 5km (3-mile) walk north to the village proper. Three-wheelers also make the trip for ¥3 (40¢/20p).

Tourist officials hope that the recent opening of some Buddhist caves here will boost revenues; the village now charges a ¥30 ($3.90/£1.95) fee to walk into the area, regardless of whether or not you'd like to see the caves. The caves have been severely damaged and all that's left of the four open to the public are small patches of cave paintings with the faces of Buddhas scratched out. Bring a flashlight for a closer look. The village itself is nice to wander through, and several courtyard homes will open their doors for you at lunchtime. The cost of a meal should be ¥15 ($1.95/£1)—make sure you agree on the price before you settle in.

WHERE TO STAY

For a town that receives so many tourists, it's a shame there aren't better hotels. You may wonder why some of the hotels below are included; it's for a lack of better options! During the peak season, discounts of 20% are standard. During the off season, discounts of 40% to 60% are possible.

Dongfang Jiudian * *Value* This no-frills two-star hotel is a good deal for budget travelers. It offers a good location next to the bazaar and bus station, comfortable beds, and clean, but cramped bathrooms. Service is kind and efficient and the environment is calmer than the well-trodden backpackers' Jiaotong Binguan a few doors down.

Lao Cheng Xi Lu 324. © **0995/626-8228.** Fax 0995/8531-1328. ¥240 ($31/£16) standard room; ¥480 ($62/£31) suite. 40% discount even in high season. No credit cards. *In room:* A/C, TV.

Hongyuan Jiudian Popular with tour groups, this place boasts a good location and decent amenities. Staff are helpful, and rooms are spacious, spotless, and have high ceilings and good bathrooms. Some of the rooms are in better shape than others, so look at a few before you pick a room. Beds can be a bit too stiff. A lively night market in front of the hotel appears at 7pm. Avoid the hotel's karaoke-sauna-massage parlor complex.

Gaochang Lu 712 (Luyou Wenhua Guangchang Xi Ce). © **0995/857-8177.** Fax 0995/857-8179. 60 units. From ¥380 ($49/£25) standard room; ¥580 ($75/£38) suite. 40% discount. No credit cards. **Amenities:** Restaurant; concierge; tour desk; business center. *In room:* A/C, TV.

Jinxin Binguan (Jinxin Hotel)   This is one of the newer establishments in town (and one of the taller buildings around); the rooms have comfy beds and passable bathrooms. The hotel is well managed, and they're used to dealing with foreigners. The one disadvantage is the karaoke parlor on the ninth floor that often reverberates with the bad sounds of government cadres well into the night; stay on the seventh floor or below.

Luzhou Zhong Lu 390. ⓒ **0995/856-0222.** Fax 0995/856-0403. 40 units. ¥380 ($49/£25) standard room; ¥688 ($89/£45) suite. 40% discount. No credit cards. **Amenities:** Restaurant; conference room; karaoke. *In room:* A/C, TV.

Luzhou Binguan (Oasis Hotel)   Managed by the same Hong Kong entrepreneur who created the Silk Road Hotel in Dunhuang, this three-star hotel set in rambling grounds is showing signs of age and group-tour syndrome. The only reason to stay here is for the Uighur-style rooms on the first floor, with low beds perched on a raised platform and richly colored rug, although these are fairly small and a little shabby. Book ahead and specify that you want a *"minzu tese fangjian"* (minority-flavored room). Service is remarkably helpful.

Qingnian Lu 41. ⓒ **0995/852-2491.** Fax 0995/852-3348. 193 units (28 with shower only). ¥280 ($36/£18) economy room; ¥580 ($75/£38) standard room; ¥1,080 ($140/£70) suite. Room rates readily reduced by 40%. AE, DC, MC, V. **Amenities:** 3 restaurants; bike rental; billiards room; concierge; tour desk (CITS); business center; 24-hr. forex; same-day laundry. *In room:* A/C, TV.

Tulufan Dafandian (Grand Turpan Hotel)   The rooms are some of the best in town, but the service could possibly be the worst in town. This hotel recently experienced a change in its management (it was formerly Hong Kong run), and as a result the front desk is terribly managed and has problems dealing with even the smallest request. Spacious rooms in the new wing with clean bathrooms meet four-star standards; dorm beds are clean if not a bit pricey. Don't get this confused with the Turpan Hotel, which is a lesser operation that is popular with backpackers.

Gaochang Zhong Lu 422. ⓒ **0995/855-3668.** Fax 0995/855-3908. xjturpanhotel.com. 154 units (38 with shower only). ¥480 ($62/£31) standard room; from ¥1,180 ($153/£77) suite. AE, DC, MC, V. **Amenities:** 2 restaurants; cafe; exercise room; large game room; concierge; business center; 24-hr. forex; same-day laundry/dry cleaning. *In room:* A/C, TV, minibar, fridge, safe.

WHERE TO DINE

Western breakfasts can be found at the Oasis Hotel for ¥25 ($3.25/£1.65), as well as at **John's Information Cafe** at the back of the Turpan Hotel on Qingnian Lu 41; John's is also a good place for a drink under the shade of grapevine trellises in the heat of the day. Hotels offer safe but boring Muslim and Chinese fare and evening performances of singing and dancing. For real food, head for the bazaar just west of the Bank of China, where you can enjoy pastries stuffed with minced lamb (*samsa, kao baozi*), kabobs, and homemade ice cream scraped from gigantic sweet orange mounds. At night, the market in front of the Hongyuan Binguan offers fantastic kabobs, Uighur dumplings, and noodles. Just point to what you want. If you want singing and dancing as well, check out the following locales.

Ataichi Canting UIGHUR   The original dinner and dance restaurant for the locals is feeling the competition from Shiji Xing (below). Although its underground location keeps it cool, there is a dungeonlike feel to it, and the print of a whole roast sheep sitting contentedly on a tablecloth in a meadow may be enough to convert you to macrobiotics. Busiest on Friday and Saturday, the banquets (minimum six people) are an excellent way to try a variety of foods without wearing out your phrasebook.

1009 Lao Cheng Lu (on the southeast side of the intersection with Gaochang Lu). © 0995/852-9775. Banquets ¥39–¥89 ($5.05–$12/£2.55–£5.80) per person. No credit cards. 8–11pm (performance starts 8:30pm).

Shiji Xing ✦✦ UIGHUR   Set amid grapevines at the edge of an unlikely looking light industrial suburb, this is a favorite among locals for carousing late into the night. Bakri, a Uighur entrepreneur, caters to the fantasies of both locals and foreigners, recruiting handsome waiters from Khotan and dancers from all over Xinjiang. Grapevines hang above the tables, and discreet fans keep you cool. Waiters shuffle on their knees across elevated platforms and somehow manage to look elegant. *Shiji xing yangpai* (lamb chops) is worth the expense, and don't miss the chance to cook your own kabobs. For the long-suffering China traveler, a real treat—dessert! Sweets *(tian-shi)* are not on the menu, but a platter of shortbread and gingerbread biscuits, many with tart apricot fillings, can be arranged. Try mulberry wine *(sangshen jiu),* less sickly sweet than most in the region. The wine will help if you get hauled up on stage.

Xin Zhan Dingzi Lukou © 0995/855-1199. Meal for 2 ¥40–¥120 ($5.20–$16/£2.60–£7.80). No credit cards. Open at 1:30pm; performance at 9:30pm. Bus: no. 202 to Xinzhan; walk 135m (450 ft.) to the northwest side of the T-junction.

12 Urumqi (Wulumuqi)

Xinjiang, 1,470km (911 miles) NE of Kashgar, 692km (429 miles) E of Yining

Early visitors gave mixed reviews. Missionary Mildred Cable thought the town "has no beauty, no style, no dignity and no architectural interest. The climate is violent, exaggerated and at no season pleasant . . ." However, acerbic American author Owen Lattimore loved Urumqi "in the spring, when along the liquescent streets the Chinese began to appear in gay colors and flowered silks and satins, and the Turkis, abandoning the reds and purples of their long winter gowns, to put on the white cotton robes of warm weather; and in the beginning of summer, when the early leafage of trees was not yet dulled with dust, and to walk on the city walls at sunset was the crowning glory of the day."

Opinions on the town are still divided, but everyone agrees that Urumqi is best avoided in winter. Ringed by factories and relying on coal heating, the town sees its first snow coated by a film of soot within hours. For those who fly in from the east, it provides a tantalizing first taste of a different culture, and there are fascinating markets to explore, all to the backdrop of snow-clad mountains that appear and vanish as the weather (and pollution) allows.

ESSENTIALS

GETTING THERE   Urumqi airport, to the north of town, has a brand-new domestic terminal and a smaller international terminal next door. Taxis into town cost around ¥35 ($4.55/£2.30), or you can lug your bags for 10 minutes to the south and catch the slow but cheap bus no. 2 for ¥2 (25¢/15p). Air tickets may be booked over the phone (© 800/893-9800), and substantial discounts are available if you book up to 10 days in advance. China Airlines handles most flights within Xinjiang and its main office (© 95539) is next to the Kempinski Hotel on Youhao Nan Lu. There is also a ticket office at the airport. Several daily flights connect with Beijing, Xi'an, Kashgar, Yining, and Dunhuang. There are also daily connections with Shanghai, Guangzhou, Chengdu, Lanzhou, and Khotan. There are also international connections with Moscow (5 hr.; Sat–Sun) and Tashkent (2½ hr.; Sat).

Urumqi's **railway station** is located in the southwest corner of town. Nearly all trains from the east and west terminate here. Tickets (for same-day travel only) may be purchased at the station in a building behind and to the right of the main entrance. To purchase sleeper tickets, either proceed through your hotel and pay around ¥30 ($3.90/£1.95) commission, or at the **railway ticket office** (7:30am–9:30pm) at Jianshe Lu 3, in the courtyard of the Laiyuan Binguan, and pay ¥5 (65¢/35p) commission. There are direct express trains to Beijing (T70; 39 hr.) at 8:20pm, and to Shanghai (T54; 45 hr.) at 6:51pm, passing through Lanzhou and Xi'an. There are also speedy connections with Lanzhou (T198; 22 hr.) at 7:12pm, and with Dunhuang (T218; 14 hr.) at 8:44pm. Sluggish trains head for Chongqing (K54; 48 hr.) at 9:54pm, and for Chengdu (454; 45 hr.) at 2:05pm.

Tickets for Almaty in Kazakhstan may be purchased in the foyer of the **Xiang You Jiudian,** next to the train station. The office is open on Mondays, Tuesdays, Fridays, and Saturdays between 10am and 1pm, 3:30 and 6pm, and 9:30 and 11pm. The more comfortable Kazakh train runs on Monday (¥708/$92/£46 in a four-berth cabin, ¥1,400/$182/£91 in a two-berth cabin) and the Chinese one on Saturday (¥489/$64/£32 hard sleeper, ¥709/$92/£46 soft sleeper). The Kazakh train leaves at 11:58pm and the Chinese train leaves at 9:46pm, arriving on Wednesday and Monday mornings respectively.

From the **main bus station** at Heilongjiang Lu 51 (© **0991/587-8895**), buses connect with Yining (692km/429 miles; 12 hr.; ¥150/$20/£9.75 lower berth, ¥140/$18/£9.10 upper berth) at 4pm, 5pm, 7pm, and 8pm; and with the border town of Tacheng (633km/392 miles; 12 hr.; ¥145/$19/£9.45 lower berth, ¥135/$18/£8.80 upper berth) at 7pm and 9pm. The **Southern Bus Station** (© **0991/286-6635**) has regular connections with Turpan from 8:40am to 8:30pm (187km/116 miles; 2½ hr.; ¥40/$5.20/£2.60); Kuqa (745km/462 miles; 14 hr.; ¥145/$19/£9.45, upper berth ¥135/$18/£8.80) every half-hour from 2 to 8pm; Kashgar (1,470km/911 miles; 30 hr.; ¥230/$30/£15 lower berth, ¥220/$29/£14 upper berth) every half-hour from 10am to 4:30pm; and Hejing (376km/233 miles; ¥70/$9.10/£4.55). Bus nos. 1, 7, and 101 all connect with this bus station. Buses across the Taklamakan Desert to Khotan (1,777km/1,101 miles; 18–22 hr.; ¥360/$47/£23 for a luxury sleeper or ¥255/$33/£17 lower berth, ¥235/$31/£15 upper berth) leave hourly between noon and 8pm.

GETTING AROUND   A legion of Santana and *Xiali* **taxis** charge ¥6 (80¢/40p) for 3km (2 miles), then ¥1.30 (15¢/10p) per kilometer; ¥2.10 (25¢/15p) midnight to 7am. For the useful **bus** nos. 1, 2, and 7, pay ¥1 (15 ¢/10p) into a box as you enter, or ¥.50 to ¥2 (5¢–25¢/5p–15p) to a conductor. Riding a **bike** through the smog and traffic snarls is not recommended.

FAST FACTS

Banks, Foreign Exchange & ATMs   The main **Bank of China** (open Mon–Fri 10am–6pm, and year-round weekends 11am–4pm) is opposite the Hoi Tak Hotel at Dongfeng Lu 1. Credit cards and traveler's checks are accepted. ATMs (left of the entrance) accept foreign cards. Another ATM is located at the Jiefang Lu branch, just west of the Xinhua Bookstore. Credit cards and traveler's checks are accepted at counter 23, and there's the added convenience of black-market dealers operating *inside* the bank. The branch is open weekdays 10am to 1:30pm and 4 to 6pm.

Consulates   Transit visas are available from the **Kazak Consulate** (© **0991/383-2324**) at Kunming Lu 31 for ¥306 ($39/£20). They are issued in 5 to 7 days, but may be available more quickly if you request. The consulate is open Monday through Thursday from 9:30am to noon for drop-offs and between noon and 1pm for collections.

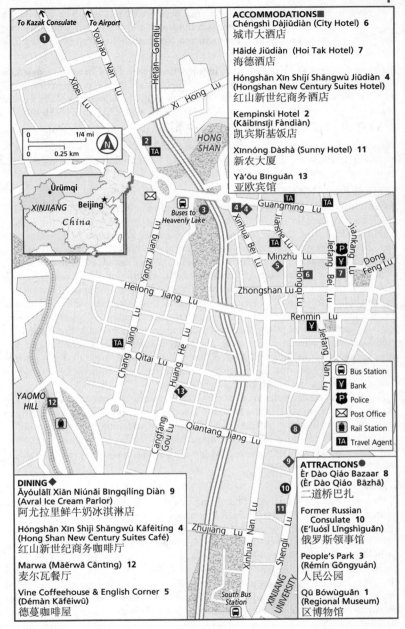

ACCOMMODATIONS

Chéngshì Dàjiǔdiàn (City Hotel) 6
城市大酒店

Hǎidé Jiǔdiàn (Hoi Tak Hotel) 7
海德酒店

Hóngshān Xīn Shíjì Shāngwù Jiǔdiàn 4
(Hongshan New Century Suites Hotel)
红山新世纪商务酒店

Kempinski Hotel 2
(Kǎibīnsījì Fàndiàn)
凯宾斯基饭店

Xīnnóng Dàshà (Sunny Hotel) 11
新农大厦

Yà'ōu Bīnguǎn 13
亚欧宾馆

To Kazak Consulate   **To Airport**

0   1/4 mi
0   0.25 km

Ürümqi
XINJIANG   Beijing ★
China

Buses to
Heavenly Lake

HONG
SHAN

Guangming   Lu

Xinhua   Bei   Lu
Jianshe   Lu
Minzhu   Lu
Jiefang   Bei   Lu
Jiankang   Lu
Dong   Feng   Lu
Zhongshan   Lu
Hongqi   Lu
Renmin   Lu

Youhao   Nan   Lu
Xibei   Lu
Hetan   Gonglu
Xi   Hong   Lu

Heilong   Jiang   Lu
Yangzi   Jiang   Lu
Chang   Jiang   Lu
Qitai   Lu
Huang   He   Lu
Jiefang   Nan   Lu

YAOMO
HILL

Cangfang   Gou   Lu
Qiantang   Jiang   Lu

Zhujiang   Lu
Xinhua   Nan   Lu
Shengli   Lu

South Bus
Station

XINJIANG   UNIVERSITY

🚌 Bus Station
¥ Bank
🅿 Police
✉ Post Office
🚉 Rail Station
TA Travel Agent

DINING

Āyóulālǐ Xiān Niúnǎi Bīngqílíng Diàn 9
(Avral Ice Cream Parlor)
阿尤拉里鲜牛奶冰淇淋店

Hóngshān Xīn Shìjì Shāngwù Kāfēitíng 4
(Hong Shan New Century Suites Café)
红山新世纪商务咖啡厅

Marwa (Māěrwǎ Cāntīng) 12
麦尔瓦餐厅

Vine Coffeehouse & English Corner 5
(Démàn Kāfēiwū)
德蔓咖啡屋

ATTRACTIONS

Èr Dào Qiáo Bazaar 8
(Èr Dào Qiáo Bāzhā)
二道桥巴扎

Former Russian
Consulate 10
(É'luósī Lǐngshìguǎn)
俄罗斯领事馆

People's Park 3
(Rémín Gōngyuán)
人民公园

Qū Bówùguǎn 1
(Regional Museum)
区博物馆

One passport photo and a photocopy of your passport are required. The consulate is not easily located, so take a taxi. Or catch bus no. 2 as far as Xiao Xigou, walk east along Suzhou Dong Lu, take the first right, and continue about 315m (1,033 ft.). The consulate is on the left (east) side.

Internet Access   There's a 24-hour Internet cafe above the **Chengshi Dajiudian** that charges ¥2 (25¢/15p) per hour, and another (same hours and cost) a few doors north of Marwa Restaurant on Huang He Lu, near the junction with Wuyi Lu and next to a Dicos fast-food restaurant—look for the net sign. Dial-up is © **16900.**

Post Office   The main post office on Yangzi Jiang Lu is open from 9:30am to 8pm.

Visa Extensions   A friendly **PSB** at Jiankang Lu 27 (© **0991/283-4489**) offers 1-month visa extensions up to 20 days in advance. The entrance is to the right of the main gate, marked ALIENS RECEPTION ROOM URUMQI.

SEEING THE SIGHTS

Qu Bowuguan (Regional Museum)   The museum underwent a full renovation in 2005, and its exhibits are now well presented in the shiny interior of this massive building. Don't miss the 12 remarkably well-preserved **mummies** ✸✸, many with Indo-European features: high cheekbones, long noses, brightly colored woolen kilts. The mummies, some of which date from 2000 B.C., were unearthed from tombs scattered around the Taklamakan in **Loulan, Astana, Hami,** and **Charchan (Qiemo).** They do little to further Han claims over Xinjiang. Add the cost of preservation and you might believe, as some suggest, that additional finds are being deliberately left in the ground. Han Chinese chauvinists point out that Uighurs, a Turkic people who migrated from western Mongolia, have nothing in common with the indigenous Indo-European Tocharians, who spoke a language that resembles a Celtic tongue. But there are enough blue- or green-eyed folk on the streets of Turpan and Kuqa (former Tocharian strongholds) to suggest that interbreeding was common. As my Uighur companion remarked, "So we killed all of them?"

Han Chinese guides make much of the relatively young mummy of General Zhang (d. A.D. 633), commander of the armies in Gaochang, whose wife rests in the Turpan Museum. Other interesting items on exhibit are lead and bronze eyeshades used in sandstorms, and a hunting boomerang unearthed in Hami.

Xi Bei Lu 581. Mon–Sat ¥30 ($3.90/£1.95); Sun free entry. Summer 9:30am–7pm (last entry 5pm); winter 10:30am–6pm (last entry 4pm). Bus: no. 7 to Bowuguan.

SHOPPING

You'll find a wide range of Uighur handicrafts on sale at **Er Dao Qiao Bazaar,** but the environment has recently been turned into a tacky tourist trap. On what used to be on airy outdoor market now stands a Hong Kong developer's interpretation of Uighur architecture, massive beige-brick buildings, complete with a Carrefour and KFC. For more of a local flavor, head to **Ribiya Dasha,** a building erected by the Uighur businesswoman Rebiya Kadeer who became famous in the Western press after being jailed by China as a political prisoner. Outside, around the perimeters of the building, bright fabrics, televisions, jewelry, and appliances are sold. Also nearby is **Baihetiya'er Huangjin Shoushidian** at Jiefang Nan Lu 197, which sells affordable gold, silver, and platinum jewelry. The necklaces are particularly elegant. Watch the Uighur women bargain, and see if you can get a similar price.

For carpets, you should avoid Er Dao Qiao Bazaar and its scary assortment of pushy salespeople who don't know the first thing about carpets. Head to the **Carpet Factory of the People's Government (Renmin Dahuitang Gongyi Lipin Xiaoshou Zhongxin)**—where government officials shop for gifts for foreign dignitaries. Here, they sell mostly new carpets, in both silk and wool varieties, fit for export. Goods can be bargained down by 50% at least. If you have trouble getting in (the store is located within the People's Government Compound), give them a call (© **0991/483-6698**) and they'll escort you from the gate. Shopping here is generally reserved for the rich and the well-connected Chinese and Uighurs; it's open from 9am to 5pm. Another area to check out carpets is Tianhaai Lu, behind Er Dao Qiao Bazaar. There are several stores here that will have some antiques, but prices are high. Those hunting for books on Buddhist art will find an excellent selection of pictorial and theoretical works at Tian Zhi Ya Shushe, in a small lane just east of Xinhua Bookstore, at Jiefang Nan Lu 348.

To stock up on snacks before a long bus or train journey, there are plenty of supermarkets around the town center; the one in the basement of the Parkson shopping center at the southern end of Youhao Nan Lu is particularly good, as is the vast and always busy Carrefour at Er Dao Qiao Bazaar.

WHERE TO STAY
VERY EXPENSIVE/EXPENSIVE
Haide Jiudian (Hoi Tak Hotel) ⓕ   The Hoi Tak benefits from aggressive Hong Kong management, rigorous staff training, and plenty of capital from its parent company for renovations. Bathrooms are opulent and the suites are superspacious. The 36-story building is the largest in town, and on the rare days when the pollution haze clears, you can enjoy a magnificent view of the Tian Shan range.

Dongfeng Lu 1. © **0991/232-2828.** Fax 0991/232-1818. www.hoitak.com. 318 units. ¥1,400–¥1,600 ($182–$208/£91–£104) standard room; from ¥2,080 ($270/£135) suite. 50% discounts are standard. 15% service charge. AE, DC, MC, V. **Amenities:** 4 restaurants; bar; cafe; nightclub; large indoor pool; health club; 8-lane bowling alley; billiards and table tennis rooms; concierge; tour desk; courtesy car; business center; 24-hr. forex; salon; 24-hr. room service; in-room massage; same-day laundry/dry cleaning. *In room:* A/C, satellite TV, broadband Internet access, minibar, fridge, hair dryer, safe.

Hongshan Xin Shiji Shangwu Jiudian (Hongshan New Century Suites Hotel) ⓕ ⓥalue   Plunked down in the middle of Urumqi is this extremely stylish hotel aimed at hipsters and business executives. The rooms are the best in Xinjiang: Plush minimalist sofas and armchairs and comfy large beds give the rooms a professional, modern feel. The bathrooms, with sparkling fixtures, come with separate shower and tub in the standard twins. The hallways and lobby buzz with a muted ambience. However, a recent change of ownership has meant that service has suffered, and until the new management finds its feet, rates here are likely to remain cheaper than at the Hoi Tak and Kempinski. The coffeehouse on the third floor offers fantastic coffee and desserts (reviewed below).

Xinhua Bei Lu 38. © **0991/887-8888.** Fax 0991/887-8546. 147 units. ¥688 ($89/£45) standard room; ¥888–¥1,288 ($115–$167/£58–£84) suite. 20% discounts. AE, DC, MC, V. **Amenities:** Restaurant. *In room:* A/C, TV, broadband Internet access, minibar, fridge.

Kempinski Hotel (Kaibinsiji Fandian) ⓕ   The Kempinski oozes class and, on clear days, its sleek, modern and tasteful rooms afford fine views over nearby Red Hill Park to the mountains beyond Urumqi. Beds are supercomfy and bathrooms have (small) tubs and separate shower. Service is attentive and friendly. While the quiet location is a little removed from Urumqi's bustling center, China Southern's main office is on-site and the hotel is close to the upmarket Parkson shopping mall.

Youhao Nan Lu 576. ℂ 0991/638-8888. Fax 0991/638-8666. www.kempinski-urumqi.com. 295 units. ¥1,280 ($166/£83) standard room; ¥3,200 ($416/£208) suite. 15% service charge. AE, DC, MC, V. **Amenities:** 3 restaurants; bar; nightclub; health club; billiards and table tennis rooms; concierge; tour desk; business center; forex; ATM; salon; 24-hr. room service; laundry. *In room:* A/C, TV, in-house movie library, broadband Internet access, minibar, fridge, hair dryer, safe.

MODERATE/INEXPENSIVE

Chengshi Dajiudian (City Hotel) ⟨★⟩
Right in the center of town, located on a busy, crowded street, the facilities and service at this three-star hotel are better than you would anticipate for the outlay. The beds are firm and the bathrooms are spotless, if a little cramped. It's worth spending a little extra for the rooms with windows, which open. Service has improved to meet the expectations of the primarily foreign clientele. Taking the elevator here feels a bit like stepping into the United Nations—you'll be sharing your space with Russians, Africans, and Americans.

Hongqi Lu 119. ℂ 0991/220-7666. Fax 0991/230-5321. 226 units. ¥322–¥522 ($42–$68/£21–£34) standard room; from ¥690 ($90/£45) suite. Discounts of 20%–40%. Rates include breakfast. AE, DC, MC, V. **Amenities:** 2 restaurants; nightclub; teahouse; billiards room; concierge; tour desk; business center; 24-hr. forex; same-day laundry/dry cleaning. *In room:* A/C, TV, minibar, fridge, safe.

Xinnong Dasha (Sunny Hotel)
A favorite with Russian traders, this two-star hotel is handy to the Uighur part of town and the South Bus Station. True to its name, rooms are bright, and recent renovations have delivered well-sprung beds and squeaky-clean bathrooms to the rooms on the fifth and sixth floors. Although the rooms higher up offer more respite from the bustle below, they have yet to be refitted and are seedily shabby.

Shengli Lu 175. ℂ 0991/285-0033, ext. 8007. Fax 0991/287-2378. 100 units. 5th–6th floors ¥260 ($34/£17) twin; 7th–12th floors ¥210 ($27/£14) twin; ¥480–¥580 ($62–$75/£31–£38) suite. 30% discounts possible for short stays; up to 60% possible for longer stays. No credit cards. **Amenities:** 2 restaurants; concierge; tour desk; business center; next-day laundry/dry cleaning. *In room:* A/C, TV, fridge.

WHERE TO DINE

The streets around Er Dao Qiao are full of Uighur restaurants serving tasty dumplings stuffed with lamb and pumpkin, lamb skewers, and *langman,* or noodles. But if you're on your way out of Xinjiang and have had your fill of Uighur food, there are also some decent Chinese and Western offerings.

Ayoulali Xian Niunai Bingqiling Dian (Avral Ice Cream Parlor) ⟨★★⟩ ⟨Moments⟩
DESSERT   Uighurs seem to enjoy the Western tradition of loving good ice cream—as evidenced in the soft-serve machines on street corners everywhere in Xinjiang. Here, ice cream is elevated to haute cuisine (though still at Uighur prices) at this parlor with wooden walls and glass tables. There are only a few flavors on offer—the trademark Avral (a butterscotch with local berries), cherry, and chocolate. It's become an institution in Urumqi.

Shengli Lu 193. ¥10 ($1.30/65p) per person. No credit cards. Bus: no. 101 to Er Dao Qiao; walk south under the overpass, keeping to the west side.

Hongshan Xin Shiji Shangwu Kafeiting (Hongshan New Century Suites Cafe) ⟨★⟩
TAIWANESE   This new restaurant, part of the Hongshan New Century Suites Hotel, is representative of the hip, new edge that's seemed to penetrate Urumqi in the past few years. The cozy booths with window views of the city are a particularly nice place to escape the hustle and bustle. You can try your luck with the entrees,

which range from Asian to Italian dishes, but it's the rich coffee and mountainous piles of ice and fruit desserts that the Taiwanese call *baobing* that stand out.

Xinhua Bei Lu 108. © **0991/887-8888**. Meal for 2 ¥100 ($13/£6.50). AE, DC, MC, V. 8am–1am.

Marwa (Maerwa Canting) 🌟 *finds* UIGHUR

To plunge straight into Uighur cuisine, this refined restaurant is a fine first choice. Smartly uniformed staff present a range of traditional dishes including *pilao* rice (served with delicious dates and raisins), chunky kabobs, and for dessert lovers, *suan nai* (milk pudding) is a real treat. The super-clean dining hall features carved wooden chairs and a vaulted ceiling and is always busy. There's no English menu but the open kitchen at the front of the restaurant means you can just point at what you want. To find the restaurant, look for the oval white sign reading Marwa in green writing.

Huang He Lu 99. Meal for 2 from ¥50 ($6.50/£3.25). No credit cards. 7am–11pm.

Vine Coffeehouse & English Corner (Deman Kafeiwu) WESTERN

A friendly Caribbean cafe is not something you expect to find in downtown Urumqi, but this oasis in a sea of blandness is a delight. The halal menu was established by the head chef of the Plaza Hotel, Curaçao. Try his signature dish, the Jacques Steak, pan-fried with green peppers, tomatoes, and onions, and served with a chunky side salad and fries. Other hits are the soup de jour, or for a quick snack, try the cookies and cakes under the front counter with a *batida* (fruit shake). "English Corner" is currently held on Sunday afternoons at 4:30pm; it's a nice way to meet locals, and possibly find a guide who isn't out to bilk you. The restaurant is down a small alley (Xinsheng Xiang) off Minzhu Lu.

Minzhu Lu 65. © **0991/230-4831**. Main courses ¥18–¥38 ($2.35–$4.95/£1.15–£2.45). No credit cards. Tues–Sun 1:30–11:30pm.

URUMQI AFTER DARK

Most Han Chinese believe that Uighurs, like all Chinese ethnic minorities, love to sing and dance *(neng ge shan wu).* As one Chinese guidebook notes, "although very few Uighurs speak Chinese well, they will often spontaneously break into song and dance to show their friendship." If you're already not exhausted by all the singing and dancing, the best-known song-and-dance troupe is the **Xinjiang Gewu Tuan** (© **0991/ 286-6901**), which performs at different venues around town. They are housed in the former Russian Consulate, at Shengli Lu 193, whose elegant, decaying buildings and grounds are a must-see for aficionados of the Great Game, a drawn-out battle of espionage fought out in central Asia between Russian (and later Soviet) diplomats and their counterparts in British India.

AROUND URUMQI

While Urumqi has improved, an explosion in domestic tourism means that **Tian Chi** (**Heavenly Lake;** admission ¥60/$7.80/£3.90) is on the way to becoming the world's largest public convenience. A "paving-the-lake" operation is underway, but it's still a more pleasant destination than **Hanas Lake** in the north of Xinjiang. If you do go, stay the night, as the lake is more tranquil after buses return to Urumqi around 5pm. Avoid Rashid's Yurt, which is listed in every guidebook—fame is not good for everyone. Buses depart for the lake from the entrance to Urumqi's **Renmin Gongyuan** at 9:30am (120km/74 miles; 1½ hr.; ¥50/$6.50/£3.25 one-way, ¥100/$13/£6.50 round-trip). A similar day trip is to **Baiyang Gou (White Poplar Gully),** where you can ride horses, stay in yurts, and enjoy lush countryside. Buses depart at 9:30am (76km/47 miles; 1½ hr.; ¥40/$7.80/£3.90) and return midafternoon.

13 Kuqa (Kuche) ⍟

Xinjiang Province, 748km (464 miles) SW of Urumqi, 723km (448 miles) E of Kashgar, 591km (366 miles) SE of Yining

A maverick Silk Route kingdom, **Kuqa** was the center of the ancient kingdom of **Qiuci.** The inhabitants were Indo-European Tocharians, who migrated down from Anatolia (Turkey) and the Caucasus. Drawing on inspiration from Gandhara and Persia, Kuqan musicians and artists were very much the fashion in the cosmopolitan capital of Chang'an. Monks adhered to Hinayana Buddhism, in contrast to other Tarim basin towns and China proper, which adhered to the more complex Mahayana tradition.

Kuqa's most famous son was **Kumarajiva** (A.D. 343–413), uniquely qualified to be a translator, with a Brahmin father and a Kuqan mother. His father wanted him to be ordained as a Buddhist monk, but his mother sent him to Kashmir and Kashgar to be instructed in Indian literature, astronomy, and Buddhism. He arrived in Chang'an in 401 as a prisoner of Chinese raiders, and soon caught the eye of the fervently Buddhist Tibetan ruling house. Kumarajiva oversaw the largest "translation team" in history. Although the Kuqan scholar was skeptical that the scriptures could ever be rendered faithfully from the Sanskrit, the team of around 1,000 scholars translated the *Diamond Sutra,* which became one of the most influential texts in Chinese Buddhism.

Present-day Kuqa is a friendly, ramshackle Uighur town with a great market. The fertile soil and relatively temperate climate yield delicious apricots, grapes, peaches, and plums. *Note:* Please turn to appendix A for Chinese translations of key locations.

ESSENTIALS

GETTING THERE   There is one flight a day from Urumqi. For times, check with **CAAC** on Wenhua Lu (© 0997/712-9390) or with the **airport** (© 0997/712-2051).

The **railway station** is on the southwest side of town. Taxis (¥10/$1.30/65p) and bus no. 6 (¥1.50/20¢/10p) take you into town. Heading west, the N887 for Kashgar (9 hr.) leaves at 2:22am or the slower 7557 (11 hr.) departs at 9:03am. Heading east, the N888 for Urumqi (14 hr.) leaves at 9:38pm; the 5808 at 7:11pm (16 hr.) and the 7558 at 8:32pm (21 hr.) all leave at more agreeable hours. The railway ticket office, open from 9am to noon, 1 to 8pm, and 9pm to midnight, sells tickets for the day of travel; your best chance of securing a sleeper ticket is CITS, which charges ¥50 ($6.50/£3.25) commission.

The **bus station** at Tian Shan Lu 125 (© 0997/712-2379) has no direct buses to Kashgar, and no guarantee of a berth on sleeper buses from Korla. However, there are buses to Aksu (275km/171 miles; 4 hr.; ¥41/$5.35/£2.65), where you'll need to take a taxi (¥5/65¢/35p) to Zhongxin Keyun Zhan in order to board a Kashgar-bound bus (8 hr.; ¥60/$7.95/£3.95). Heading east, regular buses connect with Luntai (111km/ 69 miles; 2 hr.; ¥20/$2.60/£1.30); with Korla (285km/173 miles; 5 hr.; ¥49/$6.35/ £3.20); and with Urumqi (748km/464 miles; 13 hr.; ¥135–¥145/$18–$19/£8.80– £9.45). There is one bus a day to Yining (591km/366 miles; 20–25 hr.; ¥200/ $26/£13).

GETTING AROUND   Taxis have no meters; most trips within town cost ¥5 (65¢/35p). There are **three-wheelers** and **pedicabs,** as well as six **bus** routes. Bus fare is ¥.50 (10¢/5p). Donkey-drawn **carts** for ¥1 (15¢/5p) connect the bus station with the old part of town.

TOURS   **Kuqa International Travel Service,** a branch of CITS, is located inside the Qiuci Binguan, at Tian Shan Lu 93 (© **0997/713-6016;** fax 0997/712-2524; open 9:30am–1:30pm and 4–8pm).

FAST FACTS

Banks   The **Bank of China** (open weekdays 9:30am–8pm summer, 10am–7:30pm winter), Tian Shan Lu 25, can draw money on credit cards, but it doesn't change traveler's checks.

Internet Access   There are plenty of Internet cafes on Tianshan Lu near the junction of Wuyi Lu, which charge ¥2 (25¢/15p). Dial-up is ✆ **16300.**

Post Office   The post office is at Wenhua Lu 8, open from 10am to 7:30pm.

EXPLORING KUQA

Friday is the most interesting day to be in town, as humanity pours in from the surrounding countryside for the **Kuqa Bazaar** ★★, filling the old town with unforgettable sights and smells. Eric Teichman, making the first motorized journey across Xinjiang, found himself greatly inconvenienced: "The streets were so packed with Turki peasants that it was difficult to force a passage with the trucks. . . . We lost our way in the maze of narrow streets round the bazaar of Kuchar and it was after 4 p.m. by the time we cleared the town."

There has been no attempt to "modernize" this bazaar, which spills out in front of the mosque, just across the **Kuqa River.** Get there early when the light is ideal for photography. If you're not bazaared out it's also worth making a late afternoon trip to the new city market on Wuqian Lu which stretches south off Tian Shan Lu. On any day of the week, the old town is worth exploring. Make for the **Kuqa Grand Mosque (Kuche Da Si),** the only mosque in Xinjiang that retains a religious court (ca. 17th c.). Bus no. 1 connects the old town with the bus station, or you can hail a donkey-drawn cart.

Kizil Thousand Buddha Caves (Kezi'er Qian Fo Dong)   Those without a special passion for cave temples should save themselves for Dunhuang, but for those seeking a complete picture of the transmission of Buddhist art and ideas, this site might offer some more insights. Seventy-eight kilometers (48 miles) from Kuqa, the site can be reached by arranging a tour or hiring a taxi (¥200/$26/£13 for round-trip).

The site, along with several other Xinjiang tourist spots, was recently handed over to a private company to be managed, and they've jacked up the prices of admission dramatically. You'll also have less choice over which caves you see—for visits to particular caves, you'll have to fax a letter in advance to ask for permission. Currently, only the Western Section (Xi Qu) is open to the public, and none of the caves actually have much in them except for **Cave 17,** which has several walls worth of Buddhist cave drawings intact. Even so, the blue tones in some of the caves, produced by lapis lazuli from Afghanistan (which was worth twice its weight in gold during the Middle Ages), are stunning.

The site predates Dunhuang, and painting continued until the Ming dynasty, when Islam fully displaced Buddhism. The site lies in a spectacular and remote valley beside the Muzart River, where the lack of Han influence is striking. Persian, Gandharan, Indian, and Grecian motifs dominate. Black suns, Garuda (a bird god borrowed from Indian mythology), and Apollo riding in a chariot are common decorations on the axis of the roofs. Most caves have a central pillar for perambulation, with a sleeping Buddha at the rear, presided over by mourning disciples. Buddhas and bodhisattvas are lean and muscular, with Indian features.

Unfortunately, little statuary remains, and many of the wall paintings have been removed to Europe and Japan. The eyes and mouths of most remaining images have been defaced by Muslim iconoclasts. There are also some inappropriate recent additions, particularly a ridiculous man-made lake less than 180m (600 ft.) from the caves, which depend on aridity for their preservation. **The Exhibit of Kizil Artifacts** ⟨★⟩, just inside the entrance, is worthwhile, especially if you've already made the trip out here. It features reproduction drawings from many caves that you won't be allowed to enter, and other artifacts.

ⓒ **0997/893-2235.** Fax 0997/893-2247 (fax request if you're seeking permission to visit closed caves). Admission ¥35 ($4.55/£2.30) plus ¥60 ($7.80/£3.90) for a mandatory tour guide. The price of a tour guide can be shared among several tourists, but few individual travelers visit the site. Summer 9:30am–8pm; winter 10am–6pm.

Subashi Gucheng   Originally called Jarakol (Headwater) Temple when it was established in the 4th century, this ruined town 24km (15 miles) northeast of Kuqa is evidence of Buddhist parishioners' penchant for spectacular sites. Kumarajiva and Xuanzang both preached here, the latter recording, "The images of the Buddha in these monasteries were beautiful almost beyond human skill: and the Brethren were punctilious in discipline and devoted enthusiasts." A large fire devastated the town in the 9th century, and it was gradually abandoned from the 11th century as the populace converted to Islam. There were still Buddhist relics (brought by Prince Asoka) housed in the main pagoda when the enigmatic Count Otani visited during the early 19th century.

Admission ¥25 ($3.25/£1.65). Open daylight hours. Taxi round-trip ¥80 ($10/£5.20).

WHERE TO STAY

Kuche Binguan   While the rooms are dusty and past their best, the location is central and the tariffs are low. As is often the case in this part of China, there is a selection of buildings to choose between; the one to the left of reception as you approach the hotel is the pick of them and costs only fractionally more than its shabbier neighbors. A few of the staff have a minimal grasp of English, but they are all friendly and eager to help.

Jiefang Bei Lu 17. ⓒ **0997/712-2901.** 200 units. ¥140–¥160 ($18–$21/£9.10–£10) standard room; ¥888 ($115/£58) suite. No credit cards. **Amenities:** Restaurant; tour desk; laundry. *In room:* A/C, TV.

Kuche Fandian ⟨★⟩   Although its location 3km (2 miles) from the railway station is a little isolated, this is the best place to stay in town. The hotel has plenty of choices of rooms at very reasonable prices and is popular with foreign tour groups. You can choose from rooms in buildings 8 and 9 and also the villas. Building 9 has larger bathrooms than building 8 but your best option is a standard room in the villas (if not already booked by tour groups), which offer peace within the hotel's large compound. Orchards and a lake on the premises make for relaxing strolls.

Tian Shan Dong Lu 8. ⓒ **0997/723-3156.** Fax 0997/713-1160. 340 units. ¥388–¥488 ($50–$63/£25–£32) standard room; ¥880–¥1,888 ($114–$245/£57–£123) suite. 20% discount. No credit cards. Bus: no. 6 from the railway or bus station. **Amenities:** 2 restaurants; bar; exercise room; sauna; business center; gift shop; same-day laundry. *In room:* A/C, TV.

Qiuci Binguan   Located in a compound set off of the street, the hotel looks vaguely central Asian, vaguely Communist. This is a decent budget option, with bright, airy (but dusty) rooms, and bathrooms that are in pretty good shape. Standard rooms can be bargained down to ¥120 ($16/£7.80) even in the high season. The staff is friendly and helpful.

Tian Shan Xi Lu 93. ⓒ **0997/712-2005.** Fax 0997/712-4397. 56 units. ¥280 ($36/£18) standard room; ¥360 ($47/£23) suite. No credit cards. **Amenities:** 2 restaurants; tour desk (CITS); same-day laundry. *In room:* A/C, TV.

WHERE TO DINE

For some cheap alfresco dining the pedestrianized street running east from the southern end of Tuanjie Lu (near the junction with Tian Shan Lu) has a number of atmospheric Uighur restaurants serving kabobs. If you've got kabobs coming out of your ears and feel the need for some Western food, **Best Food Burger** is, as the name suggests, Kuqa's top (and only) choice.

Wumai'erhong Meishi Cheng *食食* UIGHUR   Elsewhere, you can polish off 20 kabobs and still not be sated, but three kabobs are sufficient at Kuqa's most famous eatery. Chinese businessmen stroll in before noon and groups of Uighurs soon follow. The *pilao*, or rice pilaf, is excellent, as is the *langman* (spicy cold noodles). Other items worth trying include *laohu cai*, a spicy salad of cucumber, carrot, and red peppers; and the fruit salad *(shuiguo shala)*.

14 Tuanjie Lu. © 0997/712-4634. Meal for 2 ¥20–¥100 ($2.60–$13/£1.30–£6.50). No credit cards. 8am–11pm.

Wuqia Guoyuan Canting (Uqa Bhag Restaurant) *食* UIGHUR   At this garden restaurant, a favorite among Kuqans for special occasions, you risk becoming the guest of honor, especially if you're game to sing, dance (be prepared to make a fool of yourself attempting Uighur-style dancing), and imbibe. The *dapan ji* is an excellent value, though you'll need a party of four to polish off this tasty meal of whole chicken, peppers, potato, and tomatoes covered in thick noodles. Other dishes include spicy beef strips *(ganzha niu rou tiao)* and a cold platter of sweet cucumber *(tangban huanggua)*.

Wuqia Lu. © 0997/713-3665. Meal for 2 ¥60–¥150 ($7.80–$20/£3.90–£9.75). No credit cards. 6:30pm–12:30am. Donkey cart or motorbike ride (¥.50 (65¢/35p) south from the intersection of Tian Shan Lu and Youyi Lu.

14 Kashgar (Kashi)

Xinjiang Province, 1,470km (911 miles) SW of Urumqi, 520km (322 miles) NW of Khotan

The northern and southern Silk Routes joined at ancient **Kashgar** and bifurcated again, leading south through the **Pamirs** to Gilgit, and west through **the Ferghana Valley** to Samarkand. At the height of the Han and Tang dynasties, Kashgar was in Chinese hands. The Chinese were routed by the Arabs in 751 in the Battle of Talas River (northeast of Tashkent). This allowed Islam to spread east into the Tarim Basin, displacing Buddhism and Manichaeism. Kashgar subsequently became a center of Islamic scholarship and, but for a brief return during the Mongol Yuan dynasty, it lay outside the sphere of Chinese influence. During the Qing dynasty the Chinese reasserted control, and Kashgar became a key site for players of the **Great Game**—it boasted both a Russian and a British consulate.

Trade is the lifeblood of Kashgar, and with the opening of border crossings at **Khunjerab, Torugart,** and the **Irkeshtam route to Osh,** it is now once again an international trading center. Kashgar's strategic position has unfortunately made it a priority in efforts to "Sinicize" border areas, and with the opening of the railway line in 2000, Han settlers are arriving by the trainload, a glimpse of what's in store for Lhasa. But in spite of this, the **old town** maintains its charm. The markets are a riot of color and exotic scents, donkeys pull rickety carts laden with watermelons and cotton bales in and out of town, gray-bearded mullahs call the faithful to prayer on every street corner, and serene old men enjoy long chats over tea.

ESSENTIALS

GETTING THERE   The **airport** is 12km (7½ miles) north of downtown. Take a taxi from the airport for ¥10 ($1.30/65p), or you can take bus no. 2, which terminates to the west of the Peoples' Square. The **CAAC** airline ticket office at Jiefang Nan Lu 95 (© **0998/282-2113**) does not deliver tickets. Do your best not to resemble a separatist; bring your passport and buy your ticket on the spot. Two daily flights connect with Urumqi, and onward **flights** can also be booked. Discounts can be obtained by booking up to 15 days in advance.

The **railway station** is southeast of town. Take a 15-minute taxi ride for ¥10 ($1.30/65p), or take bus no. 28 to immediately east of the Peoples' Square. The station sells tickets up to 3 days in advance, and is open from 8:30am to 6pm, but if you want sleeper tickets in the high season it's easiest to proceed through a travel agency, or line up at the Kashi Huochezhan Shinei Shoupiao Chu (ticket office) at Jiefang Bei Lu 226. Despite a sign promising "warm service," you may witness brawls between Uighur queue jumpers and Han security guards. Tickets can be purchased 5 days in advance. The ticket office is open from 10am to 7pm in summer, 10:30am to 7:30pm in winter. The N888 for Urumqi (23 hr.) leaves at 1:06pm, and the 7558 (31 hr.) departs at 9:46am.

Most **buses** connect to the grandly named **International Bus Station (Guoji Qichezhan)** in the north of town at Jichang Lu 29 (© **0998/282-5208**). Fast, comfortable sleeper buses link with Urumqi daily between 10am and 9pm (24 hr.; ¥235/$31/£15 lower berth, ¥210/$27/£14 upper berth). There are also regular buses to Aksu (468km/ 290 miles, ¥79/$10/£5.15 lower berth, ¥73/$9.50/£4.75 upper berth, ¥62/$8.05/£4.05 seat), and three daily services (1pm, 4pm, and 6pm) to Kuqa (723km/448 miles, ¥123/ $16/£8 lower berth, ¥113/$15/£7.35 upper berth) and Korla (1,003km/622 miles, ¥170/$22/£11 lower berth, ¥157/$20/£10 upper berth). There are three departures daily for the long and scenic trip over the mountains to Yining (1,644km/1,019 miles; 2 days; ¥292/$38/£19 lower berth, ¥266/$35/£17 upper berth) at 1pm, 4pm, and 6pm. Buses

The Back Door to Lhasa

A 4-hour bus ride south of Kashgar, **Yecheng** is the main point for hitching a ride to **Ali (Shiquan He),** the main town in western Tibet. Truck drivers ask in the vicinity of ¥1,000 ($130/£65) and may be bargained down to ¥600 ($78/£39) for the 1,100km (680-mile) trip that takes at least 4 days. It is likely to take several days to arrange a lift. Aside from travelers' tales of Frenchmen freezing to death in the backs of trucks, be aware that you are putting your driver at risk. If you make it to Ali without incident, expect to be fined by the PSB (¥400–¥500/$52– $65/£26–£33) and issued with an Aliens Travel Permit (¥50/$6.50/£3.25) to continue on to Lhasa. It is now possible to undertake the journey legally, but for a price. **Kashgar Mountaineering Adventures** (© **0998/252-3660;** fax 0998/252- 2957; www.ksalpine) charges $4,300 (£2,175) for a 22-day trip and **John's Information Cafe** (© **0998/258-1186;** www.johncafe.net) runs a 15-day trip that costs $3,780 (£1,915). The **Caravan Cafe** (© **0998/298-1864;** www.caravancafe.com) was closed at press time but is due to reopen in spring 2008 and should also be able to arrange the trip. Permits, 4WD, and driver are included in all of the aforementioned.

Kashgar

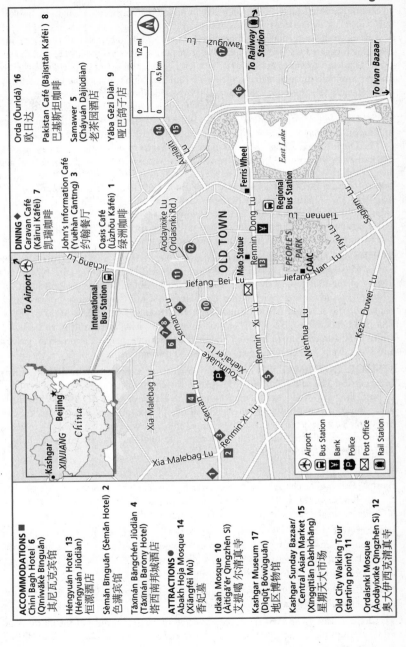

ACCOMMODATIONS ■

Chini Bagh Hotel **6**
(Qíníwǎkè Bīnguǎn)
其尼瓦克宾馆

Héngyuán Hotel **13**
(Héngyuán Jiǔdiàn)
恒源酒店

Sèmàn Bīnguǎn (Sèmàn Hotel) **2**
色满宾馆

Tǎxīnán Bāngchén Jiǔdiàn **4**
(Tǎxīnán Barony Hotel)
塔西南邦城酒店

ATTRACTIONS ●

Abakh Hoja Mosque **14**
(Xiāngfēi Mù)
香妃墓

Idkah Mosque **10**
(Àitígǎ'ěr Qīngzhēn Sì)
艾提喝 尔清真寺

Kashgar Museum **17**
(Dìqū Bówùguǎn)
地区博物馆

Kashgar Sunday Bazaar/
Central Asian Market **15**
(Xīngqītiān Dàshìchǎng)
星期天大市场

Old City Walking Tour
(starting point) **11**

Ordaisnki Mosque
(Àodàyìxīkè Qīngzhēn Sì) **12**
奥大伊西克清真寺

DINING ◆

Caravan Café
(Kǎiruì Kāfēi) **7**
凯瑞咖啡

John's Information Café
(Yuēhàn Cāntīng) **3**
约翰餐厅

Oasis Café
(Lǜzhōu Kāfēi) **1**
绿洲咖啡

Orda (Ōurìdá) **16**
欧日达

Pakistan Café (Bājīsītǎn Kāfēi) **8**
巴基斯坦咖啡

Samawer **5**
(Cháyuán Dàjiǔdiàn)
老茶园酒店

Yàba Gēzi Diàn **9**
哑巴鸽子店

To Airport ✈

International Bus Station

Jichang Lu

Jiefang Bei Lu

Xia Malebag Lu

Séman Lu

Xiéhǎi'er Lu

Youmuyake Lu

Renmin Xi-Lu

Xia Malebag Lu

Aodàyixike Lu
(Ordaisnki Rd.)

Aizirek Lu

OLD TOWN

Mao Statue

Renmin Dong-Lu

Jiefang Nan-Lu

CAAC

PEOPLE'S PARK

Wenhua Lu

Tiyu Lu

Tianan Lu

Kezi Duwei-Lu

Saglam Lu

Tawuguzi Lu

To Railway Station

To Ivan Bazaar

East Lake

Ferris Wheel

Regional Bus Station

✈ Airport
🚌 Bus Station
¥ Bank
🅿 Police
⊠ Post Office
🚆 Rail Station

0   0.5 km
0   1/2 mi

CHINA
XINJIANG
Kashgar ● ★ Beijing

321

to Sost in Pakistan (2 days; ¥270/$35/£18) at noon every day stop overnight in Tashkurgan. Note that this service only runs in summer.

Twice a week (9am Mon and Thurs) there is a direct bus to Bishkek for the scenic ride over the Torugart Pass (¥430/$56/£28), but at press time, foreigners were not allowed on it. Until the pass is upgraded to a "first level" border crossing, travelers will need to charter a vehicle through a travel agency in Kashgar. John's Information Cafe and the Caravan Cafe (due to reopen in spring 2008) provide the most reliable services.

It is now possible to take a bus to Osh in southern Kyrgyzstan via Irkeshtam for ¥420 ($55/£27). No permit is required, only a valid Kyrgyz visa. At present, the bus departs at 9am on Monday. In winter, you may need to proceed through travel agencies.

The **Diqu Keyun Zong Zhan (Regional Bus Station)** on Tiannan Lu has buses to Khotan every 90 minutes from 9:30am (520km/322 miles; ¥92/$12/£6), as well as a sleeper bus that leaves at 9:30pm (¥95/$12/£6.20 lower berth, ¥87/$11/£5.65 upper berth). There is also a daily local bus to Tashkurgan at 9:30am (294km/182 miles; ¥52/$6.70/£3.35). There are regular buses to Yecheng (¥28/$3.65/£1.80), for those considering the illegal journey to Tibet (see below).

Departure times and tickets are quoted in Beijing time (2 hr. ahead of local time), but be sure to double-check when you buy your ticket.

TOURS & GUIDES　　Those interested in adventure travel such as the popular trek out to **Mustagh Ata;** an assault on the world's second-highest mountain, **K2;** or following in the footsteps of Swedish explorer Sven Hedin into the mountains south of Khotan, should connect with either the **Caravan Cafe** (see "Visitor Information," below) or the **Kashgar Mountaineering Adventures** (© 0998/252-3660 or 0998/284-6633; fax 0998/252-2957; www.ksalpine.com) who have offices at both the Chini Bagh and the Seman hotels. They are friendly and experienced mountain guides, and if you want a trekking permit, you must go through them.

VISITOR INFORMATION　　Reliable information may be obtained from **John's Information Cafe** (©/fax 0998/258-1186; www.johncafe.net), which has branches in both the Chini Bagh and Seman hotels. The **Caravan Cafe** (© 0998/298-1864; www.caravancafe.com) was another great source of information, but it was closed at press time and expected to reopen in spring 2008. Plenty of locals are willing to act as guides for a small fee, but if you want someone qualified, try friendly and helpful **Akber Tursun** (© 0/1377-9844-021).

FAST FACTS

Banks, Foreign Exchange & ATMs　　Both traveler's checks and credit cards are accepted at counter 1 of the **Bank of China** (weekdays 9:30am–1:30pm and 4–7:30pm) on the east side of the Peoples' Square, and there's an ATM outside.

Internet Access　　Access is available at **John's Information Cafe** for ¥5 (65¢/35p) per hour (open 9am–12:30am), or at **Yimei'er Wangba** at Renmin Dong Lu 49 (on the second floor of a bathhouse immediately west of the Mao statue) for ¥3 (40¢/20p) per hour (24 hr.). Dial-up is © 16900.

Post Office　　The post office (open 9:30am–8pm) at Renmin Xi Lu 7 has a counter on the second floor for troublesome foreigners.

Visa Extensions　　The **PSB** is located about 180m (600 ft.) south of the Chini Bagh Hotel at Youmulake Xiehai'er Lu 137. They process visa extensions in half a day, but will only extend them up to 3 days before the visa expires.

EXPLORING KASHGAR

Though the wide, main streets brought in by the Han have threatened Kashgar's atmosphere, little of **old town** ✿✿✿ has changed. The dusty alleys, colorful residential doorways, and mud-brick walls remain as they have been for decades. Kids with henna-dyed feet and fingernails will approach you speaking a few words of Chinese and English; men with donkey carts trudge down narrow passages; bakers arrange round large slabs of nan in coal ovens built into the ground. At prayer time, a rush of feet shuffle toward the local mosques. A family might invite you in for a cup of tea on their carpet-lined porch within a residential courtyard. Spending time watching how citizens of Kashgar live is one of the most rewarding experiences on the Silk Road.

Unfortunately, the experience has been dampened a bit since the government turned over the management of several tourist sites to a Han company. Ticket booths now front certain neighborhoods, charging anyone who looks like a tourist ¥30 ($3.90/£1.95) for a peek. You can avoid this ridiculous fee by entering the neighborhoods from the eastern side of **Jiefang Bei Lu,** just south of the Seman Lu intersection. Working backward, you'll encounter the money-grubbers once you reach Aodayixike Lu to the south, but by that point, you'll have already been through the area deemed worthy of tourism. Turning right, or west on **Aodayixike Lu,** will put you on a busy commercial street where street vendors sell boiled lamb's heads, fresh yellow figs, Hami melon, and rotisserie chicken. You can continue south into a set of residential neighborhoods that have not been savvy enough to charge tourists yet. Proceeding west toward Jiefang Bei Lu, old men sitting on rows of old iron benches watch Uighur music videos while drinking a yogurt-and-ice concoction. Just before you reach Jiefang Bei Lu, there will be an alley to your left. Proceed south and you'll see hat vendors touting a range of eclectic styles, ranging from fluffy sheepskin caps with earflaps to tall, narrow white-and-black felt ones worn by Kyrgyzs to cowboy hats popular with Chinese tourists. Following this road down, you'll continue through a weave of streets that will eventually spit you out on **Remin Dong Lu.** Walking west on Remin Dong Lu, you'll pass Peoples' Square and the notorious, giant Mao statue that is also one of the largest in China. Note that you'll see some Uighur couples taking pictures in front of it.

Abakh Hoja Mosque (Xiangfei Mu) The tomb of one of Kashgar's most renowned kings and spiritual leader of the **Bai Shan sect** is several miles northeast of town. Five generations of his family are housed in a domed mausoleum decorated with green, blue, red, and white tiles. The cool interior houses 58 tombs draped with silks. The admission ticket means that the tomb is not a center of worship, but the adjacent mosque is active; devotees seem oblivious to police, who photograph anyone with a beard. The **Gaodi Mosque** ✿ to the left of the entrance has swastika motifs decorating its columns, trays for washing corpses, and wooden stretchers for transporting them to the graveyard. The cemetery is now cut off from the mausoleum by a high wall, hopefully not impeding the smooth passage of believers to the afterlife.

The tomb is known to the Chinese as **Xiangfei Mu,** or **Tomb of the Fragrant Concubine,** a member of the Hoja clan known for her "exceptional body aroma," probably due to the sprig of oleaster she was fond of wearing. A favorite of the Qianlong emperor (1711–99), she constantly refused his advances, but all tales have him devastated by her death. She was either murdered by Qianlong's mother, committed suicide rather than sleep with the emperor, or died naturally, depending on which account you believe. The sedan just inside the tomb is labeled as the one that brought her back to her beloved Kashgar, although her remains are almost certainly buried in the Eastern Qing Tombs in Hebei. If the ticket office tries to sell you tickets to other "attractions" involving singing and dancing minorities, hold your ground or simply walk off.

Admission to the tomb ¥15 ($1.95/£1), admission to the Gaodi Mosque ¥5 (65¢/35p). Open daylight hours. Bus: no. 20 from Peoples' Sq. to the terminus. Taxi ¥10 ($1.30/65p).

Idkah Mosque (Aitiga'er Qingzhen Si)

More of a relief from the bustling market than an attraction in itself, the prayer hall and leafy courtyard of Xinjiang's largest mosque (ca. 1442), the heart of Islamic Kashgar, can house up to 20,000 worshipers. Whether that would make a dent in the crowd outside is doubtful.

Admission ¥10 ($1.30/£0.65). Sat–Thurs 9am–2pm and 4–7pm; Fri 9am–1pm.

Kashgar Sunday Bazaar (Kashi Xingqitian Da Shichang)

You might expect the world's most famous open-air market to be safe from the meddlings of bureaucracy, if only in the name of financial gain. But you would be wrong. The Bazaar is now *two* bazaars. The original site is now a covered bazaar marked as CENTRAL ASIA INTERNATIONAL GRAND BAZAAR. But the animals are gone, and so is some of the charm. Nevertheless, if the Ivan Bazaar (see below) is all about livestock and the men who come to buy and sell them, then the Sunday Bazaar, as the market is known, is the place to see the ladies of Kashgar eagerly snapping up glistening garments. The market operates every day and is a good place to haggle over hats, pashminas, or musical instruments, but if you want to see it at its liveliest, then Sunday is the day. While the bazaar can initially seem a little touristy, the deeper you delve into its passages, the more local it feels. Bus nos. 7 and 20 serve the bazaar.

The livestock market, squeezed out by the imperatives of modernization and property development, is located several miles southeast of town, next to a four-lane motorway. Known as the **Ivan Bazaar** ★★, it still feels like a bazaar. Efforts to herd all the traders into an enclosure are cheerfully ignored by small traders, who haggle on the road outside, blocking traffic. Ignore demands for payment on entry, unless you have donkeys to trade. Bearded Uighur men in traditional blue-and-white garb sharpen their knives and trim their sheep; small boys wearing Inter Milan strips gorge themselves on Hami melons; Kyrgyz in dark fur hats pick up and drop dozens of lambs to test their weight and meatiness before settling deals with vigorous and protracted handshakes. No fewer than 10 people act as witnesses.

Arrive early while the market is setting up, and the light is perfect for some unforgettable photography. Shelter under colorful awnings during the midday heat, enjoying tea, buns stuffed with minced lamb *(samsas),* and bagels. Taxis (¥15/$1.95/£1), noisy three-wheelers (¥3/40¢/20p), and donkey carts (¥2/25¢/15p) connect the Kashgar Bazaar with the Ivan Bazaar; or simply rent a bike and follow the crowds.

Ordaisnki Mosque (Aodayixike Qingzhensi)

Islamic visitors looking for a less scrutinized place to worship can visit the oldest mosque in Kashgar (c. 1119), about 270m (900 ft.) east of Idkah Square on Ordaisnki Road. Follow your nose—the city government has so much respect for religion it has placed four huge rubbish bins outside!

SHOPPING

The lanes surrounding the **Idkah Mosque** are ideal for browsing for gifts. Just north of the mosque is a line of carpet shops with nice antique rugs from Khotan,

Afghanistan, and Turkmenistan. Prices start around ¥1,000 ($130/£65). Another great place for browsing is the **Central Asia International Grand Bazaar** (see above). Wares include embroidered fabrics, dried fruit, knives, spices, hats, musical instruments, and wooden handicrafts.

There are plenty of small supermarkets around town, although don't expect Wal-Mart; try the **Tiantianle Chaoshi** beneath the Caravan Cafe on Seman Lu.

WHERE TO STAY

Kashgar's hotels are overpriced, given the quality. Nevertheless there's something to suit most budgets and tastes and two of the most popular hotels, the Chini Bagh and the Seman, are located on the grounds of the former British and Russian consulates respectively. Indeed, the latter even offers the rare opportunity to escape the bland uniformity of mainstream hotel rooms in China.

Chini Bagh Hotel (Qiniwake Binguan)   Though the hotel is located on the grounds of the former British consulate, the consulate and any remaining character are tucked at the very back of the grounds, past the two main ugly white-tiled buildings. The hotel's location is very close to the old Uighur parts of town, which makes it a good choice. Four room choices fit a range of budgets. The cheapest rooms are located in the Jingyuan Building, located toward the back of the complex; the building has a nice patio and a bit of Uighur flavor, but rooms and bathrooms are worn and a little grimy now. The North Building (Beilou) offers slightly better rooms with cozy beds, but the bathrooms are in desperate need of renovation. Rooms in the circular Friendship Building (Youyilou), are the most popular and meet three-star standards, though bathrooms are a bit dank. Finally, for ¥1,200 ($156/£78) you can rent out the second floor of the former British consulate, which consists of three falling-apart bedrooms with bad Chinese furniture and bathrooms that look like they were last remodeled sometime before the Cultural Revolution. The first floor serves Uighur-style lunch and dinners and there's a branch of John's Information Cafe at the rear of the complex.

Seman Lu 144. ⓒ 0998/282-2103. Fax 0998/284-2299. 337 units (shower only). ¥150–¥480 ($20–$62/£9.75–£31) standard room; ¥880–¥1,200 ($114–$156/£57–£78) suite. Discounts of 30% are standard. Rates in North and Friendship buildings include breakfast. AE, DC, MC, V. **Amenities:** 3 restaurants; concierge; tour desk; business center; forex counter (8am–midnight); same-day laundry/dry cleaning. *In room:* A/C, TV (safe and fridge in Friendship bldg.).

Hengyuan Jiudian (Hengyuan Hotel) *(Value* For the budget-conscious who want modern, private rooms with clean bathrooms, this is probably the best option in town. Though its location on Peoples' Square—just steps away from the notorious Mao Zedong statue—is solidly in Han Chinese territory, the hotel also puts you within a 10-minute walk of Idkah Mosque. Rooms can be bargained down from their rack rates even during the high season, and the management is rather friendly and helpful, though little English is spoken.

Remin Dong Lu 42. ⓒ 0998/283-8000. Fax 0998/284-1988. 75 units. ¥180 ($23/£12) standard room; ¥280 ($36/£18) suite. No credit cards. **Amenities:** Restaurant; travel agency; salon. *In room:* A/C, TV.

Seman Binguan (Seman Hotel)   Although its location is farther from the old town than the Chini Bagh, the Seman has retained far more character and has helpful and friendly staff. Rooms in **buildings 1 and 3** ⓕ are some of the best in town, with a gaudy central Asian feel, intricately carved walls, beaded lampshades, and nice carpets. Bathrooms are decent, but are still a bit worn for a three-star hotel (those in building 3 are better). You could also take up residence at the former Russian consulate, though these rooms have a slightly tacky feel with "brick" wallpaper covering the walls and rather uncomfortable beds. The rest of the rooms here are only for the very budget-minded who won't fret about ugly furniture, very lumpy beds, and dingy bathrooms. If you're in a common room without bathroom (¥60/$7.80/£3.90) you'll have to share an unpleasant shower and toilet with other backpackers. The hotel is "ground-zero" for foreign tourists who frequent the travel agencies and restaurants nearby (including a branch of John's Information Cafe within the complex), but its location is not as good as the Chini Bagh's for those who want to spend time in the old quarter of town.

Seman Lu 337. 🕐 0998/255-2861. Fax 0998/255-2861. 212 units, 120 of which are Uighur-style rooms. ¥120–¥380 ($16–$49/£7.80–£25) standard room; ¥800–¥1,500 ($104–$195/£52–£98) suite. AE, DC, MC, V. **Amenities:** 4 restaurants; concierge; tour desk; business center; same-day laundry/dry cleaning. *In room:* A/C, TV.

Taxinan Bangchen Jiudian (Taxinan Barony Hotel)　Located opposite the old city wall on a stretch of road between the Seman and the Chini Bagh Hotels, this newer hotel is one of the few in town that meets four-star standards. However, it has an empty feel despite its amenities, and its claim to be "internationally managed" seems to be a hoax. Still, the bathrooms are the most modern in town, the rooms are decorated in nonoffending modern tones, and some of the better doubles have computers.

Seman Lu 242. 🕐 0998/258-6888. Fax 0998/258-5888. 108 units. ¥880 ($114/£57) standard room; ¥1,280 ($166/£83) suite. 20%–40% discounts. AE, DC, MC, V. **Amenities:** Restaurant; concierge; conference center; gift shop; gym; billiards; business center; same-day laundry/dry cleaning. *In room:* A/C, TV, broadband Internet access, minibar, safe.

WHERE TO DINE

Kashgar has plenty of culinary opportunities, from Western-style cafes serving tasty sandwiches to Uighur street food and beyond. As well as the options listed below, other good bets include the whole pigeon soup at **Yaba Gezi Dian** (🕐 **0998/222-2282**), across the street and about 300m (981 ft.) to the left of the Chini Bagh Hotel; or the extensive selection of Western and Chinese dishes at **John's Information Cafe,** which has branches in both the Chini Bagh and Seman hotels (the latter is the more pleasant of the two).

Caravan Cafe (Kairui Kafei) ★★ WESTERN　The Caravan Cafe was closed at press time due to a change of owners, but it is expected to reopen in the same vein in spring 2008. After some time in Xinjiang, the caffeine-deprived may dream of the smell of freshly ground coffee or of lattes with perfectly formed froth, perhaps accompanied by a cinnamon roll and a bowl of granola with yogurt, served by handsome and courteous waitstaff. Fortunately, this is no mirage—the coffee, the food, and the service are 100% real and 100% Western. Managed by Westerners with a passion for central Asia, and staffed by friendly English-speaking Uighurs, the Caravan Cafe can also arrange top-of-the-line adventure travel to the Taklamakan Desert, Shipton's Arch, and Mustagh Ata. If you want to know what's going on in town, make this your first port of call.

Seman Lu 120. 🕐 0998/298-1864. www.caravancafe.com. Main courses ¥19–¥33 ($2.45–$4.30/£1.25–£2.15). No credit cards. Thurs–Tues 9am–11:30pm. Closed Nov to mid-Apr.

Orda (Ourida) ★ UIGHUR　This is Uighur dining, made easy; with its kitchen in the center of the restaurant you can just point to what you want. Orders are taken at a register, and the food arrives at your table seconds later. Try the *pilao* (rice pilaf) set meal, which comes with yogurt that you can dole onto your rice to give it a creamy texture. The atmosphere is pleasant, with walls decorated in colorful tiles and Uighur musicians that play traditional instruments. If you order the fruit plate, remember to eat the watermelon first, before the grapes and the Hami melon—it's an Uighur taboo to do it in reverse!

Renmin Dong Lu (Diqu Sifa Duimian). © 0998/265-2777. Meal for 2 less than ¥50 ($6.50/£3.25). No credit cards. 10am–midnight. Bus: no. 10.

Pakistan Cafe *(finds)* PAKISTANI   Despite its slightly grubby appearance and garish posters, this tiny cafe is a gem, offering a taste of what lies just over the border in Pakistan. The menu is simple but the staff is friendly and the food is sumptuous and authentic. Try the chicken curry or *aloo palek* served with fresh-from-the-oven *chapatti* and round the meal off with a cup of sweet *chai*.

Seman Lu. No phone. Meal for 2 ¥30 ($3.90/£1.95). No credit cards. Noon–10pm.

Samawer (Chayuan Dajiudian) UIGHUR   When the locals treat themselves, they make for this eatery, an institution since 1989. Service can be frosty, and the pseudo-Arabian decor is tacky. Let the food take center stage. All dishes are well presented, often with fancy garnishes, something you don't see a lot of in southern Xinjiang. For starters, try *ban san si,* a finely sliced salad of capsicum, onion, carrot, cucumber, and noodles; or try the old favorite, roast peanuts. Recommended main courses are a tender beef stir-fry *(chaokao rou)* and the dry-fried spring chicken *(ganbian tongziji).* The local delicacy is field mushrooms steamed with bok choy, ginger, and garlic *(bachu mogu),* although their slippery texture won't be to everyone's taste. Note that there are two branches just a few shops apart on Renmin Xi Lu; unless you want a private room, head for the one marked Samawer (rather than Kona Samawar), which is the farther of the two from the roundabout.

Renmin Xi Lu 251. © 0998/282-4467. Meal for 2 ¥70–¥150 ($9.10–$20/£4.55–£9.75). No credit cards. 10am–1am.

AROUND KASHGAR

Shipton's Arch (Tushuk Tash)   The world's largest natural arch stands, largely unheralded, about 50km (31 miles) northwest of Kashgar. Located at an elevation of 3,168m (10,394 ft.), the arch towers 366m (1,200 ft.) above the canyon floor. It is composed of crumbling conglomerate and is exceedingly difficult to reach. Eric Shipton, Britain's final representative in Kashgar and an accomplished mountaineer, failed several times from the southern route via Muk and Mingyol, finally gaining access from the north via Artux and Karakum. His wife described the scene: "We found ourselves looking straight across at the immense curve of the arch. Its upper half soared above us, but the walls continued down into an unfathomable gorge below. It was as if we stood on a platform some few feet away from a giant window . . ."

John's Information Cafe and the Caravan Cafe (when it reopens) both run day tours to the arch. John's charges ¥800 ($104/£52) for a jeep that can hold up to four people and a driver.

Tomb of Mohammed Kashgari   The tomb of this eminent 11th-century translator lies 30km (19 miles) southwest of Kashgar, west of the charming Uighur town of **Opal (Wupa'er).** The scholar spent most of his years in Baghdad and is credited with compiling the first Turkic dictionary in Arabic. Hire a taxi (¥120–¥150/$16–$20/£7.60–£9.75) or take bus no. 4 (¥2.50/35¢/15p) from Kashgar's Opal bus station (a block south of the Seman Hotel) as far as Shufu, then share a taxi to Opal for ¥5 (65¢/35p). Donkey carts, charging ¥4 (50¢/25p), leave for the tomb from under a red-and-yellow arch in the center of Opal. If you haven't sated your appetite for markets after a Sunday in Kashgar, Opal's Monday market offers a smaller scale version, replete with all the usual trimmings—cattle, donkey carts, and enigmatic faces all vie for your attention.

15 Tashkurgan (Tashikuergan)

Xinjiang Province, 295km (183 miles) SW of Kashgar

Tashkurgan marked the end of the Silk Routes for Chinese traders arriving from Kashgar or Yarkand. Their goods would be transferred to Bactrian, Persian, or Sogdian caravans, which continued on to Gilgit and thence either south to the Indian Ocean along the Indus River, or west through Kabul, Herat, and Meshed, ultimately reaching the Mediterranean Sea at Antioch or Tyrus. Described by British consul Eric Teichman as the "storm centre of Asian politics," the town has a strong military presence, but it is still a Tajik town and you'll see plenty of elaborately dressed local women sporting distinctive cylindrical headgear. Those heading to Pakistan must spend the night here.

ESSENTIALS

GETTING THERE   After recent repairs, the drive from Tashkurgan to Kashgar is now a smooth 6-hour journey (bar the odd landslide). Roughly two-thirds of the way to Tashkurgan is **Karakul Lake,** over which towers the magnificent **Mustagh Ata.** Buses leave for Karakul and Tashkurgan starting at 9:30am at Kashgar's Diqu Bus Station. The cost is ¥52 ($6.70/£3.35). Or you could consider renting a taxi and driver for three people for ¥800 ($104/£52) for 2 days; **Mohammad Tursun (© 01389/ 913-3306)** is a friendly and reliable driver who speaks a little English and is usually to be found outside the Chini Bagh Hotel in Kashgar. The icy lake is surrounded by Kyrgyz yurts that take in visitors. Room and board can be negotiated for ¥40 to ¥50 ($5.20–$6.50/£2.60–£3.25) per person, but many of the locals are quite pushy. If you encounter this, just walk on; there are plenty of other yurts. The yurts that you'll come across before you get to the parking lot and official entrance of the lake are recommended and staying here will also mean you'll avoid paying the ¥50 ($6.50/£3.25) "ticket" to Karakul. You can hop on the back of a motorbike and ride around the lake for around ¥50 ($6.50/£3.25). *Warning:* Do not camp alone—recently, an Italian tourist almost met an untidy end here. Returning to Kashgar from Karakul may be a little trickier; buses are supposed to stop on their way back from Tashkurgan, but they'll often plow ahead without stopping. The bus down to Kashgar should pass by around 11am, while the bus up to Tashkurgan should arrive at around 12:30 or 1pm, but check this with the locals.

Beyond Karakul is the town of **Subash (Subashi),** starting point for hikes to Mustagh Ata. It may be possible to stay here, as a less-touristed alternative to Karakul Lake. Beyond Subash, there is a magnificent moraine valley, a highlight of the trip. A bus runs from Tashkurgan to Kashgar at 9:30am for ¥52 ($6.70/£3.35). You can continue to **Sost** for ¥225 ($29/£15); the 8-hour trip arrives in town in late afternoon after many inspections.

SEEING THE SIGHTS

Tashkurgan Fort   Dating from the 14th century, this crumbling fort is accessed by a small lane just east of the Pamir Hotel. You can enjoy an impressive view of the surrounding fields, mountains, and military complexes from the old walls, but the best view of the fort is from the pastures below in the early morning light.

Admission ¥20 ($2.60/£1.30). 8am–8pm.

WHERE TO STAY

Tashkurgan isn't a major tourist destination and most of its hotels reflect this, in terms of both price and quality; nevertheless things have picked up recently with the opening of the Crown Hotel.

Crown Inn (Taxian Huangguan Dajiudian) ⟨★⟩   It's not saying much, but the opening of the Singaporean-owned Crown has taken accommodations to new heights in Tashkurgan. Rooms and bathrooms are clean, stylish, and modern, and the hotel's location a little out of the center affords fine mountain views.

Pamir Lu. ⟨©⟩ 0998/342-2888. wwwcrowninntashkorgan.com. 30 units. ¥350 ($46/£23) standard room; ¥480 ($62/£31) suite. AE, DC, MC, V. **Amenities:** Restaurant; business center; laundry. *In room:* TV, Internet access.

Jiaotong Binguan (Traffic Hotel)   Once described by a travel guide as "the worst hotel in the world," the hotel is still stung by this assessment. On those grounds, this establishment is entitled to a "most-improved" award. Rooms facing south are the sunniest. The Muslim restaurant is often the site of the Tajik equivalent of a Scottish *ceilidh*, with plenty of drinking and dancing—all arms, wrists, and hips—that will test your sense of rhythm.

Tashikuergan Lu 50. ⟨©⟩ 0998/342-1192. 30 units. ¥120 ($16/£7.80) twin; ¥15 ($1.95/£1) dorm bed. No credit cards. **Amenities:** Restaurant; cafe; same-day laundry. *In room:* TV.

Pami'er Binguan (Pamir Hotel)   This apathetic two-star on the far side of town offers slightly more comfortable rooms than the Traffic Hotel with temperamental showers that allegedly offer hot water for 16 hours a day. Just which 16 hours is a matter of speculation. Rooms in the newer wing are worth the extra outlay.

Tashikuergan Lu 207. ⟨©⟩/fax 0998/342-1085. 66 units (30 with open shower). ¥80–¥200 ($10–$26/£5.20–£13) twin. No credit cards. **Amenities:** Restaurant; same-day laundry. *In room:* TV.

WHERE TO DINE

Tashkurgan is hardly a culinary center, but you'll find a number of basic options along Tashikuergan Lu near the junction with Hongqilapu Lu, including **Wushi Lao Huimin Canting,** which offers passable *langman,* or for something a little spicier, **Chongqing Xiaochao** turns out Sichuan favorites including *huoguo* and *gongbao jiding.*

The only upscale option is the **Silk Road Restaurant** at the Crown Inn, which offers a wide range of well-presented dishes including tasty Hainan chicken. To stock up on snacks, there's a supermarket and a bakery on the junction of Tashikuergan Lu and Hongqilapu Lu.

16 Khotan (Hetian) ⟨★★⟩

Xinjiang, 520km (322 miles) SE of Kashgar, 1,509km (936 miles) SW of Urumqi

Khotan was once a more important trading and religious center than Kashgar. From ancient times, jade was "fished" from the 24 rivers in the Khotan area, and "jade routes" to Mesopotamia and China flourished from the 3rd millennium B.C. onward. Passing through on his way to India in the 5th century, the Chinese Buddhist monk Faxian found a purely Buddhist population in the order of "several myriads." Returning to China after his adventures in India, Xuanzang found a thriving center: "the country produced rugs, fine felt, and silk of artistic texture, it also yielded black and white jade. The climate was genial, but there were whirlwinds and flying dust. The people were of gentle disposition, and had settled occupations. The nation esteemed music and the people were fond of dance and song; a few clothed themselves in woolens and furs, the majority wearing silk and calico. . . . The system of writing had been taken from that of India."

From 1901, Aurel Stein visited several sites around Khotan, concluding that the ancient capital was at **Yoktan (Yaotegan),** 9.7km (6 miles) to the west. He found Roman coins, and some delightful paintings and sculptures (ca. 2nd c.) showing Grecian influence. Unconnected by rail and thus safe from inundation by Han settlers, Khotan is a bustling commercial city, home to the liveliest **bazaar** in Xinjiang, and is a must for those hoping to experience traditional Uighur culture and markets. *Note:* Please turn to appendix A for Chinese translations of key locations.

ESSENTIALS

GETTING THERE   Khotan's **airport** (✆ **0903/293-3200**), 10km (6¼ miles) west of downtown has one daily flight to Urumqi. The airport is served by bus (¥2/25¢/15p), or taxi ¥15/$1.95/£1). The **CAAC** air ticket office at Wulumuqi Nan Lu 14 (✆ **0903/251-8999**), is open from 9:30am to 8pm.

The main **bus station** (✆ **0903/202-2688**) is at Hemo Lu 5, north of town, on the south side of Highway 315. Comfortable sleeper buses at 11am, 4pm, and 6pm cross the Taklamakan Desert Highway to Urumqi (1,509km/936 miles; 22 hr.; ¥387/ $50/£26 lower berth, ¥348/$45/£23 upper berth) and these services also stop in at Korla (¥171/$22/£11 lower berth, ¥155/$20/£10 upper berth). Cheaper, less comfortable sleeper buses (¥315/$41/£21) run every 2 hours between 11am and 9pm. For Kuqa, buy a ticket to Luntai (874km/542 miles; 10 hr.; ¥155/$20/£10). You are dropped off in the forlorn settlement of Lunnan, about 30km (19 miles) south of Luntai. A seat in a taxi to Luntai should cost ¥10 ($1.30/65p). Ask to be dropped at the bus station (qiche zhan), where buses for Kuqa (110km/68 miles; 2 hr.; ¥10/$1.30/65p) leave when full. There are plenty of buses to Kashgar (520km/322 miles; 8 hr.), both regular (¥90/$12/£5.85) and evening sleeper services (¥95/$12/£6.20 lower berth, ¥87/$11/£5.65 upper berth). Regular buses depart from the east station (Dongjiao Keyun Zhan) on Taibei Dong Lu and visit the oasis towns east of Khotan, stopping at Keriya (Yutian; 177km/110 miles; 3 hr.; ¥22/$2.85/£1.45), Niya (Minfeng; 294km/ 182 miles; 4 hr.; ¥35/$4.55/£2.30), and Charchan (Qiemo; 603km/374 miles; 9 hr.; ¥80/$10/£5.20).

GETTING AROUND   Taxis are plentiful, but seldom use their meters; ¥5 (65¢/35p) is sufficient for most journeys within town. **Bus** fare is usually ¥1 (15¢/5p), paid to the conductor.

TOURS & GUIDES   CITS is on the third floor of Tamubage Lu 23 (✆ **0903/ 251-6090;** fax 0903/202-2846). It's open from 9:30am to 1:30pm and 4 to 8pm. While rates charged for guides are reasonable, you're better off arranging your own transport.

FAST FACTS

Banks, Foreign Exchange & ATMs   If you are continuing east along the southern Silk Route, change your money in Khotan, as there are no facilities before Golmud or Dunhuang. There are several branches of the **Bank of China** around Khotan, the most convenient of which is at Beijing Xi Lu 38. The branch accepts traveler's checks and credit cards and has an ATM. It's open weekdays in summer from 9:30am to 1:30pm and 4 to 8pm; weekdays in winter from 10am to 2pm and 3:30 to 7pm.

Internet Access   There are several Internet cafes on Nawake Lu, including Crazy Boy, a little east of Gaoyang Kaorou restaurant. It's open 24 hours and charges ¥2 (25¢/15p) per hour. Dial-up is ☎ 165.

Post Office   On Beijing Xi Lu 1(☎ 0903/202-1885), a little west of the intersection with Wenhua Lu, the post office's narrow frontage belies its size. It's open in summer from 9am to 8:30pm and in winter from 9:30am to 8pm.

Visa Extensions   The **PSB** at Beijing Xi Lu 22 (☎ 0903/202-3614) offers one of the speediest visa extensions available—it takes less than half an hour! It's open weekdays from 9:30am to 1:30pm and 4 to 7:30pm.

EXPLORING KHOTAN

Sunday Market, Xingqitian Dashichang ☆☆☆ *Moments*   This is everything the

Kashgar Market once was. You'll need an early start and a lot of film stock to make the most of Xinjiang's liveliest **bazaar,** set in the heart of the Uighur part of town. The intersection between Gujiang Bei Lu and Jiamai Lu marks the center of the action, and you're unlikely to see a Han face as the streets fill with livestock and people throughout the day. Jewelers pore over gemstones, blacksmiths busy themselves shoeing horses and repairing farm tools, blanket makers beat cotton balls, rat-poison sellers proudly demonstrate the efficacy of their products—the sights and smells are overwhelming. Don't miss the **horse riding enclosure** toward the north side of the melee, where buyers test the roadworthiness of both beast and attached cart, with frequent spectacular tumbles. Head southeast from the bus station or simply follow the crowds.

SHOPPING

Jade Factory (Gongyi Meishu Youxian Gongsi)   Khotan has long been China's

source of jade (nephrite). The jade was first noticed by Zhang Qian, sent to Khotan on a reconnaissance expedition by Han Wudi, prior to the first successful Chinese invasion of the Western Regions. He believed women were adept in finding the gem, and they would dive for jade in the rivers around Khotan. Diving in the muddy and much diminished Khotan River now is not recommended, regardless of your gender. Those contemplating jade purchases should do your homework with a reputable jeweler before leaving home. While this shop is reliable, fake jade is one commodity Khotan never runs short of. Visit the dusty workshop behind the shop, where artisans turn, carve, and polish the jade. The Jade Factory is open every day from 10am to 1:30pm and 4 to 8pm, but note that you'll only see the artisans at work if you come during the week. Tanaiyi Lu 4. ☎ 0903/202-2563.

Khotan Old and New Carpet Store   In the Uighur part of town at, this little shop

has a decent selection of carpets from the surrounding areas. While the shop carries just a few hard-to-find antique carpets, this is probably the best selection you're going to get for old carpets in Khotan, as most stores only sell new ones, in fairly tacky designs, to locals. The store is a little hard to find, so if you want to make life easy, call the owner, Abdujilil, and he'll come by and pick you up. The shop is usually open 9am to 9pm. Gujiang Lu 1-1. ☎ 01367/668-9909.

WHERE TO STAY

Khotan, surprisingly enough, has plenty of decent, midrange options. Bargain hard—you can get up to 60% off rack rates.

Wild China: Yining (Gulja)

Yining, 692km (429 miles) west of Urumqi, has always been a tenuous possession of the Chinese empire, surrounded by the richest farmland in central Asia, and closer to Moscow than Beijing. During the Qing dynasty, it was the farthest point of banishment. Surrounded by high peaks and blessed with a mild climate, Yining is now a Han city with a smattering of Kazaks and Uighurs; it boasts hearty cuisine and access to the fascinating **Qapqal Xibo Autonomous County (Chab u Cha'er Xian).**

The colonization of Xinjiang began with the fierce ancestors of the current residents of **Qapqal,** 25km (16 miles) west of Yining. In 1764, 1,000 Xibo soldiers (followed "secretly" by 4,000 family members) were dispatched from Manchuria by the Qianlong emperor, with the promise that they would be allowed to return after 50 years. After putting the natives to the sword and hunting the region's animals to near extinction, the Xibo accepted the fact that there was no prospect of a return home, settled down, and took to farming.

While the **Manchu language** died out in northeast China, this outpost maintained their written and spoken language, and traditions such as the **hanging family tree** (jiapu). Most houses have one, with coins to represent the family coming into money, clubs and arrows the birth of a boy, and ribbons and boots the birth of a girl. Catch a bus from outside the Yining bus station to Cha Xian (30 min.; ¥5/65¢/35p) and take a three-wheeler (¥5/65¢/35p) onward to **Jingyuan Si** (admission ¥10/$1.30/65p). An exhibition of **Xibo** history inside this lamaist temple is fascinating, but alas, the guide speaks fluent Russian and awaits her first Russian visitor. Wander among the fields of sunflowers and wheat, dotted with light blue courtyard houses with earthen roofs.

GETTING THERE   The **airport** is connected to town by taxi (¥10/$1.30/65p) and shuttle bus (¥3/40¢/20p). **CAAC** (*©* **0999/822-1505**) is in the foyer of the **Youdian Binguan,** Jiefang Lu 162. Flights connect with Urumqi, Xi'an, and Wuhan. The **bus terminal** on Jiefang Lu in the northwest of town (*©* **0999/802-3413**) has connections with Urumqi (12 hr.) and Kashgar (52 hr.) via the wild Mongolian minority town of Bayan Bulak. Tickets for Almaty (12 hr.; ¥260/$34/£17; Mon, Wed–Thurs, and Sat) are purchased at the hotel reception

Hetian Binguan (Hotan Hotel)   If you want a retreat from the bustle of central Khotan, this spacious hotel, set amid rose gardens and grapevine-trellised walkways is a good option. While the rooms are blandly functional and service is unremarkable, outside in the grounds, the Islamic architecture lends the hotel a decidedly central Asian feel.

Wulumuqi Lu 10. *©* **0903/251-3563.** Fax 0903/251-3570. 76 units. ¥380 ($49/£25) standard room; ¥880 ($114/£57) suite. 40% discounts. No credit cards. **Amenities:** 2 restaurants; business center; laundry. *In room:* A/C, TV, Internet access.

immediately inside the bus terminal. There are abundant **taxis,** which charge ¥5 (65¢/35p) for 2km (1¼ miles), then ¥1.30 (15¢/10p) per kilometer thereafter; add ¥.20 (5¢/5p) from midnight to 5am. **Buses** charge ¥1 (15¢/5p), dropped in a box when you board. A **tandem bike** may be rented at **Diaoke Shiguang** (Jiefang Lu 64; ✆ 0999/838-2369), which also serves excellent coffee and traditional Tajik ice cream.

WHERE TO STAY & DINE **Yili Binguan** (Yingbin Lu 8; ✆ **0999/802-2794;** fax 0999/802-4964) is Yining's oldest hotel, set in the extensive (30,000-sq.-m/ 322,917-sq.-ft.) grounds of the former **Soviet consulate,** which are particularly charming in autumn. Midsize twins for ¥160 to ¥488 ($21–$63/£10–£32) in buildings 2 and 3 to the west of the complex are the best choice. Yining's swankiest three-star hotel, the **Yilite Dajiudian** (Shengli Jie 98; ✆ **0999/ 803-5600;** fax 0999/802-1819), is situated on the northeast corner of the Peoples' Square, the scene of anti-government riots in 1997. While this 12-story glass-and-tile monolith is out of place in sleepy Yining, standard rooms at ¥298 ($39/£19) are spotless and bright and suites are well-priced at ¥500 ($65/£33). Discounts of 35% are available.

For dining, **Guoyuan Canting** (Yili He Minzu Wenhua Cun Xiang Nei 500 Mi Chu; ✆ 0999/832-3580) charges less than ¥100 ($13/£6.50) for a meal set in an apple orchard on the north bank of the Yili River. (Turn left down the final road before the Yili Bridge south of town and continue for 455m/1,500 ft. The entrance is on the right.) Enjoy steamed dumplings *(you tazi),* a local version of *samsa* with three fingerprints in each bun *(yibazhua),* whole chicken with vegetables and noodles *(dapan ji),* and the filling *nang bao rou,* a huge plate of lamb and vegetable stew on a wheat pancake. Sup honeyed rye beer called *kvass (gewasi),* and make friends with the local Uighurs. Try the most renowned Kazakh dish, *naren,* at **Naren Canting** (Xinhua Xi Lu 7; ✆ **0999/803-2434).** *Naren* is roasted horse meat (taken from the waist) served on a pile of thick noodles with a side serving of nan and an appetizing salad of tomato, cucumber, and Spanish onion; it costs less than ¥40 ($5.20/£2.60). The genial owner, Talgat, will cajole you to try horse's milk or yogurt, but these sour concoctions are an acquired taste. The regular yogurt *(niunai)* is creamy and delicious.

Wenzhou Dajiudian (Wenzhou Hotel)   Once the nicest hotel in Khotan, this hotel has been supplanted by the Zhejiang Hotel next door, and if you have the extra few dollars you're better off there. While the renovated rooms are still worth the outlay, the standard rooms on the fourth (without air-conditioning) and fifth floors are only for those on a tight budget who don't mind putting up with some unsavory smells!

Beijing Xi Lu 5. ✆ 0903/203-7666. 60 units. ¥218–¥258 ($28–$34/£14–£17) standard room; ¥388 ($50/£25) suite. 40% discounts are standard. No credit cards. **Amenities:** Restaurant; concierge; business center; same-day laundry/dry cleaning. *In room:* A/C, TV, water cooler.

Zhejiang Dajiudian (Zhejiang Hotel) ★ *Value* Brought to you by coastal Chinese investors is this four-star hotel that seems to have broken out of the mold of the usual Chinese hotel with sleek, modern and well-appointed rooms that are the most comfortable in town. My only criticism would be that while the bathrooms are sparkling clean, the plumbing is starting to show its age and showers are weaker than you might hope. The location, right next to the main square in town, puts you at the Sunday market with a quick 10-minute taxi ride.

Beijing Xi Lu 75. © 0903/202-9999. Fax 0903/203-6688. 74 units. ¥418 ($54/£27) standard room; ¥785 ($102/£51) suite. 50% discounts. AE, DC, MC, V. **Amenities:** Restaurant; nightclub; concierge; business center; conference rooms. *In room:* A/C, TV, broadband Internet access (¥10/$1.30/65p per day), minibar, safe.

WHERE TO DINE

There are plenty of Uighur options in Khotan, but if you feel in need of some Western fare, there's a bakery next to the Zhejiang Hotel on Beijing Xi Lu or a unique fast-food dining opportunity at **Weilimai Burger (Weilimai Hanbao)** on the northeast corner of Tuanjie Square. From the outside this fast-food joint looks like any other, but Weilimai offers the opportunity to enjoy a decidedly mediocre burger and better fries with a beer in its unexpectedly expansive upstairs dining room surrounded by booths full of young couples, while families take in the views over the square to the Mao statue!

Nawake Lu Gaoyang Kaorou Kuaicandian ★ UIGHUR The prize for Xinjiang's best *samsa*—a package of lamb and spices baked in pastry—is safe with this delightful restaurant, distinguished by its twin chimneys and metal blue awning. You can join the ever-present line outside for takeout, or head into the atmospheric smoky, gold-wallpapered interior. The kabobs and nan are also excellent and are well followed by the slightly sweet medicinal tea which is common to many restaurants—the tea leaves (*jiankang cha*) can be purchased from the **Uighur Hospital,** Jiamai Lu 2.

Nawake Lu. © 0903/202-5132. Meal for 2 less than ¥50 ($6.50/£3.25). No credit cards. 8am–10:30pm.

Tograq Black Tea Coffee Bar (Huyang Linghong Kafeiting) UIGHUR This unpretentious little cafe is a great place to set your watch to Xinjiang time and unwind over a cup of coffee. While they only serve instant coffee, at least they have a wide range of international brands to choose from. The Uighur owners also serve a sampling of different Uighur dishes, like *samsa* and *rounan* (nan bread stuffed with minced lamb). They stay open late and serve a selection of whiskeys and beers. Come here for a drink if you'd like to escape the usual sleaziness of Chinese bars.

Wulumuqi Lu 69 (a 2-min. walk left out of the Hotan Hotel). © 0903/688-2424. Meal for 2 less than ¥40 ($5.20/£2.60). No credit cards. 8am–midnight.

AROUND KHOTAN

Carpet Factory (Ditan Chang) In the 1980s, factory inspections were an unavoidable part of any trip to China. Fortunately, you can examine the workings of this factory without listening to a cadre reciting statistics concerning output, expected turnover, and the area of the factory down to the last square foot. Workers sit outside the main carpet-making hall, their hands, feet, and hair stained red by henna dye. The gentle rattle of the looms and swoosh of the combs is almost drowned out by the banter of Uighur women—there can be as many as eight of them working on one carpet.

At the back is the inevitable shop, but much of the art of carpet weaving was lost during the Cultural Revolution, so you won't find anything to match the splendor of carpets in your average Uighur home. The factory is open Monday through Saturday from 9:30am to 1:30pm and 3:30 to 7:30pm.

Nawake Jie 6. ⓒ 0903/205-4553. Take a cab (about ¥20/$2.60/£1.30) or bus no. 2 east along Beijing Lu to the terminus, then bus no. 5 heading south, again to the end of the line.

Silk and Mulberry Research Center (Si Sang Yanjiusuo) ⚐

Khotan is said to have broken the closely guarded Chinese silk monopoly in the 5th century. According to legend, a Chinese princess was instructed by the king to smuggle silk-moth eggs in her hairpiece, as frontier guards, however zealous, would never touch a lady's hair.

The front building houses offices, and possibly someone willing to show you around, but the surest way to see the center is to arrange a tour through CITS, who will also show you "their" traditional silk makers. You can view the entire mysterious process, from sorting and boiling the cocoons, to reeling off the thread—typically 900m (2,950 ft.) long—through to the final weaving into the wavelike ikat patterns characteristic of Khotan silk. While the primitive (and deafening) technology makes for a good tour, business is not good. A sign near the gate opens with a statement of the company's bold production targets, and ends with the modest objective, DON'T LOSE MONEY *(bu kui)*. You'll find few tasteful products in the shop; buy your silk in a large city. This difference in tastes is nothing new. Chinese silk patterns were never in vogue among the Romans, who usually imported silk thread—Plinius recorded that Chinese cloth would be unraveled and rewoven.

Hemo Lu 107. Bus: no. 1 from north of the main roundabout on Hetian Lu to the terminus, then walk back about 225m (750 ft.).

Eastern Central China

by Sherisse Pham

If Shanxi Province is the cradle of Chinese civilization, then the stretch of eastern central China between the Yellow River (Huang He) and the Yangzi River (Chang Jiang)—an area covering the provinces of **Henan, Shandong, Jiangsu,** and **Anhui**—can be seen as the crucible in which Chinese culture subsequently developed and flourished. Bounded by the Yellow Sea and the East China Sea on the east, and buffered from ethnic minority influences from the north, west, and south, this swath of China is a region that, except for some Western influence late in China's history, has remained unapologetically and overwhelmingly "Han" Chinese in character.

Early Chinese civilization may have developed around the Yellow River in Henan Province with the Shang dynasty (1700–1100 B.C.), but Chinese culture as it is widely perceived today really started to take shape only some 600 years later with the birth of the most influential figure in Chinese history, Confucius, in **Qufu** in Shandong Province. By the time of the "golden age" of the Han dynasty (206 B.C.–A.D. 220), Confucianism, that quintessentially Chinese philosophical tradition, had become the official state philosophy, and would be put to the test in the subsequent 2,000 years of dynastic changes. Arguably, no region or place in China has seen the rise and fall of more dynasties than this eastern central section of the country, with the ancient capitals of **Luoyang** (capital of nine dynasties), **Kaifeng** (six dynasties), and **Nanjing**

(eight dynasties) serving as China's seat of power 23 times. Today, though none of these former capitals has retained much of their previous glory, all contain vestiges of a Chinese imperial past, and are worth visiting. Chinese history buffs may be interested as well in some lesser-known but intriguing finds such as the **miniature terra-cotta army** in Xuzhou, and the **horse and chariot funeral pits** in Zibo.

The influence of that other indigenous Chinese religious-philosophical tradition, Daoism, is also very strong in this region, which is home to two of Daoism's sacred mountains: **Tai Shan,** the most climbed mountain in China, and **Song Shan,** the central Daoist mountain. Though not indigenous to China, Buddhism's influence on Chinese culture has also been profound. Some of China's finest Buddhist art and sculpture can be seen at the magnificent **Longmen Grottoes (Longmen Shiku)** in Luoyang.

Historically, this region has also been the cultural bridge between the political center of gravity mostly in the north, and the economic center in the south, especially around the fertile lower deltas of the Yangzi River. The physical link was the great Chinese engineering feat of the **Grand Canal,** built between the Sui dynasty (581–618) and the Yuan dynasty (1206–1368) to link the Yangzi and Yellow rivers. Although much of the canal is no longer navigable, it gave rise in its heyday to many flourishing river towns, including Suzhou, Zhou Zhuang, and the

underrated but delightful **Yangzhou**, the economic and cultural capital of southern China during the Sui and Tang dynasties. The gardens that were built here by merchants and retired officials, with rocks hauled up from nearby **Tai Hu (Lake Tai)**, have created in many a mind's eye the quintessential Chinese garden. But it is at nearby **Huang Shan (Yellow Mountain)** that you find the ultimate Chinese landscape, as wispy clouds hover over a lone pine tree on a distant mountaintop.

Today, this eastern central region of China continues to function as a modern crucible of sorts. Traveling in this area, you will encounter two of China's richest provinces (Shandong and Jiangsu) bordering one of its poorest (Anhui). You will see some of China's oldest temples standing next to some of its newest skyscrapers. In the country of Laozi, this tug between such opposing forces should come as no surprise. It is, after all, quintessentially Chinese. The region sees hot, humid summers, while winters can be bone-chillingly cold; spring and fall are the best times to visit. **Note:** Unless otherwise noted, hours listed for attractions and restaurants are daily.

1 Zhengzhou

Henan Province, 689km (413 miles) SW of Beijing, 998km (599 miles) NW of Shanghai

Zhengzhou, a sprawling industrial city of six million and a major railway stop on the Beijing-Guangzhou rail lines, was once a former ancient Shang dynasty (1700–1100

B.C.) capital, though few traces of its 3,000-year history remain. Many travelers simply overnight here en route to Kaifeng and Luoyang, but there are a few lesser known but intriguing sights in the surrounding area. Zhengzhou's proximity to the Yellow River (30km/18 miles to the north) also makes it a convenient base from which to explore the river.

ESSENTIALS

GETTING THERE   Zhengzhou is connected by **air** to many major Chinese cities, including Beijing (1 hr. 30 min.), Guangzhou (2 hr. 10 min.), Hong Kong (2½ hr.), and Shanghai (1 hr. 20 min.). Tickets can be purchased at the **CAAC office** at Airport Hotel (Minhang Dajiudian) Jinshui Lu 3 (② **0371/6599-1111**). The airport is about 35km (21 miles) southeast of the city. Sofitel and Crowne Plaza have booths at the airport and can arrange transportation into the city if you contact them ahead of time. **Taxis** make the run for around ¥100 ($13/£6.50). **CAAC airport shuttles** (40 min.; ¥15/$1.95/£1; 6am–7pm) depart every hour for the airport from the Airport Hotel (Minhang Dajiudian) (② **0371/6578-1111**, ext. 6528) and also meet incoming flights.

Trains run from Zhengzhou's **railway station** (② **0371/6835-6666**) to Luoyang (2 hr.), Kaifeng (1 hr.), Xi'an (10 hr.), Beijing (12 hr.), Shanghai (14 hr.), Guangzhou (36 hr.), and a host of other cities in between. From the **long-distance bus station** (*changtu qichezhan;* ② **0371/6698-3995**) opposite the railway station, Iveco buses depart for Luoyang (every 25 min. 5:30am–9:20pm, public buses depart every 40 min. 6:50am–7:30pm; 2–2½ hr.; ¥40/$5.20/£2.60), Kaifeng (every 20 min. 6:20am–7pm; 1½ hr.; ¥12/$1.60/80p), Dengfeng (every 30 min. 6am–7:40pm; 30 min.; ¥12/$1.55/80p), and Gongyi (every half-hour 6:40am–8pm; 1½ hr.; ¥23/$3/£1.50). If you're heading to Kaifeng (every 20 min. 6:20am–8pm; 1 hr.; ¥12/$1.55/80p) it's highly recommended that you leave from the **East Bus Station (Keyun Dong Zhan)** on Jichang Lu; it will cut down your travel time significantly. If you're traveling in the summer, make sure to ask if your bus has air-conditioning *(you mei you kongtiao?).* For guaranteed air-conditioning, a private bus service, **Henan Yu An Kuaiyun** (② **0371/6638-3055**), runs air-conditioned buses to Luoyang (every hour 7:30am–7pm; 2 hr. 30 min.; ¥37/$4.80/£2.40), Beijing (9:30am, 11:30am, 1:30m, and 9:30pm; 9 hr.; ¥172–¥196/$22–$26/£12–£13).

GETTING AROUND   Taxis charge ¥6 (80¢/40p) for 2km (1¼ miles), then ¥1.50 (20¢/10p) per additional kilometer until 12km (7½ miles), after which the price rises to ¥2.25 (30¢/15p) per kilometer. From 11pm to 5am, prices rise to ¥8 ($1.05/50p) per 2km (1¼ miles). City **buses** cost ¥1 (15¢/10p) flat fare. Bus no. 26 runs from the railway station to Jinshui Lu via Renmin Lu, while bus no. 16 runs from Erma Lu to the Yellow River.

FAST FACTS

Banks, Foreign Exchange & ATMs   A convenient **Bank of China** branch (② **0371/6597-7640;** open Mon–Fri 9am–noon and 1–5pm) is across from the Crowne Plaza Hotel at Jinshui Lu 5. Counters 5 through 7 are for foreign exchange. There is an ATM at this location.

Internet Access   If you have your own computer, most hotels have in-room high-speed Internet access. Free Wi-Fi is available in the public areas of the Sofitel and the Crowne Plaza. For those without computers, Crowne Plaza's business center charges ¥1 (15¢/10p) per minute (daily 6am–11pm).

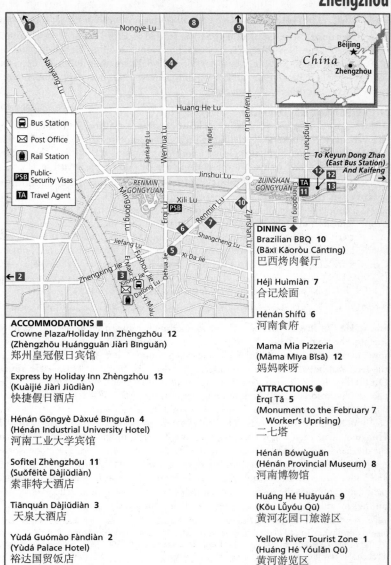

Map Legend:
- 🚌 Bus Station
- ✉ Post Office
- 🚉 Rail Station
- PSB Public-Security Visas
- TA Travel Agent

Map labels:
Nongye Lu · Nanyang Lu · Huang He Lu · Huayuan Lu · Jinshan Lu · Jiankang Lu · Wenhua Lu · Jingliu Lu · Jinshui Lu · RENMIN GONGYUAN · Xili Lu · Renmin Lu · ZIJINSHAN GONGYUAN · To Keyun Dong Zhan (East Bus Station) And Kaifeng · Minggong Lu · Erqi Lu · PSB · Shangcheng Lu · Jiefang Lu · Fushou Jie · Zijinshan Lu · Zijinshan Dong Lu · Zhengxing Jie · Er Malu · Xilong Jie · Xi Da Jie · Dehua Jie · Datong Lu · Da Yi Malu

Inset map: China · Běijīng · Zhengzhou

DINING ◆

Brazilian BBQ 10
(Bāxī Kǎoròu Cāntīng)
巴西烤肉餐厅

Héjì Huìmiàn 7
合记烩面

Hénán Shífǔ 6
河南食府

Mama Mia Pizzeria
(Māma Mīya Bǐsā) 12
妈妈咪呀

ATTRACTIONS ●

Èrqī Tǎ 5
(Monument to the February 7 Worker's Uprising)
二七塔

Hénán Bówùguǎn
(Hénán Provincial Museum) 8
河南博物馆

Huáng Hé Huāyuán 9
(Kǒu Lǚyóu Qū)
黄河花园口旅游区

Yellow River Tourist Zone 1
(Huáng Hé Yóulǎn Qū)
黄河游览区

ACCOMMODATIONS ■

Crowne Plaza/Holiday Inn Zhèngzhōu 12
(Zhèngzhōu Huángguān Jiàrì Bīnguǎn)
郑州皇冠假日宾馆

Express by Holiday Inn Zhèngzhōu 13
(Kuàijié Jiàrì Jiǔdiàn)
快捷假日酒店

Hénán Gōngyè Dàxué Bīnguǎn 4
(Hénán Industrial University Hotel)
河南工业大学宾馆

Sofitel Zhèngzhōu 11
(Suǒfēitè Dàjiǔdiàn)
索菲特大酒店

Tiānquán Dàjiǔdiàn 3
天泉大酒店

Yùdá Guómào Fàndiàn 2
(Yùdá Palace Hotel)
裕达国贸饭店

Post Office   The post office (open 8am–6:30pm) is just south of the railway station.

Visa Extensions   The **Gonganju (PSB)** is located at Erqi Lu 70 (② **0371/6962-0359;** open Sept–Nov Mon–Fri 8:30am–noon and 2–6pm, Dec–Feb Mon–Fri 8:30am–noon and 2–5:30pm, Mar–May Mon–Fri 8:30am–noon and 2–5:30pm, and June–Aug daily 8:30am–noon and 3–6:30pm). Allow 5 business days, though emergency 3-day visas can also be processed.

EXPLORING ZHENGZHOU

The 11-story twin-tower pagoda in the heart of town is the **Erqi Ta (Monument to the February 7 Workers' Uprising),** which commemorates the February 7, 1923, strike on the Beijing-Hankou rail line against the warlord authorities. The workers were fighting for their rights, but the uprising was bloodily suppressed.

Henan Bowuguan (Henan Provincial Museum) ⊙⊙⊙   Located in the northern part of town, this marvelous museum—the fourth largest in China, it claims—is well worth a couple of hours of your time. Housed in a pyramid-shaped structure, it has a strong collection of prehistoric and early Chinese artifacts such as oracle bones, tools, and pottery from the Yangshao culture, the Longshan culture, and the early Xia, Shang, and Zhou dynasties, as well as bronzes, jades, and Han dynasty funeral objects. Exhibits are well documented in English, and the English-language audio tour—¥30 ($3.90/£1.95) with a deposit of either ¥400 ($52/£26) or your passport—is quite helpful. English-speaking museum guides are available for ¥100 ($13/£6.50).

Nongye Lu 8. ② 0371/6351-1237. Admission ¥20 ($2.60/£1.30). 8:30am–6pm. Bus: no. 30, 32, 39, 42, or 61.

Huang He (Yellow River) ⊙   Prone to flooding because of silt deposits in its upper reaches, the mighty Yellow River (Huang He) has long been known as "China's Sorrow," having wreaked untold damage and taken countless lives through the ages. Here the river can be visited from two different locales. The first is at **Huang He Youlan Qu (Yellow River Tourist Zone),** a large park on the river's southern bank. You can take the hydrofoil on a 40-minute round-trip tour for ¥65 ($8.45/£4.25) per person, which includes a stop at a sandy islet in the middle of the river.

About 15km (9 miles) east of the Yellow River Tourist Zone, the **Huang He Huayuan Kou Luyou Qu** was where Chiang Kai-shek ordered his army to blow up the dikes in order to halt the advance of the Japanese troops in 1938. The tactic worked temporarily, but in the process it flooded 44 counties, killed almost a million people, and left another 12 million homeless and destitute. Today, stone tablets in this tourist park commemorate the event, as does a four-character inscription, ZHI LI HUANG HE, on the embankment by Mao Zedong, meaning "Control the Yellow River."

Yellow River Tourist Zone. ② 0371/6379-9500. Admission ¥30 ($3.90/£1.95). 7am–7pm. Bus: no. 16 (¥5/65¢/35p) from corner of Erma Lu and Zhengxing Jie to its terminus. Huayuan Kou Tourist Region of the Yellow River: ② 0371/6563-2119. Admission ¥15 ($1.95/£1). 8am–7pm. Bus: no. 220 (¥1.50/20¢/10p) from railway station; get off at Jin Shui Cun, then take a motorcycle taxi (¥8/$1.05/50p).

WHERE TO STAY
EXPENSIVE

Crowne Plaza/Holiday Inn Zhengzhou (Zhengzhou Huangguan Jiari Binguan) ⊙   Situated in the northeastern part of town, this hotel chain is in the rather unusual position of having the five-star **Crowne Plaza** and the four-star **Holiday Inn** right next to each other and sharing many of the same facilities and management. The three-star **Express by Holiday Inn Zhengzhou** (see listing below), converted from the former International Hotel, joined the party in 2005 (but does not share in the amenities). The Crowne Plaza's copious use of marble and gold trim makes it feel like you're walking through a cheesy Roman movie set. But the rooms are a good size, beds are comfortable, and bathrooms are stocked with accessories. Service is warm and helpful, and the breakfast buffet is tops. For a unique entertainment offering, they've got a driving range, added behind the Holiday Inn (2:30–10pm; ¥20/$2.60/£1.30 for one bucket of balls). Rooms at the Holiday Inn, geared more toward the business traveler looking for a less flashy, quieter environment, are smaller but were recently renovated and are very comfortable with clean and modern bathrooms. It shares the amenities of the Crowne Plaza, but you have to walk across a parking lot to get to them.

Jinshui Lu 115. ℂ **0371/6595-0055.** Fax 0371/6599-0770. www.ichotelsgroup.com. Crowne Plaza 222 units; Holiday Inn 230 units. Crowne Plaza: ¥849 ($110/£55) standard room; ¥1,588 ($206/£103) suite. Holiday Inn: ¥1,088 ($141/£71) standard room; ¥1,520 ($198/£99) suite. 35%–40% discounts possible. 15% surcharge, 5% council tax. AE, DC, MC, V. **Amenities:** 5 restaurants; bar; lounge; small indoor pool; small health club; spa; driving range; sauna; concierge; airport shuttle (incoming free; outgoing ¥40/$5/£2.50); business center; wireless Internet access in lobby; forex; shopping arcade; salon; room service; massage; laundry/dry cleaning; nonsmoking rooms; executive rooms. *In room:* A/C, satellite TV, high-speed Internet access, minibar, hair dryer, safe.

Sofitel Zhengzhou (Suofeite Dajiudian) ✶✶ As can be expected with the Sofitel name, the bedding and mattresses at this hotel are incredibly cozy and comfortable. At press time, the hotel was in the middle of a massive face-lift that should be complete by the end of 2008. The public spaces have all been redone, with new modern decor such as carpets with geometric patterns, plush chairs in purple and dark turquoise, and a funky tiered bar in the lounge area. The old desks and chipped marble counters in the bathrooms are being replaced and new rooms are now sleeker and more stylish than those at their neighbor's, the Crowne Plaza. Service is professional and impeccable; I mentioned that I had a cold and a pot of hot Coke and ginger—a cold remedy the Chinese swear by—was sent to my room. Business travelers will like the e-business rooms, which come with a fax machine, a plasma TV hooked up to a computer and wireless keyboard, and a desk stocked with tape, a stapler, and other stationery items.

Chengdong Lu 289. ℂ **0371/6595-0088.** Fax 0371/6595-0080. www.accorhotels-asia.com. 240 units. ¥1,820 ($237/£118) standard room; from ¥3,180 ($413/£207) suite. 30%–50% discounts possible. 15% surcharge, 5% council tax. AE, DC, MC, V. **Amenities:** 2 restaurants; 2 bars; lounge; small indoor pool; small health club and spa; sauna; concierge; business center; forex; shopping arcade; salon; room service; massage; laundry/dry cleaning; nonsmoking rooms; executive rooms. *In room:* A/C, satellite TV, high-speed Internet access, minibar, hair dryer, iron/ironing board, safe, scale.

Yuda Guomao Fandian (Yuda Palace Hotel) ✶✶ This handsome, modern, 45-story building is Zhengzhou's grandest and most opulent hotel, but its location in the western part of town makes it inconvenient for independent travelers. Rooms are enormous—the largest in the city—comfortable, and gorgeously furnished with classic Italian furniture and a high-tech Bose surround-sound audio system. The spacious all-marble bathrooms come with separate tub and shower, except for corner rooms.

Zhongyuan Xi Lu 220. ℂ **03716/743-8888.** Fax 0371/6742-2539. yudaeo@public2.zz.ha.cn. 365 units. ¥1,432 ($186/£93) standard room; ¥2,863 ($372/£186) suite. 30%–40% discounts possible. 15% surcharge. AE, DC, MC, V. **Amenities:** 5 restaurants; bar; lounge; disco; indoor pool; health club; sauna; concierge; business center; forex; shopping arcade; salon; room service; massage; laundry/dry cleaning; nonsmoking rooms; executive rooms. *In room:* A/C, satellite TV, high-speed Internet access, minibar, hair dryer, safe, scale.

MODERATE
Express by Holiday Inn Zhengzhou (Kuaijie Jiari Jiudian) ✶ *Value* If you'd like to stay at an internationally managed hotel but balk at the prices, this new property is

a good option. While it has a slightly institutional feel (note the staff uniforms, for example—employees look like fitness coaches), this hotel will suit any international traveler fine, if you don't require too many frills. The bathrooms are a bit small and there's no bathtub, but rooms are bright, stylish for the price, and of a good size to boot.

Jinshui Lu 114. © **0371/6595-6600.** Fax 0371/6595-1526. www.ichotelsgroup.com/h/d/6c/1/en/hd/cgoex. 269 units. ¥538 ($70/£35) standard room; ¥688 ($89/£44) suite. 40% discounts possible. AE, DC, MC, V. **Amenities:** Restaurant; high-speed Internet access; laundry facilities. *In room:* A/C, TV, high-speed Internet access, hair dryer.

Tianquan Dajiudian   Conveniently located next to the railway station, this three-star hotel offers relatively clean accommodations at reasonable prices. Guest rooms are a little dark, with forgettable furnishings, but are otherwise quite comfortable. Bathrooms are a bit old, but clean. Be sure to ask for a room in the back, as the honking taxis in the front of the square can be a rude surprise at 3am. The staff tries to be helpful.

Xi Datong Lu 1. © **0371/6698-6888.** Fax 0371/6699-1814. 214 units. ¥358–¥388 ($47–$50/£23–£25) standard room; from ¥1,298 ($169/£84) suite. Rates include Chinese breakfast. 30% discounts possible. MC, V. **Amenities:** Restaurant; bar; nightclub; exercise room; salon; business center; gift shop; room service; laundry. *In room:* A/C, TV.

INEXPENSIVE
Henan Gongye Daxue Binguan (Henan Industrial University Hotel) *Value*
Located just opposite the university's campus gates in the northeastern part of town, not far from the Henan Provincial Museum, this basic guesthouse is one of the best budget choices in town. Rooms are a little musty but well kept and the bathrooms are clean and outfitted with new fixtures. Little English is spoken at the front desk, but the receptionist says a staff member is usually on duty to help with translations.

Wenhua Lu 48. © **0371/6388-7704.** 86 units. ¥120 ($16/£7.80) standard room. No credit cards. *In room:* A/C, TV.

WHERE TO DINE
EXPENSIVE
Mama Mia Pizzeria (Mama Miya Bisa) ✦ ITALIAN/CONTINENTAL   This low-key restaurant offers many of the comfort foods of home. The ambience is casual and unpretentious, with low lighting and checkered tablecloths. Pizzas and pastas are popular here; the spaghetti carbonara is pretty good. Other favorites include the U.S. Angus T-bone steak and the grilled salmon. Service is attentive.

In the Crowne Plaza Hotel, Jinshui Lu 115. © **0371/6595-0055.** Main courses ¥40–¥160 ($5.20–$21/£2.60–£10). AE, DC, MC, V. 11:30am–2:30pm and 5:30–10pm.

MODERATE
Baxi Kaorou Canting (Brazilian BBQ) BRAZILIAN   There's nothing really Brazilian about this buffet restaurant, but the atmosphere makes for a fun night of dining. Servers wearing cowboy hats walk around tables carrying metal rods laden with roasted meat that is then doled out onto your plate. The roast duck is excellent, and the roasted lamb pieces pretty much taste like the ones at the local Xinjiang restaurant. The buffet selection is all Chinese food, mostly safe stuff like ginger pork, sautéed broccoli, fried rice, and a rather strange, ketchuplike pasta. It's a decent place to come for something in between hotel dining and hole-in-the-wall Chinese restaurant.

Zijing Shan Lu 6. © **0371/6623-9728.** Buffet ¥38-48 ($4.95–$6.25/£2.50–£3.10) per person. No credit cards. 11:30am–2pm and 6–9pm.

Henan Shifu ✦✦ HENAN   Located in a recessed courtyard off Renmin Lu in the center of town, this is one of Zhengzhou's more popular and long-standing restaurants.

The decor here is traditional Chinese and there's a festive atmosphere during peak dining hours. The food is uniformly excellent and intriguing, especially the *xiangma shaobing jia niurou* (also known as Zhengzhou's "hamburger"); it consists of marinated cold beef sandwiched in fried sesame bread—a subtle but sublime mix of cold and hot, savory and sweet. Other noteworthy dishes include *ba sushijin,* a vegetarian dish of mushrooms, seasonal greens, and bamboo shoots; and *guotie doufu,* a tofu casserole. Service is efficient and friendly but the staff doesn't speak English, nor is there an English-language menu.

Renmin Lu 22. (C) 0371/6622-2108. Meal for 2 ¥60–¥160 ($7.80–$21/£3.90–£10). AE, DC, MC, V. 11am–2:30pm and 5:30–9:30pm.

INEXPENSIVE

Heji Huimian NOODLES   The specialty at this always crowded halal restaurant in the center of town is the *teyouhuimian* (house specialty noodles), which consists of fresh coarse noodles served with a variety of mushrooms and small chunks of lamb in broth. Chilies, cilantro, and vinegar can be added at the table to taste. The first floor offers no-frills fast-food dining: Order your noodles at the counter by simply asking for a small bowl *(xiao wan)* for ¥5.50 (70¢/35p) or a large bowl *(da wan)* for ¥6 (75¢/35p); then grab a table and hand your ticket to the waitress. You'll be served within minutes. The second and third floors offer a la carte dining in a more pleasant, well-lit environment, but menus are in Chinese only.

Renmin Lu 3. (C) 0371/6622-8026. Meal for 2 ¥25–¥60 ($3.25–$7.80/£1.65–£3.90). No credit cards. 1st floor: 11am–10pm; 2nd and 3rd floors: 11am–3pm and 5–10pm.

ZHENGZHOU AFTER DARK

Target Pub (Mubiao Jiuba) at the south end of Jing Liu Lu (**(C) 0138/038-57056**), is a cool place for those in the know. You can actually have a conversation here or simply sit at the bar and let Lao Wang regale you with tales of off-roading in Lhasa, Mongolia, and the Gobi Desert.

2 Dengfeng & Song Shan

Henan Province, 63km (40 miles) SW of Zhengzhou, 87km (53 miles) SE of Luoyang

Located south of the Yellow River in northwest Henan Province, Song Shan is the central mountain of the five holy Daoist mountains. Today, it's better known as the home of the Shaolin Temple (Shaolin Si), birthplace of the eponymous brand of kung-fu martial art (Shaolin *gongfu*) that has long been popular in Asia but has only in recent years become increasingly known to the Western world. The main town serving Song Shan is Dengfeng (meaning "Ascending to Bestow Honor"), named by the Tang dynasty empress Wu Zetian who preferred Song Shan to Tai Shan (Mount Tai) in Shandong Province, traditionally the favorite mountain of most emperors. Song Shan can be visited in conjunction with Luoyang, or as a day trip from Zhengzhou.

ESSENTIALS

GETTING THERE   The nearest **airport and rail connections** are in Zhengzhou, but air tickets can be bought at **CITS** at the Guolu Dalou on Beihuan Lu Xiduan (**(C) 0371/6288-3442**). There are *luyou che* (tour buses) that connect Zhengzhou directly to Shaolin Si (Shaolin Temple). Unfortunately, you waste a lot of time waiting around because buses don't leave until they're full, there's a 30-minute stop at an uninteresting temple in Dengfeng, and another stop at a random Chinese restaurant right before the mountain (everyone on my bus put up a protest and we were able to boycott the restaurant stop). What should have been a 1½-hour trip can quickly turn into 2 or 2½ hours. You're better off taking the 30-minute bus from Zhengzhou for ¥24 ($3.10/£1.60) to Dengfeng and grabbing a 20-minute, ¥3 (40¢/20p) **minibus** ride to Shaolin Si (Shaolin Temple). Minibuses also connect Dengfeng to Luoyang (every hour 8am–noon and 2–6pm; 1½ hr.; ¥20/$2.60/£1.30) and Gongyi (7am–6pm; 1 hr.). In Dengfeng, all minibuses depart from the ramshackle **West Bus Station (Xi Kechezhan;** © **0371/6287-2049)** on Zhongyue Dajie just west of Songyang Zhong Jie. Buy your tickets on the bus. A **taxi** from Zhengzhou to Dengfeng will cost about ¥400 ($52/£26), subject to negotiation.

GETTING AROUND   The town of Dengfeng is small enough to **walk** or traverse by **bus** (¥1/15¢/10p). Bus no. 2 runs from the Songyang Academy (Songyang Shuyuan) through town to the Zhongyue Miao (temple). Bus no. 1 connects the Tianzhong Hotel with the West Bus Station.

FAST FACTS

Banks, Foreign Exchange & ATMs   The **Bank of China** (© **0371/6287-5633;** open Mon–Fri 9am–noon and 1:30–5pm) is at Shaolin Dadao 186. There's an ATM on the premises.

Post Office   The main post office (© **0371/6287-2969;** open 8am–6:30pm) is at Song Shan Lu 86 (corner of Aimin Lu).

EXPLORING THE CENTRAL MOUNTAIN

Song Shan is made up of two mountain ranges, each with 36 peaks and dotted throughout with temples and pagodas. The larger range to the east is known as **Taishi Shan,** and the lesser range to the west is **Shaoshi Shan.**

TREKKING THE MOUNTAIN   Ascending the **eastern** or greater range (**Taishi Shan**) of Song Shan is more challenging as there are no cable cars to bail out the weary. The trail typically starts behind the Songyang Academy (Songyang Shuyuan). Stone steps lead all the way up to the 1,470m-high (4,900-ft.) **Junji Feng** where, unlike at China's other sacred mountains, there is no temple or building at the summit, just patches of grass and all of Song Shan below you. Allow 4 hours to reach the top. A ¥100 ($13/£6.50) entrance fee get you into the Taishi Shan Scenic Area and is required to go up the road to the **Songyue Temple Pagoda.** You can use the same ticket to get into Shaolin Monastery.

Climbing the **western** or lesser range (**Shaoshi Shan**) is made easier by three cable cars. Just west of Tai Lin (Forest of Stupas) is the **Shaolin Suodao** (¥30/$3.90/£1.95), which runs up the northern side of the mountain and has back views of the monastery and the forest. A better option, the **Songyang Suodao,** is up the road another 150m (492 ft.). This pleasant ¥30 ($3.90/£1.95), 20-minute ride on a chairlift runs less than halfway up the mountain. The ride (or hike) back down affords some marvelous views of the Shaolin Monastery and the Forest of Stupas nestled in the foothills. The **Song Shan Shaolin Suodao** is another 300m (984 ft.) from the lower terminus of the first gondola, and is a ¥60 ($7.80/£3.90), 40-minute cable-car ride that goes past Ladder (Tizi) Gully to just below the summit. From here, trails lead to the **Song Shan Diaoqiao,** a suspension bridge stretched over a deep ravine of tall bald rocks. You can climb back down either the northern side of Shaoshi Shan underneath the cable cars, or the sheer southern face lined with steep narrow trails. At the parking lot below Sanhuang

Xinggong (Sanhuang Palace), you can hire a taxi back to Dengfeng. For the relatively fit, climbing Shaoshi Shan takes 5 to 6 hours round-trip.

SHAOSHI SHAN
Shaolin Si (Shaolin Monastery) ⊛ Most visitors these days come to Song Shan
not for the mountain climbing but for this famous monastery, better known for its martial arts than for its religious affiliations. Today's Shaolin, more loud marketplace than quiet monastery, is overrun with vendors, tourists (up to 10,000 a day in the summer), and martial-arts students.

Located 15km (9 miles) west of Dengfeng at the northern base of Shaoshi Shan, the monastery was built in A.D. 495 during the Northern Wei dynasty. Legend has it that the Indian monk Bodhidharma (Damo in Chinese), founder of the Chan (Zen) school of Mahayana Buddhism, retreated here in 527 after failing to convince the emperor of Liang in Nanjing of the "nothingness" of everything. With the Chan emphasis on meditation, Damo is said to have sat praying in a cave for 9 years. As an aid to, or perhaps relief from, meditation, Damo's disciples apparently developed a set of exercises based on the movements of certain animals like the praying mantis, monkey, and eagle, which eventually developed into a form of physical and spiritual combat known as Shaolin kung-fu (*gongfu*). In the Tang dynasty, Prince Li Shimin (later to be the Tang Taizong emperor) was rescued from a battle by 13 Shaolin monks. Thereafter the emperor decreed that the monastery always keep a troop of fighting monks, a practice that reached its apogee during the Ming dynasty (1368–1644), when 3,000 Shaolin monks were engaged in fighting Japanese pirates off the coast of China. The Shaolin monks' exploits, depicted in countless Hong Kong and Chinese films, have in recent years caught on with Western audiences. It's not unusual to see Western faces leaping and stomping at the more than 60 martial-arts schools around the monastery.

Pugilism aside, the temple itself has a number of religious relics and frescoes worth viewing. In the **Wenshu Dian (Wenshu Hall)**, visitors can squint through the protective glass casing at a piece of rock supposedly imprinted with Damo's shadow from all those months of meditation. On the base before you get to the final three halls, stop to take a look at the bas-reliefs. Instead of the same old dragon carvings seen at other temples, there are peaceful-looking monks in kung-fu and meditation poses. In the last hall, **Qian Fo Dian (Thousand Buddha Hall)**, is a gorgeous Ming dynasty fresco of 500 *arhats* (Buddhist disciples) worshiping Pilu, a celestial Buddha embodying wisdom and purity. About 400m (1,312 ft.) west of the temple is the impressive **Ta Lin (Forest of Stupas)** ⊛, the monastery's graveyard where 243 brick stupas built between the Tang (618–907) and Qing (1644–1911) dynasties contain the remains of notable monks. The oldest stupa, honoring Tang dynasty monk Fawan Chanshi, was built in 791 and features a simple stupa on a two-tiered brick pedestal. High on the mountain behind the forest is the **cave (Damo Dong)** where Damo was said to have meditated for 9 years.

Finish your visit with a free kung-fu show that takes place near the entrance at the **Shaolin Wushu Guan (Martial Arts Training Center)**. Shows take place every half-hour between 9:30am and noon and 2 and 6pm. Come at least 20 minutes in advance if you want a seat.

Shaolin Si. © **0371/6274-8276**. ¥100 ($13/£6.50) includes admission to the Forest of Stupas. 6:30am–6pm. To reach Shaolin Temple, see "Getting There," above, for directions.

Martial Arts Training

The **Shaolin Wushu Guan (Martial Arts Training Center; ℂ 0371/6274-9016)**, inside the main entrance near the Shaolin Monastery, has a very basic hostel for students and an inexpensive restaurant. Fees for foreigners average ¥125 ($16/£8.15) per day for classes and lodgings, or ¥60 ($7.80/£3.90) per person for a tourist group of 10 or more.

The **Shaolin Si Tagou Wushu Xuexiao (Shaolin Monastery Wushu Institute at Tagou; ℂ 0371/6274-9627;** www.shaolin-kungfu.com), just outside the monastery's main entrance, is one of the largest and oldest schools, with 20,000 students. The fee for foreigners is ¥250 ($33/£16) per day, including lodgings.

It is also possible to study at one of the many private schools in the area. A very unfriendly **CITS** (Beihuan Lu Xiduan, Guolu Dalou; ℂ **0371/6288-3442** or 0371/62872137; fax 0371/6287-3137) can arrange such study trips with students staying from a week to 6 months and longer. The office is open Monday through Friday from 8am to 6:30pm.

TAISHI SHAN

Songyue Ta (Songyue Pagoda) ⚐

Five kilometers (3 miles) northwest of town, nestled at the foot of the Taishi Shan Scenic Area (Fengjingqu) is the oldest surviving (A.D. 520) brick pagoda in China, originally part of the Songyue Temple built in 509 as an imperial palace for the Xuan Wu emperor of the Northern Wei. The Tang Gaozong emperor and empress Wu Zetian stayed at this temple every time they visited Song Shan. One of the few relics from the temple still stands today: The gracefully curving, 15-story hollow pagoda is 40m (131 ft.) tall. It features arched doorways and windows at its thick base, and increasingly narrow upper stories separated by layers of stepped brickwork. Today, the pagoda is still beautiful but not well kept, and it seems to attract more bats than humans. Motorcycle taxis run here from the nearby Songyang Academy for around ¥10 ($1.30/65p) each way.

Taishi Shan Scenic Area (Fengjing Qu). ℂ 0371/6287-2118. Admission: Taishi Shan Scenic Area ¥50 ($6.50/£3.25); Songyue Pagoda ¥20 ($2.60/£1.30). 7am–7pm.

Zhongyue Miao

Located about 5km (3 miles) east of Dengfeng on the road to Zhengzhou, this is the largest Daoist temple in Henan Province, and one of the oldest dating from before 110 B.C. Today's complex dates from the Qing dynasty (1644–1911). In the courtyard after the Chongsheng gate (Chongsheng Men) are four 3m-high (9¾-ft.) Song dynasty iron guards originally cast in 1064 with weapons in their hands, but these were supposedly sawed off during the Cultural Revolution (1966–76). Just before the central gate (Lingji Men) is a rather unusual 1604 **stele with carvings** of the five sacred Daoist mountains: Song Shan stands in the middle, Tai Shan in the east, Heng Shan Bei in the north, Heng Shan Nan in the south, and Hua Shan in the west. The temple's central hall, the impressive golden-roofed, double-eaved **Zhongyue Dadian,** resembles the Forbidden City's Taihe Gong and has a statue of the god of Song Shan.

Zhongyue Dajie. Admission ¥15 ($1.95/£1). 8am–6:30pm. Bus: no. 2.

A UNIQUE OBSERVATORY

Gaocheng Guanxing Tai ⚐

Located about 8km (5 miles) southeast of Dengfeng, this intriguing observatory is a welcome change for those who've had their fill of temples and pagodas. Built in 1276 by Guo Shoujing, a Yuan dynasty astronomer, this

10m-high (33-ft.) pyramidic brick structure is China's earliest surviving observatory. In Guo's time, a long stone beam from a runnel in the back wall was fitted with shadow markers and used to measure time and seasonal solstices.

Gaocheng Zhen. (℃) 0371/6295-0512. Admission ¥40 ($5.20/£2.60). 8am–6pm. From Dengfeng, catch any Gaocheng-bound minibus or *miandi* taxi (¥2–¥3/25¢–40¢/15p–20p) from the corner of Yangcheng Lu and Shaolin Dadao in the southeastern part of town.

WHERE TO STAY

Fengyuan Dajiudian   This three-star hotel is just west of the Tianzhong and has several wings with two grades of standard rooms. Opt for the more expensive rooms (¥388/$48/£24), which at least are larger, newer, and brighter—and the best rooms you'll find in town. The staff tries to be helpful.

Zhongyue Dajie 18. (℃) 0371/6286-5080. Fax 0371/6286-7090. 132 units. ¥388–¥588 ($50–$76/£25–£38) standard room; ¥1,388–¥1,888 ($180–$245/£90–£123) suite. 40%–60% discounts possible. AE, DC, MC, V. **Amenities:** Restaurant; bar; lounge; sauna; concierge; business center; forex; shopping arcade; salon; room service; massage; laundry. *In room:* A/C, TV.

Shaolin Guoji Dajiudian (Shaolin International Hotel)   The first hotel in this area to cater to Western tourists, this three-star property is still popular with independent travelers, but the facilities and service do not match those at the Fengyuan hotel. The hotel's redemption is that it puts you close to the temple. Rooms are comfortable enough, even though they're unremarkably decorated with standard-issue brown furniture and old carpets. Bathrooms could use a scrubbing.

Shaolin Dadao 16. (℃) 0371/6286-6188. Fax 0371/6285-6608. 60 units. ¥258–¥358 ($34–$47/£17–£23) standard room; ¥576 ($75/£37) suite. 20%–30% discounts possible. No credit cards. **Amenities:** Restaurant; bar; lounge; sauna; concierge; business center; shopping arcade; salon; room service; massage; laundry. *In room:* A/C, TV.

Zen International Hotel (﹩)   This new hotel is located inside the Shaolin Martial Arts Training Center. Here, you can search for your inner Zen in sophisticated, modern surroundings. The decor is minimalist, with rectangular furniture and monochrome shades of black, white, and gray in rooms and public spaces. Bedrooms are spacious, beds are comfortable, and the bathrooms are sparklingly clean. It's a popular destination for Russian and European tour groups. The location is ideal for having a leisurely stroll around the mountain (rather than the usual 1-day marathon to hit all the sights), and you get to see the monastery and temples at night, when they are all lit up.

500m (1,640 ft.) east to Shaolin Si, inside the Shaolin Wushu Guan (Martial Arts Training Center). (℃) 0371/6274-5666. Fax 0371/6274-5669. www.shaolinsi.gov.cn/hotel.asp. 69 units. ¥680 ($88/£44) standard room; ¥1,280 ($166/£83) suite. 40% discounts possible. No credit cards. **Amenities:** Restaurant; vegetarian hall; bar; tearoom; lounge; fax machine and safe in the lobby; high-speed Internet; room service; laundry/dry cleaning; nonsmoking rooms; executive rooms. *In room:* A/C, satellite TV, high-speed Internet access, minibar, hair dryer.

WHERE TO DINE

For the adventurous, there is a **night food market** in the evenings at the corner of Zhongyue Dajie and Caishi Jie, a block east of Song Shan Zhong Lu, where you can eat your fill of spicy kabobs, stir-fries, and the local noodles, *daoxiao mian*. The **Jinguan Mianbao Xidian Fang** on the western side of Song Shan Zhong Lu, just north of Shaolin Dadao, has a wide selection of breads and pastries and is open from 6:30am to 9:30pm. Just up the street from the bakery is the small **Xiangji Wang,** selling fried chicken. A favorite restaurant frequented by foreigners who live at Shaolin is **Siji Chun (Four Seasons)** (℃ **01390/381-1423** or 0371/6274-9987; 500m/1,625 ft. to the right after you leave the temple; open 6am–10pm). The proprietor, Mr. Chiu (aka

"Uncle Tom," as he's been dubbed by foreigners), makes delicious fresh-cut fries, sweet-and-sour chicken and fish, kung pao chicken, and potatoes and chicken. If you can't find the place, give him a call and he'll pick you up in his trishaw.

3 Luoyang

Henan Province, 322km (200 miles) E of Xi'an, 150km (93 miles) W of Zhengzhou

Situated in western Henan Province at the junction of the Grand Canal and the ancient Silk Road, Luoyang (literally "north of the river Luo") was the capital of nine dynasties from the Eastern Zhou (770–221 B.C.) to the Late Tang (923–36). Today, this industrial town with a population of 1.3 million is better known as home to the magnificent UNESCO World Heritage Site **Longmen Grottoes (Longmen Shiku)** ⭐⭐⭐, a must-see for anyone interested in Buddhist art and sculpture. A visit in April will allow you to take in Luoyang's famous **Peony Festival** as well.

ESSENTIALS

GETTING THERE   Luoyang's small airport is located about 11km (7 miles) north of the city center. There are daily **flights** from Luoyang to Beijing (1½ hr.) and Shanghai (1 hr. 30 min.). Tickets can be purchased at the **CAAC office (Minghang Shoupiao Chu; ℂ 0379/6231-0121)** on Jichang Lu just north of the railway station. **CITS** can arrange tickets and is at Jiudu Xi Lu 4, Luoyu Dasha (ℂ **0379/6432-5061**).

From the **railway station** (ℂ **0379/6256-1222**) just north of the city center on Daonan XiLu, trains run to Beijing (express train 8 hr.), Shanghai (14 hr.), Xi'an (5 hr.), Zhengzhou (1½ hr.), and Kaifeng (2½ hr.).

From the **long-distance bus station (changtu qichezhan; ℂ 0379/6323-9453)**, opposite the railway station on Jinguyuan Lu, buses run to Zhengzhou (every 30 min. 6:30am–7pm; 2–2½ hr.; ¥36/$4.70/£2.35), Kaifeng (hourly 7am–6pm; 3 hr.; ¥42/$5.45/£2.75), and Dengfeng (hourly; 1½ hr.; 6am–6pm; ¥20/$2.60/£1.30). High-end hotels can arrange comfortable **private cars** from Zhengzhou to Luoyang for around ¥1,500 ($195/£98). A better deal can be found by hiring a **city taxi** for ¥400 to ¥500 ($52–$65/£26–£33), subject to negotiation.

GETTING AROUND   Most **taxis** charge ¥5 (65¢/35p) for 3km (2 miles), then ¥1.50 (20¢/10p) per kilometer until 10km (6 miles), after which the price rises to ¥2.25 (30¢/15p) per kilometer. From 10pm to 5am, prices rise to ¥5.80 (75¢/35p) for 2km (1¼ miles), then ¥1.75 (20¢/10p) per kilometer thereafter. The bus costs ¥1 (15¢/10p). From the railway station, bus no. 81 runs to the Longmen Grottoes, bus no. 83 runs to the airport, and bus no. 11 runs to the western part of town via the Friendship Hotel.

FAST FACTS

Banks, Foreign Exchange & ATMs   The **Bank of China** (ℂ **0371/6332-0111;** open Mon–Fri 9am–noon and 1:30–5pm) is located at Zhongzhou Zhong Lu 439. Foreign exchange is available at counter 17. An ATM is located here.

Post Office   The main post office (ℂ **0371/6421-7261;** open 8am–9pm) at Zhongzhou Zhong Lu 216 has a Western Union in addition to the usual services.

Visa Extensions   Located at Tiyuchang Lu 1, the **Gonganju (PSB; ℂ 0379/ 6393-8397** or 0379/6313-3239; open Mon–Fri 8am–noon and 3–6:30pm in summer, 8am–noon and 2–5:30pm in winter) can process visa extensions in 5 business days.

SEEING THE SIGHTS
Longmen Shiku (Dragon Gate Grottoes) ★★★   Located 13km (8 miles) south

of the city center, along the banks of the Yi River (Yi He) which divides Xiang Shan to the east from Longmen Shan to the west, these caves are considered one of the three great sculptural treasure-troves in China. (The other two are the Mogao caves in Dunhuang, and the Yungang Grottoes in Datong, the precursor to Longmen.) In general, the limestone is harder at Longmen than at Yungang, and the caves closer to the river, making it easier to discern the details but more difficult to see the caves as a whole.

The first caves were carved in the Northern Wei dynasty in A.D. 493, when the Xiao Wen emperor moved his capital from Pingcheng (today's Datong) to Luoyang. Over the next 400 years, cave art and sculpture flourished, reaching their zenith during the Tang dynasty (618–907) and even continuing into the Northern Song. Benefactors of the Longmen Caves included imperial families, high-ranking officers, Buddhist leaders, and merchants as well as common folk, many of whom could only afford the smaller honeycomb niches. Today, there are 2,300 caves and niches with more than 2,800 inscriptions and over 100,000 Buddhist statues on both East Hill and West Hill. About 30% of the caves are from the Northern Wei dynasty (386–584); their statues are more elongated, static, and lacking in complexity and detail than the later Tang dynasty sculptures which account for about 60% of the caves, with their fuller figures, gentle features, and characteristic liveliness. The section of Longmen Shiku currently open to visitors is concentrated in a 1km-long (⅔ mile) stretch on the West Hill side of the Yi River. Morning is the best time to visit the Longmen Grottoes, which mainly face east and catch the light from the rising sun. Try to arrive before 8am to avoid the tour groups which usually descend on the caves around 9am. April, one of the peak tourist months, saw 300,000 visitors in 2007.

Following are the best caves of the lot, starting at the entrance and running south. Displays have rudimentary English captions, but even for the most independent traveler, this is one of those times when a guided tour is highly recommended. English-speaking guides are available for hire just inside the main entrance for ¥100 ($13/£6.50).

The entrance to the grottoes has recently been restructured so that you have to take a golf cart about 500m (1,625 ft.) from the parking lot to the main gate. A round-trip in the golf cart costs ¥4 (50¢/25p). Once you've toured the first side of the mountain, you will have to either walk across a long bridge to get to the other side, or take a boat for ¥20 ($2.60/£1.30) per person.

Binyang San Dong (Three Binyang Caves)   Work here began in the Northern Wei dynasty from 500 to 523, but the carver died in 523 after completing only the middle cave. The other two were finished later. All three were commissioned by the Xuan Wu emperor, who dedicated the middle cave to his father, the Xiao Wen emperor, the southern cave to his mother, and the northern cave to himself. The figures in the middle cave are comparatively longer and thinner than their fleshier, curvier Sui and Tang dynasty counterparts in the other two caves. Missing reliefs are now in the Metropolitan Museum of Art in New York and the Nelson-Atkins Museum of Art in Kansas City.

Wan Fo Dong (Ten Thousand Buddha Cave) ★   Finished in 680, this exquisite cave actually contains carvings of 15,000 Buddhas, mostly in small niches in the north and south walls, with the smallest Buddha measuring only 4 centimeters (1½ in.) high. Even more remarkable is the fact that this cave was commissioned by two women, an indication perhaps of the comparatively elevated status of females during empress Wu

Zetian's reign. The centerpiece of the cave is the Amitabha Buddha, whose delicate rounded features are said to be modeled on those of one of the cave's patrons.

Lianhua Dong (Lotus Flower Cave)   Carved during the Northern Wei dynasty around 527, this cave's highlight is a lotus flower, measuring 3m (10 ft.) in diameter, carved in high relief on the ceiling. Representing serenity and purity, lotus flowers are common motifs in Buddhist art. Surrounding the lotus are some faded but still fine apsarases (Buddhist flying nymphs).

Fengxian Si (Ancestor Worshiping Temple) 𝒜𝒜𝒜   Carved in the Tang dynasty between 672 and 675, this majestic cave is the largest and most beautiful at Longmen. Originally started by the Tang Gaozong emperor, it was expedited by empress Wu Zetian, an ardent Buddhist, who poured money (from her cosmetics budget, it is said) into its completion, no doubt because the central Buddha's face is thought be modeled on hers. This main Buddha, Vairocana, seated on a lotus flower, is a stunning 17m (56 ft.) tall, with a 4m-high (13-ft.) head, 1.9m-long (6-ft.) earlobes, a wide forehead, a full nose, and serene eyes, which were painted black at one time.

Flanking the Buddha are the disciple Kasyapa (the elder) to the left, and Sakyamuni's cousin, the clever disciple Ananda (the younger), to the right. Beside the disciples are two attending bodhisattvas (Buddhas who delay entry into nirvana in order to help others), Manjusri and Samantabhadra, who are decorated with exquisitely fine beads and ornamental drapes. It is said that this tableau of statues is a distilled replica of the Tang imperial court, with the dignified main Buddha representing the emperor (or empress), the obedient disciples representing the ministers, the heavenly kings standing in for the warriors and soldiers, the richly dressed bodhisattvas evoking the imperial concubines, and the flying devas (spirits) recalling palace maids.

Yaofang Dong (Medical Prescription Cave)   This small cave was first carved in the Northern Wei dynasty but appended in subsequent dynasties. The main Buddha here is a Northern Qi (550–77) creation, its fuller figure emblematic of the transition from the thin Wei figures to the fuller Tang sculptures. At the entrance are stelae carved with Chinese medicine prescriptions for 120 diseases, including diabetes and madness.

Guyang Dong   First carved during the Northern Wei sometime between 488 and 528, this is the oldest cave at Longmen, though additions were being made well into the Tang dynasty by different benefactors. Nineteen of the famous "Longmen Twenty" (20 pieces of calligraphy deemed especially fine and representative of their time) are found here. The central Buddha's head was restored during the Qing dynasty, and is said to resemble Daoist master Laozi.

Shiku Dong (Stone Room Cave)   This last of the major caves was carved in the Northern Wei between 516 and 528 and has the best worshiping scenes in Longmen. On both sides of the wall are niches with low-relief carvings of officials in high hats, court ladies in flowing robes carrying single lotus flowers, and servants carrying sheltering canopies, all in a procession to honor Buddha.

Luolong Lu. Admission ¥80 ($10/£5.20). Mar 1–Oct 7 7am–6:30pm; Oct 8–Nov 30 7am–5:30pm; Dec–Jan 7:30am–5pm; Feb 7:30am–5:30pm. Bus: no. 53, 60 (from the western part of town opposite the Friendship Hotel), or 81 (from the railway station) runs to the caves (35–45 min.; ¥1.50/20¢/10p). Taxi about ¥30 ($3.90/£1.95).

OTHER ATTRACTIONS

Baima Si (White Horse Temple)   It is more than likely that earlier Buddhist temples were built along the Silk Routes in what is today's Xinjiang (the path by which Buddhism entered China), but this is widely held to be the first officially sanctioned

Buddhist temple built in China proper. Located 13km (7 miles) to the east of Luoyang, this temple was built by the Eastern Han Ming Di emperor (reigned A.D. 58–76) to honor and house two Indian monks who, the story goes, came from India bearing Buddhist scriptures on two white horses. Two stone horses (likely from the Song dynasty) stand guard outside the gate to today's temple, mostly a Ming construction. Just inside the main entrance in the southeastern and southwestern corners of the complex are the tombs of the two Indian monks. In the impressive Yuan dynasty Daxiong Dian (Great Hall), there are 18 arhats (disciples) of ramie cloth.

Baima Si Lu. Admission ¥35 ($4.55/£2.30). 7:30am–7pm. Bus: no. 56 (from Xigua stop on Zhongzhou Zhong Lu).

Gumu Bowuguan (Ancient Han Tombs) ⟨★⟩ This fascinating museum features 25 reconstructed underground ancient tombs dating from the Western Han dynasty (206 B.C.–A.D. 9) to the Northern Song dynasty (960–1127). By the Eastern Han dynasty (25–220), the use of hollow bricks with painted designs gave way to larger stone vault tombs made of solid carved brick. Eleven of the tombs also have elaborate wall murals, the most famous of which is the Western Han "Expelling the Ghost Mural Tomb," which features a faded but still gorgeous fresco of celebrants holding a feast before the exorcism. The tombs are about 10km (6 miles) north of town on the road to the airport.

Jichang Lu. Admission ¥20 ($2.60/£1.30). 8am–6pm. Bus: no. 83 (Gumu Bowuguan stop).

Luoyang Bowuguan (Luoyang Museum) Standouts in this museum of local relics include a section dedicated to the Xia (2200–1700 B.C.) and Shang dynasties (1700–1100 B.C.), with an emphasis on items excavated at Erlitou (an important Shang site 30km/18 miles east of Luoyang), including jade, bronzes, and pottery artifacts; Han dynasty exhibits of painted pottery and tomb frescoes; and some fine Tang dynasty glazed pottery.

Zhongzhou Zhong Lu 298. Admission ¥20 ($2.60/£1.30). 8am–5pm. Bus: no. 4, 11, or 50.

Wangcheng Gongyuan Every April during the Luoyang Peony Festival (Apr 15–25), this park, built on the former site of a Zhou dynasty city, Wangcheng, is awash in a riot of colors: red, white, black, yellow, purple, pink, blue, green, and every shade in between. Luoyang produces the best peonies China has to offer, so don't miss paying a visit if you're in town then. For an extra ¥5 (60¢/30p) you can visit the zoo. The zoo and gardens, which open at the crack of dawn, are perfect for early risers.

Zhongzhou Zhong Lu. Admission ¥5 (65¢/35p). 5am–8:30pm. Bus: no. 2, 4, 101, 102, or 103.

WHERE TO STAY

Luoyang has several low-quality four-star-rated hotels with reasonable prices. Most hotels regularly give 20% to 30% discounts unless otherwise noted. There is usually a 5% city tax but no additional service charge. If you're going to be in town for the Peony Festival, book a room in advance.

EXPENSIVE

Huayang Guangchang Guoji Dajiudian (Huayang Plaza Hotel) ⟨★⟩ This white behemoth, which opened in 2005, looks more like a casino than a hotel. Thankfully, the tackiness of the exterior does not come indoors; guest rooms are classy with tasteful headboards, plush and comfy beds, and subtle lighting fixtures. They're the finest you'll find in town. Bathrooms can be a bit cramped but they're sparkling clean and modern. Some guests to the new hotel complain that service is a bit shaky.

Kaixuan Xi Lu 88. ⓒ 0379/6558-8123. Fax 0379/6488-4777. 530 units. ¥700–¥1,280 ($91–$166/£46–£83) standard room; ¥1,380–¥2,400 ($179–$312/£90–£156) suite. 20%–35% discounts possible. AE, DC, MC, V. **Amenities:** 2 restaurants; bar; lounge; indoor pool; health club; sauna; concierge; tour desk; business center; forex; laundry/dry cleaning. *In room:* A/C, satellite TV, minibar, hair dryer, safe.

MODERATE

Mudan Cheng Binguan (Peony Plaza) ⍟
This four-star hotel offers some of the flashiest and most modern accommodations in town. A wall of smoked blue glass on the outside, the 28-story tower has a revolving rooftop restaurant and a wide range of facilities. Guest rooms are cozy enough but the furniture is showing wear. Bathrooms are a good size and come with scales. Service is not quite up to four-star international standards but is adequate. A Western buffet breakfast is served.

Nancang Lu 2. ⓒ 0379/6468-1111. Fax 0379/6493-0303. 190 units. ¥680 ($88/£44) standard room; ¥1,280 ($166/£83) suite. 40% discounts possible. AE, DC, MC, V. **Amenities:** 3 restaurants; bar; lounge; indoor pool; health club; sauna; concierge; business center; forex; shopping arcade; salon; room service; laundry/dry cleaning. *In room:* A/C, satellite TV, minibar.

Xin Youyi Binguan (New Friendship Hotel)
Located in the western part of town, this three-star annex to the old Friendship Hotel, renovated in 2000, has pleasant, modern rooms. Units come with the usual nondescript brown furniture but beds are comfortable. Bathrooms are small but clean. The hotel also has a Western restaurant, part of its entertainment center that includes a pool table, coffee bar, and shuffleboard.

Xiyuan Xi Lu 6. ⓒ 0379/6468-6666. Fax 0379/6491-2328. 120 units. ¥358–¥458 ($47–$60/£23–£30) standard room; ¥700–¥1,500 ($91–$195/£46–£98) suite. 20% discounts possible. AE, DC, MC, V. **Amenities:** 2 restaurants; bar; lounge; sauna; concierge; business center; forex; shopping arcade; salon; room service; laundry. *In room:* A/C, satellite TV, fridge.

INEXPENSIVE

Mingyuan Dajiudian (Mingyuan Hotel) ⟨Value⟩
Not far from the railway station, this hotel, which is affiliated with Hostelling International, gets a fare share of greasy-haired foreign backpackers. The rooms, which are characterless but totally adequate, are a better bargain than the dorm beds, which come with an attached bathroom. Bathrooms, though somewhat worn, are acceptably clean. The karaoke on the lower floors of the building may give the place a slightly dodgy feel.

Jiefang Lu 20. ⓒ 0379/6319-0378. Fax 0379/6319-1269. 80 units. ¥50 ($6.50/£3.25) dorm bed; ¥218 ($28/£14) standard room. No credit cards. **Amenities:** Restaurant; sauna; karaoke. *In room:* A/C, TV.

WHERE TO DINE

For Western food, hotel dining offers the most reliable fare. The Luoyang Peony Hotel (Luoyang Mudan Dajiudian) at Zhongzhou Xi Lu 15 (ⓒ **0379/6462-0000**) has a Western dining room that serves fish and chips, pizzas, and lamb chops for dinner at ¥18 to ¥88 ($2.35–$11/£1.20–£5.70) per entree. There's a **KFC** at Zhongzhou Zhong Lu 251 and a **McDonald's** at the Shanghai Shichang Buxing Jie (pedestrian street).

MODERATE

Lao Luoyang Mianguan (Old Luoyang Noodle House) ⍟ HENAN
Bright, unpretentious, and packed with locals, this a fantastic place for a casual meal. Order the *zhajiangmian* (noodles with bean sauce) and the *tangcu liji* (sweet-and-sour fish). The place is tastefully decorated with simple Ming-dynasty-style chairs.

On Changchun Xi Lu, near the corner of Jinghua Lu (no number). ⓒ 0379/6531-5535 or 1393-790-0607. Meal for 2 ¥60 ($7.80/£3.90). No credit cards. 11am–2:30pm and 6–9pm.

Zhen Bu Tong ☆ LUOYANG   The specialty at this popular restaurant housed in a huge five-story Chinese-style building is the famous *Luoyang Shuixi* (Water Banquet), consisting of 8 cold and 16 hot dishes variously cooked in broth, soup, or juice (examples include *zhenyancai*, a soup made of ham, radish, mushrooms, and eggs; and *mizhi tudou*, sweet-potato fries in syrup). The full complement of dishes, designed for a table of 10 people, costs ¥500 ($65/£33) and up, but happily, the first-floor dining hall offers more reasonably sized four- or five-dish minibanquets. The staff is a little surly, but this is a unique local dining experience that shouldn't be missed.

Zhongzhou Dong Lu 369. ☎ 0379/6395-2338. Reservations recommended. Meal for 2 ¥40–¥80 ($5.20–$10/ £2.60–£5.20). AE, DC, MC, V. 10am–9pm.

4 Kaifeng ☆

Henan Province, 70km (43 miles) E of Zhengzhou

Located in central Henan Province, just 9km (6 miles) south of the Yellow River (Huang He), Kaifeng has a history lasting more than 2,700 years as the capital of seven dynasties. Its heyday was during the Northern Song, when it was known as East Capital (Dongjing), the most prosperous city in the world, with a population of 1.5 million. Kaifeng is also believed to be the first place the Jews settled when they arrived in China. Having survived fire, earthquake, and flooding from the Yellow River, Kaifeng today is a sleepy but charming town not yet overtaken by massive development, though the government's efforts to capitalize on tourism are kicking into high gear.

ESSENTIALS

GETTING THERE   The nearest major **airport** (☎ 0371/6851-9955) is at Zhengzhou. Frequent **trains** serve Kaifeng from Zhengzhou (40 min.), Xi'an (5 daily; 6 hr.), and Shanghai (6 daily; 11 hr.). Kaifeng's railway station is in the south part of town.

   Buses run to Zhengzhou (every 20 min. 6am–7pm; 1 hr. 20 min.; ¥17/$2.20/ £1.10) from the **Keyun Xi Zhan (West Bus Station)** on Yingbin Lu; but as this bus station seems to have some unscrupulous and dodgy drivers, go to the **long-distance bus station (Qiche Zhongxin Zhan)** across from the railway station. Private **taxi** rental between Zhengzhou and Kaifeng costs around ¥300 ($39/£20) round-trip.

GETTING AROUND   Taxis cost ¥5 (65¢/35p) for 3km (2 miles), then ¥1 (15¢/ 10p) per kilometer. Between 11pm and 6am, the rate increases to ¥5.60 (75¢/35p) for 3km (2 miles), then ¥1.20 (15¢/10p) per kilometer. All **buses** cost ¥1 (15¢/10p) per ride. **Tricycle taxis** cost ¥2 (25¢/15p) for most places within the city walls.

   Bus no. 1 runs from the railway station through the center of town to the Dragon Pavilion and Iron Pagoda. Bus no. 15 connects Po Pagoda in the southeast to the Dragon Pavilion in the northwest. Kaifeng is also an easy city to get around by **bike,** which you can rent at a small stand just north of the CITS office on Yingbin Lu for ¥10 ($1.30/65p) per day (¥100/$13/£6.50 deposit).

VISITOR INFORMATION   Kaifeng's **Tourism Bureau (Luyouju;** ☎ 0378/398-8488) can answer basic questions about accommodations and sights. For information on Kaifeng's Jewish history or to see the Jewish stelae in the museum, contact **CITS** (Yingbin Lu 98; ☎ 0378/393-9032), actually a subsidiary of the Tourism Bureau. **Tourism Complaints** can be reported by calling ☎ 0378/397-2220.

FAST FACTS

Banks, Foreign Exchange & ATMs There's a **Bank of China** (open Mar–May and Sept–Nov 8am–6pm; Dec–Feb 8am–5pm; June–Aug 8am–6:30pm), equipped with ATMs, at Zhongshan Lu 32.

Post Office The main post office (open 8am–6:30pm) is at Ziyou Lu 33.

Visa Extensions The **PSB** is at Zhongshan Lu Zhongduan 86 (ⓒ **0378/315-5561;** Mon–Thurs 8:30am–noon and 3–6pm, Fri 8:30am–noon).

EXPLORING KAIFENG

Da Xiangguo Si Originally built in A.D. 555, this temple, one of China's more famous Buddhist shrines, had its heyday during the Song dynasty (960–1279), when there were 64 Sutra Halls on the premises. Destroyed in the flood of 1642 and rebuilt in 1766, the temple's main attraction is the magnificent four-sided statue of Avalokitesvara (the male Indian bodhisattva who became transfigured over the years into the female Guanyin), with 1,000 hands and 1,000 eyes (all-seeing and compassionate), who stands surrounded by 500 arhats. Weighing 2,000 kilograms (2¼ tons), the 7m-high (23-ft.) statue was said to have been carved from the trunk of a 1,000-year-old ginkgo tree and required 58 years to complete.

Ziyou Lu 54. ⓒ **0378/566-5090.** Admission ¥30 ($3.90/£1.95). 8am–6:30pm. Bus: no. 5, 9, or 15.

Kaifeng Bowuguan (Kaifeng Museum) Located just south of Lord Bao Lake (Bao Gong Hu), this rather dilapidated and neglected museum is ordinarily not worth visiting, but the fourth floor houses three stone tablets that record early Jewish history in Kaifeng. In order to see the stelae, you should contact CITS (Yingbin Lu 98; ⓒ **0378/393-9032**) a day or two in advance to get permission to see the tablets (¥40/$5/£2.50 per person). At press time, the museum was undergoing renovations. It should be open by the time you read this, but check with your concierge or call ahead before visiting.

Yingbin Lu 26. ⓒ **0378/396-6049.** Admission ¥10 ($1.30/65p). Tues–Sun 8:30–11:30am and 3–6pm. Bus: no. 1, 7, 9, 12, or 16.

Long Ting Gongyuan (Dragon Pavilion Park) This park sits on the site of the former imperial palaces of six dynasties from the time of the Later Liang dynasty (907–23) through part of the Jin dynasty (1115–1234). The park's entrance is at the northern end of **Songdu Yujie (Imperial Street of the Song Dynasty),** once exclusively reserved for use by the emperor, imperial family, and aristocrats. Inside the park's main entrance, the imperial way continues past two lakes, Panjia Hu to the east and Yangjia Hu to the west, and ends at the foot of Long Ting (Dragon Pavilion), reconstructed in 1692 for worship of the emperor. Seventy-two steep steps to the top reward you with views of Kaifeng.

Zhongshan Lu Beiduan. ⓒ **0378/566-0142.** Admission ¥35 ($4.55/£2.30). 7am–7pm. Bus: no. 1, 15, or 20.

Po Ta (Po Pagoda) 🙀 Tucked away in a maze of alleys in the southeastern corner of town, this hexagonal pagoda, the oldest standing building in Kaifeng, was originally built in 974 with nine floors. The 37m-tall (121-ft.), three-story Ming dynasty pagoda is covered both inside and out with gray brick tiles, each meticulously carved with a Buddha image. There are 108 such images, including those of Sakyamuni, Amitabha, and various bodhisattvas and apsarases. Hiring a taxi is the easiest way to reach the pagoda.

Po Ta Xi Jie 30. Admission ¥10 ($1.30/65p). 8am–5:30pm. Bus: no. 15 (ask to be dropped off at Po Ta Xi Jie, then follow the red arrows on the walls).

Kaifeng

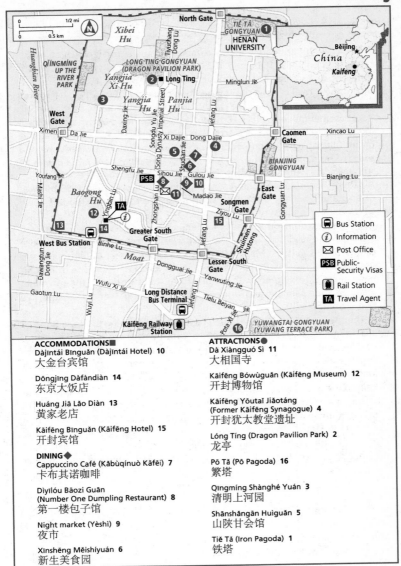

ACCOMMODATIONS ■

Dàjīntái Bīnguǎn (Dàjīntái Hotel) **10**
大金台宾馆

Dōngjīng Dàfàndiàn **14**
东京大饭店

Huáng Jiā Lǎo Diàn **13**
黄家老店

Kāifēng Bīnguǎn (Kāifēng Hotel) **15**
开封宾馆

DINING ◆

Cappuccino Café (Kǎbùqínuò Kāfēi) **7**
卡布其诺咖啡

Dìyīlóu Bāozi Guǎn
(Number One Dumpling Restaurant) **8**
第一楼包子馆

Night market (Yèshì) **9**
夜市

Xīnshēng Měishíyuán **6**
新生美食园

ATTRACTIONS ●

Dà Xiàngguó Sì **11**
大相国寺

Kāifēng Bówùguǎn (Kāifēng Museum) **12**
开封博物馆

Kāifēng Yóutài Jiàotáng
(Former Kāifēng Synagogue) **4**
开封犹太教堂遗址

Lóng Tíng (Dragon Pavilion Park) **2**
龙亭

Pó Tǎ (Pó Pagoda) **16**
繁塔

Qīngmíng Shànghé Yuán **3**
清明上河园

Shānshǎngān Huìguǎn **5**
山陕甘会馆

Tiě Tǎ (Iron Pagoda) **1**
铁塔

Kaifeng's Jews

The origins of Kaifeng's Jewish community are a mystery. Three stone tablets (dated 1489, 1663, and 1679) from Kaifeng's old synagogue record different dates of arrival. Although inscriptions on the 1663 stele points record the arrival of Jews during the Zhou dynasty (1100–221 B.C.), it is now more widely accepted that the early Jews likely came from Persia via the Silk Routes sometime in the late 10th century during the Song dynasty. According to the 1489 stele, the first arrivals were traders who were invited to stay on in Kaifeng by the Song emperor, who also bestowed his surname and those of his six ministers on the Jews who were said to have arrived with 73 surnames, and who subsequently took on the Chinese surnames of Zhao, Li, Ai, Zhang, Gao, Jin, and Shi. A synagogue was established in 1163 but was often rebuilt, usually after natural disasters like the Great Flood of 1642, which damaged much of the town.

By most accounts, the Jews in Kaifeng did not retain any contacts with other Jews outside of China. The first Western report of their existence came from Jesuit priest Matteo Ricci in 1605 when he met Ai Tian, a Kaifeng Jew who had come to Beijing seeking office. Ricci later sent one of his Chinese converts to Kaifeng, who confirmed Ai Tian's story that the town had many Israelite families and a magnificent synagogue containing the five books of Moses.

The Jewish community continued to worship in Kaifeng until the flood of 1852 again destroyed their synagogue, which was never rebuilt after that. Evidence indicates that the remaining Jews became completely assimilated. Today, with renewed interest in the Jews of Kaifeng, there are a few self-identified Chinese Jews making themselves known again, the most notable being Zhang Xingwang, who has been working with the Kaifeng Museum to preserve the history of Kaifeng's Jews. He can be contacted through CITS or the Kaifeng Tourism Bureau (Luyouju; (C) 0378/398-9388, ext. 6507). In the United States, information about Kaifeng's Jewish heritage, sometimes including special-interest tours, is available through the Sino-Judaic Institute, 232 Lexington Dr., Menlo Park, CA 94205 (www.sino-judaic.com).

Qingming Shanghe Yuan (Kids) Just west of the Long Ting Gongyuan, this manufactured theme park is modeled after painter and poet Zhang Zeduan's famous 12th-century scroll painting *Qingming Shanghe Yuan* (Festival of Pure Brightness on the River)—now hanging in the Forbidden City in Beijing—that depicts Kaifeng at its height. The park contains reconstructed traditional restaurants, shops, and bridges, and hosts performances by dancers and musicians who reenact Song dynasty rituals. An exciting show for the little ones is an action-filled reenactment of a battle between two old wooden ships held at the north end of the park. The kids can also try their hand at operating traditional flour mills or take a ride on horse- or camel-drawn carriages. Young women demonstrating traditional embroidery emulate skilled artisans in the imperial workshops who embroidered the emperor's robes using silk threads that were one-fifth the thickness of today's threads, and pulled by needles as thin as human hairs.

The highlight of the park for interested Western visitors is the **Jewish Cultural Exhibit Center (Youtai Wenhua Zhanlanguan)**, located in the western part of the park behind the Wang Yuanwai Jia building. The history of Jews in the city (see "Kaifeng's Jews," below) is documented in four rooms, with exhibits on early Jewish life in the city, as well as photographs of Jewish graves and synagogues that once stood in Kaifeng. If you're here when the center is closed, check with the Tourist Service Center just before the park's main entrance. The eager-to-please staff will often open up the Jewish Center for inquiring Western guests. For ¥5 (65¢/35p) with a ¥20 ($2.60/£1.30) deposit, the Tourist Service Center also provides an occasionally clumsy but nevertheless helpful audio tour of the park in English.

Long Ting Xi Lu 5. ℂ 0378/566-3633. Admission ¥80 ($10/£5.20); 8:30am–9pm. Dec–Feb ¥40 ($5.20/£2.60); 8:30am–8pm (last ticket sold at 6pm). Jewish Cultural Center 9am–6:30pm. Bus: no. 1, 15, or 20.

Shanshangan Huiguan ⟨★⟩   This magnificent guild hall was built during the reign of the Qianlong emperor (1736–96) by businessmen from the three provinces of Shanxi, Shaanxi and, later, Gansu, who were living in Kaifeng. All the buildings, from the stage, bell tower, and drum tower, to the double-eaved, three-gate archway and the Main Hall, are decorated with overwhelmingly vivid and exquisite wood, brick, and stone carvings.

Xufu Jie 85. Admission ¥20 ($2.60/£1.30). 8am–6pm. Bus: no. 1 or 14.

Tie Ta (Iron Pagoda) ⟨★⟩   Kaifeng's most famous landmark is located in the northeast corner of town. This beautiful 11th-century pagoda is actually a brick structure whose facade of glazed brown tiles gives the impression of cast iron. Originally built in 1049, the building has survived earthquakes, fires, and the great flood of 1642, which buried the base under several meters of silt. The 13-story, 55m-tall (180-ft.) octagonal structure has brick panels featuring exquisite designs of apsarases, *qilin* (Chinese unicorns), dragons, and flowers. For another ¥10 ($1.25/60p), you can climb the 168 steps to the top, though the experience can be a bit claustrophobic.

Jiefang Lu 175. ℂ 0378/282-6629. Admission ¥20 ($2.60/£1.30). 7am–7pm. Bus: no. 1 or 3.

WHERE TO STAY

Dajintai Binguan (Dajintai Hotel) ⟨Value⟩   This guesthouse's location and price make it a standout. Located next to the night market, the rooms are nothing special, just standard two-star fare, but you'll be saving a few bucks by opting to stay here over competitors. Bathrooms are very clean, and the tile floors in the rooms sparkle. Rooms facing the street may be noisy, especially at night when the market kicks into full gear.

Gu Lou Jie 23. ℂ 0378/255-2888. Fax 0378/595-9932. 113 units. ¥130–¥160 ($17–$21/£8.45–£10) standard room. 25% discounts. No credit cards. **Amenities:** Restaurant; tour desk. *In room:* A/C, TV.

Dongjing Dafandian   Located across from the West Bus Station, this sprawling hotel's lily pond and pavilions are charming, but the guest rooms are rather characterless, and bathrooms could be a bit cleaner. The staff doesn't speak much English but tries to be helpful. Rooms in the VIP building (presumably for such folk as former president Jiang Zemin, who is said to have stayed here) are gaudily decorated and overpriced—you're better off staying the recently renovated building 4.

Yingbin Lu 99. ℂ 0378/398-9388. Fax 0378/393-8861. 221 units. ¥120–¥800 ($16–$104/£7.80–£52) standard room. MC, V. **Amenities:** 2 restaurants; bar; lounge; indoor pool; health club; sauna; concierge; tour desk; business center; forex; shopping arcade; salon; room service; laundry/dry cleaning. *In room:* A/C, TV, fridge.

Kaifeng Binguan (Kaifeng Hotel) ⊕   This is hands-down the best choice in town. Situated in a courtyard with a variety of rooms to fit different budgets, this hotel offers a charming environment and friendly service. The building in the center of the courtyard was a Buddhist nunnery in the early 20th century and is now a protected landmark; the rooms in this building are nice, though a bit gaudy in style. The hotel's best rooms are in the slightly less historic building 5, each room recently remodeled and outfitted with sleek white armchairs and modern beds. The bathrooms are sparkling clean and feature massaging shower heads. There are no nonsmoking rooms, so some units have a very strong cigarette smell; you may want to see/smell your room beforehand. The hotel was undergoing a renovation at press time, but it should be done by the time you read this.

Ziyou Lu 66. ⓒ **0378/595-5589.** Fax 0378/595-3086. 187 plus units. ¥260–¥468 ($34–$61/£17–£30) standard room; ¥560–¥2,680 ($73–$348/£36–£174) suite. AE, DC, MC, V. **Amenities:** Restaurant; concierge; business center; bike rental; laundry. *In room:* A/C, TV, high-speed Internet access.

WHERE TO DINE

Hotels catering to foreigners all have Chinese restaurants that offer decent if forgettable fare, with a meal for two averaging ¥40 to ¥80 ($5.20–$10/£2.60–£5.20). Locals agree that the city's best *xiaolong bao,* small dumplings filled with pork and a hint of broth, is at the humble **Huang Jia Lao Dian** (Binhe Lu 1; ⓒ **0378/397-2768**). For the meat-adverse, try the *su baozi,* stuffed with vermicelli noodles, egg, carrots, mushrooms, and spring onions. A lot of tourists get sent to **Diyilou Baozi Guan (Number One Dumpling Restaurant)** at Sihou Jie 8 (ⓒ **0378/599-8655;** open 10:30am–9pm), another local institution specializing in dumplings and buns. A bit farther to the east at Gu Lou Jie 66 is the informal diner **Xinsheng Meishiyuan** (ⓒ **0378/ 597-9191;** open 11:15am–2:30pm and 6:15–9pm), which offers a wide variety of noodles, kabobs, stir-fries, pastries, and snacks. There is no English menu, but purchase your meal tickets for ¥10 ($1.30/65p) and up, then go around to the different stalls and order. For decent coffee, Western meals, and an eclectic variety of Asian fare head to **Cappuccino Cafe (Kabuqinuo Xicanting)** ⊕ (Gu Lou Jie 65; ⓒ **0378/ 597-3666;** 9am–2am; no credit cards), located near Dajintai Hotel. The cafe offers an English menu, friendly service, and live music nightly, delivered from a white grand piano in the center of the restaurant. Try the black pepper steak/fried rice, served on a hot iron plate. The Dongjing Hotel also has a **fast-food eatery** out front that offers convenient and inexpensive dining for ¥4 to ¥8 (50¢–$1.05/25p–50p) per person. Just point to choose from the many buffet dishes.

For the more adventurous, the **night market** ⊕ which starts around 7pm on Sihou Jie and closes early in the morning, offers delicious local snacks such as *wuxiang shaobing* (five-spice roasted bread) and *zhima duowei tang* (sesame soup). The shish kabobs, especially the *yangrou chuan* (spicy lamb kabob), are especially tasty. The market is located on a street filled with charming old architecture in a variety of styles, which makes for a pleasant stroll even if you're not hungry.

SHOPPING

Songdu Yujie (Imperial Street of the Song Dynasty) is lined with shops that sell souvenirs, embroidery, silk screen paintings, calligraphy, paintings, seals, and ink stones. A new touristy shopping district called Gudai Wenhua Qu (Gudai Culture Area) should be open by the time you get here. For specialty snacks from Henan, visit the **Kaifeng Tutechan Shichang** (open 8:30am–9pm), on Long Ting Xi Lu, near

Songdu Yujie. Goodies include *huasheng gao* (peanut cake) and *xingren cha* (almond tea), which is more like a gelatin than a tea.

5 Ji'nan

Shandong Province, 497km (308 miles) S of Beijing

With few tourist attractions, the capital of Shandong Province is a major rail and air junction that's best used as a base for exploring more worthwhile attractions in nearby towns such as Tai'an, Qufu, and Zibo.

ESSENTIALS

GETTING THERE Ji'nan is connected by **air** to many Chinese cities, including Beijing (1 hr.), Shanghai (1½ hr.), Xi'an (1½ hr.), Guangzhou (2½ hr.), Chongqing (2 hr.), Zhengzhou (1 hr.), and Hong Kong (2½ hr.). CAAC buses (1 hr.; ¥20/$2.60/£1.30) depart for the Yao Qiang Airport 40km (25 miles) to the east from Yu Quan Sen Xu Xin Hotel at Luoyuan Dajie 68 every hour from 6:10am to 6:10pm. Buses also meet incoming flights (last bus at 10pm) and end their run at the same hotel. Plane tickets can be purchased at the **CAAC office** (© **0531/8602-2338**) from 8:30am to 5:30pm. **China Eastern Airlines** is at Jingshi Lu 408 (© **0531/8796-4445**; open 8:30am–5pm).

From Ji'nan's main **railway station** (© **0531/8242-8862**) in the west of town, trains run to Beijing (16 trains daily, 4½–7 hr.), Shanghai (6 trains daily, 9–14 hr.), Tai'an (1 hr.), Yanzhou (2 hr.), Qufu (3 hr.), Zibo (1 hr.), Weifang (2½ hr.), Qingdao (5 hr., 2½ hr. on the new superfast D series trains, D605/D607/D609/D611/D613), and Xi'an (19 hr.). Train tickets can be bought 5 days in advance at the railway station.

From the **long-distance bus station** (*changtu qichezhan;* © **0531/96369**) in the northern part of town, buses depart for Tai'an (every 30 min. 6:10am–6:40pm; 1–1½ hr.; ¥17–¥22/$2.20–£1.10, different types of buses), Qufu (every hour 7am–5:50pm; 1½–2 hr.; ¥35/$4.55/£2.30), Qingdao (various times; 6:50am–7pm; 5 hr.; ¥70–¥99/$9.10–$13/£4.55–£6.45), Zibo (every 30 min. 6:10am–6:40pm; 1 hr. 40 min.; ¥24–¥32/$3.10–$4.15/£1.55–£2.10), and Weifang (every 40 min. 7am–6pm; 3 hr.; ¥43–¥55/$5.60–$7.15/£2.80–£3.60).

GETTING AROUND Most **taxis** charge ¥7.50 ($1/50p) for 3km (2 miles), then ¥1.50 (20¢/10p) per kilometer until 5.5km (3½ miles), after which the price rises to ¥2 (25¢/15p) per kilometer. From 10pm to 5am, the rates increase very marginally.

TOURS The **China Shandong Travel Service (Zhongguo Shandong Luxingshe)** at Lishan Lu 185 (© **0531/8260-8108**) can arrange customized tours of other Shandong destinations like Tai Shan, Qufu, Weifang, and Zibo.

FAST FACTS

Banks, Foreign Exchange & ATMs The **Bank of China** at Luoyuan Dajie 22 (Mon–Fri 9am–5pm) is open for foreign exchange.

Post Office The main post office (open May–Sept 8am–7:30pm and Oct–Apr 8am–7pm) is in the old part of town at Jing Er Lu 162 (corner of Weier Lu).

Visa Extensions The local **PSB** is in the old part of town at Jing San Lu 145 just east of Wei Wu Lu (© **0531/8508-2461;** open Mon–Fri 8–11:30am and 2–5:45pm). The surly staff at counters 2 and 3 can process visa extensions; allow 5 business days.

EXPLORING JI'NAN

Ji'nan is known for its 72 famous **springs** around town, which are really only worth visiting during the rainy season (July–Aug) when water levels are actually high enough to produce any activity. The most famous and also the first of the 72 springs is **Baotu Quan (Baotu Spring),** located in the center of town at Baotu Quan Nan Lu 1; admission is ¥15 ($1.95/£1) in the evening and ¥20 ($2.60/£1.30) during the daytime. The Qing Qianlong emperor drank from the spring waters and declared it the "First Spring Under Heaven" *(Tianxia Diyi Quan).* The park is open from 7am to 10pm. The best time to visit it is in the evenings, under a starlit sky. You can enjoy tea in the pavilion by the spring.

More interesting is a walk around the western part of town near the railway station. This area was the **old German Concession,** which came into being when Ji'nan was opened to foreign trade in 1906. There are still a number of German-style buildings around, but you'll have to look for them under webs of telephone poles and wires, and years of grime and soot.

Da Ming Hu Gong Yuan (Da Ming Hu Park) Located in the heart of town, this lake park, popular with locals, is situated by springs. The park is most famous for its lotus flowers, which are best viewed during the Lotus Festival (July–Aug). There's a memorial for the female poet Li Qingzhao, who romanticized the park's flowers 800 years ago in her poems. A sightseeing cable car whisks you to the top of hill in 13 minutes and costs ¥10 ($1.30/65p).

Minghu Lu, Li Xia District. Admission ¥15 ($1.95/£1) or ¥20 ($2.60/£1.30) (includes visit to skippable stone museum). Winter 6:30am–5:30pm; rest of year 6:30am–6:30pm. Bus: no. 41 or 66.

WHERE TO STAY

Nearly all rooms in Ji'nan come with free high-speed Internet access, either in room or in the hotel's business center. Inquire at check-in.

EXPENSIVE

Crowne Plaza Guihe Ji'nan (Guihe Huangguan Jiudian) ★★ This handsome structure with thick Western-style columns and arches sits atop six floors of the Guihe Shopping Center and offices. Arranged around a square atrium coffee shop, rooms are large and beautifully appointed, with full amenities. Marble bathrooms are brightly lit and spacious, and come with separate tub and shower. The only flaw seems to be that some of the bathrooms are already showing cracks. Service is efficient.

Tianditan Lu 3. ⓒ **0531/8602-9999.** Fax 0531/8602-3333. www.sixcontinentshotels.com. 306 units. ¥1,250 ($163/ £81) standard room; from ¥1,703 ($221/£111) and way up suite. 40%–60% discounts online. AE, DC, MC, V. **Amenities:** 4 restaurants; bar; lounge; indoor pool; health club; sauna; concierge; airport shuttle service; business center; forex; shopping arcade; salon; room service; massage; babysitting; same-day laundry/dry cleaning; nonsmoking rooms; executive rooms; rooms for those w/limited mobility. *In room:* A/C, satellite TV, high-speed Internet access, minibar, hair dryer, safe.

Longdu International Hotel (Longdu Guoji Fandian) This is a five-star hotel, Chinese-style. That means the public areas are very chintzy (think wall murals of miscellaneous Renaissance scenes) and over-the-top. The rooms, however, are pretty tasteful. Cream-colored carpets cover the floors, and beds have cozy white duvets and maroon bed skirts. Walls are done in two-tone, pale yellow stripes and it's all fairly warm and inviting, which is not the impression you get when you walk into the glitzy hotel lobby. Bathrooms are a reasonable size, with bathtubs and standard amenities. Staff is helpful, but service in English is a challenge. The rack rates at this hotel are sky high, but discounts are very common (my room was 65% off), and it's very likely you'll get it for much cheaper than either of the other five-star hotels listed here.

Beiyuan Dajie 421. © 0531/8591-8888. Fax 0531/8591-6868. www.cnlongdu.com. 142 units. ¥888–¥988 ($115–$128/£58–£64) standard room; ¥1,688–¥8,888 ($219–$1,155/£110–£578) suite. Discounts up to 40%–65%. AE, DC, MC, V. **Amenities:** 2 restaurants; bar; karaoke bar; indoor pool; health club; sauna; concierge; business center; forex; salon; laundry/dry cleaning; nonsmoking rooms. *In room:* A/C, TV, high-speed Internet access, room service.

Sofitel Silver Plaza Ji'nan (Suofeite Yinzuo Dafandian) ★★ Until the arrival
of the Crowne Plaza, this was *the* hotel at which to stay, and it continues to attract a large percentage of the foreign market with its good service and luxurious facilities. In the center of town, this modern 49-story edifice incorporates classical European elements in its decor, from chandeliers and thick columns in the lobby to traditional furniture in the rooms. Guest rooms are spacious and offer impeccable luxury and comfort, high above Ji'nan. The marble bathrooms, which come with separate tub and shower, are on the small side. The hotel is a tightly run operation with friendly and obliging staff.

Luoyuan Dajie 66. © 0531/8606-8888. Fax 0531/8606-6666. www.accorhotels.com/asia. 326 units. ¥1,725 ($224/£112) standard room; ¥2,415 ($314/£157) suite. Discounts up to 40%–60%. AE, DC, MC, V. **Amenities:** 6 restaurants; bar; lounge; nightclub; indoor pool; health club; sauna; concierge; airport shuttle service; business center; forex; shopping arcade; salon; room service; massage; laundry/dry cleaning; nonsmoking rooms; executive rooms. *In room:* A/C, satellite TV, high-speed Internet access, minibar, hair dryer, safe.

MODERATE
Qilu Binguan ★ Located in the southern part of town, this four-star outfit is rather
bland and tired on the outside, but the lobby, decorated in dark woods, is quite elegant. Guest rooms are average, aged with faded pink carpets, but otherwise functional and clean as are the clashing yellow and green marble bathrooms. The hotel has been preparing to open a five-star, 42-story wing for some time now, but no one seems to take them seriously.

Qian Fo Shan Lu 8. © 0531/8296-6888. Fax 0531/296-7676. qlhotel@public.jn.sd.cn. 255 units. ¥298–¥398 ($39–$52/£19–£26) standard room; ¥1,680 ($218/£109) suite. 40% discounts possible. AE, DC, MC, V. **Amenities:** 3 restaurants; bar; lounge; health club; sauna; bowling alley; concierge; airport shuttle service; business center; forex; shopping arcade; salon; room service; massage; laundry/dry cleaning; clinic. *In room:* A/C, satellite TV, minibar, hair dryer, safe.

Silver Plaza Quan Cheng Hotel (Yinzuo Quancheng Dajiudian) ★ This four-
star hotel in the heart of town offers modest accommodations at reasonable prices. Rooms in the south tower, renovated in 2002, are elegant and have modern furniture and comfortable beds with pristine white comforters. The marble bathrooms are on the small side, but are bright and clean. North tower rooms are larger though the furniture and carpets are worn. Service is adequate and some staff members speak a little English.

Nanmen Dajie 2. © 0531/8692-1911. Fax 0531/8692-3187. Quancheng@jn-public.sd.cninfo.net. 310 units. ¥528–¥638 ($69/£35–$83/£42) standard room; ¥748–¥968 ($97–$126/£49–£63) suite. 20%–30% discounts. 10% service charge. AE, DC, MC, V. **Amenities:** 2 restaurants; bar; lounge; nightclub; exercise room; sauna; concierge; airport shuttle service; business center; forex; shopping arcade; salon; room service; massage; laundry/dry cleaning. *In room:* A/C, satellite TV, free Internet access, minibar, hair dryer.

INEXPENSIVE
Gui Du Dajiudian Conveniently located about 1km (⅔ mile) from the railway sta-
tion, this hotel sits on a quiet street near city government offices. The rooms in the auxiliary building, which lacks an elevator, are cheaper and smaller. Rooms in the main building are a little dark and old but have decent-size bathrooms.

Sheng Ping Jie 1. ℂ **0531/8690-0888**. Fax 0531/8690-0999. www.guidu.com.cn. 236 units. ¥270–¥328 ($35–$43/ £18–£21) auxiliary building; ¥780–¥1,040 ($101–$135/£51–£68) main building. AE, DC, MC, V. **Amenities:** Restaurant; business center; concierge; airport shuttle service; massage. *In room:* A/C, TV, free Internet access in main building.

Ji'nan Tiedao Dajiudian   Well located right next to the railway and bus stations, this three-star hotel offers surprisingly plush accommodations with an elegant marble lobby. Guest rooms are more sedate and come with rather worn, unexciting brown furniture, while bathrooms are small but acceptably clean. Rooms in the front can be a little loud from the noise in the square, so avoid those if you want to sleep.

Chezhan Jie 19. ℂ **0531/8601-2118**. Fax 0531/8601-2188. 261 units. ¥368 ($48/£24) standard room; ¥400 ($52/ £26) suite. AE, DC, MC, V. **Amenities:** 2 restaurants; bar; lounge; nightclub; exercise room; sauna; concierge; business center; forex; shopping arcade; salon; room service; massage; laundry/dry cleaning. *In room:* A/C, TV, free Internet access on floors 6–8.

WHERE TO DINE

The top hotels offer reliable, if expensive, Western food. **Kentucky Fried Chicken** is at Chaoshan Jie opposite Silver Plaza, and **McDonald's** is at Quancheng Lu 180. There is a **bakery,** Dasanyuan, at Chaoshan Jie Beishou; it's open from 8am to 9pm.

Set back from Quancheng Lu's main shopping drag is **Furong Jie**, a small street redone to look like a traditional Chinese alley. It's atmospheric and not too touristy. The entrance is marked by a traditional Chinese archway at Quancheng Lu 197. Head in and take your first right. You'll find several restaurants serving standard, tasty Chinese fare and traditional Ji'nan snacks like *youxuan,* a small, flat bun with spring onions twisted and baked in the street-vendor equivalent of a coal-fired Dutch oven.

There are restaurants serving traditional Shandong cuisine on Chaoshan Jie near the heart of the town. Try the *ma popo men shuangsun* (steamed bamboo and asparagus) the various kinds of *zhou* (rice porridge) at **Lao Hangzhou Jiu Wan Ban** (Chaoshan Jie 18; ℂ **0531/8612-7228**), where a meal for two costs ¥30 to ¥50 ($4–$6.50/£1.95–£3.25). The restaurant provides special slender chopsticks that are unique to the coastal town of Hangzhou.

6 Tai Shan & Tai'an

Shandong Province, 66km (40 miles) S of Ji'nan; 68km (42 miles) N of Qufu

Inscribed on the UNESCO World Heritage List in 1987, Tai Shan (Great Mountain) is the most famous of the five Daoist sacred mountains in China, located midway between Beijing and Shanghai. Its base, in the town of Tai'an, is 150m (492 ft.) above sea level, and its summit is at 1,545m (5,068 ft.). With annual visitors numbering over four million, Tai Shan is and has always been the most climbed mountain in China. The first emperor of China scaled it. From the summit, Confucius declared that "the world is small," while Mao Zedong proclaimed that the "East is Red." Today, tourists and pilgrims, young and old, continue to make the journey, accompanied practically each step of the way by vendors peddling everything from snacks to souvenirs. Neither the highest nor the most impressive mountain in China, Tai Shan attracts visitors because of its cultural and historical significance, much of which, along with the colorful legends surrounding the different sights along the way, is lost on Westerners. However, the mountain still offers scenic vistas, interesting cultural immersion, and a good workout. During the annual International Tai Shan Climbing Festival in early September, hundreds of runners race up the mountain. Check with CITS or Tai'an Tourism (see below) for the exact dates.

Tai Shan

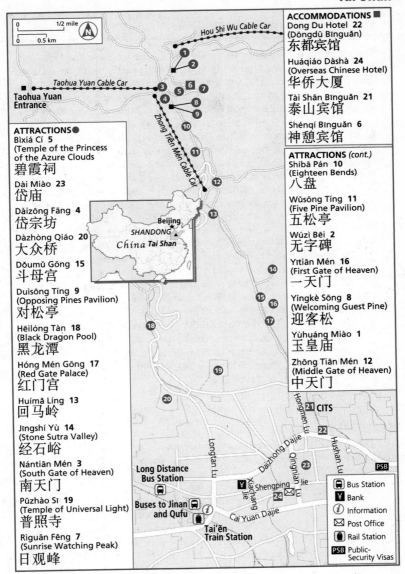

ACCOMMODATIONS ■

Dong Du Hotel **22**
(Dōngdū Bīnguǎn)
东都宾馆

Huáqiáo Dàshà **24**
(Overseas Chinese Hotel)
华侨大厦

Tài Shān Bīnguǎn **21**
泰山宾馆

Shénqí Bīnguǎn **6**
神憩宾馆

ATTRACTIONS (cont.)
Shíbā Pán **10**
(Eighteen Bends)
八盘

Wǔsōng Tíng **11**
(Five Pine Pavilion)
五松亭

Wúzì Bēi **2**
无字碑

Yītiān Mén **16**
(First Gate of Heaven)
一天门

Yíngkè Sōng **8**
(Welcoming Guest Pine)
迎客松

Yùhuáng Miào **1**
玉皇庙

Zhōng Tiān Mén **12**
(Middle Gate of Heaven)
中天门

ATTRACTIONS ●

Bìxiá Cí **5**
(Temple of the Princess
of the Azure Clouds
碧霞祠

Dài Miào **23**
岱庙

Dàizōng Fāng **4**
岱宗坊

Dàzhòng Qiáo **20**
大众桥

Dǒumǔ Gōng **15**
斗母宫

Duìsōng Tíng **9**
(Opposing Pines Pavilion)
对松亭

Hēilóng Tàn **18**
(Black Dragon Pool)
黑龙潭

Hóng Mén Gōng **17**
(Red Gate Palace)
红门宫

Huímǎ Líng **13**
回马岭

Jīngshí Yù **14**
(Stone Sutra Valley)
经石峪

Nántiān Mén **3**
(South Gate of Heaven)
南天门

Pǔzhào Sì **19**
(Temple of Universal Light)
普照寺

Rìguān Fēng **7**
(Sunrise Watching Peak)
日观峰

The Great Mountain

The significance of Tai Shan to the Chinese can be traced to their creation myth in which Pan Gu, after creating the sky and earth, died from exhaustion, his head and limbs falling to earth as five sacred mountains. Tai Shan, formed from the head and situated in the east (an auspicious direction signifying birth), became the most revered of the sacred mountains. The other four mountains are Song Shan in Henan (center), Heng Shan Bei in Shanxi (north), Heng Shan Nan in Hunan (south), and Hua Shan in Shaanxi (west). Although Tai Shan is not particularly high, the ancient Chinese came to regard it as the symbol of heaven. Historically, the Chinese emperor was considered to be the son of heaven, and many emperors, starting from China's first, the Qin Shi Huangdi emperor, climbed the mountain to perform sacrificial ceremonies to express their gratitude for being chosen to lead all below them, and to report to heaven on their progress. This also served to legitimize the emperors' power, as only those able to scale the mountain successfully were considered legitimate rulers. Today, hundreds, if not thousands, of historical relics, carved inscriptions, temples, and sacrificial altars provide a fascinating record of the imperial presence on the mountain. Countless ordinary Chinese have also made the pilgrimage to this holiest of holy mountains. They believed that the god of Tai Shan ruled the heavens and the earth and governed life and death. Although he has continued to be greatly revered through the years, his daughter Bixia (Princess of the Azure Clouds) has for many years now surpassed him in popularity. Today's pilgrims, many of them elderly, female, and peasant, scramble up the mountain paths, stopping at every altar to light incense and pray to the goddess for blessings and protection.

ESSENTIALS

GETTING THERE   The nearest major **airport** to Tai Shan is at Ji'nan, 66km (40 miles) south. From the **Tai'an railway station** (© **0538/219-6222**) located just west of the center of town, trains run to Beijing (7 hr.), Ji'nan (1 hr.), Shanghai (11 hr.), and Qingdao (6 hr.). There are also frequent **buses** to Ji'nan (every 30 min. 6am–5:30pm; 1 hr. 10 min.; ¥17–¥18/$2.20–$2.35/£1.10–£1.20) and Qufu (every 30 min. 6am–6:30pm; 1 hr. 10 min.; ¥20/$2.60/£1.30) that depart from the square in front of the railway station. From the **Tai'an long-distance bus station** (*changtu qichezhan;* © **0538/833-2656**) in the western part of town on Dongyue Dajie Xishou, buses run to Beijing (8:40am and 2:50pm; ¥130/$17/£8.45; 5 hr.), Shanghai (5:30am and 8am; ¥200/$26/£13; 12 hr.), and Ji'nan (every 30 min. 6:15am– 6:30pm; ¥17–¥21/$2.20–$2.75/£1.10–£1.40; 1 hr.).

GETTING AROUND   **Taxis** are plentiful in town and charge ¥5 (65¢/30p) for 2km (1¼ miles), then ¥1.50 (20¢/10p) per kilometer. From 10pm to 5am, the price rises to ¥5.80 (75¢/40p) for 2km (1¼ miles), then ¥1.70 (20¢/10p) per kilometer. **Bus** no. 3 (¥1/15¢/10p) runs from the railway station to Dazhong Qiao and also into town and up Hongmen Lu to the main entrance of Tai Shan.

TOURS & GUIDES **CITS,** at Hu Shan Lu 158 (© **0538/826-2456**), can arrange private guided tours of Tai Shan for around ¥700 ($91/£46), including transportation, English-speaking guide, entrance fees, and lunch. They can also arrange accommodations and book tickets.

VISITOR INFORMATION The **Tai'an Tourism Information Centre,** located just outside the railway station to the right as you exit (© **0538/688-7358;** www.sdta.cn), can answer questions and direct travelers to hotels, sights, and travel agencies.

FAST FACTS

Banks, Foreign Exchange & ATMs The **Bank of China** is located at Dongyue Dajie 48. Foreign exchange is available Monday through Friday from 8am to noon and 1:30 to 6pm. There is an ATM here.

Internet Access There are **Internet cafes** along Hongmen Lu north of Daizong Dajie. Most are open 24 hours and charge ¥2 to ¥3 (25¢–40¢/15p–20p) per hour.

Post Office The main post office (8am–5:30pm) is at Dongyue Dajie 5.

Visa Extensions The **Gonganju (PSB)** is in the eastern part of town at Dongyue Dajie Dongshou (© **0538/827-5264;** open Mon–Fri 8am–noon and 1–4:30pm). Allow 5 business days. Take a taxi or catch bus no. 4.

SEEING THE SIGHTS

Dai Miao ⟨★⟩ Chinese emperors would come to this awesome temple at the southern foot of Tai Shan to offer sacrifices and pay homage to the god of Mount Tai before tackling the mountain. The present structures date mostly from the Song dynasty (A.D. 960–1127). Built in 1009, the awesome nine-bay **Tianhuang Dian (Hall of Heavenly Gifts),** decorated with yellow glazed tiles, red pillars, and colorful brackets, houses a statue of the god of Tai Shan and a gorgeous, if faded, 62m-long (203-ft.) **Song wall mural**⟨★⟩ depicting, from right to left, the Zhenzong emperor (998–1023) as the god of Tai Shan embarking on an inspection tour. In the courtyard in front of the Hall of Heavenly Gifts, blindfolded visitors to the **Cypress of Loyalty** literally run circles around a nearby rock (three times clockwise, three times counterclockwise), after which they try to touch the fissure on the south side of the tree. It is said that those who succeed (and very few do) will have luck.

In the back of the complex is a lovely 1615 bronze pavilion, **Tong Ting,** which was formerly housed in the Bixia Temple on the mountaintop. West of the pavilion is an octagonal iron pagoda, **Tie Ta,** originally built in 1533 with 13 stories, each one cast separately, but only three survive today. The northern gate of the temple marks the beginning of Hongmen Lu and the imperial way up the mountain.

Sheng Ping Jie. Admission ¥20 ($2.60/£1.30). 7:30am–6pm. Bus: no. 1 or 4.

CLIMBING THE MOUNTAIN

Tai Shan is a challenging but manageable climb. There are two trails up to the midway point, Zhong Tian Men (Middle Gate of Heaven): a shorter but less-often hiked **western route** (7.8km/4¾ miles) which starts at Dai Miao but detours west before Hong Men; and the much more popular **eastern route** (11km/6½ miles) which runs from Dai Miao up to the main entrance on Hongmen Lu. As the former imperial way, the eastern route features more cultural and religious sights. The relatively fit should allow a total of about 4 to 5 hours to reach the summit: It's 2 hours to the halfway point, where there are some hotels and a cable car, and another 2 hours minimum to reach Nan Tian Men (South Gate of Heaven) near the summit. Water and snacks become increasingly expensive the higher you climb, so think about packing enough beforehand. A walking stick, which can be purchased in stores in town or at the mountain's entrance, can come in handy. Temperatures at the summit can differ considerably from Tai'an's, so dress in layers. Climbing Tai Shan would not be complete without viewing sunrise from the summit. Some Chinese climb at night, making it to the top just in time to catch the first rays, but this is not advisable for the average foreigner. If you plan to overnight at the top, be sure to pack warm clothing and a flashlight.

BY BUS & CABLE CAR   Those not inclined to climb day *or* night can now take one of three cable cars up to Nan Tian Men, though you'll still have to walk another 1.5km (1 mile) to the summit. The first and most popular option involves taking bus no. 3 (or a taxi) from the railway station to Dazhong Qiao (Tian Wai Cun also), where you transfer to a minibus (¥20/$2.60/£1.30) to Zhong Tian Men. You will have to purchase a ticket for entrance to Tai Shan, which costs ¥100 ($13/£6.50), here. (There are also direct buses to Zhong Tian Men from the railway station, but these only run in the morning.) From Zhong Tian Men, the 10-minute ride to Nan Tian Men on a six-person cable car costs ¥45 ($5.85/£2.95) one-way. The second cableway runs between the Tianjie Suodao Zhan and Taohua Yuan (Peach Blossom Ravine) on the western flanks of the mountain and costs ¥20 ($2.60/£1.30) one-way. The third option connects the summit to the more rural Hou Shi Wu (Rear Rock Basin) and Tianzhu Feng (Tianzhu Peak) on the northeast side of the mountain; the cost is ¥20 ($2.60/£1.30) one-way.

ENTRANCE FEES   Prices used to vary by entry point, but in early 2007 a standard ¥125 ($16/£8.15) admission was decreed, regardless of whether you enter at Hongmen Lu, Wan Xian Lou, Taohua Yuan, or Dazhong Qiao. The price drops with seasonal temperatures to ¥100/$13/£6.50 (Dec–Jan).

EASTERN ROUTE   Heading north from Dai Miao, visitors soon pass through the Ming dynasty **Daizong Fang,** a three-portal gate that leads to **Yi Tian Men (First Gate of Heaven),** which marks the beginning of the imperial ascent. Just inside is another arch commemorating the site where Confucius is said to have rested when he visited the mountain. North of the arch is **Hong Men Gong (Red Gate Palace),** which is also the main entrance to the mountain. Purchase your ticket about 200m (656 ft.) north of here. One kilometer (⅔ mile) farther is **Doumu Gong,** a Daoist nunnery whose origins are obscure, though the temple was completely renovated in 1542; it houses a statue of the goddess Doumu with 24 heads and 48 hands and eyes in the hollows of her palms. Behind Doumu Gong, a 1km (⅔-mile) detour to the east leads to **Jingshi Yu (Stone Sutra Valley),** an enormous flat piece of rock carved with the text of the Buddhist *Diamond Sutra*. Another 1.8km (1 mile) farther along the main path, an arch, **Huima Ling,** commemorates the spot where the Tang Xuanzong emperor had to dismount and continue by sedan chair when his horses could no longer navigate the steep twists and turns.

Less than a kilometer away, **Zhong Tian Men (Middle Gate of Heaven)** marks the halfway point up the mountain (elev. 850m/2,788 ft.), as well as the intersection of the eastern and western routes. There are restaurants, snack shops, and very crude hostels, as well as a cable car that runs to Nan Tian Men. A little farther on, those continuing on foot approach **Wu Song Ting (Five Pine Pavilion),** where the Qin emperor Shi Huangdi sought shelter from the rain in 219 B.C. He later conferred on the sheltering pine the title of fifth-grade official, hence the name of this spot. Just to the north, **Yingke Song (Welcoming Guest Pine)**, immortalized in countless paintings, extends a drooping branch in welcome. Recharge at **Dui Song Ting (Opposing Pines Pavilion)** before the final assault on the daunting **Shiba Pan (Eighteen Bends)**, the steepest and most perilous 1,633 steps of the mountain. Allegedly built in the Tang dynasty (618–907), the steps lie at a gradient of 80 degrees and rise over 400m (1,312 ft.) in height. Emperors used to be carried up this final stretch in sedan chairs. Today's climbers can only cling to the side railings as you straggle up the steps.

At the top, **Nan Tian Men (South Gate of Heaven)** (elev. 1,460m/4,788 ft.) is probably the most welcome and most photographed sight of Tai Shan. Originally built in 1264, this two-story red arched gate tower was completely renovated in 1984. A little farther on, the shop-lined **Tian Jie (Heavenly Lane)** brings you to a small Ming dynasty **Wen Miao (Temple to Confucius)** rebuilt in 1995, and above that the hotel Shenqi Binguan. Below, on the southern slope of the summit, is **Bixia Ci (Temple of the Princess of the Azure Clouds)**, built in 1009 and renovated and expanded during the Ming and Qing dynasties. Admission is ¥5 (65¢/35p); hours are from 8am to 6pm. The roof of the main hall is covered with copper tiles, while those on the side chambers are cast with iron to protect the buildings from the fierce elements on the summit. Elderly and female pilgrims flock here to burn incense and pray to Bixia and her different incarnations, Yanguang Nainai (Goddess of Eyesight), and Songsheng Niangniang (Goddess of Fertility).

Northeast of the temple, **Daguan Feng** is a gigantic sheer cliff face carved with inscriptions by different emperors, including the Tang Xuanzong emperor and the later Qing Kangxi and Qianlong emperors. A little farther north of here is the highest point of Tai Shan, **Yuhuang Ding** (elev. 1,545m/5,067 ft.). A temple, **Yuhuang Miao**, houses a Ming dynasty bronze statue of the Jade Emperor, considered by many Daoists to be the supreme god of heaven. Outside the temple is the 6m-high (19-ft.) **Wuzi Bei (Stele without Words)**. One version has it that the first Qin emperor had this tablet erected in A.D. 219, but years of exposure to the elements have weathered away the text. Another story tells of the stele being erected by the sixth emperor of the Han dynasty, who modestly left it blank to suggest that the virtue of the emperor was beyond words. About 200m (656 ft.) to the southeast is **Riguan Feng (Sunrise Watching Peak)**, where hundreds of bleary-eyed visitors wrapped in thick jackets congregate every morning around jutting **Tanhai Rock** to watch the sunrise. On this peak emperors such as the Tang Gaozong and Xuanzong emperors and the Song Zhenzong emperor conducted the Feng and Shan ceremonies. In 1747, two boxes of jade inscriptions by the third emperor of the Song dynasty, once thought to be lost during the Ming dynasty, were unearthed here.

If you choose this route, you should take a minibus to **Zhong Tian Men (Middle Gate of Heaven)** for ¥20 ($2.60/£1.30) and then climb to **Nan Tian Men (South Gate of Heaven)** yourself. You can then ride the cable car (¥45/$5.85/£2.95) back down to **Zhong Tian Men**, as it is rather steep to climb down.

WESTERN ROUTE   This route has fewer cultural attractions than the eastern route and emphasizes more natural sights such as pools and forests. The trail (not always clearly marked) converges at times with the main road running to Zhong Tian Men. A little over 3km (2 miles) down from Zhong Tian Men is **Shanzi Ya**, strangely shaped rock formations named for various animals they resemble. About 2km (1¼ miles) farther down past Changshou Qiao (Longevity Bridge) is the main attraction, **Heilong Tan (Black Dragon Pool)**, a pleasant enough waterfall in the summer and early fall. Another kilometer (½ mile) brings you to Dazhong Qiao and the terminus for the Zhong Tian Men buses. The path continues to **Puzhao Si (Temple of Universal Light),** a Buddhist temple built during the Northern and Southern dynasties (A.D. 420–589) and rebuilt in the Ming. Between 1932 and 1935, Feng Yuxiang (1882–1948), the "Christian General," stayed in the hall in the back of the temple complex. Born in Anhui Province, Feng was a warlord of the north who supported Sun Yat-sen but who later mounted a challenge to Chiang Kai-shek in 1929. He used to baptize his troops with a fire hose, and is buried on the southern slope of Tai Shan. From the temple, it's another 2km (1¼ miles) to the Dai Temple.

WHERE TO STAY

Dongdu Hotel (Dongdu Binguan) This three-star hotel is conveniently located about 2 blocks east of the Dai Temple, and higher floors have good views of Tai Shan. Rooms are basic, with dorm-room-style gray carpets and somewhat shabby sheets. The walls, painted sea-foam green, add a bright splash of color to the otherwise bland decor. Bathrooms are small, with no separate shower. Ask to see a room first, as some have a strong musty smell.

Daizong Dajie 279. ✆ **0538/822-7948.** Fax 0538/822-5223. 146 units. ¥320–¥480 ($42–$62/£21–£31) standard room; ¥600–¥4,888 ($78–$635/£39–£318) suite. 30%–50% discounts possible. AE, DC, MC, V. **Amenities:** Restaurant; lounge; dance hall; outdoor pool; sauna; concierge; business center; salon; room service; massage; laundry/dry cleaning. In room: A/C, TV, high-speed Internet.

Huaqiao Dasha (Overseas Chinese Hotel) This 14-story hotel is supposed to be the most luxurious in town, but it is a rather colorless place even though its rooms and facilities meet the minimum standards for a four-star hotel. Guest rooms are fitted with large twin beds and standard nondescript brown furniture, and are comfortable enough for a night or two. The decent-size bathrooms are a little dark but clean.

Dongyue Dajie Zhongduan. ✆ **0538/822-8112.** Fax 0538/822-8171. www.huaqiaohotel.com. 205 units. ¥400–¥800 ($52–$104/£26–£52) standard room; ¥720–¥1,200 ($94–$156/£47–£78) suite. 30%–60% discounts possible online. 10% service charge. AE, DC, MC, V. **Amenities:** Restaurant; bar; lounge; indoor pool; health club; sauna; bowling alley; concierge; tour desk; business center; free Internet access; forex; shopping arcade; salon; room service; massage; laundry/dry cleaning. In room: A/C, TV (in-house movies), minibar, safe (select rooms), computers (14th floor only).

Tai Shan Binguan A trusty old standby, this popular, well-located hotel between the main gate of Tai Shan and the Dai Temple is comfortable and reasonably priced. Last renovated in 1999, guest rooms come with high ceilings and basic but functional furniture. Bathrooms are clean. The whole place has a friendly feel to it and the staff seems to know what they're doing. CITS is conveniently located right next door.

Hongmen Lu 26. ✆ **0538/822-4678.** Fax 0538/822-1432. www.tsgnestandhotel.com. 110 units. ¥300–¥420 ($39–$55/£20–£27) standard room; ¥1,280–¥1,880 ($166–$244/£83–£122) suite. 30% discounts possible online. AE, DC, MC, V. **Amenities:** Restaurant; bar; lounge; exercise room; sauna; concierge; tour desk; business center; forex; shopping arcade; salon; room service; massage; laundry/dry cleaning. In room: A/C, TV, fridge, hair dryer.

ON THE MOUNTAIN

Shenqi Binguan This overpriced, overrated three-star perched atop some steep steps is nevertheless the best place to stay at the summit. It's only 30m (98 ft.) from Yuhuang Ding and 100m (328 ft.) from Riguan Feng. Rooms are somewhat dark but are clean enough and come with small twin beds and a small, clean bathroom; TVs are in place, but they receive no stations. The hotel only has hot water between 8:30 and 11pm. Thick jackets are provided for the sunrise viewing, and the staff will make sure you're awake in time. A buffet lunch or dinner starts at ¥30 ($4/£1.95).

1km (½ mile) from Nan Tian Men along Tianjie. ⓒ **0538/822-3866**. Fax 0538/833-7025. www.shenqihotel.com. 66 units. ¥680 ($88/£44) standard room. Discounts possible up to 20% except on Sat nights Apr–Oct. AE, DC, MC, V. **Amenities:** Restaurant; bar; sauna; forex (US$ only); store; salon. *In room:* A/C, TV.

WHERE TO DINE

In Tai'an, the **Baihua Canting** restaurant in the Tai Shan Binguan (ⓒ **0538/ 826-9977,** ext. 666; 7–9am, 11:30am–2pm, and 5:30–9pm) offers decent Chinese food in a clean environment. Simply point to your choices from the many dishes on display on long counters. A meal for two costs ¥60 to ¥80 ($7.80–$10/£3.90–£5.20). **Huanqiu Xishi Mianbao Fang** (Hongmen Lu 7) sells pastries and snacks for the long hike. There is a **McDonald's** at Sheng Ping Lu 2, and a **KFC** next to the railway station.

On the **mountain,** food is comparatively more expensive along the trail and on the summit than in town. Trailside vendors offer ice cream, bottled drinks, instant noodles, and boiled eggs. At the summit, **Shenqi Binguan** has a restaurant that serves basic Chinese fare *(jiachang cai)* as well as delicacies made from local ingredients such as pheasants, wild vegetables, and local medicinal herbs. A meal for two is ¥80 to ¥120 ($10–$16/£5.20–£7.80).

7 Qufu ⍟

Shandong Province, 150km (90 miles) S of Ji'nan, 68km (42 miles) S of Tai'an

Qufu, the home of Confucius, is a small town of 630,000 people, 125,000 of whom are surnamed Kong (though few are direct descendants). The town is dominated by the magnificent Temple of Confucius, the Confucian Mansion, and the Confucian Forest, all UNESCO World Heritage Sites. Qufu is often visited as a somewhat hurried day trip from Ji'nan. If you would like a more leisurely appreciation of the sights or merely wish to soak up the rarefied air, consider staying overnight and combining this with a visit to nearby Tai Shan. If you like celebrations, the ideal time to visit is on the occasion of Confucius's birthday, September 28. During this time, there are parades and musical and dance performances throughout Qufu. Book well in advance. *Note:* For Chinese translations of selected establishments listed in this section, please turn to appendix A.

ESSENTIALS

GETTING THERE The nearest major **airport** is in Ji'nan, 150km (90 miles) away. The **train** situation is a little confusing, as there are two railway stations: **Qufu Zhan,** about 5km (3 miles) southeast of the city center, where several trains a day stop between Beijing and Rizhao and between Ji'nan and Rizhao. The K51 from Beijing (9 hr.) arrives in Qufu at 7am, while the return K52 departs Qufu at 9:27pm. Bus no. 5 runs from the railway station into town, though service is infrequent. **Yanzhou Zhan** (ⓒ **0537/341-5239**), 15km (9 miles) west of Qufu, sits on the Beijing-Shanghai rail line and sees much more traffic. From Yanzhou, there are daily connections to Tai'an (1 hr.), Ji'nan (2 hr.), Beijing (5 hr.), and Shanghai (10 hr.). There are a limited number of assigned berths on trains serving both stations, so be sure to book your ongoing ticket as soon as you reach town. To avoid the hassle of running back and forth between Yanzhou and Qufu, use a ticketing agency like the **Qufu Shoupiao Chu** in the north Da Cheng Lu (Huadeng Jie) (ⓒ **0537/335-2276**). They have the only computer booking system in Qufu. The staff here is friendly and helpful.

Confucius Says . . .

Confucius's tremendous impact on Chinese society was not felt during his lifetime. Born Kong Qiu (also Kong Zhongni) to a minor noble family, Confucius (551–479 B.C.) spent most of his life wandering the country as a teacher after the various feudal lords with whom he sought positions all rejected him. Confucius himself never wrote his teachings down. It was only later, over the course of several generations, when his disciples like Zengzi and Mengzi collected and compiled his teachings in *The Analects (Lun Yu)*, that Confucianism began to take firm hold.

A philosophical tradition that has come to underpin much of Chinese society, Confucianism is a series of moral and ethical precepts about the role and conduct of an individual in society. Essentially conservative, Confucius was concerned about the breakdown in human, social, and political affairs he observed in the world around him during the Spring and Autumn Period of the Eastern Zhou dynasty (770–221 B.C.). Expounding on the traditional rites and rituals set forth during the previous Western Zhou dynasty (1100–771 B.C.), Confucius formulated a code of conduct governing what he saw as the five basic hierarchical relationships in society: between father and son, husband and wife, older and younger brothers, ruler and subject, and friend and friend. At its crux was the supreme virtue of benevolence *(ren)*, and the ideal relationship was one in which the dominant figure (always the male) would rule benevolently over the subordinate, who would in turn practice obedience and piety *(xiao)* toward the authority figure. This concept of *xiao*, which so permeates Chinese familial relations (from parents to in-laws to siblings), is the glue that holds much of Chinese society together.

After an inauspicious beginning when the Qin dynasty Shi Huangdi emperor (China's first) rejected all things Confucian and implemented a

From the **Qufu Qiche Zhan** (© **0537/441-1241**), located 1 long block south of the Temple of Confucius at the corner of Shendao Lu and Jingxuan Dong Lu, **buses** run to Ji'nan (every 20 min. 6:20am–8pm; 2½–3 hr.; ¥50/$6.50/£3.25), Tai'an (every 20 min. 6am–6pm; 1 hr. 10 min.; ¥27/$3.50/£1.75), Weifang (8:15am, 2pm; 4 hr.; ¥75/$9.75/£4.90), and Qingdao (6:45am, 10am; 7 hr.; ¥100/$13/£6.50). There are several sleeper buses to Beijing daily, but they are often booked (7am, 8am, and 10am, ¥150/$20/£9.75; noon and 1:45pm, ¥100/$13/£6.50). **Minibuses** run to the railway station at Yanzhou (every 20 min. 6am–6:15pm; 25 min.; ¥5/65¢/35p). The taxi to **Yanzhou Zhan** from town costs ¥30 ($3.90/£1.95) and takes 20 minutes.

GETTING AROUND   It is possible to tour temple, mansion, and cemetery on foot, though hiring a pedicab or horse-drawn taxi to the cemetery is an inexpensive option. Unmetered *miandi* (minivan) **taxis** cost ¥5 (65¢/35p) per 2km (1¼ miles). Around town, **horse-drawn carriages** cost ¥2 to ¥4 (25¢–50¢/15p–25p) per person, while a **tricycle taxi** costs ¥1 to ¥3 (15¢–40¢/10p–20p) per person. You can hire a tricycle taxi for 1 day for ¥20 to ¥30 ($2.60–$3.90/£1.30–£1.95), but make sure you agree on the price and what attractions you want to see before starting the ride. The

book-burning campaign in 213 B.C., Confucianism became the official state philosophy from the Han dynasty (206 B.C.–A.D. 220) until the fall of the Qing in 1911, with different rulers seizing on different aspects of Confucius's teachings to justify their rules and methods. Over the years, Confucianism underwent many changes, but Confucian temples *(wen miao)* continued to proliferate and the stature of the Kong family continued to rise; by the Qing dynasty, the Kong family had attained a status equal to that of the imperial family. To be sure, there were many detractors throughout the years, too, none more so than during the Cultural Revolution (1966–76) when, encouraged to reject tradition and authority, children openly criticized and humiliated their parents and teachers. The bonds of *xiao* were broken.

Today, Confucianism struggles to remain relevant. Some younger people scoff at it for being rigid and outdated, while a smaller group lays at its feet the onus of over 2,000 years of Chinese patriarchy. Indeed, where once the concept of *zhongnan qingnu* (the value of males over females), an extension of Confucius's emphasis on the importance of male heirs to continue the family lineage, was held absolute and paramount, today that practice is being very slowly, if not surely, challenged. Yet those fearing the imminent demise of Confucianism need only take a closer look at the family flying a kite in the park, at the crowds who show up to sweep the graves of their ancestors, at the teeming masses who burden the Chinese transportation system in the days leading up to the Spring Festival (Chun Jie) so they can all rush home to celebrate the Chinese New Year with their family, at the peasant woman who is allowed to have a second child if her first one is a girl. For good or ill, tradition is alive and well, and the family is still the strongest and most important social unit in Chinese society.

infrequent **bus** no. 1 runs from the southwest of town past the bus station all the way up Gu Lou Jie to the Confucian Forest. Bus no. 2 travels an east-west route along Jingxuan Jie.

VISITOR INFORMATION   The **Qufu Tourist Information Center** at Gu Lou Bei Jie 4 (© **0537/441-4001;** open Mon–Fri 8:30am–noon and 2–6pm) can provide information and direct travelers to sights and accommodations.

FAST FACTS

Banks, Foreign Exchange & ATMs   The **Bank of China** is at Dongmen Dajie 96 just east of Gu Lou Bei Jie. Foreign-exchange hours are Monday to Friday from 8am to noon and 3 to 6pm.

Internet Access   If you have your own laptop, there is free Internet access at most hotels around town. Otherwise, access is pretty limited. Just east of Gou Lou Nan Jie is **Xingji Wangba,** a large Internet bar with decent connections for ¥5 (65¢/35p) per hour. To get there, head east along the night market street Wumaci Jie and take your first right down the small alley. The Internet bar is about 150m (492 ft.) in on your right.

Post Office   Located north of the Drum Tower at Gu Lou Bei Jie 8–1, the post office is open from 8am to 6:30pm.

Visa Extensions   The **PSB (Shi Gonganju)** is at Wuyuntan Lu 1 (© **0537/296-0153;** open Mon–Fri 8am–noon and 2:30–6pm). Take a taxi or bus no. 3 from the Kongfu Fandian (Kongfu Hotel) at the corner of Datong Lu and Jingxuan Lu, and ask to be let off at Wuyuntan.

EXPLORING QUFU

Kong Miao (Confucius Temple) ★★★

One of the great classical Chinese architectural complexes (along with Beijing's Forbidden City and Chengde's Imperial Summer Resort), the magnificent Confucius Temple was first built in 478 B.C. by the king of Zhou, Lu Aigong, who converted three rooms from Confucius's residence into a temple to offer sacrifices to the Sage. The temple grew from the Western Han dynasty (206 B.C.–A.D. 24) onward due to the increasing number of titles conferred on Confucius. Many of today's structures, done in typical imperial fashion with red pillars and yellow-glazed tiles, and oriented on a north-south axis, date to the Ming and Qing dynasties.

Over a kilometer long (½ mile), the temple is first approached from the main south gate in Qufu's city wall. Then, a series of gates and courtyards lead eventually to **Dazhong Men,** a gate and former temple entrance (during the Song). In the next courtyard is the marvelous three-story, triple-eaved **Kuiwen Ge (Worship of Literature Pavilion),** first built in 1018 and rebuilt in 1191. This wooden building with stone pillars survived a major earthquake during the reign of the Qing dynasty Kangxi emperor (1654–1722) that destroyed much of the rest of Qufu. In the next courtyard are **13 stelae pavilions** all constructed during different periods, from the Jin (A.D. 265–420) to the Republican period (1914–19), and housing stelae recording the visits of different emperors.

The central gate, **Dacheng Men,** leads into the heart of the temple complex and the magnificent **Dacheng Dian (Hall of Great Achievements)** ★★★, originally built on this site in 1021 and rebuilt in 1724. Constructed on a two-tiered sculptured marble terrace, the building is supported by 28 carved stone pillars and majestically capped by a double-eaved, yellow-tiled roof. Individually carved from whole blocks of stone, the 10 columns in front each depict two dragons playing with pearls amid a sea of clouds. The remaining 18 octagonal pillars each bear 72 smaller dragons. Inside the temple is a statue of Confucius flanked by four of his students. These statues, destroyed during the Cultural Revolution, were replaced in 1983. Also on display is a set of bronze vessels and musical instruments that were used in ceremonial rites to honor the Great Sage, still occasionally performed here. In front is **Xing Tan (Apricot Altar),** where it is said Confucius delivered lectures to his 72 disciples. Behind the Great Hall is the **Hall of Bedroom** used to honor Confucius's wife, Lady Yuangong, who married him at the age of 19 and died 7 years before her husband.

The original Confucius's temple stands in the eastern section, only three shanties by legend. Also noteworthy is a 3m-deep (10-ft.) **well** in the eastern section of the complex from which Confucius is said to have drunk. East of the well, a screen wall, **Lu Bi,** commemorates the successful attempt by the ninth generation of Confucius's descendant Kong Fu to hide all the Confucian classics such as *The Analects* and *The Book of Rites* in the walls of Confucius's residence during Qin Shi Huangdi's book-burning campaign in 213 B.C. The books were later discovered during the Han dynasty (206 B.C.–A.D. 220), when the residence was torn down in order to enlarge the temple.

ⓒ 0537/441-4002. Admission ¥15 ($20/£9.75) for entrance to Kong Miao, Kong Fu, and Kong Lin. English-speaking guide (at temple entrance) ¥50 ($6.50/£3.25). Admission to Kong Miao only ¥90 ($12/£5.85). 8am–5:30pm.

Kong Fu (Confucian Mansion) ★★★

Until 1949 the mansion on the northeast side of the Confucius Temple had been home to 77 generations of Confucius's direct descendants, although the mansion's present location dates only from the end of the 14th century and the complex really grew to its current size (with a total of 463 halls) only in the Ming and Qing dynasties. If you've mostly been visiting temples around China, one of the most striking things about this place is the color and architecture. Temples and palaces are usually towering, majestic buildings that make you feel small and insignificant among all that red and imperial yellow. The Confucian Mansion, a residential dwelling, is a beautiful mix of gray stone walls, black columns, and black, red, and white trim throughout. It's kind of like 1950s Art Deco colors, but with a flourish of antique Chinese style. It's also smaller in scale, so you don't feel dwarfed by the surrounding architecture, and there are plenty of small passageways and paths that make this a very fun place to explore.

Here lived the Yansheng ("Continuing the Line of the Sage") duke, a title first conferred upon the 46th-generation descendant of Confucius by the Song Renzong emperor in 1055, and subsequently passed down. During the Ming dynasty, the duke's stature grew, and by the time of the Qing, he and the Kong family had attained a status equivalent to that of the imperial family. He was exempted from taxes, given power over his own court of law and subjects, and was the only one besides the emperor who could ride his horse within the Forbidden City. The Qing Qianlong emperor (reigned 1736–96) even married his daughter to a Yansheng duke in 1772, because only marriage to someone from a family equal in stature could dispel the misfortune that had been predicted for her by fortunetellers because of the mole on her face. To circumvent the law that prohibited Manchus from marrying the Chinese, Qianlong first gave her to a Chinese official, Yu Minzhong, for adoption, and her name was changed from Aixin Jueluo to Lady Yu.

The mansion is divided into three sections. The front part is reserved for formal and public business, the second serves as private family quarters, and the third is a garden. Inside the main gate is a large courtyard with the free-standing **Chongguang Men,** a gate built on eight stone drums that was only opened when emperors or imperial edicts arrived. In the three halls to the north, starting with the main hall, **Da Tang,** the Yansheng duke proclaimed imperial edicts, received visitors, and tended to business. In the second hall, where the duke received high-ranking officials, are seven tablets inscribed by various emperors, including one with the character *shou* (longevity) inscribed by the empress dowager Cixi. Northeast of the third hall is a small alley leading to a four-story **Binan Lou (Tower of Refuge),** which was meant to shelter the duke in case of attack. It was never used.

Behind the third hall, the **Neizhai Men (Gate to the Inner Apartments)** marks the beginning of the private quarters restricted to family members and a handful of trusted, mostly female servants. Even the water carrier had to pour his well water through a tiny trough in the wall just west of the gate. Behind the Front Reception Hall used for family banquets, weddings, and funeral ceremonies, the two-story **Qiantang Lou** was where the 76th duke, Kong Lingyi, lived with his wife, Madame

Tao, his two concubines, and his two daughters from Concubine Wang. After the 76th duke's death, one concubine gave birth to the 77th duke, Kong Decheng. It is widely held that Madame Tao, who produced no surviving heirs herself, poisoned his mother 17 days after she gave birth. The boy was to grow up with his sisters in relative isolation under the tyrannical Madame Tao, Qufu's equivalent of the powerful and manipulative empress dowager Cixi. As depicted in *The House of Confucius* by Decheng's sister Kong Demao and Ke Lan, life in the Confucian Mansion in those days was full of intrigue and betrayal for the adults and loneliness and sadness for the children. Decheng married and lived here until 1940, when he fled the Japanese invasion and then the Communists, ending up in Taiwan; he was the last of Confucius's descendants to occupy the mansion.

A large garden in the rear occupies the rest of the mansion grounds. A complete tour of the mansion will take 2 hours. Budget another 1 to 2 hours if you want to tour Kong Miao. It's best to do both in the morning hours, as there are fewer tourists.

Entrance opposite the back gate of Kong Miao. Admission ¥60 ($7.80/£3.90) or by combination ticket; see Kong Miao, above. 8am–5:30pm.

Kong Lin (Confucian Forest & Cemetery) 𝕲𝕲𝕲

Slightly over a kilometer (½ mile) north of the Confucian Mansion and Temple, Kong Lin is the burial ground for Confucius and his family, and is the largest and oldest cemetery park in China. Covering 2 sq. km (1¼ sq. miles), the forest has thousands of graves and over 20,000 trees, including cypresses, maples, and willows, many collected and planted by Confucius's disciples over the years. It's interesting to note that women, monks, criminals, and aborted fetuses cannot be buried here. Some 4,000 remaining gravestones span the dynasties, and the different styles make the cemetery worth visiting. It is a place both large and atmospheric enough to lose yourself in for a few hours. It can be delightfully eerie in the morning before the fog lifts. Bikes can be rented at the entrance for ¥10 ($1.30/65p).

Tip: After or between visiting the main attractions noted below, get off the main road and walk along the dirt paths to explore the myriad of gravestones and statues. You'll get away from the tour groups, flittering butterflies will keep you company, and the cicadas and warbling birds will drown out the sounds of the outside world.

The walkway leading to the forest from the south is lined with 73 trees on the right representing Confucius's age when he died, and 72 trees on the left signaling the number of his disciples. Passing through another two gates, visitors arrive at the forest proper, which is surrounded by a 3m-high (10-ft.) and 5m-thick (16-ft.) wall. To get to Confucius's grave, turn left inside the second entrance, walk along the **Imperial Carriageway** for about 200m (654 ft.), cross the Ming **Zhushui Bridge,** and continue along the "Spirit Way" *(shen sao),* which is flanked by four pairs of Song dynasty stone sculptures. At the end of the Spirit Way is **Confucius's tomb,** a mound of packed earth in front of which are two stelae. The front Ming dynasty tablet is inscribed with the characters DACHENG ZHI SHENGWEN XUAN WANG MU or "Tomb of the Ultimate Sage of Great Achievements." Local lore has it that the last two characters, *"wang mu"* (king's tomb), are partially hidden from view by the stone altar in front to reassure visiting emperors who came to pay their respects that no matter how respected and exalted the Sage was, there was only one emperor. To the right (east) of Confucius's grave is that of his son Kong Li, who died before his father. To the south lies the tomb of Confucius's grandson, Zisi, who was Mencius's (Mengzi's) teacher and the author of *The Doctrine of the Mean.*

Following the main road to the left of Confucius's grave brings you to a group of Ming Tombs. Continuing to the north eventually leads you to an archway and **tomb for Lady Yu,** the Qianlong emperor's daughter. (While Confucian wives were allowed to be buried in the forest, Confucius's female descendants were restricted to burial outside the forest.) Not far to the east is the **Tomb of Kong Shangren** (1648–1718), a 64th-generation descendant and author of the famous classical play *Taohua Shan (The Peach Blossom Fan)*. East of Kong Shangren's tomb is the Tomb of the 76th Yansheng duke, Kong Lingyi, and his wretched wife Madame Tao. Concubine Wang was also reburied here, despite laws prohibiting concubines from being buried within the forest. Following the road south brings you back to the main entrance.

Lindao Lu. Admission ¥40 ($5.20/£2.60) or by combination ticket; see Kong Miao, above. Mar–Nov 8am–6pm; Dec–Feb 8am–5pm. Bus: no. 1.

OTHER ATTRACTIONS

Kongzi Yanjiuyuan (Confucius Academy) ✵   Designed by the famous Chinese architect Wu Liangyong, this academy is a combination museum, research center, and exhibition space. Six rooms in the museum are dedicated to Confucius's life and theory, with drawings of the Sage and also some antiques from Kong Fu (Confucian Mansion) on display. Unfortunately, the place lacks English signage and English-speaking guides, but it's still worthwhile for the fantastic architecture.

Da Cheng Lu 9. Admission ¥30 ($4/£1.95), includes guide (no English-speaking guides available, though). 7:30am–5:30pm.

Shao Hao Ling (Tomb of the emperor Shao Hao) ✵   Located 4km (2½ miles) east of town, this unusually shaped tomb was built in 1111 by the Song Huizong emperor to honor Shao Hao, one of the legendary five emperors who succeeded the even more legendary first Chinese emperor, Huang Di (the Yellow Emperor). This flat-topped pyramid-shaped structure capped by a small brick altar with a yellow-tiled roof was supposedly built from 10,000 pieces of stone. Also here are two 17m-tall (56-ft.) stelae, **Wanrenchou Jubei (Sorrow of Ten Thousand Stelae),** meant to honor the Yellow Emperor, but the Song dynasty was driven from power before the stelae could be erected. Lying facedown since then, the tablets were hacked at by zealous Red Guards during the Cultural Revolution but were restored and set upright in 1992.

4km (2½ miles) northeast of Qufu in Jiuxian Village. Admission ¥10 ($1.30/65p). 8am–5pm. Shao Hao Ling is best reached by taxi (about ¥10–¥15/$1.25–$2/60p–£1) Bus: no. 2 from outside the bus station heading east on Jingxuan Dong Lu. Ask to be dropped of at Shao Hao Ling, then head north for another 400m (1,308 ft.).

SHOPPING

Popular souvenirs include the "Four Treasures of the Study": seals, ink stones, calligraphy brushes, and rice paper, all of which are available at **Chunqiu Ge** at Gu Lou Bei Jie 5 (open 8am–7:30pm). The store also sells ceramics, jewelry, cloisonné, and jade, and accepts international credit cards.

WHERE TO STAY
MODERATE
Queli Binshe (Queli Hotel) ✵   The best place to stay in town, this three-star hotel just east of the Confucius Temple has traditional Chinese buildings in a courtyard setting. Legend has it that Confucius lived nearby. Rooms, while not luxurious, are spacious, comfortable, and decorated in a style that combines traditional Chinese motifs with modern flourishes. Bathrooms have black marble walls and are small and a bit

old but acceptably clean. Most rooms have windows with views of the hotel's traditional Chinese rooftops and the central courtyards below. Service is occasionally spotty.

Queli Jie 1. ℭ 0537/486-6818. Fax 0537/441-2022. www.quelihotel.com. 160 units. ¥298 ($39/£19) single; ¥398–¥498 ($52–$65/£109–£32) standard room; ¥988 ($128/£64) suite. 10%–20% discounts possible. MC, V. **Amenities:** Restaurant; bar; bowling alley; sauna; concierge; business center; shopping arcade; salon; room service; laundry/dry cleaning. *In room:* A/C, TV w/free high-speed Internet access, fridge.

INEXPENSIVE

Qufu Youzheng Binguan (Qufu Post Hotel)   This two-star hotel just east of the Confucian Mansion is an acceptable alternative if the Queli is full. Rooms are clean and comfortable enough. Bathrooms are tired but otherwise clean. The staff doesn't speak English but tries to be helpful.

Gu Lou Bei Jie 8. ℭ 0537/448-3888. Fax 0537/442-4340. 66 units. ¥260 ($34/£17) standard room; ¥1,080 ($140/£70) suite. 20%–40% discounts possible. No credit cards. **Amenities:** Restaurant; salon; laundry/dry cleaning. *In room:* A/C, TV.

Yu Long Dajiudian (Yu Long Hotel)   Located in the north part of the old town, the quiet hotel has a good view of the city wall. It provides huge and acceptably clean rooms, though the furniture is worn. The staff are friendly, and they can book train tickets for you.

Gu Lou Bei Jie 15. ℭ 0537/441-3469. Fax 0537/441-3209. ¥280 ($36/£18) standard room; ¥800 – ¥1,180 ($104–$153/£52–£77) suite. 20%–30% discounts possible. AE, DC, MC, V. **Amenities:** Restaurant; laundry/dry cleaning. *In room:* A/C, TV, dial-up Internet access ¥.70 (10¢/5p) per minute.

WHERE TO DINE

The **Confucius Restaurant and Western Dining Room** in the Queli Hotel offers the best dining in a relatively clean environment, but watch out for shenanigans with prices. Just to the east of the Queli, the clean and well-lit **Kong Fu Dajiujia** (ℭ 0537/441-1048) has an English menu and serves local Confucian specialties like *yangguan sandie* (chicken, vegetables, and egg folded together like a fan), *daizi shangchao* (stewed pork, chicken, chestnuts, and ginseng), and *shili yinxing* (sweet ginkgo). A meal for two averages ¥40 to ¥160 ($5.20–$21/£2.60–£10); credit cards not accepted. An inexpensive choice for lunch or dinner is **Kong Fu Jia Yan Tang** (Kong Miao Dong Jie; ℭ 0537/448-8959; 8am–9:30pm; no credit cards), which provides decent Confucian food. Try *shenxian yazi* (fairy duck) and *shili yinxing* (sweet "poem" gingko). You can order half portions, which makes it ideal if you're traveling alone or as a couple. Farther east along Wumaci Jie, a lively **night market** proffers a variety of snacks, including delicious grilled kabobs, roasted nuts, and bean curd.

QUFU AFTER DARK

The Queli Hotel (see above) has nightly **Confucian musical performances.** Tickets are ¥80 ($10/£5) and are sold in the hotel lobby. From April to October, there are nightly "Confucius Dream" musical performances at 8:30pm at **Xing Tan Juchang (Apricot Altar Theater;** ℭ 0537/442-4095) where some of the rites mentioned in the *Analects (Lun Yu)* are performed. The theater is on Da Cheng Lu, about 800m (2,624 ft.) south of Kong Miao (Confucius Temple).

8 Qingdao ★★

Shandong Province, 318km (197 miles) E of Ji'nan, 890km (551 miles) SE of Beijing

Qingdao's strategic location at the mouth of a natural inlet on the south coast of the Shandong Peninsula has long made it attractive to foreign powers. When two German missionaries were killed in the Boxer Rebellion at the end of the 19th century, that was all the excuse Kaiser Wilhelm II needed to wrest Qingdao, then a small fishing town, from the weak Qing government, which ceded the port to the Germans on November 14, 1897, for 99 years. The Germans moved in, set up the Tsingtao Brewery, established churches and missions, built a railway to Ji'nan, and stationed 2,000 men in the garrison. But they were forced out at the beginning of World War I in 1914, and the Japanese took over, staying on after the 1919 Treaty of Versailles granted them authority over all ex-German territories in China. The Japanese ceded Qingdao back to the Guomindang (Nationalist Government) in 1922 but occupied the town again from 1938 to 1945 during World War II.

Today, Qingdao, which has retained much of its Teutonic architecture, remains one of China's more charming and relaxing cities. With its year-round mild climate, Qingdao also hosts many fairs and festivals throughout the year, the most famous of which is the annual Qingdao International Beer Festival, held the last 2 weeks of August and attracting upwards of a million visitors. Summers see the town packed with Chinese visitors, making spring and fall better times to visit if you hope to avoid the crowds. In recent years, Qingdao has also seen many new hotels, restaurants, and faster connections to major cities. Everything has been done to ensure that this seaside city is ready to host the watersports events of the 2008 Olympics. The Olympic Sailing Center (see below) is on the far eastern bay, with views of the central business district's sleek and glossy buildings, the international image Qingdao is eager to broadcast worldwide during the XXIX Olympiad.

ESSENTIALS

GETTING THERE   Qingdao is well connected by **air** to many Chinese cities, including Beijing (1¼ hr.), Guangzhou (2 hr. 45 min.), and Shanghai (70 min.). Tickets can be purchased at the **CAAC office (Minhang Dasha)** at Xianggang Zhong Lu 30 (© **0532/8577-5555;** open 24 hr.). International destinations served include Hong Kong, Seoul, Fukuoka, Tokyo, Pusan, and Bangkok. **Dragonair** (© **0532/8577-6159**) has an office at the Hotel Equatorial, Xianggang Zhong Lu 28, as does **Japan Airlines** (Xianggang Zhong Lu 76; © **0532/571-0088**). Qingdao's **Liu Ting Airport** (© **0532/8471-5777**) is located 30km (19 miles) north of the city; the 40-minute taxi ride costs ¥80 to ¥100 ($10–$13/£5–£6.50). Airport shuttles charging ¥15 ($1.95/£1) depart from the Haitian Fandian (Haitian Hotel), and make a stop at the Equatorial Hotel on the hour between 6am and 9pm. The bus also meets incoming flights.

The brand-new D series express trains from Beijing take 5 to 5½ hours (1:05pm D54 and 7:53am D58, 5 hr.; 5:30pm D56, 5½ hr.). The old overnight express **train** from Beijing (T26) takes 10 hours, and a slow overnight train from Shanghai (K29) takes 19½ hours. Several trains a day connect to Weifang (2 hr.), Zibo (3–4 hr.), Ji'nan (4–5½ hr.), Tai Shan (6 hr.), and Qufu/Yanzhou (7 hr.). Tickets can be bought at the railway station (© **0532/8297-5207**) at Hai'an Lu 1, 5 days in advance.

The long-distance bus station is in the northern part of town, but the **bus station** (© **0532/8371-8060**) just outside the railway station should serve most travelers'

Qingdao

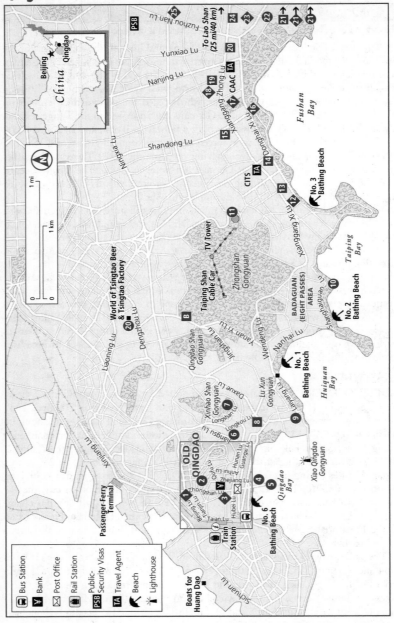

China
Beijing ★
Qingdao ★

PSB

Fuzhou Nan Lu

To Lao Shan
(25 mi/40 km)

Yunxiao Lu

Nanjing Lu

Zhong Lu

Xin

CAAC

TA

Gangao Zhong Lu

Shandong Lu

Dongxkai Xi Lu

Fushan
Bay

Ningxia Lu

N

1 mi

1 km

CITS

TA

Xianggang Xi Lu

No. 3
Bathing Beach

Taiping
Bay

Dengzhou Lu

Liaoning Lu

World of Tsingtao Beer
& Tsingtao Factory

TV Tower

Taiping Shan Cable Car

Zhongshan
Gongyuan

BADAGUAN
(EIGHT PASSES)
AREA

Shanghaiguan

No. 2
Bathing Beach

B

Qingdao Shan
Gongyuan

Jingshan Lu

Yanan Xi Lu

Wendeng Lu

Nanhai Lu

No. 1
Bathing Beach

Huiquan
Bay

Xinhao Shan
Gongyuan

Daxue Lu

Longshan Lu

Lu Xun Gongyuan

Longkou Lu

Jiangsu Lu

OLD
QINGDAO

Zhongshan Lu

Feilxing Lu

Anhui Lu

Huran Lu

Zhejiang Lu

Guangxi Lu

Hubei Lu

Taian Lu

Train
Station

No. 6
Bathing Beach

Qingdao
Bay

Xiao Qingdao
Gongyuan

Passenger Ferry Terminal

Xinjiang Lu

Boats for
Huang Dao

Sichuan Lu

Bus Station | **Bank** | **Post Office** | **Rail Station** | **PSB Public-Security Visas** | **TA Travel Agent** | **Beach** | **Lighthouse**

Qingdao Key

ACCOMMODATIONS ■

Crowne Plaza Qīngdǎo 24
(Qīngdǎo Yìzhōng Huángguān
Jiàrì Jiǔdiàn)
碌阁弥谢使诩偓站频

Dōngfāng Fàndiàn 8
东方饭店

Equatorial Hotel 19
(Guì Dū Dà Fàndiàn)
贵都大饭店

Hǎitiān Fàndiàn 13
海天饭店

Kǎilái Guójì Jiǔdià (Gloria Inn) 14
凯莱国际酒店

Qingdao Hotel 20
(Qīngdǎo Fàndiàn)
青岛饭店

Qingdao Kilin Crown Hotel 21
(Qīngdǎo Lù Lín Huángguān Dà Jiudiàn)
青岛鹿鳞皇冠大酒店

Shangri-La Hotel Qīngdǎo 15
(Qīngdǎo Xiānggélīlā Fàndiàn)
青岛香格里拉饭店

Super 8 Motel 26
(Su Bā Jǐu Diàn)
速8酒店

Surf Plaza Resort 21
(Lòng Hǎi Yuán Jiǔdiàn)
弄海园酒店

ATTRACTIONS ●

China Navy Museum 9
(Hǎijūn Bówùguǎn)
海军博物馆

Huāshí Lóu 10
花石楼

Huílán Gé 5
回澜阁

Jīdū Jiàotáng 6
(Protestant Church)
基督教堂

Qingdao Olympic Sailing Center 21
(Qīngdǎo Àolínpǐkè Fānchuán Zhōngxīn)
青岛奥林匹克帆船中心

Qīngdǎo Píijiǔ Chéng 22
(Qīngdǎo Beer Park)
青岛啤酒成
  only open during theTsingtao Beer Festival

Qīngdǎo Yíng Bīnguǎn 7
(Qīngdǎo Welcome Guesthouse)
青岛迎宾馆

Tiānzhǔ Jiàotáng 2
(Catholic Church)
天主教堂

World of Tsingtao Beer 27
(Qīngdǎo Píijiǔ Chǎng)
青岛啤酒厂

Zhàn Qiáo 4
栈桥

Zhàn Shān Sì 11
湛山寺

DINING ◆

Baeckermeister 25
(Bēimàisìtè Cānpǐn)
贝麦斯特餐品

Beida Huang Ren 21
(Běi Dà Huāng Rén)
北大黄人

Bellagio 16
(Xiānggǎng Xiǎo Zhèn)
香港小镇

Chūnhé Lóu 1
春和楼

Eden Café 3
伊甸休闲餐厅

Pasta Fresca Da Salvatore 18
(Shā Huá Yìdàlì Cāntīng)
沙华意大利餐厅

SPR Coffee 17
(Yēshì Kāfēi)
耶士咖啡

Tǔdàlì 12
土大力

Yíjǐng Lóu Hǎixiān Dàshìjiè 23
(Yíjǐng Lóu Seaview Seafood Restaurant)
怡景楼海鲜酒家

needs. Intra-province buses depart from the lot south of the railway station for Weifang (every 40 min. 6:40am–5:20pm; 2 hr. 40 min.; ¥37–¥44/$4.80–$5.70/ £2.40–£2.85) and Ji'nan (every 30 min. 6:50am–4pm; 5 hr.; ¥95–¥99/$12–$13/ £6–£6.50). Purchase your tickets at the little green kiosks. Long-distance sleeper buses depart from the front of the railway station for destinations farther afield such as Shanghai (noon, 5pm, 6pm, 7pm, 8pm; 11 hr.; ¥218/$28/£14) and Hangzhou (3:50pm; 14 hr.).

Ferries to Incheon, South Korea, run four times a week. Tickets can be bought at the **Qingdao Port Passenger Terminal (Qingdao Gang Keyun Zhan)** at Xinjiang Lu 6 (© **0532/8282-5001**).

GETTING AROUND   Downtown and the German Quarter can be toured on foot, but taxis and buses are more convenient ways to get to some of the beaches and attractions farther afield. **Taxis** charge ¥7 (85¢/40p) for 3km (2 miles), then ¥1.20 (15¢/10p) per kilometer until 6km (5 miles), when the price rises to ¥1.80 (25¢/10p) per kilometer; prices after 10pm rise to ¥1.80 (25¢/10p) per kilometer and ¥2.40 (30¢/15p) per kilometer respectively. **Bus** nos. 26 and 301 run from the railway station along the southern edge of the peninsula toward the commercial district on Xianggang Zhong Lu; the fare is ¥1 (15¢/10p).

VISITOR INFORMATION   A **Tourism and Information Service Center** (© **0532/8296-2000;** open 8:30am–5:30pm) is located 200m (656 ft.) to the left when you exit the railway station. They can provide information and direct travelers to sights and accommodations.

TOURS & GUIDES   If you haven't become frustrated enough by other **CITS** offices around the country, you can give this one a shot. It's is located at Xianggang Xi Lu 73 (© **0532/8389-3001;** fax 0532/8389-3013). For the latest information on the city and the rest of the province, look for the monthly English-language *Red Star* magazine, available at most international hotels or on the Internet at www.myredstar.com.cn.

FAST FACTS

Banks, Foreign Exchange & ATMs   The **Bank of China** at Yunxiao Lu 1 (© **0532/ 8286-1234**) has an ATM on premises and is open for foreign exchange Monday through Friday from 8:30am to 5:30pm, Saturday and Sunday from 9:30am to 4pm. Another branch at Zhongshan Lu 68 has similar hours. An **HSBC** ATM is also conveniently located inside the Crowne Plaza Hotel (Yizhong Huangguan Jiari Jiudian).

Internet Access   If you're traveling with your own laptop, most hotels offer free in-room high-speed Internet connections. There is a small **Internet cafe** across from the post office on Anhui Lu. It's open from 9am to midnight.

Post Office   Located at Anhui Lu 5 (open 8am–6pm) and another in the commercial district at Xianggang Zhong Lu 56 (open 8:30am–5:30pm).

Visa Extensions   The **PSB** office for visa extensions (© **0532/8579-2555,** ext. 2860; open Mon–Fri 8:30–11:30am and 1:30–5:30pm) is inconveniently located in the eastern part of town at Ningxia Lu 272. Bus no. 301 runs there from the railway station.

EXPLORING THE CITY
GERMAN QINGDAO

Many houses and shops in the former German Concession still retain their original European architecture. In addition to the sights that follow, other noteworthy buildings include the **Railway Station** at Tai'an Lu 2, a classical European structure built in 1901 with a 35m-high (115-ft.) bell tower; the former **Public Security Bureau** at Hubei Lu 29, built in 1904 and 1905 in the style of a medieval village church; and the **Princess House** at Juyongguan Lu 10, a villa built in 1903 by the Danish consulate general for a Danish princess.

East of the old town near the Number Two Bathing Beach, the **Ba Da Guan (Eight Passes)** area, named for the eight famous passes of the Great Wall, was and still is the toniest address in town. Unfortunately for the visitor, most of the well-preserved European mansions and villas here are hidden behind high walls and fences. Still, it's a lovely area to stroll, as the streets are wide and sheltered by a canopy of trees, with each street (or "pass") planted with a different bloom, including crab apples, peaches, pines, magnolias, and ginkgoes.

Haijun Bowuguan (China Navy Museum) 🌟🌟 (Kids)

Briefly wander through the drab indoor exhibition showing old photos and navy uniforms. Now on to the fun part: the outdoor exhibition of a torpedo boat, a surface-to-air missile, and plenty of old planes and helicopters. There are small replicas nearby that the kids can playfully scramble over (though they're pretty much allowed to run at will through the exhibition as well). You can also walk through a docked navel vessel and a jet, and for some family bonding time, take a crawl through a real submarine. It's claustrophobically tiny, so you get up close and personal with the bunkers, gauges, and inner workings of the deep-sea vessel.

Southernmost tip of Laiyang Lu. ℂ 0532/8286-6784. Admission ¥30 ($3.90/£1.95); ¥5 (65¢/35p) submarine; ¥3 (40¢/20p) jet. 8am–4pm.

Huashi Lou (Hua Shi Villa) 🌟

This Bavarian medieval castle built in 1903, with a tall round turret, chimneys, balconies, and Greek-style columns, was originally a Russian aristocrat's villa but was later taken over by the German governor general as a fishing retreat. In 1946, Chiang Kai-shek secretly retreated here to plan the Guomindang's next moves. These days, the villa, a big hit with wedding parties, can't exactly be called quiet or relaxing. Climbing to the top affords the visitor a grand view of the surrounding Ba Da Guan area.

Huanghai Lu 18. Admission ¥5 (65¢/35p). Apr–Oct 8am–6pm; Nov–Mar 8am–5pm. Bus: no. 26 or 31.

Jidu Jiaotang (Protestant Church) 🌟🌟

One of Qingdao's more attractive sights, this simple but beautiful church was designed by German Curt Rothkegel in the style of a Western medieval castle and completed in 1908. A red tile roof and a pretty green bell tower with a three-sided clock face cap the squat yellow structure. Visitors can climb the tower to see the original bells that still toll here. More popularly known to locals as Zhongbiao Lou (Clock Tower), the building was spared destruction during the Cultural Revolution, as few knew it was a church.

Jiangsu Lu 15. Admission ¥7 (90¢/45p). Mon–Sat 8am–4:30pm; Sun 1:30–4:30pm. Bus: no. 1 to Jiangsu Lu.

Qingdao Yingbinguan (Qingdao Welcome Guest House) 🌟🌟🌟

Built between 1905 and 1908 in the style of an old fortress with Tudor motifs, this magnificent building, the former residence of the German governor general, looks like it leaped from a Grimm Brothers' fairy tale. In 1934, the house became a hotel and is now a museum. Visitors can see the office where Mao Zedong slept during his month-long summer vacation in July 1957. Much of the stained glass, dark woods, and plush furnishings have survived, including an exquisite green marble fireplace with ornamental tiles in the study and an original 1876 German grand piano. There's an audio guide

Sail with Heart . . . Sail to Success . . .

That's the official (read: cheesy) motto of the Olympic watersports events Qingdao is set to host in 2008. A brand-new sailing facility covering over 50 hectares (124 acres) has been built on the far eastern side of Jiaozhou Bay. It remains closed to visitors and will be closed to spectators during the games as well. I had an opportunity to tour the center with Mei Chuntao, the man responsible for communications. He was unabashedly tired during our tour, as the center was taking care of last-minute preparations for an international regatta they were hosting the following month. The center is ultramodern, with glassy, futuristic architecture at a cost of a whopping ¥3.2 billion (about $428 million/£214 million). The main area houses the administration building, athletes' center, and the twin towers of the Olympic village (an InterContinental hotel that will be open to the public after the games). The administration building doubles as a sailing school, where Olympic silver medalist Zhang Xiaodong works as headmistress. After the games, the athletes' center will be converted into a bodybuilding center. An Olympic museum will also be somewhere on-site, but officials are undecided on where it will be.

You can view water events from one of two ultralong breakwaters. The **Main Breakwater** is 534m (1,752 ft.) long and is located at the south end of the marina. From here, you have a good view of the sailing center as well as the events. To get there, turn south from Donghai Xi Lu at Pedestrian Street, which is the street on the east side of the Jusco department store. The road (which in a slick PR move may be called Jusco Walkway during the games) leads directly to the spectator area. The other place to watch the races is from **Olympic Memorial Dock,** on the west end of the marina beside the media center. This dock is farther away from the downtown area but it has unobstructed views of the ocean, and is also closer to the podiums and medal ceremonies. Head east along Aomen Lu and follow the signs to the boardwalk, which you can then follow around to the media center and the dock behind it.

When I asked Mei what he thought was the most outstanding feature of the center, he nodded to the harbor and the pristine view of the central business district and said, "A beautiful view of New Qingdao." He talked about how the western part of town, where you find all the best old German architecture, is dubbed *Wanguo Jianzhu Bolan* (roughly "Museum of Buildings") by locals. "Old [Qingdao] is the west. But now we are *east,*" he said emphatically—a perfect metaphor for China's new place in the modern world.

for ¥20 ($2.60/£1.30) available at the information center to the left when you enter the house. The information given is pretty general, but includes facts like the height and length of the windows in the atrium.

Longshan Lu 26. Admission ¥15 ($1.95/£1); ¥10 ($1.30/65p). Apr–Oct 8:30am–5:30pm; Nov–Mar 8am–5pm. Bus: no. 25, 26, or 214 to Daxue Lu.

Tianzhu Jiaotang (Catholic Church) ✿   The former St. Michael's Cathedral was designed by German architect Pepieruch in a Gothic and Roman style and built between 1932 and 1934 with 60m-high (197-ft.) twin bell towers housing four bronze bells. Much of the church's interior was destroyed during the Cultural Revolution. Today, the inside has been given a bit of a tacky paint job and all the stained glass is new except for the small triangular panels in the round window in the eastern wall of the church. The Sunday morning 8am service is open to the public.

Zhejiang Lu 15. Admission ¥5 (65¢/35p). Mon–Sat 8am–5pm; Sun noon–5pm. Bus: no. 26.

World of Tsingtao Beer ✿   The Tsingtao beer factory was closed to the public until recently; now, it's become a must-see attraction for most visitors to Qingdao. The well-curated museum offers a history of the beer, which debuted in China in 1903 as a British-German venture. Displays of print and film advertisements from the 1930s are worth checking out as is the actual bottling assembly line. The tour ends at the Tsingtao Bar, where you'll be treated to a pitcher of beer and given a souvenir—not a bad PR pitch. English signage in the museum is adequate for explaining most of the exhibits but you can call ahead to arrange for an English-speaking guide.

Dengzhou Lu 56. ✆ 0532/383-3437. Admission ¥50 ($6.50/£3.25). 8:30am–5pm. Bus: no. 205, 2117, 221, or 604.

BEACHES

Qingdao's beaches are a top attraction for many Chinese, attractive if you're coming from any one of China's many dull, gray, overcrowded cities. Just don't expect a white-sand tropical paradise. From June to September, the beaches are packed. All the main public beaches, seven in the urban area, have changing booths where you can shower for ¥3 (40¢/20p), as well as medical stations and lifeguards on duty. Watersports range from water-skiing to parasailing.

Starting from the western tip of the peninsula, the beach nearest the railway station is the **Number Six Bathing Beach (Diliu Haishui Yuchang);** its rocky terrain makes it the least desirable for sunbathing. The big attraction here, however, is Qingdao's former pier, **Zhan Qiao** (¥2/25¢/15p; open 7am–8:30pm), originally built in 1892 for the Qing army. It now juts 440m (1,300 ft.) into the bay and is popularly considered the city's symbol. At the end of the pier is the octagonal Huilan Ge (¥4/50¢/25p), a pavilion that currently houses a small tacky aquarium with a coral exhibit.

Continuing east around the headland into the next bay past the aquarium, the 800m-long (2,624-ft.) **Number One Bathing Beach (Diyi Haishui Yuchang)** is one of Qingdao's longest, but the sand here is somewhat coarse and pebbly. Between April and June, this is where you'll find couples posing for wedding photos, with photographers and lighting equipment balanced precariously on the rocks and the stony piers that jut into the water. Around the next headland is the **Number Two Bathing Beach (Di'er Haishui Yuchang)** ✿, much nicer and more secluded than either numbers One or Six. Little wonder that this beach used to be popular with political figures like Mao Zedong and other government officials. You must pay a ¥2 (25¢/15p) entrance fee from 9am to 6pm, but at other times, it's free. In the next bay is the 400m-long (1,312-ft.) **Number Three Bathing Beach (Disan Haishui Yuchang)** ✿, also nice, quiet, and a bit out-of-the-way. **Shi Lao Ren (Old Man Rock)** ✿ is a quiet beach to the east. It's named for a rock that sits several hundred yards out from the bay and has the curved, stooped shape of an elderly man. Shi Lao Ren is far away from the business district, so things are less hectic here. It's also Qingdao's longest beach.

Far out to the west, half an hour by boat and then another half-hour by bus, is the beach of **Huang Dao** 🐦, cleaner and quieter than Qingdao's beaches, and until recently known only to locals—a real find. Take the Qingdao Huang Dao Lundu (ferry) (hourly 6:30am–9pm; 30 min.; ¥10/$1.30/65p) from the local ferry terminal (Lundu Zhan) on Sichuan Lu west of the railway station, then bus no. 1 to its terminus.

PARKS

Qingdao has a multitude of parks, some of them worth exploring. **Zhongshan Gongyuan** (Xianggang Xi Lu; ¥12/$1.60/80p 6am–5pm; ¥15/$1.95/£1 5–9:30pm) offers some pleasant strolls and is especially pretty during April and May when the cherry trees are in bloom. Northeast of the park is the **Taiping Shan Gongyuan,** where visitors can take a cable car up to a TV tower at the summit. The cable-car fare is ¥20 ($2.60/£1.30) one-way, ¥30 ($3.90/£1.95) round-trip. At the summit you can see lovely views of the city. From there, you can hike down the way you came, take the cable car, or hike down the back of the mountain to **Zhan Shan Si** (Ziquan Lu 4), the largest Buddhist temple in Qingdao. Admission to the temple is ¥5 (65¢/35p); hours are from 8:30am to 4:30pm. Note that the cable-car terminus is still a 15-minute walk to Zhan Shan Si; the fare to Zhan Shan Si is ¥20 ($2.60/£1.30) one-way, ¥30 ($3.90/£1.95) round-trip.

Xinhao Shan Gongyuan (Signal Hill Park), at Longshan Lu, just west of the Qingdao Welcome Guest House, was the location of a German navigating signal tower in 1898. Today the tower has been replaced by someone's bad idea of postmodernist architecture—three carbuncular mushroom-domed pink buildings meant to simulate signaling torches. Kitsch aside, the revolving viewing platform inside the main "mushroom" does afford some lovely views of Qingdao. Admission is ¥2 (25¢/15p) for the park only, ¥12 ($1.55/80p) including tower entrance. Hours are from 7am to 7pm (to 6pm in winter). **Qingdao Shan Gongyuan,** northwest of Zhongshan Gongyuan, has the remains of an old German fort (or rather, the underground command post). Admission is ¥8 ($1.05/50p); hours are from 8:30 to 11:30am and 2 to 5pm.

OTHER ATTRACTIONS

About 15km (9 miles) east of town, **Qingdao Pijiu Cheng** (Xianggang Dong Lu and Hai'er Lu) is a European-themed amusement park only open during the 2-week International Beer Festival in September. In this Bavarian bacchanal, there's something for everyone, from amusement park rides for kids, to drinking contests for adults, to go-karting for the kid in the adult. The beer festival also takes place closer to town at the Huiquan Guangchang, which offers a slightly more sanitized, calmer experience next to the ocean. Both are worth checking out, though you can expect a lot of kitsch at the first location. Check with CITS for exact dates.

WHERE TO STAY

Qingdao has a glut of upmarket hotels, many of which offer 20% to 30% discounts, though this probably will not be the case during the Olympics. All rooms are subject to a 15% surcharge unless otherwise noted. Also, keep your eyes open for the new **InterContinental.** It's being built right on the Olympic Sailing Center and will function as the athletes' village during the 2008 Olympic games. After that, the new five-star hotel will be available to us regular folk.

VERY EXPENSIVE/EXPENSIVE

Crowne Plaza Qingdao (Qingdao Yizhong Huangguan Jiari Jiudian) 🎭🎭

Located in the heart of the commercial and shopping district, this hotel is popular with Western independent and business travelers. Rooms have a slightly claustrophobic, dark feel as windows are small, but they are well furnished and the beds are fairly luxurious. Views of the sea are especially fine. Service here is better than at the pricier Shangri-La. With six restaurants on the premises, the hotel also has some of the most diversified dining choices; the Italian restaurant offers some of the best Western food in town.

Xianggang Zhong Lu 76. ℭ **0532/8571-8888.** Fax 0532/8571-6666. www.sixcontinentshotels.com. 388 units. ¥1,093 ($142/£71) standard room; ¥1,293 ($168/£84) suite. AE, DC, MC, V. **Amenities:** 6 restaurants; bakery; bar; lounge; indoor pool; health club and spa; sauna; bowling alley; concierge; free airport shuttle service; business center; forex; shopping arcade; salon; room service; massage; babysitting; same-day laundry/dry cleaning; newsstand; nonsmoking rooms; executive rooms. *In room:* A/C, satellite TV, high-speed Internet access, minibar, hair dryer, safe.

Haitian Fandian 🎭🎭

Located just east of the Ba Da Guan District and overlooking the sea, this five-star, 15-story, two-building Goliath of a hotel claims that all its rooms have sea views except for a few singles in the back. Rooms are comfortable and stylishly decorated with sleek modern furniture. The marble bathrooms are small but are otherwise clean and stylish, and come with dedicated potable water.

Xianggang Xi Lu 48. ℭ **0532/8387-1888.** Fax 0532/8387-1777. 606 units. ¥1,380 ($179/£90) standard room; ¥1,980 ($257/£129) suite. AE, DC, MC, V. **Amenities:** 2 restaurants; bar; lounge; indoor pool; tennis court; health club; sauna; bowling alley; concierge; tour desk; business center; forex; shopping arcade; salon; room service; massage; laundry/dry cleaning; newsstand. *In room:* A/C, satellite TV, minibar, hair dryer, safe.

Hotel Equatorial (Qingdao Guidu Da Fandian) 🎭

Attempting to snag some of the action at neighboring Shangri-La and Crowne Plaza, this hotel very recently underwent a huge renovation and hopes to achieve that all-important five-star status by the time you read this. Everything is bright and shiny and staff is very friendly. Rooms are not exactly stylish, but they are spacious and have good amenities. Bathrooms are a reasonable size, with a bathtub but no separate shower in the standard rooms.

Xianggang Zhong Lu 28. ℭ **0532/8572-1688.** Fax 0532/8571-6688. www.equatorial.com. 453 units. $138–$198 (£69–£99) standard; from $288 (£144) suite. Discounts up to 50% possible. AE, DC, MC, V. **Amenities:** 2 restaurants; bakery; bar; lounge; indoor pool w/whirlpool; small health club; sauna; concierge; business center; salon; room service; massage; babysitting; same-day laundry/dry cleaning; nonsmoking rooms; executive rooms. *In room:* A/C, satellite TV, high-speed Internet access, minibar, hair dryer, safe.

Qingdao Kilin Crown Hotel (Qingdao Lu Lin Huangguan Da Jiudian)

This five-star hotel is a franchise of the Best Western group. It attracts many Korean vacationers who are looking for a beach vacation away from the city center; the hotel is less than a 5-minute walk Old Man Rock Beach. Rooms are more functional than luxe on the lower floors, with blond furniture, forgettable carpets, and cramped bathrooms. Rooms on the 36th floor and up are much nicer, with dark wood floor entryways and pretty silk bed throws. Ask to see rooms before you commit, as they vary by floor, and some seaside views are blocked by the exposed elevator that runs the length of the hotel's front side. There's a revolving restaurant on the top floor that has top-notch views of nearby Shi Lao Ren beach.

Xianggang Lu 197. ℭ **0532/8889-1888.** Fax 0532/8889-1777. 405 units. ¥1,280–¥1,380 ($166–$179/£83–£90) standard; ¥1,880–¥3,200 ($244–$416/£122–£208) single. Discounts possible up to 50%. AE, MC, V. **Amenities:** 2 restaurants; bar; small indoor pool; exercise room; sauna; concierge; business center; forex; salon; room service; laundry. *In room:* A/C, satellite TV, high-speed Internet, minibar, hair dryer, safe.

Shangri-La Hotel Qingdao (Qingdao Xianggelila Fandian) ⟨⟩⟨⟩   Located in Qingdao's commercial center, this hotel is a top-notch choice for visitors who don't mind spending the extra cash. The rooms are spacious and have carefully designed lighting fixtures and bathrooms. The hotel is cozier and more stylish than the Crowne Plaza (see above), but often more expensive. Offering the full range of facilities and fine dining, the signature Shangri-La luxury is still very much in evidence here, though service is not up to par with the brand's other Chinese locations. The Western buffet is excellent. By the time you read this, the hotel's expansion—a giant 20-story building—should be complete, bumping up the total number of rooms to 696. Rooms in the new building will be about double the size of those currently on offer.

Xianggang Zhong Lu 9. ⟨⟩ **800/942-5050** or 0532/8388-3838. Fax 0532/8388-6868. www.shangri-la.com. 696 units. ¥1,120 ($146/£257) standard room; from ¥3,000 ($390/£195) suite. Prices for new building not available at press time. AE, DC, MC, V. **Amenities:** 2 restaurants; bakery; bar; lounge; indoor pool; outdoor tennis court; health club and spa; Jacuzzi; sauna; concierge; airport shuttle service; business center; forex; shopping arcade; salon; room service; massage; babysitting; same-day laundry/dry cleaning; newsstand; nonsmoking rooms; executive rooms. *In room:* A/C, satellite TV, DVD player (in executive rooms and suites), high-speed Internet access, minibar, hair dryer, safe.

Surf Plaza Resort Hotel (Long Hai Yuan Jiudian) ⟨⟩⟨⟩ *(Finds*   This boutique resort, also known as SPR Hotel, is the most atmospheric, charming place in town. It's not in the thick of the city's hustle and bustle like the Shangri-La or Crown Plaza, but it's not really meant for the fast-talking business folk that whirl through town. Each suite has a different theme and individual personality. I'm partial to the Colonial suite, with the master bedroom's four-poster bed and dark wood furniture, and a smaller bedroom decked out in emerald green silk. There's a huge balcony that has a fantastic view of the ocean and Laoshan Mountain. The hotel is a stone's throw from Qingdao's longest beach. The whole place has a small, exclusive feel to it; you have to enter a password to open the French doors to your floor. The resort is run by the same people who brought you SPR coffee (though the resort came first). Across the street is the huge, gleaming white SPR House, a residential complex managed by the same group. Guests can go here to access a 70m-long (230 ft.) indoor pool, a futuristic sauna room with high-backed white plastic chairs, and a small exercise room.

Xianggang Lu 316. ⟨⟩ **0532/8889-1237.** Fax 0532/8889-3647. www.spr.cc/sprhotel_en. 48 units. $250–$295 (£125–£148) standard suite; $400–$600 (£200–£300) seaside/executive suite. AE, DC, MC, V. **Amenities:** Restaurant; indoor pool; tennis court; exercise room; sauna; steam room; salon; room service; laundry/dry cleaning. *In room:* A/C, satellite TV, DVD in some suites, minibar, hair dryer, safe.

MODERATE

Dongfang Fandian ⟨⟩   For those who don't require a beach location, this four-star hotel, about a 10-minute walk from the Protestant Church, is probably the best deal around. Many Western travelers give it good marks for its comfortable, clean rooms at reasonable prices. It's not luxurious, but there's a full range of facilities and the service is quite good overall. The helpful staff speaks some English.

Daxue Lu 4. ⟨⟩ **0532/8286-5888.** Fax 0532/8286-2741. 146 units. ¥988 ($128/£64) standard room; from ¥1,888 ($245/£123) suite. AE, DC, MC, V. **Amenities:** 3 restaurants; bar; lounge; tennis court; health club; sauna; concierge; business center; forex; shopping arcade; salon; room service; laundry/dry cleaning. *In room:* A/C, satellite TV, minibar, hair dryer, safe.

Kailai Guoji Jiudian (Gloria Inn) ⟨⟩   This Hong Kong–managed three-star hotel catering mostly to Japanese, Korean, and domestic guests is the place to stay if you want to be closer to the sea and don't require luxurious amenities. An ugly white-tiled structure on the outside, the hotel has rooms that are comfortable enough. Bathrooms are bright and clean. The rooms facing the sea are bigger and a bit pricier. Views from seaside rooms are somewhat restricted by apartment blocks, but they are pleasant. Service is decent, though getting an extra towel is harder than it should be.

Donghai Xi Lu 21. © 0532/8387-8855. Fax 0532/8386-4640. 238 units. ¥880–¥1,580 ($114–$205/£57–£103) standard room; ¥2,280 ($296/£148) suite. 50%–60% discounts possible. AE, DC, MC, V. **Amenities:** 2 restaurants; bar; lounge; indoor pool; health club; sauna; salon; concierge; business center; forex; shopping arcade; airport shuttle service; room service; massage; babysitting; same-day laundry/dry cleaning; nonsmoking rooms; executive rooms. *In room:* A/C, satellite TV, minibar.

Qingdao Fandian   The best thing going for this hotel is its good location in the heart of the business district. Older rooms are quite frayed around the edges, with chips in bathroom sinks and slightly dingy carpeting. There are some renovated rooms that are cleaner and more comfortable, so ask to check things out before making a commitment.

Xianggang Zhong Lu 66. © 0532/8578-1888. Fax 0532/286-2464. www.qingdaohotel.cn. 203 units. ¥580–¥780 ($75–$101/£38–£51) standard; ¥1,280–¥1,580 ($166–$205/£83–£103) suite. Discounts possible up to 50%. MC, V. **Amenities:** 3 restaurants; bar; exercise room; sauna; ticket agency; business center; forex; salon; room service; laundry. *In room:* A/C, TV, high-speed Internet.

INEXPENSIVE

Super 8 Hotel (Su Ba Jiu Dian) 𝒱alue   This minihotel is the same chain as Motel 8 in the U.S. and Canada. The Chinese version attracts the midrange, fairly well-to-do Chinese travelers and business folk. It's super-clean and service is excellent, international-quality. Rooms are decorated like a photo from an Ikea catalog. There are plush orange or white sofas, sleek lamps, and blond wood furniture. Beds are clean and white with cozy duvets.

Yan'an Yi Lu 86. © 0532/8288-1888. Fax 0532/8271-1888. 85 units. ¥388–¥458 ($50–$60/£25–£30) standard; ¥588–¥688 ($76–$89/£38–£45). AE, DC, MC, V. **Amenities:** Restaurant; ticketing, business center; room service; laundry; nonsmoking rooms. *In room:* A/C, satellite TV, high-speed Internet.

WHERE TO DINE

Qingdao's seafood and its variations of local Shandong cuisine *(lu cai)* are all worth trying. Two long blocks east of the Shangri-La Hotel along Xianggang Zhong Lu is **Yunxiao Lu,** a lively street of bars and restaurants serving all types of Chinese cuisine into the wee hours.

McDonald's and Kentucky Fried Chicken have outlets in both the German Concession and the commercial center around Xianggang Zhong Lu. Coffee aficionados can get a fix at Starbucks on Xianggang Zhong Lu in the Sunshine Plaza (Yangguang Baihuo) or at SPR Coffee in the May 4th Square (north of the monument) on 35 Donghai Xi Lu. If you have your own computer, the SPR location also has Wi-Fi.

Backermeister (Beimaisite Canpin) 𝒻 GERMAN   This new bakery serves fresh bread and pastries and a small selection of sandwiches. Everything comes from Austria, including the baker. The interior is bright, seating is plush and cozy, and the staff is uberfriendly. This is an excellent place to come for a morning pastry and coffee, or to pick up a loaf of fresh baked bread.

Min Jiang Lu 151. © 0532/8077-0123. Pastries ¥5–¥15 (65¢–$1.95/30p–£1). AE, DC, MC, V. 11am–9:30pm.

Bei Da Huang Ren 𝒻𝒻 DONGBEI   Chinese measure the quality of a restaurant by the number of people inside and level of noise. So this place is of very serious quality! Bei Da Huang Ren is packed at dinnertime and the surrounding diners chattering away and clanking plates and chopsticks provide an atmospheric din to a tasty

Wild China: The Funeral Pits of Zibo

Once the capital of the Qi State—during the Spring and Autumn (722–481 B.C.) and Warring States periods (475–221 B.C.)—Zibo today is a dusty industrial town better known for its glass and ceramic production.

The town is located 116km (70 miles) east of Ji'nan in Shandong Province, but most of its worthwhile sights are actually in Linzi District about 35km (21 miles) east of Zibo. The **Linzi Zhongguo Guche Bowuguan (Li Museum of Chinese Ancient Chariots)** ✮✮ (Qilin Zhen, Houli Guanzhuang), is about 6km (3½ miles) from the Linzi bus station. Admission is ¥25 ($3.25/£1.65) and hours are from 8am to 6pm. Here you'll see two fascinating ancient horse-and-chariot funeral pits which predate Xi'an's terra-cotta army by more than 280 years. The horses' remains, dating from the Spring and Autumn Period, have been left as they were found. The first pit contains the remains of 10 chariots and 32 horses, all facing west. From the positions of the horses, with bronze bits still intact, archaeologists concluded that the animals were either anesthetized or otherwise rendered unconscious before burial. The second pit features the bones of four horses plus six chariots, which remain buried underneath the horses. Visitors can get a close look, which is a fascinating, if eerie, experience.

Ten minutes to the northwest, **Xun Ma Keng (Ancient Horse Relics Museum)** ✮ (Heyatou Cun; ¥10/$1.30/65p; 7:30am–6:30pm) is a series of over 20 tombs believed to have belonged to Qi Jing, the 25th monarch of the Qi State. The tombs contain the fossils of 600 horses. Only **tomb 5 (106 horses)** in the southwestern section is open, however. Unearthed in 1982, the horses are arranged in two rows with their heads facing outward. No other funerary objects were found, as the tombs were long ago robbed.

Ceramic production developed around Zibo as early as the period of the Houli culture 8,000 years ago. Four exhibit halls at the town's ceramics museum, **Zibo Zhongguo Taoci Guan** ✮ (Xincun Xi Lu; ¥20/$2.60/£1.30; May–Oct 9–11:30am and 3–6pm; Nov–Apr 9–11:30am and 2–5pm), trace the evolution of Zibo's ceramics from the Neolithic Longshan and Houli cultures to its zenith in the Tang and Song dynasties with the development of celadon ware and black glaze porcelain. Notable items on display include the dainty eggshell earthenware of the Longshan culture and the rare "Blue and Yellow Celestial Dragon" patterned porcelain reserved strictly for use

---

meal. Try their signature dish, *Bei Da Huang Kong Fu* (white fish served in a spicy broth with Sichuan peppercorns). The staff is super-friendly and efficient.

Mai Dao Meishi Lu 3-7. © **0532/8593-8888** or 0532/8593-6888. Meal for 2 ¥80–¥200 ($10–$26/£5.20–£13). No credit cards. 11am–9:30pm.

Bellagio (Xianggang Xiao Zhen) ✮ TAIWANESE   This popular chain has made its way to Qingdao city. As with their Shanghai and Beijing locations, the decor is stylish and

by the emperor. The store here (open 8–11:30am and 2:30–6pm, to 5pm in winter) sells surprisingly inexpensive locally produced vases, cups, and individual sculptures. Only cash is accepted.

GETTING THERE   From Zibo's **railway station** (© 0533/258-2522) in the southern part of town, daily trains run to Ji'nan (2 hr.), Weifang (1 hr.), Qingdao (1hr. 40 min.–3 hr.), and beyond. From Zibo's **bus station** (© 0533/288-9261), just west of the railway station, buses run to Ji'nan (every 20–30 min. 5:30am–7pm; 1½ hr., ¥25 –¥33/$3.25–$4.30/£1.65–£2.15), Qingdao (every half-hour 6:30am–5:30pm; 3½ hr., ¥70/$9.10/£4.55), Weifang (every half-hour 6:30am–6pm; 1½ hr., ¥25/$3.25/£1.65), and Tai'an (every half-hour 6:30am–6pm; 1½ hr., ¥33/$4.30/£2.15).

GETTING AROUND   Take bus no. 6 or minibus no. 20 for ¥3 (40¢/20p) from Dongyi Lu just east of the railway station to its terminus at Linzi Bus Station; then take tourist bus no. 5, which stops at all the main sights listed here (¥4/50¢/25p for the entire loop). Alternatively, a **taxi** from Zibo will cost ¥60 to ¥80 ($7.80–$10/£3.90–£5.20) one-way. In town, taxis charge ¥5 (65¢/35p) per 3km (2 miles), then ¥1.20 (15¢/10p) per kilometer thereafter.

WHERE TO STAY & DINE   Located in its own garden compound in the center of town, the four-story, four-star **Zibo Binguan** (Zhongxin Lu 189; © 0533/228-8688; fax 0533/218-4990) offers rooms that lack charm but are comfortable, with clean bathrooms. Rooms go for ¥380 ($49/£25), and can be discounted 40%. The 31-story **Zibo Fandian** ⍟ (Zhongxin Dadao 177; © 0533/218-0888; fax 0533/218-4800) was the town's first four-star hotel (1999). What it lacks in charm is made up for with a host of modern conveniences. The rack rates are absurd here, but you can bargain them down considerably. Standard rooms, with discount, cost ¥360 ($47/£23) and have large, comfortable beds and standard four-star furnishings, though the carpets are old. The spacious marble bathrooms are dark but clean. Suites can be had for ¥680 to ¥780 ($88–$101/£44–£51).The hotel's revolving restaurant on the 31st floor offers Shandong cuisine (also known as "Lu") in one of the city's more elegant settings. The Demeanor Bar serves real cappuccino and Colombian coffee, plus cocktails and imported wine. **Western fast food** is available at **McDonald's** (Zibo Shangsha at Zhongxin Lu and Meishi Jie) and at **KFC** (Meishi Jie 17).

hip. Try their signature icy desserts; I highly recommend the *huasheng bingsha* (peanut ice smoothie).

Aomen San Lu 19. © 0532/8387-0877. Meal for 2 ¥100–¥250 ($13–$33/£6.50–£16). AE, MC, V. 11am–midnight.

Chunhe Lou ⍟ SHANDONG   This long-standing institution for Shandong cuisine is located in an old two-story corner building in the German Concession. The first floor serves casual fast food while the second floor has large tables and private rooms. Despite the modest ambience, the food has its devotees. House specialties include *youbao hailuo* (fried sea snails), *songshu guiyu* (deep-fried sweet-and-sour fish), and *xiang su ji* (fragrant chicken).

Zhongshan Lu 146. (C) 0532/8282-4346. Meal for 2 ¥80–¥150 ($10–$20/£5.20–£9.75). No credit cards. 1st floor 9am–2:30pm and 5–9pm; 2nd floor 10:30am–9:30pm.

Tudali KOREAN   Located just west of the Shangri-La Hotel, this late-night Korean barbecue diner has a cozy and informal feel, with its exposed wooden beams and plenty of wall graffiti from happy and appreciative patrons. Barbecued meat and vegetable skewers are the main attractions here, along with other tasty Korean staples like kimchi fried rice and *chap chae* (stir-fried yam noodles).

Xianggang Xi Lu 52. (C) 013583229720. Picture menu. Meal for 2 ¥30–¥60 ($3.90–$7.80/£1.95–£3.90). No credit cards. 4pm–4am.

Yijing Lou Haixian Dashijie (Yijing Lou Seaview Seafood Restaurant) 𝒦𝒦 SEAFOOD/SHANDONG   Seafood doesn't get more delicious or fresh than this at this popular chain, especially when you're asked to point and choose it from the tank yourself. Ordering is supereasy here: There's no menu—just a range of aquariums and sample dishes on display. A waiter will follow you around to write down what you want. The highlight of our meal was the fresh *hualong,* a lobsterlike creature without claws, prepared three ways: served raw (brought to our table with the head still moving), deep-fried with salt and pepper, or made into a rice porridge. Other highlights included *youba gufa zheng qiezi* (steamed eggplant), *gongzhu yu* (princess fish cooked in oil and steamed), and *tieban heli kao dan* (iron plate clams with scrambled eggs). Service is good, though comically formal—they presented our Sprite the way a sommelier would show a bottle of wine before opening it. Make sure to book a private room facing the sea if you're at the Donghai Lu location, the best of the three.

Taiwan Lu. (C) 0532/8569-1111. Meal for 2 ¥300–¥500 ($39–$65/£20–£33). No credit cards. 10am–2pm and 4:30–9pm.

A NEARBY ATTRACTION

Lao Shan 𝒦𝒦   Located 40km (24 miles) east of Qingdao, Lao Shan is a mountain range that is part Daoist sanctuary, part natural wonder; with waterfalls, streams, and walking trails snaking through wooded hills; and jagged cliff faces rising dramatically from the blue sea. Daoism spread to the mountain during the Western Han dynasty (206 B.C.–A.D. 9), and emperors throughout the ages have dispatched envoys to scale the mountain in search of the elixir of life. While the water that originates from here didn't perform any miracles, today it is famous and is used in brewing Tsingtao beer.

Admission to Lao Shan is ¥80 ($10/£5.20), but thanks to greedy tourist officials you must now purchase additional tickets, ranging from ¥4 (50¢/25p) to ¥30 ($3.90/ £1.95), to gain entry to specific attractions on the mountain. The most popular sightseeing route is the **southern route,** which takes in Daoist temples, caves, and ponds, with stupendous sea views along the way. The main Daoist temple here is **Taiqing Gong,** first built in 140 B.C., now with over 140 rooms and an equally mind-boggling number of gods from the Daoist pantheon. Admission is ¥10 ($1.30/65p); hours are from 8am to 6pm. East of the temple, a trail leads up to **Yakou temple,** where you can either take a cable car or continue on foot up to Yao Lake and Mingxia Cave, where admission is ¥4 (50¢/25p). The trail down leads past **Shangqing Gong** (¥4/50¢/25p), another Daoist temple; and the impressive waterfall, **Longtan Pu.**

To get to Lao Shan, tourist buses depart from the eastern end of Qingdao's railway station square every half-hour from 6:30am to 6pm. The 1-hour trip costs ¥20 ($2.60/£1.30). Public bus no. 304 runs from the Ferry Terminal (Lundu) on Sichuan Lu all the way to Yakou. The Taiqing Gong cable car costs ¥50 ($6.50/£3.25) round-trip (¥40/$5.20/£2.60 in low season).

9 Nanjing ★★

Jiangsu Province, 306km (189 miles) NW of Shanghai

First the nation's capital in the early years of the Ming dynasty (A.D. 1368–1644), then the capital of the Republic of China from 1911 to 1937, and now capital of Jiangsu Province, this bustling city of six million is left off many China itineraries, lacking many visible reminders of what has in fact been a highly tumultuous and storied past. Except for Zhongshan Lin, the tomb of Sun Yat-sen, the scope of Nanjing's attractions do not accurately reflect the magnitude and importance of its place in China's history, which is a shame, because the city deserves at least a day or two of your time. In addition to some Ming dynasty attractions, there are reminders that Nanjing was also the seat of the Taiping Rebellion and the site of one of history's most brutal massacres. Spring and fall are the best times to visit, as Nanjing in the summer is well known as one of China's three furnaces.

ESSENTIALS

GETTING THERE   From Nanjing's **airport**, just under 50km (31 miles) southwest of the city, daily flights connect to Beijing, Guangzhou, Wuhan, Chengdu, Kunming, Guilin, and Hong Kong. There are also twice-weekly flights to Macau and Bangkok. Tickets can be purchased at hotel tour desks and at the **CAAC** at Ruijin Lu 180 (© **025/8449-9378**). **China Eastern** has a 24-hour office at Zhongshan Dong Lu 402 (© **025/8445-4325**), while **Dragonair** offices are at Hanzhong Lu 2, nos. 751–753 (© **025/8471-0181**; open 7am–11pm). CAAC airport shuttles depart from the CAAC office every 30 minutes from 6:30am to 6:30pm, and also meet arriving flights. The trip takes 50 minutes and costs ¥25 ($3.25/£1.65). *Note:* The bus leaves once full; those left behind must take taxis. A metered **taxi** into the Xinjiekou area should run about ¥140 ($18/£9.10), including toll.

Nanjing's **railway station** (Longpan Lu 264; © **025/8582-2222**) is conveniently linked to Nanjing's metro. A 5-minute ride to a central station (such as Xinjiekou) will cost ¥2 (30¢/15p). The city is an important rail junction along the Beijing-Shanghai railway line. Trains heading east to Shanghai (2 hr.) connect to Wuxi (1½–2 hr.), Suzhou (2–2½ hr.) and Hangzhou (5 hr.). Heading west, there are trains to Huang Shan (6½–10 hr.). You can buy tickets on the second floor of the three-story annex west of the station's exit. A special window selling only Shanghai tickets is marked in green; its hours are from 7 to 11am and from 11:30am to 6:30pm. You can also buy tickets at the Gu Lou ticket-booking office at Zhongshan Lu 293.

Nanjing has seven **long-distance bus stations**, but the main one, Nanjing Zhongyang Men Changtu Qiche Zongzhan, at Jianning Lu 1 (© **025/8553-1288**), just west of the Nanjing Railway Station, should serve most travelers' needs. From here, large, air-conditioned buses run to Suzhou (every 20 min.; 2 hr. 40 min.; ¥46–¥64/ $6–$8.30/£3–£4.15), Shanghai (every half-hour; 3½ hr.; ¥82–¥88/$11–$11.50/ £5.35–£5.70), and Hangzhou (hourly; 5 hr.; ¥98/$13/£6.40). The Hanfu Jie Bus Station (Changtu Qichezhan) at Changjiang Lu 296 (© **025/8454-1359**) also serves the

Nanjing

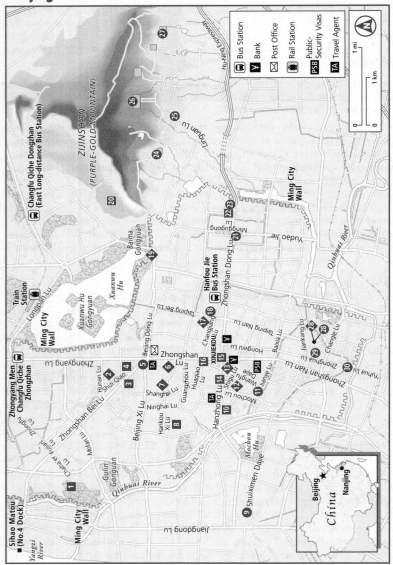

Legend:
- Bus Station
- ¥ Bank
- ⊠ Post Office
- Rail Station
- PSB Public-Security Visas
- TA Travel Agent

1 mi
1 km

Map labels:

Changfu Qiche Dongzhan (East Long-distance Bus Station)

Huning Expressway

ZIJINSHAN (PURPLE-GOLD MOUNTAIN)

Lingyuan Lu

Ming City Wall

Qinhuai River

Yudao Jie

Minggugong Lu

Hanfou Jie Bus Station

Zhongshan Dong Lu

Taiping Bei Lu

Baima Gongyuan

Xuanwu Hu

Xuanwu Hu Gongyuan

Longpan Lu

Train Station

Ming City Wall

Beijing Dong Lu

Zhongyang Lu

Zhongyang Men Changfu Qiche Zhongzhan

Zhongyang Bei Lu

Beijing Xi Lu

Hunan Lu

Shizi Qiao

Zhongshan Lu

⊠ Zhongshan

XINJIEKOU

Changjiang Lu

Hongwu Lu

Jiankang Lu

Zhongshan Nan Lu

Changle Lu

Yuhua Lu

Chang'er Lu

Fujian Lu

Zhongfu Lu

Mofan Lu

Gulin Gongyuan

Guangzhou Lu

Shanghai Lu

Ninghai Lu

Hankou Xi Lu

Huaqiao Lu

Hanzhong Lu

Mochou Lu

Shengu Lu

Wangfu Dajie

Baixia Lu

Jianye Lu

Taiping Nan Lu

PSB

Qinhuai River

Mochou Lu Mochou Hu

Shuiximen Dajie

Jiangdong Lu

Ming City Wall

Sihao Matou (No.4 Dock)

Yangzi River

Numbered markers: 1, 2, 3, 4, 5, 6, 7, 8, 9, 10, 11, 12, 13, 14, 15, 16, 17, 18, 19, 20, 21, 22, 23, 24, 25, 26, 27, 28, 29, 30

Inset map: China — Beijing, Nanjing

ACCOMMODATIONS ■

Celebrity City Hotel **4**
(Míngrén Chéngshì Jiǔdiàn)
名人城市酒店

Central Hotel (Zhōngxīn Dàjiǔdiàn) **16**
中心大酒店

Crowne Plaza Nanjing Hotels
and Suites **14**
(Qiáo Hóng Huángguàn Jiǔdiàn)
金鹰皇冠酒店

Grand Metropark Hotel Nanjing **22**
Nánjīng Wéi Jīng Guójì Dàjiǔdiàn
南京维景国际大酒店

Hotel Sheraton Nánjīng Kingsley
Hotel and Towers **10**
(Nánjīng Jīnsīlì Xǐláidēng Jiǔdiàn)
南京金斯利喜来登酒店

Jīnlíng Fàndiàn **15**
金陵饭店

Nánshān Bīnguǎn **8**
南山宾馆

Parkview Dingshan Hotel **1**
(Dīngshān Huāngguan Yuán)
丁山花园大酒店

Sofitel Galaxy Nanjing **3**
(Nánjīng Suǒfēitè Yínhé Dàjiǔdiàn)
南京索菲特银河大酒店

Sofitel Zhongshan Golf Resort **20**
(Suǒfēitè Gāo'ěrfū Jiǔdiàn)
索菲特中山高尔夫酒店

DINING ◆

Bǎinián Lǎo Fèng Xiǎochī **28**
百年老风小吃

Ciao Italia **12**
(Nǐhǎo! Yìdàlì Cāntīng)
你好! 意大利餐厅

Jīnhé Tài Cāntōng **2**
(Golden Harvest Thai Opera Café)
金禾泰餐厅

Jīnyīng Dàjiǔlóu **13**
金鹰大酒楼

Le 5 Sens **7**
(Lè Shàng Fǎguó Cāntīng)
乐尚法国餐厅

ATTRACTIONS ●

Cháotiān Gōng **11**
朝天宫

Dàzhōng Tíng **5**
大钟亭

Fūzǐ Miào (Confucian Temple) **28**
夫子庙

Gǔ Lóu **5**
鼓楼

Jiāngnán Gòngyuàn Lìshǐ Chénlièguǎn **28**
江南贡院历史陈列馆

Língǔ Sì **25**
灵谷寺

Nánjīng Dàtúshā Jìniànguǎn **9**
(Memorial to the Victims of the
Nánjīng Massacre)
南京大屠杀纪念馆

Míng Xiào Líng (Ming Filial Tomb) **24**
明孝陵

Míng Gù Gōng **21**
明故宫

Nánjīng Bówùguǎn (Nánjīng Museum) **23**
南京博物馆

Sòng Měilíng's Villa (Sòng Měilíng Gōngguǎ) **27**
宋美龄公馆

Tàipíng Tiānguó Lìshǐ Bówùguǎn **29**
(Tàipíng Heavenly Kingdom
Historical Museum)
太平天国历史博物馆

Zhōnghuá Mén Chéngbǎo **30**
中华门城堡

Zhōngshān Líng **26**
中山陵

Zǒngtǒng Fǔ (Presidential Palace) **18**
总统府

New Magazine Café (Xīn Zázhì Kāfēi) **6**
新杂志咖啡

1912/Coffee Beanery (Juéshìdǎo Kāfēi) **17**
爵士岛咖啡

Skyways Bakery and Deli **19**
(Yún Zhōng Cānpǐndiàn)
云中餐品店

same destinations. The East Long-Distance Bus Station (Changtu Qiche Dong Zhan) at Huayuan Lu 17 services Yangzhou (every half-hour; 1 hr.; ¥25/$3.25/£1.65) and Yixing (every 20 min. 6:20am–6:40pm; 2½ hr.; ¥44/$5.70/£2.85). There are also express "business" buses for ¥88 ($11/£5.70) that leave for Shanghai at 8, 9, and 10am and 2, 3:30, and 4:30pm from the back entrance of the Jinling Hotel.

GETTING AROUND   Nanjing is a sprawling city not particularly conducive to walking, with sights scattered in different directions. The rate for **taxis** is ¥8 ($1.05/50p) for 3km (2 miles), then ¥2.40 (30¢/15p) per kilometer. From 11pm to 6am, the price rises to ¥2.70 (35¢/20p) per kilometer after 3km. All taxi rides come with a ¥1 (15¢/10p) fuel surcharge. **Buses** are a convenient and cheap way to get around Nanjing, although they are almost always full. Pay ¥2 (25¢/15p) for air-conditioned buses and ¥1 (15¢/10p) for all others. No change is given. Some of the main bus routes include: no. 1: Nanjing Railway Station–Xinjiekou–Fuzi Miao; no. Y1: Nanjing Railway Station–Xinjiekou–Zhongshan Ling; no. Y2: Yuhua Tai–Zongtong Fu–Zhongshan Ling.

TOURS   **Jiangsu Zhongshan International Travel Service** (Zhongshan Bei Lu 178; ✆ 025/8342-9700) works with the major hotels to offer a standard 1-day tour of Nanjing, including visits to Zhongshan Ling (Dr. Sun Yat-sen's Mausoleum), Zong-tong Fu (the Presidential Palace), and Chaotian Gong (Worshiping Heaven Palace), among other places. The cost of ¥195 ($25/£13) includes entry fees and the use of a guide and bus driver.

VISITOR INFORMATION   *MAP,* the free local English-language monthly magazine featuring the latest on dining and entertainment in Nanjing, is available in any of the top hotels or in Western restaurants. Try the government-run **Nanjing Tourist Information Center** (**Nanjing Luyou Zixun Fuwu Zhongxin;** ✆ 025/5226-9008; 9am–5pm) in Confucius Temple for advice on sightseeing, restaurants, and hotels. The office is staffed by two very helpful employees.

FAST FACTS

Banks, Foreign Exchange & ATMs   The main branch of the **Bank of China** is located at Zhongshan Nan Lu 148. Hours for foreign exchange are Monday through Friday from 8:30am to noon and 2 to 5pm. ATMs accept international cards. Another branch is at Hongwu Lu 29 with the same hours.

Internet Access   Bring your passport or ID for Internet access at **China Telecom,** Zhongyang Lu 2 on the second floor (open 8:30am–5:30pm; ¥2/25¢/10p per hour). Free wireless laptop access is available the **Coffee Beanery** (in the 1912 restaurant/pub complex at the corner of Changjiang Hou Jie and Taiping Bei Lu) and at all locations of **New Magazine Cafe** (see "Where to Dine," later in this section).

Post Office   The main post office (8am–6:30pm) is at **Gu Lou,** Zhongshan Lu 366.

Visa Extensions   The **PSB** is located at Honggong Ci 1 (✆ 025/8442-0004; Mon–Sat 8:30–11:30am and 2–5pm). Same-day visas are possible. From Xinjiekou, walk 5 minutes south on Zhongshan Nan Lu, then head west onto Sanyuan Xiang for about 300m (980 ft.).

EXPLORING NANJING
HISTORICAL SIGHTS

Sadly, Nanjing's Ming legacy can be found in only a few buildings and ruins today. In the center of town, the drum tower **Gu Lou** was built in 1382 and contained a series of drums used to mark the night watches, welcome guests, and occasionally warn of approaching enemies (admission to grounds free, ¥5/65¢/35p to enter the second floor of tower and teahouse, metro: Gu Lou). Close by is a pavilion, **Dazhong Ting,** which houses a 23,000-kilogram (25-ton) bronze bell from 1388. Toward the eastern part of town are the ruins of the first Ming dynasty imperial palace, **Ming Gu Gong.** All that remains of the once massive palace, destroyed in the Taiping Rebellion, are the Wu Men (Meridian Gate) that once marked the front gate of the palace wall, five small marble bridges, and 12 large plinths that were once the foundation of another large gate. Sections of the Ming **city wall** are still visible.

Zhonghua Men Chengbao ✿

Located in the southern part of town, this is the biggest and best-preserved of the city wall's original 13 gates. Built by the Hongwu emperor between 1366 and 1386, the wall, at 33km (20 miles), was the longest city wall in the world, made of uniform bricks cemented with a mortar of lime, sorghum, and glutinous rice. Zhonghua Gate, first built in 1386, actually consists of four rows of gates, the first one 53m (173 ft.) long. Each gate entrance had a vertically sliding stone door lifted with a mechanical winch. Twenty-seven arched vaults inside the first gate could house up to 3,000 soldiers, who were set to ambush the enemy should the latter be so unfortunate as to be trapped within the gates. Climb to the top for some good views of the city, and to gaze at the kitschy fake guards. Along the way, watch for bricks that still bear the carvings of their maker and supervisor. In front of the walls, locals fly kites bought from vendors for ¥8 ($1.05/50p).

Zhonghua Men. Admission ¥10 ($1.30/65p). 8am–10pm.

Zongtong Fu (Presidential Palace) ✿✿

The last time I visited this fascinating site, it was worn around the edges and attracted very few visitors, but it had an authentic air of historical significance to it. Now, likely capitalizing on its location next to the big tourist attraction of 1912 (see "Where to Dine" later in this chapter), the palace has undergone a massive renovation. Columns have been repainted bright red and there are new window frames with frosted glass in place. There are also more areas on display, like the rock gardens on the west and the Taiping Lake on the east. The palace was the seat of government of the Liangjiang viceroy's office (1671–1911), the Taiping Heavenly Kingdom (1853–64), Sun Yat-sen's provisional government (1912), and the Nationalist government (1927–37 and 1946–49) . It has borne witness to all the important events and personalities in Nanjing's history. Though this presidential palace dates from the Ming dynasty, today's buildings were all built after 1870. Just inside the main entrance, the Great Hall marked by the words TIAN XIA WEI GONG (The world belongs to all) used to be the first in a series of nine magnificent halls during the Taiping Heavenly Kingdom. On January 1, 1912, provisional president of the new Chinese republic Sun Yat-sen held his inauguration here.

After the second hall, the next series of rooms were used by Chiang Kai-shek, the leader of the Nationalist Party, to receive foreign guests, among them U.S. Gen. George Marshall, who was attempting to broker a truce between Chiang and Mao Zedong. In the back, Chiang Kai-shek's former office has an interesting old-fashioned hand-operated Otis elevator, which has now been restored. In Xuyuan, the garden on the western side of the compound, a stone boat is the only remaining original artifact from the days of the Taiping Heavenly Kingdom.

Changjiang Lu 292. Admission ¥40 ($5.20/£2.60). English-speaking guides an exorbitant ¥150 ($20/£9.75). Apr–Oct 7:30am–6pm; Nov–Mar 8am–5pm. Bus: no. 1, 2, 29, 44, 65, 95, or 304.

The Taiping Heavenly Kingdom

During the mid–19th century, natural disasters, catastrophic floods and famines, Western excesses, and Qing government neglect and corruption had all coalesced to create widespread unrest in China. It was in such a setting that the largest uprising in modern Chinese history occurred. Known as the **Taiping Rebellion,** its impact continues to be felt even today.

The Taiping Rebellion started in the mind of Hong Xiuquan (born Hong Huoxiu, 1814–64), a teacher and a farmer's son from Guangdong Province. After Hong failed his civil-service exams for the third time, he had a feverish dream of a bearded man and a younger man, whom he later decided were God the Father and Jesus. Hong also kept seeing part of his own name, "Huo" in the Christian tract, which he interpreted as another divine calling. Convinced that he was God's son and Jesus' younger brother, and his mission from God was to "slash the demons"—the twin demons of the Manchu government and the traditional Chinese folk religion—Hong formulated his own ideology, a mix of Christian ideals and Confucian utopianism. He soon amassed a large anti-Manchu, anti-establishment following in the south and in 1851 led a group of 20,000 followers to establish the **Taiping Heavenly Kingdom,** with Hong himself as king. Using their army and any number of ragtag peasant militias they could muster along the way, the Taipings swept up through south and central China and established themselves in Nanjing in 1853, renaming the city Tianjing (Heavenly Capital).

The Taipings preached a new order based on the equal distribution of land, equality between the sexes, monotheism, and the existence of small communities ruled by religious leadership, an order that, save for the religious bit,

Fuzi Miao (Confucian Temple)   Kitschy it may be, but this is where you'll get a good idea of the modern interests of Nanjing's youth. Once a place of intense study and quiet contemplation, Fuzi Miao is now the site for everything from tattoo parlors to pirated music stores selling the latest Mandarin hits. To the right (east) was once the Jiangnan Gongyuan, an academy first built in 1169, which later became the largest imperial civil examination halls during the Ming and Qing dynasties, with over 20,000 cells for examinees. Today, a handful of rooms have been restored into a museum, the **Jiangnan Gongyuan Lishi Chenlieguan.** Tourists can reenact part of the examination process by donning period robes and Ming dynasty hats and sequestering themselves in the cells, which have white walls, bare concrete floors, and two boards stretched across the cells as a seat and a table.

Jiankang Lu. Confucian Temple ¥25 ($3.25/£1.65). 9am–10pm (last ticket sold at 9:30pm, Fri–Sat 10:30pm). Bus: no. 1 from Nanjing Railway Station or Xinjiekou to Fuzi Miao. Metro: Sanshan Jie.

Chaotian Gong   One of the earliest documented sites in Nanjing, this former foundry and soldier training ground during the Spring and Autumn Period (722–481 B.C.) was a temple used by the Hongwu emperor (1382–98) as a ceremonial place of worship, hence Chaotian or "heaven-worshiping." The place was rebuilt in the Qing dynasty as a Confucian temple and academy. Today, the main hall, Dacheng Dian,

was to prefigure some of the tenets of the Chinese Communist movement. Feudalism, slavery, concubinage, arranged marriages, opium smoking, foot binding, prostitution, idolatry, and alcohol were all to be abolished (at least in theory). While women under the Taiping were allowed a greater degree of freedom (there was even a Taiping army made up entirely of female troops), Taiping morals continued to stress obedience and chastity in women. Hong Xiuquan and other Taiping leaders also continued to keep harems, in that way no different from any of China's emperors or even Mao Zedong, who was known to maintain his own.

In the end, however, the Taipings were doomed by a combination of internecine struggles, corruption, defections, flawed policies, and external forces made up of a reconstituted Qing army aided by Western powers who had apparently decided they would rather deal with the devil they knew (the Qing government) than contend with the uncertainties of a strong Taiping force, even though they were closer to them in ideals. The counter-attack was brutal and merciless, and by the time the Chinese army succeeded in crushing the revolt 14 years after it began, a reported 30 million lives had been lost. Hong Xiuquan himself died of illness in 1864 but his successor, his 14-year old son, was killed by Qing troops.

It is uncanny how so many facets of the Taiping Rebellion would be echoed in later Chinese events. The ability of one man to command such a large fanatical uprising and sustain it for so long would later be paralleled in Mao's Cultural Revolution (1966–76). The effects of such large mass uprisings also help explain the current Chinese leadership's fear of them.

houses a fascinating **Six Dynasties museum.** Exhibits include a locally unearthed Roman glass, a compass vehicle, and immortality pills, which obviously didn't work. The English explanations are quite good. Outside of the temple, an antiques market sells jade knickknacks and Mao posters.

Chaotian Gong 4. Admission ¥30 ($4/£1.95). 8am–5pm. Bus: no. 4 from Fuzi Miao to Chaotian Gong.

MEMORIALS & MUSEUMS

For ¥80 ($10/£5) you can buy a combination ticket that will give you access to Zhongshan Ling, Ming Xiao Ling, and Linggu Si; a shuttle (¥3/45¢/20p) runs between these sights from morning until evening.

ZIJIN SHAN

Zijin Shan (Purple Gold Mountain), located on the eastern edge of town, got its name from the mountain's purple shales, which were said to have lent the place a mysterious purple aura at dawn and dusk. Covered with dense forests and dotted with the occasional lake, the mountain has always been a pleasant retreat for locals seeking relief from Nanjing's heat. It's also home to some important historical sites. Spend the day if you can, but if you have limited time, then the highlight is surely Zhongshan Ling.

Zhongshan Ling 𝒜𝒜 This magnificent mausoleum for Dr. Sun Yat-sen (Sun Zhongshan), widely revered as the founder of modern China, has become a mecca for Chinese tourists seeking to pay their respects. Sun Yat-sen died in Beijing in 1925 but wasn't interred here until 1929, when construction of the mausoleum was complete. (In 1912, while hunting with friends in Zijin Shan, Sun had expressed his wish to be buried here.) The tomb itself is at the end of a long, steep set of stairs beginning with a Memorial Archway made of white Fujian marble and capped by blue glazed tiles. Symbolizing the white sun on the blue background of the Guomindang flag, the colors also marked a departure from the yellow tiles used to honor all of China's previous emperors. At the top of the 392-step grand tomb passage, a white marble statue of Dr. Sun sits under the pretty mosaic roof of the Memorial Hall. The Republican government's constitution is inscribed on the side walls. Dr. Sun's marble coffin lies in the hushed domed chamber in the back. On the way down, you'll be treated to a nice view of downtown Nanjing and its surroundings. Make sure to get here early or late in the afternoon, as the place fills up like a zoo.

© 025/8444-9931. Admission ¥80 ($5.20/£10), or by ¥130 ($17/£8.45) combination ticket (see "Memorials & Museums," above). 6:30am–6:30pm. Bus: no. Y1 (from the Nanjing Railway Station) or 9 (from Xinjiekou).

Ming Xiao Ling (Ming Filial Tomb) 𝒜 More peaceful than Sun Yat-sen's mausoleum is the tomb of the founder of the Ming dynasty, Zhu Yuanzhang (1328–98), also known as the Hongwu emperor. The tomb served as a model for subsequent Ming and Qing emperors' tombs in Beijing. The site has recently been polished up with funds from UNESCO after being deemed a World Heritage Site, but the explanations of the tombs are in Chinese only with strange diagrams. Zhu Yuanzhang was the only Ming emperor to be buried in Nanjing. The Sacrificial Palace, one of the tomb's main buildings built in 1383, houses memorial tablets. The Ming Tower, a rectangular citadel, served as the command point of the tomb. Nearby, **Shixiang Lu** is a pleasant walkway half a kilometer long lined with stone carvings of 12 pairs of animals. The second half of the passageway, flanked by pairs of soldiers and mandarins, leads to Four Square Pavilion, which consists of a tall stone tablet enclosed by four walls. Built in 1413, the pavilion's tablet contains 2,000 characters inscribed with the life story of the emperor Zhu Yuangzhang, written by his son Zhu Di.

Admission ¥50 ($6.50/£3.25), or by ¥130 ($17/£8.45) combination ticket (see "Memorials & Museums," above). 6:30am–6:30pm. Bus: no. Y2 or Y3.

Linggu Si Hidden amid the tall conifers east of Zhongshan Ling, the fascinating Wuliang Dian (Beamless Hall), the only surviving edifice of this original Ming dynasty temple, is notable for having been built entirely from bricks without a single wood beam. From the outside, the building is beautiful, but unfortunately, the inside has been turned into a wax museum of key historical leaders from the early 20th century. China's Republican government erected a cemetery on the grounds of the temple in 1933 to commemorate soldiers.

Admission ¥15 ($1/£1.95), or by ¥130 ($17/£8.45) combination ticket (see "Memorials & Museums," above). 6:30am–6:30pm.

Song Meiling's Villa A beautiful, high-ceiled villa with a traditional Chinese roof, this is where Chiang Kai-shek and his wife, better known as Madame Chiang Kai-shek, often spent weekends when China's capital was located in Nanjing. The second floor consists of a massive bedroom, parlors, and a dining room decorated with large national government maps.

Admission ¥10 ($1.30/65p). 7:30am–6pm.

OTHER ATTRACTIONS

Nanjing Bowuguan (Nanjing Museum) ⚔   Situated in an impressively sleek and clean building, the Nanjing Museum is worth at least an hour or two of your time. Standouts include the **Lacquerware Hall** with an exquisitely carved Qing dynasty throne; the **Jadeware Hall** featuring an Eastern Han dynasty jade burial suit sewn together with silver from A.D. 200; and the **Fabric Embroidery Hall,** where visitors can view a demonstration of cloud-pattern brocade weaving on an old-fashioned loom. The basement level houses a nice folk-art section and earthenware from the Tang dynasty. The museum shop sells a wide selection of art and crafts.

Zhongshan Dong Lu 321. ⓒ 025/8480-2119. Admission ¥20 ($2.60/£1.30). 9am–4:30pm. Bus: no. Y1, Y2, or 9 to Zhonghua Men.

Nanjing Datusha Jinianguan (Memorial to the Victims of the Nanjing Massacre) ⚔   While worth a visit, this memorial museum, commemorating the atrocities suffered by the Chinese during the Japanese invasion of Nanjing in 1937, certainly does a heavy-handed job of explaining history, from the funerary-style orchestral music piped on the grounds to the giant statues of human limbs that greet visitors at the museum's entrance. Located at Jiang Dong Men, itself an execution and mass burial site during the invasion, the museum consists of an outdoor exhibit, a coffin-shaped viewing hall

The Nanjing Massacre

On December 13, 1937, Japanese troops invaded Nanjing. What followed were the darkest 6 weeks of Nanjing's history, as over 300,000 Chinese were bayoneted, shot, burned, drowned, beheaded, and buried alive. The city was looted and torched, and corpses were thrown into the Yangzi River. Women suffered the most: During the first month of occupation, 20,000 cases of rape were reported in the city. Many of those who survived were tortured.

During this time, a small number of Western businessmen and American missionaries, who stayed behind when their compatriots fled after the departing Chinese government, used their privileged status as foreign nationals to create a 3.9-sq.-km (1½-sq.-mile) safety zone covering today's Hanzhong Lu in the south, Zhongshan Lu in the east, Shanxi Lu in the north, and Xikang Lu in the west. Around 250,000 Chinese found safe haven in 25 refugee camps inside it. The head of the safety zone was German business-man John Rabe, chosen in part because he was a Nazi. Often described as the Oskar Schindler of China, Rabe's initial determination to save his Siemens Chinese employees eventually took on a larger purpose as he even sheltered hundreds of Chinese women in his own backyard. There were countless individual moments of courage, too, as Chinese clawed their way out of mass graves, crawled to hospitals with bullet wounds, or sheltered their brethren at great risk to themselves.

containing some excavated victims' bones, and pictures and artifacts documenting the Japanese onslaught, the massacre, and the aftermath. Photographs of tortures and executions, many taken by Japanese army photographers, are quite gruesome, as are reproductions of the blood-soaked clothing of the victims. The final room documents the reconciliation, however tenuous, between the Chinese and Japanese.

Chating Dong Jie 195, Jiang Dong Men. Free admission. 8am–5pm. Bus: no. Y4 or 7.

Taiping Tianguo Lishi Bowuguan (Taiping Heavenly Kingdom Historical Museum)   The largest uprising in modern Chinese history, the Taiping Rebellion is documented here in pictures and artifacts including Taiping maps, coins, and weapons. Unfortunately, the descriptions don't explain the rebellion particularly well. The museum itself is located in **Zhan Yuan,** a garden that was the residence of the Taiping "Eastern Prince," Yang Xiuqing, and the young "Western Prince," Xiao Youhe. Visitors can relax in the garden and ponder China's 5,000 years of history while watching goldfish in a pond.

Zhan Yuan Lu 128. Admission ¥10 ($1.30/65p). Museum 8am–5pm; park 8am–11pm. Bus: no. Y2 to Changle Lu.

SHOPPING

Nanjing's biggest **art gallery,** Jinying Yishu Zhongxin Hualang (Golden Eagle Art Center), located at Hanzhong Lu 89, 11th floor, has a large collection of traditional Chinese ink paintings, calligraphy, and modern oil paintings. Nanjing Yunjun Yanjiusuo (Brocade Research Institute) at Chating Dong Lu 240 (open 8:30am–4:30pm) sells **cloud dragon brocade** once reserved exclusively for use by emperors. Prices are high, but this is the real deal. The Nanjing Gongyi Meishu Dalou Gouwu Zhongxin at Beijing Dong Lu 31; 9am–5:40pm) has two floors of fairly expensive **handicrafts** from all over China, including jade, silk embroidery, fans, lacquerware, pottery, and jewelry. At the other end of the price and taste spectrum, shops at Fuzi Miao sell all kinds of local products, including rain flower pebbles, rain flower tea, hanging ornaments, and Nanjing salted duck.

The trendy **night market** on Hunan Lu between Zhongshan Bei Lu and Zhongyang Lu has pretty much turned into a clean and orderly shopping arcade. There's still a small night market at Yunnan Lu hosting vendors who sell ethnic batik arts, embroidered bags, jewelry, underwear, and household items.

WHERE TO STAY

The glut of upmarket hotels in Nanjing has resulted in generous discounts, averaging between 30% and 50% in low season (plus a 15% service charge). Undeterred by neither the possible market saturation nor the fact that both the Hilton and Shangri-La pulled out of Nanjing (see Parkview Dingshan and Grand Metropark hotels, below), a brand-new six-star InterContinental is being built on Zhongshan Lu. The 450-room behemoth is scheduled to open in 2010.

VERY EXPENSIVE

Parkview Dingshan Hotel (Dingshan Hua Yuan) ✦   Shangri-La ceased operation of this hotel in 2005, sadly taking with them the signature service of the Shangri-La name. Rooms remain tastefully furnished in a mix of contemporary and Asian styles, but the public spaces seem to have sprouted blinding fluorescent lights and mismatched color schemes. The hotel is also in the far western part of town, which is fine if you want to get away from it all, but is terribly inconvenient if you want to do anything in town or visit some of the major attractions in town or on Purple Mountain in the east. The hotel does have some nice perks, however, like free local calls, international calls and faxes charged at cost, complimentary laundry and dry cleaning service, and a generous 6pm late checkout.

Chahaer Lu 90. © 025/5880-2888. Fax 025/5882-1729. www.shangri-la.com. 453 units. ¥1,000 ($130/£65) standard room; from ¥2,900 ($377/£189) suite. AE, DC, MC, V. **Amenities:** 3 restaurants; bar; lounge; nightclub; indoor pool; health club and spa; sauna; concierge; shuttle service to town; free airport transfers; business center; forex; shopping arcade; salon; room service; massage; laundry/dry cleaning; executive rooms. *In room:* A/C, satellite TV, high-speed Internet access, minibar, hair dryer, safe.

Sofitel Galaxy Nanjing (Nanjing Suofeite Yinhe Dajiudian) 𝄞𝄞𝄞   This hotel

is super luxe and ultramodern. The interior decor is sleek shades of brown with accents of red and purple. Funky wall hangings like mounted Chinese scrolls, Impressionist art, or stones encased in glass against a backdrop of raw silk are in the rooms and public spaces. Ambience music piped through the hallways and elevators makes you feel like you're at a swish new lounge rather than some nameless business hotel. Concierge service, unfortunately, leaves a lot to be desired; they're pretty much clueless about what's going on around town and have next to no good recommendations. Standard rooms are spacious, with marble entryways and silky gold and yellow carpets. Beds are ultra-soft with fat duvets and pillows. Bathrooms are spacious and have stylish rectangular faucets. Showers come with a tropical rain shower, but the water pressure can be weak and the temperature finicky. I recommend having a bath in the separate tub next to the big mirror. Entertainment comes in the form widescreen, wall-mounted plasma televisions. The desk chair is butter brown leather and a plush chair with matching ottoman rests in the corner. Everything about this hotel is chic and sleek.

Shanxi Lu 9. © 025/8371-8888. Fax 025/8371-0505. www.sofitel.com/asia. 278 units. ¥1,071–¥1,241 ($139–$161/ £70–£81) standard; from ¥1,697 ($217/£108) executive/suite. Discounts possible up to 50%. AE, DC, MC, V. **Amenities:** 3 restaurants; bar; lounge; nightclub; indoor pool; tennis court; health club; spa; sauna; concierge; shuttle service to town; business center; forex; shopping arcade; salon; room service; laundry/dry cleaning; executive rooms. *In room:* A/C, satellite TV, high-speed Internet access, minibar, hair dryer, iron/ironing board, safe big enough for laptops, wireless phone, scale.

Sofitel Zhongshan Golf Resort (Nanjing Suofeite Gao'erfu Jiudian) 𝄞𝄞

Located way the heck out of town on the eastern side of Purple Mountain, this creamy white hotel with towering columns looks like an old French colonial mansion. Coincidence? I think not—this is after all a Sofitel resort. Rooms come with balconies and are as lovely and luxe as you can expect from this brand. Standard rooms are done in light blond wood (sleek dark wood for executive suites), and silk accent pillows and bed throws patterned with Chinese characters adorn the beds. Unlike its sister location, which is a popular business hotel, rates at this resort tend to be much higher on weekends when all the business folk head for the hills and the golf range.

Huanling Lu. © 025/8540-8888. Fax 025/8430-8001 www.sofitel.com/asia. 140 units. ¥1,000 ($130/£65) single room; from ¥1,017–¥1,357 ($132–$176/£66–£88) standard; from ¥1,697 ($220/£110) suite. AE, DC, MC, V. **Amenities:** 3 restaurants; bar; indoor pool; health club; mahjong rooms; concierge; business center; forex; room service; massage; laundry/dry cleaning; nonsmoking rooms. *In room:* A/C, satellite TV, high-speed Internet access, minibar, hair dryer, safe.

EXPENSIVE

Crowne Plaza Nanjing Hotels and Suites (Qiao Hong Huangguan Jiudian) 𝄞𝄞

Suites are this hotel's specialty, which accounts for its popularity with business travelers, but tourists love it, too, for its prime location a block west of Xinjiekou, right in the thick of the city. Unconventionally located in an office building, the hotel has its entrance and concierge on the first floor, its lobby and other facilities on the seventh and ninth floors, and its guest rooms on the 37th to 58th floors. Guests are treated to a personalized sit-down check-in, then whisked up to their rooms high above the city center. Look down from the city's tallest building and understand why the hotel prides itself on its views, especially at night when the daytime smog gives way to twinkling neon lights. Guest rooms are classically furnished and bathrooms have separate shower and tub.

Hanzhong Lu 89. © 025/8471-8888. Fax 025/8471-9999. www.crowneplaza.com. 300 units. ¥598 ($78/£39) standard room; ¥758–¥888 ($99–$115/£49–£58) suite. AE, DC, MC, V. **Amenities:** 4 restaurants; bar; lounge; nightclub; indoor pool; health club; sauna; concierge; airport shuttle; business center; forex; shopping arcade; salon; room service; massage; babysitting; laundry/dry cleaning; executive rooms. *In room:* A/C, TV, high-speed Internet access, dataport, minibar, hair dryer, safe.

Grand Metropark Hotel Nanjing (Nanjing Wei Jing Guoji Dajiudian) ✴

The last time we visited this place, it was a Hilton hotel and it was already showing signs of age. Looks like the Hilton family chose to abandon it rather than renovate. The rooms now have a musty smell and the decor remains bland and functional, but still quite comfortable. Unfortunately, they are not always well fitted for the modern, connected traveler (there's a distinct shortage of electrical outlets in the standard rooms, for example).

Zhongshan Dong Lu 319. © 025/8480-8888. Fax 025/8480-9999. www.hilton.com. 561 units. ¥1,800–¥2,000 ($234–$260/£117–£130) standard; ¥3,000 ($390/£195) suite. Discounts possible up to 60%. AE, DC, MC, V. **Amenities:** 4 restaurants; deli; bar; lounge; disco; indoor pool; tennis courts; health club and spa; sauna; bowling alley; concierge; business center; forex; shopping arcade; salon; room service; laundry/dry cleaning; executive rooms. *In room:* A/C, satellite TV, high-speed Internet access (executive rooms), minibar, hair dryer, safe.

Hotel Sheraton Nanjing Kingsley Hotel and Towers (Nanjing Jinsili Xilaideng Jiudian) ✴✴

Located about 1km (⅔ mile) west of Xinjiekou, this sleek and modern glass tower with a state-of-the-art elevator control system (makes a maximum of three stops per run) is a popular choice with foreign business travelers. Travelers fed up with shabby three-star accommodations in China will find the Sheraton a welcome change. The Sheraton also boasts the largest hotel swimming pool and health club in town. Rooms are tastefully decorated and comfortable, and afford good views of the city; those on executive floors come with personal butler service. Bathrooms are large and contain separate shower and tub.

Hanzhong Lu 169. © 025/8666-8888. Fax 025/8666-9999. www.Sheraton.com/Nanjing. 350 units. ¥1,580 ($205/£103) standard room; ¥1,980–¥3,280 ($257–$426/£129–£213) suite. Discounts possible up to 60%. AE, DC, MC, V. **Amenities:** 4 restaurants; bar; lounge; disco; indoor pool; tennis court; health club and spa; sauna; salon; concierge; business center; forex; shopping arcade; room service; massage; laundry/dry cleaning; executive rooms. *In room:* A/C, TV, dataport, high-speed Internet access, minibar, hair dryer, safe.

Jinling Fandian ✴

Don't let the fact that this is a state-owned hotel turn you off. The 37-story Jinling has been a local institution since it opened in 1983 and has worked to keep its reputation. Its exalted status has made it arrogant on occasion but its wide range of facilities and shops, not to mention its ideal location right at the city center, make it the place to be for many business travelers and tourists. Standard rooms run small but are functional, and come with large plasma-screen TVs that guests rave about. Rooms are decorated in a smart, minimalist style and bathrooms are sparkling clean.

Hanzhong Lu 2. © 025/8471-1888. Fax 025/8471-1666. www.jinlinghotel.com. 600 units. ¥1,535 ($200/£100) standard room; ¥2,990–¥4,650 ($389–$605/£194–£302) suite. Discounts possible up to 35%. AE, DC, MC, V. **Amenities:** 7 restaurants; bar; lounge; karaoke; disco; cigar bar; indoor pool; health club and spa; simulated golf driving range; bowling alley; concierge; business center; forex; shopping arcade; salon; room service; laundry/dry cleaning; executive rooms. *In room:* A/C, TV, high-speed Internet access, minibar, hair dryer, safe.

MODERATE

Celebrity City Hotel (Mingren Chengshi Jiudian) This hotel was meant to be a Marriott, but after negotiations fell through, it opened at the end of 2004 as a Chinese-owned four-star establishment. Rooms are tastefully decorated, and deluxe rooms come with desktop computers. One big draw is that the hotel offers free high-speed Internet access in its rooms. Bathrooms have a slight funky smell to them, but on the plus side, they come with a self-cleaning Japanese-style toilet and a massaging shower head.

Zhongshan Lu 30. ⓒ 025/8312-3333. Fax 025/8212-3888. www.yilaicch.com. 368 units. ¥1,480 ($192/£96) standard room; ¥1,880 ($244/£122) deluxe room. 40% discounts possible. AE, DC, MC, V. **Amenities:** 2 restaurants; bar; indoor swimming pool; fitness center; sauna; game room; conference center; room service; massage; karaoke; non-smoking rooms; rooms for those w/limited mobility. *In room:* A/C TV, high-speed Internet access, desktop computer (deluxe rooms and suites).

Central Hotel (Zhongxin Dajiudian) ⓕ Looking somewhat weathered on the outside, this popular four-star hotel in the round still draws visitors with its spacious, recently renovated rooms, competitive prices, and great location a block north of Xinjiekou. Amenities, however, do not seem particularly standardized in the rooms, so be sure to request rooms containing whatever specific item you may need. Bathrooms are clean.

Zhongshan Lu 75. ⓒ 025/8473-3888. Fax 0258/473-3999. 320 units. ¥1,580–¥1,880 ($205–$244/£103–£122) standard room; ¥2,880 ($374/£187) suite. 70% discounts possible. AE, DC, MC, V. **Amenities:** 5 restaurants; bar; lounge; nightclub; outdoor pool; health club; sauna; bowling alley; game room; concierge; business center; forex; shopping arcade; salon; room service; laundry. *In room:* A/C, satellite TV, high-speed Internet access (select rooms), minibar, hair dryer, safe.

INEXPENSIVE

Nanshan Binguan Located in the southwestern corner of the Nanjing Normal University campus about a 15-minute taxi ride northwest of Xinjiekou, this hotel is a no-frills budget choice that's nevertheless clean and comfortable. The hotel also houses foreign students studying at the university. Rooms are spartan but the small bathrooms are clean.

Ninghai Lu 122. ⓒ 025/8371-6440. Fax 025/8373-8174. 200 units. ¥198–¥268 ($26–$35/£13–£17) standard room; ¥368–¥558 ($48–$73/£24–£36) suite. No credit cards. **Amenities:** Cafeteria; Internet bar; ticket service; salon. *In room:* A/C, TV.

WHERE TO DINE

There are several upmarket, modern restaurants in **1912**, a restaurant and bar district on the corner of Changjiang Lu and Taiping Bei Lu. 1912 has been constructed to create an "Old China" feel: gray stone, traditional roofs, and pedestrian walkways. Everything feels a bit geared for the tourists and most restaurants are expensive or overpriced. Western standbys like KFC and Starbucks are here. For finer dining, head to the hip Taiwan chain **Bellagio** (beside Starbucks), or the popular Sichuanese chain **South Beauty,** which should be open by the time you read this. Other lively places to grab a late-night bite include **Shizi Qiao**, a popular pedestrian restaurant street off Hunan Lu, and the **Confucius Temple** area, which attracts swarms of people when it is all lit up at night.

EXPENSIVE

Jinhe Tai Canting (Golden Harvest Thai Opera Cafe) THAI Located in the Hunan Lu dining area known as Shizi Qiao, this restaurant serves decent Thai food

and is popular with Nanjing's expats. A golden Buddha statue outside greets arriving guests, while the decor inside is tasteful and subdued. Besides the typical solid curries and pad thai, Golden Harvest features several specialties, including a good fried crab with Thai curry sauce and a casserole of baked king prawns with vermicelli noodles.

Hunan Lu Shizi Qiao 2. ⓒ **025/8324-2525.** Reservations recommended. English menus with pictures. Meal for 2 ¥150–¥250 ($20–$33/£9.75–£16). AE, DC, MC, V. 11am–2:30pm and 5–10:30pm.

Jinying Dajiulou ⭐ HUAIYANG   Established in 1998 with only eight tables, this restaurant has since grown into a top restaurant with two locations. The house specialty is *Tianmuhu yutou,* a delicious white fish–head soup made with fish from nearby Tianmu Lake. Other tasty dishes here include *shuijing xiaren* (tender sautéed shrimp) and *pansi yu* (deep-fried fish-tail filets in sweet-and-sour sauce).

Wangfu Dajie 9. ⓒ **025/8452-0088.** Reservations recommended. Meal for 2 ¥120–¥250 ($16–$33/£7.80–£16). No credit cards. 11am–2pm and 6–10pm.

MODERATE

Ciao Italia (Ni hao! Yidali Canting) ITALIAN   The fine homemade pasta and wood-fired pizzas at this classic-style Italian eatery should satisfy anyone's craving for home. Naples-born chef Giuseppi Parisi recently left Bella Napoli Restaurant due to, er, artistic differences. He took his signature fresh and homemade style of cooking and opened this new outlet, which has quickly become a hit with local expats. Try the signature dish (Giuseppi's own creation), the Mezza-Luna, a half-moon pizza that's part calzone.

Shigu Lu 193-2. ⓒ **025/8660-8807.** Main courses ¥25–¥140 ($3.25–$18/£1.65–£9.10). AE, DC, MC, V. Mon–Fri 11am–2pm and 5–11pm; Sat–Sun 11am until the last customer.

Le 5 Sens (Le Shang Faguo Canting) ⭐ FRENCH   You found it—the most charming, affordable French restaurant in town. Tucked away on a small street beside Nanjing University, this intimate place serves savory, home-style French dishes. Part-owner Michael Martin originally came to Nanjing as a student and was compelled to extend his stay. He tried working at the five-star hotels, but opening his own restaurant proved to be the better path. I had the quiche Lorraine with green salad for my appetizer. The quiche was rich and flavorful while the salad, served with balsamic vinegar only, was a nice contrast. My sirloin steak was done far past my request for medium rare, so you might want to order down. I highly recommend the chocolate profiteroles. The vanilla ice cream sandwiched between puff pastries is just a way to get to the star of the dish: the warm chocolate sauce made from imported Belgian chocolate (Martin: "I can not work wit' zomething else!"). They've also got free Wi-Fi.

Hankou Lu 52-1. ⓒ **025/8359-5859.** Dinner for 2 from ¥230 ($30/£15). Credit cards should be accepted by the time you read this. 11:30am–2:30pm and 5:30–10:30pm.

INEXPENSIVE

Bainian Lao Feng Xiaochi ⭐ NANJING STREET FOOD   For a fun and authentic experience, head to this cafeteria located in Confucius Temple. It's a lively joint where diners go to the cashier to trade money for paper tickets, before heading to individual stalls where the tickets can be redeemed for an array of snacks, including steamed dumplings and glutinous rice wrapped in bamboo leaves. The best part is just being able to point to what you want. The wonton soup (¥3/40¢/20p) and the steamed buns are the most popular dishes.

122 Gongyuan Jie (on the main street near the Confucius Temple, 300m/984 ft. east of McDonald's). No phone. ¥4–¥10 (50¢–$1.30/25p–65p) per person. No credit cards. 10:30am–8:30pm.

New Magazine Cafe (Xin Zazhi Kafei) ECLECTIC   You might come here for the free wireless access but you should stay for the food, which ranges from Western-style pastas to chicken teriyaki to Sichuanese spicy noodles. Teas, in flavors from hazelnut to almond, are brought to the table in porcelain pots resting on a small fire. The cafe also features a rack of Chinese magazines for sale and a range of pastries.

Three locations. Hankou Lu 42, *C* **025/8324-8932**; Changbai Jie 488, *C* **025/8451-2013**; and Hunan Lu 18, *C* **025/5791-3508.** Main courses ¥25–¥40 ($3.25–$5.20/£1.65–£2.60). AE, DC, MC, V. 9:30am–1:30am.

Skyways Bakery and Deli *(Value)* EUROPEAN   This place serves excellent, generously sized pastries and proper homemade breads. Skyways is also a good place to meet other Nanjing expats (the Nanjing Running Club indulge themselves here after Sunday runs around the nearby lake). Deli sandwiches are a steal and done the way you like 'em. The Taipingmen Jie location is more popular, but Hankou Lu 3-6 is more centrally located.

2 locations: Taipingmen Jie 10, *C* **025/8481-2002**; Hankou Lu 3-6, *C* **025/8663-4834.** Pastries ¥5–¥15 (65¢–$1.95/35p–£1) or ¥30 ($3.90/£1.95) for an entire pie; sandwiches ¥18 ($2.35/£1.20). No credit cards. 8:30am–9:30pm.

NANJING AFTER DARK
To find out what's happening in the arts, pick up a copy of the free English-language monthly *MAP.*

Chinese *kun ju* opera is usually performed at the **Jiangnan Theater** (Yanling Xiang 5; *C* **025/440-4281**), while traditional Beijing Opera is performed at the **People's Theater** (Yanggongjing 25; *C* **025/450-1314,** ext. 8009). Performances usually begin at 7:30pm.

Around the corner from the Presidential Palace, **1912** is a district of bars, cafes, clubs, and restaurants that debuted in 2005; With it's Euro-dance music and funky interior **7 Club,** about 500m down the way from KFC, is the current hip place to grab a drink. **Danny's Irish Pub (Danni'er Ai'erlan Jiuba),** located on the fourth floor of the Sheraton Hotel, Hanzhong Lu 169 (open 6:30pm–2am) is the most popular bar with Nanjing's expatriates. For dancing, **Time Tunnel (Shiguang Suidao),** at Taiping Nan Lu 354, has the largest dance floor in Nanjing and a nightly laser show to boot. The wild **Scarlet (Luanshi Jiaren),** at Gu Lou Chezhan Dongxiang 29, has been known to give foreigners a discount on entry fees in order to entice the locals.

10 Yangzhou ★★

Jiangsu Province, 240km (149 miles) NW of Shanghai, 100km (62 miles) NE of Nanjing

Located at the junction of the Yangzi River and the Grand Canal, Yangzhou was known during the Sui and Tang dynasties as the economic and cultural center of southern China, home to scholars, painters, poets, literati, and merchants. It was also the playground of the rich and famous, starting with the 6th-century Sui Yangdi emperor, who visited courtesans here. The Qing Qianlong emperor visited six times. Today Yangzhou is a charming town with broad, tree-lined boulevards and a network of canals and lakes. Known for its handicrafts, cuisine, and landmarks, Yangzhou certainly has enough to keep you occupied for a couple of days, but it can also be a day trip from Nanjing.

ESSENTIALS

GETTING THERE The nearest **airport** is in Nanjing and the closest **railway** station is in Zhenjiang. **Buses** serve Zhenjiang (every 15 min. 6:30am–6:25pm; 1 hr.; ¥13/$1.70/85p) and Nanjing (every 20 min. 6:30am–6pm; 1½ hr.; ¥25/$3.25/£1.65) from the **West Bus Station (Yangzhou Xi Zhan;** © **0514/786-1812)** in the southwest of the city. Buses to Shanghai (7 daily 6:40am–3pm; 3–3½ hr.; ¥70–¥84/$9.10–$11/£4.55–£5.45) and Suzhou (7 daily 7:15am–4:40pm; 2 hr.; ¥57/$7.40/£3.70) depart from the **long-distance bus station** *(changtu qichezhan)* in southeast Yangzhou on Dujiang Nan Lu 27 (© **0514/781-3658**).

GETTING AROUND Most of Yangzhou's sights are clustered in the north of town. **Taxis** charge ¥6 (80¢/40p) for 3km (2 miles), then ¥1 (15¢/10p) per kilometer until 10km (6 miles), after which the price rises to ¥1.50 (20¢/10p) per kilometer. **Bus** no. 5 (¥1/15¢/10p) runs from the long-distance bus station in the southwest of town up Huaihai Lu to Daming Si.

TOURS & GUIDES **China Travel Service (CTS)** at Wenchang Zhong Lu 200 (© **0514/734-0524;** Mon–Fri 7:30am–8pm) can arrange accommodations, plane tickets, and city tours. English-speaking guides will cost around ¥200 ($26/£13) a day, transportation not included.

FAST FACTS

Banks, Foreign Exchange & ATMs The **Bank of China** at Wenchang Zhong Lu 279 conducts foreign exchange Monday to Friday from 8:30 to 11:45am and 3 to 5:30pm. An ATM is located here.

Internet Access There's a **24-hour Internet cafe** at Liuhu Lu 34. It charges ¥2 (25¢/10p) per hour.

Post Office Located at Wenchang Zhong Lu, it is open from 8am to 6:30pm.

Visa Extensions The **PSB** is at Huaihai Lu 100, © **0514/703-1111** (open Mon–Fri 8am–noon and 2:30–6pm, 2–5:30pm in winter).

EXPLORING YANGZHOU
GARDENS

Shou Xi Hu (Slender West Lake) ⟨⟨ Located in the northwest part of town, Yangzhou's premier attraction got its name during the Qing dynasty, when Hangzhou poet Wang Kang, on passing through the area, noted that it resembled a slender version of Hangzhou's West Lake (Xi Hu). The most popular photo spot is the impressive **Wu Ting Qiao (Five Pavilion Bridge),** built in 1757 by a salt merchant who, in anticipation of the Qianlong emperor's arrival, modeled the bridge after one in the imperial resort (Bishu Shanzhuang) in Chengde, Hebei. Many Qing dynasty salt merchants competed with each other to build gardens in order to impress the emperor.

   Bai Ta (White Dagoba), a white Tibetan-style stupa, was built by another ingratiating salt merchant more than 200 years ago. The story goes that during one of his six visits to the lake, the Qianlong emperor remarked on the area's resemblance to Beihai Park in Beijing and inquired if there was a similar dagoba here. Eager to please, the salt merchant said yes, then spent the whole night panicking when the emperor insisted on seeing the dagoba. Finally, the merchant hit upon the idea to have a dagoba made out of salt, a tactic that apparently worked the next day when Qianlong saw the white structure from afar. Thereafter, the merchant commissioned a real dagoba to be built. The **Diaoyu Tai (Angler's Terrace)** on **Xiao Jin Shan (Small Golden Hill)** is

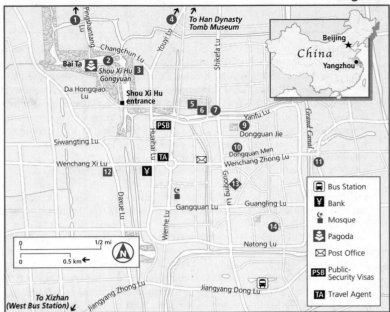

Yangzhou

ACCOMMODATIONS ■
Grand Metropole Hotel **12**
(Yángzhōu Jīnghuá Dàjiǔdiàn)
扬州京华大酒店

Xīyuán Dàjiǔdiàn **5**
西园大酒店

Yángzhōu Bīnguǎn **6**
扬州宾馆

Yángzhōu State Guesthouse **3**
(Yángzhōu Yíngbīnguā)
扬州迎宾馆

DINING ◆
Fùchūn Cháshè **13**
富春茶舍

ATTRACTIONS ●
Dàmíng Sì **1**
大明寺

Gè Yuán **9**
个园

Hàn Mù Bówùguǎn **4**
(Hàn Dynasty Tomb
Museum)
汉墓博物馆

Hé Yuán **14**
何园

Mountain Flattening Hall **1**
(Píng Shān Táng)
平山堂

Pǔhādīng Yuán **11**
普哈丁园

Shòu Xī Hú **2**
(Slender West Lake)
瘦西湖

Wāng Shì Xiǎ Yuán **10**
汪氏小园

Yángzhōu Shì
  Bówùguǎn **7**
(Yángzhōu City Museum)
扬州市博物馆

The Grand Canal

At 1,800km (1,116 miles), the Grand Canal (Da Yunhe) is the longest canal in the world. Together with the Great Wall of China, this waterway, which runs from Beijing to Hangzhou, is one of China's great engineering feats. The first 85km (52 miles) were constructed as early as 495 B.C., but the Herculean task of linking the Yellow River and Yangzi River began in earnest in the early 7th century, when the second Sui dynasty Yang Di emperor had the waterway dug from his capital at Luoyang to Beijing in the north and to the Yangzi River basin. Due to the differences in terrain and water levels, locks and dams had to be built along the way.

The original purpose of the canal was to transport the plentiful grains of the affluent south to the poorer north, but over the course of the years, the canal became a major trade conduit as commodities such as tea, silk, porcelain, lacquerware, and salt were all shipped up north. By the time of the Yuan dynasty (1206–1368), the final stretch of the canal was completed, linking Beijing all the way to Hangzhou. Many of the bricks and stones used to build Beijing's temples and palaces arrived via the canal. By the time of the Southern Song dynasty (1127–1279), political power had shifted south to Jiangsu and Zhejiang provinces, as the Song emperors moved their capital to Hangzhou and the Ming emperors established themselves in Nanjing.

The canal only fell into disuse in the early 20th century, thanks to constant flooding from the Yellow River, silting, and the development of rail lines. Today, the navigable sections are primarily south of the Yangzi River in the region known as Jiangnan, which includes the cities of Wuxi, Yangzhou, Suzhou, and Hangzhou. Even here, some sections are so shallow and narrow that they are accessible only to small, flat-bottomed boats. North of the Yangzi, much is silted up and impassable.

Tourists wanting to experience life on the canal can sail between Hangzhou and Suzhou and/or Wuxi. In Suzhou, canalboat passage can be booked at travel agencies or directly at the dock, Nan Men Lunchuan Keyun Matou, at Renmin Lu 8 (© 0512/6520-5720). Boats, which are bare-bones basic, depart from the Suzhou Boat Terminal daily at 5:30pm, arriving in Hangzhou at around 7am. The reverse voyage also departs Hangzhou at 5:30pm and gets into Suzhou at around 7am. Tickets either way cost the same and can be purchased in Hangzhou at the Wulin Men Keyun Matou (© 0571/8515-3185). For information on boats to and from Wuxi, see "Getting There" in the "Wuxi, Tai Hu & Yixing" section, below.

where Qianlong came to fish, although he was such a terrible angler that the merchants took to putting fish on his hooks in order to avoid imperial wrath.

Da Hongqiao Lu 28. Admission ¥50 ($6.50/£3.25). 6:30am–6:30pm.

Ge Yuan 🕊 This garden was built over 160 years ago as part of a salt merchant's residence. It features a ponderous rockery section quite cleverly designed according to the four seasons. "Summer," for example, features Tai Hu rocks designed to resemble clouds in the sky after a storm; magnolia trees provide welcome shade. There's also a variety of exotic bamboo here, including purple, turtle, and yellow bamboo.

Yanfu Dong Lu 10. Admission ¥30 ($3.90/£1.95). 8am–6pm.

He Yuan 🅰🅰 Smaller than Ge Yuan, this garden offers some peace and quiet. Located in the southeast part of town, it is more residence than garden but still has its share of rockeries, pavilions, and ponds. Trees, plants, and an elevated walkway are used rather ingeniously to make the garden appear much larger than it really is, a tactic employed in many classical southern Chinese gardens.

Xuningmen Jie 77. Admission ¥30 ($3.90/£1.95). 7:30am–6pm.

Wang Shi Xiao Yuan 🅰 Located in the center of town on Dong Quan Men, the street of preserved historic homes (including that of former Chinese president Jiang Zemin), this impressive late Qing dynasty residence of a local salt merchant is simple and understated from the outside but has almost 100 rooms inside, with the main rooms situated on a central axis. The furnishings are fine and reflect the wealth and status of the owner. The main Chun Hui Shi (Spring Hall), for example, contains a German chandelier, expensive marble wall panels whose patterns resemble Chinese landscapes, and a poem by Tang dynasty poet Bai Juyi.

Dongquan Men Lishi Jiequ 14. Admission ¥10 ($1.30/65p). 8am–6pm.

OTHER ATTRACTIONS

Daming Si 🅰 Built more than 1,600 years ago, this major Buddhist temple is today best known for its **Jian Zhen Memorial Hall,** dedicated to a Tang dynasty abbot of the temple, Jian Zhen (688–763), who in 742 was invited to teach in Japan. After five unsuccessful attempts to cross the ocean in a wooden boat, Jian Zhen finally made it to Japan in 753, old and blind. He spent the next 10 years introducing Chinese Buddhism, medicine, language, and architecture to the Japanese. The Jian Zhen Memorial Hall, built in 1974, is modeled after the main hall of the Toshodai Temple in Nara, Japan, which Jian Zhen built. A cedar statue of the teacher stands in the hall and there are still religious and cultural exchanges between Nara and Yangzhou.

South of the temple is **Ping Shan Tang (Mountain Flattening Hall),** where famous Song dynasty writer Ouyang Xiu (1007–72) came to drink wine and write poetry when he was governor of Yangzhou. From here, his perspective was on the same level as the nearby hills, hence the hall's name.

Ping Shan Tang 1. Admission ¥20 ($2.60/£1.30). Apr–Nov 7:30am–5:30pm; Dec–Mar 7:30am–4pm. Bus: no. 5.

Han Mu Bowuguan (Han Dynasty Tomb Museum) 🅰🅰🅰 This fascinating Western Han tomb of the king of Guangling Kingdom, Liu Xu, the fifth son of the Han Wu Di emperor (140–86 B.C.), is worth visiting. Sixty years in the making, Liu Xu's tomb is a grand five levels deep. The second airtight layer is made up of 840 *nanmu* (cedar) bricks linked to each other lengthwise by tiny hooks on the inside surfaces. These bricks could only be disassembled, and the wall breached, by locating the first brick. On the third level was the warehouse, while the living quarters occupied the fourth level; the fifth and bottom level contained a coffin on wheels. In the northwest part of the tomb, there is even a bathroom, making this the first Han tomb to contain such! Despite the seemingly impenetrable defenses, the tomb was actually robbed about 100 years later. The thieves were able to dig right down to the residential level with relative ease, suggesting that the tomb was robbed by descendants of the very people who built it. East of Liu Xu's tomb is that of his wife, who died 10 years after him. Three levels deep, the queen's tomb, also made from *nanmu,* is approached from the bottom level.

Youyi Lu 16 (3km/2 miles north of town). Admission ¥15 ($1.95/£1). 8:30am–4:30pm. Bus: no. 5.

Puhading Yuan ✿ The central tomb at this Song dynasty Muslim graveyard belongs to Puhading, 16th descendant of the prophet Muhammad, who visited Yangzhou to help spread Islam. He built the Crane Mosque (Xian E Si) in town, and was buried in this graveyard in 1275 in a simple, stepped stone grave enclosed in a rectangular structure with a vaulted roof. Also here are the tombs of Muslim traders and other Arabs from the Yuan to the Qing dynasties.

Jiefang Nan Lu 17. Admission ¥12 ($1.60/80p). 8am–5pm.

Yangzhou Shi Bowuguan (Yangzhou City Museum) Just east of the Yangzhou Hotel, this museum is housed in a temple complex dedicated to a local hero, a late Ming dynasty official named Shi Kefa, who led Yangzhou's citizenry against the advancing Qing army. Shi was killed when he refused to surrender, his body cut up into five pieces and strewn to the wind. In the 10 days after his death, which came to be known as "Ten Days in Yangzhou," Qing troops killed 80,000 Yangzhou residents. Shi's jade belt, clothes, and cap are buried in the tumulus behind the hall. The museum itself features some Han coffins, a Tang canoe, and a jade funeral suit with copper threads.

Fengle Shang Jie 2. Admission ¥10 ($1.30/65p). 8:15–11:30am and 2:30–5:30pm.

SHOPPING

Yangzhou is famous for its **lacquerware,** which has a tradition stretching from 475 B.C. Red lacquered vases, mother-of-pearl inlaid screens, ink slabs, fans, jewelry, teapots, and lacquered furniture can all be purchased at the **Yangzhou Qiqi Youxian Gongsi** at Yanhe Jie 50 (open 8:30–11:45am and 2–6pm). Prices range from the reasonable for small handicrafts to the thousands of dollars (yes, dollars) for the larger pieces of furniture. International credit cards are accepted.

WHERE TO STAY

EXPENSIVE

Grand Metropole Hotel (Yangzhou Jinghua Dajiudian) ✿ There's not much individual charm to this modern four-star outfit with joint Hong Kong management, but it does offer all the standard conveniences and comfortable, clean rooms. The staff is used to dealing with foreign business travelers and can usually handle most travelers' needs.

Wenchang Zhong Lu 1. ⓒ 0514/732-2888. Fax 0514/736-8999. 242 units. ¥900 ($117/£59) standard room; ¥1,500–¥2,000 ($195–$260/£98–£130) executive room. AE, DC, MC, V. **Amenities:** 2 restaurants; pastry shop; bar; lounge; health club; concierge; business center; forex; shopping arcade; salon; room service; laundry/dry cleaning; executive rooms. *In room:* A/C, TV, minibar, hair dryer, safe.

MODERATE

Xiyuan Dajiudian ✿ With an ideal location that will allow you to walk to many sights including Shou Xi Hu or simply stroll along the nearby canals and an interesting history—supposedly constructed on the site of Qianlong's imperial villa—this four-star hotel is the most popular choice with Western tour groups and independent travelers. Units are furnished with comfortable beds, clean bathrooms, and the usual amenities, though some rooms show signs of age. Service is acceptable, but nothing more.

Huaiyang Cuisine

As one of the four major schools in Chinese cooking, Huaiyang cuisine (referring to the region between the Yangzi River and the Huai River in northern Jiangsu) has its origins in Yangzhou, even though it has been as much influenced these days by the different regional cooking styles of Jiangsu and Zhejiang provinces. The Ming dynasty Hongwu emperor employed a chef from Yangzhou, as did the famous 20th-century Chinese opera singer Mei Lanfang. Unlike Sichuan cooking with its reliance on peppers, Huaiyang cuisine aims to preserve the basic flavor of ingredients in order to achieve balance and freshness. River fish, farm animals, birds, and vegetables feature prominently. Some of the more famous dishes include *xiefen shizitou* (lightly braised meatballs with crabmeat, also known as Lion's Head Meatballs), *chaihui lianyoutou* (stewed fish head with tofu, greens, and radish), and *bashao zheng zhutou* (stewed pig's head in a red glaze).

Fengle Shang Jie 1. ℂ **0514/780-7888.** Fax 0514/723-3870. 253 units. ¥658–¥788 ($86–$102/£43–£51) standard room; ¥1,600–¥1,800 ($208–$234/£104–£117) suite. 30%–40% discounts possible. AE, DC, MC, V. **Amenities:** 2 restaurants; bar; lounge; indoor swimming pool; tennis court; concierge; business center; forex; shopping arcade; salon; room service; laundry/dry cleaning; executive rooms. *In room:* A/C, TV, minibar, hair dryer, safe.

Yangzhou State Guesthouse (Yangzhou Yingbinguan) ⚘   Set on lovely expansive green grounds next to Slender West Lake, this hotel, which used to be closed to the public and used only for visiting high dignitaries, is the best in town. Former Chinese president Jiang Zemin, who is from Yangzhou, stays in building 1 when he is in town. Rooms are nicely decorated with colorful pillows and modern furniture. Bathrooms, impeccably clean, have a separate tub and shower.

Youyi Lu 48. ℂ **0514/780-9888.** Fax 0514/733-1674. 100 units. ¥718 ($93/£47) standard room; ¥3,800 ($494/£247) suite. 70% discounts possible. AE, DC, MC, V. **Amenities:** 2 restaurants; teahouse; bar; lounge; indoor swimming pool; tennis courts; concierge; business center; forex; salon; room service; laundry. *In room:* A/C, TV.

WHERE TO DINE

The Xiyuan and Grand Metropole hotels both have restaurants serving decent Western food. Western fast food is also available at **Kentucky Fried Chicken** (Wenhe Bei Lu 48), **McDonald's** (Wenhe Lu 3), and **Pizza Hut** (Wenhe Nan Lu 120).

INEXPENSIVE

Fuchun Chashe ⚘ TEAHOUSE/DUMPLINGS   Indulge in one of Yangzhou's favorite pastimes, drinking morning tea, at one of Yangzhou's oldest teahouses. The ritual starts with a pot of tea and a round of nine different snacks, including Yangzhou's famous *baozi* (steamed buns), which come with chicken, bamboo shoots, shrimp, crabmeat, tofu, or a variety of bean pastes. These steamed buns are also available at dinner, as are a variety of *jiaozi* (dumplings). This restaurant is so popular that it has branches in other Chinese cities and even Tokyo.

Desheng Qiao 35 (off Guoqing Lu). ℂ **0514/723-3326.** Meal for 2 ¥20–¥50 ($2.50–$6.25/£1.25–£3.15). AE, MC, V. 6:15am–1:30pm and 3:30–7:30pm.

11 Wuxi, Tai Hu & Yixing

Jiangsu Province, 128km (79 miles) NW of Shanghai

Located in the southern part of Jiangsu Province, Wuxi, literally "without tin," was once "you xi" ("has tin"). The town changed its name during the Han dynasty when nearby deposits of tin were mined out. A Grand Canal port, Wuxi itself is not an exciting city but it's the best base for a visit to Tai Hu (Lake Tai), one of China's four largest freshwater lakes and its most fabled body of water. On the west shore of Tai Hu is Yixing, famous for its purple clay pottery. ***Note:*** For Chinese translations of selected establishments listed in this section, please turn to appendix A.

ESSENTIALS

GETTING THERE   Wuxi has a small airport which is seldom used. Shanghai offers the nearest major **airline** connections. Wuxi is connected by daily **trains** to Shanghai (1–1½ hr.), Suzhou (25–35 min.), Hangzhou (4½ hr. via Shanghai), and Nanjing (2 hr.). The **railway station** (© 0510/9510-5105) is in the northern part of town (counters 7–9 sell same-day tickets for Shanghai, Suzhou, and Hangzhou).

From the **Wuxi Qichezhan (Wuxi Bus Station)** (© 0510/230-0751) just north of the railway station, buses head to Shanghai (every 30 min. 6:30am–7:30pm; 2 hr.; ¥38–¥44/$5–$5.70/£2.50–£2.90), Suzhou (every 15 min. 6:20am–7:20pm; 1–2 hr.; ¥15–¥22/$1.95–$2.80/£1–£1.40), Hangzhou (every 30 min. 6:40am–6:30pm; 3 hr.; ¥79/$10/£5.15), Yixing (every 20 min. 6:30am–7:30pm; 1–2 hr.; ¥18–¥21/$2.35–$2.75/£1.20–£1.40), Nanjing (every 20 min. 6:10am–8pm; 2 hr. 10 min.; ¥44–¥54/$5.70–$7/£2.90–£3.50), and Yangzhou (every 40 min. 6:50am–5:30pm; 2 hr. 30 min.; ¥59/$7.70/£3.85).

To get to Hangzhou along the Grand Canal, a **boat** departs daily from the Hubin Matou (Hubin Dock) on Hubin Lu at 5:30pm and arrives in Hangzhou the next morning at 7am. A berth in a standard room costs ¥114 ($14/£7); in a quad ¥82 ($10/£5). Conditions are spartan at best. Tickets can be bought at the **Hangyun Dasha** (**Ferry Building;** © 0510/586-8704; open 7:30am–5:30pm) at the dock.

GETTING AROUND   **Taxis** cost ¥8 ($1.05/50p) for 3km (2 miles), then ¥2.30 (30¢/15p) per kilometer, then ¥2.80 (35¢/20p) per kilometer after 8km (5 miles). Public **bus** no. 1 (¥1/15¢/10p) and tourist bus no. G1 (same fare) run from the railway station to Yuantouzhu. Bus no. 2 from the railway station stops at Xihui Gongyuan.

TOURS & GUIDES   **China Travel Service (CTS),** located directly across from the railway station at Chezhan Lu 88 (© 0570/8230-3366; fax 0510/230-4143), can arrange customized tours around the city and to the pottery shops and caves in Yixing County.

FAST FACTS

Banks, Foreign Exchange & ATMs   The **Bank of China** at Zhongshan Lu 258 conducts foreign exchange Monday through Friday from 8am to 5pm. There is an ATM inside the bank.

Internet Access   Broadband Internet access is available for ¥1 (15¢/15p) per hour at the library, south of Tai Hu Guang Chang. © 0510/8575-7830, ext 8401. www. wxlib.cn. 9am to 9pm. Dial-up is available at © 163.

Post Office   There's a post office (7:30am–6:30pm) on Renmin Zhong Lu, west of Zhongshan Lu.

Visa Extensions   The **Gonganju (PSB)** is located on the second floor at Chongning Lu 56 ((©) **0510/270-0123,** ext. 22215) and is open Monday through Friday from 8 to 11:30am and 1:30 to 5:30pm (2:30–5:30pm July–Sept). Allow 5 business days.

EXPLORING WUXI

Tai Hu (Lake Tai)   With its northern banks grazing the southwest edge of Wuxi, China's most fabled body of fresh water is the main attraction in town. Covering over 2,400 sq. km (950 sq. miles) with an average depth of only 2m (7 ft.), the lake is dotted with islands, fishing trawlers, low cargo boats, and small sampans. Often shrouded in mist, Tai Hu is also the source of many fantastically shaped limestone rocks that were submerged for years to achieve the desired effect, and that now decorate many a classical Chinese garden. It is said that the Huizong emperor of the Song dynasty nearly bankrupted the country's treasury in pursuit of increasingly bizarre Tai Hu rocks. For all its fabled status and storied history, however, today's lake, at least the parts accessible to tourists from Wuxi, is a bit of a disappointment, unashamedly geared as it is to the mass tourist trade.

The lake's most popular scenic spot is the peninsula **Yuantouzhu (Turtle Head Isle).** From the park's entrance, most tourists head straight for the ferry docks at the western edge of the peninsula. You can walk, take the tourist train (¥6/80¢/40p one-way, ¥10/$1.30/65p round-trip), or ride the elevated tram (¥10/$1.30/65p one-way, ¥16/$2.10/£1.05 round-trip) to the docks. The area south of the docks has some pleasant trails and is worth exploring if you have the time. A lighthouse marks the westernmost tip of the peninsula.

From the docks, ferries shuttle visitors to **San Shan Dao,** a hilly island connected by causeways to two flanking islets. The 15-minute boat ride, the highlight of a visit to Tai Hu, is usually refreshing, though you're likely to find yourself on a boat with chattering schoolchildren and loud tourists. The island itself is a tacky, commercialized affair complete with pushy vendors and wretched performing monkeys. All the structures here date from the mid-1980s, when the island was first opened to tourists.

Yuantouzhu. Admission ¥70 ($9.10/£4.55) (includes ferry ride). 6am–5pm. Bus: no. 1 or 212.

Xihui Gongyuan   This park in the northwestern part of town is dominated by two hills that have become symbols of Wuxi: **Xi Shan** after which the city was named, and **Hui Shan** to the west. It's a bit of a climb up to the seven-story octagonal brick-and-wood **Longguang Ta (Dragon Light Pagoda)** atop Xi Shan, but there are some good views of the Grand Canal snaking through the city. From 8:30am to 5pm you can also ride a chairlift (¥15/$1.95/£1 one-way, ¥22/$2.85/£1.45 round-trip) from the bottom of Xi Shan to the peak on Hui Shan. The ride offers even more commanding views of the surrounding area.

At the foot of Hui Shan is the famous Ming dynasty garden, **Jichang Yuan,** laid out in classical southern style with walkways, rockeries, ponds, and pavilions. The garden is said to have so captivated the Qianlong emperor on one of his visits south that he commissioned a copy of it to be built in the Yihe Yuan (Summer Palace) in Beijing. Just southwest of the garden is the **Second Spring Under Heaven (Tianxia Di'er Quan),** three wells containing the putative second-best water source in China for brewing tea, according to Lu Yu's Tang dynasty *Cha Jing (Tea Classic).* From May to October, nightly traditional music performances are held in the garden.

Huihe Lu. Admission to park ¥10 ($1.30/65p); Jichang Garden ¥15 ($1.95/£1) or ¥20 ($2.60/£1.30) 6–10pm. Park: Apr–Oct 5am–6pm; Nov–Mar 5:30am–5:30pm. Jichang Garden: May–Oct 7am–10pm; Nov–Apr 7am–6pm. Bus: no. 2.

SHOPPING

Wuxi's famous folk-art **Huis Han clay figurines,** which some consider rather ugly, are available at the **Hui Hhan Clay Figurine Factory** store at Xihui Lu 26 (open 8:30am–5pm). Credit cards are accepted.

WHERE TO STAY

Most hotels regularly offer 20% to 30% discounts, and add a 15% service charge.

EXPENSIVE

Hubin Fandian 🐟🐟   Set on beautiful grounds along the shores of Lake Tai, this hotel is a good place to escape the bustle of the city. A five-star hotel, this 10-story European-style luxury hotel boasts whitewashed walls, elegant marble floors, and wrought-iron balustrades and balconies. Rooms are not outstanding but they do have thick carpets, redwood furniture, and some gorgeous views of the lake. Bathrooms are small and slightly worn.

Huanhu Lu, Li Yuan. ⟨𝐶⟩ **0510/510-1888.** Fax 0510/510-2637. 281 units. ¥800–¥1,200 ($104–$156/£52–£78) standard room; ¥2,800 ($364/£182) suite. AE, DC, MC, V. **Amenities:** 3 restaurants; bar; lounge; outdoor pool; tennis court; health club and spa; sauna; bowling alley; concierge; business center; forex; shopping arcade; salon; room service; massage; laundry/dry cleaning; executive rooms. *In room:* A/C, TV, minibar, hair dryer.

Sheraton Wuxi Hotel & Towers (Xilaideng Dafandian) 🐟🐟   This five-star hotel in the center of town offers all the luxuries you'd expect in a top international hotel. Even though it's showing signs of age, it's still the best place to stay for efficient service and first-rate facilities. Rooms are spacious, comfortable, and equipped with a full range of amenities, including robe and slippers. Marble bathrooms are bright and clean. The hotel's four restaurants offer reliable fine dining. Staff is friendly and very helpful.

Zhongshan Lu 403. ⟨𝐶⟩ **0510/272-1888.** Fax 0510/275-2781. www.sheraton.com. 396 units. ¥1,495 ($195/£97) standard room; from ¥2,300 ($299/£150) suite. AE, DC, MC, V. **Amenities:** 4 restaurants; bar; lounge; cigar bar; indoor pool, health club and spa; Jacuzzi; sauna; concierge; business center; forex; shopping arcade; salon; 24-hr. room service; massage; same-day laundry/dry cleaning; executive rooms. *In room:* A/C, satellite TV, dataport, high-speed Internet access (select rooms), minibar, hair dryer, safe.

Tai Hu Fandian 🐟   Somewhat inconveniently located 10km (6 miles) west of the city center, on the northern banks of Lake Tai across from Yuantouzhu, this five-star resort offers a blissful escape from city bustle, but it's not very practical for the individual traveler. The hotel's sprawling grounds also contain private villas, landscaped gardens, and the resort's private dock, with plans underway for an 18-hole golf course. For such luxury, the standard rooms are surprisingly small and simply decorated, though all the usual amenities are here. Bathrooms are also on the small side but are clean.

Huanhu Lu, Mei Yuan. ⟨𝐶⟩ **0510/551-7888.** Fax 0510/551-7784. www.taihuhotel.com. 257 units. ¥860–¥1,580 ($112–$205/£56–£103) standard room; from ¥2,500 ($325/£163) suite. AE, DC, MC, V. **Amenities:** 4 restaurants; bar; lounge; 2 pools; 18-hole golf course; tennis courts; health club and spa; Jacuzzi; sauna; bowling alley; concierge; tour desk; business center; forex; shopping arcade; salon; room service; massage; laundry/dry cleaning. *In room:* A/C, satellite TV, minibar, hair dryer, safe.

MODERATE

New World Courtyard Wuxi (Wuxi Xinshijie Wanyi Jiudian) 🐟🐟   This hotel, without official rating, is the equivalent of a top four-star hotel catering mostly to business travelers and a few tour groups. Located in the heart of town, the hotel prides itself on having the largest standard guest rooms around. Rooms are tastefully decorated and fitted with a full range of amenities. Bathrooms are spacious and clean, and service is friendly and efficient.

Zhongshan Lu 335. ☎ **0510/276-2888.** Fax 0510/551-7784. www.courtyard.com. 266 units. ¥996 ($130/£65) standard room; ¥1,760 ($229/£114) suite. AE, DC, MC, V. **Amenities:** 3 restaurants; bar; lounge; health club and spa; sauna; concierge; tour desk; business center; forex; shopping arcade; salon; room service; massage; laundry/dry cleaning; executive rooms. *In room:* A/C, satellite TV, high-speed Internet access, minibar, hair dryer, safe.

WHERE TO DINE

The top hotels all offer reliable dining. Western fast food is readily available in the center of town, with three **KFC outlets** (9:30am–10:30pm) within a block south of Jiefang Lu, and a **Pizza Hut** at Renmin Zhong Lu 127 (10am–10:30pm). **McDonald's** is at Zhongshan Nan Lu 217 (8am–11pm). Babaiban (Yaohan Department Store) at Zhongshan Lu 168 has a **food court** on the sixth floor.

MODERATE

San Feng Jiujia ✿ WUXI   While Wuxi isn't exactly known for its cuisine, this restaurant does a superb job making the best of the regional fare. Order the *paigu,* delicious Chinese-style baby back ribs cooked in sugar and soy sauce, or the local specialty *mianjin,* which are fried balls of flour that are shredded and stir-fried with meat and vegetables. The restaurant also features fresh seafood and fresh squeezed juices.

Zhongshan Lu 240. ☎ **0510/272-5132.** Meal for 2 ¥80–¥160 ($10–$21/£5.20–£10). AE, DC, MC, V. 11am–1:30pm and 5–8:15pm.

Wuxi Kaoya Guan (Wuxi Roast Duck Restaurant) ✿✿ WUXI   This popular four-story restaurant serves its excellent signature Wuxi roast duck in two ways: with steamed bread, chives, cucumbers, and sweet sauce; and as a soup. Other specialties include *Taihu yinyu* (deep-fried Lake Tai fish) and the mouthwatering *Wuxi xiaolong* (Wuxi dumplings). Service is friendly.

Zhongshan Lu 218. ☎ **0510/272-9623.** Reservations recommended. English menu. Meal for 2 ¥90–¥200 ($12–$26/£5.85–£13). AE, DC, MC, V. 11:30am–2pm and 5–9pm.

INEXPENSIVE

Wangxing Ji DUMPLINGS   One of Wuxi's most famous and popular places for casual dining, this assembly-line cafeteria has no decor to speak of, but the crabmeat dumplings *(xiefen xiaolong)* and pork wontons *(xianrou huntun)* are pretty good. A variety of noodles are also available here. Don't expect much from the apathetic service, and try your best to grin and bear the beggars who stumble in here asking for money—or a dumpling.

Zhongshan Nan Lu 221. ☎ **0510/275-1777.** Meal for 2 ¥20–¥40 ($2.60–$5.20/£1.30–£2.60). No credit cards. 7am–9pm.

A SIDE TRIP TO YIXING

Located 60km (37 miles) southwest of Wuxi on the western shores of Tai Hu, Yixing is famous for its "Yixing ware" pottery, specifically small teapots and decorative objects made from a distinctive dark red clay (often referred to as "purple sand" due to a high level of iron in the soil). You can see a collection of Yixing pots, flasks, and urns from over 6,000 years ago, as well as the latest vases and teapots from contemporary masters, at the ceramics museum **Yixing Taoci Bowuguan** (Dingshan Bei Lu 150; ¥20/$2.60/£1.30; 7:30am–5pm) in Dingshu Town, 15km (9 miles) southwest of Yixing. Recently renovated, the museum offers coherent explanations in English and is pretty well put together for a small-town museum. It's worthwhile for visitors who are really into pottery. You can purchase a certified Yixing teapot set (teapot with six cups) for ¥200 to ¥300 ($26–$39/£13–£20) at the museum store. Outside are workshops

Wild China: The Water Village of Tongli

Now that Suzhou, once the "Venice of the East," has grown into a modern city; visitors searching for a more traditional Yangzi River delta water town should visit the Song dynasty town of **Tongli,** 20km (12 miles) southeast of Suzhou and 80km (49 miles) west of Shanghai. The entrance fee for all sights is ¥50 ($6.25/£3.15); hours are from 8am to 5pm. (Zhou Zhuang, another delta town, has unfortunately evolved into a massive tourist trap.)

The main attraction in Tongli is **Tuisi Yuan (Retreat and Reflection Garden)** , in the center of the old town. Built in 1886 by a dismissed court official, the garden contains the family's residences in the west, meeting and entertaining rooms in the center, and a small but cleverly designed landscaped garden in the east. The use of winding walkways with different-shaped windows, jutting pavilions, and a reflecting pond make the garden appear larger than it is.

West of the garden are two of the town's better-preserved traditional residences. **Jiayin Tang,** built in the 1910s as the residence of a famous local scholar, Liu Yazi, has high white walls and doorways fronted by upturned eaves. The highlight at **Chongben Tang,** also with four courtyards and three doorways, is the refined brick, stone, and wood carvings of propitious symbols such as cranes and vases. Connecting the two residences are three bridges: **Taiping Qiao (Peace Bridge), Jili (Luck) Qiao,** and **Changqing (Glory) Qiao.** It was the custom in the old days to carry a bride in her sedan chair over all three. Today, tourists can don proper wedding finery and also be carried across the bridges in an old-fashioned sedan chair.

GETTING THERE   From the bus station *(qiche zhan)* in the new part of town on Songbei Gong lu, **buses** run to Suzhou (hourly 7am–5pm; 1 hr.; ¥12/$1.60/80p). In Shanghai, the Jinjiang Optional Tours Center at Changle Lu 191 (© **021/6466-2828**) can organize a private tour with an English-speaking guide, air-conditioned car, and lunch for about ¥1,200 ($156/£78) for one person and ¥650 ($85/£42) each for two. Alternatively, a Tongli tourist bus (2 hr.; ¥110/$14/£7.15 round-trip) leaves from the Shanghai Stadium at 9am (returns at 4pm) and 10am (returns at 4:30pm).

WHERE TO DINE   Several small restaurants along **Mingqing Jie** serve basic *jiachang cai* (Chinese home-style cooking) at reasonable prices; a meal for two averages about ¥30 to ¥50 ($3.90–$6.50/£1.95–£3.25). **Nanyuan Chashe,** located in a restored Qing dynasty building, serves tea and local snacks. Local specialties include *zhuangyuan ti* (the Tongli version of braised pigs' trotters), *xiao xunyu* (small smoked fish), and *min bing* (a sweet glutinous rice pastry).

where visitors can watch ceramics artisans at work. Across the highway is a dusty pottery market, where amazing deals can be struck for a wide range of pottery ranging from ¥25 to ¥200 ($3.25–$26/£1.65–£13).

Yixing also has some karst caves near Dingshu Town. **Shanjuan Dong** (¥38/$4.95/£2.50; open 7:30am–5pm) located 25km (15 miles) southwest of Yixing, has three main chambers of oddly shaped rocks. Visitors may climb to the upper cave or take the more interesting short ride on a flat-bottomed boat in the lower cave along a 120m-long (393-ft.) underground stream that leads out to a tacky temple complex commemorating China's Romeo and Juliet, Liang Shanbo and Zhu Yingtai. Twenty-two kilometers (13 miles) southwest of town, a Daoist temple fronts the large **Zhanggong Dong** (¥30/$3.90/£1.95; 7:30am–5:30pm), which contains a labyrinthine 72 halls. The Hall of the Dragon King has wide steps that run all the way to the top of the hill, where there's a view of the dusty countryside.

From the **Yixing Bus Station (Sheng Qichezhan; ✆ 0510/794-5031)**, buses depart regularly for Wuxi (90 min.; ¥11/$1.45/70p) and Nanjing (2½ hr.; ¥44/$5.70/£2.85). Once in Yixing, tourist bus no. Y1 (¥5/65¢/30p) will take you from the bus station to the ceramics museum and Zhanggong Dong (Zhanggong Cave), while tourist bus no. Y2 heads to Shanjuan Dong (Shanjuan Cave).

Yixing is usually a day trip from Wuxi or Nanjing, but for those who wish to stay over, the renovated three-star **Yixing Guoji Fandian (Yixing International Hotel)** ✔, Tongzhengguan Lu 52 (✆ **0510/791-6888;** fax 0510/790-0767), has clean and comfortable rooms for ¥420 to ¥580 ($55–$75/£27–£38). The rooms are fitted with all new furniture, fridge, and satellite TV. The hotel has three restaurants serving decent fare.

12 Hefei

Anhui Province, 615km (381 miles) NW of Shanghai, 321km (199 miles) NW of Huang Shan

As the provincial capital of Anhui, this industrial city of 1.3 million has few attractions for the tourist but sees a constant flow of business travelers. Hefei is also home to the University of Science and Technology, where Chinese dissident Fang Lizhi was vice-president until he sought asylum in the West after the 1989 Tian'an Men Square massacre. *Note:* For Chinese translations of selected establishments listed in this section, please turn to appendix A.

ESSENTIALS

GETTING THERE   Hefei has daily **flights** to Beijing (1 hr. 10 min.), Guangzhou (1 hr. 45 min.), Shanghai (1 hr.), and Qingdao (1½ hr.), and several flights a week to Xi'an (Mon, Thurs–Sun; 2 hr. 10 min), Hangzhou (Thurs and Sun; 50 min.), Guilin (Tues and Thurs; 90 min.), Huangshan (Mon, Wed, Fri, Sun; 50 min.), Hong Kong (Mon and Fri; 2 hr.), Ji'nan (1 hr.), and Zhengzhou (1 hr.). Tickets may be purchased at the 24-hour **CAAC Booking Center (Minghang Shoupiao Zhongxin)** at Meiling Dadao 368 (✆ **0551/467-9999**). **Taxis** (20 min.; ¥20/$2.60/£1.30) are your best option for getting to Hefei's airport, which is about 10km (6 miles) south of town. There are no airport buses, but public **bus** no. 11 runs there from the railway station.

From Hefei's railway station (✆ **0551/267-6822**) in the northeast part of town, daily **trains** run to Beijing (10 hr.), Zhengzhou (11 hr.), Shanghai (8½ hr.), Huang Shan (7 hr.), Xi'an (16 hr.), and Hangzhou (7 hr.). Tickets can be purchased at the railway station or, more conveniently, at ticket outlets in town at Changjiang Zhong Lu 376 (✆ **0551/264-0000**).

Hefei has several bus stations, but the **long-distance bus station** (*changtu qichezhan;* ✆ **0551/429-9111** or 0551/429-9161) at the corner of Shengli Lu and

Mingguang Lu should serve most travelers' needs. Buses run to Shanghai (every 1 hr. 6:40am–5pm; 6 hr.; ¥150/$20/£9.75), Zhengzhou (10am, noon, and 4pm; 8 hr.; ¥150/$20/£9.75), Huang Shan (2:40pm; 5½ hr.; ¥85/$11/£5.55), and Nanjing (every 25 min. 6am–10pm; 2½ hr.; ¥44/$5.70/£2.85).

FAST FACTS

Banks, Foreign Exchange & ATMs   The **Bank of China** (© 0551/264-1756) is at Changjiang Zhong Lu 313. Foreign exchange is available at all counters Monday through Friday from 8am to noon and 3 to 6pm (2–5:30pm Nov–Apr). An ATM is located here.

Internet Access   Dial-up is © **163.**

Post Office   The post office (© **0551/267-5427;** 8am–6pm) is at Changjiang Zhong Lu 110.

Visa Extensions   The **Hefei Municipal Administration Service Center (Shi Xingzheng Fuwu Zhongxin)** is at Jiu Shiqiao Jie 45 (© **0551/262-4550**). Open year-round Monday through Friday from 8am to noon; May to October, 3 to 6pm and November to April 2:30 to 5:30pm. Allow 5 business days for processing.

EXPLORING HEFEI

Hefei's nicest park, **Bao He Gongyuan** in the center of town, has an arched bridge over a placid lake, whispering willows on the shores, and schools of fish in lily ponds, all making for some pleasant strolls. Entrance is free and the park is open 24 hours. The park is also home to **Bao Gong Muyuan (Lord Bao's Tomb)** at Wu Hu Lu 58. It commemorates one of China's most respected iconic figures, local son Bao Zheng (999–1062), a conscientious and impartial Northern Song dynasty judge who fought for the common folk. Admission to the tomb is ¥15 ($1.95/£1).

For an eclectic range of activities, head to **Xiaoyaojin Gongyuan.** It features a peaceful lake where the elderly practice tai chi, but also offers a range of tacky roller-coaster-type rides for kids, a petting zoo, a circus, paintball, and best of all, crocodile wrestling. Admission is ¥20 ($2.60/£1.30) and the cost of individual activities ranges from ¥3 to ¥20 (40¢–$2.60/20p–£1.30); the park is open from 6am to 6pm.

North of the Xiaoyaojin Gongyuan along the pedestrian street **Shangye Buxing Jie** is **Li Hongzhang Guju** (Huaihe Lu 208; ¥15/$1.95/£1; 8:30am–5:30pm), the former residence of Li Hongzhang (1823–1901), a highly successful Qing dynasty military commander who is perhaps best known as one of the chief architects of the destruction of the Taipings (p. 396). His residence has been well preserved, complete with beautiful lattice windows and Qing dynasty furniture.

The **Anhui Sheng Bowuguan (Anhui Provincial Museum),** at Anqing Lu 268 (¥10/$1.30/65p; Tues–Sun 8:30–11:30am and 2:30–5pm), is a rather forlorn place. It has a modest bronze collection, some Han tomb engravings, and a fairly comprehensive display on the Huizhou-style architecture of southern Anhui. The museum closes early if there are no visitors, which is often. There's a decent flower and bird market outside of the museum.

WHERE TO STAY
EXPENSIVE

Holiday Inn Hefei (Hefei Gujing Jiari Jiudian) 🐠🐠   Just east of the commercial heart of town, this luxurious five-star, 29-story hotel has rooms that are large, well-appointed, and decorated with classical furniture. The marble bathrooms are a bit small but very clean. Rooms on the higher floors provide panoramas of the city. Service is professional and efficient.

Changjiang Dong Lu 1104. ℭ 0551/220-6666. Fax 0551/220-1166. hihfe@mail.hf.ah.cn. 338 units. ¥760–¥1,200 ($99–$156/£49–£78) standard room; from ¥950 ($124/£62) suite. AE, DC, MC, V. **Amenities:** 4 restaurants; bar; lounge; disco; cigar bar; indoor pool; health club; concierge; business center; forex; shopping arcade; salon; room service; massage; laundry/dry cleaning; executive rooms. *In room:* A/C, satellite TV, high-speed Internet access, minibar, hair dryer, safe.

Novotel Hefei (Hefei Nuofute Qiyun Shanzhuang) 𝒢𝒢 Renovated in 2002, the trendy four-star Novotel has standard rooms that are a little small but perfectly comfortable. They are fitted with modern light-wood furniture and all the expected amenities. Bathrooms are sparkling clean. Consider upgrading to a superior room, which is spacious and refreshingly decorated with hip blue and orange futon sofas. Service is excellent, and the staff is professional and exceedingly friendly.

Wu Hu Lu 199. ℭ 0551/228-6688. Fax 0551/228-6677. www.accorhotels.com/asia. 245 units. ¥789 ($103/£51) standard room; ¥1,080 ($140/£70) superior; ¥1,460 ($190/£95) suite. Discounts possible up to 50%. AE, DC, MC, V. **Amenities:** 3 restaurants; pastry shop; bar; lounge; health club; concierge; tour desk; airport shuttle; business center; forex; shopping arcade; salon; room service; massage; laundry/dry cleaning; executive rooms. *In room:* A/C, satellite TV, high-speed Internet access, minibar, hair dryer, safe.

Sofitel Grand Park Hefei (Hefei Suofeite Mingzhu Guoji Dajiudian) 𝒢𝒢 This long, colonial white building looks like it belongs in Bavaria somewhere. But here it is, right in the middle of Hefei's technological zone. The hotel is a bit far from the city center, but it's close to the exhibition center, making it a comfy choice for business travelers. Expect luxuriously soft beds, excellent service, and a sleek decor.

Hefei Economic and Technological Development Zone, Fanhua Rd. ℭ 0551/221-6688. Fax 0551/221-6699. www.accorhotels.com/asia. 261 units. ¥765–¥988 ($99/£50) standard; from ¥1,061 ($138/£69) suite. Discounts possible up to 50%. AE, DC, MC, V. **Amenities:** 3 restaurants; 3 bars; indoor pool; health club; tennis court; tennis table; concierge; tour desk; business center; forex; shopping arcade; salon; room service; massage; laundry/dry cleaning; executive rooms. *In room:* A/C, satellite TV, high-speed Internet access, minibar, hair dryer, safe.

WHERE TO DINE

All the top hotels catering to foreigners serve very credible Western and Chinese food. For Western fast food, there's a **Pizza Hut** at Huaihe Lu 77 and a **McDonald's** at the intersection of Suzhou Lu and Changjiang Lu.

Jin Man Lou Huayuan Jiudu 𝒢 CHAOZHOU/CANTONESE This popular, clean restaurant offers reliable and tasty fare at very reasonable prices, though service is uneven. Start with a cold dish of spicy mushrooms with broad beans or the house specialty, *taiji sucai geng*, a puréed vegetable soup. Graduate to the *huishi xiaochao*, a light stir-fry mix of pork, leeks, and bean curd strips. Also try *suan zheng shanbei*, garlic steamed scallops with glass noodles.

Tongcheng Lu 96. ℭ 0551/287-7777. Meal for 2 ¥40–¥120 ($5.20–$16/£2.60–£7.80). AE, DC, MC, V. 11am–2pm and 5–9pm.

Lao Xie Longxia 𝒢𝒢 SEAFOOD Located on a street that's been dubbed *"longxia yi tiao lu"* or *"a street filled with lobsters,"* this restaurant packs them in every night of the week. *Longxia* really means Chinese-style crayfish here, which is steamed in spices and served with beer. In the warmer months, locals cram themselves on outdoor tables and enjoy grilled corn on the cob, fish, and meat-and-vegetable skewers along with the crayfish. The mustachioed Mr. Xie has been at it for more than a decade, and while

there are other restaurants on the street that serve the same thing, he keeps drawing the crowds that come until the wee hours of the morning.

Wu Hu Lu 265. ℂ 0551/288-4799. Meal for 2 ¥20–¥50 ($2.60–$6.50/£1.40–£3.25). No credit cards. 9:30am–4am.

Noodles in Chopsticks (24 Xiaoshi Mian) ⊛ NOODLES   Located in the Holiday Inn, this noodle house will satisfy your hunger pangs 24 hours a day. There's a noodle for practically every taste, from the simple Sichuan-style *dandan mian* (spicy noodles with meat sauce) to Japanese udon; egg and spinach noodles may substitute regular noodles in any of the dishes.

Holiday Inn, 2nd floor. ℂ 0551/220-6228. Meal for 2 ¥20–¥60 ($2.60–$7.80/£1.30–£3.90). AE, DC, MC, V. Open 24 hr.

13 Huang Shan ⊛⊛⊛

Anhui Province, 501km (315 miles) SW of Shanghai, 65km (40 miles) NW of Tunxi

If you climb one mountain in China, let it be Huang Shan (Yellow Mountain). Located in southern Anhui Province, and inscribed on the UNESCO World Heritage List in 1990, Huang Shan, with its 72 peaks, is China's most famous mountain for scenic beauty. Having no religious significance, the mountain is known instead for its sea of clouds, strangely shaped rocks, unusual pine trees, and bubbling hot springs—four features that have mesmerized and inspired countless painters and poets for over 1,500 years.

Huang Shan is enshrouded in mist and fog 256 days a year, while snow covers the mountain peaks 158 days a year. Trails are usually packed with hikers from May to October, so April is often cited as the best time to visit. Local tourism authorities, however, like to boast that each season highlights a uniquely different aspect of Huang Shan, and have taken to pushing Huang Shan winter tours, when hotel, restaurant, and ticket prices are at least lower. Whenever you visit, allow at least 2 days for the mountain, and another day or two for the attractions around **Tunxi.**

ESSENTIALS

GETTING THERE   The nearest **airports** and **railway stations** are at Tunxi, 65km (40 miles) and a 1½-hour bus ride away. In Tangkou, the nearest town serving the mountain, buses leave for Tunxi from the **long-distance bus station** (*changtu qichezhan;* ℂ 0559/256-6666) just before the main gate to Huang Shan and from the main bridge area in town. Slow long-distance buses also run to Hefei (every 35 min., 5:35am– 12:30pm, 1:50pm, 3:20pm, 3:40pm; 6 hr.; ¥92/$12/£6), Shanghai (5:50am, 7:10am, 8am, 8:40am, 10:20am, 11:50am, 12:30pm, 1:40pm, 3:50pm; 8 hr.; ¥110/$14/£7.15), and Hangzhou (every hour 6:50am–5:50pm; 6 hr.; ¥78/$10/£5.10).

GETTING AROUND   *Miandi* (van) taxis charge ¥3 to ¥5 (40¢–65¢/20p–35p) for trips in town. The start of the Eastern Mountain Trail (Eastern Steps) or the cable car at Yungu is another hour away by minibus (¥5/65¢/35p) or taxi (approximately ¥30/ $3.90/£1.95 per trip or ¥10/$1.30/65p per person depending on the number of people). The Peach Blossom Hot Springs area and the start of the Western Mountain Trail (Western Steps) will require a 30-minute walk or a taxi ride from the Tangkou bus station (¥10–¥15/$1.30–$1.95/65p–£1). If you want to take the cable car up the western slopes, take a minibus for ¥5 to ¥10 (65¢–$1.30/35p–65p) or a taxi for around ¥40 ($5.20/£2.60), subject to bargaining, from Tangkou to the Mercy Light Temple (Ciguang Ge).

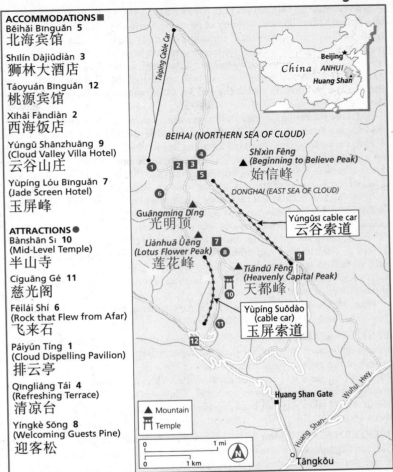

ACCOMMODATIONS ■

Běihǎi Bīnguǎn **5**
北海宾馆

Shīlín Dàjiǔdiàn **3**
狮林大酒店

Táoyuán Bīnguǎn **12**
桃源宾馆

Xīhǎi Fàndiàn **2**
西海饭店

Yúngǔ Shānzhuāng **9**
(Cloud Valley Villa Hotel)
云谷山庄

Yùpíng Lóu Bīnguǎn **7**
(Jade Screen Hotel)
玉屏楼宾馆

ATTRACTIONS ●

Bànshān Sì **10**
(Mid-Level Temple)
半山寺

Cíguāng Gé **11**
慈光阁

Fēilái Shí **6**
(Rock that Flew from Afar)
飞来石

Páiyún Tíng **1**
(Cloud Dispelling Pavilion)
排云亭

Qīngliáng Tái **4**
(Refreshing Terrace)
清凉台

Yíngkè Sōng **8**
(Welcoming Guests Pine)
迎客松

EXPLORING THE MOUNTAIN
ORIENTATION & INFORMATION

Buses from Tunxi usually drop off passengers in Tangkou by the bridge or at the bus station in upper Tangkou near the Huang Shan Front Gate.

There are two main trails up the mountain. The 7.5km-long (4½-mile) **Eastern Steps** (3–4 hr. hike) are compact and steep and are generally considered less strenuous than the 15km-long (9¼-mile) **Western Steps** (4–6 hr. hike), which are longer and steeper but which have some of Huang Shan's most spectacular vistas. For the fit, it's entirely possible to climb the mountain in the morning and descend in the afternoon in about 10 hours. But an overnight stay at the summit would allow a more leisurely appreciation of the sights and views along the way.

Sedan chairs can be hired on both routes and can cost up to ¥500 ($65/£33) for a one-way trip, though there is plenty of room for bargaining. Just be very clear beforehand on all the terms of the deal, including exact starting and ending points, and the price per passenger. If you hire a porter to tote your bags, be clear as to whether you're being charged by the piece or by weight. If the latter, insist, if you can, that the items be weighed *before* you embark so you have an idea of the total cost, and not when you're at the end, for the load at the end has an uncanny way of weighing three times more than you'd imagined.

For those preferring the path of least resistance, there are three **cable cars** going up the mountain: the Eastern Trail's **Yungu Si cable car** (Mar 15–Nov 15 6:30am–4:30pm; otherwise 8am–4pm) has a waiting line for the 6-minute ascent that can take up to 1 to 2 hours. The Western Trail's **Yuping cable car** (Mar 15–Nov 15 6:30am–5pm; otherwise 8am–4pm) runs from Ciguang Ge (Mercy Light Temple) to Yuping Lou, which is just over halfway up the western slope; the third, with a length of 3,709m (12,166 ft.) and less frequently used because it spits you west of the summit, is **Taiping cable car** (same times as above). The trip back to Tangkou takes 1 hour by taxi or infrequent minibus. The one-way cost of each cable car is ¥65 ($8.45/£4.25). When climbing the mountain, always carry layers of clothing: sweaters and raincoats as well as T-shirts. Hats and umbrellas are useful, too, as temperatures, even in summer, are subject to sudden changes due to the altitude and winds. You might also consider packing your own food and drink, as these become considerably more expensive the higher you climb.

From March 10 to November 15, the park entrance fee is ¥202 ($26/£13); from November 16 to March 9 it's ¥120 ($16/£7.80).

EASTERN STEPS　At 7.5km (4½ miles) long, these paved, cut-stone stairways are considerably easier to negotiate than the Western Steps, though this is definitely not a walk in the park. Shortly after the start of the trail, considered the Yungu Si cable car terminus, see if you can spot Eyebrow Peak (Meimao Feng) to the south, said to resemble what else but a pair of eyebrows. When you're not huffing and puffing, the climb, which takes you past bubbling streams and pretty pine and bamboo forests, is quite pleasant.

WESTERN STEPS　Most hikers begin their assault on the 15km (9-mile) Western Steps at **Ciguang Ge,** where you can burn incense and offer prayers for safe trails, not a bad idea considering that the serpentine Western Steps, hewn out of the sheer rock face, can be precipitously steep and narrow at places. There are rest stops along the way at the **Yueya Ting (Crescent Moon Pavilion)** and the **Banshan Si (Mid-Level Temple,** a misnomer—it should be the Quarter-Way Temple, for that's about where you are).

The real midpoint of the trail is **Yuping Feng (Jade Screen Peak),** with the Yuping Lou Binguan nestled like a jewel among the pointed vertical peaks. About 20 minutes by foot to the west is the upper terminus for the Yuping *suodao* (cable car). Before you reach Jade Screen Peak, however, a narrow path hewn between two large rocks named **Yi Xian Tian** (literally "A Thread of Sky" because only a sliver of sky is visible through this passage) leads to the distinctive **Yingke Song (Welcoming Guests Pine),** which extends a long tree branch as if in greeting.

South of Jade Screen Peak, an incredibly steep and exposed stairway (often called the Aoyu Bei—Carp's Backbone) snakes its way to the magnificent **Tiandu Feng** 🌸🌸🌸, the third-highest peak at 1,810m (5,937 ft.). Young lovers often bring padlocks inscribed with their names to affix to the railings at the peak in proof and hope of being "locked" together in eternal love. The **views** from this "heavenly capital" are simply extraordinary. If you suffer from vertigo or acrophobia, give this peak a pass. *Note:* The stairway to Tiandu Feng is a steep, 85-degree angle slope; CITS recommends skipping this peak on rainy days.

Past the Jade Screen Hotel is Huang Shan's highest summit, **Lianhua Feng (Lotus Flower Peak;** elev. 1,873m/6,143 ft.), so named because it resembles a lotus shoot among fronds. From here it's another 20 to 30 minutes or so to the second-highest peak, **Guangming Ding** (elev. 1,860m/6,100 ft.), where there's a weather station and a hotel. A little farther along is the famous **Feilai Shi (Rock that Flew from Afar),** a large vertical rock standing on a tapered end. Another half-hour brings you to the Beihai Binguan.

ON THE SUMMIT   The highlight at the summit is the **Beihai Sunrise** 𝕬𝕬, the only reason for overnighting on the summit. Weather permitting, the moment when the first golden ray hits and spills onto the sea of clouds is truly breathtaking. Be forewarned, however, that you'll be sharing this special moment with hundreds of other chattering tourists bundled up in the thick jackets provided by the summit hotels. The **Qingliang Tai (Refreshing Terrace),** less than 10 minutes from the Beihai Binguan, is the best place to view the sunrise. Alternatively, the **Paiyun Ting (Cloud Dispelling Pavilion)** between the Feilai Shi and the Xihai Fandian is the place to catch the equally pretty sunsets. Another popular photo op is the **Shixin Feng (Beginning to Believe Peak)** between the Beihai Binguan and the Yungu cable car terminus.

WHERE TO STAY & DINE

Tangkou's hotels are not quite up to international standards but are adequate in a pinch. Hotels at the hot springs are generally overpriced, and staying there only makes sense if you plan to indulge in the waters or if you plan an early-morning assault on the Western Trail. The Yungu Si area is more remote, and hotels there generally cater to large tour groups. Although prices are significantly higher on the summit, spending a night at the top in order to catch the famed Beihai sunrise is highly recommended. Phone ahead for reservations, particularly if you plan to visit May through October when rooms are difficult to come by.

TANGKOU

There's a **bakery,** Weitejia Mianbaofang, on Yin Shi Jie, the main street under the bridge. Next door is a tiny **supermarket** where you can stock up on snacks, groceries, and drinks for the climb.

Hongdashi Jiudian   This two-star hotel just down the street from the Zhounan Hotel has unremarkable rooms with firm beds and forgettable furniture, but at least the rooms are very clean and the furniture is still new. Bathrooms are basic but clean and there's 24-hour hot water. The staff can't muster much English, but they put on a nice game face.

Yanxi Jie. ℭ 0559/556-2577. Fax 0559/556-1888. 35 units. ¥380–¥480 ($49–$62/£25–£31) standard room. 20% discounts possible, up to 40% in low season. No credit cards. **Amenities:** 2 restaurants; lounge; concierge; salon; room service; laundry. *In room:* A/C, TV.

Mr. Cheng's Restaurant HOME-STYLE CHINESE   Currently located at Yanxi Jie, this restaurant dishes up big portions of familiar favorites like *gongbao jiding* and fried spareribs in soy sauce. For something local, try *Huang Shan erdong,* a stir-fry of winter mushrooms and bamboo shoots picked from the surrounding hills. The very friendly, English-speaking Mr. Cheng can also help with tour information and with booking accommodations and train tickets.

Yanxi Jie. © **1308/559-2603**. English menu. Meal for 2 ¥40–¥80 ($5.20–$10/£2.60–£5). No credit cards. 7:30am–11pm summer; 8:30am–11pm winter.

Zhounan Dajiudian   This two-star hotel east of the bridge has basic but clean rooms with comfortable beds and the standard no-frills amenities. But there's a hair dryer in every room! The staff speaks minimal English but tries to be helpful.

Yanxi Jie. © **0559/556-3518**. Fax 0559/556-3519. 77 units. ¥340–¥380 ($44–$49/£22–£25) standard room. 35% discounts possible. No credit cards. **Amenities:** Restaurant; tour desk; store; salon; room service; laundry. *In room:* A/C, TV, hair dryer.

WENQUAN (HOT SPRINGS)

Taoyuan Binguan   This large three-star hotel is the inn of choice and is where the Western Trail begins. Rooms were renovated in 2002, but the bathrooms are small, dark, and have sink stains. Other areas are also looking a bit worn: The batteries to my remote control were held in place by black duct tape. The staff can handle the basics, but little more.

Huang Shan Fengjingqu Wenquan. © **0559/558-5666**. Fax 0559/558-5288. 108 units. ¥720 ($94/£47) standard room; ¥2,480 ($322/£161) suite. 50% discounts possible. AE, DC, MC, V. **Amenities:** Restaurant; bar; lounge; concierge; business center; forex; shopping arcade; salon; room service; laundry. *In room:* A/C, TV.

YUNGU SI (CLOUD VALLEY TEMPLE) CABLE CAR STATION

Yungu Shanzhuang (Cloud Valley Villa Hotel)   Down the road from the Yungu Si cable car, this remote three-star hotel popular with Taiwanese tour groups is nicely designed in the traditional Huizhou architectural style, with stark white walls and gray tiled roofs. Rooms are a little dark and damp, but are otherwise furnished with the basic amenities.

Yungu Si. © **0559/558-6444**. Fax 0559/558-6018. 100 units. ¥580 ($75/£38) standard room; ¥4,880 ($634/£317) suite. 20%–40% discounts possible. AE, DC, MC, V. **Amenities:** Restaurant; bar; lounge; sauna; concierge; business center; forex (US$ only); salon; room service; laundry/dry cleaning. *In room:* A/C, TV.

SUMMIT AREA

Beihai Binguan   As the oldest hotel (1958) on the mountain, this three-star outfit has at least staked out the best position and is closest to the sunrise-viewing spot. Front rooms, which have good views of Starting To Believe Peak, are otherwise quite drab. Rooms in the back wing are newer and nicer and fitted with Chinese furniture, comfortable beds, and jackets for the sunrise-viewing. Service is uneven.

Beihai Fengjingqu. © **0559/558-2555**. Fax 0559/558-1996. 230 units. ¥1,280 ($166/£83) standard room. 10% discounts possible. AE, DC, MC, V. **Amenities:** Restaurant; bar; lounge; concierge; salon; room service. *In room:* TV, heater.

Shilin Dajiudian ⚐   This four-star hotel has rooms that are small but cozy and furnished with the usual amenities. Bathrooms are small but clean and come with showers only. The hotel's restaurant can serve Western breakfasts upon request. Service is adequate if not particularly memorable.

Beihai Fengjingqu. © **0559/558-4040**. Fax 0559/558-1888. www.shilin.com. 142 units. ¥1,280 ($166/£83) standard room. AE, DC, MC, V. **Amenities:** 2 restaurants; bar; lounge; concierge; business center; forex; shopping arcade; salon; room service; laundry; nonsmoking rooms. *In room:* A/C, TV, minibar.

Xihai Fandian 🈯   A nicer but pricier option is this four-star Swiss-designed hotel, popular with American, European, and Japanese tour groups. Rooms, resembling ship cabins, are fitted with comfortable beds and rattan furniture. Some bathrooms are a little run down. Staff is friendly and helpful. It's as comfortable as staying on the summit can be. The restaurant offers a decent breakfast buffet for ¥40 ($5/£2.50) per person.

Xihai Fengjingqu. 🕐 **0559/558-8888.** Fax 0559/558-8988. 125 units. ¥1,280 ($166/£83) standard room; ¥3,800–¥5,800 ($494–$754/£247–£377) suite. 30% discount possible. AE, DC, MC, V. **Amenities:** 2 restaurants; bar; concierge; business center; forex (US$ and yuan only); store; salon; room service. *In room:* Satellite TV, minibar, heater.

14 Tunxi

Anhui Province, 67km (41 miles) SE of Huang Shan, 27km (17 miles) W of She Xian

After arriving in Tunxi, the gateway to Huang Shan, it used to be that visitors would bypass this small town and head directly for the mountain. Nowadays, however, the beautiful countryside around Tunxi, with its paddy fields and gorgeous traditional architecture, provides a draw in its own right, and a visit here is well worth combining with your trip to Huang Shan. *Note:* For Chinese translations of selected establishments listed in this section, please see appendix A.

ESSENTIALS

GETTING THERE   Located about 8km (5 miles) northwest of town, **Tunxi airport** has daily flights to Shanghai (1 hr.), Beijing (2 hr.), and Guangzhou (1½ hr.), and less frequent flights to Hong Kong (2 hr.) and Hefei (40 min). Tickets can be bought at the **Airport Booking Office (Minghang Huang Shan Shoupiao Zhongxin)** at Huashan Lu 23 (🕐 **0559/293-4111**). Taxis to the airport cost ¥20 ($2.60/£1.30).

There are two **trains** a day connecting Tunxi to Shanghai (N204, 12 hr.; ¥252/$33/£16 soft sleeper, ¥175/$23/£11 hard sleeper). Tickets can be bought at the **railway station** (🕐 **0559/211-6222**), at CITS, or at hotel tour desks.

Tangkou-bound **buses** (1½ hr.; ¥13/$1.70/85p) regularly leave from Tunxi's bus station (*qichezhan*) and the square in front of the railway station. They start as early as 6:30am to catch arriving train passengers and run until around 6pm. Buses become less frequent in the afternoon and only depart when full.

GETTING AROUND   Taxis charge ¥5 (65¢/35p) for 3km (2 miles), then ¥1.50 (20¢/10p) per kilometer thereafter until 10km (6 miles), then ¥2.70 (35¢/20p) per kilometer. Smaller *miandi* (van) taxis charge ¥3 (40¢/20p) per 2km (1¼ miles) or ¥5 (65¢/35p) for destinations in town. Private taxi rental out to Yi Xian will run around ¥300 ($39/£20), subject to negotiation.

TOURS & GUIDES   CITS at Binjiang Xi Lu 1 (🕐 **0559/251-5303;** fax 0559/251-5255) can arrange private day trips to surrounding areas like Yi Xian and She Xian. Car rental for a day (guide not included) will run ¥300 to ¥400 ($39–$52/£20–£26) depending on your itinerary; an English-speaking guide will cost another ¥100 to ¥200 ($13–$26/£6.50–£13).

FAST FACTS

Banks, Foreign Exchange & ATMs   The **Bank of China** at Xin'an Bei Lu 9 (🕐 **0559/251-4983**) is open for foreign exchange Monday through Friday from 8am to 5:30pm. There is an ATM outside the bank.

Internet Access   There is a **24-hour Internet cafe** at the southern end of Xianren-dong Lu; it charges ¥2 (25¢/15p) per hour. If you have your own computer, the **UBC Coffee Shop** next to the Bank of China has free Wi-Fi access.

Post Office   The post office (✆ **0559/231-8875;** July–Oct 8am–noon and 3–6pm; Nov–June 8am–noon and 2:30–5:30pm) is in the southern part of town at Qianyuan Nan Lu 39.

Visa Extensions   The **PSB** is at Changgan Lu 108 (✆ **0559/232-3093;** July–Sept 8am–noon and 3–6pm; Oct–June 8am–noon and 2:30–5:30pm).

WHERE TO STAY

EXPENSIVE

Huang Shan Guoji Dajiudian (Huang Shan International Hotel) ⚘   This four-star hotel in the northwestern part of town is the choice for visiting Chinese dignitaries and the most popular choice with Western visitors, although it's starting to show signs of age. Rooms are spacious, comfortable, and equipped with extra amenities like robes, bathroom scale, and in-house movies. Bathrooms are bright and clean, and the service is quite friendly and efficient. The hotel's restaurant, featuring Anhui cuisine, is known by locals as one of the better establishments in town.

Huashan Lu 31. ✆ **0559/256-5678.** Fax 0559/251-2087. 215 units. ¥680 ($88/£44) standard room; from ¥1,280 ($166/£83) suite. 20% discounts possible; 40% discounts possible Nov–Mar. AE, DC, MC, V. **Amenities:** 2 restaurants; bar; lounge; outdoor tennis court; health club; concierge; tour desk; business center; forex; shopping arcade; salon; room service; laundry/dry cleaning. *In room:* A/C, TV, minibar, hair dryer (4th floor and up), safe (select rooms).

Huang Shan Guomai Dajiudian ⚘   Five minutes south of the railway station, this modern 11-story hotel has the most convenient in-town location of the four-star establishments. Business travelers seem to favor this hotel, which has classy rooms equipped with comfortable beds and the standard amenities. The staff speak some English and can be helpful when they're not harried.

Qianyuan Nan Lu 25. ✆ **0559/235-1188.** Fax 0559/235-1199. 153 units. ¥680 ($88/£44) standard room; ¥1,280–¥3,800 ($166–$494/£83–£247) suite. 20% discounts possible. AE, DC, MC, V. **Amenities:** 3 restaurants; bar; lounge; health club; concierge; business center; forex; shopping arcade; salon; room service; laundry/dry cleaning; executive rooms. *In room:* A/C, satellite TV, minibar, hair dryer, safe.

Jianguo Shangwu Jiudian (Jianguo Garden Hotel) ⚘   Located near the International Hotel on the road to the airport, this four-star hotel catering mostly to Asian tour groups is a modern (built in 2000) but charmless white-tiled affair on the outside. Happily, rooms are more tastefully decorated with comfortable beds and inoffensive furnishings. The clean bathrooms have bathroom scales and the basic amenities. The friendly staff speaks a little English.

Jichang Dadao 6. ✆ **0559/256-6688.** Fax 0559/235-4580. www.hs.jg.com. 130 units. ¥680–¥780 ($88–$101/£44–£51) standard room; ¥1,380–¥4,800 ($179–$624/£90–£312) suite. 20% discounts possible. AE, DC, MC, V. **Amenities:** 2 restaurants; bar; lounge; outdoor pool; outdoor tennis court; health club; concierge; business center; forex; shopping arcade; salon; room service; laundry/dry cleaning. *In room:* A/C, TV, hair dryer.

MODERATE

Huang Shan Huaxi Fandian   Located in the southwest part of town near Tunxi's Old Street, this three-star hotel used to be one of the main outfits catering to foreigners before all the new four-star hotels set up shop. Today, it still has its appeal and is often fully booked. Rooms in the main building were renovated in 2002 and are simply furnished but comfortable. Bathrooms are basic but clean.

Xizhen Jie 1. © 0559/232-8000. Fax 0559/251-4990. 282 units. ¥480–¥680 ($62–$88/£31–£44) standard room; ¥880–¥1,258 ($114–$164/£57–£82) suite. 20% discounts possible. AE, DC, MC, V. **Amenities:** Restaurant; bar; lounge; concierge; business center; shopping arcade; salon; room service; laundry. *In room:* A/C, TV.

WHERE TO DINE

Lao Jie Diyi Lou 🍴 HUIZHOU   Housed in a traditional three-story Huizhou-style building at the eastern end of Old Street, this is a clean and therefore excellent place to try Huizhou cuisine, which is typically strong and pungent, emphasizing spicy and salty flavors. Specialties include *Huang Shan suweiyuan* (stir-fried mountain vegetables, tofu, pumpkin, bamboo shoots, mushrooms, and medicinal herbs), *wucai shansi* (eel stir-fried with peppers, mushrooms, and bamboo shoots) and *chou doufu* (smelly tofu). The food is tasty but service is a bit uneven.

Lao Jie 247. © 0559/253-9797. Meal for 2 ¥50–¥100 ($6.50–$13/£3.25–£6.50). AE, DC, MC, V. 11:30am–1:30pm and 4:30–9pm.

SHOPPING

In the southwestern part of town 1 block north of the river is **Lao Jie (Old Street),** a 1.3km (¾-mile) street lined with restored Song dynasty wooden houses and shops. The usual souvenirs are here, from ethnic batik and Mao buttons to Chinese paintings and dried foodstuffs. Shops are open from 8am to 10pm. This is a fun place to stroll even if you're not in the buying mood.

Huizhou Architecture

The main courtyard in Huizhou is flanked on three sides by buildings with downward-sloping roofs, meant to aid the collection of rainwater, which symbolized wealth. This open-air courtyard provides the only illumination as there are few, if any, outside windows. Buildings typically have two or three overhanging stories; these upper floors were the havens (or prisons) of the women of the house, who had to rely on peepholes and small windows in the closed-off verandas to survey the goings-on in the courtyard below.

The average family home had a single courtyard, but those of higher status were allowed two or even three courtyards. Because building courtyards beyond one's rank was a punishable offense, many owners attempted to enhance their prestige by building more side rooms and by improving the ornamental and decorative fixtures in the house. As a result, many of Huizhou's houses have some of the best stone, brick, and wood carvings in China.

Huizhou houses are also separated from each other by high, crenelated walls called **horse-head walls (matou bi),** so named because the wall is said to look like a horse's head with its convex-shaped, black-tiled gable roof over stark white or gray stones. These walls were used both to prevent fires and to deter burglars and bandits, especially when the merchants were away on business.

Stone **memorial archways (paifang)** built to honor ancestors typically have calligraphic inscriptions detailing the reason for the arch, have two or four supporting posts, and have anywhere from two to five tiered roofs.

AROUND TUNXI

Formerly known as Huizhou (from which Anhui derived part of its name), this region was home to many wealthy salt merchants who in the Ming and Qing dynasties built many memorial arches and residences in such a unique style as to create a distinct regional *Huizhou* style of architecture. The district of Huizhou and the counties of She Xian and Yi Xian are famous for their well-preserved memorial arches *(paifang)*, memorial halls *(citang)*, and traditional villages lined with narrow streets and flowing streams.

Yi Xian is approximately 50km (30 miles) northwest of Tunxi, while the Huizhou District and She Xian are to the north and northeast. All three can easily be visited as separate day trips, but a combination of the three will be trickier. It is possible to visit both She Xian and Yi Xian in a long day, but you'll most likely only be able to visit one or two sights in each place and you won't have time to linger. You'll also have to rent a private taxi or car for the day (see "Tours & Guides," above), since public transportation to and between sights is slow and infrequent. If you have some command of Chinese or would simply like to brave it on your own, you can hire a taxi in Tunxi for the day to Xidi, Hong Cun, and Nanping in Yi Xian for ¥250 to ¥300 ($33–$39/£16–£20), and to She Xian, Qiankou, and Chengkan for around ¥280 ($36/£18). Minibuses also leave for She Xian (30 min.; ¥4/50¢/25p) and Yi Xian (1 hr.; ¥8/$1.05/50p) from the bus station and the roundabout in front of the railway station.

YI XIAN

The first village you encounter on the way to Yi Xian (7km/4 miles away) is Xidi ⚡ (¥80/$10/£5.20; open 8am–5:30pm), a UNESCO World Heritage Site famous for its over 300 well-preserved ancient residences. The houses, with their amazingly ornate stone, brick, and wood carvings, are really the highlight here at this boat-shaped village, which dates from the Northern Song dynasty (960–1127) but which developed into its present size during the Ming and Qing dynasties. The memorial archway (built in 1578) that greets visitors when you first arrive is the sole remaining archway in the village and is said to have survived the Cultural Revolution because it was covered with Mao slogans.

Another UNESCO World Heritage Site, Hong Cun ⚡⚡ (¥80/$10/£5.20; open 8am–5:30pm), located 11km (7 miles) northeast of Yi Xian town, is probably the most picturesque of the towns, with two spots in the village vying for top honors: the exterior view with an arched bridge across a large lily pond; and the crescent-shaped pond Yuezhao Tang, whose reflection of the surrounding traditional houses on a clear day is truly magnificent. If these vistas appear familiar, it is probably because the two locations were used in the movie *Crouching Tiger, Hidden Dragon*. Water is the main feature at this village, with the two large ponds connected to a series of flowing streams and canals that pass by every house, providing water for washing, cooking, and bathing, and that taken altogether are said to outline the shape of a bull.

Just over 5km (3 miles) west of Yi Xian, Nanping ⚡ (¥32/$4.15/£2.10; open 8am–5:30pm) is a late Tang, early Song dynasty town that served as the location for Zhang Yimou's 1990 film, *Ju Dou*. In fact, so many films have been made in this picturesque village that it is also unimaginatively called Movie Village of China. All the houses in the village have concave corners that bow inward, the absence of rigid sharp edges symbolizing the avoidance of quarrels in the community. With 72 lanes that seem to double back on each other like an Escher maze, the village is best visited with a local guide (included in the price of admission), even though he or she speaks practically no English. The guide also has the keys to open various halls, including the 500-year-old, 1,500-sq.-m (16,146-sq.-ft.) Ye's Ancestral Hall, where the teahouse fight scene from *Crouching Tiger, Hidden Dragon* was filmed.

SHE XIAN

Although She Xian has 94 memorial arches scattered throughout the county, **Tangyue Paifang Qun (Tangyue Memorial Arches)** ✿, with its collection of seven four-pillared arches, is the best place to view these impressive structures. Located about 6km (3¾ miles) west of She Xian, the arches may be viewed from 6:30am to 6:30pm for a fee of ¥80 ($10/£5.20). The arches were built by a salt merchant family named Bao over the course of 400 years in the Ming and Qing dynasties. If you're coming by minibus (¥4/50¢/25p) from Tunxi, ask to be dropped off at the archways. From there, it's another 1.5km (1 mile) to the arches. Walk or take a tricycle taxi for ¥5 to ¥10 (60¢–$1.20/30p–60p).

She Xian claims the only eight-pillared memorial archway in China, the **Xuguo Shifang (Xuguo Stone Archway)** ✿✿. Built in 1584 to honor a local scholar named Xu Guo, this magnificent structure has eight pillars decorated with carved lions, phoenixes, and *qilin* (Chinese unicorns). Up the hill from the archway and down a left side street is **Doushan Jie,** a narrow alley lined with traditional houses and shops.

HUIZHOU QU (HUIZHOU DISTRICT)

The highlight at **Chengkan** village ✿✿ (¥60/$7.80/£3.90; open 7am–5:30pm; 8am–4:30pm Nov 16–Mar 15), 34km (20 miles) north of Tunxi is **Baolun Ge (Baolun Hall)** ✿✿, an impressive building alone worth the trip. Located in the back of the **Luo Dongshu Ci (Luo Dongshu Ancestral Hall),** the bottom half of the structure, with stone square pillars supporting exquisitely painted (though now faded) wooden beams and brackets, was built in the Ming dynasty to honor the Luo family ancestors. The top half, with wooden windows and tiled roof, was built 70 years later to honor the emperor. At Zhongying Jie 12 is a Qing dynasty house worth visiting for its intricately carved wooden doors and panels.

Qiankou village has a Museum of Ancient Residences (¥40/$5.20/£2.60; open 7:30am–6pm), a collection of 12 Ming dynasty Huizhou-style residences formerly scattered throughout She Xian county but relocated here and restored to their original state. This museum provides a comprehensive overview of the local architecture if you don't have time to tour individual towns.

9

Shanghai

by Sharon Owyang

As China's largest city, and its economic, commercial, and financial capital, Shanghai is the heart of and key to China's future. No other supercity in China is more vibrant or fascinating, or has such a unique colonial past.

As Chinese cities go, Shanghai is comparatively young, gaining its identity only after the First Opium War in 1842 opened up this heretofore small fishing village at the mouth of the Yangzi River to foreign powers. The British, French, Americans, Germans, and Russians moved in, erecting their distinct Western-style banks, trading houses, and mansions, leaving an indelible architectural legacy to this day.

During its heyday in the 1920s and 1930s, when it grew to be Asia's leading city, Shanghai, dubbed the "Paris of the East" (and more ignominiously, the "Whore of Asia"), was a cosmopolitan and thriving commercial and financial center. It attracted legions to its shores: explorers and exploiters, gangsters and businessmen alike. In 1990, after 40 years of commercial slumber imposed by the Communist victory in 1949, Shanghai was picked to spearhead China's economic reform, and the city has not looked back or paused for breath since.

Shanghai was not always fun to tour, but it is now. After the building boom of the 1990s tore the city apart, new roads, highways, tunnels, and bridges, not to mention new hotels, restaurants, and sights, now make Shanghai a city visitors can comfortably enjoy and explore.

Today, there are neighborhoods of foreign architecture that have been preserved and restored, and are wonderful for a stroll. Shanghai's great river of commerce, the Huangpu, a tributary of the Yangzi River, is lined with a gallery of colonial architecture, known as the Bund, grander than any other in the East, much of it recently refurbished, and beckoning to the curious visitor and savvy locals alike. The mansions, garden estates, country clubs, and cathedrals of the Westerners who made their fortunes here a century ago are scattered throughout the city, and there is even a synagogue, dating from the days of an unparalleled Jewish immigration to China.

At the same time the creations of a strictly Chinese culture have not been erased. A walk through the chaotic old Chinese city turns up traditional treasures: a teahouse that epitomizes Old China; a quintessential southern-Chinese classical garden; active temples, and ancient pagodas.

But the city is not only a museum of East meeting West on Chinese soil. Overnight Shanghai has become one of the world's great modern capitals, the one city that best shows where China is headed at the dawn of the 21st century. Across the Huangpu River, Pudong, serving as the face of new Shanghai, now boasts the tallest hotel in the world, Asia's largest shopping mall, China's largest stock exchange, and one of the highest observation decks in Asia, the Oriental Pearl TV Tower.

Shanghai is also once again establishing itself as a leading trendsetter in fashion, design, culture, and the arts, and it is arguably the best city in China for dining and shopping.

Bearing the burden of all these superlatives, the Shanghainese—frank, efficient, chauvinistic, and progressive—are using their previous international exposure to create China's most outward-looking, modern, and brash metropolis, one due to host the World Expo in 2010.

Visitors dizzy from the frenzy can find, within an easy day trip, two more pastoral spots that should not be missed. To the northwest, Suzhou, with its classical gardens and canals, is known as the "Venice of China." To the southwest is Hangzhou, renowned for beautiful West Lake and the surrounding tea plantations. Winter in Shanghai is windy and chilly; summer is oppressively hot and humid, making late March or late October/early November ideal for a visit. *Note:* Unless otherwise noted, hours listed for attractions and restaurants are daily.

1 Orientation

ARRIVING

BY PLANE Shanghai has an older airport to the west, **Hongqiao International Airport,** and a newer airport to the east, **Pudong International Airport,** which began operations late in 1999. Virtually all of the international carriers use the Pudong airport, which serves all major international destinations from Amsterdam to Vancouver. Every major city in China is also served with multiple daily flights, mostly to and from Hongqiao, but the most important, such as Beijing, also have services to Pudong.

The **Pudong International Airport** (✆ 021/3848-4500), your likely point of arrival, is located about 45km (28 miles) east of downtown Shanghai. Transfers into the city take 45 minutes to 1 hour. The international arrivals hall (ground level) has hotel counters, bank counters for money exchange (directly across from the baggage-area exits), and several ATMs. There is a Tourist Information Center (TIC) counter, as well as a branch of China International Travel Service (CITS) here.

The older **Hongqiao Airport** (✆ 021/6268-8899), now largely reserved for flights within China, is located 19km (12 miles) west of the city center. There are some hotel counters here, but no money exchange, although an HSBC ATM that accepts foreign cards can be found on the second level in Departure Hall A.

GETTING INTO TOWN
FROM THE AIRPORT

Hotel Shuttles   Many of Shanghai's hotels maintain service counters along the walls in the main arrivals halls in both airports, with free or inexpensive shuttle buses offered at Hongqiao Airport. In Pudong, the hotel's airport staff will help you find a taxi or arrange for an expensive private car to take you to the hotel in the city.

Airport Taxis   The legitimate taxis are lined up just outside the arrivals halls of both airports. Taxis into town from Hongqiao Airport take anywhere from 20 to 40 minutes depending on traffic and should cost between ¥40 and ¥90 ($5–$11/£2.50–£6.50). Taxi transfers on the highway to hotels in Pudong and downtown Shanghai run between 45 minutes and 1½ hours for ¥160 ($20/£10) and up. Insist on seeing the meter started.

Metro   The world's first commercially operating maglev (magnetic levitation) line uses German technology to whisk you the 30km (19 miles) between Pudong Airport and the Longyang Lu metro station in Pudong in 8 minutes (¥50/$6/£3 one-way;

¥80/$10/£5 same-day round-trip). Maglev trains run every 15 minutes between 7am and 9pm daily. For information, call © **021/6255-6987.** From the Longyang Lu station, travelers can connect to the rest of Shanghai using metro line 2. The latter is supposed to connect directly with the old Hongqiao Airport sometime in the near (but uncertain) future, too.

Airport Buses   There are many buses making transfers from **Pudong** airport into town: Airport Bus Line no. 1 goes to Hongqiao Airport; airport Bus Line no. 2 (Jichang Er Xian) goes from Pudong to the City Air-Terminal Building (Chengshi Hangzhan Lou) at Nanjing Xi Lu 1600 every 15 to 20 minutes, from 7:20am to the last flight arrival, with taxis providing the final link to hotels. Bus no. 5 goes to the Shanghai Railway Station. Fares range from ¥18 to ¥30 ($2.25–$4/£1.12–£2). There are also shuttle buses that serve some hotels directly: Bus A serves the Jinjiang and Garden hotels; Bus B, the Hilton Hotel; Bus C, the Peace and the Sofitel Hyland; and Bus "Pudong A" makes a loop of the Pudong hotels including the Shangri-La, Grand Hyatt, and Intercontinental hotels. Hotel bus tickets are ¥30 ($3.60/£1.80). Check at the airport bus counter in the arrivals hall for the number and schedule of the bus that stops at your hotel or at the one nearest it.

From **Hongqiao,** several buses also make the run into town. A CAAC shuttle, Minhang Zhuanxian (Airport Special Line), goes to the Chengshi Hangzhan Lou (City Air-Terminal Building) at Nanjing Xi Lu 1600, every 20 minutes from 6am to 8:30pm. Tickets cost ¥4 (50¢/25p). Airport Bus Line no. 1 (Jichang Yi Xian) goes to Pudong Airport (buses depart every 20 min. from 6am–9pm). Public bus no. 941 goes to the railway station and bus no. 925 runs to People's Square (Renmin Guangchang).

BY TRAIN

Shanghai Railway Station (Shanghai Huochezhan; © **021/6354-3193** or 021/6317-9090) is massive but modern. You will have to walk a block to the metro station (follow the signs for lines 1, 3, and 4) or hail a taxi on the lower level of the terminal. Five dedicated soft-sleeper express trains (Z1, Z5, Z7, Z13, and Z21) run every evening overnight from Beijing Zhan, arriving between 7 and 7:30am. (11½ hr.; ¥478–¥499/$60–$63/£30–£32) while the return trips depart every evening between 7 and 7:30pm. Round-trip Beijing-Shanghai tickets (return trip within 3–20 days) can now be purchased up to 20 days in advance. The K100 arrives on alternate days from Hong Kong's Hung Hom Station at 4:38pm (departing from Hong Kong the day before at 3pm). There are trains to and from every other major city in China, as far away as Urumqi. There is an English-language ticket counter at the station (usually counter 41 or 43). Trains arriving from Hangzhou and select destinations south now arrive at the **Shanghai South Railway Station (Shanghai Nan Zhan;** © **021/6317-9090)** in the southwestern part of town. This station is reachable by metro lines 1 and 3 (Light Rail).

BY SHIP

International arrivals from Japan are at the **International Passenger Terminal (Guoji Keyun Matou)** at Yangshupu Lu 100, not far north of the Bund. Ships of the **Japan-China International Ferry Company (Chinajif)** line leave either Osaka or Kobe every Tuesday, arriving in Shanghai about 48 hours later; they leave Shanghai for alternately Kobe or Osaka every Saturday. See **www.fune.co.jp/chinjif/jikoku.html** for the schedule. The **Shanghai Ferry Co. Ltd.** has a weekly sailing from Osaka on Friday, and to Osaka on Tuesday; see **www.Shanghai-ferry.co.jp** (in English). Tickets are available at the terminal or at travel agencies such as CITS. Domestic ships arriving from the Yangzi River and Putuo Shan now arrive at the **Wusong Passenger Terminal (Shanghai Gang Wusong Keyun Zhongxin,** Songbao Lu 251; ℗ 021/5657-5500), at the intersection of the Huangpu and Yangzi rivers. If you arrive here as an independent traveler, you will have to hail a taxi at the passenger terminal to reach your hotel, which is likely another 30 to 45 minutes away.

VISITOR INFORMATION

The best source of visitor information is the 24-hour **Shanghai Call Center** (℗ 021/962-288) with very helpful English and Chinese-speaking university graduates providing information on almost all Shanghai-travel-related topics. There are about a dozen **Travel Information Service Centers (TIC)** in the city, and they appear to only sell tours and book hotels but, depending on who's behind the desk, you may get some guidance. The main office is at Zhongshan Xi Lu 2525, room 410 (℗ **021/6439-9806**), with smaller branch offices scattered throughout the city.

The best sources of **current information** about Shanghai events, shopping, restaurants, and nightlife are the mostly free English-language newspapers and magazines distributed to hotels, shops, and cafes around town, such as *8 Days* (www.8days.sh) *that's Shanghai* (www.thatssh.com), and *City Weekend* (www.cityweekend.com.cn). The newspaper *Shanghai Daily* (www.shanghaidaily.com) provides the sanitized official view.

CITY LAYOUT

Shanghai, with one of the largest urban populations on Earth (over 18 million residents, plus over 5 million migrant workers), is divided by the Huangpu River into Pudong (east of the river) and Puxi (west of the river).

For the traveler, the majority of Shanghai's sights are still concentrated **downtown** in Puxi, whose layout bears a distinct Western imprint. After the First Opium War in 1842 opened Shanghai up to foreign powers, the British, French, Germans, Americans, and others moved in, carving for themselves their own "concessions" where they were subject not to the laws of the Chinese government but to those established by their own governing councils. Colonial Shanghai is especially visible downtown, along the western shore of the Huangpu River up and down the **Bund (Waitan),** which has always been and still is the symbolic center of the city; from here, **downtown Shanghai** opens to the west like a fan. Today's practical and logistical center, however, is **People's Square (Renmin Guangchang),** about 1.6km (1 mile) west of the Bund. This is the meeting point of Shanghai's two main subway lines, as well as the location of the Shanghai Museum, Shanghai Art Museum, and Shanghai Grand Theatre. The Bund and People's Square are linked by several streets, none more famous than **Nanjing Lu,** historically China's number-one shopping street.

Southwest of the Bund is the historic **Nanshi District,** Shanghai's Old Chinese city. As its name suggests, here are located some typically Chinese sights, such as the quintessential Southern-Chinese Garden, Yu Yuan, the famous Huxin Ting teahouse, and several temples.

About 1.6km (1 mile) west of the Bund and south of Nanjing Lu, Shanghai's former **French Concession** is still one of Shanghai's trendiest neighborhoods, chock-full of colonial architecture and attractions. It is also home to some of the city's most glamorous shops and restaurants, as seen in the mega-development **Xin Tiandi.** Farther west still is the **Hongqiao Development Zone,** where modern commercial and industrial development was concentrated beginning in the 1980s.

North Shanghai has a scattering of interesting sights, including the Jade Buddha Temple, the Lu Xun Museum, and the Ohel Moshe Synagogue. **South Shanghai** has the Longhua Pagoda, the Shanghai Botanical Garden, and the cafes and shops of Hengshan Lu.

East of the Huangpu River, the new district of **Pudong** is today all about Shanghai's future, as epitomized by its ultramodern skyscrapers such as the Oriental Pearl TV Tower, the 88-story Jin Mao Building, and the 94-story World Financial Center, which when complete, will house the highest hotel in the world.

NEIGHBORHOODS IN BRIEF

The Shanghai municipality consists of 14 districts, 4 counties, and the Pudong New Area, and covers an area of 6,341 sq. km (2,448 sq. miles), with its urban area measuring 2,643 sq. km (1,020 sq. miles). The seven main urban districts, running from east to west, are identified here.

Pudong The Pudong New Area was formerly a backwater beginning on the east bank of the Huangpu River directly across from the Bund and downtown Shanghai. Rapid urbanization began in 1990.

Huangpu (Downtown Shanghai) The city center of old Shanghai lies in a compact sector west of the Huangpu River and south of Suzhou Creek. It extends west to Chengdu Bei Lu (the North-South Elevated Highway) along Nanjing Road and encompasses the Bund, People's Square, and the Shanghai Museum. The district now also stretches to the south to encompass **Nanshi (old town),** the old Chinese city, Yu Garden, and the Confucian Temple.

Hongkou (Northeast Shanghai) Immediately north of downtown Shanghai, across Suzhou Creek, this mostly residential sector along the upper Huangpu River was part of the International Concession in colonial days.

Luwan (French Concession) Beginning at People's Square (Xizang Lu) and continuing southwest to Shanxi (Shaanxi) Nan Lu, this was the domain of the French colonial community (up until 1949).

Jing An (Northwest Shanghai) North of the French Concession, this district has its share of colonial architecture, Chinese temples, and the modern Shanghai Centre.

Xuhui (Southwest Shanghai) West of the French Concession and south along Hengshan Lu, this is one of the city's top addresses for cafes, bars, and shops.

Changning (Hongqiao Development Zone) Starting at Huaihai Xi Lu, directly west of the Xuhui and Jing'an districts, this corridor of new international economic ventures extends far west of downtown, past the Shanghai Zoo, to the Hongqiao Airport.

2 Getting Around

BY METRO

The Shanghai metro *(ditie)* is the fastest and cheapest way to cover longer distances: rides cost ¥3–¥7 (35¢–90¢/15p–45p) depending on the number of stops. Operating from 5:30am to 11pm, the metro now has five main lines, though there are plans to extend the number to 11 lines in the next decade. Currently, **metro line 1,** the red line, winds in a roughly north-south direction connecting the Shanghai Railway Station in the north, through the French Concession to the Shanghai South Railway Station and points southwest. Its central downtown stop is People's Square (Renmin

Guangchang) near Nanjing Xi Lu, which is where it connects with **metro line 2,** the green line, which runs east-west from Pudong across downtown Shanghai. **Metro line 3,** actually more of an aboveground light rail, encircles the western outskirts of the city and also links Shanghai's two train stations, though it is seldom useful for sightseeing except for its stop near Lu Xun Park. **Metro line 4,** the purple line, forms a ring around the city and connects Pudong to the Shanghai Railway Station. **Metro line 5** runs in the far southwest reaches of the city and is not useful for most tourists. See the map on the inside back cover for all stops.

NAVIGATING THE METRO Subway platform signs in Chinese and *pinyin* indicate the station name and the name of the next station in each direction, and maps of the metro system are posted in each station and inside the subway cars. English announcements of upcoming stops are also made on trains. To determine your fare, consult the fare map posted near the ticket counters and on ticket vending kiosks. Fares range from ¥3 (35¢/15p) for the first few stops to ¥7 (90¢/45p) for the most distant ones. *Note:* Hang onto your electronic ticket, which you have to insert into the exit barrier when you leave.

BY TAXI

With over 45,000 taxis in the streets, this is the visitor's most common means of getting around Shanghai. Taxis congregate at leading hotels, but are better hailed from street corners. Your best bets for service and comfort are the turquoise-blue taxis of **Da Zhong Taxi** (© 021/6258-1688), the yellow taxis of **Qiang Sheng Taxi** (© 021/6258-0000), and the blue taxis of **Jinjiang Taxi** (© 021/6275-8800). Regardless of the company, the fare is ¥11 ($1.35/70p) for the first 3km (1¾ miles), and ¥2.10 (25¢/15p) for each additional kilometer. There's a 30% surcharge for trips after 11pm, and for bridge and tunnel tolls. Expect to pay about ¥20 to ¥35 ($2.40–$4.20/£1.20–£2.20) for most excursions in the city and up to ¥60 ($7.20/£3.60) for longer crosstown jaunts.

BY BUS

Public buses (*gonggong qiche*) charge ¥1 (15¢/5p) per ride (¥2–¥3/25¢–30¢/10p–15p if air-conditioned), but they are more difficult to use and less comfortable than taxis or the metro. Tickets are sold on board by a roving conductor, though some buses have no conductors and require exact change. Be prepared to stand and be cramped during your expedition, and take care with backpacks and purses, as these are inviting targets for thieves.

BY BRIDGE, BOAT & TUNNEL

To shift the thousands of daily visitors between east and west Shanghai, there are 10 basic routes. Three are by bridge, each handling around 45,000 vehicles a day: the 3.7km-long (2⅓-mile), harp-string-shaped **Nanpu Daqiao,** and the **Lupu Daqiao,** both in the southern part of town; and the 7.6km-long (4¾-mile) **Yangpu Daqiao** northeast of the Bund. A fourth route (and the cheapest) is by water, via the **passenger ferry** that ordinary workers favor. There are numerous ferry crossings but one of the main ones for visitors is the ferry terminal located at the southern end of the Bund on the west shore (ticket price: ¥2/25¢/10p), and at the southern end of Riverside Avenue at Dongchang Lu on the east shore. Six more routes across the river make use of tunnels. Motor vehicles make use of the Yan'an Dong Lu Tunnel (though taxis are barred 8–9:30am and 5–6:30pm), the Fuxing Lu Tunnel and the Dalian Lu Tunnel in the north; metro line 2 is filled with German-made subway cars; and the **Bund Sight-Seeing Tunnel (Waitan Guanguang Suidao)** is equipped with glassy tram cars that glide through a tacky subterranean 3-minute light show with music and narrative (8am–10:30pm; ¥30/$3.75/£1.65 one-way, ¥40/$5/£2.50 round-trip).

FAST FACTS: Shanghai

If you don't find what you're looking for in these listings, try the **Shanghai Call Center** (© 021/962-288) or inquire at your hotel desk.

American Express Holders of an American Express card can make inquiries about emergency card replacement at Nanjing Xi Lu 1376, Shanghai Centre, room 455 (© 021/6279-8082; fax 021/6279-7183; Mon–Fri 9am–5:30pm). Tickets, bookings, tours, and currency exchange are not handled directly by American Express in their Shanghai office.

Banks, Currency Exchange & ATMs The most convenient place to exchange currency is your hotel, where the rates are similar to those at the Bank of China and exchange desks are often open 24 hours. Convenient **Bank of China** locations for currency exchange and credit card cash withdrawals are located on the Bund at the Bank of China building, Zhongshan Dong Yi Lu 23 (© 021/6329-1979); at Nanjing Xi Lu 1221 (© 021/6247-1700); at Yan'an Xi Lu 2168 (© 021/6278-5060); and at Huaihai Zhong Lu 1207 (© 021/6437-8753). Bank hours are Monday to Friday from 9am to noon and 1:30 to 4:30pm, and Saturday from 9am to noon.

There are also branches of **Hongkong and Shanghai Bank (HSBC)** at the Shanghai Centre (Nanjing Xi Lu 1376) and at G/F, HSBC Tower, Yin Cheng Dong Lu 101, Pudong, that can change U.S. traveler's checks and cash. All have 24-hour **ATMs.** Although there are now many ATMs around town with international logos for Plus or Cirrus, not all of them take international cards. It's best to stick to Bank of China, HSBC, and Citibank ATMs. *Note:* You must retain your foreign exchange receipts if you wish to reconvert Chinese currency back to your home currency before you depart China.

Doctors & Dentists Shanghai has the most advanced medical treatment and facilities in China. The higher-end hotels usually have in-house or on-call doctors, but almost all hotels can refer foreign guests to dentists and doctors versed in Western medicine. The following medical clinics and hospitals specialize in treating foreigners and provide international-standard services: **World Link Medical and Dental Centers,** Nanjing Xi Lu 1376, Shanghai Centre, Suite 203 (24-hr. hot line © 021/6445-5999), have several clinics around town, 24-hour emergency services, offer Western dental care, OB-GYN services, and maintain a website (www.worldlink-shanghai.com); walk-in hours at the Nanjing Lu branch are from 9am to 7pm Monday through Friday, from 9am to 5pm on weekends. Call for times at other clinics. In addition, World Link has a Specialty and Inpatient Center at Danshui Lu 170 (© 021/6445-59999). The **Hua Shan Hospital,** Wulumuqi Zhong Lu 12, Jing'an District (© 021/6248-9999, ext. 1921), has a special Foreigner's Clinic on the 8th floor of building 1, and a 24-hour hot line (© 021/6248-3986). A representative office of **AEA International (SOS Alarm Centre),** Huaihai Xi Lu 55, Sun Tong Infoport Plaza, Unit E-G, 22nd floor (© 021/5298-9538), provides medical evacuation and repatriation throughout China on a 24-hour basis; for emergency medical evacuation, call © 021/6295-0099.

Dental care to foreign visitors and expatriates is provided by World Link Monday to Saturday (see above); and by **DDS Dental Care**, Huaihai Zhong Lu 1325, Evergo Tower, B1-05 (© 021/5465-2678; www.ddsdentalcare.com). DDS Dental Care has multilingual Western-trained dentists, a lab, and a 24-hour emergency number (© 1350-163-5171).

Embassies & Consulates The consulates of many countries are located in the French Concession and Jing'an districts several miles west of the city center. The consulates are open Monday through Friday only, and often close for lunch from noon to 1pm. The Consulate General of the **United States** is at Huaihai Zhong Lu 1469 (© 021/6433-6880; fax 021/6433-4122; www.usembassy-china. org.cn/shanghai), although U.S. citizen services are available at Nanjing Xi Lu 1038, 8th floor (© 021/3217-4650). The **Canadian** Consulate General is in the Shanghai Centre at Nanjing Xi Lu 1376, West Tower, Suites 604 and 668 (visa section, © 021/6279-8400; fax 021/6279-8401; www.shanghai.gc.ca). The **New Zealand** Consulate General is at Huaihai Zhong Lu 1375, Suite 15A (© 021/6471-1108; fax 021/6431-0226; www.nzembassy.com). The Consulate General of **Australia** is in CITIC Square at Nanjing Xi Lu 1168, 22nd floor (© 021/5292-5500; fax 021/5292-5511; www.aus-in-shanghai.com). The **British** Consulate General is in the Shanghai Centre, Nanjing Xi Lu 1376, Suite 301 (© 021/6279-8400; fax 021/6279-7651; www.britishconsulate.sh.cn).

Hospitals See "Doctors & Dentists," above.

Internet Access Business centers at most three-star and up Shanghai hotels now provide online access and e-mail services. Dial-up Internet access (© 96563, with the same user name and password) is available in any hotel room with a phone, but broadband Internet access is now commonplace in Shanghai's top hotels, many of which also offer wireless access in their lobbies and executive lounges. A number of cafes and Western-style restaurants also offer free wireless for diners. The most reliable and the cheapest Internet access can be found at the **Shanghai Library (Shanghai Tushuguan)**, Huaihai Zhong Lu 1557 (© 021/6445-2001), in a small office on the ground floor underneath the main entrance staircase. It's open from 9am to 8:30pm (¥4/50¢/25p per hour).

Maps & Books The biggest and best selection of English-language books in Shanghai, as well as the bilingual *Shanghai Tourist Map*, can be found at the **Shanghai Foreign Language Bookstore (Shanghai Waiwen Shudian)**, Fuzhou Lu 390 (© 021/6322-3200; 9:30am–6pm). **Chaterhouse Book Trader** (Shanghai Times Sq., Huaihai Zhong Lu 93, Shop B1-E; © 021/6391-8237) and **Garden Books** (Changle Lu 325; © 021/5404-8728) also have an extensive English-language book selection. The **Shanghai Museum**, Renmin Da Dao 201 (© 021/6372-3500), has selections of books on Shanghai and Chinese art and culture, as do the gift shops and kiosks in major hotels. Most hotel concierges should also be able to provide bilingual maps of the city.

Pharmacies The best outlet for Westerners is **Watson's Drug Store,** which has branches throughout town, including at Huaihai Zhong Lu 787–789 (© **021/6474-4775;** 9:30am–10pm). Prescriptions can be filled at the **World Link Medical Center,** Nanjing Xi Lu 1376, Shanghai Centre, Suite 203 (© **021/6279-7688).**

Post Office Most hotels sell postage stamps and will mail your letters and parcels, the latter for a hefty fee. The main post office (*youzhengju;* open 7am–10pm) is located at Bei Suzhou Lu 276 (© **021/6324-0069),** at Sichuan Bei Lu, in downtown Shanghai just north of Suzhou Creek; international parcels are sent from a desk in the same building, but its entrance is actually around the corner at Tiantong Lu 395. Another post office where employees can speak some English is at Shanghai Centre, Nanjing Xi Lu 1376, lower level (© **021/6279-8044).**

Taxes Most four- and five-star hotels levy a 10% to 15% tax on rooms (including a city tax), while a few restaurants and bars have taken to placing a similar service charge on bills. There is no sales tax. Airport departure taxes are now included in the price of your airline ticket.

Taxis See "Getting Around," above.

Visa Extensions The **PSB** office for visa extensions is at Minsheng Lu 1500 (© **021/2895-1900,** ext. 2; metro: Shanghai Kejiguan/Science and Technology Museum, Exit 3) in Pudong.

Weather The *China Daily* newspaper, CCTV 9 (China Central Television's English language channel), and some hotel bulletin boards furnish the next day's forecast. You can also dial Shanghai's weather number, © **121.**

3 Where to Stay

With so many international chains and new luxury hotels, Shanghai offers excellent accommodations, but few bargains. The room rates listed are rack rates, but you'll be able to negotiate much better rates in person. The top hotels all levy a service charge of 10% to 15%, though this is usually waived or included in the final negotiated price at smaller hotels. All rooms have TVs with foreign channels unless otherwise noted.

HUANGPU (DOWNTOWN)
VERY EXPENSIVE
JW Marriott (Wanhao Jiudian) ★★★   China's first JW Marriott, opened in 2003 and ideally located a short walk from both subway lines and attractions such as the Shanghai Museum, Grand Theatre, Nanjing Lu Pedestrian Mall, and Xin Tiandi, is a handsome five-star hotel lodged primarily on the 38th to 60th floors of Tomorrow Square. Boasting a penthouse library billed as the tallest library in the world by the Guinness Book of World Records, and China's first Mandara Spa, the hotel offers luxurious rooms furnished with three telephones, CD radio, laptop safe, thick bathrobes, and brilliant city views. Marble bathrooms have separate showers with power massage jets and antifog mirrors.

Nanjing Xi Lu 399 (at Huangpi Bei Lu, west side of Renmin Gongyuan). © **800/228-9290** or 021/5359-4969. Fax 021/6375-5988. www.marriott.com. 342 units. ¥3,500 ($438/£209) standard; ¥3,900 ($488/£244) executive level; from ¥4,500 ($563/£281) suite. Discounts 40%–60%. AE, DC, MC, V. Metro: Renmin Guangchang. **Amenities:** 3 restaurants; 2 lounges; indoor/outdoor pool; health club w/Jacuzzi and sauna; Mandara Spa; concierge; business center; salon;

24-hr. room service; babysitting; same-day laundry/dry cleaning; nonsmoking rooms; executive-level rooms. *In room:* A/C, satellite TV, broadband, minibar, coffeemaker, hair dryer, iron, safe.

Le Royal Meridien Shanghai (Shanghai Shimao Huangjia Aimei Jiudian) ★★

Occupying part of the tallest building in Puxi at 66 stories, Le Royal Meridien probably offers the most perfect location in town at the western end of the Nanjing Lu Pedestrian Mall, and steps from all the museums and subway stops of People's Square and People's Park. The ultramodern hotel offers luxuriously appointed rooms with floor-to-ceiling windows (with all the de rigueur breathtaking views of Puxi and Pudong farther in the distance), 42-inch plasma TV, DVD and CD player, and sofa seating in each room. All guests are also entitled to free admission to the Museum of Contemporary Art (MOCA) in nearby People's Park. Service is friendly and efficient. The hotel also boasts an excellent French restaurant, Allure.

Nanjing Dong Lu 789 (east of People's Sq., at the western end of Najing Lu Pedestrian St.). © 021/3318-9999. Fax 021/6361-3388. www.lemeridien.com/royalshanghai. 770 units. ¥3,400–¥3,800 ($425–$475/£212–£237) standard; ¥4,100 ($513/£257) executive level; from ¥4,300 ($538/£269) suite. Discounts 40%–50%. AE, DC, MC, V. Metro: Renmin Guangchang. **Amenities:** 4 restaurants; lounge; bar; juice bar; indoor heated pool; health club and spa (Le Spa) w/Jacuzzi and sauna; children's programs; concierge; 24-hr. business center; salon; 24-hr. room service; babysitting; same-day laundry/dry cleaning; nonsmoking rooms; executive-level rooms. *In room:* A/C, satellite TV, broadband, minibar, coffeemaker, hair dryer, safe.

The Westin Shanghai (Shanghai Weisiting Dafandian) ★★★ *Kids*   Located a

5-minute walk from the Bund, the award-winning 26-story Westin offers large guest rooms headlined by Westin's patented Heavenly Bed, and plushly furnished with large work desks, fax machines, high-speed Internet access, and deluxe bathrooms that include separate stalls with a "rain-forest" shower. The Westin Kids Club consists of a separate area with adjoining outdoor terrace and paddle pool. Adults meanwhile can avail themselves of the sybaritic experience at the hotel's Banyan Tree Spa. Service throughout is impeccable.

Henan Zhong Lu 88, Waitan Zhongxin (3 blocks west of the Huangpu River). © 888/WESTIN-1 or 021/6335-1888. Fax 021/6335-2888. www.westin.com. 570 units. ¥3,245 ($405/£201) standard; ¥3,970 ($496/£248) executive level; from ¥9,730 ($1,216/£613) suite (40%–50% discount). AE, DC, MC, V. Metro: Nanjing Dong Lu. **Amenities:** 3 restaurants; deli; 2 lounges; juice bar; 20m (66-ft.) indoor/outdoor pool; state-of-the-art health club and spa w/Jacuzzi and sauna; children's programs; concierge; 24-hr. business center; salon; 24-hr. room service; babysitting; same-day laundry/dry cleaning; executive-level rooms; 3 rooms for those w/limited mobility. *In room:* A/C, satellite TV, broadband, minibar, coffeemaker, hair dryer, safe.

EXPENSIVE

Radisson Hotel Shanghai New World (Shanghai Xin Shijie Lisheng Dajiudian) ★

Opened in 2005, Shanghai's second Radisson hotel is a five-star aspirant, but its service falls a little short of that at top hotels in this category such as the Westin and the JW Marriott. What it does have is one of the best hotel locations in town, right next to the Nanjing Lu Pedestrian Mall and directly across from People's Square. Furnished in a contemporary style, the average-size rooms are perfectly comfortable and appointed with all the usual five-star amenities, including free broadband Internet access. The staff tries hard to please.

Nanjing Xi Lu 88 (west of Xizang Zhong Lu). © 800/333-3333 or 021/6359-9999. Fax 021/6358-9705. www.radisson.com/shanghaicn_newworld. 520 units. ¥2,250 ($280/£140) standard; ¥2,650 ($330/£165) club room; from ¥3,500 ($437/£217) suite (30% discounts). AE, DC, MC, V. Metro: Renmin Gongyuan/Renmin Guangchang. **Amenities:** 3 restaurants; deli; lounge; bar; fitness center w/sauna; concierge; tour desk; business center; salon; 24-hr. room service; same-day laundry service/dry cleaning; executive-level rooms. *In room:* A/C, TV, broadband, minibar, coffeemaker, hair dryer, safe.

Shanghai Accommodations & Dining

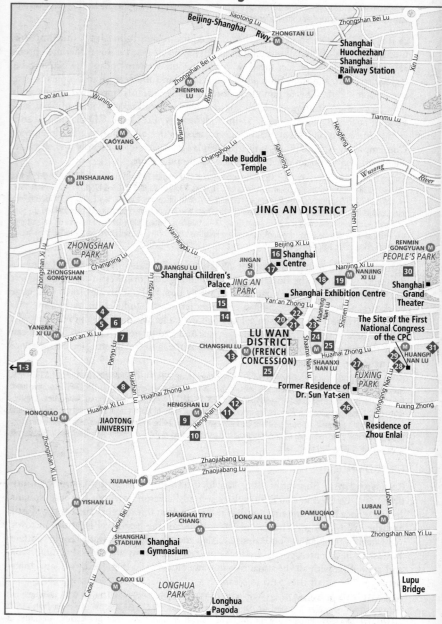

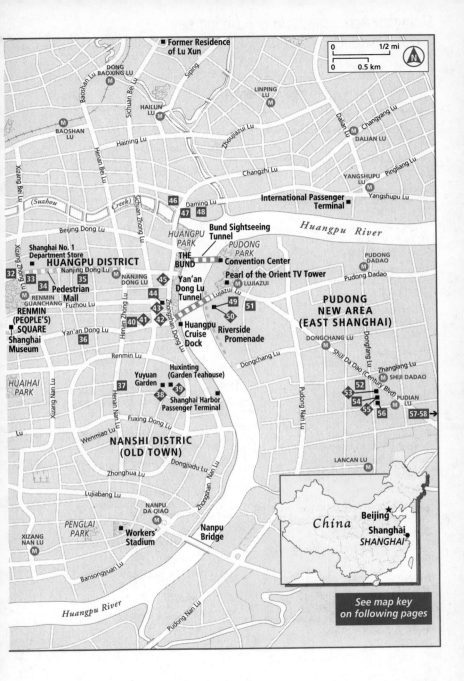

- ■ Former Residence of Lu Xun
- DONG BAOXING LU
- Ⓜ
- Baoshan Lu
- Siping
- LINPING LU
- Ⓜ
- HAILUN LU
- Ⓜ
- Sichuan Bei Lu
- DALIAN LU
- Dalian Lu
- Changyang Lu
- Ⓜ
- BAOSHAN LU
- Ⓜ
- Haining Lu
- Henan Bei Lu
- Zhoujiazui Lu
- Changzhi Lu
- YANGSHUPU LU
- Pingliang Lu
- Xizang Bei Lu
- (Suzhou Creek)
- Beijing Dong Lu
- Sichuan Zhong Lu
- 46
- 47 48
- Daming Lu
- International Passenger Terminal ■
- Yangshupu Lu
- Huangpu River
- HUANGPU PARK
- Bund Sightseeing Tunnel
- PUDONG PARK
- THE BUND
- Convention Center
- PUDONG DADAO
- Ⓜ
- Pudong Dadao
- Shanghai No. 1 Department Store ■
- HUANGPU DISTRICT
- Nanjing Dong Lu
- Ⓜ NANJING DONG LU
- 45
- Yan'an Dong Lu Tunnel
- Pearl of the Orient TV Tower
- Ⓜ LUJIAZUI
- 32
- 33
- 34
- 35
- Pedestrian Mall
- Fuzhou Lu
- Ⓜ RENMIN GUANCHANG
- 44
- 43
- Zhongshan Dong Lu
- Lujiazui Lu
- 49
- 51
- 50
- PUDONG NEW AREA (EAST SHANGHAI)
- RENMIN (PEOPLE'S) SQUARE
- 40 41
- 42
- DONGCHANG LU
- Shanghai Museum ■
- 36
- Yan'an Dong Lu
- ■ Huangpu Cruise Dock
- Riverside Promenade
- Dongchang Lu
- Shili Da Dao (Century Blvd)
- Zhanglang Lu
- HUAIHAI PARK
- Renmin Lu
- Henan Nan Lu
- Huxinting (Garden Teahouse)
- Ⓜ SHIJI DADAO
- 37
- Yuyuan Garden
- 38
- 39
- 52
- 53
- Dongfang Lu
- PUDIAN LU
- Xizang Nan Lu
- Fuxing Dong Lu
- Shanghai Harbor Passenger Terminal
- 54
- 55
- 56
- 57-58 →
- Lu
- NANSHI DISTRIC (OLD TOWN)
- Wenmiao Lu
- Dongjiadu Lu
- Pudong Nan Lu
- LANCAN LU
- Ⓜ
- Zhonghua Lu
- Zhongshan Nan Lu
- Lujiabang Lu
- NANPU DA QIAO
- PENGLAI PARK
- Nanpu Bridge
- China
- Beijing ★
- Shanghai
- SHANGHAI
- XIZANG NAN LU
- Ⓜ
- ■ Workers' Stadium
- Bansongyuan Lu
- Huangpu River
- Pudong Nan Lu
- See map key on following pages

- 0   1/2 mi
- 0   0.5 km
- N

Shanghai Accommodations & Dining Key

ACCOMMODATIONS ■

A-Line Design Hotel **10**
(Lìfǔ Gāo'ān Dàjiǔdiàn)
丽府高安大酒店

Argyle International Airport Hotel Hóngqiáo **1**
(Shànghǎi Huá Gǎng Yǎ Gé Jiǔ Diàn)
上海华港雅阁酒店

Astor House Hotel (Pǔjiāng Fàndiàn) **47**
浦江饭店

Broadway Mansions Hotel (Shànghǎi Dàshà) **46**
上海大厦

Captain Hostel **44**
(Chuánzhǎng Qīngnián Jiǔdiàn)
船长青年酒店

Courtyard by Marriott Hotel Pǔdōng **52**
(Shànghǎi Qílǔ Wànyí Dàjiǔdiàn)
上海齐鲁万怡大酒店

Four Seasons Hotel Shànghǎi **19**
(Shànghǎi Sì Jì Jiǔdiàn)
上海四季酒店

Grand Hyatt Shanghai **51**
(Jīn Mào Jūn Yuè Dàjiǔdiàn)
上海金茂君悦大酒店

Hilton Hotel **15**
(Jìng'ān Xīěrdùn Dàjiǔdiàn)
静安希尔顿大酒店

Holiday Inn Pǔdōng **56**
(Pǔdōng Jiàrì Jiǔdiàn)
上海浦东假日酒店

Hyatt On The Bund **48**
(Shànghǎi Wàitān Màoyuè Dàjiǔdiàn)
上海外滩茂悦大酒店

Jǐn Jiěng Hotel (Jǐnjiāng Fàndiàn) **25**
锦江饭店

Jǐnjiāng Inn Star Pǔdōng Airport Hotel **57**
(Jǐnjiāng Zhīxīng Pǔdōng Jōchōng Diàn)
锦江之星浦东机场店

Jǐnjiāng Star (Jǐnjiāng Zhīxīng) **36**
锦江之星

JW Marriott (Wànháo Jiǔdiàn) **30**
万豪酒店

Le Royal Meridien Shànghǎi **33**
(Shànghǎi Shìmào Huángjiā Aìměi Jiǔdiàn)
上海世茂皇家艾美酒店

Okura Garden Hotel (Huāyuán Fàndiàn) **24**
花园饭店

Old House Inn (Lǎo Shí Guā]ng Jiǔdiàn) **14**
老时光酒店

Portman Ritz-Carlton Hotel **16**
(Bōtèmàn Dàjiǔdiàn)
上海波特曼丽嘉酒店

Pǔdōng Shangri-La Hotel **49**
(Pǔdōng Xiānggélǐlā Fàndiàn)
浦东香格里拉大酒店

Radisson Hotel Shànghǎi New World **32**
(Shànghǎi Xīn Shìjiè Lìshēng Dàjiǔdiàn)
上海新世界丽笙大酒店

Ramada Pǔdōng Airport **58**
(Shànghǎi Jīchǎng Huáměidá Dàjiǔdiàn)
上海机场华美达大酒店

Regal International East Asia Hotel **9**
(Fùháo Huánqiú Dōngyà Jiǔdiàn)
富豪环球东亚酒店

Renaissance Shànghǎi Yùyuán Hotel **37**
(Shànghǎi Yùyuán Wànlì Jiǔdiàn)
上海豫园万丽酒店

Shànghǎi Marriott Hotel Hóngqiáo **2**
(Shànghǎi Wànháo Hóngqiáo Dàjiǔdiàn) **2**
上海万豪虹桥大酒店

Sheraton Grand Tài Píng Yáng **3**
(Xī Lái Dēng Háo Dá Tài Píng Yáng Dà Fàndiàn)
喜来登豪达太平洋大饭店

Sofitel Hyland Hotel (Hǎilún Bīnguǎn) **35**
海伦宾馆

St. Regis Shànghǎi (Ruìjí Hóngtǎ Dàjiǔdiàn) **54**
上海瑞吉红塔大酒店

Super Motel 168 **6**
(Mótài Yán'ān Xī Lù Diàn)
莫泰168延安西路店

The Regent Shànghǎi **7**
(Lóngzhīmèng Lìjīng Dàjiǔdiàn)
龙之梦丽晶大酒店

The Westin Shànghǎi **40**
(Shànghǎi Wīisītīng Dàfàndiàn)
上海威斯汀大饭店

Yangtze Hotel (Yángzǐ Fàndiàn) **34**
扬子饭店

DINING ◆

Renaissance Shanghai Yuyuan Hotel (Shanghai Yuyuan Wanli Jiudian) ⑅
Located a 3-minute walk from Yu Garden and its surrounding shops, and a 5-minute walk from the Bund, this is the first top-caliber modern hotel to open in the old Chinese city. The signature Renaissance whimsy is apparent in the funky blue and green color-themed rooms, which are plush and come with all the expected five-star amenities. East-facing rooms have the best views of Yu Garden and Pudong. Still undergoing a soft opening at press time, the hotel was too new to review fully, but it should draw its share of tourist travelers for its location, especially by 2009 when construction of the nearby metro line 10 is complete.

Henan Nan Lu 159 (at Fuyou Lu, just west of Yu Garden). ⓒ 021/2321-8888. Fax 021/5350-3658. www.renaissance hotels.com/shasy. 340 units. ¥2,752 ($344/£172) standard; ¥3,808 ($476/£238) executive level; from ¥8,464 ($1,058/£526) suite. Discounts 40%–50%. AE, DC, MC, V. Metro: Nanjing Dong Lu. **Amenities:** 2 restaurants; lounges; bar; 20m (66-ft.) indoor pool; 24-hr. health club; signature spa w/Jacuzzi and sauna; concierge; business center; 24-hr. room service; babysitting; same-day laundry/dry cleaning; nonsmoking rooms; executive-level rooms. *In room:* A/C, satellite TV, broadband, minibar, coffeemaker, hair dryer, safe.

Sofitel Hyland Hotel (Hailun Binguan) ⑅   This Accor-managed four-star tower in the heart of the pedestrian sector of Nanjing Lu has a superb downtown location. Recently refurbished rooms are comfortable with all the modern amenities associated with this luxury brand. Sofitel Club rooms are slightly larger and include a Western buffet breakfast. There's a European, even French feel to the hotel. Service is mostly efficient, if brusque at times.

Nanjing Dong Lu 505 (on Nanjing Lu Pedestrian Mall). ⓒ 800/221-4542 or 021/6351-5888. Fax 021/6351-4088. www.sofitel.com/asia. 401 units. ¥2,580 ($323/£161) standard; ¥3,250 ($406/£203) executive level; from ¥3,250 ($406/£203) suite (40%–50% discounts). AE, DC, MC, V. Metro: Nanjing Dong Lu. **Amenities:** 2 restaurants; deli; lounge; bar; health club w/Jacuzzi and sauna; concierge; tour desk; business center; salon; 24-hr. room service; same-day laundry/dry cleaning. *In room:* A/C, satellite TV, dataport, minibar, coffeemaker, hair dryer, safe.

MODERATE

Yangtze Hotel (Yangzi Fandian)   Located a block south of the Nanjing Lu pedestrian mall and a block east of People's Square, this striking 1934 Art Deco hotel has undergone a complete refurbishment and is today a very popular midrange choice among Chinese business travelers. Rated only three stars, the hotel offers in-room amenities that rival those at four-star outfits farther down Nanjing Lu. Rooms, a portion of which were renovated in 2002, are spacious and come with thick drapes, comfortable beds, and broadband access. The majority of the staff tries to be helpful.

Hankou Lu 740 (east of Xizang Zhong Lu, 1 block south of Nanjing Dong Lu). ⓒ 021/6351-7880. Fax 021/6351-6974. www.yangtzehotel.cn. 184 units. ¥980 ($120/£60) standard; ¥1,280 ($160/£80) executive rooms; ¥1,980 ($240/£120) suite. Discounts 30%–40%; 10% service charge. AE, DC, MC, V. Metro: Renmin Guangchang. **Amenities:** 2 restaurants; lounge; bar; business center; salon; room service; laundry service. *In room:* A/C, TV, broadband, dataport, minibar, hair dryer, safe.

INEXPENSIVE

Captain Hostel (Chuanzhang Qingnian Jiudian)   This maritime-themed hostel, lodged in a 1920s Art Deco-style building, is one of the most popular budget options in town. Among its recommendations: a superb location just off the Bund, clean "sailor bunk" dorms, comfortable if no-frills doubles with en-suite bathrooms, and a rooftop bar offering views of the Huangpu River and Pudong to rival those at the considerably more expensive bars and restaurants, but with cold beer at half the price. All the usual hostel facilities, like bike rental and a small Internet cafe, are also available.

Fuzhou Lu 37 (just west of the Bund). (C) **021/6323-5053.** Fax 021/6321-9331. www.captainhostel.com.cn. 21 units. ¥450–¥550 ($56–$69/£23–£35) standard (30% discount). Dorm beds ¥70 ($9/£4.50). AE, DC, MC, V. Metro: Nanjing Dong Lu. **Amenities:** Restaurant; bar; bike rental; business center; tour desk; self-service laundry. *In room:* A/C, TV (select rooms).

LUWAN DISTRICT (FRENCH CONCESSION)

VERY EXPENSIVE

Okura Garden Hotel Shanghai (Huayuan Fandian) ✦✦   The top hotel in the French Concession, the five-star Japanese-managed Okura was built in 1990 on the site of the 1920s French Club and Cercle Sportif. The fine Art Deco features of the original structure have been preserved in its east lobby and grand ballroom. Rooms, undergoing renovations for the next few years, are of average size, with marble bathrooms that contain automated bidets. With extensive and first-rate facilities and highly efficient service, the hotel provides little to complain about.

Maoming Nan Lu 58 (1 block north of Huaihai Zhong Lu). (C) **021/6415-1111.** Fax 021/6415-8866. www.garden hotelshanghai.com. 500 units. ¥2,300–¥2,500 ($288–$328/£144–£164) standard; ¥3,400–¥3,800 ($426–$475/£213–£237) executive level; from ¥4,500 ($563/£281) suite. Discount 40%. AE, DC, MC, V. Metro: Shanxi Nan Lu. **Amenities:** 5 restaurants; cafe; 3 bars; 25m (82-ft.) indoor swimming pool; 2 lighted outdoor tennis courts; health club w/Jacuzzi and sauna; concierge; tour desk; business center; salon; 24-hr. room service; same-day laundry/dry cleaning; nonsmoking rooms; executive-level rooms. *In room:* A/C, satellite TV, broadband, minibar, hot-water maker, hair dryer, safe.

EXPENSIVE

Jinjiang Fandian   The most famous hotel in the French Concession, the Jinjiang opened its doors in 1929 as the Cathay Mansions but is best remembered as the location for the signing of the Shanghai Communiqué by President Nixon and Zhou Enlai in 1972, reestablishing U.S.-China relations. Today's complex includes: the 1929 North Building (Bei Lou), remodeled as a five-star hotel; the central Grosvenor House (1931), with its facade an imitation of the Barclay-Vessey Building in New York City, recently redone as a five-star all-suite deluxe hotel; and the old South Building (Nan Lou), renovated in 2005 to house all executive rooms. Service, still lagging behind the international chains, is adequate though hardly exemplary. Staff still struggles occasionally with English.

Maoming Nan Lu 59 (1 block north of Huaihai Zhong Lu). (C) **021/218-9888.** Fax 021/6472-5588. www.jinjianghotel shanghai.com. 434 units. ¥2,500–¥2,900 ($312–$362/£156–£181) standard (North bldg.); ¥3,300 ($412/£206) executive room (South bldg.); from ¥4,200 ($525/£262) suite. Discount 30%. AE, DC, MC, V. Metro: Shanxi Nan Lu. **Amenities:** 5 restaurants; food street on hotel grounds; 20m (66-ft.) indoor swimming pool; health club w/Jacuzzi and sauna; concierge; tour desk; business center; shopping street; salon; 24-hr. room service; same-day laundry/dry cleaning; nonsmoking rooms; executive-level rooms. *In room:* A/C, satellite TV, dataport, minibar, coffeemaker, hair dryer, safe.

JINGAN DISTRICT (NORTHWEST SHANGHAI)

VERY EXPENSIVE

Four Seasons Hotel Shanghai (Shanghai Siji Jiudian) ✦✦✦   The 37-story Four Seasons offers top-quality pampering. Each guest room is lavishly furnished with three telephones, thick robes, and laptop safes. The patented Four Seasons bed alone is worth the stay. Marble bathrooms have separate shower and tub. Best of all, this hotel delivers impeccable service, from its 24-hour butler service for each guest to the highly efficient and friendly multilingual staff throughout the hotel. Nanjing Lu is a 5-minute walk away, the Shanghai Museum a 10-minute stroll.

Weihai Lu 500 (at Shimen Yi Lu, between Nanjing Xi Lu and Yan'an Zhong Lu). ✆ 800/819-5053 or 021/6256-8888. Fax 021/6256-5678. www.fourseasons.com. 439 units. ¥3,600–¥4,100 ($450–$513/£225–£256) standard; from ¥5,400 ($675/£337) suite; ¥500–¥700 ($62–$88/£31–£44) extra for executive lounge benefits. AE, DC, MC, V. Metro: Nanjing Xi Lu. **Amenities:** 4 restaurants; lounge; jazz bar; 20m (66-ft.) indoor pool; state-of-the-art health club and spa w/Jacuzzi and sauna; concierge; 24-hr. business center; salon; 24-hr. room service; babysitting; same-day laundry/dry cleaning; nonsmoking floors; rooms for those w/limited mobility; butler service. *In room:* A/C, satellite TV, broadband, minibar, coffeemaker, hair dryer, safe .

Hilton Hotel (Jingan Xierdun Dajiudian) ★★ Value

Shanghai's first foreign-owned hotel (1987), the Hilton still rates among the city's very best, and it's a favorite of Western business travelers. The services are top-notch, the staff competent. Guest rooms, undergoing renovations at press time, are spacious and bright and will include flatscreen TVs, bedside-controlled lighting, and broadband connection.

Huashan Lu 250 (1 block south of Yan'an Zhong Lu). ✆ 800/445-8667 or 021/6248-0000. Fax 021/6248-3848. www. hilton.com. 700 units. ¥2,910 ($364/£182) standard; ¥3,460 ($432/£216) executive level; from ¥5,930 ($741/£370) suite (up to 60% discount pending occupancy). AE, DC, MC, V. Metro: Jing An Si. **Amenities:** 6 restaurants; deli; 2 lounges; indoor swimming pool; outdoor tennis court; squash court; state-of-the-art health club and spa w/Jacuzzi and sauna; concierge; business center; 24-hr. room service; babysitting; same-day laundry/dry cleaning; nonsmoking rooms; executive-level rooms. *In room:* A/C, satellite TV, broadband, minibar, coffeemaker, hair dryer, safe.

Portman Ritz-Carlton Hotel (Boteman Dajiudian) ★★★

Despite some heavy competition, the 50-story Portman is tenaciously guarding its position as Shanghai's top choice hotel for many business travelers and world leaders. Rooms are plush, elegant, and fitted with all the amenities you could want. As expected, service is professional and excellent. The adjacent Shanghai Centre has airline offices, a medical clinic, a supermarket, a post office, automated teller machines, a performing arts theater, upscale boutiques, and a little-known cafe called Starbucks.

Nanjing Xi Lu 1376 (Shanghai Centre). ✆ 800/241-3333 or 021/6279-8888. Fax 021/6279-8800. www. ritzcarlton.com. 598 units. ¥3,320 ($415/£207) standard; ¥4,130 ($516/£258) executive level; from ¥4,700 ($588/£294) suite. AE, DC, MC, V. Metro: Jing'an Si. **Amenities:** 4 restaurants; 2 lounges; indoor/outdoor 20m (66-ft.) swimming pool; indoor tennis court; 2 indoor squash courts; indoor racquetball court; 3-story health club; Jacuzzi; sauna; concierge; 24-hr. business center; shopping arcade; grocery; salon; 24-hr. room service; babysitting; same-day laundry/dry cleaning; nonsmoking rooms; executive-level rooms; World Link Medical Center; rooms for those w/limited mobility. *In room:* A/C, satellite TV, broadband, minibar, coffeemaker, hair dryer, safe.

INEXPENSIVE

Old House Inn (Lao Shi Guang Jiudian) ★

Those nostalgic for old Shanghai Chinese style will surely love this boutique hotel in a 1930s lane house in the former French Concession. Rooms, though a bit small, are all tastefully decorated with classic Chinese furniture, four-poster beds with wispy mosquito netting and gorgeous hardwood floors. Bathrooms, however, are thoroughly modern. There is a reasonably priced Western restaurant, A Future Perfect, for those craving a taste of home.

Huashan Lu Lane 351, no. 16 (in a lane just west of Changshu Lu). ✆ 021/6248-6118. Fax 021/6249-6869. www. oldhouse.cn. 12 units. ¥720–¥1,030 ($90–$130/£45–£65) standard. AE, DC, MC, V. Metro: Jing An Si. **Amenities:** Restaurant; bar; next-day laundry service/dry cleaning. *In room:* A/C, TV, broadband, minibar, hair dryer.

CHANGNING (HONGQIAO DEVELOPMENT ZONE)
VERY EXPENSIVE

The Regent Shanghai (Longzhimeng Lijing Dajiudian) ★

Bringing a welcome dose of luxury to the western part of Shanghai, the Regent boasts some of the largest rooms in town, with wonderful city views and modern amenities including comfortable beds, 42-inch plasma-screen television, and free broadband Internet access. Bathrooms are modern and equipped with rainforest showers. The hotel also boasts a plethora of fine dining options, a Guerlain Spa, and Shanghai's biggest indoor pool. Though there's not much of interest for the tourist within walking distance, the main sights are only a 10- to 15-minute taxi ride away.

Yan'an Xi Lu 1116 (just east of Panyu Lu); see map p. 440. © **800/545-4000** or 021/6115-9988. Fax 021/6115-9977. www.regenthotels.com. 511 units. ¥2,500–¥2,800 ($312–$350/£156–£175) standard; from ¥3,550 ($444/£222) suite (30% discount). AE, DC, MC, V. No Metro. **Amenities:** 3 restaurants; deli; lounge; bar; indoor pool; health club w/Jacuzzi and sauna; L'Institut de Guerlain spa; concierge; business center; salon; 24-hr. room service; same-day laundry service/dry cleaning; executive-level rooms. *In room:* A/C, satellite TV, broadband, minibar, coffeemaker, hair dryer, safe.

Shanghai Marriott Hotel Hongqiao (Shanghai Wanhao Hongqiao Dajiudian) ⭐⭐
This grand five-star, eight-story Marriott is the top hotel address in the Hongqiao Airport neighborhood. Guest rooms are large, with comfortable beds, DVD players, and Internet broadband access. The zoo is a short walk away, but other attractions require a taxi ride to town. The hotel is often sold out during weekdays but offers substantial discounts on weekends.

Hongqiao Lu 2270 (6.4km/4 miles east of Hongqiao Airport). © **800/228-9290** or 021/6237-6000. Fax 021/6237-6222. www.marriott.com. 315 units. ¥2,650 ($331/£165) standard; ¥3,320 ($415/£207) executive level; from ¥4,150 ($518/£259) suite. Discount up to 50%. AE, DC, MC, V. **Amenities:** 3 restaurants; deli; lounge; sports bar; indoor pool; outdoor tennis court; health club w/Jacuzzi and sauna; concierge; business center; salon; 24-hr. room service; same-day laundry/dry cleaning; executive-level rooms. *In room:* A/C, satellite TV, dataport, minibar, coffeemaker, hair dryer, safe.

Sheraton Grand Taipingyang (Xilaideng Hao Da Taipingyang Da Fandian) ⭐⭐
Business travelers love this 27-story five-star Sheraton, not just for the location (halfway between the old Hongqiao Airport and downtown), but for the highly efficient service and the lush yet homey atmosphere. Rooms are a tad on the small side but are lushly decorated with rich carpeting, overstuffed chairs, and a classical roll-top desk right under Chinese artwork. Bathrooms are sleek and modern with glass sinks.

Chinese Business Motels

It may sound a bit dodgy, but for many Chinese business travelers to Shanghai, the no-frills business chain motels such as the Jinjiang Inn chain and the Super Motel chain have become popular lodging options. These motels offer basic but relatively new and clean rooms with air-conditioning, hot water, television, telephone, and even broadband Internet for the business traveler who would prefer to stay away from the backpacking hostel scene. There is usually a restaurant on the premises that serves *jia chang cai* (home-style Chinese cooking), as well as a business center that can handle airplane and train bookings. Not much English is spoken at these places, so it may be more suitable for foreigners who already have some grasp of Chinese. Still, if you're bemoaning the lack of decent but affordable lodgings in town, here are two of the better-located choices. **Jinjiang Star (Jinjiang Zhixing)**, located downtown in Huangpu District at Fujian Nan Lu (© **021/6326-0505;** www.jj-inn.com), has basic en-suite doubles for ¥269 ($34/£17); while **Super Motel 168 (Motai Yan'an Xi Lu Dian)**, located in western Shanghai at Yan'an Xi Lu 1119 (© **021/5117-7777;** www.motel168.com), across from The Regent Shanghai hotel (p. 446), has doubles for ¥298 ($37/£18).

The hotel can also arrange tee times and transportation to the Shanghai International Golf and Country Club.

Zunyi Nan Lu 5 (1 block north of Yan'an Xi Lu). © **800/325-3535** or 021/6275-8888. Fax 021/6275-5420. www. sheraton.com/shanghai. 496 units. ¥2,720 ($340/£170) standard; ¥3,230 ($404/£202) executive-level standard; from ¥3,978 ($497/£248) suite. AE, DC, MC, V. **Amenities:** 5 restaurants; deli; 3 lounges; indoor swimming pool; health club w/Jacuzzi and sauna; concierge; business center; salon; 24-hr. room service; babysitting; same-day laundry/dry cleaning; nonsmoking rooms; executive-level rooms; rooms for those w/limited mobility. *In room:* A/C, satellite TV, broadband, dataport, minibar, coffeemaker, hair dryer, iron, safe.

XUHUI (SOUTHWEST SHANGHAI)
EXPENSIVE
Regal International East Asia Hotel (Fuhao Huanqiu Dongya Jiudian) ⚐
The best luxury hotel in the district, the 22-story, internationally managed Regal has bright, modern guest rooms with bedside electronic controls, robes, slippers, and all the amenities of a five-star establishment. Its Shanghai International Tennis Center offers Shanghai's best facilities, including a center court that seats 1,200 spectators. It's located along trendy Hengshan Lu, and the metro is just a block away. Service is efficient enough, but drops off when it gets busy.

Hengshan Lu 516 (west of Wuxing Lu). © **800/222-8888** or 021/6415-5588. Fax 021/6445-8899. www.RegalShanghai. com. 318 units. ¥2,740 ($335/£167) standard; ¥3,740 ($455/£227) executive level. Discounts 30%–40% low season, otherwise 10%–20%. AE, DC, MC, V. Metro: Hengshan Lu. **Amenities:** 2 restaurants; lounge; 25m (82-ft.) indoor pool; 10 championship tennis courts; indoor squash court; extensive health club and spa w/Jacuzzi and sauna; game room; 12-lane bowling alley; concierge; tour desk; business center; salon; 24-hr. room service; babysitting; same-day laundry/dry cleaning; nonsmoking rooms; 4 executive-level floors. *In room:* A/C, satellite TV, broadband, minibar, coffeemaker, hair dryer, safe.

INEXPENSIVE
A-Line Design Hotel (Lifu Gao'an Dajiudian) Strictly a sleeping establishment, this modern hotel is as good as it gets for clean, functional accommodations in the French Concession. There isn't even a restaurant here, but the hotel's location right next to a metro station and within walking distance of a slew of restaurants and bars, shouldn't stop the budget-minded independent traveler.

Hengshan Lu 237 (at the intersection of Gao'an Lu). © 021/6433-8833. Fax 021/6433-0626. 71 units. ¥340–¥400 ($43–$50/£21–£25) standard (20% discount). MC, V. Metro: Hengshan Lu. **Amenities:** Laundry. *In room:* A/C, TV, broadband, coffeemaker.

HONGKOU DISTRICT (NORTHEAST SHANGHAI)
VERY EXPENSIVE
Hyatt on the Bund (Shanghai Jin Mao Junyue Dajiudian) ⚐⚐ The second Grand Hyatt to open in Shanghai, this new, handsome, contemporary hotel boasts a northern Bund address but is actually situated on the western bank of the Huangpu River in Hongkou, and is about a 10-minute walk from the Bund. All luxuriously appointed rooms have flatscreen LCD TVs, DVD players, and iPod docking stations. Floor-to-ceiling windows offer breathtaking views of either the Bund or Pudong, while suites give you the best of both worlds. Staff is exceedingly friendly and helpful. As Hongkou district and the western shore of the Huangpu River continue to develop, look for this hotel to be much in demand from its river location. For now, travelers can benefit from highly competitive room rates.

Huangpu Lu 199 (north of the Bund, on the northeast side of Suzhou Creek). © **021/6393-1234.** Fax 021/6393-1313. www.shanghai.bund.hyatt.com. 631 units. ¥3,800 ($475/£237) standard; ¥4,700 ($588/£294) executive-level room. AE, DC, MC, V. Metro: Nanjing Dong Lu (about 1.6km/1 mile away). **Amenities:** 4 restaurants; 2 lounges; bar;

juice bar; indoor pool; 24-hour health club w/Jacuzzi and sauna; Yuan Spa; concierge; tour desk; 24-hr. business center; salon; 24-hr. room service; babysitting; same-day laundry/dry cleaning; nonsmoking rooms; executive-level rooms. *In room:* A/C, satellite TV, broadband, minibar, coffeemaker, hair dryer, safe.

EXPENSIVE

Broadway Mansions Hotel (Shanghai Dasha)   Originally built in 1934 and once housing the Foreign Correspondents' Club, the 19-story Broadway Mansions is now a modern hotel offering spacious rooms with high ceilings, firm beds, and overhead bedside reading lights among other amenities. The rooms facing the Suzhou Creek are absolutely worth splurging on, as there are few other places where you can wake up to the creek, the Bund, *and* Pudong outside your window. Although aspiring to be a five-star hotel with its renovations in 2007, it lacks the quality of service of its competitors in the same category.

Bei Suzhou Lu 20 (north of the Bund across the Suzhou River, just west of the Waibaidu Bridge). ⓒ **021/6324-6260.** Fax 021/6306-5147. www.broadwaymansions.com. 262 units. ¥1,500 ($188/£94) standard; ¥2,000 ($250/£125) executive level; from ¥2,500 ($312/£156) suite. Discount up to 50% in low season. AE, DC, MC, V. **Amenities:** 3 restaurants; lounge; bar; health club; sauna; concierge; business center; salon; 24-hr. room service; same-day laundry/dry cleaning; executive-level rooms. *In room:* A/C, satellite TV, broadband, minibar, hair dryer, safe.

MODERATE

Astor House Hotel (Pujiang Fandian)   A cheap backpackers' favorite in the last decade, this just-north-of-the-Bund hotel, once Shanghai's oldest hotel, has upgraded into a somewhat pricey three-star outfit with executive-level rooms. Refurbished standard rooms have firm and comfortable beds, and bathrooms are large and clean. Visitors can also choose from four restored "celebrity rooms," including one occupied by Albert Einstein in 1922 (room no. 304).

Huangpu Lu 15 (northeast side of Suzhou Creek, north of the Bund). ⓒ **021/6324-6388.** Fax 021/6324-3179. www.pujianghotel.com. 116 units. ¥880 ($110/£55) standard; ¥1,580 ($198/£99) celebrity room; ¥1,580 ($198/£99) executive room (20%–40% discount); 10% service charge. AE, DC, MC, V. Metro: Nanjing Dong Lu (about 1.6km/1 mile away). **Amenities:** 2 restaurants; lounge; bar; Internet cafe; salon; tour desk; 24-hr. room service; same-day laundry/dry cleaning; executive-level rooms. *In room:* A/C, TV, broadband (select rooms), minibar (select rooms), safe (select rooms).

PUDONG (EAST OF RIVER)
VERY EXPENSIVE

Grand Hyatt Shanghai (Shanghai Jin Mao Junyue Dajiudian) ✦✦   At press time the world's tallest hotel, running from the 54th to the 88th floors of the Jin Mao Tower, but soon to be eclipsed by its sister property the Park Hyatt in the neighboring World Financial Center, the ultraluxurious Grand Hyatt is more of a novelty hotel than a practical one. The views of the Bund and Pudong are astonishing (on the increasingly rare clear day, that is), as are the lush guest rooms, which combine Art Deco and traditional Chinese motifs with high-tech designs, but the burden of renown has made the staff a bit standoffish. The hotel's highflying address means you should allow extra time to get to your destination.

Shiji Da Dao 88, 54th floor, Jin Mao Tower (southeast of the Oriental Pearl TV Tower). ⓒ **800/233-1234** or 021/5049-1234. Fax 021/5049-1111. www.hyatt.com. 555 units. ¥3,800–¥4,100 ($475–$512/£237–£256) standard; ¥4,450–¥4,800 ($556–$600/£225–£300) executive-level room; from ¥5,700 ($712/£356) suite. AE, DC, MC, V. Metro: Lujiazui. **Amenities:** 6 restaurants; food pavilion; 2 lounges; nightclub; indoor "sky pool" (world's highest swimming pool); health club w/Jacuzzi and sauna; concierge; tour desk; 24-hr. business center; salon; 24-hr. room service; same-day laundry/dry cleaning; executive-level rooms. *In room:* A/C, satellite TV, dataport, minibar, coffeemaker, hair dryer, safe.

Pudong Shangri-La Hotel (Pudong Xianggelila Fandian) ✯✯✯ With the addition of a sleek new tower annex boasting a slew of trendy designer restaurants and the Himalayan-themed Chi spa, not only is the Shangri-La currently the biggest and boldest hotel in town, it has the best location in Pudong, with unbeatable views of the Bund across the river. All Tower Two guest rooms are spacious and superbly appointed with more amenities than you know what to do with, including DVD players, fax machines, and safes equipped to recharge your laptop computer. Tower One rooms will all be renovated as well by the end of 2008. Staff is delightfully friendly and the service is of a high international caliber.

Fucheng Lu 33 (southwest of the Oriental Pearl TV Tower/Dongfang Mingzhu, adjacent to Riverside Ave/Binjiang Da Dao). ✆ 800/942-5050 or 021/6882-8888. Fax 021/6882-6688. www.shangri-la.com. 950 units. ¥2,850–¥3,150 ($356–$394/£178–£197) standard; ¥3,350 – ¥3,550 ($419–$444/£209–£222) executive level; from ¥5,150 ($644/£322) suite. Discount 40%. AE, DC, MC, V. Metro: Lujiazui. **Amenities:** 6 restaurants; deli; 2 lounges; 2 bars; 2 indoor lap pools; tennis court; 2 health clubs w/Jacuzzi and sauna; CHI spa; concierge; tour desk; large business center; 24-hr. room service; babysitting; same-day laundry service/dry cleaning; executive-level rooms. *In room:* A/C, satellite TV, broadband, minibar, fridge, coffeemaker, hair dryer, safe.

St. Regis Shanghai (Shanghai Ruiji Hongta Dajiudian) ✯✯✯ This handsome robust hotel might well be *the* luxury hotel to stay at in town were it not for its less-convenient location in Pudong. Standard rooms, the largest in the city (48 sq. m/157 sq. ft.), are gorgeously furnished with comfortable sofas, ergonomic Herman Miller "Aeron" chairs, Bose CD radios, and "rain-forest" showers in the spacious marble bathrooms. As part of their "Lifestyle Butler Service," St. Regis butlers, on call 24 hours a day, can press clothing, make dinner reservations, and even act as tour guides about town, escorting guests interested in the Chinese art scene to galleries or the private studios of local Chinese artists. Three ladies'-only floors feature women butlers and a host of special in-room amenities including toiletries by Bulgari.

Dongfang Lu 889 (south central Pudong). ✆ 800/325-3589 or 021/5050-4567. Fax 021/6875-6789. www.stregis.com. 318 units. ¥3,313–¥3,478 ($414–$435/£207–£217) standard; from ¥6,378 ($797/£398) suite. Discount up to 60%. AE, DC, MC, V. Metro: Shiji Dadao. **Amenities:** 3 restaurants; 2 lounges; indoor pool; tennis court; state-of-the-art health club and full-service spa w/Jacuzzi and sauna; concierge; tour desk; business center; salon; 24-hr. room service; babysitting; same-day laundry/dry cleaning; 24-hr. butler service; 1 room for those w/limited mobility. *In room:* A/C, satellite TV, broadband, minibar, coffeemaker, hair dryer, safe.

EXPENSIVE

Holiday Inn Pudong (Shanghai Pudong Jiari Jiudian) ✯ (Value Though appealing mostly to businesspeople, this thoroughly Western 32-story Holiday Inn offers excellent value for tourists, especially after discounts. Guest rooms are spacious and bright, with bird's-eye maple furniture, comfortable beds, and all the amenities you're likely to need. The white tile bathrooms are spotless, and service is efficient and professional. The nearby metro 4 subway station, which is within walking distance, allows easier access to the rest of Shanghai.

Dongfang Lu 899 (south central Pudong). ✆ 800/465-4329 or 021/5830-6666. Fax 021/5830-5555. www.holiday-inn.com. 318 units. ¥1,500 ($187/£93) standard; ¥2,000 ($250/£125) executive level; from ¥2,000 ($250/£125) suite. Discounts up to 50% low season. AE, DC, MC, V. Metro: Pudian Lu. **Amenities:** 3 restaurants; deli; pub; bar; indoor pool; large health club w/Jacuzzi and sauna; game room; concierge; tour desk; business center; salon; 24-hr. room service; babysitting; same-day laundry/dry cleaning; nonsmoking rooms; executive-level rooms; rooms for those w/limited mobility. *In room:* A/C, satellite TV, dataport, minibar, coffeemaker, hair dryer, safe.

MODERATE

Courtyard by Marriott Hotel Pudong (Shanghai Qilu Wanyi Dajiudian) ✯
The Courtyard is a thoroughly modern and busy four-star hotel catering to business

Airport Hotels

There are plenty of hotels with free shuttle service near Hongqiao Airport. The closest five-star hotel is the **Marriott Hotel Hongqiao** (p. 447), which is still about 6.4km (4 miles) to the east. The new Australian-managed 205-unit **Argyle International Airport Hotel Hongqiao (Hua Gang Ya Ge Jiu Dian),** Kong Gang Yi Lu 458; (?) **021/6268-7788;** fax 021/6268-5671) is the nearest major hotel within a 5-minute walk from the airport. Modern efficient doubles start at around ¥800 ($100/£50).

The two hotels currently serving Pudong Airport include the more upmarket **Ramada Pudong Airport (Shanghai Jichang Huameida Dajiudian;** Qihang Lu 1100; (?) **021/3849-4949;** fax 021/6885-2889; www.ramadaairport pd.com), a 2- to 3-minute free shuttle ride or a 10-minute walk from the airport with doubles being offered at ¥880 ($110/£55) with 15% service charge, and a 40% discount; and the no-frills **Jinjiang Star Pudong Airport (Jinjiang Zhixin Shanghai Pudong Jichang,** Qihang Lu 8; (?) **021/6835-3568),** with doubles at ¥259 ($33/£17).

travelers. The comfortable rooms are of average size, with modern furniture and the Courtyard's signature floral bedspreads. The subway is just 2 blocks away, meaning a nonbusiness traveler can stay here comfortably, especially if a bargain room rate can be secured.

Dongfang Lu 838 (at intersection with Weifang Lu). (?) 021/6886-7886. Fax 021/6886-7889. www.courtyard.com. 318 units. ¥1,495 ($180/£90) standard; ¥1,985 ($240/£120) executive level; from ¥2,315 ($280/£140) suite. Discount up to 50%. AE, DC, MC, V. Metro: Shiji Dadao. **Amenities:** 2 restaurants; lounge; fitness center w/sauna; concierge; business center; salon; 24-hr. room service; babysitting; same-day laundry/dry cleaning; executive-level rooms. *In room:* A/C, satellite TV, dataport, minibar, coffeemaker, hair dryer, safe.

4 Where to Dine

Dozens of promising, mostly upscale, international restaurants and cafes open every month, too many to keep up with. The emphasis is on Shanghai's own renowned cuisine, commonly referred to as *benbang cai.* The most celebrated Shanghai dish is hairy crab, a freshwater delicacy that reaches its prime every fall. Also popular are any number of "drunken" dishes (crab, chicken) marinated in local Shaoxing wine, and braised meat dishes such as lion's head meatballs and braised pork knuckle. Shanghai dim sum and snacks include a variety of dumplings, headlined by the local favorite *xiaolong bao,* as well as onion pancakes and leek pies, all of which deserve to be tried.

The boom in Shanghai restaurants has brought with it a dramatic increase in Japanese, Thai, European, and American restaurants, too, with the international fast-food chains, from Starbucks to McDonald's, seemingly on every corner. For restaurant locations, see the map on p. 440.

HUANGPU (DOWNTOWN)
VERY EXPENSIVE
Bund 18 INTERNATIONAL   The latest redevelopment on the Bund—in the lavishly restored Chartered Bank of India, Australia, and China building—features **Sens &**

Three on the Bund (Wai Tan San Hao)

One of the splashiest and most luxurious developments in Shanghai, **Three on the Bund** is a "lifestyle destination" that has brought some world-class swank to the Bund. Built in 1922, this former Union Insurance Company Building now houses an art gallery, exclusive fashion outlets (including a Giorgio Armani store), and a luxurious Evian spa, but it's the fine-dining restaurants, all offering stunning vistas of the Bund and Pudong, that are drawing the crowds. For even more exclusive and intimate dining, the domed **Cupola** atop the building offers private dining for two, service by a private butler, and a menu from any of the following outlets. *Note:* Reservations required at Jean Georges, Laris, Whampoa Club, and the Cupola; reservations recommended at New Heights.

Jean Georges ✸✸✸ (fourth floor; ✆ **021/6321-7733;** 11:30am–2:30pm and 6–11pm). From *amuse-bouche* to dessert, it's the finest contemporary and light French fare from world-renowned chef Jean-Georges Vongerichten. There are over 5,000 bottles of wine to choose from, and a 30-seater wine cellar private dining room, all cloaked in dark blue and deep wine hues. Expect a dinner for two to hover immodestly around ¥2,000 ($250/£125).

Whampoa Club ✸✸ (fifth floor; ✆ **021/6321-3737;** 11:30am–2pm and 5:30–10pm). Putting a creative spin on classics learned from a passel of old-time Shanghai master chefs, Chef Jerome Leung focuses on bringing out the flavors of classic Shanghai dishes. Indulge in the tasting menu, which was delicious when I was there, though there have been occasional reviews of inconsistency. A professional tea sommelier can help with selecting from over 50 teas from all over China.

Laris ✸✸✸ (sixth floor; ✆ **021/6321-9922;** 11:30am–2:30pm and 5–10:30pm). In a light breezy setting, larger-than-life Australian chef David Laris creates some wonderful "New World" cuisine inspired by his previous culinary stints in Hong Kong, Vietnam, Macau, and London (as executive chef of Mezzo). Seafood gets top billing here (seared scallops on parsnip mash with oyster lemon foam, anyone?), with a crustacean-stocked seafood bar and a special Chocolate room (which churns out the Laris signature chocolate) getting raves from guests. Save room for the Pandan Leaf Panna Cotta.

New Heights ✸ (seventh floor; ✆ **021/6321-0909;** 11:30am–3:30pm and 6–11:30pm) is the option for casual, more affordable bistro-type fare, with rooftop views of the Bund and Pudong rivaling that of M on the Bund next door. Dinner for two should be in the ¥400 ($50/£25) range. In the back of New Heights is a music lounge, **Third Degree** (7pm–2am), which serves live music with its cocktails.

Three on the Bund is located at Zhongshan Dong Yi Lu 3 (entrance on side street at Guangdong Lu 23; ✆ **021/6323-3355;** www.threeonthebund.com). Take the metro to Nanjing Dong Lu.

Bund ★★★ (sixth floor), the first China foray of Jacques and Laurent Pourcel, fresh from their three-star Michelin restaurants in France. You can expect fine haute French cuisine, with equally haute prices, and many repeat customers. Garnering more complaints, especially of rude service and only mediocre food, is the Cantonese restaurant **Tan Wai Lou** (fifth floor). **Bar Rouge** on the rooftop is still the place for the jet set to see and be seen, though the scene has gotten a little seedy of late.

Zhongshan Dong Yi Lu 18. www.bund18.com. Reservations required. AE, DC, MC, V. Sens & Bund, 6th floor, ② 021/6323-9898. Main courses ¥150–¥280 ($18–$35/£9–£17). 11:30am–2:30pm and 6:30–10:30pm. Tan Wai Lou, 5th floor, ② 021/6339-1188. Meal for 2 ¥800 ($100/£50) and up. 11am–2:30pm and 6–10:30pm. **Bar Rouge**, 7th floor, ② 021/6339-1199. 11:30am–2am. Metro: Nanjing Dong Lu.

M on the Bund (Mishi Xicanting) ★★ CONTINENTAL   Lodged atop a handsome seven-story colonial building on the Bund, this is the restaurant that 7 years ago put Shanghai dining on the world map. All Art Deco elegance, M boasts a terrace that affords unsurpassed views of the Bund, the Huangpu River, and Pudong's skyscrapers, as well as a "Glamour Room" for nightly dinner and drinks. The menu changes frequently to take advantage of fresh local ingredients, but signature dishes include the slow-baked leg of lamb and the exquisitely sublime Pavlova dessert.

Zhongshan Dong Yi Lu 5, 7th floor (entrance on side street at Guangdong Lu 20). ② 021/6350-9988. www.m-restaurantgroup.com. Reservations required. Main courses ¥150–¥280 ($18–$35/£9–£17). AE, DC, MC, V. 11:30am–2:30pm (3pm Sat–Sun) and 6–10:30pm; Sun tea 3:30–5:30pm. Metro: Nanjing Dong Lu.

EXPENSIVE

Lu Bo Lang *Overrated* SHANGHAI   Housed in a three-story traditional Chinese pavilion just south of Yu Yuan in the old Chinese city, this restaurant has become a de rigueur stop on the average tourist itinerary strictly on the basis of its celebrity guest list (Fidel Castro, President Bill Clinton). Specialties such as the seasonal *Yangcheng Hu* crab, shark's fin, and President Clinton's favorite *sansi meimao su* (eyebrow-shaped pasty stuffed with pork, bamboo, and mushrooms) sell well, though prices are generally inflated. The automatic 10% service charge is a guarantee that you won't get much in the way of service.

Yu Yuan Lu 115 (south shore of teahouse lake). ② 021/6328-0602. Reservations recommended. Meal for 2 ¥120–¥250 ($14–$30/£7–£15). AE, DC, MC, V. 7am–12:30am. Metro: Nanjing Dong Lu.

Shanghai Uncle (Haishang Ashu) ★★★ SHANGHAI   If you only get to try one Shanghainese meal, let it be at this cavernous and brash red-themed restaurant in the basement of the Bund Center where old Shanghai favorites are given a modern makeover. Menu favorites include the unbelievably tender pine seed pork rip, Shanghai traditional smoked fish, and the fusion-influenced cheese baked lobster with homemade noodles. Mezzanine booths offer the best viewing spots. There's also a Xuhui branch: Tianyaoqiao Lu 211, second floor (north of Nandan Dong Lu), ② **021/6464-6430.**

Yan'an Dong Lu 222, Waitan Zhongxin (Bund Center), Basement (between Henan Zhong Lu and Jiangxi Zhong lu). ② 021/6339-1977. Reservations highly recommended. Meal for 2 ¥160–¥250 ($20–$31/£10–£16). AE, DC, MC, V. 11am–11pm. Metro: Nanjing Dong Lu.

INEXPENSIVE

Nanxiang Mantou Dian DUMPLINGS   Tourists flock to this dumpling restaurant just west of the Bridge of Nine Turnings in old town for its award-winning *Nanxiang xiaolong* (¥10/$1.25/60p for a steamer of 16 dumplings), steamed pork dumplings with delicious broth that squirts all over the moment you bite into the wrapper. The takeout counter is on the first floor, three dining rooms are on the second, and the crowds are everywhere.

Yu Yuan Lu 85 (west shore of teahouse lake). © 021/6355-4206. Meal for 2 ¥16–¥80 ($2–$10/£1–£5). No credit cards. 7am–8pm. Metro: Nanjing Dong Lu (1.6km/1 mile away).

LUWAN DISTRICT (FRENCH CONCESSION)
VERY EXPENSIVE

Xin Tiandi Restaurant Mall 🎔🎔🎔 INTERNATIONAL   A Starbucks stands at its entrance, the First National Congress of the Communist Party at its flanks, and in its midst, brilliant restorations of Shanghai's colonial Shiku Men ("stone gate") architecture. The place is Xin Tiandi (literally "New Heaven and Earth"), an upscale cultural mall where the moneyed East meets the moneyed West. Here you'll find the city's hottest dining spots. Located downtown a block south of the Huangpi Nan Lu metro station, Xin Tiandi is a 2-block pedestrian mall with enough good eating to require weeks to experience it all. The best and the priciest are listed below.

   Crystal Jade Restaurant (Feicui Jiujia) 🎔🎔🎔 (South Block/Nanli 6–7, second floor–12A and B; © 021/6385-8752; Mon–Fri 11am–3pm and 5–11:30pm, Sat–Sun 10:30am–3pm and 5–11:30pm) serves arguably the best *xiaolong bao* (steamed dumplings with broth) and *lamian* (hand-pulled noodles) south of the Yangzi. Reserve in advance or risk a long wait.

   KABB (Kaibo Xicanting) 🎔 (North Block, House 5, Unit 1; © 021/3307-0798; Mon–Fri 9:30am–midnight, Sat–Sun 9:30am–2am), a spiffy American bar and comfort food cafe.

   La Maison (Lemeisong Faguo Canting) (North Block, House 23, Unit 1; © 021/3307-1010; 11:30am–12:30am), a strictly French cafe, with French prices and its own bakery.

   Luna 🎔 (North Block, House 15, Unit 1; © 021/6336-1717; 11:30am–1:30am), a continental cafe with heavenly surroundings.

   Paulaner Brauhaus (Baolaina) (North Block, House 19–20; © 021/6320-3935; 11am–2am), the Shanghai standby praised for its excellent German food, with authentic brews to match.

   Star East (Shanghai Dongmei) (North Block, House 17, Unit 1; © 021/6311-4991; 11:30am–2am), international film star Jackie Chan's slick five-story Cantonese restaurant and bar, where Western set meals are available as well.

   T8 🎔🎔🎔 (North Block, House 8; © 021/6355-8999; lunch Wed–Mon 11:30am–2pm, dinner daily 6:30–11pm) is the restaurant whose service and chefs have quickly rivaled those at M on the Bund, only with less attitude. Service and management are superb and unobtrusive, the decor is super chic and the food is irresistible, especially the Sichuan seared king prawns, the slow-cooked lamb, the Sichuan pie, and the to-die-for chocolate addiction plate.

   Va Bene (Hua Wan Yi) 🎔🎔 (North Block, House 7; © 021/6311-2211; 11:30am–2:30pm and 5–11:30pm), an upscale Italian diner (from the owners of Hong Kong's Gaia) with warm Tuscan decor, patio dining, and a wide range of antipasti, pasta, and gourmet pizzas, all made from the freshest ingredients.

   Xin Jishi 🎔🎔 (North Block, House 9; © 021/6336-4746; 11am–1:30pm and 5–9:30pm) *always* has a line out the door for its delectable Shanghainese specialties such as braised home-cooked pork (*hong shao rou*) and glutinous rice with red dates.

Ye Shanghai (South Block, House 6; © **021/6311-2323;** 11:30am–2:30pm and 5:30–11pm), an elegant touch of old Shanghai, which Hong Kong visitors claim is better than the original back home.

Zen (Xianggang Caidie Xuan) (South Block, House 2; © **021/6385-6395;** 11:30am–11:30pm), a modern Cantonese restaurant by way of Hong Kong, with excellent dim sum for lunch.

EXPENSIVE

Lan Na Thai (Lan Na Tai) THAI   This popular Thai restaurant is located on the second floor of a beautiful colonial mansion (the "Face" building) on the north end of the Ruijin Hotel estate. The prawn cake, satays, and papaya salad are superb and authentic, as are the soft-shell crabs. Service is discreet and gracious, making this an ideal spot for a relaxing lunch or fine candlelit dinner.

Ruijin Er Lu 118 (bldg. 4, Ruijin Guest House; south of Fuxing Zhong Lu). © **021/6466-4328.** Reservations recommended on weekends. Meal for 2 ¥200–¥320 ($25–$40/£12–£20). AE, DC, MC, V. 11:30am–2:30pm and 5:30–11pm. Metro: Shanxi Nan Lu.

MODERATE

Di Shui Dong HUNAN   Rivaling Sichuan cuisine in spiciness, the lesser-known cooking of Hunan Province can be tried at this delightful restaurant atop a flight of rickety wooden stairs inside a small French Concession storefront. Highly recommended are the *lazi jiding* (spicy chicken nuggets), *suan doujiao rouni* (diced sour beans with minced pork), *duojiao yutou* (fish head steamed with red chili), and *xiang-wei hongshu bo* (fragrant sweet potato in monk's pot). Service is no-nonsense, even occasionally impatient, but the food is superb and shouldn't be missed.

Maoming Nan Lu 56 (north of Changle Lu). © **021/6253-2689.** Meal for 2 ¥80–¥140 ($10–$18/£5–£9). No credit cards. 11am–12:30am. Metro: Shanxi Nan Lu.

Zaozi Shu VEGETARIAN   Serving some of Shanghai's best vegetarian food, this popular, health-conscious restaurant eschews alcohol, dairy, MSG, and smoking, while serving organic tea and fruit as an appetizer. The bean curd skin roll is a delicious starter, and you can't go wrong with most of the pure vegetable dishes, though the fake meat dishes don't always hold up as well.

Songshan Lu 77, 1st floor (inside the Shanghai Huanggong complex, south of Huaihai Lu, 1 block east of Huangpi Nan Lu). © **021/6384-8000.** Reservations recommended. Meal for 2 ¥60–¥100 ($7.50–$13/£3.75–£6.50). AE, DC, MC, V. 10:30am–9pm. Metro: Huangpi Nan Lu.

JINGAN DISTRICT (NORTHWEST SHANGHAI)
VERY EXPENSIVE

Shintori Null II (Xinduli Wuer Dian) JAPANESE   The crowd at this nouvelle Japanese restaurant set inside an industrial bunker is well-heeled, black-clad, and a bit precious, but the sushi and sashimi are fine and fresh. Try making a meal from a selection of appetizers such as cuttlefish in butter sauce, grilled codfish with *monomiso*, foie gras on radish, and vermicelli noodles served in an ice bowl. Service is efficient and friendly, which lends some much-needed warmth to the place.

Julu Lu 803 (west of Fumin Lu). © **021/5404-5252.** Reservations required. Meal for 2 ¥250–¥600 ($31–$75/£15–£38). AE, DC, MC, V. Mon–Fri 5:30–10:30pm; Sat–Sun 11:30am–2pm and 5:30–10:30pm. Metro: Changshu Lu.

EXPENSIVE

Meilongzhen SHANGHAI   Established in 1938, this Shanghai institution still draws the crowds after all these years. Its cuisine has evolved over time from strictly regional fare to one incorporating the spices and chilies of Sichuan cooking. Popular favorites include deep-fried eel, Mandarin fish with noodles in chili sauce, Sichuan duck, and Meilongzhen special chicken, served in small ceramic pots. Recent renovations have turned the once stodgy atmosphere into a sparkling modern restaurant. Staff alternates between attentive and harried.

Nanjing Xi Lu 1081, bldg. 22 (east of Shanghai Centre at Jiangning Lu). ⓒ 021/6253-5353. Reservations recommended. Meal for 2 ¥120–¥240 ($14–$29/£7–£15). AE, DC, MC, V. 11am–2pm and 5–10pm. Metro: Shimen Yi Lu.

Mesa (Meisa) ⭐⭐ CONTINENTAL   This modern minimalist restaurant with stark walls, floor-to-ceiling windows, and an open kitchen serves the comfort foods of home while making good use of fresh local ingredients. The menu changes frequently but established favorites include the soy-and-ginger salmon with green tea soba, the T-bone steak, and the beef pie. Wines, chosen from an impressive list, are served in specially imported glasses. Save room for the homemade desserts.

Julu Lu 748 (east of Fumin Lu). ⓒ **021/6289-9108.** Reservations required. Main courses ¥90 – ¥200 ($11–$25/£6.50–£13). AE, DC, MC, V. Mon–Fri 6–11pm; Sat–Sun 9:30am–5pm and 6–11pm. Metro: Changshu Lu.

MODERATE

Baoluo ⭐ (Value SHANGHAI   A strictly local experience, Baoluo buzzes every night with barely controlled chaos. The extensive Chinese-only menu features many local favorites given a slight twist, including *huiguo rou jiabing* (twice-cooked lamb wrapped in pancakes), *songshu luyu* (sweet-and-sour fried fish), *xiefen hui zhenjun* (braised mushroom with crabmeat), and the more unusual *qingzhen douni* (creamy mashed beans).

Fumin Lu 271 (north of Changle Lu, 1 block east of Changshu Lu). ⓒ 021/6279-2827. Reservations highly recommended. Meal for 2 ¥80–¥140 ($10–$18/£5–£9). No credit cards. 11am–6am. Metro: Changshu Lu.

INEXPENSIVE

Element Fresh (Yuan Su) ⭐ AMERICAN   This hip eatery in the Shanghai Centre serves a range of soups, sandwiches, and salads that are fresh, healthy, and an instant cure for any homesickness. Also on the menu is a slew of smoothies, fresh fruit and vegetable juices, pastas, and a handful of Asian set meals, as well as some very popular breakfast sets. The place is jampacked at lunchtime as is the patio during the warmer months. Another branch is on the fifth floor of the KWah Centre at Huaihai Zhong Lu 1028 by Dongping Lu (ⓒ **021/5403-8865**).

Nanjing Xi Lu 1376, no. 112 (ground floor, Shanghai Centre). ⓒ **021/6279-8682.** Reservations recommended. Main courses ¥35 – ¥85 ($4.50–$11/£2.25–£6.50). AE, DC, MC, V. 7am–11pm. Metro: Jing'an Si.

XUHUI DISTRICT (SOUTHWEST SHANGHAI)
EXPENSIVE

Simply Thai (Tiantai Canting) ⭐ THAI   Located in a cozy two-story cottage, Simply Thai is the top choice with many Shanghai expatriates (Thais included) for unpretentious, authentic, and reasonably priced Thai food. Especially pleasing are the refreshing pomelo (grapefruit) salad with pineapple appetizer, *tom yam* shrimp soup, panaeng pork curry, and seafood with glass noodle salad. Patio dining in the warmer months provides a lovely respite from the city bustle.

Dongping Lu 5, Unit C (between Hengshan Lu and Yueyang Lu). ⓒ 021/6445-9551. Reservations recommended. Meal for 2 ¥150–¥300 ($18–$36/£9–£18). AE, DC, MC, V. 10am–1am. Metro: Hengshan Lu or Changshu Lu.

MODERATE

Indian Kitchen (Yindu Xiaochu) ⭐ INDIAN   This small, intimate restaurant in the heart of the French Concession is a favorite with locals and expatriates for authentic

Indian food that's easy on the wallet. Besides the signature chicken tandoori, the mutton curry and the flaky spring onion *parotas* are especially fine. Staff seems a little hesitant at times, but the line at the door that forms nightly should be plenty reassuring.

Yongjia Lu 572 (between Yueyang Lu and Wulumuqi Nan Lu). ℂ 021/6473-1517. Reservations recommended. Meal for 2 ¥130–¥200 ($16–$25/£8–£13). AE, DC, MC, V. 11am–2:30pm and 5–11pm. Metro: Hengshan Lu.

Lai Fu Lou ☆ HOT POT   The sleek Lai Fu Lou offers some of the most elegant and private hot pot dining in town. There's a wide variety of soup bases to choose from. Many folks opt for the *yuanyang* version, which contains both a potent spicy stock and a more benign pork-based broth. Besides all the usual meat and vegetable ingredients, the restaurant also specializes in handmade *yuwan* (fish balls) and *danjiao* (egg-wrapped dumplings).

Huaihai Zhong Lu 1416, 2nd floor (at intersection of Fuxing Xi Lu). ℂ 021/6473-6380. Reservations recommended. Meal for 2 ¥80–¥120 ($10–$15/£5–£7.50). AE, DC, MC, V. 11am–4am. Metro: Changshu Lu.

CHANGNING DISTRICT (HONGQIAO DEVELOPMENT ZONE)
MODERATE
1221 ☆☆ SHANGHAI   Very chic, this is a popular place among resident foreigners and business travelers for reasonably priced fine Shanghai dining that's neither too greasy nor too sweet. Standouts include drunken chicken, Shanghai smoked fish, lion's head meatballs, braised pork with preserved vegetables, and stir-fried shredded beef with *youtiao* (a fried salty doughnut).

Yan'an Xi Lu 1221 (between Panyu Lu and Dingxi Lu). ℂ 021/6213-6585. Reservations recommended. Meal for 2 ¥120–¥250 ($15–$30/£7.50–£15). AE, DC, MC, V. 11am–2pm and 5:30–11pm.

Ba Guo Bu Yi ☆☆ SICHUAN   Those seeking authentic Sichuan fare can find it at this popular batik-themed eatery where chili alerts in the Chinese-only menu will let you know what you're in for. Try *lazi jiding* (chicken nuggets in a sea of red chili peppers), *huiguo rou* (twice-cooked pork with chili and scallions), *shuizhu yu* (fish slices and vegetables in a flaming spicy broth), and *dandan mian* (noodles in spicy peanut sauce), but order lots of cold beer to put out the three-alarm fire in your mouth.

Dingxi Lu 1018 (north of Yan'an Xi Lu). ℂ 021/6270-6668 or 021/5239-7779. Reservations required. Meal for 2 ¥80 –¥160 ($10–$20/£5–£10). No credit cards. 11:30am–2pm and 5–9pm.

INEXPENSIVE
Lao Tan ☆ *Finds* GUIZHOU   Miao minority cuisine from southwestern China's Guizhou Province can now be found in Shanghai in this boisterous second-floor restaurant tucked away just east of the Crowne Plaza hotel. Worth trying are *suan jiangdou larou* (sour diced long beans with chilies and smoked bacon), *huoyan niurou* (beef with red and green peppers on a bed of leeks cooked over a slow flame), *ganguoji guozi* (spicy chicken with peppers), and *ganbian tudou* (fried potato pancake)—a perfect accompaniment to just about any dish.

Xingfu Lu 42, 2nd floor (north of Fahuazhen Lu, 1 block east of Fanyu Lu). ℂ 021/6283-7843. Reservations highly recommended. Meal for 2 ¥60–¥100 ($7.50–$13/£3.75–£6.50). No credit cards. 11am–2pm and 5–11pm.

PUDONG NEW AREA
VERY EXPENSIVE
Danieli's (Danni'aili) ☆☆ ITALIAN   This fine Italian restaurant atop the St. Regis Hotel features all manner of excellent *pesci* and *carni*, but it's the pastas that fans love (giving this restaurant "the best pasta" award in a local expatriate dining magazine

competition). To top it off, the views are exquisite, the wine list extensive, and the service highly attentive.

Dongfang Lu 877 (29th floor, St. Regis Hotel). © 021/5050-4567. Reservations required. Main courses ¥90–¥250 ($11–$31/£6.50–£15). AE, DC, MC, V. 11:30am–2:30pm and 5:30–10pm. Metro: Lujiazui.

Jade on 36 🏵🏵🏵 CONTINENTAL   Fine dining with a view to match doesn't get better (or much more expensive) than at this "avant-garde" restaurant lodged on the 36th floor of the Pudong Shangri-La Hotel. Chef Paul Pairet's playful cuisine is all about treating discerning diners to wonderfully inventive and unexpected combinations like foie gras layered with passion-fruit gel and cocoa powder, a simply sublime confection well worth a special trip out to Pudong. Set dining (with six or eight dishes) is the modus operandi here, with the "Jade of Jade" set being the most popular mainstay. Staff is exceedingly attentive and can tell you stories about each course.

Fucheng Lu 33 (36th floor, Pudong Shangri-La Hotel). © 021/6882-8888, ext. 280. www.jadeon36.com. Reservations required. Meal for 2 ¥2,000 ($250/£125). AE, DC, MC, V. 6pm–midnight. Metro: Lujiazui.

MODERATE

Su Zhe Hui (Jade Garden) 🏵 SHANGHAI   This branch of one of the more highly regarded and popular Shanghai chain restaurants offers diners its signature local dishes as well as Hong Kong–style dim sum in a classy and refined setting. Menu items of note include tea-smoked duck, wine-preserved green crab, *mizhi huofang* (pork and taro in candied sauce), and *qicai dongsun* (fresh winter shoots with local greens)—something you're unlikely to get back home.

Dongfang Lu 877 (just north of the St. Regis hotel). © 021/5058-6088. Meal for 2 ¥77–¥120 ($9.60–$14/£4.80–£7). AE, DC, MC, V. 11am–11pm. Metro: Shiji Dadao.

5 Exploring Shanghai

THE BUND (WAITAN)

The Bund (Embankment) refers to Shanghai's famous waterfront running along the west shore of the Huangpu River, forming the eastern boundary of old downtown Shanghai. Once a muddy towpath for boats along the river, the Bund was where the foreign powers that entered Shanghai after the Opium War of 1842 erected their distinct Western-style banks and trading houses. Today, a wide avenue (Zhongshan Dong Yi Lu) fronts the old buildings, which date mostly from the prosperous 1920s and 1930s. On the east side of the road, a raised pedestrian promenade affords visitors pleasant strolls along the river and marvelous views of both the Bund and Pudong—its modern skyscrapers constituting Shanghai's "21st Century Bund"—across the river.

The Bund, stretching for 1.6km (1 mile) from Suzhou Creek in the north to Jinling Lu in the south, is well worth strolling by day or at night. The chief colonial buildings, running north to south, include: the **former British Consulate** (No. 33–53), its two remaining faded but still stately buildings part of a compound slated for redevelopment; **Banque de L'Indo-Chine** (No. 29), built in 1911; **Glen Line Building** (No. 28), built in 1922 and briefly the American Consulate after World War II; **Jardine Matheson** (No. 27), 1922, one of the first and most powerful foreign trading offices in Shanghai; **Yangtze Insurance Building** (No. 26), 1916, with a fine restored lobby; **Bank of China** (No. 23), dating from 1937; **Peace Hotel** (No. 20), the former Cathay Hotel (1929), famous for its spectacular Art Deco interiors, but now closed for renovation until 2010; the former **Palace Hotel** (No. 19), 1906, built by the Sassoon family and now part of the Peace Hotel; **Chartered Bank of India,**

Australia, and China (No. 18), 1923, newly restored into a stunning high-end restaurant and retail complex; **North China Daily News Building** (No. 17), built in 1921; **Bank of Taiwan Building** (No. 16), built in 1924 as a Japanese bank; **Russo-Chinese Bank Building** (No. 15), dating from 1901; **Bank of Communications Building** (No. 14), a 1940 edifice with an entrance framed in copper sheets; **Shanghai Customs House** (No. 13), dating from 1927 and still housing some dank offices and apartments; **Hongkong and Shanghai Bank** (No. 12), dedicated in 1923, with its not-to-be-missed restored lobby dome just inside; **Hospital of the Shanghai Navigation Co.** (No. 7), built in 1906 and the site of China's first switchboard; **China Merchants Bank** (No. 6), built in 1906; the former **Nishin Navigation Company** (No. 5), 1925, its seventh floor now housing the restaurant M on the Bund; **Union Insurance Company Building** (No. 3), 1922, also known as Three on the Bund, one of Shanghai's hippest "lifestyle destinations" complete with international caliber restaurants and luxury shops (see box on p. 452); and **Shanghai Club** (No. 2), 1910, former home of the legendary Long Bar.

YU GARDEN (YU YUAN)

Yu Yuan is a pleasant enough, well-contained classical Chinese garden, if not quite the loveliest of its kind, as local boosters would have you believe. Bearing the burden of being the most complete classical garden in urban Shanghai and therefore a must-see for every tourist, this overexposed garden overflows daily with hordes of visitors, and is no longer the pastoral haven it once was. Built between 1559 and 1577 by local official Pan Yunduan as the private estate for his father, Yu Yuan (meaning Garden of Peace and Comfort) is a maze of Ming dynasty pavilions, elaborate rockeries, arched bridges, and goldfish ponds, all encircled by an undulating dragon wall. Occupying just 2 hectares (5 acres), it nevertheless appears quite expansive, with room for 30 pavilions.

Located in the heart of the old Chinese city, a few blocks southwest of the Bund in downtown Shanghai (nearest metro: Nanjing Dong Lu, which is still 1.6km/1 mile away), Yu Yuan has a ticket window on the north shore of the Huxin Ting Teahouse pond. The garden is open from 8:30am to 5pm; admission is ¥40 ($5/£2.50).

The layout of Yu Yuan, which contains several gardens-within-gardens, can make strolling here a bit confusing, but if you stick to a general clockwise path from the main entrance, you should get around most of the estate and arrive eventually at the Inner Garden (Nei Yuan) and final exit.

Halls and pavilions of note (in clockwise order from the north entrance) include the **Hall for Viewing the Grand Rockery (Yang Shan Tang)**, a graceful two-story tower serving as the entrance to the marvelous rock garden behind, which consists of 2,000 tons of rare yellow stones pasted together with rice glue and designed by a famous garden artist of the Ming dynasty, Zhang Nanyang; the **Hall of Heralding Spring (Dian Chun Tang)**, the most famous historical building in the garden, where in 1853 the secret Small Sword Society (Xiaodao Hui) plotted to join the peasant-led Taiping Rebellion and help overthrow the Qing dynasty; and the **Hall of Jade Magnificence (Yu Hua Tang)**, opening to the most celebrated stone sculpture in the garden, the **Exquisite Jade (Yu Ling Long)**, which was originally procured by the Huizong emperor of the Northern Song (reigned 1100–26) from the waters of Tai Hu (Lake Tai) where many of the bizarre rocks and rockeries found in classical Chinese gardens were submerged to be naturally carved by the currents. Such rocks represent mountain peaks in classical Chinese garden design. Just before the **Inner Garden (Nei**

Shanghai Attractions

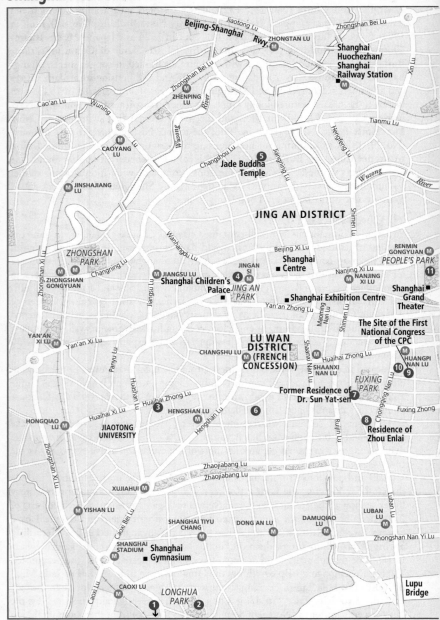

Beijing-Shanghai Rwy.

ZHONGTAN LU

Jiaotong Lu

Zhongshan Bei Lu

Xin Lu

Shanghai Huochezhan/ Shanghai Railway Station

Cao'an Lu

Wuning Lu

Zhongshan Bei Lu

Wusong River

ZHENPING LU

Tianmu Lu

Tienmu Lu

Hengfeng Lu

CAOYANG LU

Changphou Lu

Jiangning Lu

Jade Buddha Temple 5

Wusong River

JINSHAJIANG LU

JING AN DISTRICT

Wanhangdou Lu

Beijing Xi Lu

Shimen Lu

RENMIN GONGYUAN
PEOPLE'S PARK

ZHONGSHAN PARK

Changning Lu

JIANGSU LU

JINGAN SI

Shanghai Centre

Nanjing Xi Lu

NANJING XI LU

11

ZHONGSHAN GONGYUAN

Shanghai Children's Palace

4 *JING AN PARK*

Shanghai Exhibition Centre

Yan'an Zhong Lu

Maoming Nan Lu

Shimen Lu

Shanghai Grand Theater

The Site of the First National Congress of the CPC

YAN'AN XI LU

Yan'an Xi Lu

LU WAN DISTRICT (FRENCH CONCESSION)

CHANGSHU LU

Shaanxi Nan Lu

Huaihai Zhong Lu

SHAANXI NAN LU

FUXING PARK

HUANGPI NAN LU

10   9

Panyu Lu

Huashan Lu

Huaihai Xi Lu

Huaihai Zhong Lu

3

HENGSHAN LU

Hengshan Lu

6

Former Residence of Dr. Sun Yat-sen 7

Chongqing Nan Lu

Fuxing Zhong

HONGQIAO LU

JIAOTONG UNIVERSITY

Hengshan Lu

Ruijin Lu

8 **Residence of Zhou Enlai**

Zhongshan Xi Lu

Zhaojiabang Lu

Zhaojiabang Lu

XUJIAHUI

Luban Lu

YISHAN LU

Caoxi Bei Lu

SHANGHAI TIYU CHANG

DONG AN LU

DAMUQIAO LU

LUBAN LU

Zhongshan Nan Yi Lu

SHANGHAI STADIUM

Shanghai Gymnasium

Caoxi Lu

CAOXI LU

1   *LONGHUA PARK*   2

Lupu Bridge

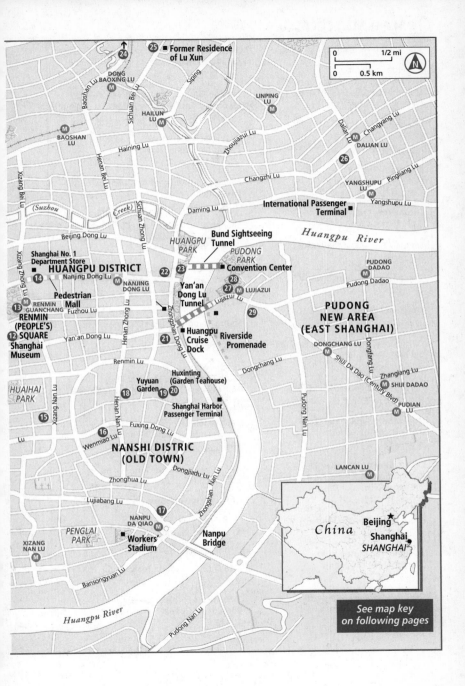

Former Residence
of Lu Xun

DGNG
BAOXING LU

Baoshan Lu

LINPING
LU

HAILUN
LU

Sichuan Bei Lu

Siping

Zhoujiazui Lu

Changyang Lu

Dalian Lu

DALIAN LU

BAOSHAN
LU

Henan Bei Lu

Haining Lu

YANGSHUPU
LU

Pingliang Lu

Changzhi Lu

Xizang Bei Lu

(Suzhou

Creek)

Sichuan Zhong Lu

Daming Lu

International Passenger
Terminal

Yangshupu Lu

Beijing Dong Lu

Huangpu River

Bund Sightseeing
Tunnel

Shanghai No. 1
Department Store

HUANGPU
PARK

PUDONG
PARK

Convention Center

PUDONG
DADAO

HUANGPU DISTRICT

Nanjing Dong Lu

NANJING
DONG LU

Yan'an
Dong Lu
Tunnel

LUJIAZUI

Pudong Dadao

Xizang Zhong Lu

Pedestrian
Mall

RENMIN
GUANCHANG

Fuzhou Lu

Henan Zhong Lu

Lujiazui Lu

PUDONG
NEW AREA
(EAST SHANGHAI)

RENMIN
(PEOPLE'S)
SQUARE

Yan'an Dong Lu

Shanghai
Museum

Zhongshan Dong Lu

Huangpu
Cruise
Dock

Riverside
Promenade

DONGCHANG LU

Shiji Da Dao (Century Blvd)

Renmin Lu

Dongfang Lu

SHIJI DADAO

Zhanglang Lu

HUAIHAI
PARK

Xizang Nan Lu

Henan Nan Lu

Yuyuan
Garden

Huxinting
(Garden Teahouse)

Dongchang Lu

Pudong Nan Lu

PUDIAN
LU

Shanghai Harbor
Passenger Terminal

Lu

Fuxing Dong Lu

Wenmiao Lu

NANSHI DISTRIC
(OLD TOWN)

Dongjiadu Lu

Zhonghua Lu

Zhongshan Nan Lu

LANCAN LU

Lujiabang Lu

NANPU
DA QIAO

China

Beijing ★

XIZANG
NAN LU

PENGLAI
PARK

Workers'
Stadium

Nanpu
Bridge

Shanghai
SHANGHAI

Bansongyuan Lu

Huangpu River

Pudong Nan Lu

See map key
on following pages

Shanghai Attractions Key

The Bund (Wài Tān) **23**
外滩

Dōngtái Lù Antiques Market
(Dōngtái Lù Gǔwán Shìchǎng) **15**
东台路古玩市场

Friendship Store
(Yǒuyì Shāngdiàn) **21**
友谊商店

Fúyòu Market **18**
福佑市场

Húxīn Tíng Teahouse **20**
(Húxīn Tíng Cháshè)
湖心亭茶社

Jīn Mào Tower (Jīn Mào Dàshà) **29**
金茂大厦

Jìng'ān Temple (Jìng'ān Sì) **4**
静安寺

Lónghuá Temple (Lónghuá Sì) **2**
龙华寺

Lǔ Xùn Park and Memorial Hall **25**
(Lǔ Xùn Jìniànguǎn)
鲁迅纪念馆

Nánjīng Road Pedestrian Mall **14**
南京路步行街

Ohel Moshe Synagogue **26**
(Móxī Huìtáng)
摩西会堂

Oriental Pearl TV Tower **28**
(Dōngfāng Míngzhū
    Guǎngbō Diànshì Tǎ)
东方明珠广播电视塔

Peace Hotel (Hépíng Fàndiàn) **22**
和平饭店

Shànghǎi Art Museum **11**
(Shànghǎi Měishùguǎn)
上海美术馆

Shànghǎi Botanical Gardens
(Shànghǎi Zhíwùyuán) **1**
上海植物园

Shànghǎi Circus World **24**
(Shànghǎi Mǎxì Chéng)
上海马戏城

Shànghǎi Municipal History Museum **27**
(Shànghǎi Shì Lìshǐ Bówùguǎn)
上海市历史博物馆

Shànghǎi Museum **12**
(Shanghai Bówùguǎn)
上海博物馆

Shànghǎi Museum of Arts and Crafts **6**
(Shànghǎi Gōngyì Měishù Bówùguǎn)
上海工艺美术博物馆

Shànghǎi Urban Planning Centre **13**
(Shànghǎi Chéngshì Guīhuà Zhǎnshìguǎn)
上海城市规划展示馆

Site of the First National
    Congress of the Communist Party **9**
(Zhōnggòng Yīdà Huìzhǐ)
中共一大会址

Soong Ching-ling's Former Residence **3**
(Sòng Qīnglíng Gùjū)
宋庆龄故居

South Bund Fabric Market **17**
(Nán Wàitān Qīng Fáng Miánliào Shìchǎng)
南外滩轻纺面料市场

Sun Yat-sen's Former Residence **7**
(Sūn Zhōngshān Gùjū Jìniànguǎn)
孙中山故居纪念馆

Wén Miào (Confucius Temple) **16**
文庙

Xīntiāndì (New Heaven and Earth) **10**
新天地

Yù Yuán (Yù Garden) **19**
豫园

Yùfó Sì (Jade Buddha Temple) **5**
玉佛寺

Zhōu Enlái's Former Residence **8**
(Zhōu Gōng Guǎn)
周公馆

Yuan), where local artists and calligraphers often display and sell their works, is the garden's main exit.

SHANGHAI BOWUGUAN ✮✮✮

Frequently cited as the best museum in China, the Shanghai Museum has 11 state-of-the-art galleries and three special exhibition halls arranged on four floors, all encircling a spacious cylindrical atrium. The exhibits are tastefully displayed and well lit, and explanatory signs are in English as well as Chinese. For size, the museum's 120,000 historic artifacts cannot match the world-renowned Chinese collections in Beijing, Taipei, and Xi'an, but are more than enough to fill the galleries on any given day with outstanding treasures.

Located downtown on the south side of People's Square (Renmin Guangchang) at Renmin Da Dao 201 (**© 021/6372-3500**), the museum has its main entrance on the north side of the building, facing the three monumental structures that now occupy the north half of the square (Grand Theatre to the west, City Hall in the middle, Shanghai Urban Planning Exhibition Center to the east). Metro lines 1 and 2 both have their main stations on the northeast corner of People's Square. The museum is open 9am to 5pm (no tickets sold after 4pm). Admission is ¥20 ($2.50/£1.25). Audio phones providing narratives of the major exhibits in English, French, Japanese, Spanish, German, and Italian are available for rent (¥40/$5/£2.50 plus a deposit of ¥400/$50/£25 or your passport) to your left as you enter the lobby.

The first floor contains major galleries displaying bronzes and stone sculptures. The second floor has wonderful displays of ceramic ware. The third floor has separate galleries for paintings, calligraphy, and personal seals. The fourth floor has exhibits of jade, coins, furniture, and minority cultures. Though visitors all have their individual favorites, the Bronze Gallery and the Stone Sculpture Gallery on the first floor, the Painting Gallery on the third floor, and the Jade Gallery on the fourth are generally considered the most impressive.

HUANGPU RIVER CRUISE

The Huangpu River (Huangpu Jiang) is the city's shipping artery both to the East China Sea and to the mouth of the Yangzi River, which the Huangpu joins 29km (18 miles) north of downtown Shanghai. It has also become a demarcating line between two Shanghais, east and west, past and future. On its western shore, the colonial landmarks of the Bund serve as a reminder of Shanghai's 19th-century struggle to reclaim a waterfront from the bogs of this river (which originates in nearby Dianshan Hu or Lake Dianshan); on the eastern shore, the steel-and-glass skyscrapers of the Pudong New Area point to a burgeoning financial empire of the future.

The Huangpu's wharves are the most fascinating in China. The port handles the cargo coming out of the interior from Nanjing, Wuhan, and other Yangzi River ports, including Chongqing, 2,415km (1,500 miles) deep into Sichuan Province. From Shanghai, which produces plenty of industrial and commercial products of its own, as much as a third of China's trade with the rest of the world is conducted each year.

Several boat companies offer cruises, but the main one is the **Shanghai Huangpu River Cruise Company (Shanghai Pujiang Youlan),** at Zhongshan Dong Er Lu 219 (**© 021/6374-4461**), located on the southern end of the Bund Promenade; there's another office farther north at Zhongshan Dong Er Lu 153. They have a daily full 3½-hour afternoon cruise (2–5:30pm) with the possibility of a full morning cruise during the summer. Cost is ¥150 ($19/£9.50). There are also hour-long cruises during the day (¥50/$6.25/£3.10) starting around 9:30am, and at night (¥70/$9/£4.50) until 10pm.

The granite offices, banks, consulates, and hotels of Shanghai's past colonial masters form a stately panorama along the Bund, while the Oriental Pearl TV Tower, the Jin Mao Tower, the World Financial Tower, and other new skyscrapers soar on the Pudong side. As the ship heads north of the Bund, hugging the west shore are the old "go-downs" or warehouses of the many foreign trading firms. This area, known as Hongkou District, and the district to the east, Yangpu District, have been marked for rapid development after Pudong, though new modern towers have already started to stake out the skyline. Eventually, all of this waterfront will be developed into a series of marinas and a combination of industrial and recreational areas.

As the Huangpu slowly curves northward again, you'll pass the **Yangpu Cable Bridge,** which, like the **Nanpu Cable Bridge** to the south, is one of the largest such structures in the world. Boasting the longest span in the world, some 602m (1,975 ft.), the Yangpu Bridge is considered the world's first "slant-stretched" bridge. Its total length is about 7.6km (4¾ miles), and 50,000 vehicles pass over it daily.

What overwhelms river passengers even more than the long industrial shoreline is the traffic slinking up and down the waterway from the flotilla of river barges to the large rusting hulls of cargo ships. The Huangpu is, on the average, just 183m (600 ft.) wide, but more than 2,000 oceangoing ships compete with the 20,000 barges, fishing junks, and rowboats that ply the Huangpu every year.

The Huangpu eventually empties into the mighty Yangzi River at **Wusong Kou,** where the water during high tide turns three distinct colors, marking the confluence of the Yangzi (yellow), the Huangpu (gray), and the South China Sea (green). Before this, there's an ancient **Wusong Fort,** from which the Chinese fought the British in 1842. The passenger terminal for Yangzi River cruises is also here. This marks the end of Shanghai's little river and the beginning of China's largest one. As your tour boat pivots slowly back into the narrowing passageway of the Huangpu, you can look forward to a return trip that should be more relaxed.

TEMPLES

Jing'an Si (Jing'an Temple)   Always lively and crowded, this garishly decorated and recently renovated temple has the longest history of any shrine in Shanghai: about 17 centuries. Its chief antiquities are a Ming dynasty copper bell (the Hongwu Bell) that weighs in at 3,175 kilograms (3½ tons), and stone Buddhas from the Northern and Southern States Period (A.D. 420–589).

Nanjing Xi Lu 1686, Jing An (corner of Huashan Lu). ⓒ **021/6256-6366.** Admission ¥10 ($1.25/60p). 7:30am–5pm. Metro: Jing An Si.

Longhua Si (Longhua Temple) 🕬🕬   Shanghai's largest temple features the city's premier pagoda (Longhua Ta). The seven-story, eight-sided, 1,000-year-old wood-and-brick pagoda is pretty, but it is not open for visits. The temple is active, its main halls impressive, its courtyards crowded with incense-bearing supplicants. Longhua is also famous for its midnight bell-ringing every New Year's Eve (Dec 31–Jan 1). The Bell Tower's 3,000-kilogram (3⅓-ton) bronze bell, cast in 1894, is struck 108 times to dispel all the worries said to be afflicting mankind. For a small fee, you, too, can strike the bell, but three times only.

Longhua Lu 2853, Xuhui. ⓒ **021/6456-6085.** Admission ¥10 ($1.25/60p). 7am–5pm. Metro: Shanghai Tiyuguan (a long, unpleasant walk; easier to reach by taxi).

Wen Miao (Confucius Temple)   Built in 1855 on the site of an earlier temple, and restored in 1999 to celebrate the 2,550th birthday of Confucius, this temple honoring

China's Great Sage offers quiet refuge from the crowded streets of the old Chinese city. Inside are statues of Confucius flanked by his two disciples, Mencius (Mengzi) and Yanhui; the Zunjing Ge, a former library now containing a display of unusually shaped rocks; and, near the entrance, Kuixing Ge, a three-story, 20m-high (66-ft.) pagoda dedicated to the god of liberal arts, the only original structure left. A lively book market is held here Sunday mornings.

Wenmiao Lu 215, Huangpu (north side of Wenmiao Lu, 1 block east of Zhonghua Lu). ✆ 021/6377-1815. Admission ¥10 ($1.25/60p). 8:30am–4:30pm.

Yufo Si (Jade Buddha Temple) ★ *Overrated*   Though an active Buddhist monastery today, the real emphasis at Shanghai's most popular temple is squarely on tourism. The chief attractions are two gorgeous white jade Buddhas, each carved from an individual slab of Burmese jade and brought to Shanghai in 1881 by the monk Huigen. The first—a lustrous seated Buddha weighing 205 kilograms (455 lb.), measuring 1.9m (6 ft. 5 in.), and adorned with jewels and stones—can be found in the Cangjing Lou in the northeast of the compound, while a smaller 1m-long (3 ft. 4 in.) sleeping Buddha is in the Wofo Si, northwest of the main hall.

Anyuan Lu 170, Putuo (northwest Shanghai, west of Jiangning Lu, 6 long blocks north of Beijing Xi Lu). ✆ 021/6266-3668. Admission ¥20 ($2.50/£1.25). 8am–4:30pm.

PARKS & GARDENS

Shanghai Botanical Gardens (Shanghai Zhiwuyuan) ★ *Kids*   Located in the far southwest of town, the city's premier garden, covering 81 hectares (200 acres), is divided into different sections featuring peonies, roses, bamboo, azaleas, maples, osmanthus, magnolias, and orchids (considered the best in China). The hallmark section is the Penjing Yuan (Bonsai Garden), which requires a separate admission (¥7/90¢/45p), with hundreds of bonsai displayed in a large complex of corridors, courtyards, pools, and rockeries.

Longwu Lu 1111, Xuhui. ✆ 021/5436-3369. Admission ¥15 ($1.80/90p) garden only; ¥40 ($5/£2.50) includes Bonsai Garden and 3 other sections. 7am–5pm.

MUSEUMS & MANSIONS

Lu Xun Park and Memorial Hall/Former Residence of Lu Xun (Lu Xun Gongyuan/Lu Xun Guju)   Named for China's best-known 20th-century writer, Lu Xun (1881–1936), who lived in this neighborhood from 1927 until his death, this park contains Lu Xun's mausoleum and a museum devoted to his life, the Lu Xun Memorial Hall. A 10-minute walk east of the park, **Lu Xun's Former Residence** is a brick house where he lived from 1933 to his death, largely decorated as it was then.

Jiangwan Dong Lu 146, Hongkou. Park admission ¥2 (25¢/10p) includes Lu Xun's tomb. 6am–6pm. Lu Xun Memorial Hall (inside park on east side; ✆ 021/6540-2288); admission ¥8 ($1/50p); 9am–4pm. **The Former Residence of Lu Xun**, Shanyin Lu 9 Lane 132, Hongkou (from park, take a left out the main entrance, follow Tian'ai Lu south until it curves left onto Shanyin Lu); admission ¥8 ($1/50p); 9am–4pm. Light Rail: Hongkou Zuqiu Chang.

Ohel Moshe Synagogue (Moxi Huitang)   Shanghai experienced several waves of Jewish immigration, beginning with the arrival of Sephardic Jews in the late 1840s, and lasting into the 1930s with a wave of European Jews fleeing Hitler. This synagogue, built in 1927 by the Ashkenazi Jewish community of Shanghai, no longer serves as a synagogue, but as a museum devoted to the Jews in Shanghai (whose number topped 30,000 just before World War II). The best way to visit this, as well as other sites in the Hongkou District that formed Shanghai's "Little Vienna," is on the

"Tour of Jewish Shanghai" 🔍 conducted by appointment with Dvir Bar-Gal (📞 **1300-214-6702;** www.shanghai-jews.com).

Changyang Lu 62, Hongkou District. Admission ¥50 ($6.25/£3.10) donation. Mon–Fri 9am–4pm.

Shanghai Art Museum (Shanghai Meishuguan) 🔍

Relocated in 2000 to the historic clock tower building on the northwest end of People's Park, the museum is more to be seen for its monumental interior architecture than for its art. The fastidiously restored interiors of this 1933 five-story landmark recall colonial times when People's Park was a racecourse and the grandstand (1863) stood where this museum is now. Today, in addition to the artwork, there is a nice American restaurant, Kathleen's 5, on the fifth floor.

Nanjing Xi Lu 325, Huangpu (northwest edge of People's Park at Huangpi Lu). 📞 021/6327-2829. www.sh-art museum.org.cn. Admission ¥20 ($2.50/£1.25). 9am–5pm (last tickets sold 4pm). Metro: Renmin Gongyuan.

Shanghai Municipal History Museum (Shanghai Shi Lishi Bowuguan) 🔍🔍

This excellent museum tells the history of Shanghai with special emphasis on the colonial period from 1860 to 1949. Exhibits include dioramas of the Huangpu River, the Bund, and foreign concessions, evoking the street life and lost trades of the period; dozens of models of Shanghai's classic avenues and famous buildings; and intriguing artifacts such as an ornate wedding palanquin, and visiting chits used in brothels. Signs are in English and Chinese.

Lujiazui Lu 2, Oriental Pearl TV Tower basement, Pudong. 📞 021/5879-3003. Admission ¥35 ($4.25/£2.15). 9am–9pm. Metro: Lujiazui.

Shanghai Museum of Arts and Crafts (Shanghai Gongyi Meishu Yanjiusuo Jiugongyipin Xiufu Bu)

With its expansive lawns, stained-glass windows, and dark wooden paneling, this 1905 French Concession mansion gives a fine picture of how the colonials lived in old Shanghai. After 1960, this became the Shanghai Arts and Crafts Research Center, and its many rooms were converted to studios where visitors could watch artisans work at traditional handicrafts. Today, a few artists' studios remain, along with a formal museum of the crafts produced in Shanghai over the past 100 years. A salesroom is attached, of course.

Fenyang Lu 79, Luwan District (at intersection of Yueyang Lu and Taojiang Lu). 📞 021/6431-1431. Admission ¥8 ($1/50p). 9am–5pm (last ticket sold 4pm). Metro: Changshu Lu.

Shanghai Urban Planning Exhibition Centre (Shanghai Chengshi Guihua Zhanshiguan 🔍🔍 Finds

One of the world's largest museums showcasing urban development, this exhibit is far more interesting than its dry name suggests. On the third floor is a showstopper: an awesome vast scale model of urban Shanghai as it will look in 2020, a master plan of endless skyscrapers punctuated by patches of green. See this and understand how and why Shanghai is going to be *the* city of the future.

Renmin Da Dao 100, Huangpu (northeast of the Shanghai Museum; entrance on east side). 📞 021/6372-2077. Admission ¥30 ($3.75/£1.85). 9am–4pm (to 5pm Fri–Sun). Metro: Renmin Guangchang.

Site of the First National Congress of the Communist Party (Zhonggong Yida Huizhi)

This historic building of brick and marble—a quintessential example of the traditional Shanghai style of *shiku men* (stone-framed) houses built in the 1920s and 1930s—contains the room where on July 23, 1921, Mao Zedong and 12 other Chinese revolutionaries founded the Chinese Communist Party. Supposedly the original teacups and ashtrays remain on the organizing table.

Xingye Lu 76, Luwan (south end of Xin Tiandi). ℂ 021/5383-2171. Admission ¥3 (35¢/15p). 9am–4pm. Metro: Huangpi Nan Lu.

Soong Ching-ling's Former Residence (Song Qingling Guju)   Soong Ching-ling (1893–1981) is revered throughout China as a loyalist to the Communist cause. Born in Shanghai to a wealthy family, she married the founder of the Chinese Republic, Dr. Sun Yat-sen, in 1915. This house was her residence from 1948 to 1963. The 1920s villa is little changed; the rooms are much as Soong left them. There is also a collection of her personal letters, photos, and books from her college days at Wesleyan College.

Huaihai Zhong Lu 1843, Xujiahui (east of Tianping Lu). ℂ 021/6437-6268. Admission ¥20 ($2.50/£1.25). 9am–4:30pm.

Sun Yat-sen's Former Residence (Sun Zhongshan Guju)   Sun Yat-sen (1866–1925), beloved founder of the Chinese Republic (1911), lived here with his wife Soong Ching-ling from 1918 to 1924, when the address would have been 29 Rue de Molière. Here Sun's wife later met with such literary stars as Lu Xun and George Bernard Shaw, and political leaders including Vietnam's Ho Chi Minh. An English-speaking guide leads visitors through the house. The backyard has a charming garden.

Xiangshan Lu 7, Luwan (west of Fuxing Park at Sinan Lu). ℂ 021/6437-2954 or 021/6385-0217. www.sh-sun yat-sen.com. Admission ¥20 ($2.50/£1.25). 9am–4pm. Metro: Shanxi Nan Lu.

Zhou Enlai's Former Residence (Zhou Gong Guan)   China's most revered leader during the Mao years, Premier Zhou Enlai (1898–1976), used to stay at this ivy-covered house when he visited Shanghai in 1946. Used more as office than residence, the house served before 1949 as the Communist Party's Shanghai office. Zhou's old black Buick is still parked in the garage.

Sinan Lu 73, Luwan (2 blocks south of Fuxing Zhong Lu). ℂ 021/6473-0420. Admission ¥2 (25¢/10p). 9am–4pm. Metro: Shanxi Nan Lu.

SPECIAL ATTRACTIONS
Huxin Ting Teahouse (Huxin Ting Chashi)   Shanghai's quintessential teahouse has floated atop the lake at the heart of old town, in front of Yu Yuan, since 1784. Believed to be the original model for Blue Willow tableware, the two-story pavilion with uplifted black-tiled eaves is a relaxing place to idle over a cup of tea and escape the old-town crowds.

Yuyuan Lu 257, Nanshi (at pond in the center of the Old Town Bazaar). ℂ 021/6373-6950. Free admission. 8:30am–9pm. Metro: Nanjing Dong Lu.

Jin Mao Tower (Jin Mao Dasha) ★★   Built in 1998 as a Sino-American joint venture, at press time the second tallest building in China (to its neighbor the World Financial Center) at 421m (1,379 ft.), is sublime, blending traditional Chinese and modern Western tower designs. Offices occupy the first 50 floors, the Grand Hyatt hotel the 51st to the 88th floors, while a public observation deck on the 88th floor offers views to rival those of the nearby Oriental Pearl TV Tower (its admission charge is also lower). Enter the building through entrance 4.

Shiji Da Dao 2, Pudong (3 blocks southeast of Oriental Pearl TV Tower). ℂ 021/5047-5101. Admission ¥70 ($8.75/£4.40). 8:30am–9:30pm (last ticket sold 9pm). Metro: Lujiazui (Exit 5).

Oriental Pearl TV Tower (Dongfang Mingzhu Dianshi Ta) ★   Built in 1994 at a height of 468m (1,550 ft.), this hideous gray tower with three tapering levels of pink spheres (meant to resemble pearls) is hailed as Asia's tallest TV tower and the third-tallest in the world. For most visitors, the observation deck in the middle sphere

---

F1 Fever

Formula One racing officially roared into China with the **Shanghai Grand Prix** in 2004. Located in the northwestern suburb of Anting in Jiading County, about 40 minutes from People's Square, the Shanghai International Circuit (Shanghai Guoji Saichechang), which will host F1 races in China until 2010, features a stunning track in the contours of a Chinese character, and a 10-story glass-and-steel grandstand. Tickets range from ¥160 ($19/£9.50) for practice sessions to ¥3,980 ($527/£263) for top seats overlooking the finish line on the last day. Tourist bus line no. 6B (¥4/50¢/25p) makes the run to Anting from the Shanghai Stadium. For more information, call ℂ **021/9682-6999** or 021/6330-5555 or visit www.icsh.sh.cn.

(elev. 263m/870 ft.), reached by high-speed elevators, is just the right height to take in panoramas of Shanghai (when the clouds and smog cooperate, that is).

Lujiazui Lu 2, Pudong. ℂ **021/5879-1888**. Admission ¥85–¥135 ($11–$17/£5.30–£8.50), depending on sections visited. 8am–9:30pm. Metro: Lujiazui (Exit 1).

Peace Hotel (Heping Fandian) ★★★ As the ultimate symbol of romantic colonial Shanghai, this Art Deco palace was built in 1929 by Victor Sassoon as part office and residence (Sassoon House) and part hotel (the Cathay Hotel), the latter becoming one of the world's finest hotels in the 1930s. Renowned for its Art Deco interiors, the Peace Hotel is closed for renovation until 2010 but if you're around the area, you might still be able to catch a glimpse of its famous green pyramid roof.

Nanjing Dong Lu 20, Huangpu (on the Bund). ℂ **021/6321-6888**. Free admission. 24 hr. Metro: Nanjing Dong Lu.

TOURS

Most Shanghai hotels have tour desks that can arrange a variety of day tours for guests. These tour desks are often extensions of **China International Travel Service (CITS)**, with its head offices near the Shanghai Centre at Beijing Xi Lu 1277, Guolu Dasha (ℂ **021/6289-4510** or 021/6289-8899, ext. 263; www.scits.com). The FIT (Family and Independent Travelers) department can be reached at fax 021/6289-7838. There's another branch at the Bund at Jinling Dong Lu 2 (ℂ **021/6323-8770**) where you can purchase airline and train tickets.

If you have little time, **group tours** are convenient, efficiently organized, and considerably less expensive than private tours. These tours cost about ¥250 to ¥400 ($30–$48/£15–£24) per person. The **Jinjiang Optional Tours Center,** which has its head office in the CITS building (Beijing Xi Lu 1277, room 611; ℂ **021/6445-9525;** fax 021/6472-0184; www.jjtravel.com) and a desk in the Jinjiang Tower Hotel at Changle Lu 161 (ℂ **021/6415-1188,** ext. 80160) offers a typical group tour of Shanghai by bus, with English-speaking guide and lunch, for ¥350 ($44/£22); sites include Yu Yuan, the Bund, Jade Buddha Temple, Xin Tiandi, People's Square, the Shanghai Museum, and a quick drive-by of Pudong. Hotel desks have a wider range of group tour itineraries to select from, but at higher prices than those offered by the Jinjiang Optional Tours Center. Another option is **Gray Line Shanghai,** located at Hanzhong Lu 188, Youth Center Plaza, second floor, A9 (ℂ **021/6150-8061;** www.grayline.com), part of the international chain that offers a 1-day tour of Shanghai for around ¥390 ($49/£24).

6 Shopping

Shanghai's top street to shop has always been **Nanjing Lu,** enhanced recently by the creation of the **Nanjing Lu Pedestrian Mall** downtown, where the most modern and the most traditional modes of retailing commingle. More popular with locals, however, is **Huaihai Zhong Lu,** the wide avenue south of Nanjing Road and parallel to it. The modern shopping malls here have better prices than you'll find on Nanjing Road.

Some of the most interesting clothes and shoes shopping in the French Concession is concentrated in the **Maoming Lu/Changle Lu** area, while the **Old Town Bazaar** in Yu Yuan is the best place to shop for local arts and crafts, and antiques.

To preview what's available and for last-minute purchases, try the **Friendship Store (Youyi Shangdian)** at Jinling Dong Lu 68 (© **021/6337-3555;** metro: Nanjing Dong Lu). It's open from 9:30am to 9:30pm.

There are 250 **antiques** stalls located in the basement of the **Hua Bao Lou** on "Shanghai Old Street" near the Temple of the Town God at Fangbang Zhong Lu 265, Nanshi (© **021/6355-2272;** metro: Nanjing Dong Lu), but the chances of buying something authentic are as slim as anywhere else in China. Still, it's worth a browse.

For **ceramics,** the **Shanghai Jingde Zhen Porcelain Artware,** is at Nanjing Xi Lu 1185 (© **021/6253-3178;** metro: Jing An Temple) and is open from 10am to 10pm. Or try the **Shanghai Arts and Crafts Museum (Shanghai Gongyi Meishuguan),** open from 8:30am to 4:30pm, at Fenyang Lu 79, Xujiahui (© **021/6437-0509;** metro: Changshu Lu).

Pearls, jade, gold, and silver jewelry can be found at **Amy's Pearls** in Gubei, open from 9am to 7pm at Yili Nan Lu 39 (by Guyang Lu; © **021/6275-3954**); and at Nanjing Xi Lu 580 (© **021/5228-2372**); and at **Lao Feng Xiang Jewelers** on the north side of the Nanjing Lu Pedestrian Mall, open from 9:30am to 10pm at Nanjing Dong Lu 432 (© **021/6322-0033;** metro: Nanjing Dong Lu). **Pearl Village (Zhenzhu Cun),** located in the Old Town Bazaar at Fuyou Lu 288, Yayi Jindian, third floor (© **021/6355-3418;** metro: Nanjing Dong Lu) has over 50 vendors representing pearl dealers, farms, and factories from throughout China.

Silk and wool yardage, along with a wide selection of shirts, blouses, skirts, dresses, ties, and other finished silk goods, have make **Silk King (Zhensi Da Wang)** the top silk retailer in Shanghai. Silk or wool suits can be custom tailored in as little as 24 hours. Two of the more conveniently located branches are at Nanjing Dong Lu 66 (© **021/ 6321-2193;** metro: Nanjing Dong Lu) and Huaihai Zhong Lu 550 (© **021/5383- 0561;** metro: Huangpi Nan Lu).

Those interested in purchasing **Chinese contemporary art** have a mind-boggling number of galleries and artists' studios to choose from. Must-visits include the galleries at **Moganshan Lu 50** just south of the Suzhou Creek in the northern part of town, and at **Taikang Lu 210** in the southern part of the French Concession.

MARKETS & BAZAARS

DONGTAI ANTIQUES MARKET (DONGTAI LU GUWAN SHICHANG) ☆
Located on Dongtai Lu and Liuhe Lu, 1 block west of Xizang Nan Lu, Luwan, this market features dealers specializing in antiques, curios, porcelain, furniture, jewelry, baskets, bamboo and wood carvings, birds, flowers, goldfish, and colonial-era bric-a-brac. Open from 9am to 5pm.

FUYOU MARKET Still the best place to rummage through lots of junk for the chance to find the rare real nugget, this favorite for weekend antique and curio hunting is located in the Cangbao Lou (building) at Fangbang Zhong Lu 457 and Henan Nan Lu (in the Old Town Bazaar, Nanshi). Come as early as possible on Saturday or Sunday morning, preferably the latter, when vendors come in from the surrounding countryside and display goods ranging from porcelains, old jade pendants, and used furniture, to old Russian cameras, Buddhist statues, and carved wooden screens. Open 9am to 5pm; the weekend market (on the third and fourth floors) runs from 5am to 6pm, but tapers off by noon.

SOUTH BUND FABRIC MARKET (NAN WAITAN QING FANG MIANLIAO SHICHANG) ⭐ This popular fabric market, formerly the Dongjiadu Fabric Market, moved in 2006 to Lujiabang Lu 399 (intersection with Nancang Jie; ✆ 021/6377-5858) in the southeastern corner of the old Chinese city. Hundreds of stalls still sell bales of fabric (silk, cotton, linen, wool, and cashmere) at ridiculously low prices. Many stalls have their own in-house tailors who can stitch you a suit, or anything else you want, at rates that are less than half what you'd pay at retail outlets like Silk King. Turnaround is usually a week or more but can be expedited for an extra fee. Open 9am to 5pm.

7 Shanghai After Dark

Well into the 1990s, visitors retired to their hotels after dark, unless they were part of a group tour that had arranged an evening's outing to see the Shanghai acrobats. In the last few years, however, the possibilities for an evening on the town have multiplied exponentially, and Shanghai, once dubbed the "Whore of Asia" for its debauchery, is fast becoming again a city that never sleeps.

THE PERFORMING ARTS

Shanghai acrobatics are world renowned, and a performance by one of the local troupes makes for a diverting evening. These days the juggling, contortionism, unicycling, chair-stacking, and plate-spinning have entered the age of modern staging; performances are beginning to resemble the high-tech shows of a Las Vegas–style variety act. That's exactly what you'll see at the **Shanghai Circus World (Shanghai Maxituan),** Gonghe Xin Lu 2266 (✆ 021/5665-6622, ext. 2027), a circus of many acts, headlined by acrobats. The Shanghai Acrobatic Troupe, one of the world's best, tours the world, but can often be found performing at the **Shanghai Centre Theatre (Shanghai Shangcheng Juyuan),** at Nanjing Xi Lu 1376 (✆ 021/6279-8663), in a 2-hour variety show with about 30 acts. Check with the box office as performance schedules vary seasonally.

Shanghai has its own **Chinese opera** troupe that performs Beijing opera *(Jing Ju)* regularly at the Yifu Theatre at Fuzhou Lu 701, Huangpu (✆ 021/6351-4668). Most opera performances these days consist of abridgements lasting 2 hours or less (as opposed to 5 hr. or more in the old days), and with their martial arts choreography, spirited acrobatics, and brilliant costumes, these performances can be a delight even to the unaccustomed, untrained eye. Regional operas, including the Kun Ju form, are also performed in Shanghai. Check with your hotel desk for schedules.

JAZZ BARS

Shanghai was China's jazz city in the prerevolutionary days (before 1949), and it is once again becoming the home of some of the most creative and exciting jazz heard on the mainland. Most of the top-end hotel lounges and bars offer jazz performances, albeit of the easy-listening variety, by international artists. The famous **Peace Hotel Old Jazz Bar Band** now performs at 8pm nightly at the Huating Hotel and Towers (Huating Binguan) in Xujiahui at Cao Xi Bei Lu 1200 (✆ **021/6439-1000**), while the Peace Hotel undergoes renovation until 2010. For more modern and improvisational sounds, check out the following spots: the long-running **Cotton Club**, Fuxing Xi Lu 8 (✆ **021/6437-7110**); the stylish **House of Blues and Jazz**, Maoming Nan Lu 158 (✆ **021/6437-5280**); and the jamming and jampacked **Club JZ**, Fuxing Xi Lu 46 (✆ **021/6415-5255**). The **Shanghai International Jazz Concert Series** has been held the second week of November since 1996; ask your hotel concierge for details.

DANCE CLUBS, DISCOS & BARS

Some of the top spots to dance the night away are the always popular **California Club** (Gaolang Lu 2, Lan Kwai Fong at Park 97, Fuxing Gongyuan); the Bund-located **Attica** (Zhongshan Dong Er4 Lu 15, 11th floor); **Babyface** (Maoming Nan Lu 180, Luwan), an ultrapretentious but popular club; **Bon Bon,** popular with young expats (Huaihai Zhong Lu 1331, Yunhai Tower, 1st floor); **Club dkd** (Huaihai Zhong Lu 438), popular for its DJs; the trendy **4Live** (Jianguo Zhong Lu 8), with excellent acoustics and dance floor; **Guandii** (Gaolan Lu 2, inside Fuxing Gongyuan, Luwan), attracting a Taiwan, Hong Kong, and hip local crowd in a garden setting; and the spectacular nightspot complex in the Grand Hyatt Hotel on the Pudong side, **Pu-J's** (Podium 3, Jin Mao Tower).

Among the best bars are the romantic **Face** (building 4, Ruijin Er Lu 118) in the heart of the French Concession; **Glamour Room** (in M on the Bund, Guangdong Lu 20, seventh floor), with great views; **Bar Rouge** (Zhongshan Dong Yi Lu 18, seventh floor), with its Bund views and creative drinks though the scene has become a bit seedy of late; the Moroccan-themed **Barbarossa** in the middle of People's Park (Nanjing Xi Lu 231); the classy **Manifesto** (Julu Lu 748); **Malone's** (Tongren Lu 255 near Shanghai Centre), Shanghai's earliest American-style pub still going strong; and **O'Malley's** (Taojiang Lu 42, off Hengshan Lu), China's best Irish-style pub, with good food, too. In Pudong, **Jade on 36** (Fucheng Lu 33) on the 36th floor of the Shangri-La Hotel, offers the best views of the Bund and Puxi at night.

Gay-friendly nightspots (subject to change, as the scene shifts but never disappears) include **Eddy's**, Huaihai Zhong Lu 1877, by Tianping Lu (✆ **021/6282-0521**); **PinkHome,** Gaolan Lu 18, west of Sinan Lu; and **Kevin's,** Changle Lu 946, no. 4, at Wulumuqi Bei Lu (✆ **021/6248-8985**).

8 Suzhou

81km (50 miles) NW of Shanghai

Suzhou's interlocking canals, which have led it to be called the "Venice of the East," its classic gardens, and its embroidery and silk factories, are the chief surviving elements of a cultural center that dominated China's artistic scene for long periods during the Ming and Qing dynasties. Rapid modernization in the last decade has robbed the city of much of its mystique, but enough beauty remains to merit at least a day of your time.

GETTING THERE

There are a plethora of trains plying the Shanghai-Suzhou route, with "D" trains making the journey in just over 30 minutes. At press time, the most popular **trains** for day-trippers from Shanghai include the D406 which leaves Shanghai at 7:48am and arrives at 8:24am; and the T764, which departs at 8am and arrives at 8:45am. There are plenty of return trains as well in the afternoon and evening. You can now purchase your return ticket in Shanghai. There is also an express direct train between Suzhou and Beijing (11½ hr.), Z85/Z86, leaving each city nightly around 7:30pm. The **railway station, Suzhou Huoche Zhan** (© 0512/6753-2831), is in the northern part of town on Chezhan Lu, just west of the Renmin Lu intersection.

Suzhou is also well connected by **bus** to Shanghai, Wuxi, and Hangzhou. There are two main bus stations: the **Qiche Bei Zhan** (© 0512/6577-6577) in the north; and the **Qiche Nan Zhan** (© 0512/6520-4867) in the south. From the North Bus Station, buses depart for Shanghai (every 20 min. 6:30am–7:30pm; 90 min.; ¥30/$3.75/£1.90), Wuxi (every 30 min. 7:15am–5:50pm; 1 hr.; ¥20/$2.45/£1.20), and Hangzhou (every hour 5:30am–6:50pm; 2–3 hr.; ¥65/$8/£4).

Check with your hotel tour desk to book a bus tour of Suzhou. In Shanghai, the **Jinjiang Optional Tours Center,** Changle Lu 161, in the lobby of the Jin Jiang Tower Hotel (© 021/6445-9525 or 021/6415-1188, ext. 80160), offers a day group bus tour with an English-speaking guide and lunch, departing Wednesday and Saturday between 8am and 9am and returning in the late afternoon. The price is ¥550 ($69/£35) for adults. In Suzhou itself, **China International Travel Service (CITS),** at Dajing Xiang 18, off Guanqian Jie (© 0512/6515-2401), can provide an English-speaking guide and vehicle for the day at ¥400 ($50/£25) each (lunch and entrance tickets not included) but it's just as easy, and a whole lot cheaper, to see the town on your own via **taxi,** with trips about town averaging between ¥10 and¥20 ($1.25–$2.50/65p–£1.25).

EXPLORING SUZHOU

Central Suzhou, surrounded by remnants of a moat and canals linked to the Grand Canal, has become a protected historical district, 3×5km (2×3 miles) across, in which little tampering and no skyscrapers are allowed. More than 170 bridges arch over the 32km (20 miles) of slim waterways within the moated city. The poetic private gardens number about 70, with a dozen of the finest open to public view. No other Chinese city contains such a concentration of canals and gardens.

CLASSIC GARDENS

Suzhou's magnificent formerly private gardens are small, exquisite jewels of landscaping art, often choked with visitors, making a slow, meditative tour difficult. Designed on principles different from those of the West, these gardens aimed to create the illusion of the universe in a limited setting by borrowing from nature and integrating such elements as water, plants, rocks, and buildings. Poetry and calligraphy were added as the final touches. Listed below are some classic gardens worth visiting.

FOREST OF LIONS GARDEN (SHIZI LIN YUAN) 🐪🐪 Built in 1342 by a Buddhist monk and reportedly last owned (privately) by relatives of renowned American architect I. M. Pei, this large garden consists of four small lakes, a multitude of buildings, and Suzhou's largest and most elaborate collection of tortured rockeries, here said to resemble lions. Many of these oddly shaped rocks come from nearby Tai Hu (Lake Tai), where they've been submerged for a very long time to achieve the desired shapes and effects. The garden is located at Yuanlin Lu 23 (© 0512/6727-2428). It's open 7:30am to 5:30pm; admission is ¥30 ($3.75/£1.85).

HUMBLE ADMINISTRATOR'S GARDEN (ZHUO ZHENG YUAN) 𝍅𝍅 Usually translated as "Humble Administrator's Garden," but also translatable tongue-in-cheek as "Garden of the Stupid Officials," this largest of Suzhou's gardens, which dates from 1513, makes complex use of the element of water. Linked by zigzag bridges, the maze of connected pools and islands seems endless. The creation of multiple vistas and the dividing of spaces into distinct segments are the garden artist's means of expanding the compressed spaces of the estate. As visitors stroll through the garden, new spaces and vistas open up at every turn. The garden is located at Dong Bei Jie 178 (© 0512/6751-0286). It's open 7:30am to 5pm; admission is ¥70 ($8.75/£4.40) (¥50/$6.25/£3.15 Oct–Apr).

LINGERING GARDEN (LIU YUAN) 𝍅𝍅 This garden in the northwest part of town is the setting for the finest Tai Hu rock in China, a 6m-high (20-ft.), 5-ton castle of stone called Crown of Clouds Peak (Juyun Feng). Liu Yuan is also notable for its viewing pavilions, particularly its **Mandarin Duck Hall,** which is divided into two sides: an ornate southern chamber for men, and a plain northern chamber for women. Lingering Garden is located at Liuyuan Lu 80 (© 0512/6533-7940). It's open 7:30am to 5:30pm; admission is ¥40 ($5/£2.50).

MASTER OF THE NETS GARDEN (WANG SHI YUAN) 𝍅𝍅𝍅 Considered to be the most perfect, and also smallest, of Suzhou's gardens, this a masterpiece of landscape compression. Hidden at the end of a blind alley, its tiny grounds have been cleverly expanded by the placement of walls, screens, and pavilion halls, producing a maze that seems endless. In the northwest of the garden, don't miss the lavish **Dianchun Yi (Hall for Keeping the Spring),** the former owner's study furnished with lanterns and hanging scrolls. This was the model for Ming Xuan, the Astor Chinese Garden Court and Ming Furniture Room in the Metropolitan Museum of Art in New York City. Master of the Nets Garden is located at Kuojie Tou Xiang, off Shiquan Jie (© 0512/6529-3190). It's open 7:30am to 5:30pm; admission is ¥30 ($3.75/£1.90). In the summer, daily performances of traditional music and dance are staged in the garden (7:30pm; ¥80/$10/£5).

TIGER HILL (HU QIU SHAN) 𝍅 This multipurpose theme park can be garishly tacky in parts, but it's also home to some local historic sights, chief among them the remarkable leaning **Yunyan Ta (Cloud Rock Pagoda)** at the top of the hill. Now safely shored up by modern engineering (although it still leans), this seven-story octagonal pagoda dating from A.D. 961 is thought to be sitting on top of the legendary grave of He Lu, the 6th-century-B.C. king of Wu, and also Suzhou's founder. His tomb, thought to include his arsenal of 3,000 swords, is said to be guarded by a white tiger (hence the name of the hill). Partway up Tiger Hill is a natural ledge of rocks, the **Ten Thousand People Rock (Wanren Shi),** where according to legend a rebel delivered an oratory so fiery that the rocks lined up to listen. Tiger Hill is located 3km (2 miles) northwest of the city at Huqiu Shan 8 (© 0512/6532-3488). It's open 7:30am to 6pm; admission is ¥60 ($7.50/£3.75).

WATER GATES & CANALS

Suzhou is not only the city of gardens, but of canals. In the southern part of town in the scenic area just south of the Sheraton Hotel known as **Gusu Yuan (Gusu Garden),** you'll find in the southwestern corner **Pan Men (Pan Gate),** built in A.D. 1351, and the only major piece of the Suzhou city wall to survive. **Pan Men** once operated as a water gate and fortress when the Grand Canal was the most important route linking

Suzhou to the rest of China. To the south is a large arched bridge, **Wumen Qiao,** a fine place to view the ever-changing canal traffic. Near the main garden entrance in the east is **Ruiguang Ta,** a seven-story, 37m-high (122-ft.) pagoda built in A.D. 1119 that affords some excellent views of the old city from its top floors. The rest of the grounds are not very interesting. Gusu Yuan is located at Dong Da Jie 1. It's open 7:30am to 5pm; admission is ¥25 ($3.15/£1.60).

In the northwest part of town near Liu Yuan, **Shantang Jie (Shantang Street),** chock-full of Suzhou's old houses, narrow alleyways, arched bridges, and canals, is being slowly developed for tourists and pedestrians, with entrance to seven mansions and community halls of note being included in the ¥45 ($5.60/£2.80) entrance fee (open 8am–9pm; ℭ **0512/6723-6980**). You can also take the de rigueur canalboat ride here (¥25/$3.15/£1.60 per person).

MUSEUMS

Suzhou is synonymous not only with gardens and canals, but also with silk. Its silk fabrics have been among the most prized in China for centuries, and the art of silk embroidery is still practiced at the highest levels. The **Suzhou Silk Museum (Suzhou Sichou Bowuguan),** Renmin Lu 2001 (ℭ **0512/6753-6538**), just south of the railway station, takes visitors through the history of silk in China, with an interesting section on sericulture complete with silkworms, cocoons, and mulberry leaves. Weavers demonstrate on traditional looms. The museum is open 9am to 5pm; admission is ¥15 ($1.90/95p).

Opened in October 2006, the new I. M. Pei–designed **Suzhou Museum (Suzhou Bowuguan)** just west of the Humble Administrator's Garden at Dongbei Jie 204 (ℭ **0512/6757-5666**), and reportedly the last design of his career, combines characteristics of a typical Suzhou garden with modern geometric designs, and is worth a visit both for the building and its well-laid-out collection of locally discovered cultural relics including an exquisite Pearl Pillar of the Buddhist Shrine from the Northern Song dynasty. The museum is open 9am to 5pm (last ticket sold at 4pm); admission is ¥20 ($2.50/£1.25).

WHERE TO STAY & DINE

If you plan to spend the night in Suzhou, a perennial favorite is the five-star **Sheraton Suzhou Hotel & Tower (Suzhou Wugong Xilaideng Dajiudian),** Xin Shi Lu 259, near Pan Men in southwest Suzhou (ℭ **800/325-3535** or 0512/6510-3388; fax 0512/6510-0888; www.sheraton.com/suzhou). With 407 rooms starting at ¥1,660 ($200/£100; usually no more than 10%–20% discount) for a standard room, this luxury hotel receives rave reviews for its quality service and its Chinese-style buildings. Another excellent choice is the newly opened (2007) **Shangri-La Hotel Suzhou (Suzhou Xianggelila Fandian,** Tayuan Lu 168; ℭ **0512/6808-0168;** fax 0512/6808-1168; www.shangri-la.com), located less conveniently in the Suzhou Hi-Tech Industrial Development Zone about 20 minutes west of the old town. Delightfully luxurious rooms (¥1,880/$235/£117; 30% discount) offer high ceilings and panoramic views of the city. Another relative newcomer is the centrally located **Sofitel Suzhou (Suzhou Xuanmiao Suofeite Dajiudian),** Ganjiang Dong Lu 818 (ℭ **0512/6801-9888;** fax 0512/6801-1218; www.sofitel.com/asia) with plush doubles (with free Internet access) starting at ¥1,488 ($186/£93; up to 50% discount). For those on a budget, the lovely 37-unit **Scholars Inn (Shuxiang Mendi Shangwu Jiudian)** in the center of town at Jingde Lu 277 (ℭ **0512/6521-7388;** fax 0512/6521-7326;

www.sscholarsin@163.com) offers simple but clean standard rooms with air-conditioning, phone, TV, and showers for ¥300 to ¥520 ($38–$65/£19–£33).

Although hotel restaurants offer the most reliable fare and accept credit cards, Suzhou has a number of good restaurants that deserve to be tried, many of which are located on Taijian Nong (Taijian Lane), also known as Gourmet Street, around the Guanqian Jie area. One of the most famous local restaurants on this street is the over 200-year-old **Song He Lou (Pine and Crane Restaurant)** at Taijian Nong 72 (© **0512/ 6727-2285;** 8am–9pm), which serves Suzhou specialties such as *Songshu Guiyu* (squirrel-shaped Mandarin fish), *Gusu Luya* (Gusu marinated duck), and *Huangmen Heman* (braised river eel). Dinner for two ranges from ¥100 to ¥200 ($13–$25/ £7.50–£13).

9 Hangzhou

185km (115 miles) SW of Shanghai

Seven centuries ago, Marco Polo pronounced Hangzhou "the finest, most splendid city in the world . . . where so many pleasures may be found that one fancies oneself to be in Paradise." Hangzhou's claim to paradise has always been centered on its famous **West Lake (Xi Hu),** surrounded on three sides by verdant hills. The islets and temples, pavilions and gardens, causeways, and arched bridges of this small lake (about 5km/3 miles across and 14km/9 miles around) have constituted the supreme example of lakeside beauty in China ever since the Tang dynasty when Hangzhou came into its own with the completion of the Grand Canal (Da Yunhe) in 609. Hangzhou reached its zenith during the Southern Song dynasty (A.D. 1127–1279), when it served as China's capital. In 2003, much to the horror of purists, Xi Hu was enlarged in the western section with an additional causeway along its new western shoreline. New sights, shops, and restaurants were added to the eastern and southern shores. ***Note:*** For Chinese translations of selected establishments listed in this section, please turn to appendix A.

GETTING THERE

Hangzhou has an **airport** (© **0571/8666-1234** or 0571/8666-2999) about a 30-minute drive from downtown, with international connections to Hong Kong, Macau, Singapore, Bangkok, Osaka, Tokyo, and to Beijing and other major Chinese cities, but not Shanghai. A taxi into town costs around ¥130 ($16/£8) while an air-conditioned bus (© **0571/8666-2539;** ¥15/$1.90/95p) runs to the railway station and the Marco Polo Hotel (nearest stop to the Shangri-La Hotel).

By **train,** the "bullet" D653 leaves the **Shanghai South Railway Station (Shanghai Nan Zhan;** © **021/6317-9090)** at 7:50am, arriving in Hangzhou at 9:08am. The D657 leaves Shanghai at 9:30am and arrives at 10:48am; there are return journeys during the day including the D680 which departs Hangzhou at 6:18pm and arrives Shanghai at 7:36pm. Soft-seat train tickets cost ¥50 ($6/£3) plus a typical ¥20 ($2.50/ £1.25) service charge if purchased from hotel tour desks. There is also an express direct train between Hangzhou and Beijing (about 11 hr.), with the Z10 leaving Hangzhou nightly at 6:30pm. The no. 7 bus connects the railway station to downtown and to the Shangri-La Hotel for ¥1 (15¢/5p), and its air-conditioned version, the K7, connects them for ¥2 (25¢/15p). For train information, call © **0571/5672-0222;** ticket booking is from 8am to 5pm (© **0571/8782-9983**). **Bus** service is quicker and more frequent. There are regular departures from the East Bus Station to Shanghai until

7pm. There are also connections with Suzhou, Shaoxing Ningbo, and Wenzhou. There is also a direct bus to Hangzhou from Shanghai Pudong International Airport (© 021/6834-5743) that runs between 10:30am and 7pm.

Check with your hotel tour desk to book a **bus tour** of Hangzhou. The **Jin Jiang Optional Tours Center,** Changle Lu 161, in the lobby of the Jin Jiang Tower Hotel (© 021/6445-9525 or 021/6415-1188, ext. 80160), offers a convenient if expensive 1-day group bus tour with an English-speaking guide and lunch, departing at 8am every day except Monday and Wednesday, and returning in the late afternoon. The price is ¥680 ($85/£45) for adults. The same tour operator can also arrange a private 1- or 2-day tour with a guide, air-conditioned car, lunch, and door-to-door service for significantly more. If you're staying at the Shangri-La Hotel (see below) in Hangzhou, their business center can also organize half- or full-day city tours.

EXPLORING HANGZHOU

The city surrounds the shores of West Lake, with modern Hangzhou spread to the north and east. The lake is best explored on foot and by boat, while sights farther afield will require a taxi or bus. Taxis cost ¥10 ($1.25/60p) for 3km (13/4 miles), then ¥2 (25¢/15p) per kilometer until 10km (6 miles) and ¥3 (30¢/15p) per kilometer after that. Buses cost ¥1 to ¥2 (15¢–25¢/5p–15p) depending on whether they have air-conditioning. Bus no. K7 runs from the railway station to Lingyin Si via the northern shore of the lake (Beishan Lu) and the Shangri-La Hotel, while bus no. 27 runs along Beishan Lu to Longjing Cun (Dragon Well Village), and bus no. Y1 makes a loop of the lake starting from Lingyin Si. Bicycles are available for rental around the lake (¥10/$1.25/60p per hour, ¥300/$38/£19 deposit).

XI HU (WEST LAKE)

Strolling the shores and causeways of West Lake and visiting the tiny islands by tour boat should not be missed. A **Lakeshore Promenade** (★—a combination walkway and roadway—encircles the lake, with the busiest parts along the eastern edge of the lake. The once-busy thoroughfare Hubin Lu has now become a pedestrian walkway home to such outlets as Starbucks and Häagen-Dazs, while the area immediately to the south around Nanshan Lu and Xihu Da Dao is now known as Xi Hu Tiandi (West Lake Heaven and Earth), a miniature version of Shanghai's Xin Tiandi, right down to the *shiku men* (stone-frame) style housing and with some of the exact same restaurants. Following are the top attractions around the lake:

SOLITARY ISLAND (GUSHAN DAO) ★   Situated just off the lake's northwest shore, this big island is accessible via the **Xiling Bridge** in the west. A roadway sweeps across the island, which is home to a number of minor sights including Hangzhou's famous restaurant, Lou Wai Lou, and the large **Zhejiang Provincial Museum (Zhejiang Sheng Bowuguan; © 0571/8798-0281)**, which contains the oldest grains of cultivated rice in the world (developed 7,000 years ago in a nearby Hemudu village). The museum is open from 9am to 4pm; admission is free.

BAI CAUSEWAY (BAI DI) ★★   Solitary Island is connected in the east to downtown Hangzhou by Bai Di, a man-made causeway providing some of the finest walking around West Lake. It runs east for half a mile, rejoining the north shore road (Beishan Lu) at **Duan Qiao (Broken Bridge),** so named because when winter snows first melt, the bridge appears from a distance to be broken.

CRUISING WEST LAKE ★★   All along the lakeshore, but particularly on Hubin Lu and near Gushan Dao (northwest corner of the lake), there are boats for hire, from

3m (10-ft.), heavy wooden rowboats (where you take the oars) to small junks propelled by the owner's single oar to full-fledged ferries—flat-bottomed launches seating 20 under an awning. To tour the lake in a small junk costs ¥80 ($10/£5) for an hour. Larger passenger ferries sell tickets for ¥30 ($3.75/£1.90) (80-min. cruise with no stops), and ¥45 ($5.60/£2.80), which includes entrance to the Island of Small Seas (below). There are ticket booths across the street from the Shangri-La Hotel and along the east side of the lake.

ISLAND OF SMALL SEAS (XIAO YING ZHOU) 🏮🏮🏮 Make sure your boat docks on this island at the center of West Lake. The **Island of Small Seas** was formed during a silt-dredging operation in 1607. As a Chinese saying goes, this is "an island within a lake, a lake within an island." Its form is that of a wheel with four spokes, its bridges and dikes creating four enclosed lotus-laden ponds. The main route into the hub of this wheel is the **Bridge of Nine-Turnings,** built in 1727. Occupying the center is the magnificent **Flower and Bird Pavilion,** an exceedingly graceful structure that is notable for its intricate wooden railings, lattices, and moon gates, though it only dates from 1959. It's open 8am to 5pm; admission is ¥20 ($2.50/£1.25).

THREE POOLS MIRRORING THE MOON (SAN TAN YIN YUE) 🏮🏮 Located just off the southern shore of the Island of Small Seas are three little water pagodas, each about 2m (6 ft.) tall that have "floated" like buoys on the surface of West Lake since 1621. On evenings when the full moon shines on the lake, candles are placed inside. The effect is of four moons shimmering on the waters. Even by daylight, the three floating pagodas are quite striking.

SU CAUSEWAY (SU DI) 🏮🏮 The best land view of the Three Pools Mirroring the Moon is from the Su Causeway, the great dike that connects the north and south shores along the western side of West Lake. (A third causeway added in 2003, the Yanggong Di running parallel to Su Di in the west, is primarily for vehicles and is not as scenic.) Running nearly 3km (2 miles), Su Di is lined with weeping willows, peach trees, and shady nooks and crosses six arched stone bridges.

LEI FENG TA (LEI FENG PAGODA) Completely rebuilt in 2003 on the south bank of West Lake, this modern steel-and-copper pagoda affords some of the best panoramic views of the lake. Beneath the modern construction are the brick foundations of the original Leifeng Pagoda built in 977. The bricks you see were part of an underground vault used to store precious Buddhist relics, including a rare woodcut sutra, which was found among the ruins. The pagoda and surrounding gardens are open daily from 7:30am to 9pm (to 5:30pm Dec–Mar); admission is ¥40 ($5/£2.50).

OTHER ATTRACTIONS

LINGYIN SI (LINGYIN TEMPLE) 🏮 Located in the lush hills just west of West Lake, Lingyin Si (Temple of the Soul's Retreat) has been rebuilt a dozen times since its creation in A.D. 326. More of an amusement park than quiet temple, the whole complex is open from 7am to 5:30pm; admission is ¥35 ($4.40/£2.20), while entrance to the temple itself is a separate ¥30 ($3.75/£1.90).

The main attraction on the way to the temple is a limestone cliff, called **Feilai Feng (Peak That Flew from Afar),** so named because it resembles a holy mountain in India seemingly transported to China. The peak, nearly 150m high (500 ft.), contains four caves and about 380 Buddhist rock carvings. The most famous carving is of a Laughing Buddha from the year A.D. 1000. Scholars have deemed these stone carvings the most important of their kind in southern China.

The present temple buildings go back decades rather than centuries. The main Daxiong Baodian (Great Hall) contains a gigantic statue of Buddha carved in 1956 from 24 sections of camphor and gilded with nearly 3,000 grams (104 oz.) of gold—not a bad modern re-creation.

LONGJING WENCHA (DRAGON WELL TEA VILLAGE)   West of West Lake is the village of **Longjing (Dragon Well),** the source of Hangzhou's famous **Longjing tea,** grown only on these hillsides and revered throughout China as a supreme vintage for its fine fragrance and smoothness. The best tea here is still picked and processed by hand. A popular stop near the village is the **Zhongguo Chaye Bowuguan (Chinese Tea Museum),** open 8:30am to 4:30pm. Here you can comb through the extensive displays of Chinese teas, pots, cups, and ceremonial tea implements. Admission is free.

ZHONGGUO SICHOU BOWUGUAN (CHINA SILK MUSEUM)   Though Suzhou may be better known as a silk capital, Hangzhou, too, produced its share of this much sought-after commodity. This large museum south of West Lake boasts a surprisingly comprehensive exhibit with displays ranging from mulberry bushes and silkworms to traditional looms and exquisite pieces of damask brocades, all well annotated in English. The museum is located at Yuhuang Shan Lu 73–1 and is open 8:30am to 4:30pm; admission is free.

CHINESE MEDICINE MUSEUM (QING HEFANG/HUQINGYUTANG ZHONGYAO BOWUGUAN)   Located east of West Lake in downtown Hangzhou, Qing Hefang Lishi Jie (Qing Hefang Historical Street) has been the commercial center of Hangzhou since the late 6th century. Restored in 2001 with Ming and Qing dynasty–style buildings, this pedestrian mall has your usual quota of teahouses, restaurants, specialty stores, and also a few small museums. The most interesting of the lot is the Huqingyutang Chinese Medicine Museum on Dajing Xiang 95. Established in 1874, the original apothecary has a striking dispensary hall with Chinese lanterns, and finely carved wooden pillars and brackets. There are English explanations throughout. The museum is open daily from 8am to 5pm; admission is ¥10 ($1.25/65p).

WHERE TO STAY & DINE

If you're spending the night, the most atmospheric hotel is still the fine five-star, 384-unit **Shangri-La Hotel Hangzhou (Hangzhou Xianggelila Fandian),** Beishan Lu 78, on the north shore of West Lake (© **0571/8797-7951;** fax 0571/8799-6637), though it is running a little old these days. Standard rooms cost ¥1,650 to ¥2,250 ($200–$270/£100–£135), depending on whether they have garden or lake views. You can expect a 35% discount off the rack rate. Another top choice is the classy **Hyatt Regency Hangzhou (Kaiyue Dajiudian),** Hubin Lu 28, on the northeastern shore of West Lake (© **0571/8779-1234;** fax 0571/8779-1818; www.hangzhou.regency. hyatt.com). Rooms are plush and modern with standard doubles ranging from ¥1,600 to ¥2,050 ($200–$256/£100–£128) before the typical 20% discount. A little farther south on the eastern shore of the lake is the slightly faded 200-unit **Sofitel Westlake Hangzhou (Hangzhou Suofeite Xihu Dajiudian),** Xihu Da Dao 333 (© **800/ 221-4542** or 0571-8707-5858; fax 0571/8707-8383; www.sofitel.com). Standard rooms start at ¥1,200 ($145/£70), while lake-view rooms cost ¥1,736 ($210/£105) before the average 40% discounts. For a cheaper alternative, the 60-unit **Jiexin Century Hotel (Jiexin Shiji Jiudian),** also known as the Yiyuan Binguan, Nanshan Lu 220 (© **0571/8707-0100;** fax 0571/8708-7010), on the eastern edges of the lake is affiliated with the China Academy of Fine Arts and offers clean, renovated (2005) doubles from ¥680 ($85/£44) (discounted in low season to around ¥300/$38/£19).

For dining, try the Hangzhou institution **Lou Wai Lou,** Gushan Lu 30 (© **0571/ 8796-9023**), on Solitary Hill Island, between the Xiling Seal Engraving Society and the Zhejiang Library. Hours are 11:30am to 2pm and from 5 to 8pm; local specialties, such as Beggar's Chicken *(jiaohua ji),* which costs about ¥140 ($18/£8.75) here, and the excellent local *dongpo* pork, and Longjing shrimp can all be tried here. A meal for two will cost ¥120 to ¥150 ($15–$19/£7.50–£9.50). The Shangri-La Hotel's signature restaurant, **Shang Palace** (© **0571/8797-7951**), is more elegant and also more expensive, with a meal for two costing ¥200 ($25/£12) and up. The international restaurants at the new development **Xi Hu Tiandi (West Lake Heaven and Earth)** on the southeastern shore of the lake should provide plenty of comfort food.

10

The Southeast

by Christopher D. Winnan

A quick glance at the topography of this area speaks volumes. Apart from a few scattered river deltas, this is harsh and unforgiving mountain country, with just a narrow ribbon of land next to the sea, into which most of China's modern coastal cities are all tightly squeezed.

Although the indigenous peoples of this area were assimilated by Han colonists long ago, the isolated terrain has fostered a strong feeling of independence in the coastal dwellers, forever aware that "the mountains are high and the emperor far away." In fact, it was probably their relative isolation and the establishment of small cell network economies that led to their early successes.

Few people realize that this was the part of the world that Columbus sought when he first set sail for the East Indies. While Europe had been blindly staggering through the Dark Ages, some of the foremost trading ports of their time had developed in this region. From then on it was only a matter of time before the industrialization that swept across 18th-century Europe was to have similar disastrous effects in China. China's xenophobia, which appears currently to be aimed at Japan, was earlier focused on England, and China lay blame for the subsequent "Opium Wars" firmly on the British, rather than on the emerging global economy and its corporate mercenaries, like the East India Company. Endless statues, museums, and memorials illustrate the "humiliations" of the Opium Wars to maximum effect for propaganda purposes, and yet nobody would dream of starting a cigarette war in retaliation for the 10,000 Chinese who now die from smoking-related illnesses every week. Still, beyond the misguided nationalism, this region is a treasure-trove of history for those willing to dig just a little bit further than the official media mouthpieces.

The relentless pressure and pace of the modern economy in business cities like Guangzhou and Wenzhou can make them appear harsh and unfriendly. Tourists are relatively few compared to the unending stream of businessmen, here to put yet more Chinese to work in factories. It is hardly surprising that foreigners are often treated with such mistrust and suspicion. Mass migration from the hinterland has put even more pressure on rapidly expanding urban areas until they now suffer the same problems that plague oversize cities all over the world: terrifying levels of pollution, rising crime, and social misery. The region now resembles a huge cargo ship in which the load is concentrated on only one side, and it is listing dangerously.

Traveling throughout the region provides an excellent opportunity to see the process in action. Industrialization in the cities destroys the traditional economies of the hinterlands, which then takes its revenge via mass migration to the cities, crowding them further and making them even more unmanageable. The flat delta areas have become toxic rats' nests of

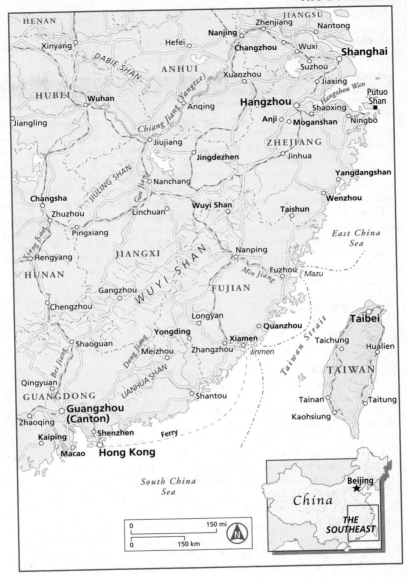

industrialization, as more and more rice paddies are paved over to build ever more factories and express highways. Only the old and infirm remain in the rural areas, and with less and less land to cultivate every year, it is difficult to imagine how China can continue to feed itself.

Summers are hot and extremely humid around the coast; the mild months of October through March are the best times to visit, although some offshore islands are appreciated year-round for their breezes. Inland Jiangxi suffers from drier but furnacelike summers and chilly dank winters, making spring and autumn the best times to travel. *Note:* Unless otherwise noted, hours listed for attractions and restaurants are daily.

1 Anji & Moganshan

Zhejiang Province, 58km (36 miles) SE of Hangzhou

Tourism has exploded in and around Anji during the last 5 years, partly due to the lip service that China is currently paying to the newly introduced concept of ecotourism, but mainly due to the fact that a handful of scenes from the movie *Crouching Tiger, Hidden Dragon* were filmed here in 1999.

There are some who contend that the vast swaths of bamboo have only appeared in the last few decades and that before the mass deforestation of the Great Leap Forward, this area was mainly mountainous stretches of majestic pine forest. It is clear that the influence of foreign missionaries on Moganshan had a significant impact, as many of the mountain smallholders still hold quasi-Christian beliefs, and this might even stretch back as far as the Taiping Rebellion, when heavenly troops used these inaccessible areas as a stronghold against the imperial forces. More recently, the tortuous mountain passes provided safe havens for refugees fleeing the Japanese occupation of Shanghai and other large cities.

The most popular sights lie south of the city, although the rest of the county would be great for extended exploration if you have the time and inclination to get away from other travelers.

ANJI

ESSENTIALS

GETTING THERE   Thanks to the newly constructed highway, Anji now has rapid access to Hangzhou and Shanghai. The nearest airport is Xiaoshan airport on the other side of Hangzhou.

Anji Bus Station (© 0572/522-9571) is well served with comfortable modern coaches to and from Hangzhou (63km/34 miles) almost every half-hour from 5:30am to 6:20pm. On this route, try to notice how the environment changes slowly from an ocean of green to dirty concrete as you leave Anji's vast swathes of bamboo and approach Hangzhou. The ticket price is ¥23 ($3/£1.50) and the buses arrive at Hangzhou North Station on Moganshan Lu 758 (© 0571/8809-7761). Buses also run to Shanghai (220km/136 miles) at 6:25am, 7:10am, 8:30am, 1pm, and 1:30pm; Nanjing (240km/149 miles) at 7:45am; Yiwu at 6:30am; and Suzhou at 6:45am and 12:30pm.

GETTING AROUND   The downtown area of Anji is well served by *sanlunche* (cycle rickshaws) that will happily ferry you short distances for ¥2 to ¥5 (25¢–65¢/15p–35p). For getting out of town, metered taxis are a better option, with flagfalls starting at ¥5 (65¢/35p); after that, it's ¥2.20 (30¢/15p) per kilometer. City bus lines run across the downtown with the no. 1 and no. 3 lines being the most useful for tourists. All have a flat fee of ¥1 (15¢/10p).

VISITOR INFORMATION   The travel agent behind the ticket office next to the main bus station has a good selection of glossy brochures highlighting sights in the area. Unfortunately most of them are in Chinese only and none of the staff speak any English.

Fast Facts

Banks, Foreign Exchange & ATMs   The main **Bank of China** (open 8am–5pm) is on Sheng Li Xi Lu and offers currency exchange. They also have an ATM for international credit cards.

Internet Access   Apart from the typically large *wangba* that are springing up everywhere, the library, located on Tian Mu Zhong Lu, is quieter and cleaner than most and is open from 9 to 11:30am and 1:30 to 5pm.

Post Office   The post office (open 7:30am–9:30pm) is at Shengli Dong Lu (© 0572/502-3957). Only one city map is available at the moment and that is Chinese only. It costs ¥5 (65¢/35p) and is available from the post office or shops around the bus station.

Public Security Bureau   The officers at the PSB (© 0572/502-2341) are friendly but extensions are probably better handled back at Hangzhou, where there are plenty of excellent English-speakers.

EXPLORING ANJI

The city itself is little more than furniture factories and construction, with most of the real sights a short bus ride outside of the town. Be on your best behavior with the locals, as a surprisingly large number of them seem to have *chu tou* (bamboo-cutting billhooks) hanging on the back of their belts.

Bamboo Museum and Gardens (Zhu Bo Yuan) 🛪   A taxi from the bus station will cost around ¥15 ($1.95/£1), but the budget conscious can hop on to any of the minibuses that head south for ¥3 (40¢/20p). Just ask to be dropped off outside the Dakang Furniture Factory (Dakang Jia Ju Gong Chang). From there cross the road, go over the bridge, and then walk another 500m (1,640 ft.) past the Sunny Holiday Resort until to reach the museum bus stop on the left, and the parking lot on the right.

The museum itself has half a dozen different display halls, all of which are fascinating in their own way. One deals with all the hundreds of different species of bamboo, another reveals some of the many products that can be made from bamboo, while a third focuses solely on musical instruments fashioned from bamboo.

Even so, aficionados may be disappointed at the limited scope of some of the displays. There is no mention anywhere, for example, of the work of specialist bamboo architects such as Simon Velez or Darrel Deboer. Even Buckminster Fuller's work on geodesic domes fails to make an appearance. A recent article in *Time Asia* stated that manufacturing in the area had reached a major bottleneck thanks to a serious deficiency in research and development. A visit to the bamboo museum makes this sad state of affairs very clear.

Bamboo Museum and Gardens, Ling Feng Scenic Zone. © 0572/533-8988. www.cnbamboo.cn. Admission ¥38 ($4.95/£2.50). 10am–5pm.

Hidden Dragon Falls (Chan Long Pu Bu) 🛪   If you are staying up in one of the farmer's guesthouses, you can enter Hidden Dragon Falls from the very top late in the afternoon and save the ¥30 ($3.90/£1.95) entrance fee. This is probably a good idea as it is a very steep climb up from the main gate, especially on some of the more precarious scaffolding walkways, where the sides of the gullies are simply too steep for rock-hewn steps.

Back up at the top is a superb lookout point that provides amazing views over the entire valley. It is also a great spot to spend the early evening if you are lucky enough to be staying up here.

Hidden Dragon Falls, south of Tian Huang Ping. ℂ 0572/511-2357. Admission ¥30 ($3.90/£1.95). 10am–5pm.

Big Bamboo Sea (Da Zhu Hai) ★★ A ¥30 ($3.90/£1.95) ticket gains you access to plenty of anachronistic reinforced concrete structures including a teahouse and a five-story lookout tower, but that all rather pales in comparison to the magnificent culms of the giant bamboo that grows in the area. While the Big Bamboo Sea tourist attraction is probably only worth an hour of your time, it is a good starting point for exploring the rest of this green ocean. In summer, the groves are cool and shaded. In winter, the mountain breezes bring forth a mysterious chanting as the huge plants move rhythmically back and forth. For those short on time, take a walk back to the nearby village of Gangkou, and see the bamboo being harvested and processed in fields along the side of the road. The more serious hikers can take their bearings from the lookout tower and strike out to find a path that leads southwest, to Tianhuangping.

Gangkou County. ℂ 0572/501-5999. Admission ¥30 ($3.90/£1.95). 10am–5pm.

Tian Huang Ping Hydro Electric Facility (Tian Huang Ping Dian Zhan) ★★ I like to take the bus up from Anji station for ¥10 ($1.30/65p), do a short circuit around the mountaintop reservoir (with perhaps the world's largest dirty bathtub ring), make a short stop at the visitor center, and them make my way back down to Tian Huang Ping town by foot. In summer, the mountains are cool, with waterfalls jumping out in all directions. In winter, these same cataracts are frozen in time, hanging like huge abstract sculptures on the side of the road. Once you are through the tunnel (which always makes me want to burst into song) you can continue down to the guts of the power plant, for a look at the inner workings.

Tian Huang Ping. ℂ 0572/504-1888. Admission ¥30 ($3.90/£1.95). 10am–5pm.

SHOPPING

What appears at first glance to be a wholesale bamboo market at Tian Huang Ping Lu (open 10am–4pm) is actually a shopping stop for package tour day-trippers, although there are a few shops worth looking at. Our favorite was the **Tianzhuzhuang Bamboo Fiber Company** (ℂ 0572/502-9911), which has an extensive clothing stock, all made from 100% bamboo fiber, everything from socks and tennis sneakers to bath towels and winter long johns. We also like the outlet of the **Bamboo Charcoal Factory** (ℂ 0572/520-9588), which sells bamboo shampoo, soap, and other toiletries.

WHERE TO STAY

Up in the mountains surrounding Anji, there are literally hundreds of small guesthouses to choose from, all offering basic accommodations at reasonable prices. A good example is the **Mountain Clan House (Gao San Ren Jia Ke Zhan;** Daxi Village, Chan Long Mountain; ℂ 0572/511-2505 or 1356/727-6184; twin ¥80/$10/£5.20), easily distinguishable by its two red lanterns. The owner, Miss Zhang, is a local bamboo farmer and will happily take guests out into forest to instruct them in the art of cutting new shoots and picking white tea. She also provides meals of healthy local fare for between ¥20 and ¥30 ($2.60–$3.90/£1.30–£1.95), including local specialties such as spicy cuckoo *(la wei bu gu niao)* and meat and potato stew *(rou shao tu dou li).*

Golden Leaf Hotel (Xiang Yi Jin Ye Da Jiu Dian) While there seem to be a dozen small business hotels on almost every street, the only downtown place we would recommend is the Golden Leaf Hotel next to the river. The best rooms are up on the ninth floor and even these are only a modest ¥200 ($26/£13) on weekdays and ¥280 ($36/£18) on weekends. On the opposite side of the road to the main entrance is a very unusual piece of street furniture. While many cities have large digital signs displaying the temperature, Anji's version is a decibel meter. Usually it comes to rest at about 55 to 60 decibels until a group of cheeky youngsters ride past, screaming at the top of their lungs to see who can make the sign register the highest. Bearing this in mind, it might be better to get a room at the rear of the hotel.

Sheng Li Lu 158. ⓒ **0572/502-6068.** Fax 0572/502-3967. 132 units. ¥200 ($26/£13) single; ¥550 ($72/£36) standard room; ¥900 ($117/£59) suite. Rates include breakfast. MC, V. **Amenities:** Restaurant; fitness room; business center. In room: A/C, TV, fridge.

Sunny Land Resort (Xiang Yi Du Jia Cun) ★★ About 10 minutes south of the city, beside the Bamboo Museum and Gardens is the beautiful Sunny Land Resort. Officially it's a four-star resort but it usually has standard rooms available at under ¥300 ($39/£20) at many times of the year. The grounds are perfectly manicured and there is a pontoon bridge over the weir, leading to the miniature Mount Lingfeng, complete with twisting staircases up to the summit. Furnishings are typically unimaginative, but this is made up for the large windows which give the rooms a light and airy feel as well as excellent views out over the grounds.

Anji Munt Lingfeng Scenic Spot. ⓒ **0572/533-8888.** Fax 0572/512-5798. www.zjsunny.com. 149 units ¥300 ($39/£20) standard room; ¥648 ($84/£42) suite. AE, DC, MC, V. **Amenities:** 2 restaurants; bar; pool; exercise room; tour desk; business center. In room: A/C, TV, fridge, hair dryer, safe.

WHERE TO DINE

Both of the larger hotels mentioned above have a selection of reasonable restaurants to choose from. Downtown both a McDonald's and a KFC have opened along with a string of Western-style coffee shops that have sprung up opposite the post office. These serve both local dishes and rough approximations of Western food. Just next door to the post office is UES (United Easy Systems) a local fast-food outlet serving burgers, juices, and hot drinks as well as passable bento-style lunchboxes for ¥12 ($1.55/80p).

On the opposite side of the river from the Sunny Land Resort is the **Gu Long Ke Zhan (Ling Feng Scenic Spot;** ⓒ 0572/**533-2388**), where most of the regular visitors are well-herded tour groups, so do not expect much in the way of personal services. Even so, they can provide tasty local fare; be sure to ask for the local bamboo beer (Anji Bamboo Science Beer), which is served in shallow pottery bowls and might in fact turn out to be one of the best finds on your trip.

Other local specialties to look out for are *sha bing*, savory unleavened breads cooked in the same way that Indians fire chapattis, and delicious at only ¥.50 (5¢/5p) each. The area is famous for its hickory nuts (*shan xing ren*) and its walnuts (*shan he tao*) with both deserving their well-earned reputations. You should also try the dried sweet potatoes (*hong shu gan*) that are wonderfully tender and the dried sliced kiwis (*qi yi guo*) that taste sweeter than most factory-produced candies.

MOGANSHAN

Mount Moganshan (719m/2,360 ft. high) was first built as a vacation destination in 1890 for Western missionaries and their families to escape the Shanghai summer furnace. By its peak in 1930, some 160 Western-style stone retreats dotted the cool bamboo glades, including 32 occupied by wealthy Chinese, and even Generalissimo Chiang Kai-shek bought his new bride Soong Mei-ling to Moganshan for their honeymoon in 1927. The Nationalists, never far behind, established their own resort called Wuling on the northeast side of the mountain.

The area's architecture is of an impressive variety, from the over-the-top Western opulence of the Chiangs' villa and the sprawling Chinese-style compound of Du Yuesheng ("Pock-marked Du," the notorious Green Gang boss from Shanghai who helped Chiang massacre the Shanghai workers' movement in 1927), to the simpler elegance of the Western vacationers' stone mansions. There were two churches, a swimming pool fed by icy water, seven tennis courts, and an amateur dramatics society. Many of the original houses, built by Western architects using the local gray dressed stone, still survive.

Mao Zedong was a frequent visitor to the area, and used a group of old stone foreign villas throughout the 1960s. By then Moganshan was a secret retreat for "the leadership" in case of war, with air-raid shelters for the Big Potatoes. Some of the houses even have secret tunnels that go right down to the valley.

ESSENTIALS

GETTING THERE   Air-conditioned **buses** to Moganshan's nearest town, Deqing (also known as Wukang) leave every morning at 10:10am from Shanghai's **New North Bus Station** (Hengfeng Lu 258, at Gonghe Lu; ✆ **021/5663-0230**), costing ¥31 ($4/£2) and taking 4 hours. Alternatively, take the bus or train to Hangzhou (approximately an hour and a half) and then catch a bus to Wukang. Buses leave daily from Shanghai **Old North Bus Station (Lao Bei Zhan)** at Gongxing Lu 80 near Baoshan Lu metro station, direct for Wukang. Departure times are 6:30am, 11:50am, and 12:40pm. Ticket price ¥53 ($6.90/£3.45) one-way. The journey takes about 4 hours via Huzhou. An alternative is to jump on one of the semiofficial buses from Shanghai **South Railway Station** to Hangzhou; touts are all over the place. The cost last time we looked was ¥50 ($6.50/£3.25). Then make your way by bus or taxi from Hangzhou.

Regular buses leave from Hangzhou North Bus Station, on Moganshan Lu, at least every hour, and take about 40 minutes to Wukang bus station ¥13 ($1.60/80p). A taxi from Hangzhou will run to about ¥200 ($26/£13) and takes 1½ hours.

At least four trains run daily from Shanghai South Station (Mei Long; ✆ **021/ 5110-5110**) to Hangzhou with a journey time of 2 hours; soft seats costs ¥40 ($5.20/ £2.60), hard seats ¥25 ($3.25/£1.65). (**Note:** The new South Station is still under construction. Currently the old south station, beside Jinjiang Leyuan, is still in use.)

Note: In the early 1990s, an Iveco passenger vehicle's brakes failed and it plummeted off the road on its way back down to the village you pass through on the 13km (8-mile), short and steep road. There were no survivors. Now, Ivecos and large buses are banned from the road and are relegated to the 30km (19-mile) route around the back of the mountain.

From Deqing, negotiate with a taxi or minivan outside the bus station to take you up to Mogan Mountain. Taxis are normally ¥50 ($6.50/£3.25), while a minivan can be had for ¥40 ($5.20/£2.60). Insist that you go to the top of the mountain, not the village at the foot of the mountain or the ticket gate. Entrance tickets are now a hefty ¥80 ($10/£5.20). Usually at a location like this I would suggest a back entrance in order to avoid unjustified entrance costs, but scaling the vertical walls of Moganshan is out of the

---

> **Tips   Cabbing It**
>
> If coming by taxi from Hangzhou, get the driver to drop you at Wukang bus station and catch a local cab from there. It won't cost any extra. Try to get the Hangzhou driver to go by the meter and offer to pay the tolls both ways (¥30/$3.90/£1.95). Price should work out at about ¥160 ($21/£10) total to Wukang. A taxi from Wukang Bus Station up to the top of the mountain is normally ¥50 ($6.50/£3.25).

---

question, unless you enjoy taking your life in your hands. There is an interesting-looking path leading up to the right about 45m (150 ft.) before the ticket office, and while it does eventually lead to the very highest peak, it will take at least 90 minutes and you will literally have to haul yourself up vertical inclines using the bamboo like a cost-conscious orangutan. You are much better off getting a lift up and saving your energy to enjoy the adventurous paths and trails nearer the top of the mountain. In addition, there is a very high-security *lao gai* (labor camp) at the base of the mountain where members of the Falun Gong, a spiritual sect outlawed in China, are being kept, and it's probably best avoided.

VISITOR INFORMATION   Talk to Mark or Joanna at Moganshan Lodge for historical details, suggested walking routes, and even a couple of cross-country paths over to Anji.

The official **Moganshan Travel Service** number is © **0572/803-3402.**

The only local map available can be picked up at the bus station, but the map is in Chinese only, focuses more on Huzhou to the north, and only has a tiny insert map for Moganshan.

FAST FACTS
Post Office   The post office (open 8am–4:30pm) is on Yinshanjie.

Public Security Bureau   The officers at the PSB (© **0572/803-3303**) are friendly but as with Anji, extensions are probably better handled back at Hangzhou, where there are plenty of excellent English-speakers.

EXPLORING MOGANSHAN
Moganshan is crisscrossed with a maze of stone pathways and steps, and away from the ravages of its small tourism industry, there is plenty of wonderfully isolated mountain wandering to be had. Stone steps laid with expert precision over a century ago wind through the mountains. Flower gardens laid by generations of foreigners have gone wild, resulting in a mad cacophony of brilliant colors between the bamboo. And of course the imposing villas themselves: One of my own favorites is the impressive entrance to the China International Tea Culture Institute Communication Centre, where huge blocks of stone lock together to create walls, stairs, and floors, all set into the mountain itself like a geological mosaic.

The Mao Museum   This is more a bizarre cultural keepsake than a museum, as the place is largely empty. The only furniture is an iron bedstead, where Mao supposedly spent the night. Not true. He ventured up for a day with an old war comrade, and after lunch, he had an afternoon nap in this house.

Qingliang Ting   As you climb the steep, windy road, down near the Radisson's Du Yue Sheng Villa, there is a great lookout point from which to view the surrounding sea of bamboo. Views down to the plain and across the hillside are spectacular on clear days.

Sword Forging Pool (Jian Chi)   Legend (or local tourism PR, at least) has it that Mo Xie and Gan Jiang, a pair of married sword smiths who lived in the 5th century B.C. after whom the mountain is named, devoted their lives to making two incomparably beautiful swords for the emperor. Supposedly they would sit by this pool fed by three waterfalls and polish the swords they had just forged. The local administration bureau has done a remarkably good job of building walkways, wooden pagodas, and viewing points.

Steep steps lead down from the main Yinshanjie area but more interesting is the small **pagoda** about 100m (328 ft.) up and away to the left of the falls. What at first looks like simple ornamental pagoda sits atop a cave that appears to be an early interrogation chamber complete with bars in the ceiling. Moganshan has many similar dark secrets to be discovered, secrets that give the place a feel of part Disneyland, part concentration camp.

WHERE TO STAY

Hotels abound in Moganshan, and prices range by season, with the peak in July and August and medium rates from April to June and from September to October.

Bai Yun Hotel   This hotel is located at the end of a road running along the top of the mountain, with great views. Once the residence of a Kuomintang foreign minister, Huang Fu, one of the villas is where Chiang Kai-shek spent a few days on his honeymoon with Soong Mei-ling, in 1927. Ten years later Chiang returned here to meet Zhou Enlai. They discussed how the Kuomintang and the Communists might cooperate against the Japanese. The museum is pretty spartan in its artifacts, but compared to the Mao museum, it is positively cluttered. For contemporary overnight guests, these are lovely old buildings but fairly basic rooms, which may make you feel that you are staying in a museum display area rather than a midrange hotel.

Lu Hua Dang Gong Yuan 502. (℃) 0572/803-3382. Fax 0572/803-3274. www.mogan-mountain.com. 100 units. ¥240 ($31/£16) standard room; ¥648 ($84/£42) suite. 10% tax (usually not charged). No credit cards. **Amenities:** Restaurant; bar; lounge; game room; meeting room. *In room:* A/C, TV.

Moganshan Castle (Moganshan Zhuang)   Originally called Mount Clare by foreigners, this spur of the mountain was the site of some of the earliest houses, in the very late 1800s. Its popularity is explained by the fact that there is a gully on the north side that sucks up a constant draft, which in the days before air-conditioning was the choicest spot on the mountain (Moganshan can be as much as 7° cooler than Shanghai in summer). These days the hotel is still impressive from the outside but retains a country-village feel to some of the rooms, which may be a little rural for some visitors, especially considering the high prices.

Wuling Cun, bldg. no 7. (℃) 0572/803-3421. Fax 0572/803-3209. 30 units. ¥550 ($72/£36) standard room; ¥900–¥2,600 ($117–$338/£59–£169) suite. Rates include breakfast. Discounts 30% or 40% (no breakfast). AE, DC, MC, V. **Amenities:** Restaurant; coffee shop; meeting room; game room. *In room:* A/C, TV.

Radisson Du Yue Sheng and Priest Villas   If you're looking for the five-star experience, the Radisson Hangzhou rents out two villas on the mountain, the Du Yue Sheng Villa, which was once owned by its namesake, the famous 1930s Shanghai gangster, and a former missionary retreat. Both houses have been completely overhauled to five-star standards. Ironically it is the missionary who ended up with the sauna. Be warned that existing reports on standards and service have not been very promising so far.

Moganshan Mountain 329. ℭ **0572/803-3601**, ext. 801. 2 units. ¥1,100 ($143/£72) standard room; ¥11,100 ($1,430/£715) villa. AE, DC, MC, V. *In room:* A/C, TV, fridge, hair dryer, safe.

Wuling Hotel (Songyue Ting)   The Western-style Song Yue Mansion, built in 1933, which was home to Chiang Kai-shek and Soong Mei-ling, is now the Wuling Hotel. The interior has been badly redecorated many times, and Art Deco door handles give the only testimony to its former flair. Chiang's old bedroom and study, complete with command phone and ostentatiously expensive mahogany furniture, are preserved in one wing. Another is dedicated to detailing with photographs and letters concerning Chiang and Soong's activities in Moganshan, from their 1927 honeymoon to their final visit in 1948. Guest rooms share the same musty smell as the display areas and may be a disappointment for those used to staying in more modern facilities.

Wuling Cun, bldg. no. 550. ℭ **0572/803-3132**. 35 units. ¥280 ($36/£18) standard room; ¥680 ($101/£51) suite. MC, V. **Amenities:** Restaurant. *In room:* A/C, TV, fridge.

WHERE TO DINE

In Yinshanjie you can find several restaurants, hotels, and a Western-run coffee shop/restaurant. The local restaurants are in the village center. Here you'll be served tasty home-style food; be sure to try the local delicacies, including wild partridge, celery, mushrooms, and tea—all hunted down in the area's bamboo forests.

Moganshan Lodge (Song Liang Shan Zhuang) ★★ *Finds*   Mark Kitto, the founder of China's most popular English-language magazine, is enjoying his retirement immensely up in Moganshan, after the Shanghai government forcibly nationalized his publishing company (the phrase "to be kittoed" has quickly entered the expat vernacular, meaning to be screwed by the Chinese authorities). Now he and his wife (along with two youngsters and two dogs) welcome escapees from the Shanghai cosmopolis. The mouthwatering Full Fry Up includes all the usuals along with mushrooms, kidneys, and home-cured bacon, and lunch and dinner options (for example, three-course pork stroganoff a la Moganshan) are also available if booked in advance. Mark himself is a mine of information both for this area and the rest of China, and can make very good recommendations on local accommodations and transportation.

Yinshanjie. ℭ **0572/803-3011**. www.moganshanlodge.com. Meal for 2 ¥200 ($26/£13). No credit cards. 11am–11pm.

2 Yandangshan ★★★

Zhejiang Province, on the coast, 80km (116 miles) N of Wenzhou, 378km (233 miles) SW of Hangzhou, 470km (292 miles) S of Shanghai

Although most Chinese have heard of these famous religious peaks, very few have actually been here. Subsequently, although as impressive as its counterparts, it is far less commercialized than the Five Sacred Mountains, with lower ticket prices, better-value hotels, and few rip-offs. Yandang Mountain was named a World Geopark by UNESCO in 2005.

Named after the flocks of wild geese that gather in the marshes around the lake at the top of the mountain, Yandang Mountains are situated in the southeast of Zhejiang Province. This is the largest among the 44 key scenic resorts of the country, covering an area of 450 sq. km (176 sq. miles). The mountain range was formed 120 million years ago, and belongs to a complete and typical rhyolitic paleovolcano dating from the Cretaceous Period of the Mesozoic Era, in the edge of the volcanic belt of Asia surrounding the Pacific Ocean. The belt is older than the Andes and the western part of the United States.

Master Xu Xiake, renowned monk/geographer, visited Yandangshan twice and it became widely known during the Song dynasty (960–1279). He wrote that "to fully appreciate the beauty of Yandangshan, you would have to be a flying spirit!"

The mountain used to be serene with various natural brooks. However, excessive extraction of groundwater has drained many of the those.

ESSENTIALS

GETTING THERE   The nearest airport is at Wenzhou, 80km (50 miles) away, and is well served by domestic flights. My preference is to arrive early in the morning on one of the overnight trains from Hangzhou or Shanghai (hard sleeper ¥140/$18/£9.10) and disembark at about 6:30am. I then cross the Wenzhou Da Dao, Huochezhan Xi Shou road from the railway station, and jump on the 7am bus to North Yandangshan (¥28/$3.60/£1.80) at the Xinnan Bus Station. This way, I arrive at my hotel by about 8:30am and can be out exploring the cascades and cataracts by 10am. In Hangzhou, you can also take a bus at East Station at 7am or 2pm (¥85/$11/£5.50; 5 hr.). In Shanghai, take a bus at Zhiqing Bus Station at 2pm directly (¥150/$20/£9.75).

From Wenzhou, make sure that you are heading for North Yandangshan rather than east or south. The bus drives through a depressing repetition of anonymous factories until the bus turns off the main highway to the Lower Yandangshan Bus Station. This is a good place to purchase a map of the area for ¥5 (65¢/35p) as well as check your bearings on the excellent wall map. There are usually a few local loiterers offering overpriced (¥15/$1.95/£1) taxi rides to the resort area, known officially as Xianglintou. If you would like to check out some of the locals' proffered accommodations, simply take the ¥2 (25¢/15p) ride up to the main bridge in the resort area and have a scout around.

For direct buses away from Yandangshan, Hangzhou has more than 40 buses per day starting at 6:40am and finishing at 7:30pm (¥140/$18/£9.10) as well as regular buses back to Wenzhou.

GETTING AROUND   In the resort there are simple minibuses whose fare ranges from ¥2 to ¥10 (25¢–$1.30/15p–65p) depending on location. These are well marked and the stops are noted in English. In addition there are a number of venerated gentlemen zipping around in *sanlunche* (cycle rickshaws) that have been converted to battery power. Rates are negotiable (about ¥5/65¢/35p to Ling Feng) but poor suspension makes the local roads bone-jarring.

VISITOR INFORMATION   There are a number of commercial travel agencies posing as visitor information offices but we finally tracked down the official **Wenzhou Yandangshan Holiday Agency** (Xiao Xia Lu 6; ⓒ **0577/6224-4111;** www.ydjr.com). Unfortunately it is only open until 5:30pm and the staff cannot speak any English.

FAST FACTS

Banks, Foreign Exchange & ATMs   Yandangshan only has an Agricultural Bank with only a Union Pay ATM rather than a Bank of China, so it is best to bring a good supply of cash with you. There is also a forex service at the Yandangshan Villas.

Internet Access   There was as yet no *wangba* in the resort area at press time, although a number of hotels (such as the Sunshine) had broadband access in the rooms.

Post Office   The main post office (open 8:30am–6pm) is in the Xianglingtou resort area, on the corner of Xue Xiao Xiang and the main road

Visa Extensions   There is a tiny PSB office on Bu Xing Jie, but extensions are better taken care of back in the larger cities.

SEEING THE SIGHTS

Rising to 1,056m (3,464 ft.), Yandangshan is my favorite mountain park in China, a feeling that is heightened by the knowledge that I am one of the few foreigners to have explored here, even though accessibility is good and prices are, for the time being, reasonable. The peaks themselves are magnificent works of natural beauty, combining danger and elegance, seclusion and mystery. Unfortunately, the man-made structures are less impressive, and as usual, propaganda centers such as the Revolutionary Martyrs' Memorial (Le Qing Ge Ming Lie Shi Ji Liang Guan) on Jingming Lu can safely be skipped.

There is much more to explore. The **Wild Goose Lake (Yan Hu Gang)** at the summit (¥10/$1.30/65p) has fantastic sunrises. There's an amazing stone arch locally known as **The Immortal Bridge (Xian Qiao)**, while the **Xiansheng Gate (Xiangsheng Men; ¥10/$1.30/65p)** is a temptation to any serious climber. The **Three-Step Waterfall (San Zhi Pu; ¥10/$1.30/65p)** with its extinct volcano also has a cable car.

Spiritual Peaks (Ling Feng Jing Qu) ✦✦✦   Within easy walking distance of the resort area, 10 minutes past the Chaoyang Holiday Villas, this area is open during both the daytime and the evening when the delicate pattern of stellar embroidery matches the splendor of the mountains.

Towering behind Spirits Peak Temple (Ling Feng Si) is the 270m-high (886 ft.) Husband and Wife Peak (Fu Qi Feng) which does actually resemble a couple in each other's arms. The real showstopper here though is **The Goddess of Mercy Cave (Guan Yin Dong).** I am usually rather blasé about temples, having seen so many reconstructions and fakes around China. This, on the other hand, was a very impressive experience: 10 stories of wooden timbers measuring 113m (371 ft.) high, 14m (46 ft.) wide, and 76m (249 ft.) deep built inside the long vertical crevasse, He Zhang Feng, that reaches into the rock face. Look out for the small outcropping of rock that resembles Lao Shou Xing (the Chinese god of longevity) and prepare to be amazed in the top level of the cave, where hundreds of small Buddhas perch on tiny ledges. The rest of the park deserves plenty of attention. The Fruit Box Bridge (Guo He Qiao) is especially charming, although the Plough Cave (Bei Dou Dong) could not really live up to Guan Yin Dong. Wandering around the park, I really liked the aptly named "air-condition cave," which had clouds of cold mist gushing out of it.

Ling Feng Jing Qu. Admission ¥30 ($3.90/£1.95). 8am–10:30pm.

The Spiritual Rocks (Ling Yan Jing Qu)   This is a beautiful but limited section of the peaks and seemingly one of the most crowded, especially when the trapeze artist appears 260m (853 ft.) above the Lingyan Temple courtyard (10:30am and 3pm on weekdays; 10:30am, 1:30pm, and 4pm on weekends). Surrounding cafes fill rapidly as tour groups converge to see how locals once used their free climbing skills to collect rare traditional herbs for religious and medical practices. These days it is just a bit of abseiling and a tightrope act, but I bet some of the Yangshuo sport climbers would give their back teeth to know about this place.

Up past the Xiaolong (small dragon) waterfall is a concrete elevator shaft built into the cliff side, which takes visitors up about 10 stories to another hanging wire walkway and on to a number of schemes designed to separate tourists from their small change. These include bows and arrows at the Cave of Dragon Nose (Longbidong Cave), pellet guns in the Cave of Clerestory (Tianchuangdong) and wishing pools in the Valley of Double Pearls (Shuangzhugu Valley). There are a few other paths to explore, but with the lift and the show and the carnival booths, you might feel (as I did) the need to get away to quieter parts of the park.

The best aspect of this attraction was the food in the parking lot outside: lightly boiled new potatoes by the pound at ¥1 (15¢/10p), big egg and chives pancakes at ¥3 (40¢/20p), and pool ball–size waxberries that were just coming into season.

Ling Yan. Admission ¥30 ($3.90/£1.95). 8am–4:30pm.

The Chaoyang Cave (Chaoyang Dong) ★★★

Behind the resort coach park (the one with the ornate public restroom—why is it that public restrooms showcase some of the best architecture in China?), a road leads up into a strange concrete spiral and onto a ticket office for the Jade Peak. The rocky ledge just behind the ribbon cascade is my favorite place to chill out. The pool is a great spot for some meditation and contemplation as the falling torrent sways rhythmically back and forth between the pair of stone monks. Steps down to the outer rim even encourage some paddling. The path rises another 2 hours up to the double bamboo peaks, but be warned that none of these paths seem to have guardrails and some areas are not in the best condition.

Chaoyang Dong. Admission ¥30 ($3.90/£1.95). 8am–4:30pm.

The Big Dragon Waterfall (Da Long Qiu Jing Qu) ★

Falling from Lianyun Peak, 190m (623 ft.) high, the Big Dragon Waterfall runs into the Qingjiang River and makes the tourists below look like marauding army ants. The famous Qing dynasty (1644–1911) poet Jiang Shi exclaimed that "the beauty of the Big Dragon Waterfall cannot be expressed in words," but of course that has not stopped anybody from building a massive car park, and a long stretch of vendors where you can proclaim your financial piety. I especially enjoyed the local minority snack of sweet sticky black rice, served in a handy-size basket *(she zu wu mi fan)*, but the bats wing nuts *(suan jiao)* are good, too.

Da Long Qiu Jing Chu. Admission ¥30 ($3.90/£1.95). 8am–4:30pm.

Feng Cloud Cliffs (Xuan Yan Zhan Dao) ★★★

Getting up here can be half the fun. Of course, the minibus is the easy way but on weekdays when the traffic is not so bad, this can be a nice stroll up the river. About halfway up the road's ascent into the peaks, go past the barracks, under the cable car, and off the road to the right. You'll find a path that comes out at a beautifully isolated waterfall, followed by the cable car station 50m (164 ft.) or so later.

The pathway has been carved into the cliff face and while there are metal guardrails, the precipice beyond can be nerve-racking. The Happy Immortals Attic is a chimney formation—you can attempt the stairs to the top, but they were too steep for me. Views back on the walkway are spectacular. The pathway leads out over a testing suspension bridge but this is where tour groups tend to head back to their coaches, after purchasing padlocks, having them engraved, and then hanging them on the cables. My advice is to follow the path down past the teahouse and the unfortunately disused hotel. Ignore the oddly named rock formations as the signage becomes more and more bizarre, including A SIDE VIEW OF AN UPSIDE DOWN PEACOCK and DOUBLE CHICKENS CONTEND FOR HEGEMONY. Turn right, to go over the steps and past a small pagoda down to yet another locked-up guesthouse. Here you'll find an alternate route (without a

Tips   Touring or Exploring?

While weekend crowds from Wenzhou and the rest of Zhejiang arrive in startling numbers, they generally stay with their tour groups and stick to the designated paths. That means it is easy to get away and explore. Be warned that paths up and down rock cliff faces can be treacherous in the wet season. To escape the hordes up at Da Long Qiu Jing Qu, put your money back in your pocket and walk out of the car park, back toward Yandangshan. There is a road that forks off to the left, up into a tiny village of maybe a dozen houses. Follow the stream up through the back yards to the left and then on beyond the concrete reservoir. Here it starts to get interesting: The track switches sharply back and forth across the mountain stream well up into the clouds. At one point the track splits just below a waterfall. I checked the path leading away over the side of the gorge, but I wanted to leave something for next time and continued up to the left. I stumbled under a collapsing watchtower, slowly being consumed by the vegetation. Then perhaps 100m (328 ft.) on the plateau beyond, the ruined remains of a very early stone settlement appeared out of the mists. Parts of the buildings remain, but it is the deep terraces both above and below that are most impressive. I tried to descend on the eastern side of the mountain but the terraces disappear after about 100m (328 ft.) and all that remains is the equivalent of a toboggan training run; if you are lucky, the sheer number of spiders' webs will slow you down. Eventually the track emerges onto a stone path that leads down to the ticket office.

ticket office) that leads down to the Long Dong Temple at the bottom of the mountain road.

Feng Clond Cliffs. Admission ¥30 ($3.90/£1.95). 8am–4:30pm.

WHERE TO STAY

The largest place in town, the three-star **Yandangshan Shan Zhuang (Yandangshan Mountain Villa),** is way overpriced for unattractive low-standard rooms that look much older than 13 years, while the **Bai Le Da Jiu Dian** has obviously seen much better eras, too. Here are three alternative choices.

Jing Yuan Holiday Village (Jing Yuan Du Jia Cun)   While not in tiptop condition, this collection of 24 log cabins and 18 wooden bungalows manages to retain some charm with lots of timber verandas and split-levels. But it would all be even better if management paid some attention to the very visible undersides of their properties. The entrance to the Forest Park is just to the rear of the complex, while more adventurous types might like to try the wire ladder that the acrobats use to get up to the Heavenly Peaks.

Jing Ming Lu 16. © 0577/6224-6111. Fax 0577/6224/2521. 42 units. ¥188 ($24/£12) standard room; ¥480 ($63/£31) suite. No credit cards. **Amenities:** Dining lodges; lobby bar; teahouse. *In room:* A/C, TV.

Sunshine Hotel (Chaoyang Shan Zhuang)   While the rooms are comfortable enough, it is the setting that I really like here. Nestled into the cliffs, with the Pingxiang stream bubbling out front, the hotel is only 2 minutes' walk from the Sunshine Cave and the spiritual peaks and has an extensive range of sports and games facilities.

Chaoyang Lu 56. (✆ 0577/6224-5999. Fax 0577/6224-5998. 100 units. ¥280 ($36/£18) standard room; ¥520 ($68/£34) suite. MC, V. **Amenities:** Restaurant; bar; outdoor tennis court; fitness room; sauna; game room; concierge; business center, salon. *In room:* A/C, fridge, Internet, hair dryer, safe.

Tian Yi Bie Ye   Located at the back of the school, this small guesthouse gives a more professional impression than most, probably because it is only just over a year old. Still, the marble lobby and spotless rooms are head and shoulders above anything else at this price, even though roll technology has not yet arrived in Yandangshan and toilet paper is still dispensed from flat metal boxes. For a look at where you could have been staying, check out the medieval toilets at the top of the street.

Xing Jie Xiang Yang Lu 36. (✆ 0577/6224-8999. Fax 0577/6224-2588. 25 units. ¥100 ($13/£6.50) standard room. No credit cards. **Amenities:** Lobby bar. *In room:* A/C, TV, kettle.

WHERE TO DINE

The coast is not very far away, so there is still a good deal of seafood to had in the mountains at small family-run restaurants in the resort area. I enjoyed eating a selection of local dishes at the **Yandang Te Se Xiao Chi,** a few doors along from the post office, including toadstools and chrysanthemum flowers *(ping gu chao huang hua cai)* and mountain peonies fried with meat *(shan shao chao rou shi).* In addition, *maofeng* tea grows in places of high altitude and abundant fog and is one of the treasures of this area.

3 Wenzhou

Zhejiang Province, 470km (294 miles) S of Hangzhou, 436km (272 miles) N of Fuzhou

Hemmed in by mountains and looking to the sea, Wenzhou, with its own peculiar local dialect, is a modern trading hub based on an early treaty port. It sits on a small seaside plain laced with canals, but it is no Hangzhou. Opened by an Anglo-Chinese convention of 1876, it never amounted to much.

Apart from being a useful starting point to visit Yandangshan (see above), Wenzhou is also a fascinating place to see what deplorable damage the modern economy can do to an ancient agrarian culture. From the designer boutiques and European car dealers downtown, through the poverty of the surrounding shanty towns to the utter hopelessness of those left behind in the surrounding villages, visitors can see very clearly how dual economies are tearing the nation apart. Nowhere else is the wealth gap more pronounced than here, in a city that the propagandists have made famous for its concentration of millionaires. The official media constantly lauds "the Wenzhou model," which, like "socialism with Chinese characteristics," is a way of talking about raw capitalism without having to admit to the Communist Party's U-turn. In reality, the city is simply home to innumerable sweatshops which churn out cheap plastic goods ranging from disposable lighters to adult novelties. Visitors to Wenzhou may be alarmed by the high concentration of beggars, or the frequency with which some local men tend to urinate in public.

Note: For Chinese translations of selected establishments listed in this section, please turn to appendix A.

ESSENTIALS

GETTING THERE   Wenzhou is connected by **air** to 38 Chinese cities as far-flung as Urumqi, including Beijing (two to three flights daily), Guangzhou (four or five flights),

Hangzhou (four or five flights), Shanghai (both airports six or seven flights), and Shenzhen (three to five flights). There are also five flights a week from Hong Kong. The main **CAAC ticket office (Wenzhou Minhang Shoupiao Chu)** is at the junction of Minhang Lu and Jinxiu Lu (② **0577/96555** domestic, or 0577/883-24311 international—only Hong Kong from Wenzhou). Prices include ticket delivery. The airport is 25km (16 miles) east of town, served by an airport bus that makes 13 trips from 5:40am to 8pm for a fare of ¥10 ($1.30/65p).

Wenzhou has a **railway station** but not many useful connections; these are all to the interior, such as sleeper trains to Hangzhou and Shanghai. The ticket office (open 8am–7pm) is at the far left side as you face the station. Left luggage is to the right; it's open from 6am to 11:40pm and charges ¥5 (65¢/35p) per piece.

The fastest way along the coast north or south is by luxury **bus** on the new coastal highways. Buses from Ningbo (4 hr.) mostly arrive at the **Xincheng Keyun Zhongxin Zhan** (② **0577/8891-1927**), well to the southeast of the center and northeast of the railway station. This is the main station for the excellent Zhejiang Quik company's connections with Ningbo (13 departures 7:30am–5:10pm; ¥116/$15/£7.50), Shaoxing (9:30am and 2:40pm; ¥108/$15/£7), and Hangzhou (25 departures 6:40am–6:20pm; ¥120/$13/£6.65). The **Wenzhou Keyun Zhongxin Zhan** (② **0137/678-8822**), south of the center, has buses to Taishun, a tortuous, winding 191km (119 miles) away (5 hr.; ¥54/$7/£3.50), with departures at 7am, 9am, 1:30pm, and 3:30pm. The ticket windows are to the left of the entrance. The **Xin Nan Zhan,** just west of the railway station, has buses to Fujian Province, but as elsewhere in China, cross-border services are more limited. The best bus to Fuzhou is a luxury daytime sleeper bus at 8:30am (8 hr.; ¥154/$20/£10). The bus station automatically adds ¥2 (25¢/15p) in insurance. There's also an overnight sleeper service. Shoes must be taken off and placed in a bag provided. Berth allocation is random, so come early. There are also services from here to Nanjing, Shanghai, Guangzhou, and beyond.

GETTING AROUND   Taxis have a flagfall of ¥10 ($1.30/65p), which includes 4km (2½ miles); after that, it's ¥1.50 (20¢/10p) per kilometer, and 50% more after 6km (33/4 miles). Add another 20% from midnight to 5am. Public **buses** have a minimum fare of ¥1 (15¢/10p); most charge that as their flat fare. Buses serve all parts of the city and while the signs at stops do not have any English, route maps give very useful visual representations. For shorter distances there are lots of *sanlunche,* which make a surprisingly ecofriendly alternative to the usual traffic fumes. There are **ferries** to Jiangxin Island (see below) from the Jiangxin Matou (dock), well marked in English on Wang Jiang Dong Lu. From the dock there are also **tourist river trips** for ¥50 ($6.50/£3.25) at 6:30pm (② **0577/8819-9073**).

FAST FACTS

Banks, Foreign Exchange & ATMs   The main branch of the **Bank of China** (open 8am–6pm) is at the east end of Renmin Xi Lu at Xinhe Jie. Go to counter 4/5 *opposite* the foreign-exchange sign.

Internet Access   *Wangba* are almost everywhere but the library on Gong Yuan Lu (② **0577/8882-4163**) offers cleaner, quieter facilities.

Post Office   The main post office branch (open 7:30am–5:30pm) is at Xu Shan Lu 73. There's also a branch just east of the railway station, beyond the Wanhao Grand Hotel.

Visa Extensions   The city **PSB** Aliens Entry-Exit Bureau (⟨ **0577/8808-9888;** open Mon–Fri 8:30am–noon and 2–5:30pm) is at the end of an alley on the west side of Renmin Guangchang at Guangchang Lu Xi Gongxie 86.

AROUND CENTRAL WENZHOU

The warren of streets north of **Wu Ma Jie,** particularly between (and along) Jiefang Bei Lu and Fuqian Jie, has a number of ancient facades and a labyrinth of girly shopping. Bored heiresses arrive in Porsches, and leave with an armful of designer carrier bags. Wu Ma Jie itself has been pedestrianized and received a heavy-handed restoration, although several faintly Art Deco buildings sport slightly unlikely mid-19th-century dates.

Jiangxin Gu Yu ("solitary island in the heart of the river" in a very literal translation) makes for a pleasant stroll despite the piped music from speakers in the trees and, in the evenings, the howls of the damned from the opposite shore. Or it may just be karaoke.

Small as the island is, it has a central lake and is dotted with pavilions outlined in gaudy lights, a Song dynasty well, a temple or two, Soviet-style heroic monuments to the People's Liberation Army, and two pagodas. The **Dong Ta,** at the eastern end, built in 869 and restored in the Ming and Qing dynasties, reportedly owes its topless state to a consular complaint about the noise of roosting birds. The local mandarin simply removed the roof. The lighthouse here, established by foreign residents, was included by the International Association of Lighthouse Authorities in 1997 on a world list of 100 historical lighthouses, and is still in service. In roughly the middle of the island's southern side, the **Xi Ta** was built in 969 and its most recent restoration was in 1982. Its seven six-sided stories look like freshly poured concrete. Ferries leave for the island every 30 minutes from the Jiangxin Matou in Wenzhou, from 8am to 11:30pm for ¥10 ($1.30/65p) round-trip.

WHERE TO STAY

There are plain and simple budget accommodations to the left and right of the railway station for about ¥200 ($26/£13). Across the Wenzhou Da Dao, Huochezhan Xi Shou road, beside the Xinnan bus station are even cheaper places in the ¥100 ($13/£6.50) range.

City Inn Bandao (Bandao Huan Cheng Shang Wu Jiudian) ⟨★★ *(Finds*   This downtown hotel is aimed at the Chinese businessman who enjoys a little four-star luxury but at realistic three-star prices. It still has a very modern feeling to it, with polite and friendly staff. I like the little extras designed to make a stay that little bit more comfortable, such as recliner-type chairs and footrests. My only complaint was that the corridors are a little claustrophobic.

Feixia Bei Lu. ⟨ 0577/8808-8889. Fax 0577/8806-8222. 56 units. ¥280 ($36/£18) standard room. AE, DC, MC, V. **Amenities:** Restaurant; coffee shop; business center; foot massage; laundry. *In room:* A/C, Star TV, Internet, safe.

Fan Dong Binguan   An relatively unappealing hotel in a white-tile building, Fan Dong Binguan happens to have an excellent location directly opposite the Xinnan Bus Station, just west of the railway station. It also happens to be among the better budget accommodations in this neighborhood, and will do just fine for those merely passing through. Modest, functional guest rooms have decent bathrooms with shower cubicles. There is cheap point-to-order fast food on one side of the hotel and a convenience store on the other, and even a fake McDonald's (Maidanglao) and KFC (Kendeji) combination called Maikenji nearby.

Wenzhou Da Dao, Huochezhan Xi Shou. ✆ **0577/8678-5588**. Fax 0577/8678-3732. 60 units. ¥228 ($30/£16) standard room; ¥358 ($47/£23) triple. Discounts up to ¥110 ($15/£7.15). No credit cards. **Amenities:** Restaurant. *In room:* A/C, TV.

Zhong Cheng Hotel (Zhong Cheng Da Jiu Dian)   While the interiors are large

and satisfactory, it is the heavy red eaves and pagoda structure of this hotel that I really like. I personally prefer the Standard B rooms with the bamboo floors to the more pricey but less interesting rooms.

Duan Deng Qiao Lu 92. ✆ **0577/8806-7777**. Fax 0577/88067255. 45 units. ¥208 ($27/£14) standard room; ¥508 ($66/£33) suite. No credit cards. **Amenities:** Restaurant; Karaoke bar; business center; meeting rooms. *In room:* A/C, TV, Internet.

WHERE TO DINE

Despite all their wealth, Wenzhounese are still decidedly provincial when it comes to eating. A couple of the flashier hotels recently imported celebrity chefs from Hong Kong, but the locals simply turned their noses up at Cantonese and sent the disappointed chefs back to the swankier eateries of Central with their tails between their legs. The Taiwanese coffee shop and snack chain **Shangdao Kafei** has six branches across Wenzhou, including the one at Wendi Lu, Chengkai Huayuan 10 (✆ **0577/8865-3063**). **KFC** and **McDonald's** outlets are dotted around town, and there's a **Pizza Hut** on Wu Ma Lu.

Fruit Restaurant (Chun Song Lang Shuiguo Fang) ☆ *(Finds)* FUSION   Tucked

away on a little side street next to the Chocolate Club, this initially appears to be a simple juice bar but is much more than that. Sure, you can try all kinds of exotic juices (star fruit, papaya, even the dreaded, foul-smelling durian), but there is a great selection of food on the English menu, too. My favorite was the stir-fried rice with mango and frogs' legs, but the steak set with papaya sauce ran a close second—all washed down with a refreshing kiwi and lemon juice. Not only one of the best places in Wenzhou, but surely one of my personal favorites on the entire east coast.

Chun Song Lang Shuiguo Fang, Cai Qiao Xiang, off Shengli Lu. No phone. Meal for 2 ¥80 ($10/£5.20). No credit cards. 11am–11pm.

4 Wuyi Shan

Fujian Province, 369km (231 miles) NW of Fuzhou, 364km (228 miles) SE of Nanchang

The mountains of Wuyi Shan are just as beautiful as anywhere in Yunnan or Guangxi; in fact, choose the right time of year, get away from the domestic tourists, and you'll find one of the best places in China for hiking, climbing, and exploring. The resort area has a well-deserved reputation for rip-offs, but there are ways to avoid the scams and enjoy one of the most spectacular parts of China.

It's the resort area you'll want to spend time in, rather than the town, and the airport and the railway station are between the two. While the surrounding scenery is gorgeous, the resort itself is an unsightly sprawl of restaurants and guesthouses clustered alongside a highway that stretches back to the main town. Most of the hotels are on the east bank of the Chongyang Xi, with a little spillover onto the west bank, where the Fengjingqu (scenic area) can be found. This is prime Chinese tourist territory, especially the "ganbu" variety—those who do not mind being herded around in Day-Glo baseball caps. Avoid summers, the weeklong public holidays at the beginning of May and October, and weekends between those two holidays. But in November, daytime temperatures are a pleasant 59°F (15°C), just right for walking, and the trees change color prettily. ***Note:***

For Chinese translations of selected establishments listed in this section, please turn to appendix A.

ESSENTIALS

GETTING THERE   The **airport** is served by flights from Beijing (at least one daily), Fuzhou (once daily), Guangzhou (at least one daily), Shanghai (two daily), and Xiamen (once daily). There are occasional flights from other cities. Bus no. 6 passes the airport entrance and runs the 8km (5 miles) to the resort for ¥1 (15¢/10p). The **railway station** is a little farther from the resort, also passed by bus no. 6, and three-wheelers run a shuttle the few hundred meters to the main road. There are useful train services from Hangzhou (509km/318 miles; ¥215/$27/£14 soft sleeper), Nanchang (364km/221 miles; ¥165/$21/£11), Jiujiang (499km/312 miles; ¥205/$27/£14), Shanghai (710km/444 miles; ¥288/$37/£19), Xiamen (590km/369 miles; ¥241/$31/£16), Quanzhou (593km/371 miles; ¥241/$31/£16), and other cities. Ticket offices are open from 3:30 to 5:30am, 8:30am to noon, 1:30 to 5:30pm, and 8:30 to 11:30pm. Agents in Wuyi Shan want a ¥35 ($4.55/£ 2.30) commission for rail tickets. The station's left-luggage facility is open only at from 6:30am to noon and 2:30 to 11pm.

GETTING AROUND   Within the resort, everything is walkable. **Bus** no. 6 is the most useful of all; coming from Wuyi Shan town, it passes both the railway station and the airport, runs through the middle of the resort down Chongyang Dao, turns west along Wangfeng Dao, crosses the Chongyang Xi (river), and continues to Xing Cun. Minibuses in fairly good condition with air-conditioning cost a little more, but rides are typically ¥1 (15¢/10p). *Miandi* (minivans) to most destinations are ¥2 (25¢/15p) if you use them like buses, with others hopping on and off; you can use them to get to Xing-cun for the *zhufa* (bamboo rafts), to get to the airport, or to get to the railway station. Bus no. 5 runs to the railway station when trains are scheduled, but not frequently. *San-lunche* three-wheelers that charge ¥1 (15¢/10p) are everywhere but they do not understand that visitors might want to walk anywhere. If you try to take one any distance, they will be straight onto one of their taxi friends to take over. It is generally assumed that you want to get wherever you are going as quickly as possible, when really the three-wheelers offer the chance to see and hear nature up close, something that most domestic tourists miss as they zip from sight to sight in their air-conditioned coaches.

FAST FACTS

Banks, Foreign Exchange & ATMs   The **Bank of China** (open 8am–5:30pm), with an ATM outside, is at San Gu Jie.

Internet Access   There are *wangba* (open 8am–midnight; ¥2/25¢/15p per hour) in back streets south of Wangfeng Dao. As you walk east from the river, look for the *wangba* characters on your left.

Post Office   The post office (open 7:50am–9pm summer; 8am–5:30pm winter) is on Wang Feng Lu.

WUYI SHAN FENGJING QU

The scenic area spreads across the river west of the resort, and is best appreciated either from the top of one of the peaks or from a bamboo raft *(zhufa* or *zhupai)* on **Jiu Qu Xi (Nine Bend Stream).**

There's a constant stream of buses (¥1 (15¢/10p) and minivans (¥2 (25¢/15p) from Chongyang Dao or Wangfeng Lu to the village of **Xing Cun;** they drop you off either in the village center or at the dock itself. If you are dropped off in the center, fork right, follow the road to the left, and take the first major right turn down toward the river. The ticket office is down on the right, about 5 minutes' walk altogether. The overpriced *zhufa* depart in groups intermittently between 7:30am and 4pm. Tickets are on sale about 20 minutes before each departure; they cost ¥115 ($15/£7.50) plus an optional ¥1 (15¢/10p) for insurance.

The river ride of about 9.5km (6 miles) takes an hour and 40 minutes, a lot of it right next to the main highway. The river is only a meter deep in some parts, and is clear enough to let you see the bottom. It's at its highest in July, and if it rises to a 2m (5½-ft.) height, trips are suspended.

The scenery is a slightly scaled-down version of that around Guilin, but more interesting due to the tilted strata that give the cliffs the look of a sandwich with everything on it. Various rocks are said to resemble an elephant trunk, a turtle, a frog, and two lions playing with a ball, but you'd never be able to say which was which without assistance. In common with the Yangzi trip, there are cliff-side burial places. Two large caves high up, which supposedly contain 3,800-year-old tombs along with some wooden remains, can be seen protruding from the cliffs, more easily visible than those elsewhere. As the river winds sinuously around its nine bends, bird song echoes between the cliffs, the metal tips of the bamboo poles rattle against the river bottom, flights of wigeon whir past, and there's the occasional brilliant flash of a kingfisher. Some of the more still water is supposed to run deep indeed—down to 28m (92 ft.).

The disembarkation point is just before the river's confluence with the Chongyang Xi, in manicured gardens a short walk from the base of **Da Wang Feng.** You have the option of returning to the road to flag down a passing bus back to the resort, or you can walk toward the peak past various (slightly tawdry) shopping opportunities and purchase one of two *tao piao.* One of the tickets is for the immediate area, which includes the two most commonly climbed peaks; it's valid for 2 days and costs ¥120 ($16/£8). The other ticket offers wider access around the scenic area from 6am to 8pm.

Climbing **Da Wang Feng** officially takes 1½ hours, but it can be scaled by the moderately fit in an hour. At the top, the views are principally over the confluence of the rivers and the not particularly attractive sprawl of the resort. As you climb, you have several choices of route, which all lead eventually to the top; the routes include two horizontal galleries cut into the rock, the higher of which involves slightly less bending. It can be slippery when wet. The lower stairways wind wonderfully, but in some cases they are only wide enough for one—awkward when you encounter tour groups. At some points, the only thing that will catch you if you fall is a stand of bamboo.

You'll probably want to climb **Tianyou Shan,** farther east and included in your ticket, on another day. The turnoff is about halfway to Xing Cun, and the entrance to the mountain about 5km (3 miles) from the resort. A *miandi* will bring you here for ¥10 ($1.30/65p), dropping you a 10 to 15-minute walk from the gate. If you're fit, the climb will not take more than about 30 minutes.

The slogan "If you haven't climbed Tianyou Shan, you haven't seen Wuyi Shan" is much bandied about, and this is the one peak all the tour groups climb, mostly in the morning—so leave it until the afternoon. The paths are more solid, are broader, and have more handholds than the paths of Wuyi Shan. Views are pretty, and you look down to the loop of the river's fifth and sixth bends, around which might drift some rafts. Halfway up, a pretty waterfall, multithreaded and glued to the cliff face, seemingly moves in slow motion. Near the top are a house built for Chiang Kai-shek's wife, Soong Mei-ling, and a flat open space with teahouses. As you jostle your way to the top, the views show you why you should consider extending your stay—the peak opposite also has a staircase snaking up it, but no sign of modern concrete additions, and no crowds.

SHOPPING

Various gift shops around town sell mountain produce such as dried roots, berries, and mushrooms, and specialist shops sell supposedly medicinal products (yes, including snake oil), but everything is priced ridiculously. When I inquired about a painting nearly identical to one I picked up in Guangzhou for ¥50 ($6.50/£3.25), the guy took one look at me and asked for ¥5,000 ($650/£325.)

WHERE TO STAY

Hotels are legion (more than 60 in the resort area alone), most of them the elevator-free four-story kind. Those that date from a building boom in 1995 are run down and worth avoiding, but some others just 2 or 3 years old are not much better. Generally speaking the resort is overpriced, almost two or three times the price of somewhere like Yandan-gshan. The resort is very busy at Spring Festival (Chinese New Year) and during the first weeks of May and October. But on weekdays for the remainder of the May-to-October period, supply still outstrips demand, and you can pay half price. Outside those times you need not pay more than a third of the first asking price. Almost all the hotels have two or three stars; in addition to the choices below, glance into a few others. Avoid those with "beauty parlors" too full of beauties and those that offer karaoke. Although temperatures are well above freezing even in December, make sure that your hotel has the heat turned on and has hot water 24 hours during low season.

Wuyi Shanzhuang (Wuyi Mountain Villa; ℂ 0599/525-1888; www.wysvilla.com) is the resort's most prestigious hotel but service is poor unless you arrive in a cavalcade of red-flag limousines. Budget options are out there but require some seeking out.

Baodao Dajiudian   Centrally located next to the bank, this property has recently been upgraded to four-star standing, with an odd circular central atrium that allows the wail of karaoke to drift up from the basement. The lobby is full of furniture carved from tree trunks, but the guest rooms are less imaginative. The hotel has expanded along the main street and now has even more rooms and facilities than before.

Wangfeng Lu. ℂ 0599/523-4567. Fax 0599/525-5555. 220 units. ¥780 ($101/£50) single; ¥880 ($114/£57) standard room; from ¥1,800 ($234/£117) suite. 60% discount off season. AE, DC, MC, V. **Amenities:** 2 restaurants; business center; game rooms; conference facilities; forex. In room: A/C, TV, fridge.

Fa Ting Jie Dai Chu   Located in the greenest part of the resort that I could find, this guesthouse shares with the court building and therefore the parking lot is always full of police cars. Next door is the Yue Yi Hotel, which is not actually a hotel but a restaurant. Staff seem to be scarce, but at this price it is worthwhile seeking out some help.

Next to Yue Yi Hotel, Wuyi Gong. ℂ 1351/508-2933. 30 units. ¥120 ($16/£7.80) standard room. No credit cards. In room: A/C, TV.

Gu Yue Shan Zhuang   On the same side of the river as Wuyi Mountain Villa, the guesthouses here are not as nice as some of those mentioned above in the resort area proper, but rooms are generally quieter and it is lovely to look out over the mountains rather than more white tiles.

Wuyi Gong. ℂ 0599/525-2916. 30 units. ¥100 ($13/£6.50) standard room. No credit cards. In room: A/C, TV.

Jin Gu Yuan Da Jiudian   One of the newer hotels in town (opened May 2005), this three-star property has been decorated in a sophisticated, modern style—modern for

---

Tips Cheap Eats on the Street

The cheapest and probably the best food can be found at a handful of *you zha* stalls outside the Baodao Hotel. These nocturnal street eateries, frequented mainly by local foot-massage girls, offer a wide range of pan-fried meat and vegetables on kabob sticks. The small pumpkin cakes are delicious, and fried banana with ketchup seems to be a popular if strange local specialty.

Wuyi Shan at least. The staff is a friendly bunch, but do not expect any English to be spoken. The location is close to the center of the resort, and this currently offers the best value around.

Da Wangfeng Lu. © **0599/523-9888.** Fax 0599/523-5866. 52 units. ¥480–¥690 ($64–$90/£32–£45) standard room; ¥1,698 ($220/£110) suite. 70% discount off season; 40% otherwise. No credit cards. **Amenities:** Restaurant. *In room:* A/C, TV, fridge.

WHERE TO DINE

Restaurants in tourist areas like this typically offer low-quality cuisine at extortionate prices; Wuyi Shan is no exception. All the restaurants have the same exotic displays of mushrooms, snakes, and bee larvae as well as standard meat and vegetables. Proprietors are especially keen to take advantage of rich but scarce foreigners. I only met one other non-Chinese during my entire stay, a Chicagoan who was beating himself up for letting this resort of con men and tricksters turn him into an angry "ugly American," hardly surprising when he had just been charged ¥450 ($59/£29) for a simple meal that would have been overpriced at ¥45 ($5.85/£2.90).

Ultimately, in terms of the quality of service, Wuyi Shan resort is not yet ready for overseas visitors. There are no English menus, and Westerners are seen as money trees to be shaken endlessly. This is a shame because the mountains are definitely some of the most spectacular in the country, but returning to the resort area in the evenings is a tribulation that most travelers could do without. The most comfortable dining is inside hotels, overpriced and of modest, if acceptable, quality. (Most three-star hotels charge under ¥100/$13/£6.50 for a meal for two.)

SIDE TRIPS FROM WUYI SHAN

The Wuyi mountains deserve a lot more time than most people give them, usually because they tire quickly of the mercenary resort or the endless streams of tourists at the main attractions. Independent travelers are so unusual that incredulous locals will constantly ask, *"Ni shi yi ge ren ma?"* ("Are you traveling alone?"). Following are three memorable day trips.

DA HONG PAO

For ¥5 (65¢/35p) you can hire a three-wheeler to take you to the small parking lot just below the stone Buddha; then walk the last 5 minutes up to the ticket office. For ¥22 ($2.80/£1.40), you can follow the official route to visit three small tea bushes, known as Da Hong Pao, which purportedly yield the rarest and most expensive tea in China. When you actually arrive at the trees you may walk past them, as I did, without even noticing—rather disappointing after treks up seemingly endless flights of steps and back down deep terraced gorges. At the bottom of the stairs that lead back up to the tea trees, look for a sign that points out an alternative route to the water curtain cave (Shui Lian Dong), as well as the intriguing words NON TOUR ROUTE. *This* is where the real adventure begins. The path is far from virgin as the plastic bags and empty bottles quickly attest, but after a 15-minute stroll you will be rewarded with a hidden valley, draped at one end by a splashing ribbon of water cascading down 30m (98 ft.) into an icy cold rock pool. The path has just about disappeared by this point, but old campfires show that you are not the first one; you'll probably have to try a few routes across the bare rocks to get to the flowing water, but I recommend that you persevere and jump in. I was exhilarated when I finally made it to the base of what I quickly christened Frommer's Falls.

A number of paths continue up through the small tea plantations, each one almost begging to be explored. Along the way are caves, waterfalls, and the occasional tea farmer to greet. The paths are sturdy rock steps and are sometimes carved into the very cliff faces themselves. All the time new vistas and views appear, each one seemingly more spectacular than the last.

Backtrack to the NON TOUR ROUTE sign and head for the water curtain cave. The path forks, one way heading to the cave the other passing China's greediest cold drinks vendor, selling bottles of water at ¥10 ($1.30/65p) each, 10 times the usual price. Continue toward the cave and the path will deposit you at the rear of the newly constructed Ever Happy Temple (Tian Xing Yong Le), populated with even more grabby vendors, this time posing as monks. Follow the stairs that lead down to the parking lot and ticket office, and you have inadvertently discovered a sneaky back entrance where you can avoid the exorbitant ticket prices.

FORGOTTEN GORGE

Another favorite place where I like to take first-time visitors is what I call the forgotten gorge. Guaranteed, no herds of local tourists—only perhaps an odd tea farmer if you are really lucky.

From the main resort area, cross the bridge and turn right. A 30-minute walk will take you to a left-hand junction marked with a large stone gate. A moto-taxi will bring you here for ¥5 (65¢/35p), and you might even be able to persuade a *sanluche* to come this far for ¥10 ($2.30/65p), which is a much more relaxing way to travel. From the turnout on the left, follow the road up past the huge laughing Buddha until you reach the parking lot for Da Hong Pao. Just opposite are some stones steps leading up. Follow these up to the still unfinished Ever Happy reproduction temple, although even on this short climb there are a few gorges leading away that are tempting to explore. Walk straight past the temple complex and follow the road up, passing between the memorial on the right and the traditional wooden house structure on the left. The road leads up to even more construction, but there are some stone steps leading down to the left, which lead down to the forgotten gorge. Due to the path's disuse, the footing can be tricky in places, but it is well worth it. From just a few yards down you can see all the way down to the resort. There are plenty of caves and extra staircases leading away to be explored and thanks to the wonderful perspective lines of the walls of the gorge, photographers will be snapping away like Ansel Adams. If you hot-foot it down the trail, you can be back on the road in under an hour, but my advice is to bring a book or a picnic or a sketchbook, and spend some time in the solitude offered by these magnificent mountains.

WUYI SHAN VIRGIN FOREST

The Wuyishan Virgin Forest (Yuanshi Senlin Gongyuan; © **0599/523-3808**), 48km (30 miles) east of Wuyi Shan and past the village of Xingcun, is no longer worth the effort of seeking out. Motorbike taxis will happily offer to take you up there for just ¥2 (25¢/15p), but this is only because they get a hefty commission from the ¥100 ($13/£6.50) ticket price that is now charged to get inside. There are rope bridges and white-water rafting and even paintball shootouts, but the place is overrun with busloads of Chinese tourists and the charm of this area is long gone.

Instead make your way up past Xing Cun town to the small of village of Hong Xing and asked to be dropped off at the water wheel just on the other side of the old bridge. This should cost about ¥8 ($1/50p) on the public bus or about ¥20 ($1.25–$2.50/65p–£1.25) by motorbike taxi. Continue walking for about 10 minutes until you see the antique hydroelectric station on the far bank. There is a new hotel that was just finishing construction as we passed, and the wooden timbers smelled glorious so this may well be worth further investigation when you arrive (**Jin Gu Long Zhuang,** Jing Qu San You; © **1385/949-6696**). There are some steps down to the river here but the power plant churns up the water and makes it a bit murky. Better to keep walking down to the next bend where tire tracks lead down to a pebble beach, which makes a great spot for a bit of skinny-dipping in the summer months. True, it is visible from the road, but drivers are far too busy craning to see around the blind bend to watch you taking a quick dip. If you are not that brave, there are rocks galore where you can perch to dangle your feet into the water, and mini waterfalls across the eddies that seem to attract wildlife, with loads of species of birds on display here. One thousand shades of green surround bubbling rapids, punctuated by rocks of every size from small pebbles to boulders the size of small houses. I was especially interested to see the way that the flow had carved natural bowls into the stone.

From here it is a short stroll into the village, a quaint little hamlet that has been virtually unharmed by the throngs of the nearby main resort. Actually, the whole valley has a somewhat alpine appearance and this only adds to its charm. Look out for the clay brick tobacco drying kilns, which smell like roasted sweet potatoes as the leaves are gently roasted before the big cigarette manufacturers coat them with all those toxic addictive chemicals. In the center of town, take a peak inside the old Communist Party meeting hall that has now been converted into a tea processing factory, a first-class example of Communist stone architecture long past its sell-by date. Keep walking past the duck ponds and rice paddies and explore some of the side roads and enjoy some of Fujian's finest nature. Look into some traditional wooden houses where basket weavers can still be seen at work before hopping on a bus back to the hotel resort area. All in all, an excellent afternoon out.

5 Quanzhou ⍟

Fujian Province, 593km (371 miles) SE of Wuyi Shan, 109km (68 miles) N of Xiamen

Quanzhou was once Zaytun, "one of the two greatest havens in the world for commerce," according to Marco Polo. "Twice as great as Bologna," said Franciscan friar Odoric da Pordenone, who was in China from 1323 to 1327. "The harbour of Citong is one of the greatest in the world—I am wrong; it is *the* greatest. I have seen there about a hundred first-class junks together; as for small craft, they were past counting," said Moroccan Ibn Battuta, who visited the area in 1345 to 1346. The Franciscan bishop of Zaytun wrote of Genoese merchants in 1326, and the city had other foreigners, including many Arabs.

But after the Ming expulsion of the Mongol Yuan dynasty in 1368, China gradually closed itself up, and by the time of Europe's next contact, via the Portuguese in the 16th century, Zaytun had withered. In the 19th and 20th centuries, while almost all its neighbors became treaty ports with resident foreigners and trading, Quanzhou was overlooked.

Today Quanzhou's center has been overtaken by a different kind of commerce, mainly cheap sneakers and plastic sandals. The suburbs are filled with factories and white-tiled blocks of apartments. The downtown area is even more depressing, with Wenling Nan Lu, the main drag, consisting primarily of karaoke clubs interspersed with sleazy short-time hotels, along with a few large brothels thinly disguised as hotels. Still, Quanzhou's interesting history does manage to surface and receive the attention it deserves, and the city has two fairly new museums and a host of sites to explore outside of town. Just be prepared—it seems that at the moment, more money is earmarked for propaganda than for serious archaeological study.

ESSENTIALS

GETTING THERE   The nearest **airport** is at Xiamen, 40km (25 miles) away, and many bus services there pick up and drop off at its entrance. The railway line down to Quanzhou is new, and the **railway station** is in the northeast suburbs. Bus nos. 19 and 23 run from the railway station to the center of town. Train tickets are on sale from 6:30 to 11:30am, 1:30 to 5pm, and 6:30 to 8:30pm. Trains to Zhejiang and elsewhere in coastal Fujian have to perform long loops. There are no longer any sleeper trains for Wuyi Shan For that you have to travel to Xiamen, but the early riser can enjoy the winding mountain line by taking the K955 at 6:32am and arriving at 4:53pm (K9856 and K955; 594km/368 miles; ¥149/$19/£9.70 hard sleeper, ¥232/$30/£15 soft sleeper).

The main bus station, the **Keyun Xin Zhan,** is full of yelling louts and has buses to Wuyi Shan (but the train is better); to Xiamen (20 departures 6:35am–5:40pm; luxury bus ¥38/$4.90/£2.50); and to Fuzhou (12 departures 8:05am–5:25pm; ¥41/$5.30/£2.70). There are also sleeper buses to Jiangxi destinations, Taishun, Wenzhou, and Hangzhou. Some express buses to Xiamen drop off passengers at the airport entrance. Some luxury services from and to Fuzhou terminate next to the **Huaqiao Dasha,** as do luxury buses to Shenzhen (② **0595/2228-7158**) and a daily bus to Guangzhou and Zhuhai for Macau (② **0139/6022-9688**). The same Huaqiao Dasha office has tickets for **flights** from Xiamen (② **0595/2218-2573**).

GETTING AROUND   While most youngsters seem to have bicycles with strange plastic spokes, older motorcyclists will beep at you and wave spare helmets until you want to hit them. Jetta **taxis** are ¥6 (80¢/40p) for 2km (11/4 miles), then ¥1.60 (30¢/15p) per kilometer up to 4km (21/2 miles), then ¥1.80 (25¢/15p) per kilometer up to 30km (19 miles), then ¥2 (25¢/15p) per kilometer up to 50km (31 miles), and after that, ¥2.20 (30¢/15p) per kilometer. At night, from 11pm to 5am, rates begin at ¥1.80 (25¢/15p) per kilometer. To get to the suburbs, **buses** charge a flat fare of ¥1 (15¢/10p) on entry; buses without air-conditioning but with conductors charge ¥2 (25¢/15p).

VISITOR INFORMATION   The **Quanzhou International Club (Quanzhou Guo Ji Ju Le Bu;** ② **1379/950-3010;** www.qzintlclub.com) is organized by David Zeng (david@jinshow.com) of the Puppet Museum, who is a great source of local information. **CITS** is now on the 15th floor of the Zhenxing Building (② **0595/ 223-1259;** fax 0595/223-1260). CTS's sales manager **Jackie Cai** (Cai Jian Jing) has also been reported as being very helpful. His office is in the Overseas Chinese Hotel, Baiyuan Road 362000 (② **0595/598-5940;** fax 228-2366).

Quanzhou

DINING ◆
Měicān Shí Jiē **11**
(The Delicacy Street)
美餐食街
Qing Qí Shén **6**
清其神
Sān Dé Sù Shí Guǎn **3**
(Three Virtues
Vegetarian
Restaurant)
三德素食馆

RIVERSIDE
PARK

Jin River

ACCOMMODATIONS ■
Háo Dì Fān Shāng Wù Jiǔ Diàn **4**
(GP Hotel)
好地方商务酒店

Jiàn Fú Shāng Wù Jiǔdiàn **10**
(Jian Fu Business Hotel)
建福商务酒店

Quánzhōu Hángkōng Jiǔdiàn **12**
(Xiàmén Airlines Quánzhōu Hotel)
泉州航空酒店

Quánzhōu Jiǔdiàn **8**
泉州酒店

🚌 Bus Station
¥ Bank
🅿 Police
✉ Post Office

ATTRACTIONS ●
Guāndì Miào **7**
关帝庙
Kāiyuán Sì **2**
开元寺
Luòyáng Qiáo **14**
洛阳桥
Maritime Museum **15**
(Hǎiwài Jiāotōng Shǐ Bówùguǎn)
海外交通史博物馆
Mùòu Bówùguǎn (Puppet Museum) **5**
木偶博物馆
Quánzhōu Museum **1**
(Quánzhōu Bówùguǎn)
泉州博物馆
Quán Zhōu Mǐn Taí Bó Wù Guǎn
(Quánzhōu Táiwān Friendship Museum)
泉州闽台博物馆
Statue of Zhèng Chénggōng **13**
郑成功
Tiānhòu Gōng **9**
天后宫

China
Beijing ★
EAST-LAKE
PARK
Quánzhōu

FAST FACTS

Banks, Foreign Exchange & ATMs   The main branch of the **Bank of China** (8–11am and 2:30–6pm) is in Fengze Jie just west of the Xiamen Airlines Hotel. Counter 14 handles checks and credit card withdrawals; it also handles cash exchanges during the same hours. ATMs at branches around town all accept foreign cards.

Internet Access   The **Dadi Wangba** (open 8am–3am; ¥2–¥3/25¢–40¢/15p–20p per hour) is just east of the PSB on Dong Lu. The **Huanqiu Wangba** is at Zhuangyuan Jie 127, and another *wangba* is opposite it at no. 138. Both are full of chain-smoking youngsters hurling obscenities at each other. A quieter alternative, with two dozen or so PCs, is the public library at Donghu Lu 752 (open 8–11:30am and 2:30–10pm; ¥2/25¢/15p per hour). Dial-up is ⓒ **8163.**

Post Office   The main post office (open 8am–8pm) is at Wenling Bei Lu 209, at the junction of Jiuyi Lu.

Visa Extensions   Extensions are harder to obtain here than in most places. The **PSB** on Dong Hu Lu (© **0591/2218-0323;** open Mon–Fri 8–11am and 3–6pm) requires evidence of the possession of $100 per day, for a single extension of up to 30 days.

EXPLORING QUANZHOU

Quanzhou has its fair share of the hideous white-tiled buildings that infest most cities; in fact, the tallest building in the city is already derelict, and new chunks of concrete masonry litter the sidewalk below every day—well worth avoiding. Other tour books drone on about saintly tombs and Arab mosques but the really interesting spots are to be found elsewhere.

Maritime Museum (Haiwai Jiaotong Shi Bowuguan) ★★   The Maritime Museum, east of the library on Dong Hu Lu, used to be one of the most interesting museums in China, especially for anybody who already has a penchant for the sea. Unfortunately ongoing budgets for these places never match the sums put aside for construction and the result is often rapid deterioration. The first floor displays the sort of ranting xenophobia that is par for the course in most Chinese museums, with exhibits that explain how Taiwan was "recovered from the greedy grasp of Dutch invaders" and how Quanzhou was infested with Japanese pirates, spitefully described as "pygmy bandits." The real gems are on the second floor: a priceless collection of hundreds of intricate scale models representing the whole of China's seafaring history. Each ship was handmade by master craftsman Chen Yanhong, and the level of detail is extraordinary. Highlights include imperial warships, caterpillar-like articulated vessels, and battleships that conceal secret launches. The English labels are better than you might expect, although, as so often seems to be the case, the authors claim to the Chinese invented anything worth inventing long before the West. In this particular field, this includes anchors, rudders, watertight compartments, paddlewheels, and even catamarans. Despite this pomposity, the construction of the models is of excellent quality and nobody leaves unimpressed. Unfortunately, much of the money for repairs, cleaning, and maintenance has been siphoned away to support other local museums, and many of the now-dusty exhibits are damaged, masts snapped by over-enthusiastic visitors and sails ripped by grabbing youngsters.

Back on the first floor directly below the seafaring exhibit visitors will find a collection of carved stonework, dating from the peak of Quanzhou's heyday. The displays are a lot less accessible for the casual visitor than the model ships but their significance is attested to by the fact that UNESCO funds are being used to help save these historical artifacts. Some of the inscriptions are carved in Syriac script, the written form of Aramaic, the language that was supposedly spoken by Jesus. During my visit, the stones were being examined in detail by academics from Cambridge in England and Macquarie in Australia. Five hundred years ago, this place was already a magnet for travelers of the world. Even though he ended up on the other side of the world, Columbus risked everything to find this already mythical city that had been made famous long before in the seven voyages of Sinbad, the tales of Marco Polo, and maybe even the mystical Christendom of Prester John.

Donghu Lu. © **0595/2210-0561.** Admission ¥10 ($1.30/65p). Tues–Sun 8:30am–5:30pm.

Quanzhou Museum (Quanzhou Bowuguan)   The brand-new Minnan-style Quanzhou Museum is so new that you may be the only visitor in the place. The museum provides the usual political propaganda, but this is made up for by a very interesting *National Geographic*–style documentary, describing the *Taixing* wreck and how treasure hunters salvaged more than 350,000 pieces of porcelain from the ocean floor.

During my visit, not all exhibits were open and the shops were just in the process of stocking their shelves, but one item caught my eye, the *Guide to Quanzhou Tourism*, a strangely translated book that talks about "interflow between Quanzhou and the alien countries." Although the descriptions are very brief and overly official, at just ¥15 ($1.95/£1) it is a useful book to have if you plan to explore this area further.

North section of Xihu Lu. ✆ **0595/2228-3914.** Admission ¥10 ($1.30/65p). 9am–5:30pm.

Quanzhou Taiwan Friendship Museum (Quanzhou Ming Tai Bowuguan)   Both inside and outside, the design of this museum is equally impressive. The exterior seems to spread to fill as much area as possible while inside are three galleries of exquisite Minnan mosaic designs. The content of the displays, though, is just laughable. Here are a few examples, just so you are not expecting any objective descriptions: "[Fujian Migrants] turned Taiwan from a wasteland into a rich and popular island"; "Taiwan has been part of China's territory from everlasting." And the Japanese: "A handful of scum of a nation who betrayed their ancestors and country." Similar venomous, racist comments fill all the displays. In the main foyer, is an 18m-high (59-ft.) gunpowder painting by a local artist that was created for the opening ceremony in May 2007, with the legend "Same wood, same seed, same root." My advice? Ignore the propaganda and enjoy the art.

North section of Bei Qing Lu. ✆ **0595/2275-1800.** Free admission with ID. 9am–4pm.

Cai Family Residence (Minnan Jian Zhu Da Guan Yuan)   About 30 minutes out of the main town, this well-preserved complex of 16 complete examples of Southern Fujian Qing dynasty residences is an interesting contrast to the conditions at nearby Chongwu (see below). Complexity abounds with fantastic relief carvings decorating almost every nook and cranny, as well as large wide boulevards that give a feeling of spaciousness. Look out for lots of building surprises such as drainpipes in the style of shubunkin and the large hollow Indian coral tree at the rear that has been adopted as home by a local stray. From Quanzhou bus station take a no. 9 bus to Guan Qiao and then change onto a bus that heads out to Nan'an and get off outside the Yilida Hotel. Turn right off the main road and continue walking for about 10 minutes.

Nan'an City, Guan Qiao Town, Zhang Li Village. ✆ **0595/8689-2290.** Admission ¥15 ($1.95/£1).

Statue of Zheng Chenggong   At 38m (125 ft.) high, 42m (138 ft.) long, and weighing in at 500 tons, this huge monument to Chinese propaganda is visible from just about any part of the city. Atop a mountain beyond the northern suburbs, this enormous statue portrays Zheng Chenggong, a Ming pirate who routed the Dutch from Taiwan and who, unlike most other pirates from around the world, has been a national hero ever since. The best way to get to this massive monolith is as a side trip on the way back from Chongwu. Once the general, who is seated astride an equally gigantic stallion, comes into view, jump off the bus and hail a moto-taxi to take you the rest of the way for ¥5 to ¥10 (65¢–$1.30/35p–65p). Up close, however, the monster statue of the great patriot on horseback is rather disappointing, being of a hollow metal-plate construction rather than local stone as one might have expected. Still, the views of Quanzhou are excellent.

Muou Bowuguan (Puppet Museum)   While the idea of a puppet museum may sound a little dull, Quanzhou is full of surprises. Have you ever seen a puppet disrobe, smoke, or pour itself a drink? The marionettes in this small private museum have up to 30 strings and can be manipulated in the most fascinating ways. Ask the proprietor David Zeng to show you around as he can explain all the fascinating carving and outfit embroidery techniques. The range of puppets available for sale is equally impressive at very reasonable prices. There is also a second shop with lots more of interesting souvenir opportunities at Jin Xiu Zhuang, Li Cheng Qu, Da Xi Jie 124 (© **0595/2228-6924**).

Hou Cheng Wen Hua Jie 6, behind the Ashab Mosque. © 0595/2216-3286. www.jinshow.com. Free admission. 9am–9pm.

A WALK AROUND THE WALLS OF CHONGWU ✦✦

A little over 50km (30 miles) from Quanzhou, Chongwu has one of the best-preserved city walls in China. Measuring 2.5km (1½ miles) long and dating from 1387, it is not yet the victim of much official recognition, and consequently is more natural than walls at Pingyao (p. 241).

The bus ride there departs from the main bus station every 30 minutes from 7am, with the last one heading back at 6pm; the fare is ¥9.50 ($1.25/60p). The often crowded minibus takes an indirect 90-minute route through towns and villages almost entirely devoted to stonemasonry. Stone is the traditional building material in this area and is still used in preference to concrete, the mountainsides gashed like raw meat; stacked beams everywhere look like a giant's rough-hewn Jenga tower. Houses are blockish, plain, and flat-roofed, with the occasional external stairway giving them a decidedly Middle Eastern look, reinforced by the tendency of local women to wear headscarves.

Before you even arrive at the old town, get off the bus and walk the last part of the way to see the amazing output of all the local **stone factories.** Alight at the round-about with the three laughing Buddhas (known in Chinese as Mi Le Fo) and the huge triangular billboard. From there on in, not only do statues of every description line the road, but the front lots of the factories have thousands more. Apart from a complete pantheon of Asian deities, there are local celebrities of every age, right up to modern times with Mickey Mouse, Pokemon, and Hello Kitty. The biggest factories are clustered together and we particularly recommend these sites. Start out at Haoxiang Stone (Shan Xia Industrial Zone; © **0595/8761-9999;** www.haoxiang.cc); Shi Xing Stone, which is almost next door (© **0595/8760-9999;** www.cn-shixing.com); and then maybe ask for Miss Ye, who speaks a little bit of English at the Hua Feng Sheng Stone Carving Company (Shan Xia Chi Hu Gong Ye Qu (Shan Xia Industrial Zone; © **0595/8760-6210;** www.hfs-stone.come). The stockyards of these places are amazing, with everything from aliens and snowboarders to sumo wrestlers and copulating porcines. Many of the designs are semi-abstract and some even downright erotic. Unfortunately, this wonderland of stonework may make the statue park a little drab when you finally arrive at Chongwu. And if you fancy a 6m (20 ft.) granite representation of yourself then expect to pay around ¥60,000 ($7,800/£3,900) excluding shipping.

Modern Chongwu, reached after 1½ hours, is typically hideous, but walk straight from the bus terminus, and where the road swings right, go straight on up the narrower street of small shops. Continue uphill until you arrive in less than 10 minutes at the modest east gate of the old walls, its enceinte still intact. Through that gate, turn immediately right into an alley called Cui Shi Xiang, which is barely wider than your shoulders, and find steps up. Turn right and walk clockwise.

The wall is very solid, with varied construction styles much less regular than walls elsewhere. It's sometimes overgrown, but accessible. At each gate in the wall the enceinte is entered from one side with a turn forcing you to pass through the wall itself. You can look down on the passage of beeping motorbikes, and on meat sold from open trestles in the shade. Elsewhere, geese, ducks, and hens in backyards look up startled at your passage.

This makes an interesting contrast to other old towns such as Lijiang and Dali, where the whole layout has been expanded to make it more accessible for tourists. Inside Chongwu, conditions are cramped and claustrophobic. The stench of open sewers pervades the narrow alleys and yet motorbikes scream though the dark confines pinning pedestrians up against the walls, assuming that they manage to sidestep the sewers. Here is an authentic view of what really happens when an ancient Chinese town meets the 21st century head on.

After the north gate the wall has been cleared a little and rises to views of the sea across the roofscape. There's a modern statue of a heroic defender looking out to sea, and a little temple on the wall topped with marvelous dragons with green bodies and red tails and faces. Firecracker residue and incense ash indicate the temple's popularity. Another temple below is worth descending to see, its walls papered with lists of contributors to its restoration, and its hall again topped with rampant polychromic dragons.

Below the east gate, a group of bad modern statuary looks out over broad sand beaches, and there's a modern lighthouse at the southeast corner. Actually the **statue park** (¥25/$3/£1.50) is worth a visit if you have not been to any of the statue factories, as it contains a truly bizarre sight, the 24 virtues of filial piety. Taken from a collection of popular Chinese folk tales available in every bookstore, the statues are great examples of weirdness. Madam Tang breastfeeds her grandmother for she has no teeth, Guo Ju buries his own son alive because he is too poor to feed him. I'll leave you to check out the tiger strangling and dung eating for yourself.

On the south side there's more beach, neat topiary-lined pathways, and sun shades. At the south gate, the **Nan Men Guandi Miao** is a new but remarkably elaborate temple, its stone pillars carved fantastically into dragons. The ceiling inside is finely carved and gilded, and interior pillars are fabulously carved with birds and figures giving great liveliness to dead stone.

A ticket office at the base of the gate is unmanned but would attempt to charge ¥2 (25¢/15p) to visitors entering from the beach side if anyone could be bothered. The exterior of the wall here is bearded with creeper, and beyond it are cold-drink and ice-cream sellers, sly seafood restaurants, horse rides, lookout points labeled as suitable for photography, and more bad statuary.

The final section is more overgrown but there's a clear path, where you scatter crickets underfoot while ducking under branches.

WHERE TO STAY

Hotels in Quanzhou are unexceptional, and many at the three- and four-star levels are overpriced considering their dowdiness. Much renovation and new construction are going on, and there may be more choices by the time you arrive.

GP Hotel (Hao Di Fan Shang Wu Jiu Dian)   While the corridors up on the guest floors still resemble the labyrinthine antechambers of a darkened karaoke club, the rooms, especially those at the front, are surprising comfortable. I particularly like the original open space planning of the bathrooms. Best of all this is a great location, literally at the rear of the Puppet Museum. By the way, GP stands for Good Place.

Bai Yuan Lu 1, Zhong Nan Shang Xia. ✆ **0595/2806-0000.** Fax 0595/2805-9928. hdf0595@163.com. 124 units. ¥180 ($23/£12) standard room; ¥280 ($36/£18) business room. AE, DC, MC, V. **Amenities:** Karaoke bar; business center; salon. In room: A/C, cable TV, broadband Internet access.

Jian Fu Shangwu Jiudian (Jian Fu Business Hotel)

Renamed and redecorated about 5 years ago, the hotel's unbeatable location makes this an excellent value for money, although it is starting to need a makeover these days. On the downside, like most Quanzhou hotels, Jian Fu has a very active "massage" service. The boss here must have some kind of automatic war-dialer software, as the phone rings in your room almost every 10 minutes. Simply unplug the phone when you arrive. Watch out for falling masonry from the abandoned Hua Lian Guang Chang next door, and listen for the melodic chimes from the clock tower across the road.

Wenling Lu Nan Duan. ✆ **0595/2298-7999.** Fax 0595/2298-0889. 80 units. ¥168 ($22/£11) standard room. 10% service fee not charged. AE, DC, MC, V. **Amenities:** Restaurant; karaoke bar; therapeutic massage (including in-room). In room: A/C, TV, fridge.

Quanzhou Hangkong Jiudian (Xiamen Airlines Quanzhou Hotel)

An upper-end three-star hotel, with a free shuttle bus to Xiamen Airport, this fresh, modern, 16-story tower with well-maintained rooms has above-average service, except in the first-floor coffee shop, with its awful coffee, which is understandably always empty. This is a typical businessman's hotel where conformity to general standards is more important than imaginative design. Still, the bathrooms are slightly larger than would otherwise be expected, though on the downside the beds seemed much harder than the general standard. Larger and with more facilities than the Jian Fu, it has higher prices to match.

Fengze Jie 339. ✆ **0595/2216-4888.** Fax 0595/2216-4777. 177 units. ¥560 ($73/£36) standard room; ¥998 ($130/£65) suite. Rates include breakfast. 10% service fee not charged. 40%–50% discounts available. AE, DC, MC, V. **Amenities:** 2 restaurants; fitness room; business center. In room: A/C, TV, video on demand, broadband Internet access, minibar, fridge, hair dryer, safe.

WHERE TO DINE

The liveliest eating is in the **Meican Shi Jie (The Delicacy Street)** running north from the arch on Jinhuai Jie, 1 block east and parallel to Wenling Bei Lu. Here rows of food stalls with tables and chairs in the open air or in air-conditioned interiors compete for your business until the small hours. There's seafood in buckets, *niupai* (beefsteak—a local favorite), dumplings, kabobs, hot pot, Sichuan food, and even Lanzhou "pulled" noodles. Especially interesting are the army-themed restaurants with pictures of aircraft carriers and stealth bombers on the walls. For more budget options such as rice boxes and barbecue, have a stroll up and down Yin Jin Jie opposite the Xinhua Bookstore. The excellent local wheat beer, Huiquan, will please anyone fond of Hoegaarden.

Those craving Western food will find **McDonald's, KFC,** and **Pizza Hut** around the city center, as well as a lot of smaller places trying to fake it until they make it. These include a CKF, a Just Loving Blue and Sea (obviously a McDonald's and Blue and White combo), and even an imitation of the Filipino Jollibee brand, here called Jallie Bee.

Qing Qi Shen, near the GP Hotel, behind the Guandi Miao in Tumen Jie, is a very pleasant teahouse in a traditional multicourtyard setting, where people sit playing board games beneath caged songbirds or watch the performance of a storyteller (in local Minnan dialect), and order snacks and tea from a bamboo slat menu: Oolong (Wulong) is ¥70 ($9.10/£4.55) per pot; ordinary tea from ¥8 ($1/50p). The **Red**

Rock French Restaurant (© **0595/2218-7273;** open 10am–1am) next door to the Puppet Museum is full of faux rococo furniture that Chinese seem to love, but the menu is interesting with temptations such as smoked salmon with asparagus rolls and baked taro and ribs with rice and cheese.

Three Virtues Vegetarian Restaurant (San De Su Shi Guan; © **0595/2291-0599),** opened by a locally based Hong Konger, has all the style, comfort, and imagination that you would expect of establishments at the midlevel. The menu includes vegetarian sushi *(ri shi su ci shen),* deep-fried crab claws with minced vegetarian squid *(bai hua zha rang su xie qian),* vegetarian spareribs with sweet osmanthus sauce *(gui hua su wu pai),* and the huge durian pastries *(gan si liu lian su).*

6 Xiamen ⟨★⟨★

Fujian Province, 109km (68 miles) S of Quanzhou, 770km (481 miles) E of Guangzhou

The island of Xiamen, then better known to foreigners by its Fujian name of Amoy, became a foreign concession in 1903, with most of the foreigners living on the tiny islet of Gulang Yu just off Xiamen itself. By the 1930s there were about 500 resident foreigners and nine consulates, several of which still stand, as do the vast, European-style mansions of Chinese who returned wealthy from overseas.

Here, more than at any other former treaty port including Shanghai, there seems to be something left of the foreign presence and the colonial era. Xiamen is home to the largest and best-preserved warren of colonial-era shop-houses in mainland China, and on Gulang Yu, you'll find the largest and best-preserved collection of colonial mansions. People also seem remarkably relaxed and law-abiding—there's little spitting, little shouting at foreigners, and an unusual tendency to obey road signs.

Much of the island is a hideous white-tiled wasteland to match anything else in China, but even so, the odd turret and spire reflect the city's pride in its stock of original European-style architecture. The rest of the island is a refreshing change and full of character—narrow alleys connecting sinuous streets are laced together with power and telephone cables, and house DVD shops, noodle restaurants, and hair salons where no hair is ever cut. Vehicle-free Gulang Yu, a few minutes away by ferry, was until recently all pleasant strolls and quiet back streets full of mansions overgrown with brilliant bougainvillea. Be warned that this is now one of the busiest tourist locations in China.

ESSENTIALS

GETTING THERE   Xiamen's **Gaoqi International Airport** (© **0592/602-8940)** is on the north side of the island only 20 minutes from the downtown area. Airport taxis cost little more than ¥30 ($3.90/£1.95) to downtown, and there's a shuttle to the railway station from the right of the terminal as you leave that charges ¥6 (75¢/40p). Marco Polo and the other big hotels have free shuttles for guests. There are international connections to Bangkok, Hong Kong, Kuala Lumpur, Manila, Osaka, Singapore, and Tokyo, with an assortment of domestic and foreign airlines including JAL, Philippine, ANA, and Dragonair; and regular flights to all major Chinese cities, including Beijing (five or six flights daily), Guangzhou (five or six daily), and Shanghai (nine flights daily). While most airlines maintain offices in the Crowne Plaza or Marco Polo hotels, or in the Yinhang Zhongxin at the corner of Hubin Xi Lu and Xiahe Lu, you are better off purchasing your tickets from independent agencies, preferably away from your hotel. **Xiamen Airlines** (© **0592/222-6666;** www.xiamen air.com.cn) has a 24-hour ticketing and check-in desk for its own passengers and those of China Southern in the Jinyan Jiudian. It also sells tickets for other airlines with reasonable discounts. Its shuttle service is free for guests and for Xiamen/China Southern passengers; there are eight departures from 5:20am to 7:20pm. Reserve a seat on the shuttle in advance at ⓒ **0592/221-8888,** ext. 34 or 6110.

At the airport, an **ATM** that accepts foreign cards is upstairs at international departures, as is a **Bank of China** forex counter open from 8:30am to 4:30pm. Just outside the airport is a bus station and no. 27 goes all the way to Gulang Yu Ferry for ¥1 (15¢/10p), which is a good alternative to a ¥50 ($6.50/£3.25) taxi.

On routes to neighboring coastal cities and to Hong Kong, luxury long-distance bus services are quickest, but there are useful **train** connections from Wuyi Shan (K985/988; Shanghai (K175; 1,395km/872 miles; ¥472/$61/£31), Guangzhou (K297; 746km/389 miles; ¥261/$40/£16). There is also a useful sleeper service to Wuyi Shan (K198) leaving at 10:14pm (¥155/$20/£10 hard sleeper), arriving in Wuyi Shan at 7am the next morning. The mostly single-track route through mountainous Fujian Province is pretty and winding, passing sugar-cane plantations and banana palms with bags tied over the fruit to help them ripen. There are also direct services from Beijing, Nanjing, and Xi'an. For **train inquiries,** call ⓒ **0592/581-4340;** for **bookings,** ⓒ **0592/398-8662,** up to 12 days in advance. The railway station is a 10-minute cab ride east of the ferry dock, which can also be reached on bus no. 1. Ticket windows are open from 8am to 8:30pm, with tickets available up to 5 days in advance including day of travel. As you face the railway station, booking and left luggage are to the right of the entrance. The **Nanfang Luxingshe** inside the Heping Wharf has computer access to the railway system, and charges a ¥10 ($1.30/65p) service fee per ticket. Bus no. 17 goes from the railway station to Pearl Harbor near Xiamen University for ¥2 (25¢/15p).

Southern China's new highway system is now cruised by air-conditioned **buses** with frequent services, many of them luxury foreign makes with attendants and lavatories. For all coastal destinations north in Fujian and into Zhejiang, as well as south into neighboring Guangdong Province, these buses are far quicker than trains.

You can board most bus lines at the **Songbai changtu qichezhan** (Lian Yue Lu; ⓒ **0592/508-9328**). Services include Wenzhou (¥163/$21/£11); Wuyi Shan (¥124/$16/£8) at 8:10am and 1:50pm; Guangzhou (17 departures; ¥180/$23/£12) from 7:50am to 10:10pm; Shenzhen (14 departures; ¥200/$13–$26/£13) from 8am to 10:30pm; and Quanzhou (more than 50 departures; ¥32/$4.50/£2.10) from 6:20am to 9:10pm.

From Songbai there is there is a free shuttle bus service (no. 816) to the other **long-distance bus station (changtu qichezhan;** ⓒ **0592/221-5238**), officially described as the Xiamen Travel Distribution Centre, is on Hubin Nan Lu 59, just north of downtown. It sells tickets from 5:30 to 10pm. Buses depart for Longyan every 30 minutes and cost ¥72 ($9.50/£4.70). However, many of the best services also have agencies located conveniently opposite the main ferry terminal to Gulang Yu. Try **Lundu Shoupiao Chu** (ⓒ **0592/213-5051**), next to the Spring Sunlight Hotel, where several services pick up passengers and which has a small waiting room. Sample bus routes: Guangzhou (770km/481 miles; ¥220/$29/£14), Shenzhen (680km/425 miles; ¥180/$23/£12). There's even a direct bus route to Hong Kong (830km/519 miles; ¥350/$46/£23).

Although most coastal **ferry** routes are long gone, the service to Hong Kong survives just barely. Service is now restricted to a once-a-month trip that takes place at the end of the month, usually on the 29th, 30th, or 31st. Services leave Xiamen at 4pm on Thursday and arrive in Tsim Sha Tsui, Hong Kong, at 10am to noon the next day. The route is unfortunately one-way and there is no return available from Hong

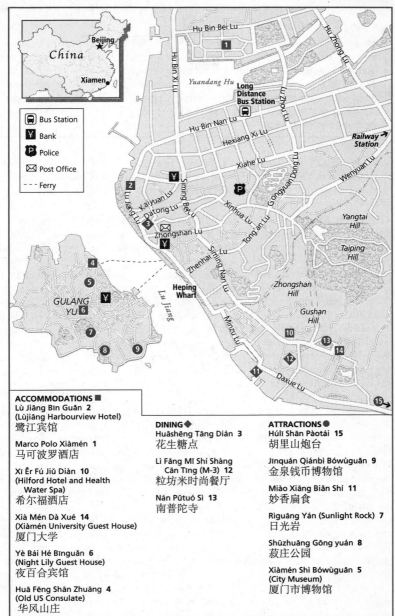

> ⸢*Tips* **A Good Seat**
>
> Although not double-deckers, many of the coaches in this part of the country are split-level with the driver sitting below and the passengers all in luxury seats on a slightly higher level. It pays to know that the three final seat nos. 36, 37, and 38 are actually at the front rather than the rear. This means that these front seats with great panoramic windows are the very last to fill up. If you don't luck out by getting those seats but the coach is not full, feel free to head up front and spread out.

Kong to Xiamen. One-way fares for cabin berths range from ¥320 ($42/£21) for a regular cabin to ¥352 ($46/£23) for a deluxe berth. Call ⓒ **0592/202-2517** for up-to-date schedule details. Xiamen departures are from the Heping Wharf (Heping Matou), just south of the Gulang Yu ferry terminal.

GETTING AROUND   Both the old town and Gulang Yu are easily explored **on foot,** and the other main sights are short **taxi** rides away although taxis in Xiamen are rather more old and battered than other cities. Flagfall for taxis is ¥8 ($1/50p) including 3km (2 miles), then ¥2 (25¢/15p) per kilometer up to 8km (5 miles), then ¥3 (40¢/20p) per kilometer. Add 20% from 11pm to 5am. **Buses** are frequent and reliable, with fare boxes into which you deposit ¥2 (25¢/15p) for air-conditioned service, ¥1 (15¢/10p) without. A few non-air-conditioned buses have conductors. There are several **ferry** routes between the **Ferry Dock (Lundu Matou)** and Gulang Yu. The 5-minute main route is free outbound, but ¥3 (40¢/20p) to return. There's an optional ¥1 (15¢/10p) charge to sit on the top deck in either direction. Ferries run roughly every 10 to 15 minutes from 5:45am, every 20 to 30 minutes after 9pm; the last sailing is at 12:30am. To the right of the ferry boarding point are windows for a **daytime cruise** around Gulang Yu and to see Taiwanese Jinmen Dao. The 35-minute cruise departs roughly every 30 minutes from 7:40am to 5pm; call ⓒ **0592/202-3493.** The next windows offer a **night cruise** (ⓒ **0592/210-4896;** 1 hr., 50 min.; ¥118/$15 including snacks). There are also night trips to see the Haicang Da Qiao, a large, illuminated suspension bridge just to the north; the 40-minute trip is offered May through October from 8 to 8:45pm for ¥10 ($1.30/65p) to ¥20 ($1.25–$2.50/60p–£1.25). At the end farthest to the right is a second ferry service to Gulang Yu, running to San Qiu Tian, a little east of Gulang Yu's main dock, beneath the former U.S. consulate. Ferries depart every 30 minutes from 7:15am to 9:40pm; throughout the night, they depart roughly every hour.

On any given summer weekend, Xiamen expats head to the ferry terminal, following a quick trip to the supermarket to buy supplies of wine, beer, meat, and salads. With overflowing shopping bags, they pile onto a small wooden boat, crank up the engine, and head deeper into the archipelago. These boats are usually owned by local fishing couples who make extra money on the weekends taking hedonistic sun-lovers out to sea. For ¥300 ($39/£20), 15 to 20 people can spend the day sun baking on deck while exploring smaller islands near Xiamen. The driver knows the best places to throw in the anchor. Dive into the ocean, fill up your glass, and soak up the sun. Most boats have a small barbecue, but if it seems like too much trouble, let the driver know and he'll find a restaurant to moor at. Needless to say, Sunday evenings back in Xiamen are often lit by happy sunburned faces. Official tour boats also cruise the harbor, taking tourists close to the Taiwan island of Jinmen. These bigger, fancier boats cost around ¥100 ($13/£6.50) per person for a 2- to 3-hour cruise.

A **tourist bus** now stops at the major tourist sites and charges ¥58 ($6.20/£3.10) a day and includes lunch (© **0592/335-2833** or 0592/333-2702). The commentary is in Chinese, so take a good guidebook or carry an illustrated map with photos so you will know what you are seeing.

Hog fans may notice a large numbers of large Chinese 750 military-style motorcycles with sidecars, very similar to the prewar BMW R71. As yet, there is nowhere to rent one of these monsters, but background details can be seen at the manufacturer's website, **www.chang-jiang.com/lsc.**

VISITOR INFORMATION   For travel complaints, call © **0592/505-6777.** American Express has an office in the Crowne Plaza, room 212 (© **0592/212-0268;** Mon–Fri 9am–5pm). The staff isn't terribly helpful, but with some prodding they can at least tell you where to find the check-cashing service. For more details about new developments in the area, check the *What's on Xiamen* website at **www.whatson xiamen.com.** There is also a book called *Amoy Magic* that cannot be recommended due to the inane humor, amateurish style, and constant party brown-nosing of the author. Even so, it covers a lot more locations than most Western guidebooks, but you may end up chucking it out of a train window in disgust after reading some of the writer's ridiculous comments.

Xiamen Travel Service says it has 10 English-speaking guides. It's at Lianhua Nan Lu 5 (© **0592/512-8855;** xm_travel@xiamenair.com.cn); ask for Chen Yu Cheng, Vice G. Manager, Foreign Liaison Center.

FAST FACTS

Banks, Foreign Exchange & ATMs   All **Bank of China** ATMs take foreign cards, from the airport, via Gulang Yu (at Haitan Lu 2), to the convenient Zhongshan Lu branch (open 8:30am–noon and 2:30–5:30pm) close to the Gulang Yu ferry dock in the center of town, which also has forex at counters 2 to 6. There's another Bank of China with forex and ATM in the Yinhang Zhongxin on the corner of Hubin Xi Lu and Xiahe Lu. Just next door is a branch of the **Hongkong and Shanghai Bank (HSBC),** whose ATMs take almost any card invented.

Internet Access   There are Internet cafes located around the old town, including one on Kaiyuan Lu. A much quieter option is the third floor of Xiamen Library at Gong Yuan Nan Lu 2; it's open 8 to 11:30am and 2:30 to 5:30pm. Dial-up is © **8163.**

Post Office   The main post office (open 7:30am–7:30pm) is in Zhongshan Lu opposite the Bank of China. There's also a useful branch in Longtou Lu on Gulang Yu.

Visa Extensions   The **PSB (Gong'anju;** open Mon–Sat 8–11:45am and 3–5:45pm) is in Chu Mi Yan (© **0592/2262-2207).**

EXPLORING XIAMEN

The narrow streets of the **old quarter,** which has the mainland's largest and best-preserved area of treaty port–era shop-houses in a labyrinth of curling streets and narrow lanes, is bounded to the north by Xiahe Lu and to the south by Zhongshan Lu, which leads to the ferry docks.

GULANG YU

Amoy, as Xiamen was then known, was one of the first five treaty ports to be opened to foreign residence and trade after the First Opium War, and a British consulate was

Smuggling Kingpin or Local Boy Made Good?

Some say that Xiamen owes its economic head start to local hero (but pub-lic enemy number one) Lai Cai Xing. Currently under house arrest in Vancou-ver, Lai escaped the mainland when it was discovered that he had built up his billion-dollar business on bribes and smuggling. At the time, he ran an empire so powerful that locals used to joke that Xiamen should change its name to the name of his company, Yuanhua. Lai earned a reputation as a modern-day Robin Hood, a big-hearted billionaire who helped out folks far more than most stingy government cadres ever did. The trickle-down bene-fits of the operation were immense. In the city and its suburbs, Lai built hotels, residences, a port, and a full-scale model of Beijing's Tian'an Men Gate. He opened homes for the elderly and showered associates and gov-ernment officials and their relatives with gifts, money, and trips abroad. Investigators reckon he spent $2.5 million on gifts during the 1997 lunar New Year celebration alone. For his generosity, Lai was charged as the mas-termind behind China's largest-ever smuggling ring. In the ensuing investi-gation, 14 officials were executed and another 300 imprisoned.

According to a recent online poll, more than 80% of Chinese university students believe China's biggest companies are corrupt. Even Lai admits, "The whole system in China is corrupt. To get ahead, you have to become part of that system." Xiamen residents are bitter that their city has been tar-geted, when, they say, corruption is equally rampant in other Chinese cities. More resentment has followed as this has opened the door for rich investors from other cities such as Wenzhou, to force up property prices in Xiamen.

With dozens of police, Customs, and mayoral staff in jail, Xiamen quickly became a pariah in the eyes of domestic and foreign investors. Yuanhua, it turned out, was intertwined with hundreds of local companies from tour agencies to flower shops, many of which were closed, turning one of China's more prosperous and promising cities into a place of financial and social gloom. The only companies that were excluded from the effects of this city-wide crackdown were, unsurprisingly, those operated by the People's Liber-ation Army. What for many years had been one of China's most prosperous

opened in 1843. The first foreign settlements were on Amoy proper, but the town was then famously noisome, its alleys, some too narrow to allow the opening of an umbrella, funneling an extravagant palette of aromas from sewers inadequately con-cealed beneath the pavements. Surprisingly clean now, Xiamen was then reputed to be the filthiest city in China.

The foreign community therefore moved to the 1.7-sq.-km (¾-sq.-mile) Gulang Yu but grew slowly (37 residents in 1836), although in 1852 the site became the first of the "concessions"—areas of land formally set aside for foreign residence, then parceled out to British citizens. By 1880, the now multinational foreign population was around 300 and sustained a daily English newspaper, an ice factory, a club, and tiger shoot-ing (25 were bagged at the beginning of the 1890s alone). Amoy's main export was workers, the British having forced the Qing to permit Chinese emigration, and

and free-spirited cities became a gloomy wreck of halted building projects and shuttered nightclubs. Xiamen recorded blistering growth of 17% a year in the second half of the 1990s. Most worrying for local officials is that foreign investment plunged precipitously—down 23% in the first year after Lai's arrest.

To recover some of the losses, government officials tried without success to auction Lai's holdings, including the Tong 'An Forbidden City Film Studio and the 88-story Yuanhua International Hotel, where a lake of stagnant water had begun to fester. Eventually the downtown location was sold to a Hangzhou tycoon who now operates a Sheraton on the site at Jiahe Lu.

The only evidence that remains is Lai's notorious pleasure palace. From the outside, the infamous Red Chamber (Hong Lou) on Hua Xing Lu, Near Yong Shen New City (bus no. 109) looks like any other office building in Xiamen—a drab and dusty complex covered in red tiles. Leased to Lai by the local Public Security Bureau in 1996, the building held four opulent dining rooms for the culinary amusement of his friends. On the third floor, the sensual pleasures became more dizzying: four massage rooms, two Jacuzzis, a sauna, a steam room. The fourth floor boasted a 40-seat movie theater, a karaoke parlor, a bar, and three mini dance halls. Both the fifth floor and sixth floors were made up of guest rooms, including several presidential suites where top officials could slip in through secret entrances for trysts with procured entertainment.

The Red Chamber reopened briefly as an anticorruption museum but was quickly shuttered when tourists seemed to take its opulence as an inspiration instead of a warning. In its first 4 days, more than 8,500 people paid about ¥10 ($1.30/65p) each to see how their homegrown Al Capone did business. **Tong 'An Film City** is located in Wu Xian Town of Tong 'An district (© 0592/730-2870) and can be reached on bus no. 67 leaving from the harbor near the Lujiang Hotel for ¥6 (80¢/40p). For more background on this captivating character try reading *Inside the Red Mansion: On the Trail of China's Most Wanted Man* by Oliver August.

between 1883 and 1897 an estimated 167,000 left for labor overseas, founding Chinatowns around Asia and North America.

More recently, the population of this island has dropped to about 15,000 from 25,000 as the government returns houses to original owners. Its houses are being transformed into multistoried resorts and apartments.

In treaty port days all transport was on foot, and no wheeled vehicles were allowed—a rule still enforced with the exception of some quiet electric carts used sometimes to take tourists on a circuit round the island (¥50 ($6.50/£3.25) but mostly to quietly sneak up and scare the bejeesus out of them.

First impressions of the island are not very favorable. The ferry disembarkation area consists of huge sliding steel gates that would be more at home on Alcatraz rather than a tourist hot spot. Once through the maximum security–type entrance, the first thing that visitors see is a huge ad for McDonald's.

As you alight from the ferry, an office straight ahead as you dock offers a ¥80 ($10/£5.20) ticket giving entrance to a variety of tawdry modern entertainments such as a fun fair and a laser show, so turn left instead to where the electric cars are parked. Proceed uphill straight to the area of finest mansions, on serpentine Fujian Lu and Lujiao Lu. The best examples are signposted, yet marked with unhelpful plaques giving construction dates and little more information; the former Japanese consulate is marked, however. Look out for the Catholic church of 1917 at Lujiao Lu 34. Some sources claim that 30% of the island's 20,000 residents are still practicing Christians. It's also a tradition that there are more pianos here than anywhere else in China, and tourism promoters claim that Gulang Yu is known as "Piano Island," Directly opposite Sunlight Rock is Asia's largest Piano Museum, testimony to the island's long love affair with the piano. There are over 70 historic pianos including the world's first square piano. A selection of them is used at the two major piano competitions held on the island, Gulang Yu Piano Festival and the National Competition for Young Pianists. Bach and Clementi can often be heard being hammered out rhythmically if unimaginatively, but that is only because the local high school uses concerto snippets instead of the usual school bells.

Fujian Lu 32 is particularly impressive—a vast porticoed mansion built in 1928 by a Vietnamese-Chinese real estate tycoon; the mansion later served as a hospital during the Japanese occupation of World War II, and today is the Art Vocation University of Xiamen. Dozens of families now occupy a range of such mansions and have bricked up entrances, walled in balconies to add floor space, and left gardens to turn wild. Pretty winding paths between mansions are now overgrown with hawthorn, but despite the sometimes dismaying crush on the ferry, the island has generous amounts of what China generally lacks—peace and quiet.

Farther on, clockwise around the island, is the **Jinquan Qianbi Bowuguan,** a museum of ancient coins housed in the handsome British consulate, originally built in 1843 and the earliest foreign building on the island. Recently opened, its hours and entrance fee seem not yet set, but beyond the building is one of the best lookout points back to Xiamen.

Follow signs down to the beach below. Chinese now paddle where foreigners once held bathing parties that inexplicably involved eating ginger cookies and drinking cherry brandy. Just past the beach are shady benches beneath the trees, beyond which a short tunnel takes you through to the next beach. Immediately after that on the left, steps lead up the hillside through gardens to **Riguang Yan (Sunlight Rock),** a lookout point perhaps used by pirate and Ming loyalist Zheng Chenggong (1624–62), also known as Kongxia, a Dutch corruption of a title awarded him by the expiring Ming. He's an official state hero for being the first Han to invade Taiwan, which he did mainly for its silk and sugar, but is idolized for having kicked the Dutch off Taiwan in 1624. A dull museum to his memory is laced with the usual propaganda about how Taiwan has always been "an inseparable part of the motherland." It's a stiff climb (although there's a cable car alternative) and the entrance fee is a hefty ¥60 ($7.80/£3.90). The view is very overrated, just a busy shipping lane and some ugly container-handling facilities over on the opposite island. Unfortunately the world's biggest amplifier is not visible this far away.

Past the beach, a right turn before a farther tunnel leads you into a maze of old mansions, but signs will direct you to the **Xiamen Shi Bowuguan (City Museum)** at

Guxin Lu 43 (open 8:30am–5pm; ¥10/$1.30/65p). The museum is located in possi-bly the grandest of all the mansions, the swaggering, three-story, cupola-topped Bagua Lou or Eight Trigrams Building of 1907, designed by an American for a Taiwanese businessman. The ground floor has early examples of the Min Nan region (Quanzhou/ Zhengzhou/Xiamen) specialty ware, *blanc de chine,* mostly Qing. There's other mate-rial on the Opium War and the Japanese occupation, as well as on the Communist forces' drive to Xiamen, which forced the Nationalists to Taiwan. The small matter of Jinmen Island, which sits uncaptured less than 2km (1¼ miles) from the mainland (despite being the subject of two major offensives and the fact that the Chinese shelled the island nonstop for 44 days back in '58), receives no comment. The museum is dusty, echoing, forgotten, and rarely visited, but there are good views from upper bal-conies (hung with the attendants' washing) for a fraction of the cost of views from Sunlight Rock. A new building to one side has well-presented displays on fishing, local customs, and tea.

AROUND XIAMEN

Southeast of the center, a series of sites make a pleasant excursion when seen together. Start by taking a taxi or bus no. 2 or 22 from Siming Lu to the **Huli Shan Paotai,** a platform (open 8:30am–5pm; ¥25/$3.30/£1.60) with a vast Krupp 280-millimeter cannon overlooking the island-dotted ocean and offering a different kind of seashell. The huge gun, one of two originally sited here in 1893, sits on a vast rotating chain-driven mechanism and is credited with sinking a Japanese warship in 1937. When it was first fired, several nearby houses collapsed, too. The other gun emplacement now houses a tacky souvenir shop. There are plenty descriptions in English but they include the usual nationalist claptrap about "British aggressors" and "brave Chinese soldiers." The surrounding sunken barracks area has been turned over to the exhibi-tion of peculiar stones and ancient weaponry that includes a rusty pistol said to have belonged to Opium warrior Lin Zexu. A boat at the pier below offers 1-hour trips to see Jinmen and Little Jinmen islands for ¥96 ($13/£6.20); call © **0592/208-3759** for information.

Cross the road opposite the cannon and turn left until you find the gate to the uni-versity, **Xiamen Daxue.** Even the footbridge here is worth a closer look as this inno-vative tension structure is millennia ahead of almost any other construction in China. Street furniture is very interesting, with a huge musical stave decorating the center of the road and with oversize sculpted computer mice down on the beach.

This is one of China's older and most pleasant campuses, founded around 90 years ago and heavily funded by donations from Chinese overseas. Wander straight on past substantial brick buildings to a major left turn to the main gate—students will point you in the right direction if you look lost.

The recently completed island ring road begins at Bai Cheng Beach outside the gates to Xiamen University and incorporates a substantial lane purely for cyclists, run-ners, and strollers. Bicycles can be rented from several outlets along Huang Dao Lu (the ocean ring road) but like everything else in Xiamen prices are high and rentals begin at ¥10 ($1.30/65p) per hour.

Just outside the campus, on the right, is **Nan Putuo Si** (open 3am–6:30pm; ¥3/40¢/20p). It's a temple of little antiquity but fully functional as a place of worship, with the devout on their knees reading scriptures and surely nearly asphyxiated by all the incense smoke. Monks bustle about, and wooden blocks are tossed to obtain the answers to important questions. There are also rock-cut calligraphy, modern stupas containing the remains of recently interred monks, 18 particularly animated *luohan* statues, a "thousand-armed" Guanyin, and an excellent vegetarian restaurant. On the cable car ride from the gardens over the South Putuo Temple, you will be treated to a stunning panoramic view over Xiamen, Gulang Yu, and the surrounding waters.

WHERE TO STAY

Xiamen has a variety of shiny business hotels scattered around the island. For those on expenses, the two to choose from are the Marco Polo and the Sofitel, although new additions such as the Hilford and the Black Lily have much more character for more adventurous tourists. We no longer recommend the Xiamen University Guest House, whose prices have doubled since the last edition even though levels of service and comfort have dropped like a stone. Upmarket hotels add a 10% to 15% service charge and there is now an additional 4% local government tax.

You'll find abundant budget accommodations on the waterfront north of the Lujiang Binguan and some (much quieter) on Gulang Yu, including a former American consulate. Just outside the railway station, if you are just passing through, is the **Yijing Hotel (Yi Jing Jiu Dian;** He Xiang Dong Lu 108; © **0592/385-8999;** ¥248/$32/£16).

Xiamen holds its annual marathon on the last Saturday of March when almost 20,000 athletes compete for a first prize of $25,000, so don't expect any hotel discounts that particular weekend. Xiamen tourism is busy March through May, after which Chinese tourism drops to almost nothing, and only the odd foreigner is seen midsummer; it picks up again September through early October for a trade fair. Typically, 40% discounts are available in nonpeak periods, more in lower-level accommodations.

EXPENSIVE

Lujiang Bing Guan (Lujiang Harbourview Hotel)   One of the oldest buildings in the city looks much better after its recent refurbishment, but don't expect perfection. This hotel has the best views over Gulang Yu and is located in the center of town. The travel agent downstairs gives excellent advice. It has an American breakfast, but no buffet, for ¥25 ($3.25/£1.65), while Chinese breakfast costs ¥15 ($1.95/£1) but does not include coffee. Up a hard-to-find, dirty, narrow staircase, the business center charges ¥10 ($1.30/65p) for 10 minutes of e-mail and is open from 9am to 11pm.

Lujiang Dao 54. © **0592/202-2922.** Fax 0592/202-4644. www.lujiang-hotel.com. 180 units. ¥410–¥700 ($52–$91/ £26–£46) deluxe room; ¥830–¥1,360 ($108–$176/£54–£88) suite. 30% discounts available. 15% service charge. AE, DC, MC, V. **Amenities:** 2 restaurants; 3 bars including a pool bar and cigar bar; spa; concierge; tour desk; airport shuttle; business center; forex; salon. *In room:* A/C, TV, Internet access, fridge, hair dryer, safe.

Marco Polo Xiamen 𝒜   Many of the rooms are arranged on eight floors around a central atrium with sandstone carvings of Marco Polo's travels, but a wing off to one side is a better choice for peace and quiet. Set on the lakeside, it's a short walk from coffee shops, restaurants, parks, and gardens. It has a complimentary shuttle from the airport 14 times a day. On Saturdays and Sundays, it has a shuttle to the main tourist attractions four times a day. The concierge desk is particularly well staffed with good English-speakers, both eager to help and capable of doing so. The center of town is only a few minutes away by taxi.

Jianye Lu 8 (off Hubin Bei Lu on the north shore of Yuandang Lake). © **0592/509-1888.** Fax 0592/509-2888. www. marcopolohotels.com. 350 units. ¥1,280–¥2,000 ($166–$260/£83–£130) standard room; ¥1,600–¥7,840 ($208– $1,019/£104–£509) suite. 15% service charge. AE, DC, MC, V. **Amenities:** 3 restaurants; lobby lounge; poolside bar w/views across the lake to the city skyline; outdoor swimming pool; fitness room; sauna; concierge; tour desk; free airport shuttle; business center; forex; shopping arcade; salon; 24-hr. room service; babysitting; same-day laundry/dry cleaning; executive-level rooms. *In room:* A/C, satellite TV, minibar, fridge, hair dryer, safe.

MODERATE

Hua Feng Shan Zhuang *(Overrated)*   Here's a chance to sleep in a former U.S. consulate, built in 1928 with bricks imported from the States at a cost of $200,000 (the first consulate burned down). The neoclassical portico (with an oddly Egyptian touch to the tops of its pillars) has been glassed in and the upper floor extended into the space. The building was refitted and opened as a hotel in 1999. Unfortunately, nobody speaks a word of English, and the only decent views are from the much more expensive suites. The standard rooms I saw were cramped and stuffy, outfitted in far too much beige. The gardens and tennis courts are perfectly manicured, so it is perhaps better to come here for a little sun in the afternoon but sleep somewhere else.

Sanming Lu 26 (on Gulang Yu, a short walk to the right from the main ferry dock, and served less frequently by ferries to a dock immediately beneath it). ☎ 0592/206-5621. Fax 0592/206-9762. 29 units. ¥450 ($59/£29) standard room; ¥660 ($86/£43) suite. 30% discounts typical. ¥280 ($36/£18) simple standard rooms in separate newer building. No credit cards. **Amenities:** Restaurant (open intermittently); 2 outdoor tennis courts. *In room:* A/C, TV, fridge.

Xi Er Fu Jiu Dian (Hilford Hotel and Health Water Spa) ★★★ *(Finds)*   While the university guesthouse may have dropped its standards, the Hilford is an excellent alternative. Rooms are opulent but not extravagant, with ancient Chinese designs translated into modern luxuries, so that even a standard room here would please an imperial prince and his consorts. The huge wooden doors are a breath of fresh air after so much flimsy plywood in cheap business hotels. Surprise extras include a balcony, a kitchen, and even a coffeemaker. Guests also have free access to the spa next door.

Siming Nan Lu 495. ☎ 0592/208-2222. Fax 0592/209-2222. www.hilford.com.cn. 165 units. ¥438 ($57/£29) standard room; ¥738 ($96/£48) suite. Rates include Chinese breakfast. MC, V. **Amenities:** 2 restaurants; concierge; tour desk; airport shuttle; business center; salon. *In room:* A/C, TV, Internet access, kitchen, fridge, hair dryer.

Ye Baihe Binguan (Night Lily Guest House) ★★ *(Finds)*   This is just the kind of accommodations that China needs. Two forward-thinking foreigners have converted this 1930s colonial mansion on Gulang Yu into what can only be described as a boutique hotel. There are five guest suites done in wonderfully eclectic styles that mix and match antique Chinese furniture with modern designer bathrooms. The view across to the city is breathtaking, but actually finding the place in the maze of higgledy-piggledy streets is a nightmare. Better to call one of the owners in advance who will arrange to pick you up from the docks.

Bishan Lu 11, Gulang Yu. ☎ 0592/206-0920 or 1359/992-4474. yyzpec@soho.com. 53 units. ¥450 ($59/£29) standard room; ¥500 ($65/£33) triple room. Rates include breakfast. No credit cards.

WHERE TO DINE

Unsurprisingly for a port city, Xiamen is known for its fresh fish, and seafood can be found for next to nothing in the back streets of the old quarter or at small, hole-in-the-wall restaurants just up from the dock on Gulang Yu. Lunch will still be swimming or crawling in plastic tubs set out in the street, and is priced by weight. A waterfront **Pizza Hut** on the 24th floor of a tower in Lujiang Dao, visible for miles, has correspondingly excellent views once you get up there.

Popular with university students in the Siming part of town, **M-3** (Li Fang Mi Shi Shang Canting, Xia Da Xi Cun Ding, Wo Zai Lu 14–18; ☎ 0592/899-1820) offers an eclectic range of New York–Tokyo fusion food. Sushi fans will love the creativity that these guys put into their dishes. Highlights include golden dragon roll (salmon roll with cheese; *san wen zi shi juan*) and green dragon roll (eel, cucumber, and avocado; *man yu za xia juan*). Do not forget to finish with a helping of fried ice cream (*zha xue gao*).

Huang Ze He, or peanut soup, from the **Huasheng Tang Dian** (peanut snack bar) on Zhongshan Lu, seems to be the local dish that most tourists seek out, but you will have to battle through crowds of red and white baseball caps to get any. A more relaxing option is to head down to the old harbor where a small eatery turns out equally delicious peanut-based dishes. My favorite was the local-style wonton soup *(bia nshi)* and the tasty noodles *(ban mian)* at Miao Xiang Bian Shi located on Daxue Lu 102 (© **0592/899-1820**), open from 6am to 10:30pm.

The owners of The House, Baihe Lu 10-1 (© **0592/204-4368**), have renovated an original 1920s French-style building and now have a stylish restaurant and bar serving Californian cuisine. Courtyard tables, fine wines, fresh pastas, and some of the best steak in town, as well as chill-out music to go with a chilled-out atmosphere.

YONGDING

About 205km (128 miles) inland from Xiamen, Yongding is a heartland of the **Hakka** people—Han who migrated south from near Kaifeng in five waves beginning more than 1,000 years ago, and who were kept moving around southern China by civil war, famine, and discrimination by earlier Han arrivals. They often ended up with the worst farming land on the highest ground. Unlike other Han, their women did not bind their feet and worked alongside men in the fields, and so tended to marry only other Hakka. They also maintained what they claim is something close to early Chinese but is unintelligible to speakers of Mandarin, Cantonese, and Min Nan Hua.

Now an officially recognized minority, known as the **Kejia** or "guest people," their long exile and continued sense of being outsiders has produced both tangible and intangible benefits for visitors. The Hakka claim to be more hospitable to outsiders than other Chinese, but the need to protect themselves against others has produced the magnificent multistory fortresses called *tulou* or "earth buildings," some home to hundreds, all sharing a single family name.

The *tulou* are spread around nearly 50 counties on the Guangdong-Fujian-Jiangxi border. The concentration easiest to reach, and nowadays, the most commercialized, is at **Hukeng,** where a bus will drop you right outside the ticket office, although you will need to transfer buses at least twice if traveling from Xiamen. A fee of ¥60 ($9/£4.55) includes access to four officially open major *tulou* and another containing a museum, although no one seems to mind if you wander in anywhere else. Helpful English signs are quite common, and there's a primitive hotel in the middle of the village (summer only), but you would be better off having the full experience by staying in an actual *tulou*. Residents with rooms to let (typically for ¥20/$2.60/£1.30 or so) will persistently approach you, as will motorbike and *sanlunche* owners wanting to take you to other villages.

The vast fortresses nestle together on either side of a river in a narrow green valley, and in autumn their khaki tones have splashes of color as crops of plums and persimmons are spread out to dry on flat surfaces. The "earth" is in fact a tamped mixture of sand, lime, and dirt, giving the walls a textured surface. The best-known building is the marvelous circular **Zhencheng Lou** of 1912, consisting of an outer four-story ring with each floor divided into 44 rooms and two halls; an inner, two-story ring divided into eight sections; and two tobacco workshops outside, bringing the total number of rooms to 222. As with other *tulou,* windows to the outside world begin two stories up. Balconies run around the interiors, providing access and light. The inner ring joins at a hall for worshiping ancestors, marriage ceremonies, greeting distinguished guests, and other events. What used to be authentic living space has largely been replaced by tacky souvenir shops selling the same junk as Yangshuo and Li Jiang.

The battered **Huanxing Lou** is not an official sight, but it dates from around 1550 and is the oldest in this village. It has walls more than 1.8m (5 ft.) thick, and two sets of vast and heavy wooden doors, the first secured by a set of wooden beams, and the second by stone ones. The squealing of tussling pigs reveals that the inner ring retains its original use, but it has gaps caused by past flooding. An earthquake a century ago also destroyed one section of the outer ring, and another has lost its inner surface and interior floors. A hole through one section was blasted during the Taiping Rebellion (p. 396). One resident claims that the occupants, numbering 500 only 20 years ago, could survive for a year under siege. There are still 200 residents, all called Li. Persimmons, plums, and vegetables hang out to dry over the balconies of the upper stories, having been washed in the stream outside. The ground floors contain the kitchens, the rooms above are for storage, and the upper two floors are for living and sleeping. But there are few people around under 40—they've already left for accommodations in the new town, or become part of the drifting migrant economy of 150 million or so.

Tulou also come in half-moon, pentangle, "five phoenix," and other shapes. The square, fortresslike **Kuiju Lou**, dating from 1834, is, at 6,000 sq. m (64,583 sq. ft.) even bigger than the circular buildings. It has an interior of brick and wood more like that of a conventional mansion. The 7,000-sq.-m (75,347-sq.-ft.) **Fuyu Lou** of 1880, whose residents are all called Lin, has multiple axes, and a five-story earthen tower at the rear. Its beams and pillars are beautifully carved, and it also has some fine inlaid screens, as well as a teahouse and rooms to let.

The last official *tulou* (although residents don't mind if you wander into several others) is the charming **Rusheng Lou**, built sometime between 1875 and 1908. It's a single 23m (63-ft.) diameter ring-shaped dollhouse in comparison to the others, which have three stories each of 16 rooms. Finally, the **museum** occupies a rectangular *tulou*, where the music of traditional instruments echoes around the two floors of one courtyard, given over to displays of tobacco knives, tools used in building, and photographs of festivals and other *tulou* that may have you planning trips to other villages. You may see dried persimmons being roasted and pressed into cakes—a local specialty called *shibing*.

GETTING THERE   The best route is by **bus** from Xiamen, first to **Longyan** (4 hr.; ¥72/$9.40/£4.70) every 45 minutes from 7am to 6:30pm, and then by Iveco minibus to **Hukeng** (13 departures; 2 hr.; ¥20/$2.60/£1.30) from 7am to 4:50pm. Bear in mind that buses for Longyan depart from the Hubin Bus Station in Xiamen. There is a free shuttle bus (no. 816) to Hubin Lu from the more popular Songbai Bus Station. There is a free shuttle bus from Hukeng to the main entrance of the Earth Houses. There are limited **train** services to **Yongding**, 37km (37km/23 miles) and ¥7 (90¢/45p) by minibus from modern Hukeng, and then a short taxi ride to the old town. But timings are highly inconvenient. The roundhouses are particularly popular with Japanese tourists, and so for those seeking a more comfortable alternative we recommend one of the companies used regularly by the Marco Polo. The example schedule includes 2 days and 1 night. If you should get stuck in Hukeng, there is a standard business hotel called the **Xing He Bing Guan**, Hu Xing Bei Lu, near Zi Ning Bridge, Hukeng Zhen (© 0597/553-1355; ¥80/$10/£5.20). A far better alternative is to stay in one of the Earth Houses themselves such as the Ke Lai Deng Hotel (② **0597/ 553-5286;** www.keldeng.com).

TOURS   Guided tours are available; following are two recommended agencies. For two to three travelers, the **Xiamen Overseas Tourist Co China** (② **0592/212-7638,** 0592/212-7738, or 0592/213-4038; LJW@xmotc.com) charges flat fees for transportation from Xiamen (¥1,600/$200/£100), a guide (¥300/$38/£19), and guesthouse accommodations (¥250/$31/£15 per room). Meals cost ¥50 ($6.50/£3.25) per person per meal, and entry to the *tulou* costs about ¥100 ($13/£6.50) per person. Rates do not apply for Spring Festival, National Day, or the Labor Day holiday. Ask for Mr. Liu Jingwe or Ms. Huo Lufang when booking.

The **Xiamen C&D Travel Agency** (② **0592/211-0294**) offers a similar package that costs ¥1,400 ($182/£91) per person and includes transportation, guesthouse accommodations, guide, and meals for individuals or groups smaller than 10. Contact Ms. Zeng for more information.

WHERE TO STAY & DINE   Owners of lodgings will find you, and you get what you pay for. Insist on clean bedding, but expect a single light bulb, a thermos of boiling water, and a chamber pot to be the sum total of facilities. Make careful note of the locations of the pit toilet and a tap with running water, both down at ground level, before it gets dark. Simple food will be offered, to be eaten in the ground-floor room. Three plain dishes, cooked over wood fires, will cost around ¥20 ($2.60/£1.30). Take supplementary snacks from Xiamen. After dark it's eerily quiet, especially in the now sparsely inhabited **Zhencheng Lou.** Lin Hongyuan (② **0130/6245-7844**) is among those with rooms there; Lin Qinming also has rooms at the **Fuyu Lou** (② **0130/ 6245-7844**). Slightly less basic accommodations can be found in the new town 5km (3 miles) away.

7 Jingde Zhen

Jiangxi Province, 280km (174 miles) NE of Nanchang, 430km (267 miles) E of Wuhan

Did you know that the English word "china" probably derives from Jingde Zhen's former name, Changnan? The place got its big break in the first year in Jingde Reign of Song dynasty (1004–07), when the potters of the town, then known as Changnan, picked up a juicy commission from the emperor Zhen Zong. The royal court decreed that local artisans stamp their bowls and vases with the wording "Made during the Jingde Reign" printed on the bottom of every piece. Hence the city assumed the name of its imperial patron "Jingde Zhen."

By the Ming dynasty, Jingde Zhen had become a major export center. Several hundred kilns turned out hundreds of thousands of pieces each year and, conveniently located not far from the original Ming capital at Nanjing, it continued to keep the emperor and his concubines in teacups. When the capital moved north to Beijing, Jingde Zhen maintained its connection to the court via the waterways of Poyang Lake, the Yangtze, and the Grand Canal. Porcelain now runs deep in Jingde Zhen's history. The layer of discarded porcelain shards and kiln debris under its streets is said to be 9m (30 ft.) thick in places.

Although 17th-century Manchu riots destroyed much of the town, the Yangzi to the north, and river systems leading south to Guangzhou, enabled Jingde Zhen to get its wares around China for sale, and later, via the treaty ports, to an increasingly enthusiastic European market. Imperial support also helped—some kilns were employed solely for the making of wares for the emperors and their officials. The first kiln site to produce white china and to use certain underglaze painting techniques, Jingdezhen reached its peak of technical brilliance during the mid–17th to late 18th century with the gaudy full-colored enamel overglaze illustrations of *famille vert* and *famille rose* china.

The secret, as Jingde Zhen potters had known for more than 1,000 years, lay in using the right combination of clays and feldspars. The most famous of these was kaolin, or china clay, which got its name from the high ridge, or Gao Ling, just north of Jingde Zhen combined with the timber from the surrounding hills as coal caused yellowing in the glaze. Industrialization of the area, which employed around half the town's workforce, soon stripped the hills bare and enough coal was fired to turn the skies black. Just 10 years ago, mass-production kilns began to be converted from coal to gas. The air is much better now and even the porcelain quality has improved thanks to this change in technology.

With Jiang Zemin (he was born nearby) as its champion, Jingde Zhen attracted huge amounts of investment in the 1990s and early 2000s but since big brother lost power, the city has withered as presidential focus has returned to Zhejiang. The best example of this is the enormous museum at the end of Changnan Lu, which is already derelict and falling into disrepair although the old bus station is a depressing reminder that the future of Jingde Zhen is unclear. Rising real estate prices have forced many factories to relocate and the town's reputation as a wholesale center has rapidly been eclipsed by the rising star of Yiwu, in nearby Zhejiang. Much of the city is now run down and depressing, although places like the Sanbao Ceramic Institute definitely seem to be moving in the right direction.

ESSENTIALS

GETTING THERE   The **airport** is only 8km (5 miles) out of town, but it has a very limited number of flights only to Shanghai, Beijing, Xiamen, Chongqing, and Shenzhen. A **shuttle bus** runs to the Jichang Shoupiao Zhongxin (© **0798/822-3907;** ticket office, 8am–5:30pm), in the center of town at Zhu Shan Lu 127. The shuttle fare is ¥5 (65¢/35p) and it leaves for the airport 1½ hours before each flight. A taxi ride costs about ¥20 ($2.60/£1.30). For more choices, head to Nanchang's Changbei Airport, 6 hours north of Jingdezhen.

Rail services are less limited than you might expect for its remote central location: Guangzhou (K221), Kunming (K155), three trains daily from Beijing Xi (West) (K46), one from Beijing, two from Shanghai (2181), two from Xiamen (2521), and two from Fuzhou (K60). However, none start at Jingde Zhen, so ticket availability is limited. Nanchang and Jiujiang, both best reached by express bus from Jingde Zhen, have far more trains. Ticket windows at the station are open from 7:45am to 8pm, with brief breaks.

The **Main Bus Station (Keyun Zhongxin;** © **0798/858-8787)** is on the northwest side of town and is open from 6am to 7pm. Express buses using the highway to Jiujiang and beyond, arrive and depart from here. Destinations include Jiujiang (134km/ 84 miles; 12 departures 7:30am–6:30pm; ¥30/$3.90/£1.95), Nanchang (280km/175 miles; 14 departures 6:30am–7:10pm; ¥60/$9.10/£4.55 for the best bus), and Wuhan (430km/269 miles; four departures 7:30am–4:30pm; ¥100/$13/£6.50), as well as Wenzhou, Hangzhou, and Nanjing. Left luggage doubles as a small store outside the ticket office, charges ¥3 (40¢/20p) per piece, and closes at 6pm. Another bus station (© **0798/ 820-8156**) opposite the railway station, open from 6:20am to 5:30pm, also serves Jiujiang and Nanchang.

GETTING AROUND   **Taxis** are incredibly ugly locally made boxlike Suzukis. Flag-fall of ¥5 (65¢/35p) includes 2km (1¼ miles), after which the fare is ¥1 (15¢/10p) per kilometer up to 6km (3¾ miles), then ¥1.50 (20¢/10p) per kilometer thereafter. From 11pm to 5am the fare is ¥1.80 (25¢/10p). **Buses** charge a ¥1 (15¢/10p) flat fare deposited in the slot. Bus no. K35 starts at the Keyun Zhongxin and goes south past the Jinye Dajiudian and then east along Zhu Shan Zhong Lu. On Zhongshan Nan Lu there are a few cycle shops such as the one owned by Mr. Deng at number 92 (② **0798/ 851-0687**), who will rent out bikes by the day.

FAST FACTS

Banks, Foreign Exchange & ATMs   There's a useful **Bank of China** (open 8am–6pm, to 5:30pm winter) just outside Kaimenzi Hotel on Xing Feng Lu.

Internet Access   *Wangba,* such as the one on the south side of Zhu Shan Lu near the junction of Cidu Da Dao, usually charge ¥2 (25¢/15p) per hour.

Post Office   The main post office (open 8am–7pm summer, to 6:30pm winter) is on Zhu Shan Lu.

Visa Extensions   The **PSB** (open Mon–Fri 8:30–11:30am and 2:50–5:30pm) is on the west side of Cidu Da Dao well south of the Zhu Shan Lu junction, in a tall white building with pink steps.

POTTERING AROUND TOWN

Local authorities are starting to recognize the importance of tourism and, in 2004, first celebrated the area's 1,000th anniversary as an imperial kiln-production center. There is now a ceramics festival every October and a locally maintained website at www.jingdezhen.cov.cn.

Taoci Wenhua Bolanqu (Pottery Culture Exhibition) ⑨   Although run down and desperately in need of a new coat of paint, this is still the best of several exhibi-tions devoted to ceramics, and includes several old kilns, areas demonstrating the pro-duction process, and ancient houses and temples. The site is down a winding country lane called Guyao Lu off an urban main street, providing an abrupt transition from town to countryside. The entrance to the left of the ticket office leads to rebuilt ancient kiln types in reddish brick, and a fine old mansion in local style, with black pillars, white walls, and richly carved and gilded interior beams. Glass cases in its three courtyards hold modest displays of ceramics. English signs guide you around the site, and visitors can even have a try at the ceramics process themselves.

A second entrance to the right of the ticket office leads to an area where, in theory, you can watch the production process in a series of sheds, which begins with pools of clay and continues with racks of pieces in various stages of preparation. But the kiln is no longer fired, there are weeds growing from the clay pits, and this is all for show and shopping. I was especially interested to see that in a location famed for its techni-cal expertise, potters still used hand-driven wheels to throw their clay.

Behind this area, what looks at first like a dry-stone wall is a large pile of firewood built into the shape of a cottage. Pine wood was carefully cut and stacked this way to guard against rain and spontaneous combustion, and to save the cost of building stor-age sheds, but the result is a work of art. The duck's-egg-shaped kiln to the right, one of Jingde Zhen's oldest, occupies only about a quarter of the area of a large barnlike building. The ground floor is a small forest of curved pillars that seem to be largely unfashioned tree trunks, between which are stacked piles of saggars, the rough ceramic outer cases into which pieces were placed for firing. A series of wall-mounted illustrations shows the process.

At the end of the low-ceilinged hall there's a ramp up through a narrow entrance into the arched brickwork of the kiln space itself, where the firewood would have been stacked in patterns depending on the effect required, and saggars containing porcelain requiring different temperatures would have been placed in different positions.

Guyao Lu, Exhibition area (just off Cidu Da Dao). Admission ¥50 ($6.50/£3.25). 8am–5pm. Bus: no. 19 to the end of the route.

San Bao Shuidui (Water-powered Hammers) ✪   A short way into the countryside, some fascinating primitive technology can be seen. Take bus no. K35 (¥1/15¢/10p) to the east (look out for all the porcelain lamp posts and even traffic lights) and alight at the Hutian stop on Hangkong Lu, shortly before the terminus where the bus swings right outside the large red Ri Xin General Merchandise Store; walk on for 2.5km (1½ miles), or take a taxi. The route leads past a development of abandoned half-finished villas (the developer committed suicide in summer 2007) and smokeless chimneys peeping from among the green hills. The *shuidui* can be heard before they are seen, an irregular solid clunking from beneath a thatched hut to the left. In the middle of the town look for the peoples' center with the Chinese opera stage inside; follow a path that crosses a stream and then swings around to the left of the hut. Inside, four giant wooden mallets with long heads and pointed noses, ingeniously driven by a small water wheel and among the last of their kind, pound soggy masses of clay.

Bus: no. K35 to Hutian; follow directions above.

Guan Yao Bowuguan (Imperial Porcelain Museum)   This shabby old museum contains three floors of broken porcelain, all of which is extremely unimpressive. The top floor on the other hand offers a great bird's-eye view on what remains of the old city. For now, small areas of ramshackle housing still survive behind the typical white-tile shopping streets, but are clearly not due to be around much longer.

Zhonghua Bei, near Sheng Li Lu. ✆ 0798/822-3580. Admission ¥15 ($1.95/£1). 9am–5pm.

SHOPPING

Long-distance sleeper buses of the cheaper, more primitive kind leave groaning with vast quantities of rope-bound packages of china. In fact, the North Bus Station is surrounded by wholesale shops. Most hotels and museums sell it, too. Even the KFC has it on display.

Just to the south of Renmin Square (Jing Chang Li Chi Mao Da Sha, Zhu Shan Zhong Lu) is a large five-floor **ceramics market** with some very creative artists among the mass-produced stuff. I was particularly impressed by the deities and mythical figures in **Shang Ping Studio** (✆ 0798/822-2081) on the third floor, as well as the some of the porcelain paintings in **Tan Qing Xuan Zhi** (✆ 0798/823-5677) on the fourth floor.

Even more interesting are the back streets behind Zhejiang Lu. From the train station, head left for the Wen Yuan Business Hotel (Wen Yuan Shang Wu Da Jiu Dian, Tong Zhan Lu 36) with the golden Thai-style temple roof. On the opposite side of the road, venture into one of the small alleys to find yourself in a rabbit warren of side streets and small wholesalers. Here you will find the more exotic lines such as the Cultural Revolution reproductions, where the Red Guards stand atop kneeling intellectuals wearing dunce caps and placards, with slogans such as "Kill the Capitalist."

For all China's claims of development, the sheer number of coolies dragging back-breaking carts of pots and plates shows that technology has not reached many areas of logistics and distribution at least.

WHERE TO STAY

The largest and most expensive hotel in town is the four-star **Kaimenzi Dajiudian** (© **0798/857-77770;** it's the same company that supplies all the gas in Jingde Zhen) located in the old Telecom Building on Xing Feng Lu, but it would not be my first choice. Newer and more centrally located is the **Holy Mountain Hotel (Sheng Shan Jiudian;** Zhu Shan Xi Lu 5; © **0798/838-8888;** fax 0798/852-6666), which looks like a Bauhaus box hospital from the outside but has nicely appointed rooms inside. Standard rooms are ¥366 ($48/£24), and suites ¥788 to ¥1,588 ($102–$206/£51–£103). The usual credit cards are accepted, but there's no foreign exchange.

Of the many budget options along the main street, Zhu Shan Xi Lu, the soon-to-be three-star **Binjiang Binguan** at no. 19 (© **0798/703-2288;** fax 0798/703-2266) is the best choice, refurbished in summer 2007. Due to the construction I got a the bargain price of ¥60 ($9/£4.55) for a standard room, but this will probably double by the time you read this. This hotel has a nice riverside location; look out for the local opera sessions that take place outside under the bridge during the evenings. April through November is the busy season.

Sanbao Ceramic Art Institute (San Bao Tao Yi Yan Xiu Yuan) ★★★ (Finds   This

is an artists' retreat more than a hotel, but the rural location is fantastic and the owner, Jackson Li, is an expert in porcelain, ready to answer any and all questions. The institute stretches across a restored porcelain workshop complete with ancient kilns, water hammers, and duck pond. At one end Jackson has his own impressive office and studio. In the center are various workshops and studios for visiting artists, and at the other end are simple but authentic accommodations with shared facilities. Book early, as this place is very popular due to its reasonable prices (¥150/$20/£9.75 per night per person, full board) and is often filled with creative types from all over the world.

Sanbao Taoyi Cun, near Hutian (¥5/65¢/35p from the bus station by moto taxi). © **0798/849-7505.** www.china sanbao.org.

WHERE TO DINE

Small eateries abound, but hygiene does not seem to be a priority and even I—with a cast-iron stomach from 10 years of being in China—did not have the guts to try any of them. **Yilong Dajiudian** (Cidu Da Dao 908; © **0798/833-3333;** open 6:30–9:30am, 5–9pm, and 9:30pm–2am), next to the Customs Office, looks more like a hotel than a restaurant but offers a wide selection of *Gan cai* (Jiangxi dishes) and Chinese standards. The hot dishes (Jiangxi food is spicy) are labeled *huo la*—fiery hot. Try *sangna niurou,* "sauna" beef—tender slices in a garlicky, peppery oil, served in a clay pot and cooked by putting small heated stones in the liquid. The first floor has plenty of other dishes on display to make choosing easier, but bear in mind that this is not a cheap place and a bill of ¥200 ($26/£13) for two should be expected. **KFC** is now on Zhu Shan Lu, as is the copycat **CFC** or China's Fried Chicken, with identical typeface on the logo and I think even better chicken wraps than the original.

UNDC (Di Ou) Coffee Shop (Changnan Da Dao; © **0798/851-8768;** www. diocoffee.com; open 11am–2am) has free wireless for customers and a huge menu of Chinese and Western dishes to choose from with the business sets seeming to be the best value. The staff here are outstanding, with one little waitress running after me in the street to return the tip that I had left, explaining that in China "this is not the custom." Statues at the end of Zhu Shan Jie on the opposite corner show the process of working the local clay, blowing on glazes, carrying items to kilns, and more.

8 Guangzhou

Guangdong Province, 163km (102 miles) NW of Hong Kong, 165km (103 miles) NE of Macau

Guangzhou has recently become the workshop of the world. In and around its satellite cities, there are more assembly lines, factories, and mass production than anywhere else on the planet. Visitors seeking nature, history, or even culture are going to be sorely disappointed as Guangzhou is all about one thing—profit. Even so, this massive concentration of commerce provides plenty of interesting color for those who know where to look. Ignore all those remarkably dull sights glorifying the revolutionary credentials of the city and seek out instead what the Cantonese currently have passions for: business and food.

ESSENTIALS

GETTING THERE   Guangzhou's New **Baiyun International Airport** (CAN) has been in operation since August 5, 2004, but is barely in Guangzhou anymore. It's way out in the sticks, in a white-tiled cluster called **Hua Du,** 28km (17 miles) away from Haizhu Square, the center of Guangzhou City. Don't be surprised if your taxi driver asks for the ridiculous sum of ¥150 ($20/£9.75) just to get out of town. If you are arriving later than 10pm, taxis are particularly bad about not wanting to run on the meter and charging exorbitant amounts.

Fortunately, there are plenty of regular **airport buses** to dozens of locations within the city. Seven main bus routes traverse Guangzhou but nos. 1 and 2 will probably satisfy the short-term visitor. No. 1 goes to the old station and no. 2 goes through Tian He and past the big hotels on Huanshi Lu. Fares range from ¥10 ($1.30/65p) to ¥30 ($3.90/£1.95) by distance. There are direct buses heading for Zhuhai at ¥80 ($10/£5.20) per person, running approximately every 2½ hours. The last bus leaves at about 8:30pm. For more information, contact the **Baiyun Port Bus Service** (© 020/3129-8077; http://newsgd.com/specials/airportguide/airportqna/200407300080.htm). The no. 3 metro line connecting the airport with the city might be open when you read this; then again, this is China.

Tip: For those heading to Hong Kong from elsewhere in China, it's often considerably cheaper to fly here or (even better) to Shenzhen instead, and then take a bus, train, or boat.

Guangzhou is also connected internationally to more than 70 domestic cities and over 20 international cities. Direct international flights are to Singapore, Kuala Lumpur, Melbourne, Bangkok, Osaka and Hong Kong Amsterdam, Bangkok, Fukuoka, Jakarta, Los Angeles, Melbourne, Osaka, Phnom Penh, Seoul, Singapore, Sydney, and Tokyo.

Since March 2007, passengers who pass directly through the territory of China on an international service or stay in Guangzhou less than 24 hours do not need a visa. They must however have a connecting flight and a booked seat.

As elsewhere, tickets are best bought from agents rather than directly from airlines. **CITS** (© 020/8669-0179 air tickets, or 020/8666-4661 train tickets; Mon–Fri 8:30am–6:30pm, Sat–Sun 9am–5pm) to the right of the main railway station as you face it, is unusually helpful, with some English spoken. Air ticket prices can be bargained down.

Guangzhou

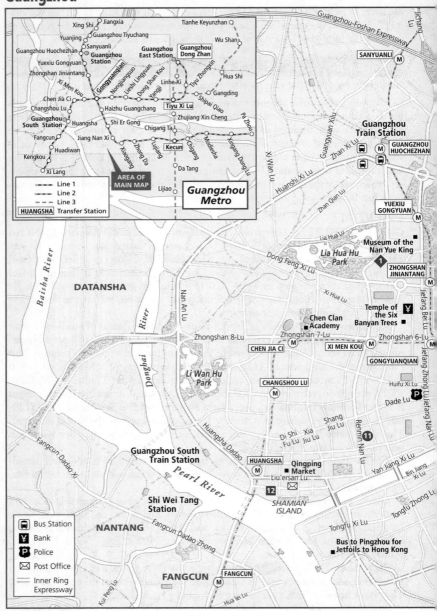

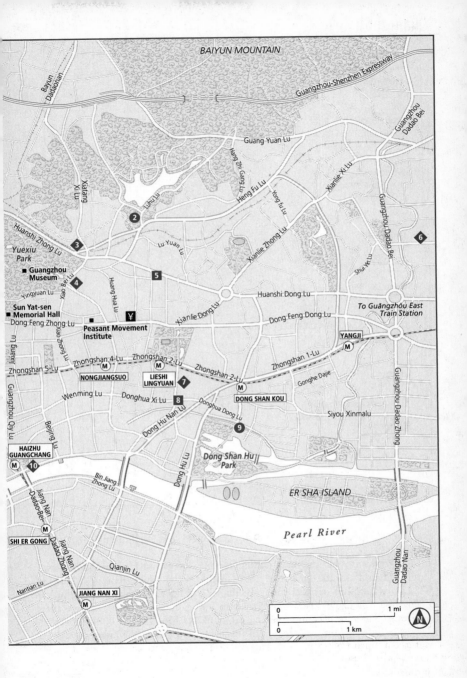

BAIYUN MOUNTAIN

Guangzhou-Shenzhen Expressway

Bayun Dadaohan

Guang Yuan Lu

Guangzhou Dadao Bei

Xiatang Xi Lu

Hang Zhi Gang Lu

Heng Fu Lu

Yong Fu Lu

Xianlie Xi Lu

Luhu Lu ②

Huanshi Zhong Lu

③ Lu Yuan Lu

Xianlie Zhong Lu

Shui Yin Lu

⑥

Yuexiu Park

■ **Guangzhou Museum** ④

Xiao Bei Lu

Huang Hua Lu

⑤

Huanshi Dong Lu

Yingyuan Lu

■ **Sun Yat-sen Memorial Hall**

Dong Feng Zhong Lu

Xianlie Dong Lu

Dong Feng Dong Lu

To Guǎngzhōu East Train Station

¥

■ **Peasant Movement Institute**

Beijing Lu

YANGJI Ⓜ

Zhongshan 4-Lu

Zhongshan 2-Lu Ⓜ

Zhongshan 2-Lu

Zhongshan 1-Lu

Guangzhou Dadao Zhong

Zhongshan 5-Lu

NONGJIANGSUO Ⓜ

LIESHI LINGYUAN Ⓜ ⑦

Gonghe Dajie

Wenming Lu

Donghua Xi Lu ⑧

DONG SHAN KOU

Donghua Dong Lu

Guangzhou Qiy Lu

Dong Hu Nan Lu

Siyou Xinmalu

⑨

HAIZHU GUANGCHANG Ⓜ ⑩

Dong Shan Hu Park

Jiang Nan Dadao Bei

Bin Jiang Zhong Lu

ER SHA ISLAND

SHI ER GONG Ⓜ

Jiang Nan Dadao Zhong

Pearl River

Guangzhou Dadao Nan

Qianjin Lu

Nantian Lu

JIANG NAN XI Ⓜ

0   1 mi

0   1 km

N

Guangzhou Key

ACCOMMODATIONS ■

The Garden Hotel 5
(Huāyuán Jiǔdiàn)
花园酒店

Globelink Hotel) 8
(Quán Qiú Tong Dà Jiǔdiàn
全球通大酒店

White Swan Hotel 12
(Bái Tiānēé Bnguǎn)
白天鹅宾馆

DINING ◆

Běi Yuán Jiǔjiā 4
北园酒家

Dōng Běi Rén 1
东北人

Dōng Jiāng Haǐ Xiān Dà Jiǔ Loú 3 10
东江海鲜大酒楼

Japan Fusion 6
中森名菜日本料理

Suì Yín Cháng Fěn Diàn 7
(Cháng Fěn Fast Food Shop)
穗银肠粉店

ATTRACTIONS ●

Guǎngzhōu Art Museum 2
广州艺术博物馆

Hé Qún Dà Shà 9
(Hé Qún Building)
合群大厦

Zhuàng Yuán Fǎng 11
状元坊

For general airport inquiries in Mandarin, Cantonese, and English, call ☏ **020/360-66999.**

Most **trains** arrive at the main railway station **Guangzhou Huochezhan** (known locally as Lao Zhan, the old station 159, Huanshi Xi Lu, Guangzhou; ☏ **020/613-57222**), which has services from Beijing Xi, Chengdu, Xi'an, Shijiazhuang, Zhengzhou, Chongqing, Lanzhou, Wenzhou, and many more cities. There are a few services to Shenzhen. For information, call ☏ **020/6135-7412** or 020/6135-8952. There's an information counter toward the right-hand end of the railway station as you face it, open from 5am to midnight. The 24-hour ticket windows are at the far right-hand end. Buy up to 12 days in advance. The 24-hour left-luggage windows are in the middle.

Direct trains from **Hong Kong** arrive at **Guangzhou Dong Zhan (East Station;** Linhe Zhong Lu, Tianhe District; © **020/6134-6222**), which is conveniently at the end of the first metro line (exit D). This station is on the express line from Beijing Xi through Jiujiang with direct trains that continue to Hong Kong on alternate days. There are also direct services to Changchun, Tianjin, Qingdao, Nanchang, and other cities. There are seven train departures a day for **Hong Kong** between 9:50am and 5:20pm; the trip takes 1½ to 2 hours and costs from HK$190 (US$23/£11). For more information, see www.kcrc.com/eng/services/services/itts_shedule.asp. There's also a very high-speed train service to **Shenzhen,** with departures every few minutes, some of which cover the 139km (87 miles) in under an hour and drop you right next to the border crossing to Hong Kong at Luo Hu/Lo Wu. (A few slower services run to and from the main railway station.) The railway station has a customer service center (open 5:30am–11:40pm), a number of air ticket agents (some surprisingly competitive), and a counter selling tickets for Shanghai, Taiyuan, Jiujiang, and Beijing Xi (West). The main ticket windows, open from 5:50am to 9:40pm with short breaks, are set back on the right, while the left-luggage office (open 8:30am–6:30pm) has moved to the central concourse. The Hong Kong ticket office (open 7:30am–6pm) is at the far end of the concourse, upstairs on the right. The entrance to Hong Kong trains, via Customs, is just beyond that.

Guangzhou has multiple **long-distance bus stations.** The **Liuhua Chezhan** (open 5am–10:30pm) is reached by an underpass across the station forecourt and to the right. It has buses to Shenzhen (15 departures 6am–10:30pm; ¥60/$7.80/£3.90; and a few more expensive services); and to Zhuhai (60 departures 5:45am–10pm; ¥65/$8.50/£4.20). From the far right-hand corner of the station forecourt as you leave it, turn right along Huanshi Xi Lu, and the 24-hour **Sheng Qiche Keyun Zhan (Guangdong Provincial Long-distance Bus Station)** is a couple of minutes farther on the right. Buses here are generally bound for Hunan, Jiangxi, Fujian, and Guangxi and cities in Guangdong Province. It has services to Shenzhen (¥60/$7.80/£3.90) every 12 minutes from 6:15am to 11pm; to Zhuhai Gong Bei for Macau (¥55/$7.20/£3.60) every 20 minutes from 6:30am to 8:30pm; and to Kaiping (¥45/$5.90/£2.90) every 40 minutes from 6:30am to 7pm. There are also services to Guilin, Nanning, and Beihai. The **Shi Qiche Keyun Zhan** opposite, over the footbridge, has more departures to the same destinations.

There are also direct bus services to **Hong Kong airport,** picking up at the China Hotel, White Swan, Garden Hotel, International Hotel, Holiday Inn, and other hotels (eight services 5:45am–4:25pm; HK$250/US$33/£16; buses to Guangzhou depart 10:05am–5:15pm from the CTS counter at Hong Kong Airport; call © **020/8333-6888,** ext. 5384, or 852/2764 9803 in Hong Kong). Buses also run from the Garden Hotel to Hung Hom Station or Prince Edward MTR in Hong Kong; there are 16 departures from 8am to 7:15pm, and the cost is HK$120 ($16/£7.80). There are also services to Macau two to three times daily for HK$53 (US$7/£3.50).

Unfortunately, nearly all of the **ferry services** to and from Hong Kong have been discontinued, even though the roads become more and more congested every day. Boats no longer depart from Guangzhou, only from some of the satellite towns such as Nansha, Panyu, and Shunde. The Garden Hotel still has shuttles to Nanhai where there is still a boat to Hong Kong that takes about 2½ hours. Shuttle buses leave the Garden Hotel at 9am and 4pm and the cost of the service is ¥170 ($22/£11), ¥180 ($16/£7.80) for first class. Call the Garden Hotel for more information (© **020/8333-8989**).

GETTING AROUND   Taxi fares are among China's most expensive with a flagfall of ¥7 (90¢/50p) including 2.3km (1¼ miles), then ¥2.60 (30¢/15p) per kilometer up to 15km (9 miles), then 50% more. There are no extra nighttime charges, but beware the 5-to-7pm rush hour, which will add significantly to your costs.

The **metro** is the most convenient way to get through Guangzhou's heavy traffic but due to pathetic political wranglings, it completely misses many key areas of the city, notably the mainly Hong Kong–invested downtown area around the Garden Hotel. Much of the new development has simply been added on to the original lines, with new stations and extensions becoming very confusing. The useful line no. 1 (yellow on maps) runs from Xilang in the Fangcun District in southwest Guangzhou, passes Shamian Island (Huangsha Station) and two or three other major sights, and ends up at Guangzhou East railway station. Line no. 2 (yellow) opened in 2003, runs from Sanyuanli in the Baiyun District to Wanshengwei in the Haizhu District and will eventually reach the current airport. It passes the main railway station and one or two useful hotels. Line 3 (gold) runs from the East Railway Station to Panyu Square; with a branch that runs from Tianhe Bus Station to West Tiyu Road via Gangding. Subway Line 4 (green) runs from Wanshengwei to Huangge including the Daxue Cheng (University Town) Special Section which has only five stops from Wanshengwei to Xinzao. The mayor recently announced that he planned to have a whopping 255km (158 miles) of new lines by 2010.

Tickets cost ¥2 to ¥8 (25¢–$1/10p–50p) according to the distance to be traveled, as shown on a color-coded sign above ticket machines. Stored-value Yang Cheng Tong cards allowing multiple journeys are strangely unavailable from the metro station ticket desks, but can be found at the laundry chain that is always close by. The system runs from around 6am to 11pm. Oddly, the metro stations are fairly well signposted, but the entrances are overly discreet. There are on-board announcements that sometimes resemble English; for example "Please mind the doors" has become "Please take care not to be nipped!" Ordinary buses charge a flat fare of ¥1 (15¢/10p); newer air-conditioned versions charge a flat fare of ¥2 (25¢/15p).

In April 2007, six water buses began to run along the channel of the Pearl River in Guangzhou, supplying residents and tourists with a more convenient transport service. There are four ports along the line: Zhongda Passenger Port, Tianzi Passenger Port, Xidi Passenger Port, and Fangcun Passenger Port. The whole journey only takes 25 minutes; the ticket is ¥1 (15¢/10p) to ¥2 (25¢/15p).

VISITOR INFORMATION   Guangzhou supports several free magazines that tend to be more advertorial than useful information, obtainable from hotel lobbies and expat hangouts. They contain reviews of new restaurants, clubs, and bars (usually paid for), and intermittently accurate listings. *That's Guangzhou* is marginally better than *South China City Talk,* but not much since the English owner was pushed out in a very hostile takeover by the Chinese authorities. *Guangzhou Today* is advertorials from cover to cover.

A locally run agency used to dealing with the needs of foreigners is **Xpat Travel Planners,** Flat E, 20/F, Regent House, Taojin Lu 50 (© 020/8358-6961; xpats@ public.guangzhou.gd.cn).

American Express (© 020/8331-1311; fax 020/8331-1616) has a branch in the office building of the Guangdong International Hotel. It's open Monday through Friday from 9am to 5pm. For official tourist information, call © 020/8668-7051; for complaints call © 020/8667-8043; and for "emergency rescue" (not to worry, that's

just the unfortunate Chinese to English translation for "emergency services") call
© **020/8666-6330.**

FAST FACTS

Banks, Foreign Exchange & ATMs   Most of the many branches of the **Bank of
China** (open 9am–noon and 2–5pm) have forex services and ATMs accepting foreign
cards, including the branch inside the Garden Hotel and the nearby Friendship Store.
But be prepared to wait. Nearly all banks now have a ticket system like you find at a
cheese counter. Just take a number and wait your turn. There's a newly opened branch
of the **Hongkong and Shanghai Bank** at the front of the Garden Hotel on.

Consulates   The consulate of **Australia** is now on the 12/F Zhujiang New City
Development Centre, 3, Linjiang Lu (© **020/3814-0111;** fax 020/3814-0112). The
consulate of **Canada** is in Suite 801, Wing C in the China Hotel (© **020/8666-0569,**
ext. 0; fax 020/8667-2421). The **U.K.** consulate is on the second floor of the Guangdong International Hotel, Huan Shi Dong Lu 339 (© **020/8335-1354;** www.uk.
cn/gz). The **U.S. Consulate** has moved to 5/F Phase 2, Tian Yu Gardens, 136-142 Lin
He Zhong Lu 1 (© **020/8620-8121**). Onward visas for **Vietnam** are available on the
second floor of B Building North at the Landmark Hotel, Qiaoguang Lu 8 (© **020/
8330-5910**); hours are Monday through Friday from 9am to noon and 2 to 5pm.
Cambodia, Denmark, France, Italy, Japan, Korea, Malaysia, The Philippines, Poland,
Thailand, and The Netherlands also have consulates in Guangzhou.

Internet Access   There are Internet cafes everywhere, but most of them are dark,
dingy places populated by sad locals. A far cleaner alternative is on the second floor of
the Guangzhou library, just outside the Lieshi Lingyuan subway stop. No smoking is
allowed and the keyboards are still legible—all for just ¥2 (25¢/15p) per hour. Deposit
is (¥50/$6.50/£3.30); have your passport with you in case its requested. It's open
Thursday to Tuesday (9am–5pm) and gets very busy on the second Monday of the
month when access is free between 9am and noon; on Wednesdays, you can head to
the nearby Zhongshan library (Zhongshan Lu 4) instead. Dial-up is © **163,** or the
faster © **96169.**

Post Office   There's a useful post office (open Mon–Sat 9am–5pm) in San Jie on
Shamian if you happen to be staying in that part of town, but for sending anything
bulky, try the branch outside the old railway station, where both of the packing guys
are extremely helpful and speak excellent English.

Visa Extensions   The **PSB** is at Jiefang Nan Lu 155 (© **020/8311-5808;** open
Mon–Fri 8:50–11:30am and 2:30–5pm) at the corner of Dade Lu. Pick up an application form upstairs on floor M1 (open 8–11:15am and 2:20–4:45pm) then continue
past various travel agencies mostly selling overseas travel to Chinese (air tickets from
Guangzhou and Hong Kong airports) to the fourth floor, where there can be long
lines. Extensions take 5 working days to obtain.

EXPLORING GUANGZHOU

History buffs and culture vultures may well be disappointed in Guangzhou as this city
moves to a very different beat, the vibrant pulse of international trade. The art museum
is one of the best in the country and is definitely worth a visit, but apart from that the
real highlights are the markets, the vast bazaars, and the huge numbers of people
crammed into this small river delta. Those making a brief trip to Guangzhou from Hong
Kong should concentrate on the commerce rather than the culture. The Provincial

Museum, the Sun Yat-sen Memorial Hall, the Peasant Movement Institute, and other revolutionary sites are all dull and avoidable.

SHAMIAN ISLAND ⚑

Forced to relinquish a permanent trading base to the hated barbarians (Westerners) at the end of the First Opium War in 1841, the Guangzhou authorities probably snickered as they palmed off a sandbar to the British and French. Perhaps they snickered less when it was promptly bunded (made secure with artificial embankments); was provided with proper streets, drainage, and imposing buildings; and became home to a prosperous foreign enclave with everything from tennis courts to a yacht club. The rest of Guangzhou lacked even properly surfaced roads well into the 20th century. Resentment from the local authorities manifested itself in dictatorial regulations, restricting traders solely to the island (barely half the size it is today and resulting in the word "cantonment") and forbidding wives or families. There was a death penalty for anybody attempting to learn Chinese, and the only time that the foreigners were allowed to leave the island was by rowboat to visit the notorious flower boats upriver, lucrative sidelines for the same Cantonese merchants who monopolized the vast opium networks that quickly brought China to its knees.

Shamian (metro: Huangsha on line no. 1) still retains some of its former grandeur in the mansions which served as foreign residences, business premises, banks, and consulates. The mansions were taken over by dozens of families after 1949, but they were recently restored, in many cases to their former splendor, with each major building labeled as to its former purpose. Now partly pedestrianized, its broader boulevards are like long thin gardens with a lot of topiary. A line of bars and cafes on the southwest side with views over the Pearl River serves modern expats. Dozens of small businesses close to the modern White Swan Hotel aim to entrap those on organized tours who wander out of the hotel by themselves and think they are being brave. Souvenir stalls, tailoring stores, and teahouses all have inflated prices, and all offer "special discounts" to those with children—the U.S. consulate on the island is the one specializing in adoption matters, and adoptive parents fan out from here to collect their new daughters (almost always daughters) and return to do the paperwork. One or two of the old mansions are roofless and boarded up, but others are open as restaurants, shops, or hotels.

CD Graveyard (Gou Wu Zhong Xing) ⚑⚑ *Finds*   While many Western tourists

like to stock up here on pirated CDs and DVDs, little realizing that they are funding the same crime gangs that smuggle immigrants in containers and sell women into slavery, locals prefer to purchase the real thing at even lower prices. Gou Wu Zhong Xing, for example, has about 30 such shops on the fourth floor and has been popularized in the last few years by anti-copyright activists working to undermine the RIAA and the MPAA. The big recording companies take any surplus stock, and cook the books so that they can profit at least three times, first cheating the IRS by claiming tax breaks on supposedly destroyed stock, second by charging the original artists for product unsold, and third by illegally selling the same stock to Chinese jobbers who buy in container quantities. For a long time now, these *Dakou* (this means "big mouth" and reflects the way that some CDs are notched or cut) CD markets, as they are known locally, have become veritable Aladdin's caves for politically active eBayers. Music and movies arrive regularly from all over the world and yet on average most cost between only ¥5 (65¢/35p) and ¥10 ($1.30/65p.)

Shi Pai, Gou Wu Zhong Xing 4/F. Metro: Gangding on line no. 4. Walk east from the subway past the large hospital and over the pedestrian footbridge. The entrance to Gou Wu Zhong Xing is between the Watson's and the McDonald's.

Haizhu Square Wholesale Market

What was once a stronghold of revolutionary fervor (as can be seen from the rifle-thrusting monument in the center of the round-about) has succumbed entirely to the forces of the free market and is now one of the most colorful markets in Asia, a vast area that stretches from Haizhu Square almost as far down as Shamian Island. Apart from the usual toys, furnishings, and electronics, this is a great place to find many of those souvenirs found in tourist shops around the rest of the country, but here at wholesale prices. A short walk to the west along Yide Lu brings you to even more markets, with vast areas specializing in stationery, toys, and even dried foods. It is a shame that most people stop off in Guangzhou at the beginning of their trip into China, as this is the ultimate shopping stop and would be much more suitable on the return journey.

Metro: Haizhu Sq. on line no. 1.

Zhuang Yuan Fang

Many visitors come to China and focus solely on relics and artifacts from the purported 5,000 years of history. Here instead is a chance to see China's youth, the so-called Q generation, up close and personal. Originally filled with shops devoted to costumes, instruments, and props for Cantonese opera, only one or two of this kind of emporium remains. The rest have been taken over by innumerable fashion stores, and this street is now the place where many trends and fads are started. Unfortunately, the current fashions seem to be West Coast hip-hop–meets–East Coast bag lady. Spiky-haired teenagers puff on orange and strawberry cigarettes while others chomp on stinky fried tofu or even stinkier durian ice cream. Don't be ashamed by the fact that you are probably the oldest person in a 5km (3-mile) radius.

Look for the large new gateway on the left as you head south from Huifu Lu on Renmin Nan Lu.

Guangzhou Old Railway Station

Here is a rare chance to see what China is undoubtedly most famous for: its enormous population. While other tourist high-lights such as Tian'an Men Square are usually devoid of life, here is a large public square that perpetually teems with humanity. Certainly one of the best opportunities to visualize what a population of 1.6 billion really looks like. At Chinese New Year, this square is awash with more than 100,000 people a day, and ticket queues stretch kilometers away into the suburbs. Even at the nonpeak times, being in this area is like being outside the stadium doors as a rock concert finishes and the audience pours out. The area has a bad reputation for crime but this is rather undeserved, especially compared to the new East Station and the central business district of Tian He, where gangs of pickpockets roam openly and arrogant motorists make the simple act of crossing the road one of the most high-risk events of your entire holiday. Here at the old station, there are at least 18 kinds of uniformed security as well as patrol cars ranging from converted golf carts to oversize SUVs. Business people from all over the province and much of the rest of the country converge here at the vast wholesale clothing markets nearby. Just opposite is Bai Ma, probably one of the largest ladies' clothing whole-sale markets in the world; and close by around the corner from the Provincial Bus Station is the fake-watch market, the source of all those shady, conspiratorial vendors that whisper "Copy Rolex, sir?" Simply find a vantage point and look on in awe, as immense flows of human traffic surge endlessly by.

Huadiwan Few tourists venture south of the river, but those who do are always impressed with Huadiwan in the Fangcun District. As you emerge from the subway, head for the furniture stores that feature carving and carpentry from all over the country. This soon transforms into specialist aquaria stores, then more conventional pet stores, and across the road into the bird market. This merges toward the main road with a horticultural section that includes exquisite bonsai trees (known locally as *penjing*, the original Chinese name), and a large number of stores featuring "viewing stones," oddly shaped rocks and stones that often resemble dragons, deities, and wild animals.

Huadiwan Subway Station on line no. 1.

THE LEANING TOWERS OF KAIPING ★★

Much of southern Guangdong is a sprawl of untidy and often grim manufacturing, where sweated labor produces the world's toys and other sundries. But Kaiping, 140km (85 miles) southwest of Guangzhou, 164km (102 miles) from the Macau border, and also reachable by sea directly from Hong Kong, is a step back in time. Peasants in conical straw hats bend over their plants, and position hand-powered threshing machines on shoulder poles, much as in other provinces. But here they often toil beneath the gaze of extraordinary towers called *diaolou*, which are partly Portuguese Gothic, like *Citizen Kane's* Xanadu broken into nearly 2,000 fragments and sprinkled across the county. Some squat brick fortresses dating from the 17th century were intended as places of refuge for whole villages. But more alien watchtowers were mostly built by Chinese who traveled out through the treaty ports and returned wealthy in the late 19th and early 20th centuries to buy land, build a house, and marry. Simple concrete towers were merely lookout points intended to provide warning of approaching bandits, but by the 1920s these had evolved into massive fortified residences up to nine stories high, sprouting turrets and loopholes, balconies and cupolas, borrowed from half-understood European styles encountered everywhere from Macau to Manila. Of around 3,000 originals, 1,833 still stand, towering over almost every village. A representative sample can be visited in a day by taxi, or Kaiping town can used as a base for exploring by public transport and on foot.

There are around 50 buses daily to Kaiping from Guangzhou (about 2 hr.; last bus back at 6pm; ¥40/$5.20/£2.60), and eight from the Macau border at Zhuhai Gong Bei (2½ hr.; last bus back at 6:30pm; ¥45/$7.20/£3.60). A representative sample of towers can be seen in a day by chartering a taxi in Kaiping or, with an early start, en route between Macau and Guangzhou. There are also nine bus services from Shenzhen (299km/187 miles; ¥65/$8.50/£4.20). Kaiping makes a far more pleasant entry point to the mainland from Hong Kong than Shenzhen does, and there's a daily high-speed **catamaran** service from Hong Kong's China (HK) Ferry Terminal at 8:30pm (4 hr 10 min.; from HK$192/US$25/£13) to Kaiping's Sanbu port, just east of the center (taxi around ¥15/$1.95/£1), with the return to Hong Kong at 1:30am. See **www. cksp.com.hk** for more information.

The oldest surviving *diaolou* is the **Yinglong Lou** at **San Men Li,** 15 minutes west on the main road and passed by many local buses. A narrow pine-lined path leads to the village, and the tower is through a narrow passage between ancient houses. It's a three-story solid brick place of refuge, the lower two reddish stories built sometime between 1436 and 1449, and the upper gray one added in 1919. The villagers suffered serious flooding in 1884 and 1908, took refuge in the upper stories, and survived. Their descendants are pleased by your interest and very proud that they kept their

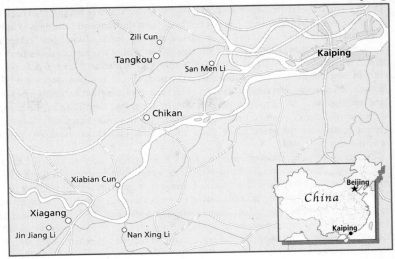

diaolou when everyone else knocked theirs down (brick can be recycled for other uses—concrete cannot, so most survivors are of later date); they may unlock the tower so you can climb the bare interior.

The largest single collection of *diaolou* is at **Zili Cun.** Almost any bus passing San Men Li will drop you at the right-hand turn toward **Tangkou,** where there's a convenience store and some small restaurants. Motorbikes here will take you to Zili Cun, turning right again where there's a gas station after 4km (2½ miles), and then going through Tangkou. Most buses from Kaiping drop you at the gas station (every 20 min.; ¥4/50¢/25p), from where it's a 5-minute walk into Tangkou and a 45-minute walk beyond that on a country lane that swings left into Zili Cun at the last moment. Or you can stay on the bus until a closer stop, when you'll be pointed vaguely across the paddies and duck ponds to a visible cluster of towers. Taxis from Kaiping charge about ¥70 ($9.10/£4.55) per hour. They can also take you to Zili Cun and wait for 1 hour for ¥80 ($10/£5.20). There is now an entrance fee of ¥30 ($3.90/£1.95), as well as separate fees for some of the individual towers.

The 15 towers that are close together here, like a miniature city, are scheduled to be the first developed for tourism—a new road big enough to handle tour buses is being built. This is a very impressive group of towers, with little stone paths weaving through the marshy ground on which they stand; the marsh no doubt contributes to the slight lean some of them display. Wooden signs indicate a viewing route, but you won't exactly be elbowing your way through hordes of other visitors, although there's sometimes a pause as a gaggle of ducks crosses from one damp patch to another. Villagers chop sugar cane, geese seek shade beneath banana palms, and crabs cluster beneath bridges. Most of the towers are three or four stories high, made of concrete, their top stories decked with arches and balustrades, ornamental urns, and turreted corners. Perhaps the most elegant is the taller **Mingshi Lou,** on the right toward the rear of the village, which has been opened as a museum, as it retains late-Qing furnishings and a top-floor ancestral shrine. The original Chinese owner had three wives, one of them a Westerner. When he died in the U.S., his relatives bought him back to be buried here in a glass coffin. The last bus back from the Tangkou turning is at 6pm.

Li Garden (¥60/$7.80/£3.90) is located in the rich fields of Genghua village of Tangkou town 20km (12 miles) from the downtown area of Kaiping, and was built in 1926 the late Mr. Xie Weili, an overseas Chinese who resided in the United States; it takes in much of the Chinese traditional garden architecture and integrates it with the features of European and American villas of its time, a successful combination of Chinese and the West. In October 1999 Ms. Xie Yu Yaoqiong, the widow of the garden owner, wrote a letter to entrust the People's Government of Kaiping City to administer the garden for 50 years. Since then, the famous garden has been completely renewed and expanded.

Farther southwest, about 35 minutes from Kaiping on buses heading to **Chikan** (¥8/$1/50p), **Xiabian Cun** has a rather different tower, the five-story **Shi Lu** of 1924, to the left as you enter the village. Cement, unknown in mainland China, had to be imported from Hong Kong at considerable expense, and the ingenious alternative was to make a tower of rammed earth, sugar, lime, and sticky rice. The clayey red soil has left its warm color in the pink-ocher walls, and the pits left by its extraction are now fishponds beside a row of ancient housing. Limited supplies of cement were reserved for the tower's top, with its balcony, pepper-potted corners, and domed pavilion.

Farther southwest at **Xiangang**, 50 minutes and ¥4 (50¢/25p) from Kaiping, are perhaps the oddest tower and the most impressive tower of all. Motorbikes meet buses, but it's much more enjoyable to do this on foot. The first tower is about a 2.5km (1½-mile) walk. Cross the river bridge with views of river-going vessels, homes to their owners, with firewood stacked on their decks, and turn left onto Dong Long Lu (East Dragon St.). After a short distance, the path passes a gate and shrinks to a track before reaching the unspoiled and friendly little village of Dong Xi Cun. The third narrow alley between the traditional houses leads to a vast European-influenced mansion, whose owners went back overseas again and are now said by the villagers to be in San Francisco. Carry straight on and descend to a decent paved road. Turn left, making a note of where to turn off on your return. Passing the occasional armchair grave, water buffalo wallowing in the paddies, rice, and buffalo dung laid out to dry on the road, you reach the first major village on the left; the village of **Nan Xing Li** is beyond this one on the right. Here's China's answer to Italy's Torre di Pisa, a slender six-story concrete finger called the **Nan Xing Xie Lou (Leaning Tower of Nan Xing),** 20m (60 ft.) high and inclined severely but very photogenically to one side. It is reflected attractively in the village pond. The tower's top is out of alignment, with an annual lean increase of 2 centimeters (⅘ in.)—so though it has survived since 1902, you'd better see it while you can. Even when just completed, it was already leaning so far the watchman had to put bricks under one side of his bed.

Returning to Xiangang, turn right and recross the bridge, then turn left and walk straight out the other side of town; the narrow road wriggles between other *diaolou* en route. Once you're in the fields, fork left. There are optional diversions into other villages, but swing left at a junction with a modern pavilion, and the **Ruishi Lou** in **Jin Jiang Li** will shortly appear on the right across the waterlogged fields. The road leads past it to the village entrance and across the open area at the entrance, where people shoo pigeons away from drying rice. Any narrow alley between the ancient houses where shoeless children scurry among the chickens will take you to the tower's base. This is perhaps the most magnificent *diaolou* of all, built by a man who ran a bank and herbal medicine store in Hong Kong. Completed in 1925, it took 3 years to construct using local labor but imported materials. The nine-story tower dominates the village, with its corners and windows decorated from top to bottom, a gallery with domed corners running around all four sides, 28 Roman arches, and a two-story octagonal folly at the top. Nearly as elaborate, the neighboring **Shengfeng Lou,** completed in 1925 by a returnee from the U.S., has bizarre columns running up two stories of elevated galleries. A motorbike ride out to this village and back will cost around ¥4 (50¢/25p), and to the two sites about ¥10 ($1.30/65p).

There's much pleasure to be had just by rambling at will through the countryside, heading toward any toothy towers visible on the skyline. Few are still occupied, but many are used for storage, and sometimes the remarkably friendly local people, seeing your curiosity, will invite you to inspect the tower and climb to the roof for a panoramic view of the countryside. A small local government team is working to obtain UNESCO World Heritage listing for the towers, and they have already placed plaques with good English at these sites. But they are proceeding cautiously with tourism development, and for now, roads cannot accommodate tour buses. Schemes to control entry to the narrow spaces in the towers are being considered before any are opened as museums.

GETTING AROUND   **Taxis** in Kaiping are mostly Jettas or Santanas with a ¥5 (65¢/35p) flagfall that includes 2km (1¼ miles), then a fare of ¥2 (25¢/15p) per kilometer. From 11pm to 5am, flagfall is ¥6 (75¢/40p). Rentals for trips out of town should not involve the meter, however. Bargain down from the first asking price of ¥70 ($9.10/£4.55) per hour, especially if you plan to be out for a few hours. The first price for Tangkou, a 1-hour wait, and return is ¥80 ($10/£5.20). **Buses** to Tangkou, Xiangang, and Chikan leave from two green-arched parking bays at the rear of the bus station. The left is for Tangkou and the right for the other towns; there are about one to three buses an hour between about 6:30am and 5:30pm.

For those who want to stay overnight, Kaiping is a pleasant small town at the confluence of two rivers. There are still sizable communities of émigré Kaipingren who return regularly, and many who retire here (buying specially built apartments rather than constructing towers). The five-star **Ever Joint Hotel (Tan Jiang Bandao Jiudian)** at Zhongyin Lu 2 (© **0750/233-3333;** fax 0750/233-8333; www.jmtour.org/tanjiang) doesn't quite deserve its grade but, run by the White Swan people from Guangzhou, it is surprisingly glitzy for such a small town, and is full of "overseas Chinese." Its tower, positioned at the tip of an island dividing the Tan River, has excellent views; standard rooms cost from ¥800 ($104/£52) to ¥1,250 ($162/£81), suites from ¥1,200 to ¥8,000 ($156–$1,040/£78–£520). A 10% service charge is not usually added. Discounts of 20% are available year-round, and you can usually bargain from there. A short walk along Xi Jiao Lu (opposite the bus station entrance) past a KFC, the **Guangshi Jiudian** (© **0750/221-2213;** fax 0750/229-8409) is a modest two-star hotel whose best guest rooms and bathrooms have had a recent refit. "Luxury" rooms can be bargained from ¥173 to ¥138 ($18–$23/£9–£12), and surprisingly contain a DVD player, for which the hotel will loan free disks. This is the best of the budget hotels. The **Shiji Zhi Zhou Canting (Ship of the Century),** Yan Jiang Xi Lu 18 (© **0750/222-2988;** open 9am–2am), is a two-story boat-shaped restaurant/cafe/bar on the river itself whose "sails" form an awning over a platform with pleasant views. There's an English menu, local and Western dishes (including breakfast), very cold beer, and decent coffee. Main dishes are around ¥20 ($2.60/£1.30).

WHERE TO STAY

Guangzhou can be quite expensive. Don't visit in April or October when the main trade fairs are on, as you may have to pay even above rack rates. Sweltering July and August are popular with tour groups. However, from November to March, rates drop, with a further dip in December and after Chinese New Year.

This is one of the last cities where cavernous hotels with innumerable rooms and endless facilities have survived in any numbers. These are designed to serve the vast numbers of business people attending the main trade fairs in the last 2 weeks of October and April. These have an effect on room rates as far away as Hong Kong, and the major hotels, despite their cavernous size, are likely to be full in that period and offering no discounts. Otherwise, expect to cut 20% to 50% from the prices quoted, although major hotels also add a 10% service charge and a 5% city tax. Lesser hotels conform to normal Chinese standards by not adding service and including city tax in the quoted price.

EXPENSIVE

Shangri-La Pazhou (Guangzhou Xiang Ge Li La)   This is the chain's 50th property and its first new opening since 1983. Touted as the first true international hotel in Guangzhou, Shangri-La will have its work cut out as all the super-luxury brands start to arrive in Guangzhou at once. There will be a Hyatt, a Westin, a Sofitel, and a Mandarin Oriental opening in 2008, to say nothing of the 25 other five-stars that are opening in the province before 2010. Shangri-La is currently fending off the competition and rates as the biggest and best so far in the city. Rooms are some of the largest you'll find in Guanzhou, and each has fantastic views of the Pearl River. Ostentatious gold-leaf and hardwoods give the rooms a traditional Chinese air. Still, ultra-modern features such as large flatscreen TVs and sleek leather swivel chairs ensure that international travelers will feel right at home.

Haizhu Qu, Hui Zhan Dong Lu 1 (near Pa Zhou Hui Zhan Zhong Xing). ⓒ 020/8197-8889. Fax 020/8917-8899. www.shangri-la.com. 708 units. ¥1,160 – ¥2,080 ($150–$270/£75–£135) standard room; ¥2,740 – ¥4,980 ($356–$647/£178–£323) suite. AE, DC, MC, V. **Amenities:** 8 restaurants and bars; indoor and outdoor swimming pool; tennis and squash courts; fitness room; sauna; children's playground; tour and ticket desk; limousine service; forex; 2 conference centers; shopping arcade; salon; babysitting; dry cleaning; valet. *In room:* A/C, satellite TV, minibar, fridge.

White Swan Hotel (Bai Tian'er Binguan) *(Kids)*   This was one of China's first luxury hotels (1982)—an ugly, labyrinthine monster whose dominating location on Shamian Island and views over the Pearl River have all but destroyed the island's colonial atmosphere. The more you pay, the higher your room. Refurbishment is a continuous process, and the hotel is unusual among long-standing hotels in keeping up standards and adding facilities. Some slightly larger rooms come with dataport, some with broadband Internet access, high ceilings, and new furniture. The tacky lobby features a waterfall and fish-stocked pools crossed by bridges. Former guests include Queen Elizabeth II and former U.S. president George H. W. Bush. Many agencies organizing adoptions use the White Swan: Every floor is fully stocked with diaper service, parents get a free toy for their kids, and the hotel goes quiet at nap time—no wonder it has been nicknamed the White Stork. In early 2007, every single guest was kicked out with just 1 night's notice, when North Korean dictator Kim Jong-Il paid a flying visit and was given the run of the entire hotel for the weekend. With customers like that, this is good reason to stay somewhere else.

Shamian Nan Jie 1 (on Shamian Island). © 020/8188-6968. Fax 020/8186-1188. www.white-swan-hotel.com. 843 units. ¥2,320–¥2,800 ($301–$364/£150–£182) standard room; ¥2,960–¥3,440 ($384–$447/£192–£223) suite. Rack rates are halved outside trade fair periods, and can often be bargained down by a further 30%. AE, DC, MC, V. **Amenities:** Multiple restaurants; nightclub; 2 pools; golf driving range; 10 tennis courts; squash court; fitness room; sauna; extensive children's facilities; tour desk; business center; forex; extensive shopping arcade w/bakery, florist, bookshop, and pharmacy; salon. *In room:* A/C, satellite TV, dataport, broadband Internet access (select rooms: ¥150/$19/£9 per 24 hr.), minibar, fridge.

MODERATE/INEXPENSIVE

Globelink Hotel (Quanqiu Tong Dajiudian) ⍟   It is surprising that so few Western tourists stay at the Globelink, as it has by far the largest rooms in the city. Its location is very central, with easy access to the subway as well as large shopping areas such as Beijing Road, China Plaza, and Haiyin Electronics Market. The staff are friendly and helpful; a few even speak English. Best of all, the discounted prices for this four-star hotel are unbeatable.

Yuexiu Nan Lu 208. © 020/8389-8138. Fax 020/8389-8899. globalh@public.guangzhou.gd.cn. 406 units. ¥480 ($62/£31) standard room; ¥580–¥680 ($75–$88/£37–£44) suite. AE, DC, MC, V. **Amenities:** 3 restaurants; lobby lounge bar; nightclub; health club; sauna; business center; forex; salon; health clinic; valet. *In room:* A/C, cable TV, broadband Internet access, minibar.

Peoples' Liberation Army Kindergarten Teachers' Hotel (Hequn Dasha) *(Finds)*
This bizarrely named hotel has large well-appointed rooms and yet retains a number of uniquely Chinese features such as steel thermoses of boiling water. Located just on the edge of the sprawling military district, most of its clients are either trainee teachers or army officers, with the occasional foreign tour group. Watch out for all the army-licensed SUVs that charge around nearby, immune to the law and seemingly unaware of pedestrians.

Hequn Yi Ma Lu 43. © 020/8716-1858. Fax 020/8776-3818. 180 units. ¥228 ($30/£15) standard room; ¥588 ($76/£38) suite. No credit cards. **Amenities:** Business center; salon; therapeutic massage; ticketing office. *In room:* A/C, TV.

WHERE TO DINE

According to a national survey, the average Cantonese spends ¥4,413 ($573/£286) on dining out annually, which is three times as much as the average Shanghainese, and a whopping seven times more than the national average. While it is Cantonese cuisine that captures the headlines, the local passion for eating has ensured that an eclectic mix of international flavors has established a presence here. Not only does Guangzhou provide the chance to sample many provincial cuisines, an abundance of Asian, Middle Eastern, and even European creativity can now be tasted here. Guangzhou's expat community has changed rapidly in the last few years and this can be seen in the number of international cuisines available. Overpriced generic brands such as the Hard Rock Cafe were not able to survive here but have been replaced with a wide variety of flavors, from Caribbean to Syrian.

Bei Yuan Jiujia CANTONESE   The Cantonese seem to be the most raucous of all Chinese, and the main restaurant choices for classic Cantonese food, or for dim sum, are bedlam. The Bei Yuan dates from the 1920s, although the current two-story building with courtyards is newer, built around a garden and pond. There's dim sum here all day (about ¥4/50¢/25p per steamer) and a generous menu of Cantonese classics, with some English translations. Try *huadiao zhu ji* (chicken cooked in yellow wine— although some might argue this is really a Zhejiang dish), *tang cu su rou* (sweet-and-sour pork), and *jiuhuang rou si* (sliced pork with yellow chives). The typically garish carpets, screens, and chandeliers are in odd contrast to a central green space. There are twin entrances—the left is for the traditional Cantonese dishes; the right is for a Chaozhou (Chiu Chow) restaurant, with the roast goose dishes typical of that area of northeast Guangdong.

Xiao Bei Lu 202. Ⓒ 020/8356-3365. Meal for 2 about ¥80 ($10/£5.20). No credit cards. 6:50am–4:30pm and 5:30pm–12:10am.

Dong Bei Ren MANCHURIAN   One of the most successful chains in the region, Dong Bei Ren offers the opportunity to try northern cuisine in a southern city. I highly recommend that you sample as many different kinds of *jiaozi* (resembling miniature ravioli) as possible. So many carts will come wheeling past your table that you may not even need to consult a menu; rest assured that you will not be disappointed by the selection. Accompany it with great-value fresh fruit juices or even a sweet red wine that might surprise with its potency. The bright flowery uniforms and decor should make branches easy to spot, but watch out for the copycats that are springing up. Additional branches at Tian He Nan Er Lu 36 (Ⓒ **020/8750-1711**), Taojin Bei Lu 2/F (Ⓒ **020/8357-1576**), and Lanbaoshi building of Renmin Bei Lu (Ⓒ **020/8135-1711**).

He Qun Y1i Ma Lu 65-7. Ⓒ 020/8760 0688. Main courses ¥30–¥50 ($3.90–$6.50/£1.95–£3.25). No credit cards. 10:30am–10:30pm.

Dong Jiang Haixian Da Jiulou CANTONESE SEAFOOD   While Cantonese food can now be found all over the world, the enormous, multistory, football field–size restaurants remain something than can only be seen in Guangzhou. Many places compete to be the largest (the title is currently held by Fishermans' City, more the size of a theme park than a restaurant, in the suburb of Panyu) but most branches of the Dong Jiang chain are vast enough to impress. This particular location stretches over five floors and even spills out on to the sidewalk later in the evening. Huge tanks of seafood fill the first floor with many obscure, strange-looking varieties available at higher prices. Beginners may want to start with a plate full of steamed shrimp and another of steamed crab, and practice eating with their fingers before they proceed onto local exotica such as water beetles and horseshoe crabs. Restaurant rush hour is early Sunday evening, when it seems like every family in the city is heading out to eat. If you can even find a seat, the noise will be deafening (when eating, Cantonese seem to use a speaking volume that Brits would only ever use to shout at their children), but it will be an experience that you will be unable to replicate elsewhere on the planet. Also at Huanshi Zhong Lu 276, opposite the children's activity center (Ⓒ **020/ 8322-9188**).

Yanjiang Lu 2, beside Haizhu Sq. Ⓒ 020/8318-4901. Meal for 2 about ¥80–¥200 ($10–$26/£5.20–£13). AE, DC, MC, V. 7am–4am.

Gao Li Jiu Jia Korean Restaurant KOREAN   A strong Korean expat community means that cuisine from the hermit kingdom is especially well represented in Guangzhou. This newly opened establishment is the best of four in the immediate vicinity and serves authentic fare without the noisy crowds of more established Korean places. A short but succinct picture menu shows all the national favorites without 4drowning the reader with too much variety. Every meal is accompanied with delicious barley tea and a selection of appetizer dishes including fresh kimchi and delicious pumpkin purée.

26 Song Bai Dong Lu, 4th floor. C 020/8657-3168. Photo menu. Main courses ¥30–¥80 ($3.90–$10/£2–£5.20). No credit cards. 11am–11pm.

Hui Ying Chang Fen Dian CANTONESE

Just 5 minutes' walk from China Plaza, Hui Ying is perhaps the best place on the planet to sample the most delicious Chang Fen, a kind of steamed rice-flour pasty served in soy sauce. Although it is massively popular with locals and busy at all times of the day and night, the only other foreigner that you will ever see here is the author. Ask for *xian xia ji dan chang* and you will get a tasty shrimp and egg dish that is the epitome of Guangzhou. Ask for some *jok* and *you tiao* and you will get some thick rice broth and tasty fried bread sticks for dipping. Fantastic fare at ultra-low prices and a secret that few other tourists will ever find.

Dong Chuan Lu 94, on the left just past the Provincial Cardiovascular Hospital opposite the Songsha air conditioner store. C 020/8386-1967. Meal for 2 about ¥5–¥10 (65¢–$1.30/35p–65p). No credit cards. 6:15am–1:15am.

Japan Fusion JAPANESE/CANTONESE

Reputedly the largest Japanese restaurant in Asia, but the equally huge menu reveals a strong inclination toward Cantonese flavors. At lunchtime, the vast expanse of tables, teppanyaki plates, and sashimi bars is flooded to capacity, hardly a surprise considering the choice of excellent-value set lunches available. Great for lunch on the way to or from the station, but watch out in the evening when prices rise sharply.

2/F Metro Plaza, Tian He Bei Lu 358–378. C 020/83884-5109. Set lunches ¥20–¥100 ($2.60–$13/£1.30–£6.50); specialty dishes can be much, much higher. AE, DC, MC, V. 11am–11pm.

1920 EUROPEAN

Conveniently located next to the Pearl River, 1920 is ideal for lunch after a morning browsing the markets or before an afternoon stroll around Shamian. This small cafe-style eatery has an outdoor seating area and an upstairs section with live jazz in the evening and a Sunday jazz brunch (10:30am–4pm). Although now under Filipino management, there is still a strong German influence to the menu and the place is popular with tourists and expats alike. On the way out, make sure to check just around the corner to see what Oliver Twist is eating at the bizarrely named Village of Gruel.

Haizhu Sq. Subway Station, Exit D, Yanjiang Zhong Lu 183. C 020/8333-6156. www.1920cn.com. Main courses ¥20–¥100 ($2.60–$13/£1.30–£6.50). AE, DC, MC, V. 11am–2am.

Zheng Gong Fu–Kung Fu CANTONESE

With Chinese authorities growing increasingly nationalistic and the rest of the population following suit, locally branded fast-food chains are making an impromptu resurgence. Rather surprisingly, given what a huge hit Western chains were when they first opened in China, the passion for McDonald's is beginning to wane and some KFCs are even closing down. But fast-food fans need not fear, as the Kung Fu chain is quickly taking up the slack. Kung Fu, which opened its first branch in 1994, now operates 200 restaurants in the mainland, predicts 500 outlets in 2008, and hopes to become the top Chinese fast-food chain in the country within 5 years. Relying heavily on the Bruce Lee brand, the menu consists of steamed dishes with fresh ingredients and simple seasoning, such as pork ribs with soybean sauce, chicken with mushroom, beef with pickled vegetable, Taiwanstyle minced pork, and eel, all priced between ¥22 ($2.80/£1.40) and ¥29 ($3.80/£1.90). The restaurant chain believes that a Cantonese-style steamed meal is a healthier alternative for customers—they're probably right. All dishes are accompanied by Chinese a choice of herbal soup such as chicken with ginseng (¥13/$1.70/85p), dried bok choy steamed with pig bones soup (¥11/$1.40/70p), or mushroom steamed with duck soup (¥12/$1.55/80p).

7/F, China Plaza. © 020/8386-8999. Meal for 2 about ¥80 ($10/£5.20). No credit cards. 6:50am–4:30pm and 5:30pm–12:10am.

9 Shenzhen

Guangdong Province on the border with Hong Kong, 163km (102 miles) SE of Guangzhou

In the 1980s, Shenzhen grew seemingly overnight from nothing to a metropolis. The growth spurt came at the instigation of then-supreme leader Deng Xiaoping, and remains the primary symbol of the reform and opening policy he initiated. It's equally a symbol of everything that's wrong with what China has become—a jostle of shanty-towers with a rootless, money-grubbing, gone-in-a-day atmosphere. Hardly anyone's a native, and many Chinese are here illegally. Far from finding the get-rich-quick scheme of their dreams, often many of these workers end up in sweatshops or prosti-tution. Seemingly oblivious to the city's terrifying growth in violent crime, the author-ities seem to believe that even more expansion will cure all ills. To this end, Shenzhen is trying to remake itself, attempting to disassociate itself from the fake handbag shops that line the border and focusing instead on a spanking new Central Business District in Futian.

If you're in Hong Kong and are considering Shenzhen as a side trip, then be aware that shopping is the main activity. Otherwise, the main point of visiting here is to use its airport to get somewhere else. *Warning:* Although Hong Kong has "returned to the motherland," this is a full-scale **international border crossing**, open from 6:30am to midnight, and is prohibited even to Chinese who don't have the right documenta-tion. Lines can be long, especially during holiday periods. In either direction, allow *at least* an hour, and whether you're coming or going, be sure to collect immigration cards and fill them in while waiting in line. There are lines for Hong Kong residents, mainland Chinese, and foreigners—you'll be sent to the back again if you join the wrong one. Full Chinese tourist **visas** cannot be obtained here. A 5-day permit allow-ing access *only* to Shenzhen can be purchased at the border by citizens of most devel-oped nations for ¥100 ($13/£6.50), but the list of favored nations changes as high-level diplomatic spats eventually filter down to the ordinary traveler. Last year it was the British who were out of favor; this year it is the Americans who are in the dog-house. *Note:* For Chinese translations of selected establishments listed in this section, please turn to appendix A.

ESSENTIALS

GETTING THERE   It is usually much cheaper to **fly** into Shenzhen from other mainland cities than it is to fly directly to Hong Kong, and there are around 60 Chi-nese cities to choose from, including Beijing (18 flights daily), Chengdu (seven flights), Guilin (four flights), Hangzhou (six flights), Kunming (five flights), Shang-hai (17 flights), Xiamen (12 flights), and Xi'an (four flights).

Shenzhen Airport is the main airport for tourists planning further travel in China, with water, land and air transport easily accessible. Well known as **Shenzhen Bao'an International Airport** (SZX), it also is the fourth-largest airport in China. At present, there are about 107 internal and international airlines opened, connecting Shenzhen and 80 other cities both home and abroad. The daily flights from such famous tourist cities of China as Beijing, Shanghai, Xian, Qingdao, and Hangzhou can take you to

Shenzhen easily. Daily international lines from London, Los Angeles, Vancouver, and Paris via transfer in Shanghai can be used. Flights from Manila, Bangkok, Singapore, and Tokyo depart to Shenzhen directly every day. Finally, there are frequent flights between Shenzhen and Macau every day.

Additionally, there is a convenient bus shuttle between Hong Kong International Airport and Shenzhen Airport every 20 minutes from 8:20am to 9:20pm and a return shuttle every 45 minutes starting at Shenzhen Airport at 9:45am and finishing at 6:15pm costing HK$180 per adult and HK$100 per child.

Hong Kong can be reached directly from the airport using TurboCAT (jetfoil/ catamaran) services to Kowloon (six sailings, 9am–5:15pm) and the Macau Ferry Terminal on Hong Kong Island (4:30, 6:30, and 7:45pm; HK$189–HK$289/US$25–US$38, can be paid in yuan on the Chinese side). Shuttle buses take passengers the short distance to the pier, and the total journey time is around 55 minutes. There are also services to **Macau** at 9:30am and 1:30pm (HK$171–HK$271/US$22–US$34; can be paid in yuan or Macanese patacas). For current times and services in each direction, see **www.turbocat.com/turbojet_sailing_rev.htm**. There's talk of helicopter service between Macao and Shenzhen later this year. Its port should be near the Crowne Plaza Hotel.

Airport bus no. 330 (✆ **0755/99788**) runs from the airport to the Hualian Dasha (a hotel and department store), just west of the center on Shen Nan Zhong Lu. The ride takes 40 minutes and costs ¥20 ($2.60/£1.30); the buses run every 15 minutes from 6:20am to 9pm.

When work on an extension to the KCR East Rail line is complete, buses will run to the railway station. For now it's a ¥20 ($2.60/£1.30) taxi ride farther. (Coming from Hong Kong, ignore touts at Luo Hu, and make for the signposted taxi rank.)

The **railway station** (✆ **0755/8326-5043**) is 2 minutes' walk north of the Luo Hu/Lo Wu border and connected by elevated walkway. Tickets for Guangzhou are on sale at this level, and for elsewhere on the floor below, from 7am to 8pm. The express trains directly from Kowloon to Beijing and Shanghai pass through but do not stop here. Shenzhen has its own services from Beijing Xi, of which the best is the T107 at 8:30pm, passing through Jiujiang and Nanchang, and arriving at 9:10pm the next day—not bad for 2,373km (1,483 miles). The cost is ¥467 ($60/£30) hard sleeper, ¥720 ($93/£47) soft sleeper. To Beijing, the T108 leaves at 1:08pm. Tickets for this and many other **trains** from Shenzhen can be bought at CTS in Hong Kong, but there's a much greater choice of services and destinations from Guangzhou. Departures by 200kmph express trains to Guangzhou Dong (East) leave 45 times a day from 7:18am to 8:45pm. They occasionally continue to the main station.

About 30 long-distance bus stations operate out of Shenzhen, but it is the **Luo Hu Qichezhan** (✆ **0755/8232-1670**) that visitors will find most useful as buses here depart to most cities of Guangdong Province. Buses for Guangzhou leave every 5 minutes and cost ¥60 ($7.80/£3.90).

From **Hong Kong,** the easiest train route is via the KCR East Rail line from Hung Hom or Kowloon Tong to Lo Wu. The first train from Hung Hom is at 5:30am and the last at 11:07pm. *Only stay on for Lo Wu if you plan to cross the border, or you may be fined.* The long-distance bus station, **Luo Hu Qichezhan,** is beneath Luo Hu Commercial City, to your right as you leave Customs. There are rapid bus connections with Guangzhou, Zhuhai Gong Bei (the Macau border crossing, every 15 min. 7am–8:30pm), Kaiping, and most other corners of Guangdong Province. A cross-border coach service runs to the Shangri-La hotel directly from Hong Kong Airport's arrivals hall counter 4B; 16 services make the 2-hour trip from 10:30am to 8:30pm for HK$100 (US$13/£6.50). In the other direction, 10 services operate from 7:30am to 5:50pm. *Warning:* Access to Shenzhen is subject to extra controls. Have your passport ready if you're arriving or leaving by bus.

GETTING AROUND   Few people get farther than Luo Hu, with its border station, railway station, bus station, shopping, restaurants, and hotels, all close together. **Red Taxi** fares are among China's most expensive with a flagfall of ¥13 ($1.60/80p) including 2.3km (1¼ miles), then ¥2.40 (30¢/15p) per kilometer up to 15km (9 miles), then 50% more. **Green Taxis,** on the other hand, are a much more reasonable ¥7 (90¢/50p) including 2.3km (1¼ miles), then ¥1.60 (20¢/10p) per kilometer. *Never* deal with touts who approach you at the border. The taxi stand is signposted beyond Luo Hu Commercial City to your right. At the north end of the plaza, with the border on the south side and the station on the west, stands the Shangri-La hotel. The street leading north on the left side is Jianshe Lu, and the street on the right side is Renmin Nan Lu; between the two of them, they lead to everything you might want.

There is a **tour bus** that makes a comfortable 2-hour trip around the city that leaves the front of the bus station every 10 minutes, but thanks to all the construction it can be a little difficult to locate. Get directions from the English-speaking staff at the information desk, which is located next to the ticket counter on the first floor in section B. Tickets are ¥10 ($1.30/65p), but do not catch this bus at rush hour or you will just end up sitting in one of the city's infamous traffic jams.

The new **metro** is currently limited to two lines. Line no. 1 (green on maps) runs 15 stations from Luo Hu 17km (11m) to Window on the World (Shi Jie Zhi Chuang). Line no. 4 (blue on maps) runs five stations from Huang Gang to the Children's Palace (Xiao Nian Gang). Tickets cost ¥2 to ¥8 (25¢/15p–65¢/35p) according to the distance to be traveled.

FAST FACTS

Banks, Foreign Exchange & ATMs   There's a branch of the **Hongkong and Shanghai Bank** on the Renmin Nan Lu side of the Century Plaza Hotel—you can't change money here but you can use its ATM outside. A branch of the **Bank of China** (open Mon–Fri 8:30am–5:30pm; Sat–Sun and holidays 9am–4pm), which has foreign-exchange service and an outside ATM, is nearby to the right and beyond the Shangri-La hotel.

Internet Access   The 24-hour **PC-War E-Cafe** even has a nonsmoking area. It's on the fourth floor of the Cybermart at Renmin Nan Lu 3005 and charges ¥2 (25¢/15p) per hour. Use the side entrance from 7pm to 9am. Dial-up is ✆ **169.**

Post Office   There's a useful post office (open 9am–noon and 12:30–5pm) at the ground-floor level of the north end of Luo Hu Commercial City.

Visa Extensions   Cross into Hong Kong and purchase a brand-new 3-month visa within 24 hours if you need one. (see chapter 11).

EXPLORING SHENZHEN

Newly minted Shenzhen has only the face of modern China to show you, including tawdry and occasionally offensive theme parks. The *Minsk,* certainly out of the ordinary, can be seen as a day trip from Hong Kong.

Minsk **World (Mingsike Hangmu Shijie)** 🌟 *Kids*   Throughout mainland China there's a slightly chilling admiration for military power and for weaponry both high- and low-tech. Much of the admiration for the West (when admitted) is for its ownership of the kinds of munitions that, if our own generals are to be believed, double-check the address, knock politely, and ask for ID before deciding whether or not to explode. The Russian aircraft carrier *Minsk,* launched in 1978 and once the flagship of the Soviet Union's Pacific Fleet, is of a more clockwork era, with not a microchip in sight, but its sheer scale and power are still impressive, as is the relentless marketing to which visitors are subjected from the moment they pass the monument to peace at the entrance, a-flutter with doves, to enter what is a large-scale celebration of the weapons of war.

The ticket office is in a vaguely St. Petersburgian fake palace, behind which are a shooting range where you can fire tennis balls at assorted objects, stalls selling animated military dolls, a row of MIG fighter planes, a tank or two, an inflatable Russian bear presiding over a number of centrifugal rides, and a Soyuz space capsule (the genuine article).

The carrier itself has been substantially refitted, with stirring Russian military music playing through a PA system. Your visit commences with a compulsory 10-minute cinema show on the history of aircraft carriers, into which you are ushered by pretty young women in naval uniforms. Next, you'll follow a clearly marked route through the torpedo hall, bridge, deck, anchor room, missile elevators, and just about every other corner, with informative signage in good English. At every turn there's a souvenir stall (¥15/$1.90/£1 for a postcard!), or a stall selling obsolete military equipment, or another stall selling radio-controlled toys. The deck has occasional reenactments of Russian military parades; the officers' mess is a restaurant serving black bread and imitations of Russian food; and the main aircraft hanger is a disco with neon signs shaped like weaponry, flight-simulator rides, and a stall selling popcorn. If you survive all this, then for ¥30 ($3.90/£1.95) you can be whizzed around the ship at water level in a small motorboat.

Shatoujiao. Adults ¥110 ($14/£7.20), children ¥55 ($7.20/£3.60). 9am–7:30pm. Minibus: no. 430, from a local bus terminal just north of Luo Hu Commercial City on the east side of Renmin Nan Lu; it drops you at the gate of *Minsk* World in 30 min. for ¥4 (50¢/25p). Walk a short distance back up to main road to catch returning buses, however. Alternative buses include the nos. 103, 202, 205, and 430.

SHOPPING

It's an increasingly popular view among residents of Hong Kong that Shenzhen is a cheap place to shop. Compared to Hong Kong, it *is* cheap, of course, at least for domestic items, but many proclaiming this view have never been anywhere else in China (and many Hong Kong people have never been to the mainland at all). Those who do go to shop often get no farther than the overrated **Luo Hu Shangye Cheng (Luo Hu Commercial City),** five stories of shopping (open 8:30am–11pm) above the bus station to the right as you leave the border, where you find luggage, shoes, bags, CDs, clothes, toys, Chinese medicine, tea, tailoring services, portrait photography, bed linens, quilts, electrical goods, leather goods, pearls, jewelry, wigs, massages, pedicures, and even a Cantonese opera house. Of course, as elsewhere in the mainland, nearly everything is a fake. "Where else can you get a cotton tailored shirt for around $9?" enthuses one shopping guide. To which the answer might be, "Name a mainland city where you can't—and usually cheaper." This mall's very proximity to rich Hong Kong, almost inside the border post, ought to warn you off in the first place.

WHERE TO STAY

Business-oriented Shenzhen tends to be expensive. But if you must spend a night, the best place to stay is the five-star **Shangri-La (Xianggelila Dajiudian)** at Jianshe Lu

1002 (℃ **0755/8233-0888;** fax 0755/8233-9878; www.shangri-la.com), visible straight ahead as you leave the border crossing, and 2 minutes from the railway station. This is a luxurious and fully outfitted business hotel with excellent service, four restaurants, and cozy, recently refurbished rooms fitted with everything that you could possibly want in order to shut out the bedlam of Shenzhen, including broadband Internet access, satellite TV channels, and in-house movies. Rack rates are from ¥1,865 to ¥4,420 ($242–$574/£121–£287), but special offers and on-the-spot bargaining can produce rates under $100 (all plus 15%).

Of the budget hotels up Renmin Nan Lu, the best is probably the **Guangxin Jiudian,** on the west side, north of Chunfeng Lu (℃ **0755/8223-8945**). The lobby is modern and stylish, which makes the grubby corridors beyond a bit of a shock, but refurbishment may have reached that far by the time you visit. Battered guest rooms and bathrooms are clean enough and larger than average, although they have few amenities. Standard rooms are ¥308 ($40/£20), usually reduced to ¥228 ($30/£15); triple rooms are ¥400 ($52/£26), usually reduced to ¥350 ($46/£23).

WHERE TO DINE

Street-level dim sum from 6 to 10:30am, outside the **Yang Xi Jiudian** and just around the corner from the Shangri-La in Jianshe Lu, makes a good and very cheap start to the day. There's Kejia food, *jiaozi,* and familiar Hong Kong fast-food names such as Fairwood in the Luo Hu Commercial City. Keep clear of the restaurants in the railway station building, however, where the food and portions are both miserable, and where there's a 10% charge for nonexistent service. Venture farther up Jianshe Lu or Renmin Lu to find an assortment of standard Chinese restaurants and Western fast-food chains. The rotating **Tiara** restaurant on the top (31st) floor of the Shangri-La has an excellent international buffet for around ¥150 ($20/£9.75) per person, as well as constantly changing views that include the one across the barbed wire to the green New Territories of Hong Kong. The hotel's signature **Shang Palace** restaurant has top-of-the-line Cantonese food at fair prices for the quality; a meal for two costs around ¥400 ($65/£23). For burger and steak enthusiasts, the hotel also has a branch of the American chain **Henry J. Bean's,** with main courses for ¥100 ($13/£6.50).

For a change of pace from the rather predictable five-star hotels, I would suggest the **Shenzhen Number One Production Team,** Hong Hui Lu (℃ **0755/8247-6222;** metro station Dai Ju Yuan). Step back in time into the midst of Maoist revolutionary fervor and sample popular dishes from the time of the Long March such as "Third battalion steam eggs and pork in an earthenware pot," served by staff in authentic Red Guard uniforms.

Hong Kong

by Beth Reiber

Viewed from Victoria Peak, Hong Kong surely rates as one of the most stunning cities in Asia, if not the world. In the foreground rise the skyscrapers of Hong Kong Island, while beyond them is the incredible bustle of Victoria Harbour, where all manner of watercraft—from the historic Star Ferries to cruise liners, cargo ships, and wooden fishing vessels—compete for space. On the other side is the Kowloon Peninsula, growing by the minute with ambitious land-reclamation projects, housing estates, and ever-taller buildings, all set against a dramatic backdrop of gently rounded mountains.

Today's Hong Kong is a blend of the exotic and the familiar forged during its 156 years as a British colony—from 1842, when Britain acquired Hong Kong Island as a spoil of the first Opium War, to its 1997 handover to the Chinese. The Chinese government has given Hong Kong status as a Special Administrative Region (SAR), guaranteeing its capitalist lifestyle and social system for 50 years, so to the casual observer little seems changed. English is still an official language, the Hong Kong dollar remains legal tender, and entry formalities are largely the same. Although it's pricier than most other Asian destinations, many travelers find Hong Kong a welcome respite, with all the creature comforts of home.

Hong Kong boasts what is arguably the greatest concentration of Chinese restaurants in the world, along with top-notch restaurants serving dishes from around the globe. The city has also revved up its sightseeing attractions, offering museums, parks, temples, and other amusements. And Macau, with its fascinating blend of Portuguese and Chinese cultures, is just an hour's boat ride away.

Note: Unless otherwise noted, hours listed in this chapter are the same everyday.

1 Orientation

ARRIVING
BY PLANE

Hong Kong International Airport (© **852/2181 0000;** www.hongkongairport.com) is located about 32km (20 miles) from Hong Kong's central business district. In the arrivals hall, just past Customs, visitors can pick up English-language maps and sightseeing brochures and get directions to their hotel at the **Hong Kong Tourist Board (HKTB),** open 7am to 11pm. Also in the arrivals hall are the **Hong Kong Hotel Association** (www.hkha.com.hk), open from 6am to midnight, with a free booking service to some 60 member hotels; and the **Macau Government Tourist Office,** open from 9am to 1pm, 1:30 to 6pm, and 6:30 to 10pm. You can also exchange money in the arrivals hall, although because of the unfavorable rates, it's best to change only what's needed to get into town—about US$50/£27 should do it. Otherwise, it's much

Hong Kong

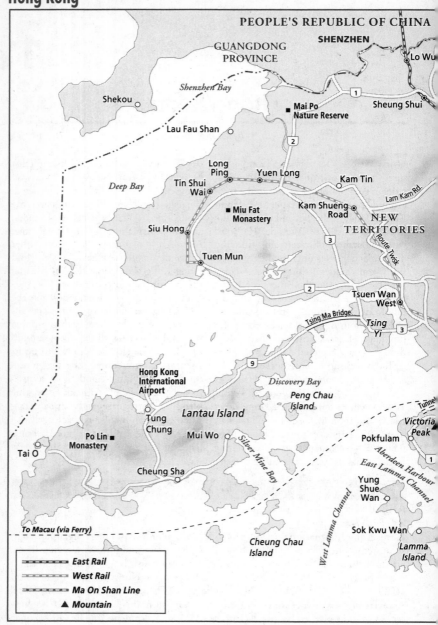

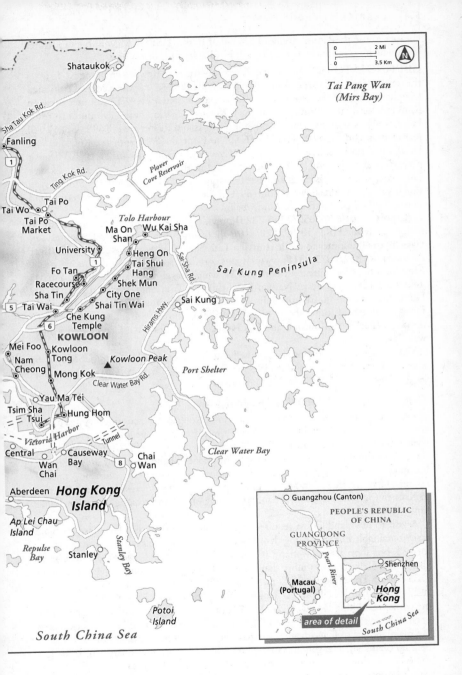

cheaper to use the **Hongkong and Shanghai Bank (HSBC)** ATM at the departures level, which takes almost any card—ask HKTB staff for directions.

GETTING INTO TOWN   The quickest way to get to downtown Hong Kong is via the sleek **Airport Express Line** (© 852/2881 8888; www.mtr.com.hk), located straight ahead past the arrivals hall. Trains, which depart every 12 minutes between 6am and 1am, take 20 minutes to reach Kowloon Station and 24 minutes to reach Hong Kong Station (in Central on Hong Kong Island). Fares are HK$90 (US$12/£6) to Kowloon and HK$100 (US$13/£6.50) to Central. From both the Kowloon and Hong Kong stations, free shuttle buses (every 12–24 min. 6:18am–11:10pm) deposit passengers at major hotels. If you're returning to the airport via the Airport Express Line, consider purchasing a **Tourist Transport Pass** for HK$300 (US$39/£20), a stored-value pass that allows unlimited travel for 3 days and includes the trip from and to the airport (see "Getting Around," below).

Airport Shuttle (© 852/2735 7823) provides door-to-door airport bus service to major hotels for HK$150 (US$20/£10); the shuttle departs every 30 minutes and takes 30 to 40 minutes to reach Tsim Sha Tsui. Slower, with more stops, are **Cityflyer Airbuses** (© 852/2873 0818; www.citybus.com.hk), serving major downtown areas. Most important for tourists are **Airbus A21,** which travels through Mongkok, Yau Ma Tei, and Jordan, and down Nathan Road through Tsim Sha Tsui on its way to the Hung Hom Kowloon–Canton Railway Station; and **Airbuses A11,** which travels to Hong Kong Island. Buses depart every 10 to 30 minutes, with fares costing HK$33 (US$4.30/£2.15) to Kowloon and HK$40 (US$5.20/£2.60) to Central and Causeway Bay.

On average, a **taxi** to Tsim Sha Tsui will cost approximately HK$300 (US$39/£20); a taxi to Central will cost about HK$365 (US$47/£24). Expect to pay an extra luggage charge of HK$5 (US65¢/35p) per piece.

TRAVELING TO & FROM THE MAINLAND

If you plan to spend most of your time in Hong Kong and are considering just a brief trip to the mainland, avoid the massively overpriced tours peddled by Hong Kong agents—trips to Guangzhou and Shenzhen are easy to arrange for yourself. Neither of these cities should be picked as your sole experience of the mainland, however; nor, for longer stays, should they be your first choice as a point of entry. Instead, consider taking a ferry service to rural Kaiping, or a proper oceangoing vessel around the coast to Xiamen (perhaps providing the softest landing of all), and making easy connections up the coast.

A visit to mainland China requires advance purchase of a **visa,** but these are more easily obtainable in Hong Kong than anywhere else. Numerous agents are eager to act for you, but shop around—many agents within the tourist districts are also eager to charge you 50% to 100% more than you need to pay. The Hong Kong operation of **CTS (China Travel Service)** has more than 30 branches, the best known of which is at 27–33 Nathan Rd., Tsim Sha Tsui (one floor up in Alpha House, entrance around the corner on Peking Rd.; © 852/2315 7188; fax 852/2315 7292; www.ctshk.com), open 365 days a year. Come here for commission-free ferry, train, and bus tickets to the mainland, as well as advance-purchase tickets for a limited selection of trains to Beijing, Shanghai, Hangzhou, Guangzhou, Xi'an, Guilin, and Shenzhen. Visa purchase here is slow and expensive, however. It's best to make your visa application at least 4 business days prior to departure; cost of a single-entry visa (valid for 30 days) is HK$210 (US$27/£14). However, if you're in a hurry, you can obtain a visa more quickly by paying more: For HK$360 (US$47/£23), your visa will be processed and available for pickup by 2pm the next day; for HK$480 (US$62/£31), visa applications made before noon will be available by 5:30pm the same day. Note, however, that at press time, Americans applying for visas were required to pay HK$450 (US$58) for a single-entry visa; HK$650 and HK$850 (US$84 and US$110) for the expedited services. U.K. residents pay HK$500, HK$700, and HK$900 (£33, £46, and £59) respectively. Double-entry and multiple-entry 6-month visas are also easily available.

For air tickets, shop around the many budget-travel agents in the area, such as **Shoestring Travel,** also in the Alpha House, fourth floor (© **852/2723 2306;** fax 852/2721 2085; www.shoestringtravel.com.hk). Entry visas are cheaper here, too, but agents farther away from the main shopping streets are even cheaper still.

BY PLANE

Various Chinese airlines fly to and from Beihai, Beijing, Changchun, Changsha, Chengdu, Chongqing, Dalian, Fuzhou, Guangzhou, Guilin, Guiyang, Haikou, Hangzhou, Harbin, Hefei, Huang Shan, Ji'nan, Kunming, Nanchang, Nanjing, Nanning, Ningbo, Qingdao, Sanya, Shanghai, Shenyang, Shijiazhuang, Tianjin, Wenzhou, Wuhan, Xiamen, Xi'an, Zhengzhou, and other minor destinations. Hong Kong's more expensive **Dragonair** flies to Beijing, Changsha, Chengdu, Chongqing, Dalian, Fuzhou, Guilin, Hangzhou, Kunming, Nanjing, Ningbo, Qingdao, Sanya, Shanghai, Wuhan, Xiamen, and Xi'an. Shop around with travel agencies and bargain for discount fares. Do *not* book with Hong Kong agents in advance online—prices are outrageous. With the exception of rare special offers, it is almost always cheaper to fly from **Shenzhen** or Guangzhou to domestic destinations. Be sure to factor in transportation costs to Hong Kong International Airport and to Shenzhen or Guangzhou, as well as the mainland domestic departure tax of ¥50 ($6.50/£3.25), when making comparisons.

Shenzhen Airport has service to 57 Chinese cities and can be reached from Hong Kong International Airport via **TurboJET Sea Express** (© **852/2859 333;** www.turbojetseaexpress.com.hk) with seven sailings (10:45am–7:50pm) to Shenzhen's Fu Yong Ferry Terminal, followed by a 5-minute shuttle bus to Shenzhen Airport. Fares range from HK$230 to HK$330 (US$30–US$43/£15–£21). Transfers to the Sea Express are made *before* Hong Kong Customs, thereby eliminating Hong Kong immigration formalities. In Hong Kong, there are also TurboJET services (www.turbojet.com.hk) from Kowloon's China HK Ferry Terminal (six sailings, 7:30am–6pm) and the Macau Ferry Terminal on Hong Kong Island (one sailing, 8am), for HK$200 to HK$300 (US$26–US$39/£13–£20). Passengers should plan on about 1 hour for the total journey time.

BY TRAIN

The T98 leaves for Beijing at 3:16pm on alternate days, stopping at Dongguan (Changping), Guangzhou East, Shaoguan, Changsha, Wuchang, Hankou, Zhengzhou, and Shijiazhuang before arriving in Beijing West at 3:41pm the next day. The T100 leaves for Shanghai at 3:16pm on alternate days, calling at Dongguan (Changping), Guangzhou East, Shaoguan, and Hangzhou East before arriving in Shanghai at 11:10am the next day. Tickets can be bought at Hung Hom or any KCR East Rail station, or through travel agents (with no commission payable). Online agents overcharge by as much as 70%. To find out whether your train is departing on odd or even days of the month, go to www.kcrc.com or call the **Intercity Passenger Services Hotline** at © **852/2947 7888,** which also has details on Guangzhou services.

From Beijing, fares are HK$1,191 (US$155/£82) for *gaoji ruanwo*—a bed in a two-bed cabin—HK$934 (US$121/£60) for a soft sleeper, and HK$574 to HK$601 (US$75–US$78/£37–£39) for a hard sleeper. From Shanghai, fares are HK$508 to HK$1,039 (US$66–US$135/£33–£65).

There are 12 daily services to and from **Guangzhou Dong Zhan (East Station)** for HK$190 to HK$230 (US$25–US$30/£12–£15); the trip takes a little less than 2 hours.

From Beijing and Shanghai, passengers are required to alight with all baggage and go through Customs and Immigration procedures about an hour out from Kowloon's Hung Hom Station, at Changping (Dongguan). Leaving Hong Kong, don't bother to stow heavy baggage until after you reboard the train. To and from Guangzhou, formalities are conducted at Guangzhou Dong station and on the train. Hong Kong Customs and Immigration procedures (including yet another X-ray of baggage) take place at Hung Hom station. Expect to spend about HK$30 (US$3.90/£2) for a taxi to a hotel in Tsim Sha Tsui or Tsim Sha Tsui East.

There are also services every few minutes to and from Lo Wu, Hong Kong's border crossing to Shenzhen, the last stop on the KCR East Rail. See "Getting Around," below, and "Shenzhen" (p. 546) for details. You should proceed as far as Lo Wu only if you intend to cross the border, which is open from 6:30am to midnight. Lines can be long—allow an hour.

BY FERRY

Up-to-date schedules of TurboJET jetfoil sailings from Hong Kong can be found at www.turbojet.com.hk or by calling © **852/2859 3333** in Hong Kong, or © **853/790 7039** in Macau. In addition to the round-the-clock services to Macau from the Macau Ferry Terminal on Hong Kong Island and nine daily sailings from the China (HK) Ferry Terminal in Tsim Sha Tsui in Kowloon (see "A Side Trip to Macau," later in this chapter), there are seven daily sailings to Shenzhen (six on weekends) from Kowloon and one from Hong Kong, complete with free bus link to the Shenzhen airport (about 55 min.,altogether). Tickets to Shenzhen cost HK$200 to HK$300 (US$26–US$39/£13–£20). There are also direct sailings from Hong Kong International Airport to Shenzhen and Macau, as well as three daily sailings from Macau to Shenzhen (four on weekends) for HK$171 to HK$271 (US$22–US$35/£11–£17). Tickets are sold at ferry terminals and at the Shun Tak Centre 3/F (200 Connaught Rd. Central, Hong Kong), the TurboJET Service Counter (Sheung Wan MTR Station, exit D), Hong Kong and Macau airports, and China Travel Service branches. Telephone reservations via credit card can be made up to 28 days in advance at © **852/2921 6688.**

The **Chu Kong Passenger Transport Co.** operates a catamaran service to various ports in **Guangzhou** from the China HK Ferry Terminal. See www.cksp.com.hk or call © **852/2858 3876** for details.

BY BUS

CTS sells tickets for a variety of cross-border bus services to destinations around Guangdong Province and beyond, including Guangxi's Yangshuo and Guilin (many more than appear on their website). There are services from Causeway Bay (Metro Park Hotel), Wan Chai ferry pier, and Prince Edward MTR station to the China Hotel in Guangzhou for HK$100 (US$13/£6.50); and direct services from Hong

Kong airport to Shenzhen (Shangri-La Hotel) and to Guangzhou (White Swan, Garden Hotel, and several others).

VISITOR INFORMATION

In addition to its tourist counter in the arrivals hall of Hong Kong International Airport and at Lo Wu Arrival Hall (8am–6pm), the **Hong Kong Tourist Board (HKTB)** maintains two offices in town, on both sides of the harbor. On the Kowloon side, there's a convenient office in Tsim Sha Tsui right in the Star Ferry concourse, and another on Hong Kong Island in the Causeway Bay MTR subway station near exit F. Both offices are open from 8am to 8pm. Otherwise, if you have a question about Hong Kong, you can call the **HKTB Visitor Hotline (© 852/2508 1234)** from 8am to 6pm.

The HKTB publishes a wealth of excellent free literature, maps, and the weekly *What's On—Hong Kong*. *Where Hong Kong* and *bc* are other free monthly giveaways with event listings.

THE LAY OF THE LAND

The Hong Kong Special Administrative Region (SAR) is located at the southeastern tip of the People's Republic of China, some 2,000km (1,240 miles) south of Beijing. Hong Kong can be divided into four distinct parts: **Hong Kong Island;** the **Kowloon Peninsula;** the **New Territories,** which stretch north from Kowloon all the way to the mainland border; and 260 **outlying islands,** most of which are barren and uninhabited.

HONG KONG NEIGHBORHOODS IN BRIEF

Hong Kong Island

CENTRAL DISTRICT Central serves as Hong Kong's nerve center for banking, business, and administration. It also boasts some of Hong Kong's most innovative architecture, some of the city's poshest hotels, high-end shopping centers, and restaurants and bars catering to Hong Kong's white-collar workers.

LAN KWAI FONG Named after an L-shaped street in Central, this is Hong Kong's premier nightlife and entertainment district, occupying not only Lan Kwai Fong but overflowing into neighboring streets like D'Aguilar and Wyndham.

MID-LEVELS Located above Central on the slope of Victoria Peak, the Mid-Levels is a popular residential area with swank apartment buildings, sweeping views of Central, lush vegetation, and slightly cooler temperatures. Serving white-collar workers who commute to

Central is the Central–Mid-Levels Escalator, the world's longest people mover.

SOHO This up-and-coming dining and nightlife district, flanking the Central–Mid-Levels Escalator, is named for being "South of Hollywood Road." It has blossomed into an ever-growing neighborhood of cafe-bars and intimate restaurants specializing in ethnic and innovative cuisine, centered mostly on Elgin, Shelley, and Staunton streets.

WESTERN DISTRICT The Western District is a fascinating neighborhood of shops selling medicinal herbs, ginseng, medicines, dried seafood, and other Chinese products. It's also famous for Hollywood Road (long popular for its many antiques and curio shops) and for Man Mo Temple, one of Hong Kong's oldest.

WAN CHAI Notorious for its sleazy bars and easy women, Wan Chai has become a little more respectable with new, mostly business-style hotels, the huge Hong Kong Convention and Exhibition Centre, and a small but revitalized nightlife scene.

CAUSEWAY BAY Just east of Wan Chai, Causeway Bay is popular as a shopping destination, with Japanese department stores; clothing, shoe, and accessory boutiques; and restaurants. On its eastern perimeter is the large Victoria Park.

ABERDEEN Aberdeen, on the south side of Hong Kong Island, was once a fishing village but is now studded with high-rises and housing projects. It remains famous for its hundreds of sampans and junks, and for a huge floating restaurant.

STANLEY Located on the quiet south side of Hong Kong Island, this former fishing village is home to Hong Kong's most famous market, selling everything from silk suits to name-brand shoes, casual wear, and souvenirs.

Kowloon Peninsula

KOWLOON North of Hong Kong Island, across Victoria Harbour, is Kowloon, 7.7 sq. km (4¾ sq. miles) that were ceded to Britain in 1860. Kowloon includes the districts of Tsim Sha Tsui, Tsim Sha Tsui East, Yau Ma Tei, Hung Hom, and Mongkok. Boundary Street in the north separates it from the New Territories.

TSIM SHA TSUI Tsim Sha Tsui boasts an excellent art museum, a cultural center for the performing arts, Kowloon Park, one of the world's largest shopping malls, a broad selection of international restaurants, a jumping nightlife, Hong Kong's largest concentration of hotels, and Nathan Road, nicknamed the "Golden Mile of Shopping."

TSIM SHA TSUI EAST This area was built entirely on reclaimed land and is home to several hotels, shopping and restaurant complexes, museums, and the new KCR East Tsim Sha Tsui Station, with train service to the New Territories and China and connections to the Mass Transit Railway (MTR) subway system.

YAU MA TEI Just north of Tsim Sha Tsui, Yau Ma Tei has an interesting produce market, a jade market, and the fascinating Temple Street Night Market. It also has several moderately priced hotels.

MONGKOK This district north of Yau Ma Tei is a residential and industrial area, home of the Bird Market and the Ladies' Market on Tung Choi Street.

2 Getting Around

Hong Kong is compact and easy to navigate, with street, bus, and subway signs clearly marked in English. Each mode of transportation—bus, ferry, tram, and train/subway—has its own fare system and requires a new ticket each time you transfer from one to another. However, if you're going to be in Hong Kong for a few days, consider purchasing the **Octopus** smart card, which allows users to hop on and off trains, trams, subways, and most buses and ferries without worrying about purchasing tickets each time. Sold at all MTR subway stations and at some ferry piers, it costs a minimum of HK$150 (US$19/£10), including a HK$50 (US$6.50/£3.25) refundable deposit, and can be reloaded as necessary. For information, call the Octopus Hotline at ℂ **852/2266 2222** or check its website at www.octopuscards.com.

Otherwise, transportation on buses and trams requires exact fare, making it imperative to carry lots of loose change wherever you go.

BY SUBWAY   Hong Kong's **Mass Transit Railway (MTR)** is modern, easy to use, and very fast, consisting of six color-coded lines. Single-ticket, one-way fares range from HK$4 to HK$26 (US50¢–US$3.40/25p–£1.60), depending on the distance. Credit card–size plastic tickets are inserted into slots at entry turnstiles, retrieved, and inserted again at exits. The MTR operates from 6am to 1am, and there are no public restrooms at any of the stations or on the trains. For general inquiries, call the **MTR Hotline** at ℂ **852/2881 8888** or check www.mtr.com.hk.

BY TRAIN   The **Kowloon-Canton Railway (KCR) Corporation** (ℂ **852/2929 3399;** www.kcrc.com.hk) operates three rail lines in the New Territories as well as trains to China. Most useful for visitors is the **East Rail,** which offers local commuter travel from the KCR East Tsim Sha Tsui Station in Kowloon up to Sheung Shui in the New Territories. That is, Sheung Shui is where you get off if you don't plan on traveling onward to China. Departing every 3 to 8 minutes from 5:28am to midnight, the commuter train from East Tsim Sha Tsui in Kowloon to Sheung Shui takes only 38 minutes, with a one-way ticket costing HK$13 (US$1.60/80p) for ordinary (second) class and HK$25 (US$3.25/£1.60) for first class. If you plan on visiting Shenzhen, you can continue to the border station of Lo Wu and cross the border on foot. Or, if you have a visa, you can travel onward to Guangzhou, Shanghai, and Beijing.

BY BUS   HKTB has individual leaflets showing bus routes. Depending on the route, buses run from about 6am to midnight, with fares ranging from HK$1.20 to HK$45 (US15¢–US$5.85/10p–£2.90)—exact fares required. Few drivers speak English, so you may want to have someone at your hotel write your destination in Chinese. In rural areas, you must flag down a bus to make it stop.

BY TRAM   Tram lines, found only along the north side of Hong Kong Island, are a nostalgic way to travel through the Western District, Central, Wan Chai, and Causeway Bay. Established in 1904, these old, narrow, double-decker affairs clank their way from Kennedy Town in the west to Shaukeiwan in the east, with one branch making a detour to Happy Valley. Regardless of how far you go, you pay the exact fare of HK$2 (US25¢/15p) or use an Octopus card as you exit. Trams run from 6am to 1am.

BY FERRY   A 5-minute trip across Victoria Harbour on one of the white-and-green ferries of the **Star Ferry Company** (ℂ **852/2367 7065;** www.starferry.com.hk), in operation since 1898, is one of Hong Kong's top attractions. It costs only HK$1.70 (US20¢/10p) for ordinary (second) class or HK$2.20 (US30¢/15p) in first class on the upper deck. Ferries ply the waters between Central and Tsim Sha Tsui from 6:30am to 11:30pm, with departures every 4 to 10 minutes. Besides the Central-to-Tsim Sha Tsui route, Star Ferries also run between Central and Hung Hom and between Tsim Sha Tsui and Wan Chai; hover ferries run between Central and Tsim Sha Tsui East.

   A large fleet also serves the many outlying islands and the northern part of the mainland, with most ferries departing from the Central Ferry Pier (home also of the Star Ferry). The HKTB has ferry schedules, or call **First Ferry** at ℂ **852/2131 8181** or check its website at www.nwff.com.hk for travel to Cheung Chau and Lantau. For Lamma, call ℂ **852/2815 6063** or visit www.hkkf.com.hk.

BY TAXI   Taxi drivers in Hong Kong are strictly controlled and as a rule are fairly honest. Fares start at HK$15 (US$1.95/£1) for the first 2km (1¼ miles), then HK$1.40 (US20¢/10p) for each 200m (656 ft.). Luggage costs an extra HK$5 (US65¢/30p) per piece, and taxis ordered by phone add a HK$5 (US65¢/30p) surcharge. Extra charges are also permitted for trips through harbor tunnels and Aberdeen Tunnel. At major taxi stands, there are separate lines for Kowloon and Island-side taxis. A 24-hour hot line handles complaints about taxis (© **852/2889 9999**).

BY MINIBUS These small, 16-passenger buses are the poor person's taxis. There are two types of vehicles: The green-and-yellow public "light buses," which follow fixed routes, charge fixed rates ranging from HK$2 to HK$20 (US25¢–US$2.60/15p–£1.30) depending on the distance, and require the exact fare as you enter (many also accept Octopus cards); the red-and-yellow **minibuses** will stop wherever you hail them and do not follow fixed routes. Fares for these range from HK$2 to HK$23 (US25¢–US$2.90/15p–£1.50), and you pay as you exit. Just yell when you want to get off.

FAST FACTS: Hong Kong

American Express American Express offices (Mon–Fri 9am–5pm and Sat 9am–12:30pm) are located up on the first floor of the Henley Building, 5 Queen's Rd. Central, in the Central District (© **852/3192 7788**); and at 48 Cameron Rd. (© **852/3191 3838**) in Tsim Sha Tsui.

Banks, Foreign Exchange & ATMs Although opening hours may vary among banks, banking hours are generally Monday through Friday from 9am to 4:30pm and Saturday from 9am to 12:30pm. Some banks stop their transactions an hour before closing time. ATMs are everywhere, and almost all accept foreign cards.

Doctors & Dentists Most first-class hotels have medical clinics with registered nurses, as well as doctors on duty at specified hours or on call 24 hours (see individual hotel listings below). Otherwise, your concierge or the U.S. consulate can refer you to a doctor or dentist. In an emergency, dial © **999** or call one of the recommendations under "Hospitals," below.

Embassies & Consulates The consulate of the **United States** is at 26 Garden Rd., Central District (© **852/2523 9011**, or 852/2841 2211 for the American Citizens Service; www.hongkong.usconsulate.gov). The consulate of **Canada** is on the 11th to 14th floors of Tower One, Exchange Square, 8 Connaught Place, Central District (© **852/2867 7348**; www.dfait-maeci.gc.ca/asia/hongkong). The consulate of the **U.K.** is at 1 Supreme Court Rd., Central District (© **852/2901 3000**, or 852/2901 3222 for passport inquiries; www.britishconsulate.org.hk). The consulate of **Australia** is on the 23rd and 24th floors of Harbour Centre, 25 Harbour Rd., Wan Chai, on Hong Kong Island (© **852/2827 8881**; www. Australia.org.hk). The consulate of **New Zealand** is on the 65th floor of Central Plaza, 18 Harbour Rd., Wan Chai (© **852/2525 5044**; www.nzembassy.com/ hongkong). Most other nations, including all of China's neighbors—even hermit kingdoms like North Korea and Bhutan—also have representation in Hong Kong. Collect onward visas here.

Hospitals Try **Queen Mary Hospital**, 102 Pokfulam Rd., Hong Kong Island (© **852/2855 3838**); and **Queen Elizabeth Hospital**, 30 Gascoigne Rd., Kowloon (© **852/2958 8888**).

Internet Access **Shadowman**, 21A Ashley Rd., Tsim Sha Tsui (© **852/2366 5262**) is a small cybercafe open Monday to Thursday 8am to midnight, Friday and Saturday from 8am to 1am, and Sunday from 10am to midnight. It offers free Internet access for 20 minutes with the purchase of a drink or snack and charges HK$10 (US1.30/65p) per 15 minutes beyond that. **Pacific Coffee (www.pacificcoffee.com)** is a chain of coffee shops, several with computers offering free Internet access. Its shop no. 1022 in the International Finance Center (IFC), above Hong Kong Station in Central (© **852/2868 5100**), is open Sunday through Thursday from 7am to 11pm and Friday and Saturday from 7am to midnight.

Newspapers The *South China Morning Post* and *The Standard* are the two local English-language daily newspapers. The *Asian Wall Street Journal, Financial Times, International Herald Tribune,* and *USA Today International* are also available.

Pharmacies There are no 24-hour drugstores in Hong Kong. One of the best-known pharmacies in Hong Kong is **Watson's,** with more than 100 branches, most of them open from 9am to 10pm.

Police You can reach the police for an emergency by dialing © **999,** the same number as for a fire or an ambulance.

Post Offices Airmail letters up to 20 grams (.7 ounces) and postcards cost HK$3 (US40¢/20p) to the United States or Europe. Most hotels have stamps and can mail your letters for you. Otherwise, most post offices are open Monday through Friday from 9:30am to 5pm and Saturday from 9:30am to 1pm. The main post office is at 2 Connaught Place, Central District, Hong Kong Island (© **852/2921 2222**). You can have your mail sent here "Poste Restante," where it will be held for 2 months; be sure to bring along your passport for identification. On the Kowloon side, the main post office is at 10 Middle Rd., which is 1 block north of Salisbury Road (© **852/2366 4111**). Both are open Monday through Saturday from 8am to 6pm and Sunday from 9am to 2pm.

Weather If you want to check the day's temperature and humidity level or the 2-day forecast, dial © **187 8200** or 187 8066.

3 Where to Stay

Hotel rates listed below are the hotels' official or "rack" rates, which you might end up paying if you come during peak season (Chinese New Year, Mar–May, Oct–Nov, major trade fairs). Otherwise, you should be able to get a room for much less by calling the hotel directly to ask whether any promotional rates are available, or by checking the hotel's website.

Hong Kong's top hotels are among the best in the world, many with sweeping views of Victoria Harbour (for which you'll pay dearly) and superb service and amenities. Although the greatest concentration of hotels is on the Kowloon side, Hong Kong is so compact and easily traversed by public transportation that location is not the issue it is in larger, more sprawling metropolises. Moderate hotels comprise the majority of hotels in Hong Kong, with smaller rooms compared to their American counterparts and catering largely to the burgeoning growth of tourists from mainland China.

Inexpensive hotels offer just the basics. A 10% service charge and 3% government tax will be added to prices quoted below.

KOWLOON
EXPENSIVE

Hotel Inter-Continental Hong Kong ★★★   The stylish Inter-Continental, located on the water's edge, boasts the best views of Victoria Harbour from Tsim Sha Tsui, with about 70% of its rooms commanding sweeping views of the harbor with floor-to-ceiling and wall-to-wall windows. Other notable features here are the highly rated restaurants; state-of-the-art spa renowned for its healing treatments; free tai chi and yoga classes; contemporary rooms with 37-inch LCD TVs, iPod docking stations, air purification systems, and spacious bathrooms (each fitted in Italian marble with a sunken bathtub, separate shower, and adjoining walk-in closets); and wireless broadband that enables guests to access the Internet even from poolside.

18 Salisbury Rd., Tsim Sha Tsui, Kowloon, Hong Kong. ⓒ 800/327-0200 in the U.S. and Canada, or 852/2721 1211. Fax 852/2739 4546. www.hongkong-ic.intercontinental.com. 495 units. HK$3,900–HK$5,400 (US$506–US$701/ £279–£386) single or double; HK$700 (US$91/£50) extra for Club lounge; from HK$8,000 (US$1,039/£571) suite. Children under 12 stay free in parent's room. AE, DC, MC, V. MTR: Tsim Sha Tsui. **Amenities:** 5 restaurants; bar; lounge; outdoor pool; whirlpools overlooking Victoria Harbour; fitness room (open 24 hr.); spa; concierge; limousine service; business center; upscale shopping arcade; 24-hr. room service; massage; babysitting; same-day laundry service/dry cleaning; house doctor. *In room:* A/C, satellite TV w/keyboard for Internet access and on-demand pay movies, wireless Internet access, minibar, coffeemaker, hair dryer, safe.

The Peninsula Hotel ★★★ *(Value*   This is Hong Kong's most famous hotel and *the* place to stay. Built in 1928, it exudes elegance, from its white-gloved doormen to one of the largest limousine fleets of Rolls-Royces in the world. Its lobby, with high gilded ceilings, pillars, and palms, has long been Hong Kong's foremost spot for afternoon tea and people-watching. Its restaurants are among the city's best, classes are offered on everything from tai chi and feng shui to cooking, and its spa offers harbor views even from its sauna. A magnificent 32-story tower added in 1993 provides fantastic views also from guest rooms and its top-floor restaurant, Felix, designed by Philippe Starck. Spacious rooms are so wonderfully equipped that even jaded travelers are likely to be impressed.

Salisbury Rd., Tsim Sha Tsui, Kowloon, Hong Kong. ⓒ 800/462-7899 in the U.S. and Canada, or 852/2920 2888. Fax 852/2722 4170. www.peninsula.com. 300 units. HK$2,900–HK$4,200 (US$377–US$545/£207–£300) single or double; from HK$4,600 (US$597/£329) suite. AE, DC, MC, V. MTR: Tsim Sha Tsui. **Amenities:** 6 restaurants; 2 bars; lounge; gorgeous indoor pool w/sun terrace overlooking the harbor; health club; spa; concierge; limousine service; business center; designer-brand shopping arcade; salon; 24-hr. room service; massage; babysitting; same-day laundry service/dry cleaning; in-house nurse. *In room:* A/C, cable/satellite TV w/CD/DVD player (free in-house movies), fax, free high-speed dataport, minibar, hair dryer, safe.

MODERATE

Eaton Hotel ★★ *(Finds*   This property has more class and facilities than most in its price range. A handsome, 21-story brick building, it's located above a shopping complex not far from the Temple Street Night Market. The lobby lounge is bright and cheerful, with a four-story glass-enclosed atrium that overlooks a garden terrace with a water cascade, where you can sit outside with drinks in nice weather. Other pluses are the small but nicely done rooftop pool with sunning terrace, free daily guided tours of the night market, and small but welcoming guest rooms with all the basic creature comforts.

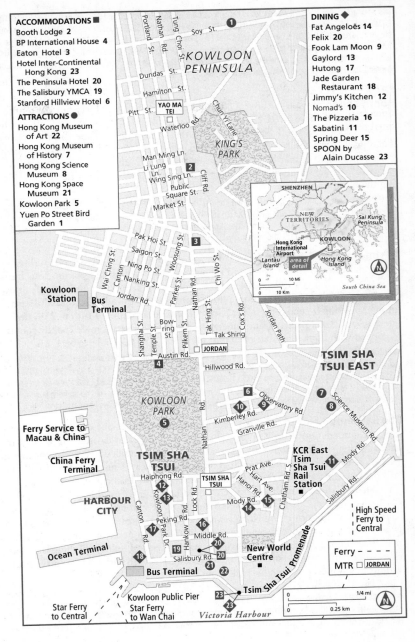

Kowloon

ACCOMMODATIONS ■
Booth Lodge **2**
BP International House **4**
Eaton Hotel **3**
Hotel Inter-Continental
  Hong Kong **23**
The Peninsula Hotel **20**
The Salisbury YMCA **19**
Stanford Hillview Hotel **6**

ATTRACTIONS ●
Hong Kong Museum
  of Art **22**
Hong Kong Museum
  of History **7**
Hong Kong Science
  Museum **8**
Hong Kong Space
  Museum **21**
Kowloon Park **5**
Yuen Po Street Bird
  Garden **1**

DINING ◆
Fat Angeloës **14**
Felix **20**
Fook Lam Moon **9**
Gaylord **13**
Hutong **17**
Jade Garden
  Restaurant **18**
Jimmy's Kitchen **12**
Nomad's **10**
The Pizzeria **16**
Sabatini **11**
Spring Deer **15**
SPOON by
  Alain Ducasse **23**

380 Nathan Rd., Yau Ma Tei, Kowloon, Hong Kong. © 800/223-5652 in the U.S. and Canada, or 852/2782 1818. Fax 852/2782 5563. www.eaton-hotel.com. 460 units. HK$1,950–HK$2,150 (US$253–US$279/£139–£154) single or double; HK$2,470–HK$2,670 (US$356–US$347/£176–£190) executive room. AE, DC, MC, V. MTR: Jordan. **Amenities:** 3 restaurants; bar; lounge; small outdoor pool; exercise room; concierge; 24-hr. business center; shopping arcade; 24-hr. room service; babysitting; same-day laundry service/dry cleaning. *In room:* A/C, satellite TV w/pay movies on demand, dataport, minibar, coffeemaker, hair dryer, safe.

INEXPENSIVE

Booth Lodge ⌘ *(Finds)*   About a 30-minute walk to the Star Ferry but close to the Jade Market, Temple Street Night Market, Ladies' Market, and MTR station, Booth Lodge is located just off Nathan Road on the seventh floor of the Salvation Army building. It has a comfortable lobby and an adjacent coffee shop offering reasonably priced lunch and dinner buffets. Rooms, all twins or doubles and either standard or larger deluxe, are spotlessly clean. Some face the madness of Nathan Road; those facing the hillside are quieter.

11 Wing Sing Lane, Yau Ma Tei, Kowloon, Hong Kong. © 852/2771 9266. Fax 852/2385 1140. http://boothlodge. salvation.org.hk. 53 units. HK$620–HK$1,500 (US$81–US$195/£44–£107) single or double. Rates include buffet breakfast. AE, MC, V. MTR: Yau Ma Tei. **Amenities:** Coffee shop; tour desk; laundry service/dry cleaning. *In room:* A/C, satellite TV, free local phone calls, fridge, hair dryer.

BP International House *(Kids)*   This 25-story hotel has a spacious but utilitarian lobby and caters mainly to tour and school groups as well as budget-conscious business travelers. Built in 1993 at the north end of Kowloon Park, it's just a stone's throw from the park's indoor and outdoor public swimming pools and a short walk to a playground, making it good for families. Guest rooms, located on the 14th to 25th floors, are tiny but clean, pleasant, and modern. There are also very simple "family rooms" equipped with bunk beds that sleep four for HK$1,350 (US$175/£96).

8 Austin Rd., Tsim Sha Tsui, Kowloon, Hong Kong. © 800/223-5652 in the U.S. and Canada, or 852/2376 1111. Fax 852/2376 1333. www.bpih.com.hk. 529 units. HK$1,100 (US$143/£79) standard; HK$1,400–HK$2,100 (US$180–US$270/£100–£150) corporate room; from HK$3,100 (US$403/£221) suite. Children under 12 stay free in parent's room. AE, DC, MC, V. MTR: Jordan. **Amenities:** Coffee shop; lounge; tour desk; babysitting; coin-op laundry; laundry service/dry cleaning; executive-level rooms. *In room:* A/C, satellite TV w/pay movies, wireless Internet access, fridge, safe.

The Salisbury YMCA ⌘⌘⌘ *(Kids)*   For decades the number-one choice among low-cost accommodations, this YMCA right next to The Peninsula near the waterfront offers 19 single rooms (none with harbor view) and more than 250 doubles and twins (the most expensive provide great harbor views), as well as suites with and without harbor views that are perfect for families. Although simple in decor, these rooms are on a par with those at more expensively priced hotels in terms of in-room amenities. For budget travelers, there are also seven dormitory-style rooms, available only to visitors who have been in Hong Kong fewer than 7 days. Great for families is its sports facility boasting two indoor swimming pools (one a lap pool, the other a children's pool, free to hotel guests), a fitness gym, squash courts, and indoor climbing wall (fees charged). Because this is Tsim Sha Tsui's cheapest hotel with harbor views, make reservations in advance, especially in peak times.

Salisbury Rd., Tsim Sha Tsui, Kowloon, Hong Kong. © 800/537-8483 in the U.S. and Canada, or 852/2268 7000 (852/2268 7888 for reservations). Fax 852/2739 9315. www.ymcahk.org.hk. 368 units. HK$950 (US$123/£68) single; HK$1,050–HK$1,250 (US$136–US$162/£75–£89) standard; from HK$1,600 (US$208/£114) suite. Dormitory bed HK$230 (US$30/£16). AE, DC, MC, V. MTR: Tsim Sha Tsui. **Amenities:** 2 restaurants; 2 indoor pools; exercise room; Jacuzzi; sauna; squash courts; badminton; climbing wall; tour desk; salon; room service 7am–10pm; babysitting; coin-op laundry; laundry service/dry cleaning; bookstore. *In room:* A/C, satellite/cable TV, wireless Internet access, minibar, coffeemaker, hair dryer, safe.

Stanford Hillview Hotel ⭐ *Finds* This small, intimate hotel is near the heart of Tsim Sha Tsui and yet a world away, located on top of a hill in the shade of some huge banyan trees, next to the Royal Observatory with its colonial building and greenery. Knutsford Terrace, an alley with trendy bars and restaurants, is just around the corner. Its lobby is quiet and subdued (quite a contrast to those in most Hong Kong hotels) and its staff friendly and accommodating. Rooms are basic and small.

13–17 Observatory Rd., Tsim Sha Tsui, Kowloon, Hong Kong. ⓒ 852/2722 7822. Fax 852/2723 3718. www. stanfordhillview.com. 163 units. HK$1,000–HK$1,680 (US$130–US$218/£71–£120) single or double. AE, DC, MC, V. MTR: Tsim Sha Tsui. **Amenities:** Restaurant; lounge; outdoor golf-driving nets; exercise room; business center; 24-hr. room service; babysitting; same-day laundry/dry cleaning. *In room:* A/C, cable TV w/pay movies, wireless Internet access, minibar, coffeemaker, hair dryer.

CENTRAL
EXPENSIVE

Four Seasons Hotel Hong Kong ⭐⭐⭐ Opened in 2005 just a stone's throw from the Central Ferry Piers, ifc mall, and Hong Kong Station, this gorgeous, 45-story property is a cool urban oasis, buffered from the city's inherent bustle and providing a polished service that rises above even Hong Kong's legendary pampering. It boasts a luxurious spa, outdoor lap and infinity pools with great harbor views, and one of the hottest French restaurants in town. Its rooms are to die for, decorated in either contemporary Western style or a modern take on traditional Chinese design and featuring city or harbor views, 42-inch plasma TVs, and spacious marbled bathrooms with two sinks, shower stalls, and deep soaking tubs.

8 Finance St., Central, Hong Kong. ⓒ 800/819-5053 in the U.S. and Canada, or 852/3196 8888. Fax 852/3196 8899. www.fourseasons.com/hongkong. 399 units. HK$3,800–HK$4,200 (US$494–US$545/£271–£300) single or double; extra HK$700 (US$91/£50) single or HK$900 (US$117/£64) double for executive lounge; from HK$5,500 (US$714/£393) suite. AE, DC, MC, V. MTR: Central. **Amenities:** 2 restaurants; bar; lounge; 2 outdoor heated pools w/whirlpool, open year-round; 24-hr. health club; spa; sauna; concierge; tour desk; limousine service; 24-hr. business center; connected to shopping arcade; salon; 24-hr. room service; babysitting; same-day laundry service/dry cleaning. *In room:* A/C, satellite TV w/keyboard for Internet access and on-demand pay movies, DVD/CD players, wireless Internet access, minibar, coffeemaker, hair dryer, safe.

Island Shangri-La Hong Kong ⭐⭐⭐ *Finds* With Hong Kong Park on one side and the upscale Pacific Place shopping mall on the other, Hong Kong Island's tallest hotel offers the ultimate in extravagance and luxury, rivaling the grand hotels of Europe with its Viennese chandeliers, lush Tai Ping carpets, and artwork throughout. The 17-story atrium, which stretches from the 39th to the 56th floors, features a marvelous 16-story-high Chinese painting, drawn by 40 artists from Beijing and believed to be the largest landscape painting in the world. Also in the atrium are a private lounge open only to hotel guests, and a two-story old-world-style library. Elegant rooms, among the largest in Hong Kong, face either Victoria Peak or spectacular Victoria Harbour.

Pacific Place, Supreme Court Rd., Central, Hong Kong. ⓒ 866/565-5050 in the U.S., or 852/2877 3838. Fax 852/2521 8742. www.shangri-la.com. 565 units. HK$3,000–HK$4,300 (US$389–US$558/£214–£307) single; HK$3,300–HK$4,700 (US$428–US$610/£236–£336) double; from HK$6,600 (US$857/£471) suite. Children under 12 stay free in parent's room. AE, DC, MC, V. MTR: Admiralty. **Amenities:** 6 restaurants; lounge; outdoor heated pool; 24-hr. health club; spa; Jacuzzi; sauna; steam bath; concierge; tour desk; limousine service; 24-hr. business center; adjoining shopping arcade; salon; 24-hr. room service; massage; babysitting; same-day laundry service/dry cleaning; medical clinic; free shuttle to Queen's Pier in Central and Convention Centre. *In room:* A/C, satellite TV w/pay movies on demand, DVD players, fax/printer/scanner, dataport, minibar, coffeemaker, hair dryer, safe.

MID-LEVELS
MODERATE
Bishop Lei International House ★★ *Finds*   Located about halfway up Victoria Peak in a residential area favored by expats, this hotel makes up for its out-of-the-way location with free shuttle service to Central, Admiralty, and Wan Chai; a half-dozen city buses stop outside its door, and the Central–Mid-Levels Escalator is nearby. It offers tiny standard rooms (with even tinier bathrooms, most with showers instead of tubs) that have large windows letting in lots of sunshine but that face inland. If you can, spring for a more expensive room with fantastic harbor views.

4 Robinson Rd., Mid-Levels, Hong Kong. © 852/2868 0828. Fax 852/2868 1551. www.bishopleihtl.com.hk. 203 units. HK$1,280 (US$166/£91) single; HK$1,480 (US$192/£106) double; HK$1,880–HK$2,080 (US$244–US$270/£134–£149) twin; from HK$2,480 (US$322/£177) suite. 1 child under 12 can stay free in parent's room. AE, DC, MC, V. Bus: no. 3B, 12, 12M, 23, 23A, or 40 to Robinson Rd. **Amenities:** Coffee shop; small outdoor pool; small exercise room; business center; 24-hr. room service; babysitting; same-day laundry service/dry cleaning; free shuttle bus. *In room:* A/C, cable TV, high-speed dataport, minibar, coffeemaker (but no coffee), hair dryer, safe.

CAUSEWAY BAY/WAN CHAI
MODERATE
Jia ★★ *Finds*   Hong Kong's hippest boutique hotel, designed by Philippe Starck and opened in 2004, goes out of its way to prove it's no ordinary place of abode, with a staff decked out in chic Shanghai Tang–designed uniforms and stylish rooms bathed in white. Studios and one- and two-bedroom suites are available, complete with kitchens and home entertainment centers. Add a bunch of freebies—like local complimentary telephone calls, Internet access, breakfast, cocktail hour, and access to a local gym—and it seems well positioned for both business and tourist markets.

1–5 Irving St., Causeway Bay, Hong Kong. © 852/3196 9000. Fax 852/3196 9001. www.jiahongkong.com. 54 units. HK$1,800 (US$234/£129) single or double; from HK$2,600 (US$338/£186) suite. Rates include continental breakfast. AE, DC, MC, V. MTR: Causeway Bay. **Amenities:** 2 restaurants; bar; free access to nearby health club; sun deck; room service noon–10pm; same-day laundry service/dry cleaning. *In room:* A/C, satellite/cable TV w/DVD/CD player, dataport, kitchen, hair dryer, safe.

Lanson Place Boutique Hotel & Residences ★★★ *Value*   Following close on Jia's heels (and just down the street), this stylish boutique hotel caters to long-staying guests with upbeat, contemporary rooms and one-and two-bedroom residences, all with kitchenettes, home theater systems (you can check out DVDs for free at reception), and mobile phones you can carry to breakfast or the gym. While in-house facilities are limited, this is a perfect home-away-from-home for weary road warriors, and the staff, which runs operations from sit-down desks, couldn't be nicer.

133 Leighton Rd., Causeway Bay, Hong Kong. © 852/3477 6888. Fax 852/3477 6999. www.lansonplace.com. 194 units. HK$1,500–HK$3,200 (US$195–US$415/£107–£229) single or double; from HK$4,200 (US$545/£300) suite. Rates include continental breakfast. Children under 12 stay free in parent's room. AE, DC, MC, V. MTR: Causeway Bay. **Amenities:** Bar; small gym; limousine service; business center; coin-operated laundry; same-day laundry service/dry cleaning. *In room:* A/C, satellite TV w/DVD/CD player, free wireless Internet access, kitchen, hair dryer, safe.

Metropark Hotel ★   Although not as centrally located as other Causeway Bay hotels, this property makes up for it with free shuttle service to the Causeway Bay shopping district and the convention center (MTR and tram lines are just outside the door). It's cheerier and more colorful than most hotels, with a contemporary, fun design that extends through the lobby and into the rooms, the most expensive of which have great views over Victoria Park to the harbor (the cheapest rooms face

Central Hong Kong

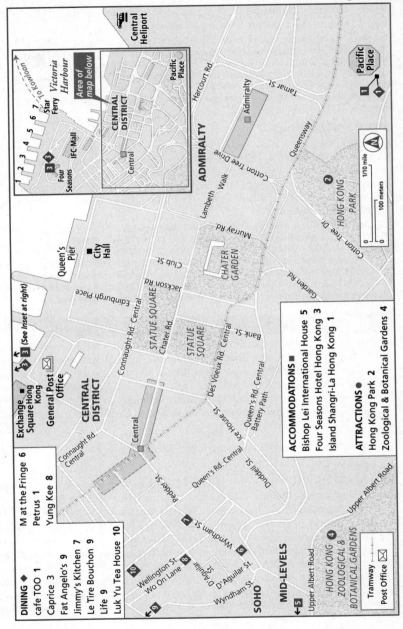

DINING ◆
cafe TOO 1
Caprice 3
Fat Angelo's 9
Jimmy's Kitchen 7
Le Tire Bouchon 9
Life 9
Luk Yu Tea House 10
M at the Fringe 6
Petrus 1
Yung Kee 8

ACCOMMODATIONS ■
Bishop Lei International House 5
Four Seasons Hotel Hong Kong 3
Island Shangri-La Hong Kong 1

ATTRACTIONS ●
Hong Kong Park 2
Zoological & Botanical Gardens 4

Tramway
Post Office ⊠

another building). Bathrooms, however, are small, with showers instead of tubs and limited counter space, but the rooftop pool has great views.

148 Tung Lo Wan Rd., Causeway Bay, Hong Kong. © 800/223-5652 in the U.S. and Canada, or 852/2600 1000. Fax 852/2600 1111. www.metroparkhotel.com. 266 units. HK$900 (US$117/£64) single; HK$1,500–HK$1,800 (US$195–US$234/£107–£129) double; from HK$2,600 (US$338/£186) suite. Children under 12 stay free in parent's room. AE, DC, MC, V. MTR: Tin Hau. **Amenities:** Coffee shop; bar; outdoor pool; exercise room; Jacuzzi; sauna; tour desk; business center; 24-hr. room service; same-day laundry service/dry cleaning; free shuttle to Wan Chai and Causeway Bay. *In room:* A/C, cable/satellite TV w/pay movies on demand, free Internet access, minibar, coffeemaker, hair dryer, safe.

NEAR THE AIRPORT
EXPENSIVE

Regal Airport Hotel ✦   Opened in 1998, this is the only hotel at Hong Kong International Airport, a 5-minute walk from the terminal via covered walkway. Guest rooms are large and soundproof, with modern furniture in eye-popping colors of purple, red, or lime green, but there's no mistaking that this is an airport hotel, functional but rather characterless.

9 Cheong Tat Rd., Chek Lap Kok, Hong Kong. © 800/457-4000 in the U.S. and Canada, or 852/2286 8888. Fax 852/2286 8686. www.regalhotel.com. 1,100 units. HK$2,400–HK$3,700 (US$312–US$481/£165–£255) single or double; from HK$3,700 (US$481/£255) Regal Class; from HK$4,500 (US$584/£310) Regal Club. Children under 13 stay free in parent's room (maximum 3 persons per room). AE, DC, MC, V. Airport Express Liner: Hong Kong International Airport. **Amenities:** 5 restaurants; lounge; indoor and outdoor pools; health club and spa; concierge; limousine service; 24-hr. business center; shopping arcade; salon; 24-hr. room service; babysitting; same-day laundry/dry-cleaning service; house doctor. *In room:* A/C, satellite TV w/pay movies, minibar, coffeemaker, hair dryer, safe.

4 Where to Dine

With more than 11,000 restaurants from which to choose, in a few short days you can take a culinary tour of China, dining on Cantonese, Sichuan, Shanghainese, Beijing, Chiu Chow, and other Chinese specialties. Other national cuisines are also popular, including French, Italian, American, Thai, Indian, and Japanese. A welcome trend has seen talented chefs opening neighborhood establishments in ever greater numbers. Avoid dining from 1 to 2pm on weekdays, the traditional lunch hour for office workers.

KOWLOON

For Kowloon restaurant locations, see the map on page 563.

EXPENSIVE

Felix ✦✦✦ *Value* PACIFIC RIM FUSION   Designer Philippe Starck has made sure that Felix is not your ordinary dining experience, beginning with the elevator's wavy walls and continuing inside the restaurant, where a huge aluminum wall and two glass facades reveal stunning views of Kowloon and Hong Kong Island. The food, featuring Pacific Rim ingredients brought together in East-meets-West combinations, rarely disappoints. You might start with seafood pot stickers, followed by the Mongolian-style barbecued rack of lamb. Bargain hunters can dine before 7pm and opt for a three-course fixed-price dinner for HK$38 (US$50/£25). Or just come by for a drink.

In The Peninsula Hotel, Salisbury Rd., Tsim Sha Tsui. © 852/2315 3188. www.peninsula.com. Reservations required. Main courses HK$225–HK$350 (US$29–US$45/£16–£25). AE, DC, MC, V. 6pm–2am (last order 10:30pm). MTR: Tsim Sha Tsui.

Fook Lam Moon ✦✦✦ CANTONESE   Upon entering this restaurant you immediately feel as if you've stepped back a couple of decades. The decor is outdated, and, unless you're a regular, the waiters are indifferent. Yet this remains *the* place to go for exotic dishes, including shark's fin, bird's nest, and abalone. Some Hong Kong old-timers swear this restaurant serves the best Cantonese food in the world, but you can dine more cheaply here on dim sum for lunch.

There's another branch in Wan Chai at 35–45 Johnston Rd. (© **852/2866 0663;** MTR: Wan Chai), with the same hours.

53–59 Kimberley Rd., Tsim Sha Tsui. © 852/2366 0286. www.fooklammoon-grp.com. Reservations recommended for dinner. Main dishes HK$100–HK$240 (US$13–US$31/£7–£17). AE, DC, MC, V. 11:30am–2:30pm and 6–11:30pm. MTR: Tsim Sha Tsui.

Sabatini ★★ *Finds* ITALIAN   The dining hall here is rustic and cozy yet refined, with live guitar music in the evenings. An offshoot of the original restaurant opened by the Sabatini brothers in Rome in 1954, its menu is a faithful replica of the fare served there, with liberal doses of olive oil, garlic, and peppers and including hand-made pasta. Popular dishes include Dover sole with Prosecco, green and black olives, and herbed lemon butter; and veal with morel sauce. The list of mostly Italian wines is seemingly endless.

In the Royal Garden hotel, 69 Mody Rd., Tsim Sha Tsui East. © 852/2733 2000. www.rghk.com.hk. Reservations required. Main courses HK$278–HK$408 (US$36–US$53/£20–£29); fixed-price lunch Mon–Sat HK$125–HK$148 (US$16–US$19/£8.90–£11); Sun and holiday buffet HK$388 (US$50/£28). AE, DC, MC, V. Noon–2:30pm and 6–11pm. MTR: Tsim Sha Tsui.

SPOON by Alain Ducasse ★★★ FRENCH   Dinner at this sophisticated venue is more than just a meal—it's an experience. The focal point of the dining room is the ceiling, where 550 handblown Murano glass spoons are lined up like a landing strip, directing one's attention to the open kitchen and to the stunning harbor view just beyond the massive windows. The menu, featuring the contemporary cuisine inspired by chef and restaurateur Alain Ducasse, gives diners the freedom to mix and match food and cooking styles by selecting an entree (the steak is superb), its sauce, and accompanying vegetables. You might, therefore, pair Chilean sea bass with pistachio and macadamia nuts with a coconut/lemon-grass condiment, served with a baby spinach bamboo salad. Or, your entire group may opt for the Sexy Spoon, a menu created for your table for HK$750 (US$97/£54) per person.

In the Hotel Inter-Continental Hong Kong, Salisbury Rd., Tsim Sha Tsui. © 852/2721 1211, ext. 2323. www.hongkong-ic.intercontinental.com. Reservations required. Main courses HK$235–HK$495 (US$31–US$64/£17–£35). AE, DC, MC, V. 6pm–midnight. MTR: Tsim Sha Tsui.

MODERATE

Gaylord ★ INDIAN   This long-established, first-floor restaurant in the heart of Tsim Sha Tsui is popular for its authentic North Indian classics, including tandoori, lamb curry cooked in North Indian spices and herbs, chicken cooked in fiery-hot vin-daloo curry, prawns cooked with green pepper and spices, and fish with potatoes and tomatoes. There are also a dozen vegetarian dishes. The lunchtime buffet, served every day except Sunday and public holidays until 2:30pm, is a winner. There are also fixed-price dinners, along with a dinner buffet available until 9:30pm.

23–25 Ashley Rd., Tsim Sha Tsui. © 852/2376 1001. Main dishes HK$88–HK$168 (US$11–US$22/£6.30–£12); lunch buffet HK$88 (US$11/£6.30); dinner buffet HK$138 (US$18/£9.85); fixed-price dinner HK$160–HK$210 (US$21–US$27/£11–£15). AE, DC, MC, V. Noon–2:30pm and 6:30–11pm. MTR: Tsim Sha Tsui.

Hutong ★★★ *Finds* NORTHERN CHINESE   This stunning restaurant is about as far from a real *hutong* (ancient Beijing alleyway) as one can get, since it's located on the 28th floor of a strikingly modern high-rise. Still, the restaurant is to be commended for its down-to-earth yet dramatic setting, with red lanterns providing the only splash of color against a dark, muted interior with fantastic views of Hong Kong. The cuisine uses new ingredients and combinations to create its own trademark dishes, along with classic north Chinese fare, including drunken raw crab (an appetizer marinated 3 days in Chinese wine), the crispy deboned lamb ribs, and crispy soft-shelled crab with Sichuan red chili. Dim sum is available for lunch.

1 Peking Rd. (28th floor), Tsim Sha Tsui. © 852/3428 8342. www.aqua.com.hk. Reservations required for dinner. Main dishes HK$120–HK$288 (US$16–US$37/£8.55–£21). AE, DC, MC, V. Noon–3pm and 6–11:30pm. MTR: Tsim Sha Tsui.

Jade Garden Restaurant CANTONESE   Jade Garden is popular with Chinese families and is the place to go if you don't know much about Chinese food but want to try it. The view of the harbor afforded by some of the window-side tables is a major plus. Dim sum is available for lunch from an English menu; or, you might consider drunken shrimp boiled in rice wine, deep-fried boneless chicken with lemon sauce, or stir-fried minced pigeon served with lemon leaves. Also at 1 Hysan Ave., Causeway Bay (© **852/2577 9332**). Open 7:30am–midnight.

Star House (4th floor), 3 Salisbury Rd., Tsim Sha Tsui. © **852/2730 6888**. Main dishes HK$68–HK$168 (US$8.85–US$22/£4.85–£12). AE, DC, MC, V. Mon–Sat 11am–11:30pm; Sun and holidays 10am–11:30pm. MTR: Tsim Sha Tsui.

The Pizzeria ⟨★⟨Value ITALIAN   Located on the second floor of the Kowloon Hotel (just behind The Peninsula), this casual and bustling dining hall offers relaxed meals at good prices. It offers a dozen different combinations of pizza, as well as pasta dishes like herbed pasta with homemade Italian sausage, porcini mushrooms and pecorino cheese, and main courses that include fish dishes.

In the Kowloon Hotel, 19–21 Nathan Rd., Tsim Sha Tsui. © 852/2929 2888, ext. 3322. www.thekowloonhotel.com. Pasta and pizza HK$128–HK$158 (US$17–US$21/£9.15–£11); main courses HK$188–HK$238 (US$24–US$31/£13–£17); fixed-price lunch HK$98 (US$13/£7) Mon–Fri, HK$210 (US$27/£15) Sat–Sun. AE, DC, MC, V. Noon–3pm and 6–11pm. MTR: Tsim Sha.

INEXPENSIVE

Fat Angelo's ⟨Value ITALIAN   This local chain offers good value with its hearty, American renditions of Italian food, including pastas ranging from traditional spaghetti marinara to fettuccine with salmon and main courses that include rosemary roasted chicken, grilled salmon with pesto, and eggplant Parmesan, all of which come with salad and homemade bread. The emphasis is on quantity, not quality, though the food isn't bad. And they really pack 'em in; this place is bustling and loud. Also at the Elizabeth House, 250 Gloucester Rd. in Causeway Bay (© **852/2574 6263;** MTR: Causeway Bay), Wu Chung House, 213 Queen's Rd. E., Wan Chai (© **852/2126 7020**), and 49A-C Elgin St., Central (© **852/2973 6808;** MTR: Central), all open noon to midnight.

33 Ashley Rd., Tsim Sha Tsui. © 852/2730 4788. www.fatangelos.com. Reservations recommended. Pasta HK$88–HK$178 (US$11–US$23/£6.30–£13); main courses HK$128–HK$218 (US$17–US$28/£9.15–£16). AE, DC, MC, V. Noon–midnight. MTR: Tsim Sha Tsui.

Nomads ⟨★⟨Finds ASIAN   This very popular Mongolian restaurant allows diners to select their own raw ingredients for one-dish meals that are then stir-fried by short-order cooks. All-you-can-eat lunches and dinners give choices of vegetables, meats, seafood, sauces, noodles, rice, and spices, spread buffet-style along a counter together with salads and dessert. Sheepskin-draped chairs, rawhide lampshades, animal skins, and tribal weaponry hung on walls transport this restaurant straight into the Mongolia of our fantasies.

55 Kimberley Rd., Tsim Sha Tsui. ℂ 852/2722 0733. www.igors.com. Lunch buffet HK$58 (US$7.55/£4.15) Mon–Thurs, HK$68 (US$8.85/£4.85) Fri–Sat; dinner buffet HK$168 (US$22/£12). AE, DC, MC, V. Noon–2:30pm and 6:30–10:30pm. MTR: Tsim Sha Tsui.

Spring Deer Restaurant *Finds* BEIJING   This long-established restaurant offers excellent Beijing food at reasonable prices. Your tablecloth may have holes in it, but it will be clean—and the place is usually packed. Best on the menu is its specialty—honey-glazed Peking duck, which costs HK$280 (US$36/£20). You'll probably have to wait 40 minutes for the duck if you order it during peak time (7:30–9:30pm). Chicken dishes are also excellent, as are the handmade noodles. Most dishes come in small, medium, and large sizes; the small dishes are suitable for two people to share.

42 Mody Rd., Tsim Sha Tsui. ℂ 852/2366 4012. Reservations recommended. Small dishes HK$54–HK$90 (US$7–US$12/£3.85–£6.40). AE, MC, V. 11:30am–3pm and 6–11pm. MTR: Tsim Sha Tsui.

CENTRAL

For Central Hong Kong restaurant locations, see the map on p. 567.

EXPENSIVE

Caprice ✸✸✸ FRENCH   Ensconced in the sleek Four Seasons Hotel Hong Kong, this is *the* restaurant of the moment. Under the skilled guidance of chef Vincent Thiery, brought from Le Cinq in the Four Seasons George V Paris, Caprice garners high marks for its innovative take on French classics and gorgeous setting affording dramatic views of Victoria Harbour. The menu, orchestrated around the seasons and drawing inspiration from provincial influences throughout France, may include the likes of sautéed scallops with black truffles, nest of capellini pasta, butternut squash, and Parmesan cream; or warm duck foie gras with Granny Smith compote, beets, and dry sherry. If making a decision is too painful, there's a fixed-price tasting menu for HK$1,080 (US$140/£77) per person.

In the Four Seasons Hotel Hong Kong, 8 Finance St., Central. ℂ 852/3196 8888. www.fourseasons.com/hongkong. Reservations required. Main courses HK$330–HK$690 (US$43–US$90/£24–£49). AE, DC, MC, V. Noon–2:30pm and 6–10:30pm. MTR: Central.

M at the Fringe ✸✸✸ *Finds* CONTINENTAL   A meal here is a treat in more ways than one—the artsy furnishings are a feast for the eyes, while the food, influenced by cuisines along the Mediterranean, is consistently spot on. The handwritten menu changes every 3 months but is always creative and always includes lamb and vegetarian selections. An example of the former is a salt-encased, slowly baked leg of lamb served with roasted beets. For dessert, don't pass up the Pavlova—fresh fruits with house-made sorbets and ice creams.

2 Lower Albert Rd., Central. ℂ 852/2877 4000. www.m-atthefringe.com. Reservations strongly recommended. Main courses HK$208–HK$256 (US$27–US$33/£15–£18). AE, MC, V. Mon–Fri noon–2:30pm; daily 7–10:30pm. MTR: Central.

Petrus ✸✸✸ *Finds* FRENCH   Simply put, the views from this 56th-floor restaurant are breathtaking, probably the best of any hotel restaurant on the Hong Kong side. The restaurant is decorated like a French castle, with the obligatory crystal chandeliers, statues, thick draperies, and murals gracing dome-shaped ceilings. The cuisine emphasizes contemporary Mediterranean/French seasonal ingredients, and the menu changes often but has included such intriguing choices as gooseliver confit ravioli with black truffles or poached salmon with garlic, black olives, and artichokes.

In the Island Shangri-La (56th floor), Pacific Place, Supreme Court Rd., Central. © **852/2820 8590.** www.shangri-la.com. Reservations recommended. Jacket required for men. Main courses HK$350–HK$800 (US$45–US$104/£25–£57); fixed-price lunch HK$338–HK$388 (US$44–US$50/£24–£27); fixed-price dinner HK$980 (US$127/£70). AE, DC, MC, V. Noon–3pm and 6:30–11pm. MTR: Admiralty.

MODERATE

cafe TOO *★★★ Finds* INTERNATIONAL   The most interesting buffet in Hong Kong, cafe TOO features open kitchens and seven "stations" of food presentations spread throughout the restaurant, thereby giving it a theatrical touch. Browse the appetizer and salad table; a cold seafood counter with sushi, fresh oysters, crab, and other delights; and a Chinese section with dim sum and main courses. Other stations serve Western hot entrees, pastas that are prepared to order (and run the gamut from Chinese to Italian), and Asian dishes from Thai curries to Indian tandoori. The dessert table is the crowning glory.

In the Island Shangri-La Hotel, Pacific Place, Supreme Court Rd., Central. © **852/2820 8571.** www.shangri-la.com. Reservations recommended. Lunch buffet HK$258 (US$34/£18) Mon–Sat, HK$298 (US$37/£21) Sun and holidays; dinner buffet HK$358 (US$46/£26) Mon–Thurs, HK$388 (US$58/£28) Fri–Sun and holidays. AE, DC, MC, V. Mon–Fri noon–2:30pm; Sat–Sun noon–3pm; Mon–Thurs 6:30–10pm; Fri–Sun 6–11pm. MTR: Admiralty.

Jimmy's Kitchen *★* CONTINENTAL   Opened in 1928, this restaurant, a replica of a similar, American-owned restaurant in Shanghai, has an atmosphere reminiscent of an American steakhouse, with white tablecloths, dark-wood paneling, and elevator music. The daily specials are written on a blackboard, and an extensive a la carte menu offers salads and soups, steaks, chicken, Indian curries, German fare, and a seafood selection that includes sole, scallops, and the local garoupa. Also at 29 Ashley Rd., Tsim Sha Tsui (© **852/2376 0327**); noon–11pm.

1 Wyndham St., Central. © 852/2526 5293. www.jimmys.com. Main courses HK$116–HK$268 (US$15–US$35); fixed-price lunch HK$88–HK$158 (US$11–US$21/£5.50–£10). AE, DC, MC, V. 11:30am–3pm and 6–11pm. MTR: Central.

Le Tire Bouchon *★★ Finds* FRENCH   This dark, cozy restaurant near the Central–Mid-Levels Escalator was established in 1986 and claims to be Hong Kong's oldest independent restaurant with a French chef. It serves classic French food heavy on the sauces, like beef filet in port and shallot sauce with fresh duck liver, or steak with black peppercorn sauce. Fatten up even more on one of the sumptuous desserts.

48 Graham St., Central. © 852/2523 5459. www.hkdining.com. Reservations recommended. Main courses HK$160–HK$280 (US$21–US$36/£11–£20); fixed-price lunch HK$98–HK$118 (US$13–US$15/£7–£8.40). AE, DC, MC, V. Mon–Sat noon–2:30pm and 6:30–10:30pm. MTR: Central.

Luk Yu Tea House *★★* CANTONESE   Luk Yu, first opened in 1933, is the most famous teahouse remaining in Hong Kong, a wonderful Art Deco–era Cantonese restaurant with ceiling fans, spittoons, individual wooden booths for couples, marble tabletops, and stained-glass windows. It's one of the best places to try Chinese teas like *lung ching* (a green tea) or *sui sin* (narcissus or daffodil), but Luk Yu is most famous for its dim sum, served from 7am to 5:30pm. The problem for foreigners, however, is that the place is always packed with regulars who have their own special places to sit, and the staff is sometimes surly to newcomers. In addition, if you come after 11am, dim sum is no longer served by cart but from an English menu with pictures but no prices, which could end up being quite expensive unless you ask before ordering.

Bring along a Chinese friend, or consider coming for dinner, when it's not nearly so hectic and there's an English menu listing more than 200 items, including all the Cantonese favorites.

24–26 Stanley St., Central. © 852/2523 5464. Main dishes HK$110–HK$280 (US$14–US$36/£7.85–£20); dim sum HK$25–HK$55 (US$3.25–US$7.15/£1.80–£3.90). MC, V. 7am–10pm. MTR: Central.

Yung Kee ✿ CANTONESE   Popular for decades, Yung Kee started out in 1942 as a street stall selling roast goose. Its specialty is still roast goose with plum sauce, cooked to perfection with tender meat on the inside and crispy skin on the outside and available only for dinner (a half bird, enough for five or six people, costs HK$180/US$23/£11). Other specialties include roast suckling pig or duck, cold steamed chicken, barbecued pork, bean curd combined with prawns, sautéed filet of garoupa, and thousand-year-old eggs (eggs preserved in a mixture of lime, clay, and salt and rice straw for several weeks or even months). Dining is on one of the upper three floors, but if all you want is a bowl of congee or takeout, join the office workers who pour in for a quick meal on the informal ground floor.

32–40 Wellington St., Central. © 852/2522 1624. www.yungkee.com.hk. Main dishes HK$78–HK$180 (US$10–US$23/£5.55–£13). AE, DC, MC, V. 11am–11:30pm. MTR: Central.

INEXPENSIVE

Life ✿ *Finds* VEGETARIAN   Located beside the Central–Mid-Levels Escalator, Life is a godsend to travelers seeking vegetarian and vegan alternatives, as well as those with dietary restrictions (the restaurant will prepare dishes that are free of yeast, gluten, garlic, onion, or wheat). Occupying the second story above a health-foods store and with rooftop dining available in the evening, this down-to-earth venue serves salads, samosas made with tofu and veggies, quiche, noodles, vegetable lasagna, and daily specials, along with juices, power and protein shakes, teas, and organic wine and beer.

10 Shelley St., Central. © 852/2810 9777. Main dishes HK$80–HK$110 (US$10–US$14/£5.70–£7.85). AE, MC, V. 10am–midnight. MTR: Central.

CAUSEWAY BAY
MODERATE

Red Pepper ✿ SICHUAN   Open since 1970, the Red Pepper has a large following among the city's expats. Specialties include fried prawns with chili sauce served on a sizzling platter, fried garoupa with sweet-and-sour sauce, smoked duck marinated with oranges, and shredded chicken with hot garlic sauce and dry-fried string beans. Most dishes are available in two sizes, with the small dishes suitable for two people.

7 Lan Fong Rd., Causeway Bay. © 852/2577 3811. Reservations recommended, especially at dinner. Small dishes HK$90–HK$220 (US$12–US$29/£6.40–£16); fixed-price lunch HK$48–HK$68 (US$6.25–US$8.85/£3.40–£4.85). AE, DC, MC, V. 11:30am–11:15pm (last order). MTR: Causeway Bay.

Wasabisabi ✿✿ JAPANESE   This contemporary restaurant looks like it was airlifted straight out of Tokyo, and as in that huge metropolis, it's easy to get lost here. Luckily, staff is on hand to lead diners past the mirrors and corridors to the dark and cozy dining room, where diners are faced with all the usual choices like sashimi, sushi, temaki (hand-rolled sushi), grilled dishes (like grilled salmon), and tempura, as well as the Japanese chef's own creations. Top off your meal with a drink at the restaurant's popular bar.

Times Sq. (13th floor), 1 Matheson St., Causeway Bay. © 852/2506 0009. www.aqua.com.hk. Sushi (2 pieces) HK$50–HK$160 (US$6.50–US$21/£3.55–£11); main dishes HK$98–HK$178 (US$13–US$23/£7–£13). AE, DC, MC, V. Noon–3pm and 6pm–midnight. MTR: Causeway Bay.

VICTORIA PEAK

MODERATE

Cafe Deco ⚓ *Overrated* INTERNATIONAL   This chic, airy restaurant boasts the best views in town. To assure a ringside window seat, be sure to make reservations for the second floor at least 2 weeks in advance, emphasizing that you don't want your view obstructed by the Peak Tower, or opt for one of the outdoor tables, which are often easier to get. The food is as trendy as the restaurant, with an eclectic mix of international dishes and ingredients, including tandoori kabobs and dishes, Asian noodles, sushi, grilled steaks and chops, pizzas, create-your-own pastas, soups, and salads. Unfortunately, main dishes occasionally fall short of expectations. What you're really paying for here is the view.

Peak Galleria, Victoria Peak. © 852/2849 5111. www.cafedecogroup.com. Reservations recommended for dinner (request window seat with view). Pizzas and pastas HK$98–HK$148 (US$13–US$19/£7–£11); main courses HK$118–HK$278 (US$15–US$36/£8.40–£20); fixed-price lunch (Mon–Fri only) HK$178 (US$23/£13); Sun brunch HK$298 (US$39/£21). AE, DC, MC, V. Mon–Thurs 11:30am–11pm (last order); Fri 11:30am–11:30pm; Sat 9:30am–11:30pm; Sun 9:30am–11pm. Peak tram.

The Peak Lookout ⚓⚓ INTERNATIONAL   Although it's on the Peak, across the street from the Peak Tram terminus, there are only limited views of the South China Sea from The Peak Lookout's terrace. A former tram station, it's a delightful place for a meal, with exposed granite walls, a tall, timber-trussed ceiling, an open fireplace, wooden floors, and a greenhouselike room that extends into the garden. You can also sit outdoors amid the lush growth where you may actually hear birds singing—it's one of the best outdoor dining opportunities in Hong Kong on a glorious day. The menu is eclectic, offering a combination of American, Chinese, Indian, and Southeast Asian dishes, including tandoori chicken tikka, Thai noodles, penne with prawns, grilled steaks and salmon, and curries like Thai green chicken curry with coconut milk.

121 Peak Rd., Victoria Peak. © **852/2849 1000.** www.peaklookout.com.hk. Reservations required for dinner and all weekend meals. Main courses HK$128–HK$258 (US$17–US$33/£9.15–£18). AE, DC, MC, V. Mon–Thurs 10:30am–11pm; Fri 10:30am–1am; Sat 8:30am–1am; Sun 8:30am–11:30pm. Peak tram.

ABERDEEN

MODERATE

Jumbo Kingdom ⚓ CANTONESE   There are many other restaurants that are more authentic and more affordable, but this floating restaurant has been in operation for more than a quarter of a century and attracts a bustling crowd with its claims to be the largest in the world. Simply take the bus to Aberdeen and then board one of the restaurant's own free shuttle boats, which depart every few minutes. The floating venue specializes in fresh seafood and changing seasonal dishes, as well as dim sum available from an English menu (from carts on Sun and holidays) until 4pm. On the roof of Jumbo Kingdom is **Top Deck, at the Jumbo** (© **852/2553 3331;** www.cafedecogroup.com), an alfresco venue where an open kitchen turns out excellent platters of seafood and international dishes ranging from sushi and Asian curries to pasta, as well as an excellent Sunday seafood brunch, making this a great place to chill.

Main dishes HK$60–HK$450 (US$7.80–US$58/£4.30–£32); dim sum HK$17–HK$23 (US$2.20–US$3/£1.20–£1.65). Table charge HK$12 (US$1.55/85p) per person. AE, MC, V. Mon–Sat 11:30am–10:30pm; Sun 7am–10:30pm. Bus: no. 7 or 70 from Central, 72 or 77 from Causeway Bay, or 973 from Tsim Sha Tsui to Aberdeen, then the restaurant's free shuttle boat.

5 Exploring Hong Kong

Every visitor to Hong Kong should eat dim sum in a typical Cantonese restaurant, ride the Star Ferry across Victoria Harbour, and, if the weather is clear, take the Peak Tram for the glorious views from Victoria Peak.

VICTORIA PEAK

At 392m (1,308 ft.), Victoria Peak is Hong Kong Island's tallest mountain and offers spectacular views. Since the Peak is typically cooler than the sweltering city below, it has always been one of Hong Kong's most exclusive places to live. More than a century ago, the rich reached the Peak via a 3-hour trip in sedan chairs, transported to the top by coolies. In 1888 the **Peak Tram** began operating, cutting the journey to a mere 8 minutes.

The easiest way to reach the Peak Tram Station, located in Central on Garden Road, is to take the no. 15C open-top shuttle bus that operates between the tram terminal and the Star Ferry in Central. Otherwise, the tram terminal is about a 10-minute walk from the MTR Central Station. Trams depart from Peak Tram Station every 15 minutes between 7am and midnight. Round-trip tickets cost HK$30 (US$3.90/£2.15) for adults, HK$14 (US$1.80/£1) for seniors, and HK$9 (US$1.15/65p) for children.

Upon reaching the Peak, you'll find yourself at the very modern **Peak Tower** (© 852/ **2849 7654;** www.thepeak.com.hk). Head straight for the rooftop viewing deck, where you have one of the world's most breathtaking views: the South China Sea, the skyscrapers of Central, the boats plying Victoria Harbour, Kowloon, and the many hills of the New Territories undulating in the background.

The best thing to do atop Victoria Peak, however, is to take an hour-long **circular hike** on Lugard Road and Harlech Road, located just a stone's throw from the Peak Tower. Mainly a footpath overhung with banyan trees and passing through lush vegetation (with glimpses of secluded mansions), the road snakes along the cliff side, offering views of Central District below, the harbor, Kowloon, and then Aberdeen and the outlying islands on the other side. This is one of the best walks in Hong Kong.

MUSEUMS

Municipal museums are closed December 25 and 26, January 1, and the first 3 days of Chinese New Year.

Hong Kong Heritage Museum ★★ *(Kids)*   Presenting both the history and culture of the New Territories, this museum is probably the best reason to take the KCR to Sha Tin in the New Territories. Come here to learn about the customs, religions, and lifestyles of the early fishermen and settlers and how they have changed over the centuries. See a barge loaded for market, traditional clothing, models of Sha Tin showing its mind-numbing growth since the 1930s, musical instruments, elaborate costumes

---

⌐Tips A Money-Saving Museum Pass

The Museum Pass, available at HKTB for HK$30 (US$3.90/£2.15), is valid for 1 week and allows entry to the Hong Kong Museum of Art, Hong Kong Museum of History, Hong Kong Space Museum, Hong Kong Science Museum, Hong Kong Museum of Coastal Defence, and Hong Kong Heritage Museum. Note, however, that admission to all six museums is free on Wednesdays.

used in Chinese opera, porcelains, bronzes, jade, and other works of Chinese art dating from the Neolithic period to the 20th century. At the Children's Discovery Gallery, youngsters can practice being archaeologists, wear traditional costumes, and learn about marshes. Plan on spending 2 hours here.

1 Man Lam Rd., Sha Tin. © 852/2180 8188. http://hk.heritage.museum. Admission HK$10 (US$1.30/65p) for adults, HK$5 (US65¢/35p) for children, students, and seniors. Free admission Wed. Mon and Wed–Sat 10am–6pm; Sun and holidays 10am–7pm. KCR: Tai Wai or Sha Tin, about a 15-min. walk from either.

Hong Kong Museum of Art ★★★   Because of its location on the Tsim Sha Tsui waterfront just a 2-minute walk from the Star Ferry terminus, this museum is the most convenient and worthwhile if your time is limited. Feast your eyes on ceramics, bronzes, jade, cloisonné, lacquerware, bamboo carvings, and textiles, as well as paintings, wall hangings, scrolls, and calligraphy dating from the 16th century to the present. The Historical Pictures Gallery provides a visual account of life in Hong Kong, Macau, and Guangzhou in the late 18th and 19th centuries. Another gallery displays contemporary Hong Kong works by local artists. You'll want to spend at least an hour here, though art aficionados can devote more time by renting audio guides for HK$10 (US$1.30/65p).

Hong Kong Cultural Centre Complex, 10 Salisbury Rd., Tsim Sha Tsui. © **852/2721 0116.** www.hk.art.museum. Admission HK$10 (US$1.30/70p) adults, HK$5 (US65¢/35p) children, students, and seniors. Free admission Wed. Fri–Wed 10am–6pm. MTR: Tsim Sha Tsui.

Hong Kong Museum of History ★★★   If you visit only one museum in Hong Kong, this should be it. Opened in 2001, it's Hong Kong's ambitious attempt to chronicle 6,000 years of history. Through displays that include life-size dioramas, replica fishing boats, reconstructed traditional housing, furniture, clothing, and items from daily life, the museum introduces Hong Kong's ethnic groups, traditional means of livelihood, customs, and beliefs. You can peer inside a fishing junk, see what Kowloon Walled City looked like before it became a park, view the backstage of a Chinese opera, read about the arrival of European traders and the Opium Wars, and study a map showing land reclamation since the 1840s. One of my favorite parts of the museum is a re-created street of old Hong Kong, complete with an original Chinese herbal medicine shop located in Central until 1980 and reconstructed here. There are also 19th- and early-20th-century photographs, poignantly showing how much Hong Kong has changed through the decades. You can easily spend 2 hours here.

100 Chatham Rd. S., Tsim Sha Tsui East. **852/2724 9042.** http://hk.history.museum. Admission HK$10 (US$1.30/70p) adults, HK$5 (US65¢/35p) children and seniors. Free admission Wed. Mon and Wed–Sat 10am–6pm; Sun and holidays 10am–7pm. MTR: Tsim Sha Tsui (a 20-min. walk from exit B2). Bus: no. 5 or 5C from Star Ferry bus terminus.

Sam Tung Uk Museum ★★   Located in the New Territories but easily accessible from either Central or Tsim Sha Tsui in about 25 minutes via MTR, this is actually a restored Hakka walled village, built in the 18th century by members of the farming Chan clan. It consists of tiny lanes lined with tiny tile-roofed homes, four houses that have been restored to their original condition, an ancestral hall, two rows of side houses, an exhibition hall depicting Tsuen Wan's history, and an adjacent landscaped garden. The four windowless restored houses are furnished much as they would have been when occupied, with traditional Chinese furniture (including elegant blackwood furniture). Although as many as 300 clan members once lived here, the village was abandoned in 1980. Today the museum is a tiny oasis in the midst of high-rise housing projects.

2 Kwu Uk Lane, Tsuen Wan. (C) 852/2411 2001. Free admission. Wed–Mon 9am–5pm. MTR: Tsuen Wan (a few minutes' walk from exit E).

TEMPLES

Man Mo Temple ✿   Hong Kong Island's oldest and most important temple was built in the 1840s and is named after its two principal deities: Man, the god of literature, and Mo, the god of war. Two ornately carved sedan chairs in the temple were once used during festivals to carry the statues of the gods around the neighborhood. But what makes the temple particularly memorable are the giant incense coils hanging from the ceiling, imparting a fragrant, smoky haze—these are purchased by patrons seeking good health or a successful business deal, and may burn as long as 3 weeks.

Hollywood Rd. and Ladder St., Western District. (C) 852/2803 2916. Free admission. 8am–6pm. Bus: no. 26 from Des Voeux Rd. Central (in front of the Hongkong Bank headquarters) to the 2nd stop on Hollywood Rd., across from the temple. Or, take the Central–Mid-Levels Escalator to Hollywood Rd.

Wong Tai Sin ✿✿   Located six subway stops northeast of Yau Ma Tei in the far north end of Kowloon Peninsula, Wong Tai Sin is Hong Kong's most popular Daoist temple and attracts worshipers from the Daoist, Buddhism, and Confucianism religions, most of whom come to seek information about their fortunes. Although the temple is less than 100 years old, it adheres to traditional Chinese architectural principles with its red pillars, two-tiered golden roof, blue friezes, yellow latticework, and multicolored carvings. On the temple grounds are halls dedicated to the Buddhist Goddess of Mercy and to Confucius; a clinic with both Western medical services and traditional Chinese herbal treatments; and the Nine Dragon Garden, a Chinese garden with ponds, an artificial waterfall, a Nine Dragons relief, and circular, square, octagonal, and fan-shaped pavilions, ponds.

Wong Tai Sin Estate. (C) 852/2327 8141. www.siksikyuen.org.hk. Free admission to temple, though donations of about HK$1 (US15¢/5p) are expected at the temple's entrance, with an additional HK$2 (US25¢/15p) donation at the Good Wish Garden. Temple 7am–5:30pm; garden 9am–4pm. MTR: Wong Tai Sin (exit B2) and then a 3-min. walk (follow the signs).

ORGANIZED TOURS & CULTURAL ACTIVITIES

For information and pamphlets on the following tours, stop by HKTB; most hotels also have tour desks.

CITY TOURS   For general sightseeing, the **Gray Line** ((C) **852/2368 7111;** www.grayline.com.hk) offers a variety of tours to such locations as Man Mo Temple, Victoria Peak, Aberdeen, Stanley, Po Lin Monastery on Lantau island, and the New Territories, as well as sunset cruises and visits to the horse races. **Splendid Tours & Travel** ((C) **852/2316 2151;** www.splendidtours.com) also offers a general city tour, excursions to Lantau and the New Territories, night tours, cruises, and organized visits to the horse races.

"MEET THE PEOPLE" _Finds_   Through this unique program of free, 1-hour tours, lectures, classes, and seminars, visitors can meet local specialists and gain in-depth knowledge of Hong Kong's traditions. Programs are updated and revised annually; past offerings have covered Chinese antiques, Cantonese opera, jade, feng shui (geomancy), Chinese tea, and _taijiquan_ (shadow boxing), with something going on virtually every day of the week. Reservations are not necessary. For details on what, when, and where, pick up a _Cultural Kaleidoscope_ brochure at HKTB or go to HKTB's website, www.discoverhongkong.com.

OUTDOOR PURSUITS

PARKS & GARDENS

Hong Kong Park ★★ (Kids   Opened in 1991, Hong Kong Park, Supreme Court Road and Cotton Tree Drive, Central, features a dancing fountain at its entrance, Southeast Asia's largest greenhouse with more than 2,000 rare plant species, an aviary housing 800 exotic birds in a tropical rainforest setting, various gardens, a children's playground, and a viewing platform reached by climbing 105 stairs. The most famous building on the park grounds is the **Flagstaff House Museum of Tea Ware** (© 852/ 2869 0690; www.lcsd.gov.hk/hkma), the oldest colonial building in Hong Kong. Completed in 1846 in Greek Revival style for the commander of the British forces, it now displays some 150 items of tea ware on a rotating basis from its 600-piece collection, primarily of Chinese origin and dating from the 7th century to the present day. The park is open from 6am to 11pm, the greenhouse and aviary are open from 9am to 5pm, and the museum of tea ware is open Wednesday through Monday from 10am to 5pm. Admission is free to everything. Take the MTR to Admiralty Station (exit C1), then follow the signs through Pacific Place and up the escalators.

Yuen Po Street Bird Garden ★★★ (Kids   Birds are favorite pets in Chinese households; perhaps you've noticed wooden bird cages hanging outside shops or from apartment balconies, or perhaps you've even seen someone taking his bird for an outing in its cage. To see more of these prized songbirds, visit the fascinating Yuen Po Street Bird Garden, Prince Edward Road West, Mongkok, which consists of a series of Chinese-style moon gates and courtyards lined with stalls selling songbirds, beautifully crafted wood and bamboo cages, live crickets and mealy worms, and tiny porcelain food bowls. Young children love it here. Take the MTR to Prince Edward Road station (exit B1) and walk 10 minutes east on Prince Edward Road West, turning left at the overhead railway onto Yuen Po Street. Admission to the garden is free and it's open from 7am to 8pm. (**Note:** Because of concerns about avian flu, signs warn against touching bird droppings and there are hand sanitizers at the exits.)

Zoological & Botanical Gardens ★ (Kids   Established in 1864, the Zoological and Botanical Gardens, Upper Albert Road, Central, are spread on the slope of Victoria Peak, making them a popular respite for Hong Kong residents. Arrive early around 7am to see Chinese residents going through the slow motions of *taijiquan*. The gardens retain some of their Victorian charm, and of the 1,000 species of plants, something is almost always in bloom, from azaleas in the spring to wisteria and bauhinea in the summer and fall. The small zoo houses 600 birds, 90 mammals, and 20 reptiles from around Asia. There's also a children's playground. Admission is free. The eastern part of the park, containing most of the botanical gardens and the aviaries, is open from 6am to 10pm, while the western half, with its reptiles and mammals, is open from 6am to 7pm. Take the MTR to Central and then walk 15 minutes up Garden Road to the corner of Upper Albert Road. Or take bus no. 3B or 12 from Queen's Road Central in front of the HSBC bank building in Central.

TAI CHI

Taijiquan (shadow boxing), called "tai chi" in the West, is an ancient Chinese regimen designed to balance body and soul and thereby release energy from within. Visitors can join free, 1-hour **lessons** in English, offered by HKTB's "Meet the People" cultural program, every Monday, Wednesday, Thursday, and Friday at 8am on the Tsim

Sha Tsui waterfront near Avenue of Stars, and every Saturday at 9am on the Peak Tower rooftop. For more information, stop by or call HKTB (© **852/2508 1234**).

HIKING

With 23 country parks—amounting to more than 40% of Hong Kong's space—there are many trails of varying levels of difficulty throughout Hong Kong, including hiking trails, nature trails, and family trails. Serious hikers may want to consider the famous **MacLehose Trail** in the New Territories, which stretches about 100km (62 miles) through eight country parks, while the **Lantau Trail** is a 70km (43-mile) circular trail on **Lantau island** that begins and ends at Mui Wo (also called Silvermine Bay). Easier to reach is the 50km (31-mile) Hong Kong Trail, which spans Hong Kong Island's five country parks. The HKTB has trail maps and a hiking and wildlife guidebook called *Exploring Hong Kong Countryside: A Visitor's Companion*. Its website, www.discoverhongkong.com, also lists recommended hikes.

HORSE RACING

If you're here anytime from September to mid-June, join the rest of Hong Kong at the horse races. Introduced by the British more than 150 years ago, horse racing is by far the most popular sporting event in Hong Kong, due to the fact that, aside from the local lottery, racing is the only legal form of gambling in Hong Kong. Winnings are tax-free.

There are two tracks—**Happy Valley** on Hong Kong Island, which you can reach by taking the tram to Happy Valley or the MTR to Causeway Bay; and **Sha Tin** in the New Territories, reached by taking the KCR railway to Racecourse Station. Races are held Wednesday evenings and some Saturday and Sunday afternoons. The lowest admission price is HK$10 (US$1.30/70p), which is for the general public and is standing room only. If you want to watch from the more exclusive Hong Kong Jockey Club members' enclosure, are at least 18 years old, and are a bona fide tourist, you can purchase a temporary member's badge for HK$100 (US$13/£6.50) for most races and HK$150 (US$19/£12) on rare special race days. It's available on a first-come, first-served basis by showing your passport at either the Badge Enquiry Office at the main entrance to the members' private enclosure (at either track), or at designated off-course betting centers like the ones at 10-12 Stanley in Central and 4 Prat Ave. in Tsim Sha Tsui.

You can also see the races by joining an organized tour offered by Gray Line or Splendid Tours (see "Organized Tours & Cultural Activities," above).

SWIMMING

There are numerous public swimming pools, including those at **Kowloon Park,** with admission costing around HK$19 (US$2.45/£1.35) for adults and HK$9 (US$1.15/65p) for children and seniors. About 40 **beaches** are free for public use, most with lifeguards on duty April through October, changing rooms, and snack stands or restaurants. On Hong Kong Island, beaches include Big Wave Bay and Shek O on the east coast, and Stanley, Deep Water Bay, South Beach (popular with the gay crowd), and Repulse Bay on the southern coast. There are prettier beaches on the outlying islands, including Hung Shing Ye and Lo So Shing on Lamma, Tung Wan on Cheung Chau, and Cheung Sha on Lantau.

OUTLYING ISLANDS

An excursion to an outlying island provides not only an opportunity to experience rural Hong Kong but also the chance to view Hong Kong's skyline and harbor by ferry, and very cheaply at that. I recommend either Lantau, famous for its giant outdoor Buddha, monastery serving vegetarian meals, and other attractions, or Cheung Chau, popular with families for its unhurried, small-village atmosphere and beach. Both islands are reached in an hour or less via ferries that depart approximately every hour or so from the Central Ferry Piers, location also of the Star Ferry (pick up a free timetable at HKTB). Tickets range from HK$11 to HK$32 (US$1.40–US$4.15/ 75p–£2.30) depending on the day (weekdays are cheaper), class (ordinary and deluxe), and boat (regular ferry or quicker Fast Ferry). Upper-deck deluxe class entitles you to sit on an open deck out back on some ferries.

In addition to the ferries above, there is also infrequent ferry service from Tsim Sha Tsui's Star Ferry concourse on Saturday afternoon and Sunday. You can also reach Lantau via the Tung Chung MTR Line, with a connecting cable car that delivers passengers directly to the Giant Buddha in just 17 minutes.

LANTAU

Hong Kong's largest island and twice the size of Hong Kong Island, Lantau has a population of 84,000 and is home to Hong Kong's international airport. Luckily, more than half of the mountainous and lush island remains preserved in country parks. For a change of scenery, you might want to arrive at Lantau via the ferry from Central to Silvermine Bay (called *Mui Wo* in Cantonese), then bus no. 2 to Ngong Ping Plateau. On the return trip, take the Ngong Ping Skyrail cable car to Tung Chung, where you can board the MTR. In any case, you should allow for at least 5 hours for a visit to Lantau.

At the plateau of Ngong Ping, with an elevation of 750m (2,460 ft.), is Lantau's biggest attraction, the **Giant Tian Tan Buddha,** erected in 1993 as the largest seated outdoor bronze Buddha in the world. It's more than 30m (100 ft.) tall and weighs 220 metric tonnes (243 tons); it's reached via 268 steps and offers great views of the surrounding countryside. Admission to the viewing platform is free and it's open from 10am to 6pm.

Here, too, is **Ngong Ping Village** (℗ 852/2109 9898; www.np360.com.hk), which contains shops, restaurants, a teahouse, a museum called **Walking with Buddha** that chronicles Siddhartha Gautama's path to enlightenment, and the **Monkey's Tale Theatre,** which presents a computer-animated comical story about a selfish monkey who learns about greed, humility, friendship, and kindness. Ngong Ping Village is open Monday to Friday from 10am to 6pm and Saturday and Sunday from 10am to 6:30pm. Admission to the museum and theater is HK$65 (US$8.45/£4.65) for adults and HK$35 (US$4.55/£2.50) for children.

For dining, **Po Lin Monastery** (℗ 852/2985 5248) is famous for its vegetarian meals. Be sure to explore the grounds of the colorful monastery, established near the turn of the 20th century by reclusive Buddhist monks.

Also on Lantau is **Hong Kong Disneyland** (℗ 852/1830 830; www.hongkongdisneyland.com), a 126-hectare (311-acre) theme park reached via the Tung Chung MTR line. Open hours vary with the season, with admission priced at HK$295 (US$38/£21) for adults, HK$210 (US$27/£15) for children, and HK$170 (US$22/£12) for seniors. During peak times (weekends, holidays, and school vacation), admission costs HK$350 (US$45/£25), HK$250 (US$32/£18), and HK$200 (US$26/£14), respectively.

CHEUNG CHAU

If you have only a few hours to spare and don't want to worry about catching buses and finding your way around, Cheung Chau is your best bet. It's a tiny island (only 2.5 sq. km/1 sq. mile), with more than 25,000 people in its thriving fishing village. There are no cars on the island, making it a delightful place for walking around and exploring. The island is especially popular with Chinese families for its rental bicycles and beach, but my favorite thing to do here is to walk the tiny, narrow lanes of Cheung Chau village.

Inhabited for at least 2,500 years by fisher folk, Cheung Chau still supports a sizable population of fishing families, and fishing remains the island's main industry. Inhabited junks are moored in the harbor, and the waterfront where the ferry lands, known as the **Praya,** buzzes with activity as vendors sell live fish and vegetables. The village is a fascinating warren of narrow alleyways, food stalls, open markets, and shops selling everything from medicinal herbs to toys.

About a 3-minute walk from the ferry pier is **Pak Tai Temple,** near a playground on Pak She Fourth Street. Built in 1783, it's dedicated to the "Supreme Emperor of the Dark Heaven," long worshiped as a Daoist god of the sea. As you roam the village, you'll pass open-fronted shops selling incense, paper funeral objects such as cars (cremated with the deceased to accompany him or her to the next life), medicinal herbs, jade, rattan, vegetables, rice, sun hats, sunglasses, and beach toys. On the other side of the island (directly opposite from the ferry pier and less than a 10-min. walk away) is **Tung Wan Beach.**

6 Shopping

Shopping is one of the main reasons people come to Hong Kong, and at first glance the city does seem to be one huge department store. Good buys include Chinese antiques, clothing, shoes, jewelry, furniture, carpets, leather goods, luggage, handbags, briefcases, Chinese herbs, watches, toys, and eyeglasses. Electronic goods and cameras are not the bargains they once were, though good deals can be found in recently discontinued models. Hong Kong is a duty-free port, so there is no sales tax.

BEST SHOPPING AREAS

Tsim Sha Tsui boasts the greatest concentration of shops in Hong Kong, particularly along Nathan Road, with its many electronics stores (which should be avoided in favor of the reliable chain Fortress). Be sure to explore its side streets for shops specializing in washable silk, casual clothing, and luggage. Harbour City, one of the largest malls in the world, stretches along Canton Road.

For upscale shopping, **Central** is where you'll find international designer labels, in boutiques located in the Landmark and Prince's Building. For one-stop shopping, there's the upscale Pacific Place at Admiralty and the ifc mall beside Hong Kong Station. **Causeway Bay** caters more to the local market, with lower prices, small shops selling everything from shoes and clothing to Chinese herbs, several Japanese department stores, and a large shopping complex called Times Square.

Antiques and curio lovers usually head for **Hollywood Road** and **Cat Street** on Hong Kong Island, where everything from snuff bottles to jade carvings is for sale. Finally, one of my favorite places to shop is **Stanley Market,** on the southern end of Hong Kong Island, where vendors sell business and casual wear, as well as Chinese crafts and products. Another good place to shop for Chinese imports and souvenirs is

> **Tips Buyer Beware**
>
> Hong Kong is a buyer-beware market. To be on the safe side, try to make your major purchases at HKTB member stores, which display the HKTB logo (a gold circle with black Chinese calligraphy in the middle and the words "Quality Tourism Services"). Member stores are listed in a directory called "A Guide to Quality Merchants," free at HKTB, and at www.discoverhongkong.comqts. Still, it's always a good idea to obtain a receipt from the shopkeeper with a description of your purchase, including the brand name, model number, serial number, and price for electronic and photographic equipment. For jewelry and gold watches, there should be a description of the precious stones and the metal content. If you're making a purchase using a credit card, ask for the customer's copy of the credit card slip, and make sure "HK$" appears before the monetary total.

one of several Chinese **craft emporiums.** Finally, another good stamping ground is **Horizon Plaza**, 2 Lee Wing St., a huge warehouse with more than a dozen shops selling antiques, as well as outlet designer stores.

Because shopping is such big business in Hong Kong, most stores are open 7 days a week, closing only for 2 or 3 days during the Chinese New Year. Most stores open at 10am, closing at 7:30pm in Central, 9 or 10pm in Tsim Sha Tsui, and 9:30pm in Causeway Bay. Street markets are open every day.

SHOPPING A TO Z
ANTIQUES & COLLECTIBLES

The most famous area for antiques and chinoiserie is around **Hollywood Road** and **Cat Street,** both above the Central District on Hong Kong Island. Hollywood Road twists along for a little more than half a mile, with shops selling original and reproduction Qing and Ming dynasty Chinese furniture, original prints, scrolls, porcelain, clay figurines, silver, and rosewood and blackwood furniture, as well as fakes and curios. Near the western end is Upper Lascar Row, popularly known as Cat Street, where sidewalk vendors sell snuff bottles, reproductions, and other curios.

Arch Angel Antiques   Established in 1988, this is one of Hollywood Road's largest shops for Asian antiques and art, including museum-quality ceramics, furniture, Ming dynasty figurines, terra-cotta animals, boxes, and collectibles. In addition to this three-story main shop, nearby galleries showcase ancient ceramics, bronze Buddhas, terra-cotta figures, and contemporary Vietnamese art. Every antique item for sale is accompanied by a detailed certificate of authenticity. Open from 9:30am to 6:30pm. 53–55 Hollywood Rd., Central. ℂ 852/2851 6848. MTR: Central.

Cat Street Galleries   Cat Street Galleries, on Cat Street, houses several individually owned booths of arts and crafts and expensive antiques from the various dynasties, making it a good place to begin an antiques shopping odyssey. It's open Monday to Friday from 11am to 6pm and Saturday from 10am to 6pm. 38 Lok Ku Rd., Central. ℂ 852/2543 1609. MTR: Shueng Wan. Bus: no. 26 (from Des Voeux Rd. Central in front of the Hongkong Bank) to the 2nd stop on Hollywood Rd., at Man Mo Temple.

China Art   The mixed displays of furniture and art give this family-owned shop the elegance of an art gallery. It's one of Hong Kong's best for antique Chinese furniture, including chairs, folding screens, chests, and more, mostly from the Ming dynasty (1368–1644). Located across from the Central Police Station, it's open Monday through Saturday from 10am to 6pm and Sunday and holidays from 1 to 5pm. 15 Hollywood Rd., Central. © 852/2542 0982. www.chinaart.com.hk. MTR: Central. Bus: no. 26 (from Des Voeux Rd. Central in front of the Hongkong Bank) to Hollywood Rd.

Dragon Culture *Finds* All serious fans of Chinese antiques eventually end up here. One of the largest and most knowledgeable purveyors of antiques in Hong Kong, Victor Choi began collecting Chinese antiques in the 1970s, traveling throughout China. He shares his expertise in three books, which you can purchase in his shop. With another gallery in New York, Choi carries Neolithic pottery, three-color glazed pottery horses from the Tang dynasty, Ming porcelains, bronzes, jade, woodcarvings, snuff bottles, calligraphy, paintings, brush pots, stone carvings, and more, and also provides a certificate of authenticity. He's open Monday through Saturday from 10am to 6pm. 231 Hollywood Rd., Sheung Wan. © 852/2545 8098. www.dragonculture.com.hk. MTR: Shueng Wan. Bus: no. 26 (from Des Voeux Rd. Central in front of the Hongkong Bank) to the 2nd stop on Hollywood Rd., at Man Mo Temple.

True Arts & Curios *Finds* This tiny shop is so packed with antiques and curios that there's barely room for customers. Although everything, from snuff bottles, porcelain, antique silver, earrings, and hairpins, to children's shoes (impractical but darling, with curled toes), is stocked, the true finds here are some 2,000 intricate woodcarvings, pried from the doors and windows of dismantled temples and homes. The shop is open Monday through Saturday from 10:30am to 6:30pm and Sunday from 2 to 6pm. 89–91 Hollywood Rd., Central. © 852/2559 1485. MTR: Sheung Wan.

CHINESE CRAFT EMPORIUMS

In addition to the shops listed here, which specialize in traditional and contemporary arts, crafts, souvenirs, and gift items from China, there are souvenir shops at Stanley Market, located in Stanley on the southern end of Hong Kong Island, that carry lacquered boxes, china, embroidered tablecloths, figurines, and other mainland imports. All these items will be much cheaper across the border, of course.

Chinese Arts and Crafts Ltd. In business for more than 40 years, this is the best upscale chain for Chinese arts and crafts and is one of the safest places to purchase jade. You can also buy silk clothing, arts and crafts, antiques, jewelry, watches, carpets, cloisonné, furs, Chinese herbs and medicine, rosewood furniture, chinaware, Chinese teas, and embroidered tablecloths or pillowcases—in short, virtually all the upmarket items produced by China. It's a great place for gifts, though prices are high. Open from 10am to 9:30pm. The shop is located in Star House near the Star Ferry at 3 Salisbury Rd., Tsim Sha Tsui (© 852/2735 4061; www.crcretail.com; MTR: Tsim Sha Tsui). Other branches are at Pacific Place, 88 Queensway, Central (© 852/2523 3933; MTR: Admiralty); and in the China Resources Building, 26 Harbour Rd., Wan Chai (© 852/2827 6667; MTR: Wan Chai).

Shanghai Tang *Finds* Step back into 1930s Shanghai at this upscale, two-level store with its gleaming wooden and tiled floors, raised cashier cubicles, and ceiling fans. This is Chinese chic at its best, with neatly stacked rows of updated versions of traditional Chinese clothing ranging from cheongsams and silk pajamas to padded jackets, caps, and shoes—all in bright, contemporary colors and styles. If you're looking for a lime-green or shocking-pink padded jacket, this is the place for you. It's open Monday to Saturday from 10am to 8pm and Sunday from 11am to 7pm. There are small branches in The Peninsula Hotel ((C) **852/2537 2888**) and Hotel Inter-Continental ((C) **852/2721 1211**), both on Salisbury Road in Tsim Sha Tsui; MTR: Tsim Sha Tsui). Pedder Building, 12 Pedder St., Central. (C) 852/2525 7333. www.shanghaitang.com. MTR: Central.

FASHION

Hong Kong has been a center for the fashion industry ever since the influx of Shanghainese tailors fleeing the 1949 Communist revolution in China. If you're looking for international designer brands and money is no object, the **Landmark,** located on Des Voeux Road Central, Central, is an ultra-chic shopping complex boasting the highest concentration of international brand names in Hong Kong, including Gucci, Tiffany & Co., Polo/Ralph Lauren, Manolo Blahnik, Marc Jacobs, Versace, Michel Kors, Sonia Rykiel, Louis Vuitton, Lanvin, and Christian Dior. Other shopping arcades with well-known international designer boutiques include the **Prince's Building,** next to the Mandarin Hotel, and **The Peninsula Hotel,** on Salisbury Road in Tsim Sha Tsui.

For trendier designs catering to an upwardly mobile younger crowd, check out the **Joyce Boutique** chain, established in the 1970s by Joyce Ma to satisfy Hong Kong women's cravings for European designs. Today her stores carry clothing by Issey Miyake, John Galliano, Stella McCartney, Yohji Yamamoto, Rei Kawakubo (Comme des Garçons), and others on the cutting edge of fashion. You'll find Joyce shops at 18 Queen's Rd. Central, Central District ((C) **852/2810 1120;** MTR: Central); 334 Pacific Place, 88 Queensway, Central ((C) **852/2523 5944;** MTR: Admiralty); and Shop G106 in The Gateway, Canton Rd., Tsim Sha Tsui ((C) **852/2367 8128;** MTR: Tsim Sha Tsui). For bargains, head to the Joyce Warehouse, Horizon Plaza, 2 Lee Wing St., Ap Lei Chau ((C) **852/2814 8313;** bus no. M590 from Exchange Square in Central).

FACTORY OUTLETS Hong Kong's factory outlets offer excess stock, overruns, and quality-control rejects. Because these items have been made for the export market, the sizes are Western. Bargains include clothes made of silk, cashmere, cotton, linen, knitwear, and wool. Most outlets are located in **Hung Hom,** clustered in a large group of warehouse buildings called **Kaiser Estates** on Man Yue Street (take bus no. 5C from the Tsim Sha Tsui Star Ferry bus terminal to Ma Tau Wai Rd., the third stop after the KCR Kowloon Railway Station). On Hong Kong Island, the best-known building housing factory-outlet showrooms is the **Pedder Building,** 12 Pedder St., Central. For a list of factory outlets, along with their addresses, telephone numbers, and types of clothing, pick up the free pamphlet "Clothing & Accessories" at HKTB offices. Most outlets are open from 10 or 11am to 7pm Monday through Friday, with shorter hours on Saturday. Some are open Sunday as well.

MARKETS

Jade Market Jade is available in all sizes, colors, and prices at this market at the junction of Kansu Street and Battery Street, in two temporary structures in the Yau Ma Tei District. Unless you really know your jade and pearls, you won't want to make any expensive purchases here. It's open from 10am to about 4pm (mornings are best), though some vendors stay until 6pm on busy days like Sunday. The market is located near the Jordan MTR station or less than a 30-minute walk from the Star Ferry.

Ladies' Market Stretching along Tung Choi Street (between Argyle and Dundas sts.) in Mongkok, Kowloon, Ladies' Market specializes in inexpensive women's and children's fashions, shoes, jewelry, sunglasses, watches, handbags (including fake designer bags), and other accessories. Some men's clothing is also sold. Although many of the products are geared more to local tastes and sizes, an increase in tourism has brought more fashionable clothing and T-shirts in larger sizes and you may find a few bargains. In any case, the atmosphere is fun and festive, especially at night. The nearest MTR station is Mongkok. Vendors' hours are from 12:30 to 10:30pm.

Li Yuen Street East & West   These two streets are parallel pedestrian lanes in the heart of Central, very narrow and often congested with human traffic. Stalls are packed with Chinese jackets, handbags, clothes, scarves, sweaters, toys, baby clothes, watches, makeup, umbrellas, needles and thread, knickknacks, and even brassieres. Don't neglect the open-fronted shops behind the stalls. These two streets are located just a couple minutes' walk from the Central MTR station, between Des Voeux Road Central and Queen's Road Central. Vendors' hours are from 10am to 7pm.

Stanley   Stanley Market is probably the most popular and best-known market in Hong Kong. Located on the southern coast of Hong Kong Island, it's a fun place to buy inexpensive clothing, especially sportswear, cashmere sweaters, silk blouses and dresses, and women's suits. Men's, women's, and children's clothing are available. The inventory changes continuously—one year it seems everyone is selling washable silk; the next year it's Chinese traditional jackets or Gore-Tex coats. The market also has souvenir shops selling paintings, embroidered linen, beaded purses, handicrafts, and other products from mainland China.

To reach Stanley, take bus no. 6, 6A, 6X, or 260 from Central's Exchange Square bus terminal (bus no. 260 also makes stops in front of Pacific Place) or Minibus no. 40 from Causeway Bay. The bus ride to Stanley takes approximately 30 minutes. From Kowloon, take bus no. 973 from Mody Road in Tsim Sha Tsui East or from Canton Road in Tsim Sha Tsui. Shops are open from 9:30 or 10am to about 6:30pm.

Temple Street Night Market   Temple Street in the Yau Ma Tei district of Kowloon is a night market that comes to life when the sun goes down. It offers T-shirts, jeans, menswear, watches, jewelry, CDs, mobile phones, electronic gadgets, alarm clocks, luggage, and imitation designer watches and handbags. Bargain fiercely, and check the products carefully to make sure they're not faulty or poorly made. The night market is great entertainment, a must during your visit to Hong Kong though the surge of shoppers can be overwhelming. North of Temple Street, near Tin Hau Temple, are fortunetellers and sometimes street performers singing Chinese opera. Although some vendors begin setting up shop at 4pm, the night market is busiest from about 7 until the 10pm closing; it's located near the Jordan MTR station.

7 Hong Kong After Dark

Hong Kong's nightlife is concentrated in Tsim Sha Tsui, in Central's entertainment areas of Lan Kwai Fong and SoHo, and in Wan Chai. If you're watching your Hong Kong dollars, take advantage of happy hour, when many bars offer two drinks for the price of one or drinks at reduced prices. Furthermore, many pubs, bars, and lounges offer live entertainment, from jazz to Filipino combos, which you can enjoy simply for the price of a beer. Remember, however, that a 10% service charge will be added to your bill.

In addition to the recommendations below, be sure to watch the nightly "Symphony of Lights" show from 8 to 8:18pm, when an impressive laser and light show is projected from approximately 30 buildings on both sides of the harbor. The best vantage points? From the Tsim Sha Tsui waterfront's Avenue of Stars and Bauhinia Square in Wan Chai.

To obtain tickets for the Hong Kong Chinese Orchestra, Chinese opera, rock and pop concerts, and other major events, call the **Urban Council Ticketing Office (URBTIX)** at ✆ **852/2734 9009,** or drop by outlets located in City Hall, Low Block, 7 Edinburgh Place in Central, or in the Hong Kong Cultural Centre, 10 Salisbury Rd. in Tsim Sha Tsui. Both are open from 10am to 9:30pm. You can also reserve tickets before arriving in Hong Kong, either by calling the Credit Card Hotline at ✆ **852/ 2111 5999** or through the website, www.urbtix.gov.hk.

PERFORMING ARTS
CHINESE OPERA

The most popular regional styles of Chinese opera in Hong Kong are Peking-style opera, with its spectacular costumes, elaborate makeup, and feats of acrobatics and swordsmanship; and the less flamboyant but more readily understood Cantonese-style opera. For visitors, the easiest way to see a Chinese opera is during a festival, such as the Hong Kong Arts Festival, held from about mid-February through early March. Otherwise, Cantonese opera is performed fairly regularly at town halls in the New Territories, as well as in City Hall in Central and at the Hong Kong Cultural Centre in Tsim Sha Tsui. Tickets, ranging from HK$100 to HK$300 (US$13–US$39/£6.50– £21), usually sell out well in advance, so book before arriving in Hong Kong. Contact HKTB for an updated schedule.

HONG KONG CHINESE ORCHESTRA

Established in 1977, the Hong Kong Chinese Orchestra (www.hkco.org) is the world's largest professional Chinese-instrument orchestra, with 80-some musicians performing both new and traditional works using traditional and modern Chinese instruments and combining them with Western and Chinese orchestrations. Performances are held at the Hong Kong Cultural Centre, 10 Salisbury Rd., Tsim Sha Tsui (✆ **852/ 2734 2009**), and at City Hall, Edinburgh Place, Central District (✆ **852/2921 2840**). Tickets range from HK$100 to HK$200 (US$13–US$26/£6.50/£13).

DANCE CLUBS/DISCOS

C Club   With a seductive interior of velvet sofas and a curved bar, all bathed in red lighting, this basement club packs them in with what management calls "sexy house" music, including funk, R&B, soul, and Latino. If you come on a weekend, be prepared to wait in the queue of beautiful people lined up outside. It's open Monday to Thursday from 6pm to 2am, Friday from 6pm to 4:30am, and Saturday from 9pm to 4:30am. California Tower, 30–32 D'Aguilar, Lan Kwai Fong, Central. ✆ 852/2526 1139. www.lankwai-fong.com. No cover Mon–Thurs; cover HK$200 (US$26/£13) Fri–Sat, including 1 drink. MTR: Central.

Propaganda   Hong Kong's longest-standing and most popular gay disco, Propaganda moved into upgraded quarters a few years back in the new SoHo nightlife district, with a discreet entrance in a back alley (off Pottinger St.). The crowd is 95% gay, but everyone is welcome. Come late on a weekend if you want to see this alternative hot spot at its most crowded. It's open Tuesday through Thursday from 9pm to 3:30am, Friday and Saturday from 9pm to 5am. 1 Hollywood Rd., Central. ✆ 852/2868 1316. No cover Tues–Thurs; cover HK$120 (US$16/£8.50) Fri–Sat. MTR: Central.

THE BAR SCENE
KOWLOON

Aqua Spirit   This glam newcomer is one of Hong Kong's hottest bars, due in no small part to its unbeatable location on the 30th floor of a Tsim Sha Tsui high-rise, where slanted, soaring windows give an incredible bird's-eye-view of the city. Circular booths shrouded behind strung beads, designer drinks, and a voyeur's dream location on an open mezzanine overlooking a restaurant on the 29th floor make this one of Kowloon's trendiest venues. There's a HK$120 (US$16/£8.50) drink minimum, and it's open Sunday to Thursday from 5pm to 2am and Friday and Saturday from 5pm to 3am. 1 Peking Rd., Tsim Sha Tsui. ℭ 852/3427 2288. MTR: Tsim Sha Tsui.

Bahama Mama's   One of many bars lining Knutsford Terrace, this one is decorated in a kitschy Caribbean theme and offers a few tables outside from which to watch the passing parade, as well as a small dance floor. It's open Monday through Thursday from 4pm to 3am, Friday and Saturday from 4pm to 4am, and Sunday from 4pm to 2am. 4–5 Knutsford Terrace, Tsim Sha Tsui. ℭ 852/2368 2121. MTR: Tsim Sha Tsui.

Delaney's   This upmarket Irish pub with a convivial atmosphere gets an extra boost from a Tuesday quiz night with prizes for winners and DJ Friday nights, both free of charge, as well as big soccer and rugby events shown on a big screen. An a la carte menu features Irish stew and other national favorites. Happy hour is from 5 to 9pm; regular hours are from 8am to 2:30am. There's another Delaney's in Wan Chai at 18 Luard Rd. (ℭ **852/2804 2880**). 71–77 Peking Rd., Tsim Sha Tsui. ℭ **852/2301 3980**. MTR: Tsim Sha Tsui.

Lobby Lounge   This comfortable cocktail lounge boasts gorgeous, water-level views of Victoria Harbour and Hong Kong Island. You'll fall in love all over again (with Hong Kong, your companion, or both) as you take in one of the world's most famous views (this is a very civilized place for watching the nightly Symphony of Lights laser show) and listen to a live jazz band (from 6pm–midnight). It's open from 8am to 2am. In Hotel Inter-Continental Hong Kong, 18 Salisbury Rd., Tsim Sha Tsui. ℭ **852/2721 1211**. MTR: Tsim Sha Tsui.

Ned Kelly's Last Stand   This lively Aussie saloon attracts a largely middle-aged crowd with free live Dixieland jazz from 9:30pm to 1am. It serves Australian chow and pub grub, and is open from 11:30am to 2am (happy hour until 9pm). 11A Ashley Rd., Tsim Sha Tsui. ℭ 852/2376 0562. MTR: Tsim Sha Tsui.

CENTRAL DISTRICT

California   This was once *the* place to see and be seen—the haunt of young nouveaux riches in search of definition—and it remains a respected and sophisticated restaurant/bar. Consider starting your night on the town here with dinner and drinks; the menu exalts Californian cuisine, though hamburgers (the house specialty) remain hugely popular. On Friday and Saturday night from 11pm to 4am, the California becomes a happening disco. It's open Monday to Thursday from noon to midnight, Friday and Saturday from noon to 4am, and Sunday from 6pm to midnight. 24–26 Lan Kwai Fong St., Central. ℭ 852/2521 1345. MTR: Central.

The Cavern   This sophisticated live-music venue attracts a slightly older crowd with its casual-chic dress code, large outdoor seating area, and sexy interior bathed in red lights. The house band, silhouetted on stage, plays unplugged, easy-listening acoustics from 8 to 11pm, then switches to electric and turns up the volume, transforming The

Cavern into a dance club (admission of HK$100/US$13/£6.50, which includes one drink, is charged Fri–Sat from 11pm). It's open Sunday through Thursday from 5pm to 2am and Friday and Saturday from 5pm to 4am or later. Lan Kwai Fong Tower, Ground Floor, 55 D'Aguilar St., Central. © 852/2121 8969. MTR: Central.

Club 97   Opened more than 20 years ago as a disco, this well-known club is now a sophisticated lounge, a reflection of an aging clientele more prone to drinking and conversation than to dancing. Weekly events to watch for are the Friday gay happy hour, complete with drag shows, and the Sunday reggae night. The club is open Monday to Thursday from 6pm to 2am (happy hour 6–9pm), Friday from 6pm to 4am (happy hour 6–10pm), Saturday from 8pm to 4am (happy hour 8–9pm), and Sunday from 8pm to 3am (happy hour 8–10pm). 9 Lan Kwai Fong, Central. © 852/2810 933. MTR: Central.

CAUSEWAY BAY/WAN CHAI

Dusk til Dawn   This laid-back bar attracts a mostly expat and Southeast Asian clientele, who take advantage of its 5-to-11pm happy hour, food and snack menu served until 5am, and nightly free live music starting at 10pm. Open Monday through Saturday from noon to 6am and Sunday from 3pm to 6am. 76–84 Jaffe Rd., Wan Chai. © 852/2528 4689. MTR: Wan Chai.

Klong Bar & Grill   Wishing to evoke steamy, sensual Bangkok, this establishment takes its name from the many canals that lace Thailand's capital. Its open-fronted ground-floor bar and grill, with an open kitchen turning out delectable Thai barbecue, looks like any Asian bar, dark and slightly rough around the edges, but go upstairs and it's a whole different place, very posh and with well-dressed urbanites crowded around a huge U-shaped bar and lounging in the corner "opium den." Things do get crazy however, especially when a DJ hits the scene on Friday and Saturday nights and both professionals and amateurs are encouraged to hop on the bar and perform an exotic pole dance, which probably happens most on Wednesday nights when ladies are served free vodka. Still, it's a long cry from Bangkok's nightlife scene. It's open from 11:30am until 3am or later, with happy hour until 3 to 9pm. The Broadway, 54–62 Lockhart Rd., Wan Chai. © 852/2217 8330. MTR: Wan Chai.

8 A Side Trip to Macau

Macau was established as a Portuguese colony in 1557, centuries before the British acquired Hong Kong. Just 64km (40 miles) west of Hong Kong, across the Pearl River Estuary, Macau is Lilliputian, only 28 sq. km (11 sq. miles) in area. Once a sleepy backwater, it has experienced tremendous growth since the turn of the millennium, with spanking-new boutiques and restaurants and an explosion of world-class hotels and casinos that have transformed it into Asia's hottest gambling mecca. The number of tourists to Macau—20 million a year, mostly from mainland China—has doubled since 2001.

While much has been lost in the flurry of development, Macau is still a unique destination in the world, an intriguing mix of Chinese and Portuguese traditions and culture. On December 20, 1999, Portugal's 400 years of rule came to an end when Macau was handed back to China. Like Hong Kong, Macau is a Special Administrative Region of China, permitted its own internal government and economic system for another 50 years after the Chinese assumed control. As with Hong Kong, no advance visa is required.

Macau

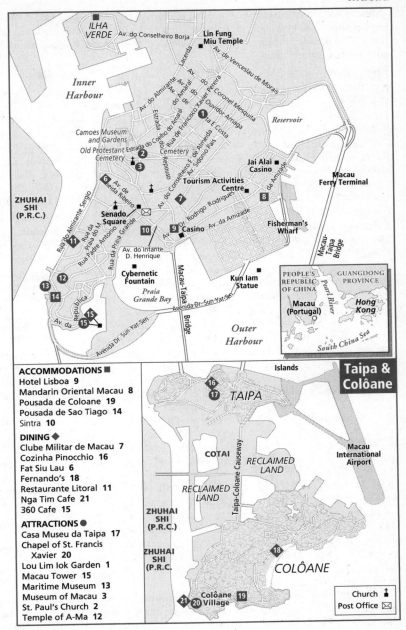

ILHA VERDE

Av. do Conselheiro Borja

Lin Fung Miu Temple

Av. de Venceslau de Morais

Inner Harbour

Av. do Almirante Lacerda

Av. do Amaral

Av. do Coronel Mesquita

Estrada do Coelho do Amaral

Rua de Francisco Xavier Pereira

Av. do Ouvidor Arriaga

❶

Ta E Costa

Reservoir

Camoes Museum and Gardens

Old Protestant Cemetery

Estrada do Coelho do Amaral

Av. Sidónio Pais

❷

❸

Av. do Conselheiro F. de Almeida

Jai Alai Casino

da Amizade

Macau Ferry Terminal

ZHUHAI SHI (P.R.C.)

Rua da Almirante Sergio

Av. de Almeida Ribeiro

❻

✝

Tourism Activities Centre

❼

Av. do Dr. Rodrigo Rodrigues

❽

Senado Square

✉

❿

❾ **Casino**

Av. da Amizade

Fisherman's Wharf

Rua do M

Rua da Praia do M

Rua Padre Antonio

Rua da Praia Grande

⓫

Av. do Infante D. Henrique

Cybernetic Fountain

Praia Grande Bay

Kun Iam Statue

Macau-Taipa Bridge

⓬

⓭

⓮

Av. da República

Avenida Dr.-Sun-Yat-Sen

⓯

⓯

Avenida Dr.-Sun-Yat-Sen

Macau-Taipa Bridge

Outer Harbour

Macau-Taipa Bridge

PEOPLE'S REPUBLIC OF CHINA

GUANGDONG PROVINCE

Pearl River

Macau (Portugal)

Hong Kong

South China Sea

Islands

Taipa & Colôane

⓰

⓱

TAIPA

Macau International Airport

COTAI

RECLAIMED LAND

Taipa-Coloane Causeway

RECLAIMED LAND

ZHUHAI SHI (P.R.C.)

ZHUHAI SHI (P.R.C.

⓲

COLÔANE

㉑

⓳

㉒

Colôane Village

Church ✝

Post Office ✉

ACCOMMODATIONS ■
Hotel Lisboa **9**
Mandarin Oriental Macau **8**
Pousada de Coloane **19**
Pousada de Sao Tiago **14**
Sintra **10**

DINING ◆
Clube Militar de Macau **7**
Cozinha Pinocchio **16**
Fat Siu Lau **6**
Fernando's **18**
Restaurante Litoral **11**
Nga Tim Cafe **21**
360 Cafe **15**

ATTRACTIONS ●
Casa Museu da Taipa **17**
Chapel of St. Francis Xavier **20**
Lou Lim Iok Garden **1**
Macau Tower **15**
Maritime Museum **13**
Museum of Macau **3**
St. Paul's Church **2**
Temple of A-Ma **12**

Macau has beaches, churches, fortresses, temples, gardens, museums, and fascinating neighborhoods to explore, as well as restaurants serving wonderful Macanese cuisine. What's more, Macau's prices are cheaper than Hong Kong's, including accommodations and dining.

ARRIVING

BY PLANE **Macau International Airport** (© 853/2886 1111; macauairport.gov.mo), located on Taipa Island and connected to the mainland by bridge, has international connections to Taipei, Singapore, Seoul, Tokyo, Manila, and Bangkok. It also has flights with Chinese airlines to Fuzhou, Hangzhou, Shanghai, and Xiamen; and flights with Air Macau to Beijing, Guilin, Haikou, Hangzhou, Kunming, Nanjing, Chengdu, Shanghai, and Xiamen. Several first-class hotels offer complimentary transfers on request. Otherwise, airport bus AP1 travels from the airport to the ferry terminal and Hotel Lisboa; the fare, in Macau pataca currency, is MOP$3.30 (US45¢/20p). A taxi to the Lisboa costs approximately MOP$40 (US$5.20/£2.80). Airport-departure tax is included in the price of plane tickets.

BY BOAT Macau is easily accessible from Hong Kong by **high-speed jetfoil,** with most departures from the **Macau Ferry Terminal,** located just west of the Central District in the Shun Tak Centre, 200 Connaught Rd., on Hong Kong Island. Situated above Sheung Wan MTR station, the terminal houses jetfoil ticket offices, as well as the Macau Government Tourist Office (room 336, on the same floor as boats departing for Macau). Limited service is also available from Kowloon, from the newer China Hong Kong Terminal on Canton Road, Tsim Sha Tsui.

The fastest, most convenient way to travel to Macau is via a 55-minute ride on jetfoils operated by **TurboJET** (© 852/2859 3333 in Hong Kong, or 853/790 7039 in Macau; www.turbojetc.com.hk), with departures from the Macau Ferry Terminal every 15 to 30 minutes, 24 hours a day. One-way fares Monday through Friday are HK$243 (US$32/£17) for super class and HK$141 (US$18/£10) for economy class; fares on weekends and holidays are HK$259 (US$34/£10) in super class and HK$153 (US$20/£11) in economy. Fares for night service (6:15pm–6am) are HK$274 (US$36/£20) and HK$175 (US$23/£13) respectively. Seniors older than 60 and children younger than 12 receive a HK$15 (US$1.95/£1.05) discount.

Tickets can be purchased at the Macau Ferry Terminal on Hong Kong Island, the China Ferry Terminal in Kowloon, all China Travel Service branches in Hong Kong, and the TurboJET Service Counter at Sheung Wan MTR Station, exit D. You can also book by credit card by calling © 852/2921 6688. Note that passengers are allowed only one hand-carried bag, not to exceed 20 kilograms (44 lb.), with one additional piece checked in 20 minutes prior to departure for a fee ranging from HK$20 to HK$40 (US$2.60–US$5.20/£1.40–£2.85), depending on weight.

There is also TurboJET Sea Express service directly from Hong Kong International Airport (transfers are made without passing through Hong Kong Customs), with four sailings daily costing HK$180 (US$23/£13) for economy class and HK$280 (US$36/£20) for super class.

In Macau, you'll arrive at the **Macau Ferry Terminal,** on the main peninsula. After going through Customs, stop by the Macau Government Tourist Office for a map and brochures. In the arrivals hall is also a counter for free shuttle buses to major hotels. Otherwise, city bus nos. 3, 3A, and 10 travel from the terminal to Avenida Almeida Ribeiro, the main downtown street, for MOP$2.50 (US30¢/15p).

TO THE MAINLAND

Travel to the mainland (on foot across the border to Zhuhai, by jetfoil to Shenzhen, or by plane) requires a Chinese visa. For all but land crossings, buy visas in Hong Kong (see "Traveling to & from the Mainland" in the Hong Kong section, earlier in this chapter). The **border crossing** is open from 7am to midnight, but arrive by 11:30pm.

Guangzhou can be reached by bus from Zhuhai Gong Bei bus station, ahead and slightly to the right as you emerge from the Macau/Zhuhai border crossing. There are departures every 15 minutes or so between 8am and 8pm to Guangzhou Station, from where there's a choice of taxi, bus, or metro to take you the 8km (5 miles) to the airport. There are also frequent services to **Shenzhen** and **Kaiping** between 8:30am and 7:30pm.

VISITOR INFORMATION

There are two **Macau Government Tourist Offices (MGTO)** in Hong Kong—at counter A06 in the arrivals lobby of the International Airport (© **852/2769 7970;** www.macautourism.gov.mo), open from 9am to 10pm (closed for lunch 1–1:30pm and dinner 6–6:30pm); and in room 336 on the third floor of the Macau Ferry Terminal, Shun Tak Centre, in Central (© **852/2857 2287**), open 9am to 1pm and 2:15 to 5:30pm.

In Macau, you'll find an MGTO at the Macau Ferry Terminal, open from 9am to 10pm; there is also an MGTO at Macau International Airport, open for all incoming flights. For complete information, stop by the main Macau Government Tourist Office, Largo do Senado, located in the center of town on the main plaza just off Avenida Almeida Ribeiro and open from 9am to 6pm. Other tourist information offices are located at **Fisherman's Wharf,** open from 10am to 1pm and 2 to 6pm; **Guia Fort and Lighthouse,** open from 9am to 1pm and 2:15 to 5:30pm; and the **Border Gate** (also called Barrier Gate and serving visitors from the mainland), open from 9:15am to 1pm and 2:30 to 6pm. Be sure to pick up a free city map, brochures on everything from churches to fortresses, and the tourist tabloid *Macau Travel Talk.* For information by telephone, call the **Tourist Hotline** at © **853/2833 3000.**

GETTING AROUND

Macau comprises a small peninsula and Taipa and Colôane, two islands that have merged due to land reclamation and are linked to the mainland by bridges. The peninsula—referred to simply as Macau and surrounded by an Inner and an Outer Harbour—is where you'll find the city of Macau, as well as the ferry terminal and most of its hotels, shops, and attractions. Macau's main road is **Avenida Almeida Ribeiro;** about halfway down its length is the attractive **Largo do Senado (Senate Square),** Macau's main plaza.

Because the peninsula is less than 8.9 sq. km (about 3½ sq. miles), you can walk most everywhere. If you get tired, jump into a metered **taxi,** which charges MOP$11 (US$1.45/75p) at flagfall for the first 1.5km (1 mile), then MOP$1 (US15¢/5p) for each subsequent 180m (594 ft.). **Public buses** run from 7am to midnight, with fares costing MOP$2.50 (US30¢/15p) for travel within the Macau Peninsula, MOP$3.30 (US45¢/20) for travel to Taipa, and MOP$4 to MOP$5 (US50¢–US65¢/30p–35p) to Colôane. Buses heading for Taipa and Colôane make a stop in front of Hotel Lisboa, located on the peninsula near the Macau-Taipa Bridge. MGTO has a free map with bus routes.

WHERE TO STAY

In addition to the rack rates given below (quoted in Hong Kong dollars; be sure to bargain for a better rate, especially in the off season), there's a 10% hotel service charge and a 5% government tax. If you plan on coming during Chinese New Year, Easter, July, August, or late November when the Grand Prix is held, book well in advance.

EXPENSIVE

Mandarin Oriental Macau ★★★ *(Kids)*   This is a companion hotel of the Mandarin Oriental in Hong Kong, but with room rates much lower than you'd pay in Hong Kong. Located about a 7-minute walk from the ferry terminal in the direction of downtown, a huge land-reclamation project has robbed the hotel of much of its waterfront view, but on the plus side the hotel claimed a small portion of the new land for its state-of-the-art resort facility, which includes an outdoor swimming pool; waterfall; water slide, pool, playground, and children's center; and a gorgeous spa. Although the hotel's exterior is rather nondescript, if not downright ugly, its interior is beautifully designed and elegantly decorated throughout with imports from Portugal.

Av. da Amizade 956–1110, Macau. © 800/526-6566 in the U.S. and Canada, 853/2856 7888, or 852/2881 1288 for reservations in Hong Kong. Fax 853/2859 4589. www.mandarinoriental.com/macau. 435 units. HK$2,000–HK$2,600 (US$260–US$337/£143–£186) single or double; HK$3,300–HK$3,900 (US$428–US$506/£236–£279) Mandarin floors; from HK$5,300 (US$688/£379) suite. AE, DC, MC, V. Free shuttle bus from ferry terminal or bus no. 10A or 10B from ferry terminal. **Amenities:** 4 restaurants (Italian, Cantonese, international, Thai); bar; 24-hr. casino; outdoor heated pool open year-round; kids' pool; 4 outdoor floodlit tennis courts; 2 indoor squash courts; health club and spa; outdoor Jacuzzi; playground; children's day-care center for ages 3–12; concierge; business center; shopping arcade; salon; 24-hr. room service; massage; babysitting; same-day laundry service/dry cleaning; executive-level rooms; doctor on call. *In room:* A/C, satellite TV w/pay movies, high-speed dataport, minibar, coffeemaker, hair dryer, safe.

Pousada de São Tiago ★★★ *(Finds)*   Built around the ruins of the Portuguese Fortress da Barra, which dates from 1629, this delightful small inn on the tip of the peninsula is guaranteed to charm even the most jaded of travelers. The entrance is dramatic—a flight of stone stairs leading through a cavelike tunnel that was once part of the fort, with water trickling in small rivulets on one side of the stairs. Once inside, guests are treated to the hospitality of a Portuguese inn, with ornately carved wooden bedroom furniture imported from Portugal and the use of stone, brick, and Portuguese blue tile throughout. A terrace restaurant is shaded by banyan trees, and most of the rooms, all of which face the sea, have balconies.

Av. da Republica, Fortaleza de São Tiago da Barra, Macau. © 853/2837 8111, or 800/969 153 for reservations in Hong Kong. Fax 853/2855 2170. www.saotiago.com.mo. 24 units. HK$2,600–HK$3,200 (US$337–US$415/£186–£229) single or double; from HK$4,200 (US$545/£300) suite. Sun–Thurs discounts available. AE, DC, MC, V. Free shuttle bus (on request) or bus no. 28B from ferry terminal. **Amenities:** Restaurant (international); lounge; outdoor pool; room service 7:30am–11pm; babysitting; same-day laundry service/dry cleaning. *In room:* A/C, cable TV, minibar, hair dryer, bathroom scale.

MODERATE

Hotel Lisboa *(Finds)*   The Lisboa is in a class by itself. Built in 1969, it's a Chinese version of Las Vegas—huge, flashy, and with a bewildering array of facilities that make it almost a city within a city, and its 24-hour casino has long been one of the most popular in Macau. It has countless restaurants, shops, and nighttime diversions. The rooms are located in an older east wing and a tower that was completed in 1993 (a 49-story sister hotel, the Grand Lisboa, opened across the street in late 2007). The tower, which added 14 floors, offers the best—and most expensive—harbor views, including rooms with traditional Chinese architecture and furniture. Otherwise, rooms seem rather small and old-fashioned. In short, this is the place to be if you want to be in the thick of it. Buses traveling to the outlying islands and other parts of Macau stop right outside the front door, and downtown Macau is only a 5-minute walk away.

Av. de Lisboa 2–4, Macau. (C) 853/2837 7666, or 800/969 130 for reservations in Hong Kong. Fax 853/2856 7193. www.hotelisboa.com. 927 units. HK$1,650–HK$3,000 (US$214–US$389/£118–£214) single or double; from HK$3,800 (US$494/£271) suite. Children under 13 stay free in parent's room. AE, DC, MC, V. Free shuttle bus or bus no. 3, 3A, 10, 10A, 10B, 12, 28A, 28B, 28BX, 32, or AP1 from the ferry terminal. **Amenities:** 15 restaurants (some 24 hr.); bar; lounge; 24-hr. casino; outdoor heated pool; health club; shopping arcade; salon; 24-hr. room service; same-day laundry service/dry cleaning. *In room:* A/C, satellite TV w/free movies, free high-speed dataport, minibar w/free drinks, coffeemaker, hair dryer, safe.

Sintra With the best central location of any of the moderately priced hotels, the Sintra, under the same management as Hotel Lisboa, enjoys a prime spot in the heart of Macau, within easy walking distance of Avenida de Almeida Ribeiro and Largo do Senado. Originally built in 1975 but completely overhauled in the mid-1990s, it looks good for its age and the staff is friendly. Standard rooms face another building but are large. Even roomier are the higher-priced rooms occupying higher floors, some with high-speed Internet connections; individual bookings (not through a travel agency) are often upgraded to one of these rooms if space is available. Of note for night owls is the hotel's one restaurant, open 24 hours.

Av. de D. João IV, Macau. (C) 853/2871 0111, or 800/969 145 for reservations in Hong Kong. Fax 853/2856 7769. www.hotelsintra.com. 240 units. HK$1,160–HK$1,760 (US$151–US$228/£83–£126) single or double; executive floor; from HK$1,780–HK$2,080 (US$231–US$270/£127–£149) executive floor; from HK$2,360 (US$306/£169) suite. Children under 13 stay free in parent's room. AE, DC, MC, V. Free shuttle bus or bus no. 3, 3A, 10A, from the ferry terminal. **Amenities:** Restaurant (international/Cantonese); sauna (men only); business center; 24-hr. room service; same-day laundry service/dry cleaning; executive-level rooms. *In room:* A/C, satellite TV w/pay movies, minibar, hair dryer, safe, free distilled water.

INEXPENSIVE

Pousada de Colôane ⭐ *Finds* This small, family-owned property, perched on a hill above Cheoc Van Beach with views of the sea, is ideal for couples and families in search of a reasonably priced isolated retreat. More than 30 years old but recently renovated, it's a relaxing, rather rustic place, with modestly furnished rooms, all of which have balconies facing the sea and a popular public beach. There's an outdoor terrace where you can relax over drinks, and the inn's Portuguese restaurant is especially popular for the Sunday lunch buffet offered during peak season. The main drawback is one of access, but buses to Macau pass by frequently; when you arrive at the Macau ferry terminal, you're best off traveling to the hotel by taxi.

Praia de Cheoc Van, Colôane Island, Macau. (C) 853/2888 2144. Fax 853/2888 2251. www.hotelpcoloane.com.mo. 30 units. HK$750–HK$880 (US$97–US$114/£54–£63) single or double. Weekday discounts available. MC, V. Bus: no. 21A, 25, or 26A from Lisboa Hotel (tell the bus driver you want to get off at the hotel). **Amenities:** Restaurant (Portuguese); bar; outdoor pool; children's pool; babysitting; laundry service. *In room:* A/C, TV, minibar.

WHERE TO DINE
EXPENSIVE

Clube Militar de Macau ⭐⭐ *Finds* MACANESE/PORTUGUESE With its tall ceilings, whirring ceiling fans, arched windows, wooden floor, and displays of antique Chinese dishware, this is one of Macau's most atmospheric dining halls. It's located in a striking pink colonial building, built in 1870 for military officers and opened to the public in 1995. It's best to stick to the classics, such as roasted codfish with hot olive oil and garlic, roasted beef filet with Portuguese sauce, or African chicken. The lunch buffet is a downtown favorite, and the list of Portuguese wines is among the best in town.

Av. da Praia Grande 795. © **853/2871 4009.** Reservations recommended for lunch. Main courses HK$99–HK$163 (US$13–US$21/£7.05–£12); fixed-price lunch or dinner HK$90–HK$99 (US$12–US$13/£6.40–£7.05); lunch buffet HK$90 (US$12/£6.40). AE, DC, MC, V. Noon–3pm and 7–11pm. Bus: no. 3, 3A, 8, 8A, 9, 9A, 10, 10A, 10B, 11, 12, 21, 21A, 22, 23, 25, 26, 26A, 28A, 32, 33, or AP1.

360 Cafe ⊛ INTERNATIONAL   This is Macau's most conspicuous restaurant, more than 219m (730 ft.) above reclaimed ground in the soaring Macau Tower. Opened in 2001, the tower contains an observation deck and lounge, with an admission of HK$70 (US$9.10/£4.55). Head instead to the tower's revolving restaurant, where for the price of a buffet you have an equally good view. It takes 1½ hours for a complete spin, giving you ample time to sample the various Southeast Asian, Chinese, Macanese, and Continental dishes available as you soak in the view.

In the Macau Tower, Lago Sai Van. © **853/28988 8660.** www.macautower.com.mo. Reservations recommended weekends. Buffet lunch HK$168 (US$22/£12); buffet dinner HK$248 (US$32/£18). AE, DC, MC, V. 11:30am–3pm and 7–10:30pm. Bus: no. 9A, 18, 21, 23 or 32.

MODERATE

Cozinha Pinocchio PORTUGUESE/MACANESE   Opened in 1977, Taipa Island's first Portuguese restaurant is still going strong, though some who have known it since its early days claim that the atmosphere became more staid when a roof was added to the original roofless two-story brick warehouse. Nevertheless, things are still hopping—people crowd its doors for specialties like curried crab, king prawns, charcoal-grilled sardines, fried codfish cakes, grilled spareribs, roast veal, roast quail, and Portuguese-style cooked fish.

Rua do Sol, Taipa Village, Taipa Island. © **853/2882 7128.** Main courses HK$52–HK$160 (US$6.75–US$21/£3.70–£11). DC, MC, V. Noon–midnight. Bus: no. 11, 22, 28A, 30, 33, or 34.

Fat Siu Lau MACANESE   This is Macau's oldest restaurant (dating from 1903). Its three floors of dining have been updated, but its exterior matches all the other storefronts on this revamped street—whitewashed walls and red shutters and doors. Dishes include roast pigeon marinated according to a 90-year-old secret recipe; spicy African chicken; curried crab; garoupa stewed with tomatoes, bell pepper, onion, and potatoes; and grilled king prawns. A branch is located at the Docks nightlife district, Avenida Dr. Sun Yat-sen (© **853/2872 2922**), open noon to 3pm and 6:30pm to midnight.

Rua da Felicidade 64. © **853/2857 3580.** www.fatsiulau.com.mo. Main courses HK$50–HK$142 (US$6.50–US$18/£3.55–£10). AE, MC, V. 11:30am–11:30pm. Bus: no. 3, 3A, 5, 6, 7, 8, 10, 11, 18, 19, 21, or 21A.

Fernando's ⊛ (finds) PORTUGUESE   For years Fernando's was just another shack on Hac Sa Beach, hardly distinguishable from the others (it's the brick one closest to the beach, below the vines). But then a brick pavilion was added out back, complete with ceiling fans and an adjacent open-air bar with outdoor seating (a good place to wait for a table; reservations are not accepted), and now everyone knows the place. The strictly Portuguese menu includes prawns, crabs, mussels, codfish, *feijoada* (a Brazilian stew), veal, chicken, pork ribs, suckling pig, beef, and salads. Only Portuguese wine is served, stocked on a shelf for customer perusal (there is no wine list). The place is very informal and not for those who demand pristine conditions—there is no air-conditioning, not even in the kitchen.

Praia de Hac Sa, 9, Colôane. © 853/2888 2264 or 853/2888 2531. Reservations not accepted. Main courses HK$66–HK$148 (US$8.55–US$19/£4.70–£11). No credit cards. Noon–9:30pm (last order). Bus: no. 15, 21A, 25, or 26A.

Restaurante Litoral 𝒦𝒦 MACANESE   Exactly which restaurant serves the most "authentic" Macanese food in town is a hotly contested subject, but this attractive restaurant, with its dark-gleaming woods, whitewashed walls, and stone floor, can certainly lay claim to the title. All the traditional favorites are here, including curry crab, curry prawns, African chicken, feijoada, and *minchi,* a Macanese dish prepared with pork cubes, potatoes, onion, and garlic. Still, Portuguese specialties like codfish baked with potato and garlic, roast Portuguese sausage, and Portuguese green soup are not to be overlooked. Wash it all down with Portuguese wine or beer. The restaurant is located along the covered sidewalk not far from the Maritime Museum and A-Ma Temple.

Rua do Almirante Sergio 261A. © 853/2896 7878. Main courses HK$95–HK$180 (US$12–US$23/£6.75–£13). AE, MC, V. Noon–3pm and 6:30–10:30pm. Bus: no. 1, 1A, 2, 5, 6, 7, 9, 10, 10A, 11, 18, 21, 21A, 28B, or 34.

INEXPENSIVE

Nga Tim Cafe *finds* CHINESE/MACANESE   This lively, open-air pavilion restaurant is a good place to rub elbows with the natives. It's situated on the tiny main square of Colôane Village, dominated by the charming Chapel of St. Francis Xavier. Its popularity with the locals lends it a festive atmosphere. The food, which combines Chinese and Macanese styles of cooking and ingredients, is in a category all its own, with many dishes not available elsewhere. Try the salt-and-pepper shrimp, baked chicken in a fresh coconut, grilled prawns with curry, or the barbecued spring chicken.

Rua Caetano 8, Colôane Village, Colôane Island. © 853/2888 2086. Main courses HK$15–HK$98 (US$1.95–US$13/£1.05–£7). MC, V. 11:30am–1am. Bus: no. 15, 21A, 25, 26, or 26A.

SEEING THE SIGHTS

St. Paul's Church 𝒦𝒦   The church crowns a hill in the center of the city and is approached by a grand sweep of stairs. However, only its ornate facade and some excavated sites remain. Designed by an Italian Jesuit, it was built in 1602 with the help of Japanese Christians who had fled persecution in Nagasaki. In 1835, the church caught fire during a typhoon and burned to the ground, leaving its now-famous facade, adorned with carvings and statues depicting Christianity in Asia—an intriguing mix of images that includes a Virgin Mary flanked by a peony (representing China) and a chrysanthemum (representing Japan). Beyond the facade is the excavated crypt, where glass-fronted cases hold the bones of 17th-century Christian martyrs from Japan and Vietnam. Here, too, is the tomb of Father Allesandro Valignano, founder of the Church of St. Paul and instrumental in establishing Christianity in Japan. Next to the crypt is the underground Museum of Sacred Art, with religious works of art produced in Macau from the 17th to 20th centuries, including 17th-century oil paintings by exiled Japanese Christian artists, crucifixes of filigree silver, and wooden saints.

Rua de São Paulo. © 853/2835 8444. Free admission. Grounds 24 hr.; museum Wed–Mon 9am–6pm. Bus: no. 8A, 17, 18, 19, or 26. Or a 10-min. walk northwest of Senado Sq.

Museum of Macau 𝒦𝒦𝒦   A must-see, this very ambitious project beside St. Paul's Church in the bowels of ancient Monte Fortress provides an excellent overview of Macau's history, local traditions, and arts and crafts. Displays, arranged chronologically, start with the beginnings of Macau and the arrival of Portuguese traders and

Jesuit missionaries. Particularly interesting is the room comparing Chinese and European civilizations at the time of their encounter in the 16th century, including descriptions of their different writing systems, philosophies, and religions. Other displays deal with the daily life and traditions of old Macau, such as festivals, wedding ceremonies, and industries ranging from fishing to fireworks factories. Displays include paintings and photographs of Macau through the centuries, traditional games and toys, an explanation of Macanese cuisine and architecture, and a re-created Macau street.

Citadel of São Paulo do Monte (St. Paul Monte Fortress). ℂ 853/2835 7911. www.macaumuseum.gov.mo. Admission MOP$15 (US$1.90/£1) adults, MOP$8 (US$1/55p) seniors and children. Tues–Sun 10am–6pm. Located next to St. Paul's Church.

Temple of A-Ma *★★*   Macau's oldest temple is situated at the bottom of Barra Hill at the entrance to the Inner Harbour, across from the Maritime Museum. With parts of it more than 600 years old, it's dedicated to A-Ma, goddess of seafarers. The temple was already here when the Portuguese arrived, and they named their city A-Ma-Gao (Bay of A-Ma) after it. The temple contains images of A-Ma and stone carvings of the boat that carried her to Macau, as well as several shrines set on a rocky hillside linked by winding paths through moon gates and affording good views of the Inner Harbour.

Rua de S. Tiago da Barra. Free admission. 6:30am–6pm. Bus: no. 1, 1A, 2, 5, 6, 7, 9, 10, 10A, 11, 18, 21, 21A, 28B, or 34.

Macau Tower *Overrated*   Does the world really need another tower? Since admission to the observation deck is rather exorbitant by Macau standards, I personally think you are best off coming for a meal in the revolving **360 Cafe** (p. 594). However, thrill seekers take note: Daredevils can tour the observation deck's *outside* ramparts with the safety of harnesses and ropes, which costs MOP$198 (US$25/£13), half price for children and seniors. Other ways to have fun with Macau Tower: climbing the mast (a 2-hr. ordeal); climbing 32m (106 ft.) up the tower's concrete shaft on what may be the world's highest artificial climbing wall; bungee jumping 233m (769 ft.); and more.

Lago Sai Van. ℂ 853/2893 3339. www.macautower.com.mo. Admission to observatory MOP$70 (US$8.75/£4.65) adults, MOP$35 (US$4.40/£2.30) children and seniors. 10am–9pm. Bus: no. 9A, 18, 21, 23, or 32.

MACAU AFTER DARK

Several hotels have casinos, including the **Mandarin Oriental** and **Hotel Lisboa,** open 24 hours. In the past couple of years, several themed, Las Vegas–style casinos have opened their doors, including **Sands Macau,** near the ferry terminal and Fisherman's Wharf (ℂ 853/2888 3388; www.sands.com.mo); **Wynn Macau,** across from the Lisboa near the center of town on Avenida Da Amizade (ℂ 853/2888 9966; www.wynnmacau.com); and **MGM Grand Macau,** which made its debut in late 2007. But the biggest developments are taking shape on COTAI (the strip of reclaimed land between Taipa and Colôane), where the **Venetian Macao-Resort-Hotel** (ℂ 853/2882 8888; www.venetianmacao.com) boasts a 50,725-sq.-m (546,000-sq.-ft.) casino and serves as the anchor of several resort hotels, meeting and convention spaces, shopping complexes, and more. For a glimpse of gambling Chinese-style, none is more interesting than the ornately decorated **Floating Macau Palace Casino,** moored in the Outer Harbour not far from the Mandarin Oriental Hotel.

One of the few benefits to have arisen from reclaimed-land development on the Outer Harbour is the Docks, a string of sidewalk cafes and bars lining Avenida Dr. Sun Yat-Sen near the Kun Iam Statue; they are busiest from 10pm to 1am.

East Meets West

The Historic Centre of Macau, a World Heritage Site, celebrates more than 400 years of cultural exchange between the East and the West. Encompassing most of the historic old town, it ensures the preservation of both traditional Chinese architecture and the oldest Western structures on Chinese soil, with forts, temples, churches, mansions, squares, a library, cemetery, and a garden among 25 protected sites. Two of the most famous attractions—A-Ma Temple and the ruins of St. Paul's—are described here, but for a complete list of protected structures and a map, stop by the Macau Government Tourist Office for its *Macau World Heritage* pamphlet. Among my favorites: the Moorish Barracks, Mandarin's House, Leal Senado Building, Senado Square, Lou Kau Mansion, the Protestant Cemetery, and Guia Fortress.

At the other end of the spectrum is another "town," **Fisherman's Wharf** (*©* 853/2829 9330; www.fishermanswharf.com), which opened in 2004 on reclaimed land in the Outer Harbour, just a few minutes' walk from the ferry terminal. With replica Tang dynasty, North American, European, and South African architecture, it contains upscale shops, restaurants, and regularly scheduled street performances and other events, making for an interesting stroll.

TAIPA & COLÔANE ISLANDS

Closest to the mainland, **Taipa** has exploded with new construction in recent years, but it's still worth coming to see **Taipa Village,** a small, traditional community with narrow lanes; two-story colonial buildings painted in yellows, blues, and greens; and hanging baskets of flowers. There are a number of fine, inexpensive restaurants here, making dining reason enough to come. For sightseeing, don't miss the **Casa Museu da Taipa (Taipa House Museum),** on Avenida da Praia (*©* 853/2882 7088). It's one of five colonial-style homes lining the banyan-shaded street that once belonged to Macanese families in the early 1900s. Combining both European and Chinese designs and furnishings as a reflection of the families' Eurasian heritage, the Casa Museu displays a dining and living room, kitchen, and upstairs bedrooms filled with period furniture. A couple of the other former homes contain displays relating to the history of Taipa and traditional regional costumes of Portugal. Hours are Tuesday through Sunday from 10am to 6pm, and admission is MOP$5 (US65¢/35p). Bus nos. 11, 15, 22, 28A, 30, 33, and 34 all go to Taipa Village.

Farther away and connected to Taipa via causeway and a huge strip of reclaimed land, **Coloane** is less developed than Taipa and is known for its **beaches,** particularly Cheoc Van and Hac Sa, both with lifeguards. To reach them, take bus no. 21A or 26A. Farther along the coast is the quaint, laid-back community of **Coloane Village,** with its sweet **Chapel of St. Francis Xavier,** built in 1928 and dedicated to the Catholic missionary.

For more information on Taipa and Coloane, pick up a free pamphlet from the Macau tourist office called *Macau, Outlying Islands.*

The Southwest:
Mountains & Minorities

by Christopher D. Winnan

"The most interesting part of China, from a geographical and ethnological point of view, is the West—geographically, because its recesses have not yet been thoroughly explored, and ethnologically, because a great part of it is peopled by races which are non-Chinese." In describing the attraction of southwest China for a few iconoclastic foreigners in 1889, British consul Alexander Hosie may as well be describing the region's appeal today for hundreds of thousands of travelers, both foreign and Chinese. Considerably more explored than in Hosie's day but still retaining large swaths of undiscovered territory, today's splendid southwest is beginning to attract its deserved share of attention, and will be one of China's major tourist destinations in the years to come.

For starters, this region, encompassing the provinces of **Yunnan, Guizhou, and Guangxi,** is home to some of China's most spectacular mountain scenery. As the Himalayan mountain range in northwest Yunnan gives way to the Yunnan-Guizhou plateau to the southeast, the scenery changes from the awesome 5,000m-high (16,400-ft.) glacier peaks of the **Jade Dragon Snow Mountain range** to the lower, but no less beautiful, famed limestone hills of eastern Guangxi. Three of Asia's mighty rivers—the Salween, the Mekong, and the Yangzi—cut parallel paths all within 150km (90 miles) of each other in the northwest mountains before they flow their separate ways, creating in their passage some of the most breathtaking gorges and lush river valleys in the country.

Even more appealing is the fact that this region is easily the most ethnically diverse in China. Twenty-six of China's 56 ethnic groups can be found in the southwest, which claims about 45 million of China's 100-million-strong minority population. If geography is destiny, then this inhospitable mountainous terrain, to which many ethnic minorities were historically displaced by earlier expanding Chinese empires, has not only helped create a vibrant kaleidoscope of peoples, languages, and cultures, but it has helped some of these cultures maintain their unique traditional ways in the face of encroaching modernization. At the same time, shared borders with Sichuan, Tibet, Myanmar (Burma), Laos, and Vietnam have allowed the region to absorb and integrate the colorful and diverse influences of its neighbors. From the Mosu at **Lugu Lake** to the Dai in **Xishuangbanna,** and the Miao around **Kaili San Jiang,** you will have multiple opportunities to encounter different minorities.

Historically, this area has undertones of the Wild West, with the Miao and other minorities replacing the American

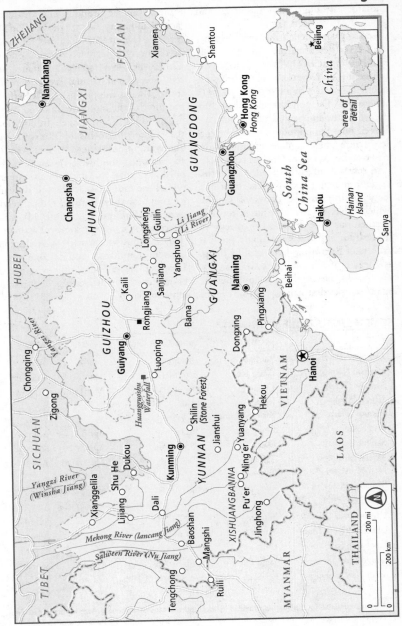

The Southwest Region

Indians. Although the massacres and genocide have been going on for hundreds of years, French missionary Father Paul Perry described the situation coldly and bluntly in 1871. "The Chinese government is determined to obliterate these aboriginal peoples by a systematic policy of repression." The policy seems to have succeeded as the indigenous populations are indeed now the minorities, driven relentlessly into these remote mountains by never-ending waves of Chinese colonists.

A traveler can easily spend years in this region and not exhaust its offerings. Between the obvious draws of **Guilin,** which ranks as one of China's top five destinations, the backpacker mecca of **Yangshuo,** and the increasingly popular trifecta of **Kunming, Dali,** and **Li Jiang,** is a legion of other delights awaiting discovery. To be sure, travel outside the major tourist destinations and provincial capitals can be arduous and distinctly lacking in luxury, but for those willing to forego a few creature comforts for heaps of discovery, Guizhou Province, one of China's best-kept secrets, contains not only spectacular natural scenery in the form of karst mountains and waterfalls, but some of the most dynamic and colorful minority life in China. In addition, the still-quaint towns of **Jianshui and Yuanyang** promise new delights even for the seasoned southwest traveler. In the north, the road to Tibet, which remains one of the most spectacular and difficult journeys, passes through the newly crowned **Shangri-La,** while in other directions we unveil some new names that are touting themselves as destinations of tomorrow such as **Bama** and **Luoping.** *Note:* Unless otherwise noted, hours listed for attractions and restaurants are daily.

SOME FESTIVALS IN THE SOUTHWEST

Festival	Location	Lunar Calendar	2008	2009
Dragon Lantern (Miao)	Tai Jiang	15th of 1st	Feb 21	Feb 9
Huapao (Dong)	Cong Jiang	28th of 1st	Mar 5	Feb 23
Sanduo (Naxi)	Li Jiang	8th of 2nd	Mar 15	Mar 4
Water Splashing Festival (Dai)	Jinghong Xishuangbanna	(Apr 13–15 fixed in Western calendar)		
Sanyuesan	Dong areas	3rd of 3rd	Apr 8	Mar 29
Sanyue Jie (Bai)	Dali	15th of 3rd	Apr 18	Apr 10
Sisters' Meal Festival (Miao)	Tai Jiang/ Shidong	15th–17th of 3rd	Apr 18–20	Apr 10–12
Siyueba (Miao)	Huangping	8th of 4th	May 12	May 2
Raosanling (Bai)	Dali	23rd–25th of 4th	May 27–29	May 17–19
Dragon Boat (Miao)	Shidong	25th of 5th	June 28	June 17
Chabai Singing (Buyi)	Xingyi	21st of 6th	July 23	Aug 11
Huoba Jie (Bai)	Dali	24th of 6th	July 26	Aug 15
Zhuan Shan Jie	Lugu Hu	25th of 7th	Aug 25	Sept 13
Miao New Year	Lei Shan	last 10 days of 10th	4th week Nov	2nd week Oct

**Dates are based on information provided by local tourism sources. However, there are many date fluctuations, especially with festivals like the Miao New Year. Check with the local CITS or other local sources before setting off.

1 Guilin ⭐

Guangxi Province, 500km (310 miles) NW of Hong Kong, 1,675km (1,039 miles) SW of Beijing

One of the most-visited Chinese cities, Guilin (pop. 630,000), located in the north-eastern part of the Guangxi Zhuang Autonomous Region, has long been famous for its limestone karst hills. Formed more than 200 million years ago when the oceans receded from this area, the towers sprout from a patchwork of paddy fields and flow-ing streams, creating a dreamy, seductive landscape that leaves few souls unstirred. Time and space meet here to produce a masterpiece of nature's handiwork. Though there are a few hills in the city that can be explored, and the Li River cruise from Guilin to Yangshuo remains one of top river journeys in the world, Guilin is also being used as a base to visit the Yao, Miao, and Dong minority villages to the northwest. Unfortunately, the cost of Guilin's overwhelming popularity is a degree of unrelenting exploitation and extortion audacious even by Chinese standards; foreigners especially are overcharged for everything.

With summer's heat and humidity and winter's low rainfall affecting water levels in the Li River, April, May, September, and October are the best months for cruising. April to August also marks the rainy season, however, so be prepared with rain gear. Avoid the first weeks of May and October, when China celebrates national holidays, the Li River becomes even more congested with tourist boats than usual, and the price of everything doubles at the very least. July can become unbearably hot, and this is the last place on earth that you want to be holed up in your hotel room, clinging to the air conditioner.

ESSENTIALS

GETTING THERE   From Guilin's airport 30km (19 miles) west of town (located on Nixon Rd. in honor of the U.S. president who visited in 1971), **flights** connect to Guangzhou (1 hr.), Beijing (2½ hr.), Shanghai (2 hr.), Kunming (1½ hr.), and Chengdu (70 min.). There are also international flights to Seoul (4 hr.), Bangkok (2 hr.) and Hong Kong (1½ hr.). Tickets can be purchased at the **Minhang Dasha** on Shanghai Lu (© 0773/384-3922), and also at travel agencies or hotel tour desks. **Dragonair** has an office at the Guilin Bravo Hotel, Ronghu Nan Lu 15 (© 0773/282-3950, ext. 1150). Airport shuttles depart from the CAAC office every half-hour from 6:30am to 8pm for ¥25 ($3.25/£1.65); they also meet incoming flights. Taxis to the airport cost around ¥120 ($16/£7.80). Many expats simply skip Guilin altogether in preference for a weekend in Yangshuo as the taxi fare is only ¥200 ($26/£13) direct from the airport.

Train travel to and from Guilin is very convenient, although the surrounding mountainous topography means that destinations farther afield often require several days' travel; also, sleeper tickets for those destinations are often difficult to come by. The city has two railway stations, though the main one used by most travelers is the **Guilin Huochezhan** (© 0773/383-3124) in the southern part of town. The T6 to Beijing (24 hr.) departs at 5:23pm, the K38 to Guangzhou (13 hr.) at 8:30pm, the K150 to Shanghai (26 hr.) at 4:28pm, and the K155 to Kunming (via Guiyang, 30 hr.) at 2:08pm. The route from Guilin to Guangzhou is recognized as being a flagship journey for overseas tourists and so the staff are handpicked and the carriages are spot-less. If you want to try the comforts of a Chinese train, then this is one of the best routes to choose. For Chengdu and Chongqing, change trains at Guiyang (18 hr.).

There are trains throughout the day to Nanning (7–8 hr.). The T5/905 from Beijing to **Hanoi** stops in Guilin (only four sleeper berths are available from Guilin). It's best to have a travel agent or your hotel tour desk arrange tickets because they are extremely difficult to come by.

The **Guilin Bus Station (Guilin Qichezhan;** © 0773/382-2153), just north of the railway station, is in an appalling condition. One would have expected the road transport hub of China's most popular tourist city to be an architectural and logistical showpiece. In reality, it is dirty and run down, with overcrowded waiting rooms full of tin spittoons looking out on a snarled-up bus yard. From here large, air-conditioned direct *(zhida)* **buses** go to Beihai (7 hr.; ¥150/$20/£9.75) at 8:30am, 9:20am, and 10:20am; to Longsheng (3 hr.; ¥35/$4.55/£2.30) every 40 minutes from 7am to 7pm; to Nanning (5 hr.; ¥80/$10/£5.20) every half-hour from 7am to 7pm; and to Guangzhou (9 hr.; ¥150/$20/£9.75) at 9am, 11am, 9pm, 10pm, and 11pm. Regular minibuses run to Yangshuo (1 hr.; ¥15/$1.95/£1) from the bus station and outside the railway station. A luxury air-conditioned bus to Hong Kong (© 0773/585-7088) now runs every Friday evening, charging ¥350 ($46/£23) one-way, ¥600 ($91/£46) round-trip. It departs from the Guilin Guishan Hotel on Chuanshan Lu at 7pm, stops at the Yangshuo Paradise Hotel at 8pm, and arrives at Huanggang in Shenzhen at 7am. After passengers go through Customs and Immigration, the bus continues onto Sha Tin, Kowloon Tong, and Tsimshatsui in Hong Kong. For the return, the bus simply retraces the route, departing from Hong Kong's Tsimshatsui at 4pm and arriving in Guilin the next morning around 7am. There are plans to increase the frequency of this service, but beware, for the moment, this is an arduous and treacherous night's travel, with road conditions and driving skills that you may not be used to.

GETTING AROUND   Guilin is a compact area and is easy to get around by foot or bicycle. **Bikes** can be rented at most hotels, including the Bravo Hotel and the Sheraton, for ¥25 ($3.25/£1.65) to ¥50 ($6.50/£3.25) per day plus a deposit of ¥400 ($52/£26).

Taxis cost ¥7 (90¢/45p) for 2km (1¼ miles), then ¥1.60 (20¢/10p) per kilometer. After 4km (2½ miles), the price jumps to ¥2 (25¢/15p) per kilometer. From 11pm to 7am, the fare is ¥7.80 ($1.05/50p) for 2km (1¼ miles), then ¥2.40 (30¢/15p) per kilometer until 4km (2½ miles), and ¥3 (40¢/20p) per kilometer after that.

There are also several **buses** geared toward tourists: The free bus no. 58 from 8:30am to 4:30pm runs from Nanxi Park in the south to Reed Flute Cave, stopping along the way at Elephant Hill, Seven Star Park, Fubo Hill, and Diecai Hill. Another free sightseeing minibus travels a similar loop from Seven Star Park to Reed Flute Cave between 8:40am and 4pm, but passengers are required to show their entrance tickets to at least one of the sights.

TOURS   CITS at Binjiang Lu 41 (© 0773/286-1623; fax 0773/282-7424) has full-day city tours with English-speaking guides for ¥200 ($26/£13) per person. The CITS Panda Bus picks up daily from the Fubo, Sheraton, Bravo, and Royal Garden hotels. CITS can also organize Li River cruises for ¥460 ($60/£30), day trips to Yangshuo by bus for ¥280 ($36/£18) per person, and overnight trips to Longsheng Minority Village and Terrace Fields for ¥550 ($68/£29) per person. The concierge at the Sheraton Hotel, Binjiang Nan Lu (© 0773/282-5588), can arrange all of the above, as well as nighttime cormorant fishing trips for ¥120 ($16/£7.80) and evening cultural performances for around ¥180 ($23/£12).

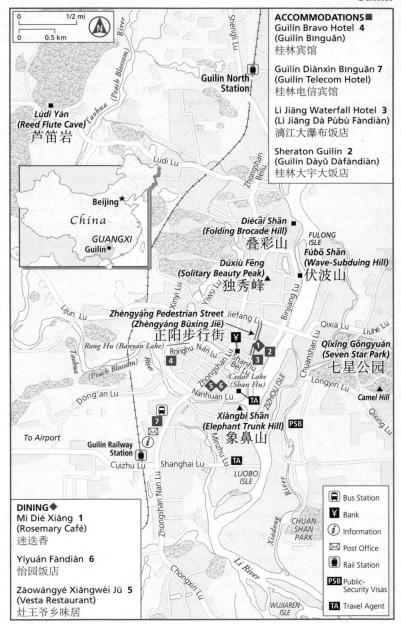

Guilin

ACCOMMODATIONS ■
Guìlín Bravo Hotel 4
(Guìlín Bīnguǎn)
桂林宾馆

Guìlín Diànxìn Bīnguǎn 7
(Guìlín Telecom Hotel)
桂林电信宾馆

Lì Jiāng Waterfall Hotel 3
(Lì Jiāng Dà Pùbù Fàndiàn)
漓江大瀑布饭店

Sheraton Guìlín 2
(Guìlín Dàyǔ Dàfàndiàn)
桂林大宇大饭店

DINING◆
Mi Dié Xiāng 1
(Rosemary Café)
迷迭香

Yíyuán Fàndiàn 6
怡园饭店

Zàowángyé Xiāngwèi Jū 5
(Vesta Restaurant)
灶王爷乡味居

Bus Station
Bank
Information
Post Office
Rail Station
PSB Public-Security Visas
TA Travel Agent

VISITOR INFORMATION For information on hotels and sights, there are **Guilin Tourism Information Service** centers around town, most noticeably outside the railway station (© **0773/382-7391**) and in the Central Square (Zhongxin Guangchang; © **0773/285-4318**).

FAST FACTS

Banks, Foreign Exchange & ATMs **Bank of China** (open Mon–Fri 8am–noon and 3–6pm) is at Shanhu Bei Lu 5. It offers forex and an ATM.

Internet Access Visit the third floor of **Lequn Shouji Cheng** at Zhongshan Zhong Lu 49, corner of Lequn Lu. Internet access is 24 hours, at ¥2 (25¢/15p) per hour. Dial-up is © **96163.**

Post Office The main post office (open 8am–8pm) is at Zhongshan Zhong Lu 249.

Visa Extensions The **Gonganju** (**PSB;** © **0773/582-9930;** open Mon–Fri 8:30am–noon and 3–6pm) is on the east side of the Li River south off Longyin Lu.

EXPLORING GUILIN

In the center of town are two of Guilin's main lakes left over from the moat that ringed the city in the Tang dynasty. To the western side of Zhongshan Lu is **Rong Hu (Banyan Lake),** named after an 800-year-old banyan tree on its shore. On the eastern side is **Shan Hu (Cedar Lake),** with its newly erected twin pagodas. A **Liang Jiang Si Hu (Two Rivers and Four Lakes) boat tour** offers visitors a chance to tour these lakes together with Gui Hu (Osmanthus Lake), Mulong Hu (Wooden Dragon Lake), and parts of the Li Jiang and Taohua Jiang (Peach Blossom) rivers, all of which are now connected by newly dredged waterways. Day sailings for ¥90 ($12/£5.85) from 9:30am to 4pm, and evening sailings for ¥120 ($16/£7.80) from 7:30 to 9:30pm, depart from the Jiefang Qiao Matou (pier) on Binjiang Lu near Jiefang Qiao, and from the Zhiyin Tai Matou on the eastern side of Cedar Lake. Buy tickets at hotel tour desks and at Shizi Jie next to the Dashijie Bridge (© **0773/282-2666**).

MOUNTAINS & CAVES

Diecai Shan (Folding Brocade Hill) Named for its striated layers of rock, which resemble folded brocade, this hill was most popular with poets and painters in the Ming and Qing dynasties, whose visits were commemorated by scores of inscriptions carved in the rock face. Halfway up the hill is the Wind Cave, a breeze-cooled tunnel that extends right through the mountain. The city's highest peak (elev. 223m/731 ft.) has some unobstructed views of the Li River.

Diecai Lu. Admission ¥48 ($6.25/£3.10). 6:30am–6:30pm (cave 7am–4pm). Bus: no. 2 or 58.

Duxiu Feng (Solitary Beauty Peak) ✿ Tapering to a pavilion-capped peak, this 152m-high (498-ft.) limestone beauty in the middle of town is the most dramatic of Guilin's hills. A set of steep stairs winds to the top, where awaiting you is a spectacular panorama of Folding Brocade Hill to the north, Wave Subduing Hill to the east, and Seven Star Crag to the southeast. The hill is actually located on the grounds of the 14th-century former palace *(wangcheng)* of a Ming dynasty prince, occupied today by the Guangxi Normal University. A gallery sells works by local artists at exorbitant prices.

Wangcheng 1. Admission ¥35 ($4.55/£2.30). Apr–Oct 7am–7pm; Nov–Mar 7:30am–6:30pm. Bus: no. 1 (Lequn Lu stop); from Zhongshan Lu, take a right onto Xihua Lu for about 150m (490 ft.). The park entrance is on your left.

Guilin's Darker Days

Although the basement-level CD store of the Xinhua Bookstore on Zhongshan Bei Lu is not particularly well stocked, it does offer an insight into Guilin's past. Check out the heavy steel bomb doors at the entrance, remnants from a paranoid time when every building had such an installation for fear of Soviet attack.

Ludi Yan (Reed Flute Cave) ★★   Located a pleasant 45-minute bike ride northwest of town, Reed Flute Cave, whose name derives from the reeds that used to cover the entrance and were used to make flutes, is the most impressive and most popular of Guilin's caves. Going first thing in the morning or late in the afternoon helps you avoid the overwhelming crowds. At any time, however, individual visitors may have to wait for a group of 20 or more tourists to amass before you can take the 40-minute tour of the cave—and then only with a Chinese-speaking guide. The highlight is the cavernous Crystal Palace of the Dragon King (Shuijing Gong) with a dense collection of limestone mounds reflected in pools of water, all lit by hundreds of colored lights. Despite the blatantly tacky artifice of it all, most visitors can't help but gasp at the scene before them. This grotto is said to have been an air-raid shelter during World War II.

Ludi Lu. (If you're biking from the Guilin Bravo Hotel, go north on Xinyi Lu, take a left on Lijun Lu, and continue as it becomes Xishan Lu; bear right as the road changes to Taohua Jiang Lu, and continue all the way to Ludi Lu; take a right onto the bridge crossing the Peach Blossom River [Taohua Jiang] until you reach the park entrance.) Admission ¥120 ($16/£7.80). Bus: no. 3.

Qixing Gongyuan (Seven Star Park) ★   Named for its seven hills whose configuration is said to resemble the Big Dipper, this extremely popular park's most famous attraction is the gargantuan **Qixing Yan (Seven Star Cave)**, which requires about 40 minutes to tour and is full of brightly lit, bizarrely shaped rock outcroppings. Exiting the cave puts you in the vicinity of the aptly named **Luotuo Shan (Camel Hill).** In the south of the park is the Crescent Moon Peak with its **Longyin Dong (Dragon Darkness Cave)** and **Guihai Beilin (Forest of Stelae),** which has thousands of stone tablet inscriptions from the last 1,600 years. There's plenty of room for some pleasant strolls away from the crowds.

Ziyou Lu. Admission ¥50 ($6.50/£3.25) park, ¥35 ($4.55/£2.30) cave. Park 6am–10pm; cave 8am–5:30pm. Bus: no. 10, 11, 14, 28, 52, or 58.

Guilin Wholesale Carving Market ★   For an afternoon away from the other tourists, I like to have a stroll among the craftsman up at the Guilin Commercial Carving Market, out past Wa Yao wholesale area. Here you can see huge mural-size woodcarvings, from massive root systems transformed into giant peacocks to large fungus growths turned in likenesses of famous Chinese historical characters such as Da Mo, Mi Le Fo, and Kong Zi. At the rear, there are dozen of stone warehouses, and while some seem to be little more than looters' stockpiles, others such as the Hua Nan Jing Ti Guan (Wa Yao Lao Dian Chang; © 0773/355-7080) make the geological collections of major world museums seem inadequate and unimpressive.

Ping Shan Da Cun. Bus: no. 4 (30 min.).

SHOPPING

With generally overinflated prices, Guilin is no place for bargains. Snacks and candies that make nice gifts include *guihua su* (a crisp, sweet osmanthus cracker) and *guihua wangcha* (osmanthus flower tea). The newest attraction, the **Zhengyang Pedestrian Street,** has a plethora of shops and stalls selling everything from teapots and jade to clothing and overpriced minority handicrafts and embroidery. The **Guilin Weixiao Tang Shangsha (Guilin Niko Niko Do Co, Ltd.)** at Zhongshan Zhong Lu 187, open from 9am to 10:30pm, is the largest **department store** in town.

WHERE TO STAY

Unlike Yangshuo, there are not any really good accommodations choices in Guilin. The big players have such a monopoly that it is difficult for smaller, more innovative places to get a foothold. Hotels are often heavily booked in May, June, September, and October, so plan ahead if want to visit then. Many Guilin hotels tack on a 15% service charge and a ¥8 ($1.05/£50p) per-person, per-night government tax, which rises to ¥25 ($3.25/£1.65) during the second to sixth days of the Lunar New Year and also during the May and October national holidays. This is all on top of the usual holiday period price hikes, all of which give good reason to head straight out of town.

EXPENSIVE

Guilin Bravo Hotel (Guilin Binguan)   Catering to foreigners since 1988, this former Holiday Inn, located on the northwestern bank of Banyan Lake, is still the best four-star hotel in town. Rooms are comfortably furnished with large twin beds and soft chairs. Ninth-floor rooms have high ceilings and marvelous views of the lake. Bathrooms are bright and clean.

Ronghu Nan Lu 14. ✆ 0773/282-3950. Fax 0773/282-2101. www.glbravohtl.com. 274 units. ¥960 ($121/£61) standard room; from ¥1,360 ($177/£88) suite. 20%–30% discounts. AE, DC, MC, V. **Amenities:** 3 restaurants; bar; lounge; outdoor swimming pool; rooftop tennis courts; health club; Jacuzzi; sauna; bike rental; concierge; tour desk; business center; forex; shopping arcade; salon; room service; laundry/dry cleaning; nonsmoking rooms. *In room:* A/C, TV, minibar, hair dryer, safe.

Li Jiang Waterfall Hotel (Li Jiang Da Pubu Fandian) ✯   This extravagantly over-the-top—note the enormous man-made waterfall (72m/236 ft. wide by 45m/148 ft. high)—five-star hotel aims to be Guilin's first choice in accommodations. Rooms are large and luxurious enough, but the service is not yet up to the standard of its Western-managed competitors. For now it caters more to northeast Asian tour groups, but special deals are often good enough to entice independent Westerners away from the Bravo and the Sheraton.

North Sanhu Lu 1. ✆ 0773/282-2881. Fax 0773/282-2891. www.waterfallguilin.com. 646 units. ¥1,480–¥2,480 ($192–$322/£96–£161) standard room; from ¥3,150 ($410/£205) suite. 10%–20% discounts. AE, DC, MC, V. **Amenities:** 4 restaurants; bar; lounge; teahouse; nightly minority cultural show; indoor swimming pool; sauna; concierge; business center; forex; shopping arcade; salon; 24-hr. room service; laundry/dry cleaning; 24-hr. medical clinic. *In room:* A/C, TV, broadband Internet access, minibar, hair dryer, safe.

MODERATE

Guilin Dianxin Binguan (Guilin Telecom Hotel)   This is a slightly cheaper alternative to the dreary Osmanthus Hotel just up the road, which while having benefited from a number of interior refurbishments, still looks like an asylum from the outside. The Telecom is simpler, but much closer to the station, and is a good choice if you are stuck in Guilin for the evening but do not want to blow your budget on a five-star. The rooms are spartan but clean, sufficient for an overnight if heading elsewhere.

Zhongshan Nan Lu 57. ✆ 0773/383-9898. Fax 0773/383-5558. www.gldx.com. 64 units. ¥220–¥380 ($29–$49/£14–£25) standard room; ¥680 ($102/£51) suite. Up to 40% discount. AE, DC, MC, V. **Amenities:** 2 restaurants; karaoke and dance hall; forex; room service; laundry/dry cleaning. *In room:* A/C, TV, broadband Internet access, fridge.

WHERE TO DINE

Guilin's most famous local dish is *Guilin mifen* (Guilin rice noodles), served at practically every street-corner eatery. Order it dry or in broth, with chicken, beef, even horse meat *(marou),* or plain, then add chives, chili, and pickled sour green beans. Other local favorites, including snake, dog, seafood, and a variety of wild animals sometimes too exotic for foreign tastes, are available in many local restaurants, which usually don't have English menus. For Western food, stick to the international hotel restaurants such as the Sheraton's **Studio Cafe** and the Guilin Bravo's **Patio Cafe.** **McDonald's** and **KFC** are both on Yiren Lu off the Zhengyang pedestrian street.

Midiexiang (Rosemary Cafe) ⊛ WESTERN   While the usual traveler's fare such as banana pancakes is ubiquitous in Yangshuo, this is one of the few places in Guilin to have a reliable Western menu. Conveniently located near the Sheraton and just off the pedestrian walking street, Rosemary's is a hit with the overseas tourists that stumble across it. The only downside is that that there are only half a dozen tables and it soon fills up with European package tourists enjoying extended breakfasts or sipping ice-cold watermelon juice to escape the summer heat outside.

Yiren Lu 1–1. ⓒ 0773/281-0063. Meal for 2 ¥80 ($10/£5.20). No credit cards. 11am–midnight.

Yiyuan Fandian SICHUAN   Garnering consistently high marks from travelers, this restaurant serves some excellent spicy dishes, including the tear-inducing diced chicken stir-fried with loads of chilies and garlic; and the *shuizhu niurou* (tender beef slices and vegetables in a chili sauce). Calm the palate with *tangcu cuipi yu* (crispy sweet-and-sour fish), then rev back up to a spicy finish with the *dandan mian* (noodles in spicy peanut sauce). The decor is pleasant, and the service is friendly and efficient.

Nanhuan Lu 106. ⓒ 0773/282-0470. English menu. Meal for 2 ¥80–¥100 ($10–$13/£5.20–£6.50). No credit cards. 11:20am–2pm and 5:20–9pm.

Zaowangye Xiangwei Ju (Vesta Restaurant) YAO/ZHUANG   The emphasis at this pleasant restaurant serving authentic Yao and Zhuang minority cuisines is on spices and fresh ingredients gathered from the countryside. Specialties include *shancun tuji* (free-range chicken soup), *zaliang zhutong fan* (bamboo cooked rice), and *shancun larou zheng yupian* (steamed taro with smoked meat).

Nanhuan Lu 96. ⓒ 0773/282-7769. Meal for 2 ¥80 ($10.40/£5.20). No credit cards. 11am–2:30pm and 4:30–9:30pm.

GUILIN AFTER DARK

Minority song and dance performances are held nightly at the **Li Jiang Theatre (Li Jiang Juyuan),** Binjiang Lu (ⓒ **0773/286-0288**). Performances cost ¥60 to ¥100 ($7.80–$13/£3.90–£6.50) and run from 8 to 9:15pm. The **Guilin Folk Customs Center (Guilin Minsu Fengqing Yuan)** at Linjiang Lu (ⓒ **0773/581-5678**) charges ¥60 ($7.80/£3.90) for shows from 7 to 9:30pm. **The Guilin Spring Theatre (Chuntian Juchang)** at Xinyi Lu 31 (ⓒ **0773/285-6290**) offers 7:30pm performances for ¥80 ($10/£5.20) that are only fractionally better than the other two.

A POPULAR BOAT TRIP: LI JIANG (LI RIVER)

A boat cruise from Guilin to Yangshuo along the 432km (270-mile) Li River is usually sold as the highlight of a Guilin visit, and indeed, the 83km (52-mile) stretch between the two towns affords some of the country's most breathtaking scenery as the river snakes gracefully through tall karst mountains, gigantic bamboo sprays, and picturesque villages—sights that have inspired countless poets and painters for generations.

Unfortunately, such inspiration these days costs a lot more than it used to and, inevitably, monopoly and price-gouging have become the trademarks of this cruise. Foreigners, segregated onto "foreigner boats," pay ¥460 to ¥480 ($60–$62/£30–£31), which is especially insulting considering that Chinese tourists pay less than half that amount. Unfortunately, there is no other way to travel this stretch of the Li River except on these official tourist authority–sanctioned boats. If time and convenience are your priorities, then take the cruise by all means. Otherwise, if you plan to spend some time in Yangshuo, consider bypassing the cruise; more beautiful karst scenery can be better toured on foot, by bike, or by boat from Yangshuo.

Currently, river trips for foreigners depart from Zhu Jiang Matou (Zhu Jiang Pier) 24km (15 miles) and a half-hour bus ride south of Guilin at around 8:30am. The first 1½ hours of the cruise to the town of Yangdi is serene and comparatively unexciting but for names of hills along the way, such as a woman yearning for her husband's return, the Eight Immortals, even a calligraphy brush. Visual highlights are clustered between **Yangdi** and the picturesque town of **Xingping. Jiuma Hua Shan (Nine Horses Fresco Hill)** is a steep cliff face with shadings and markings said to resemble a fresco of nine horses. A little farther on, **Huangbu Daoying,** a series of karst peaks and their reflections, is the tableau burnished on the back of a Chinese ¥20 note.

Boats arrive in Yangshuo in the early afternoon after 4 or 5 hours of sailing. There's a stop for shopping, after which tour buses transport passengers back to Guilin (1 hr.). Tickets for the cruise can be bought at hotel tour desks or at CITS, and include round-trip transportation to Zhu Jiang Pier, an English-speaking guide, and a Chinese lunch.

Note: See appendix A for Chinese translations of key locations listed above.

2 Yangshuo ★★★

Guangxi Province, 65km (40 miles) S of Guilin

Located at the terminus of the Li River cruise from Guilin, the small town of Yangshuo has long been a mecca for backpackers, but even before that, it was a geomancer's delight, too. Here the vast landscape is reduced to a garden scale, nature in microcosm, where hills, mountains, oceans, and rivers are reduced to rocks, karsts, streams, and pools. Set amid an awesome cluster of limestone pinnacles—a zigzag, serrated skyline superior even to that of Manhattan—Yangshuo is more beautiful, less expensive, and significantly less crowded than Guilin. Some of the most accessible karst scenery in Guangxi can be found just a short bike ride outside town. With its inexpensive hostels and Western-style cafes, some foreigners have been known to stay for months, sometimes even years. Once a sleepy little town, today's Yangshuo is being overtaken by upscale hotels, new shops and bazaars, and hordes of eager tourists. While the town is undergoing massive growth, there is precious little in the way of actual development. Five-star hotels are now moving in and will inevitably push prices even higher. It remains to be seen how long this sleepy little town can retain its charm with so many business arriving to squeeze profits out and so few putting anything back in.

I like to spend 3 or 4 months of the year chilling out in Yangshuo, so I've included a few of my own secret hideaways in this edition as alternatives to the more well-worn sights.

Yangshuo

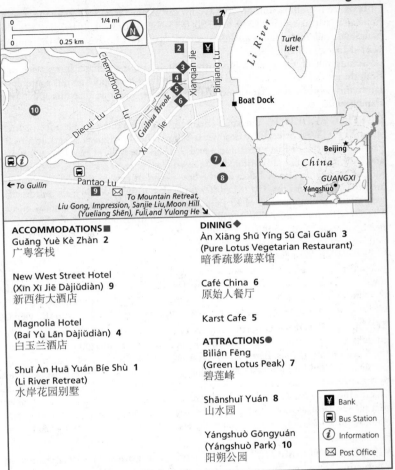

ACCOMMODATIONS ■
Guǎng Yuè Kè Zhàn **2**
广粤客栈

New West Street Hotel
(Xīn Xī Jiē Dàjiǔdiàn) **9**
新西街大酒店

Magnolia Hotel
(Baí Yù Lǎn Dàjiǔdiàn) **4**
白玉兰酒店

Shuǐ Àn Huā Yuán Bíe Shù **1**
(Li River Retreat)
水岸花园别墅

DINING ◆
Àn Xiāng Shū Yíng Sū Cai Guǎn **3**
(Pure Lotus Vegetarian Restaurant)
暗香疏影蔬菜馆

Café China **6**
原始人餐厅

Karst Cafe **5**

ATTRACTIONS ●
Bìlián Fēng
(Green Lotus Peak) **7**
碧莲峰

Shānshuǐ Yuán **8**
山水园

Yángshuò Gōngyuán
(Yángshuò Park) **10**
阳朔公园

¥ Bank
🚌 Bus Station
ⓘ Information
✉ Post Office

ESSENTIALS

GETTING THERE   The nearest **rail and air** connections are in Guilin, but tickets can be purchased here from CITS. From the bus station on Pantao Lu, **buses** depart for Guilin (70 min. travel time but leave at least 2 hr. before your train departs to allow for traffic in Guilin; ¥15/$1.95/£1) every 10 to 15 minutes from 7:30am to 8pm; for Xingping (1 hr.; ¥10/$1.30/65p) every 15 minutes from 6am to 7:30pm; for Fuli (20 min.; ¥10/$1.30/65p) every 15 minutes from 6am to 7:30pm; and for Gaotian (a half-hour; ¥10/$1.30/65p) every 15 minutes from 6:30am to 7pm. Direct buses with very poor reputations for safety run to Guangzhou (8 hr.; ¥150/$20/£9.75) at 10am, noon, 4pm, and 10pm; and to Shenzhen (10 hr.; ¥180/$23/£12) at 5:30pm and 9pm.

Taxis from Guilin (your hotel in Guilin can arrange this) will make the trip in an hour at a cost of around ¥250 to ¥300 ($33–$39/£16–£20). If heading straight to Yangshuo, call ahead and your hotel can arrange a taxi for between ¥160 and ¥180 ($21–$23/£10–£12).

Getting out of Yangshuo is less convenient. There is no direct bus service to and from the airport, so that local taxis can maintain their monopoly on this route. It's certainly not good from an environmental perspective; we hope that this situation will change soon.

GETTING AROUND   Yangshuo's main thoroughfare is the cobblestone pedestrian street **Xi Jie (West Street),** also known as Yangren Jie (Foreigner's Street). It runs from Pantao Lu to the Li River boat docks and is where the bulk of travelers' cafes, shops, and basic guesthouses are clustered. The town itself is small enough to be traversed by foot in less than an hour. **Bikes** are the best means of getting to outlying sights, and are available for rent for ¥10 ($1.30/65p) per day at many Xi Jie cafes and hotels, as well as at the southern end of Xi Jie toward Pantao Lu. **Motorcycle taxis,** normally ¥3 (40¢/20p) for 3km (2 miles), will offer to take tourists out to Moon Mountain and nearby caves for ¥30 ($3.90/£1.95), but be sure to agree on all the desired destinations and cost beforehand.

Note: While West Street remains pretty much crime free (although this is due more to the threat of vigilantes than due to the organized security apparatus), not all of the town is so lucky. Groups of pickpockets are familiar sights up around the fruit market, the petrol station, and some of the newer Chinese hotels, where they employ long thin tweezers to remove valuables while their accomplices distract the victim. Be vigilant.

TOURS & GUIDES   Unfortunately in Yangshuo, as in other tourist spots, a tour guide is simply someone who takes you to the most common sights where he can get the biggest commissions. Better to save your money and buy a good map. Rather then get steamrollered into a tour by some stranger you meet on the street, ask your hotel to organize something for you. Talk to Jasmine at the Magnolia Hotel, Alf at Buffalo Guest House, or Angel at Mountain Retreat (see "Where to Stay," below). Be aware that all specialist agents in Yangshuo are now charging a ridiculous booking fee of ¥50 ($6.50/£3.25) for train and plane tickets, so plan ahead and arrange to get these yourself.

VISITOR INFORMATION   The friendly **Yangshuo Luyou Zixun Fuwu Zhongxin (Yangshuo Tourism Information Service Center)** just south of the bus station on Pantao Lu (© 0773/882-7922) can answer basic questions on accommodations, local sights, and tours.

FAST FACTS

Banks, Foreign Exchange & ATMs   The **Bank of China** is located at Binjiang Lu 11. Forex hours are Monday to Friday from 9am to 5pm.

Internet Access   Internet access is available at most cafes, and wireless users should be able to find a few unsecured nodes just about wherever they are in the town.

Post Office   The post office (open 9am–9:30pm) is at Pantao Lu 28.

Visa Extensions   The Yangshuo **PSB** office at Chengbei Lu 39 now tells foreigners that they have to go to Guilin to renew their visas.

EXPLORING YANGSHUO

The majority of Yangshuo's treasures are located a bike ride out of town. **Xi Jie (West Street)**, with its souvenir shops and travelers' cafes, has become a bona fide tourist attraction for Chinese visitors, who completely take over the street starting in the early afternoon when boats from Guilin pull in.

In the southeastern part of town along the western banks of the Li River, the **Shan-shui Yuan** park (¥21/$2.75/£1.35; open 8:30am–6pm) is home to the impressive karst mountain **Bilian Feng (Green Lotus Peak)**, which towers over the town and the harbor. In the western part of town next to the bus station, **Yangshuo Gongyuan (Yangshuo Park)** (Diecui Lu 22; ¥10/$1.30/65p; open 6:30am–7pm) sees few foreign visitors but is full of loafing locals who pay nothing to enter. You can hike to the top of Xilang Shan for some arresting views of the countryside.

OUTDOOR ACTIVITIES

With so many karst hills and caves around the area, Yangshuo has become a little mecca for **rock climbing,** boasting some 70 climbing circuits. English-speaking Echo at the **Karst Cafe,** Xianqian Jie 42 (© 0773/882-8482), helps organize and lead both half-day trips for ¥150 ($20/£9.75) and 1- to 3-day trips for ¥300 ($39/£20) per person per day. During the summer months, Richard and George (© 1350/783-9490 or 1355/766-4617) organize some of the best **rafting** and **kayaking** trips on the Li River and on smaller rivers like the Yulong He (Jade Dragon River). Those preferring something more sedate can take courses on tai chi, Chinese cooking, Chinese calligraphy, Chinese medicine, or Mandarin at various outfits in town, including the **Chinese Culture and Art Promotion Workshop,** Diecui Jie 2 (© 0773/881-1121).

SHOPPING

While much of the souvenir junk in Yangshuo can be found at much better prices elsewhere, the two chopsticks stores in town, **Jiu Mu Tang Kuai Zi Fang,** Xi Jie 63 (© 0773/886-3000), and **Quan Yi Kuai Zi Fang,** Xin Xi Jie (© 0773/298-1771), do deserve serious attention. Both shops have a fair selection of travel sticks that are a great investment for the environmentally conscious traveler who does not want to be responsible for even more deforestation through the daily use of disposable chopsticks. A selection of models are available from ¥10 to ¥100 ($1.30–$13/65p–£6.50); they also make beautiful gifts for other ecologically minded friends, either at home or on the road.

WHERE TO STAY

Xi Jie, once a backpacker's dream with its cheap hostels and guesthouses, has grown steadily but improved little over the last 5 years. While there are always new places opening, often they show little imagination and close quite quickly again. We suggest avoiding the larger hotels along Pantao Lu—such as the monstrous, overpriced **New West Street Hotel** (Xin Xi Jie Dajiudian; © 0773/881-8888)—and find something more on a human scale, just on the outskirts of the town, or better yet, well outside. Some seriously offensive price gouging occurs during holidays (first week in May and Oct) and peak periods (summer), when rooms can cost up to four times the usual price.

Yangshuo has been in a constant state of flux for some 10 years, and some complain that the town has become crass and overcommercialized. While few tourists would gripe about the arrival of air-conditioning, techno nightclubs like Babyface and blaring hip-hop chants from bars like Si-if have really spoiled the atmosphere. See Mountain Retreat in the Yulong He section below if you are looking to escape the scene.

Guang Yue Ke Zhan *(Value)*   While there are still a few 10-yuan dorm beds around the town, I prefer a little more privacy and so prefer the simple wooden doubles provided here. Although there is no English sign outside, look for the owners' motocross bike parked outside. There are two free Internet-enabled PCs in the lobby, and it's only a few short steps from the busiest part of the town without having to listen to it.

Xianqian Jie 7. ⓒ 0773/881-3365. 24 units. ¥50–¥100 ($6.50–$13/£3.25–£6.50) standard room. No credit cards. **Amenities:** Coffee shop; free Internet access; self-service laundry. *In room:* A/C, TV.

Li River Retreat (Shui An Hua Yuan Bie Shu) *令*   Just a short stroll out of town, another Australian has taken his experience from running the local bar and now has done a really good job of turning an old kung-fu/krav maga school into a peaceful, out-of-the-way guesthouse. The views from most of the clean, modernized rooms are stunning.

Shuang Dui Cun, 10-min. walk beyond Long Tou Shan Ma Tou. ⓒ 0773/873-5681. www.yangers.com. 28 units. ¥250 ($32/£16) standard room; ¥350 ($46/£23) deluxe room. V, MC. **Amenities:** Teahouse; bike rental; limited room service; next-day laundry. *In room:* A/C, TV.

Magnolia Hotel *令令*   One of the newest and definitely the best choice of accommodations in Yangshuo town at the moment. Formerly a run-down student dormitory, the Magnolia has been transformed into a great-value boutique hotel by an Australian entrepreneur with an eye for detail and a knack for getting the best out of local staff. Four floors are built around a bright, spacious atrium, with rooms that are equally bright, and outfitted with supercomfortable king-size beds, which is why this is the favorite among organized tour groups. *Tip:* Ask Jasmine, the charming manager, for room no. 307; it's much larger than the rest and boasts it own private patio garden.

Diecui Lu 7. ⓒ 0773/881-9288. Fax 0773/881-9218. www.yangshuoren.com. 30 units. ¥200–¥300 ($26–$39/£13–£20) standard room. AE, DC, MC, V. **Amenities:** Laundry/dry cleaning. *In room:* A/C, TV, hair dryer.

Yangshuo Shengdi (Mountain Retreat) *令令令*   Built by a successful American businessman, this is one of China's true gems and has possibly the best location in the entire province. Rooms are a good size with massive picture windows and balconies to take advantage of views that are both amazing and inspiring. The retreat itself has a

---

(Moments **Taking a Dip in the Yulong**

For those who'd prefer not to float down the entire length of the Yulong, there is an alternative. Mountain Retreat's public relations manager led me down to the riverbank where boatmen were noisily bragging. For ¥10 ($1.30/65p), one of them agreed to pole us the 100m (328 ft.) or so to the next weir, where we promptly jumped off the raft and spent the rest of the afternoon swimming. Even the boatman stripped down to his skivvies and jumped in with us. So many tourists float down this stretch of water that two rafts even feature an onboard PC and printer, with locals taking digital pictures for a small fee. Mountain Retreat's manager told me that swimming like this was her summertime morning routine, a half-hour dip before returning for breakfast and fresh orange juice. Certainly one of my China highlights!

Confucian academy feel to it and is especially popular with corporate groups who find that the stunning location works wonders for the training seminars and personal development courses. Located a good half-hour outside the town, it remains my number-one choice for the ultimate Yangshuo experience.

Wang Gong Shan Jiao in Gaotian, Yangshuo. ⓒ 0773/877-7091. Fax 0773/877-709. www.yangshuomountainretreat. com. 28 units. ¥200 ($26/£13) standard room; ¥500 ($65/£33) deluxe room. MC, V. **Amenities:** Restaurant; coffee shop; boutique; bike rental; wireless Internet access; laundry. *In room:* A/C.

WHERE TO DINE

There are plenty of bars, restaurants, and eateries on Xi Jie but most have the same tired menu offering the usual copycat Western, Chinese, and local dishes. Unfortunately, such alfresco dining is also a lot less fun now that customers are incessantly harassed midbite by overeager vendors or would-be English practitioners offering their services as tour guides.

On the plus side, Yangshuo still abounds with great cafe food if you choose the right places. The **Karst Cafe** ★★★ (Xianqian Jie 42; ⓒ **0773/882-8482**) still hangs on the title of best pizza in town, with a bacon, egg, and blue cheese creation. In addition, the enormous "Full Monty" breakfast takes the award for largest breakfast in town. Just a little farther up the street, the **Fresh Juice** (Xianqian Jie 51; ⓒ **0773/882-1993**) has some fantastically imaginative combinations such as snow pear and passion fruit, and kiwi and strawberry. At the corner of West Street and Xianqian Jie, **Cafe China's** (ⓒ **0773/882-7744**) rooftop is one of the best locations in town, with excellent mountain views. Local specialties such as delicious *pijiu yu* (fish cooked in beer and spices) and *baochao tianluo* (Li River snails stuffed with pork) are extremely reliable here, but it might be wise to book a table in advance as this is the number-one choice for Western tour groups.

In answer to requests from visitors for more fine-Chinese dining, the owner at Cafe China opened a restaurant in the small village of Liu Gong. Ask at Cafe China or the Magnolia Hotel and staff will organize a boat (¥100–¥150/$13–$20/£6.50–£9.75) to take you to this converted village watch tower, less than an hour downstream from Yangshuo. Tourist boats rarely come down this far, so you may have the entire Li River to yourself as you pass the abandoned sugar refinery that still sits nestled between riverside peaks. **Liu Gong Pavilion (Zhi Huan Xuan)** ★★★ (www.yangshuoren. com) overlooks the river with a backdrop of mountains so spectacular that it almost answers the question of divine existence. Recommended are the stir-fried sweet-potato shoots and the Yao minority-style braised pork wrapped in rice stalks. Two people can eat here very well for less than ¥100 ($13/£6.50) and even a pot of fresh coffee is only ¥22 ($2.85/£1.45). You may want to take your bikes with you on the boat and then ride home via Fuli. Don't leave too late, though: Only a few houses in Liu Gong village have electricity, and one of the Pavilion staffers might have to guide you over the cobbles by flashlight.

In the meantime, his latest venture, **Pure Lotus Vegetarian Restaurant (An Xiang Su Ying Su Cai Guan;** Diecui Lu 7; ⓒ **0773/881-9079)** is a very reliable dining experience, and apart from the relaxing ambience, we really enjoyed the almond roll (*shi su xing ren quan*), the taro and egg yolk balls (*li yu dan huang wan*), and the sweet-and-sour eggplant (*tang chu qie gua*).

To eat where the locals eat, head 1 block north of Xi Jie to **Diecui Lu.** Walk down past the Magnolia and turn left where there are still a few old buildings facing the new shopping development. The third shop along is a scary-looking noodle store that's popular with local waitresses. Few locals eat banana pancakes, but with these *spicy snail noodles (luo si fen)* this is an opportunity to see what people really eat in Yangshuo, and for just ¥2.50 (35¢/15p). Up at the night market, the pulled noodles outdoor store at the main entrance is always popular. It is great fun to watch the owner stretching the delicate noodles out by hand and then tossing them into the pot. Just across the road, I really like the **Small Confused Produce Rice,** in between China Tobacco and Garden Hotel (✆ **1347115390**), not only because of its cute mistranslation, but for the good selection of vegetables that they fry up to go with baked rice pots. Great value at just ¥5 (65¢/35p) per dish.

AROUND YANGSHUO

See appendix A for Chinese translations of key locations.

RIVER TRIPS

There are plenty of opportunities to take shorter and significantly less expensive river trips from the Yangshuo area—check with the travel agencies and backpackers' cafes on Xi Jie for your options. The Li River patrol authorities have a stranglehold on all river traffic, and there are strict laws about the kinds of boats foreigners can ride on (boat licenses can cost up to a million yuan), so stick with the legitimate outfits rather than with the random touts who approach you, no matter how friendly they are.

One of the more popular trips is downriver to the umbrella and fan town of **Fuli** (see below), but boats only ply this route during the summer and early fall. Another trip is to the town of **Xingping,** about 3 hours upstream from Yangshuo. Official boats make the run in summer for about ¥60 to ¥80 ($7.80–$10/£3.90–£5.20) per person. Rather than sail upstream, some tourists prefer to cycle or take a bus to Xingping and catch a boat downstream back to Yangshuo. Some tour operators come up with creative combinations of hiking/river-trip tours, which involve traveling to Xingping by bus or bike, then hiking along the river for part of the way before hopping onto a boat for the rest of the journey.

MOON MOUNTAIN (YUELIANG SHAN) AREA

A bike trip out along the main highway with endless trucks and coaches involves riding 8km (5 miles) out to **Moon Mountain (Yueliang Shan)** in the direction of Gaotian. Follow Pantao Lu in the opposite direction from Guilin until the traffic circle, and bear right onto Kangzhan Lu. Once you leave town, you'll be greeted around each bend with unbelievably scenic vistas of karst pinnacles stretching as far as your eyes can see. (It's just a shame that the authorities have not spent any of their profits on road maintenance!)

Along the road to Moon Mountain are several recently built attractions geared strictly toward Chinese tour groups that can be safely missed. About 6km (4 miles) from Yangshuo, the **Gurong Gongyuan** (¥18/$2.35/£1.15; open 6am–sunset) has an intriguing 17m-tall (56-ft.), over 1,500-year-old banyan tree that looks like a collection of entwined snakes up close and like a giant umbrella from afar. Unlike most alleged antiquities that tourists see, this is the real deal, easily as old as any American redwood. The whole area is now a bit of a circus so it is better to view the tree just as easily from atop **Moon Hill,** 1km (⅔ mile) away (¥15/$1.95/£1; open 7am–6pm), so named because of the large moon-shaped arch under its peak. A series of steep steps winds through thick bamboo brush all the way to the top, where there are some marvelous views. Unfortunately, you will be trailed from top to bottom by persistent vendors who employ high-pressure sales tactics and quickly get abusive if you do not buy anything.

If there's an adventurous spelunker in you waiting to break free, there are several interesting caves around here worth exploring. However, some of these are suitable only for the fit, as none have paved paths and all will require you to get down-and-dirty by crawling through holes and climbing rickety ladders. **Buddha Cave**, where entry now costs a whopping (¥128/$17/£8.50; open 8am–6pm summer, 9am–5pm winter), and the **Water Cave (Shuiyan)** both have underground pools and rivers on which you can paddle and get that mud bath you've always wanted.

A more civilized alternative is 90 minutes south at the magnificent **Silver Cave (Yinzi Yan;** www.glyinzicave.com) situated in spectacular parkland about 20km (13 miles) south of Yangshuo. Any local agency will arrange tickets and transportation for around ¥80 ($10/£5) per person, which is perhaps a safer option than public transport. We missed the last bus back to town and had to flag down an archaic vehicle (half-tractor, half-tricycle), whose maximum speed turned out to be about half my normal walking pace. After a painfully slow half-hour, we asked how long it would take to get back to Yangshuo. The young peasant girl at the wheel simply shrugged her shoulders; she had never been that far from her village before!

FULI

Located along the Li River downstream from Yangshuo, the village of Fuli, first established over 1,300 years ago during the Tang dynasty, is a popular excursion either by boat or bike. Most travelers seem to prefer the latter for the gorgeous scenery along the 6km (4-mile) ride, especially now that the Pavilion has opened at Liu Gong. Fuli holds a **market** every 3 days, and while there's not much to buy for tourists there's enough local color here to take an hour or so of your time. Just before the market is a lane that winds past traditional stone houses down to the river. To cycle to Fuli, head east on Pantao Lu past the traffic circle and follow the road across the bridge. You can also take a bus from the station on Pantao Lu.

XINGPING ★★

Surrounded by a jungle of karst pinnacles, the charming, as yet unspoiled village of Xingping about 25km (15 miles) upstream of Yangshuo is being touted by some as the next Yangshuo, meaning the next backpackers' haven, now that Yangshuo has become more of a commercialized circus. Cobblestone streets wend their ways through this quaint village of stone houses that's refreshingly free of souvenir stores, and residents go about their daily business with nary a glance spared for the visitor. The most scenic area is the riverfront; on market days you'll see villagers from the surrounding areas boarding boats laden with everything from live chickens to new aluminum woks. A few cafes and backpackers' hostels have sprung up here, but accommodations and dining are still fairly basic. There are regular buses to Xingping from the Yangshuo bus station, or you can ride your bike here in 3 to 4 hours.

An interesting side trip from Xingping is to **Yucun** (literally "Fishing Village"), a tiny, picturesque Ming dynasty village (1506–21) 20 minutes downstream along the Li River, whose more famous visitors have included Sun Yat-sen in 1921 and Bill Clinton in 1998. Full of traditional Ming and Qing dynasty houses with white walls and gray-tiled roofs with upturned eaves, as well as the occasional ancestral hall, the village requires a ¥5 (65¢/35p) entrance fee which includes a tour by a Chinese-speaking local. Daily boats make the 20-minute trip to Yucun for ¥250 ($32/£16) per boat round-trip—20 times the original price. They depart Xingping's waterfront between 8am and 5:30pm (the ticket booth is to the right at the end of the main street), but boats only depart with a quorum of 10, which sometimes can mean a wait of hours in low season. The gorgeous boat ride between Xingping and Yucun, however, is generally worth the bit of hassle in getting there.

YULONG HE (JADE DRAGON RIVER) ✸✸✸

One of the loveliest trips outside Yangshuo, this river, sometimes dubbed **Xiao Li Jiang (Lesser Li River),** is, if anything, even more beautiful and certainly quieter than the Li. The river's more famous landmarks may be its bridges, in particular the 59m-long (194-ft.) Ming dynasty **Yulong Qiao (Jade Dragon Bridge)** found in the town of **Baisha,** but it's the scenery of small villages nestled at the foot of karst hills surrounded by rice paddies and a lazy winding river that most visitors remember long after they've left. Many of the travelers' cafes offer full-day tours of the river and surrounding sights, but it's entirely possible to visit on your own. Just pack a picnic, plenty of film, and rain gear, check your bike's tire pressure, and you're off.

There are several routes by which to explore the river. From Yangshuo, head out toward Moon Hill. Before the bridge crossing the Yulong He, head right on the dirt trail which can, with several deviations, take you all the way up to Baisha and the Jade Dragon Bridge. You can return along these back paths, or head back from Baisha on the main Guilin-Yangshuo highway. Or reverse the order and take the highway to Baisha (9km/6 miles of noisy main raid from Yangshuo), then cycle back down through the villages. Chances are you'll get lost on some of these paths, which can narrow to the width of your bicycle (so get off and walk carefully or you may end up face first in a rice paddy!), but that's half the fun. Not to worry, the villagers around here are more than happy to set you right, and there are enough paths between the river and the highway that you won't be lost for long.

The full journey to Yulong Qiao may be a bit much for some, especially in the summer when heat stroke and sunburn are serious threats on a journey as long as this. A less exhausting alternative is to stop off at Mountain Retreat for some lunch and then explore the bridges and side roads from there.

Alternately, some travelers have sailed back down the Yulong He on narrow bamboo rafts. This used to be very pleasant when the boatmen would ask for ¥100 to ¥200 ($13–$26/£6.50–£13). These days the raft operators have learned to squeeze every last yuan from international tourist; one Englishman we met this year was charged more than ¥600 ($78/£39) for a brief 450m (1,500 ft.) and refused to accept this kind of extortion. Some travelers have settled for sailing down a very short, relatively smooth stretch of the river from Baisha, but even this involves having to get off the raft occasionally so it can be poled down the bigger bumps.

LI JIANG AFTER DARK

Every night from July through September, 2,000 spectators are herded into the purpose-built riverside amphitheater for acclaimed director Zhang Yimou's waterborne spectacular, **"Impression, Sanjie Liu."** The celebrity connection is tenuous but it helps bring in the crowds, while the show itself is on such a grand scale with over 200 bamboo rafts in the water at once and a total production crew of 600 that it can hardly fail to impress. In fact, with such a spectacular backdrop as the Li River and the mix of floodlights, singing, and minority processions it would be difficult to execute anything less than magical, but the acclaimed director gets all the credit all the same. Tickets start at ¥180 ($23/£12) and can be arranged through most hotels, although very little of that actually goes to the local performers. The show starts at 8pm but best to get there half-hour early, leaving time to wander Liu San Jie Park. Bring binoculars or rent them for ¥5 (65¢/35p); insect repellent is also a good idea. At the bottom of West Street in Yangshuo, there is an endless succession of boat owners who will happily take you to an alternative viewing point on the river for just ¥20 to ¥30 ($2.60–$3.90/£1.30–£1.95); but at this price you will be paying mostly for the mosquitoes. For more info, visit **www.yxlsj.com**.

While many of the bars on Xianqian Jie seem to be full of Chinese youngsters looking for a bit of vacation romance "yan yu," an interesting alternative might be **Monkey Janes' Guest House Rooftop Bar** (© **0773/882-1603**), where there is a quiet pool table and the barman Finnegan makes awesome tequila sunrises for only ¥20 ($2.60/£1.30), especially on Sundays, when it is two-for-one happy hour all night long.

THREE SECRET SPOTS ✶✶✶

While much of Yangshuo is now overcrowded year-round, here are three of my own secret locations, where you can get away from the endless busloads of tourists.

Rent a bike and head out of Yangshuo on the Guilin road until you come to end of the residential development and the last large electric pylon on the left-hand side. Look for a sign that directs you to the rheumatism clinic and follow this path down through the village and out past the two disused quarries that are on either side of the track as you ride farther into the countryside. Just after the large fish farm on the left, cross the stone bridge and follow the path that goes along the left-hand bank of the stream, until you come to another even smaller stone bridge that recrosses the water. On the far side, haul your bikes up over the small stone wall that surrounds the copse on the left, lock them up around a tree and continue from here on foot. Look for a natural stone staircase that rises up from the woods. It is only a 10-minute climb, but pay attention to the steps themselves as some of them are fragments of an old temple that was torn down here by Red Guards during the Cultural Revolution.

As you emerge into the first of a series of hidden valleys, you will probably hear the bleating of goats. The pint-size Mr. Jiang keeps a herd of around 200 goats up here that sleep in a barn about three times the size of his own shack, which he shares with a couple of scaredy-cat dogs. To the right of the valley are some beautiful stone outcroppings, but if you continue to the left and then skirt around to the right of a sunken forest, it will lead you down through an area of pomelo trees and sinkholes. Continue up the hill until you reach a clump of pine trees that form a natural canopy from which a variety of local birds sing. To the right, the wary can venture into a depression of mold-covered thorn trees, an ideal location for a slasher movie, but up to the left is a charming boulder-strewn paddock, surrounded on all sides by wonderfully symmetrical shaped karsts. Although the grass is cropped tight like a super-exclusive fairway, this natural pasture has a very urgent sense of growth with nature pushing out in all directions. After a while, despite the beauty, the noise of so many different kinds of insects can become a little oppressive and I like to head back to the shade of pine trees for lunch.

Once you are back down with your bicycles, recross the stone bridge and continue along the bank path to the Yangshuo-to-Baisha back road. Take a right onto the tarmac and ride until the road takes a sharp right with a fork off to the left. Follow the fork through two villages and past the Giggling Tree Farm Guest House on the left. By now you should be able to see that you are on the bank of the Yulong River somewhere away to the right. It takes another 15 or 20 minutes to Mountain Retreat where you can stop for a rest and a cold drink, and then continue down the hill and around the bend. The road forks off to the right and fords the river. The recklessly brave can pedal across at any time of year but the more timid might want to remove their shoes and wheel their bikes across. Zigzag quickly through the village on the other side, and then once you are past the large karst on the left, take a sharp right into the grounds of the secondary school. Exit at the left and follow the path, watching out for the cobbles, all the way through the village until you reach the water's edge. This is the Jin Bao River, and the weir at the edge of Feng Huang (Phoenix) Village is my favorite swimming spot in the area. While 20 bamboo rafts a minute now squeeze down the Yulong River, you'll be luck if you see more than half a dozen all afternoon here. There are a few sharp stones at the bottom of the weir but after that, the water drops to about 3m (9ft)and is ideal for cooling off. Directly below the falls, the current is strong enough that it'll feel like you have your own personal swimming trainer, something which millionaires fork out thousands of dollars to re-create in their expensive personal gyms. Best of all, the view upstream is fantastic and apart from a few local farmers and their water buffalo crossing the weir, you'll probably remain undisturbed all afternoon.

If you are looking for a quick dip closer to town, then head up Long Tou Shan Mat Tou to where the boats from Guilin dock in the afternoon. Some choose to take the plunge here but they do not realize that the city garbage dump is in a valley just to the left of the river and that all kinds of unpleasant chemicals are seeping into the Li Jiang here. My advice is to continue on upstream, and once you pass the first bend after the Buffalo Guest House, make you way back down to the river's edge. Depending on the time of year there is usually a small beach down here, with a gentle slope that makes it ideal for even beginning swimmers. The more confident can go right across to the other side to explore the cave, but be warned that the rocks there are sharp and jagged. The best time of day to come here is about 3pm, when all the boats have passed by and the water is still nice and warm.

3 Bama ✱✱✱

Guangxi Province, 410km (317 miles) N of Nanning, 222km (138 miles) SW of Baise

Bama is a wonderful alternative for those who feel that Yangshuo has lost its charm. Although it is much more difficult to reach, the rewards are many. In fact, some might describe Bama as being what they imagine Yangshuo may have been 20 years ago, before tourism arrived en masse. Still, this is no pristine wilderness. The Chinese economic miracle has taken its heavy toll even in this remote corner of the country. The town center is a hideous hodgepodge of half finished cinder-block boxes and yet a few miles away karsts, caves, and clear waters rival anything in Yangshuo. Best of all, apart from a few intrepid speleologists, both Western and domestic tourists are still a rarity here.

In China, Bama's claim to fame is that out of a population of just over 300,000, it has 73 centenarians, one of the highest ratios in the world. Scores more nonagenarians and octogenarians fill the surrounding villages. Many of these elderly residents attribute the secret of their longevity to the *huo ma you,* a soup made from the oily seeds of the cannabis plant, ironic in a country where this ancient medicinal weed is still vilified as an evil deserving execution. Still, many of these extremely senior citizens, some of them veterans of the Long March, take a dim view of tourists and dislike being stared at like zoo animals, which is why I prefer to focus on the amazing scenery of this area. The Panyang River, for example, is still the bright aquamarine that the Li Jiang must have once been before it was polluted by scores of tour boats churning up and down every day.

ESSENTIALS

GETTING THERE   The fact that there is no railway connection or airport means that Bama has not yet been overrun by either Western or Chinese tourists. At present the only public transportation option is a coach from Nanning in the South. The first coach departs from Anji Road Long Distance Bus Station (Anji Qi Che Zhan) at 7:50am and takes 4½ hours to reach Bama, costing ¥75 ($9.75/£4.90). If you arrive late in Nanning, it might be wise to spend the evening in the unimpressive but conveniently located Kang Du Bing Guan, just 200m (656 ft.) north of the station (© **0771/ 380-1808**). The first bus for the return journey leaves Bama at 7:30am and costs only ¥60 ($9.10/£4.55), but it arrives at the North Station (Bei Zhan Ke Yun Zhong Xing) instead of Anji Station. *Be warned:* Bama residents taking this journey are not all that widely traveled and this was the first bus that I had traveled on where they dispersed complimentary travel sickness pills. Buses also leave Bama at the following times: 9:10am, 11:30am, 1:20pm, 2:30pm, and 4:10pm.

GETTING AROUND   Although there are a few Xiali taxis at the bus station, the most common forms of transportation in Bama are the small silver Wuling micro buses (made to comfortably seat seven but more often crammed with 10-plus kids and livestock) and converted motorbike taxis. These are simply small motorbikes with the back wheel chopped off and a welded metal box put in its place. The micro buses are slightly more expensive than the public buses, while the customized motorbikes charge ¥2 (25¢/15p) for trips within the confines of the town. Practically speaking they are too slow and too uncomfortable for any distance is beyond that.

At the moment, there are no bicycle rental facilities, although there are least two bike shops in town where cheap bicycles can be purchased in the region of ¥200 to 300 ($26–$39/£13–£20). The alternative is to explore using a combination of public buses and walking. Just as Yangshuo must have been before all the coach parks, there is plenty to explore.

TOURS & GUIDES   **Bama Long Life Halidom of Travel Service Company** organizes plenty of local Chinese language–only tours, but their level of English can be gauged from their bizarre company name.

VISITOR INFORMATION   There is Chinese language–only hot line at (© **0778/ 621-8152**). There is also a website at **www.bamasd.com**, but again this is still Chinese only.

FAST FACTS

Banks, Foreign Exchange & ATMs   Stock up with Renminbi before you arrive in Bama as Bank of China does not yet have an office here at the agricultural bank, and the Rural Credit cooperative only operates domestic ATM networks. There are no capabilities for exchanging foreign currency or traveler's checks.

Internet Access   Net cafes are still few and far between in Bama, and the public library only has eight machines on the first floor and they are invariably in use. There is a small Internet cafe just off the main streets in an alley between the furniture shop and Dancing With Wolves men's clothing shop, with about 25 machines and access costing ¥2 (25¢/15p) per hour. For some reason the tops of the black monitors attract plagues of flies of biblical proportions.

Post Office   There is a small post office (open 9am–6pm) on Shou Xiang Da Dao, the main street.

Visa Extensions   The PSB office is at the north end of Gu Cheng Lu, but it cannot handle visa extensions and will refer you to the provincial capital.

EXPLORING BAMA

The town has a small Peoples' Park on Gong Yuan Lu with a few pagodas dotting karst outcrops, but watch out as the caves have been taken over by beggar squatters. Anyway, there are far better sights outside of town.

WHERE TO STAY

Bama currently only has one really good hotel, but the low costs and high quality certainly make up for the lack of variety.

There are a number of small family-run guesthouses operating in various side streets, but with squat toilets and poor facilities they are no comparison or competition for the Shou Xiang (below).

Long Life Hotel (Shou Xiang Da Jiu Dian) ★★★ *(Finds*   Opened in February 2007, this four-star is one of the best bargains in China. Luxurious twin rooms are priced at ¥108 ($14/£7) per night including Guangxi-style breakfast that consists of rice porridge, picked vegetables, a boiled egg, and a glass of hot milk. Standard rooms are ¥158 ($20/£9.75) per night but are located on the front side of the hotel and are therefore disturbed by the noisy music and dancing that takes place in the main square every evening. Best of all, price increases during national holidays are minimal. When I was there for the May Day celebrations, rooms increased by only ¥20 ($2.60/£1.30) as opposed to tripling or quadrupling as they do in Guilin and Yangshuo.

Shou Xiang Da Dao 488. ✆ 0778/622-1818. Fax 0778/622-8688. www.bmsxdjd.com. 80 units. ¥108–¥158 ($14–$20/£7–£9.75) standard room; from ¥388 ($50/£25) suite. No credit cards. **Amenities:** Restaurant; bar; lounge; salon; room service; next-day laundry/dry cleaning. *In room:* A/C, TV, minibar.

Sheng Di Da Jiu Dian   Located just outside the bus station, this sad old dinosaur is in desperate need of a makeover. At ¥100 ($13/£6.50) per night for a twin, it's is exorbitantly overpriced, especially considering that the bathrooms do not even have sink plugs and the curtains are tissue-paper thin. This is a real shame as the staff are super friendly and very helpful (the security guard lent me his bicycle for the afternoon as there were no rental facilities in town), and the hotel is the only place in town that has a map of the area for sale. It also has an interesting photo album of local sights and a souvenir DVD for sale at ¥20 ($2.60/£1.30).

Shou Xiang Da Dao 2. ✆ 0778/621-2062. 70 units. ¥100 ($13/£6.50) standard room; ¥400 ($52/£26) suite. No credit cards. **Amenities:** Restaurant; bar; concierge; room service; laundry. *In room:* TV.

WHERE TO DINE

This is currently one of Bama's main problems. Small noodle shops abound, but they are not always so hygienic. On the main square there are two local burger copycats, one called **MKJ** and the other **Happy Burger.** There is also a small place just behind the Shou Xiang hotel that serves tasty steamed baozi on kindergarten-size chairs and tables.

AROUND BAMA

See appendix A for Chinese translations of key locations.

BAINIAO YAN ✿✿✿

A good starting place is Bainiao cave (© **0778/622-1515**), about half an hour out of town. The bus will drop you off just below a small hydro station where you cross the bridge and follow the track on the right-hand side of the river. Boat tours for this spectacular cavern begin at an especially constructed wharf, and are still a very reasonable ¥40 ($5.20/£2.60) for a 1-hour trip. Above their blaring techno music, the country boys who have been left in charge may try to convince you that at least four customers are necessary before they can depart. Simply play dumb (as I did), speaking no Chinese, and you can soon get past this minor obstacle rather than sit around waiting while they smoke and scratch their heads.

The cave itself is one of the most spectacular I have ever seen. There are no psychedelic lights and a flat-bottomed pontoon with a single oarsman keeps the noise to a minimum. Even the approach is inspiring, a gaping cleft in the rock face just waiting to swallow unwary tourists. Just inside the mouth there are colonies of bats and swallows, but their chirps and squeaks soon fade into the distance, leaving only the rhythmic sound of the oar against its rubber grommets. There are places where the rocks can be seen plunging away into the 20m (66-ft.) inky depths, although this drops as far as 50m (164 ft.) in some parts. Best of all, there are no ripples to disturb the wonderful silence.

Back out on the main drag, follow the main road up the hill through the village, until you see a small turn that leads down into a tunnel. The recently constructed main road heads up around the mountains, but walking down through the tunnel leads to a number of wonderful surprises. The first is a scree slope that falls away down to the Panyang River. Follow the road down the side of the ravine and then backtrack along the water buffalo path, which will take you to the point where the rapids plunge into the water cave that you just visited half an hour before.

Back out in the valley is a stone-and-iron suspension bridge that is a perfect gateway for hard-core trekkers wanting to get into the real wealth of this area. Continue alongside the beautiful turquoise waters through a small cluster of houses each with a good selection of Bama ancient residents, and after an hour or so you will reach the main road, where you can flag a bus back to Bama or onto Poyue for Baimo dong.

POYUE ✿✿✿

Continue on the same Feng Shan bus that stops off at Bainiao Cave to the small village of Poyue. Look for a large, rocky, exposed section of the riverbed as the bus comes around a right-hand bend into the village. There should be caves by the roadside and all along the edge of the river. Alight from the bus where all the motorcyclists congregate and follow the road that leads away to the right, which leads to one of the most spectacular public caves in the world.

BAIMO DONG ✿✿✿

The asphalt road follows the river for about 200m (656 ft.) and then zigzags away to the left between a small power station the only tree for miles around. Every single square inch of ground has been planted with sweet corn, even high up into the rocky hillsides. After about a 10-minute walk, the newly constructed car park and toilets can be seen on the right. Just around the corner from here, Baimo dong (② **0778/622-1527**) opens up like a enormous gaping rift in the mountainside.

The entrance fee is ¥30 ($3.90/£1.95), and there is at least one young local guide with a smattering of English. Helmets are available but an extra torch is more useful. Surprisingly, the cave begins with a steep climb of 70m (230 ft.) rather than a sharp descent. Many of the formations are gigantic in proportion and completely alien to anything seen on the outer surface of this planet. Look out for small blind, white cave worms that wriggle around on slowly forming stalagmites. In places the ceiling reaches a height of some 200m (656 ft.), and the middle section opens up into a vast *Tiankeng* or doline, where the cave collapsed, leaving it open to the elements. Beyond this, the path is unfinished and there is no lighting, but the guide can easily be persuaded to take visitors all the way to the end. In places the silence is as still as an isolation tank and the darkness as black as pitch. It's quite possibly the best underground experience in all of China.

AROUND POYUE ✿✿✿

Just before the throng of motorcyclists, there is a concrete bridge that leads across the river. Follow this to the left and look for tan alley on the right-hand side that winds up into the mountains. There is not much of a path, but it will take you around the back of the few houses and between some pigsties, easily noticeable by their noise and odor, until it becomes little more than a mule trail. Sometimes the outlines of farmers climbing this route can be made out from the paved road across the river which earlier led you to and from Baimo dong. Follow it around the mountain until a fork is reached (about a 40-min. climb), where a small garden of Guinness-colored rocks sprout from the earth. To the right, the trail leads up to a natural water cistern that has been cut from the living rock, with steep steps leading down to who knows where. Rest here for a while and look out over the natural amphitheater that has been formed from the hundreds of terraces that dominate this beautiful, isolated valley. Yet another spectacular wonder of the amazing Bama region.

The left fork rises up through the village (if a small cluster of 10 dwellings can be called a village) past a number of man-made cisterns and along the edge of the Baimo Valley where peasants graze their horses and cattle. The cows here are particularly charismatic, with their friendly demeanor and long fluttering eyelashes. It is also a good idea to bring along some sugar cubes for the ponies. On my visit, I only had bananas left over from my packed lunch, but the young gelding enjoyed the treat so much that he promptly ate the skin, too.

Back down on the main track, the gravel road takes a long arcing loop to the right until it reaches a gorge known as Long Men Ao. From here there is the chance to explore far beyond into this magical topographic realm. Short of time, I simply climbed the rise on the left and perched myself at the top, to look out on the comings and goings of the villagers below.

Returning through the "dragons' gate" rather than following the road all the way around, look out for the old path that cuts across the north side of the valley. This is a series of rock steps that go up and down, and unless you possess the floating footwork of Muhammad Ali, I would recommend a strong pair of ankle-supporting walking boots. Back down at the bottom of the valley, surprise surprise, a new hydroelectric plant is under construction at the mouth of Baimo dong. Even so, where the river emerges from underground the water is crystal clear, and the local children will quickly point of the best spots for a quick dip.

Back in Poyue village, head in the opposite direction from the cave, across the main road, and down past the market, look for the noodle shop next to the headstone mason. The noodles are passable but do not let him persuade you to purchase any of the plum spirit; it is only ¥1 (15¢/10p) per *jin* but tastes about half that price. As I sat slurping my noodles, the owner came over and gave the big pot next to my table a stir. When asked what was inside, he pulled out some hideous alien artifact that I quickly identified by the dangling eyeballs and lolling tongue to be a deskulled pig's head. Needless to say, I did not get to finish my noodles.

Back on the cave side of the village is the **Yan Nian Shan Zhuang Guest House** (© **0778/614-0311**), a rather ugly six-story Chinese house but with friendly owners and decent rooms for ¥40 ($5.20/£2.60), making it a suitable base for further exploring the surrounding mountains.

CHI FU LAKE
To the west of the city, the lake is one of the few disappointments in the area. Yet another artificial reservoir, the section between Bama and the main expanse shows a history of heavy industrialization, with lots of disused derricks and smelters, while in recent times the lake has been filled with fish farms. Far more interesting would be an exploratory trip in the opposite direction up to the next large town of Fengshan to find some of the longest natural stone arches in the world, some bridging rivers and others crossing roads. I did not have time to go that far, but there are plenty of clues around town, so I shall save that expedition for you.

4 Beihai

Guangxi Province, 580km (360 miles) W of Hong Kong, 229km (142 miles) S of Nanning

Located at the southeastern tip of Guangxi, Beihai is a sleepy coastal town famous for its beaches and pearls. First settled over 2,000 years ago, this fishing community was opened up to Western powers after the Yantai Agreement of 1876; Westerners moved in and established consulates and businesses here. With a relaxed pace of life and a subtropical climate offering plenty of sunshine, Beihai makes for a pleasant escape from the nonstop frenzy of many Chinese cities. *Note:* Please turn to appendix A for Chinese translations of key locations.

ESSENTIALS
GETTING THERE Beihai is connected by **flights** to Beijing (3 hr.), Guangzhou (50 min.), Guilin (45 min.), Shenzhen (1 hr.), Shanghai (2 hr.), Hong Kong (1 hr. 20 min.), Guiyang (1 hr.), and Kunming (1½ hr.). Tickets can be purchased at the **CAAC** office at Beibuwan Xi Lu, second floor of Minhang Dasha (© **0779/303-3757**) from 8:30am to 8:30pm. Buses depart from here for the airport (30 min.; ¥10/$1.30/65p), which is 24km (9 miles) east of town, 2 hours before scheduled departures and also meet incoming flights. Taxis to the airport should run ¥50 ($6.50/£3.25).

From the **railway station** (© **0779/320-9898**) located between downtown and Silver Beach, twice-daily trains run to Nanning (3 hr.), where there are more extensive connections to the rest of China's rail network.

From the **long-distance bus station** (© **0779/202-2094**) on Beibuwan Lu, air-conditioned luxury buses run to Nanning (2½–3 hr.; ¥50/$6.50/£3.25) every half-hour from 6:50am to 9pm. Express buses also run to Shenzhen (11 hr.; ¥230/$30/£15) at 8:20pm; to Guangzhou (10 hr.; ¥180/$23/£12) at 8:45am and 8:55pm; and to Guilin (7 hr.; ¥150/$20/£9.75) at 8:40am and 9:10pm.

A daily 10-hour **ferry** to Haikou on Hainan Island departs at 6pm from the Beihai Guoji Keyun Gang (International Ferry Terminal; © **0779/388-0711**). A standard room with shared bathroom costs ¥233 ($30/£15). A daily boat also runs to Weizhou Dao (2½ hr.) at 8:30am and returns at 3pm. A sleeper berth costs ¥70 ($9.10/£4.55), while seats in second and third class cost ¥40 ($5.20/£2.60) and ¥35 ($4.55/£2.30) respectively. During high season, a fast boat, the *Jinghai Hao,* leaves at 8:30am. The fare is ¥120 ($16/£8).

GETTING AROUND   Santana **taxis** cost ¥7 (90¢/45p) for 3km (2 miles), then ¥1.60 (20¢/10p) per kilometer. Motorcycle taxis charge ¥3 (40¢/20p) around town and ¥6 to ¥8 (80¢–$1.05/40p–50p) to Silver Beach.

Bus no. 3 (¥2/25¢/15p) runs from downtown to Yin Tan (Silver Beach), while bus no. 2 runs from the railway station north past Waisha to the ferry docks in the western part of town.

Bike rentals at Ba Da Bike Club, Bei Bu a Zhong Lu, Opposite Yin Bing Guan (© **0779/203-2334**).

FAST FACTS

Banks, Foreign Exchange & ATMs   The **Bank of China** (open Mon–Fri 8am–noon and 2:30–5:30pm) is located on Beihai Dadao between Guizhou Lu and Sichuan Lu. An ATM is available.

Internet Access   The Beihai Library at Min Zu Da Dao 61 (© **0779/562-3636**) is an impressive 50m-tall (164-ft.) geodesic dome. Unfortunately, the design is the only impressive thing about it: The glass invariably leaks and the bookshelves are about as well stocked as a thrift shop. Still, they do have a quiet **Wangba,** charging ¥2 (25¢/15p) per hour, just west of the Guotong Gouwu Zhongxin (Guotong Shopping Center). Dial-up is © **163.**

Post Office   The main post office (open 8am–8pm) is at the southwestern corner of Jiefang Lu and Woping Lu.

Visa Extension   The **Shi Gonganju (PSB)** is located at Zhongshan Lu 213 (© **0779/209-1811;** Mon and Fri 2:30–5:30pm and Tues–Thurs 8am–noon and 2:30–5:30pm, 3–6pm June–Sept).

EXPLORING THE TOWN

The consulates, trading firms, and homes built by foreign powers after the Yantai Agreement of 1876 can still be seen in Beihai's **old town** around Zhuhai Lu and Zhongshan Lu. Three long blocks south of Zhongshan Lu on Jiefang Lu is the former German Consulate, a two-story yellow structure with graceful arches, now on the grounds of the Nanzhu Binguan. Across the road is the old British Consulate, which has fallen into a state of disrepair and is now part of a local school.

Beihai now has two **aquariums.** The original down in the waterfront park next to the Shangri-La Hotel is old and dated, while there is a new center up on Sichuan Nan Lu Zhong Duan (© **0779/320-2238**). Ticket prices are a stiff ¥98 ($13/£6.40) for adults and ¥58 ($7.55/£3.75) for children, but I was much more curious to have a look around the warehouse across the street, whose sign announced that it was a wholesale outlet for "Fisherman's Pyrotechnic Supplies."

Yin Tan (Silver Beach) ⊘★★ Beihai's premier attraction, located 10km (6 miles) south of downtown, offers a 24km (16-mile) stretch of dull, gun-metal gray sand, murky water, and thousands of jellyfish the size of small satellites. Supposedly Chinese tourists throng here for volleyball, sunbathing, and sandcastle building, but the only time I saw lots of people on the beach was in Photoshopped posters that adorned the walls of hotel lobbies. Unfortunately, more than half the worlds' supertankers make their way through the Gulf of Tonkin, and excessive tank washing, ballast dumping, and undersea pipelines have all led to a severe deterioration in the water quality both here and in Hainan, with even a number of red tides. The local practice of fishing using TNT blasting and cyanide poisoning, although banned, has not helped either. Still, there are plenty of entrepreneurs who will rent out motorized skiffs, speedboats, horses, and even the obligatory camel. Officially there is an entrance fee, but I was never able to find a ticket booth.

Yin Tan. Admission ¥30 ($3.90/£1.95). 6am–9pm. Bus: no. 3.

SHOPPING

Beihai is famous for its pearls and the shops are full of them. For less-expensive souvenirs, try the **night market** that goes south from Fu Gui Lu past the Ming Du Hotel.

WHERE TO STAY

Like much of the town, many hotels are run down and in poor condition. This is hardly surprising as many of the investors who made money on the first wave of property speculation then used the money to emigrate. There is a well-worn Shangri-La, but it looks like an old warehouse from the outside and is located on one of the dirtiest parts of the beach. Only mollycoddled overseas groups with no other idea stay here any more.

Gofar Garden Paris Hotel (Ye Ba Li Jiudian) ⊘★★ This is my favorite hotel in town, with eager-to-please English-speaking staff and elegant rooms with very spacious shower areas. I especially enjoyed researching the next part of my trip in their small garden, a spot that none of the other guests seemed to know about.

Bei Bu Wan Zhong Lu 8. ⓒ **0779/202-2788.** Fax 0779/202-6980. www.gofarhotel.com. 108 units. ¥420 ($55/£27) standard room; from ¥680 ($88/£44) suite. AE, DC, MC, V. **Amenities:** Restaurant; bar; lounge; health club; sauna; teahouse; concierge; salon; room service; massage; laundry. *In room:* A/C, TV, minibar, hair dryer.

Zhong Long Hai Bing Guan Just a few minutes off the main road, this budget option is a plain Jane, but the rooms are more than satisfactory. New and clean, the bathrooms are spotless, but I am unsure why the shaving light has red-and-white LEDs that would be more suitable on the dashboard of a custom car.

Guang Dong Lu 18. ⓒ **0779/208-5888.** Fax 0779/202-3960. 72 units. ¥168 ($22/£11) standard room. No credit cards. **Amenities:** Therapeutic massage; laundry. *In room:* A/C, TV.

WHERE TO DINE

For the best seafood, albeit at extortionate prices, head out to **Waisha,** a thin strip of land connected by a bridge to the northwest part of town where new restaurants have replaced the 72 informal "no-name" food stalls that used to be here. Local specialties worth trying include sandworms, abalone, snails, crayfish, and sea cucumber. To eat where the locals eat, look for the night market at the rear of Chang Qin Park on Chang Qin Lu.

Golden Horse Food Street (Jin Ma Mei Shi Cheng) CHINESE Underground and to the rear of the very visible KFC, this Chinese-style food court has a massive selection of over 700 different dishes to choose from. Simply park yourself at a table, let the waitress supply you with tea and an order form, and then go peruse the glass counters for something that you fancy.

Bei Bu Wan Guang Chang, basement. ℂ **0779/399-8818**. ¥20–¥80 ($2.60–$10/£1.30–£5.20) per person. No credit cards. 11:30am–1am.

Tommy's SEAFOOD Among all the seafood rip-off joints aimed at gullible daytrippers, here is a haven of sanity. Tommy serves a nice selection of Western food (including some interesting steaks such as kangaroo, ostrich, and crocodile) mainly to expats, but can also let you know which of the nearby seafood emporiums still treat their customers like guests rather than cash machines.

Wai Sha Dao, Yue Nan Jie, D-Dong. ℂ **0779/208-7202**. Meal for 2 ¥100 ($13/£6.50) and up. No credit cards. 10am–2am.

AROUND BEIHAI

The highlight of **Weizhou Dao** ✿, apart from leaving, is an unusual 21m (69-ft.) high **French Cathedral** built here shortly after the 1876 Yantai Agreement, constructed entirely of local materials (rocks, coral, sand, limestone, and bamboo). Unfortunately, the island, 36 nautical miles (56km/35 miles) from Beihai, has seen much better days, especially since a 2-million-ton refinery opened up on the south of the island and polluted all 300 freshwater wells, killing off much of the natural vegetation. There is now the nasty shock of a ¥50 ($6.50/£3.25) entrance fee to leave the docks while the rest of the island lacks any decent accommodations and smells like a stinking fish-packing plant. There is also a volcanic museum that demands an excessive ¥40 ($5.20/£2.60) for just two rooms of displays. Daily boats leave Beihai in the morning at 8:30am (see "Getting There," above) and return from Weizhou at 3pm. Check with your hotel tour desk about 1-day tours of the island.

5 Pingxiang ✿

Guangxi Province, 230km (143 miles) S of Nanning

Unfortunately Pingxiang has traditionally been a town that is passed through, not a place where people often choose to stay. Even though it is surrounded by spectacular karst scenery on all sides, development for tourism is only just now getting underway. Guangdong merchants were originally drawn here in the mid-1800s by the booming opium trade, and there followed a number of Miao suppressions that all but wiped out the original inhabitants. The recently completed Nan You highway, which brings the 230km (143-mile) trip from Nanning down to less than 3 hours, should help boost its popularity, although at the moment there are still many more soldiers and policemen than tourists.

ESSENTIALS

GETTING THERE The first express bus to Nanning leaves for Jiang Nan station at 6am and then every 30 minutes until 6pm; it costs ¥60 ($7.80/£3.90) and takes about 3 hours, passing through some very spectacular scenery. The bus station (© 0771/ 852-0958) also has services to Haiphong over the border in Vietnam at 12:30pm and to Hanoi at 10:20am and 4pm. Tortuous sleeper buses run to Guangzhou at 6:10, 7, 7:30, 8:10, and 8:50pm, and to Shenzhen at 4:30pm.

The town has two railway stations, north and south. The north station (© 0771/ 8522-060) is just off the main square but is easily missed. Its front entrance is well concealed just next to a large billboard reading THE FIELD OF COMMERCE. Only two trains stop here every day. One is the 7312 to Nanning at 10:07am, arriving at 3:25pm; and the other is the 7311, which leaves Nanning at 10:30am and arrives in Pingxiang at 3:50pm.

The south station is approximately 4km (2½ miles) out of town toward the Vietnam border. It is a brand-new silver building that is usually kept locked up 90% of the time. Tickets can be purchased in a scruffy converted stable just outside that houses the most irritable ticket seller in the whole country. Unsurprisingly, the only choice of train is to Nanning. The road to the south train station is notable only for the cement factory, where it can be seen how a limestone peak that took millions of years to form can be completely annihilated just a couple of decades.

GETTING AROUND Although there is a Giant dealership in town, they do not rent bicycles, and this instead has to be done the hard way. I asked an old bicycle repair man just a few doors down from my hotel, and the shoe shiner who was working alongside him offered me his rickety old runabout at ¥10 ($1.30/65p) for the whole day with just a ¥100 ($13/£6.50) deposit. It turned out that there was so little to see that I returned the bicycle after just 2 hours.

Santana **taxis** cost ¥5 (65¢/35p) for 3km (2 miles), then ¥1.60 (20¢/10p) per kilometer. Motorcycle taxis charge ¥3 (40¢/20p) around town.

FAST FACTS

Banks, Foreign Exchange & ATMs The **Bank of China** (open 9am–5pm) has a branch with an ATM on the corner of Bei Huan Lu and Ji Zhou Lu

Internet Access There are a number of small **wang ba** on Bei Huan Lu, just up from the post office on the opposite side of the road, all charging ¥2 (25¢/15p) per hour.

Post Office The post office (open 8am–6pm) is on the corner of the main square adjoining Bei Huan Lu.

Visa Extensions The Pingxiang **PSB** office at the bottom of Bei Huan Lu politely informed us that foreigners must go to Nanning or Guilin to renew their visas.

WHERE TO STAY

Long Yuan Bing Guan A cheaper option for those on a budget, this is a very conveniently located family-run guesthouse, just through the new shopping area, across from the bus station. Rooms at the rear are rather claustrophobic compared to those in front.

Pingxiang Lu 115. © 0771/853-0618. 20 units. ¥50 ($6.50/£3.25), standard room. No credit cards. *In room:* A/C, TV.

Zhong Yue Guo Ji Da Jiu Dian It's a typical Chinese business hotel, but as of yet it offers the best rooms in town. The standard, unimaginative rooms are clean and reasonably priced.

Xin Hua Lu 3. © 0771/853-9888. Fax 0771/853-8733. 125 units. ¥150 ($20/£9.75) standard room; from ¥358 ($47/£23) suite. No credit cards. **Amenities:** 2 restaurants; bar; lounge; concierge; business center; sauna, salon; room service; next-day laundry/dry cleaning. *In room:* A/C, TV, Internet.

WHERE TO DINE

Mei Jia Hui fast food (© **0771/853-3996**) is opposite the main indoor market, just over the river, and can be spotted by its big yellow FAST FOOD sign. They serve a tasty Chinese-style buffet that is dished out on metal trays along with soup and boiled rice for ¥5 (65¢/35p), ¥7 (90¢/45p), or ¥10 ($1.30/65p) depending on how many different items you select.

The large wet market has a wide range of noodle stores as well as a few fresh fruit juice places that will knock up a quick orange and lemon or passion-fruit juice for just ¥1 to ¥2 (15¢–25¢/10p–15p). There is also a lady close by who will put together Vietnamese-style pork sandwiches that are useful as a packed lunch on a day trip to Huashan—she is up by the bridge to the poultry market.

AROUND PINGXIANG

See appendix A for Chinese translations of key locations.

HUASHAN CLIFF PAINTINGS (HUASHAN BIHUA)

Adorning the cliffs that rise alongside the Zuo River are what are alleged to be the largest Shamanic murals in the world. Although buses leave Pingxiang station for Ningming every 15 minutes, starting at 6:50am and costing ¥10 ($1.30/65p), a more interesting alternative route utilizes the daily slow train to Nanning, which leaves at 10:07am and covers the 40km (25-mile) journey in 70 minutes and costs just ¥2.50 (35¢/15p).

From Ningming station, head out of the main door and walk 200m (656 ft.) down to the Tuolongqiao bridge. Invariably a boat tout will stop you on the way and escort you down under the bridge where a number of decidedly troll-like fellows keep some poor excuses for boats. From here to the best paintings are almost another 40km (25 miles) and will take a good 6 hours there and back. There is a visitor's lodge at the site but at ¥300 ($39/£20), it is inordinately overpriced for a night of discomfort and mosquitoes. Hold out for ¥80 ($10/£5.20) for the round-trip getting back to Ningming around 6pm. The first hour is spent acclimatizing to the incredible din of the outboard engine, which is only occasionally drowned out by dynamite blasting from some of the local limestone quarries along the riverbank. It takes about 1 hour to reach the first few examples and then approximately another hour to reach the main viewing area, with the best spot being on the East Bank of the adjoining Mingjiang River. Although these paintings are claimed to be some 2,000 years old, I find it rather suspicious that they have not faded over time, nor have the rock faces been darkened and weathered.

The last train from Ningming leaves at 3:25pm, but for ¥2 (25¢/15p) one of the little converted Moto taxis will take you to Ningming bus station, where buses for Pingxiang leave every 15 minutes, costing ¥10 ($1.30/65p).

FRIENDSHIP BORDER (YOUYIGUAN)

Rather a strange name for the site of one of the worlds' bloodiest pyrrhic victories of recent times. At the end of the 1970s, the Chinese government decided that Vietnam was cozying up far too nicely with the Soviet Union and deserved punishing for such disloyal behavior. Deng Xiaoping then boldly announced that PLA troops would be sent across the border and of course the Vietnamese were waiting patiently for them, mowing down the first 20,000 with heavy machine guns. There is a museum is located at the border that conveniently makes no reference to this face-losing episode.

Buses leave Pingxiang station at 7:30am, 10:20am, and 1:30pm with the 20km (12-mile) journey costing ¥10 ($1.30/65p). While the natural surroundings are truly spectacular much of the valley is still a half-finished parking lot. A ticket office charges ¥30 ($3.90/£1.95) admission to gullible tourists, but foreigners can safely stroll by, as if they are walking up to the border. The gatehouse consists of three floors of propaganda stating how the brave imperial forces (a mere 5,000 Zhuang peasants without modern weapons and heavily outnumbered) under the leadership of Feng Zicai held out against the French colonists, a defeat that eventually bought down the French government, but unsurprisingly makes no mention of the 1979 incident. Crumbling stone steps lead up on either side to fortifications, tunnels, and gun emplacements and despite the numerous signs asking visitors to "take care of the cultural relics please," they are in such appalling condition that the entire site would be closed for safety reasons if it were in the West.

Taxis and motorbikes loiter conspiratorially back down near the ticket office, asking ¥30 ($3.90/£1.95) to go back to Pingxiang.

6 Guiyang

Guizhou Province, 450km (270 miles) NE of Kunming

Guiyang, the capital of Guizhou Province, is a natural fortress. The capricious weather and the hostile topography, giving Guiyang the resemblance of a castle in the mist, would seem more at home in Transylvania. Few Han Chinese even knew these strange lands existed before the famed geographer Xu Xiake traveled here in 1636 as part of his 30-year trek exploring China's sacred mountains (on foot and unescorted!). Again and again he was confronted by "massive, labyrinthine heaps of rock towering wave-like into crests or busting out like petals, dizzying in their effect as they jostle and surge toward the sky!"

"Imagine a series of quaintly shaped hillocks littering a landscape that is also pockmarked with deep depressions," explained 17th-century explorer Francis Garnier. "No valleys or mountain ranges. No general sense of direction. The streams flow to all points on the compass. Every step would have led us up against some impossible piece of terrain."

By that time the empire had relocated so many eastern Chinese colonists to this unforgiving land that the province's population had soared from 65 million to 150 million. A series of rebellions was dealt with mercilessly by succeeding generations of Tunpuren, or Han military colonists. Eighteen thousand Miao were killed in 1732, with almost the same number executed and a similar number enslaved. More than 100 years later the scenario was repeated. The governor of Guizhou wrote that the province had lost nine-tenths of its entire population in just 2 decades, either massacred or exiled to the hills of northern Laos, Burma, and Thailand.

Guiyang remains an important strategic possession in a land where even the locals claim that there are "never three days of sun in a row, never three acres of flat land and never three people with any money." Despite some development, Guizhou has remained an impoverished backwater compared to its neighbors. Incomes and literacy rates are well below the national averages, and many villages still lack basic infrastructures such as roads and electricity.

A closer look at the map reveals how these proud, defiant peoples have been dominated and humiliated by Chinese colonists. Name after name stands out like marker flags on a campaign plan: Anshun (Peace and Submission); Liping (Pacification of the Li); Zhenyuan (Pacification of the Distant Tribes); Guiding (Pacification of Guizhou); Luodian (Extension of Imperial Power); and Kaili (Village of the Victory Song).

As for the Han Chinese contribution, Guiyang itself is a place many travelers can't wait to get out of, if they make it here at all. Today, gray, dreary buildings still dominate the disarray of so-called development, and the city is staggering to cope with its growing population of over a million people. Happily for visitors interested in exploring Guizhou's ethnic minority cultures, having to stay over is not as dreaded as it once was. The city is now an essential jumping-off point to see the unique native cultures, as different to the Han Chinese as the Native Americans are to the 21st-century descendants of their European conquerors.

ESSENTIALS

GETTING THERE Daily **flights** connect Guiyang to Beijing, Shanghai, Guangzhou, Chengdu, Xi'an, Kunming, Guilin, Nanning, Chongqing, and Hong Kong. Tickets can be purchased at the **CAAC** office at Zunyi Lu 264 (© **0855/597-7777**) from 8:30am to 8pm. A **China Southwest Airlines** office, located in the Taiwan Dasha at Zhonghua Nan Lu (© **0851/581-1222**), is open from 8am to 10pm. The 12km (8-mile) **taxi** ride to the airport should cost ¥50 ($6.50/£3.25). **Airport buses** depart from the CAAC office every half-hour for a fare of ¥10 ($1.30/65p); the CAAC office is open from 8:30am to 6:30pm. Getting to the airport is more of a problem. Most drivers demand ¥50 ($6.50/£3.25) for what is actually a ¥25 ($3.25/£1.65) journey, but it is an unavoidable rip-off that is almost worth it if you get to go on the notorious shortcut.

Guiyang's **railway station** (© **0851/818-1222**) in the southern part of town is a modern building with computerized ticketing and all your usual touts. From here, several **trains** a day run to Kaili (3–4 hr.; ¥25/$3.25/£1.65). Theoretically it's much faster to take the 2-hour bus, but poor driving skills mean that buses are often involved in minor collisions that double the journey time as drivers argue incessantly about who was to blame. The K946 originates in Guiyang at 7:40am, so it's easier to get an assigned seat on it. The 2079 departs for Kunming (12½ hr.; ¥234/$30/£15 soft sleeper) at 6:50pm; the K922 leaves for Chengdu (17 hr.; ¥226/$23/£15 soft sleeper) at 4pm; and the 5608 departs for Chongqing (10 hr.; ¥150/$20/£9.75 soft sleeper) at 7:40pm. The T88 departing at 10:36pm is the quickest option for getting to Beijing (32 hr.; ¥754/$98/£49 soft sleeper). The K112 runs to Shanghai (33 hr.; ¥556/$72/£36) at 9:30pm; and the 1688 heads for Guangzhou (33 hr.; ¥337/$54/£22) at 9am, stopping at Guilin (17 hr.) along the way.

Guiyang has several bus stations, but the main one that should serve most travelers' needs is the **Sports Stadium Bus Station (Tiyuguan Keyun Zhan)** near the railway station at Zunyi Lu and Jiefang Lu (© **0851/579-3381**). **Buses** run to Kaili (2 hr.; ¥35/$4.55/£2.30) every half-hour from 7:30am to 7:30pm; to Anshun (1½ hr.; ¥15/$1.95/£1) every 20 minutes from 7:05am to 7:30pm; and to Rong Jiang (7 hr.; ¥70/$9.10/£4.55) at 1:50pm. Tour buses to Huangguoshu Falls and Dragon Palace Cave depart from the bus stand just outside the railway station (see "Tours & Guides," below).

GETTING AROUND **Taxis** cost ¥10 ($1.30/65p) for 3km (2 miles), then ¥1.60 (20¢/10p) per kilometer, and ¥1.90 (25¢/10p) per kilometer after 10km (6 miles).

Guiyang

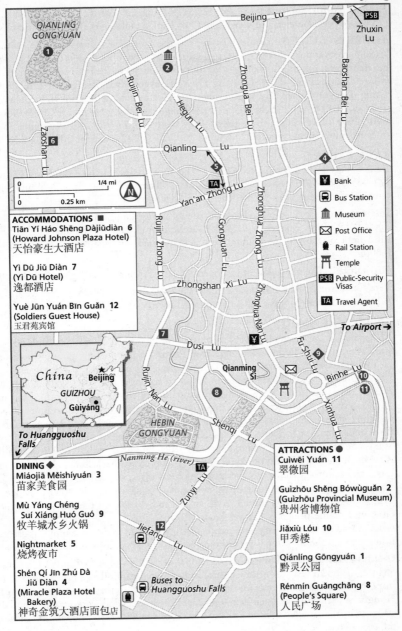

QIANLING GONGYUAN

1

Beijing Lu

3 PSB Zhuxin Lu

Ruijin Bei Lu

Hegun Lu

Zhonghua Bei Lu

Baoshan Bei Lu

Zaoshan Lu

6

Qianling Lu

5

TA

Yan'an Zhong Lu

4

Gongyuan Lu

Zhonghua Zhong Lu

	Bank
	Bus Station
	Museum
	Post Office
	Rail Station
	Temple
PSB	Public-Security Visas
TA	Travel Agent

0 ———— 1/4 mi
0 ———— 0.25 km
N

ACCOMMODATIONS ■
Tiān Yí Háo Shēng Dàjiǔdiàn 6
(Howard Johnson Plaza Hotel)
天怡豪生大酒店

Yì Dū Jiǔ Diàn 7
(Yì Dū Hotel)
逸都酒店

Yuè Jūn Yuán Bīn Guǎn 12
(Soldiers Guest House)
玉君苑宾馆

Ruijin Zhong Lu

Zhongshan Xi Lu

Zhonghua Nan Lu

To Airport →

7

Dusi Lu

Qianming Si

Fu Shui Lu

9

Binhe Lu

10

11

Xinhua Lu

Ruijin Nan Lu

8

Shenqi Lu

HEBIN GONGYUAN

China
Beijing
GUIZHOU
Gùiyáng

To Huangguoshu Falls

Nanming He (river)

TA

DINING ◆
Miáojiā Měishíyuán 3
苗家美食园

Mù Yáng Chéng
Suí Xiáng Huó Guó 9
牧羊城水乡火锅

Nightmarket 5
烧烤夜市

Shén Qí Jīn Zhú Dà
Jiǔ Diàn 4
(Miracle Plaza Hotel
Bakery)
神奇金筑大酒店面包店

Zunyi Lu

Jiefang Lu

12

**Buses to
Huangguoshu Falls**

ATTRACTIONS ●
Cuìwēi Yuán 11
翠微园

Guìzhōu Shěng Bówùguǎn 2
(Guizhou Provincial Museum)
贵州省博物馆

Jiǎxiù Lóu 10
甲秀楼

Qiánlíng Gōngyuán 1
黔灵公园

Rénmín Guǎngchǎng 8
(People's Square)
人民广场

From 10pm to 7am, prices rise to ¥12 ($1.55/80p) for 3km (2 miles), then ¥1.90 (25¢/10p) per kilometer, and then ¥2.40 (30¢/15p) per kilometer after 10km (6 miles).

TOURS & GUIDES   Companies outside the Tongda Fandian near the railway station offer various tours of the Huangguoshu Falls. For about ¥200 ($26/£13), you get transportation, meals, and a guided tour (in Chinese) of the falls, as well as a Miao village. You also get either **Tianxing Qiao (Heavenly Star Bridge)** or **Longgong Dong (Dragon Palace Caves).** Another option is a round-trip bus ride to the falls for ¥60 ($9.10/£4.55). **CITS**, at Hequn Lu 1, Longquan Dasha, seventh floor (© 0851/ 690-1660), can arrange private tours of the same with English-speaking guides, but rates are much higher (starting at around ¥800/$104/£42 a day for car and guide).

FAST FACTS

Banks, Foreign Exchange & ATMs   The main branch of the **Bank of China** (© 0851/586-9790; open Mon–Fri 8:30–11:30am and 2:30–6pm/2–5:30pm in winter) is located at Dusi Lu 30. The branch has an ATM.

Internet Access   A 24-hour Internet cafe at Yan'an Dong Lu 20, just east of the Trade Point Hotel, charges ¥2 (25¢/15p) an hour. A cleaner, quieter alternative is the third floor of the provincial library on Beijing Road, which is open from 9am to 8:30pm.

Post Office   The main post office (open 8:30am–7pm) is at Zhonghua Nan Lu 68.

Visa Extensions   The **PSB** is at Zhuxin Lu 5 (© 0851/676-5230; open Mon–Fri 8:30am–noon and 2–5pm). Allow 5 business days for a month-long extension.

SEEING THE SIGHTS

The stretch of the Nanming River southeast of the city center is worth a couple hours' stroll at most. From **Renmin Guangchang (People's Sq.)** on Zunyi Lu (now housing an underground Wal-Mart beneath Louvre-style glass pyramids), a giant gleaming white statue of Mao Zedong stands in his usual hailing a cab pose. Walk along the river to the Fuyu Bridge on which sits **Jiaxiu Lou** (open 8:30am–5:30pm). Built in 1598 as a meeting place for scholars attending the provincial Confucian examinations, this three-story pavilion has three tiers of soaring eaves supported by 12 stone pillars. The pavilion currently houses a teahouse and a small exhibit of the building's history as it is one of the few remaining traditional wooden buildings in the city. The real find is the open-air **secondhand bookstore** on the ground level that sells rare, hard-to-find travel and nature guides, great for exploring local caves, or reading up on the local flora and minority cultures at well below the usual tourist prices in other provinces. This is a must visit if you intend to do any extended travel in the province. At the other end of the bridge is **Cuiwei Yuan** (¥3/40¢/20p; open 8:30am–midnight), a series of traditional buildings once part of a Ming dynasty Buddhist temple. Today, it is home to a teahouse favored by mahjong players; pricey shops sell minority goods.

Qianling Gongyuan   Located on the slopes of 1,395m-high (4,576-ft.) Qianling Shan in the northwest part of town, this lushly forested park offers a pleasant reprieve from the urban jungle. A hike up the steep winding path to the 17th-century temple **Hongfu Si** (¥1/15¢/10p; open 8am–6pm) will give you a good workout and a bird's-eye view of the city. A cable car (¥12 ($1.55/80p) up; ¥8/$1/50p down) also makes the trip. Avoid the zoo at all costs.

Zao Shan Lu. Admission ¥5 (65¢/35p). 6:30am–10pm.

Jinyang Stone Valley (Jinyang Shi Lin) About 30 minutes west of the town center on the no. 29 bus, nestled among the mushrooming construction, is a miniature but quiet and relaxing stone forest. The ticket office seems to be permanently unmanned, although the day I visited, three PLA soldiers were sprawled out on the grass next to a heavy machine gun, a dozen K47s, and a pile of grenades, which seemed ample security for such a quiet scenic spot. At the front of the attraction is the nicely designed Qian Feng Yuan Restaurant.

Shi Lin Lu, get off the bus at Jin Yang Da Dao 3 Hao Zhan. Free admission. 8:30am–10pm.

SHOPPING

You're better off buying minority handicrafts in the outlying villages, although the **Duocai** shop (© 0851/687-3382) on the ground floor of the library has some very knowledgeable English-speaking staff and is a good place to begin your research. Guizhou is home to China's most famous alcohol, Maotai, an appallingly awful 106-proof liquor that most foreigners can take only in extremely small or extremely large quantities.

WHERE TO STAY

Budget options are difficult to find in Guiyang. Avoid all the touts who congregate on the corner of Jiefang Lu and Zunyi Lu, as the rooms that they offer are dismal. Tucked away on the opposite corner in an alley behind Telecom office is the **Yu Jun Yuan Hotel** in converted army quarters. On the ground floor, they have some very spartan, concrete-floor rooms that I would dismiss in any other city. Here, though, they represent pretty good value at just ¥80 ($10/£5.20). Choose one of the ex-officers' rooms on the ground floor that have private bathrooms, but do not expect air-conditioning.

Howard Johnson Plaza Hotel (Tian Yi Hao Sheng Da Jiu Dian) Although Guizhou is still a province of extreme poverty, much of which can be witnessed in the streets of Guiyang, the wealthy are well looked after at five-star hotels such as this and the army-patronized Sheraton downtown. There, promotion material describes their location as being "in the lovely forest city of Guizhou," which just goes to show how far from reality they must be.

Zaoshan Lu 298. © 0851/651-8888. Fax 0851/651-7777. www.hojochina.com. 310 units. ¥1,080–¥1,600 ($140–$208/ £70–£104) standard room; ¥1,800 ($234/£117) suite. AE, DC, MC, V. **Amenities:** 3 restaurants; bar; lounge; health club; sauna; concierge; business center; forex; shopping arcade; room service; laundry/dry cleaning; nonsmoking floor; executive rooms. *In room:* A/C, satellite TV, minibar, hair dryer, safe.

Yidu Hotel ★ (Value) Just around the corner from a sauna that features 4m-high (13-ft.) Thai deities, this unassuming hotel provides very adequate midrange accommodations. Corridors are bright and clean, unlike most hotels, and the rooms (while small) are quite acceptable. On the lower floors, there are a number of IYHF three-, four-, and six-room dorms ranging from ¥50 to ¥70 ($6.50–$9.10/£3.25–£4.55).

Zhi Yue Lu 9. © 0851/864-9777. Fax 0851/863-1788. www.gyyd08.51.com. 112 units. ¥278 ($36/£18) standard room; ¥578 ($75/£38) suite. AE, DC, MC, V. **Amenities:** Restaurant; bar; lounge; health club; sauna; concierge; business center; forex; shopping arcade; salon; room service; laundry/dry cleaning; executive rooms. *In room:* A/C, satellite TV, minibar, hair dryer, safe.

WHERE TO DINE

The best Western dining is offered in high-end hotels like the **Sheraton,** which has a Western buffet. Less exalted fare like **KFC** (open 9am–11pm) is available at

Zhonghua Nan Lu 246. For local dining, an extremely lively **night market** on Hequn Lu just north of Yan'an Zhong Lu proffers kabobs, grilled meats and vegetables, noodles, dumplings, stir-fries, and hot pot and is, for adventurous patrons, one of the more interesting dining experiences in town. Dog meat is very popular here.

Miaojia Meishi Yuan MIAO   Located down a set of dark steps in a traditional courtyard setting, this casual Miao restaurant serves some incredibly spicy food. Try, if you dare, the fiery *yang lajiao* (hot peppers and chilies that have been blanched, sundried, and fried), *Miaojia anyu* (Miao sour fish), or the delicious *Miaowei paigu* (spicy Miao spareribs). For something more benign, the *Miaojia tudou pian* (deep-fried potato coins) and *rousi chaomian* (stir-fry noodles with pork) should be comfortingly familiar.
Baoshan Bei Lu 433 (opposite Holiday Inn). *(C)* **0855/675-1451.** ¥25–¥70 ($3.25–$9.10/£1.65–£4.55). No credit cards. 11am–2:30pm and 5–9:30pm.

Miracle Plaza Hotel Bakery WESTERN   While the hotel it's located in is overpriced, the in-house bakery is a pleasant surprise, with a reasonable selection of Western-style breads and delicious cream napoleons. A great place to stock up for lunch if you are heading out to visit minority villages or if you are doing an overnight train journey.
Bao Shan Bei Lu 219. *(C)* **0851/682-5888.** No credit cards. 9am–8pm.

Mu Yang Cheng Shuixiang Huoguo *Value* HOT POT   While many have seen the latest craze in sushi bars where dishes are pulled around on toy trains with narrow-gauge tracks, here is an improvement on even that idea. All tables (each equipped with its own gas stove) are located alongside a small stream. A succession of small boats floats along and you choose the ingredients that you would like to parboil in your table-top soup dish. There are plenty of safe choices such as lotus root, potato, duck, and quail eggs; for the more adventurous there is stomach (which strangely resembles bathroom carpet, in both texture and taste) and fresh pigs' brains. Best of all it costs ¥38 ($4.95/£2.45) for all you can eat, including soft drinks. Definitely one of the best deals in town. See the special hot pot glossary in appendix B for more ingredients.
Fu Shui Nan Lu 198. *(C)* **0851/580-9118.** ¥38 ($4.95/£2.45). No credit cards. 11am–4am.

SIDE TRIPS FROM GUIYANG

A new highway between Guiyang and the Huangguoshu Falls enables visitors to make the trip in a day. Those short on time would do well to hire a private car, which your hotel or, in a pinch, CITS, can help arrange. *Note:* Please turn to appendix A for Chinese translations of key locations below.

HUANGGUOSHU PUBU (HUANGGUOSHU FALLS) *Overrated*

Asia's largest waterfall, located 150km (90 miles) and just over 2 hours on the highway southwest of Guiyang, has become a tourist trap of immense proportions. Many foreigners have reported being underwhelmed by the falls (named for the indigenous *huangguoshu* or yellow fruit tree), possibly because they visited during the dry season (Nov–Apr), when the usual torrents are reduced to a mere trickle. Others complain about the huge amounts of trash floating in the water, aggressive vendors, and ill-mannered domestic tourists, as well as the fact that all the trekking paths away from the falls have now been blocked.

Fed by the Baishui River (Baishui He), the main waterfall spans 81m (266 ft.) and plunges down a precipitous 74m (243 ft.) into **Rhinoceros Pool.** The **Water Curtain Cave,** a 100m-long (328-ft.) walkway behind the falls, is currently closed off to visitors.

There are three entrances to the falls: just south of Huangguoshu town, next to the Huangguoshu Binguan, and next to the cable car. Admission to the falls is now a ridiculous ¥180 ($23/£12).

During the rainy season, other falls to visit include **Doubotang Pubu** (about 1km/⅔ mile upstream from the main falls) and **Luositan Pubu** (about 1km/⅔ mile downstream). The latest attraction for Chinese tourists is **Tianxing Qiao Jingqu (Heavenly Star Bridge Scenic Area;** ¥80 ($10/£5.20) about 8km (5 miles) below the main falls. Highlights include a large cave full of the usual karst formations, a wonderful tableau of steppingstones rising from the water, and a waterfall. It's nice, if you can explore away from the crowds.

The falls are very well lit in the evenings, which makes an overnight stay worthwhile to go with the rainbows that you saw during the day. If you want to spend the night, the three-star **Xin Huangguoshu Binguan** (© 0853/359-2110) offers the nicest accommodations and a Chinese restaurant. Up a driveway off the main road south of the village, the hotel has large, bright, and comfortable standard rooms with sparkling new bathrooms (shower only) for ¥480 ($62/£31).

LONGGONG DONG (DRAGON PALACE CAVES)

About 132km (79 miles) west of Guiyang is a string of 90 karst caves that stretch for over 15km (9 miles) through some 20 hills. Until recently, only 840m (2,755 ft.) of the main **Dragon Palace Cave** (¥120/$16/£7.80; open 8am–6:30pm/5:30pm in winter) is open to the public, although the newly opened Guanyin Cave houses 32 Buddha statues, the largest being 13m (41 ft.). Rowboats take visitors through five chambers of colorfully lit, wonderfully weird karst formations, as tacky Muzak plays in the background. When the water levels are low, you'll have to return by boat, but during the rainy season, visitors can climb stone ladders in the last chamber to Tiger's Den, then slowly meander back to the entrance through a stone forest park. Private car hire and an organized tour from Guiyang are the most convenient ways to visit.

MINORITY VILLAGES

The area southwest of Guiyang around Anshun is home to the **Bouyi,** one of the original peoples of southwest China, who number around 2.5 million today. Related to the Zhuang, the poorer Bouyi are skilled stonemasons, forced by the rocky karst terrain to build entire hillside villages out of stone. One such village worth visiting is **Shitou Zhai (Stone Village)** ☞ where, not surprisingly, all the walls, bridges, roads, and houses are made of stone. Home to about 200 households, the village sits along the river Baishui He and is surrounded by pretty green paddies. You can pick up some of the Bouyi's famous batik here, since everyone seems to have a batik workshop in their house. Discerning buyers should look for hyperrealistic and even erotic motifs. Shitou Zhai is off the main highway about 15km (9 miles) beyond the Longgong turnoff and 5km (3 miles) before Huangguoshu. Watch for the turnoff and travel another kilometer or so along the dirt road to the village.

7 Kaili & the Miao & Dong Autonomous Prefecture

Guizhou Province, 184km (110 miles) E of Guiyang

As the capital of the Qian Dongnan Autonomous Prefecture of the Miao and Dong nationalities in eastern Guizhou, Kaili is the gateway to some of the most fascinating minority villages you're likely to encounter in China. About 65% of the prefecture's

The Miao

The Miao, also called Hmong, trace their history back 4,000 years to what is now the Yellow River area in central China. As the first Chinese dynasty (221–207 B.C.) came into being and the Chinese empire expanded, the Miao were driven into the outlying mountain regions. The subsequent south-westerly migration splintered the Miao into different subgroups with their own dialects, dress, and customs, making them one of the most diversified ethnic groups in China. Black, Red, White, Long-Horned, Flowery, Mountain, and Long-Skirt Miao are just some names that the Han Chinese gave to the Miao, based on their appearance or locale. Those who continued their southerly migration into Laos, Myanmar, Thailand, and Vietnam are generally known as Hmong. Today there are about eight million Hmong worldwide.

Miao festivals such as the Miao New Year, the Sisters' Meal Festival (Zimeifan Jie), and the Lusheng Festival (dates vary by village) are occasions for young men and women to socialize and find marriage partners. Traditional Han Chinese consider attracting attention invites misfortune. The events are marked by dancing, the playing of *lusheng* (a musical instrument made of pipes), buffalo fighting (not as bad as you might imagine), and horse racing. If at all possible, time your visit during one of these occasions. The Miao are generally very hospitable and will greet visitors with cups of locally brewed rice wine, the ultimate sign of respect from some of the hardiest drinkers around.

population is Miao, clustered to the east and northeast of Kaili. The Dong are to the southeast. This entire region hosts more than 100 festivals (see chart on p. 600) each year, with the greatest concentration around February/March and October/November, making these excellent months to visit. Be warned that travel around the Miao areas can be difficult due to their narrow, winding roads, but this is often light-years ahead of traveling through some of the Dong region's backwaters, where a farmer's truck or your own feet might be the only means of navigating pothole-ridden mud paths. In truth, half the fun of traveling in this part of the country is getting there in the first place, so bring your sense of adventure and don't forget the seat cushion. *Note:* Please turn to appendix A for Chinese translations of key locations in this section.

ESSENTIALS

GETTING THERE   Traveling by **train** to Guiyang (3½ hr.) has become less popular now that buses can whisk travelers there in 2 hours. The faster trains leave Kaili in the middle of the night, though there's a 10am train (K192) that gets in at 1:51pm and a 4:10pm train (K79) that gets in at 7:47pm. Tickets (hard seats only) can be bought at a counter inside the **Bank of China** at Beijing Dong Lu 9–11 (© 0855/822-1065; open 8:30am–noon and 2–5:30pm). A taxi ride to town from the **railway station** (© 0855/381-2222) costs ¥10 ($1.30/65p). For destinations farther afield like Kunming (the T61 departs at 11:59pm and arrives in Kunming at 3:17pm), purchase your tickets in Guiyang if you want anything more than a hard seat. Inside the train station, the left luggage area is not signposted but is actually a small room hidden away behind the shop, opposite the main ticket counter. Opening times are 8am until 8pm and the cost is ¥3 (40¢/20p) per item.

From the **bus station** at Wenhua Bei Lu (© **0855/823-8035**), **buses** run to Guiyang (2 hr.; ¥35/$4.55/£2.30) every half-hour from 6am to 7:15pm; to Rong Jiang (6 hr.; ¥35/$4.55/£2.30) from 6:40am to 3pm; to Cong Jiang (9 hr.; ¥68/$8.45/£4.25) at 6:50am, 8am, and 9am; to Leishan (1 hr.; ¥20/$2.60/£1.30) every half-hour from 7am to 5:30pm; to Tai Jiang (1 hr.; ¥20/$2.60/£1.30) every 40 minutes from 8:30am to 6pm; and to Shidong (2½ hr.; ¥15/$1.95/£1) from 8am to 2:50pm. Left luggage opens at 6am and closes at 8pm.

GETTING AROUND   Taxis charge ¥4 (50¢/25p) for in-town destinations, but ¥5 (65¢/35p) if you catch one inside the bus station. Add an additional ¥1 (15¢/10p) to all fares from midnight to 7am. **Bus** no. 2 makes a loop from the railway station in the north down past the main traffic circle on Beijing Lu and then down Zhaoshan Nan Lu, before it returns to the railway station via Ningbo Lu. The bus fare is ¥.70 ($9 /£4.50). Unfortunately there do seem to be any bikes for rent at the moment. If you bring your own, make sure that you pack a spare pair of legs because if Guizhou does in fact have any flat roads they keep them very well hidden. There are a number of motorbike shops at the east end of Ningbo Lu that might be persuaded to hire out a motocross bike, but do not expect any bargain prices.

TOURS & GUIDES   **CITS,** at Yingpan Dong Lu 53 (© **0855/822-2506;** www. qdncits.com; open Mon–Fri 9am–6pm) can customize private trips to the Miao and Dong regions, especially if you're looking to explore remote villages, but none of it comes cheap. Rates start at around ¥800 ($104/£52) a day for a guide and driver. Bargain hard. The office's top English-speaking guide, the friendly Mr. Li Maoqing, can answer questions regarding nearby sights.

FAST FACTS

Banks, Foreign Exchange & ATMs   The main branch of the **Bank of China** is at Zhaoshan Nan Lu 6 (open Mon–Fri, 8am–noon and 2:30–6:30pm/2–6pm in winter).

Internet Access   The **Tengxun Wangba** at the intersection of Beijing Dong Lu and Wenhua Lu (look for the green sign) charges ¥2 (25¢/15p) an hour. Dial-up is © **163.**

Post Office   The post office (open 8am–6:30pm, until 6pm Oct–Apr) is at Beijing Dong Lu 1.

Visa Extension   The **PSB** is at Yongle Lu 26 (© **0855/853-6113;** open Mon–Fri 8:30–11:30am and 2–5:30pm). Allow 5 working days.

SEEING THE SIGHTS

Kaili's highlights are undoubtedly in the villages outside of town. You will see plenty of minorities in the city proper but rather depressingly most of them seem to be sweeping the streets, hauling away garbage, or shining the shoes of Han Chinese immigrants. Here in the urban areas only the very old women still wear traditional dress. You can have an interesting morning at the **Sunday Market,** where minorities from nearby villages sell all manner of goods around Ximen Jie and surrounding side streets. Live water buffalo can often go for under ¥500 ($65/£33), but a smarter and more portable option is traditional clothing. Minority girls learn to embroider at the same time that they learn to read and write, and a festival costume may take up to

5 years' continuous work. If you are not in town at the weekend then head up to Dong Men Jie (Lao Gai in local dialect) in the old town with its wooden house and cobbled streets. There are some great deals here on embroidered baby carriers starting at just ¥30 ($3.90/£1.95) each, or see the shops where they make every possible size of Chinese weighing scales.

Laborers toting their own tools are found sitting on every corner waiting for a day's work. By far the highest concentration of workers is found on the corner of Shaoshan Lu and Yingpan Lu where plasters, carpenters, and bricklayers all sit patiently with their tool boxes on display. Dog lovers might notice the large number of strange albino mutts with pink noses that I have been unable to identify as a particular breed.

WHERE TO STAY

Crown Plaza (Jing Guan Jiu Dian)   While definitely not the Holiday Inn variety, this new four-star opposite the Miao-inspired stadium currently gets all the affluent foreign tour groups. Guest rooms are nothing special and the bathrooms are about 2 decades out of date. Try to get a room at the rear as the new minority-style stadium seems to be the nightly meeting point for a group of motocross enthusiasts who work on their wheelies and other Evel Knievel abilities.

You Zhuang Lu 18. ☎ **0855/806-8888**. Fax 0855/806-0678. 103 units. ¥218–¥278 ($36/£18) standard room; ¥308–¥688 ($40–$102/£20–£51) suite. No credit cards. **Amenities:** Restaurant; bar; karaoke bar; gym; concierge; meeting rooms; salon; room service; laundry. *In room:* A/C, TV.

Yiran Hotel   This is a brand-new, budget guesthouse just to the west of People's Square. The Yiran is hidden away in a new residential area, opposite Da Donghai massage parlor with the large pictures of ancient Chinese beauties. Rooms are clean, and the staff is friendly and at least tries to be helpful.

Ningbo Xi Lu 1 (opposite Tao Ran Ju Sichuan Restaurant). ☎ **0855/806-5980**. 12 units. ¥70 ($9.10/£4.55) standard room. No credit cards. *In room:* A/C, kettle, TV.

WHERE TO DINE

Hotels still offer the best dining options, but restaurants serving a variety of Chinese cuisine are popping up along **Shangmao Jie** in the newly developing southern part of town. These spots are geared toward locals, so don't expect English menus. But do venture here if you're tired of hotel food. Make sure you recognize the characters for dog meat *(gourou)* if that's not something you're game for. For thrill seekers there is a row of specialist dog eateries on the old museum road (Bowuguan Xi Lu) that leads off Beijing Xi Lu between the Wan Bo Underground Shopping Arcade and the Guizhou Power Supply Bureau. Across on the square, listen for the cracks of whips as locals play with wooden tops.

A lively **night market** on the Shaoshan Road above the tunnel on offers barbecue, noodles, dumplings *(jiaozi)*, meat buns *(baozi)*, and fresh fruit.

The closest approximation to Western food can be found at **Victoria,** located at You Zhuang Lu 168, although the service and choice may be disappointing.

After a day exploring the countryside, my favorite experience was calling in at the local market on Lian Hua Xiang, where a Miao lady with a big red plastic bucket sold me a large plastic bag of the most delicious sour soup *(suan tang),* a local delicacy that goes for ¥1 (15¢/10p) per *jing* (half kilo). It tastes very much like a consommé filled with lightly pickled vegetables. I also picked up a couple of roast sweet potatoes and some local pancakes to take home with me. What was most surprising was how peoples' attitudes changed when they saw me carrying a big bag of the local soup. A population that had just the day before seemed surly and suspicious was now all smiles. This is useful tip anywhere in China: Walk around sampling the local fare and it suddenly becomes much easier to make friends.

AROUND KAILI

If you're short on time, several Miao villages around Kaili can comfortably be visited as day trips. One of the most popular is **Langde** ⋆, a lovely traditional Miao village of about 600 people (all surnamed Chen), located 31km (19 miles) and a 45-minute ride south of Kaili. Dating from the late Yuan/early Ming dynasty, the village is divided into two sections. If your visit coincides with a tour group's, you may be greeted with songs and rice wine and treated to a bronze-drum dance performance in the upper village square, although you will also be asked to contribute ¥20 ($2.60/£1.30) for the experience. With its water wheels and wooden stilt houses made from local cedar, it is very interesting to climb up and down the steep paths within the village. Some find the place fascinating while others might think it claustrophobic and dirty. To get there, take the Leishan-bound bus for ¥6 (80¢/40p) and ask to be let off at Langde. From the main road, it's still around a 1.2km (1-mile) walk along the charming Bala River, through a number of smaller hamlets into the upper village.

More experienced travelers might find Langde to be a little bit too touristy and prefer to spend the day hiking the 20km (12-mile) loop into the mountains behind Langde and back around to the Bala River. Just below Upper Langde, a spectacular Miao-style bridge has been constructed across the river. This is a favorite swimming spot with local boys as well as with water buffalo. In fact if you go across to the rocks on the far side of the river, you can see the metal rings that have been driven into the stone so that that these beasts of burden can spend the sunny afternoons cooling off in the fast-flowing currents. About 4km (2½ miles) farther upstream, a small limestone-diluted tributary the color of lemon sherbet joins the main clear blue stream, turning it into a delicious shade of honeydew-melon sorbet. The road (now more of a track) continues another 5km (3 miles) up to Nan Meng and all around, mini cascades surge down from on high to feed the river. Alerted to the presence of a passerby, cicadas go off like exotic car alarms, competing with the rushing waters below. Another couple of clicks will bring you to the tiny hamlet of Jao Meng. Here it is clear to see that the locals, in their shoes cut from recycled tires and hand-me-down clothes, are almost a world away from the overfed performers at Langde with their baskets of silver and fancy costumes. Up past the Mao River, you will emerge back onto the main road and can jump on a passing bus to go the 5 minutes back down to Lower Langde. There is even a reasonable hotel down here if you would like to stay the night rather than return to the big-city blight of Kaili.

Fifteen kilometers (9 miles) southwest of Kaili, the small village of **Zhouxi** is host to a grand *lusheng* festival every year around the 20th day of the first lunar month, when melodious pipes resound through a sea of silver headdresses. To reach Zhouxi, take a minivan taxi for ¥3 to ¥4 (40¢–50¢/20p–25p) from the corner of Huancheng Xi Lu and Beijing Xi Lu.

About 19km (11 miles) northwest of Kaili, the village of **Matang** ⋆⋆ is home to about 400 members of the **Gejia** people (the other Gejia stronghold is in **Huangping Village**). Once lumped in with the Miao, the Gejia were formally recognized only in 1993. Unlike the Miao, who are known to have strong constitutions, the Gejia toast with rice, not wine. Another distinguishing custom is the Caiqing dance (Caiqing Wu), with its characteristic stomping. The harder the stomp, the deeper the love between the man and the woman. Known for their batik and embroidery, the Matang Gejia are friendly and hospitable. Thanks to new highway construction, the road conditions out to Matang are more like a rigorous section of the Camel Trophy 4x4 race. What is left of the original road has been destroyed by overladen coal and quarry trucks. To get here, take a minivan taxi for ¥15 ($1.95/£1) bound for Longchang, as the road to Yudong is temporarily impassable. These can be found up at the junction of Da Qiao Lu and Guang Ming Da Dao opposite the Kaili Fa Dian Chang, next to the Industrial and Commercial Bank. The trip, while only 19km (11 miles) in theory, may take up to 3 hours as the bus heads down past the swage farm, the power station, and the coal gas refinery and then makes a huge loop to avoid an army of bulldozers and workers. We were stopped by three landslides and an overturned coal truck on this journey alone, so plenty of patience is required. Ask to be dropped off at Matang; it's a 15-minute walk to the village.

XI JIANG 🌟🌟

Located about 75km (45 miles) southeast of Kaili in Leishan County, Xi Jiang is the largest Miao village in China, with about 1,000 households. Nestled in a valley surrounded by lush bamboo forests, the village has hundreds of dark brown wooden stilt houses built into the side of a hill and, unfortunately for purists, a white concrete building (Xi Jiang's new school) smack in the middle of it all. No matter how deep you venture into the countryside, there is always ready cash available to build a school and a police station. Never mind that the peasants do not have running water or sanitation, as long as the youngsters can be indoctrinated and the adults watched over, the authorities are happy. Xi Jiang hosts a massive celebration during the **Miao New Year Festival** in the 10th lunar month with dances, bullfights, *lusheng* competitions, and other festivities around the buffalo pillar on the dancing ground but these days are mostly clustered around the basketball court. On the sixth day of the sixth lunar month (usually July or Aug), the **New Rice Tasting Festival** is another raucous celebration. **Market** days in Xi Jiang (every 7 days for the large market, every 5 days for a smaller market) are also very colorful, as villagers hawk everything from fish to fake hair.

Xi Jiang can be visited as a day trip with private car hire or overnight if you travel by bus. From Kaili, there are very infrequent direct buses. More reliable is the bus to Leishan (1 hr.; ¥30/$3.90/£1.95); from there, transfer to a bus for Xi Jiang (1 hr.; ¥15/$1.95/£1).

The best option among the town's very basic accommodations is the relatively new, relatively clean **Cangzhen Lou** (𝄢 **0855/334-8068**), located down the main street

---

Tips Local Recipes Best Avoided

Curses, evil eyes, and other forms of witchcraft are still common in these primitive surroundings. One popular concoction to look out for is "gu," a slow-acting poison. To create it, a selection of scorpions, lizards, and snakes are dropped into a jar without any food so that they devour each other. Next, the body of the lone survivor, supposedly gorged with poison, is then crushed to make a mysterious toxin that will kill only the unrepentant.

Fun Fact **Sisters' Rice Speaks to Suitors**

Sisters' Meal rice is stained bright colors using wild berries and is then wrapped in an indigo cloth, together with a small item that conveys a message. A pair of chopsticks signifies acceptance for a marriage proposal, while a single stick denotes refusal. Garlic shoots or pepper mean "Please look elsewhere," while pine needles remind a suitor that a girl's heart can sometimes be won with satin or silk.

---

from the old and decrepit Zhengfu Zhaodaisuo (Government Guesthouse). It has 30 beds at ¥30 ($3.90/£1.95) each, in different room combinations with bare concrete floors and communal showers and toilets.

SHIDONG

About 94km (56 miles) northeast of Kaili, this little Miao village along the banks of the Qingshui River hosts two big festivals. The 3-day **Longzhou Jie (Dragon Boat Festival)**, in the middle of the fifth lunar month, features dragon boats made from hollowed-out tree trunks that are decorated with a dragon's head and hold up to 30 rowers. Each of the nearby villages enters a boat in the race. This is certainly the place to see **Zimeifan Jie (Sisters' Meal Festival)**, during the fourth lunar month, which is celebrated with *lusheng* dances, antiphonal singing, and plenty of opportunities for young Miao women, gorgeously bedecked with elaborate silver headdresses, to socialize with erstwhile suitors. Several months before the festival, many Shidong households will be engaged in making silver ornaments for the festival. Silver aficionados may wish to visit here at any time, as Shidong (in particular the neighboring hamlet of Tanglong) is renowned for excellent-quality silver. Traditional Chinese consider that attracting attention invites misfortune, but not the Miao. Some of these girls will wear more than 20 kilograms (44 lb.) of silver, engraved, embossed, stippled, and assembled into set pieces. While these ornaments are mostly for private use, it's possible to purchase pieces from enterprising villagers. Ask around.

For now, visit Shidong as a day trip from Kaili; the local accommodations currently available would make sleeping in one of those dragon boats seem like a night at the Ritz. Return buses to Kaili stop running around 2pm.

DONG REGION

The southeastern part of Guizhou is squarely Dong territory, with over 400 Dong roofed bridges in Liping, Rong Jiang, and Cong Jiang counties. On the southeastern border across from Guangxi Province, Zhaoxing is the largest Dong village, while the area around Rong Jiang and Cong Jiang is dotted with smaller villages awaiting discovery.

RONG JIANG & CONG JIANG

The only reason to stay in Rong Jiang is its famous and incredibly colorful **Sunday Market,** which spills onto several streets east of the main road. Unless you want to explore the Dong villages around here, many travelers heading south from Kaili end up overnighting or changing buses in Cong Jiang, which serves as more of a gateway to both Zhaoxing in the east and Guangxi Province in the south.

The Dong

Accounts differ as to the origins of the Dong people—some say they came from the Yangzi River (Chang Jiang) region, and others argue that they migrated north from Thailand—but now they are firmly planted in southeast Guizhou (2.5 million Dong residents) and in northeast Guangxi Province, where they gravitate toward lush river valleys.

Famed for their (fir) wooden architecture, Dong villages typically have a Wind and Rain Bridge *(fengyu qiao)*, which serves not only as a meeting place for villagers but to ward off inauspicious energies from the village. Each village also has one or several drum towers *(gulou)*, each built for a clan with the same surname.

In addition to the many Han festivals such as Spring Festival and Festival of the Ghosts, the primarily animist Dong celebrate many of their own, including one of the biggest, Sanyuesan, held on the third day of the third lunar month and celebrated with fireworks, dances, sporting competitions, bullfights, and abundant feasting. The Taiguanren Festival, which coincides with the Han Spring Festival, has visitors from neighboring villages dressed up as bandits, goblins, and strange animals, while a man dressed as a government official *(guanren)* parades through town dispensing money as a gift to the village. The Firecracker Festival (Huapao), celebrated in Guangxi's San Jiang on the third day of the second month, has participants competing to catch an iron ring that's been blasted out of a small cannon.

Rong Jiang

173km (104 miles) SE of Kaili

GETTING THERE   From the **Main Bus Station (Qichezhan)** in the north of town, **buses,** including minibuses, large air-conditioned buses, and sleepers, run to Kaili (6–7 hr.; ¥35/$4.55/£2.30) from 6:30am to 4pm; and to Cong Jiang (3 hr.; ¥20/$2.60/£1.30) from 6:40am to 4:30pm.

WHERE TO STAY & DINE   The best place to stay is the **Rong Jiang Binguan** at Guzhou Zhong Lu 47 (© **0855/662-4188;** fax 0855/662-4223), which has basic but comfortable enough standard rooms for ¥160 ($21/£10) with private bathrooms. There's also a restaurant.

Cong Jiang

79km (47 miles) SE of Rong Jiang, 252km (151 miles) SE of Kaili

Like Rong Jiang, there's little to recommend Cong Jiang itself, but about 7km (4 miles) before the town, on the road from Rong Jiang, the unusual village of **Basha** 𝒓𝒓 makes for a fascinating visit. Although recognized as members of the Miao, the Basha Miao are practically a tribe unto themselves. They cling to unique traditions such as the men's *hugun* hairstyle, which is created by shaving off all the hair except for what grows on the crown, and coiling what's left into a topknot never to be cut, as hair is considered the lifeline given by ancestors. Wandering through the village, you can hear the pounding of indigo grass and dyed cloth and see swags of glutinous rice hanging on giant racks to dry. Barefoot boys play hide-and-seek, and dogs bark at approaching visitors while pigs snort and wallow deeper in the mud. Living a simple and extremely poor existence, the Basha are understandably wary of cadres of tourists tramping through their village. You can only hope that the entrance fees of ¥10 ($1.30/65p) for foreigners and ¥6 (80¢/40p) for Chinese are actually going to the village and not padding some tourist official's pockets. If you're visiting on your own, tread softly and sensitively.

As you leave Cong Jiang in the direction of Zhaoxing, cutting a dashing sight on the left are the three drum towers of **Gaozeng** village. Two of the drum towers are the tallest in the region, at 17 stories and almost 30m (98 ft.) high. The road between Cong Jiang and Zhaoxing offers some of the most picturesque pastoral scenes of terrace fields cut into gently rolling hills.

GETTING THERE   From the **Cong Jiang Bus Station (Qichezhan; © 0855/641-3957)** on the eastern side of the river, **buses** run to Rong Jiang (3 hr.; ¥15/$1.95/£1/) every hour from 7am to 5:20pm; to Kaili (10 hr.; ¥53/$6.60/£3.30) at 6am, 8am, and 9:20am; and to San Jiang in Guangxi Province (3½–4 hr.; ¥15/$1.95/£1), with nine departures from 6:30am to 3:30pm via Baluo and Fulu. To get to Zhaoxing, take a Liping-bound bus for ¥20 ($2.60/£1.30) from 6:30am to 1:40pm and change at Pilin. You can also change at Luoxiang, but connecting buses are infrequent; at press time, the dirt road (if it can be called that) between Luoxiang and Zhaoxing consisted a series of never-ending potholes.

WHERE TO STAY & DINE   The newest place to stay is the **Yueliang Shan Binguan** on Jiang Dongnan Lu (© 0855/641-4888), on the eastern side of the river just next to the bus station. Standard rooms with air-conditioning, TV, phone, and 24-hour hot water cost ¥120 ($16/£7.80). The hotel also has a Chinese restaurant. No English is spoken. Across from the bus station are food stalls that serve basic stir-fries (point to the vegetables you want and say *"chao rou"* if you want them with pork) and noodles to get you through the night. Off the main street west of the river is a small **night market** of barbecue stalls, north of the post office.

ZHAOXING 𝕮𝕮𝕮

Zhaoxing, the biggest Dong village in China with a population of 3,500 people (all surnamed Lu!), is one of those places where the rewards that await you are in direct proportion to the difficulty in getting there. And it is very difficult to get to Zhaoxing. With a history of over 700 years, this picturesque village of fishponds and rice paddies is extremely welcoming (but largely free of tourists) and boasts the single greatest collection of drum towers (five) in China, ranging from 7 to 13 stories high. With many settlements around the area ripe for exploration, there's enough to occupy you for at least a couple of days; allow an equal amount of time to get here and away. Though Zhaoxing can be approached from both Kaili and San Jiang in Guangxi Province, the latter has more direct buses.

GETTING THERE   The most hassle-free way to get to Zhaoxing is by private car/taxi hire. From San Jiang in Guangxi Province, the 3-hour-plus ride will run between ¥200 and ¥300 ($26–$39/£13–£20) depending on your bargaining powers. The most reliable public bus leaves at 6:50am, costs ¥14 ($1.95/£1), and takes about 4 hours. Unfortunately much of the road is currently under construction so it is probably better to allow 6 hours and perhaps bring a face mask to filter out the incredible amounts of dust. From Zhaoxing to San Jiang by bus (4–4½ hr.), an early morning bus departs at 7:30am and another less reliable bus around 9:30am. The quickest way to Kaili (10 hr.) is to take the 7am bus to Liping and transfer to the 11:40am bus to Kaili. At press time, there were no direct buses to Cong Jiang. The best option is to take a bus to Pilin (2½ hr.), then transfer to a Cong Jiang bus that's coming from Liping (3 hr.). Alternately, some folks have hiked an hour to Luoxiang; or they have taken a local farmer's truck for ¥30 ($3.90/£1.95) along a wretched pothole-riddled dirt road and transferred to a Cong Jiang-bound (¥11/$1.45/70p) bus, which runs every half-hour to hour from 7:30am to around 4pm.

Exploring the Village & Beyond

The main attraction is the village itself, which is divided into five sections organized by clan, each with its own all-wooden **drum tower, wind and rain bridge,** and **theater stage.** Ranging from 7 to 13 stories (the tallest is 25m/82 ft. high), the drum towers have all been rebuilt since they were destroyed by Red Guards during the Cultural Revolution (1966–76). Desperately in need of a fresh coat of paint, the structures are still impressive and continue to play host to large events like weddings, festivals, and funerals, and to less-momentous occasions like a villager's afternoon nap. The rest of the place is filled with photo ops of villagers dyeing cloth, sifting rice, weaving baskets, and building houses.

There are also several villages around Zhaoxing worth visiting. Three kilometers (2 miles) or an hour's invigorating climb to the south, the village of **Jitang** ⊛ has three well-preserved original drum towers that escaped destruction during the Cultural Revolution. The largest, in the middle of the village square, has 11 tiers of eaves and is held up by 16 original stone pedestals. Wander this lovely village, where bales of indigo cloth hang from beautiful traditional wooden houses and friendly children try their Chinese (usually limited to *"nihao"* meaning "hello") on you. To get there, follow the main street in the direction of Luoxiang and bear left as the road winds uphill. The village of **Tang'an** about 4km (2½ miles) to the southeast has some stone terraces worth hiking out to see if you have time.

Where to Stay & Dine

The nicest and most popular place to stay is the all-wooden **Wenhuazhan Zhaodaisuo** right in the center of town off the main road, just under 50m (164 ft.) from the informal bus stop. The spartan rooms come with nothing more than beds and fans but are otherwise clean, as are the communal showers and toilets. A bed costs ¥20 ($2.60/£1.30) and a standard room ¥50 ($6.50/£3.25). The owners don't speak much English but are very friendly and can cook Chinese and Dong meals as well as pancakes for breakfast. Deeper inside the village, **Lulu's Homestay (Fengqing Luyou Shewai Minju Luguan; ℭ 0855/613-0112)** offers six rooms on the second level of the owner's (Lu Xinfeng) house, but a new wooden guesthouse was being constructed next door at press time. The new rooms should be basic but clean, with beds averaging ¥25 ($3.25/£1.65) each. Mr. Lu's wife cooks delicious Dong meals for ¥10 to ¥20 ($1.30–$2.60/65p–£1.30) per person, and instant coffee is available. Mr. Lu, with his smattering of English, often leads hikes in the surrounding hills.

Around Zhaoxing

If you're traveling the road between Zhaoxing and San Jiang in Guangxi Province, you'll notice about 1½ hours south of Zhaoxing at the hamlet of **Diping** a three-tower

wind and rain bridge stretching 56m (184 ft.) across the river. Guizhou's most impressive bridge of its kind, the structure was built as early as 1883. Keep your eyes peeled for a lovely set of four stamps issued in 1997, featuring the Diping Bridge and three other splendid examples of Dong architecture.

8 Kunming ⊛

Yunnan Province, 1,200km (744 miles) NW of Hong Kong, 450km (270 miles) SW of Guiyang

As the capital of Yunnan Province, Kunming, also known as the "city of eternal spring," was once one of the most pleasant and relaxed cities in China. These days it is quickly becoming as crowded as Shenzhen and Guangzhou. In addition that rapidly growing number of private cars, combined with the city's elevation, is making pollution a very serious problem. Though it was founded over 2,000 years ago, the city did not gain prominence until it became the eastern capital of the Nanzhao Kingdom in the 8th century. By the time the Mongols swept through in 1274, Kunming, or Yachi as it was then known, was enough of a flourishing town to have attracted the attention of Marco Polo, who described it as a "very great and noble" capital city. The city's bloodiest period occurred during the Qing dynasty, with a series of Muslim rebellions. In the late 19th century, foreign influence appeared in the form of the French, who built a narrow-gauge rail line to Vietnam still in use today. During World War II, Kunming played an important role as the terminus of a major supply line (the famous Burma Road) in the Allies' Asian theater of operations.

Today, Kunming's wide streets, towering office blocks, and giant shopping centers all convey the impression of a modern, 21st-century city. Sadly, much of the development of recent years, most of it on account of the 1999 International Horticultural Exhibition, has come at the expense of traditional wooden dwellings and artisan workshops, which have all been razed in the process, taking much of the city's original charm with them. Still, Kunming remains a useful starting point even if its offerings do not match some of Yunnan's other treasures. A subtropical location and high elevation (1,864m/6,213 ft.) give Kunming a temperate climate year-round. Its days are filled with sunshine, making almost any time good for a visit, though the balmy months of September and October are especially fine.

ESSENTIALS

GETTING THERE   By Plane   Kunming is connected by daily flights to Beijing (2½ hr.), Chengdu (1 hr.), Guilin (1½ hr.), Shanghai (2½ hr.), Dali (½ hr.), Li Jiang (40 min.), Xianggelila (1 hr.), Baoshan (40 min.), Mangshi (40 min.), and Xishuangbanna (40 min.). There are twice-weekly flights to Lhasa via Xianggelila. Tickets can be purchased at the **CAAC/Yunnan Airlines** office at Tuodong Lu 28 (© **0871/ 316-4270** domestic, or 0871/312-1220 international). Tickets can also be purchased at the airport, at CITS and other travel agencies, and at hotel tour desks. On the international front, Yunnan Airlines and several international carriers serve Hong Kong, Bangkok, Chiang Mai, Yangon, Mandalay, Vientiane, Osaka, Singapore, and Hanoi. Foreign airline offices include: **Dragonair** (Beijing Lu 157; © 0871/356-2828); **Lao Aviation** (Camellia Hotel, Dongfeng Dong Lu 96; © 0871/316-3000, ext. 5166); **Thai Airways** (Beijing Lu 98, second floor, King World Hotel annex; © 0871/351-2269); **Silk Air/Singapore Airlines** (Dongfeng Dong Lu 25; © 0871/315-7125); **Japan Airlines** (Bank Hotel, Qingnian Lu 399; third floor; © 0871/315-8111); and **Vietnam**

Kunming

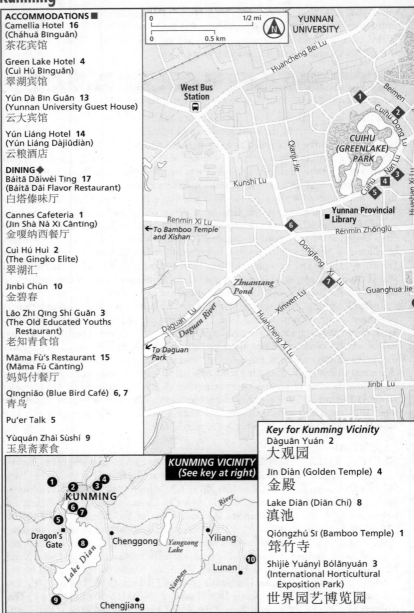

ACCOMMODATIONS ■

Camellia Hotel **16**
(Cháhuā Bīnguǎn)
茶花宾馆

Green Lake Hotel **4**
(Cuì Hú Bīnguǎn)
翠湖宾馆

Yún Dà Bīn Guǎn **13**
(Yunnan University Guest House)
云大宾馆

Yún Liáng Hotel **14**
(Yún Liáng Dàjiǔdiàn)
云粮酒店

DINING ◆

Báitǎ Dǎiwèi Tīng **17**
(Báitǎ Dǎi Flavor Restaurant)
白塔傣味厅

Cannes Cafeteria **1**
(Jīn Shà Nà Xī Cāntīng)
金嘎纳西餐厅

Cuì Hú Huì **2**
(The Gingko Elite)
翠湖汇

Jīnbì Chūn **10**
金碧春

Lǎo Zhī Qīng Shí Guǎn **3**
(The Old Educated Youths
Restaurant)
老知青食馆

Māma Fù's Restaurant **15**
(Māma Fù Cāntīng)
妈妈付餐厅

Qīngniǎo (Blue Bird Café) **6, 7**
青鸟

Pu'er Talk **5**

Yùquán Zhāi Sùshí **9**
玉泉斋素食

West Bus Station

YUNNAN UNIVERSITY

Huancheng Bei Lu

Beimen Jie

Cuihu Dong Lu

CUIHU (GREENLAKE) PARK

Qianju Jie

Cuihu Nan Lu

Huashan Xi Lu

Kunshi Lu

Yunnan Provincial Library

Rénmín Xī Lu
←To Bamboo Temple
and Xishan

Rénmín Zhōnglù

Dongfeng

Zhuantang Pond

Dongfeng Xī Lu

Guanghua Jie

Xinwen Lu

Daguan Lu

Daguan River

Huancheng Xī Lu

←To Daguan
Park

Jinbi Lu

KUNMING VICINITY
(See key at right)

KUNMING

River

Dragon's Gate

Chenggong

Yangzong Lake

Yiliang

Lake Diān

Nampan

Lunan

Chengjiang

Key for Kunming Vicinity

Dàguān Yuán **2**
大观园

Jīn Diàn (Golden Temple) **4**
金殿

Lake Diān (Diān Chí) **8**
滇池

Qióngzhú Sī (Bamboo Temple) **1**
筇竹寺

Shìjiè Yuányì Bólǎnyuán **3**
(International Horticultural
Exposition Park)
世界园艺博览园

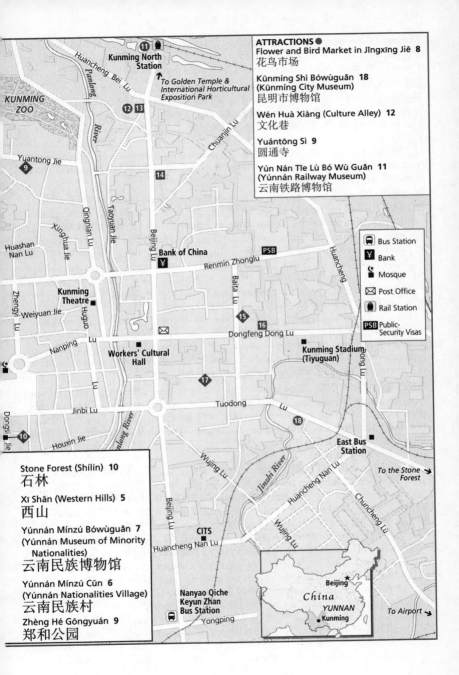

KUNMING ZOO

Kunming North Station

To Golden Temple & International Horticultural Exposition Park

Huancheng Bei Lu

Panlong River

Yuantong Jie

Chuanjin Lu

Qingnian Lu

Taoyuan Jie

Beijing Lu

ATTRACTIONS ●
Flower and Bird Market in Jīngxīng Jiē **8**
花鸟市场

Kūnmíng Shì Bówùguǎn **18**
(Kūnmíng City Museum)
昆明市博物馆

Wén Huà Xiàng (Culture Alley) **12**
文化巷

Yuántōng Sì **9**
圆通寺

Yún Nán Tiě Lù Bó Wù Guǎn **11**
(Yúnnán Railway Museum)
云南铁路博物馆

Bank of China

PSB

Renmin Zhonglu

Huancheng

Baita Lu

Huashan Nan Lu

Xinghua Jie

Zhengyi Lu

Weiyuan Jie

Huguo Lu

Nanping

Kunming Theatre

Workers' Cultural Hall

Dongfeng Dong Lu

15

16

Kunming Stadium (Tiyuguan)

Dong Lu

Jinbi Lu

17

Tuodong

Lu

18

East Bus Station

To the Stone Forest

Panlong River

Dongsi Jie

10

Houxin Jie

Wujing Lu

Jinbi River

Huancheng Nan Lu

Wujing Lu

Chuncheng Lù

Bus Station

¥ **Bank**

☪ **Mosque**

✉ **Post Office**

🏛 **Rail Station**

PSB Public-Security Visas

Stone Forest (Shílín) **10**
石林

Xī Shān (Western Hills) **5**
西山

Yúnnán Mínzú Bówùguǎn **7**
(Yúnnán Museum of Minority Nationalities)
云南民族博物馆

Yúnnán Mínzú Cūn **6**
(Yúnnán Nationalities Village)
云南民族村

Zhèng Hé Gōngyuán **9**
郑和公园

Beijing Lu

CITS

Huancheng Nan Lu

Nanyao Qiche Keyun Zhan Bus Station

Yongping

China

Beijing ★

YUNNAN

Kunming

To Airport

Airlines (Tuodong Lu 80; © 0871/315-7175). The airport is 5km (3 miles) south of city center, a quick ¥30 ($3.90/£1.95) taxi ride depending on your destination in town. There are no CAAC airport buses, but public bus nos. 67 and 52 also serve the airport at ¥1 (15¢/10p).

By Train   Kunming is well connected by rail to many major Chinese cities, but these trips can require several days and nights and therefore require some preparation. Trains run to Beijing (T62, 42 hr.), Shanghai (K80, 46 hr.), Guangzhou (1166, 26 hr.), Guilin (K182, 17½ hr.), Nanning (2006, 12½ hr.), Guiyang (K156, 11 hr.), Chengdu (K114, 18 hr.), Dali (K446 or K732, 8 hr.), and Shilin/Stone Forest (K440, 90 min.). Tickets can be purchased at the **railway station** (© **0871/612-2492**) south of town from 6:30am to 11:30pm.

By Bus   Kunming has a number of long-distance bus stations, all within 5 minutes of each other and the railway station, but the main one that should serve most travelers' needs is the **Nanyao Qiche Keyun Zhan** at Beijing Lu 60 (© 0871/351-0617), at the northwest corner of Beijing Lu and Yongping Lu. From here, buses go to Xiaguan (17 buses; 5 hr.; ¥119/$16/£7.75) from 7:30am to 7:30pm; to Li Jiang (9 hr.; ¥150/$20/£9.75) at 7:30am, 9:30am, 11:30am, and 2pm); to Xianggelila/Zhongdian (12 hr.; ¥174/$23/£11) at 8:20am; to Ruili (16 hr.; ¥204/$27/£13) at 3:30pm; to Jinghong (16 hr.; ¥150/$20/£9.75) at 2pm, 4pm, 6pm, 7pm, and 8pm; and to Jianshui (4½ hr.; ¥54/$7.10/£3.55) every half-hour from 7:20am to 9pm.

For the really adventurous, or those who are allergic to Chinese sleeper buses, cycling into Southern Yunnan from Kunming deserves serious consideration. Not only are there some beautiful back roads, but it is downhill all the way. For further inspiration and a day-to-day report from somebody who has already done this, check out **www.pratyeka.org/bike/southern-yunnan.html**.

GETTING AROUND   Downtown sights can be toured on foot or by bike. If your hotel does not offer bike rental, the Camellia Hotel (see "Where to Stay," below) rents them for ¥2 (25¢/15p) an hour or ¥15/$1.95/£1 for the day. For a choice of mountain bikes for rent, visit **Fattire Fun Mountain Bike Club** at Beimen Jie 1 hao, Qianju Lu 61, off Cui Hu Nan Lu (© **0871/530-1755;** owner Xiong Jinwu's e-mail: bear_bike@hotmail.com).

Flagfall for Xiali and smaller **taxis** is ¥7 (90¢/45p) for 3km (2 miles), then ¥1.60 (20¢/10p) per kilometer until 10km (6 miles), when it goes up to ¥2.40 (30¢/15p) per kilometer. From 10pm to 6am, the cost is ¥8.40 ($1/50p) for 3km (2 miles), then ¥1.90 (25¢/10p) per kilometer until 10km (6 miles), then ¥2.70 (35¢/15p) per kilometer. Santana taxis cost ¥8 ($1.05/50p) for 3km (2 miles) and ¥1.80 (25¢/10p) per kilometer after that; from 10pm to 6am, flagfall is ¥9.60 ($1.25/65p) for 3km (2 miles).

While many of the outlying sights such as the Bamboo Temple and Dragon's Gate can be reached most conveniently by taxi, public **buses** also travel most of these routes. Bus no. 52 runs from the airport to Da Guan Yuan via the railway station. Bus no. 47 runs from the railway station to the International Horticultural Exposition Park, from where you can either take the cable car or bus no. 10 to the Golden Temple. Bus no. 44 goes from a block north of the railway station to the Yunnan Nationalities Village. The fare for each bus is ¥1 (15¢/10p). Unlike other cities in China, buses have special access to the innermost lane rather than the outside lane. This is a very effective innovation and makes buses the fast way to get around the city, especially during rush hour.

CONSULATES **Laos** The **Laos consulate** (© 0871/317-6624) is in room 120 of the Camellia Hotel at Dongfeng Dong Lu 96 (open Mon–Fri 8:30–11:30am and 1:30–4:30pm). Transit visas (5–7 days) and standard 15-day tourist visas (valid within 2 months of issue) can be issued in 3 working days (ordinary service) or by the next working day (express service). Fees vary from ¥270 to ¥378 ($35–$49/£18–£25) for ordinary service and from ¥400 to ¥500 ($52–$65/£26–£33) for express service. You cannot currently get a Laos visa at the border. Bring two photos and complete two application forms.

Myanmar The **Myanmar consulate** (© 0871/316-3000, ext. 6225; fax 0871/317-6309) is located in room 225 of the Camellia Hotel (open Mon–Fri 8:30am–noon and 1–2pm). Standard 28-day travel visas costing ¥285 ($37/£19) and valid within 3 months of issue can be issued in 3 working days; for same-day service, expect to pay an extra ¥150/$20/£9.75) . This visa is only good for flying into Yangon or Mandalay. For overland crossing at the Ruili border, see "Tours," below.

Thailand The **Thai consulate** (© 0871/316-2033, ext. 62105; fax 0871/316-6891) is located on the grounds of the Kunming Hotel at Dongfeng Dong Lu 50–52 (open Mon–Fri 9am–1:30pm). Note that travelers from most countries won't need Thai visas.

Vietnam There is no Vietnamese consulate here, but you can apply for 30-day Vietnamese visas for ¥400 ($52/£26) at the **Vietnam Airlines** office, Tuodong Lu 80 (© 0871/315-7175). Bring your passport and photo.

OUTDOOR ACTIVITIES Golfers can head to the **Spring City Golf and Lake Resort** located 48km (29 miles) southeast of Kunming; it has a championship 18-hole golf course designed by Jack Nicklaus and another by Robert Trent Jones, Jr. Standard rooms at the five-star resort (© 0871/767-1188; www.springcitygolf.com) cost ¥1,504 ($196/£98), while a round of golf will set you back ¥1,760 ($229/£114).

For a more exhilarating afternoon, you might try **Kunming Blue Angels Para-sailing Club** (© 0871/622-7788; www.kmlts.com). A two-person jump from over 1,000m (3,280 ft.) and lasting 30 minutes costs just ¥400 ($52/£26).

TOURS **CITS** at Huancheng Nan Lu 285 (© 0871/353-5448; fax 0871/316-9240; www.kmcits.com.cn; open Mon–Fri 8:30am–noon and 2–6pm) is often busy juggling international tour groups but can be very helpful with arranging accommodations, ongoing transportation, or customized tours throughout Yunnan for individual travelers. The **Camellia Travel Service** on the ground floor of the Camellia Hotel is the rudest and most unhelpful agency in town and worth avoiding.

For overland travel to **Myanmar** at the Ruili border, you will have to be accompanied all the way to Mandalay by an official travel agency–sponsored guide. Jenny in the travel agency (© 0871/316-0003) in room 208 of the Camellia Hotel just before the Myanmar consulate can handle all the arrangements for you, including the visa. Expect to pay about ¥1,500 ($195/£98) per person for a day trip as far as Lasio, more if you want to travel farther.

FAST FACTS
Banks, Foreign Exchange & ATMs The main branch of the **Bank of China** (open Mon–Fri 8:30am–noon and 2–5pm) is at Renmin Dong Lu 448. ATMs here accept international cards.

Internet Access   The imposing Yunnan Provincial Library on Cui Hu Nan Lu 141 has a large number of machines on the third floor (open 9am–5pm) and the fourth (open 9am–8pm); ¥1.40 (20¢/10p) per hour.

Post Office   The main post office (open 8am–8pm) is at Dongfeng Dong Lu 14, and another (open 9am–8pm) is west of the railway station.

Visa Extensions   The visa office is located at counter 57 of the **People's Service Center** of Kunming Municipality (Kunming Shizhengfu Bianmin Zhongxin), Renmin Dong Lu 196 (*©* **0871/319-6540**; open Mon–Fri 8:30–11:30am and 1–5:30pm).

EXPLORING KUNMING

Cui Hu (Green Lake) *◈*   Kunming's nicest park is a pleasant retreat from the bustling city even though it can get quite crowded on weekends. Bridges and pavilions connect the various islands on the lake, and sipping tea at a lakeside teahouse is one of the more pleasant activities here. The park is home to the Siberian black-headed gulls, which migrate here during the winter. There are also some great restaurants and accommodations.

Cui Hu Nan Lu. Free admission. Bus: no. 4, 59, 22, 74, 78, 85, or 101.

Kunming Shi Bowuguan (Kunming City Museum)   Only worth a visit if you've exhausted the city's other offerings, this museum focuses on the bronzes, drums, jewelry, swords, and other artifacts of the Dian nation unearthed around the Lake Dian area, including a seven-story octagonal Sutra Stone Incantation Pillar built during the Dali Kingdom (938–1254) to release the soul from suffering. Just opposite is the Museum of Urban Planning, which has some great scale models that give you a bird's-eye view of the city but not a word of English in sight. Still, at least entrance is free.

Tuodong Lu 120. Admission ¥5 (65¢/35p). Tues–Sun 10am–4:30pm.

Yunnan Tie Lu Bowuguan (Yunnan Railway Museum)   Well designed and packed with information for the rail history buff, the majority of displays describe the construction and eventual demise of the French-built narrow-gauge rail network in the province, which at one time led all the way to Hanoi and beyond. Many of the aging photos make clear the hardships and obstacles faced when trying to build 3,422 bridges and tunnels without any of the huge modern extraction tools.

The locomotives and carriages (including a very strange Michelin model with pneumatic tires) are kept in an annex just down the road. This is great spot for travelers who prefer to climb all over the displays rather than simply stand and look.

North Station, Beijing Lu. *©* **0871/613-8610**. Admission ¥10 ($1.30/65p). Tues–Sun 10am–4pm.

Yuantong Si   This unusual temple, the largest Buddhist shrine in Kunming, combines elements from Mahayana, Hinayana (or Theravada), and Tibetan Buddhism (Lamaism). Originally built between 780 and 807, and rebuilt during the Qing dynasty, the temple is dedicated to the worship of Avalokitesvara (the original male Buddha who was later transfigured into the female Guanyin in Chinese Mahayana Buddhism). In the back of the complex is a Hinayana-style hall with a bronze statue of Sakyamuni donated by the Buddhist Association of Thailand. To the east is an altar hall of the Lama sect.

Yuantong Jie. Admission ¥4 (50¢/25p). 8am–5pm.

SHOPPING

The area around Zhengyi Lu and Nanping Lu has turned into Kunming's main shopping district. The Guwan Cheng (open 8:30am–7:30pm) at the southwest corner of Huguo Lu and Nanping Lu has a collection of stores selling **antiques,** curios, and ceramics. The Flower and Bird Market in Jingxing Jie is worth a browse for **souvenirs** and minor, mostly fake, antiques, but do not expect anything much different from all the other souvenir markets. For something more original, head down Beijing road past the Jinda Hotel and the PLA Headquarters. There are plenty of army surplus shops here that sell everything from fur caps (¥20/$2.60/£1.30) to military police ID wallets (¥25/$3.25/£1.65), all of which make very unusual gifts.

WHERE TO STAY

Camellia Hotel (Chahua Binguan)   Still popular among budget travelers but only because of apathy. This two-star is old and run down but thrives on its long-standing reputation. There are older budget standard rooms that are smaller and more run down, and basic dorms with shared showers that are in high demand among backpackers. The hotel offers a budget ¥10 ($1.30/65p) Western buffet breakfast. The staff speaks some English and can be helpful when pressed, but the travel agency is, sadly, not helpful in the least.

Dongfeng Dong Lu 96. (?) **0871/316-3000.** Fax 0871/314-7033. 180 units. ¥30 ($3.90/£1.95) dorm bed; ¥200 ($26/£13) standard room. AE, DC, MC, V. **Amenities:** 2 restaurants; bar; lounge; bike rental; concierge; tour desk; business center; forex; laundry. *In room:* A/C, TV.

Green Lake Hotel (Cui Hu Binguan) 🏵🏵🏵   Originally opened by the Hongta tobacco group in 1956, and later by Hilton, this was Kunming's very first hotel to be opened to foreigners. The location easily surpasses any of the downtown five-stars, and its two new wings make it a tempting new choice. The rooms are very well maintained and luxuriously appointed with huge king-size beds, making this one of the few locally run five-stars that can give the multinationals a run for their money. The lake is wonderful area to stroll, as is the university, although the military academy can safely be ignored.

South Cui Hu Nan Lu 6. (?) **0871/515-888.** Fax 0871/515-3286. 302 units. ¥1,180 ($154/£77) standard room; from ¥1,380 ($179/£90) suite. 35% discounts. AE, DC, MC, V. **Amenities:** 2 restaurants; teahouse; nightclub; indoor pool; health club; driving range; sauna; concierge; tour desk; free shuttle to city center; business center; forex; shopping arcade; salon; 24-hr. butler service; same-day laundry/dry cleaning. *In room:* A/C, satellite TV, broadband Internet access, DVD player, minibar, hair dryer, safe.

Yun Liang Hotel (Yun Liang Dajiudian) 🏵 *Value*   Near the Yuantong Temple and Green Lake, this is a very well-located business hotel that's a much better choice than the Camellia for budget-minded travelers. Rooms are clean and simple (although the beds are a little hard), while staffers are friendly, but not linguists.

Beijing Lu 623. (?) **0871/617-7188.** Fax 0871/515-5730. 65 units. ¥288 ($38/£19) standard room; from ¥688 ($90/£45) suite. 35% discount. AE, DC, MC, V. **Amenities:** Tour center; salon; in-room massage; karaoke. *In room:* A/C, TV.

Yunnan University Guest House (Yun Da Bing Guan) 🏵🏵🏵   Located conveniently for Green Lake, this is by far the best value hotel in the city. The rooms might be described as a little too beige, but they are very clean and comfortable with a staff that is far more efficient than most five-stars. Best of all it leads out onto what is quickly developing into Kunming's international bar street, Wen Hua Xiang.

121 St., Tian Jun Dian Xiang. (?) **0871/503-4181.** Fax 0871/503-4190. 84 units. ¥150 ($20/£9.75) standard room. AE, DC, MC, V. **Amenities:** 2 restaurants; bar; lounge; laundry. *In room:* A/C, satellite TV, minibar, Internet.

WHERE TO DINE

The most famous Yunnan dish is **"crossing the bridge noodles"** *(guoqiao mixian)*, a hot pot consisting of steaming chicken broth to which you add thinly sliced chicken, pork, fish, other meats, vegetables, mushrooms, and rice noodles, all seasoned with peppers and chilies to taste. The oil on top keeps the simmering food hot enough to scald tongues, so be careful with your first bites! According to legend, the dish was invented over a century ago by the wife of a scholar who discovered that a layer of oil on top of her husband's food could keep it warm all the way from her kitchen across the bridge to a pavilion where he was studying for his imperial examinations, hence the dish's name. Another popular local dish is *qiguo ji* (chicken stewed with medicinal herbs). Along with a pharmacopoeia of allegedly healthful herbs and spices that are often used in many local dishes, Yunnan mushrooms are also valued for their medicinal qualities. Fried goat cheese, Yunnan sweet ham, and Yunnan coffee are some other local favorites.

Cannes Cafeteria (Jin Ga Na Xicanting) ★★★ MEDITERRANEAN   While
this may not be Las Ramblas, Green Lake Park does have a relaxing Latin feel to it at times, especially with all the pavement cafes. The owner of Cannes lived in Spain for more than 20 years and his extensive knowledge of the country's cuisine is reflected in the menu. The second floor is a great place to spend a lazy afternoon; the staff is friendly and the prices reasonable.

Cui Hu Bei Lu 78, Green Lake. ⓒ **0871/519-9696**. Main courses ¥18–¥50 ($2.35–$6.50/£1.15–£3.25). No credit cards. 11am–midnight.

The Gingko Elite (Cui Hu Hui) WESTERN/CHINESE   The Gingko just goes to
show how stylish and elegant Kunming can be. Certainly the most unique building on the lakeside, the food that it serves is a step above, too. Recommended are the fried lily and asparagus *(bai he chao lu sun)* for ¥28 ($3.65/£1.80), and crispy fragrant chicken *(cui pi yan ju ji)* for ¥33 ($4.30/£2.15). A variety of local and imported beers and wines are available to complement your meal.

Dong Hu Lu 16. ⓒ **0871/516-6972**. Main courses ¥30–¥150 ($3.90–$20/£1.95–£9.75). AE, DC, MC, V. 9am–2am.

The Old Educated Youths Restaurant (Lao Zhi Qing Shi Guan) DAI   For a
refreshing change of palate, this ethnic Dai restaurant, decorated comfortably with rattan furniture and batik prints, serves delicious a selection of the hot and crispy dishes that it is famous for such a fried beef skin and baked dried beef, but also a deliciously soft and sweet steamed corn fish in pineapple.

Cui Hu Nan Lu 4. ⓒ **0871/514-0231**. Main courses ¥15–¥40 ($2–$5.20/£1–£2.60). No credit cards. 8:30am–11pm.

Pu'er Talk   In an interesting twist on the fruit juice stalls that are now popular along
the side of the lake, we also enjoyed this little place where they have a different take

---

ⓘ Tips Local Flavors

Just on the other side of the Yuantong Bridge are a number of holes in the wall serving excellent roast duck. The dish is so popular among locals that whole racks of birds are lined up for the oven every single day. Combined with a couple of fresh fruit juices (¥4–¥6/50¢–80¢/25p–40p) from Fresh, just around the corner opposite the river, this makes an excellent choice for lunch.

on the famous Pu'er tea, now served with a selection of sweet fruit flavors including blueberry, lemon, ginger, and orange.

Cui Hu Nan Lu Zhong Duan. © 0871/516-2526. Open 24 hr.

Yuquan Zhai Sushi ⚜ VEGETARIAN   The largest vegetarian restaurant in town, located diagonally across from the Yuantong Si, is a clean, low-key, and foreigner-friendly place where Buddhist chants play softly in the background. All the dishes here are made from vegetables, tofu, or soy products but have been known to fool even the most discerning of meat eaters. Try *hongshao shiziqiu* (a mushroom ball in soy sauce), *cuipi ya* (crispy fried mock duck), and *cuipi ruyi yu* (crispy mock fish in sweet-and-sour sauce). Although mentioned in most guidebooks, the place is never overly busy and retains a sense of peace and orderliness that many more popular venues have lost.

Pingzheng Jie 88, 2nd floor. © 0871/511-16572. English menu. Main courses ¥30–¥120 ($3.90–$16/£1.95–£7.80). No credit cards. 9am–9pm.

KUNMING AFTER DARK

The 24-hour **Aoma Meili Restaurant** at Dongfeng Lu 60 (© **0871/312-6036**) is a laid-back bar with a good selection of liqueurs, beers, wines, sake, and the usual coffees and teas. The popular **Camel Bar (Luotuo Jiuba)** at Baita Lu 274 (© **0871/337-6255**) serves inexpensive beer and has live music on weekends. The local bar scene thrives at dark but trendy **The Hump** (© **0871/364-4197**; open noon–2am or until last customer) has a full bar and posters of American pop and movie stars but attracts highly budget-conscious backpackers rather than regular independent travelers. For more sophisticated venues, try some of the bars around Green Lake.

AROUND KUNMING

Jin Dian (Golden Temple) ⚜   The centerpiece of this gorgeous Daoist temple complex, located 10km (6 miles) northeast of town, is the small but exquisite Golden Temple, built in 1671 on a two-tiered marble platform ringed by beautifully carved balustrades. The weathered 6.7m-high (22-ft.), 7.8m-wide (25-ft.), 250-ton hall has a double-eaved roof with gables, beams, columns, lattice doors, and lattice windows, all cast in bronze. Inside is a 1.5m-tall (5-ft.) bronze statue of Zhen Wu, the legendary God of the North, flanked by a girl and a boy servant. Beyond the Golden Temple at the summit of the hill is the **Bell Tower (Zhong Lou)**, a 36m-high (118-ft.), three-story square structure with a total of 36 flying eaves evoking flying phoenixes that was built only in 1983. Inside hangs a 14-ton bronze bell, used to signal time as well as to sound the alarm at the city's southern gate. A ¥15 ($1.95/£1) cable car now runs from the temple to the World Horticultural Expo Garden.

Jin Dian Gongyuan. Admission ¥20 ($2.60/£1.30). 7am–8pm. Bus: no. 10 or 71 (from Jinri Gongyuan).

Qiongzhu Si (Bamboo Temple) ⚜   Built in 639 and rebuilt from 1422 to 1428, this temple houses an incredibly vivid tableau of 500 arhats carved between 1883 and 1890 by Sichuanese sculptor Li Guangxiu and his six apprentices, who gave to each arhat a different and incredibly naturalistic facial expression and pose. It is thought that some of these arhats, who range from the emaciated to the pot-bellied, the angry to the contemplative, were carved in the images of the sculptor's contemporaries, friends, and foes. A wildly fantastical element dominates the main hall, where an arhat surfs a wave on the back of a unicorn, while another stretches a 3m (10-ft.) arm upward to pierce the ceiling.

12km (7 miles) northwest of town. Admission ¥40 ($5.20/£2.60). 7:30am–5pm. Bus: no. 1 from Nanping Jie and Zhengyi Lu to Huangtu Po; transfer to *miandi* (van) taxis (¥10/$1.30/65p) for Qiongzhu Si.

Dounan Flower Market (Dou Nan Hua Hui Si Chang)   Back in 1979 when Kunming's population was just still well under one million, the government removed many of the strict "household responsibility system" regulations that required locals to grow only sugar and rice. While the change may have been with good intentions, it immediately resulted in a mass conversion to vegetables and a subsequent massive price drop.

As the rush to grow vegetables swept through the region, some decided to go a different route, and were rewarded handsomely. Beginning in 1983 farmers in the city of Dounan moved toward flowers after seeing the success of a local man named Hua Zhongyi, who got the idea on a trip to Guangzhou. The results were tremendous and the industry rocketed, quickly making the city the richest in the region.

Now, more than half of China's flowers come from Yunnan, with 80% of those passing through Dounan's market of 5,000 individual flower shops. More than 3 billion stems a year of over 600 different varieties go through the once-poor city. In fact, estimates indicate that flowers have lifted at least 20,000 farmers out of poverty.

18km (11 miles) southeast of Kunming, via a ¥80 ($10/£5) bus into Ju Hua Village or ¥5 (65¢/35p) bus from Dong Bu bus station to Chen Gong town.

LAKE DIAN (DIAN CHI)

China's sixth-largest freshwater lake, located southwest of Kunming, is 40km (25 miles) from north to south and covers an area of 300 sq. km (186 sq. miles). Fishing boats still trawl the lake, but serious pollution has made it difficult for many families to continue to make their living this way. Bordered by hills to the west and industrial settlements to the south and east, the lake has a number of attractions.

Da Guan Yuan   This pleasant park on the northern shore of Lake Dian boasts nurseries, gardens, and walkways, but it is most famous for its triple-eaved **Grand View Tower (Da Guan Lou)**, first built in 1682 and rebuilt in 1883. The tower offers unobstructed views of the lake.

Daguan Lu (3km/2 miles south of Kunming). Admission ¥10 ($1.30/65p). 8:30am–6pm. Bus: no. 4 or 52 (from airport).

Xi Shan (Western Hills)   Sometimes called the Sleeping Beauty Hills—their contours are said to resemble the outline of a sleeping maiden when viewed from afar—this densely forested range of hills on the western banks of Lake Dian is home to a number of Buddhist and Daoist temples and pavilions carved into the sheer rock face.

From the park's entrance, it's a 5km (3-mile) hike uphill to the parking lot and cable-car station, though most visitors prefer to take the bus from Gaoyao directly to the parking lot. Along the way, the first major temple is the large and impressive Ming dynasty **Huating Si** (¥20/$2.60/£1.30; open 7:20am–6:30pm), which has statues of 500 arhats. About 2km (1¼ miles) later is another Ming temple, **Taihua Si** (¥3/40¢/20p; open 8am–6pm), which was built in 1306 and boasts large gardens that contain camellia, plum, and osmanthus trees.

At the minibus and cable-car terminus is **Nie Er Zhi Mu** (free entrance; open 8am–6:30pm), the tomb of the famous Yunnan musician Nie Er, who composed China's national anthem before he drowned prematurely at sea in Japan in 1935. From here, you can take a chairlift for ¥45 ($5.85/£2.95) to the summit at Dragon Gate (Long Men), or you can take a tram for ¥20 ($2.60/£1.30) to **Sanqing Ge**, a Daoist temple dedicated to the three main Daoist Gods that marks the beginning of the climb to the Dragon Gate Grottoes (¥30/$3.90/£1.95). This series of grottoes containing various deities was carved by a local Daoist monk, Wu Laiqing, and his band of monks between 1781 and 1795, all of whom must have been hanging by their fingertips as they painstakingly hacked away at the sheer rock face. The path on the cliff edge leading to **Dragon Gate** is so narrow that only one person can pass at a time. Below is a precipitous drop of about 600m (2,000 ft.) to the shores of Lake Dian. Those with vertigo should avoid this path. But the views from here of the lake and Kunming in the distance are quite stunning and worth the trip.

To get to Xi Shan, take a taxi for ¥100 ($13/£6.50), or take local bus no. 5 from the Kunming Hotel to its terminus at the Liu Lu Chechang. Change to bus no. 6, which will take you to the village of Gaoyao, where minibuses and van taxis will run you up to the tomb of Nie Er for ¥15 ($1.95/£1). Minibuses also make the run to the tomb from the Liu Lu Chechang, but these are unreliable. You can also leave Dragon Gate by cable car for ¥60 ($9.10/£4.55) one-way, ¥100 ($13/£6.50) round-trip. It crosses Lake Dian down to Haigeng Park and the Yunnan Nationalities Village. The cable-car terminus is at the tomb of Nie Er.

15km (9 miles) west of Kunming.

STONE FOREST (SHI LIN) ☆☆

Located 90km (55 miles) southeast of Kunming in the Lunan Yi Autonomous County, Shi Lin is Kunming's most famous attraction—a giant forest of limestone rocks formed 270 million years ago when the ocean receded from this area. Millions of years of tectonic shifts and erosion from wind and rain have resulted in today's maze of sharp-edged fissures and sky-piercing pinnacles, which are punctuated by walkways, ponds, and pavilion lookouts. Fed by subterranean rivers, **Jianfeng Chi** is the only natural body of water in the forest. The reflection of the blue sky, white clouds, and sword-like stone peaks in the pond makes this one of the most photographed locales in the forest. **Shizi Ting (Lion Pavilion),** the highest point in the Stone Forest, and **Wangfeng Ting (Peak Viewing Pavilion)** offer the best panoramas.

This geological wonder is quite a sight if you've never before seen a petrified forest, but some visitors are more amazed at the immense parking lots and long lines at the ticket offices. It could be the hordes of tourists that tramp through here during the day, for the forest takes on a much more ethereal and mysterious quality only in the evening after the tour groups have left. The Stone Forest can be comfortably navigated in a 2½- to 3-hour loop with plenty of opportunities to get off the trodden path. An English-speaking tour guide can be hired for ¥80 ($10/£5.20) but is not really necessary.

⟨Tips⟩ Another, Quieter Stone Forest

About 8km (5 miles) northeast of the Stone Forest is the 300-hectare (741-acre) **Naigu Shilin Black Pine Stone Forest** (¥25/$3.25/£1.65), which predates the Stone Forest by about 2 million years. The park is a much quieter option; in fact, I only saw two other Western tourists the entire day that I was there. There are some interesting geological signs in English and the terrain varies from underground karst caves to magnificent black volcanic lookout points. On your own, catch a horse and cart for ¥15 ($1.95/£1) from the main road outside the Stone Forest.

This area is also home to the Sani branch of the Yi minority group. Young Sani men and women (allegedly) in colorful costumes greet all arriving visitors and act as tour guides through the forest, while Sani vendors sell a variety of handicrafts and some very nice batiks. There are also Sani song and dance performances during the day and on most nights at the Minor Stone Forest (Xiao Shi Lin) right next to the Stone Forest. For early risers, the route down through the Sani village bypasses the ticket gates and means free entrance if you arrive before 8am.

Another side trip worth considering is the 96m-high (315-ft.), 54m-wide (177-ft.) **Dadieshui Feilong Pu** (¥18/$2.35/£1.15), Yunnan's largest waterfall. Hiring a taxi for ¥100 ($13/£6.50) directly from the Stone Forest is the most convenient way to get here.

GETTING THERE   The best way to reach the Stone Forest is via the direct K440 train (90 min.; ¥20/$2.60/£1.30 one-way, ¥30/$3.90/£1.95 round-trip), which departs Kunming at 8:10am and returns from the Stone Forest at 4:30pm. Train tickets for the forest are sold from 7:30 to 8:10am at a special booth at the southeast corner of the railway station next to the gate for the Stone Forest train. During other times, purchase Stone Forest train tickets at counter 3 in the main station or from travel agencies or hotel desks. Entrance tickets for the Stone Forest can be purchased for ¥80 ($10/£5.20) on the train, where attendants may also try to sell you organized tours taking in nearby sights. Naigu Stone Forest costs an additional ¥40 ($5.20/£2.60) including lunch, and the Dadieshui Waterfall costs an additional ¥50 ($6.50/£3.25) including lunch. If you decide to join one of these tours, usually conducted in Chinese only, they will send you to the railway station in time for the return train to Kunming at 4:30pm. If you do not wish to wait for the 4:30pm return train, you can catch other, earlier Kunming-bound trains for ¥17 ($2.10/£1.05) that stop at the Stone Forest on the way (the 1165 leaves Shi Lin at 1:47pm and arrives in Kunming at 3:30pm), although there are no reserved seats. Avoid anyone who tries to sell you bus rides for ¥30 ($3.90/£1.95) round-trip, unless you want to spend all your time shopping along the way and only reach the forest in the afternoon. Trips from the Camellia are especially overrated; your ¥90 ($12/£5.85) includes nothing but a ride in a cramped microbus with a surly driver, who pretends to speak no English. Rather than drive through ghastly industrial towns like "Developing Yiliang," the train is a much more scenic option.

WHERE TO STAY & DINE   The sprawling three-star **Stone Forest Xingya Fengqing Garden** (© 0871/771-0599; fax 0871/771-1599) offers guest rooms that are spacious and comfortable, if a little worn. Rates can easily be discounted to ¥250 ($33/£16); no credit cards accepted.

9 Dali

Yunnan Province, 392km (243 miles) NW of Kunming, 15km (9 miles) N of Xiaguan, 150km (90 miles) S of Li Jiang

The charming town of Dali, traditionally one of the best places in China to tune in, turn on, and drop out for a while, remains a wonderful place to visit despite the increasing commercialization brought by tour groups. Its small size belies its important place in Yunnan's history: During the Tang dynasty (609–960), Dali was the capital of the Nanzhao Kingdom, and during the Song dynasty (960–1079), it was the capital of the Dali kingdom. Deserted after Kublai Khan overran Dali in 1252, it was

Dali

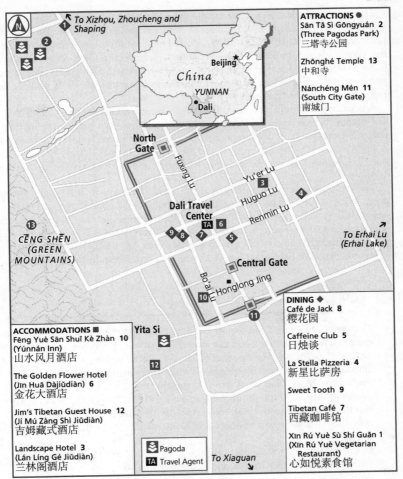

ATTRACTIONS ●

Sān Tǎ Sì Gōngyuán **2**
(Three Pagodas Park)
三塔寺公园

Zhōnghé Temple **13**
中和寺

Nánchéng Mén **11**
(South City Gate)
南城门

To Xizhou, Zhoucheng and Shaping

China
YUNNAN
Dali
Beijing

North Gate

Dali Travel Center

CĒNG SHĒN (GREEN MOUNTAINS)

Central Gate

To Erhai Lu (Erhai Lake)

ACCOMMODATIONS ■
Fēng Yuè Sān Shuǐ Kè Zhàn **10**
(Yúnnán Inn)
山水风月酒店

The Golden Flower Hotel
(Jīn Huā Dàjiǔdiàn) **6**
金花大酒店

Jim's Tibetan Guest House **12**
(Jí Mú Zàng Shì Jiǔdiàn)
吉姆藏式酒店

Landscape Hotel **3**
(Lán Líng Gé Jiǔdiàn)
兰林阁酒店

Yita Si

Pagoda
TA Travel Agent

To Xiaguan

DINING ◆
Café de Jack **8**
樱花园

Caffeine Club **5**
日烛谈

La Stella Pizzeria **4**
新星比萨房

Sweet Tooth **9**

Tibetan Café **7**
西藏咖啡馆

Xīn Rú Yuè Sù Shí Guǎn **1**
(Xīn Rú Yuè Vegetarian Restaurant)
心如悦素食馆

reconstructed during the Ming dynasty (1382). Today's Dali is the capital of the Bai Autonomous Prefecture (although it's run from Xiaguan). Located in a mountain valley at an elevation of 1,948m (6,496 ft.), Dali is sunny year-round, though winter nights can be chilly. The best times to visit are between February and October, when the majority of festivals take place.

ESSENTIALS
GETTING THERE Dali's transportation hub is **Xiaguan,** 15km (9 miles) to the south. From the Dali Airport another 15km (9 miles) northeast of Xiaguan, there are daily **flights** to Kunming (40 min.) and Xishuangbanna (50 min.). From the airport to Dali is about a 1-hour taxi ride, which will cost up to ¥100 ($13/£6.50). If you

need to purchase additional plane tickets, take a taxi into Xiaguan for about ¥40 to ¥50 ($5.20–$6.50/£2.60–£3.25) (or see the buses below) and go to the **Yunnan Airlines** ticket office (© 0872/231-5339), located next to the railway station across from the China Telecom building. There is another outlet in the Cang Shan Fandian at Cang Shan Lu 118. Travel agencies or your hotel concierge in Dali may be able to help you purchase airline tickets, but give them as much advance notice as possible and expect to pay a fee for the service.

A popular **train** route is the overnight sleeper from Kunming (8 hr.; ¥161/$20/£10 soft sleeper), which leaves Kunming at 10:34pm and arrives in Xiaguan at 6:22am. A later train departs at 11:16pm and arrives at 7:30am. From the railway station, bus no. 8 (45 min.; ¥3/40¢/20p) runs to the West Gate of the old city in Dali, while bus no. 10 runs into Xiaguan. Returning to Kunming, trains depart Xiaguan at 9pm and 10:02pm.

The expressway between Kunming and Xiaguan has brought the 9-hour journey down to just 4 hours. Back in the 1980s, this route took a good 2 days, although for Marco Polo it was nearly 2 weeks. Most Dali-bound buses actually stop in Xiaguan, which has several bus stations, but the main one that travelers will likely use the most is the confusingly named **Dali Qiche Keyun Zhan** (© 0872/218-9330) opposite Minsheng Plaza, on Jianshe Lu east of Renmin Lu. From here, luxury air-conditioned

The Bai

Occupying the Er Hai Lake region for some 3,000 to 4,000 years, the Bai people are among the oldest and the second-largest minority group in Yunnan. Over 80% of the Bai, now numbering close to 1.4 million, live in Dali and the surrounding villages and countryside in what is known as the Bai Autonomous Prefecture. More than most minority groups, the Bai, who've had a long illustrious history throughout the Nanzhao and Dali kingdoms, are one of the best adapted to the Han majority. The Bai—the "white"—revere the color, which is regarded as noble and is the main color of their traditional dress.

The Bai celebrate many festivals, the largest of which is Sanyue Jie (Third Month Festival), which had its origins more than 1,000 years ago when Buddhist monks and adherents gathered to celebrate Guanyin's (the Goddess of Mercy) appearance to the Bai. Today's festival, which starts on the 15th day of the third lunar month (usually Apr or early May), has become more secular as the Bai and other minorities from around the area gather in the foothills of Cang Shan (Green Mountains) for 5 days and nights of singing, dancing, wrestling, horse racing, and large-scale trading of everything from Tibetan-made felt hats and silk floss to horses and medicinal herbs. Raosanling, which involves a procession to three nearby temples, is held between the 23rd and the 25th days of the fourth lunar month (usually May). Huoba Jie (the Torch Festival) is held on the 24th day of the sixth lunar month (usually July) and involves the parading of flaming torches through homes and fields. There are also fireworks and dragon boat races.

Horse Trekking Takes Its Toll

The horse trek up the mountain to **Zhonghe Temple** has gone downhill. It is easy to feel sorry for these worn-out horses, but perhaps worse is the damage that is being done to the paths by constant erosion. Look closely as you pass overhead on the chairlift; notice how the paths have been worn more than 1m (3 ft.) deep in many places.

buses depart for Kunming (5 hr.; ¥104/$14/£6.75) every half-hour from 7:30am to 8:30pm; for Li Jiang (3 hr.; ¥55/$7.15/£3.60) at 8:30am, 2pm, 7pm, and 7:30pm; and for Xianggelila/Zhongdian (6 hr.; ¥88/$11/£5.70) at 9am and 3pm. There are also regular buses to Li Jiang (3 hr.; ¥55/$7.15/£3.60) every half-hour from 7:20am to 7:30pm; and to Jinghong (9 hr.; ¥168/$22/£11) at 7:30pm. A private bus company, **YNTAC** (© 0872/212-5221), operates luxury, air-conditioned, nonsmoking buses from Xiaguan's Cang Shan Fandian (Cang Shan Lu 118). The buses go to Kunming (4 hr.; ¥119/$16/£7.75) at 8:30am, 10:30am, 12:30pm, 1pm, 2:30pm, and 7:30pm; and to Li Jiang (3 hr.; ¥55/$7.15/£3.60) at 8:20am, 1:40pm, 2:40pm, and 7pm. From the center of Xiaguan to Dali, take bus no. 4 for ¥2 (25¢/15p) from the corner of Jianshe Lu and Renmin Lu.

In Dali, it's best to have a tourist cafe arrange your Dali-Kunming bus for ¥120 ($16/£7.80), as they will take care of sending you to Xiaguan for the transfer. There is usually a ¥5 (65¢/35p) fee for this service. Buses to Li Jiang also mostly originate out of Xiaguan. Again, the most hassle-free option is to have a travel agency or cafe book your ticket.

Note: If you get stuck in Xiaguan en route to Dali, the modern four-star **Manwan Dajiudian** at Canglang Lu (© 0872/218-8188; fax 0872/218-1742) is the nicest place to stay in town, with large comfortable rooms and bright, clean bathrooms. Standard rooms cost ¥500 ($65/£33); suites are ¥780 ($89/£44).

GETTING AROUND   The beauty of Dali is that the old town is so small that it's possible to walk from the North Gate (Bei Men) to the South Gate (Nan Men) in half an hour. To explore farther afield, **bikes** are the best way to get around and can be rented all along Bo'ai Lu for around ¥10 ($1.30/65p) a day. A **taxi** to nearby sights such as the Three Pagoda Park or the Cang Shan chairlift will run between ¥5 (65¢/35p) and ¥10 ($1.30/65p). Bus no. 2 runs from the Yaxing (Asia Star) Hotel to the dock at Cai Cun.

TOURS & GUIDES   Many of the Dali cafes provide a variety of tours, including a **boat trip** on Er Hai Lake which costs ¥20 ($2.60/£1.30) to ¥40 ($5.20/£2.60) per person, depending on group size; or **horseback riding** to a mountain monastery or local Bai village for about ¥40 ($5.20/£2.60) to ¥60 ($9.10/£4.55) per person. Local English-speaking guides can be hired through cafes for about ¥30 ($3.90/£1.95) to ¥50 ($6.50/£3.25) per hour, or around ¥200 ($26/£13) per day. The **Dali Travel Center,** next to the Golden Flower Hotel (Huguo Lu 76; © 0872/267-1282), offers the above services and also sells bus tickets to local destinations.

FAST FACTS

Banks, Foreign Exchange & ATMs   The **Bank of China** (open Mon–Fri 8am–6pm) is at Fuxing Lu 333. It has an outside ATM.

Value Free Maps

An American company produces excellent free maps for Dali, Yangshuo, and Guilin. Check out their website at **www.trax2.com** for details.

Internet Access Many cafes offer Internet access, mostly with free DSL, including the **Tibetan Cafe** at Renmin Lu 58. Dial-up is ✆ **163.**

Post Office The post office (open 8am–6pm) is at the corner of Fuxing Lu and Huguo Lu.

Visa Extension These are available in Xiaguan at the **Gonganju (PSB),** located at Tianbao Jie 21 (✆ **0872/216-6090;** open Mon–Fri 8:30–11am and 2:30–5pm).

EXPLORING DALI

Old town Dali, with its 9m-high (30-ft.) battlements, dates from the Ming dynasty (1368–1644), but the current wall was restored and extended only in 1998 as part of a project to gentrify Dali and attract tourists. From the top of the freshly painted Nan Cheng Men (South City Gate; ¥2/25¢/15p; open 8am–9pm), there are some lovely views of the town and the Cang Shan Mountains to the west. You can also walk along the restored city wall to Xi Men (Western Gate) and if you climb the stairs at the southwestern corner, you can avoid the small entrance fee.

Unlike Li Jiang, Dali's charm is that visitors still can see the original residents slowly going about their daily business, as if traveling back in time. Old people especially move slowly through the main thoroughfares like unwilling immigrants from a long-gone era, seeing things very differently from the way we do, but always responding positively to any attempt we might make to interact with them.

Foreigner Street is a photo-op must for domestic tourists and has expanded rapidly, but if you prefer not to be on display, **Renmin Lu** is a little more laid-back. The recently completed **Hong Longjing** is certainly the most photogenic part of the town while those looking for a little solitude might try the west wall, where local and international students practice their tai chi.

San Ta Si Gongyuan (Three Pagodas Park) ✈ About 2km (1¼ miles) northwest of town at the foot of the Cang Shan Mountains, Dali's most famous landmark has unfortunately become a massive tourist trap. Apart from the pagodas, a new temple and a museum have been added to the rear of the park but there is very little of interest inside them; nonetheless, in 5 years, ticket prices have increased more than tenfold, from ¥10 to ¥120 ($1.30–$16/65p–£7.80). This once open and informal garden is now sequestered behind thick red walls. The three pagodas were originally part of Chongwen Si monastery and have withstood several earthquakes through the years. The monastery itself was destroyed in the Qing dynasty, and what you see today dates only from 1999. The central pagoda, the statuesque 16-story, 69m-high (226-ft.) **Qianxun Ta,** resembling Xi'an's Small Goose Pagoda, was built first between 824 and 859 and is a hollow square brick structure with graceful eaves. Each floor has windows and niches containing Buddhist statues, many of them now defaced if not completely destroyed. The two smaller flanking octagonal pagodas were built later during the 12th century, and have 10 tiers each for a total height of 42m (138 ft.). The pagoda's doors and windows have been filled with concrete to prevent visitors from climbing inside. A popular photo op is from a small lake in the northeast corner of the park that captures the reflections of all three pagodas in a stunning tableau. Apart from that one particular vista, the rest of the site is overrated.

San Ta Gongyuan. Admission ¥120 ($16/£7.80). 8am–7pm.

SHOPPING

There seems to be an alarming trend in tourist towns like Dali toward fashion shops that sell only **military clothing,** usually with AK47s or M16s as display pieces— hardly surprising when you see that most children here start off with a wooden sword and soon graduate to plastic pistols and rifles.

Dali's growing season is almost never ending and **fruit** here is nothing like you see in the average supermarket. Watch out for peaches so large that they would frighten even Roald Dahl, sweet syrupy figs, and dozens of different apple-pear combinations.

Hundreds of shops in town sell Dali **marble,** famous for its beautiful cloudlike patterns and anticorrosive nature; the marble is now even more in demand because the practice of quarrying from the Cang Shan mountains has been officially prohibited. For now most of it comes in the unfortunate form of cheap tacky ashtrays, but a growing number of sculptors are setting up studios in the area, which could be promising. Other local specialties include **sliced walnut vases and lampshades,** but a block of **Pu'er tea** might be a little wiser. As always, comparison shop before you commit to anything: A piece of batik on Huguo Lu can sometimes cost 10% to 20% more than another along Fuxing Lu (or vice versa). For **batiks,** you can usually get better prices in the wholesale factories and workshops in Zhou Cheng (see below). In stores, it's not uncommon to bargain to half or two-thirds of the asking price.

MARKETS

A market visit is highly recommended for a sense of local color. Many of the markets around Dali are scheduled according to the lunar calendar, so check with the local cafes before you set out. Dali itself has a market every 7 days (usually on the 2nd, 9th, 16th, and 23rd days of the lunar month). Once the most popular, the Shaping market, held every Monday, has become a bit of a commercialized circus. The town of Wase on the eastern shores of Er Hai Lake also has a popular market held every 5 days from 9:30am to 4pm. Foodstuffs and agricultural produce are the main goods here, as the market still caters to locals instead of tourists. The easiest way to visit is to sign up with a local cafe that will arrange round-trip transportation for around ¥50 ($6.50/ £3.25) per person.

WHERE TO STAY

Accommodations can be scarce during festivals and also in June and July, so be sure to book your hotel ahead of time if you plan to visit then. Many guidebooks only list a handful of hideous backpacker haunts such as the MCA Guesthouse and the notorious numbered guesthouses. Although there have been many new developments including four- and five-star contenders on Bo'ai Lu, we are not all that impressed, finding only poor design and lack of character.

Feng Yue San Shui Kezhan (Yunnan Inn) *(Finds)* Just as the resident mongrel Big Diamond (Da Bao) is looking a bit shabby these days, this nonconformist guesthouse is starting to need some attention, too. Opened in 2003 by a successful Beijing-based artist, this eclectic selection of rooms clings to the surrounds of a converted studio by means of steel walkways and metal girders. And while most Chinese hotel rooms are arranged neatly off central corridors, rooms here go off in all different directions. There are few government-approved amenities, but this is more than made up for by eccentric touches, such as being able to watch the fish under your feet as you check your e-mail, or being treated to the unparalleled views from the enormous rooftop. Best of all **Hong Longjing** is right on your doorstep.

Hong Longjing 3, next to the Yu Yuan Hotel. (C) 0872/266-3741. 10 units. ¥80–¥120 ($10–$16/£5.20–£7.80) standard room. No credit cards. *In room:* TV.

The Golden Flower Hotel (Jin Hua Dajiudian)

Still the best location in town, but with dated, ugly rooms and poor service, it no longer deserves to be the first choice for foreign study groups, which now prefer Jim's Tibetan Guest House after long field expeditions in the wilds of Yunnan. Room nos. 2023 or 3023 are a decent size, but the furniture is dark and clunky with uncomfortable marble inlays.

Fuxing Lu 349. (C) 0872/267-3343. Fax 0872/267-0573. www.goldenflowerhotel.com. 150 units. ¥288–¥388 ($38–$50/£19–£25) standard room. Up to 50% discounts (low season). No credit cards. **Amenities:** Ticket service; laundry. *In room:* A/C, TV.

Jim's Tibetan Guest House (Ji Mu Zang Shi Jiudian) 🌟🌟🌟

At press time, this was one of the best hotel choices in town. The location, a bit off the beaten track, is more than made up for by the levels of service, interior decoration, and imagination on the part of the owners, one Kampa Tibetan, and the other Dutch. Rooms are bright and colorful as well as comfortable, but often booked solid with Western tour groups. This is also a great place to eat. For four people or more, go for the Tibetan smorgasbord at ¥30 ($3.90/£1.95) per person. We counted at least 16 dishes as well as a delicious dessert. You may want to keep away from Jim's No. 1 Whiskey, a local moonshine whose harshness is disguised by a few local herbs, but would probably be better in a tractor carburetor than in some unwary tourist's stomach.

Yu Xiu Lu Zhong Duan 13, Lu Yu Xiaoqu. (C) 0872/267-7824. Fax 0872/266-1822. www.china-travel.nl. 30 units. ¥180 ($23/£12) standard room. No credit cards.

Landscape Hotel (Lan Ling Ge Jiudian)

A slightly more expensive option than the Golden Flower, the beautiful Landscape is an agglomeration of old city houses that have been joined together to form a 163-room hotel incorporating a number of traditional Bai construction styles. With some of the most ornately decorated screen walls in the town, the Landscape offers designs surprises at every turn, from a bubbling stream to a functioning well. This is a very popular option with the more upmarket tour groups.

Yu' er Lu 96. (C) 0872/266-6188. Fax 0872/266-6189. 163 units. ¥600 ($91/£46) standard room; ¥1,080 ($136/£68) suite. Up to 45% discount (low season). All rates subject to 15% service charge. AE, DC, MC, V. **Amenities:** Laundry. *In room:* A/C, TV, minibar (select rooms), hair dryer.

WHERE TO DINE

Baba is sold all around northwest Yunnan, where it mostly consists of a piece of flat rice dough that's grilled or fried and flavored with salty and spicy seasonings. In Dali, the dough is stuffed with salted vegetables, sweet sauce, chili sauce, crushed peanuts, and *youtiao* (fried, salty doughnut) and grilled to tender perfection. This "Dali calzone" is one of the most popular breakfast items, often sold on street corners like Huguo Lu and Fuxing Lu. Other typical local dishes include *shaguo yu* (stewed fish casserole) and the Bai specialty, *rushan* (milk fan), a delicious local goat's cheese sliced in thin layers and fried until "rubbery."

The foreigners' cafes clustered along Huguo Lu and Bo'ai Lu serve inexpensive and generally tasty Western, Chinese, Bai, and Tibetan meals. **Cafe de Jack** at Bo'ai Lu 82 (© **0872/267-1572**) has recently been refurbished but as yet the reliability of the menu does not match the new decor. Jack is also the owner of **La Stella Pizzeria** at Huguo Lu 58 (© **0872/266-2881**), which serves an excellent pizza focaccia and does a very generous goat's cheese and tomato salad.

Also popular is the **Tibetan Cafe** on Renmin Lu (© **0872/266-4177**), which used to be a lot cozier until they recently invested in a row of PCs to supply free Internet. Even so, this is still the best place to start the day; the unbeatable Dalai Lama's Breakfast Slam consists of Tibetan oats, fresh fruit, yogurt, and jasmine tea. New to the scene, **Sweet Tooth,** at the corner of Renmin Lu and Bo'ai Lu (open Mon–Sat 10am–10pm), is wildly popular with foreigners but sees very few domestic customers. Set up by an American entrepreneur to provide jobs for Dali's deaf community, Sweet Tooth's traditional chocolate chip cookies are just what a stressed traveler needs; their ugly brownies and huge slabs of Oreo cheesecake will make you wonder if you are still in China.

While generally we were not impressed by many of the copycat eateries on the local Foreigner's Street, the one exception was the newly opened **Clock Tower** on Yang Ren Jie Zhong Xin Guang Chang (© **0872/267-1883**). Three stories consisting of a ground floor kitchen, a second floor dining area overlooking the local croquet ground and a rooftop bar. Western breakfasts are reliable and the salads full of local produce are very refreshing.

To get away from the tourist crowds, take a taxi for ¥10 ($1.30/65p) or the no. 19 bus for ¥1 (15¢/10p) up to the rear ticket office of the Three Pagodas (San Ta Gongyuan), where the Xin Ru Yue Vegetarian Restaurant (© **0872/266-6516**), owned by Taiwanese TV celebrity, Lin Xin Ru hosts lunchtime tour buses for its bread and butter, and so the place is very quiet in the evening, with plenty of surplus staff, all willing to bend over backward. The English translations on the menu are clear and accurate, and although the exterior is a very pleasing Bai courtyard, the interior is stark but efficient Cantonese style. I especially liked the orange sauce to go with the deep-fried dishes, such as the vegetarian shrimp balls or the banana spring rolls.

AROUND DALI

Please turn to appendix A for Chinese translations of key locations.

CANG SHAN (GREEN MOUNTAINS)

Running down the west side of Dali, the 42km-long (25-mile) Cang Shan mountain range with its 19 peaks (a number of them permanently snow-covered), 18 streams, and acres of verdant forests, is well worth exploring. The easiest way to ascend the mountain is by chairlift, a lovely ride ¥28 ($3.65/£1.80) up, ¥20 ($2.60/£1.30) down, that offers some of the loveliest vistas of the old town and the shimmering blue Er Hai Lake in the distance. (From the western gate of the old town, head north until you see the sign for the chairlift; or take a taxi for ¥10/$1.30/65p.) At the chairlift's upper terminus is **Zhonghe Si,** a not particularly memorable temple. The sign for the **Highlander Guest House** (© **0872/266-1599;** www.higherland.com/index2.htm) says 100m (328 ft.), what it doesn't say is that it's 100m (328 ft.) straight up. At the

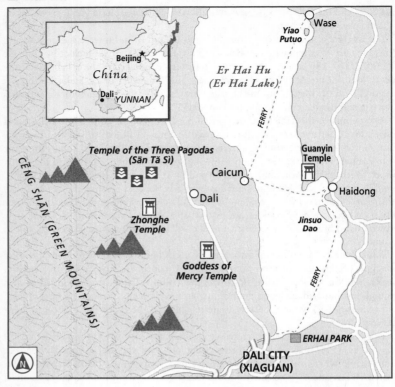

moment the place has superb potential and will one day be a star attraction, but not yet. Several trails branch out from Zhonghe Si. One option if you don't have time to make a day of it is the trek through pretty terrain to **Fengyan Dong (Phoenix Cave),** which takes you through the back of Longquan Mountain (about an hour each way). There's also a vigorous 11km (7-mile), 4½- to 5-hour hike to **Gantong Si,** a temple first built in 900 on the southern slope of Yingsheng Peak. The road down the mountain from Gantong Temple will take you back to the main road, from where you can take a taxi or bus no. 4 back to Dali. Another trail leads to the lovely **Qingbi Xi** in the valley between Malong and Shengying peaks. Flowing through three large ponds, this stream eventually empties into Er Hai.

ER HAI HU (ER HAI LAKE)

East of Dali and north of Xiaguan, Er Hai Hu, literally named after its resemblance to a human ear *(er),* is one of the seven largest freshwater lakes in China and the second largest in Yunnan after Dian Chi in Kunming. Originating in the Heigu Shan mountains to the northwest and fed partially by the 18 streams of Cang Shan, the lake spans 42km (25 miles) from north to south, and 7km (4 miles) from east to west, and has an average depth of 10m (33 ft.). There are many settlements and towns scattered around the lake, along with some tourist traps on the eastern side. **Warning:** Some recent travelers have reported that the lake was unsafe for swimming as it contained the schistosomiasis (bilharzia) parasite; unfortunately, accurate up-to-date information on the situation is hard to come by.

However, a **boat ride** ✈ on the beautiful lake is one of the highlights of a visit to Dali. Several ferries cross the lake, from Longkan to Haidong, Cai Cun to Wase, and Xiaguan to Jinsuo Dao. Giant tourist boats charge ¥90 ($11/£5.50) to make a 3½- to 4-hour run of the lake from the Taoyuan Matou (dock) in Zhou Cheng to Xiaguan, stopping along the way at **Putuo Dao, Guanyin Ge (Guanyin Pavilion)**, and **Jinsuo Dao**, an island full of caves and caverns and inhabited by Bai fishermen. You can also negotiate with smaller private boats, which charge an average of ¥100 ($13/£6.50) to ¥200 ($26/£13) for the round-trip; or get a travelers' cafe in town to help you with any special arrangements.

About 7km (4 miles) north of Xizhou, the village of **Zhou Cheng** is famous for its **tie-dyed batiks** ✈. The minute you step off the bus, you'll be approached by Bai women who will invite you to visit their batik workshops. This is worth considering, as you can often pick up batik tablecloths or shirts for considerably less than you would pay in the shops in Dali—subject to bargaining, of course. There is also a local **market** in the center of town; uphill from there, part of the old town is worth exploring. Catch an Eryuan-bound bus from either Dali or Xizhou.

10 Li Jiang ✈✈

Yunnan Province, 527km (316 miles) NW of Kunming, 150km (90 miles) NW of Dali

Located in the northwest part of Yunnan Province, this capital of the Li Jiang Naxi Autonomous County (pop. 302,000) is home to the Naxi people (who constitute almost 60% of its population) and to a smaller number of Bai, Tibetan, Yi, Mosu, and Han peoples. Though its history dates from the Warring States (475–221 B.C.), its most influential period was when it was governed by Naxi chieftains during the Ming dynasty (1368–1644).

In February 1996, an earthquake hit Li Jiang, killing over 300 people, injuring 17,000 more, and destroying 186,000 homes, much of the city. Amazingly, many of the traditional Naxi houses held up quite well, leading the government in its reconstruction process to pour millions of yuan into replacing concrete buildings with traditional wooden Naxi architecture. The World Bank came up with rebuilding funds, and Li Jiang was conferred with the ultimate imprimatur (some would say the kiss of death) as a UNESCO World Heritage town in 1999. All this attention plus the construction of a new airport and hotels has turned it into a major tourist destination with outrageous prices at every turn. Li Jiang's old town, with its cobblestone streets, gurgling streams, and Naxi architecture, thankfully preserves a modicum of traditional ways, but as Han merchants move in to cater to hordes of stampeding tourists, many of the Naxi who still live there (about 6,000 households) are finding their old way of life being challenged.

Located on the road to Tibet in a region widely regarded as being one of the most beautiful in the world, Li Jiang also offers a plethora of fascinating side trips that can easily take up to a week or more of your time. Li Jiang (elev. 2,340m/7,800 ft.) has a pleasant climate year-round with average temperatures in the spring, summer, and fall ranging between 60°F and 80°F (16°C–27°C). Spring and fall are the best times to visit, as the summer months are unbelievably crowded with Chinese tourists, busier even than the big-city shopping areas.

ESSENTIALS

GETTING THERE From Li Jiang's airport, 24km (15 miles) and a 30-minute taxi ride (around ¥80/$10/£5.20) southwest of town, there are daily **flights** to Kunming (50 min.) as well as weekly flights to Guangzhou (3 hr.), Shanghai (4½ hr.), and Xishuangbanna (30 min.). Tickets can be bought at the **CAAC/Yunnan Airlines** ticket office at Fuhui Lu, Minhang Zhan (✆ **0888/516-1289**). CAAC airport buses (¥10/$1.30/65p) depart from the office 90 minutes before scheduled departures. There is another CAAC office on the first floor of the Li Jiang Dajiudian at Xin Dajie (✆ **0888/518-0280;** open 8:30am–6:30pm).

Though the flight from Kunming to Li Jiang only takes a half-hour or so, road transportation in last decade has improved exponentially, reducing a 20-hour journey to just 5 hours once the new Dali bypass opens in spring 2006. From the main **long-distance bus station** at the southern end of Minzu Lu (✆ **0888/512-1106**), **buses** run to Xiaguan (3 hr.; ¥55/$7.15/£3.60) every half-hour from 7:10am to 6:30pm; express buses to Xiaguan depart at 8:20am, 11:30am, and 2:30pm. Express buses run to Kunming (6 hr.; ¥168/$22/£11) at 8:20am, 9:20am, 11:20am, and 3:20pm; a sleeper bus to Kunming (9 hr.; ¥145/$19/£9.45) runs every half-hour from 5:30 to 8:30pm. Buses also run to Zhongdian/Xianggelila, passing Qiaotou (3 hr.; ¥35/$4.55/£2.30) every hour from 7:30am to 4pm; to Jinjiang/Sichuan (9 hr.; ¥88/$11/£5.70) at 7:10am, 8:30am, 12:30pm, 2pm, and 6pm; and to Ninglang (4 hr.; ¥42/$6.75/£3.40) every hour from 7:50am to 3:30pm. A private bus company, **YNTAC** (✆ **0888/512-5492**), operates luxury air-conditioned buses to Xiaguan (3 hr.; ¥50/$6.50/£3.25) at 8:30am, 9am, 10:30am, and 5pm; and to Kunming (6 hr.; ¥168/$22/£11) at 8:30am, 9am, and 10:30am. YNTAC buses depart from the Naxi Dajiudian, at Nan Guojing Lu about 1km (⅔ mile) west of the bus station.

GETTING AROUND The old town, off-limits to motor traffic, can be comfortably toured on foot. **Taxis** cost ¥6 (80¢/40p) for 3km (2 miles), then ¥1.60 (20¢/10p) per kilometer. From midnight to 7am, in-town taxis charge ¥10 ($1.30/65p) per trip. **Bikes** can be rented from several cafes in the old town and also in Mao Square at Ali Baba (✆ **0139/8704-7896**) for around ¥15/$1.95/£1 a day.

TOURS & GUIDES Many of the cafes and hostels in old Li Jiang have travel agencies that provide day tours and air and bus tickets. **The Nice Hiking Club,** Xinyi Jie, Jishan Xiang 17 (✆ **0888/517-5432**), has photocopied maps of the locale that can help with backpackers' routes. **Yunnan International Travel Service,** across the way at Jishan Xiang 47 (✆ **0888/512-0653**), frequently organizes hikes to Tiger Leaping Gorge and Wen Hai, skiing trips to nearby Haba Mountain and Jade Dragon Snow Mountain, and overland trips by Land Cruiser into Tibet (approximately ¥4,500/$585/£293 per person for transportation and Tibet permit, based on four-person minimum). For the less adventurous, Old Li Jiang has a **Tourist Consultation Service** just inside the northern entrance on Xinyi Jie (✆ **0888/511-6666**), which offers more sedate day tours of the surrounding areas (in Chinese only).

FAST FACTS

Banks, Foreign Exchange & ATMs The main branch of the **Bank of China** (open Mon–Fri 8:30am–5:30pm) is on Xin Daje south of Fuhui Lu and has an ATM. In the old town, the **Industrial and Commercial Bank of China (ICBC)** across from the post office (open Mon–Fri 8:30am–5pm) can exchange cash and traveler's checks.

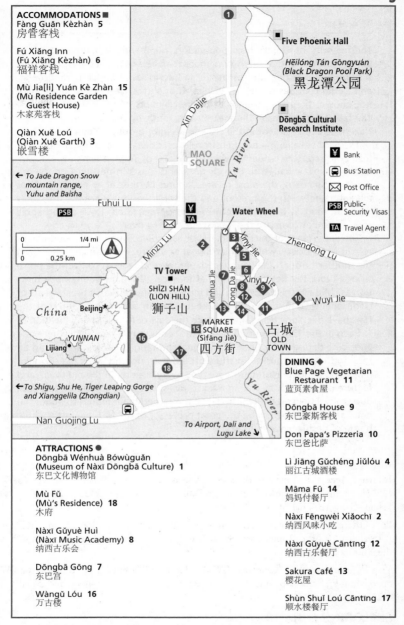

The Naxi

The majority of China's Naxi population, numbering just under 290,000, lives in Yunnan, and of this group, more than half reside in the Li Jiang Naxi Autonomous County; the rest reside in Zhongdian, Ninglang, Yongsheng, and Deqin counties to the northwest. Though the Naxi's exact origins are not known, they are thought to be descendants of the ancient nomadic Tibetan Qiang tribes of Qinghai. Driven south by northern invaders, the Naxi have been resident in the Li Jiang area for around 1,400 years.

The Naxi believe in a polytheistic religion called *dongba* (meaning "wise man" or "scripture reader"), which is a blend of Tibetan lamaism, Daoism, and shamanistic beliefs in various gods and spirits in nature. *Dongba* are also Naxi shamans, the most revered figures because they not only act as mediators between the present and the spirit world but are the only ones who can read, write, and interpret the approximately 1,400 pictographic characters that comprise the Naxi script created over 1,000 years ago.

The importance of the shaman notwithstanding, women play a dominant role in Naxi society, which is matrilineal in nature. Inheritance passes from the mother through the youngest daughter, and women control the purse strings, work the fields, and trade at markets. The men traditionally function as child-raisers, gardeners, and musicians. The revival in recent years of traditional Naxi music has helped keep alive an ancient art form that the Naxi have been practicing since before the days of Kublai Khan's invasion of Li Jiang in the 13th century. Many of the songs, rarely heard anywhere else and some dating as far back as the Song and Tang dynasties, are played on rare and unusual musical instruments several hundred years old. Dongba music and dance performances are held every evening in the old town, and feature prominently as well in Naxi festivals, including the traditional Sanduo Festival held on the eighth day of the second lunar month to honor the god Sanduo, believed to be the great protector of the Naxi against a whole horde of pestilence and disasters.

Internet Access   A number of cafes in the old town offer Internet service for ¥2 (25¢/15p) an hour. One of the most reliable is the **Dongba House Inn,** Xinyi Jie Jishan Xiang 16. Dial-up is © **163.**

Post Office   The main post office in new Li Jiang (open 8am–8pm) is on Xin Dajie. A smaller post office (open 8am–8pm) is in the old town at Sifang Jie just south of the Xinhua Bookstore.

Visa Extensions   The **Gonganju (PSB)** is located at Fuhui Lu (© **0888/518-8437;** open Mon–Fri 8am–noon and 2:30–5:30pm in summer, 8:30am–noon and 2–5:30pm otherwise).

EXPLORING LI JIANG
OLD TOWN ★★

When visitors and travel guide writers gush about Li Jiang, they're really referring to its raison d'être, the **old town** *(gucheng),* built over 800 years ago during the Southern

---

Tips **Lost in Li Jiang**

If you ever get lost in the old town, just find a stream and walk against the current, as it will invariably lead you back to an entrance of the town.

Song dynasty. A delightful maze of twisting cobblestone streets and Naxi-style homes but more and more shops, usually of the souvenir variety, the old town still affords glimpses of traditional Naxi life as residents go about their daily lives despite the staggering crowds and the increasingly commercial tenor of the whole place.

Unlike many ancient towns in China, Li Jiang does not have a city wall. It is said that the first ruling family of Li Jiang, surnamed Mu, prohibited the building of a wall around the old town because drawing a box around the character of *mu* turned it into the character *kun*, meaning "difficulty," and was therefore not auspicious. What the old town does have, however, is a web of flowing canals fed by the Yuquan springs in today's Black Dragon Pool to the north. These streams often flow into several three-pit **wells** scattered around the old town with designated pits for drinking, washing vegetables, and washing clothes. You can see such a well at the **Baima Long Tan** in the south of town. The **Yican Quan,** for drinking water only, can be found on Mishi Xiang next to the Blue Page Vegetarian Restaurant. The old town used to have several water mills as well, but the only one standing today is a reconstructed **water wheel** at the old town entrance. In the center of town is **Market Square (Sifang Jie),** ringed with shops and restaurants. During the day, Naxi women come here to trade, and on certain evenings, residents will gather here and break into spontaneous circle dances.

From Market Square, a cobblestone path leads uphill along the eastern flanks of **Shizi Shan (Lion Hill),** which separates the old town from the new. This area, known as Huang Shan, is one of the region's oldest neighborhoods and is a lovely place to wander, as it's a relatively tourist-free zone. At the top of the hill is the 33m-tall (108-ft.) **Wangu Lou;** admission is ¥15 ($1.95/£1) and it's open from dawn to dusk. Each meter represents 10,000 of Li Jiang's 330,000 people; it is said to be the tallest wooden pagoda in China. Supported by 16 massive 22m-high (72-ft.) pillars made from old local wood, the square pagoda has 13 soaring eaves (representing the 13 peaks of the Jade Dragon Snow Mountain range) and over 2,300 Dongba designs carved into the structure. There are some stunning **views** ★★ of the old town, new town, and majestic Jade Dragon Snow Mountain range from the top.

Anchoring the southern part of the old town is **Mu Fu (Mu's Residence; ¥35/ $4.55/£2.30; open 9am–6pm).** The former home of the Naxi ruling family, which ruled Li Jiang for 22 generations until 1723, the residence was actually completely destroyed in the Qing dynasty (1644–1911) and, until the earthquake of 1996, the houses of ordinary Naxi stood in the palace's stead. Post-earthquake authorities apparently determined that World Bank rebuilding funds would be better justified by an imperial residence that could attract legions of tourists rather than by banal domestic housing; the result is the sprawling residence you see today. Stepped into the side of Lion Hill are six main halls separated by courtyards said to resemble those of the Forbidden City, including a meeting hall where the clan chiefs met and a library of Dongba writings. From the back of the residence, steps lead up the hill to Wangu Lou.

Dongba Wenhua Bowuguan (Museum of Naxi Dongba Culture) ★ This museum features exhibits of Naxi clothing and jewelry, Dongba pictographic script, unearthed artifacts from old Li Jiang, and a display claiming the region is the real Shangri-La. Explanations are in English. At the museum shop you can have a piece of Dongba calligraphy drawn for you by an 85-year-old Dongba shaman for about ¥100 ($13/£6.50).

Heilong Tan. Admission ¥5 (65¢/35p). 8:30am–6pm.

Heilong Tan Gongyuan (Black Dragon Pool Park) 🏛 About 1.5km (1 mile)

north of the old town, this park, which contains the source of much of the old town's water, also offers Li Jiang's most famous photo op: the distant snowcapped Jade Dragon Snow Mountain fronted by the park's Deyue Lou (Moon Embracing Pavilion), and Wukong Qiao (Five Arch Bridge). In the eastern section is the three-story Ming dynasty Wufeng Lou (Five Phoenix Hall), with soaring eaves meant to resemble flying phoenixes. Also here is the Dongba Cultural Research Institute (Dongba Wenhua Yanjiusuo), where you can see experts translating Dongba pictographs.

Xin Daje. Admission ¥60 ($9.10/£4.55). 6:30am–8:30pm.

WHERE TO STAY

While new Li Jiang has more upscale hotels with modern facilities, none of them can match the charming ambience and coziness of the old town's traditional Naxi guesthouses and hotels. There are plenty of inns offering basic dormitory-style accommodations, but a notch above these guesthouses are several hotels also housed in traditional Naxi buildings, although the lack of windows makes them feel a bit dark. The **Fu Xiang Inn (Fu Xiang Kezhan)** 🏛 at Jishan Xiang 24, Xinyi Jie (ⓒ **0888/ 515-2525;** fax 0888/515-2526), is one such property. Situated just beyond a small stream that seems to be the center of activity for the whole neighborhood, this courtyard inn has 25 passable rooms (¥180/$23/£12), but with big, wide internal balconies. Some rooms even have Jacuzzis, but even this luxury does not match the pleasure of sipping tea under the crimson glow of traditional *denglong* lanterns. Operated by the same owners is the **Fang Guan Kezhan** at Jishan Xiang 58, Xinyi Jie (ⓒ **0888/510- 2118**); its 19 comfortable rooms have air-conditioning (and central heating during the winter) and private bathrooms for ¥280 ($38/£19).

Mu Jia Yuan Ke Zhan 🏛 Tucked away near the fire station, the staff here was

extremely welcoming, even though business seemed to be only just making it. Although rooms are a little dark as is the Naxi courtyard style, all rooms have their own PC and there is a fantastic rooftop patio that looks out on the old town. There is a free airport pickup for reserved guests

Guang Yi Jie, Guang Bi Xiang 1 (Next to Mu Fu Residence). ⓒ 0888/518-1816. www.ljmjy.com. 33 units. ¥130 ($17/£8.45) standard room. No credit cards.

Qian Xue Lou (Qian Xue Garth) 🏛 With its imposing location, the Garth seems

to dominate the entire main square, and it is difficult to find any courtyards more pleasant than these. Rooms are clean and comfortable, but it is the courtyards where you can sit outside that are more important in Li Jiang. Staff can be somewhat elusive, spread out among all the courtyards, private dining rooms, and small gardens. The best part is the viewing terrace that looks directly out over the water wheels and the main square.

Shuang Shi Duan, Xin Hua Jie (north entrance of old town Li Jiang). ⓒ 0888/515-1816. Fax 0888/515-1789. 123 units. ¥480 ($62/£31) standard room; ¥640 ($83/£42) deluxe room; from ¥960 ($125/£62) suite. 20%–30% discounts. AE, DC, MC, V. **Amenities:** 2 restaurants; bar; lounge; concierge; business center; forex; shopping arcade; salon; 24-hr. room service; laundry/dry cleaning. *In room:* A/C, satellite TV, minibar, hair dryer, safe.

WHERE TO DINE

Old town Li Jiang offers plenty of friendly cafes and family-operated restaurants catering to foreign travelers with Western, Chinese, and Naxi food at prices that have recently increased so much they almost match those of the big cities. The classic **Mama Fu** (© 0888/512-2285), located on Xinyi Jie just north of the Market Square, serves some of the best pizza around and is also famous for its homemade breads and apple pie. Sit outside by the running stream and watch old Li Jiang go by. The **Blue Page Vegetarian Restaurant** at Xinyi Jie, Mishi Xiang 69 (© 0888/518-5206), is a quiet, cozy place with fresh flowers that serves excellent vegetarian fare such as a mushroom and vegetable pie, vegetarian burgers, and apple crumble. The **Dongba House** at Xinyi Jie, Jishan Xiang 16 (© 0888/517-5431), offers Tibetan cuisine along with Naxi, Chinese, and Western food, and some of the best people-watching in the old town. On the west side of the old town, the always-crowded **Sakura Cafe** at Xinhua Jie, Cuiwen Duan 123 (© 0888/518-7619), has everything from delicious Korean *bibimbap* (rice with vegetables and meat) to an Israeli chicken-cutlet dinner.

Don Papa's Pizzeria ★★★ *Finds* WESTERN   This is an oasis of sweetness for those who have overloaded themselves on goat cheese, yak butter, and that local specialty, deep-fried insects. Run by a French expat with excellent culinary skills, this somewhat hidden corner store has a great balcony upon which to enjoy a reliable Western breakfast. For the rest of the day, customers can choose from strawberry tartlets, chocolate croissants, and fresh fruit Danish. At dinnertime, among the excellent Italian entrees is a delicious four-cheese pizza, featuring goat cheese, Li Jiang cheese, mozzarella, and Parmesan.

Xinyi Jie, Jishan Xiang 3 © 0888/518-3967. Meal for 2 ¥50–¥150 ($6.50–$20/£3.25–£9.75). No credit cards. 8:30am–11:30pm.

Naxi Fengwei Xiaochi ★ NAXI   This no-frills restaurant serves some of the best local fare in all of Li Jiang; witness the crowds that throng here every night. You can dine outdoors by a running stream or on the second floor. Naxi favorites include *jidou chao mifan* (fried rice with soy bean), *Li Jiang baba* (a local baked pastry that can be ordered sweet or salty), and *zha rubing* (fried goat cheese). If you're with a group of five or more, ask for the *fengwei can,* which consists of 10 to 16 special Naxi dishes. Service is brusque during peak meal times from 6 to 8pm. The restaurant has a second outlet two doors down.

Xinhua Jie, Shuang Shi Duan 22. © 0888/518-9591. Meal for 2 ¥20–¥40 ($2.60–$5.20/£1.30–£2.60). No credit cards. 7:30am–11pm.

Shun Shui Lou Canting NAXI   This is one of the best locations that we found in town, right beside one of the numerous streams, and yet another good choice for experimenting with the more bizarre tastes of Naxi food such as *shu wa* (frog-skin fungus) or the numerous types of deep-fried insects that are available here. The English menu is a starting point, but as this place is popular among Cantonese diners, see what everybody else is trying before making your own choices.

Bai Sui Fang, 80, Xinyi Jie. © 0888/5129029. Meal for 2 ¥40–¥80 ($5.20–$10/£2.60–£5.20). No credit cards. 7:30am–11:30pm.

LI JIANG AFTER DARK

Attending a Naxi concert is one of the more popular evening activities in Li Jiang. The original Naxi Orchestra at the **Naxi Guyue Hui (Naxi Music Academy)** is led by esteemed Naxi ethnomusicologist Xuan Ke, who delivers introductions and explanations to the music and instruments in both English and Chinese. Nightly performances are held at the Naxi Concert Hall (Dong Dajie) from 8 to 9:30pm. Purchase tickets for ¥120 ($16/£7.80) to ¥160 ($21/£10) ahead of time; performances are frequently sold out. Directly across the street, the **Dongba Gong** offers a second option for Naxi song and dance performances at 8pm. Tickets are ¥35 ($4.55/£2.30) or ¥50 ($6.50/£3.25)

AROUND LI JIANG

Please turn to appendix A for Chinese translations of key locations.

YUFENG SI

Located about 13km (8 miles) northwest of Li Jiang at the foot of Jade Dragon Snow Mountain, this small lamasery belonging to the Scarlet Sect of Tibetan Buddhism was first built in 1660. Today it is best known for its *wanduo shancha* (10,000-flower camellia tree). Formed from the merger of two trees planted by monks between 1465 and 1487, the camellia tree is said to bloom 20 times between March and June, bearing a total of 20,000 blossoms! If you're cycling here (2 hr.), follow Xianggelila Da Dao out of town. About 5km (3 miles) past the town of Baisha, take a left at **Yushui Zhai (Jade Water Village)**, go past the **Dongba Village,** and continue on to Yufeng Temple.

YU HU (NGULUKO) 𝒶𝒶

Just before the Dongba Village is the turnoff for the lovely, quiet, tour group–free village that was Joseph Rock's home in the 1920s and 1930s. The Austrian-born botanist and anthropologist, whose *Ancient Nakhi Kingdom of Southwest China* is the definitive account of Naxi culture and language, is a local legend who lived in Li Jiang for 27 years. Following the turnoff—which you can't miss, as large letters proclaim FOLLOW ROCKER'S TRAIL TO SHANGRI-LA (the misspelled name turns out to be an English transliteration of the literal Chinese pronunciation of "Rock," or "Luoke")—take a right at the first fork for about 3km (2 miles), then follow signs directing you to the village where all the houses are built entirely from large stones and rocks. **Joseph Rock's former residence (Luoke Guju Chenlieguan;** ¥10/$1.30/65p; open 8am–6pm) is a two-story wooden house where Rock lived with his Naxi assistant Li Siyu. Rock's quarters on the second floor contain his original twin bed, his suitcase, a folding table, two chairs, and kerosene lamps. A newly built exhibition hall next to the residence has displays of Rock's gun, clothing, pictographic cards used to help Rock learn the Dongba language, and Rock's own photographs of Naxi funeral ceremonies and festivals.

BAISHA 𝒶

Ten kilometers (6 miles) northwest of Li Jiang, 1km (½ mile) off the main road to Jade Dragon Snow Mountain, this dusty historic town is most famous these days for its Ming- and Qing-dynasty **temple frescoes,** which were painted by Naxi, Tibetan, Bai, and Han artists and hence incorporate elements of Buddhism, Lamaism, and Daoism. The largest fresco, found on the front wall of the **Dabaoji Palace** (¥8/$1/50p; open 7:30am–6pm), is a gorgeous Ming dynasty mural of Buddha preaching to his disciples.

In the street behind the Dabaoji Palace, visitors can also find Baisha's most famous personality, Dr. Ho (He), at his Chinese herbal clinic. Immortalized by travel writer Bruce Chatwin as the "Taoist physician in the Jade-Dragon Mountains of Li Jiang," and visited by countless journalists and curious travelers ever since, Dr. Ho can dispense herbs for any ailment and will happily sell you some of his special tea made from homegrown herbs, which has many fans if you believe all the scrapbooks of letters from grateful patients.

For those more interested in local history than local celebrity, the plain that the bus crosses to get to the village conceals the remains of the airstrip used by the Flying Tigers. Unfortunately, there is not much left to look at, but a nose around might inspire the amateur archaeologist in you.

YULONG XUESHAN (JADE DRAGON SNOW MOUNTAIN) ✦✦✦

This magnificent 35km-long (21-mile) mountain range framing Li Jiang has become an expensive day out. The tallest of the mountain's 13 peaks is the daunting **Shanzifeng** (**Fan Peak;** elev. 5,596m/18,355 ft.), perennially snowcapped and climbed for the first time only in 1963 by a research team from Beijing. Today's visitors have a number of options for exploring the mountain. All require you to pay a ¥120 ($16/£7.80) entrance fee to the Jade Dragon Snow Mountain Scenic Area, about 30km (20 miles) north of town. Many tourists visit as part of an organized tour. To get out here on your own, take a bus for Baoshan or Daju. The no. 7 bus goes from Red Sun Square (Hong Tai Yang Guang Chang) opposite the Mao statue to Jade Dragon Mountain but the correct price is ¥7 (90¢/50p), not the ¥10 ($1.30/65p) that they try to wring out of ignorant tourists.

The most popular visit is a round-trip cable-car ride for ¥180 ($23/£12) from the village just inside the main gate to **Bingchuan Gongyuan (Glacier Park).** If possible, purchase your ticket in town the day before at the Jade Dragon Snow Mountain ticket office at Xianggelila Da Dao and Xiangshan Dong Lu, as ornery ticket attendants at the reception center will sometimes insist you cannot purchase a ticket on the spot. Buses for ¥10 ($1.30/65p) round-trip will transport you the 4km (2½ miles) from the reception center to the cable car terminus. From here it's a two-section ride on a chairlift to the foot of Fan Peak. You can climb a walkway all the way up to 4,480m (14,700 ft.), where visitors are greeted with a stunning view of glaciers and with ice caverns. If you feel any altitude sickness, Chinese vendors will happily sell you an oxygen bag for around ¥30 ($3.90/£1.95).

About 20 minutes north of the reception center past the Baishui He River, a 10-minute ride on a chairlift for ¥60 ($9.10/£4.55) round-trip and a 30-minute ramble through groves of spruce and pine trees leads you to **Yunshan Ping (Spruce Meadow,** elev. 3,206m/10,515 ft.). During the annual Torch Festival, young Naxi men and women come here to pray for eternal love.

The third cable car, which costs ¥120 ($16/£7.80) round-trip and takes you another 20km (12 miles) north, arrives at **Maoniu Ping (Yak Meadow,** elev. 3,500m/11,480 ft.), the least visited of the three spots. The meadow has grazing yaks, blooming flowers (in spring and summer), and a number of hiking possibilities. One of the more popular routes leads to Xuehua Hu (Snow Flake Lake), which brilliantly captures the crystalline reflection of the surrounding mountains.

TIGER LEAPING GORGE (HUTIAO XIA) ✦

Often billed as one of the most spectacular sights in Li Jiang and a must-hike for trekkers, the 30km-long (18-mile) Tiger Leaping Gorge, which sits between the Jade Dragon Snow Mountain of Li Jiang and the Haba Snow Mountain of Zhongdian to the north, is a tad overrated. To be sure, this canyon, reaching a depth of over 3,000m (9,842 ft.), is pretty enough, and occasionally breathtaking; as treks go, it is a moderately interesting, occasionally strenuous, and infrequently dangerous trek taking 2 to 3 days, but by no stretch of the imagination is it the ultimate of sights, as its renown may have led some to expect.

The gorge is divided into upper *(shang hutiao)*, middle *(zhong hutiao)*, and lower *(xia hutiao)* sections, with two main entrances, one at the town of Qiaotou at the upper gorge and the other at the town of Daju at the end of the lower gorge (¥50/$6.50/£3.25; open 8am–7pm). Most hikers now start from Qiaotou, as all foreigners traveling on buses from Li Jiang to Daju are required to pay the ¥120 ($16/£7.80) entrance fee to the Jade Dragon Snow Mountain Scenic Area between Li Jiang and Daju. For most visitors short on time, the gorge can be visited as a day trip from Li Jiang or on the way to Shangri-La. Recently, instead of going all the way to Qiaotou, many private-hire taxis and tour buses like to drop off visitors at a newly constructed parking lot on the south side of the gorge across from the town of Qiaotou. After paying the entrance fee, it's a 2.6km (1½-mile) walk along a wide paved path to the gorge's most famous sight, the **Tiger Leaping Stone (Hutiao Shi),** a large rock in the middle of the raging river which gave the gorge its name. The legend goes that a tiger being chased by a hunter escaped capture by leaping over the river with the help of this rock.

On the north side of the gorge, a new road for buses and cars has been built all the way from Qiaotou to Tiger Leaping Stone, allowing for even more busloads of tourists to disembark on the northern side of the stone; by the time you read this, the road from Tiger Leaping Stone to Walnut Grove that marks the end of the middle section of the gorge should be paved, which means more exhaust-spewing cars reaching ever deeper into the gorge.

For trekkers approaching from Qiaotou, there are two paths: the lower path used by buses and cars as described above, which is a relatively easy and flat, if exhaust-filled, hike; and the higher path, which is longer, more strenuous, and more dangerous because of falling rocks and narrower paths. Check with the travelers' cafes in Li Jiang beforehand for the latest hiking conditions. It is possible but not advisable to do the hike in a day. Basic but charming guesthouses along the way, all with hot water and restaurants, make overnighting at the gorge a relatively painless affair. In general, hikers on the high path can overnight at **Nuoyu** village, 6.3km (4 miles) and 2 hours from Qiaotou, where the Naxi Family Guesthouse charges ¥30 ($3.90/£1.95) per bed. Or you can stay at **Bendiwan** village, 17km (10 miles) and 4 to 8 hours from Qiaotou, which has several guesthouses; the Halfway Guesthouse (Zhongtu Kezhan) has beds for ¥20 to ¥50 ($2.60–$6.50/£1.30–£3.25), and some of the best views. Some hikers even manage to get to **Walnut Grove (Hetao Yuan),** 23km (14 miles) from Qiaotou and 2 to 4 hours from Bendiwan, in 1 day. However, the middle rapids between Tina's Guesthouse on the lower path and Walnut Grove is one of the prettiest sections of the gorge, so you may want to take your time through there. Guesthouses at Walnut Grove include the very social Sean's Spring Guesthouse (Shanquan Kezhan) with beds for ¥15 to ¥20 ($1.95–$2.60/£1–£1.30); and the quieter Château Woody (Shanbailian Luguan), with beds for ¥10 ($1.30/65p), clean toilets, and great views. From Walnut Grove, you can either hike back to Qiaotou via the 4- to 5-hour lower path, or you can take a taxi back to Qiaotou for ¥10 ($1.30/65p). Another option is to continue on to Daju, a section considerably less scenic that requires crossing the river; the old ferry costs ¥10 ($1.30/65p), the new ferry ¥12 ($1.55/80p).

To get to Qiaotou from Li Jiang, take a Zhongdian-bound bus (2½ hr.; ¥18/ $2.35/£1.20), which runs every half-hour to hour from 7:30am to 3pm, and ask to be let off at Qiaotou. From Qiaotou, the last bus to Li Jiang passes at around 6:30pm, while the last bus to Zhongdian passes at around 5pm. The last bus (3 hr.; ¥35/$4.55/ £2.30) from Daju to Li Jiang leaves at 1:30pm. Frequent minibuses, running until 5pm, take 2½ hours and cost ¥28 ($3.65/£1.80) to get from Daju to Zhongdian.

A FASCINATING SIDE TRIP
LUGU HU (LUGU LAKE) ✸✸

Located about 210km (126 miles) northeast of Li Jiang in the Ninglang Autonomous County (Ninglang Xian) at the juncture of Yunnan and Sichuan provinces, the pristine and breathtaking **Lugu Hu (Lugu Lake)** is the home of the Mosu ("Mosuo" in Mandarin)—the only practicing matriarchal society in the world, with a population of 36,000—and a smaller number of Tibetans and Yi. The relatively remote lake is at least a 5-hour trip by car (up to 8 hr. by minibus with a change in Ninglang) from Li Jiang, and it used to be that only anthropologists and a handful of curious travelers would make the trip. However, as word got out about the unusual Mosu, new roads were built and Chinese visitors have been arriving by the busloads, usually as part of a 2-day tour from Li Jiang. It's an interesting world, where women do *all* of the work, from child raising to cooking, from planting to governing, and the men are defined by their roles not as fathers but as uncles to the children in their mother's household. On the 25th day of the seventh lunar month (Aug or Sept), the Mosu celebrate their biggest festival, Zhuan Shan Jie (Mountain-Circling Festival) at the Gemu Nushen Shan (Goddess Gemu Mountain) on the shores of Lugu Lake.

Despite the increasingly crass commercialization and crowds, Lugu Lake is still worth visiting, though an overnight stay is required. Most of the Chinese tour groups arrive in the afternoon and depart after breakfast the next morning, leaving you a good part of the day to explore, take a boat ride on the lake, or engage a Mosu in conversation, all in relative peace before the next batch of tourists arrives in the afternoon.

The 70-sq.-km (27-sq.-mile) freshwater lake (admission ¥80/$10/£5.10) is dotted with many Mosu log cabins, though these have been replaced by three- and four-story hotels in the main village of **Luoshui Cun** on the western shore. The lake is surrounded by mountains, with the **Gemu Nushen Shan** in the north and the hills of Sichuan's Yanyuan County across the lake in the east. Colorfully clothed Mosu women can row visitors in "pig-trough" *(zhucao)* boats, for approximately ¥40 ($5.20/£2.60) per person, out to the two major islands in the lake: **Liwubi Dao** and **Heiwae Dao.** A small **museum** next to the bus station on the main strip has displays (in Chinese only) of Mosu artifacts and hosts evening Mosu song and dance performances. The owners of the **Husi Teahouse,** transplants from Chongqing themselves, are a great source of information on local activities and often lead hikes around the lake. Farther on, **Yongning** is home to several more Mosu villages worth exploring.

Little-Known History

While many books and brochures talk about the Mosu, this area is also home to the Yi tribe, especially the infamous Norzu clan, slavers who made regular raids into the surrounding lowlands. A fascinating account of life is presented in Alan Winnington's book *Slaves of the Cool Mountains*. The practice was only abolished in 1956.

GETTING THERE Short of joining an organized tour (which travel agencies in Li Jiang can arrange), the easiest way to get out to the lake on your own is by private car or taxi hire (5½ hr.; ¥500/$65/£33)–¥600/$91/£46 round-trip); you'll have to pay for the driver's food and accommodations separately. Otherwise, take a Ninglang-bound bus from Li Jiang's main bus station, then transfer to a Luoshui-bound minibus (2–2½ hr.; ¥20/$2.60/£1.30). Leaving Luoshui, a Li Jiang-bound bus (¥48/$6.25/£3.10) leaves the bus station *(keyun zhan)* along the lakeshore at 7:30am. Alternatively, take a minivan taxi to Ninglang for ¥20 ($2.60/£1.30), and then catch a connecting bus back to Li Jiang (every hour 7am–3pm).

WHERE TO STAY & DINE A decent option close to the lake is the relatively new **Axia Nongjia Yuan (Axia Farmer's House; © 0888/588-6066)**, located behind the museum between the lake and the main road. It has 12 clean standard rooms with attached bathrooms for ¥200 ($26/£13), with a 50% discount in low season. Staying along the waterfront is the most pleasant option, but the log cabin guesthouses for ¥10 ($1.30/65p) per bed are very basic, with communal showers and toilets. The **Mosuo Yuan (© 0888/588-1188)** along the lakeshore is one of the larger guesthouses and is relatively clean. Guesthouse owners can cook you dinner for about ¥20 ($2.60/£1.30). In the evenings, barbecue stalls set up along the waterfront, where you can get any variety of grilled meats and vegetables. The **Husi Teahouse** along the waterfront offers coffees, teas, juices, and basic but tasty Chinese fare.

11 Xianggelila (Zhongdian)

Yunnan Province, 651km (390 miles) NW of Kunming, 198km (119 miles) NW of Li Jiang

To its majority Tibetan residents, the capital of the Diqing Tibetan Autonomous Prefecture, a small town on the road between Li Jiang and Tibet, is known as Gyalthang. To the town's smaller Han population, it's still called Zhongdian. To tourist authorities, hotel owners, and tour operators around the country, the town is now the earthly paradise of Xianggelila (that's Shangri-La to you). A rose never had it so difficult, and we'll continue to refer to the destination as "Zhongdian" in practical information.

Though Zhongdian was officially renamed Xianggelila in May 2002 (see sidebar below), you'll be sorely disappointed if you arrive here expecting paradise. Tourist authorities are working hard to build new hotels and roads, but for now this is still a small, dusty town (elev. 3,380m/11,092 ft.) to be visited mostly for its Tibetan monastery if you aren't going to make it to Tibet. The surrounding area, however, does offer some spectacular scenery. *Note:* Please turn to appendix A for Chinese translations of key locations.

ESSENTIALS

GETTING THERE Zhongdian is connected by **flights** to Kunming (50 min.; daily), Chengdu (1 hr., 10 min.; three or four flights a week), and Lhasa (1 hr., 45 min.; one or two flights a week depending on season). To fly to Lhasa, you must have your Tibet travel permit in order. Tickets can be purchased at the **Yunnan Airlines/CAAC** office at Wenming Jie next to the Guanguang Hotel (© 0887/822-9901); it's open from 8:30am to noon and 3 to 8pm (2–5:30pm in winter). Taxi fare to the airport about 6km (4 miles) south of town will cost ¥20 ($2.60/£1.30).

Paradise Found?

In 1933, the word *Shangri-La* was introduced into the world's lexicon by novelist James Hilton, who wrote in *Lost Horizon* of four Westerners stranded by a plane crash in an idyllic mountain paradise in the Himalayas called Shangri-La. In this earthly Eden, peace and harmony prevailed. Hilton, who never set foot in China, later hinted that the inspiration for his mythical paradise may well have derived from Joseph Rock's many *National Geographic* articles about northwest China in the 1920s and 1930s. By then, this "magical place" with the lush valley, a monastery, a village, and Mount Karakal, "an almost perfect cone of snow," had stirred the soul of many an explorer, Chinese and Western alike, and the search for the "real" Shangri-La was on.

For the last 70 years, countries like Nepal and Bhutan have laid claim to the title. Within China, some have posited that Li Jiang, after all Rock's hometown for 27 years, was the real Shangri-La, while Sichuan Province claimed that its Yading Nature Reserve in the Konkaling Mountains was the true site. Then, in 1997, the Yunnan government declared that they had, with "certainty," found Shangri-La—the Diqing Plateau, 100km (60 miles) north of Li Jiang. Citing many similarities to Hilton's description, Zhongdian County, the capital of the Diqing Tibetan Autonomous Prefecture, officially changed its name to Xianggelila (Shangri-La) in 2002. Was paradise found after all? Zhongdian may have the official imprimatur, but several rebel experts believe that the real inspiration for Shangri-La can actually be found some 320km (200 miles) to the southeast in the ancient kingdom of Muli, an area the size of Wales between Daocheng, Zhongdian, and Jiulong.

From the **Bus Station (Keyun Zhan)** on Changzheng Lu (© **0887/822-2972**), **buses** run to Kunming (9–10 hr.; ¥180/$23/£12) at 9am, and then hourly from 11am to 8pm; to Xiaguan (5 hr.; ¥85/$11/£5.55) every hour from 7am to 8pm; to Li Jiang (3½–4 hr.; ¥35/$4.55/£2.30) every half-hour to hour from 7:10am to 5pm; to Deqin (7 hr.; ¥35/$4.55/£2.30) at 7:20am, 8:20am, and 9:20am; to Xiangcheng (9 hr.) at 7:30am; to Jinjiang (10 hr.) at 3:30pm and 5pm; and to Sanba (5–6 hr; ¥20/$2.60/£1.30) at 8:30am. The 3:30pm bus to Jinjiang will get you there in time to connect with the train to Chengdu. There has been talk of moving the bus station to the northern part of town along Zhongxiang Lu, so check beforehand.

To Tibet   You can only travel overland to Tibet by Land Cruiser as part of an official travel agency group with all the requisite Tibet travel permits. If you haven't made prior reservations by the time you arrive in Zhongdian, check first at the travelers' cafes. During the summer, there may be enough interest to pull together a group, but it'll likely cost around ¥5,000 ($650/£325) per person just for transportation and the permit. From Zhongdian, the overland route passes through Deqin, the last border town in Yunnan, another 6 to 8 hours away by car. Any questions about Tibet travel permits can be referred to Mr. Lin at the Tibet Tourism Office (see below).

To Sichuan   The back roads into Sichuan from Zhongdian are no less scenic or any more comfortable than the road to Tibet, but at least you won't have to worry about permits. Busing it to Chengdu will take at least 6 to 7 days over some very high altitudes (above 4,000m/13,120 ft.) and incredibly gorgeous terrain. Hiring a private car will cost around ¥1,000 ($130/£65). From Zhongdian, a 7:30am bus departs every 2 to 3 days for Xiangcheng in Sichuan; the trip takes 10 hours. From Xiangcheng, the route continues to Daocheng or Litang, depending on weather and road conditions, then to Kanding (11 hr. from Litang), and finally to Chengdu (a further 8 hr.).

Return to Dali 𝄞   The alternate route back to Dali that does not stop at Li Jiang, is an interesting option for those heading back south. Leaving at 12:30pm and costing ¥48 ($6.25/£3.10), the 6-hour journey starts on the Tibetan plateau and passes a surprising number of breeding centers for the shaggy Tibetan Mastiff, perhaps the only dog in the world with a hardier constitution than a St. Bernard. The road then drops away and descends through endless forest switchbacks, past numerous new hydro plants. After some breathtaking precipices, the surroundings turn agricultural once more and the roads turn to yellow as local farmers spread their rice husks across the road, to be conveniently winnowed by passing minibuses such as yours. Most travelers are very surprised by the huge amounts of one particular crop that grows in this province—opium's natural successor, tobacco.

GETTING AROUND   Around town, **taxis** (unmetered) cost ¥5 (65¢/35p) per trip. Bus no. 3 (¥1/15¢/10p) runs from the Tibet Hotel up the main thoroughfare, Changzheng Lu, all the way to Songzanlin Si.

TOURS   **CITS** at Changzheng Lu (✆ 0887/823-0152) just north of the bus station offers day tours (in Chinese only) to the surrounding areas. A group package to Songzanlin Si, Bita Hai, and Napa Hai will run to ¥150 ($20/£9.75). Information on local sights and travel to Tibet and Sichuan can be picked up at the **Tibet Cafe** at Changzheng Lu (✆ 0887/823-0282). Mr. Lin at the **Tibet Tourism Office** (✆ 0887/688-3996; mobile 013988717676688) in the Xiangbala Hotel can arrange Tibet travel permits.

FAST FACTS

Banks, Foreign Exchange & ATMs   The **People's Bank of China (Zhou Renmin Yinhang;** open Mon–Tues and Thurs–Fri, 8:30am–noon and 2:30–5:30pm) is on Changzheng Lu. It offers forex, but it won't give cash advances on credit cards.

Internet Access   **China Telecom** on Changzheng Lu 9 has Internet service from 9am to 9pm, at ¥3 (40¢/20p) per hour. Dial-up is ✆ 163.

Post Office   The post office (open 8:30am–8:30pm, 9am–8pm in the winter) is at the corner of Chengzheng Lu and Xiangyang Lu and has a nice collection of stamps and cards at very low prices.

Visa Extensions   The visa section of the **Gonganju (PSB;** Mon–Fri: 8:30–11:30am and 2:30–6pm summer; 9am–noon and 2–5:30pm winter) is located at Changzheng Lu 72 just south of the Diqing Binguan.

EXPLORING THE TOWN

The largest Tibetan Buddhist temple in southwest China, **Ganden Sumtseling Gompa (Songzanlin Si)** 𝄞𝄞𝄞 (¥10/$1.30/65p; open 7:30am–6:30pm), is located 3km (2 miles) north of town. The Gelukpa (Yellow Hat) monastery was built in 1679 by the fifth Dalai Lama. Modeled on the Potala Palace in Lhasa, the temple was shelled by the Chinese army in 1959 and officially reopened in 1981. About 700 monks currently reside here. The main temple at the top of the hill, a four-story structure with a gold-plated roof reached by climbing a series of steps (or you can have your taxi drive you up to the north entrance *[beimen]*), has a solemn main hall with 108 red pillars and scores of colorful *thangka* hanging from the ceiling. Ascend to the roof, where a simply glorious panorama of Zhongdian awaits you. In the living quarters of the Living Buddha, check out the smooth marks along the floor, where thousands have prostrated themselves in front of the Lama. You may even be able to find a monk who can point out the nearby mountain to the south used for Tibetan sky burials.

Returning to town on Changzheng Lu, you'll see a large white **chorten** (Tibetan stupa) on a hill to the west. There is typically a stupa at the entrance to every Tibetan town which, as a symbol of protection, is usually decorated with prayer flags and jewels, and ringed with stones laid by pilgrims as expressions of particular wishes or prayers. Pilgrims entering town are required to circumambulate the stupa three times.

To the south, Zhongdian's **old town** is worth a tour. From the Tibet Hotel, head east on Tuanjie Lu until it curves south onto Cangfang Jie. You'll soon come to the **Old Town Scripture Chamber (Gucheng Zangjing Tang).** Admission is ¥5 (65¢/35p) and hours are from 7am to 8pm. The 300-year-old temple housed part of the Red Army on their Long March in 1936. The triple-eaved main hall contains a statue of an all-seeing and omnipotent Buddha with a thousand heads and hands (*qianshou qianyan*).

WHERE TO STAY

The **Tibet Cafe** has reasonable rooms at perhaps the best prices in town, although the main road can be a little noisy. The Tibet Hotel on the other hand has an impressive reception area but awful rooms and some brainless staff whose entire knowledge of local history could be written on a postage stamp. The rooms are even worse and to be avoided at all costs.

Cobbler's Hill Inn (Pi Jiang Cheng Lao Ke Zhan)   One of the few guesthouses in town that decided to restore rather than rebuild, with interesting results. Although the rooms on the front balcony are a little musty, there are some good-value standard roomson the second floor. Up on the third floor are two special rooms, one with a large Tibetan-style bed and the other with an antique Chinese bed. With their spectacular balconies and thoughtful little extras such as electric shoe driers, these are the best choice for a short stay.

Gu Cheng Bei Men Jie 16. © 0887/828 9894. 20 units. ¥100 ($13/£6.50) standard room; ¥200 ($26/£13) deluxe room. No credit cards.

Tian Jie Shen Chuan Dajiudian (Paradise Hotel)   At last, Zhongdian has its first five-star hotel. Arranged around a huge tropical, indoor pool, featuring rock cascades and steppingstones, this must be one of the most out-of-place hotels in China. Rooms are suitably luxurious, especially the designer bathrooms, but do you really want to experience Guangdong accommodations when you are so close to the kingdom on the roof of the world?

Changzheng Lu, Zhong Duan. © 0887/822-8008. Fax 0887/822-3776. 300 units. ¥880–¥1,380 ($114–$179/£57–£90) standard room; ¥1,980 ($257/£129) suite. 20%–30% discounts possible. AE, DC, MC, V. **Amenities:** 3 restaurants; bar; lounge; teahouse; indoor swimming pool; sauna; karaoke bar; concierge; business center; forex; shopping arcade; salon; 24-hr. room service; laundry/dry cleaning. *In room:* A/C, satellite TV, broadband Internet access.

WHERE TO DINE

For decent and inexpensive local and Western fare, head to the traveler's cafes in the southern part of town. The most popular of the lot is the cozy **Tibet Cafe** ⭐ at Changzheng Lu near the Martyr's Cemetery (© **0887/823-0282**). It serves Western staples like pancakes, pasta, and pizza, along with Naxi and Tibetan specialties (try the yak steak or the hearty fried bread stuffed with yak meat). Main courses cost about ¥20 ($2.60/£1.30). The Snowland Restaurant (Xue Yu Kafeiting), near the Tibet Hotel, has now changed names to **The Puppet Restaurant** (© **0887/887-8225485**) but still does very reliable breakfasts, and the owners are a mine of information for places to visit both in and outside the town. Around Heping Lu and Jiantang Lu are a number of food stalls and small restaurants that serve Hui Muslim, Sichuan, and home-style *(jiachang cai)* Chinese food; none, however, have English menus.

The fabulous Arro Khampa Restaurant (A Luo Kang Ba), located on Gu Cheng Pi Jiang Po (© **0773/822-6442**), employs chefs from Tibet, India, Nepal and China to create a wide and varied menu. Apart from the stylish surroundings of carved beams and colorful *thangkas,* we really enjoyed the potato and pumpkin slices as well as the yak meat stew at only ¥10 ($1.30/65p).

In the evenings, nocturnal activities begin at 7:30pm when locals and tourists alike congregate in the main square for Tibetan dancing in the old town main square that is even more fun that the dancing in Li Jiang and Shuhe. In addition there are plenty of local bars, our favorites being the Google Bar with its huge balcony and the Raven Bar for its wide selection of music.

AROUND XIANGGELILA

The most popular day trip is to **Baishui Tai (White Water Terraces)** ⭐ (¥80/$10/£5.20; open 8am–6pm), a limestone-deposit plateau at the town of Sanba about 108km (67 miles) southeast of Xianggelila. These seemingly sculpted terraces, actually formed from calcium carbonate deposits over hundreds of years, are quite beautiful. It has become de rigueur for visitors to walk barefoot on the terraces, which appear slippery but are actually not. Nearby is the village of Baidi, the cradle of Naxi Dongba culture. To get there, it's best to hire a private car for ¥600 ($91/£46); or join a day tour organized by the travelers' cafes or your hotel concierge desk.

Many tourists combine their Baishui Tai visit with a stop at **Bita Hai (Bita Lake;** ¥60/$9.10/£4.55; open 8am–5pm, 6pm summer) a nature reserve some 25km (15 miles) east of town whose centerpiece freshwater lake is awash in azalea blooms in June and a riot of autumn colors in September. There are two entrances to the lake: one in the west which is still several kilometers (a half-hour by pony) from the lake; and another in the south, on the road to Baishui Tai. From the southern entrance, it's a 2km (1¼-mile) walk down a log-lined path or a 20-minute pony ride for ¥20 ($2.60/£1.30) to the lake. Many visitors tend to walk down and ride up, because the walk uphill at this altitude can be quite taxing. The main paths are full of tourists but there are plenty of opportunities to get away for more private hikes.

12 Jinghong & Xishuangbanna

Yunnan Province, 590km (366 miles) SW of Kunming, 646km (401 miles) SW of Dali

The Xishuangbanna Dai Autonomous Prefecture is situated at the subtropical southwestern tip of Yunnan and shares a border with Myanmar (Burma) and Laos. About a third of its 800,000-strong population is Dai, another third is Han, and the rest

The Dai

Historically, the Dai (also known as the "Tai") are said to have appeared in the Yangzi River valley around the 1st century A.D. but were driven south by the expansion of the Chinese empire. The majority of the Dai moved into the northern parts of Southeast Asia and are found today in Thailand, Laos, northeast Myanmar (Burma), and northern Vietnam. The majority of China's Dai population of over one million live in the Xishuangbanna region and in Dehong Prefecture. *Dai* means "peace and freedom loving," and it is no coincidence that the Dai/Thai are often regarded as being some of the most gracious people in the world.

The Dai mostly inhabit the plains areas around rivers and lakes. To keep away from the damp earth, they live in bamboo stilt houses, with the second floor given over to the living quarters and the first floor reserved for livestock.

The Dai practice Theravada Buddhism, and there are Buddhist temples and pagodas in every village, though individual villages are not beyond their own animistic beliefs and spirit worship. The Water Splashing Festival (Poshui Jie), a huge tourist attraction, also marks the Dai New Year. According to legend, the Dai were once terrorized by a sadistic demon who took for himself seven consorts. In an *in vino veritas* moment, the youngest of the consorts, who was plying the demon with strong libations, discovered that he would die if hung by his own hair. As soon as the demon fell into a drunken stupor, she grabbed a strand of his hair and strangled him. The demon's head fell off but burst into unquenchable flames as it rolled through the land wreaking havoc. The seven consorts took turns dousing the ball of fire with water. To this day, water is splashed on everyone in gratitude for deliverance from the demon, and to wash away your own sins as well as any disasters or diseases. The wetter you are, the more luck you're likely to receive in the coming year. The lively festival is also marked by dragon boat races, group dances, temple visits, and rocket launching.

comprises minorities such as the Hani, Lahu, Bulang, Jinuo, Yao, and Yi. With its tropical forests, perennial sunshine, and laid-back lifestyle, the place has always felt more like Southeast Asia than China. Today, with domestic tourists able to travel more easily to the real Thailand and Myanmar, Xishuangbanna, a Chinese approximation of the original Thai *Sip Sawng Panna* ("Twelve Rice-Growing Districts"), is no longer the much-ballyhooed destination it once was, and much of the main town of Jinghong has fallen into a kind of romantic decay. Still, it remains a useful alternative embarkation point for those wishing to travel down the Mekong to Laos, Burma, Northern Thailand, and beyond. The wildly popular Dai Water Splashing Festival (Apr 13–15) can be an interesting time to visit, but book well in advance, as flights and accommodations are notoriously scarce at this time. Otherwise, the most pleasant times to visit are between October and February. ***Note:*** Please turn to appendix A for Chinese translations of key locations in this section.

ESSENTIALS

GETTING THERE   Jinghong is connected by **flights** to Shanghai (4 hr. 30 min.), Chengdu (3 hr. 15 min.), Kunming (40 min.), Dali (45 min.), Li Jiang (50 min.), and Bangkok (30 min.). Tickets can be purchased at the **Yunnan Airlines/CAAC** office located at Jingde Xi Lu 8 (© **0691/212-7040**). There is also a **Bangkok Airways** office at Jingde Xi Lu 8 (© **0691/212-1881**). Minibuses charge ¥2 (25¢/15p), or ¥3 (40¢/20p) after 10pm; they make runs to the airport every 10 minutes from 7am to 11:30pm. The airport is located about 5km (3 miles) southwest of town, and the minibuses depart from the corner of Jingde Xi Lu and Minzu Nan Lu. A taxi ride between the airport and town will cost around ¥30 ($3.90/£1.95).

For destinations such as Kunming or Dali, bus trips are still interminably long and smoke-filled, and you may find yourself caught in floods, mudslides, or bus break-downs. Still, for the intrepid (or the foolish), there's the **Bus Station (Qiche Keyun Zhan)** on Minzu Bei Lu (© **0691/212-3570**). Express buses run to Kunming (9 hr.; ¥180/$23/£12) at 10:30am, 12:30pm, 5pm, 5:40pm, 6pm, 6:20pm, 7:05pm, 7:20pm, 8pm, and 8:20pm. In addition, buses run to Xiaguan (14 hr.; ¥180/$23/£12) at 4:40pm and 7pm. Buses also leave for Kunming and Xiaguan from the new and some-what forlorn **South Bus Station (Nan Zhan;** © **0691/212-4884** or 0691/213-7105) on Nonglin Lu. A bus leaves here for Laos but only on alternative days so it is best to check at Mei Mei's Cafe for further details first. Additional buses leave from the **City Bus Station,** also known locally as the Banna Bus Station (**Shi Keyun Zhan;** © **0691/ 212-4427** or 0691/898-3666) for Ganlanba (a half-hour; ¥8/$1.05/50p) every 20 minutes from 6:30am to 7pm; for Menglun (2 hr.; ¥14/$1.95/£1) every 20 minutes from 6:30am to 7pm; for Menghai (¥11/$1.45/70p) every 20 minutes from 7am to 6:40pm; for Mengyang every half-hour from 8am to 6:30pm; and for Mengla (5–7 hr.; ¥55/$7.15/£3.60); every hour), Ning Er (3 hr.; ¥42/$5.45/£2.65) every 20 min-utes, and Pu'er (2 hr.; ¥55/$7.15/£3.60) every 30 minutes.

There is an official **boat** service running between Jinghong and Chiang Saen, Thai-land. The Golden Peacock office is located at Jingde Xi Lu 8 (© **0691/222-1555;** www.tian-da.com.cn), but they rarely answer their phone and we found it more expe-dient to book tickets through Orchid's contact at Mei Mei Cafe. From December to May (the dry season), the low level of water only allows express boats to hydroplane the 200km (124 miles) up and down to the Golden Triangle, and although the deaf-ening engine noise is not much different from a 747, most relish the chance to sit on deck and view the jungle scenery that runs up between Laos and Myanmar. Travel at this time of the year gives an especially good view of this great Asian waterway, with shoals, rapids, and craggy outcrops dotting the thoroughfare. Boats leave from the Jinghong Dock at 7am (look for other confused passengers in the Customs hall rather than dockside) every Monday, Wednesday, and Friday, take about 10 hours and cost ¥880 ($114/£57). A Chinese rice lunchbox is served, but you might want to take some extra food and drinks for the trip.

Where passengers board and alight depends on the height of the water in the Mekong, which has about as much flow as a urinal these days thanks to the frenzy of Chinese dam building upstream. We were taken by minibus to a jetty about an hour downstream and then had the displeasure of disembarking at Guan Lei, a hole-in-the-wall Chinese border post that is not even on most maps. The whole place reeks of gar-lic as there are boatloads full of the stuff passing through. The ferry company offered us all accommodations beside the immigration office, but the filthy prefabs they referred to were not recommendable. Try this place instead: **Guan Lei Lu San Jiao Jiu Dian** (© **0691/878-6318;** ¥50/$6.50/£3.25). It's just outside the Customs House and very basic but still the best in town.

Come May through December, there is a slow-boat option available. The same Golden Peacock line plies its way up and down stream on a triple deck cruiser with berths for up to 80 people as well as the usual Chinese function areas including tea drinking and mahjong rooms. This option takes 3 days and 2 nights as opposed to 10 hours on the fast boats. Disembarkation at the golden triangle offers many interesting options. Chiang Mai and Chiang Rai are only a few hours away by luxury VIP coach. Luang Prabang and Vientianne in Laos invite those who wish to continue their river odyssey while the mysterious Myanmar interior awaits the truly intrepid.

For the return journey, the ticket office is just past the immigration office on the riverside road in Chiang Saen, just next to the Fresh Mart and they even have a Jinghong number (© **0691/2221-5555**). Between September 2 and May 31, boats leave at 7am on Tuesdays, Thursdays, and Saturdays.

GETTING AROUND   Taxis cost ¥7 (90¢/45p) for 2km (1¼ miles), then ¥1.50 (20¢/10p) per kilometer until 20km (12 miles), when the cost rises to ¥2.30 (30¢/15p) per kilometer. From 10pm to 6am, the cost is ¥8.40 ($1.10/55p) for 2km (1¼ miles). **You Qi Bicycle Shop** at Manting Lu (© **0691/216-1189**), opposite the dark and depressing Zhong Yu Hotel, rents good-quality mountain bikes at ¥20 ($2.60/£1.30) and also arranges tours.

TOURS & GUIDES   CITS at Luyou Dujiaqu, Sanhao Lu (© **0691/214-8520;** Mon–Fri 8:30–11:30am and 3–6pm), can arrange day tours to the surrounding areas, with car hire for a day costing around ¥300 ($39/£20), and an English-speaking guide for another ¥200 ($26/£13) or so, though there's room for bargaining. Travelers' cafes such as the Mei Mei Cafe and the Mekong Cafe can also organize treks to nearby villages and are generally much better options.

FAST FACTS

Banks, Foreign Exchange & ATMs   The **Bank of China** (open Mon–Fri 8–11:30am and 3–6pm) is at Minzu Nan Lu and Jingde Xi Lu.

Internet Access   Manting Lu has several Internet cafes, including one below the Mekong Cafe (¥2/25¢/15p per hour) at Manting Lu 111.

Post Office   The post office (open 8am–8:30pm) is at Jinghong Xi Lu 2. The attached postcard outlet around the corner is often overlooked but also worth a look in.

Visa Extensions   The **Gonganju (PSB)** is at Jinghong Dong Lu 5 (© **0691/ 213-0366;** open Mon–Fri 8–11:30am and 3–5:30pm).

EXPLORING JINGHONG

There is not much to see in Jinghong itself. **Manting Gongyuan** (admission 7:30am–7pm, ¥40/$5.20/£2.60; 7–10:30pm, ¥80/$10/£5.20) in the southeastern part of town, once an imperial garden for the Dai kings, hosts the annual Dai Water Splashing Festival. Those who can't make it to the real festival can now be splashed in a faux daily ceremony as meaningless as your clothes are wet. In the rear of the park is the **Zongfo Si,** a Theravada-style temple complex that is the center of Dai Buddhism, but the stupas and the temples complete with gilded statues of Sakyamuni all

---

Tips Dai Etiquette

Always take off your shoes before entering a Dai temple or household, as a sign of respect. Dress appropriately in temples, don't take photos of the monks or the interiors without permission, don't raise yourself higher than a Buddha figure, and never sit with your feet pointing at the Buddha or at anyone else.

---

date only from the late 1980s. Many of the monks here have studied in Thailand and seem to be experts in lolling around on the park grass. There is an exhilarating rope slide across the lake for ¥15 ($1.95/£1) and an enclosure with dozens of greedy peacocks that love to pose for pictures and be fed by hand.

The **Tropical Flower and Plants Garden (Redai Huahuiyuan)** ⋆ (¥80/$10/£5.20; open 8am–6pm), in the western part of town, has garnered good reviews from green thumbs impressed with the collection of over 1,000 plants from Yunnan's tropical forests but is probably not worth a visit if you are heading farther south to Thailand. Descriptions are mostly in Chinese.

SHOPPING

An interesting nightly market on Mengpeng Lu is much better than the regular tourist market in the city center on Mengla Da Dao. Our favorite shops were located a bit farther out at Min Zu Gong Yi Ping Shi Chang (Minority Crafts Market) with the best of the bunch being the **Xi Nan Min Zu Bu Luo (South West Minority Tribe Shop;** ℂ **0691/213-9650**), where the owner travels extensively in the region carefully selecting Yi, Hani, and Jinuo handmade fabrics, clothes, and crafts.

WHERE TO STAY

Kingland Hotel (Jin Lan Da Jiu Dian)   This hotel is gaudy to excess with plaster elephants adorning every possible inch of space. Plenty of extras in the room such as a flashlight and even a pair of bathroom scales, but this hardly justifies ¥680 ($88/£44) per night when most other hotels in the area are a tenth of that price. If you arrived overland in a company SUV, then this is probably the place for you.

Jin De Lu 6. ℂ **0691/212-9999.** Fax 0691/219-9198. 212 units. ¥680 ($83/£41) standard room; from ¥1,380 ($179/£90) suite. 20%–40% discounts. AE, DC, MC, V. **Amenities:** 2 restaurants (Western dining available); bar; lounge; health club; concierge; business center; forex; shopping arcade; room service; laundry/dry cleaning; executive rooms. *In room:* A/C, TV, hair dryer.

Thai City Hotel (Xishuangbanna Tai Du Da Jiu Dian)   Located in its own compound with a full range of facilities, this is the most luxurious hotel in town, but it's somewhat inconveniently situated in the southwest part of town. Guest rooms are fairly plush, comfortable, and well-appointed, with large beds; bathrooms run a little small but are otherwise clean. The staff here is friendly and efficient.

Min Hang Lu4 26. ℂ **0691/213-7888.** Fax 0691/219-7509. 172 units. www.thaicityhotel.com. ¥670 ($87/£43) standard room; from ¥1,200 ($156/£78) suite. 20%–40% discounts. AE, DC, MC, V. **Amenities:** Restaurant; bar; lounge; sauna; concierge; business center; forex; room service; laundry. *In room:* A/C, TV (Thailand and Hong Kong satellite channels only), hair dryer.

WHERE TO DINE

Though all five tastes are represented in Dai cuisine, the emphasis is on the sour, the pungent, and the fragrant. Famous Dai dishes include *kao yu* (grilled fish) and *kao sunzi* (grilled bamboo shoots), often wrapped in banana leaves or lemon grass; *xiangzhu fan* (fragrant bamboo rice, or glutinous rice stuffed inside a hollowed bamboo that is then cooked over an open fire), and *suansun zhu yu* (fish boiled with sour bamboo shoots).

Informal Dai and Western food can be had at the traveler's cafes concentrated around Manting Lu, with prices about ¥10 to ¥30 ($3.90/£1.95) per dish. The best of these is the **Mei Mei Cafe** at Manting Lu 5 (© **0691/216-1221**), with a good selection of pizzas and pastas, juices, and coffees. The big slabs of whole-grain bread that they serve with their breakfasts are especially tasty. Staffed by A-chun and Orchid, both girls are founts of local knowledge and can help out with just about anything. The **Mekong Cafe (Meigong Canguan)**, at Manting Lu 111 (© **0691/212-8895;** open 8am–1am), has gone downhill since our last visit but they still prepare some reasonably priced food such as Dai-style steamed pineapple sticky rice to a Hani set meal. **Banna Cafe** at the corner of Manting Lu is best worth avoiding; continental breakfast consisted of burned coffee, fried bread rather than toast, and ill-tasting and -looking butter. The **Dongguan Jiaozi Guan** (© **0691/214-9346**) on Jingde Dong Lu (open 7am–10pm) serves your basic northern staples like dumplings, noodles, and steamed buns.

Cai Chun Qing ⊛ THAI   This clean and informal restaurant along lively Manting Lu serves authentic and flavorful food, courtesy of the restaurant's Thai chef. Menu highlights include green papaya salad, *tom yum kung* (spicy shrimp) soup, and steamed fish with chili and lemon. The staff is friendly.

Manting Lu 193. © **0691/216-1758**. English menu. Meal for 2 ¥40–¥80 ($5.20–$10/£2.60–£5.20). No credit cards. 9am–9:30pm.

Dai Jia Meishi Cun ⊛ DAI   Located in traditional bamboo buildings on the grounds of the Banna Binguan, this restaurant offers excellent Dai specialties like *kao yu* and *kao sunzi*. The *zhutong fan* (glutinous rice cooked in bamboo) and the *suansun zhu ji* (chicken cooked with pickled bamboo) are also worth trying. The costumed staff is friendly and there is a nightly Dai song-and-dance performance.

Ganlan Zhong Lu 11. © **0691/212-3679**. Main courses ¥20–¥40 ($2.60–$5.20/£1.30–£2.60). No credit cards. 6:30–9pm.

JINGHONG AFTER DARK

The **Municipal Art Theatre** in the southwestern part of town (Galanzhong Lu 6) hosts Dai and Jinuo song-and-dance performances at ¥120 ($16/£7.80) per person. The performance starts at 8:30pm and is followed by a barbecue, drinking, and audience participation in group dances and games, which may just make you want to run away. **Manting Gongyuan** features a similar program from 7 to 10pm but both are ridiculously overpriced and we much prefer the almost identical show in Ning Er.

AROUND JINGHONG
GANLANBA (MENGHAN)

Ganlanba (Olive Plain) lies on the Mekong River about 27km (16 miles) southeast of Jinghong. It used to be that you could sail down the Mekong (known in Yunnan as the Lancang Jiang) to Ganlanba, but few boats make the trip anymore and it's more convenient to take the minibus from Jinghong's city bus station. The main attraction here is the **Dai Minority Folk Customs Park** (**Daizu Yuan;** ¥80/$10/£5.20; open 7:30am–6:30pm). The collection of five pleasant Dai villages has now been "preserved" for tourists, which essentially means it has become a human zoo for Chinese tourists in golf carts. The first village of **Manchunman** has the Manchunman Fo Si, a regal temple first built in 1126. There is a gorgeous golden Burmese stupa here surrounded by four smaller golden stupas. Farther in, **Manting** village has another impressive temple and white pagoda worth exploring, the **Manting Fo Si Da Du Ta,** built in 669, which now houses Buddha statues donated by a Thai philanthropist.

MENGLUN

About 42km (25 miles) east of Ganlanba, the town of Menglun is home to China's largest botanical garden, the 900-hectare (2,223-acre) **Xishuangbanna Redai Zhiwuyuan** (¥80/$10/£5.20; open 24 hr.), which boasts around 7,000 species of tropical and subtropical plants from China and abroad. The sprawling grounds are divided into many sections, including a rubber and tea plantation, a stretch of natural tropical rainforest, and a bamboo forest. To get there, take a minibus from the city bus station. From the Menglun bus station, turn left and walk to the corner of the second block. Turn left and walk down the road flanked by hawkers; follow this road until you come to a ticket booth in front of a footbridge across the Luosuo River. This is the western entrance to the garden. If you're coming by taxi, the entrance is way over in the east, but taxis should be able to let you off close to the Tourist Information Center (Youke Fuwu Zhongxin) in the middle of the park.

About 8km (5 miles) west of Menglun (at the 63km marker on the Jinghong-Menglun road) is the **Banna Rainforest Valley (Banna Yulin Gu;** ¥80/$10/£5.20; open 8am–6:30pm), a pleasant enough primary rainforest park. It has several aerial walkways and a number of ancient trees that include a giant strangling fig with long, gnarled roots.

MENGYANG

One of the highlights at this town 20km (12 miles) northeast of Jinghong is an elephant-shaped banyan tree, **Xiangxing Rongshu,** that is a magnet for Chinese tourists. Considerably more interesting is the **Jinuo Folk Custom Village (Jinuo Minsu Shanzhai),** about 6km (4 miles) east of Mengyang near Jinuo Shan, home of the Jinuo people. Though the main village of Bapo Zhai has been spruced up to become your usual tour group–friendly folk-custom village, it at least affords visitors a friendly introduction to the Jinuo, who have not always been so welcoming toward individual travelers in the past.

Officially recognized as a minority group only in 1979, the Jinuo have a population of just over 20,000, all living in 46 villages east of Jinghong. Jinuo men are famous hunters, while the women are known for their elaborately decorated earlobes and black teeth, caused by a local medicinal plant used to prevent tooth decay. The Jinuo's biggest festival is celebrated every February 6 to February 8 with their characteristic solar drum dance, which visitors can now view upon entering the village. You can also visit a typical Jinuo house, which is built 1m (3 ft.) aboveground and often houses four generations of a family. Admission to the village is ¥35 ($4.55/£2.30) and includes entry to the Banna Wild Elephant Valley, as both are managed by the same company.

About 28km (17 miles) north of Mengyang, the **Banna Wild Elephant Valley (Banna Yexiang Gu;** ¥80/$10/£5.20; open 8am–5:30pm) is part of the 1.5-million-hectare (3.7-million-acre) **Sanchahe Nature Reserve (Sanchahe Ziran Baohuqu).** There are hiking trails and a 2,063m (6,766-ft.) chairlift ride (¥40/$5/£2.50) over the forest canopy, all designed to help visitors spot the roughly 40 wild elephants that live here. If you don't manage a sighting, there are wretched performances by more domesticated elephants near the eastern exit at 1:30 and 3:30pm. By the southern entrance are some tacky hotels with permanently damp bedding and clouds of starved mosquitoes.

To get to the nature reserve, take any Simao-bound bus (1 hr.; ¥10/$1.30/65p) from Jinghong that passes the reserve. A daily tour that takes in the Elephant Valley and Jinuo village costs ¥120 ($16/£7.80), and includes admission, transportation, and lunch. The tour bus departs daily at 8:40am from the entrance to Peacock Lake (Jinghong Dong Lu) and returns around 5pm.

XIDING SUNDAY MARKET

More interesting than the market at Menghan, this makes an interesting morning trip. First take the 8am bus to Menghai (smaller than Jinghong, without the pollution and the palm trees) for about 1 hour and 50 minutes, which should get you into town to catch the 10:30am bus to Xiding which takes another 90 minutes. The market sets up well before dawn and gets going around 8am; it is especially good for fabrics and minority food, and if you are really lucky you might see some of the rare shaven-headed Lahu minority women. It is tempting to cycle to Menghai as it is downhill all the way, but getting back might be a struggle unless you have thighs like Lance Armstrong.

HAIKOU

Hainan Island, 520km (322 miles) SW of Guangzhou, 480km (288 miles) SW of Hong Kong

As the capital of Hainan Island, Haikou, formerly a treaty port in the late 1800s, is the transportation hub and center of all government and commercial services. In recent years, the town has developed into another modern Chinese city with large shops and colorful restaurants, but there's little for the average tourist here. Many take the first bus out to Sanya.

Few guidebooks mention that China's gender imbalance is at its peak here with an astonishing estimated 135 men for every 100 women. In Haikou, renowned through the country for its sex industry, these numbers are boosted even higher by Chinese sex tourists. The area around Wuzhishan Lu is especially intimidating, with almost every shop being a liquor store. Street fights are common and the whole area has a distinct air of malice in the evenings. Everywhere in Hainan, the huge surplus of men sit around idly, usually in restaurants with pink plastic chairs, sipping tea while women run around doing all the work. Truly a feminist's nightmare.

ESSENTIALS

GETTING THERE   From Haikou's Meilan Airport (© **0898/6575-1333**), 25km (15 miles) southeast of town, daily **flights** connect to Beihai, Beijing, Guangzhou, Shanghai, and Shenzhèn. There's a daily flight to Hong Kong and weekly flights to Bangkok, Macau, and Singapore. Tickets can be purchased at the **CAAC office** at Xisha Lu 22 (© **0898/6676-3166**) from 8am to 7pm. **Dragon Air** flies to Hong Kong and Gaoxiong (Kaoshiung in Taiwan), and has an office at the Hainan Mandarin Hotel at Wenhua Lu 18 (© 0898/6855-**0312**). CAAC buses (¥15/$1.95/£1) depart from the Minhang Binguan on Haixiu Lu every half-hour from 5:30am to 8pm. A taxi to the airport costs around ¥50 ($6.50/£3.25).

New air-conditioned express **buses** with lots of leg room run to Sanya (3–3½ hr., ¥70/$9.10/£4.55) every 30 minutes from 6:45am to 18:45am; they depart from the **South Bus Station (Qiche Nan Zhan)** at Xin Hua Qu Long Kun Nan Lu, Li Jiao

Qiao Xia (© **0898/6676-9671**). The **Long-Distance Bus Station (Changtu Qiche Zongzhan)** on Nanbao Lu (© **0898/6677-2791**) has ferry/sleeper buses to Guangzhou (15 hr.; ¥190/$25/£12) from 9am to 8pm.

From the **Xiuying Matou** (© **0898/6866-1943**) 8km (5 miles) west of town, daily **boats** sail across the Qiongzhou Straits to Beihai (10 hr.; ¥ 211/$27/£14 double) at 6pm; and to Shenzhèn (18 hr.; ¥390/$51/£25 for first class) at 3:30pm. A boat to Guangzhou (21 hr.; ¥303/$39/£20) departs at 3pm every Monday, Wednesday, and Friday. Tickets can be bought at the dock. A taxi out to Xiuying Dock costs around ¥20 ($2.60/£1.30).

GETTING AROUND   Taxis charge ¥10 ($1.30/65p) for 3km (2miles), then ¥2 (25¢/15p) per kilometer thereafter. Gas prices are 30% higher here than on the island and road transportation reflects this. Also there are a surprisingly large number of Do Not Drink and Drive signs, which should tell you something.

There are at least two choices for **bike rental.** The first is just outside the Xin Jia Yuan Hotel, at the **517 Bike Club,** Nanbao Lu (© **0898/6669-8989;** www. 517bike.com; open 9am–8pm), which only has a relatively small selection compared to the much larger **Tianya Bike Club** on Jiefang Dong Lu 40 (© **0898/6624-9551**). Both places have good quality mountain bikes for ¥20 ($2.60/£1.30) per day. Be warned, though, that riding in Haikou gets tiresome quickly as road conditions are poor and local drivers incompetent at best.

FAST FACTS

Banks, Foreign Exchange & ATMs   The **Bank of China** (open Mon–Fri, 8:30am–5:30pm) is behind the International Finance Center at Datong Lu 33.

Post Office   The 24-hour post office is at Jiefang Xi Lu 9.

Visa Extensions   The **PSB** is in the western part of town at Jinlong Lu 43 (© **0898/ 6859-3666;** open Mon–Fri 8am–noon and 2:30–5:30pm).

EXPLORING THE TOWN

Haikou's **old town,** just north of the negligible **Haikou Gongyuan (Haikou Park),** around Xinhua Lu to Jiefang Lu and Zhongshan Lu would likely be more interesting if it wasn't in such a sorry state of disrepair and now hidden under years of soot and grime. There are a few memorial halls (**Wugong Ci,** or **Five Officials Temple,** in the eastern part of town) and a tomb (**Hairui Mu** in the western part of town) dedicated to various Chinese historical figures who were banished to Hainan. However, these are usually of interest to Chinese tourists only.

WHERE TO STAY

Sun Herton Hotel (Ming Yang He Tai Jiu Dian)   Conveniently located right in the downtown has some very good value standard rooms for just ¥100 ($13/£6.50) on the fifth floor, but these are invariably taken. Still, standards on the ninth floor are still very new and some even have balconies for just ¥188 ($24/£12), which can sometimes be negotiated down to ¥150 ($20/£9.75). The staff are very friendly and bend over backwards to be of assistance.

Hai Xiu Da Dao 25. © 0898/6679-5199. Fax 0898/6658-1099. 212 units. ¥188 ($24/£12) standard room; from ¥488 ($63/£32) suite. **Amenities:** Restaurants; bar; business center; massage; laundry. *In room:* A/C, hair dryer.

Xin Jia Yuan Jiu Dian   On the corner with Nanbao Lu, the polka-dotted sheets and chrome bathrooms give rooms here are light, airy feel. There is comfortable Internet bar on the second floor, and the small pond and waterfall at the lift entrance is charming, although locals prefer to use it as a spittoon. Do not be tempted by the disco across the street as I saw gang fights outside every night I was in residence.

Lantian Lu 25. © 0898/3634-9001. Fax 0898/3634-9009. 78 units. ¥100 ($13/£6.50) standard room; from ¥388 ($50/£25) suite. **Amenities:** Bar; lounge; Internet bar; salon, massage; laundry. *In room:* A/C, hair dryer.

WHERE TO DINE
Australian Geoff's Western City Cafe Bar BURGERS Opposite Hainan
Teachers' University, in a desolate part of town with seemingly even more Lanweilou (unfinished office towers) this local expat hangout resides in what used to be the penthouse of the Xi Long Hotel. Geoff does thick juicy burgers and steaks of a wide variety while the few remaining expats sit around sharing tales of woe.

Long Kun Nan Lu, Top Floor, Xi Long Business Hotel. © 0898/6588-9955. No credit cards. Thurs–Fri 5pm till late, Sat–Sun noon to late.

Lao Xin Jiang Tian Shan Zhi Zi Fan Dian UIGHUR On the corner of Yelin Lu,
the interior of this Xinjiang eatery is a bit murky, but by 8pm they fill the pavement with tables and chairs for some pleasant early evening alfresco dining. Although there is an extensive picture menu, I was quite content to choose from the selection of breads, kebabs, and delicious lamb pilaf that was on display behind their large ornate barbecue stand.

Wuzhishan Lu 23. © 0898/6537-5027. Photo menu. Meal for 2 ¥40–¥80 ($5.20–$10/£2.60–£5.20). No credit cards. 11:30am–11:30pm.

AROUND HAIKOU
While local guidebooks mention dozens of fascinating day trips, the only one that I could personally recommend is a one-way trip back to the airport. The Yantian salt flats (Qian Nian Gu Yan Tian) at Yangpu on the NW coast were the filthiest part of the island that I visited, although that was quite an achievement in itself here in Hainan.

Surfers should head across to Longlou on the east coast where conditions are said to be acceptable. Boards are available for hire at the Haikou Banana Hostel (© 0898/ 6628-6780), tucked away off Renmin Lu.

The old **crystal mines** at Tunchang (Tunchang Shui Jing Kuang) were a semi-interesting day trip, although by the time you read this the whole area might have been turned into a theme park. Buses leave every hour from the West Bus Station for charging ¥87 ($13/£6.30) for the 3-hour trip. From the bus station, head along Dong Feing Zhong Lu and then out along town on Changshèng Nan Lu. Pass the Mingyuan Hotel and turn right just before the Sinopec gas station. A stroll will show that most of the crystal mine workshops have been converted in pig sties or left to rot. Up on the left is the entrance to the old quarry where crystals and shards litter the ground. There are usually a few locals scrounging around for some nice examples although the signs state that the whole area is about to be developed into a new "Huangshan Park."

I made the mistake of crossing the road to explore the rest of the area. After trudging around acres of slash-and-burn wasteland, all I discovered were leeches and mosquitoes. Worst of all when I sat down for lunch, I was immediately harassed by a pair of king cobras, the larger one being at least 3m long. Now I understand why most visitors to Haikou never step out of their resort hotels.

SANYA

Hainan Island, 285km (171 miles) S of Haikou

Sanya's white-sand beaches are the nicest in China, but that is not saying much. Even if the resorts here were half the price they would still be able to compete with a beach holiday in Thailand. In fact, there's not much to do here, and the town itself very dirty and unfriendly for a supposed tourist town. The majority of foreign tourists here are Russians, a surly bunch that do not seem to mind the equally miserable locals. Other Europeans tend rarely set foot out of their expensive resorts, which seems to defeat the object of coming all the way to China in the first place. December through February is the peak season.

ESSENTIALS

GETTING THERE   From Sanya's **Phoenix Airport** (© 0898/8889-5961) 20km (12 miles) northwest of downtown, daily **flights** connect to Beijing, Guangzhou, Shenzhèn, Shanghai, and Hong Kong. There are now direct flights to a number of European airports including Heathrow as well as a selection of ex soviet airports. Tickets can be bought at the **Hainan Airlines** office at Shangpin Jie, Dongfang Dasha, 1st floor (© 0898/8827-9487). A taxi to the airport costs around ¥45 ($5.85/£2.95).

From the **bus station** on Jiefang Èr Lu (© 0898/8827-2440), express buses run to Haikou (3–3½ hr.; ¥65/$9.75/£4.90) every 20 minutes from 7am to 11pm; and minibuses run to Tongzha (2½ hr.; ¥20/$2.60/£1.30) from 6:15am to 5pm. Long-distance buses run to Guangzhou (16 hr.; ¥271/$35/£18) from 11am to 4:10pm; and to Shenzhèn (15 hr.; ¥ 271/$35/£18) at 11:50am. There are currently no passenger **boats** departing from Sanya.

Sanya now has a brand-new train station (© 0898/3188-7222) with direct trains to Guangzhou leaving at 4:50pm, 7:35pm, and 11:55pm.

GETTING AROUND   **Taxis** cost ¥10 ($1.30/65p) for in-town destinations, and around ¥40 ($5.20/£2.60) to Yalong Wan. **Buses** depart for Tianya Haijiao (¥4/50¢/25p) from the eastern side of Jiefang Lu. Minibus no. 102 (30 min., ¥6/80¢/40p) ostensibly runs every half0hour from Yuya Dadao to Yalong Wan but is not very consistent. Otherwise, take a minibus to Tiandu from just east of the traffic circle on Gangmen Lu and transfer to a motorcycle taxi (¥10/$1.30/65p), which will take you the rest of the way. A large, blue double-decker open top tourist bus runs from the furthest extent of Yalong Bay all the way back across Sanya Bay for just ¥5 (65¢/35p).

Bikes can be hired for ¥20 ($2.60/£1.30) per day at the **Wild Green Outdoor Club** (Lu Ye Hu Wai Ju Lè Bu; Sanya Wan Lu (© 0898/8836-9968).

Fast Facts

Banks, Foreign Exchange & ATMs   The **Bank of China** (open Mon–Fri 8am–5:30pm) is on Jiefang Èr Lu but does not have a ATM that accepts foreign cards.

Internet Access   There's a spot (¥2/25¢/15p per hr.) on the opposite corner of the Jinhong Resort.

Post Office   The post office (open 8am–6pm) is on Jiefang San Lu just north of Xinfeng Lu.

Visa Extensions   Visas can be renewed only in Haikou.

EXPLORING SANYA & BEYOND

For sun and sand lovers, **Yalong Wan (Yalong Bay)** is rather a disappointment. About 15km (10 miles) or a half-hour bus ride east of Sanya, this 7km (4-mile) stretch of sand edging the South Sea used to be perfect for walking, sunbathing, and swimming. Nowadays it has to contend with lying beside one of the busiest shipping routes in the world where huge polluting supertankers regularly flush their ballast tanks. Closer to town, the crescent-shaped **Da Donghai Beach,** about 3km (2 miles) southeast of town, is another alternative, but it would be useful if you can speak Russian in this area. The beach is smaller and more crowded than Yalong Bay's but you can engage in all the same activities here, including snorkeling, boating, and scuba diving. Be warned that safety standards are nonexistent; locals rush into half-hour scuba dives with almost no training or preparation, and a little American girl was killed here in a parasailing accident just last year. The beach at **Tianya Haijiao** (¥46/$6/£3), 23km (13 miles) to the west, is often considered to be the end of the earth (literally "edge of the sky, mouth of the sea"); it is best left to Chinese tourists who tramp through the sand in their patent-leather shoes to see Chinese calligraphy carved on giant boulders and fend off the persistent hawkers. A popular but expensive day trip is to **Xi Dao (West Island),** about a 10-minute boat ride off the coast of Tianya Haijiao, where you can dive, fish, or ride buggies in the sand dunes. Boats leave from the dock (✆ **0898/8834-3516**) just east of the Tianya Haijiao Tourist Area and cost ¥120 ($16/£7.80) round-trip.

OUTDOOR ACTIVITIES

Besides **swimming,** a plethora of water sports awaits the active. Several dive operations, including **Global Divers** (✆ **0898/8822-6600**) at Xiao Donghai Beach, organize **scuba diving** trips out to nearby reefs. **Sailing, windsurfing,** and **kayaking** are available at any of the resort hotels, and you can rent water-skis and motorized skiffs from the beaches at Yalong Bay and Da Donghai. There are now even **underwater scooters** (*ping tai hai di mo tuo*) at ¥128 ($17/£8.30) per hour. Your hotel can arrange trips out to local **golf** courses. The **Olympic Shooting and Entertainment Center** (Ao Lin Pi Kè Shè Ji Yu Lè Zhong Xing) on Yu Ya Lu 557 (✆ **0898/8822-1820**) has large stocks of AK47s and live chickens, giving new meaning to the word entertainment and pause for thought concerning the Beijing 2008 games.

WHERE TO STAY

Almost every multi-national hotel chain is now represented here, in the hope that getting a foothold here will give them easier access to other Chinese cities. While some actually claim to be environmentally conscious, the ones I spoke to were too busy guzzling resources and destroying natural ecologies to have even heard of the phrase "carbon footprint." The Hilton boasts the largest set of collection of swimming pools in the country and local water shortages go to prove it. The Kempinski, not to be outdone in wasting water, ensure that every one of their rooms have king-sized double bath on the balcony, not to mention its fleet of hideously ugly lime-green limousines. In addition, their unending staff requirements mean that the rest of the island is now almost devoid of English-speaking staff.

Donggang Seaview Hotel (Donggang Hai Jing Jiu Dian)   While I would not

recommend this place, it is interesting to see what the average Mr. and Mrs. Li have to put up with on their holidays. The walls of the reception area are adorned with exquisite ocean vistas as per the hotel name, while the rooms themselves look out onto gas tanks and rusty derricks. Most rooms seem to have a majiang table and the hotel is attached to the "Fei Poh" Fat Lady Seafood Restaurant. Just across the road, the Hilton house their staff in airless concrete dorms, well out of sight of resort guests.

Shèng Li Lu ✆ **0898/3189-8888**. Fax 0898/3198-8889. www.donggangsesview.com. 88 units. ¥150 ($20/£9.75) standard room. In room: A/C, mahjong table, TV, hair dryer.

Sanya Jinhong Resort (Jinhong Du Jia Jiu Dian)　Just inside from the snake bridge is the friendly and clean Sanya Jinhong Resort is a resort in name only. In fact it is a small city center hotel that is well located for eateries and evening strolls along the river (as long as you choose the bank that is not one long red light stretch). Rooms are well maintained and comfortable.

Heng Yi Lu 2, off Heping Lu opposite Tian Shan Da Sha ✆ **0898/3825-4888**. Fax 0898/3825-8080. 62 units. ¥148 (21/£10) standard room; ¥ 358 ($49/£25) suite. **Amenities:** Tea shop. In room: A/C, TV, hair dryer.

WHERE TO DINE

DayuTeppenyaki, DaDonghai Food Square　Translated into Chinglish as the "Summer Gastronomy Square," this is locally known as Red Square because of the number of Russians who congregate here for dinner. It is an outdoor food hall with a selection of vendors, our favorite being the friendly girls at Dayu who do everything from budget plates of seafood fried rice all the way up to lobster and abalone.

Mei Shi Guang Chang. ✆ **0898/6388-9855**. No credit cards. 5pm till late.

Mediterranean Restaurant, Cafe and Shisha Lounge　Owned and managed by an affable Italian who originally came to Hainan to lecture in molecular biology, this stylish eatery is a diamond lying among the garbage that makes up most of Sanya. Delicious pizzas, succulent pastas and crisp fresh salads that suit the sunny weather ten times better than the usual array of spicy Chinese hot pots

2nd Floor, Xi He Xi Lu. ✆ **0898/8825-2548**. No credit cards. 11:30am–11pm.

13

Yangzi & Beyond

by Lee Wing-sze

In addition to shared borders, the land-locked provinces of Sichuan, Hubei, and Hunan and the municipality of Chongqing have in common the world's third-longest river, the Chang Jiang ("Long River," aka Yangzi), whose navigable reaches start in Sichuan, thread through Chongqing, and roughly define the border between Hubei and Hunan. Now China's heartland, this region—home to the Chu, Ba, and Shu cultures—was for centuries a land of exile and colonization for the ruling kingdoms of the North China Plain. The Qin (221–206 B.C.) banished thousands to faraway, inhospitable Shu (present-day Sichuan), and China's most famous martyr, Qu Yuan, was exiled to the southern edges of his own Chu kingdom where he drowned himself in the Miluo River (in present-day northern Hunan).

Five hundred years later, this same swath of central China was the battlefield on which the rulers of Wei, Shu, and Wu contended for complete dominion over China. Many sights along the Yangzi commemorate the heroes of those 60 years of turmoil known simply as the Three Kingdoms Period (220–80). By the 3rd century, Buddhism and Daoism were spreading rapidly through the region, and many of the hundreds of temples that dot the sacred mountains of Sichuan, Hubei, and Hunan were first constructed at this time.

In addition to being the home of five holy Buddhist and/or Daoist mountains, this area contains some of China's most beautiful scenery—in northern Sichuan and northern Hunan—and lays claim to seven World Heritage Sites.

Until recently, most foreign travelers came to this part of central China to see the Three Gorges—the spectacular 242km (150-mile) channel comprising Qutang, Wu, and Xiling gorges—but with China's equivalent of the New Deal underway, new airports, rail lines, and expressways are opening all the time, making travel to remote areas much less painful.

If the Three Gorges are on your itinerary, try to leave yourself a few days on either end to explore Chongqing and Wuhan. And a day trip from Chongqing to the Buddhist grottoes at Dazu is well worth the time. Sichuan is best explored over 2 or 3 weeks. Use Chengdu as a place to leave extra luggage and to return to for a break and some urban sightseeing before going out again. In Hunan, do the same with Changsha. *Note:* Unless otherwise noted, hours listed for attractions and restaurants are daily.

The Yangzi Region

1 Chengdu ⭐

Sichuan Province, 504km (313 miles) NW of Chongqing, 842km (523 miles) SW of Xi'an

Ask a resident of Beijing or Shanghai what to do in Sichuan's capital of Chengdu, and 9 times out of 10 they'll tell you to drink tea and eat hot pot, such is the city's reputation as a culinary capital that knows how to take it easy. Indeed, Chengdu's cuisine is irresistible and tea drinking is a custom that took hold here 1,300 years ago and never let go. With few genuine ancient sights within the city proper (Du Fu's cottage is only a replica; Wuhou Temple is ho-hum), drinking tea may be Chengdu's most durable link to the past. But what Chengdu lacks in ancient sites, it makes up for in charm and atmosphere. Like so many cities in central China, Chengdu has a pretty little river running through it. The narrow Fu He and its southern tributary form a sort of moat around the city, sections of which are lined with attractive restaurants and teahouses. The city is also in the midst of a building boom, but a few old ramshackle warrens and outdoor markets still survive just west of the city square.

Chengdu is the gateway to scenic Jiuzhai Gou, the Buddhist mountains of Emei Shan and Le Shan, and one of the most important panda breeding centers. It's also a traveler's haven and a place to gather information between trips. People are friendly

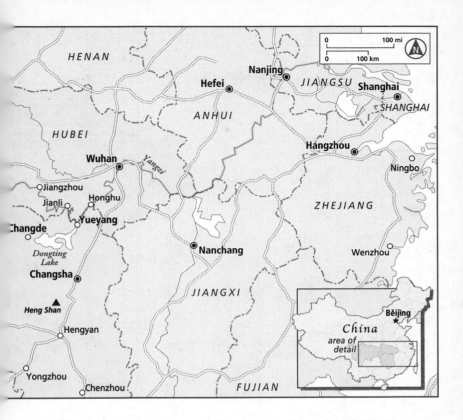

and the pace unrushed. And because Chengdu is one of the few cities with daily flights to Lhasa, many travelers come here to arrange transportation to Tibet.

ESSENTIALS

GETTING THERE   Shuangliu Airport is 17km (11 miles) south of Chengdu. Destinations include Beijing (eight or nine flights daily); Guangzhou (eight or nine flights daily); Hong Kong (one or two flights daily); and Kunming (8–10 flights daily). To Lhasa, there are one to four flights daily, but it's always best to book the 6am flight; later flights are often canceled or delayed. Travelers are no longer required to enter Tibet with a group of five or more, but Tibet Tourism Bureau (TTB) permits are, for the time being, still required. It takes 3 to 7 days to obtain a permit. The price of a one-way flight to Tibet, TTB permit, and airport transfer in Chengdu is around ¥2,000 ($260/£130). All flights can be booked with any of the several English-speaking travel agents at and near the Traffic Hotel. **Dragonair** has an office in the Sheraton Lido (© **028/8676-8828**) at Renmin Zhong Lu 15, 1 Duan. An **airport shuttle** from the China Southwest office on Renmin Nan Lu (next to Min Shan Fandian) takes 45 minutes and costs ¥10 ($1.30/65p); it departs every half-hour. A less direct CAAC shuttle (Minhang Banche), no. 303, leaves every half-hour from 7am to 7pm

Chengdu

Sānxīng Duī Bówùguǎn
(Sānxīng Duī Museum)
三星堆博物馆

Xióngmāo Jīdì/
Dàxióngmāo Fánzhí Zhōngxīn
(Panda Research Base/
Giant Panda Breeding Center)
熊猫基地/大熊猫繁殖中心

¥ Bank
🏛 Rail Station
🛕 Temple
PSB Public-Security Visas
TA Travel Agent

Wǔguì Qiáo Qìchēzhàn
(Wǔguì Qiáo Bus Station)
五桂桥汽车站

BUS STATIONS ▼
Xīn Nán Mén Qìchē Zhàn
(Xīn Nán Mén Bus Station)
新南门汽车站

Zhāojué Sì Qìchē Zhàn **1**
(Zhāojué Temple Bus Stati
昭觉寺汽车站

from the CAAC office at the North Railway Station. The 22km (14-mile) ride takes 70 minutes and costs ¥6 (80¢/40p). A **taxi** from the city center to the airport costs ¥50 to ¥75 ($6.50–$9.75/£3.25–£4.90), including a ¥10 ($1.30/65p) toll.

The main **railway station** is at the northern end of Renmin Bei Lu, 8km (5 miles) north of the Mao statue in the city center. The ticket office, open 24 hours, is to the right of the main building. Try to purchase tickets at least 2 days in advance. Major destinations include Beijing (fast trains; 26 hr.; hard sleeper ¥420/$55/£27), Kunming (fast trains 18½ hr.; ¥257/$33/£17), and Shanghai (36½ hr.; hard sleeper ¥467/$61/£30).

Xin Nan Men Bus Station (Xin Nan Men Qichezhan), at the corner of Xin Nan Lu and Linjiang Zhong Lu and next to the Traffic Hotel, is clean, efficient, and tourist-friendly (has signs in English). Air-conditioned buses leave from here for Le Shan (2 hr.; ¥38–¥42/$4.95–$5.45/£2.45–£2.70) and for Emei Shan (2 hr. 15 min.; ¥34/$4.40/£2.20); to Jiuzhai Gou (12 hr.; ¥108–¥121/$14–$16/£7–£8), Dujiang Yan and Qingcheng Shan (¥25/$3.25/£1.65).

Air-conditioned buses to Chongqing leave throughout the day from the equally clean, efficient **Wu Gui Qiao Bus Station (Wu Gui Qiao Qichezhan)** southeast of the city center on Yinghui Lu (4¼ hr.; ¥125/$16/£8). Buses to Wolong now leave from the **Chadianzi Keyun Zhan** in Chengdu's western suburbs near the Third Ring Road (San Huan Lu).

VISITOR INFORMATION   Pick up the free monthly English-language *Go West Magazine* in hotels and Western-style restaurants for its listings of entertainment and shopping in Chengdu and Chongqing.

GETTING AROUND   Chengdu's flat terrain and many bike lanes make walking and biking easy, but blocks are long, and crossing the river can require a trek before reaching a bridge. Renmin Lu bisects the city on the north-south axis. Its east-west counterpart is less straightforward: At the heart of the city (Tianfu Sq.), Renmin Xi Lu runs west from the square and Renmin Dong Lu runs east; after a block in either direction, the names change every block or so. Unfortunately, most of Chengdu's avenues have a multitude of names, making a street map essential.

Traffic Hotel (Jiaotong Binguan) at Linjiang Zhong Lu 77 rents **bicycles** for ¥15 ($1.95/£1) per day with a ¥300 ($39/£20) deposit. Take bus no. 6, 49, 50, or 55 and get off at the Xin Nan Men stop. City **buses** (¥1/15¢/10p; air-conditioned ¥2/20¢/10p) serve all parts of the city. Some buses charge ¥1 (15¢/10p) extra at night. Routes are on city maps. Both bus no. 16 and minibus no. 5 (not the full-size no. 5) running the length of Renmin Lu from the North Railway Station to the South Railway Station are useful lines. The most common **taxi** is the midrange Jetta. Taxi rates are ¥5 (65¢/35p) for the first kilometer, then ¥1.40 (20¢/10p) per kilometer thereafter; the rate increases to ¥2.10 (25¢/15p) per kilometer above 7km (4⅓ miles). From 10pm to 6am the first kilometer costs ¥6 (80¢/40p); after that the fare is ¥1.70 (20¢/10p) per kilometer for the first 7km and ¥2.55 (35¢/15p) after that.

At the moment, the city is building the underground railway, Chengdu Metro, to be opened in 2010. Many roads are now blocked because of the construction work, and traffic is unpleasantly chaotic most of the time. Some of the bus routes may be affected.

TOURS   Chengdu has enough good, English-speaking **independent travel agents** that you needn't bother with CITS and its generally higher rates. The best deals can be found inside and in the vicinity of the Jiaotong Binguan (Traffic Hotel). The **Traffic Travel Service** (inside the hotel) and **Tianfu International Travel Service** at the entrance to the hotel both book air and train tickets and offer a variety of tour packages. For a **private guide,** Mr. Tray Lee is a highly recommended freelance guide. His prices are competitive, his English excellent, and he's always reachable by mobile phone (✆ **0139/8160-5307;** message only 028/8555-4250; fax 028/8556-4952; lee_tray@ hotmail.com). His "Sichuan Opera" tour (see "Chengdu After Dark," later in this chapter) costs ¥80 ($10/£5.20) for admission, a backstage visit, one-way transportation, and an English-speaking guide. Die-hards stay for the whole 4 hours, but that's not required. **BikeChina Adventures** (www.bikechina.com), an American company based in Chengdu, arranges adventure bicycle tours through any part of China.

FAST FACTS

Banks, Foreign Exchange & ATMs   The **Bank of China** (open Mon–Fri 8:30am–noon and 2–6pm), Zhimin Lu 36 near the Traffic Hotel and Xin Nan Men Bus Station, has full foreign-exchange facilities and an ATM. The branch at Renmin Nan Lu opposite the Min Shan Fandian also has an ATM, and is open the same hours.

Consulates   The U.S. Consulate is at Lingshiguan Lu 4 (✆ **028/8558-3992;** open Mon–Thurs 1:30–5:30pm, Fri 9am–noon and 1:30–4pm; consular.chengdu@ state.gov). Take bus no. 16, 61, 49, or 50 to Lingshiguan Lu.

Internet Access   Try the **Qilin Wangba** and **Jin Shou Wangba,** which both charge ¥2 (25¢/10p) per hour. Both are halfway down the alley off Lingshiguan Lu near the U.S. Consulate. There is also an Internet cafe on the second floor above **Xin Nan Men Bus Station** that is surrounded by computer game machines. It also charges ¥2 (25¢/10p) per hour. Otherwise, you can find Internet cafes around the university, the U.S. Consulate, and the Jiaotong Binguan, most of them open 24 hours. Dial-up is ✆ 163.

Post Office   The Jinjiang Hotel post office (open 8am–noon and 2:30–5:30pm) at Renmin Nan Lu 80, 2 Duan, opposite the Min Shan Fandian, is reliable and conveniently located.

Visa Extensions   The Exit-Entry Office of the **PSB (Jingwai Renyuan Banzheng Qianzheng Ting)** is at Wenwu Lu 144 (✆ **028/8640-7067;** open Mon–Fri 9am–noon and 1–5pm). The entrance is at 391 Shuncheng Dajie. Processing time is officially 5 days, but 3 days seems to be the average, and it's even speedier if you show an ongoing ticket. Take bus no. 55, 62, or 73 from railway stations 16 or 64; get off at the junction of Renmin Zhong Lu and Wenwu Lu and walk east.

EXPLORING CHENGDU

The best way to enjoy Chengdu is to take long walks or cycle through the city, relax in a few teahouses and hot pot restaurants, and spread your visits to the best sights over a few days—or longer if you're using Chengdu as a base from which to visit out-of-town attractions. Here are some of my favorite strolls:

- Much of Chengdu's Tibetan community lives southeast of the Wuhou Temple, and the area around the Southwest Minority Nationalities College and the Tibetan Hospital is interesting for its bookstores, Tibetan shops, and people. **Wuhou Ci Heng Jie,** in particular, has lots of shops selling Tibetan and minority goods. Have lunch at **Xizang Fengqing Wu** (p. 707).

- Directly to the east of Wuhou Temple is Chengdu's entertainment landscape, **Jinli Gu Jie (Jinli Ancient Street).** Completed in early 2005, this narrow strip of restaurants, bars, and souvenir stores is built in the style of traditional Eastern Sichuan architecture and is surprisingly tastefully done. Catering more to locals than tourists, the walk is as interesting for the architecture as it is for the opportunity to just mingle with middle-class Chinese. The strip is also well worth visiting for its alley of traditional Sichuan street food—an infinitely more hygienic environment than where you'll usually find it.

- To truly experience local people's lifestyle, one of the best ways is heading to **Kuan/Zhaixiangzi (Wide/Narrow Lane),** located in the west of the city center. The streets are full of teahouses and traditional Chinese architecture erected back in the Ming and Qing dynasties. However, the area is not as bustling as the old days because of the redevelopment plan aiming to turn the then-residential area to a commercial tourist spot. On Zhaixiangzi, though most residents have been evacuated and old buildings were demolished, locals still love to spend their day here, enjoying a cup of tea, playing cards and mahjong on Kuanxiangzi.

- Chengdu's art students used to sell their work on the roads leading into their campus, but the art trade has since been institutionalized and moved into the government building **Songxian Qiao Yishu Cheng (Songshan Bridge Art City)** on Huanhua Bei Lu. While all this might make the complex seem tragically bereft of bohemian spirit, it is worth taking an afternoon to wander through the stalls of "antiques" (both new and old), old party propaganda, Chinese handicrafts, and art. While much of what is on offer is indistinguishable from the pap passed off as Chinese culture in every city you are likely to visit, there are enough gems to warrant some of your time. Of particular interest is the **Zhongchuan Shoucang (Zhongchuan Collection)** (A Qu, second floor no. 53), run by Yang Xiguang, a former cadre selling off his extensive personal collection of Cultural Revolution propaganda. Mr. Yang does not speak English, but the collection more than speaks for itself.

Qingyang Gong (Green Ram Monastery)

Directly west of the city center, this Daoist monastery is culturally and historically the most important sight in the city. It's said that at Qingyang Fair (its first incarnation), Laozi attained immortality. And it was here that he revealed the *Daode Jing (Classic of the Dao)* to Yin Xi, frontier guardian at the Hangu Pass and last man to see Laozi before he left the world of men for Mount Kunlun, gateway to the Western Paradise. Today Qingyang Gong is one of the most active and important Daoist monasteries in China. Among its treasures, of greatest historical significance is a set of rare and elegant pear-wood printing plates of abstracts of scriptures in the Daoist canon. The grounds contain six halls on a central axis, a room for printing Daoist texts that stands to the east, and a room for worshiping Daoist sages that stands to the west. The **Hall of Three Purities (Sanqing Dian)** is the monastery's main building, but the most emblematic has to be the **Bagua Ting (Pavilion of the Eight Trigrams).** This octagonal building sitting on a square pedestal (symbolic of the earth) rises 20m (65 ft.) and has two flounces of upturned roofs covered in yellow, green, and purple ceramic tiles. Between the roofs, each facet of the octagon has at its center a plaque of the eight trigrams set off by a pattern of swastikas, symbolic of the sun or the movement of fire. The 81 carved dragons are said to symbolize the 81 incarnations of Laozi, but the number has closer associations with Chinese numerology and the belief in nine as the most "accomplished" of numbers. A bookstore in the **Hunyuan Dian (Hall of Chaotic Origin)** sells souvenirs alongside Mao bookmarks, Daoist study guides, and a fortunetelling manual called "Unlocking the Secrets of the *Book of Changes.*" If you buy one of the likenesses of Laozi that comes in a cloth envelope and hand it to the Daoist priest behind the counter, he'll burn incense over it to *kaiguang* or "open its light."

Escape the din of the city at the partially covered outdoor **teahouse,** where you can sit in a bamboo chair and watch other customers play mahjong and chat with friends (albeit sometimes on cellphones). Next door is a **vegetarian restaurant,** open 9am to 2pm.

Yi Huan Lu Xi, 2 Duan (at Yi Huan Lu and Qingyang Zheng Jie intersection, on the grounds of Wenhua Gongyuan/ Cultural Park). Admission ¥5 (65¢/35p). 8am–5:30pm. Bus: no. 11, 42, 47, 59 or 302.

Sanxing Dui Bowuguan ✪

This modern, spiral-shaped museum, opened in 1997, houses one of the most remarkable collections of ancient sculpture, masks, and ritual bronzes in China—don't miss it. Discovered in 1986, these otherworldly, artistically sophisticated tomb relics have sparked debate about the origins of the culture that produced them (as far back as the 14th c. B.C.) and its connection, if any, to the later Shu culture. The museum brochure equates the Sanxing Dui civilization with the Shu, but some scholars doubt this, and there are many unanswered questions. For example, why is there no mention of this culture in historical records? When and why did the civilization disappear? Why do many of the masks and human busts seem to have been burned and deliberately shattered—quite possibly by the very people who created them?

Still, it's a marvelous collection. Highlights include a delightful ornament-bearing bronze holy tree supported by three kneeling guards and crowned with hawk-beaked birds. The piece most emblematic of the Sanxing Dui is a 2.4m (8-ft.) standing bronze figure thought to be a sorcerer. Barefoot and standing on a pedestal of zoomorphic design, the creature has a long forehead, oversize eyes, and ears shaped like butterfly wings. Many of the bronze heads wear masks of pure gold. There is also an impressive gold-covered stick believed to be the ritual wand of a shaman. There are photos of the excavation process, English labels and, supposedly, an English-speaking guide on duty for ¥100 ($13/£6.50). Give yourself about 2 hours to explore the museum.

Guanghan, 40km (25 miles) north of Chengdu. www.sxd.cn. Admission ¥80 ($10/£5.20). 8:30am–5pm. Direct buses (¥12/$1.55/80p) leave Chengdu Tourist Transportation and Service Center at 8:30am and 3pm. From Zhaojue Si Qichezhan (Zhaojue Temple bus station) near the zoo to Guanghan. Frequent departures throughout the day. Deluxe A/C bus (¥10/$1.30/65p), 20-min. ride. Bus no. 6 leaves Guanghan for Sanxing Dui every 20 min. for ¥2 (25¢/10p).

Jinsha Yizhi Bowuguan (Jinsha Site Museum)

Jinsha Yizhi, northwest of the city center, is another major ancient relic discovered in Sichuan after Sanxing Dui. Opened in 2007, the new museum has collections including gold wares, bronze, jade, ivory, and stone statues of human portraits and animals evacuated from the site, which was discovered in 2001. Like Sanxing Dui, it is believed to be part of the ancient Shu Kingdom 3,000 years ago. Some of the collections are quite similar to that of Sanxing Dui. An English-speaking guide charges ¥100 ($13/£6.50) each person.

Jinsha Relics Lu 2 (west of Chengdu city). www.jinshasitemuseum.com. Admission ¥80 ($10/£5.20). 8am–6pm. Bus: no. 7, 14, 82, 96, 311, 401, or 502 to Qingyang Dadao Bei or 901 to Jinsha Yizhi Lu.

Sichuan Daxue Bowuguan (Sichuan University Museum) ✪

Construction of a new provincial museum is underway, but it will be hard to match Sichuan University's fascinating, well-presented collection, which includes Han and Tang dynasty Buddhist carvings; important Daoist documents, ritual instruments, talisman blocks, and clothing worn by shamans from the Eastern Han dynasty (25–220) to the Qing dynasty (1644–1912); bronzes from Ba and Shu cultures; a shadow puppet theater; and an ethnology collection featuring artifacts from a dozen central China minorities. Rarely are costumes displayed in such a dignified manner and without mannequins.

On the first floor, in the **Hall of Stone Carvings,** look for the exquisite 2m (7-ft.) carved Tang dynasty figure of a **bodhisattva** draped in cloth and jewels. On the second floor, there are several standouts. In the small room of ancient pottery from the Eastern Han dynasty, look for the life-size **clay dog** with hanging jowls and bulbous nose. The **Tibetan trumpet** made of a human femur can be found in the Exhibition Hall of Tibetan Artifacts. In the Daoist room, don't miss the **stone certificate of purchase** for a piece of subterranean real estate. In the bureaucratic netherworld, these funerary land deeds were taken to the grave as the deceased's proof of ownership of the land in which he or she was buried. Lastly, located in the same room is a circular **jade disk** *(bi)* from the Shang dynasty, symbol of Heaven (thought to be round), which was used in worship and burial (when it was probably placed beneath the corpse's back).

Enter through east gate from Wangjiang Lu; walk to end, turn right; look for the lotus pond; the museum is adjacent. ⓒ **028/8541-2451.** Admission ¥10 ($1.30/65p). Mon–Fri 8:30am–5:30pm. Bus: no. 3, 35, 19, or 27.

Wang Anting Xiaoxiao Zhanlanguan ⋒ *Finds*   Informally known as the **Mao Museum,** this very small exhibition hall/apartment is the most eccentric museum you're likely to find in China. The 57,000 badges and Mao pins, along with two more tons of Mao memorabilia still boxed in the attic, were all collected by the museum's owner, Wang Anting—who said that Mao came to him in a dream instructing him to share his collection with the world. In addition to badges, there are busts, buttons, posters, magazines from the 1960s, and photographs from the same era. At the apartment's center, where a dining room table should be, is a large framed sepia-toned portrait of a beatific Mao. In front of it are burning incense and offerings of packages of instant noodles, and usually a plate of pears or a dish of candies. Other photos include one of a decrepit-looking Mao as he shakes the hand of Julie Nixon Eisenhower.

The best day to visit is December 26, when the museum and its small street are packed with people who've come to celebrate Mao's birthday.

Wufu Jie 23, northwest of the Mao statue; facing Mao, walk left (west). Turn right at the big street with a traffic light; pass Jinjiaba (lane with a market); turn at the 2nd left down Pingan Xiang; the entrance to Wufu Jie is on the right. Admission is free; however, the proprietor will encourage donations to support the museum. 9am–5pm.

Wenshu Yuan   The best things about this active, Tang-founded Buddhist monastery are neither its gilded statues nor its relatively youthful buildings, but its teahouse filled with people reading, knitting, and just relaxing, and its excellent vegetarian restaurant with tables for two and windows overlooking the gardens. Outside, the street is lined with shops selling incense, paper money, and other Buddhist paraphernalia. Inside, locals come to worship and burn incense. The 1st and 15th days of the lunar month are the most active. Another day that draws large crowds is the 19th day of the second lunar month, when the monastery celebrates the birthday of China's favorite bodhisattva, Guanyin, Goddess of Mercy. The Huayan Scripture, written in human blood, and the cranial bones of the monk Xuanzang are among the treasures housed at Wenshu. A pleasing and unusual Song fresco of a child worshiping Guanyin can be found near the gold-plated bronze Guanyin.

Wenshu Yuan Jie, just off Renmin Zhong Lu. Admission ¥5 (65¢/35p). 8am–5:40pm; restaurant 10:30am–10:30pm. Enter to the right of main entrance. Bus: no. 16 or 55.

Xiongmao Jidi/Daxiongmao Fanzhi Zhongxin (Panda Research Base/Giant Panda Breeding Center) ⭑   This research base, which has elements of a veterinary lab, a park, a panda habitat, and a zoo, is one of the best places to see giant pandas. The much more wild and natural Wolong Nature Reserve (p. 716) would be better, but—except in its panda enclosures—panda sightings are few and far between. The stated purpose of the breeding center is to increase the captive population of pandas in order to reintroduce some to the wild. The grounds of the research base, covered with trees, flowers, and 14 species of bamboo, are lovely and, at the very least, provide a pleasant escape from the noise and congestion of Chengdu proper. As you follow pathways through the reserve you may see not only giant pandas but red pandas (closer to a raccoon than a panda), black-necked cranes, and white storks. You might also run into visiting field researchers. Your best chance of seeing pandas is at feeding time, 8:30 to 10am, although a few, mostly those for breeding, are in cages. Ask if there are cubs around—a mother panda with babe in arms is a sight not to be missed. Allow an hour to get to the base, two to stroll the grounds. Alternately you can take a tour cart for ¥10 ($1.25/60p) and reduce the visit to about 50 minutes; the tour is conducted in Chinese, but at least you go straight to the pandas.

Xiongmao Da Dao, northern suburb, northeast of the zoo. ⓒ 028/8351-6748. Admission ¥30 ($3.90/£1.95). 8am–6pm. Bus: no. 902 outside Traffic Hotel or no. 107 or 532 from Zhaojue Si Qichezhan (Zhaojue Temple bus station).

SHOPPING
Chengdu abounds in supermarkets, including three **Carrefour (Jialefu)** stores (open 9am–10pm). Thanks to discounts and a broad selection of Chinese and imported products, shopping here always feels like the day before Christmas—festive, but impossibly crowded. If you abhor body contact with perfect strangers, go elsewhere. If you don't mind it, the most accessible location is at Babao Jie 1 (ⓒ **028/8626-6789**). Take bus no. 4, 56, or 76 to Babao Jie. **Trust-mart (Haoyouduo Chaoshi),** located at Jinxiu Lu 2 near the corner of Kehua Bei Lu on the south side of town, is a block long, next to McDonald's and almost opposite KFC. Open from 9am to 10pm, it's a grocery store, drug store, and department store in one, and one of the few stores in China to carry tampons. Take bus no. 6, 76, or 77. The best, most convenient supermarket at which to buy snacks for a long train journey is the huge **Renmin Shangchang (People's Market)** opposite the main railway station. It also has a bakery and a fast-food restaurant that serves a Chinese breakfast for ¥1 to ¥4 (15¢–50¢/5p–25p). Open 7:30am to 9:30pm. **Chunxi Lu** is the most lively shopping and dinning area. It has restaurants of different cuisines and major shopping malls such as Ito Yokado, New Asia Plaza, and the newly open Japanese brand Isetan. Take bus no. 58 or 81.

WHERE TO STAY
EXPENSIVE
Holiday Inn Crowne Plaza (Zongfu Huangguan Jiari Jiudian)   Located a few blocks from the city center and next door to Parkson, this five-star international hotel used to be the best in Chengdu. It still is quite good, with clean bathrooms and pleasant staff, but the Sheraton (see below) is a notch above and no more expensive. If you stay here, rooms with a single king-size bed rather than twins are slightly bigger.

Zongfu Jie 31 (4 blocks east of the Mao statue). ⓒ **800/968-688** or 028/8678-6666. Fax 028/8678-9789. www.ichotelsgroup. com. 434 units. ¥1,623 ($211/£106) standard room. Most rates include breakfast. 40% discount standard; add 15% service charge. AE, DC, MC, V. Bus: no. 3, 4, 7, 45, 58, or 98. **Amenities:** 2 restaurants; 2 bars; deli; indoor pool; health club; sauna; airline, train, and bus ticketing; business center; forex; 24-hr. room service; laundry/dry cleaning. *In room:* A/C, satellite TV, dataport, broadband Internet access, minibar, fridge, hair dryer, safe.

Shangri-la Chengdu (Xianggelila Dafandian) ⭑⭑ Opened in mid-2007, Shangri-la Chengdu is the newest five-star hotel in the city. Located beside the Jiajiang River, the hotel enjoys a spectacular view of the Hejiang Pavilion and the beautiful garden along the riverside. Guest rooms are spacious and stylish, equipped with plasma TVs. The bathrooms are large, with separate tub and shower. The hotel, with its excellent service, is now the best choice in Chengdu.

Binjiang Dong Lu 9 (near Tianxianqiao Binhe Lu). ⓒ **028/8888-9999**. Fax 028/8888-6666. www.shangri-la.com. 594 units. ¥988–¥1,088 ($128–$141/£64–£71) standard room. 15% service charge. AE, DC, MC, V. **Amenities:** Restaurant; bar; indoor pool; tennis court; health club; spa; salon; airline, train, and bus ticketing; business center; forex; 24-hr. room service; same-day laundry/dry cleaning. *In room:* A/C, satellite TV, dataport, broadband Internet access, minibar, fridge, hair dryer, safe.

Sheraton Chengdu Lido (Tianfu Lidu Xilaideng Fandian) ⭑ Located 1km (½ mile) north of the city center, the Sheraton is one of the most attractive luxury hotels in Chengdu. The lobby's fountain and large floral arrangement give this spot a warmer ambience than the standard hotel, and the front desk staff is amiable and efficient. Although the standard rooms aren't as spacious as those at the Holiday Inn, the cozy decor is more inviting.

Renmin Zhong Lu, 1 Duan 15. ⓒ **028/8676-8999**. Fax 028/8676-8888. www.sheraton.com/chengdu. 402 units. ¥800–¥930 ($104–$121/£52–£60) standard room. Most rates include breakfast. 15% service charge. AE, DC, MC, V. Bus: no. 16. Minibus: no. 5 from railway station. **Amenities:** 2 restaurants; 2 bars; indoor heated pool; health club, Jacuzzi; sauna; airline, train, and bus ticketing; business center; forex; 24-hr. room service; massage; laundry/dry cleaning. *In room:* A/C, satellite TV, dataport, minibar, fridge, hair dryer, safe.

MODERATE

Jinli Renjia Kezhan (Jinli Home Hotel) This Sichuan-themed hotel is one of the new economical choices in Chengdu. It is close to Jinli Gu Jie and Wuhou. Rooms are clean and simple with red decor. Beds are comfy enough, but bathrooms are a bit small, with shower only. Noise from the strip of Chinese restaurants across the street can be heard inside the room, but it's an acceptable level.

Jiang Cheng Hua, Daosangshu Jie, Wuhou District. ⓒ **028/8559-5111**. Fax 028/8555-5111. 80 units. ¥238–¥288 ($31–$37/£15–£19) standard room. 20%–30% discount is standard. No credit cards. **Amenities:** Restaurant; business center; airline, train, and bus ticketing; limited room service; laundry. *In room:* A/C, TV.

Xinzu Binguan (Sunjoy Inn) Located just a short walk from the U.S. Consulate, this three-star hotel was renovated in 2004. Management and staff pride themselves on continued maintenance of the building and guest rooms; clean hallway carpets and unstained sinks—rarities in all but the priciest hotels—attest to their sincerity. Guest rooms and bathrooms are medium in size. Furnishings are run-of-the-mill but better maintained than most in this range. The hotel is connected to one of the best non-Chinese restaurants in Chengdu, **Tandoor Indian Cuisine** (p. 707).

Renmin Nan Lu, 4 Duan 34. ⓒ **028/8557-1660**. Fax 028/8554-6598. www.sunjoy-inn.com. 189 units. ¥400–¥460 ($52–$60/£26–£30) standard room. Rates include breakfast. 20% discount is standard. AE, DC, MC, V. Bus: no. 16, 19, or 72. Minibus: no. 5. **Amenities:** 3 restaurants; bar; exercise room; sauna; salon; airline, train, and bus ticketing; small business center; forex; 24-hr. room service; laundry/dry cleaning. *In room:* A/C, TV, broadband Internet access, minibar, fridge.

INEXPENSIVE

Guanhua Qingnian Youshe (Sim's Cozy Guesthouse) The cheapest of Chengdu's budget offerings, Sim's is spartan but clean and well situated—a good starting point for exploring the city. Staying here is also a great way to mingle with

Chengdu locals: It is located on a side street that is not only close to Wenshu Temple, one of the more lively temples in town, but is also filled with seniors playing mahjong on the side of the road. The hotel has communal bathrooms, a common room with a TV and an extensive DVD collection, and a leafy outdoor area with tables and chairs—ideal in summer to meet fellow travelers. To account for the vagaries of the seasons, ¥20 ($2.60/£1.30) extra will buy you air-conditioning and ¥5 (65¢/35p) will get you an electric blanket. The hotel staff and the in-house travel agent all speak English.

Xi Zhushi Jie 42 (just down from Wenshu Yuan, on the east side). © 028/8691-4422. www.gogosc.com. 24 units. ¥70 ($9.10/£4.55) standard room. No credit cards. Bus: no. 16, 64, 55, or 80. **Amenities:** Restaurant; airline and train ticketing; laundry/dry-cleaning service; Internet access; bike rental.

Jiaotong Binguan (Traffic Hotel) *Value* Catering to independent travelers and backpackers, this one-star hotel puts Internet access, Tibet travel news, rental bikes, and bag storage at your fingertips. Equally important, room rates range from inexpensive to moderate. The staff is friendly and helpful (most speak some English), and the **Anchor Bar** (see below) in front is *the* place to meet other like-minded travelers. Although the elevator has a disturbing rattle, rooms are clean and sort of cozy.

Linjiang Zhong Lu 6 (next to the Xin Nan Men Bus Station). © 028/8545-1017. Fax 028/8544-0977. www.traffichotel. com. 151 units. ¥240 ($31/£16) standard room; ¥290 ($38/£19) triple with bathroom; ¥40 ($5.20/£2.60) bed in 3-person room with A/C and communal shower/toilet. No credit cards. Bus: no. 15, 16, 28, or 55. **Amenities:** 2 restaurants; bar; airline, train, and bus ticketing; bike rental; business center; laundry/dry cleaning. *In room:* A/C, TV.

WHERE TO DINE

Anchor Bar (An Ba) *Value* HOME-STYLE WESTERN/CHINESE Situated in front of the Traffic Hotel, this cozy little bar is a great place to relax over a cold beer; plus, Internet access is free if you buy a meal there. For the most part, the menu lacks imagination—both in the Chinese and Western offerings—with the exception of an excellent hot Western breakfast. But all is forgiven when you sink into one of the soft, welcoming couches that are a godsend after a day spent pounding city streets. The rest of the decor is Tibetan-inspired with warm, earthy colors. The staff speaks limited English but is a friendly lot and will burn your pictures onto a CD, and let you use the TV to watch a DVD after 8pm.

Linjiang Zhong Lu 6. © 028/8545-4520. Main courses ¥15–¥30 ($1.95–$3.90/£1–£1.95). No credit cards. 9am until the last customer goes home. Book exchange. Bus: no. 15, 16, 28, or 55.

Baguo Buyi *★★* *Value* SICHUAN Delicious local fare made with fresh, natural ingredients is served here in artfully rustic surroundings—dried corn stalks and red peppers hang between photographs of farmhouses and peasant life. A spiral wooden staircase wrapped around a large artificial tree leads to second-floor tables with views of the open kitchen. There's enough space for privacy, and service is excellent. House specialties include the gelatinous green turtle stewed with taro (*yuer shao jiayu*)—a regional delicacy, but not to everyone's taste. More reliable would be *huiguo houpi cai* (twice-cooked thick-skinned greens), a leafy green vegetable boiled and stir-fried in a delicious broad bean sauce, and more inspired than its name suggests. Also try *yecai ba* (steamed glutinous rice bread with wild vegetables wrapped in corn husks), and *doufu jiyu* (tofu and golden carp). The tasty sauce, made of tomato, spring onion, chilies, and beans, makes this a particular favorite with locals.

Renmin Nan Lu 20, 4 Duan (near Lingshiguan Lu). © 028/8553-1688. English menu. Meal for 2 ¥50–¥100 ($6.50–$13/£3.25–£6.50). No credit cards. 11:30am–2:30pm and 5–10pm. Bus: no. 16 or 99.

Caigen Xiang ★ SICHUAN With four outlets and a cooking school, this is one of Chengdu's most popular restaurants. Specializing in dishes made with traditional pickled vegetables *(pao cai)*, the restaurant has won awards for its *paojiao moyu zai* (pickled pepper with baby squid). Two other distinctive dishes are Caigen Xiang spareribs *(Caigen Xiang paigu)*, which fall off the bone and are cooked in a delicious sauce that renders them juicy and tender, and fish with pickled vegetables *(paocai jiayu)*. This is a whole fish served in a red sauce with a variety of fresh and pickled vegetables. Bones have to be dealt with, but the fish is delicate and tasty.

Renmin Nan Lu (near corner of Tongzi Lin Bei Lu). ⓒ 028/8518-5967. Photo menu. Meal for 2 ¥40–¥200 ($5.20–$26/£2.60–£13). No credit cards. 9:30am–9:30pm. Bus: no. 16 or 99 to Jinxiu Huayuan.

Dave's Pizzeria (Bisafong) PIZZA If you're lonely for friendly faces or other travelers, you'll find both in this cheerful restaurant serving pizzas, salads, and pastas. Opened in 2007 by the owner of Dave's Oasis hostel, the joint is managed by a chef from England. The pizzas are tasty, with a satisfying selection, and the portion is just right. You can also enjoy the free Internet and wireless access at the same time. Staff is friendly and speaks English.

Remin Nan Lu, Sector 2, no. 19. ⓒ 028/6655-9988. English menu. Pizza ¥30–¥60 ($3.90–$7.80/£1.95–£3.90). No credit cards. 10am until late.

Fiesta Thai (Feichang Tai Taiguo Fengwei Canting) ★ THAI Nestled in next to the Anchor Bar, the food at Fiesta isn't exactly authentic—suffering from the Sichuan tendency to make everything a little hotter than necessary—but the service and environment more than compensate. The polished wooden floor boards and elegantly dressed serving staff add a touch of class, and the high ceilings add a breezy feeling that makes the restaurant a pleasant escape from the summer heat.

Linjiang Zhong Lu 6 (just in front of the Traffic Hotel). ⓒ 028/8545-4530. English menu. Meal for 2 ¥65–¥80 ($8.45–$10/£4.25–£5.20). No credit cards. 5–10:30pm. Bus: no. 15, 16, 28, or 55.

Grandma's Kitchen (Zumu de Chufang) AMERICAN HOME COOKING Farm-style chandeliers and wall lamps, straight-back wooden chairs with gingham cushions, and framed photos on the wall give this split-level restaurant an appropriately homey atmosphere—and goes a long way toward explaining how Grandma's is turning itself into a booming franchise with two locations in Chengdu and two in Beijing. The menu might not be entirely familiar—tuna-fish pizza is undoubtedly the result of a recipe confused in the translation—but the rest of the menu, which includes fried chicken, a variety of steaks, and much more, is a prayer answered for any U.S. resident craving a taste of home. The pies and desserts are made at **Grandma's Deli,** next door to the Kehua Bei Lu premises, which specializes in sandwiches and homemade desserts. A comfortable atmosphere with small libraries containing donated English-language paperbacks make either Grandma's location a perfect place to hole up on a rainy day and write postcards. There's another location at Renmin Nan Duan Lu 22 (ⓒ **028/8555-3856**).

Grandma's Kitchen and Grandma's Deli at Kehua Bei Lu 75. ⓒ 028/8524-2835. Main courses ¥35–¥50 ($4.55–$6.50/£2.30–£3.25). No credit cards. English spoken. Mon–Fri 8:30am–midnight; Sat–Sun 8am–midnight. Bus: no. 55, 110, 49, or 6.

Rome Restaurant (Luoma Yidali Xicanting) ITALIAN Formerly a French restaurant, it has made the transition to Italian seamlessly. Service in this small restaurant is friendly and efficient, design is modern and comfortably minimalist, and prices are affordable. The menu is mammoth with something for everyone, but the pork medallions in white wine and lemon sauce are highly recommended. Desserts include chocolate mousse and tiramisu. A small selection of Western wines and liqueurs is available, but more importantly, the restaurant shares the same coffee supplier as the top hotels in town. Not far from Grandma's (see above).

Kehua Bei Lu 115 (just north of the west gate of Sichuan University). ⊘ 028/8524-4968. Meal for 2 ¥50–¥100 ($6.50–$13/£3.25–£6.50). No credit cards. 10:30am–10:30pm. Bus: no. 55.

Tandoor Indian Cuisine (Tengduer Yindu Canting) 🖈🖈 NORTHERN INDIAN

Tandoor's Indian chef clearly takes care in buying and preparing ingredients to make authentic dishes from chiefly the north, but also from southern India. The food and service are equally superb. A delicious specialty from Goa is the Portuguese-influenced pork vindaloo. This very hot dish is made with Indian spices, vinegar, and chilies. One of the best northern specialties is *murgh malai* kabob, chunks of chicken marinated in ginger-garlic paste, then mixed with cheese, cream, coriander, chili, cinnamon, and anisette, and cooked in a tandoori oven. Connected to the Xinzu Binguan (Sunjoy Inn), Tandoor, designed by an Indian architect, is airy and handsome; elegant wooden rafters give it flair, and soft Indian music enhances an already pleasing ambience. Traditional Indian dance performances run nightly from 7 to 8pm.

Renmin Nan Lu 34, 4 Duan (directly behind the Xinzu Binguan). ⊘ 028/8555-1958. Reservations recommended. Set meals ¥48–¥110 ($6.25–$14/£3.10–£7.15). AE, DC, MC, V. 11:30am–2pm and 5:30–10:30pm. Bus: no. 99 or 16.

Tanyoto 🖈 HOT POT

You'll appreciate this hot pot restaurant as much for its good food as for its warmly lit, inviting dining room. The space is large and airy and affords privacy at every table. Ambience aside, the keys to great hot pot are the broth—here it is rich and flavorful—and the dipping sauce. Ingredients vary, but are likely to include bean sprouts, leeks, a variety of mushrooms, sausages, seafood, organ meats, and/or duck tongues. Fish heads, which may sound exotic, are the signature ingredient of the shop. There are different kinds of fish heads that you can pick. They are fresh and very nice to go with the spicy broth. I recommend the *ma la* (hot and numbing) hot pots, but a handful selection of nonchili broth is also available. *Bin tofu* (frozen tofu), which absorbs the essence of the soup, is a must-have item.

Qingyang Zheng Jie 227 (south of Qingyang Gong, 5-min. walk from the temple). ⊘ 028/8777-7789. Meal for 2 ¥80–¥150 ($10–$20/£5.20–£9.75). No credit cards. 8:30am–9pm. Bus: no. 11, 42, 47, 59, 302 to Qingyang Gong, 5-min. walk from there.

Xizang Fengqing Wu 〈Value〉 TIBETAN

Situated in a Tibetan neighborhood and frequented by Tibetans (many Khampas from western Sichuan), this intimate three-room restaurant (with four to six tables in each room) serves top-quality dishes in a warm, cheerful environment. Tibetan music usually plays in the background, and almost any time of day you'll find monks at several of the tables, eating snacks and drinking milk tea. Three great dishes are *jiarong suancai kaobing* (jiarong Tibetan bread stuffed with pickled cabbage and barbecued pork), *maoniu roubao* (yak meat *baozi*) and *suan luobo chao maoniurou* (pickled cabbage with fried yak meat). For a snack, try Tibetan bread with milk tea. A large pot of tea costs ¥10 ($1.25/60p).

Wuhou Ci Dong Jie 3, Fu 2 (look for painting of yak on an ocher-yellow building with Tibetan script in blue, red, orange, and yellow). ⊘ 028/8551-0112. Menu has some English. Meal for 2 ¥30 ($3.90/£1.95). No credit cards. 8am–10:30pm. Bus: no. 82 from Traffic Hotel.

The Ways of Tea

In the 8th-century *Classic of Tea,* author and tea sage Lu Yu says that there are "nine ways by which man must tax himself when he deals with tea."

1. He must manufacture it.
2. He must develop a sense of selectivity and discrimination about it.
3. He must provide the proper implements.
4. He must prepare the right kind of fire.
5. He must select a suitable water.
6. He must roast the tea to a turn.
7. He must grind it well.
8. He must brew it to its ultimate perfection.
9. He must, finally, drink it.

In modern China, there are still many ways to drink tea, from the highly ritualized, heavy-on-equipage style prescribed by Lu Yu, to the style favored on long-distance trains (toss a pinch of tea leaves into a glass jar with a screw-top and keep adding water and drinking until you reach your destination). The Chengdu way doesn't use a teapot or a glass jar: The typical setting is the riverside, a park, or temple grounds—in an outdoor teahouse with bamboo tables and chairs. Here, patrons sip tea from 3-ounce cups that sit on saucers small enough to rest in the palm of the hand while protecting it from the heat of the cup. A lid keeps the tea hot and can be used to sweep aside tea leaves that rise to the top as you drink. Melon seeds, boiled peanuts, or dried squid are typical snack accompaniments.

TEAHOUSES

For the typical Chengdu experience, go to Qingyang Gong or Wenshu Yuan monasteries (see "Exploring Chengdu," earlier in this chapter). For something trendier, Chengdu has upmarket teahouses for the connoisseur or connoisseur-in-training. The best of the bunch is **Guanghe Chalou,** on the river at Linjiang Zhong Lu 16 (© 028/8550-1688). Rattan chairs, palm trees, lots of large potted plants, and blonde wood lend a clean, spalike atmosphere to this teahouse. The Chinese/English menu has pages of teas, some medicinal or therapeutic, others special for the locale in which they're grown. Under "Teas for Women" are "Aloe Beauty Face Tea," "Heart Tea," and "Chinese Yew Tea for Lady." A small pot of "Rose Love Things" is ¥48 ($6.25/£3.10), but my favorite is always Wulong, of which there are many kinds. The best come from the high mountains of Taiwan and Fujian Province. A pot of tea costs ¥38 to ¥68 ($4.95–$8.85/£2.45–£4.40). The teahouse is open from 9am to midnight.

CHENGDU AFTER DARK

Unlike many Chinese cities, Chengdu offers a variety of ways to pass the evening. **Sichuan opera** is a favorite for foreign and Chinese tourists alike. Known for its humor and dynamism, an integral part of every performance is *bianlian* or "changing faces." The character is often a villain who changes his face to escape recognition. The reputed record is 14 changes in 24 seconds. Over its 300-year tradition, the trick has changed, but it has always been a closely guarded secret within the operatic community. Traditional stick puppets and flame balancing are also incorporated into the drama. Performances are at the teahouse next to the Jin Jiang Theater on Huaxing Zheng Lu on Saturday for ¥15 ($1.95/£1). Performances are also held at the strictly-for-tourists **Shufeng Yayun** (© **028/8776-4530**; www.shufengyayun.com; 8–9:30pm) in Wenhua Gongyuan; the fee is ¥120 ($16/£7.80) and performances are held nightly. Take bus no. 25, 46, or 103 to Wenhua Gongyuan.

The highlight of Chengdu's nightlife is unquestionably the **Lotus Palace Bar and Restaurant (Lianhua fudi;** © **028/8553-7676;** 3pm–3am). Nestled halfway down Jinli Ancient Street, you'll first notice the red-and-black lacquered traditional-style tables and chairs in a small courtyard to your left. The entrance to the bar itself is hidden behind two heavy black doors and walled in by a granite facade in the traditional Sichuan style. But once inside the designers have tweaked the traditional design with some modern license: red decor throughout the bar, a Perspex ceiling above the dance floor to see the night sky, silver faux bamboo hanging from the ceiling. Drink prices are reasonable (¥30/$3.75/£1.85 for a beer or mixed drink) and, if you go early in the evening, the music is sufficiently loungey and good for enjoying a quiet drink; go later and the music gives way to heavier dance mix enjoyed by Chengdu's young, bright things. Even if the bar is not busy, it is worth a visit to see how China is trying to reclaim its cultural heritage—without giving into kitsch.

If you are interested to explore the mainland underground music scene, go to **Little Bar (Xiaojiuguan,** Fangxin Jie 87; © **028/8515-8790;** 5pm until late), on the east of Yongfeng Stereo Bridge. You won't miss the red table and chair hung on exterior wall next to the glass door. First established by local musician Tang Lei in 1997, the Fangxin bar is the second branch of Little Bar. Being a popular stage for local and overseas bands, the bar organizes band shows almost every Saturday night. You can also find a large variety of mainland underground acts' CDs on a big shelf inside.

2 Emei Shan ✶

Sichuan Province, 143km (89 miles) SW of Chengdu, 36km (22 miles) E of Le Shan

Emei means "lofty eyebrows," but it's also a pun on a poetic expression referring to the delicate brows of a beautiful woman. The mountain was named for two of its high adjacent peaks, whose outlines, according to 6th-century commentary on the "Book of Waterways," did indeed conjure the image of two long, thin, graceful eyebrows. Once richly endowed with both flora and fauna, this sacred Buddhist mountain is still home to 10% of China's plant species; fauna have fared less well. Threatened species include Asiatic black bear, giant salamander (the famous "crying fish," or *wawa yu* in Chinese), gray-hooded parrotbill, and Asiatic golden cat. You'll also bump into monkeys that want a handout, but try to resist—they already suffer from obesity and hypertension. As of 2002, park wardens have put them on a diet. *Note:* For Chinese translations of selected establishments listed in this section, please turn to appendix A.

Come here for scenic hiking and active Buddhist shrines and monasteries (where the monk and nun population was once as threatened as the golden cat but has now returned, albeit in smaller numbers). Nature enthusiasts will delight in the exotic insects and butterflies along the way.

Altitudes on the mountain range from 500 to 3,099m (1,640–10,167 ft.) at the Wanfo Ding summit. Not surprisingly, average yearly temperatures vary significantly

A Proper Visit to Emei Shan

The Chinese say a proper visit to Emei Shan involves at least one of the following:

- Watching the **sunrise** from the summit (which requires staying the night on or near it—the earliest shuttle arrives after sunup).
- Standing in the **Cloud Sea.** Like many a Chinese mountain, Emei is famous for its clouds and mists. The classic experience happens when layers of clouds gather between Jiulao Dong and Xi Xiang Chi (Elephant Bathing Pool). You see the clouds above, climb through them, then look down to see clouds billowing and surging at your feet like the sea. Of course, conditions aren't always right.
- Witnessing **Buddha's Halo.** When the sun shines through misty clouds, and you're standing between the clouds and the sun, you can see your shadow outlined by a halo-shaped rainbow. Optimal time: 2 to 5pm. Optimal place: Sheshen Yan.
- Seeing the **"Strange Lamps" (Guai Deng).** Photos and witnesses are both scarce, but supposedly in the evening when the moon is waning, especially after it has rained and the sky has cleared, those looking down from Sheshen Yan at the layers of mountains in the distance can see thousands of floating orbs of light.

from one part of the mountain to another. In the subtropical zone at the bottom, the average is 63°F (17°C); at the summit, 37°F (3°C). Bring layers of clothes, and adjust them as you climb and descend. The best months to visit are late August through early October. The busiest months are July and August. Avoid national holidays.

Emei Shan. ℂ **028/8737-1405.** www.ems517.com. Admission ¥120 ($16/£7.80), (¥100/$13/£6.50 Dec 1–Jan 31), student discount ¥60 ($7.80/£3.90). Entrance to monasteries ¥6–¥10 (80¢–$1.30/40p–65p).

ESSENTIALS

GETTING THERE   There are several **trains** from Chengdu to Emei Shanon on the Chengdu-Kunming line. The trip takes 2 to 3 hours and costs ¥22 ($2.85/£1.45). Minibuses and taxis connect the **Emei Railway Station** (3.2km/2 miles east of town) with the mountain entrance at Baoguo. The fare is ¥16 ($2.10/£1.05) and it's a 20-minute drive. The bus is faster and more direct than the train.

In Chengdu, most **buses** to Emei Shan depart from Xin Nan Men; the first leaves at 6:40am. Buses terminate at Baoguo Town, where the mountain trails begin. The Emei Bus Station is connected to Baoguo Si, the monastery at Emei's entrance, by **minibuses** that make the 20-minute, 6.4km (4-mile) drive for ¥10 ($1.40/70p). You can also take one of the public buses leaving every 5 minutes; the fare is ¥2 (25¢/15p). The bus from Chengdu costs ¥34 ($4.40/£2.20) each way and takes 2½ hours. Buses also run between Emei Shan and Le Shan bus stations every few minutes. Buy your ticket for the half-hour trip inside the terminal for ¥8 ($1.05/50p). Buses unload at Le Shan's north gate. You can also hop on one of the many Le Shan–bound minibuses that wait outside the Emei gate. They don't depart until every seat is taken; the fare is ¥4 (50¢/25p).

VISITOR INFORMATION   The very modern and helpful **Emei Shan Tourist Center (Luren Zhongxin)**, near Baoguo Temple (© **0833/559-0111**), provides free information and materials about Mount Emei. Guides can be hired here, although you're sure to pay less if you hire one of the many freelance guides (whose English may not be as good) outside Baoguo Temple. For quiet and tranquillity, you may opt to go it alone.

Bilingual maps are sold at the tourist center and at any of the many postcard and book stands near the entrance and along the trail. The map costs ¥3.50 (45¢/20p); one side of the map shows Emei Shan, the other Le Shan (see below).

EXPLORING EMEI SHAN

There are two main **hiking routes** up Emei Shan to the Jin Ding summit, and two involving bus and/or cable car. Both hiking routes follow the same path from **Baoguo Si** (at the entrance) to **Niuxin Ting**. At Niuxin Ting, they split into a higher and a lower trail, which meet up again at **Xi Xiang Chi**, where they merge into a single path that leads to **Jin Ding Peak**. Since there are 80km (50 miles) of trails to the peak, a combination of hiking, buses, and cable car is recommended.

You can take a **bus** from Baoguo Si to Leidong Ping; from there, take a **cable car** to the top. Buses travel between Baoguo Si and Leidong Ping all day (5am–5pm golden weeks; 7am–4pm Nov–Apr; and 6:30am–5pm May–Oct). The trip each way takes 2 hours and costs ¥70 ($9.10/£4.55). The cable car runs the 500m (1,666-ft.) leg between the last parking lot, at Jieyin Dian (next to Leidong Ping), and Jin Ding (Golden Peak); round-trip fare is ¥70 ($9.10/£4.55); 5:30am–6pm.

An option is to take the bus as far as **Wannian Cable Car Station (Wannian Chechang)**. Begin your trek there or take the 8-minute cable car ride to Wannian Si and start climbing from there. The cable car ride costs ¥40 ($5.20/£2.60) for the ascent, ¥30 ($3.90/£1.95) for the descent, and ¥60 ($7.80/£3.90) round-trip, from 6:40am to 6pm.

All roads lead to Jin Ding, but the highest peaks are **Qianfo Ding** and **Wanfo Ding**. These can be reached by a **monorail** that runs between Jin Ding and Wanfo Ding. The round-trip takes 20 minutes and costs ¥60 ($7.80/£3.90); 8am–6pm.

Note: If you get caught without enough warm clothing, rent a Chinese army jacket for ¥10 ($1.30/65p) at several spots on the mountain, including the Leidong Ping (Leidong parking lot).

WHERE TO STAY

For the most comfort, stay in one of the several full-service hotels near the entrance to Emei Shan. At the summit, the **Jin Ding Dajiudian** is quite comfortable (see below). Other than that, if you want to overnight on the mountain, be prepared for relatively spartan accommodations. Beginning at Baoguo Si—the first temple you encounter upon entering the Emei Shan scenic area—and continuing to the summit, all the monasteries have guesthouses with rates ranging from ¥20 to ¥160 ($2.60–$21/£1.30–£10) per night. Accommodations are as basic as the rates suggest: The least expensive have dorm-style rooms for four to six people, limited or no hot water, and a hallway bathroom. In the $10-and-higher range, expect air-conditioning and limited hot water. Meals can consist of vegetarian, mock-meat dishes or a simple bowl of noodles for around ¥6 (80¢/40p). Two popular monasteries are **Xianfeng Si** and **Xi Xiang Chi.** Guesthouses at the peak and in the vicinity of the cable-car terminus at

Jing Shui offer more comfortable lodging (with TV, air-conditioning, and hot showers) for a bit more—but not all of them accept foreigners. They charge ¥150 to ¥250 ($20–$33/£9.75–£16).

Emei Shan Fandian (Emei Shan Hotel) 🍴   Completed in 2002, the hotel in Emei continues to be fresh and sparkling. Each deluxe standard room is spacious and comfortably furnished with a sofa, chair, and coffee table. Some rooms have picture windows with a garden view. Located next to the bus station, the hotel is convenient for late arrivals or early departures, but it's about 8km (5 miles) from Emei Shan. To get to the mountain, catch a bus in front of the station for ¥2 (25¢/10p) or take a taxi for ¥12 ($1.50/75p) or less.

Baoguo Si (by the Emei Shan Bus Station, 8km/5 miles from Baoguo Si). ℂ 0833/5529-0518. Fax 0833/559-1399. 210 units. ¥300–¥580 ($37–$72/£19–£36) standard room. 20%–30% discounts. Rates include Chinese breakfast. AE, DC, MC, V. **Amenities:** Restaurant; bar; business center; limited room service; Internet access. *In room:* A/C, TV, fridge/minibar in some rooms.

Hongzhu Shan Binguan 🍴🍴   Located on park grounds with a lake and surrounded by dense forest, this is the most beautiful place to stay at Emei Shan, and the choice of visiting dignitaries. Several buildings comprise the hotel, but no matter where you stay, you're guaranteed a gorgeous, wooded view. Guest rooms and bathrooms are large, with tastefully appointed furnishings. Wing nos. 7 and 8 are three-star standard; they're clean and comfortable, but the rooms are a little on the small side.

Emei Shan Baoguo Si Zuoce (approaching Emei Shan from town, after passing Emei Museum on the right, and just before reaching Baoguo Si, turn left and follow road to end). ℂ 0833/552-5888. Fax 0833/552-5666. www.hzshotel. com. 500 units. ¥680–¥1,580 ($88–$205/£44–£103) standard room; ¥2,200–¥3,200 ($286–$416/£143–£208) suite. Rates include breakfast. 20%–50% discounts. AE, DC, MC, V. **Amenities:** 3 restaurants; 2 bars; hot spring; health club; outdoor tennis court; outdoor badminton court; airline, train, and bus ticketing; business center; forex; limited room service; laundry/dry cleaning; nonsmoking floors. *In room:* A/C, satellite TV, broadband Internet access, minibar/fridge, hair dryer, safe.

Jin Ding Dajiudian (Golden Summit Hotel)   If you'd like to see the sunrise, this three-star hotel close to the summit is the place to stay. The rooms may be standard issue, but the views are incredible.

Jin Ding (at the Jin Ding summit). ℂ 0833/509-8088. 70 units. ¥600–¥800 ($78–$104/£39–£52) standard room. 20%–30% discounts. No credit cards. **Amenities:** Restaurant; limited room service. *In room:* A/C, TV.

WHERE TO DINE

The two restaurants at **Hongzhu Shan Binguan** serve excellent food. The prices are higher than usual, but basic meat and vegetable dishes are still quite reasonable. There are a number of restaurants along the road leading to Baoguo Si. The biggest draw for Western tourists is **Teddy Bear Cafe** (ℂ 0833/559-0135), which serves Chinese and Western dishes and has an English menu. Next door is the Teddy Bear Hotel, whose English-speaking staff is extremely useful in organizing tours and booking tickets.

3 Le Shan

Sichuan Province, 154km (96 miles) SW of Chengdu, 36km (22 miles) W of Emei Shan

The carved stone statue of the Great Buddha (Da Fo) at Le Shan is one of Sichuan's top tourist destinations, but whether it's worth a day in a tight travel schedule is debatable. The thrill of Le Shan is in your first sighting of the Great Buddha. Whether that's from the top looking down, from a boat looking straight up, or from the path of nine switchbacks (Lingyun Zhandao) looking somewhere in between, the moment it dawns on you that the large, gracefully curved, stone wall (for example) that you're looking at is actually the lobe of a colossal ear, and that the ear is only a small slice of a well-proportioned giant—that moment is thrilling. But after you've marveled at the Great Buddha from all the various angles, what's left to explore is not much more than an overcrowded theme park.

The town of Le Shan is not without charm, but with a 2,300-year history and situated as it is at a confluence of rivers, it should offer much more than it does. Mass demolition and reconstruction have rendered it indistinguishable (except for its pretty waterways) from a thousand others undergoing the same process. I suggest you skip the town and go directly to the mountain. Le Shan is best done as a day trip from Chengdu or as a stopover on the way to Emei Shan from Chengdu. Two to 3 hours is plenty of time to enjoy it. Admission to the mountain is ¥70 ($5/£2.50) and includes all the sights. It's open from 7:30am to 7:30pm, May through September; and from 8am to 6pm, October through April. *Note:* For Chinese translations of selected establishments listed in this section, please turn to appendix A.

ESSENTIALS

GETTING THERE   Air-conditioned **buses** depart for Le Shan from Chengdu's Xin Nan Men Bus Station every 20 to 30 minutes from 7am to 7pm for ¥38 to ¥42 ($4.95–$5.45/£2.45–£2.75); the ride takes 2 hours. They arrive at the Le Shan Xiao Ba Lu Bus Station. Return buses for Chengdu leave from the bus station every half-hour or so. The last bus returning to Chengdu from the entrance leaves between 5:30 and 6pm (whenever it fills up). Buses run between Emei Shan and Le Shan bus stations every few minutes for ¥8 ($1.05/50p). On the return leg to Chengdu, be aware of which bus station you are being taken to. **Taxi** fare between Emei and Le Shan is about ¥60 ($7.80/£3.90).

GETTING AROUND   Buses arrive in the Le Shan Xiao Ba Lu Zhan. From the bus stop, you can take a taxi (¥15/$1.95/£1), or take bus no. 3 or 13 (¥1/15¢/10p) to the Great Buddha. What should be a 10-minute drive stretches to a half-hour as the bus driver trawls for passengers along a circuitous route. The bus unloads at Le Shan's north gate. It's a 7-minute walk to the park entrance, or you can hitch a motorcycle lift for a few yuan. Pedicabs are an option that will shave time off the journey between the bus stop and Le Shan scenic area; they charge ¥8 to ¥10 ($1.05–$1.30/50p–65p). By taxi from the bus stop to the Le Shan scenic area, expect to pay ¥12 to ¥15 ($1.55–$1.95/80p–£1). A round-trip **tour boat** or **motorboat** from the north gate to Wuyou Temple costs ¥50 ($6.50/£3.25) and allows time for photos of the Great Buddha. **Ferries** run between the Le Shan City dock and both Lingyun Shan and Wuyou Si for ¥5 (65¢/35p); the last boat leaves Le Shan at 6pm.

At the entrance to Le Shan scenic area, vendors sell **maps** of the mountain for ¥3.50 (45¢/25p). Maps are also sold at the small stands near the head of the Great Buddha. One side of this bilingual map shows Le Shan; the other shows Emei Shan.

EXPLORING LE SHAN

On foot from the entrance, it's a 10-minute walk along a stone path to the Great Buddha. When the road forks into two staircases, take the staircase to the right. This leads around the side of the mountain looking back at the town. It also affords a panoramic view of the three converging rivers, the Min Jiang, the Dadu He (Chang Jiang), and the Qingyi Jiang. The path leads to a terrace and souvenir area beside and around the back of the Buddha's head. From here you can look into his ear and over his shoulder.

For a variety of views of Da Fo, descend the zigzag staircase called **Jiuqu Zhandao (Path of Nine Switchbacks)** by the statue's right side. This leads to a large viewing platform that puts visitors at toe level.

Da Fo (The Great Buddha) ⟨✦⟩   At 71m (233 ft.) tall, Le Shan's Da Fo—hewn out of a mountain—is similar in size, subject, and artistic medium to the recently demolished Bamiyan Buddhas in the Hindu Kush. Carved some 500 years later, between 713 and 803, Da Fo is one of the world's largest stone sculptures of Buddha. It was the inspiration of the Buddhist monk Hai Tong, abbot of Lingyun Monastery, who hoped that a giant Maitreya Buddha (Future Buddha) overlooking the water might subdue floods and violent currents. In 1996 it was added to UNESCO's World Heritage List, and in 2001 large-scale repairs were started: The Buddha's head, shoulders, and torso were cleaned up and repaired and a cement coating (added in modern times) was removed. The next stage took 10 months and was completed in 2002. Repairs were made to the statue's ingenious, hidden drainage system that slowed, but could not stop, erosion; and cracks as deep as 4m (13 ft.) in the base of the Buddha were filled in. For an idea of how massive this statue is: Each eye is 3m (11 ft.) long; each ear 7m (23 ft.); and his middle finger is 8m (27 ft.) long. His head is covered with 1,021 buns of coiled hair, carved out of tapered stone blocks that fit into his head like pegs in a cribbage board.

Wuyou Shan   After viewing the Great Buddha, there isn't a lot more to do, except stroll the park grounds and enjoy the views. To reach the adjacent southern hill, Wuyou Shan, cross the **Haoshang Da Qiao** footbridge on the south side of the Great Buddha. The plain, six-hall monastery by the same name, built in the Tang dynasty and rebuilt many times since, sits atop the hill. The Luohan Tang contains an army of terra-cotta arhats, each in a different pose. Most impressive is the view of the rivers from the top of the complex.

WHERE TO STAY & DINE

The best stays in Le Shan were once within the park itself, but they have all since closed down. A nice alternative is the **Xiandao Dajiudian (Xiandao Hotel)** which is only a 2-minute walk to the back entrance of the park. Out of the city on Dao Long Island, it is surrounded by waterways and greenery. Although the rooms can be a little damp, it makes for a pleasant escape from the dust and general blandness of Le Shan itself. Standard rooms cost ¥268 to ¥388 ($33–$46/£16–£23), but management is open to negotiation. The most comfortable place to stay in downtown Le Shan is the **Jia Zhou Binguan,** Baita Jie 19 (✆ **0833/213-9888;** fax 0833/213-3233). It's as three-star hotel with basic modern rooms for ¥360 ($45/£22) and a restaurant. A number of good small restaurants are also in the vicinity of this hotel. **Yang's** is inexpensive, with Chinese and Western food and an English menu; it's located at Baita Jie 49 (✆ **0833/211-2046**). Richard Yang, the proprietor, has a wealth of local knowledge and personal anecdotes. A vegetarian restaurant specializing in faux meat dishes is on Wuyou Shan behind Daxiong Temple.

4 Dujianyan & Qingcheng Shan ⟨✦⟩

Sichuan Province, 55km (34 miles) NW of Chengdu, 16km (10 miles) SW of Dujiang Yan

As a convenient subalpine getaway, Qingcheng Shan is better than all the other mountains in this chapter. It offers solitary climbing on stone steps and wooden paths through dense forests of pine, fir, and cypress. Along the way are caves, ponds, a pedestrian bridge, ancient ginkgoes, and 16 Daoist and Buddhist monasteries housing statues dating from as far back as the 6th century.

More important (though it may have slim bearing on the travel plans of most Westerners), Mount Qingcheng is considered the birthplace of China's only indigenous religion, Daoism—that is, "organized" Daoism, which gelled a half century after Laozi. It was to this mountainous part of western Sichuan (the Shu Kingdom) that the pilgrim Zhang Daoling came to cultivate the *Dao*. Some years later, in A.D. 142, the deified Laozi appeared at Heming Shan (just south of Qingcheng) and made Zhang the first Celestial Master. Zhang went on to establish 24 peasant communities throughout Shu, whose customs included confession and the regular payment of 5 pecks of rice to a communal grain reserve.

Less awe-inspiring than other World Heritage mountains, Qingcheng Shan nevertheless makes an invigorating day trip from Chengdu. If you wish to stay longer, there is lodging in monasteries and inns on the mountain. Escape crowds and high guesthouse rates by coming midweek. Summer is considered the best time to visit, but it's also the busiest, as Chengdu residents flee the city heat.

ESSENTIALS
GETTING THERE   **Buses** depart Chengdu's Xin Nan Men Bus Station frequently from 8:40am to noon (1 hr.; ¥25/$3.50/£1.75); they run in the afternoon as well but are more sporadic. Return buses leave every 30 minutes from 3 to 5pm, from Qingcheng's main entrance. An option is to take a bus to Dujiang Yan and transfer to a Qingcheng Qian Shan bus. Buses make the 16km (10-mile) trip between Dujiang Yan and Qingcheng every half-hour from 6:20am to 5:30pm for ¥4.50 (60¢/30p); to Qingcheng rare mountain for ¥10 ($1.30/65p).

GETTING AROUND   The hike to the 1,260m (4,133-ft.) summit is less strenuous than the Emei trail, but it includes a few short, steep sections. At a leisurely pace, Shangqing Gong can be reached in about 2 hours. It's possible to cut that time in half by taking the ferry across Yuecheng Hu and from there a cable car to just below Shangqing Gong. Passage is ¥30 ($3.90/£1.95) one-way; ¥50 ($6.50/£3.25) roundtrip. The cable shuts at 5:30pm. It's a fun way to go, but you sacrifice seeing the sights. Admission is ¥90 ($12/£5.85).

EXPLORING QINGCHENG SHAN
SUGGESTED ROUTE (3–4 HR.)
From the entrance, follow the main trail, keeping to the left. Pass **Yile Wo (Nest of Pleasures);** continue to **Tianshi Dong (Celestial Master Cave).** This is the core site of Qingcheng Shan. The six surrounding peaks were to act as natural inner and outer walls that would protect the area from the world of men. A temple first built in 730 now stands in the spot where Zhang Daoling is supposed to have built a hut for himself. It's said that he planted the **ancient ginkgo tree** that grows here—which would make it about 1,700 years old. Continue on to **Zushi Dian (Hall of the Celestial Master Founder)** and **Chaoyang Dong (Facing the Dawn Cave).** The narrow section of path between these two sights passes through beautiful dark forest and thick undergrowth. Continue on the path; after veering right and passing a couple of viewing pavilions, it leads to **Shangqing Gong (Temple of Highest Clarity).** First built in the 4th century, the present building is considerably newer. The tearoom here also sells snacks. From here to the summit at **Laojun Ge (Lord Lao Pavilion)** is a short but steep climb.

Return Hike: Coming back down the mountain, the road forks at Shangqing Gong. The left trail leads to the cable car. The ride down takes you to the small **Yuecheng Hu (Moon Wall Lake).** From here, boats ferry people across for ¥5 (65¢/35p) If you don't take the cable car, it's only about a half-hour walk through pine forest to the lake.

WHERE TO STAY & DINE

If you've come to watch the sunrise, you'll need to spend the night on the mountain. Tianshi Dong and Shangqing Gong both have basic but clean lodgings for ¥40 to ¥100 ($5.20–$13/£2.60–£6.50), depending on the season. These monasteries also serve vegetarian meals. The **Lingyun Shanzhuang (Lingyun Mountain Inn)** near the top cable-car station has lodgings and a restaurant.

5 Wolong Nature Reserve (Wolong Ziran Baohu Qu)

Sichuan Province, 135km (84 miles) NW of Chengdu, 50km (31 miles) NW of Dujiang Yan

Established in 1963, Wolong isn't the only place to see giant pandas, nor is it the most convenient. (And erase any notion of observing pandas in the wild.) But scientists here have made more advances in artificial breeding and raising pandas in captivity than anywhere in the world. The Wolong Breeding Center currently has about 30 giant pandas ranging in age from newborn to adult, and it is almost always possible to see panda cubs here.

Another aspect of Wolong's appeal is location. Situated in the high, densely forested mountains between the Sichuan Basin and the Qinghai-Tibetan Plateau, the area has a diverse topography that supports a broad range of vegetation and animal life—not that you're likely to see any of the panthers, macaques, white-lipped deer, or takins purported to live on the reserve. Nonetheless, the area is unspoiled and the flora is magnificent (and much more apparent than the fauna). You also have the chance to climb a mountain sans stairs—good news to some. The population is mostly Tibetan and Qiang farmers who work the fields and make and sell handicrafts.

The best months to visit are May, August, and September. Allow 2 days to see the sights; add another day or two if you want to hike the several marked trails. *Note:* For Chinese translations of selected establishments listed in this section, please turn to appendix A.

ESSENTIALS

GETTING THERE   At least one bus leaves Chengdu's Chadianzi Bus Station daily at 9am (3½ hr.; ¥40/$5.20/£2.60); from Dujiangyan (2 hr.; ¥13/$1.70/85p). The return bus passes through Shawan (also called Wolong Zhen) between 8 and 9am daily; the fare is ¥40 ($5.20/£2.60). Catch it on the main street or at the Panda Museum parking lot.

GETTING AROUND   Getting around the three main sights must usually be done either on foot or by hiring a private taxi (without a meter). The exception is if you hit it just right and for a few yuan can hop on a passing bus from Chengdu. Hetao Ping—where the breeding center is—and Shawan (Wolong Town), where the museum and most of the hotels are, are on the same road some 6.5km (4 miles) apart.

Tourist and administrative offices share the **Panda Museum** building in Shawan, on the road from Chengdu. The museum's parking lot is the terminus for buses from

Chengdu. The **tourist office** can answer questions in English and provide an English-speaking guide to the mountain.

Be sure to carry yuan. There are no foreign exchange services, and credit cards are not accepted.

Buy **maps** of the reserve at the Panda Museum in Shawan or at the Panda Breeding Station in Hetao Ping for ¥5 (65¢/30p).

EXPLORING WOLONG

Most tourists to Wolong come for the **Giant Panda Protection and Research Center** in Hetao Ping, which is good enough reason, but there are so few chances in China to enjoy nature, free of crowds, that you may want to do some hiking while you're here. If so, be prepared for temperature fluctuations and rain, especially in summer. Also consider hiring a guide at the Panda Museum if you plan to hike very far. Trails can be faint and muddy, and descents at times slippery (the downside of not having stairs).

A viable **2-day plan** is to arrive in Shawan in the afternoon. After checking into your hotel, visit the museum for an hour or so and roam around the very small town before dinner. The next morning, get up early and visit the breeding center in Hetao Ping. Spend the late morning and afternoon hiking. Depart the next morning.

Baohu Daxiongmao Ziran Zhongxin (Giant Panda Protection and Research Center) ⊛ (Kids)   The pandas are housed either in enclosures or in seminatural habitats—if they're being prepared to return to the open reserve. Unfortunately, Wolong has had less success with reintroducing pandas to the wild than with captive breeding, so the majority of pandas are in large enclosures that include an indoor room and an outdoor courtyard. For bird's-eye views of the pandas in open-air pens, an elevated trail runs along an adjacent cliff face above the enclosures.

Opposite are the **Lesser Panda Enclosures (Xiaoxiongmao Shengtai Guan).** Although the smaller red pandas—related to the raccoon—don't get nearly as much press, they are undeniably appealing and usually more playful.

The best time to visit is between 8:30 and 10:30am, while the pandas feed.

In the town of Hetao Ping, 5km (3 miles) before Shawan on the road from Chengdu. Buses go to Shawan. If you want to get off here, notify the driver in advance. Admission ¥60 ($7.80/£3.90). 8:30am–noon and 1–5pm.

Wuyipeng Shengtai Guance Zhan (Wuyipeng Field Observation Station)

This used to be an active station for researching and monitoring the giant panda, but it is no longer in use. A visit here makes a nice 1- to 2-hour hike on a steep trail that flattens out the last mile or so. The habitat behind the station is prime forest, and Darjeeling woodpeckers and various species of pheasants have been sighted here.

The cost of a guide from the Panda Museum's Tourist Desk is ¥100 ($13/£6.50) for the round-trip trek (¥100/$13/£6.50 with lunch) and ¥40 ($5.20/£2.60) for the taxi to and from the beginning of the trail, which is about 9km (5½ miles) southwest of the museum. Hire your own taxi round-trip for ¥15 to ¥20 ($1.95–$2.60/£1–£1.30), but you'll have to agree on a pickup time. Allow about 3 hours. Pay at the end.

To go on your own from Shawan, walk south on the main road until you reach a small village. Look for a large sign by the road with two big Chinese characters (for "Distillery"). Cross the wooden bridge on your left and follow it to the mountain. If at that point you regret not hiring a guide, you may be able to persuade one of the farmers on this patch of land to lead you. Unless you speak Chinese, you'll need the

Chinese characters to indicate your destination and a calculator to settle on a fee. Expect to pay around ¥20 ($2.60/£1.30)—more if weather conditions are poor or if the farmer has something else to do.

WHERE TO STAY

Before China's push to join the WTO, Chinese and foreigners were commonly charged different prices for the same service or merchandise. Now, the two-tiered pricing approach has virtually disappeared in large cities. Not so in Wolong. Hotels make no attempt to hide the fact that they charge "foreign guests" a few dollars more for a room.

Panda Inn (Xiongmao Shanzhuang)   More upscale than Shawan's hotels, this pleasant inn has close connections with the Giant Panda Breeding Center, conveniently nearby. Rooms are well maintained and clean, and pleasant views through picture windows make up for the bland interiors. Although there's no town to explore, tour groups are better managed here than in Shawan, and the inn has the best restaurant in town.

Hetao Ping (next to the Panda Breeding Station). © **0837/624-3028.** Fax 0837/624-3014. 69 units. ¥320 ($42/£21). 30%–50% discounts. No credit cards. **Amenities:** Restaurant; limited room service. *In room:* TV, 24-hr. hot water.

Wolong Shanzhuang (Wolong Hotel)   Situated in the Wolong Nature Reserve, this expansive hotel is a nice escape from the town. The view from your window will give you the sense of getting back to nature. The rooms are fairly small and simply appointed, but also have a rustic and cozy feel to them. Although the main driveway into the hotel suggests delusions of grandeur, it is a reasonable alternative to the Panda Inn.

Wolong Ziran Baohu Qu (Wolong Nature Reserve). © **0837/624-6888.** Fax 0837/624-6111. 323 units. ¥280–¥350 ($36–$46/£18–£23) standard room. No credit cards. **Amenities:** Restaurant; teahouse; swimming pool; sauna; limited room service. *In room:* TV.

WHERE TO DINE

The **Wolong Hotel** prepares good, simple dishes, but the Panda Inn offers a greater variety. There are also a couple of small restaurants and stands on Shawan's main street.

6 Jiuzhai Gou (Valley of Nine Villages)

Sichuan Province, 450km (280 miles) N of Chengdu, 102km (63 miles) NE of Songpan

Photographs of this World Heritage nature site look retouched. The lakes are too "jewel-like," the pools too "limpid," the fall colors too "flaming." Surprisingly, the brochures aren't lying; they aren't even exaggerating. For sheer scenic beauty and variety, Jiuzhai Gou has it all: dense forest, green meadow, rivers, rapids, ribbon lakes in various shades of blue and green, chalky shoals, and waterfalls of every kind—long and narrow, short and wide, terraced, rushing, and cascading. Of cultural interest are the six remaining Tibetan villages of the original nine from which this valley gets its name. Some 1,000 Tibetans, of 130 families, live within the site. And to facilitate sightseeing, so-called "green buses" run along special highways within the valley delivering passengers to various scenic spots. Another aid to tourism is a network of raised plank paths and wooden pavilions that afford visitors a proximity to natural wonders that would otherwise be unapproachable.

Still, you may lose your will to visit just getting to Jiuzhai Gou from Chengdu; you must then face the honking, belching traffic along the strip of hotels outside the main gate, not to mention the contagion of avarice that seems to have infected the town. Cabbies are in cahoots with the hotels; hotel managers beg bribes; the PSB is on the take; the place claims to be "green," but the air is polluted. It's not a pretty sight.

Jiuzhai Gou gets three stars for its scenery and is docked four for everything else. But despite the cons, few places on earth have prettier scenery, and except for a few photo-taking forays, the majority of tourists stay on the bus, so it's not hard to find solitude along the plank paths. In the end, as much as I loathed the 12-hour ride on a smoke-filled bus and the tacky town outside the gate, the 2 days spent inside the reserve were absolutely worth it. Jiuzhai Gou can be seen in 1 day, but 2 days is optimal.

The best time to go is from July to November, before the weather cools down significantly. Even at the height of summer, have a jacket on hand for rain and sudden temperature drops. To avoid crowds and get the best hotel discounts, come midweek. Busy times are Chinese New Year, Labor Day week (first week of May), and National Day week (first week of Oct). Some hotels close between November and March. *Note:* For Chinese translations of selected establishments listed in this section, please turn to appendix A.

ESSENTIALS

GETTING THERE The **Jiuhuang Airport,** just northeast of Jiuzhai Gou, has greatly increased the park's accessibility, putting the park within striking distance of tourists from all neighboring provinces. However, the most convenient launching point is still likely to be Chengdu, and ¥1,500 ($195/£98) will get you a round-trip ticket for the 45-minute flight. From the airport, you can take a bus to Jiuzhai Gou (1½ hr.; ¥30/$3.90/£1.95).

Air-conditioned **buses** (¥121/$16/£7.85) depart Chengdu every hour from 8am from the Xin Nan Men Bus Station and arrive approximately 12 hours later in Zhangzha Zhen at the Long-Distance Bus Station (Changtu Qiche Keyun Zhan) behind the Jiutong Binguan—leaving you the evening to check into a hotel and have dinner. Four return buses leave at 6:20am, 7am, 8am and 1pm. Buy tickets at least a day in advance. Buses also leaves Chengdu from the less convenient Chadianzi Keyun Zhan west of the city center, dropping passengers near the Jiuzhai Gou entrance for ¥120 ($16/£7.80).

GETTING AROUND Jiuzhai Gou's five designated scenic zones run along a Y-shaped route. Over 200 **shuttle buses** travel the 58km (36-mile) route from 7am until 6pm. The best sights and most of the plank paths are along the right branch, so if you haven't time to trace the entire route, go to the right first. If you're tempted to walk the full length, bear in mind that the distance from the entrance to the last scenic spot on this route—Yuanshi Senlin (Primeval Forest)—is about 32km (20 miles). For the best views, take the bus to the end and walk back. You can reboard at bus stops along the way. Very useful bilingual **tourist maps** are available for ¥5 (65¢/30p) at the **Tourist's Center (Youke Zhongxin)** near the ticket office.

Note: Be sure to carry Chinese currency. Only the five-star hotels accept credit cards. None accept traveler's checks, and only a few change U.S. dollars.

EXPLORING THE VALLEYS

With 2 days, using a combination of shuttle bus and walking, you can see all five scenic zones. For a more relaxed pace or extended walking, add a third day. Of the scenic zones, the two with the highest concentration of natural wonders are **Shuzheng Jingqu** and **Rize Jingqu.** Each zone covers several miles and has wooden planks or stone paths that lead the visitor right up to waterfalls, across shoals, or to the edge of turquoise waters. These can be done in a day if that's all you have, or they can be spread over 2 days, leaving half of each day for wandering in the less-visited areas beyond **Panda Lake (Xiongmao Hai)** to the right or beyond **Wucai Chi (Five-color Pool)** to the left. Admission to Jiuzhai Gou, which is open from 7am to 6pm, is ¥220 ($29/£14) April to mid-November and ¥80 ($10/£5.20) mid-November to March per person, for 2 days. The shuttle bus costs ¥90 ($12/£5.85); ¥80 ($10/£5.20) from mid-November to March.

WHERE TO STAY

For now, officials who say that tourists may not stay inside the park seem to be winning their battle with villagers who offer basic beds for around ¥20 ($2.60/£1.30), and simple meals for ¥10 to ¥25 ($1.30–$3.25/65p–£1.65). Rooms have limited plumbing and no hot water, but some are in Tibetan style with brightly painted tables and window frames. If that appeals, inquire at the Zharu Si and at villages on the west side of the main road. You'll probably be asked to arrive after 6pm and leave before 7am, to avoid problems with officials.

Most visitors stay in one of the many hotels lining the 11km (7-mile) stretch of road outside Jiuzhai Gou Goukou (Jiuzhai Gou Entrance), identified on the map as Zhangzha Town.

EXPENSIVE

Jiuzhai Gou Xilaideng Dajiudian (Sheraton Jiuzhai Gou Resort) ⟨⟩ This huge complex is arguably the best five-star option in Jiuzhai Gou. The rooms are elegantly appointed and infused with a Tibetan quality, all the more notable considering the Chinese propensity for reducing minority cultures into kitsch. The hotel has more restaurants and amenities than any other in town and, for now, is the only one with a swimming pool and sauna. The grounds include a 500-seat theater with revolving stage for nightly Tibetan song and dance performances.

Jiuzhai Gou Scenic Area (1.5km/1 mile from entrance to Jiuzhai Gou). ⟨⟩ 0837/773-9988. Fax 0837/773-9666. www.sheraton.com/jiuzhaigou. 482 units. ¥1,100–¥1,300 ($143–$169/£72–£85) standard room. Rates include breakfast. 15% service charge. AE, DC, MC, V. **Amenities:** 3 restaurants; deli; bar; indoor pool; gym; spa; sauna; salon; electronic game room; airline, train, and bus ticketing; concierge; business center; clinic; limited forex; 24-hr. room service; laundry/dry cleaning; nonsmoking rooms. In room: A/C, satellite TV, dataport, minibar, fridge, hair dryer, safe.

Xingyu Guoji Dajiudian (Xingyu International Hotel) This perfectly comfortable four-star hotel shows some signs of wear. There are a few Tibetan touches, but for the most part, the rooms, lobby, and restaurants hold no surprises. Discounted prices are reasonable, and staff is friendly and professional. For the comfort of a pricier hotel (but without some of the five-star luxuries), this hotel serves well.

Jiuzhai Gou Scenic Area (under 1.5km/1 mile from entrance to Jiuzhai Gou). ⟨⟩ 0837/776-6888. Fax 0837/773-9773. www.scxingyu.com. 190 units. ¥980 ($127/£64) standard room. Rates include breakfast. 20%–40% discounts. 15% service charge. No credit cards. Closed Nov–Dec. **Amenities:** 2 restaurants; airline, train, and bus ticketing; business center; limited room service; laundry/dry cleaning. In room: Limited hours of A/C, TV, fridge in some rooms.

INEXPENSIVE

Yinyuan Binguan ⟨Value⟩ Renovated in 2004, this small, low-frills hotel used to be Jiuzhai Gou's best—which says lots about how much building has taken place here in the last few years. Clean, good value, and staffed with cordial, conscientious people, it still doesn't come close to being the best anymore. Still, with only 60 rooms, it feels homier than most.

Jiuzhai Gou Scenic Area (150m/492 ft. from Jiuzhai Gou entrance). (*) 0837/773-4890. Fax 0837/773-4114. 60 units. ¥260–¥500 ($34–$65/£17–£33) standard room; ¥1,880 ($244/£122) suite. 20%–50% discounts, depending on occupancy. No credit cards. **Amenities:** Restaurant; airline, train, and bus ticketing; limited room service; laundry/dry cleaning. *In room:* Limited hours A/C, TV, 24-hr. hot water.

WHERE TO DINE

Except for hotel restaurants, there aren't lots of dining choices. For inexpensive (but still overpriced) local food, try one of the several identical *huoguo* (hot pot) restaurants on the main street of Zhangzha Town. Another option is to pay ¥160 ($21/£10) for dinner and a performance of Qiang and Tibetan folk entertainment, which includes dancing, singing, and audience participation. Tibetan-style barbecued mutton, Tibetan tea, and a ritual welcoming liqueur are included in the ticket price. The **Gesangla Art Troupe (Gesangla Yishu Tuan)** performs nightly at 7:30pm at Jiuxin Shanzhuang (Jiuxin Mountain Villa), on the hotel strip 1km (½ mile) east of the Jiuzhai Gou entrance. For information, call (*) 0837/773-9588.

A snack bar selling kabobs, watermelon juice, pearl milk tea (a Taiwanese-style drink made of tea, milk, and sago palm starch), and tofu on a stick is outside the Jiuzhai Gou entrance, next to the tourist center. Snacks are also sold inside the reserve, but they're overpriced and not very good.

7 Chongqing

Chongqing Municipality, 334km (208 miles) SE of Chengdu, 1,346km (836 miles) S of Xi'an, 1,000km (620 miles) upstream of Three Gorges Dam

If other major cities in China are undergoing face-lifts, Chongqing is having radical reconstructive surgery: In 1997, it became the fourth city to achieve the status of municipality (after Beijing, Tianjin, and Shanghai). With summers so hot it's been dubbed one of China's Three Furnaces, and streets so steep that no one rides a bike, terrain and weather were once its chief claims to fame. Now, this cliff-side city overlooking the confluence of the Chang and Jialing rivers has much to boast about. Chongqing is the biggest metropolitan area in the world (surpassing Tokyo); it's got the world's biggest dam site downriver; and it's in the midst of building the world's tallest skyscraper (the Chongqing Tower). But whether all this development is a boom or a binge is yet to be seen.

As recently as the 19th century, Chongqing was a remote walled city. Even after the steam engine eased passage through the Three Gorges, few Easterners had any reason or desire to make the trip. That all changed in 1938, when Hankou fell to the Japanese and downriver residents made a mass exodus up the Chang Jiang (Yangzi River). Chongqing became China's last wartime capital, and after withstanding 3 years of Japanese bombing, the city never looked back. Very few of the old ramshackle neighborhoods rebuilt after the war have survived "urban improvement," and except for an old prison complex and a few small museums and memorials there is little evidence of earlier eras.

Most travelers come to Chongqing because it's the first or last stop on a Three Gorges cruise. But until recently, levels of sulfur dioxide and suspended air particles were so high that visitors couldn't wait to leave. As the city implements pollution control programs, that seems to be gradually changing. Chongqing's pleasures are modest, but there's enough here to make a 2- or 3-day stay enjoyable. The city is also just a 2-hour bus ride from the Buddhist Grottoes at Dazu. *Note:* For Chinese translations of selected establishments listed in this section, please turn to appendix A.

ESSENTIALS

GETTING THERE   Jiangbei Airport is 25km (15 miles) north of Chongqing, and 30 minutes by taxi (around ¥65/$8/£4). It offers daily domestic service to Beijing, Chengdu, Guilin, Hong Kong, Kunming, Shanghai, and Xi'an; it offers service to Lhasa twice a week. International destinations include Tokyo, Seoul, Bangkok, and Düsseldorf. The Minhang (CAAC) **airport shuttle bus** (© 023/6386-5824) leaves every half-hour from 6am to 6pm from Shangqing Si for ¥15 ($1.95/£1). Domestic and international air tickets are also on sale here from 7:30am to 6:30pm. **Dragonair** has offices in the Metropolis Building (Daduhui Shangsha), Zourong Lu 68 (© 023/ 6372-9900).

The **Main Railway Station** and **Long-Distance Bus Station** are next to each other on Nanqu Lu, near the Yangzi River. **Trains** from Shanghai and Beijing take approximately 28 and 25 hours, respectively. Trains from Chongqing Bei Zhan (Chongqing North) to Chengdu take 3½ hours, costing ¥51 ($6.65/£3.30). The soft-seat waiting lounge is on the far right of the station complex.

Luxury **buses** with a uniformed attendant and bathroom onboard connect Chongqing to Chengdu; the 4-hour trip costs ¥125 ($16/£8). The bus makes two stops in Chongqing: the first, at Chenjia Ping, for those going to the wharf; the second, at the Fuyuan Binguan, next to the Long-Distance Bus Station. As you exit, ignore the throng of private drivers vying to overcharge you. Walk across the parking lot to the taxi queue in front of the railway station. Insist on using the meter. The ride to any of the major hotels is ¥5 to ¥10 (65¢–$1.30/35p–65p). Large Volvo and Mercedes buses leave the Long-Distance Bus Station for Chengdu every half-hour throughout the day for ¥125 ($16/£8). Buses to Le Shan leave from the Jiefang Bei Qiche Keyun Zhan (Liberation Monument Bus Station) at Linjiang Lu 60. (For Yangzi River travel, see section 9, "Middle Reaches of the Chang Jiang.")

GETTING AROUND   There are three types of **taxis.** Rates for midrange Xiali are ¥5 (65¢/35p) for 3km (2 miles), then ¥1.80 (25¢/10p) per kilometer thereafter. The rate increases to ¥2.30 (30¢/15p) from 10pm to 7am. In addition to the 10 bridges that span the Jialing and Yangzi rivers, there is a cable car line across each river. Leave from Xinhua Lu to cross the Yangzi for ¥2 (25¢/15p), or leave from Cangbai Lu to cross the Jialing for ¥1.50 (20¢/10p). Cable cars run from 6:30am to 10:30pm. **Buses/trolleys** serve all parts of the city. Rides with air-conditioning are ¥1.50 to ¥2.50 (20¢–35¢/10p–15p); rides without are ¥1 to ¥1.50 (15¢–20¢/10p). Cable cars and some buses/trolleys have attendants. At the moment, the **light rail** only has one line running from Yuzhong District center (Jiao Chang Kou) to the Jialing River side, to Jiulongpo District, and ending at Dadukou District's Xinshancun. Fare is ¥2 to ¥5 (25¢–65¢/15p–35p); from 6:30am to 10pm. Two more lines—one connecting Chaotianmen and Shapingba—are scheduled to be completed in 2010.

VISITOR INFORMATION   CITS is located near the People's Square (Renmin Guangchang). This branch, at Zaozi Lanya Zheng Jie 120, second floor (© 023/ 6385-0693; fax 023/6385-0196; citscq@cta.cq.cn.), is particularly helpful.

Chongqing

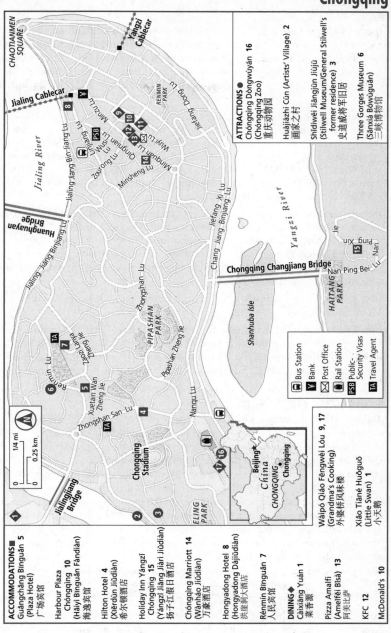

ATTRACTIONS ●
Chóngqìng Dòngwùyuán **16**
(Chongqing Zoo)
重庆动物园

Huàjiāzhì Cūn (Artists' Village) **2**
画家之村

Shǐdíwēi Jiāngjūn Jiùjū
(Stilwell Museum/General Stilwell's
former residence) **3**
史迪威将军旧居

Three Gorges Museum **6**
(Sānxiá Bówùguǎn)
三峡博物馆

Legend:
- Bus Station
- ¥ Bank
- Post Office
- Rail Station
- **PSB** Public-Security Visas
- **TA** Travel Agent

ACCOMMODATIONS ■
Guǎngchǎng Bīnguǎn **5**
(Plaza Hotel)
广场宾馆

Harbour Plaza
Chóngqìng **10**
(Hǎiyì Bīnguǎn Fàndiàn)
海逸宾馆

Hilton Hotel **4**
(Xīěrdùn Jiǔdiàn)
希尔顿酒店

Holiday Inn Yángzǐ
Chóngqìng **15**
(Yángzǐ Jiāng Jiàrì Jiǔdiàn)
扬子江假日酒店

Chóngqìng Marriott **14**
(Wànháo Jiǔdiàn)
万豪酒店

Hongyadong Hotel **8**
(Hóngyádòng Dàjiǔdiàn)
洪崖洞大酒店

Rénmín Bīnguǎn **7**
人民宾馆

DINING ◆
Càixiāng Yuán **1**
菜香源

Pizza Amalfi
(Āmèifēi Bǐsà) **13**
阿美比萨

KFC **12**

McDonald's **10**

Wàipó Qiáo Fēngwèi Lóu **9, 17**
(Grandma's Cooking)
外婆桥风味楼

Xiǎo Tiāné Huǒguō
(Little Swan) **1**
小天鹅

723

FAST FACTS

Banks, Foreign Exchange & ATMs   The main branch of **Bank of China** (open Mon–Fri 9am–noon and 2–5:30pm), north of Liberation Monument on the north side of Minzu Lu, has full foreign-exchange services and an ATM. The branch cater-cornered from Harbour Plaza Hotel, Zourong Lu at Bayi Lu, has a 24-hour ATM and offers foreign-exchange service, although limited to cash and U.S. dollar traveler's checks.

Consulates   Both the Canadian and United Kingdom consulates are in the Metropolitan Plaza building (Daduhui Shangsha) on Wuyi Lu, and are open Monday through Friday from 8:30am to 5:30pm. The **Canadian Consulate** is in Suite 1705 (© **023/6373-8007;** chonq@dfait-acci.gc.ca), and the **United Kingdom Consulate** is in Suite 2802 (© **023/6381-0321**). Take bus no. 306, 402, 413, or 601 to the Jiefang Bei stop. From there, walk southeast on Zourong Lu to Wuyi Lu. Metropolitan Plaza is next to the Harbour Plaza Hotel.

Internet Access   The area around Liberation Monument has lots of Internet bars, including **Reader's Club (Duzhe Julebu),** open 24 hours and located on the third floor of the Xinhua Bookstore at Minsheng Lu 181 (opposite Nuren Guangchang; © **023/6371-6364**). Rates are ¥2 (25¢/15p) per hour; less with membership card. Coffee and tea are served. Enter from Xinhua Shudian or from the side door of the adjacent bank. Dial-up is © **163.**

Post Office   The main post office is near Jiefang Bei (Liberation Monument), at Minquan Lu 3.

Visa Extensions   The **Administrative Division of Exit-Entry (Churujing Guanli Chu)** processes visa extensions in 5 working days. Located at Wusi Lu 48, Fu 1 (© **028/ 8640-7067;** open Mon–Fri 9–11:30am and 2–5pm), it's next to the Municipal PSB; enter on Shuncheng Dajie. Take bus no. 16 or 64 to the Renmin Zhong Lu and Wenwu Lu junction.

EXPLORING CHONGQING

Artists' Village (Huajia Zhi Cun)   Seventeen state-sponsored artists—some of them renowned—live in this complex of cottages overlooking the Jialing River. This sight is a favorite with tour groups who roll in for a quick buying frenzy before or after their Three Gorges tour. Even if you're not prepared to spend lots of money, the vine-covered studios and residences, connected by stone walkways and surrounded by small gardens, provide a more interesting respite from the traffic than just another city park. Each artist has a small studio, and visitors roam the grounds from one to the next. The colony dates from the days when the function of art was to serve the state. There are few other places where the casual traveler can rub elbows with people who were part of that movement. Look for Niu Wen's pre- and post-1949 woodblock prints, which are rare finds.

Hualong Qiao Jie, Hua Cun 24 (south bank of Jialing River near Hua Cun bus stop; look for English sign at bus stop). © 023/6331-3735. 9am–6pm. Bus: no. 104, 215, or 261 to Hua Cun. Taxi from People's Sq. about ¥10 ($1.30/65p). You will have to go through a guarded gate, so have the characters (from the map key, p. 723) ready to show the guard.

Chongqing Zoo (Chongqing Dongwuyuan)   If you're going to Chengdu and have time to visit one of the panda breeding centers (in the northern suburbs or at Wolong), then don't bother with the Chongqing Zoo. But if this is your only chance to see pandas, consider spending part of a morning at the giant panda and red panda enclosures. To get to the red pandas, go to the left of the English introduction board and down the stairs. The outdoor enclosure has a half-dozen extremely active small red pandas. Don't bother with the rest of the zoo; it will only depress you.

Tip: The best chance of seeing pandas is during feeding—between 8:30 and 10:30am. If the pandas aren't out, poke your head in the office behind the English introduction board and ask the zoo warden if he'll feed them. Sometimes that's all it takes.

Jiulong Po Qu, Xijiao Yi Cun 1, in city's southeast quadrant. ℂ 023/6843-3494. Admission ¥20 ($2.60/£1.30). Zoo summer 6:30am–9pm; winter 7am–9pm. Panda enclosures 8:30–10:30am and 3:30–4:30pm. Light rail or bus: no. 463 to Dongwuyuan.

Ciqikou 🖈

This small neighborhood with cobblestone streets in the Shaping District is popular with travelers who have a few days in Chongqing; however, it has somewhat turned into a theme park. The two main streets—lined with modest eastern Sichuan–style buildings—form a T from the entrance. Shops on the first street sell paintings, batik clothing, and other items geared mainly for tourists.

At the top of the T, a right turn leads to the wharf. Along the way are several teahouses and restaurants. One teahouse, Qingdai Minju, has a nice courtyard just off the main thoroughfare where you can enjoy performances on traditional Chinese instruments. Farther along at Lingyun Minyue in another tearoom, a small ensemble of musicians gathers most days to play traditional music.

Take the light rail to Daiping Station, then take bus no. 467 on Daiping Zheng Jie for Ciqikou.

Gele Shan/Baigong Guan/SACO (Gele Hill)

Standing in a lovely setting with trees, shrubs, stone walkways, and a babbling brook, Baigong Guan was originally a Sichuan warlord's *pied-à-terre*, but it was taken over by the notoriously brutal Dai Li— head of the Nationalist (KMT) secret police and guerrilla forces—and turned into a prison in 1939. Two years later, the U.S. spy agency SACO (Sino-American Cooperation Organization), which trained secret agents for the KMT, housed its servicemen here. It reverted to a prison in 1945, and it was here that the KMT slaughtered several hundred Communists and dissidents before retreating to Taiwan in 1949. The incident is known as the Bloodbath of 11/27, and many locals still come here to pay homage on that date.

The wooden buildings that were used as a prison are open to visitors. Photos of prisoners are displayed on the walls with poems and excerpts from letters—some in English translation—reflecting the political idealism of an earlier age.

Shapingba Qu (3.2km/2 miles west of Hongyan Cun). Admission ¥25 ($3.25/£1.65). 8:30am–7pm. Bus: no. 280 or 215.

Sanxia Bowuguan (Three Gorges Museum)

Originally called the Chongqing Municipal Museum, this museum moved to its more modern and spacious location mid-2005. While still lacking a certain charisma, several items in this museum make the trip worthwhile. First is its lovely collection of Tang and Song heads carved out of stone. Most are of Buddha, Guanyin, and various bodhisattvas, but what distinguishes them are their human rather than heavenly miens. A fine collection of terra-cotta sculptures from an Eastern Han tomb is also on the display. Discovered in Chongqing north of the Yangzi, they are small, whimsical figurines of musicians, dancers, singers, and storytellers—a lively group to spend eternity with. The museum also boasts collections that stretch as far as the Shang dynasty (ca. 1600–1045 B.C.). Of particular interest are the paulownia-wood "boat coffins" of the ancient Ba culture.

Renmin Lu, north side of the People's Sq. (Renmin Guangchang). Admission ¥10 ($1.30/65p). 8:30am–5pm. Bus: no. 129, 215, 22, 111, 103, or 104.

Stilwell Museum/Former Residence of General Stilwell (Shidiwei Jiangjun Jiuju) After Pearl Harbor, President Roosevelt sent Gen. Joseph Stilwell (1883–1946) to Chongqing as commander in chief of Allied forces in the China-Burma-India theater of the war. Unfortunately, "Vinegar Joe" and the KMT general he was supposed to advise—Chiang Kai-shek—had rather different agendas, not to mention temperaments, and in 1944, at Chiang's urging, Stilwell was relieved of his post. Nonetheless, his contribution to the Burma Road campaign was significant—reason enough for the local government to continue to maintain a museum honoring him. His disdain for Chiang must also have endeared him to the party. The museum, housed in Stilwell's Chongqing residence, has a collection of newspaper clippings, photographs, letters, and Stilwell's personal belongings. A video tells the Chinese version of Stilwell's tour of duty and includes rare clips. Explanations are in English and Chinese. The Stilwell and Flying Tiger T-shirts sold here make unique gifts.

Jialing Xin Cun 63. ✆ 023/6387-2794. Admission ¥5 (65¢/35p). No regular hours; doorman always on duty (or so it's claimed). Bus: no. 104, 215, or 261 to Liziba stop.

SHOPPING

Carrefour Supermarket (Jialefu Chaoshi) is inside the Xin Chongqing Building. It's open from 9am to 10:30pm; take bus no. 111 or 166 to the Xiao Shizi stop. The supermarket is absolutely crammed with customers because you can get anything here—and cheaply. **KFC** is inside the same building. A **Watson** drugstore is on the first floor of Metropolitan Plaza (Daduhui Guangchang), next to the Harbour Plaza on Wuyi Lu, 1 block southeast of Jiefang Bei. This seven-floor indoor mall has restaurants, upscale and international clothing stores, and even an ice-skating rink on the sixth floor.

WHERE TO STAY
EXPENSIVE

Chongqing Marriott (Wanhao Jiudian) With its high-ceilinged lobby flanked by two sweeping staircases, palm trees, a steakhouse overlooking the rivers, and a Japanese restaurant with traditional architecture and decor, the Marriott is the most elegant choice in town. Ask for one of the rooms above the 19th floor, which are slightly bigger and have separate bathroom and shower.

Qingnian Lu 77 (corner of Qingnian Lu and Minsheng Lu), Yuzhong. ✆ 023/6388-8888. Fax 023/6399-9999. www. marriott.com. 436 units. ¥1,702–¥2,047 ($221–$266/£111–£133) standard room. 50%–60% discounts year-round; 15% service charge. AE, DC, MC, V. Bus: no. 306, 402, 413, or 601 to Jiefang Bei. **Amenities:** 4 restaurants; indoor pool; health club; airline, train, and bus ticketing; business center; wireless Internet access; 24-hr. room service; laundry/dry cleaning. In room: A/C, TV w/satellite channels, dataport, broadband Internet access, minibar, fridge, hair dryer, iron, safe.

Harbour Plaza Chongqing (Haiyi Fandian) This five-star luxury hotel has a convenient downtown location (next to deluxe shopping on the city's pedestrian mall) that's cater-cornered to a 24-hour ATM. The new, enlarged reception area is open and airy. Guest rooms are decorated in rich blues and golds, and most have views of the cityscape. Bathrooms are spacious and most have separate tub and shower. Though less glamorous than the Marriott, the Harbour Plaza still meets international standards in every way.

Wuyi Lu (at Zourong Lu, 1 block southeast of Liberation Monument). ✆ 023/6370-0888. Fax 023/6370-0778. www.harbour-plaza.com/hpcq. 388 units. ¥1,200–¥1,400 ($156–$182/£78–£91) standard room; ¥2,300–¥2,576 ($299–$335/£150–£167) suite. 50%–65% discounts year-round; 15% service charge. AE, DC, MC, V. Bus: no. 306,

402, 413, or 601 to Jiefang Bei. **Amenities:** 2 restaurants; 4 bars; indoor pool; health club; airline and train ticketing; business center; forex; 24-hr. room service; laundry/dry cleaning. *In room:* A/C, TV w/satellite channels, international direct dialing, dataport, minibar, fridge, hair dryer, safe.

Hilton (Xierdun Jiudian) ⚡ *(Kids)*　Opened in 2002, this five-star hotel is one of Chongqing's finest, and highly recommended. Views are of the rivers and the Datianwan Sport Stadium; rooms are attractively decorated. There are also playground and activities for children. The hotel is well located near the business district and less than 3km (2 miles) from the railway station. It's also a short, interesting walk from Pipa Shan Gongyuan and the City Museum.

Zhongshan San Lu 139 (near Datianwan Sport Stadium). ℂ 800/820-0600 or 023/8903-9999. Fax 023/8903-8700. www.hilton.com**http://www.hilton.com**. 443 units. ¥1,494 – ¥1,921 ($194–$250/£97–£125) standard room; ¥2,392 – ¥2,680 ($311–$348/£155–£174) suite. 65% discounts year-round; 15% service charge. AE, DC, MC, V. Bus: no. 224, 368, 402, 411, or 605 to Liang Lukou stop. **Amenities:** 3 restaurants; bar; indoor pool; health club; spa; airline, train, and bus ticketing; business center; forex; 24-hr. room service; laundry/dry cleaning. *In room:* A/C, satellite TV, dataport, broadband Internet access, minibar, fridge, hair dryer, safe.

Holiday Inn Yangtze Chongqing (Yangzi Jiang Jiari Fandian)　Compared to the five-star Harbour, Hilton, and Marriott properties, this four-star isn't nearly as posh, nor can it boast a central location. But it does have beautiful views all around—on one side, the Chang Jiang, on the other, mountains. To compensate for the inconvenient location, a free shuttle service runs several times a day between the hotel and the French supermarket, Carrefour. The rooms are clean but slightly run down; bathrooms are small. The hotel feels like a Western budget inn, but even with the standard 50% discount, the rates aren't much better than those of a five-star property.

Nanping Bei Lu 15 (in Nan'an District south of the Yangzi). ℂ 023/6280-3380. Fax 023/6280-0884. www.holiday-inn. com. 424 units. ¥1,290 ($168/£84) standard room; ¥1,800 – ¥2,100 ($234–$273/£117–£137) suite. Most rates include breakfast. Over 50% discounts year-round; 15% service charge. AE, DC, MC, V. **Amenities:** 4 restaurants; bar; outdoor pool; health club; sauna; airline, train, and bus ticketing; business center; forex; ATM; 24-hr. room service; laundry/ dry cleaning. *In room:* A/C, satellite TV, dataport, broadband Internet access, minibar, fridge, hair dryer, iron, safe.

MODERATE/INEXPENSIVE

Guangchang Binguan (Plaza Hotel)　Located opposite Renmin Guangchang, this midsize three-star hotel is particularly good value for three people traveling together, even without the hefty discounts that are standard. Despite renovations in 2004, prices have remained unchanged and, with the discounts, all rooms are very reasonably priced. Room decor and furnishings are standard and forgettable, but the staff, outfitted in crisp uniforms, is warm and welcoming, despite (or perhaps, due to) the fact that few foreigners have discovered this hotel. There are two standard room types—A and B. "A" rooms are slightly bigger and the bathroom ceilings slightly higher, but standard "B" rooms are perfectly acceptable. The difference isn't enough to warrant the additional $17 for an "A" room. The location puts guests within walking distance of the Municipal Museum, People's Square, People's Auditorium, and CITS.

Xuetianwan Zheng Jie 2. ℂ 023/6355-8989. Fax 023/6355-9000. www.cqghotel.com. 129 units. ¥328 – ¥468 ($43–$61/£21–£30) standard room; ¥980 – ¥1,588 ($127–$206/£64–£103) suite. 20%–30% discounts year-round. AE, DC, MC, V. Bus: no. 103, 162, 181, or 261. **Amenities:** 2 restaurants; bar; airline, train, and bus ticketing; small business center; forex; room service; laundry/dry cleaning. *In room:* A/C, TV, minibar/fridge (suites only).

Hongyadong Hotel ⚡　This four-star hotel, opened in 2006, is highly recommended and good value. The hotel, which sits beside the Jialing River, is part of the traditional Chinese-style Hongyadong complex comprised of shopping malls, restaurants, and bars. Some of the guest rooms overlook the river and Jiangbei District. The entire hotel is decorated with classy wooden furniture, modern Chinese-style decor, and tasteful Chinese paintings. Rooms are large and charming and beds are plush. Bathrooms have showers only; the wash basin has a traditional Chinese pattern. The staff speaks English.

Cangbai Lu 56, Yuzhong District. © 023/6399-2888. Fax 023/6399-2999. 176 units. ¥398–¥768 ($52–$100/ £26–£50) standard room; ¥818–¥1,588 ($106–$206/£53–£103) suite. Rates include breakfast. 40% discount is standard. AE, DC, MC, V. **Amenities:** 3 restaurants; bar; sauna; airline, train, and bus ticketing; limited room service; laundry/ dry cleaning. *In room:* A/C, TV, broadband Internet access, minibar, fridge, safe.

WHERE TO DINE

One of the dishes most identified with Sichuan cooking (though it may have come from Mongolia) is hot pot or *huoguo* (fire pot). It is so popular here that a block of Wuyi Lu (just off Minzu Lu) is called **Huoguo Jie (Hot Pot Street).** Street stalls and small restaurants serving this dish line the street, recognizable by their dining tables, the centers of which have a cooking pot with boiling broth and hot oil. Diners add meat, fish, sprouts, scallions, and any other ingredients they like to the pot. Once the submerged meat or vegetables are cooked, diners pluck pieces out with chopsticks and eat them plain or with a spicy dipping sauce. By tradition in both Sichuan and Inner Mongolia, locals favor organ meats, intestines, brains, and chicken feet for this poor-man's stew, but these days, in restaurants, choices abound. Like the best meals, the best hot pots use ingredients that combine a variety of tastes, textures, shapes, and colors.

Near Liberation Monument there's a **McDonald's** on the corner of Zourong Lu and Wuyi Lu, cater-cornered from Harbour Plaza, and a **KFC** on Minquan Lu at Jiefang Bei. There is also a **Starbucks** at Hongyadong.

Caixiang Yuan ↺ SICHUAN   Very popular with locals, this place serves traditional and nouveau Sichuan. Strange-flavored duck (*guaiwei Yazi*), with its perfect blend of salty, sweet, tingling, hot, sour, savory, and fragrant flavors, is a favorite here, and for good reason.

Building C-4 Jiazhou Huayuan (Jiazhou Garden in Yubei District). © 023/6762-9325. Meal for 2 ¥20–¥52 ($2.60–$6.75/ £1.30–£3.40). No credit cards. 11:30am–2:30pm and 5:30–10pm. Bus: no. 465 or 602 to Jiazhou Huayuan.

Pizza Amalfi (Ameifei Bisa) PIZZA   Though some might find the act of topping pizza with raisins and oranges sacrilegious, the menu here is varied enough to please every palate. Highly recommended, though, is pizza topped with goat cheese.

Minquan 3, 3rd floor, opposite the Liberation Monument, above the ground-floor Unicom store. © 023/6381-7868. Meal for 2 ¥40–¥80 ($5.20–$10/£2.60–£5.20). No credit cards. 9am–10:30pm.

Waipo Qiao Fengwei Lou (Grandma's Cooking) ↺↺ SICHUAN   This extremely popular restaurant, now with two locations, is more evidence that nostalgia is selling well in China. One manager, lumping over 500 years together, defined the cuisine as "Ming-Qing," and a real *waipo* (grandmother), dressed in simple garb, greets customers. The larger restaurant, in the Metropolitan Plaza, has a separate hot pot dining room next door that does an equally rousing business. Three of the best entrees in the main restaurant are *tieban shao zhi yinxueyu* (silver snow fish cooked on an iron plate), serves six; the slightly hot *qingjiao bao ziji* (baby chicken quick-fried with green pepper); and *guoba roupian* (pork with bamboo shoots over crispy rice). Faintly sweet corn cakes (*yumi bing*) complement the latter two dishes well. There's a second location at Taodu Chengshi Jiudian er Lou (Taodu City Hotel, second floor) Yangjiaping, Xijiao Lu 21 (near the zoo) (© 023/6878-1818; bus no. 413 or 148).

Zourong Lu 68, Daduhui Guangchang 7 lou (Metropolitan Plaza, 7th floor near Jiefang Bei and next to Harbour Plaza Hotel). © 023/6383-5988. Reservations accepted. The Metropolitan Plaza location has an English menu. Meal for 2 ¥100 ($13/£6.50). No credit cards. 10:30am–2pm and 5–9pm. Bus: no. 306, 413, or 601 to Jiefang Bei.

Xiao Tian'e Huoguo (Little Swan) ★★ HOT POT   One of the most popular hot pot restaurants in Sichuan and beyond is a chain of 126 stores, the first of which opened over 20 years ago in Chongqing. Little Swan continues to be one of the best in town. This self-serve restaurant gives patrons a choice of hot or mild broth, and its buffet table of ingredients allows non-Mandarin speakers more control than usual over what goes into the pot.

Jianxin Bei Lu 78. © 023/6785-5328. Meal for 2 ¥30–¥80 ($3.90–$10/£1.95–£5.20). No credit cards. 11am–10pm. Bus: no. 181, 411, 601, or 902 to Haiguan.

8 Dazu (Dazu Buddhist Grottoes) ★★★

Chongqing Municipality, 83km (52 miles) W of Chongqing, 251km (156 miles) SE of Chengdu

Among the most impressive and affecting artistic monuments that have survived through the ages are the extensive Buddhist cave paintings, sculptures, and carvings of Datong, Luoyang, Dunhuang, and Dazu. Of the four sites, **Dazu's stone carvings,** executed between 892 and 1249, are among the subtlest and most sophisticated, and worth going out of your way to see.

An unusual aspect of Dazu is that in addition to Buddhist images, it contains Daoist and Confucian statues and themes—not only in separate areas but, in rare instances, in the same cave. Initiated outside the monastic establishment, the Dazu carvings also commemorate historical figures as well as the project's benefactors, including commoners, warriors, monks, and nuns. In addition to what these carvings reveal about artistic advances made from the late Tang to the late Song, the garments and ornaments, along with garden and architectural settings, shed much light on everyday life in ancient China.

Of the six largest sites scattered around the county seat of Dazu, two are most worth a visit—**Bei Shan,** completed in the late Tang dynasty (618–907); and **Baoding Shan,** started and completed in the Song dynasty (960–1279). If you have time or interest for only one, make it Baoding Shan.

ESSENTIALS

GETTING THERE   Buses leave Chongqing for Dazu from the Caiyuanba Long-Distance Bus Station (next to the railway station) every 20 minutes. The earliest bus is at 5:30am; the last return bus is scheduled to leave at 6pm. It's best to be at the Dazu bus station by 5pm for the return trip to Chongqing. The 1½-hour drive from Chongqing to Dazu Xian Bus Station costs ¥40 ($5.20/£2.60). From the Dazu Bus Station, catch a **minibus** for Baoding Shan. Buses depart every half-hour. The half-hour ride costs ¥3.50 to ¥4.50 (45¢–60¢/25p–30p) each way. Buses also depart from the small bus station in the north part of town for ¥4.50 (60¢/30p). A **taxi** from Dazu Xian to Baoding Shan is about ¥30 ($3.90/£1.95).

Taking the **train** to Dazu is slow and requires first going to Youting; from Youting, transfer to a bus going to the bus station. From the station, transfer to another bus to the grottoes. Whether coming from Chengdu or Chongqing, the bus is considerably faster and more convenient.

TOURS & GUIDES   Guided trips to Baoding Shan can be arranged at Chongqing **CITS,** Zaozi Lanya Zheng Jie 120, second floor (✆ **023/6385-0693;** fax 023/6385-0196; citscq@cta.cq.cn). The ¥1,300 ($162/£81) fee for one or two people includes admission to Baoding and Bei Shan, a guide, transportation, and lunch. Alternately, English-language books give brief explanations of the more important carvings.

FAST FACTS
There are no useful services for visitors in Dazu. Exchange money before you leave Chongqing.

EXPLORING DAZU
Video cameras are permitted for a fee of ¥100 ($13/£6.50), plus a ¥50 ($6.50/£3.25) deposit for a permit. Plainclothes guards are stationed throughout the grotto area, so don't be tempted to tape without a permit. Still photography is allowed inside the grottoes except where signs indicate otherwise.

Baoding Shan ✦✦✦   Carvings of the cliff-side grottoes known as Da Fo Wan (Big Buddha Cove) were initiated and directed by Zhao Zhifeng, a self-styled Buddhist monk whose brand of Esoteric Buddhism incorporated current religious ideas and popular beliefs. Beginning in 1178 with the construction of Shengshou Temple at Xiao Fo Wan (Little Buddha Cove)—just north of Da Fo Wan—the Baoding Shan project continued for 71 years, possibly halted by the Mongol offensive in Sichuan. If Zhao lived that long (he'd have been 90) it would explain the unity of design and absence of repetition that mark Baoding Shan. The carvings are a series of instructive and cautionary scriptural stories arranged in order around a U-shaped cove with interludes of inscriptions and caves devoted to Buddhist deities. At the bottom curve of the U is a massive carving of a reclining **Sakyamuni Buddha** as he enters Nirvana (no. 11). It is just one of the many imposing sculptures at Baoding Shan. Others that should be noted include the stories of **parental devotion** (no. 15) and **Sakyamuni's filial piety** (no. 17). Local guides usually say these attest to the merging of Confucianism and Buddhism during the Song. But scholars see their inclusion as either a concession to Confucianism—when you want government endorsement, there's no point alienating folks—or, possibly, an answer to it from Buddhist scriptures. (In the parental devotion story, look for the nursing boy at the far right wearing the same split pants Chinese toddlers still wear today instead of diapers.) The gruesome **Hell of Knee-Chopping** (no. 20) captures the many faces of drunkenness (none flattering) without crossing the line into kitsch. These carvings are first and foremost works of art. The last story in the cove (no. 30) depicts the taming of a water buffalo and is meant to be a metaphor for taming the mind in meditation. One of the most accomplished carvings in this cove is no. 8, the **Thousand-arm Avalokitesvara** (aka Guanyin), said to be the only Thousand-arm Avalokitesvara that really has a thousand arms (1,007, actually). Remarkably, each of its hands is in a different pose. Expect to spend 1½ to 2 hours if you're exploring on your own, another hour if you've hired a guide.

Tip: The greatest obstacle to enjoying these caves is the crowds. The best time to visit Baoding Shan is at noon, when they go to lunch. Go to Bei Shan (below) anytime—tours usually skip it.

15km (9 miles) northeast of the town of Longgang Zhen (often called Dazu Xian). It's about .5km (¼ mile) from the drop-off point (where the restaurants and souvenir stands are) to the entrance. Mini-trolley shuttle between parking lot and entrance ¥3 (35¢/20p). There's a private pay bathroom by the parking lot (5 mao/5¢/3p) and another, cleaner restroom halfway to the entrance. No restrooms inside. Admission ¥80 ($10/£5). Combination ticket for Baoding Shan and Bei Shan ¥120 ($15/£7.50). 8:30am–6pm.

Bei Shan ⊛   The problem with visiting Bei Shan after Baoding Shan is that it's a bit of a letdown. If you visit it first, though, you risk being glutted before properly feasting on the best. That said, Fo Wan (Buddha Cove), the cove at the top of Bei Shan, offers a fine series of religious and commemorative carvings, if somewhat less dazzling than the Song carvings. In 892, Wei Junjing, a military commander and imperial envoy, began carving Buddha images in what, at that time, was his encampment atop Bei Shan. That started a 250-year trend that resulted in the completion of nearly 10,000 statues scattered over the county by the end of the Song dynasty. Highlights of Bei Shan include the story of **Amitabha Buddha and his Pure Land** in Cave 245, which contains exquisite carved heads that look remarkably alive. Another is the statue of the **Bodhisattva Manjusri** in the largest cave at Fo Wan (no. 136). He appears high-minded and lofty, but it's the touch of self-satisfaction in his expression that captures his humanity and sets this statue apart.

2km (1¼ miles) north of the town of Longgang Zhen (often called Dazu Xian). Admission ¥60 ($6.50/£3.25). 8:30am–6pm. Buses leave regularly from Dazu Bus Station for ¥1 (15¢/10p). A taxi from Dazu Xian to Bei Shan is about ¥5 (65¢/35p).

WHERE TO STAY

Dazu Binguan   This hotel and the Bei Sha Binguan accept foreign visitors, but the Dazu, with comparable rates, is so far superior (and cleaner) that it's the only recommendation I'll make. Rooms are decorated without imagination and contain the usual twin beds with cheap colored bedspreads, but there is a range of rooms for two, making this hotel affordable for most. Rooms in the back wing are small and show wear; bigger, more recently renovated standards are in the front. Both have bathrooms with tub/shower combo.

In the town of Longgang Zhen, Dazu County, Gong Long Lu 47. From the Dazu Bus Station, turn left (north) as you exit the station; cross the bridge over the Lai Xi River to its junction with Gong Long Lu. Turn right (east). The hotel is about 275m (900 ft.) ahead on the right. ☏ **023/4372-1888.** Fax 023/4372-2967. 122 units. ¥298–¥498 ($36–$57/£18–£29) standard room. Rates include breakfast. No credit cards. **Amenities:** Restaurant; room service. *In room:* A/C, TV.

WHERE TO DINE

The tourist town of Baoding Shan outside the entrance gate has a number of small restaurants, noodle shops, and kabob stands serving good, simple dishes at inflated (but still inexpensive) prices. It's usually the Qingdao or imported beer that hikes the bill up; unless you ask for local, that's what you'll get.

9 Middle Reaches of the Chang Jiang ⊛

THE THREE GORGES DAM (SANXIA BA)

The dream of constructing an enormous dam to harness and utilize the power of the Chang Jiang (Yangzi River) originally belonged to Sun Yat-sen in the early 1920s, but every Chinese leader since—including Mao and Deng Xiaoping—has shared it. The appeal of this massive project to premiers and presidents may have more to do with classical Chinese flood myths than engineering logic. The most enduring is the story of Yu, who was born out of the belly of his father's corpse. Through superhuman feats of repositioning mountains and changing the courses of rivers, Yu quelled the great flood of the world and restored natural order. Selfless and moral, his efforts left his body half-withered, yet he went on to found the (semimythical) Xia dynasty (ca. 21st–16th c. B.C.). There are also historical models of men who tamed rivers: Shu governor Li Bing supervised ancient China's largest irrigation project (256 B.C.) and is still admired for it; and the Sui Yangdi emperor (reigned 604–617) completed the building of the Grand Canal linking the north and south. Latest to see himself in the role of a new Yu out to suppress floods is the former premier Li Peng (best remembered for suppressing the student democracy movement), who pushed approval of the dam through the National People's Congress in 1992, and with whom the dam is most identified, though he no longer holds office.

If all goes according to plan, the massive project will be finished in 2009, but whether it ensures Li's fame or infamy is yet to be seen. It breaks so many records in terms of size, manpower utilized in its construction, volume of building materials (including 10 million lb. of cement), and projected energy output (equal to "10 nuclear power stations"), that there is no real precedent by which to assess the short-term, let alone long-term, effects. But that hasn't stopped pundits (and nonpundits) from trying.

The chief aims of the dam are flood control, power generation, safer navigation, and increased river shipping, but critics of the project cite more than a few concerns, such as the resettlement of one million to two million people; the destruction of wildlife habitats, archaeological sites, and historical relics; and the environmental threat of trapped sewage and industrial waste.

DAM EFFECTS ALONG THE THREE GORGES ROUTE

Following are some of the immediate effects the 135m (443-ft.) water level is expected to have on sites along the Three Gorges route:

- The residents of Fengdu have already been moved to the new city built across the river on higher ground. The mountain and kitsch, ghoulish temple complex with its sculptures of bug-eyed demons and "scenes of hell" will remain, but the mountain will be a semi-island.
- A tall weir has been built surrounding the town of Shibao Zhai. The intriguing old town and temples inside are preserved.
- Zhangfei Temple has been moved to higher ground across the river. The temple commemorates the upright Shu warrior who was beheaded by two dastardly commanders in his own army. The bulk of the temple and its collection were destroyed during the Cultural Revolution. What stands is the restored building.
- Baidi Cheng (White Emperor City) will be half submerged. Trackers' paths carved into the cliffs of Qutang Gorge will be submerged.
- Three-quarters of Wan Xian will be inundated. The last quarter, renovated and developed, has become the new downtown.
- Fuling (site of ancient royal tombs of the Ba Kingdom and the port town of 150,000 people that is the setting of *River Town,* Peter Hessler's fine personal account) will be inundated. Excavation of the tombs is underway.
- The building of the underwater viewing chamber for the ancient stone carvings at White Crane Ridge is still underway at press time. At the time this book went to press, it was scheduled to be completed before 2008.
- The Daning and Shennong gorges will be slightly diminished, but naturally not enough to stop tours. Boats will be able to venture farther into these narrow gorges and provide a closer look at the ancient hanging coffins—among them a cluster of 24.
- The western part of Xiling Gorge will be submerged.
- The population of Badong has been moved upstream to the opposite side of the river. Landslide-prevention projects veil the nearby slopes.

The River by Any Other Name

The name "Yangtze" is troublesome. English dictionaries usually give it two or three accepted pronunciations and an equal number of ways to spell it: Yangtze, Yangtse, Yangzi. The irony of it is that Chinese almost never use that name. As far back as the Zhou dynasty (1045 B.C.–246 B.C.), China's longest river was simply called Jiang, meaning "River." ("He," also meaning "River," was used to refer to the Yellow River, China's other great waterway.) Sometime in the 3rd century, Chinese started calling it the Chang Jiang (meaning "Long River"), and that's what it's called today. Theories abound on how the name Yangzi came about. Some say it came from Cantonese; others that it was a Western invention. In fact, in the 6th century the name Yangzi Jiang started showing up in poetry to refer to a short stretch of the river near Yangzhou. By the 19th century the name was applied to the whole river; and for a time, under the Republic, Yangzi Jiang was even the official name. But it returned to Chang Jiang under the People's Republic, and that is the river's proper name.

TO CRUISE OR NOT TO CRUISE

Debate rages around the question of whether the **Three Gorges cruise** is the thrill of a lifetime or an overrated, overpriced yawn. Members of tour groups invariably rave about their luxury trip. The boats are plusher than they expected; the cabins roomier; the food better. If the scenery comes as a bit of a letdown—well, they weren't expecting *A Single Pebble*. And if the excursions aren't all they're cracked up to be, at least they're short. Perhaps one reason tour members find their Three Gorges cruise so delightful is that it puts a halt to the mania of touring for a few days.

While it's true that other parts of China have better scenery, prettiness isn't everything. The best part of these cruises is watching life on the river as it is today—in flux. A new city springs up on high, and a few hundred yards below it, the old city sits like a sloughed-off shell. If you choose to take an excursion, as most do, see "The Top Excursions," below, for the very best.

If you'd like to take the excursion but can't afford the steep cruise prices, cheaper tourist ferries and dirt-cheap passenger boats also make the trip. There are boats that sail all the way to Shanghai, but unless you're fanatical about river travel, limit your journey to the stretch between Chongqing and Yichang/Wuhan. From there eastward, the river widens and the scenery becomes decidedly prosaic, and train, bus, or plane is preferable.

The best times to go are September and October. In terms of weather, May, early June, and early November are risky, but they can be lovely. Summer is the rainy season, and winter is usually dry but quite cold. Fewer ships sail off season, and schedules are less reliable.

CRUISING INDUSTRY BE DAMMED?

No one, including cruise directors and travel agents, is entirely sure how the flooding of the Three Gorges all the way upstream to Chongqing will affect the Yangzi cruising industry—although, the fact that cruise lines such as Viking (see below) are adding the Three Gorges to their cruise roster suggests a certain optimism for the time being. June 2003 marked the end of Phase Two in construction and witnessed a rise in water level by 40m (85 ft.); at the end of the third and final phase in 2009 the expected rise will be an additional 50m (106 ft.). As a result, the peaks towering above the river are not as high, nor is bottom of the ravine as narrow. The ghost towns that now dot the banks of the Yangzi, evacuated in anticipation of the rising water level, make for an novel if unintended tourist curiosity, but the majesty of the Gorges themselves has definitely been compromised. In the meantime the Gorges might still be worth a visit, but 2009 will likely mark the end of the love affair.

THE CRUISE LINES

The following liners have the best English-speaking guides and the best ships. And after years of experience with foreign passengers, most have removed from their itineraries excursions that require a thorough familiarity with characters and events of the Three Kingdoms in order to enjoy them. Take advantage of off-season rates; book and buy in China; compare prices; bargain; and ask what the excursions are. The prices quoted here are rack rates, but 50% discounts are standard even during high season.

The cruising high seasons are April, May, September, and October. Shoulder seasons are late March, June, July, August, November, and early December. Some cruise ships offer specials in December, January, February, and March.

Orient Royal Cruises   Until the appearance of Viking River Cruises (below), Orient's *East King* and *East Queen* were arguably the plushest ships on the Yangzi—built to five-star standards and tied with the *Yellow Crane* (see Presidential Cruises, below) for the best food. Their cruise directors, both from the Philippines, do a superior job of attending to passenger needs and special requests, and their Chinese river guides deliver expert commentary in well-spoken English. Standard cabins have twin beds, a desk, and small fridge. Orient Royal offers 4-day route from Chongqing to Yichang and 5-day, from Yichang to Chongqing.

Orient Royal Cruise, Wuhan office. Xinhua Lu 316, 14th floor, E Zuo (Block E), Liangyou bldg. ℂ 027/8576-9988. Fax 027/8576-6688. www.orientroyalcruise.com. 96 cabins. ¥6,230–¥6,720 ($760–$980/£380–£490) per person, standard cabin. Shore excursions ¥560 ($70/£35) per person. AE, DC, MC, V. **Amenities:** 2 restaurants; 2 bars; exercise room; salon; massage; library; business center; 24-hr. room service; laundry. *In room:* A/C, TV, minibar/fridge, safe, hair dryer on request.

Presidential Cruises   Presidential, run by CITS, has five ships currently operating on the Yangzi, imaginatively named MV1, MV3, and so on. The *Yangzi Paradise* (aka MV6) is built to China's four-star standard, and its cabins aren't as spacious as those of Viking and Orient Royal, but the ship is attractively appointed and well-staffed with an English-speaking crew. While the *Yellow Crane* lacks the slick promotion of Victoria and Orient Royal, the ship itself serves better food, is more luxurious than Victoria's ships, and very nearly meets the five-star standard of the *East King* and *East Queen*. Standard rooms are comparable in size and furnishing to those in Victoria Cruises' fleet.

The *Yellow Crane* travels between Chongqing and Yichang (4 days downriver, 5 days upriver). CITS in Wuhan and Chongqing usually offer great savings on these tours; see contact information below under "Lower-Cost Cruise Alternatives: Local Passenger Boats & Tourist Ferries."

Contact Wuhan Empress Travel, Huiji Lu 15, 7th floor Changhang Dajiudian, Wuhan. ℂ 027/8286-5977. Fax 027/8286-6351. www.cits.net. 84–94 cabins. ¥2,740–¥3,120 ($335–$385/£168–£193) per person, standard cabin. 50% discounts. AE, DC, MC, V. **Amenities:** 2 restaurants; bar; exercise room; salon; massage; business center; reading room; laundry. *In room:* A/C, satellite TV, hair dryer on request.

Victoria Cruises   Based in New York, this is one of the few Western-managed lines. At one time, Victoria had the most luxurious liners on the Yangzi. While they still offer first-rate cruises with some of the best English-speaking cruise directors and river guides, other cruise lines equal or surpass their ships' cabins, kitchen, and facilities, and are equally well staffed. Standard cabins have twin beds and writing desk, but are slightly smaller than Orient Royal's *East King* and *East Queen*.

Victoria offers two routes: between Chongqing and Yichang (downriver 4 days, upriver 6 days); and between Chongqing and Shanghai (downriver 7 days, upriver 9 days).

57–08 39th Ave., Woodside, NY 11377. ℂ 800/348-8084 or 212/818-1680. Fax 212/818-9889. www.victoriacruises. com. 74–87 cabins. Cruise between Chongqing and Yichang: $675–$920 (£358–£488) per person, standard cabin; $1,850–$2,250 (£980–£1,193) per person largest suite. Shore excursion $80 (£42) per person. Cruise between Chongqing and Shanghai: $1,400–$1,500 (£742–£795) per person, standard cabin; $3,200–$3,600 (£1,696–£1,908) per person largest suite. Shore excursion $225 (£119) per person. 50%–60% discounts year-round. AE, DC, MC, V. **Amenities:** Restaurant; bar; exercise room; forex; salon; massage; acupuncture; laundry. *In room:* A/C, TV, hair dryer on request.

Viking River Cruises   Not only the most recent cruise line to start plying the Three Gorges, Viking's two liners, the *Viking Century Sky* and the *Viking Century Star*, comfortably float above the competition as the top way to see the river. Effortlessly five-star, every room is spacious and tastefully appointed with blond woods. The food is excellent and plentiful—to the extent that it sometimes feels as though you are living from meal to meal—and the staff has a working grasp of English and is extremely friendly. Although the Viking's main route runs between Chongqing and Yichang (3–4 nights), the company also offers trips that go all the way to Shanghai (9 nights). The cost of the cruise covers daily (but optional) shore visits, including the Three Gorges Dam, the Lesser Three Gorges, and Shi Bao Zhai Temple. However, the day trips are little more than a distraction from the cruise itself. Viking cruises are usually sold as part of package tours visiting China's other key tourist meccas: Xi'an, Beijing, Hong Kong, and Shanghai. Prices vary according to package, time of year, and type of cabin you choose, so check the website for current rates.

5700 Canoga Ave., Suite 200, Woodland Hills, CA 91367. ℂ 818/227-1234. www.vikingrivercruises.com. 153 cabins (*Century Sky*), 93 cabins (*Century Star*). Check website for current rates. AE, DC, MC, V. **Amenities:** Restaurant; 2 bars; exercise room; gym; sauna; salon; massage; laundry; Internet access. *In room:* A/C, closed-circuit/satellite TV, minibar, fridge, hair dryer.

The Top Excursions

One of the best excursions is to **Shi Bao Zhai (Stone Treasure Fortress).** This square-edged **red pagoda** built in the 18th century hugs the cliff and is an elegant vision from the river. The climb up its 12 narrow staircases is only difficult when other tour groups are pressing from behind or blocking the way in front. Since the descent is down a back staircase, just let them all go ahead. Inside, look for the two "magic" holes. The first is the **Hole of the Greedy Monk.** As the story goes, when monks lived in the tower, the hole spouted just enough rice for their daily rations. One monk, thinking he'd like rations to sell in the market, tried to make the hole bigger. His avarice shut the source for good. Of the second hole, it is said that if you drop a duck down it **(Duck Tossing Hole),** within seconds you'll see the duck floating far below on the river.

Close to the top of the pagoda, if you peek under the **arched bridge** (which is meant to be crossed in three steps or less), you'll get a good look at a *wawa yu*—the

giant Chinese salamander that supposedly cries like a baby. This one has been here for years—how it survives is a mystery.

For impressive scenery, the half-day trip up **Shennong Stream** (near Badong) is the best of the excursions. Cruise passengers board a ferry that takes you to Shenong Xi. There, you climb into "peapod" boats that are rowed and pulled upstream by trackers (in shorts and handmade sandals), most of whom are farmers in the off season. Each boat has a female guide whose English isn't always up to the task, but she makes up for it by singing a Tujia minority song for the group on the return trip. If the trackers are in the mood, one or two will join in. The scenery on this narrow stream is probably closer to what most travelers expect of the Three Gorges. **Towering cliffs** rise on either bank, and the water is crystal clear. On rare occasions, passengers catch sight of **monkeys** along the cliffs. The trackers used to go only far enough to glimpse the first **hanging coffin,** but now that the water level has risen, they may continue farther (though time is a factor, too). Depending on the ship and water conditions, you may go instead to the small gorges of the **Daning River** (near Wu Shan), where the scenery is equally beautiful and monkeys are more often sighted.

Whether or not you have any interest in engineering or construction, the sheer immensity of the **Three Gorges Dam Site** at **San Dou Ping** makes this worth a visit. Not only is it a unique photo opportunity, its monumental size lends it the visual (if not yet the historical) power of the Great Wall or Xi'an's Terra-Cotta Warriors. The luxury cruise ships usually include it on their itineraries, while local tourist ferries don't. Before booking, make sure it's included. Its absence from the itinerary is reason enough to look elsewhere.

LOWER-COST CRUISE ALTERNATIVES: LOCAL PASSENGER BOATS & TOURIST FERRIES

Yangzi River supercheap **passenger boats** depart from Wuhan (for upriver trips) and from Chongqing (for downriver trips) year-round, but their facilities are terribly foul, and so is the food. Their raison d'être is transport, not tourism, so they make no effort to go through the gorges in the light of day, and naturally there are no tourist excursions.

Numerous Chinese **tourist ferries** operate on the Yangzi, some of them with quite comfortable cabins and facilities. Management and staff are not used to foreign travelers and they rarely speak English, but the price, even for first class, is considerably less than the price on a luxury ship. These boats will invariably only take you as far as Yichang. The remaining leg on to Wuhan is best accomplished on the air-conditioned buses that travel the recently completed freeway that connects the two cities; in fact, the option to sail to Wuhan is becoming less available. Fourth-class passage from **Chongqing to Yichang** starts at ¥249 ($32/£16) and isn't much better than ferry accommodations—a bunk in an eight-person dorm with a filthy toilet down the hall. Prices for first-class passage (two-bed cabin with private shower/toilet), excluding meals and excursions, start at ¥1,042 ($135/£68) per person. Since you can pay on board or at the site for excursions, make sure they're *not* included in your ticket price, giving you more flexibility. Typically, excursions are to Fengdu, Shi Bao Zhai, and the Little Three Gorges, but these ships do not stop at the Three Gorges Dam construction site. Tickets can be booked in Chongqing inside the Navigation Office Building at Chaotian Men near the Chaotian Men Hotel, but you probably won't find an English-speaker. Beware of so-called "government-run tour agencies" along the wharf; they are likely to charge much higher fees than the actual ticket cost. And be sure to ask which pier your boat will depart from.

In this instance, the better way to book is through **China International Travel Service (CITS)** in Wuhan, Taibei Yi Lu 26, seventh floor, Xiao Nan Hu Building (*(C)* **027-8578-4100;** fax 027-8578-4089; citswuh@public.wh.hb.cn). In Chongqing, CITS is at Zaozi Lanya Zheng Jie 120 (*(C)* **023-6385-0693;** fax 023-6385-0196; citscq@cta.cq.cn). The booking fee of ¥50 ($6.25/£3.15) is worth every cent. The agents in the international division of both these offices are unusually well-informed and helpful, and speak excellent English.

10 Wuhan

Hubei Province, 1,125km (699 miles) W of Shanghai, 1,354km (841 miles) E of Chongqing, 1,047km (650 miles) SE of Xi'an

Wuhan is primarily an industrial and business center. Were it not for the fact that many of the Three Gorges tours traditionally begin or terminate in Wuhan, few Western tourists would ever make it here. However, trisected by the Yangzi River and its longest tributary, the Hanshui, and dotted with a hundred-plus lakes and scores of parks, this city of 4.8 million urban residents is an agreeable place to spend a couple of days. Three districts—Wuchang, Hanyang, and Hankou—which used to be separate cities, comprise present-day Wuhan. Avoid summers when the city inevitably lives up to its reputation as one of China's Three Furnaces.

Wuhan is also the gateway to the Daoist mountain Wudang Shan.

ESSENTIALS

GETTING THERE Tianhe International Airport is 26km (16 miles) northwest of Wuhan. Destinations include Beijing (six or seven flights daily); Guangzhou (at least seven flights daily); Hong Kong (one flight daily); Shanghai (seven flights daily); Chengdu (four or five flights daily); Chongqing (four or five flights daily); and Fukuoka and Tokyo (two flights weekly).

An **airport bus** between the airport and Hankou (¥15/$1.95/£1), Hanyang (¥20/$2.60/£1.30), and Wuchang (¥30/$3.90/£1.95) departs when full; board near the airport entrance. The trip takes 1 hour and the bus stops at Hangkong Lu, The Yangtze Plaza, and terminates at Fujiapo Bus Station. A **taxi** to Hankou should be ¥50 to ¥70 ($6.50–$9.10/£3.25–£4.55), plus a ¥15 ($1.95/£1) toll. Stand in the taxi line and use the meter. Ignore independent drivers who will offer to drive you for hundreds of yuan.

Wuhan has a number of **railway stations,** but the two major terminals are **Hankou Huochezhan** (mostly northbound) and **Wuchang Huochezhan** (mostly southbound). Major connections from Wuchang Station are Beijing (Z12, Z38; 10 hr.; soft sleeper only ¥411/$53/£27); Guangzhou (T95, T96; 10½ hr.; hard sleeper ¥281/$37/£18); Kunming (K109/K110; 35 hr.; hard sleeper ¥399/$52/£26); and Shanghai (Z25/28; 9 hr.; soft sleeper only ¥400/$52/£26). Major connections with Hankou Station are fewer: Beijing (D122/D123; 6½ hr.; ¥373/$48/£24); and Chongqing (T257/T258; 15 hr.; hard sleeper ¥281/$37/£18).

Tickets can be booked 5 days in advance at the respective stations. Hotels and CITS will book tickets for a ¥50 ($6.25/£3.15) fee.

The two main **long-distance bus stations** are the **Hankou Changtu Qichezhan** on Jiefang Da Dao at the Youyi Lu intersection (mostly northbound), and the **Wuchang Changtu Qichezhan,** northeast of the railway station on Wuluo Lu (mostly southbound). Buses for Shanghai leave from both stations (12 hr.; ¥307/$40/£20). It's best to buy tickets a day in advance.

A **light rail** line, began operating at the end of 2004, is currently exclusive to Hankou but is being extended to Wuchang. It runs along the old rail line on Jing-Han Da Dao, making stops every kilometer. It is operational between 6:30am and 9:30pm, and tickets cost ¥3 (40¢/20p)

GETTING AROUND   Standard **taxi** rates are ¥8 ($1.05/50p) for 3km (2 miles), then ¥1.40 (20¢/10p) for each additional kilometer up to 7km. Above 7km (4⅓ miles), add 50% per kilometer.

FAST FACTS

Banks, Foreign Exchange & ATMs   There's a large **Bank of China** just off the pedestrian street at Zhongshan Da Dao 593 (at the junction with Jianghan Lu; look for a stately old European concession building near the overhead walkway) and it has an ATM out the front. Foreign exchange is Monday through Friday from 8:30am to noon and 1:30 to 5pm.

Internet Access   There are several Internet cafes on Jianghan Street, charging ¥2 to ¥4 (25¢–50¢/15p–25p) per hour. Dial-up is ℂ **163.**

Post Office   A useful post office is at the west side of the railway station opposite the city bus terminal. There's another one on Jianghan Da Dao Pedestrian Street, no. 134, which is open from 8:30am to 10pm.

Tours   China International Travel Service (CITS) is exceptionally helpful and straightforward about prices. They book flights, train rides, and cruises, and arrange guided tours. CITS is located at Zhongshan Da Dao 909, near the intersection with Yiyuan Lu (ℂ **027/8277-0344;** fax 027/8284-5833; citswuh@public.wh.hb.cn).

Visa Extensions   Applications are available at the **Gonganju Waishi Ke (PSB Department of Foreign Affairs)** at Zhang Zizhong Lu (ℂ **027/8539-5394),** which is open Monday through Friday from 9 to noon and 2 to 5pm. The process takes 3 working days.

EXPLORING WUHAN

Guiyuan (Chan) Si (Guiyuan Buddhist Temple)   Best known for its hall of 500

gilded *luohan* (enlightened disciples), each in a different posture and having distinct features, this temple was founded in the mid–17th century by the monk Bai Guang. The present buildings date from the late Qing dynasty to the beginning of the Republican era (1911–49), but the *luohan* were sculpted between 1822 and 1831. Men proceed to the left and women to the right, counting one *luohan* until the number equals their age. They note the number that designates that statue and, on their way out, for ¥3 (35¢/15p) they buy the corresponding "*luohan* card," which tells their fortune. In the sutra library at the far end of the complex is a pretty jade Buddha with Indian influence that dates from the Northern Wei dynasty (4th–5th c.).

Cuiwei Heng Lu 20. ℂ 027/8243-5212. Admission ¥20 ($2.60/£1.30). 8am–4:30pm. Bus: no. 401 is the only bus that can enter the narrow Cuiwei Heng Lu, but bus nos. 6 and 528 run along Yingwu Da Dao, which intersects Cuiwei Heng Lu. From this intersection, it's a short walk to Guiyuan.

Hubei Sheng Bowuguan (Hubei Provincial Museum) 🏮🏮   "When the Master

was in Qi he heard the Shao [ceremonial music] and for three months was oblivious to the taste of food. He marveled, 'I never expected music to do this to me'" (from *The Analects,* Confucius).

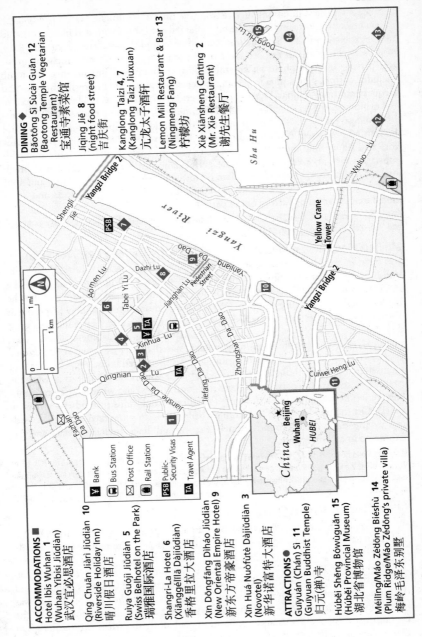

Wuhan

739

DINING ◆
Bǎotōng Sì Sùcài Guǎn **12**
(Baotong Temple Vegetarian
Restaurant)
宝通寺素菜馆

Jíqìng Jiē **8**
(night food street)
吉庆街

Kanglong Taizi **4, 7**
(Kanglong Taizi Jiuxuan)
亢龙太子酒轩

Lemon Mill Restaurant & Bar **13**
(Ningmeng Fang)
柠檬坊

Xiè Xiānsheng Cāntīng **2**
(Mr. Xiè Restaurant)
谢先生餐厅

ACCOMMODATIONS ■
Hotel Ibis Wuhan **1**
(Wuhan Yíbìsì Jiǔdiàn)
武汉宜必思酒店

Qíng Chuān Jiàrì Jiǔdiàn **10**
(Riverside Holiday Inn)
晴川假日酒店

Ruìyǎ Guójì Jiǔdiàn **5**
(Swiss Belhotel on the Park)
瑞雅国际酒店

Shangri-La Hotel **6**
(Xiānggélǐlā Dàjiǔdiàn)
香格里拉大酒店

Xīn Dōngfāng Dìháo Jiǔdiàn **9**
(New Oriental Empire Hotel)
新东方帝豪酒店

Xīn Huá Nuòfùtè Dàjiǔdiàn **3**
(Novotel)
新华诺富特大酒店

ATTRACTIONS ●
Guīyuán (Chán) Sì **11**
(Guiyuan Buddhist Temple)
归元(禅)寺

Húběi Shěng Bówùguǎn **15**
(Húběi Provincial Museum)
湖北省博物馆

Méilǐng/Máo Zédōng Biéshù **14**
(Plum Ridge/Máo Zédōng's private villa)
梅岭毛泽东别墅

■ Bank
■ Bus Station
✉ Post Office
🚆 Rail Station
PSB Public-
Security Visas
TA Travel Agent

Since no musical notations survive from the time of Confucius (ca. 551–479 B.C.), there's no way of knowing what the music he refers to above sounded like, but thanks to the excavation in 1978 of the intact tomb of Marquis Yi of Zeng (d. ca. 433 B.C.), visitors to this museum can see some of the actual instruments on which the music was played. In addition to an ensemble of ancient musical instruments, the tomb included coffins, gold and jade decorative items, weapons, and impressive bronze- and lacquerware from China's Warring States period (474–221 B.C.). The centerpiece of the exhibition is a huge set of 65 bronze chime bells, said to be the heaviest and possibly oldest extant musical instrument in the world. Inscriptions on the bells and hooks that hold them constitute the earliest known work on musicology. To give visitors an idea of how the bells were played and how their pentatonic scale sounded, musicians give an excellent 20-minute performance on classical instruments, which include replicas of the bronze bells. Two performances are scheduled at 11am and 4pm each day. Two new halls, completed in 2006, feature Bronze Age artifacts and additional items from the Warring States period.

Wuchang, Dong Hu Lu 156. (C) 027/8679-4127. www.hubeimuseum.net. Admission ¥30 ($3.90/£1.95). 9–11:30am and 1:30–4:30pm. Bus: no. 14, 402, or 578.

Meiling/Mao Zedong Bieshu ("Plum Ridge"/Mao Zedong's Private Villa)

If you have an extra hour or so after visiting the Provincial Museum (above), Mao's second-favorite *pied-à-terre* (after Beidai He) is a pleasant 10-minute walk from the museum. Built in 1958 as one of Mao's several private retreats, it was here that he hosted notables as diverse as labor activist Anna Louise Strong and U.S. president Richard Nixon. There are no English signs or explanations, but they're not necessary. The separate bedrooms of Mao and his wife, Jiang Qing, are as interesting for their plainness as Mao's private swimming pool is noted for its excessive size. Personal effects, such as Mao's blood-pressure gauge and his cherry-red house slippers, speak for themselves. However, those who don't read Chinese will miss such tidbits as what the chairman liked to eat (coarse multigrains and local snacks) and what Jiang Qing's hobbies were (photography, and that favored pastime of ambitious first ladies—amassing shoes). Off the porch outside Jiang Qing's bedroom is an unmarked vault-door leading to the dank underground tunnels that would have sheltered Mao and his entourage in an emergency.

Wuchang, Dong hu Lu no. 56. (C) 027/8679-6106. Admission ¥20 ($1.25/60p). 8am–5pm. Bus: no. 578, 709, 14, or 701; get off at the Provincial Museum, then follow the tree-lined drive behind the old museum building several hundred yards (a 10- to 15-min. walk). Alternately enter by the main entrance on Dong Hu Lu, a 10-min. walk to the left of the museum. The entrance is mark by a uniformed soldier. Follow the signs for Meiling Yi Hao through the grounds.

SHOPPING & STROLLING

A few years ago, a 1km (½-mile) stretch of **Jianghan Street** (between Jianghan Da Dao and the wharf) was closed to motor traffic, and old stores were replaced with trendy new ones.

The street is a popular place to stroll, especially on hot summer evenings. If you walk south from Jianghan Street to the wharf, you'll get to the Customs Building and the former **foreign concession** area of Hankou, which under the Treaty of Tianjin was forced open to British trade in 1859. The dozen or so remaining buildings in the European style of the 1920s and 1930s are spread along the wharf on **Yanjiang Da Dao** (a left turn off the pedestrian street). A number of the buildings (which include the Russian police station, the former German and U.S. consulates, several banks, businesses, and living quarters) are identified by signs in English. In efforts to entice foreign investors, Wuhan's mayor has invited overseas businesses to set up offices in these historical buildings.

The **Xin Shijie Baihuo Shangchang (New World Department Store)** on Jianshe Da Dao (around the corner from Novotel Hotel) has a large supermarket on the basement level. There is also a Carrefour in each of the three districts of Wuhan. The one in Hankou is on Wusheng Lu.

WHERE TO STAY
EXPENSIVE
Shangri-La Hotel (Xianggelila Dafandian)   Whatever the time of day, the lobby and cafe of this international hotel are abuzz with businesspeople and tourists. The Shangri-La's guest rooms are large, comfortable, and attractive—but nothing out of the ordinary for this level of hotel. Bathrooms are large and well designed, with separate shower cubicles.

Jianshe Da Dao 700, Hankou. ✆ 027/8580-6868. Fax 027/8577-6868. www.shangri-la.com. 448 units. ¥808 – ¥1,438 ($105–$187/£53–£93) standard room. Rates include breakfast. 20%–30% discount available; 15% service charge. AE, DC, MC, V. **Amenities:** 3 restaurants; 2 bars; indoor pool; health club; tennis court; sauna; salon; airline, train, and bus ticketing; business center; forex; 24-hr. room service; laundry/dry cleaning; executive floor. *In room:* A/C, satellite TV, dataport, broadband Internet access, minibar, fridge, hair dryer, safe.

MODERATE
Qing Chuan Jiari Jiudian (Riverside Holiday Inn) *(Kids*   Perched on the west bank of the Yangzi River across from the Yellow Crane Tower—emblem of Wuhan—this four-star hotel has the best views in the city. The rooms themselves are immaculate and comfortably appointed even if the decor isn't inspired. Hefty discounts, a children's center, weekend barbecues by the river, and a Western buffet breakfast make this a good choice for families. Rooms overlooking the Yellow Crane Tower are slightly more expensive, but all rooms have comparable river views. One possible disadvantage of the Riverside's location is that it's across the Han River from Hankou; but the actual distance to the city center is only about 4km (2½ miles).

Xima Chang Jie 88 (next to Qing Chuan Pavilion), Wuhan. ✆ 027/8471-6688. Fax 027/8471-1808. www.hirw.com. 336 units. ¥946 ($123/£61) standard room; ¥1,240 ($161/£81) standard room with river view; ¥1,527 ($199/£99) business suite. Most rates include breakfast. 50% discount standard; 15% service charge. AE, DC, MC, V. **Amenities:** 2 restaurants; 3 bars; tennis court; exercise room; sauna; reflexology center; children's center; airline, train, and bus ticketing; business center; forex; limited room service; laundry/dry cleaning. *In room:* A/C, satellite TV, fax (in some rooms), dataport, broadband Internet access, minibar, fridge, coffeemaker, hair dryer, safe.

Ruiya Guoji Jiudian (Swiss Belhotel on the Park) *(Value*   Situated on a relatively sleepy lane in the center of Hankou, the Swiss Belhotel (formerly the New World Courtyard) is within walking distance of major shops and parks. The staff is used to repeat and extended-stay business guests, which may account for the genuine and universal warmth with which they treat even short-term guests. The Swiss Belhotel meets many of the standards of a much pricier hotel with amenities such as English TV programming and a Western-style breakfast buffet. Yet while the rooms are pleasant enough and very well maintained, they're not large, and the beds and furniture show wear. This is the best bargain in town, but its popularity makes reservations advised.

Taibei Yi Lu 9 (between Taibei Lu and Xinhua Lu). ✆ 027/6885-1888. Fax 027/6885-1808. www.swiss-belhotel.com. 138 units. ¥595 ($77/£39) standard room; ¥1,080 –¥1,245 ($140–$162/£70–£81) suite. Most rates include breakfast. Discount can be up to 50%; 15% service charge. AE, DC, MC, V. Cab from airport ¥65 ($8.45/£4.25). **Amenities:** 2 restaurants; bar; exercise room; sauna; airline, train, and bus ticketing; business center; forex; limited room service; laundry/dry cleaning. *In room:* A/C, satellite TV, dataport, broadband Internet access, minibar, fridge, hair dryer, iron, safe.

Xinhua Nuofute Dajiudian (Novotel)   Touted as bringing "the European touch" to Wuhan, this new French joint-venture (part of the Accor group) distinguishes itself from the pack of four-star hotels with its creative decor. In the guest rooms, cone-shaped bed lamps are set against blonde wood; the look is smart and streamlined. Though standard rooms are on the small side, they still feel light and airy. And small-ish bathrooms are made to feel roomier by a black marble counter that is big enough to accommodate a travel case and toiletries and looks elegant against white tiled walls. Novotel's central location between the concession area and the Hankou railway station is convenient for both shopping and sightseeing.

Jianshe Da Dao 558 (next to New World Department Store Xin Shijie Baihuo Shangchang). ℂ 800/221-4542 in the U.S. and Canada, or 027/8555-1188. Fax 027/8555-1177. www.novotel.com. 303 units. ¥676–¥780 ($88–$101/£44–£51) standard room; ¥736–¥840 ($96–$109/£48–£55) deluxe standard room; ¥1,120–¥1,920 ($146–$250/£73–£125) suite. 20%–40% discount; 15% service charge. AE, DC, MC, V. Bus: no. 509 from railway station. Cab from airport ¥65 ($8/£4). **Amenities:** 2 restaurants; bar; health club; indoor pool; sauna; Jacuzzi; business center; forex; 24-hr. room service; laundry/dry cleaning; executive floors. *In room:* A/C, satellite TV, fax in some executive rooms, dataport, wireless Internet access, minibar, fridge, hair dryer, safe.

INEXPENSIVE

Hotel Ibis Wuhan *(Value)*   This relaxing hotel—part of the French franchise—opened in Wuhan in 2006 and is a great budget choice. Rooms are clean and cozy, though standard. Staff are helpful and friendly.

Jianshe Da Dao 539, Hankou. ℂ 027/8362-3188. Fax 027/8368-3177. www.ibishotel.com. 243 units. ¥158 ($21/£10) standard room. AE, DC, MC, V. **Amenities:** Restaurant; bar; wireless Internet access. *In room:* A/C, TV.

Xin Dongfang Dihao Jiudian (New Oriental Empire Hotel)   The Swiss Belhotel is a better value, but this is a good choice if you want to be on the wharf. The staff is friendly and the royal blue carpets in the guest rooms haven't been damaged yet by cigarette burns and discarded tea leaves. Rooms are the standard model, but the view makes the difference. Try for a corner room, which overlooks the street and has two windows instead of one. Avoid rooms at the back, which face the back of a dark building and smell of mold. The price is the same, so it's only a matter of asking.

Yanjiang Da Dao 136 (between Shanghai Jie and Nanjing Lu; opposite Wuhan Port). ℂ 027/8221-1881. Fax 027/8277-5912. 68 units. ¥218–¥278 ($28–$36/£14–£18) standard room; ¥338 ($44/£22) suite. Rates include breakfast. 20% discount available. No credit cards. Bus: no. 9 from railway station; another dozen city buses start and terminate from the bus station opposite the hotel. **Amenities:** 2 restaurants; bar; business center; forex; limited room service; laundry/dry cleaning. *In room:* A/C, TV.

WHERE TO DINE

If you're after a meal that's *not* Chinese, the coffee shop at the Shangri-La hotel serves the best **Western buffet breakfast** in town. The **deli** at Tianhe Holiday Inn sells European cheeses, French bread, and good hard rolls. **Pizza Hut, McDonald's,** and **KFC** are all concentrated on the same intersection on Jianghan Lu 1 block northwest of the overhead walkway at the Zhongshan Da Dao intersection. **Faguo Jie (French Street),** a street full of Western restaurants, coffee shops, and pubs, was opened by foreigners living in Wuhan, in Jinse Gangwan (Golden Harbour), Sanjiao Hu, Hanyang, an expat community; take bus no. 202, 204, 205, or 208. For some local flavor, go to **Hubuxiang** (bus no. 542 to Simenkou), which is called the Breakfast Street. Stalls sell local street food such as *reganmian* (Wuhan-style dry noodles), a wide range of *baozi* (steam buns), and pastry. If you like spicy food and are adventurous enough, you must try Wuhan's famous snack spot, **Jing Wu Ren Jia,** located on the Jingwu Road of

Hankou (bus no. 522 to Xinhua Lu); you won't miss the red signs and neon lights of this franchise's original shop. It's open 24 hours, but there's always a long line here. Be warned that it's so spicy that it will bring you to tears.

Baotong Si Sucai Guan (Baotong Temple Vegetarian Restaurant) ✿

BUDDHIST VEGETARIAN   Almost as popular with nonvegetarians, this restaurant prepares *zhaicai* (Buddhist cuisine) in the temple tradition, specializing in faux meat, fish, and fowl dishes. A delicious appetizer is *wuxiang niurou* (faux beef with blended spices). Made from *doufu pi* (the top, most nutritious layer of the tofu), this cold dish is served with hot sesame oil and soy sauce. Another *doufu pi* main dish is *hongshao fuzhu* (braised *doufu pi* rolls with bamboo shoots and green pepper). Two dishes that don't pretend to be anything else are *quanjiafu* (several kinds of mushroom sautéed with dates) and sautéed *youmaicai*, which is a dark-green leafy vegetable similar to spinach. Both dishes are delicate and tasty.

Wuluo Lu no. 289 (next to the temple entrance). No phone. Meal for 2 ¥100 ($13/£6.50). No credit cards. 9am–8pm. Bus: no. 18, 25, 518, 519, 577, or 710 to Hong Shan Gongyuan stop.

Jiqing Jie (Night Food Street) HUBEI

The street used to be a crowded area consisting of outdoor restaurants, making it an evening of dining and enjoying roving singers, musicians, sketch artists, flower sellers, photographers, and shoe shiners. However, the place has been overwhelmingly commercialized and some of the restaurants charge tourists unreasonably, which earned the area a bad reputation. Since then, fewer people go there. All the restaurants on this street serve similar fare and mainly seafood, which is generally satisfying. Like Sichuan cuisine, Hubei dishes incorporate a lot of pepper—but not all the dishes are fiery.

Jiqing Jie starting from Dazhi Jie. Meal for 2 ¥60–¥100 ($7.80–$13/£3.90–£6.50). No credit cards. From 6:30pm until everyone goes home; liveliest time is after 10pm.

Kanglong Taizi ✿ VARIOUS CHINESE

This franchise, with five locations, makes for one of Wuhan's more popular dinning places. Nearly always packed, the restaurants don't claim to offer any particular type of Chinese cuisine, although Hunan and Hubei dishes feature prominently. The food is generally good and the place is clean. It features new and seasonal dishes from time to time. In any case, the picture menu will help you order. Also at Hankou, Yanjiang Da Dao 226 (© 027/8271-2228).

Jianshe Da Dao 711, Hankou (10-min. walk west from the Novotel). © 027/8576-8666. Photo menu. Meal for 2 ¥50–¥100 ($6.50–$13/£3.25–£6.50). No credit cards. 10am–10pm.

Lemon Mill Restaurant & Bar (Ningmeng Fang) ✿ *Value* VIETNAMESE

This small restaurant, located near Wuhan University, offers some good Vietnamese dishes. The pool table hung upside down on the ceiling adds a humorous touch to this cozy restaurant. The veggie crepe served with a special sauce is fresh and the thickness of the crepe is just right. I also recommend the beef noodles and fried rice.

Bayi Lu Nan Duan no. 59, Hongshan District, Wuchang (east of the Wuhan University entrance). © 027/8765-2690. English menu. Meal for 2 ¥60–¥100 ($7.80–$13/£3.90–£6.50). No credit cards. 10am–10pm. Bus: no. 413, 519, or 724 to Luojia Shan.

WUHAN AFTER DARK

Along the Yanjiang Da Dao, there are loads of bars and clubs. **SOHO**, at Nanjing Lu intersection (© 027/5223-3668), and **CASH**, Shanghai Lu 19 (© 132/6066-9282), are two of the most popular ones. **Take Five**, located next to the Zhong Binguan on

Xinhua Xiao Lu, features great live jazz from 9pm every night. Check out **VOX** in Wuchang, at Luxiang Lumo Lu Caojiawan Chezhan Guoguang Daxia (© **027/ 5076-1020;** bus no. 59, 709, or 401), for local underground music and shows during weekends.

11 Wudang Shan

Hubei Province, 500km (311 miles) NW of Wuhan

In the hierarchy of sacred Daoist mountains, Wudang is number one because of its association with the popular god Zhenwu (Perfected Warrior). In the 7th century, a cult developed around him, and his popularity continued to grow for the next 7 centuries. By the Ming dynasty, Zhenwu was considered the 82nd transformation of Laozi, and even supplanted the deified Laozi as the most important of the Daoist gods. Visitors to Wudang have the Perfected Warrior to thank for many of the monasteries and temples that still stand on the mountain. It was in his honor that the Yongle emperor ordered a massive building campaign on Wudang Shan in 1412. Several of the extant buildings date back to that time.

Unlike Emei Shan, Qingcheng Shan, and Nan Yue Heng Shan, Wudang receives relatively few tourists, and it has preserved its temples and its Daoist tradition more successfully than the less-remote mountains. The price of preservation for the traveler is a longer journey and less-comfortable lodging. However, the mountain's rugged peaks covered in old-growth forest, along with its ancient monasteries—some built to fit the contours of the cliffs, others to mirror them—are well worth the sacrifice.

Another name associated with these mountains is Zhang Sanfeng, the Daoist Immortal credited with inventing the discipline of *taijiquan* in the late 14th century. Though less well known overseas, Wudang's "internal" form of *wushu* (martial arts) is as highly regarded as Shaolin Temple's "external" form (p. 345). Students come from all parts of China to study at the many martial arts schools in town and on the mountain. The famous swords used in the Wudang style are for sale everywhere.

The best times to visit are April through June and September through October, when the leaves turn as red as the gorgeous temple walls.

Note: For Chinese translations of selected establishments listed in this section, please turn to appendix A.

ESSENTIALS

GETTING THERE The best way is take the **train** from Wuchang at 9am to Wudang Shan (T672673; 5 hr. 10 min; hard sleeper ¥127/$17/£8.25). Unless you're staying more than a few days, buy your return ticket as soon as you arrive. The return train leaves at 4:45pm each day. At press time, an express rail between Wuhan and Shiyan was under construction. The expressway, scheduled to be completed in 2009, will cut the long journey to 3 hours.

Less convenient, **buses** from Wuchang go to Shiyan (9 hr.), where you transfer to a minibus to Wudang Shan. Buses wait for passengers in front of the railway station and depart when full. The ride takes 30 to 45 minutes and costs ¥10 ($1.25/60p).

EXPLORING THE MOUNTAIN

The entrance to the mountain is less than a mile east of Wudang Shan Town. **Tour vans** pick up passengers outside the railway station and drop them at the entrance of the mountain (¥1/15¢/10p).

From there to the main temples and trail head is another 12km (7 miles). The peak can be reached **on foot** in 2½ hours up stone stairs. The views are magnificent. Save energy for the final very steep leg to the peak. The Round-trip by **sedan chair** is ¥120 ($15/£7.50). Or you can just get on the **tour buses** at the tourist service center to different scenic spots in the mountain. A **cable car,** which starts at Qiongtai, goes to Taihe Gong (near the peak). The 25-minute trip costs ¥50 ($6.50/£3.25) up, ¥45 ($5.85/£2.95 down), ¥80 ($10/£5.20) round-trip.

Best preserved from the Ming dynasty building boom is Wudang Shan's **Zixiao Gong (Purple Mist Palace),** located on **Zhanqi Peak** (below the cliff Taizi Yan). This large, still very active monastery was built in 1413. Its striking red halls often bustle with priests and pilgrims. You may also come upon a *taijiquan* class practicing on one of the open terraces. Famous among its relics is a series of statues of Zhenwu at various stages of his life.

The most dramatic of the existing temples, **Nanyan Gong (Southern Cliff Palace),** is built into the side of a sheer cliff, recalling Northern Heng Shan's Xuankong Si—another Daoist temple that seems to defy gravity (p. 219). From Zixiao Gong, follow the trail up the mountain (southwest) to Wuya Ling (about 2.5km/ 1½ miles); Nanyan is just after Nantian Men. **Jin Dian (Golden Hall),** which sits on **Tianzhu Feng,** highest of Wudang's 72 peaks (1,612m/1 mile high), is part of the 15th-century **Taihe Gong (Palace of Supreme Harmony)** complex. Its two-tiered roof, covered in gilded bronze, is, naturally, best viewed on a clear day when it sparkles. To reach Jin Dian from Nanyan Gong, continue up the path to Huanglong Dong (Yellow Dragon Cave). From here, both ascending paths lead to the Golden Hall. The steeper route is to the right through the three "Heaven Gates."

Admission to the scenic area is ¥180 ($23/£12); the fee includes admission to the mountain, transportation from the entrance to main temples, and entrance to all but **Jin Dian** and **Zixiao Gong,** which charge an extra ¥20 ($2.60/£1.30) and ¥15 ($1.95/£1) respectively.

WHERE TO STAY & DINE

The best two places to stay are on the mountain near Tianzhu Peak. **Taihe Gong** offers very basic accommodations in their **Jinding Guibin Zhaodaishi** (© 0719/568-7155). The cost of ¥200 ($26/£13) each person includes a room with twin beds, shared bathroom, and limited hot water. The **Jingui Jiudian** (© 0719/568-9198) just down the hill from the Wuya Ling parking lot is basic and satisfactory, and costs ¥280 ($36/£18) for a standard room, with discounts of up to 40% available. None of the hotels in Wudang Shan have the charm, views, or quiet of the mountain. The **Wudang Shan Binguan** (Tequ Yongle Lu 33; © 0719/566-5548) is the most comfortable and cleanest. Furniture and bedspreads show wear, and the bathroom sink is a bit dingy but acceptable. There's a Chinese restaurant on the premises. The price of a standard room ranges from ¥120 to ¥200 ($16–$26/£7.80–£13).

12 Changsha

Hunan Province, 1,419km (882 miles) SE of Chongqing, 707km (440 miles) N of Guangzhou

Changsha is another hazy, congested, modern Chinese city hurrying to divest itself of any architectural trace of its past. But it is the capital of Hunan Province and gateway to one of the Five Sacred Mountains of Daoism and the gorgeous scenic area of the

World Heritage Site, Wu Ling Yuan. It is also home to one of the most exciting tomb collections in China—the Mawang Dui, which dates from the Western Han dynasty.

The city itself—most often associated with Mao and the model worker Lei Feng—receives few foreign tourists. While Western visitors are fairly common, most come here not to see sights, but to research dissertations or adopt babies from Changsha's orphanage. In the international hotels, it's not unusual to see a large table of wide-eyed European couples, each cradling a new Chinese baby girl.

ESSENTIALS

GETTING THERE   The **Changsha Huanghua Airport** is 34km (21 miles) east of town. Destinations include Beijing (six or more flights daily); Guangzhou (five flights daily); Hong Kong (daily); Kunming (six flights daily); Chengdu (four flights daily); Shanghai (five or more flights daily); and Xi'an (two or three flights daily). An **airport shuttle** from Minhang Dajiudian (Minhang Hotel) at Wuyi Da Dao 5 (cross street Chaoyang Lu) ((C) **0731/417-0288**) takes about 40 minutes and costs ¥15 ($1.95/£1); it departs the hotel every half-hour. A taxi to the airport is around ¥100 ($13/£6.50). **Changsha Huochezhan (Changsha Railway Station)** is at the east end of Wuyi Da Dao. The city is on the Beijing-Guangzhou railway line. Major connections include Beijing (T1, T2; 15½ hr.; hard sleeper ¥345/$45/£22); Guangzhou (5361, 5362; 9 hr.; hard sleeper ¥108/$14/£7); Shanghai (D101/104, D106/107; 8 hr.; ¥365/$47/£24); and Wuchang (D149, D150; 3 hr.; ¥112/$15/£7.30). Changsha has three main **bus stations: Qiche Nan Zhan (South Station), Qiche Dong Zhan (East Station),** and **Qiche Xi Zhan (West Station).** Buses to Nan Yue Heng Shan, Shao Shan, Xiamen, and Guilin leave from the South Station. Buses to Hankou (Wuhan), Guangzhou, and Nanjing leave from the East Station. Buses to Zhang Jia Jie and Yichang leave from the West Station.

GETTING AROUND   Air-conditioned **public buses** cost ¥2 (25¢/15p); non-air-conditioned buses cost ¥1 (15¢/10p). Standard **taxi** rates are ¥8 ($1.05/50p) for 3km (2 miles), then ¥1.80 (25¢/10p) per kilometer up to 10km (6 miles). Beyond that, add 50% per kilometer.

FAST FACTS

Banks, Foreign Exchange & ATMs   The main **Bank of China** is at Furong Lu 593, near Ba Yi Qiao (8-1 Bridge) and opposite Carrefour. It has full foreign-exchange services Monday through Friday from 8:30am to noon and 2 to 5pm, and an ATM. It also gives cash advances on credit cards. There's an **ATM** in the lobby of Huatian Dajiudian.

Internet Access   Internet cafes are fairly prolific between along the stretch of Zhongshan Lu, near the corner of Huangguang Lu, conveniently located to most of the hotels listed in this section. Alternately Shan Nan Lu, near Hunan University, has inexpensive Internet cafes on every block, but getting there requires crossing the Xiang River. Dial-up is (C) **163,** 165, or 169.

Post Office   The main post office is on the east side of the pedestrian block of Huangxing Lu. Another is just north of the railway on Zhong Bei Lu. It's open from 8am to noon and 2:30 to 5:30pm.

Changsha

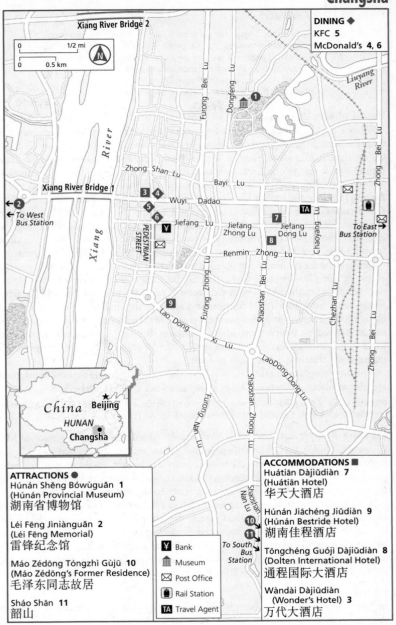

DINING ◆
KFC **5**
McDonald's **4, 6**

Xiang River Bridge 2

Liuyang River

Furong Bei Lu

Dongfeng Lu

Zhong Shan Lu

Bayi Lu

Xiang River Bridge 1

2
← To West
Bus Station

Wuyi Dadao

Zhong Bei Lu

3 **4**

5

6

¥

Jiefang Lu

Jiefang Zhong Lu

TA

Chaoyang Lu

To East
Bus Station

7

Jiefang Dong Lu

8

Renmin Zhong Lu

Furong Zhong Lu

Shaoshan Bei Lu

Chezhan Lu

PEDESTRIAN STREET

9

Lao Dong Xi Lu

LaoDong Dong Lu

Shaoshan Zhong Lu

Furong Nan Lu

China
★ **Beijing**
HUNAN
Changsha

Shaoshan Nan Lu

To South
Bus
Station

10
11

ATTRACTIONS ●

Húnán Shěng Bówùguǎn **1**
(Húnán Provincial Museum)
湖南省博物馆

Léi Fēng Jìniànguǎn **2**
(Léi Fēng Memorial)
雷锋纪念馆

Máo Zédōng Tóngzhì Gùjū **10**
(Máo Zédōng's Former Residence)
毛泽东同志故居

Sháo Shān **11**
韶山

¥ Bank
🏛 Museum
⊠ Post Office
🏢 Rail Station
TA Travel Agent

ACCOMMODATIONS ■

Huátiān Dàjiǔdiàn **7**
(Huátiān Hotel)
华天大酒店

Húnán Jiāchéng Jiǔdiàn **9**
(Húnán Bestride Hotel)
湖南佳程酒店

Tōngchéng Guójì Dàjiǔdiàn **8**
(Dolten International Hotel)
通程国际大酒店

Wàndài Dàjiǔdiàn
(Wonder's Hotel) **3**
万代大酒店

EXPLORING CHANGSHA

> *"Watered by the Yangtze and the Han, Chu is a land of lakes and rivers, of well-forested mountains. . . . The people live on fish and rice. Because there is always enough to eat, they are a lazy and improvident folk. . . . They believe in the power of shamans and spirits and are much addicted to lewd religious rites."*
> —1st-century historian Ban Gu concluding his survey of Chu history.

Hunan Sheng Bowuguan (Hunan Provincial Museum) ⍟   Between 1972 and 1974, the family plot of the chancellor to the prince of Changsha (which was in the Chu Kingdom) was excavated at **Mawang Dui** in the eastern suburbs of Changsha. Of the three tombs—one each for the husband, wife, and son—only wife Xin Zhui's tomb was left undisturbed. Inside her tomb and her son's tomb (the chancellor's was looted) were thousands of funeral objects and hitherto lost classics copied on silk. Among them are the earliest known text of the Zhou *Book of Changes* and two important versions of the *Daode Jing (The Laozi)*. But the bulk of the manuscripts concern the quest for immortality through meditation, exercises, sexual practices, drugs, and alchemy. These rare records attesting to one family's search for the Dao are invaluable for what they reveal about the actual practice of religion in the early Han dynasty.

Perhaps the most astonishing object discovered in the tombs was the well-preserved corpse of Xin Zhui herself—who, after all, did achieve immortality of a kind. At the time of her death, she was 50 years old, stood 1.5m (5 ft.) tall, and weighed 75 pounds. She suffered from a variety of illnesses and ailments that included tuberculosis, hardening of the arteries, and lead poisoning; and her death was probably from a heart attack induced by an acute episode of gallstones. Reading her litany of ailments and looking at the intact corpse, it would appear that 50 years of life took a far greater toll on her body than did 2,100 years of death.

The new wing, completed in 2005, hosts the temporary exhibitions. English guides are now available if you book 1 day in advance; call ℭ **0731/451-5566.**

Dongfeng Lu 50. ℭ **0731/451-4630.** www.humuseum.com Admission ¥50 ($6.50/£3.25). Apr–Oct 8am–6pm; Oct–Mar 8:30am–5:30pm. Last ticket sold 1 hr. before closing. Bus: no. 113 or 303.

Lei Feng Jinianguan (Lei Feng Memorial)   Those looking for a trace of Mao's China will find it here. The selfless soldier whose only ambition was to be "a little screw that would never rust in the revolutionary machinery" ended up getting a whole memorial to himself, not to mention the Lei Feng Hospital, the Lei Feng Hotel, and the big statue of Lei Feng that flanks the street to the museum. Unfortunately, there are no English signs in this monument to a past era, but much of the collection is self-explanatory. It includes propaganda posters that trace the life of Lei Feng and his family members, some obviously retouched photographs, and a number of Lei Feng's personal effects. Give yourself about 45 minutes to an hour here.

Lei Feng Zhen 9, across Xiang River, about 10km (6 miles) beyond the West Bus Station. ℭ **0731/810-7918.** Admission ¥16 ($2.10/£1.05). 8am–6pm. Bus: no. 315 or 913 to terminus.

SHAO SHAN

In 1893, Mao Zedong was born in this village 98km (60 miles) south of Changsha. Beginning with the frenzied early years of the Cultural Revolution (1966–76) and continuing into the early 1990s, Shao Shan was a mecca of sorts to millions of Chinese who made the pilgrimage here for reasons that changed over the years—from revolutionary zeal to coercion to, finally, nostalgia. Today the crowds have thinned out considerably, though they increase on holidays and on Mao's birthday, December 6. The sights include the house Mao grew up in, a memorial exhibition, the Mao Library, and the family ancestral home, but the latter two will be of little interest without knowledge of written Chinese. This is an easy day trip from Changsha.

Mao Zedong Tongzhi Guju (Comrade Mao Zedong's Former Residence)

Best of the two main sights, Mao's former home doesn't look that different from some of the present farmhouses in Hunan and Sichuan. The spartan but attractive brick buildings with curved wooden shingles have signs in Chinese and English that identify each room and contain a variety of intriguing implements, such as a large wok in the kitchen, grain-milling bowls, and equipment for hulling rice. Photos of Mao's family grace the walls. The barn is part of the house, and the bedroom of Mao's brother, Zetan, is right next to the pig pen. Give yourself 45 minutes to see the house and stroll the bucolic grounds.

Free admission. 8am–5pm. Buses (Iveco) between Changsha's South Station (Nan Zhan) and Shao Shan leave both places every half-hour 8am–5pm for ¥24 ($3/£1.50); the ride takes 1 hr. 40 min. The ride from Shao Shan Bus Station to Mao's old home is 6km (3¾ miles). By motorcycle the trip costs ¥5 (65¢/30p); by bus ¥1 (15¢/10p).

Shao Shan Mao Zedong Tongzhi Jinianguan (Shao Shan Mao Zedong Museum)

The highlight of the museum, built in 2003, is undoubtedly the third-floor collection of items used by Mao during his life. The museum replaces a more extensive, stand-alone exhibition of Mao's personal items that was on the same site, but it still offers an interesting insight into the idiosyncrasies of the Great Helmsman, such as the bed that permanently slants to one side. The rest of the exhibition is concerned with Mao's exploits until liberation.

Admission ¥30 ($3.90/£1.95). Summer 7:30am–5:30pm; winter 8am–5pm. From Mao's former residence, follow the path past the souvenir stands; to the left is the gravesite of Mao's parents; turn right and walk through long, narrow, dank tunnel. At the end go up to the right (pond on your left); at bottom of drive, Mao Library, ¥10 ($1.30/65p), will be to the left; walk to street and turn right, then left through parking lot.

Mao's Roots

Mao's father was a poor peasant compelled out of poverty to join the army. Years later he returned to Shao Shan with ambitions of bettering his lot. When Mao was born, his father owned 15 hectares (37 acres) of land and was a "middle peasant." By the time Mao was a teenager, his father had 22 hectares (55 acres) and the status of "rich peasant." Mao spent his childhood in Shao Shan working in his father's rice paddies and, from age 8, studying the Confucian *Analects* and *The Five Classics*—meaning the most modern of his textbooks (the *Analects*) was from the 3rd century B.C.

In his interviews with Edgar Snow, Mao described a strict upbringing by a father he perceived as oppressive. What isn't often mentioned is that his mother was a devout Buddhist who raised her children in the religion. It wasn't until Mao broadened his reading that he lost his religious faith. Though Mao's family never went hungry, it was in Shao Shan that he witnessed famine and the oppression of the poor. He claimed that such incidents and a natural rebelliousness inclined him toward revolution.

WHERE TO STAY

EXPENSIVE

Huatian Dajiudian   This five-star hotel is Changsha's biggest and most luxurious. It's also one of the most expensive, but with the 40%-to-50% discounts that are standard here, the rates become reasonable. Conformity usually defines hotel design in China, but the bold-colored fresco behind the reception counter of this hotel sets a tone of originality that carries throughout. For example, on the way to the elevator, guests cross a glass bridge that spans a fishpond full of goldfish. The guest rooms, too, have original touches. Bathroom sinks look like elegant glass bowls. In plusher rooms, a walk-in closet connects with both the bathroom and the bedroom. Business suites have huge bathrooms with bidets and very attractive separate shower and tub.

Jiefang Dong Lu 300. ℂ 0731/444-2888. Fax 0731/444-2270. www.huatian-hotel.com. 700 units. ¥858–¥1,138 ($112–$148/£56–£74) standard room; ¥1,798 – ¥3,038 ($148–$224/£74–£117) suite. Rates include breakfast. 40%–50% discount is standard. AE, DC, MC, V. **Amenities:** 4 restaurants; bar; indoor pool; health club, airline, train, and bus ticketing; business center; forex; ATM; 24-hr. room service; laundry/dry cleaning. *In room:* A/C, satellite TV, dataport, broadband Internet access, minibar, fridge, hair dryer, safe.

Hunan Jiacheng Jiudian (Hunan Bestride Hotel)   The competent staff and management of this midsize, Hong Kong–managed hotel go out of their way to make guests feel comfortable and appreciated. While it lacks some of the facilities of a five-star hotel, such as a pool and full-scale gym, the hotel is one of the best in town in terms of service, furnishings, upkeep, and comfort. Guest rooms were renovated in 2001 and still look well maintained. The rooms are airy and clean and have views of the city, which by night are stunning. The Chinese restaurant on the fourth floor serves outstanding food.

Laodong Xi Lu 386. ℂ 0731/511-8888. Fax 0731/511-1888. www.hnbrhotel.com. 238 units. ¥580–¥820 ($75–$107/ £38–£53) standard room; ¥1,080–¥1,480 ($140–$192/£70–£96) suite. Rates include breakfast. 35%–50% discount is standard. 15% service charge. AE, DC, MC, V. Bus: no. 139 from railway, 202, or 314. **Amenities:** 4 restaurants; 2 bars; spa; airline, train, and bus ticketing; business center; forex; 24-hr. room service; therapeutic massage; laundry/dry cleaning. *In room:* A/C, TV w/pay movies, broadband Internet access, minibar, fridge, hair dryer, safe.

Tongcheng Guoji Dajiudian (Dolten International Hotel)   This popular hotel competes with the Huatian for the title of Changsha's plushest; yet despite its recent renovations late in 2004 it still comes in second. The guest rooms are spacious, the bedspreads and furnishings are tasteful. Service is efficient and this staff is friendly and professional—nothing is missing here. But there's nothing extra, either. The Dolten is a standard five-star hotel, and for that it can be counted on.

Shao Shan Bei Lu 159. ℂ 0731/416-8888. Fax 0731/412-6688. www.dolton-hotel.com. 450 units. ¥918–¥1,118 ($115–$140/£58–£70) standard room; ¥1,380–¥1,688 ($170–$208/£85–£104) suite. Rates include breakfast. 35% discount is standard. 15% service charge. AE, DC, MC, V. Bus: no. 7 or 139 from railway. **Amenities:** 2 restaurants; 3 bars; gym, indoor pool; airline, train, and bus ticketing; business center; forex; 24-hr. room service; laundry/dry cleaning. *In room:* A/C, satellite TV, dataport, broadband Internet access, safe, minibar, fridge, hair dryer.

MODERATE

Wandai Dajiudian (Wonder Hotel)   This four-star hotel, which opened in 2002, occupies floors 7 to 15 in an office building. Guest rooms frame the indoor garden plaza, but the best views are on the east side, overlooking Wuyi Square, and on the west side, facing the river. Each standard room is clean and comfortable, with a Japanese-inspired wooden screen between the bed and the living area that gives the illusion of two rooms.

Huangxing Zhong Lu 101 (at Wuyi Da Dao; reception on 7th floor). ℂ 0731/488-2333. Fax 0731/488-2111. 321 units. ¥528–¥588 ($69–$76/£34–£38) standard room; ¥1,800–¥2,800 ($234–$364/£117–£182) suite. Rates include

breakfast. 15%–20% discount is standard. AE, DC, MC, V. Bus: no. 132 from railway to Wuyi Guangchang stop.
Amenities: 2 restaurants; bar; exercise room; airline, train, and bus ticketing; business center; limited forex; 24-hr. room service; laundry/dry cleaning. *In room:* A/C, TV, dataport, hair dryer.

WHERE TO DINE

In the vicinity of Wuyi Lu and Huangxing Zhong Lu, there's a **KFC** on the southwest corner of that intersection. A large **McDonald's** is on the northeast corner of Wuyi Guangchang; in fact, McDonald's has reached near saturation point in Changsha, making it all too easy to get your fix. A **Pizza Hut** has also appeared on Huangxing Lu between Zhongshan Lu and Jiefang Lu. The **Shennong Dajiudian (Grand Sun City Hotel) coffee shop** and **City Pub** both serve plausible Western fare.

Xiang Garden *®®* HUNAN   The head chef of this fine restaurant on the fourth floor of the Bestride Hotel (Jiacheng Jiudian) was once a chef in China's embassy in Germany. Here his kitchen puts out perfectly executed dishes that are beautifully presented and delicious. A few of the delicacies are *lingjiao* (water chestnuts); *hong zaozi* (red dates); *qiang qincai xiaguo* (baby celery and pearl onions sautéed with macadamia nuts); *qingjiao qiezi* (eggplant sautéed with green pepper); and *mitang sigua* (rice soup with silk gourd).

Laodong Xi Lu 386, Jiacheng Jiudian (Bestride Hotel), 3rd floor. ℂ **0731/511-8888.** Meal for 2 ¥50–¥160 ($6–$20/£3–£10). AE, DC, MC, V. 11:30am–3pm and 5–11pm. Bus: no. 139 from railway, 202, or 314.

13 Nan Yue Heng Shan

Hunan Province, 137km (85 miles) S of Changsha

> *"Those who mix medicines, who are avoiding political turmoil,
> or who seek quietude in order to practice the Way, have always
> gone into the mountains."*
> —from *The Master Who Embraces Simplicity,* Ge Hong (283–343)

Located on the southwestern bank of the Xiang River in the middle of Hunan Province, Nan Yue Heng Shan—known locally as Nan Yue (Southern Mountain) *or* Heng Shan—is one of the five sacred peaks (symbolizing the four directions and the center) of Daoism. It was believed that these peaks were supernatural channels connecting heaven and earth. For Daoists, mountains were the sites where *qi* (cosmic energy) was at its most refined; herbs and minerals—the ingredients of health and longevity elixirs—were found on mountains; and it was on mountains and in mountain caverns that seekers were most likely to find transcendent beings.

As far back as the 6th century, Nan Yue was also a place of Buddhist worship; and it is the birthplace of the Nan Yue school of Southern Chan (Zen) Buddhism, which got its start here in the 8th century.

Late summer and fall are the best times to visit. Locals warn visitors to resist the temptation of shortcuts on overgrown and little-used paths, where you're likely to encounter snakes.

ESSENTIALS

GETTING THERE   Direct **buses** (Iveco or Turbo) depart from Changsha's South Bus Station every half-hour from 6:30am to 6pm for the 2¼-hour drive; the fare is ¥38 ($4.50/£2.25). Buses leave the station when they're full. Return buses leave every 20 minutes from the same drop-off point in the town of Nan Yue. If you take an early bus, it is possible to make this a day trip. You'll have time to enjoy the mountain and its temples if you combine hiking with cable car, bus, or motorcycle taxi. A **train** also runs between Changsha and Nan Yue Railway Station, but the trip takes 3 hours, plus another 30 to 40 minutes from the railway station to the town of Nan Yue.

GETTING AROUND   The bus from Changsha drops passengers off at the west end of town. To get to the mountain, walk east on the same road (Hengshan Lu) to the memorial archway *(paifang)* on Zhurong Lu. Inside the archway, **minibuses** take passengers to the entrance for ¥1 (15¢/10p). If the bus is slow to fill up, you can pay a bit more to be taxied there alone. Price is negotiable, but ¥5 (65¢/35p) is about right. The distance is 1.5km (just under a mile). The **mountain park entrance** is at the north end of the village. Admission is ¥80 ($10/£5.20) and covers entrance to all the sites and temples on the mountain. **Buses** charging ¥12 ($1.55/80p) to the mid-section of the mountain depart every 10 minutes from the park entrance. Another bus for ¥12 ($1.55/80p) from the midway station goes to the top; ¥8 ($1.05/50p) down-hill. A mile-long **cable car** also operates from the midway point. The ride to **Nantian Men,** three-quarters of the way to the summit, takes 5 minutes; the round-trip costs ¥50 ($6.50/£3.25); ¥100 ($13/£6.50) in winter. From Nantian Men, **minibuses** go to the summit, charging ¥5 (65¢/35p). The footpath from bottom to top is 14km (9 miles) long and takes about 4 hours to walk at a comfortable but steady clip.

NAN YUE SIGHTS

The best preserved and most famous of the mountain temples is **Nan Yue Da Miao** at the southern foot of the mountain. Originally built in the Tang dynasty (618–907), it was destroyed by fire a number of times. The present temple dates to the Qing dynasty (1644–1911). The main hall is noteworthy for its double roof, which is supported by 72 columns representing the inevitable 72 peaks of Nan Yue. Admission to the temple is ¥40 ($5.20/£2.60). Halfway up the mountain, past the cable car entrance, is the Daoist monastery Xuandu Guan. Here, worshipers light firecrackers, kowtow in front of the white marble statues of three Daoist Celestial Masters, or cast their fortunes by throwing two halves of a wooden oval on the ground. Eleven Daoist priests live in this monastery. Lodging is available for up to 3 days here. There is also a vegetarian restaurant.

Daoist and Buddhist monasteries and temples are scattered over the mountain. Most are small and worth a peek, but they don't need lots of time. **Zhurong Hall** is at Nan Yue's highest peak, **Zhurong Feng** (1,290m/4,232 ft.), where the views are magnificent.

WHERE TO STAY & DINE

To better preserve the natural environment of the mountain, the authority has ordered that buildings and inns that don't blend in with the landscape be torn down. Approximately 80% of the existing buildings will be torn down. But lodging can still be found at the summit near Zhurong Dian and midway up the mountain just above the bus parking lot, in the vicinity of the cable car. Directly opposite the Xuandu Guan (Xuandu Monastery) is the **Ban Shan Ting Shanzhuang (Ban Shan Ting Mountain Inn;** ℰ **0734/567-6239).** Rooms are basic but very clean, and those on the south side have views of the mountain. The front-desk and kitchen staffs are friendly and eager to make guests comfortable. Guest rooms have private bathrooms, 24-hour hot water, and TV. A standard room costs ¥208 ($27/£14); a room with older furniture and fix-tures costs ¥148 ($19/£9.60). Discounts of 40% are standard, even in high season, but not during holidays.

The best accommodations on the mountain are at the **Caifu Mountain Villa (Caifu Shanzhuang; © 0734/622-3301)**, built in 2000. To date, its primary claim to fame is that Jiang Zemin stayed here while visiting the mountain in 2003. The unimaginatively furnished standard rooms go for ¥388 ($50/£25), but it does offer the most comfortable stay on the mountain by far.

In the summertime, it is also possible to stay in monasteries on the mountain for only a few dollars.

All of the inns on the mountain have small dining rooms and kitchens. Since there are no English menus, you may have to go to the kitchen and point to your order. Settle on a price in advance or you may end up getting the most expensive dish on the menu—or the largest serving. On average, each dish should cost about ¥10 to ¥20 ($1.30–$2.60/65p–£1.30). In town, Deng Shan Lu, running from the memorial archway through the center of town, has lots of restaurants serving local food.

14 Wu Ling Yuan/Zhang Jia Jie ⓕ

Hunan Province, 269km (167 miles) NW of Changsha, 480km (298 miles) SW of Wuhan

> *"O soul, go not to the south! In the south are a hundred leagues of*
> *flaming fire and coiling cobras; the mountains rise sheer and steep;*
> *tigers and leopards slink; the cow-fish is there, and the spit-sand,*
> *and the rearing python. O soul, go not to the south! There are*
> *monsters there that will harm you."*
> —from the 3rd-century poem "Great Summons," *Songs of Chu*

Wu Ling Yuan's landscape might well have inspired the shamanistic poems of the classic collection *Songs of Chu.* Unlike most famous sights in China, the area remained remote and little visited until relatively late. To the ancients, that part of northwestern Hunan (at the southern periphery of the Chu Kingdom) was an inhospitable wilderness—mountainous terrain populated by wild animals. And unlike the sacred Buddhist and Daoist mountains, it did not draw pilgrims.

But that's all changed. Wu Ling Yuan Scenic and Historic Interest Area (also called Zhang Jia Jie) became China's first National Forest Park in 1983, and in 1992, its core zone was inscribed as a World Heritage Site. Prior to that, whatever damage humans inadvertently spared this wild region over the centuries, they undid in a few decades of poaching, land clearing, tree felling, and polluting. Despite that, the natural beauty of the region—dominated by quartzite sandstone peaks and pillars—remains stunning and unusual; and opportunities to see rare plants and insects in this dense, subtropical forest still abound. What's more, restrictions on construction and pollution, as well as a total fire ban, are just a few of the measures now in place to protect this singular environment.

ESSENTIALS
GETTING THERE   Changsha is the gateway city to Zhang Jia Jie. With the completion of the expressway in late 2005, the bus has become the most convenient way to travel between the two spots. **Hehua Airport** is 5km (3 miles) from Zhang Jia Jie City (formerly called Dayong) and 37km (23 miles) from Zhang Jia Jie National Forest Park. It has flights connecting with many major cities in China, including Beijing, Shanghai, Guangzhou, and Wuhan. It also has air service from Hong Kong. If you arrive by plane, there's no reason to bother with charmless Zhang Jia Jie City (Zhang

Jia Jie Shi). Go directly to **Wu Ling Yuan,** which is located just outside the entrance to the national park. By taxi, it's ¥70 ($9.10/£4.55).

The **Zhang Jia Jie Railway Station** is 8km (5 miles) southeast of town. Short of flying, the overnight train from Changsha is the most comfortable choice. The N569/572 leaves Changsha at 8:18pm and arrives in Zhang Jia Jie the next morning at 7:23am; the N571/570 leaves Zhang Jia Jie at 7pm and arrives in Changsha at 6:10am the next morning. Hard and soft sleepers cost ¥183 to ¥276 ($24–$36/£12–£18). The railway station is also 45km (28 miles) southeast of Zhang Jia Jie Village, which is at the main park entrance and is the best place to find lodging. As you exit the station, taxi drivers, porters, and kids selling maps will pounce, but just keep walking. A bus from the railway station to Zhang Jia Jie Village departs from the square when it's full (an hour-plus wait sometimes). An alternative is a bus for ¥1 (15¢/10p) leaving from the middle of the railway square to the bus station in town. From there, catch one of the many buses for the 1-hour trip to Wu Ling Yuan; the fare is ¥10 ($1.30/65p). To National Forest Park, the buses charge ¥8 ($1.05/50p); to Tianzi Shan, ¥15 ($1.95/£1). Or you can take a taxi directly to Wu Ling Yuan for about ¥70 ($9.10/£4.55). As you exit, go to the **taxi stand** at the left end of the railway square. Taxi rates are ¥3 (65¢/35p) for 2km (1¼ miles), then ¥1.50 (20¢/10p) per kilometer. After 10km (6 miles), add 50% per kilometer.

The expressway between Changsha and Zhang Jia Jie, completed in late 2005, cuts the bus ride to 3½ hours. Bus fare is ¥60 ($7.80/£3.90) and buses run from 8:30am to 5pm, departing Changsha from the terminal opposite the railway station every 1½ hours.

GETTING AROUND   Vehicular and hiking paths provide access to some 240 designated scenic spots within Wu Ling Yuan. The scenic area comprises the three adjoining parklands of **Zhang Jia Jie National Forest Park** to the south, **Tianzi Shan Nature Reserve** to the north, and **Suo Xi Yu Nature Reserve** to the east. **Cable cars** for ¥48 ($6.25/£3.10) lead to viewing platforms from Huangshi Zhai in the Zhang Jia Jie forest area and from the eastern edge of Tianzi Shan. A local **bus** connects Suo Xi Yu Village, located at the southeast entrance to the park, and Zhang Jia Jie City Bus Station. The 32km (20-mile) trip costs ¥8 ($1.05/25p). Once you're inside the park, free buses will take you between designated stops, allowing you the freedom to alternate between walking and taking a ride.

In terms of lodging and proximity to the most sights, **Wu Ling Yuan** makes the best base. The village has one main street, Jinbian Da Dao, which is lined with hotels and leads to the National Forest Park entrance. As you approach the park, you'll see a small street to the left; it leads to the Xiangdian Mountain Villa and a few restaurants and Internet cafes.

TOURS   For most of the sightseeing within the park, there's no need for a guide. But you must join a tour to go river rafting. This can be organized by **Zhang Jia Jie National Forest Park Travel Service,** which is conveniently located and much more customer-oriented than the CITS branches in either Zhang Jia Jie City or Village. Their office is in Zhang Jia Jie City and they are willing to either meet you at the train, or come out to the park (© **0744/822-7088;** fax 0744/822-8488).

The freelance guides near the park entrance charge considerably less than the travel agencies, but you need to bargain. Price depends on the season and where you go, but generally the asking price for an English-speaking guide starts at ¥100 ($13/£6.50) a day. Be sure the person you hire has a guide's license; otherwise, you'll have to pay their entry fee.

HIKING   Exploring the mountain means following stone paths through spectacular forests of bamboo, oak, and pine to scenic spots and terraces that afford breathtaking views. Since every tour group takes these paths, you won't be alone, but the crowds can be part of the fun. For solitude, take the less-traveled paths, where the setting and scenery can be as dramatic as the popular sights. Admission is ¥248 ($32/£16), good for 2 days.

FAST FACTS
Internet Access   Zhang Jia Jie Village has several Internet cafes on the side street near the park. Turn left off the main street just before the park. The cafes usually charge ¥2 (25¢/15p) per hour. Dial-up is ⓒ **163.**

TOP SPOTS IN THE THREE PARKLANDS
In Zhang Jia Jie National Forest Park: Huangshi Zhai. At the first fork after the entrance to the park, take the left road; hike 2 hours to this former mountain stronghold that is 1,080m (4,542 ft.) high and affords a panoramic view of forested peaks and jagged sandstone pillars. A cable car also goes to the plateau (see "Getting Around," above). Another path that leads through beautiful jade-green forest and passes a tight cluster of sandstone columns is reached by taking the right road at the first fork. Follow the path along Jinbian Stream. At the next fork, either take the left to Mihun Tai (and return the same way), or take the more traveled right-hand path to Zicao Tan. From there, take the right-hand path at the next two forks to return to the entrance.

Yuanjiajie, located on the north of the park, is another scenic spot that shouldn't be missed. Head to the right path of the park, where the Jinbian Si (Golden Whip Stream) starts. Follow the path; there is a small road going up to Yuanjiajie. The hike takes another 2½ hours. Or you can walk farther to Shui Rao Xi Men (Stream Winding Around Four Gates). From there, take a bus to the Bailong Tianti (Bailong Tourist Lift), which runs 356m (1068ft) vertically and costs ¥56 ($7.30/£3.60). During 2-minute journey, you can enjoy the magnificent panoramic view of hundreds of sandstone pillars. After that, take a bus from Bailong Tianti to Mihuntai (the Platform of Lost Mind) of Yuanjiajie. The huge quartz sandstone mountain has breathtaking landscapes of sandstone pillars.

In Tianzi Shan Nature Reserve: Located just southeast of the cable car platform at Tianzi Shan, **Yubi Feng** and **Tianzi Ge** are two of the most famous spots for their imposing views of forested peaks and jutting sandstone pillars.

In Suo Xi Yu Nature Reserve: Baofeng Hu (Baofeng Lake). A boat ride on this lovely clear lake surrounded by lush forest is included in the admission fee of ¥74 ($10/£4.80).

Huanglong Dong (Huanglong Cave): The colored lights that illuminate famous Chinese caves are an acquired taste, but they shouldn't get in the way of appreciating this 11km-long (7-mile) cave that contains spectacular calcite deposits as well as a waterfall 50m (164 ft.) high. Entrance is ¥80 ($10/£5.20). Take bus no.1 from Wu Ling Yuan Qiche Zhan (Wu Ling Yuan Bus Station) to the entrance; ¥1 (15¢/10p); 20 min.

WHERE TO STAY

In Zhang Jia Jie City, the only four-star hotel is the **Dragon International Hotel (Xianglong Guoji Dajiudian)**, Jiefang Lu 46 (© **0744/571-2999;** fax 0744/571-2266). Standard rooms are ¥630 ($75/£37). Although the Dragon is the best the town has to offer, it doesn't deserve its rating—for facilities or services—but the rooms are clean. Hotels in Wu Ling Yuan are attractive and close to the park, and room rates are the most reasonable in the area.

Pipa Xi Binguan   This hotel and the Xiangdian Mountain Villa are the best in Wu Ling Yuan. The majority of guests are with tour groups, and on holidays it's full. Rooms are clean but unadorned, and most have picture windows overlooking gardens and/or mountains. Some standard rooms have balconies. From the hotel, it's a 10-minute walk along the main street (Jinbian Da Dao) to the park entrance. Whether you call first or just turn up, do negotiate for a substantial discount.

Jinbian Da Dao. © **0744/571-8888.** Fax 0744/571-2257. www.pipaxi-hotel.com. 180 units. ¥548 – ¥648 ($71–$84/£36–£42) standard room. Rates include breakfast. 20% discounts. AE, DC, MC, V. **Amenities:** 2 restaurants; business center; limited forex; laundry. *In room:* A/C, TV, broadband Internet access, minibar, fridge, hair dryer.

Xiangdian Shanzhuang (Xiangdian International Hotel) 🏵   Visiting dignitaries usually stay at the Pipa Xi Hotel (above), but that should change now that this hotel has upgraded to four stars. Rooms are simple but pleasant and bright. Bathrooms combine tub and shower in a small, spotless space. The grounds have been beautifully landscaped and include lawns, a pond, and a pagoda; classical Chinese music plays faintly in the background—all to wonderful effect. Many of the rooms have close-up views of the mountains.

As you approach the National Forest Park on the main street, turn left on the small lane just before you reach the park. The hotel is about 300m (984 ft.) ahead. © **0744/571-2999.** Fax 0744/571-2266. www.xiangdianhotel.com.cn. 156 units. ¥880 – ¥1,080 ($114–$140/£57–£70) standard room. Rates include breakfast. 20%–30% discounts. AE, DC, MC, V. **Amenities:** Restaurant; business center; health center; bowling center; sauna and massage; limited forex; laundry/dry cleaning. *In room:* A/C, TV, broadband Internet access, minibar, fridge, hair dryer, safe.

WHERE TO DINE

Zhang Jia Jie City and Village, Tianzi Shan, and Suo Xi Yu all have inexpensive restaurants featuring spicy Hunan dishes, but the food is not outstanding, nor are English-language menus available. The best in Zhang Jia Jie City is Hushifu Sanxiaguo. Sanxiaguo is a special local cuisine similar to hot pot but without broth. All the ingredients, including meat and vegetables, are cooked together with chili and garlic in a small wok. Try *hetao ruo* (a kind of pork) and *ganbian changzi* (sausage). The pork is tender while the sausage is tasty. Take circular bus route no. 10 to Fengwan Daqiao. A meal for two costs between ¥20 and ¥30 ($2.60–$3.90/£1.30–£1.95); it's open from 11am to 9pm. The restaurant, which has an open area, is always packed during lunch and dinner.

Small restaurants serving Tujia dishes can be found all along the main street of Zhang Jia Jie Village. Tujia cuisine specializes in fresh game (such as rabbit and various guinea-pig and weasel-like mammals), reptiles (including poisonous snakes), crayfish, eel, and crab, so if you're feeling adventurous, point to the creature that interests you, and they'll cook it for you. Settle on a price, first, though; these dishes can be expensive. The hotels have restaurants that are more accessible to foreign travelers, but the food is mediocre. The best I found was inside **Xiangdian Shanzhuang.** For a simple repast, on the main street about 150m (500 ft.) before the entrance to the park, across the stream, there's a row of small **noodle restaurants.** You can sit outside, watch the stream, and eat a bowl of noodles for under a dollar.

14

The Tibetan World

by Simon Foster

Less than half of the world's Tibetans reside in the **Tibetan Autonomous Region (TAR)**, established in 1965. Tibetans form the majority in large regions of neighboring Nepal, India, Sikkim, and Bhutan, as well as in the adjacent provinces of **Qinghai, Gansu, Sichuan,** and **Yunnan.** Disagreement over where Tibet begins and ends is an ongoing stumbling block in negotiations between the Tibetan government-in-exile, based in Dharamsala (India), and the Chinese government.

For this guide, **Qinghai** has been included, as it is part of the Tibetan plateau, and most of its area—which covers much of **Amdo** (northern Tibet) and **Kham** (eastern Tibet)—is culturally and ethnically Tibetan. In many ways a better destination than the TAR, it has yet to be overwhelmed by Han migration, and restrictions on both locals and travelers are less onerous.

Tibet may be the "roof of the world," but it became that only recently, when the Indian subcontinent collided with the Eurasian landmass 35 million years ago. Prior to that, the Himalayas formed the seabed of the Tethys Sea. Mollusks are still found throughout the region.

Tibet is dominated by the vast, dry Tibetan plateau, a region roughly the size of western Europe, with an average elevation of 4,700m (15,400 ft.). Ringed by vast mountain ranges, such as the **Kunlun range** to the north and the **Himalayas** to the south, the plateau's west side features high plains, and the north is dominated by the deserts of the **Changtang** and the **Tsaidam Basin.** China's great rivers—the Yellow River and the Yangzi—rise in the east, carving out steep gorges. The greatest diversity in landscape, vegetation, and wildlife is found in the broad and fertile valleys of the Himalayas, but most of the border regions are closed to individual travel.

Most Tibetans still look back to the "heroic age" (7th–9th c.) of their history, when their armies dominated the Silk Routes and much of western China, assimilating the culture and technology of these regions. At the same time, Buddhism was introduced to Tibet from northern India. With the disappearance of Buddhism from India around the 13th century, Tibet became the new bearer of a complex faith, which combined a strict monastic code with Tantric Buddhism (with a strong emphasis on ritual). It is often characterized as "complete Buddhism."

The Tibetans went on to convert an entire people—the Mongols—despite being weakened by civil war and fighting between different schools of Tibetan Buddhism.

Just as China was often characterized as "closed" until it was "opened" by the West, the idea of Tibet as an inherently inward-looking Shangri-la is a long-standing myth. Isolationism was encouraged by the Manchu rulers from the 18th century onward, with some success.

⟨Tips⟩ Dealing with Altitude Sickness

It's likely that you'll suffer from a headache and shortness of breath upon your arrival in Tibet—they are both common signs of altitude sickness. Other visitors have complained of sleeplessness, fatigue, and even vomiting. So take it easy and let yourself get acclimated to the altitude during your first days in Tibet, certainly before you venture to any higher altitudes. Altitude sickness pills called Diamox (acetazolamide) can also help; they can be taken a few hours before your arrival in Tibet. In Lhasa, you can pick up a Chinese medicine alternative called Hongjingpian at the local pharmacies. Oxygen canisters are available at many hotels, and there is also a doctor on duty 24 hours at the Lhasa Hotel in case you're really having trouble.

Most visitors to Tibet get through the trip with just a few minor symptoms, and cases of altitude sickness typically go away after a couple of days. There are a few danger signs, however, such as a deep liquidlike cough accompanied by a fever, that you should watch out for that may indicate your case is more serious. For more information, go to **www.high-altitude-medicine.com**.

Regents backed by the Manchus held sway over young Dalai Lamas who often died mysteriously before they were old enough to rule.

Dalai Lama XIII (1876–1934) tried to reverse the policy of isolation, but encountered resistance from the conservative monastic hierarchy. Troubled by the destruction of Mongolia by Russian Communists during the 1920s, he prophesied, "The officers of the state, ecclesiastical and secular, will find their lands seized and their other property confiscated, and they themselves forced to serve their enemies, or wander about the country as beggars do. All beings will be sunk in great hardship and in overpowering fear."

In 1951, Chinese Communist armies entered Lhasa, and the prophecy began to unfold. A revolt against Chinese rule rose in Kham (eastern Tibet) 5 years later, and Dalai Lama XIV (b. 1935) fled for India in March 1959, soon after the **Great Prayer (Monlam)** was celebrated in Lhasa. Tibet's darkest hour was the Cultural Revolution (1966–76), known to the Tibetans as the time when "the sky fell to earth." Monks and nuns were tortured, executed, and imprisoned. Monasteries were looted and razed, and a vast body of Tibetan art was lost. Adding to the pain is the fact that many Tibetans, either willingly or coerced, participated in the destruction.

A revival of Tibetan culture and religion throughout the 1980s was checked after pro-independence protests, led by monks from **Drepung Monastery,** resulted in the declaration of martial law in March 1989, signed by chief of the local Communist Party Hu Jintao, now president of China. With the completion of the rail line to Tibet in 2006, Lhasa is now more accessible than ever, but increased political sensitivity in the run-up to the Olympics has made travel within the TAR troublesome for individual foreign travelers.

Travel in Tibet should not be taken lightly. Not only are there restrictions on travel to and within the TAR, there are wide variations in temperature throughout the day, and many visitors experience altitude sickness (see box above), particularly those who fly directly to Lhasa. The northern and western regions of Tibet are cold and arid, with an annual average

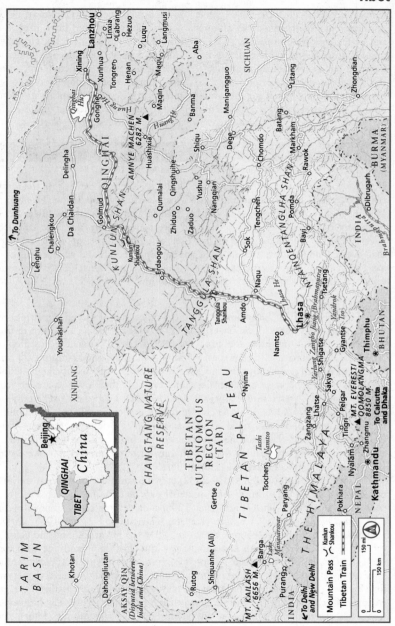

temperature of about 32°F (0°C), while southern and eastern regions are warmer and wetter. Peak season runs from May to mid-October. Winter in Lhasa is cozy, but transport out can be difficult to arrange— the Friendship Highway from Nepal to Lhasa is effectively closed for the winter months. The last half of this chapter, from the section on Shigatse onward, covers towns on the Friendship Highway, a loose way of describing the dusty road built from Lhasa, passing near the Himalayas and Mt. Everest, to the Nepali border. In spite of increasing restrictions on travel, the trip has become a popular one among foreign travelers in recent years. *Note:* Unless otherwise noted, hours listed for attractions and restaurants are daily.

1 Xining

232km (144 miles) W of Lanzhou, 781km (484 miles) E of Golmud. Altitude: 2,300m (7,544 ft.)

Once a key trading post on the southern Silk Route, Xining is perched on the northern edge of the Tibetan plateau and boasts a sizable Muslim population. Tibetan and Mongol monks and pilgrims may still be spied, drawn by **Kumbum (Ta'er Si)** ⍟ monastery to the south. A recent boom in the economy from the discovery of oil reserves and the city's attempt to market itself as a "summer resort" with its cooler-than-average temperatures has increased the supply of hotels and amenities the city has to offer. Still, there's little of interest in the city itself, but it's a useful base for exploring the **Amdo** and **Kham** regions to the south.

ESSENTIALS

GETTING THERE　The **airport** is 29km (18 miles) east of Xining. An airport bus runs to the **CAAC** ticket office, Bayi Lu 34 (✆ **0971/813-3333**). The bus trip from the airport takes 40 minutes and costs ¥21 ($2.75/£1.35). From the bus drop-off point, the Zhongfayuan Binguan is a 15-minute walk west; or take bus no. 28 from Bayi Lu to the railway and bus stations. CAAC delivers tickets free of charge. Oddly, discounts are possible during the peak season, but not in the off season. Other ticket offices are at the Qinghai Binguan (✆ **0971/613-2222**) and at the Wusi Dajie Shoupiao Chu (✆ **0971/612-2555**). There are flights to Beijing, Shanghai, Kunming, Urumqi, Chengdu, Dunhuang, Golmud, and Xi'an. Previously there were direct flights to Lhasa, but these had been suspended indefinitely at the time of writing, although flights via Chengdu or Xi'an (with a mandatory overnight stay) were available at reasonable prices (around ¥1,300/$195/£98).

　　The **railway station** (✆ **0971/819-2832**) is at the north end of town, at the junction of Jianguo Lu and Huzhu Xi Lu. Counters 1 to 5 are for normal ticket sales. Trains connect with Lanzhou (3 hr.) at 12:17pm (T208) and 7:43pm (T210). Trains also connect with Beijing (T152; 25 hr.) at 11:29am; Chengdu at 8:13am (1050; 26 hr.); Shanghai (K378; 33 hr.) at 9:56pm; Yinchuan (K916; 13 hr.) at 5:45pm; and Golmud (N911; 13 hr.) at 7:35pm. All Lhasa trains pass through Xining and one train daily (N917; 26 hr.) at 8:28pm starts in Xining. However, while it's easy to get tickets heading east, if you're planning on heading from Xining (or Golmud) to Lhasa, be prepared for a long wait, some backhand payments, or maybe even resorting to flying; it's far easier to get a ticket coming down from Lhasa than for the journey up. The problem in Qinghai is that the bulk of the tickets are snapped up by local hoods the moment they become available. These tickets are then sold to well-connected travel agents to provide tickets for the army of baseball cap–clad Chinese tourists you'll see in Lhasa. So, unless you come with a group, order your tickets well in advance, or are very lucky, the

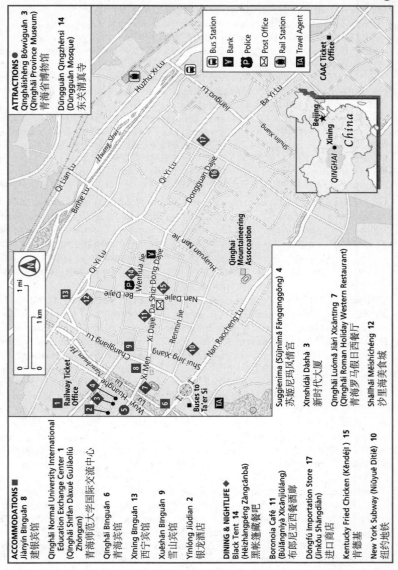

ATTRACTIONS ●

Qīnghǎishěng Bówùguǎn **3**
(Qinghai Province Museum)
青海省博物馆

Dùngguān Qīngzhēnsì **14**
(Dùngguān Mosque)
东关清真寺

Bus Station 🚌
Bank ¥
Police Ⓟ
Post Office ⊠
Rail Station 🚉
Travel Agent ▣

CAAC Ticket Office ■

China map inset: Beijing ★, Xining ●, QINGHAI

Railway Ticket Office

Qinghai Mountaineering Assocoation

Buses to Ta'er Si

ACCOMMODATIONS ■

Jiànyín Bīnguǎn **8**
建银宾馆

Qīnghǎi Normal University International
Education Exchange Center **1**
(Qīnghǎi Shīfàn Dàxué Guójiāoliú
Zhōngxīn)
青海师范大学国际交流中心

Qīnghǎi Bīnguǎn **6**
青海宾馆

Xīníng Bīnguǎn **13**
西宁宾馆

Xuěshān Bīnguǎn **9**
雪山宾馆

Yínlóng Jiǔdiàn **2**
银龙酒店

DINING & NIGHTLIFE ◆

Black Tent **14**
(Hēizhàngpéng Zàngcānbā)
黑帐蓬藏餐吧

Boronoia Café **11**
(Bùlǎngníyà Xīcānjiǔláng)
布朗尼亚西餐酒廊

Dōngfú Importation Store **17**
(Jìnkǒu Shāngdiàn)
进口商店

Kentucky Fried Chicken (Kěndéjī) **15**
肯德基

New York Subway (Niǔyuè Dìtiě) **10**
纽约地铁

Sugienima (Sùjínímǎ Fàngqínggōng) **4**
苏姬尼玛风情宫

Xīnshídài Dàshà **3**
新时代大厦

Qīnghǎi Luómǎ Jiàrì Xīcāntīng **7**
(Qīnghǎi Roman Holiday Western Restaurant)
青海罗马假日西餐厅

Shālǐhǎi Měishíchéng **12**
沙里海美食城

---

chances of getting any kind of ticket in Xining, let alone a sleeper, are slim. And of course, before you even consider how you're going to try and secure a berth, you'll need to get your hands on a Tibet Travel Permit (TTP; see "Permit Purgatory," p. 780).

All ticket offices, including those at the station, sell tickets up to 10 days in advance. The easiest place to buy tickets is from the **Huoche Shoupiao Chu** (open 8am–noon and 2–6pm) at Wusi Dajie 40 (© **0971/614-5203**). A ¥5 (65¢/35p) commission is charged. Take bus no. 9 from the railway station to Shangye Xiang.

The **Long-Distance Bus Station** (© **0971/814-9611**) is just south of the railway station. Buses service Lanzhou (3 hr.; ¥53/$6.90/£3.45) every half-hour between 7:20am and 6:30pm; Tongren (4 hr.; ¥30/$3.90/£1.95) hourly between 7:30am and 5pm; Linxia (5 hr.; ¥44/$5.70/£2.85); Liujia Xia (4 hr.; ¥31/$4.05/£2) at 11am; Hezuo (6 hr.; ¥53/$6.90/£3.45) at 7:45am; Golmud express service (9 hr.; ¥148/19/£9.60) at 8:30am and 11am, and sleeper (11 hr.; ¥131/$17/£8.60) at 5:30pm; Tianshui (9 hr.; ¥70/$9.10/£4.55) at 6pm; Dunhuang (20 hr.; ¥181/$24/£12) at 2pm; Maqin (12 hr.; ¥105/$14/£6.85 express service, ¥79/$10/£5.15 sleeper) is served by four buses daily; Banma (14 hr.; ¥95/$12/£6.20 seat, ¥143/$19/£9.30 sleeper) at 9:45am; Yushu (17 hr.; ¥115/$15/£7.50 seat, ¥150/$20/£9.75 sleeper) at 11am and 3pm (seat), and at 5 and 6pm (sleeper)—take the newer Nangqian bus if you can; Nangqian (25 hr.; ¥190/$25/£13) at 10:30am.

GETTING AROUND   Both Santana and Xiali **taxis** come in two varieties and cost ¥6 (80¢/40p) for 3km (2 miles), ¥1.30 (15¢/10p) per kilometer thereafter. From 10pm to 5am they charge ¥1.50 (20¢/10p) per kilometer. **Buses** require you to pop ¥1 (15¢/5p) in a box. Bus no. 1 runs from the railway station to the main intersection *(da shizi)*, passing the Bank of China. Bus no. 9 departs from opposite the railway station, passing the Haiyi Holiday Hotel, the railway ticket office, and the Boronia Cafe.

TOURS & GUIDES   There are several branches of **CITS** in Xining. Good English is spoken at the branch outside the Qinghai Binguan (© **0971/613-8444**), although staff isn't particularly helpful. A more competent branch is on the first floor of Xining Dasha (© **0971/814-9254;** fax 0971/812-9842). Get far more reliable info and service from the refreshingly professional **Qinghai Mountaineering Association,** Tiyu Xiang 7 (© **0971/823-8922;** fax 0971/823-8933; www.qma.org.cn; open 8am–noon and 2:30–6pm May to mid-Oct; closed winter weekends). Take bus no. 33 to Nan Men Tiyuchang. Tashi Phuntsok of **Wind Horse Adventure Tours** (Nan Dajie 4; © **0971/613-1358** or 139-9712-4471; www.windhorseadventuretours.com) can arrange customized trekking trips in Qinghai and the surrounding areas. He's a former monk who lived in India for 10 years, speaks great English, and is a great resource for any questions about Tibet and Qinghai. **Tibetan Connections** (© **0971/820-3271;** www.tibetanconnections.com) at on the 15th floor of building 5 at Guojicun Gongyu (upstairs from the Lete Youth Hostel), is another great resource that operates tours to Yushu and beyond and can also help with getting a Tibet permit.

To buy a train or plane ticket to Lhasa, you will need to buy a Tibet travel permit (and possibly a tour) unless you are a Chinese national (see "Permit Purgatory," p. 780 for more). The **Tibet Tourism Bureau of Xining** at room 2109 in the Xining Binguan (© **0971/845-9840** or 138-9725-9919; qxhotel@public.cn.qh.cn or xnhotel@sina.com) can help you arrange this annoying and costly bureaucratic nonsense. A 14-day permit costs ¥500 ($65/£33). The office is open Monday through Friday from 8:30am to noon and 2:30 to 6pm. Some agencies will only sell you a permit (and plane ticket) as part of a tour, but **Tibetan Connections** (see above) and **Qinghai Xinjun Travel Service** (© **0971/616-7130**) on the sixth floor of Shenbao Dasha on Shengli Lu can both get you a good deal on permits and flights.

FAST FACTS

Banks, Foreign Exchange & ATMs   Xining is overrun with branches of the **Bank of China.** Traveler's checks and cash may be changed and most branches have ATMs which accept foreign credit cards. The main branch is at Yinma Jie 23 (Mon–Fri 8:30am–6pm; Sat–Sun 10am–4pm).

Internet Access   The 24-hour **Man Jiahong Wangba,** Renmin Jie 3–6, is a 5-minute walk south from Da Shizi. In the west of town, **Wangchong Julebu** is at Shengli Lu 25. Near the station, **Liuxingyu Wangba** is downstairs at Zhan Dong Xiang 9. Dial-up is *C* **165.**

Post Office   The main post office is on the southwest corner of the main crossroads (second floor; open 8:30am–6pm).

Visa Extensions   The **PSB** at Bei Dajie 35 (*C* **0971/825-1758;** Mon–Fri 8:30am–noon and 2:30–6pm) will arrange visa extensions in a couple of days.

AROUND XINING

Dongguan Qingzhensi (Dongguan Mosque)   Located in the center of a bustling Muslim district, this is where some of Qinghai's 800,000 Muslims gather for the call to prayer. The buildings here aren't much to look at, but if you come during prayer times, you'll get an interesting glimpse into the lives of Chinese Muslims. During other times, elderly men sit in the square and gossip. Behind the mosque, there's a crowded produce market and next to the mosque are stores selling Muslim wares.

On Dongguan Dajie. Admission ¥10 ($1.30/65p). 8am–9pm.

Kumbum (Ta'er Si) 🐾   Jesuit missionary Emmanuel Huc, who visited in 1860, recorded, "On either side of the ravine, and up the edges of the mountains, rise, in amphitheatrical form, the white dwellings of the Lamas, each with its little white terrace and wall of enclosure, adorned only by cleanliness, while here and there tower far above them the Buddhist temples, with their gilt roofs glittering with a thousand colours and surrounded by elegant peristyles . . ."

One of the six largest **Geluk (Yellow Hat)** monasteries, Kumbum was established in 1560 to mark the birthplace of **Tsongkapa (Zongkaba),** founder of the Geluk School (described later in this chapter). The image of Tsongkapa is easily recognized by his pointed cap with long earflaps. Guides charging ¥50 ($6.50/£3.25) cluster around the entrance, but as there are English signs, a guide is not essential. Facing away from the ticket office, a path leads up the hill from the left side of a row of eight white *chorten* (Tibetan stupas). Keep your ticket: It will be punched by bored monks lounging around the major temples. Shrill guides, huge Chinese tour groups, and glassed-in relics lend Kumbum the feel of a museum, but Han visitors are more respectful than in the past.

The most striking building is **Serdong Chenmo (Da Jinwa Dian)** 🐾, at the heart of the complex, with its aquamarine tiles. The original structure is said to have been built by Tsongkapa's mother, around a sandalwood tree that sprouted from Tsongkapa's fertile placenta. The **Butter Sculpture Exhibition (Suyouhua Zhanlanguan),** farther up the slope, is popular with the locals. These sculptures were once only made for festivals, after which they would be destroyed.

Festivals are held the 8th to the 15th of the first **(Monlam)** and fourth **(Saka Dawa)** lunar months, as well as the 3rd to 8th of the sixth lunar month, and the 20th to the 26th of the ninth lunar month, which celebrates **Tsongkapa's birthday.** Call

Tsongkapa: Tibet's First Catholic?

While many portray **Tsongkapa** as a reformer or even a revolutionary, in the history of Tibetan Buddhism he was actually a conservative who appealed to existing (but neglected) monastic precepts. Drawing on his prodigious knowledge of the Mahayana Buddhist canon, Tsongkapa emphasized monastic discipline, insisting on abstinence from sex and intoxicants. The Jesuit missionary Emmanuel Huc believed he saw a touch of Catholicism about the man, and hypothesized that "a premature death did not permit the Catholic missionary to complete the religious education of his disciple [Tsongkapa], who himself, when afterwards he became an apostle, merely applied himself . . . to the introduction of a new Buddhist liturgy."

ahead to check exact dates. Religious dancing, mass chanting, and "sunning the Buddha" can be seen, as well as crowds of Tibetans who, in missionary Huc's day, "sang till they were fairly out of breath; they danced; they pushed each other about; they tumbled head over heels: and shouted till one might have thought that they had all gone crazy." Current festivals may be tamer.

© **0971/223-2357.** Admission ¥80 ($10/£5.20). 8:30am–5:30pm. Buses (28km/17 miles; 1 hr.; ¥4/50¢/25p) have their destination marked as HUANGZHONG, and depart after 6am from south of Kunlun Qiao (bus no. 3 from station). The last bus returns at 7:30pm. A round-trip taxi ride from the leagues of drivers waiting at the bus stop should only cost ¥50 ($6.50/£3.25), but if you hail a regular cab they'll charge ¥140 ($18/£9.10), including a couple of hours waiting time.

Qinghai Sheng Bowuguan (Qinghai Province Museum) 🏮 If you don't have much time to travel the rural parts of Qinghai, this recently opened museum is definitely worth a visit for its collection of relics that includes Mongolian pottery, Tibetan *mani* stones (stones carved with religious script and images), and bronze coins from the Han dynasty. The permanent exhibition also features a display of traditional clothing and architecture from minority ethnic groups in Qinghai, including Tibetans, Mongolians, and Hui, and the lesser-known groups like the Tu and Sala. English descriptions are decent, though the explanations do little to explain each group's religious beliefs and cultural habits. Still, the museum far exceeds the quality of most of its provincial counterparts.

Xining Guangchang. Admission ¥15 ($1.95/£1). 9am–4pm.

Qinghai Hu (Lake Kokonor) Large, high, salty, and stunningly blue, the lake that gave Qinghai (Blue Lake) Province its name provides an ornithological spectacle in April and early July, and wild vistas year-round. Over 100,000 birds migrate from the Indian Ocean to feed on spawn of Lake Kokonor's one variety of fish, the slow-growing scaly carp *(huangyu),* which swims up the Buka He each spring. The fattened birds crowd onto tiny **Niao Dao (Bird Island),** actually a peninsula situated on the northwest side of the lake. Tibetans consider this island as the plug for the lake. In 2005, a bird flu scare closed down the lake for several weeks, when hundreds of migratory birds were found dead near the shore.

Most hotels in Xining offer tours to Lake Kokonor, starting from ¥100 ($13/ £6.50). Be clear about what your tour includes. To come independently you can take a morning bus (5 hr.; ¥43/$5.60/£2.80) from the long-distance station. Bird-watchers should head for **Niao Dao Binguan** (© **0970/865-2447**) on Bird Island, which has basic twins for ¥120 ($16/£7.80) and dorm beds for ¥20 ($2.60/£1.30). Alternatively you can rent tents around the island for around ¥20 ($2.60/£1.30) per person, but bear in mind that it gets very cold up here.

Better tented accommodations are available at the **Tibetan Tent Guesthouse** (**Zangfang Binguan;** © **0974/851-9688;** fax 0974/851-9658) on the east side of the lake. This three-star guesthouse has decent accommodations in tents for ¥280 ($36/£18) and standard rooms for ¥360 ($47/£23). You can stay here for a night or have a meal before hiking around a small inlet of the lake, which should take at least half a day.

Admission to Bird Island Sanctuary ¥118 ($15/£7.65) plus ¥10 ($1.30/65p) for the electric car from the entrance. 8:30am–5:30pm.

SHOPPING

The **Dongfu Importation Store** on Gonghe Lu, between Qiyi Lu and Dongguan Dajie, has a small selection of hard-to-find Western goods including cheese, Pop-Tarts, cereal, and granola bars. Food supplies may also be picked up from the basement level of the **Wantong Guowu Guangchang,** which features a huge assortment of grocery items and toiletries. One of Qinghai's special exports is caterpillar fungus, called *dongchongxiacao,* which can be soaked in vodka like a worm in tequila or brewed with soup. You can purchase the fungus at the stores to the right of the gate of **Xining Binguan,** with prices ranging from ¥50 to ¥1,000 ($6.50–$130/£3.25–£65). Qinghai has a long history of carpet making, an art form that **Meiya Rugs** (© **0971/801-1098;** www.meiyarugs.com) is trying to keep alive, with several factories in Xining and another in the pipeline in Yushu. The factories turn out top-quality Tibetan carpets in contemporary designs. You can see the rugs at the Meiya shop at Huzhu Dong Lu 12.

WHERE TO STAY

For a city of its size, Xining has a wide choice of hotels. A 20% to 30% discount is standard at most establishments.

VERY EXPENSIVE

Yinlong Jiudian   To date, the monstrous monolith of the Yinlong is Qinghai's only five-star hotel, and as such it is definitely worthy of a mention. However, while service is friendly, it isn't always efficient, and though the rooms are spacious and comfortable, they feature an eclectic hodgepodge of colors and styles. In fact, the bathrooms are just about the only aspect of the rooms which are undeniably five-star. Nevertheless, if money is no object and you're looking for comfort and a central location, you won't find a better option.

Huanghe Lu 38. © 0971/616-6666. Fax 0971/612-7885. 316 units. ¥1,380 ($179/£90) standard room; from ¥2,380 ($309/£155) suite. Rates include 1 breakfast. 30% discount. AE, DC, MC, V. **Amenities:** 3 restaurants; cafe; sauna; business center; conference center; health center. *In room:* A/C, satellite TV, broadband Internet access, minibar, fridge, safe.

EXPENSIVE

Jianyin Binguan   This hotel, owned by the China Construction Bank, used to be one of the few places that allowed foreign tourists, and in spite of increased opposition its central location and recent renovations still make it a decent choice. Once the tallest building in town, the Jianyin is now overshadowed by a building across the street. The comfortable rooms feature pleasant decor, large beds, and good bathrooms.

A revolving restaurant on the 28th floor with Western food is popular with Chinese businessmen and tourists.

Xi Dajie 55. ⓒ **0971/826-1888.** Fax 0971/826-1551. 100 units. ¥468 ($61/£30) standard room; from ¥698 ($91/£45) suite. AE, DC, MC, V. **Amenities:** 2 restaurants; sauna; business center; conference center; bowling; travel agent. *In room:* A/C, TV, broadband Internet access (¥7.80/$1/50p per hour), minibar, fridge.

Qinghai Binguan ⚔ Popular with tour groups, this four-star hotel's renovated upper floors offer comfortable rooms and good city views, although they are starting to show their age. These rooms are tastefully decked out in simple wood furnishings and have large, clean bathrooms. Rooms below the 13th floor are a different story and are well past showing their age—avoid them at all costs.

Huanghe Lu 20. ⓒ **0971/614-8999.** Fax 0971/614-4145. 423 units. ¥324–¥386 ($42–$50/£21–£25) standard room; ¥908 ($118/£59) suite. Rates include breakfast. 20% discount. AE, DC, MC, V. **Amenities:** 4 restaurants; teahouse; concierge; business center; same-day laundry/dry cleaning; safe. *In room:* A/C, TV w/video on demand, broadband Internet access, fridge.

MODERATE

Xining Binguan ⚔ Located on pleasant grounds away from the bustle of the city traffic, this hotel boasts better-than-average service for a three-star, state-owned hotel. The Soviet-style architecture adds character, and the high ceilings and recent room renovations make for an enjoyable stay. Furnishings in the rooms match the dark, albeit fake, redwood floors; the bathrooms are spotless. The single rooms, while somewhat cramped, feature a larger-than-average twin bed and are ideal if you're traveling alone. Skip the Chinese breakfast buffet, unless you want last night's leftovers.

Qiyi Lu 348. ⓒ **0971/846-3333.** Fax 0971/845-0798. 327 units. ¥220 ($29/£14) single room; ¥298 ($39/£19) standard room; from ¥688 ($89/£45) suite. 20% discount possible. AE, DC, MC, V. **Amenities:** Restaurant; business center; travel agency; salon; concierge; laundry/dry cleaning. *In room:* TV, broadband, water filter.

INEXPENSIVE

Qinghai Normal University International Education Exchange Center (Qinghai Shifan Daxue Guoji Jiaoliu Zhongxin) ⚔⚔ *Finds* Located on the campus of one of Qinghai's biggest universities, this hotel offers a quiet environment away from the bustle of city traffic. You'll have to drag your bags a few hundred feet to the entrance of the guesthouse (taxis aren't allowed on campus), but the cheap rates and clean rooms and bathrooms make the effort worthwhile.

Qinghai Shifan Daxue Zhengmen. ⓒ **0971/630-3779.** 20 units. ¥120 ($16/£7.80) standard room; ¥280 ($36/£18) suite. No credit cards. *In room:* TV.

Xueshan Binguan ⚔ *Value* This hotel isn't much different from the usual two-star hotel, but its remarkable service and good price make it a standout. Not only are the comfortable rooms kept very clean, but after check-in a housekeeper comes around to ask if you need any laundry done—free of charge. The room also includes a fruit bowl that is refreshed every day, and broadband Internet access for ¥10 ($1.30/65p) for the entire day.

Jiefang Lu 24. ⓒ **0971/823-1010.** 32 units. ¥120 ($16/£7.80) standard room. No credit cards. **Amenities:** Free laundry. *In room:* TV, broadband Internet access.

WHERE TO DINE

Black Tent NEPALESE/TIBETAN When it opened a few years ago, Black Tent was an instant hit with Tibetans and the foreign community (consisting of English teachers, nongovernmental organization workers, and missionaries). The restaurant has since moved locations, but has retained the same relaxed ambience, friendly (but slow) service, and decent Nepalese and Tibetan fare. The vegetable pakora and chicken curry are tasty, although the chicken was a little chewy.

2nd floor, Wenmiaoguangchang, Wenhua Jie. ℂ 0971/823-4029. Meal for 2 less than ¥100 ($13/£6.50). English menu. No credit cards. 9:30am–11:30pm.

Boronia Cafe (Bulangniya Xicanjiulang) WESTERN   If you've been on the yak butter road for too long and are in need of some Western sustenance, Boronia is a good bet. The atmosphere inside is sophisticated, with a pianist during the day and occasional live music in the evenings, and the walls are adorned with modern art. But it's the quality coffee and Western set meals that keep the regulars coming back. There's another branch on Wusi Dajie (ℂ **0971-631-0679**).

North side of Xi Dajie. ℂ 0971/821-1588. Meal for 2 from ¥80 ($10/£5.20). English menu. No credit cards. 11am–11pm.

Shalihai Meishicheng 𝒜 *Value* MUSLIM/SICHUAN   It might take a slight adjustment to appreciate the noisy and fluorescent-lit dining room, but the food keeps this place packed nearly 24 hours a day. The *chao mianpian,* small pieces of noodles stir-fried with green squash, beef, and peppers, is a steal at ¥3 (40¢/20p) a bowl and incredibly satisfying—kind of like a spicy Chinese version of pasta primavera (with meat). After 6pm, the chefs fire up the front grill to serve *yangrouchuan* (lamb skewers).

Bei Dajie 4. ℂ 0971/823-2039. Meal for 2 ¥40–¥100 ($5.20–$13/£2.60–£6.50). No credit cards. Open 24 hr. Bus: no. 102, 35, 14, or 15.

Suggienima (Sujinima Fangqinggong) 𝒜 TIBETAN   This atmospheric restaurant serves a host of tasty Tibetan specialties including momos and yak steak, and also does a decent curry. The dimly lit interior is beautifully decked out with Tibetan furnishings, and there's live Tibetan music from 7:30pm onward.

Huanghe Lu. ℂ 0971/610-2282. Meal for 2 from ¥60 ($7.80/£3.90). No credit cards. 10am–11pm.

XINING AFTER DARK

In the summer months, one of the most popular things to do at night is to eat on one of Xining's renowned **"eat streets."** The biggest one is on **Daxin Jie,** where touts sell everything from barbecued fish to fried dumplings. *Warning:* This isn't the most hygienic environment; make sure you use disposable chopsticks.

You'll have to walk down a flight of stairs to get to the subterranean **New York Subway (Niuyue Ditie),** on Nanguan Jie 57, Xining's hippest nightclub. Owned by an American, the venue features a DJ spinning decent Western techno music while young women in tight bikini bottoms and bra tops dance around a stage. For a more sedate drinking spot, try **Soho** (ℂ **0971/822-3299;** open 6pm–2am), behind the Sports Center on Ximen, which features R&B most nights. Another popular nighttime activity is a visit to a Tibetan *nangma,* a variety show with singing and dancing. One of the most popular, for both Tibetan and Han Chinese, is on the seventh floor of the **Xinshidai Dasha** (ℂ **0971/610-8758**). The entertainment runs nightly from 9:30pm to 1:30am.

2 Tongren (Rebkong)

181km (112 miles) S of Xining, 107km (66 miles) NW of Xiahe. Altitude: 2,400m (4,872 ft.)

Tongren is at the center of a major revival in Tibetan art, particularly in sculpture and the painting of appliquéd *thangkas* (silk paintings). Although viewed by both Lhasa and Beijing as being on the periphery of the Tibetan world, the locals remember their crucial role in the Sino-Tibetan peace treaty, signed in 822. This is still marked by the **Lurol Festival,** held in the middle of the sixth lunar month. With fertility dances and body piercing, it has a pagan feel. Monks are *not* allowed to attend. The major **Buddhist festival** is held from the 5th to the 12th days of the first lunar month, with debates, religious dancing, and the unveiling of large *thangkas* moving between the main temples of **Sengeshong Gompa, Gomar Gompa,** and **Rongpo Gompa.** The town itself is drab; nearly all the sites of interest are located several miles north.

ESSENTIALS

GETTING THERE   The **Tongren Bus Station** (© 0973/872-2014) connects Tongren with Xining (14 buses; 4 hr.; ¥30/$3.90/£1.95) between 7:20am and 4:30pm; with Lanzhou (7 hr.; ¥55/$7.15/£3.60) at 6:50am; with Xiahe (4 hr.; ¥21/$2.75/£1.35) at 8am; with Liujia Xia (3 hr.; ¥16/$2.10/£1.05) at 9:30am; and with Linxia (4 hr.; ¥34/$4.40/£2.20) at 8am. Uphill from the bus station is a large roundabout. To the right is Zhongshan Lu, the main street, which runs west to Xiaqiong Lu.

TOURS & GUIDES   The **Rebgong Cultural Center** at Fengwu Zhonglu 217 (© 0973/879-7139; rebgonglibrary@yahoo.com) is the town's community center. The center features a library of Tibetan, Chinese, and English books, and can help arrange art classes and an English-speaking tour guide. Sherab, the director, is a jolly ex-monk who knows everyone in town.

FAST FACTS

Banks, Foreign Exchange & ATMs   None available.

Internet Access   Immediately east of the entrance to the Telecom Hotel is the non-smoking **Huangnan Dianxin Fengongsi Wangba** (© 0973/872-4196; open 8am–midnight) which charges ¥3 (40¢/20p). Dial-up is © 165.

Post Office   The main post office (Mon–Fri 8:30am–5:30pm; Sat–Sun 10am–4pm) is located on Xiaqiong Zhong Lu, next to the junction with Zhongshan Lu. Unless you read Chinese the post office has nothing to sign itself and is without the familiar logo; it's the yellow building with a small China Telecom plaque outside.

EXPLORING THE REGION

The main Geluk monastery of the region, **Rongpo Gompa (Longwu Si;** ¥18/$2.35/£1.15), is to the south of town. But the most popular outing for those interested in Tibetan art is a visit to the villages of **Shang Wutun (Upper Wutun)** and **Xia Wutun (Lower Wutun),** located 6.4km (4 miles) north of Tongren. The villages are filled with monks and laypeople turning out masses of Buddhist art for temples as far away as western Tibet; each village charges a ¥10 ($1.25) admission. The monks from **Sengeshong Yagotsang** (© 0973/872-9227; ¥10/$1.30/65p) in the upper village are exceptionally friendly, and happy to show their work. Thanghkas can be purchased for ¥80 to ¥3,000 ($10–$390/£5.20–£195), depending on the size of the piece, how intricately drawn the artwork is, and how much gold paint is used. Don't be afraid to bargain, even if you are buying from a monk! The most celebrated painter of this village is **Shawu Tsering** (© 0973/872-5032), who is very sprightly for an octogenarian.

Minivans charging ¥2 (25¢/15p) depart when full for **Shang Wutun** and **Xia Wutun** from the roundabout near the Tongren bus station, or hail a three-wheeler for ¥8 ($1/50p). You can hire a taxi to make the round-trip for around ¥20 ($2.60/£1.30). Directly across the river (Longwu He) is **Gomar Gompa (Guomari Si;** ¥10/$1.30/65p), marked by a spectacular five-tiered chorten (stupa). The climb to the top of the 38m (125-ft.) structure is a nervy one, as the ledges get narrower closer to the apex. The reward is a spectacular view down the valley. The monks are Tu, not Tibetan—even those fluent in the Amdo dialect won't understand a word they say.

WHERE TO STAY
Unfortunately, Tongren lacks any fashionable guesthouses; they're run-of-the-mill in this town.

Dianxin Binguan (Telecom Hotel)   If there is any truth in the rumor that CCP leaders get kickbacks on the sale of titanium dioxide, then they cleaned up with this white-tiled edifice that can only be viewed with eye protection under the midday sun. Inside are clean, simple, functionally furnished rooms with blue bathrooms, and refreshingly efficient service.

Zhongshan Lu 38 (on the north side, halfway down the main road). © 0973/872-6888. 33 units (shower only). ¥136 ($18/£8.85) standard room; ¥286 ($37/£19) suite. No credit cards. **Amenities:** Bowling alley. *In room:* TV.

Huangnan Binguan   Slightly cheaper than the Telecom Hotel, this establishment, located across the street, is your average traveler's hotel. Avoid the front building rooms with squat toilets and televisions that are relics from the 1950s. Spend a few more dollars to stay in the back wing, as the rooms are a significant improvement.

Zhongshan Lu 8. © 0973/872-2293. 100 units. ¥116–¥158 ($15–$21/£7.55–£10) standard room; ¥240 ($31/£16) suite. Discount of 30%. No credit cards. **Amenities:** Restaurant. *In room:* TV.

WHERE TO DINE
Homeland of Rebkong Artist Restaurant (Regong Yishuke) ✚ TIBETAN
The ambience doesn't get better than this at one of Tongren's few Tibetan restaurants. Monks and Tibetan government officials stroll in to sip yak butter tea and eat *momos* (yak dumplings). Try the *chao yangrou* (stir-fried mutton), the *tsampa* (barley flour mixed with yak butter, tea, and sugar), and the *renshenguo mifan* (ginseng rice). It's also a good place to relax with a cup of tea or a beer.

Zhongshan Lu (just west of the Huangnan Binguan). © 0973/872-7666. Meal for 2 ¥40 ($5.20/£2.60). No credit cards. 7:30am–8:30pm.

Taishan Mianshiguan ✚ *Value* MUSLIM   Popular with the few foreigners who live in town and the local community alike, this recommended restaurant serves an excellent *chao mianpian* (stir-fried noodle pieces with squash, beef, and onions). You can opt for the *qingtang mianpian*, which is a variation of the dish with soup. A counter with a variety of cold dishes sits at the front of the restaurant, including spicy cauliflower and cold seaweed. All you have to do is point to what you want.

On Zhongshan Lu, just east of the Dianxin Binguan. © 0/139-0973-6677. Meal for 2 ¥20 ($2.60/£1.30). No credit cards. 7:30am–9:30pm.

TONGREN AFTER DARK

Weekend nights, the most happening place in town is **Meinaxia** (Xiaqiong Zhong Lu 37), a Tibetan *nangma,* or nightclub. Entering via a fire escape on the side of the building felt like going to a club on New York's Lower East Side. Inside, young men in black sleeveless T-shirts take over the dance floor, grooving to a Chinese version of Kylie Minogue only to be edged out by couples (straight and gay) slow dancing to sappy love songs. For me, the highlight of the night was watching the performance of dancers in slinky off-the-shoulder dresses made of colorful wool shimmying to traditional Tibetan music.

3 Yushu (Jyekundo) ★★

819km (508 miles) SW of Xining. Altitude: 3,700m (12,136 ft.)

Because the Kham region inside the **Tibetan Autonomous Region (TAR)** is closed to individual travel, **Yushu** is your best opportunity to visit a large, thriving Khampa town. Though named for the **Jyekundo Gompa,** which looms above the town, Yushu has always been more trading center than monastic town.

The fierce reputation of the Khampas keeps Han migration down (aside from the odd Sichuan restaurant). Housing has improved, and locals are extremely friendly; strangers may rise and grasp your hand before you join them for a meal. The week-long spectacular **Horse Festival** is free of the vagaries of the lunar calendar and commences on July 25, on a grassy plain south of town.

ESSENTIALS

GETTING THERE   Yushu's often-talked-about plan for an **airport** is actually coming into being. The groundbreaking ceremony was held in 2005, and the project is scheduled for completion in 2009. It is expected that there will be weekly flights to both Xining and Lhasa. Check with CAAC in Xining for the latest details.

The normal **bus** trip from Xining should take around 17 hours, though if your bus breaks down, it could take double this! The road climbs steeply out of Xining, passing through **Yueri Shan** into vast grassland country. There are few towns along the way; take plenty of provisions. After **Maduo,** you enter an expanse of alpine lakes and gradually ascend to a pass at 5,082m (16,670 ft.). If you aren't overcome by altitude sickness, stop for fresh yogurt and perhaps some filling *tsampa* (roasted barley flour mixed with tea) in grasslands south of Qingshui He. The last major town, 48km (30 miles) before Yushu, is **Xiewu,** where a dirt road branches east to **Shiqu** (95km/60 miles) and **Manigange** in Sichuan. If several passengers for Sichuan disembark, a minibus can be arranged at the Xiewu crossroads.

The bus station is on Shengli Lu. Turning left (north) as you exit the station, you pass the post office on your left; it's a 10-minute walk from there to the main T-junction with Minzhu Lu, which runs left (west) toward the Yushu Hotel and Zhiduo, and east toward Xiwu and Xining. Jiegu Si commands a hill northeast of the T-junction.

Xining buses offer either separate hard seat (not recommended) or sleeper service. Hard-seat buses, ¥95 ($12/£6.20), depart throughout the day. There are four sleeper buses, ¥152 ($20/£9.90) per day. Book your ticket at least a couple of days in advance—you *don't* want to be stuck at the back of the bus. A minivan to Shiqu can be negotiated for ¥300 ($39/£20), but most drivers are reluctant to go farther. The cheapest option is to get up early and hitch a lift on a truck to Shiqu (¥30/$3.90/£1.95) or Ganzi

(¥70/$9.10/£4.55). The trucks depart from near the large yak statue, just west of the main T-junction.

FAST FACTS

Banks, Foreign Exchange & ATMs   None are available.

Internet Access   Qingzang Wangba is two storefronts east of the Yushu Hotel (open 24 hr.; ¥3/40¢/20p) per hour). The **Dongwangjiao Wangba,** located next to the Jiegu Hotel, offers similar 24-hour service for the same rate. Dial-up is ℰ **16300.**

Post Office   The main post office (ℰ **0976/8825024;** open Mon–Fri 9:30am–5:30pm, Sat–Sun 11am–4pm) is just north of the bus station. Overseas calls can be made from the **Dianxinju,** west of Yushu Binguan on the south side of the street.

EXPLORING YUSHU

At the **market** *(shangchang)* ✯ on the southwest corner of the main T-junction, you can enjoy some of the sights, gestures, and attitudes described by Dutch missionary Susie Rijnhart, one of Tibet's earliest and most astute observers: "The men are mainly dressed in *pulu,* or colored drilling, have their hair mainly done in a great queue about which they adorn with bright rings and twist about their heads. . . .The women often wear a large disk of silver on their forehead and sometimes on the back of their head, and both sexes carry from their girdles silver needle cases, flint and steel boxes and occasionally an embroidered cloth case for their *tsamba* bowl . . ."

Religious paraphernalia—including bells, prayer wheels, incense, and chanting tapes—is sold alongside knives, snuff from India, and bundles of tea wrapped in bamboo. Prayer flags *(tar-choks)* handmade by printers from Dege, and tailor-made *chubas* (Tibetan jackets) make excellent purchases. Kham is renowned for its richly colored carpets, but many are inferior weaves from Sichuan. Better carpets are usually Nepalese imports, but the craft is being revived locally; a **carpet factory** (www.meiya rugs.com) opened in 2003, although it has yet to produce a carpet! To buy a Meiya rug, you'll need to check out their shop in Xining (p. 765). A huge **open-air local crafts market,** 100m (330 ft.) southeast of the T-junction, is under construction and slated to open by 2008.

Jiegu Si (Jyekundo Gompa)   The striking red, gray, and deep-blue walls of this monastery dominate Yushu. Built in the characteristic tapering farmhouse style of Tibetan architecture, it was established in 1398 by the Sakya School on the site of a small Bon temple. It still houses some very dedicated practitioners. One monk housed adjacent to the temple has yet to see the light of day, and is well into his forties. So keep the noise down! Evening chanting sessions are regularly held in the golden-roofed red temple. *Note:* Remove your shoes before entering. The *dzong* (fortress), whose ruins lie above the temple, once commanded an unassailable position, looking out over river valleys to the east, west, and south. A stroll beyond the ruins up the ridge gives you a stunning panorama of Yushu, and eventually of the surrounding peaks.

Free admission. Minivan ¥15 ($1.95/£1), or walk up along the river east of the Dragon King Hotel.

Mani Shi Cheng ✯✯   *Mani* **stones** *(mani shi)* usually carry the most popular Buddhist mantra, *om mane padme hum,* while others are more intricate, containing entire scriptures carved with gold lettering. Tibet's largest collection of *mani* stones stands 5km (3 miles) west of Yushu. In 1955, there were optimistically estimated to be over two billion stones surrounding the temple, and although some now grace toilets in the area, the site has been resanctified and the pile is growing once more. The mass of stones and prayer flags towers over pilgrims who circumambulate the 1-sq.-km (½-sq.-mile) complex. It's a prodigious symbol of faith, especially when you consider that the temple is believed to have been established a little over 800 years ago. Stones were placed here by thankful pilgrims and traders from Sichuan, Lhasa, and Xining, who would rest in Yushu for several weeks. If you forgot to bring a *mani* stone, you can purchase one from some women of remarkable antiquity and persistence. On the road back to Yushu, you may notice other stones by the side of the road, which have a less holy purpose and reflect the strength of Bon animistic traditions in the region. "Mouth stones" have the character for "mouth" inscribed one hundred times in a spiral pattern to seal the curse (usually against a business rival) on the reverse side. Understandably, these stones are carved and placed covertly.

Free admission. Open daylight hours. Taxi ¥10 ($1.30/65p), bus ¥1 (15¢/5p).

Vairocana Temple or Wencheng Gongzhu Miao (Temple of Princess Wencheng)   Situated 20km (12 miles) south of town, just to the left (east) of the road to Nangqian, lies a temple associated with Princess Wencheng, who married King Songtsen Ganpo in a bid to halt Tibetan raids. Han commentators credit her with bringing all manner of spiritual and agricultural advancements to the Tibetans. On her way to Lhasa, the princess stopped with her retinue for a month in this remote gorge, and carved statues of **Vairocana Buddha** (one of the five transcendent or Tathagata Buddhas, said to transform delusion and ignorance) and the eight bodhisattvas into the naked rock. Some commentators suggest the delay was due to a miscarriage, and that Wencheng's child is housed within the central effigy. The hall sheltering the images was added in 710 by the next Tang princess, Jincheng. These political marriages were to no avail: The Tibetans sacked Chang'an in 763. Behind the temple is a great deal of Tibetan and Chinese script, but the passage of time makes it difficult to decipher. A spectacular view of the recently renovated temple is gained by climbing the hill opposite, but the climb is a steep 2 hours.

Free admission. Open daylight hours. Return trip by minivan ¥100 ($13/£6.50).

WHERE TO STAY

Yushu lacks quality accommodations, and prices at all establishments tend to double during the Horse Festival, when it is best to book months in advance (with a firm agreement on the price). If you are staying at a place that doesn't offer baths, there are two recommended bathhouses: the **Hongwei Lu Linyu,** east of the T-junction and next to the Longwang Hotel, and the **Jie Shuanglin,** opposite the Labu Si Hotel. The price at each should be ¥5 (65¢/35p). *Warning:* Some bathhouses offer "extra services."

Longwang Binguan *Ⓡ*   This recently opened gem sits at the foot of the Jiegu Monastery, at the top of Hongwei Lu, and to the east of the T-junction. Limited to 20 rooms, the service is exceptional and many of the attendants speak impressive English. The Longwang boasts clean rooms, double-paned windows, and a second-floor snack shop. The downsides? Hot water is only available from 8pm to midnight (though the neighboring Hongwei Bathhouse [see above] can meet this need) and the absence of private toilets, though there is one on premises.

Hongwei Lu. Ⓒ **0976/881-0222** or 0976/864-7233. 20 units (4 with bathroom). ¥80 ($10/£5.20) single without bathroom; ¥120 ($16/£7.80) single with bathroom. No credit cards. *In room:* TV.

Yushu Binguan   Lying about 200m (654 ft.) west of the main T-junction, on the right (north) side of the road, this is Yushu's best three-star lodging. The hotel was recently completely renovated and now features comfortable Tibetan furnished rooms and competent English-speaking Tibetan staff.

Minzhu Lu 12. ☏ 0976/882-2999. Fax 0976/882-2428. 89 units (41 without bathroom); ¥288 ($37/£19) standard room; ¥688 ($89/£45) suite. No credit cards. **Amenities:** Restaurant; sauna (¥25/$3.25/£1.65); tour desk. *In room:* TV.

WHERE TO DINE

Xiao Hongniu Meishi Cheng ☞ SICHUAN   Dining in Jyekundo's most upmarket eatery is done in private rooms—not really suited to the solo traveler. But those with a few friends will enjoy lavishly painted rooms, friendly service, and (if you wish) karaoke. A famished tour group might try tackling the *hao kao quanyang* (roast lamb) at ¥350 ($46/£23), or perhaps would just settle for a *kao yangtui* (roast leg of lamb) for ¥80 ($10/£5.20). Other local favorites include the *suanla fentiao* (sour and spicy vermicelli), *yangpai* (rack of lamb), and *huayu* (a river fish).

400m (1,312 ft.) west of the Yushu Binguan. ☏ 0976/882-4822. Meal for 2 ¥80–¥160 ($10–$21/£5.20–£10). No credit cards. 8am–11pm.

Ya Fanguan ☞ *Finds* MUSLIM   Noodles are the specialty of this perpetually full Hui-run establishment, found east of the main T-junction, just up the hill on the left (north) side. Easily identifiable by the yellow sign boasting two yaks, this strictly meat-and-pasta affair offers good value with such dishes as cold mutton and beef ribs, ¥18 ($2.35/£1.15) and ¥20 ($2.60/£1.30) per half-kilo (1.1 lb.) respectively. The delicious *paozhang* and *ganban* are similar spaghetti-like dishes, both covered in a beef-and-vegetable sauce. Local traders taking a break from the nearby caterpillar fungus market frequently stop in, offering you an excellent chance to observe the art of Kham debate up close and loud.

Hongwei Lu 7. ☏ 0976/882-7568. Meal for 2 less than ¥20 ($2.60/£1.30). No credit cards. 8am–10pm.

AROUND YUSHU

Travel to the five county towns around Yushu—**Chengduo, Nangqian, Qumalai, Zaduo,** and **Zhiduo**—no longer requires a permit. Thriving monasteries, remote nature reserves, and bumpy roads await the intrepid. You should be able to negotiate a minivan to take you around for ¥300 ($39/£20) per day, but more extensive tours are best arranged through **Tibetan Connections** or the **Qinghai Mountaineering Association** (p. 762) in Xining. The Mountaineering Association is willing to arrange tours to Lhasa via Yushu, following the traditional trade route along riverbeds for much of the way. Give them at least 2 weeks' notice.

4 Maqin (Dawu)

552km (342 miles) S of Xining, 525km (326 miles) NW of Aba. Altitude: 3,700m (12,136 ft.)

Few capital cities are one-street towns, but **Maqin,** the capital of Golok Tibetan Autonomous Prefecture, is just that. Efforts to "settle" nomads are rarely successful (see below), and the town has a Wild West ambience. Nomads wander around for a few hours, and then amble out again. North of town is a picturesque **Mani temple,** choked with *tar-choks* (prayer flags), and the bustling **market** to the left of the bus station is worth a look. But the main reason to come here is to visit **Amnye Machen,** Amdo's holiest mountain. *Warning:* Maqin is one of the coldest towns in Qinghai— and Qinghai is a cold place.

The Panchen Lama's Letter

The Great Leap Forward (1959–61) killed an estimated 30 million Chinese, but the horror of Qinghai was unparalleled. The leftist policies of the city's radical governor, Gao Feng, are said to have wiped out up to half the population. Starvation claimed most lives, while the PLA's policy of "fighting the rebellion on a broad front" *(pingpan kuoda)* saw countless monks and nuns murdered. The Panchen Lama, viewed as a puppet of Beijing, was sent to Qinghai on a fact-finding mission in 1962. Upon his return, he penned a 70,000-word tract—*The Panchen Lama's Letter*—which implied genocide: "The population of [greater] Tibet has been seriously reduced. . . . it poses a grave danger to the very existence of the Tibetan race and could even push the Tibetans to the last breath." Mao was enraged, the "puppet" was put under house arrest, and he was only rehabilitated by the Party in 1988. Ending nomadism, of which Marxism takes a dim view, is still official government policy.

ESSENTIALS

GETTING THERE   Compared to the trek out to Tibet's other renowned holy mountain, Kailash, getting to Amnye Machen is straightforward. The **bus** from Xining passes **Lajia Si,** a charming Geluk monastery on the upper reaches of the Yellow River, at daybreak, and arrives at Maqin midmorning. The **bus station** at Tuanjie Lu 137 (© 0975/838-2665), open from 7am to 5:30pm, has services to Xining (12 hr.; ¥105/$14/£6.85 express service, ¥79/$10/£5.15 sleeper) at 8am (seat) and 4pm (sleeper). To continue south, you will need to arrange permits in Xining. There are buses for Dari (4 hr.; ¥28/$3.65/£1.80) at 7:30am; and on odd-numbered dates for Banma (10 hr.; ¥54/$7/£3.50) and thence to Aba (1½ days; ¥94/$12/£6.10) in Sichuan, departing at 8am. Hiring a Beijing **jeep** through CITS, you can connect directly with Maduo (¥1,000/$130/£65), Aba (¥1,500/$195/£98), and Yushu (¥2,000/$260/£130). Facing out from the bus station, you are on Tuanjie Lu. As major streets go, that's it. The direction to your left is roughly north.

TOURS & GUIDES   CITS (© 0975/838-3368; fax 0975/838-3431; whitesnow lion@88yahoo.com) is in the lobby of **Dawu Binguan,** and goes by the name Amdo & Kham International Travel Service (open 9am–noon and 3:30–5:30pm). While they are friendly enough and can rent jeeps for ¥500 ($65/£33) per day, you're better off arranging the trip to Amnye Machen through the Qinghai Mountaineering Association or Tibetan Connections in Xining.

FAST FACTS

Banks, Foreign Exchange & ATMs   None are available.

Internet Access   **Hong Niu Wangba** is across the road, just north of the bus station, on the second floor of a music shop (open 10am–10pm; ¥4/50¢/25p per hour). Dial-up is © 16300.

Post Office   The main post office (Mon–Fri 9:30am–5:30pm; Sat–Sun 10:30am–4:30pm) is a 5-minute walk north of the bus station.

WHERE TO STAY

Dawu Binguan Located just south (right) of the bus station, this is Maqin's premier hotel. That's not a big claim. Midsize rooms in building 2 (*er lou*) are sunny, beds are comfy, but in spite of new electric showers, the tubs are grubby and the plumbing is shoddy. The reception staff is so indolent that they will ask *you* to go tell the maid to check your room, rather than pick up the phone in front of them.

Tuanjie Lu 109. Ⓒ 0975/838-2142. 58 units (40 without bathroom). ¥16 ($2.10/£1.05) dorm bed; ¥160 ($21/£10) standard room. No credit cards. **Amenities:** Tour desk. *In room:* TV.

Oxeye Binguan To the left of the bus station, on the first corner, is this white-tiled, blue-glass monolith. Guest rooms are narrow, but bathrooms are spacious with deep tubs, reversing the usual formula. Diagonally opposite is the **Dianxin Binguan,** a similar property with dingier bathrooms.

Tuanjie Lu. Ⓒ 0975/838-1889. 78 units (54 without bathroom). ¥20–¥26 ($2.60–$3.40/£1.30–£1.70) dorm bed; ¥96 ($13/£6.25) twin. 20% discount possible. No credit cards. **Amenities:** Restaurant. *In room:* TV.

WHERE TO DINE

The **Oxeye** offers decent dining, and there are plenty of Sichuan canteens near the Ghoul Hotel on Tuanjie Lu. Stock up on food supplies in town if you're heading out for a hike.

A NEARBY HOLY MOUNTAIN

About 86km (53 miles) from Maqin stands **Amnye Machen (Magi Gantry)** ☀☀☀. In 1929, American botanist Joseph Rock incorrectly measured its height at over 9,000m (30,000 ft.), making it (for a while) the world's highest peak. It actually comes in well short, at 6,282m (20,605 ft.), but it was unconquered until 1981 (partly because an earlier Chinese expedition climbed the wrong peak). One of the first Western visitors was the French adventurer Gerard, who was impressed by "a prodigious and resplendent mass of snow and ice, which strikes any man, however accustomed to mountains, with admiration and astonishment." The protector deity who resides in the mountain, **Machen Parma,** is popular with Bongos (followers of the Bon faith) and is also revered by Buddhists.

Many pilgrims start the trek from **Santiago (Thelma Chemo),** where the road meets the pilgrimage circuit. Farther down the motor road is **Baita (Chowan),** the traditional starting point for the trek where yaks or horses (and drivers) may be hired from ¥100 ($13/£6.50) per day. The full circuit is a hefty 132km (82 miles), and there is no way of retracing your steps without incurring the wrath of Machen Parma! It is possible to walk only part of the loop by starting further around the mountain; 4-day, 7-day or the complete 10-day circuit are all options. Alternatively, riding on horseback should take no more than 3 days. The atmosphere of the *okra* is pious and social. Entire villages or families make the trip, coming from all corners of the Tibetan world for a pilgrimage that is equal to Kailash in significance. The scenery is unsurpassed.

A permit (obtainable through CITS, Qinghai Mountaineering Association, or Tibetan Connections), tent, a sleeping bag, food and fuel, and a spare pair of light shoes or sandals for the numerous stream crossings are all essential. A sturdy water filter would also be an idea—there is a lot of glacial silt in the streams. Most pilgrims abstain from meat during the *okra*—a real sacrifice for the meat-loving Tibetans. June through September are the best months, after the deadly cold of winter.

A **pilgrim bus** to Santiago and Baita crawls by at 8am, but a **Beijing jeep** (2½ hr.; ¥20/$2.60/£1.30 per person) is quicker. *Warning:* The road is rough—windows are often broken from the *inside.*

5 Golmud (Ge'ermu)

1,165km (722 miles) N of Lhasa, 781km (484 miles) W of Xining, 524km (325 miles) S of Dunhuang. Altitude: 3,000m (9,840 ft.)

Unless you're heading to Lhasa from the Southern Silk Road, there is no reason to visit this blot on the wild and gloomy landscape of the **Tsaidam Basin.** Golmud used to be the only option for the overland journey to Lhasa, but these days you have the infinitely preferable option of passing straight through the town on the new Qinghai-Tibet rail line. *Note:* For Chinese translations of selected establishments listed in this section, please turn to appendix A.

ESSENTIALS
GETTING THERE   The **airport** is 20km (12 miles) west of Golmud. A bus making the 30-minute trip for ¥10 ($1.30/65p) connects with the **CAAC** office, just east of the PSB, at Chasidim Lu 66 (① **0979/842-3333**, ext. 8808). There are daily flights to Xining and three weekly connections with Xi'an (Tues, Thurs, and Sat). Golmud is connected by **rail** to Lhasa (K917; 7:33am; 27 hr.), Xining (12½ hr., N904, 9:05pm; N910, 6:24pm) and Lanzhou (14 hr.) by the T221, which leaves at 12:39am. Golmud has a relatively small sleeper ticket allocation for Lhasa-bound trains; nevertheless, you should be able to get a berth within a couple of days, and seat tickets are readily available. The left-luggage room is to the right (east). The **Golmud Bus Station** (① **0979/845-3688**) is directly opposite the train station, with buses to Dunhuang (8 hr.; ¥88/$11/£5.70 seat, ¥100/$13/£6.50 sleeper) at 9am and 6pm; and to Xining (10 hr.; ¥150/$20/£9.75) at 9am and 11am.

Heading to Lhasa, a Tibet Travel Permit (see "Permit Purgatory," p. 780) is required, although a few wily travelers have managed to take the bus or train without one. Travel permits can be arranged through the **Tibet Tourism Bureau** at Yanqiao Lu 79 (① **0979-848-3532**).

GETTING AROUND   Taxis charge ¥5 to ¥6 (65¢–80¢/35p–40p). **Buses** cost ¥1 (15¢/5p), paid to the conductor. The key bus is no. 2, which runs from the railway station to the center of town.

FAST FACTS
Banks, Foreign Exchange & ATMs   The **Bank of China** (Mon–Fri 8:30am–6:30pm; Sat–Sun 9:30am–4pm), Chaidamu Lu 19, changes cash and traveler's checks only.

Internet Access   **"Ai wo ba" Wangba** (open 9am–midnight) is above a grocery store, on the corner of Xi Shichang San Lu and Zhanqian Er Lu. Dial-up is ① **165.**

Post Office   The main post office (open 9am–6pm summer; 9am–5pm winter) is on the northeast corner of Kunlun Lu and Chaidamu Lu.

Visa Extensions   The **PSB** (open Mon–Fri, 8:30am–noon and 2:30–6pm) at Chaidamu Lu 68 (① **0979/844-2550**) grants 1-month extensions in 2 days. Permits for closed areas of the Tsaidam Basin are arranged here.

WHERE TO STAY

Foreigners were once forced to stay at the **Ge'ermu Binguan** (© **0979/842-4288**), where the standard greeting is "Passport" and the ¥288 ($37/£19) standard rooms are passable, but no more. Fortunately discounts of 20% are standard at other establishments.

Wei'ershi Dajiudian   Tucked in a quiet location between town and railway station, this two-star hotel has clean and comfortable furnished rooms; service is efficient and unobtrusive. Well-scrubbed dormitory rooms are at the back *(hou lou)*, but there are no common showers.

Jiangyuan Nan Lu 26. © **0979/843-1208**. Fax 0979/842-4888. 64 units (12 without bathroom). ¥120 ($16/£7.80) standard room; ¥388 ($50/£25) suite; ¥30–¥45 ($3.90–$5.85/£1.95–£2.95) dorm bed. Rates include breakfast. No credit cards. **Amenities:** Concierge; business center; same-day laundry/dry cleaning. *In room:* TV.

Youzheng Binguan (Post Hotel)   This clean and friendly three-star establishment opened in 2002. Rooms vary in size; a larger room is worth paying more for. The friendly travel agency provides free information.

Yingbin Lu (directly opposite railway station). © **0979/845-7000**. Fax 0979/845-7020. 59 units (51 with shower only). ¥80 ($10/£5.20) bed in a shared room; ¥128–¥168 ($17–$22/£8.30–£11) standard room; ¥388 ($50/£25) suite. No credit cards. **Amenities:** Restaurant; bike rental; concierge; tour desk; business center; same-day laundry/dry cleaning. *In room:* TV.

WHERE TO DINE

Liuyi Shou HOT POT   If you don't speak Chinese, a waiter will lead you straight to the kitchen, where you can select all the meat and vegetables you want. A *yuanyang huoguo* (yinyang hot pot consisting of both a spicy and a nonspicy broth), is then brought to your table so you can do the cooking yourself. As an added bonus, you get a bib to protect your shirt from any unforeseen splashes of spicy soup.

Chaidamu Lu 59. © **0979/841-5333**. Meal for 2 ¥50–¥80 ($6.50–$10/£3.25–£5.40). No credit cards. 11am–4pm and 6–10pm.

6 Lhasa (Lasa)

1,165km (722 miles) S of Golmud, 278km (172 miles) E of Shigatse. Altitude: 3,600m (11,808 ft.)

The religious and political heart of the Tibetan world, Lhasa sits on the north bank of the Kyi Chu, surrounded by colossal mountain ranges to the north and south. The first hint that you are entering the traditional capital of Tibet is the red and white palaces of the **Potala** 𝒜𝒜, home to Tibet's spiritual and temporal leaders, the Dalai Lamas, since the 17th century. Most Western visitors, however, are disillusioned to find a Chinese city. The Dalai Lama, the other enduring symbol of Tibetan purity and mystery, fled the grounds of his summer residence, the **Norbulingka,** more than 40 years ago.

Nowhere is the grip of Chinese rule tighter. The effects of martial law, declared in March 1989, are still felt in Lhasa, particularly in the nearby Geluk monasteries of **Drepung** 𝒜 and **Sera.** Hu Yaobang, general secretary of the CCP during the early 1980s, compared Chinese policies and attitudes in Tibet to colonialism, and this feeling is still hard to shake. Since the 1980s, waves of Han migration from poor neighboring provinces have made Tibetans a minority in their own capital and the opening of the Qinghai-Tibet rail line has only exacerbated the situation. Ironically, Hu Yaobang's policy of opening Tibet to migration and trade led to this influx of Han migrants, which most Tibetans consider the most odious aspect of Chinese rule.

Lhasa

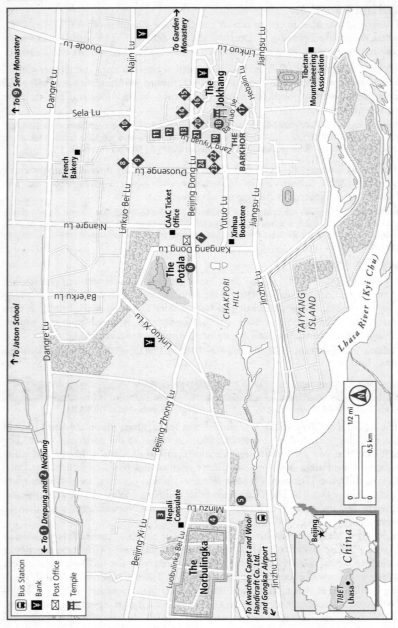

ACCOMMODATIONS ■
Dhod Gu Hotel (Dūngù Bīnguǎn) **20**
敦固宾馆

Kerry Hotel (Jírì Fàndiàn) **16**
吉日饭店

Kyichu Hotel(Jíqū Fàndiàn) **24**
吉曲饭店

Lhasa Hotel(Lāsà Fàndiàn) **3**
拉萨饭店

Oh Dan Guesthouse (Oudān Bīnguǎn) **12**
欧丹宾馆

Pilgrimages Inn **11**
(Miàojíxiáng Lǚguǎn)
妙吉祥旅馆

Yak Hotel(Yǎkè Bīnguǎn) **13**
亚宾馆

ATTRACTIONS ●
Drepung Monastery (Zhébàng Sì) **1**
哲蚌寺

Jokhang Temple (Dàzhāo Sì) **18**
大昭寺

Nechung Monastery (Nǎiqióng Sì) **2**
乃琼寺

Norbulingka (Luóbùlínkǎ) **4**
罗布林卡

Potala Palace (Bùdálā Gōng) **6**
布达拉宫

Sera Monastery(Sèlā Sì) **9**
色拉寺

Tibet Museum
(Xīzàng Bówùguǎn) **5**
西藏博物馆

DINING ◆
Alu Cang Restaurant
(Aēuáāng Cāntīng) **23**
阿罗仓餐厅

Dunya Restaurant and Bar **14**

(Dūnyà Jiǔbā)
敦亚酒吧

Holy Land Vegetarian Restaurant
(GāoyuánhóngShūcàiguǎn) **10**
高原红蔬菜馆

Mayke Ame (Mǎjí A'mǐ) **17**
玛吉阿米

Naga Restaurant (Naga Xī Cāntīng) **15**
西餐厅

Niúwěi **8**
牛尾

Shānchéng Míng Xiǎochī **21**
山城名小吃

Shangrila Restaurant
(Xiānggélǐlā Zàngshí) **16**
香格里拉藏食

Snowlands Restaurant (Xuěyù Cāntīng) **19**
雪域餐厅

Summit Cafe **9, 22**

Xīnshìjì Bīnguǎn **7**
新世纪宾馆

All Tibetan Buddhists aim to visit Lhasa at least once in their lives, drawn by the sacred **Jokhang Temple** ★★★, which forms the heart of the Tibetan quarter. It is recommended that you spend most of your time exploring this captivating neighborhood, also known as the **Barkhor District.**

ESSENTIALS

GETTING THERE   Aside from the problems of securing a travel permit (see "Permit Purgatory," below) getting to Lhasa is now far more straightforward since the opening of the railway, and there are flights from various major cities throughout China. Those arriving by **air** from Kathmandu can obtain a standard 1-month tourist (L) visa and a TTB permit only by joining a group tour through a travel agency. Two good choices are **Royal Mt. Trekking,** P.O. Box 10798, Durbar Marg, Kathmandu (© 977-1/421-5364; fax 977-1/421-5372; www.royal-mt-trek.com); and **Green Hill Tours & Treks,** P.O. Box 5072, Kathmandu (© 977-1/442-2467; fax 977-1/441-9985; www.greenhill-tours.com). **Gongkar Airport** is 97km (60 miles) southeast of Lhasa. Buses (1½ hr.; ¥25/$3.25/£1.65) connect the airport with the **CAAC** ticket office in Lhasa at Niangre Lu 1 (© 0891/683-3446). The buses depart the office for the airport about 3 hours before flights. Check when purchasing your ticket, or call © 0891/682-6282.

Permit Purgatory

As well as the current problem of actually getting a train ticket to Lhasa, there has always been the inconvenience of getting the relevant permits to visit the TAR. Permit restrictions, a subject long shrouded in mystery, appeared to be relaxing and, in recent years, independent foreign travelers found themselves able to visit the TAR as individuals rather than part of a mandatory group (which most visitors then abandoned as soon as they reached Lhasa). But restrictions have always been subject to change at short notice, and an incident at Everest Base in April 2007 has led to vigorous enforcement of laws that were once loosely applied. The "incident" involved a group of Americans unfurling a "Free Tibet" flag, singing the banned Tibetan national anthem, and burning a Chinese flag. The perpetrators were quickly removed and held for a couple of days before being expelled to Nepal. This action did nothing to help Tibetans in Tibet and increased restrictions for all Tibetans involved in tourism and foreign travelers alike.

Many agencies in Beijing, Shanghai, and Xi'an now once again require travelers to travel in groups of five in order to secure a permit. These group tours include a permit, transport (by plane or train) and transfers, hotel accommodations, and a city tour in Lhasa and cost from ¥1,500 ($195/£98) for the train. However, the Everest incident may be merely an excuse for the agents to make more money, as you can still find some agents (such as Tibetan Connections—see p. 762) who offer permits and plane tickets without a tour.

In order to buy a plane or train ticket you must be in possession of a valid Tibet Travel Permit (TTP), which costs anything from ¥300 to ¥1,500 ($39–$104/£20–£52) depending upon the agent, duration, and where you apply.

For tickets, fill out a form obtained from the information desk to the left, join a line to book your flight, swap your passport for an invoice (which you pay at the counter to the right), and finally pick up the ticket from the front of the original line. There are daily flights to Beijing, Chengdu, Chongqing, Xi'an, and Zhongdian. Flights from Chengdu connect to most destinations in China. There are Guangzhou flights on Mondays, Wednesdays, and Fridays, and international flights to Kathmandu on Tuesdays, Thursdays, and Saturdays.

The brand-new **rail station** is 10km (6 miles) southwest of town, reached by an equally new stretch of road. Taxis should charge ¥15 ($1.95/£1), but will try for double that. There are also public buses for ¥2 (25¢/15p) that connect with Tibet University on Jiangsu Lu. At the station you'll find ticket offices, left luggage, and shopping opportunities aplenty if you like paying over the odds for tack. All trains leave in the morning. There are direct trains for Beijing (T28; 8:30am; 47 hr.), Chengdu (T23; 9:05am; 48 hr.), Chongqing (T224; 10:30am; 49 hr.), Shanghai (T166; 10am; 24 hr.), Guangzhou (T266; 10am; 57 hr.), and Xi'an (T221/T224; 10:42am; 36 hr.), all of which pass through Golmud (13 hr.), Xining (24 hr.), and Lanzhou (30 hr.). There's also a specific train for Golmud, Xining, and Lanzhou (K918; 11:20am).

Permits are valid for between 6 days and 1 month depending upon where you get them and how much you pay; check before you buy. There are official **Tibet Tourist Bureaus (TTBs)** in Beijing (© 010/844-77899), Golmud (© 0979/848-3532), Guangzhou (© 020/3874-2948), Hong Kong (© 00852/283-83391), Shanghai (© 021/622-88845), Xi'an (© 029/781-5987), and Xining (© 0971/845-9840); processing usually takes a couple of days. Once you have your TTP, you are free to buy a Lhasa ticket.

The next hurdle to overcome, and the one that has certainly been affected by the recent Everest incident, is traveling outside of Lhasa. While the surrounding monasteries of Sera, Drepung, and Ganden are all visitable on a TTP, for travel beyond Lhasa an Alien Travel Permit (ATP) and a guide are now required. Foreigners aren't allowed to travel on public transport anywhere outside of Lhasa, and to this end, bus details have been omitted from this edition. The situation becomes yet more complex if you wish to travel to sensitive regions such as Kailash, for which a Military Permit (¥100/$13/£6.50) is required.

Of course, all of these permits require time and money to process, but given that you have no option but to travel with a guide in a group, they are all arranged fairly easily. As always there are stories of those who slip through the net; on this research trip, I met a Serbian who reached Lhasa by train from Golmud without a TTP, and I managed to get to Shigatse without an ATP. However, the exceptions are far fewer than those who get turned back (and fined). As always, there is hope that the regulations will relax again, but this seems highly unlikely before the 2008 Olympics.

The **bus station** (© 0891/682-4469) is at the south end of town, although it has become somewhat obsolete to foreign travelers with the opening of the train and the current restrictions on independent travel in the TAR. You might be able to sneak onto a Shigatse-bound bus (4 hr.; ¥50/$6.50/£3.25; every half-hour from 8:30am), but getting onto other buses is currently out of the question.

GETTING AROUND   Taxis within town are ¥10 ($1.30/65p) for any destination. **Minibuses** charging ¥2 (25¢/15p) and **buses** (with conductors) charging ¥1 (15¢/5p) are plentiful.

TOURS & GUIDES   If you arrive in Lhasa without a tour arranged, and you wish to visit anywhere else in the TAR, you will need an **Aliens' Travel Permit,** a tour guide, and a vehicle. These can only be obtained by joining a tour through **Foreign Individual Traveler (FIT)** branches in the Snowland Hotel at Zang Yiyuan Lu 4 (© **0891/634-9239;** fax 0891/634-3854) and in the Banak Shol Hotel at Beijing Zhong Lu 8 (©/fax **0891/634-4397**). The latter currently enjoys the better reputation. Restrictions are very tight at the moment (see "Permit Purgatory," above), but also tend to increase around certain dates, particularly the Monlam Festival (sometime mid-Jan to mid-Feb), the Saka Dawa Festival (sometime mid-May to mid-June), and

Railway on the Roof of the World

China (and the world's) highest and most ambitious railway link opened to great fanfare on July 1, 2006. The rail line took 6 years to build and passes through some of the harshest, most inhospitable and beautiful landscapes on the planet. Most of the 1,142km (709-mile) track lies at an altitude above 4,000m (13,123 ft.), and the highest pass is a staggering 5,072m (16,636 ft.). The line also claims another record: the highest rail tunnel in the world at 4,905m (16,088 ft.). Oxygen is pumped into all carriages and additional supplies are available for those who are really suffering. Aside from these special features, the trains are much like any other you'll travel on in China, albeit more modern. The proposed Tangula Train, a five-star rail experience operated by the Kempinski group, is expected to start operating in 2008.

While such altitude may seem like a scary prospect, taking the train actually offers the opportunity to acclimatize more easily than flying directly to Lhasa (3,700m/12,136 ft.). Critics are quick to point out the environmental and social impact of the rail line, which passes through pristine habitats and is currently bringing at least 3,000 Han visitors to Lhasa every day (during the summer). Indeed, Tibetan culture in Lhasa is being further diluted day by day, and the TAR's minerals are efficiently being converted into cash, all of which makes visiting the Tibetan world outside of the TAR a more appealing proposition. However, most Han visitors limit themselves to taking the train up to Lhasa and flying out a few days later, leaving the rest of the TAR relatively unaffected (although the rail line is due to reach Shigatse by 2009 and ultimately is planned to stretch all the way to Nepal). If you ask most Tibetans how they feel about the rail line, the answers usually include something about the increased wealth brought by tourists, and the ease of travel that it affords, meaning students can return home for the holidays and businessmen can bolster profits by saving on airfares. Also, in spite of all the hoo-ha about the environment, the railway is infinitely preferable to the emissions caused by aircraft. Whatever you think of the rail line, it's here to stay and the trip is one of the most incredible journeys China has to offer.

the Dalai Lama's birthday on July 6. If you're planning an extensive trip and have limited time you should organize your tour through other agencies well before you arrive. Of the Lhasa-based tour operators, **Shigatse Travels,** located inside the Yak Hotel (© **0891/633-0489;** fax 0891/633-0482; www.shigatsetravels.com), is highly recommended. For off-the-beaten-track trips **Tibet Wind Horse Adventure** (© **0891/683-3009;** www.windhorsetibet.com) offers a range of options, but specializes in whitewater rafting tours. Longer tours are best arranged a few months in advance but they also operate half-day ($75) and day ($95) tours, which can be put together at shorter notice. Their main office is at Lingkor Road 26 but they have a branch on Zang Yiyuan Lu.

The most popular trip in the TAR is the 5- to 6-day tour from Lhasa to Zhangmu on the Nepali border. This trip should cost between ¥4,500 and ¥6,000 ($585–$780/£293–£390), which includes a Land Cruiser that will comfortably seat four, a guide, and Alien Travel Permits (ATP) for all passengers; meals and accommodations are extra. If you're looking to share a ride with other passengers, check out the bulletin-board postings at Snowlands, the Pentoc, and the Kerry Hotel. Be sure to draw up a contract with the driver stating where you will visit and how long the trip will last; make a deposit and try to negotiate withholding the balance (ideally 25%) until your tour is completed—some travelers have been left stranded. Also be sure to check out the vehicle before you embark on your trip—you may even want to take the car and driver on a test drive on the streets of Lhasa to see how the car performs before agreeing to embark into the wilderness. Once you do arrive at your destination, and if you're happy with the service, tip your driver ¥50 to ¥100 ($6.50–$13/£3.25–£6.50) per person. Gifts of music cassettes are also highly appreciated.

Those planning mountaineering expeditions must obtain permits from the **Tibetan Mountaineering Association** (© **0891/633-3720**), housed in a building immediately north of the Himalaya Hotel. Whatever difficulties you face, you won't be the first traveler in Tibet to have his or her way blocked by the authorities.

FAST FACTS

Banks, Foreign Exchange & ATMs   The main branch of the **Bank of China,** west of the Potala Palace at Linkuo Xi Lu 28, accepts traveler's checks and credit cards at counters 6 to 10. There are several international ATMs. Hours are weekdays from 9am to 1pm and 3:30 to 6pm; weekends 10am to 4:30pm. There are several other branches of the bank throughout town, including one on the northeast side of town, at Najin Lu 188 and another just west of the Banak Shol Hotel on Beijing Dong Lu. Hours are the same for all branches.

Consulates   North of the Norbulinka Palace, the **Nepalese Consulate-General** at Luobulinka Bei Lu 13 (© **0891/682-2881;** fax 0891/683-6890) is open from 10am to noon on weekdays. Visas are processed in 2 days, cost ¥255 ($33/£17), and are valid for 6 months. Non-Chinese nationals can arrange 60-day visas at the border (Zhangmu) for $30. You can get a transit visa for $5 if you're staying in Nepal for less than 48 hours. Consular officials joke that this may be the only example of preferential treatment for foreigners in the TAR.

Internet Access   The 24-hour Jinma Wangba offers broadband Internet access for ¥3 (40¢/20p) per hour. The **Summit Cafe** has branches in the courtyard of the Shangbala Hotel on Zang Yiyuan Lu and another opposite Niuwei on Linkuo Bei Lu and offers comfortable broadband and wireless access for ¥8 ($1.05/50p) per hour. Many hotels and guesthouses also offer Internet access; the **Snowlands Guesthouse** (© **0891/633-7323**) has several computer terminals that cost ¥5 (65¢/35p) per hour. Dial-up is © **165.**

Post Office   The main post office is at Beijing Dong Lu 33. Summer hours are from 9am to 8pm; winter hours are from 9:30am to 6:30pm. The counter to the far left designated INTERNATIONAL POST BUSINESS is efficient; it's open from 9am to noon and 3:30 to 5:30pm.

Visa Extensions   You can't miss the imposing PSB on Linkuo Bei Lu (© **0891/632-4528**). In spite of a recent change of address, attitudes remain the same and visa officers spit out the term "individual traveler" as through it's a disfiguring and contagious affliction. They offer extensions of up to 5 days, usually processed in half a day. Hours are weekdays from 9am to 12:30pm and 3:30 to 6:30pm. Longer extensions are possible if you have an onward air ticket or have already arranged a tour.

EXPLORING LHASA

Drepung Monastery (Zhebang Si) 🏵 Founded in 1416 by Tsongkapa's disciple Jamyang Choeje, Drepung was once Tibet's largest and most influential monastery, with over 10,000 monks, a number which now stands at a paltry 700. The seat of the Dalai Lamas before the "Great Fifth" Dalai Lama built the Potala Palace, many of its buildings survived the Cultural Revolution, but the order now pays a price for its prominent role in the pro-independence demonstrations of 1987. On September 27, 1987, about 20 Drepung monks unfurled banners and the Tibetan flag, and marched around the Barkhor before being arrested in front of the TAR Government HQ. This politicization of the monks is remarkable, as they were once loyal to their college first, and country second. Monks at Loseling College fought *against* Tibetan independence after the fall of the Qing. The effects of a program of political indoctrination undertaken in 1996 are still felt. A PSB compound sits below the monastery, and "cadre monks" keep a close eye on day-to-day activities.

A circuit of the monastery begins with **Ganden Podrang (Ganden Palace),** and continues on to **Tsokchen (Assembly Hall), Ngakpa Tratsang (College of Tantric Studies), Jamyang Drubpuk** (Jamyang Choeje's **meditation cave,** attached to the east wall of the Assembly Hall), **Loseling Tratsang (College of Dialectics),** and **Tashi Gomang Tratsang.** The pilgrimage trail continues southeast down to the shadowy and enthralling **Nechung Monastery (Naiqiong Si)** 🏵, home of the Nechung Oracle, who is consulted by the Dalai Lama on important matters of state. Separate admission to Nechung is ¥10 ($1.30/65p).

To the left (west) of Drepung's Assembly Hall is the **kitchen,** where butter tea is prepared in huge wooden vats. Make much-needed donations to the monastery here. With the passing of the charismatic teacher Gen Lamrim in 1997, Drepung lost a major source of income. This master's lectures once drew devotees from all over the Tibetan world. The first floor of the **Assembly Hall** 🏵🏵 holds a striking statue of Dalai Lama XIII, magnificently lit by filtered sunshine and pungent yak butter lamps. Readings of the scriptures are often held at midday; it is hoped that you will be able to enjoy the spectacle of novices tumbling over one another in the race to fetch tea from the kitchen for their elders. Also popular with pilgrims is a chapel to the north of the second floor, which houses a mirror said to cure the facial diseases of those who gaze into it. The most revered image is a 15m-tall (49-ft.) statue of the 8-year-old **Maitreya Buddha,** designed by Tsongkapa and housed in the northwest section of the building, usually viewed from the third floor. You will be offered holy water: Cup your right hand above your left, take a quick sip, and splash the rest on your head.

© 0891/686-3149. Admission ¥55 ($7.15/£3.60). 9am–5pm (Nechung closes at 4pm). Morning buses (10km/6¼ miles; 30 min.; ¥3/40¢/20p) depart from west of the Jokhang. Returning to Lhasa, take bus no. 302 from Nechung Monastery, or bus no. 301 from the bottom of the hill. Taxis charge ¥20 ($2.60/£1.30) each way.

Jokhang Temple (Dazhao Si) 🏵🏵🏵 To fully explore Tibet's spiritual heart, visit this temple twice. From 8am, pilgrims line up to enter the Jokhang. You'll have no trouble singling the eager out-of-towners from the more detached city folk. In the morning, the rooms are unlocked, allowing pilgrims to rub their foreheads furiously against the sacred images. Your visit can be a painfully slow shuffle, lasting up to 2 hours, but it can be a moving experience.

Don't miss the image of **Palden Lhamo** 🏵 on the third floor. The fierce protector of both Lhasa and the Dalai Lama, she is said to have murdered her own child to bring her husband and king to his senses and put an end to his endless military campaigns.

Note the exquisite **deer and wheel motifs** on the roof. Both symbols allude to Sakyamuni's first sermon, "Turning the Wheel of the Doctrine," delivered in a deer park in Benares (Varanasi, India). Sakyamuni was initially reluctant to expound his teachings, believing they would be incomprehensible to most, but the god Brahma intervened. The deer and the wheel hark back to a time when believers respectfully avoided depicting the Buddha. A bodhi tree and a solitary footprint were also common symbols.

In the afternoon, a gate to the right of the main entrance admits tourists, and gives you an opportunity to view the ancient statuary and woodwork in relative peace, strident Chinese tour guides notwithstanding. The most revered object in Tibet is **Jowo Rinpoche** 𝕽𝕽𝕽, a 1.5m (5-ft.) image of the young Buddha, which originated in India and was brought with Princess Wencheng as dowry. Many credit her with selecting the temple's location according to the principles of geomancy *(feng shui)*. Without the bustle of the morning crowd, take time to appreciate the ancient Newari door frames, columns, and finials (7th and 8th c.). Note the more recent *yab-yum* images of sexual union in a chapel to the south. Many mistakenly believe tantric practice has no place in the "reformed" Geluk School, but Tsongkapa simply restated the principle that only advanced practitioners should engage in tantric sex.

𝄆 **0891/633-6858.** Admission ¥70 ($9.10/£4.55). 8am–6:30pm.

Norbulingka (Luobulinka)

Whatever traits the various manifestations of the Dalai Lama share, architectural taste is not one of them. The manicured gardens of the summer residence are pleasant—especially on weekends when locals gather for picnics—but the buildings, added by the 7th (who choose the site for its medicinal springs), 8th, 13th, and 14th incarnations, do not sit well together. The most interesting is **Takten Podrang,** commissioned by Dalai Lama XIV in 1954, 5 years before he fled to India. As at the Potala Palace, the lack of luxuries is striking, but the rooms give a distinctly human insight to the Dalai Lama, particularly the grubby bathtub, full of financial offerings. On the second floor is a fascinating **mural** 𝕽 depicting the history of Tibet, from the legendary union of a wild ogre with a monkey (an emanation of Avalokiteshvara), to the final frame of the young Dalai and Panchen Lamas meeting with Mao Zedong and Zhou Enlai. Duck under the rope to get a good look.

𝄆 **0891/682-6274.** Admission ¥70 ($9.10/£4.55). Mon–Sat 9am–1pm and 2:30–6pm.

Potala Palace (Budala Gong) 𝕽𝕽

Commissioned by Dalai Lama V (17th c.), the Potala was built around the fortress of King Songtsen Gampo, which had stood on **Mount Mapori** for a millennium. "Potala" refers to a mountain in south India, the abode of Tibet's patron deity, Avalokiteshvara (Chenresik). Both the ancient kings and the Dalai Lamas are said to be manifestations of this bodhisattva, feminized in the Chinese Buddhist pantheon as Guanyin, the goddess of mercy. A monastery, a palace, and a prison, it symbolizes the fusion of secular and religious power in Tibet. Early Tibetan temples, such as Samye Monastery, followed the Indian practice of modest locations, allowing temples to adhere to a mandala design. The Great Fifth, the last significant Dalai Lama before Dalai Lama XIII, was fond of imposing hilltop locations, making adherence to the mandala pattern impossible. Tibetologist Guiseppe Tucci saw the Potala as an "outgrowth of the rock underlying it, as irregular and whimsical as nature's work," and it was not a simple project. **Podrang Marpo (Red Palace)** was completed under the regent Desi Sangye Gyatso, 15 years after the then–Dalai Lama's death in 1682, and involved over 8,000 workers and artisans.

Most visitors enter the palace via the central staircase up to the **Eastern Courtyard (Deyang Shar)**. Buildings are denoted numerically. You first reach the **Eastern Apartments** of the Dalai Lama XIV (3). Portraits of Dalai Lamas XIV and XIII once hung above the entrance, but they were removed in 1996. Inside the entrance is a splendid mural of Wutai Shan in northeast China, the earthly Pure Land of Manjusri, a bodhisattva who symbolizes wisdom. The simplicity of the present Dalai Lama's personal chambers, with prayer beads still resting by the bed, is moving, particularly for those who have met His Holiness. You next enter the **Red Palace**, the spiritual center and home to the remains of all the Dalai Lamas (except Dalai Lama VI, who was fonder of wenches than worship, and was eventually chased into exile by the Mongols). The throne room of Dalai Lama VII, **Sasum Lhakang** (6), contains an exquisite silver statue of Avalokiteshvara and an inscription on the north wall, dated 1722, wishing that the Chinese emperor would reign for 10 thousand years. The Kangxi emperor died in 1722. The most sacred chapel is **Phakpa Lhakang** ✿ (10), part of the original 7th-century palace and housing a "self-arising" image of Avalokiteshvara. Even Chinese visitors are awed. As Tucci observed in the 1950s, "The crowds of pilgrims daily ascending the stairs of the Potala were a tangible proof of devotion. Rich or poor, dignitaries or peasants, they kneeled before each image: faith and ecstasy could be read on their faces. Holding copper pitchers full of clarified butter, they went to feed the temple lamps."

A meditation cave, **Chogyel Drupuk** (17), contains an image of Songtsen Gampo, with his Nepali and Chinese wives; it dates from the 7th or 8th century. The Dalai Lama V's death was kept secret for 12 years; his reliquary stupa is the most magnificent structure in the palace, containing over 3,000 kilograms (6,600 lb.) of gold, encrusted in jewels, and disappearing into the darkness of **Serdung Lhakang** (21).

The Potala is firmly entrenched on Lhasa's must-see list, but it's hardly the most stalwart of structures, which has led authorities to limit the number of visitors per day to 2,500. Sounds like a lot, but if you come during one of the major Chinese holidays you'll struggle to get a ticket. Plans to build a museum housing the Potala's greatest treasures below the building and cease visits to the palace itself are as yet unsubstantiated.

Warning: Visits to the Potala are best made *after* you are accustomed to the altitude.

Beijing Zhong Lu. ✆ 0891/683-4362. Admission ¥100 ($13/£6.50). You must make a reservation a few hours to 1 day in advance; at the ticket counter you will be assigned a time to return for entry. Admission to relics museum and roof additional ¥10 ($1.30/£65p) each. 9am–4pm.

Sera Monastery (Sela Si)

This major Geluk monastery was founded in the early 15th century by Sakya Yeshe, a disciple of Tsongkapa. A pilgrimage circuit of the complex passes the colleges **Sera Me Tratsang, Ngakpa Tratsang,** and **Sera Je Tratsang** before reaching **Tsokchen,** the huge assembly hall (ca. 18th c.), which houses an image of Sakya Yeshe. The path continues up to **Sera Utse,** a hermitage that predates the monastery, a stiff 1½-hour hike up the mountain. Most visitors are drawn to Sera by the lively **debates** ✿✿✿ held in the Sera Je Tratsang Courtyard Monday to Saturday from 3 to 5pm.

Debates provide an opportunity for monks to demonstrate their scholarship and rise through the ranks. A prodigious body of religious literature must be digested before a monk can become a useful sophist. Visitors usually are struck by the physicality of the debates, with one monk sitting down, biding his time, while the other launches a verbal and physical attack. One monk noted that they were instructed that "the foot must come down so strongly that the door of hell may be broken open; and that the hands must make so great a noise that the voice of knowledge may frighten the devils all the world over."

© 0891/638-3639. Admission ¥50 ($6.50/£3.25). 9am–5pm. Bus: no. 502 from northwest corner of Beijing Dong Lu and Duosenge Lu. Taxis charge ¥15 ($1.95/£1) each way.

Tibet Museum (Xizang Bowuguan)   While the Communist Party's propaganda ranges from laughable to downright offensive in this museum, it's still worth a visit for its extensive displays of *thangkas* (Tibetan scrolls), instruments, and gold copper statues of Buddhas. The museum also houses the gold seal of the vaunted 5th Dalai Lama, who is credited with unifying Tibet in the 17th century (though this isn't mentioned in the museum). A spiffy audio tour is included in the price of admission. The third floor isn't worth visiting, unless you like stuffed-animal dioramas. Be sure to pick up the free pamphlet issued by the Information Office of the State Council, which recalls "the four glorious decades of regional ethnic autonomy in Tibet."

Admission ¥30 ($3.90/£1.95). May–Oct 9am–6:30pm; Nov–Apr 10:30am–5pm.

SHOPPING

There are plenty of supermarkets to be found along Beijing Dong Lu, including **Baiyi Chaoshi** opposite the post office and **Hongyan Chaoshi**, a few minutes walk farther east. **Saikang Dasha** is a fancy department store, 1 block east of the post office, open from 10am to 9pm. If you're heading out into the wilds of the TAR and haven't got the necessary kit, Lhasa has lots of outdoor stores, but if you're going to be relying on your gear, don't believe the brand names you'll see in many of these stores. For genuine outdoor gear, head for Toread at Beijing Zhong Lu 182.

Tibetan art is seeing something of a renaissance and *thangka* shops seem to be all over Lhasa now, although many sell items of questionable quality produced over the border in Kathmandu. If quality and authenticity are important to you, it's worth heading into a shop where you can see the craftsmen at work, painting the tiny details onto the Tibetan scroll that is used for meditation. Prices can range from several dollars to several thousand. The **Tibet Thangka Art House** (Zang Yiyuan Lu 75; © 0891/671-5338 or 1364-898-2836; riverintibet@sina.com.cn) and the **Ancient Fine Art General Restoration Company** (© 0891/632-2860) at Caigang Road 11, opposite Dropenling (see below) are both recommended for *thangka*.

Dropenling *Finds*   Taking its name from a Tibetan word that means "giving back for the betterment of all mankind," this store, tucked away near the Muslim quarter of Lhasa, gives all its profits back to the Tibetan artisans who make the store's handicrafts in an attempt to help Tibetan artisans compete with the Nepalese, whose goods have flooded Tibetan markets in recent years. The emphasis here is on quality—from fine-woven rugs to handbags and jewelry, which also comes with a hefty price tag. The store's goods have inspired pirates to make knockoffs for sale on the pilgrim's circuit of Jokhang, but they aren't of the same quality.

Chak Tsal Gang Rd. 11 (just north of the Lhasa Mosque, about a 10-min. walk from Jokhang Monastery). © 0891/636-0558. www.tibetcraft.com. AE, DC, MC, V. 10am–6pm.

Jatson School (Caiquan Fuli Teshu Xuexiao) *Finds Kids*   By shopping here, you are helping Tibet's handicrafts tradition to survive, and giving poor, orphaned, and disabled children a shot at life. They don't receive a *fen* from the government, so your support is valued. Shopping doesn't have to be a guilty pleasure. The store, tucked away to the right of the entrance, sells traditional Tibetan clothing, paper, incense, mandala *thangkas,* yak-hide boots, dolls, door hangings, and more. Prices are more than fair, and you'll probably want to give more. The quality of work is astounding, and as nearly everything is made on-site, you can watch how it's done. Store hours are Monday through Saturday from 9:30am to 5:30pm.

Xue Xin Er Cun, 101 Xinxiang. (C) 0891/681-5382. www.jatson.tibet Bus: no. 97 to Xue Sancun; walk south, and the school is on the right-hand (west) side.

Khawachen Carpet and Wool Handicraft Co. Ltd (Kawajian Ditan He Yang-mao Gongyipin Youxian Gongsi) (Value

The hardy sheep of the Changtang produce wool that is ideal for carpet making. Unfortunately, most new Tibetan carpets or Han-inspired rugs use frightening themes or colors. This U.S.-Tibetan joint venture in the west of town gets it right: rich but tasteful shades woven into delightful traditional patterns. (See the designs at www.innerasiarugs.com.) You'll be able to pick them up a lot cheaper here than from the New York headquarters or the Lufthansa Center in Beijing. Carpets can be made to order; allow a week for an average-size carpet. You're free to inspect the entire process from dyeing and drying to weaving and cutting. Unlike Lhasa's main Han-run factory (where 14-hr. shifts are common), conditions here are excellent. A courtesy car to the factory is provided for visitors, credit cards are accepted, and shipping can be arranged. Hours are Monday to Saturday from 9am to 1pm and 3 to 7pm.

Jinzhu Xi Lu 103. (C) 0891/683-3257.

WHERE TO STAY

From December to March, Lhasa sees very few tourists, and most hoteliers halve their prices.

VERY EXPENSIVE

Lhasa Hotel (Lasa Fandian)

Situated in the Han part of town, north of the Norbulinka Palace, the former Holiday Inn Lhasa is no longer a well-run property. Although many well-trained staff remain, you run the risk of dying a slow death waiting for service. The enormous block-shaped hotel is disintegrating and most of the bathrooms could do with a refit. The Tibetan-style rooms are more appealing and tend to be heavily booked.

Minzu Lu 1. (C) 0891/683-2221. Fax 0891/683-5796. 455 units. ¥1,051 ($137/£68) standard room; from ¥2,120 ($276/£138) suite. Rates include breakfast. 20% discounts; 15% service charge. AE, DC, MC, V. **Amenities:** 5 restaurants; bar; cafe; health club; concierge; tour desk; business center; forex (9:30am–8:30pm); shopping arcade; room service; same-day laundry/dry cleaning. *In room:* A/C, satellite TV, hair dryer.

MODERATE

Dhod Gu Hotel

A Nepalese-owned venture, this hotel gets rave reviews from American tourists. It's conveniently located in the Tibetan quarter, the staff speaks English, and the rooms are very comfortable. Furnished with a sensory overload of tasteful Tibetan decorations, each room is uniquely designed, and some have views of the Potala, although lighting could be better. Bathrooms, though a bit worn, are squeaky-clean.

Xialasu Lu 19. (C) 0891/632-2555. Fax 0891/632-3555. www.dhodghuhotel.com. 61 units. ¥400 ($52/£26) single room; ¥520 ($68/£34) standard room; ¥600 ($78/£39) suite. AE, DC, MC, V. **Amenities:** 2 restaurants; bakery; business center; laundry service; doctor on call; safe deposit; forex. *In room:* A/C, satellite TV.

Kyichu Hotel (Jiqu Fandian)

Located in the Tibetan quarter, the Kyichu combines Western comfort with a welcoming Tibetan atmosphere. Rooms in the south wing opened in 2001. Overlooking an incongruous lawn with white outdoor furniture, these midsize rooms boast clean wooden floors, simple furnishings, and spotless bathrooms with deep tubs. Tourists rave about the excellent service here, saying that the staff members are the nicest people in all of Tibet. The solar-heated hot water can be unreliable. The restaurant on the first floor prepares a superb buffet breakfast for ¥30 ($3.90/£1.95).

Beijing Dong Lu 149. © 0891/633-1347. Fax 0891/633-5728. www.kyichuhotel.com. 52 units (22 with shower only). ¥480 ($62/£31) standard room. 25% discounts. AE, DC, MC, V. **Amenities:** Restaurant; bike rental; concierge; business center; same-day laundry. *In room:* TV.

Yak Hotel (Yake Binguan)   Popular with both tour groups and individual travelers, this hotel is several notches up from some of the decrepit guesthouses that line Beijing Dong Lu. Rooms are decorated with Tibetan furnishings and the bathrooms are very clean and showers are inviting. The Yak is considered a "hub" where tourists gather and share information. Next door is the ever-popular Dunya restaurant. The staff here is decent, though unwilling to give much of a discount as the place is often booked. Reserve ahead of time.

Beijing Dong Lu 100. © 0891/632-3496. 100 units. ¥550 ($72/£36) standard room. No credit cards. **Amenities:** Restaurant; travel agent; business center; same-day laundry. *In room:* A/C, TV.

INEXPENSIVE

Oh Dan Guesthouse (Oudan Binguan) ⭐ *(Finds*   Tucked away on a street that runs past Ramonche Monastery just north of Beijing Dong Lu, this guesthouse offers immaculately clean and fresh rooms and bathrooms. It's near enough to the Barkhor but its location on a typical Tibetan street is so far devoid of the trappings of backpacker development. The rooftop patio offers stunning view of Potala Palace.

Xiaozhao Si Lu 15. © 0891/634-4999. Fax 0891/636-3992. ohdan_guesthouse@yahoo.com. 40 units. ¥180 ($23/£12) standard room without bathroom; ¥288 ($37/£19) standard room with bathroom. Up to 50% discount. No credit cards. **Amenities:** Restaurant; travel agent; business center; laundry. *In room:* TV.

Pilgrimages Inn (Miaojixiang Luguan)   If you can put up with some atmospheric street noise (during the day only), then the Pilgrimages is one of the best budget bets in Lhasa. Just a few doors up from the Oh Dan, this new guesthouse offers clean and spacious (if bland) twins with bathrooms which front busy Ramonche Lam (Xiaozhao Si Lu) and smaller, quieter common rooms without bathrooms. The welcoming Taiwanese owner is a devout Buddhist and the staff is friendly and efficient.

Xiaozhao Si Lu. © 0891/634-1999. 26 units ¥80 ($10/£5.20) common room; ¥180–¥220 ($23–$29/£12–£14) standard room. 40% discount. No credit cards. *In room:* TV.

WHERE TO DINE

Lhasa's dining options are ever more diverse and present everything from excellent Tibetan to decent Chinese and good Western fare. If you can't face any of the above at 3,600m (11,808 ft.), there are even branches of the Chinese burger joint **Dicos,** one of which is opposite the Jokhang. For a fine cup of coffee or *chai* and a good cake selection while you surf the Net, **The Summit Cafe** has branches in the courtyard of the Shambala Hotel on Zang Yiyuan Lu and another opposite Niuwei on Linkuo Bei Lu.

Alu Cang Restaurant (A'luocang Canting) ⭐ TIBETAN   On the western edge of the Tibetan quarter, this restaurant is a longtime favorite with locals, who appreciate its unpretentious style and hearty cuisine. The second floor is packed at most hours. The English menu is unreliable, with beef and lamb often translated as yak.

Specialties include radish with yak meat (lamb) and fried mutton spareribs. The simple curry rice is an excellent choice for those on the run.

Duosenge Lu 21–32. © 0891/633-8826. Meal for 2 ¥30–¥70 ($3.90–$9.10/£1.95–£4.55). No credit cards. 9am–11pm.

Dunya Restaurant and Bar 🔑 WESTERN
Located on the east side of the Yak Hotel, Dunya serves decent if uninspired Western cuisine that's enhanced a lively atmosphere replete with happily singing staff. The menu offers pizza, pasta, and a range of Asian dishes, from Malaysian noodles to vegetable dumplings. If you've just landed in Lhasa, get the "altitude relax tea." Who knows if it actually works, but it tastes good. The convivial bar and terrace upstairs, open late, is a favorite with Lhasa's growing expat community, and the kitchen is supposedly one of the cleanest in town.

Beijing Dong Lu 100. © 0891/633-3374. www.dunyarestaurant.com. Reservations recommended. English menu. Main courses ¥12–¥45 ($1.55–$5.85/80p–£2.95). No credit cards. Apr–Oct only: 8am–10pm; bar open noon–2am.

Holy Land Vegetarian Restaurant 🔑🔑 *Finds* VEGETARIAN/SICHUAN
Not far from the dreaded PSB, this restaurant may be owned by a local monk, but the culinary delights within are far from frugal. Waitresses greet you with a light tea and a watermelon slice, and then the gluttony begins. Fake meats tend to creep some people out, but the wheat gluten and tofu replicas of chicken, sausage, and even intestines, are more delicious than the real thing. Try to *gongbao jiding* (kung pao chicken), *qingchao maodou* (beans with soy beef), *ganbian suchang* (soy pork slices with green pepper), *songren yumi* (pine nuts, carrots, and sweet corn), and the *chang xiangsi* (sliced soy-pork sausages). If you prefer less spicy dishes, let the kitchen know. The restaurant, simply decorated with wooden tables, is popular with health-conscious Tibetans.

Linkuo Bei Lu Waibanshang Pingfang 10. © 0891/636-3851. Meal for 2 ¥60–¥80 ($7.80–$10/£3.80–£5.20). No credit cards. 9am–10pm.

Mayke Ame (Maji A'mi) 🔑 NEPALI/TIBETAN
On the southeast corner of the Barkhor circuit stands Lhasa's most enchanting eatery, Makye Ame, which can be translated as Holy Mother. This may be the first Tibetan chain restaurant—they have two outlets in Beijing and another in Kunming. If it's chilly, take a seat on the second floor, with its comfy sofas and relaxing Tibetan folk music. On a sunny day, soak up the spectacle of the *kora* (circuit) from the third-floor balcony. The manners of the staff are strained by the Han clientele—the most popular Chinese guidebook lists one restaurant, and this is it. There are many excellent vegetarian choices, including spinach-tofu ravioli smothered in tomato basil sauce, and the vegetable curry set with chapati.

Bajiao Jie Dongnan Jiao. © 0891/632-8608. English menu. Main courses ¥15–¥35 ($1.90–$4.40/£85p–£2.20). No credit cards. 10am–11:30pm.

Naga Restaurant 🔑 TIBETAN/NEPALI/CONTINENTAL
This quiet and cozy Tibetan-owned restaurant offers a subtle environment to enjoy a variety of dishes from French ratatouille to Nepalese paneer curry. The ¥25 ($3.25/£1.65) breakfast of bacon, eggs, delicious damper bread, jam, and coffee is a tasty deal. Service can be lackadaisical; order a masala tea or a lassi while you wait for your food.

Beijing Dong Lu 11. © 0891/632-7509. puntso12@hotmail.com. English menu. Meal for 2 ¥50–¥100 ($6–$12/£3–£6). No credit cards. 8am–11pm.

Shancheng Ming Xiaochi 🔑 *Value* SICHUAN
Most of Lhasa's best Chinese restaurants are located in the gaudy bathroom-tiled part of town, but why make the effort when you can get delicious Sichuanese food right next to Barkhor Square? Popular with

Tibetan pilgrims and backpackers, this unassuming joint with stools and grubby tables serves spicy, juicy dumplings in soup and a good twice-cooked pork. The steamed buns with pork *(baozi)* deserve a special mention.

Zang Yiyuan Lu 9. ℂ 0891/671-1719. English menu. Meal for 2 ¥20 ($2.60/£1.30). No credit cards. 8am–11pm.

Snowland Restaurant ℱ INTERNATIONAL/TIBETAN Tibetan restaurant meets New York diner seems an unlikely combo, but Snowland manages to feel just like that and is frequented by Tibetan elites and international travelers alike. You're not going to get earth-shattering fare here, but the variety of options, from Japanese teriyaki to Indian curries, is at least decent if not pretty good. The Yak pepper steak, croquette-like potato momos, nan, dumplings, and crêpes suzette are all recommended.

Zang Yiyuan Lu (near Barkhor Sq.). ℂ 0891/633-7323. English menu. Meal for 2 ¥100 ($13/£6.50). No credit cards. 7:30am–10:30pm.

LHASA AFTER DARK
It's doubtful whether the tongue-in-cheek performance offered by the **Shangrila Restaurant (Xianggelila Zangshi)** inside the Kirey Hotel (ℂ **0891/636-3880**) qualifies as art, but it's certainly entertainment—and kids love it! The campy pantomime is held nearly every night, and without giving away too much, watch out for the yak! The restaurant is open from 7:30am to 10:30pm, and the performance starts at 8pm. Reservations are recommended from July to September. An excellent Tibetan buffet can be enjoyed for ¥50 ($6.50/£3.25).

The hottest *nangma* (Tibetan nightclub) around is **Niuwei** (Linkou Bei Lu 13; ℂ **0891/655-8383**), where booths of Tibetans down beers and groove to Tibetan singers that perform on a stage with a picture backdrop of Potala Palace; get here by 10pm to ensure good seats. There are new bars springing up all over Lhasa, but the best ones are to be found in the Tibetan quarter. The Dunya restaurant and bar (see above; open until 2am) is a hub for expats, and the surrounding streets hold plenty of smaller, more intimate bars.

AROUND LHASA
Ganden Monastery (Gandan Si) Shelled by the Chinese army during the peaceful liberation of Tibet and further damaged during the Cultural Revolution, the most significant monastery of the **Geluk School** is slowly undergoing a revival. Dramatically perched on a mountain east of Lhasa, to the south of the Kyi Chu, it was built in 1409 by **Tsongkapa**. Drawing on support from monks of the older schools, as well as laypeople, the school rapidly expanded, with disciples opening Drepung and Sera monasteries in 1416 and 1419 respectively. Mongol support during the 17th century eventually assured their status as the preeminent school of Tibetan Buddhism, and more than 3,000 monks lived here prior to 1950.

Food and lodging at Ganden are basic, and both are provided by the guesthouse to the left (west) of the parking lot. In front of this decaying two-story building, peddlers hawk yak butter and fragrant grass *(sang)* to pilgrims. The **Meditation Hall (Ngachokhang)** ℱ, to the right (east) of the path beyond the bus stop, is atmospheric. Tsongkapa instructed his first disciples here. Chanting and the creation of *torma* (butter sculptures) take place throughout the day. Inside, to the left, is one of several dark and gruesome protector deity shrines that are off-limits to women. Other notable buildings are the **Assembly Hall,** behind and to the right of a prominent white chorten, where a jolly monk is likely to thwack you on the head with the shoes and hat of Tsongkapa. On the opposite side of a courtyard is a printing house, and above it stands **Tsongkapa's Reliquary (Serdung Lhakang)**, which was devastated during the Cultural Revolution. Tsongkapa's tooth remains. Pilgrims waste little time in undertaking a spectacular *lingkhor* **(pilgrimage circuit)** ✿✿. The pilgrimage path commences from a tangle of *tar-choks* (prayer flags) to the left of the monastery. Allow at least an hour—you are above 4,000m (13,120 ft.). For the fit and acclimatized, the peak to the west offers spectacular views of the lush surrounding countryside.

ⓒ **0891/614-2077.** Admission ¥25 ($3.25/£1.65). Buses for Ganden depart from west of Barkor Sq. 6:30am and 7am (45km/28 miles; 2 hr.; ¥20/$2.50/£1.25 round-trip, ¥10/$1.25/65p one-way). Buses return at 3pm.

Samye Monastery (Sangye Si) ✿✿

About 39km (24 miles) west of Tsetang, on the northern banks of the **Yarlung Tsangpo (Brahmaputra River),** stands Tibet's first monastery (late 8th c.), famous for its striking mandala design and as the site of the "Great Debate" (792–94) between the Indian Mahayanists and Chan (Japanese: Zen) Buddhists from China. This intriguing and protracted religious debate, held in the **Western Temple (Jampa Ling),** ended in victory for the Mahayanists. A predictable result, as Tibet was at war with China on several fronts. Chinese records claim that they won the theological battle, but the numerous Chinese monks and translators were nonetheless expelled from Tibet, and Mahayanist orthodoxy was established. Although Samye has been razed several times, the mandala symmetry is intact. The main temple, **Samye Utse,** symbolizes Mount Meru, the center of the universe, surrounded by the four temples of the continents, the eight temples of each subcontinent, and the sun (south, ruined) and moon (north) temples. The best view is gained from **Hepo-Ri** to the east of Samye, where Padmasambhava (Guru Rinpoche) is said to have subdued the local demons, making the site safe for construction. The secular support of King Trisong Detsen, who proclaimed Buddhism the state religion in 779, was perhaps more crucial.

Samye Utse demonstrates the classic principles of Tibetan architecture. A solid barnlike first floor tapers to refined and intricate upper tiers. To left of the entrance is an original 5m-tall (16-ft.) obelisk that proclaims Buddhism to be the state religion and urges future generations to obey Buddhist law and support the temple. Many of the murals on the first and second floors are original, but the lighting is poor, so bring a flashlight.

Basic dorm beds are available at the **Samye Monastery Guesthouse** (ⓒ **0891/736-2086**) for ¥30 ($3.90/£1.95) and the **East Friendship Hotel** for ¥40 ($5.20/£2.60). English menus and adequate fare are offered at both.

Admission ¥45 ($5.85/£2.95). Buses for Samye depart from Barkhor Sq. at 6:30am, but at the time of writing foreigners required an ATP, driver, and guide to visit the monastery. Jeeps charge around ¥500 ($65/£33) for the trip if you have a permit. Daily 9am–6pm.

Chimpu Caves (Qingpu Shandong)

The Chimpu retreat caves gave monks relief from constant study, but were also crucial in maintaining Buddhist traditions during periods of persecution, and in transmitting teachings before formal monasteries were established.

A warren of caves set in a lush U-shaped valley, Chimpu boasts some of the most sacred pilgrimage destinations in Tibet, including the cave where Guru Rinpoche first instructed his Tibetan disciples. Below is **Guruta Rock,** where Guru Rinpoche displayed his yogic prowess by leaving an enormous footprint. Above and to the left is the **meditation cave of Vairocana,** where the master translator dwelt for 12 years, eating the naked rock and thus solving the twin dilemmas of food and shelter. Grains and beans are appreciated as gifts by less-gifted retreatants; to understand why, imagine subsisting on *tsampa* for a year. It is possible to camp here (far from PSB checkpoints), and there is a small store.

Northeast of Samye Monastery (which you'll need a permit to get to). Free admission. A truck (15km/9¼ miles; 1 hr.; ¥10/$1.30/65p) departs Samye Monastery Guesthouse about 8am, and returns early afternoon. The walk takes 4 hr.

A TRIP TO A NEARBY LAKE

Namtso Lake ✿✿ can be done as a 2- or 3-day trip, depending on how much peace and nature you want. The crystal-blue waters surrounded by snowcapped mountains are stunning and a nice change from the (relatively) bustling pace of Lhasa, although the lake's popularity has recently led to something of a building spree. You can visit Namtso as a 1-day bus trip through most agents in town for ¥120 ($16/£7.80), or for ¥150 ($20/£9.75), you can give the lake its due and stay overnight. Better still, rent a Land Cruiser for a night or two (¥1,500–¥2,000/$195–$260/£98–£130). Jeeps can take up to four travelers. It's a 4-hour journey from Lhasa, and at an altitude of 4,700m (15,416 ft.), you should definitely acclimatize in Lhasa for a few days before attempting the journey here. Admission to the lake is ¥80 ($10/£5.20); save your ticket, it may be checked during your stay.

You can stay in mock nomad tents at the lake for around ¥30 ($3.90/£1.95) or at the **Namucuo Kezhan** (📞 **0891/651-1390**), which offers basic dorm beds for ¥50 ($6.50/£3.25) each (credit cards not accepted). Rooms come in an array of sizes from standards to quads. By the time you get here there will probably be more options. The Namucuo Kezhan restaurant serves decent Sichuan fare, and basic meals are usually available at the tents.

7 Shigatse (Rikaze)

278km (172 miles) W of Lhasa, 91km (56 miles) NW of Gyantse. Altitude: 3,900m (12,792 ft.)

Set to the south of the confluence of the Brahmaputra River and the Nyang Chu, the second-largest town in Tibet is considerably smaller than Lhasa, its ancient rival for political power. For a period between the 16th and 17th centuries, **Shigatse** was the capital of Tibet, and even after the capital shifted to Lhasa, it maintained influence both as the center of the **Tsang region** and as the home of the **Panchen Lama,** who traditionally resides in **Tashilhunpo Monastery.** Unfortunately, Chinese-style development has taken over the town, and the extension of the train line to Shigatse, which is due for completion by 2009, will only obscure the small and touristy Tibetan quarter further. *Note:* For Chinese translations of selected establishments listed in this section, please turn to appendix A.

ESSENTIALS

GETTING THERE   At the time of writing permits and a guide were supposedly required for travel to anywhere in the TAR outside of Lhasa (see "Permit Purgatory," p. 780), Shigatse included. However, on my recent trip, it was easy enough to buy a bus ticket to Shigatse and if you don't intend to travel any farther, you may well get away without a permit or guide, but you will certainly need them beyond here. **Air** tickets may be purchased from the **CAAC** office inside the Bank of China on Zhufeng Lu (📞 **0892/882-4252**), open from 4 to 5pm.

For the time being, foreign travelers are unable to take buses onward from Shigatse; the following details are included in the hope that legislation will change in the future. The **bus station** is on Shanghai Lu (*©* **0892/882-2903**), just north of the Shigatse Hotel. Buses connect with Lhasa (4 hr.; ¥50/$6.50/£3.25) at 8am, 9:30am, and 10am and minibuses depart throughout the morning.

FAST FACTS

Banks, Foreign Exchange & ATMs   Cash and traveler's checks may be changed at counter 5 of the **Bank of China,** immediately south of the Shigatse Hotel, at Shanghai Lu 7. Credit card advances can also be made (open weekdays 9am–1pm and 3:30–6:30pm, weekends 10:30am–4:30pm).

Internet Access   *Avoid* China Telecom, with their WELCOME TO INTERNET sign. The welcome involves being fleeced. Continue north to **Guangsu Zaixian Wangba** at Shanghai Zhong Lu 41, where you'll pay the same price the locals do (¥4/50¢/25p per hour) and enjoy a cup of jasmine tea. Dial-up is *©* **165.**

Post Office   The main post office (open 9am–7pm) is at Zhufeng Xi Lu 12.

Visa Extensions   The **PSB** (*©* **0892/882-2056**) used to offer 1-month extensions a week before expiration (open 9am–1pm and 4–7pm summer; 10am–1pm and 3–6:30pm winter). Due to the recent tightening of restrictions on travel outside of Lhasa, the Shigatse office was issuing neither visa extensions nor travel permits. It is hoped this will have changed by the time you arrive—check in Lhasa before you leave.

EXPLORING SHIGATSE

When Tibetologist Guiseppe Tucci visited, he found the *dzong* (fortress) in the north of town (a model for the Potala) to be "huge and dreary," but he needn't have worried. A few years later, PLA artillery did a thorough job: It is difficult to discern any structures, and the *dzong* does not appear on Chinese maps. The ruins are honeycombed with secret tunnels, but killjoys have barred up most of these.

Tashilhunpo Monastery (Zhashilunbu Si)   This vast monastery of the **Geluk School** was established by the first Dalai Lama in 1447. The monastery gained standing when Panchen Lama IV, head abbot of Tashilhunpo and teacher of Dalai Lama V, was accepted as the personification of Amitabha Buddha, the Buddha of Longevity, thus becoming the "number two" lama in Tibet. The Mongols, Han, and British have exploited this division to good effect. Due to the size of the complex, start early in the morning, as all the temples are locked at midday. In the afternoon, you are more likely to enjoy chanting in the ancient **Assembly Hall (Dukhang).**

The pilgrimage circuit begins at **Jamkhang Chenmo,** at the west end of the complex, which houses a massive 26m (85-ft.) Maitreya (ca. 1914), a mass of gold around a wood and metal core. It was built by hand; around 900 artisans dedicated 4 years of their lives to it. But from an artistic perspective, Tashilhunpo is mediocre. As Tucci noted, "Everything was new and garish here. The collected composure of the primitives had been succeeded by baroque pomposity." Some composure remains in the gorgeous murals of Tsongkapa and his disciples that surround the reliquary stupa of Panchen Lama IV **(Kundung Lhakhang),** in the narrow cobblestone paths, and in the Assembly Hall, erected around an ancient sky-burial slab. The adjacent courtyard, with its striking flagpole, is the heart of the temple and the focus of religious dances.

Where Is the Panchen Lama?

In 1995, the world was stunned to learn that China's Marxist leaders were authorities on Tibetan Buddhism. Shortly after the Panchen Lama's death in 1989, then-premier Li Peng declared that "outsiders" would not be allowed "to meddle with the selection process." It was clear Beijing wanted to minimize the Dalai Lama's role in the selection of the child who will eventually become the teacher of the next Dalai Lama. The list of candidates was leaked to Dharamsala and the Dalai Lama announced his choice in May, catching the Chinese authorities by surprise. Predictably, the 6-year-old candidate disappeared a month later and has not been seen since. Gyaltsen Norbu, the "official" Panchen Lama XI, was chosen in a clandestine ceremony held in the **Jokhang** in November 1995, and recently made his first public appearance at **Tashilhunpo Monastery.** Tibet's religious leaders, with a few brave exceptions, recognize Gyaltsen as the Panchen Lama. But Beijing wasn't the only side playing politics with a young boy's life. As one of the few levelheaded commentators on this tragedy noted, "The two protagonists in the dispute were clearly swayed by their eagerness to use the issue to gain maximum propaganda value." Norbu's public appearance at the 2006 World Buddhist Forum in Hangzhou was intended to cement the puppet Panchen's status, and his short speech (to an international audience) focused on the need for ethnic Chinese unity and patriotism. Neither the Dalai Lama nor the Karmapa Lama were invited to the forum, and the location of the real Panchen Lama remains a mystery.

A small new museum has opened on the grounds of Tashilhunpo, but houses little more than a few black-and-white photos taken at the monastery and a small display of *thangkas* and costumes. Admission to the museum is ¥5 (65¢/35p).

Admission ¥55 ($7.15/£3.60). Summer Mon–Sat 9am–12:30pm and 3:30–6:30pm; winter Mon–Sat 10am–noon and 3–6pm.

SHOPPING

Shigatse bazaar stands in the shadow of the ruins, and aside from catering to the tourists, it has changed little. Khampa and Hui vendors hawk large knives, wooden tea bowls, prayer wheels, "bronze" statues, "ancient" coins, Tibetan medicine, incense from Calcutta, and cowboy hats and boots. The best-stocked supermarket is **Sifang Chaoshi** on Zhufeng Lu, open from 9am to 11pm.

WHERE TO STAY

Shenhu Jiudian (Hotel Manasarovar) ✦ Owned by the manager of the Yak Hotel, the Manasarovar is tidy and well run. Staff is well trained and foreigner-friendly. Simple and functionally furnished rooms have polished wooden floors and even sport potted plants. While the dormitories and communal showers are the cleanest in Tibet, the asking price is ludicrous. The breakfast and lunch buffets in the attached Nepali restaurant are recommended.

Qingdao Dong Lu 20. ⓒ **0892/883-2085.** Fax 0892/882-8111. www.hotelmanasarovartibet.com. 49 units (35 with bathroom). ¥340 ($44/£22) standard; ¥688 ($89/£45) suite. 40% discount. No credit cards. **Amenities:** 2 restaurants; cafe; nightclub; concierge; business center; same-day laundry/dry cleaning. *In room:* A/C, TV.

Tenzin Hotel (Dan Zeng Binguan) 𝕉 *Value*   This recently refurbished guesthouse offers some of the best standard rooms in town, for less than half the cost of rooms at the ugly three-star Chinese hotels. Rooms are nicely decorated with Tibetan furnishings and the bathrooms are very clean. Service is better than average. The only minor annoyance is the flies that buzz around in the hallways and some of the dorm rooms, which are popular with backpackers.

Bang Jia Ling 8. ⓒ **0892/882-2018.** Fax 0892/883-1565. 30 units. ¥35 ($4.55/£2.30) dorm bed; ¥180 ($23/£12) standard room with bathroom. No credit cards. **Amenities:** Restaurant; laundry. *In room:* TV.

Wuzi Dajiudian (Wutse Hotel)   Located in a quiet Tibetan residential area to the southeast, this three-star hotel, run by the owners of the Wutse Hotel in Gyantse, has recently renovated its spacious rooms. The bathrooms are immaculate, but the hot water takes a while to warm up. The competent, English-speaking staff works long hours.

Sichuan Nan Lu. ⓒ **0892/883-8666,** ext. 8888. 60 units. ¥280 ($36/£18) standard room; ¥750 ($98/£49) suite. 20% discounts. No credit cards. **Amenities:** Restaurant; bar; concierge; business center; same-day laundry. *In room:* TV, minibar.

WHERE TO DINE

Following FIT's lead, many restaurants in Shigatse, such as Shigatse Kitchen, have separate Chinese and English menus, with different prices.

Laoyou Leyuan 𝕉 *Value* NOODLES   Wedged in between furniture stores on the pedestrian street *(buxing jie)* that leads to the Tashilhunpo, this unassuming noodle shop run by a family from coastal Zhejiang province might be a bit hard to spot, but it's worth the effort. With little decor to speak of—just plastic blue-and-white chairs and tables that are nailed to the ground—and no menu, there's little to look at other than the food. But that seems to suit the diners just fine—just specify what you'd like from the three-dish menu: *mian tiao* (noodles with pork), *baozi* (steamed buns with pork), or *jiaozi* (dumplings in soup). Noodles and dumplings can be prepared spicy *(la)* or not *(bula)*, with vinegar *(cu)* or without *(buyao cu)*. We ordered all three of the items and our bill came to a whopping ¥10 ($1.25/60p)!

Buxing Jie. No phone. Meal for 2 ¥10 ($1.30/65p). No credit cards. 7am–11pm.

Yak Head Restaurant (Niutou Zangcan) TIBETAN   You'd think a picture menu would help in most restaurants, but in this restaurant's case, it does more to hinder the ordering process with its obscenely blurry photos tucked neatly into an album. But no worries, a plucky waitress will do her best to explain what each photo is in broken English. Try the potato dumplings, the *renshenguo* (fried ginseng), or if you're feeling particularly adventurous, the yak head for a mere ¥30 ($3.90/£1.95). The ambience can't be beat—a comfy outdoor patio beckons on warm afternoons, while the cramped and cozy main room feels like a living room for monks, who hang out and watch TV at all hours of the day.

Buxing Jie. ⓒ **0892/883-7186** or 1398/992-1574. Picture menu. Meal for 2 ¥30–¥60 ($3.90–$7.80/£1.95–£3.90). No credit cards. 8:30am–midnight.

Yalu Zang Canting 𝕉 TIBETAN/CHINESE   The dilemma that many travelers encounter when in Tibet is wanting to support Tibetan establishments, though the taste of tsampa and yak butter tea tends to drive them away. Yaluzang offers a happy solution: delicious Chinese food in a Tibetan-owned restaurant. Unfortunately, the Chinese dishes only appear on the Chinese menu, and the English menu is full of the standard backpacker fare. Ask for *chao bocai* (stir-fried spinach), *tieban niurou* (iron plate beef), *chao mianpian* (stir-fried noodle pieces), *qingjiao niurou* (green peppers and beef), and *gali tudou* (curry potatoes). The environment is traditional Tibetan, which means benches covered with wool carpets and low tables. Be patient with the slow service.

Shandong Lu. (℃) **0892/883-3638**. Meal for 2 ¥40 ($5.20/£2.60). No credit cards. 9am–midnight.

SHIGATSE AFTER DARK

If you haven't had a chance to hit a *nangma* yet in Tibet, Shigatse gives you an opportunity with **Huaiyu Minzu Biaoyi Zhongxin** (on Shanghai Lu just south of Zhufeng Lu; ℃ **1398/902-2888**). A lively performance with dancers dressed in yak costumes leaping on stage to techno-Tibetan music begins at 11pm and continues to the small hours.

8 Gyantse (Jiangzi) (★(★(★

67km (42 miles) SE of Shigatse, 255km (158 miles) SW of Lhasa. Altitude: 3,900m (11,700 ft.)

Presided over by the spectacular **Gyantse Dzong**, and once the third-largest town in Tibet, **Gyantse** is the only substantial settlement in the TAR to retain its vernacular architecture of sturdy two- and three-story farmhouses. Offering a rare and beautiful glimpse of Tibetan rural life, Gyantse should not be missed by any visitor to the TAR. Historically, it was a trading town for goods from Nepal, Sikkim, and Bhutan, and the closure of the border at Dromo (Yadong) has saved Gyantse from the ravages of development and Han colonization. Most members of Tibet's current generation of political leaders hail from Gyantse.

ESSENTIALS

GETTING THERE   At the time of writing, the only way for foreigners to get to Gyantse was in a private vehicle with a guide. The journey from Lhasa takes about 6 hours; from Shigatse, the journey is 2 hours.

FAST FACTS

Banks, Foreign Exchange & ATMs   None available.

Internet Access   The fastest connection is at the **Dashijie Wangba** (℃ **0892/898-2258**). Located next to the Gyantse Hotel, they're open from 9:30am to midnight and charge ¥5 (65¢/35p) per hour. Dial-up is ℃ **165.**

Post Office   The main post office (open 9am–12:30pm and 3:30–7pm) is a few minutes' walk east of the main intersection on the corner of Weiguo Lu and Jianghong Lu.

Visitor Information   The tourism bureau's complaint number is ℃ **0892/899-6667** or 1390/892-2542.

EXPLORING GYANTSE

Gyantse Dzong (Jiangzi Zong Shan)   Towering above the settlement, this awesome fortress (ca. 13th c.) immediately catches your eye as you approach Gyantse. It's a stiff hike up, but views of Pelkhor Choede, the ancient alleyways, and the jagged surrounding peaks are breathtaking. The **Hall of Anti-British** provides entertainment for fans of the Chinese practice of "using the past to serve the present." Pick your favorite saying, though it's hard to beat "They [the British] tried to occupy the fertile land of Tibet" (so why did they leave?). Another says that the Tibetan troops were fighting for the unity of the [Chinese] motherland, of which "Tibet has always been an inseparable part." The Tibetans drove disunited Chinese forces out of Tibet less than 10 years later, and the Seventeen-Point Agreement signed in 1951 provides recognition that Tibet had strayed from the fold of the motherland. Beyond the crude propaganda, a photo of Tibetan soldiers clasping spears and clad in medieval armor shows why they were butchered by the poorly conceived Younghusband expedition. Next is an exhibit of the torture methods of "Old Tibet," said to include tearing out a man's intestines and forcing him to eat them. In New Tibet, more sophisticated methods, such as the electric baton, are preferred.

Admission ¥35 ($4.55/£2.30). 9am–5:30pm. Closed Nov–Mar.

Pelkhor Choede (Baiju Si) The once-mighty temple complex of Gyantse (ca. 1418) used to house several different orders under the one roof. While restoration is ongoing, only the **main temple,** a huge *thangka* **wall,** and **Gyantse Kumbum** stand intact. Many of the chapels in the main temple are locked; if you persist, one of the 30 remaining monks may open them. The different orders bequeathed different artistic styles, shown in the chapels of the second floor. To the right (east) is the bizarre **Neten Lhakhang,** decorated in Chinese style with leaping tigers and dragons, floating clouds, and pagodas, representing Manjusri's Pure Land in Wutai Shan.

The nine-story **Kumbum** 𝕬𝕬𝕬, the largest chorten in Tibet, towers to a height of 42m (140 ft.). The first five floors are four-sided, while the upper floors are circular, forming a huge three-dimensional mandala. Kumbum means "the hundred thousand images," and while the actual number of Buddhist images is around one-third of that estimate, even the most dedicated pilgrim won't have time to properly inspect all the chapels. They house the finest art preserved in Tibet. Vibrant color and a lively, naturalistic style characterize the murals, while the broad faces of the statues point to Chinese influence. The mandalas of the upper levels are exquisite, though an extra fee may be required to gain access to the seventh through ninth floors. Bring a flashlight.

Admission ¥30 ($3.90/£1.95). Photography ¥10 ($1.30/65p). 10am–1pm and 3–7pm.

SHOPPING

Gyantse is famous for its carpets. **The Carpet Factory** (© 0892/817-2004; open Mon–Sat, 9am–1pm and 3–7:30pm) is tucked away on the north side of Gyantse Dzong. The sales room is to the left of the entrance, but garish designs are prevalent. Near the factory, many people weave at home; you may be treated to a cup of sweet tea and a quick exhibition.

WHERE TO STAY

Look for rooms away from the road; mangy curs and nervous Han soldiers bark through the night. Discounts of 50% are negotiable, and prices seem to have come down in the past few years.

Jian Zang Fandian Just south of the Wutse Hotel, this small, orderly guesthouse was recently opened by a genial Tibetan doctor, Jian Zang. His pharmacy still operates north of the hostel. Rooms are well lit and the beds are comfortable, but bathrooms are showing signs of decay. The dorms here are popular with backpackers, and additional dormitories and single rooms should be available when you arrive.

Yingxiong Lu. © **0892/817-2324.** Fax 0892/817-3910. 17 units. ¥40 ($5.20/£2.60) dorm bed; ¥150 ($20/£9.75) twin. No credit cards. **Amenities:** Restaurant; TV; next-day laundry. *In room:* TV.

Jiangzi Binguan (Gyantse Hotel) ⚑ This hotel offers Gyantse's best accommodations, though the competition in the town isn't that stiff. You have your choice of three-star Western-style or Tibetan rooms. Opt for the Tibetan one if you'd like more character; they're outfitted with colorful furniture and *thangkas* on the walls. The one drawback is that the beds in the Tibetan rooms aren't as comfortable as those in the Western rooms. Bathrooms in either style are shiny and welcoming and include amenities like a hair dryer and a magnifying mirror, which you won't find elsewhere in town.

Yingxiong Nan Lu 8. © **0892/817-2222.** Fax 0892/817-2366. 106 units. ¥460 ($60/£30) twin. 30% discounts possible. AE, DC, MC, V. **Amenities:** 2 restaurants; cafe; fitness center; bike rental; business center; salon; massage; doctor's clinic. *In room:* Satellite TV, hair dryer.

Wuzi Fandian (Wutse Hotel) Just south of the main intersection, this guesthouse has the feel of a Motel 6 (evidenced in the balconies), but is a notch up in terms of comfort from Jian Zang's rooms. Rooms were recently renovated and bathrooms feature 24-hour hot water. The restaurant on the first floor serves decent banana pancakes and masala tea. A buffet dinner is served nightly.

Yingxiong Nan Lu 8. © **0892/817-2888.** Fax 0892/817-2880. wutse_deji888@yahoo.com.cn. 48 units (40 with bathroom). ¥40 ($5.20/£2.60) dorm bed; ¥210 ($27/£14) standard room. No credit cards. **Amenities:** Restaurant; next-day laundry. *In room:* TV, hair dryer.

WHERE TO DINE

Tashi's (Zhaxi Zangcan) ⚑ NEPALI/WESTERN Located on the northwest side of the main intersection, at the foot of Gyantse Dzong, this is the final outpost of a Tibetan restaurant chain based in Lhasa. If the restaurant is quiet, ask the chef to show off and prepare something off the menu. Chicken Whitehouse, crumbed chicken breast stuffed with lamb mince, mushroom, ginger, and garlic, is his specialty. On the menu, the filling chicken curry set, creamy dal, and fresh flavored lassi are recommended.

Baiju Lu. © **0892/882-7512.** Meal for 2 ¥50–¥130 ($6.50–$17/£3.25–8.45). No credit cards. 7am–11pm. Closed Nov 20–Mar 1.

Zhuang Yuan Restaurant ⚑ CHINESE Originally from Sichuan, Mr. Zhuang is one of the few restaurateurs in all of Tibet that gets the importance of customer service. He and his brother greeted us with an unpushy "hello" and beckoned us with a smile; they further tempted us with a look inside their fridge, stocked with fresh veggies. The food is not particularly authentic or stunning (one of his best-selling dishes is sweet-and-sour chicken, though, and the owner will invite you into the kitchen to watch flames shoot high into the air), and prices are aimed at foreigners. But Mr. Zhuang's congeniality and fresh manners won us over anyway.

Yingxiong Nan Lu. © **1367/802-0792.** Meal for 2 ¥80 ($10/£5.20). No credit cards. 7am–11pm.

9 Sakya (Sajia)

150km (93 miles) SW of Shigatse, 55km (34 miles) SE of Lhatse. Altitude: 4,200m (13,776 ft.)

This remote Tibetan township boasts one of the most magnificent and best-preserved monasteries in the TAR, and is the home of the **Sakya** school of Buddhism. Founded by Konchok Gyalpo in 1073, it is similar to the Kagyu order in being heavily influenced by Indian Tantric Buddhism, but it differs in that its lineage is hereditary, passed down through the **Khon family.** In 1247, Kodan Khan offered the head lama, Sakya Pandita, absolute power to rule over Tibet, in exchange for submission to Mongol rule. Mindful of the fate of the Xixia Kingdom to the north of Tibet, annihilated 20 years previously by the hordes of Genghis Khan, Sakya Pandita readily agreed. At this point, theocratic rule in Tibet was born, and the concept of "priest and patron," used to this day to justify Chinese rule in Tibet, was developed. Marco Polo noted that the magical powers of the Sakya lamas were highly regarded, and it is said they won over Kublai Khan when they triumphed in a battle of supernatural powers with Daoists and Nestorian Christians. You wonder what Sakyamuni would have made of this. He once reprimanded a follower who levitated above a crowd, likening him to a prostitute showing herself for a few coins. While the influence of Sakya faded with the Mongols, they produced stunning religious paintings during the 15th and 16th centuries, and the monastery houses some remarkable statuary.

GETTING THERE   Land Cruisers make the trip from Lhatse, 50km (31 miles) away, in 1½ hours; a trip from Shigatse, 130km (81 miles) away, takes 4 hours.

GETTING AROUND   There are no street addresses in the simple two-street town of Sakya, but everything is easy enough to locate.

A 13TH-CENTURY MONASTERY

Sakya Monastery (Sajia Si) ☆☆   The massive 35m (115-ft.) windowless gray walls of **Lhakhang Chenmo** tower above the village and fields on the southern bank of the Trum Chu. Completed in 1274, this monastery fort was largely funded by Kublai Khan, and unlike the older temples of north Sakya, it survived the Cultural Revolution. Little was left standing on the north side of the river, although a **nunnery** to the northeast is being revived.

Unlike the rich and confusing pantheon seen in most Geluk temples, most images in the **Assembly Hall (Dukhang)** ☆☆ are of the historical Buddha, Sakyamuni. You'll need a flashlight to see the exquisite statuary and murals. Look for a striking 11th-century image of the **"speaking" Buddha,** third from the left on the back wall, with its cheeky grin. Other great works include an image of the bodhisattva **Manjushri,** second from the right on the back wall, leaning gently to one side, suggesting a sympathetic ear to believers. Walk around the monastery's walls, which offer fantastic views of the surrounding areas. Only 170 monks remain, but they're a young, friendly bunch. They may show you the monastery's greatest treasure—a white **conch shell,** said to have housed a very early incarnation of Sakyamuni. Mountains of white *kata* (silk cloths) give away its location. Just south of the monastery stands a modern-looking museum that is still awaiting its collection—ask at the monastery for the latest.

ⓒ 0892/884-2428. Admission ¥55 ($7.15/£3.60). 8am–4pm.

WHERE TO STAY

Sakya Family Hotel (Luwa Sajia Binguan)   Run by a friendly Tibetan family, this cozy guesthouse has great atmosphere and nice budget rooms. A labyrinth of hallways will lead to the family's living room, where they'll invite you for a cup of tea. Toilets are of the pit kind and there are no showers, but if you can do without the amenities, choose this place over the Sakya Manasarovar Hotel and the rest of the shabby guesthouses in town.

ⓒ 0892/890-4555. 20 beds. ¥40 ($5.20/£2.60) dorm bed; ¥150 ($20/£9.75) standard room (just 1 in the guesthouse). No credit cards. *In room:* TV, no phone.

Sakya Manasarovar Hotel (Shenhu Sajia Binguan) As you push out farther into the hinterlands of Tibet, modern amenities like hot water and flush toilets become harder to find. This hotel has the illusion of having those things, but bad plumbing means that the toilets give off a stench that wafts into all areas of the high-ceilinged floors; the solar heating system means that hot water is only available in day-light, when it's sunny. Still, if you're after such amenities, this is your best option in town. Rooms are new, beds are comfortable, and if you keep your door closed, you'll be saved from the smell of septic tanks. For the budget conscious, there are several dorm rooms; the fewer beds in the room the more they cost. The restaurant serves decent Nepalese food, including nan and chicken tikka masala.

Ⓒ 0892/824-2222. 30 units. ¥25 ($3/£1.50) dorm bed without bathroom; ¥20–¥40 ($2.60–$5.20/£1.30–£2.60) dorm bed; ¥180 ($23/£12) standard room. No credit cards. **Amenities:** Restaurant. *In room:* TV, no phone.

WHERE TO DINE

The **Sakya Manasarovar Hotel** and the **Sakya Monastery Restaurant** serve decent cuisine. For Sichuanese, go to **Gaoyuan Chuancai,** 1 block south and east of the Sakya Monastery Guesthouse (Ⓒ **0892/824-2479;** meal for two ¥30–¥60/$3.90–$7.80/£1.95–£3.90; 8am–10pm). Dishes to try include *mapo doufu* (spicy tofu with chopped meat), *yuxiang qiezi* (literally "fish-flavored" eggplant, although there's no fish in the dish), and *gongbao jiding* (spicy chicken with cashews).

10 Lhatse (Lazi)

148km (92 miles) W of Shigatse, 325km (202 miles) NE of Zhangmu. Altitude: 4,000m (13,120 ft.)

Stretching for 1.6km (1 mile) along the Friendship Highway, **Lhatse** is the jumping-off point for trips to **Mount Kailash** (p. 804) and **Ali,** or it can be an overnight stop between Lhasa and the Nepali border.

ESSENTIALS

GETTING THERE   Traveling by Land Cruiser, the journey from Shigatse (80km/ 50 miles away) should take about 3 hours—if the road conditions are normal, that is. The journey to Pelbar, 90km (56 miles) away, also takes about 3 hours.

FAST FACTS

Banks, Foreign Exchange & ATMs   None available.

Internet Access   Sitong Wangba (Ⓒ 0892/832-3528 or 0/1364-892-4982), on the main drag, charges ¥5 (65¢/35p) per hour for a good connection. It's open from 11am until midnight. Dial-up is Ⓒ **165.**

Post Office   The post office is located east of the intersection, on the south side.

WHERE TO STAY

If you're staying at a hotel without running hot water (read: no showers), Da Shang-hai Yushi (Ⓒ 0892/832-2868), north of the intersection, will let you take a hot shower for ¥10 ($1.30/65p).

Lazi Binguan (Lazi Hotel)   This is one of the nicer accommodations in Lhatse, which really isn't saying much. Rooms are clean enough, but there's only a common pit toilet (like everywhere else in Lhatse) and no showers. A restaurant called Tashi 2, which has no relation to the other Tashi restaurants in Tibet, adjoins the hotel; you can get decent backpacker fare and Chinese food here.

No formal address. ⓒ **0892/832-2208.** 14 units (no bathroom). ¥25 ($3.25/£1.65) dorm room; ¥80 ($10/£5.20) single or standard room; ¥150 ($20/£9.75) triple room. No credit cards. *In room:* TV, no phone.

Nongmin Yule Luguan (Tibetan Farmer's Adventure Hotel)   A 5-minute walk east of the main intersection on the north side of the highway, this Tibetan-run place is fly-infested and a little grubby, but still manages to offer a decent atmosphere. Set around a sunny courtyard, this hotel offers your last shot at a warm shower if you are bound for the Kailash region. The restaurant serves decent yak-fried noodles and other simple dishes.

Zhongni Lu 8. ⓒ **0892/832-2333.** 38 units (with shared bathroom). ¥20–¥45 ($2.60–$5.85/£1.30–£2.95) dorm bed. No credit cards. **Amenities:** Restaurant; bike rental; limited room service. *In room:* TV, no phone.

WHERE TO DINE

For Chinese food, try **Yuechuan Caiguan** (no formal address; ⓒ **0892/832-2929;** May–Oct 7:30am–11:30pm), which offers Cantonese specialties like vermicelli clay pot *(zacha fensi bao),* beef-fried rice *(niurou chaofan),* and salty chicken *(chiyou ji).* The Tibetan Farmer's guesthouse does decent fried noodles with yak meat.

11 Pelbar (Dingri)

228km (141 miles) SW of Shigatse, 255km (158 miles) NE of Zhangmu. Altitude: 4,000m (13,120 ft.)

Confusingly, there are three towns known as **Dingri.** The county capital town of **Shelkar,** 7km (4⅓ miles) farther west from **Pelbar (Dingri),** is referred to as **Xin Dingri (New Tingri). Tingri,** the other base for treks in the Everest region, 60km (37 miles) farther west, is called **Lao Dingri (Old Tingri).** Other than dodging children peddling mollusks and demanding pens—will the idiots who give them away *please* do something more useful with their consciences and money?—there is little of interest in Pelbar. Pick up your permit for the **Qomolangma Nature Reserve** (see "Everest Trekking," p. 803) at the Qomolangma Service Center, on your right, set off the road, just after the turnoff.

GETTING THERE   By Land Cruiser, the journey from Shigatse takes around 6 hours. On the 3-hour drive from Lhatse to Dingri, you'll drive past the Gyantsola Pass at 5,200m (17,056 ft.), a great place for your first view of the Himalayas.

VISITOR INFORMATION   The **Qomolangma Service Center** offers information, permits, and superclean restrooms round-the-clock.

WHERE TO STAY & DINE

Xueyu Fandian (Snowlands Hotel)   Located at the turnoff to Shelkar, this is the best of several grimy budget options. Unadorned and relatively clean rooms are set around a sun-drenched courtyard, but the pit toilets are diabolical. The cozy attached restaurant has an English menu, and the staff is incredibly gracious and helpful.

ⓒ **0892/826-2848.** 15 units. ¥30 ($3.90/£1.95) dorm bed; ¥100 ($13/£6.50) standard room. No credit cards. **Amenities:** Restaurant. *In room:* No phone.

Zhufeng Zonghe Fuwu Zhongxin (Qomolangma Service Center) *Value*   Set off the road on your right, just after the turnoff, the service center, where you get your permit for the nature reserve, offers the best-priced rooms in town. Get a suite here, which is a bargain, and you'll be relaxing in a room with a lounge, two beds, and a mahjong table. The standard rooms are much smaller and only a tiny bit less in price.

Bathrooms (private ones!) are clean and have flush toilets, something you won't take for granted after spending time in Tibet.

Ⓒ **0892/826-2833.** 30 units. ¥100 ($13/£6.50) standard room; ¥150 ($20/£9.75) triple. No credit cards. **Amenities:** Restaurant; bar; business center.

12 Tingri (Lao Dingri)

289km (179 miles) SW of Shigatse, 184km (114 miles) NE of Zhangmu. Altitude: 4,300m (14,104 ft.)

An impoverished settlement with a breathtaking view of the world's highest peaks, **Tingri** is the favored starting point for those wishing to walk to **Everest Base Camp,** and a common overnight stop between Kathmandu and Lhasa. A row of white-tiled houses and shops to the west of town represents the Han section of the settlement. Magnificent views of Everest may be gained from the ruins of the late-18th-century **Tingri Dzong,** spread across a hill south of town.

WHERE TO STAY & DINE

Be forewarned: All the guesthouses in town are dumps and look like truck stops, so bringing a sleeping bag to put over your bed is highly recommended and keep your expectations low on the cleanliness, plumbing, and electricity fronts. The honest and shabby **Lhasa Fandian (Lhasa Hotel;** Ⓒ **0892/826-2703)** has grubby dorm rooms (¥10/$1.30/65p) but very friendly staff, and much-needed hot showers are available

---

Everest Trekking

The trek out to **Everest Base Camp** follows two main routes—from **Pelbar** via the wretchedly poor village of Chay, and from **Tingri** via Lungjiang. The former route (113km/70 miles) is usually traveled by 4WD in 3 hours along a much-improved road. The latter is a tough 3- to 4-day journey, and the path is hard to follow in places. Gary McCue's *Trekking in Tibet* is a reliable guide for this route and for other hikes in the Qomolangma Nature Preserve. At ¥400 ($52/£26) per jeep plus another ¥180 ($23/£11) per person, the permit price matches the steepness of the mountain. Permits can be purchased at Pelbar, Tingri, or Chay. Accommodations are available in tents at **Base Camp** (¥25/$3.25/£1.65) at an elevation of 5,150m (16,890 ft.). The "real" Base Camp with real expeditions and mountaineers is a couple of kilometers farther on. There are also basic rooms at **Rongbuk Monastery** (¥40/$5.20/£2.60) and a new guesthouse right next door (¥40–¥60/$5.20–$7.80/£2.60–£3.90), both of which lie at an elevation of 4,980m (16,330 ft.).

The height of Mount Everest was recently fixed at 8,846m (29,015 ft.), somewhat lower than first believed, and a fact which some experts are blaming on global warming and the mountain's shrinking icecap. However, a few yards is invisible to the naked eye and on a clear day it presents an astounding vista, particularly from Pang La and Lamma La. Insistence on the use of Qomolangma (Zhumulangma) rather than Mount Everest to label the world's highest peak would have pleased Sir George Everest, who staunchly believed in using local place-names.

Wild China: Mount Kailash & Lake Manasarovar

Worshiped by the followers of no less than four religions—Tibetan Buddhists, Bonpos, Hindus, and Jains—**Mount Kailash (Gangdise)** draws pilgrims from the Tibetan world and beyond. For Tibetan Buddhists, it is Mount Meru, the center of the universe, and many aim to circumambulate the mountain 108 times, thus attaining Buddhahood in this lifetime. For Hindu pilgrims, who are allowed to cross the border at **Purang (Pulan)**, it is the abode of Shiva, one of the three supreme gods. The beauty of the 6,714m (22,028-ft.) peak, jutting up from the surrounding arid plain, is astounding, and the sight of **Lake Manasarovar** under a full moon is enough to have even the most cynical visitor believing in supernatural possibilities.

The **Saka Dawa Festival,** the traditional pilgrimage holiday held from late May to early June, is the most spectacular time to visit, but access (even for prebooked tours) is often restricted during this festival. Regardless, try to time your visit to coincide with the full moon.

To reach Kailash, Western visitors need a guide, vehicle, driver, and a military permit (¥100/$13/£6.50, which will be arranged by the agency). Short tours, from either Lhasa or Kathmandu, last 14 days and cost around ¥15,000 ($1,950/£975). More extensive tours of the region run for 21 days and cost about ¥17,000 ($2,210/£1,105). Costs can be split between four travelers. Check out the FIT branches at the Banak Shol (© 0891/634-4397) or the Snowlands Guesthouse (© 0891/632-3687) in Lhasa. Beyond Zhongba, the road is in poor shape. Inspect your vehicle before you leave. The trip is not feasible from November to mid-April.

Accommodations along the route are usually ¥30 ($3.90/£1.95) per bed. Even basic amenities, such as hot showers, are usually unavailable. Dishes at restaurants tend to cost more than they would in Lhasa, so figure that you'll spend around ¥80 ($10/£5.20) per day on food, unless you're okay with instant noodles.

The traditional gateway to the mountain is the village of **Darchen (Dajin),** which sits on the southern edge of the pilgrimage circuit, although you can't see the mountain from here. Admission to the Kailash area is ¥100 ($13/£6.50), collected at a checkpoint at the entrance to town. Foreigners must register with the PSB in Darchen upon arrival. Accommodations range

for the same price as a bed. **The Xuebao Fandian (Everest Snow Leopard Hotel;** © 0892/826-2775) offers the best accommodations in town, but the price is expensive (¥40/$5.20/£2.60 dorm bed, ¥200/$26/£13 standard room), compared to other local guesthouses, and the service staff is indifferent. Hot water in the clean showers allegedly runs 24 hours. For those en route to Everest Base Camp, you can get your permit for the Qomolangma Nature Reserve here. The **Amdo Restaurant,** located on the north side of the road in the middle of town, is popular with locals and has an English-language menu.

in price from ¥25 ($3.25/£1.65) to ¥80 ($10/£5.20) for a dorm bed, and popular places include the Yak Hotel and the Darchen Guesthouse. At the **Gangdisi Binguan** private standard rooms and triples with decent bathrooms go for ¥240 ($31/£16) and ¥300 ($39/£20) respectively. Some travelers have attempted to camp in the courtyard of some hotels, but they often wake up covered with human feces and broken glass. The nearest bearable site to camp is a 1½-hour walk on the kora at Darpoche (marked with a flagpole). Outside the eastern entrance of the Gangdisi Binguan is the **Lhasa Restaurant**, run by a charming retired teacher from Tsetang.

Most people take 3 days to complete the 53km (33-mile) circuit. Buddhists undertake the journey in a clockwise direction, while a handful of Bonpos walk counterclockwise. Stick with the majority. Do *not* count on finding accommodations in monasteries along the route—bring a tent! Waterproof hiking boots (or a change of shoes) are a must, as there are numerous small river crossings. Bring all the food you think you'll need, as you'll only find instant noodles and a few other snacks for sale on the circuit. Even if you intend to hire a yak and driver at ¥150 ($20/£9.75) per day, you should be very fit, as the trek is above 4,500m (14,760 ft.), rising to over 5,600m (18,370 ft.) on the second day.

Hor Qu (Huo'er Qu), 39km (24 miles) southeast of Darchen, is the most common jumping-off point for **Lake Manasarovar** (4,560m/14,957 ft.). Here you can enjoy unparalleled views of the Himalayas across turquoise waters which freeze over in winter, visit monasteries carved from the naked rock of the lakeshore, and even attempt the 90km (56-mile) circuit of the lake. **Chiu Gompa**, 35km (22 miles) south of Darchen and 8km (5 miles) south of the main road, has a few unmarked guesthouses that will rent you a bed for ¥40 ($5.20/£2.60). A wash in the bathhouse that has unlimited hot-springs water costs ¥20 ($2.60/£1.30). Entrance to the Chiu Monastery is free, and its setting, on a crag facing Lake Manasarovar, is the perfect place to relax and enjoy the view. If you go to Chiu Gompa, bring food from Darchen or Hor Qu. The **Indian Pilgrims Resthouse** by the lakeshore, where you can spend the night for ¥100 ($13/£6.50), serves a few minimal dishes like egg-fried rice.

13 Zhangmu (Dram)

473km (293 miles) SW of Shigatse. Altitude: 1,900m (6,232 ft.)

The Friendship Highway drops 1,400m (4,600 ft.) during the treacherous 30km (19 miles) of road between **Nyalam** and the border town of **Zhangmu**. The arid Tibetan plateau gives way to lush greenery and deliciously damp air. Nepalis complain about the cold, but you'll be shedding layers if you've arrived from Lhasa. A tiny collection of wooden houses before the border opened in 1980, Zhangmu is now one of the wealthiest towns in Tibet, due to licit and illicit trade in gold, clothing, and footwear.

Zhangmu stretches for several miles through a series of switchbacks toward the border. Buildings are referred to in this section as though you are facing downhill.

ESSENTIALS

GETTING THERE   In a Land Cruiser, the drive from Tingri to Zhangmu, 180km (112 miles), takes about 6 hours. At present, arriving overland from Nepal involves arranging a "group visa" of 15 to 20 days through a travel agency in Kathmandu. Once in Lhasa you're not obliged to stay with the group, and can extend the visa elsewhere in China.

The border is open from 9:30am to 6:30pm on the Chinese side, and from 10am to 6pm on the Nepali side, with a time difference of 2¼ hours. If you've hired a vehicle from Lhasa, many of the drivers are not allowed to take you the extra 8km (5 miles) to Nepali Customs, but taxis wait beyond the immigration building and the price is cheap (¥10/$1.30/65p per person).

GETTING AROUND   Taxis are ¥10 ($1.30/65p).

FAST FACTS

Banks, Foreign Exchange & ATMs   The **Bank of China** (open Mon–Sat 9:30am–1pm and 3–6:30pm) is toward the top of the hill on the right-hand side. They accept traveler's checks, but not credit cards. There is no ATM.

Internet Access   The **Zhangmu Wangba** (© 0892/874-2492), on the right-hand side, just down from the Premchi Guesthouse, charges ¥5 (65¢/35p) per hour. It's open from 10am to 11pm. Dial-up is © 165.

Post Office   The main post office (open weekdays 10am–1pm and 3:30–6pm; weekends 10:30am–12:30pm) is located on the left-hand side at the top of town. A more convenient branch is located just up from the Gangyen Hotel.

Visa Extensions   On the left-hand side, just up from the border, the **PSB** (© 0892/874-2264 or 0892/882-2241; open 9am–6pm) is located on the third floor of a wooden building. Knock loudly to rouse them. As the border is in sight, you're unlikely to need to extend your visa and, at present, you're unable to enter from Nepal overland without joining a tour group.

WHERE TO STAY & DINE

The best choice in town is the recently renovated, two-star **Zhangmu Binguan** (© 0892/874-2221), located on the right-hand side just before the border. It's got clean bathrooms (with hot water 9:30–11:30pm) and two restaurants. Rooms go for ¥380 to ¥400 ($49–$52/£25–£26). Foreign visitors are also drawn to the **Gangyen Hotel**, opposite the Zhangmu Binguan at Duo er Ji Gang Lin 280 (**Gangjian Binguan;** © 0892/874-2323; ¥150/$20/£9.75 standard room without bathroom, ¥300/$39/£20 standard room with bathroom). The lower floors are a little damp, so ask for a room on the sixth floor—these are brighter and have large windows. The **Himalaya Restaurant,** near Zhangmu Binguan (© 0892/874-3068), is pricey, but a nice place to relax before and after a trip to Nepal. The fresh yogurt and fried noodles with yak meat were delicious. The owners also offer decent exchange for Chinese yuan, Nepalese rupees, and American dollars. A meal for two is about ¥80 to ¥100 ($10–$13/£5.20–£6.50).

Appendix A:
The Chinese Language

Chinese is not as difficult a language to learn as it may first appear to be—at least not once you've decided what kind of Chinese to learn. There are six major languages called Chinese. Speakers of each are unintelligible to speakers of the others, and there are, in addition, a host of dialects. The Chinese you are likely to hear spoken in your local Chinatown, in your local Chinese restaurant, or used by your friends of Chinese descent when they speak to their parents, is more than likely to be Cantonese, which is the version of Chinese used in Hong Kong and in much of southern China. But the official national language of China is **Mandarin** (**Pǔtōnghuà**—"common speech"), sometimes called Modern Standard Chinese, and viewed in mainland China as the language of administration, of the classics, and of the educated. While throughout much of mainland China people speak their own local flavor of Chinese for everyday communication, they've all been educated in Mandarin, which in general terms is the language of Beijing and the north. Mandarin is less well known in Hong Kong and Macau, but is also spoken in Taiwan and Singapore, and among growing communities of recent immigrants to North America and Europe.

Chinese grammar is considerably more straightforward than that of English or other European languages, even Spanish or Italian. There are no genders, so there is no need to remember long lists of endings for adjectives and to make them agree, with variations according to case. There are no equivalents for the definite and indefinite articles ("the," "a," "an"), so there is no need to make those agree either. Singular and plural nouns are the same. Best of all, verbs cannot be declined. The verb "to be" is *shì*. The same sound also covers "am," "are," "is," "was," "will be," and so on, since there are also no tenses. Instead of past, present, and future, Chinese is more concerned with whether an action is continuing or has been completed, and with the order in which events take place. To make matters of time clear, Chinese depends on simple expressions such as "yesterday," "before," "originally," "next year," and the like. "Tomorrow I go New York," is clear enough, as is "Yesterday I go New York." It's a little more complicated than these brief notes can suggest, but not much.

There are a few sounds in Mandarin that are not used in English (see the rough pronunciation guide below), but the main difficulty for foreigners lies in tones. Most sounds in Mandarin begin with a consonant and end in a vowel (or -n, or -ng), which leaves the language with very few distinct noises compared to English. Originally, one sound equaled one idea and one word. Even now, each of these monosyllables is represented by a single character, but often words have been made by putting two characters together, sometimes both of the same meaning, thus reinforcing one another. The solution to this phonetic poverty is to multiply the available sounds by making them tonal—speaking them at different pitches, thereby giving them different meanings. *Mā* spoken on a high level tone (first tone) offers a set of possible meanings different to those of *má* spoken with a rising tone (second tone), *mǎ* with a dipping then rising tone (third tone), or *mà* with an abruptly falling tone (fourth tone). There's also a different meaning for the neutral, toneless *ma*.

In the average sentence, context is your friend (there are not many occasions in which the third-tone *mǎ* or "horse" might be mistaken for the fourth-tone *mà* or "grasshopper," for instance), but without tone, there is essentially no meaning. The novice best sing his or her Mandarin very clearly, as Chinese children do—a chanted singsong can be heard emerging from the windows of primary schools across China. With experience, the student learns to give particular emphasis to the tones on words essential to a sentence's meaning, and to treat the others more lightly. Sadly, most books using modern Romanized Chinese, called *Hànyǔ pīnyīn* ("Hàn language spell-the-sounds"), do not mark the tones, nor do these appear on **pīnyīn** signs in China. But in this book, the authors, most of whom speak Mandarin, have added tones to the maps, so you can have a go at saying street names, hotels, restaurants, and place names for yourself. And we've included the tones in these appendices.

Cantonese has *eight* tones plus the neutral, but its grammatical structure is largely the same, as is that of all versions of Chinese. Even Chinese people who can barely understand each other's speech can at least write to each other, since written forms are similar. Mainland China, with the aim of increasing literacy (or perhaps of distancing the supposedly now thoroughly modern and socialist population from its Confucian heritage), instituted a ham-fisted simplification program in the 1950s, which reduced some characters originally taking 14 strokes of the brush, for instance, to as few as three strokes. Hong Kong, separated from the mainland and under British control until 1997, went its own way, kept the original full-form characters, and invented lots of new ones, too. Nevertheless, many characters remain the same, and some of the simplified forms are merely familiar shorthand for the full-form ones. But however many different meanings for each tone of *ma* there may be, for each meaning there's a different character. This makes the written form a far more successful communication medium than the spoken one, which leads to misunderstandings even between native speakers, who can often be seen sketching characters on their palms during conversation to confirm which one is meant.

The thought of learning 3,000 to 5,000 individual characters (at least 2,500 are needed to read a newspaper) also daunts many beginners. But look carefully at the ones below, and you'll notice many common elements. In fact, a rather limited number of smaller shapes are combined in different ways, much as we combine letters to make words. Admittedly, the characters only offer general hints as to their pronunciation, and that's often misleading—the system is not a phonetic one, so each new Mandarin word has to be learned as both a sound and a shape (or a group of them). But soon it's the similarities among the characters, not their differences, that begin to bother the student. English, a far more subtle language with a far larger vocabulary, and with so many pointless inconsistencies and exceptions to what are laughingly called its rules, is much more of a struggle for the Chinese than Mandarin should be for us.

But no knowledge of the language is needed to get around China, and it's almost a plus that Chinese take it for granted that outlandish foreigners (that's you and me unless you're of Chinese descent) can speak not a word (poor things) and must use whatever other limited means we have to communicate—this book and a phrase book, for instance. For help with navigation to sights, simply point to the characters below. When leaving your hotel, take one of its cards with you, and show it to the taxi driver when you want to return. At the end of this section, there's a limited list of useful words and phrases, which is best supplemented with a proper phrase book. If you have a Mandarin-speaking friend from the north (Cantonese speakers who know Mandarin as a second language tend to have fairly heavy accents), ask him or her to pronounce the greetings and words of thanks from the list below, so you can repeat after him and practice. While you are as much likely to be laughed *at* as *with* in China, such efforts are always appreciated.

1 A Guide to Pīnyīn Pronunciation

Letters in pīnyīn mostly have the values any English speaker would expect, with the following exceptions:

c ts as in bits

q *ch* as in *ch*in, but much harder and more forward, made with tongue and teeth

r has no true equivalent in English, but the *r* of *r*eed is close, although the tip of the tongue should be near the top of the mouth, and the teeth together

x also has no true equivalent, but is nearest to the *sh* of *sh*eep, although the tongue should be parallel to the roof of the mouth and the teeth together

zh is a soft j, like the *dge* in ju*dge*

The vowels are pronounced roughly as follows:

a as in f*a*ther

e as in *e*rr (*leng* is pronounced as English "lung")

i is pronounced *ee* after most consonants, but after c, ch, r, s, sh, z, and zh is a buzz at the front of the mouth behind the closed teeth

o as in s*o*ng

u as in t*oo*

ü is the purer, lips-pursed u of French t*u* and German *ü*. Confusingly, u after j, x, q, and y is always ü, but in these cases the accent over "ü" does not appear.

ai sounds like *eye*

ao as in *ou*ch

ei as in h*ay*

ia as in *ya*k

ian sounds like *yen*

iang sounds like *yang*

iu sounds like *you*

ou as in t*oe*

ua as in g*ua*va

ui sounds like *way*

uo sounds like *or*, but is more abrupt

Note that when two or more third-tone "ˇ" sounds follow one another, they should all, except the last, be pronounced as second-tone "ˊ."

2 Mandarin Bare Essentials

GREETINGS & INTRODUCTIONS

ENGLISH	PINYIN CHINESE	
Hello	Nǐ hǎo	你好
How are you?	Nǐ hǎo ma?	你好吗？
Fine. And you?	Wǒ hěn hǎo. Nǐ ne?	我很好你呢？
I'm not too well/ things aren't going well	Bù hǎo	不好

ENGLISH	PINYIN	CHINESE
What is your name? (very polite)	Nín guì xìng?	您贵姓
My (family) name is . . .	Wǒ xìng . . .	我姓...
I'm known as (family, then given name)	Wǒ jiào . . .	我叫...
I'm [American]	Wǒ shì [Měiguó] rén	我是美国人
[Australian]	[Àodàlìyà]	澳大利亚
[British]	[Yīngguó]	英国
[Canadian]	[Jiānádà]	加拿大
[Irish]	[Àiěrlán]	爱尔兰
[New Zealander]	[Xīnxīlán]	新西兰
I'm from [America]	Wǒ shì cóng [Měiguó] lái de	我是从美国来的
Excuse me/I'm sorry	Duìbùqǐ	对不起
I don't understand	Wǒ tīng bù dǒng	我听不懂
Thank you	Xièxie nǐ	谢谢你
Correct (yes)	Duì	对
Not correct	Bú duì	不对
No, I don't want	Wǒ bú yào	我不要
Not acceptable	Bù xíng	不行

BASIC QUESTIONS & PROBLEMS

ENGLISH	PINYIN	CHINESE
Excuse me/I'd like to ask	Qǐng wènyíxià	请问一下
Where is . . . ?	. . . zài nǎr?	. . . 在哪儿?
How much is . . . ?	. . . duōshǎo qián?	. . . 多少钱?
. . . this one?	Zhèi/Zhè ge . . .	这个...
. . . that one?	Nèi/Nà ge . . .	那个...
Do you have . . . ?	Nǐ yǒu méi yǒu	你有没有...?
What time does/is . . . ?	. . . jǐ diǎn?	...几点?
What time is it now?	Xiànzài jǐ diǎn?	现在几点?
When is . . . ?	. . . shénme shíhou?	...什么时候?
Why?	Wèishénme?	为什么?
Who?	Shéi?	谁?
Is that okay?	Xíng bù xíng?	行不行?
I'm feeling ill	Wǒ shēng bìng le	我生病了

TRAVEL

ENGLISH	PINYIN	CHINESE
luxury (bus, hotel rooms)	háohuá	豪华
high-speed (buses, expressways)	gāosù	高速
air-conditioned	kōngtiáo	空调

NUMBERS

Note that more complicated forms of numbers are often used on official documents and receipts to prevent fraud—see how easily 1 can be changed to 2, 3, or even 10. Familiar Arabic numerals appear on bank notes, most signs, taxi meters, and other places. Be particularly careful with *4* and *10*, which sound very alike in many regions—hold up fingers to make sure. Note, too, that *yī*, meaning "one," tends to change its tone all the time depending on what it precedes. Don't worry about this— once you've started talking about money, almost any kind of squeak for "one" will do. Finally note that "two" alters when being used with expressions of quantity.

ENGLISH	PINYIN	CHINESE
0	líng	零
1	yī	一
2	èr	二
2 (of them)	liǎng ge	两个
3	sān	三
4	sì	四
5	wǔ	五
6	liù	六
7	qī	七
8	bā	八
9	jiǔ	九
10	shí	十
11	shí yī	十一
12	shí èr	十二
21	èr shí yī	二十一
22	èr shí èr	二十二
51	wǔ shí yī	五十一
100	yì bǎi	一百
101	yì bǎi líng yī	一百零一
110	yì bǎi yī (shí)	一百一（十）
111	yì bǎi yī shí yī	一百一十一
1,000	yì qiān	一千
1,500	yì qiān wǔ (bǎi)	一千五百
5,678	wǔ qiān liù bǎi qī shí bāi	五千六百七十八
10,000	yí wàn	一万

MONEY

The word *yuan* (¥) is rarely spoken, nor is *jiao*, the written form for ¹/₁₀th of a *yuan*, equivalent to 10 *fen* (there are 100 *fen* in a *yuan*). Instead, the Chinese speak of "pieces of money," *kuai qian*, usually abbreviated just to *kuai*, and they speak of *mao* for ¹/₁₀th of a *kuai*. *Fen* have been overtaken by inflation and are almost useless. Often all zeros after the last whole number are simply omitted, along with *kuai qian*, which is taken as read, especially in direct reply to the question *duoshao qian*—"How much?"

ENGLISH	PINYIN	CHINESE
¥ 1	yí kuài qián	一块钱
¥ 2	liǎng kuài qián	两块钱
¥ .30	sān máo qián	三毛钱

ENGLISH	PINYIN	CHINESE
¥ 5.05	wǔ kuài líng wǔ fēn	五块零五分
¥ 5.50	wǔ kuài wǔ	五块五
¥ 550	wǔ bǎi wǔ shí kuài	五百五十块
¥ 5,500	wǔ qiān wǔ bǎi kuài	五千五百块
Small change	língqián	零钱

BANKING & SHOPPING

ENGLISH	PINYIN	CHINESE
I want to change money (foreign exchange)	Wǒ xiǎng huàn qián	我想换钱
credit card	Xìnyòngkǎ	信用卡
traveler's check	lǚxíng zhīpiào	旅行支票
department store	bǎihuò shāngdiàn	百货商店
	gòuwù zhōngxīn	购物中心
convenience store	xiǎomàibù	小卖部
market	shìchǎng	市场
May I have a look?	Wǒ Kànyíxia, hǎo ma?	我看一下，好吗？
I want to buy . . .	Wǒ xiǎng mǎi . . .	我想买...
How many do you want?	Nǐ yào jǐ ge?	你要几个？
Two of them	liǎng ge	两个
Three of them	sān ge	三个
1 kilo	yì gōngjīn	一公斤
Half a kilo	yì jīn	一斤
or	bàn gōngjīn	公斤
1m	yì mǐ	一米
Too expensive!	Tài guì le!	太贵了
Do you have change?	Yǒu língqián ma?	有零钱吗

TIME

ENGLISH	PINYIN	CHINESE
morning	shàngwǔ	上午
afternoon	xiàwǔ	下午
evening	wǎnshang	晚上
8:20am	shàngwǔ bā diǎn èr shí fēn	上午八点二十分
9:30am	shàngwǔ jiǔ diǎn bàn	上午九点半
noon	zhōngwǔ	中午
4:15pm	xiàwǔ sì diǎn yí kè	下午四点一刻
midnight	wǔ yè	午夜
1 hour	yí ge xiǎoshí	一个小时
8 hours	bā ge xiǎoshí	八个小时
today	jīntiān	今天
yesterday	zuótiān	昨天

ENGLISH	PINYIN	CHINESE
tomorrow	míngtiān	明天
Monday	Xīngqī yī	星期一
Tuesday	Xīngqī èr	星期二
Wednesday	Xīngqī sān	星期三
Thursday	Xīngqī sì	星期四
Friday	Xīngqī wǔ	星期五
Saturday	Xīngqī liù	星期六
Sunday	Xīngqī tiān	星期天

TRANSPORT

ENGLISH	PINYIN	CHINESE
I want to go to . . .	Wǒ xiǎng qù . . .	我想去 . . .
plane	fēijī	飞机
train	huǒchē	火车
bus	gōnggòng qìchē	公共汽车
long-distance bus	chángtú qìchē	长途汽车
taxi	chūzū chē	出租车
airport	fēijīchǎng	飞机场
stop or station (bus or train)	zhàn	站
(plane/train/bus) ticket	piào	票

NAVIGATION

ENGLISH	PINYIN	CHINESE
north	Běi	北
south	Nán	南
east	Dōng	东
west	Xī	西
Turn left	zuǒ guǎi	左拐
Turn right	yòu guǎi	右拐
Go straight on	yìzhí zǒu	一直走
crossroads	shízì lùkǒu	十字路口
10km	shí gōnglǐ	十公里
I'm lost	Wǒ diū le	我丢了

HOTEL

ENGLISH	PINYIN	CHINESE
How many days?	Zhù jǐ tiān?	住几天？
standard room (twin or double with private bathroom)	biāozhǔn jiān	标准间
passport	hùzhào	护照
deposit	yājīn	押金
I want to check out	Wǒ tuì fáng	我退房

RESTAURANT

ENGLISH	PINYIN	CHINESE
How many people?	Jǐ wèi?	几位
waiter/waitress	fúwùyuán	服务员
menu	càidān	菜单
I'm vegetarian	Wǒ shì chī sù de	我是吃素的
Do you have . . . ?	Yǒu méi yǒu . . . ?	有没有 . . . ?
Please bring a portion of . . .	Qǐng lái yí fènr . . .	请来一份儿 . . .
beer	píjiǔ	啤酒
mineral water	kuàngquán shuǐ	矿泉水
Bill, please	jiézhàng	结帐

SIGNS

Here's a list of common signs and notices to help you identify what you are looking for, from restaurants to condiments, and to help you choose the right door at the public restroom. These are the simplified characters in everyday use in China, but note that it's increasingly fashionable for larger businesses, and those with a long history, to use more complicated traditional characters, so not all may match what's below. Hong Kong and Macau also use traditional characters, and sometimes use different terms altogether, especially for modern inventions. Also, very old restaurants and temples across China tend to write their signs from right to left.

ENGLISH	PINYIN	CHINESE
hotel	bīnguǎn	宾馆
	dàjiǔdiàn	大酒店
	jiǔdiàn	酒店
	fàndiàn	饭店
restaurant	fànguǎn	饭馆
	jiǔdiàn	酒店
	jiǔjiā	酒家
vinegar	cù	醋
soy sauce	Jiàngyóu	酱油
bar	jiǔbā	酒吧
Internet bar	wǎngbā	网吧
cafe	kāfēiguǎn	咖啡馆
teahouse	cháguǎn	茶馆
department store	bǎihuò shāngdiàn	百货商店
	gòuwù zhōngxīn	购物中心
market	shìchǎng	市场
bookstore	shūdiàn	书店
police (Public Security Bureau)	gōng'ānjú	公安局
Bank of China	Zhōngguó Yínháng	中国银行

ENGLISH	PINYIN	CHINESE
public telephone	gōngyòng diànhuà	公用电话
public restroom	gōngyòng cèsuǒ	公用厕所
male	nán	男
female	nǚ	女
entrance	rùkǒu	入口
exit	chūkǒu	出口
bus stop/station	qìchē zhàn	汽车站
long-distance bus station	chángtú qìchē zhàn	长途汽车站
luxury	háohuá	豪华
railway station	huǒchēzhàn	火车站
hard seat	yìng zuò	硬座
soft seat	ruǎn zuò	软座
hard sleeper	yìng wò	硬卧
soft sleeper	ruǎn wò	软卧
metro/subway station	dìtiězhàn	地铁站
airport	fēijīchǎng	飞机场
dock/wharf	mǎtóu	码头
passenger terminal (bus, boat, and so on)	kèyùn zhàn	客运站
up/get on	shàng	上
down/get off	xià	下
ticket hall	shòupiào tīng	售票厅
ticket office	shòupiào chù	售票处
left-luggage office	xíngli jìcún chù	行李寄存处
temple	sì	寺
	miào	庙
museum	bówùguǎn	博物馆
memorial hall	jìniànguǎn	纪念馆
park	gōngyuán	公园
hospital	yīyuàn	医院
clinic	zhěnsuǒ	诊所
pharmacy	yàofáng/yàodiàn	药房/药店
travel agency	lǚxíngshè	旅行社

3 Selected Destinations by City

Following are some translations for destinations not covered in maps in this book. Just point to the characters when asking a cabdriver to take you to the specific destination.

BĚIJĪNG & HÉBĚI (CHAPTER 4)
SHĀNHǍI GUĀN
山海关

ACCOMMODATIONS & DINING

Jīguān Zhāodàisuǒ	机关招待所
Lónghuá Dàjiǔdiàn	龙华大酒店
Sì Tiáo Bāoziguǎn	四条包子馆
Wàng Yáng Lóu Fànzhuāng	望洋楼饭庄
Yìhé Jiǔdiàn (Friendly Cooperate Hotel)	谊合酒店

ATTRACTIONS

Jiǎo Shān	角山
Lǎo Lóng Tóu	老龙头
Mèngjiāngnǚ Miào	孟姜女庙
Tiānxià Dìyī Guān	天下第一关
Wáng Jiā Dàyuàn	王家大院

SHIÍJIĀZHUĀNG

ACCOMMODATIONS & DINING

Héběi Shìjì Dàfàndiàn (Héběi Century Hotel)	河北世纪大饭店
Huìwén Jiǔdiàn	汇文酒店
Quánjùdé	全聚德
Shāo'ézǎi	烧鹅仔
Shìmào Guǎngchǎng Jiǔdiàn (World Trade Plaza Hotel)	世贸广场酒店
Yànchūn Huāyuán Jiǔdiàn (Yànchūn Garden Hotel)	燕春花园酒店

ATTRACTIONS

Bǎilín Sì	柏林寺
Cāngyán Shān	苍岩山
Zhàozhōu Qiáo	赵州桥
Zhèngdìng	正定

THE NORTHEAST (CHAPTER 5)
CHÁNGBÁI SHĀN
长白山

ACCOMMODATIONS & DINING

Xìndá Bīnguǎn	信达宾馆
Fúbǎi Bīnguǎn)	福柏宾馆
Yùndòngyúan Cūn (Athlete's Village)	运动员村
Chángbái Shān Guójì Bīnguǎn	长白山国际宾馆
(Chángbái Shān International Hotel)	
Chángbái Shān Dàyǔ Fàndiàn (Chángbái Shān Daewoo)	长白山大宇饭店

ATTRACTIONS

Tiān Chí (Heavenly Lake) Èrdào Bái Hé	二道白河
(Bái Hé for short)	
Běi Pō (North Shore)	北坡
Wēnquán Yù	温泉峪
Dìxià Sēnlín (Underground Forest)	地下森林
Měirén Sōng Sēnlín (Sylvan Pine Forest)	美人松森林
Sōngjiāng Hé	松江河
Xī Pō Shān Mén (West Slope Mountain Gate)	西坡山门
Sōngjiāng Hé Bīnguǎn	松江河宾馆

YANBIAN　　　　　　　　　　　　　　　　　　　　延边
ACCOMMODATIONS & DINING
　Dazhou Jiǔdiàn (Dazhou Hotel)　　　　　　　　　大洲酒店
　Yánbiān Dàyǔ Fàndiàn (Yánbiān International Hotel)　延边国际饭店
　Jīndálái Fàndiàn　　　　　　　　　　　　　　　金大莱饭店
　Mozhate Kuaicandian　　　　　　　　　　　　　莫扎特快餐店

MANZHOULI　　　　　　　　　　　　　　　　　满洲里
ACCOMMODATIONS & DINING
　Mǎnzhōulǐ Yǒuyì Bīnguǎn (Friendship Hotel)　　　满洲里友谊宾馆
　Jiāngnán Dàjiǔdiàn　　　　　　　　　　　　　　江南大酒店
　Jiayi Jiǔdiàn (Home 1 Hotel)　　　　　　　　　家易酒店
　Mengxiangyuan Huǒguō　　　　　　　　　　　　蒙祥原火锅
　Xīnmǎnyuán Xīcāntīng　　　　　　　　　　　　新满园西餐厅
　Beijiaerhu Xīcāntīng　　　　　　　　　　　　　贝加尔湖西餐厅
　Dàmòfáng (Délifrance)　　　　　　　　　　　　大磨坊

ATTRACTIONS
　Guó Mén (Sino-Russian Border Crossing)　　　　国门
　Eluosi Taowa Guangchang　　　　　　　　　　　俄罗斯套娃广场
　　(Russian Matryoshka Dolls Plaza)
　Dálài Hú (Hūlún Hú)　　　　　　　　　　　　　呼伦湖
　Hūlúnbèi'ěr Cǎoyuán (Hulun Buir Grasslands)　　呼伦贝尔草原

ALONG THE YELLOW RIVER (CHAPTER 6)
DATONG
ACCOMMODATIONS & DINING
　Fēitiān Bīnguǎn　　　　　　　　　　　　　　　飞天宾馆
　Mr. Lee's (Měiguó Jiāzhōu Niūrōumiàn Dàwáng)　美国加州牛肉面大王
　Yǒnghé Měishíchéng　　　　　　　　　　　　　永和美食城

HOHHOT
ACCOMMODATIONS & DINING
　Jiāyuán Bīnguǎn　　　　　　　　　　　　　　　家源商务宾馆

YÁN'ĀN　　　　　　　　　　　　　　　　　　延安
ACCOMMODATIONS & DINING
　Yán'ān Bīnguǎn　　　　　　　　　　　　　　　延安宾馆
　Yàshèng Dàjiǔdiàn　　　　　　　　　　　　　　亚圣大酒店
　Yínhǎi Guójì Dàjiǔdiàn　　　　　　　　　　　　银海国际大酒店
　Wúqǐ Dàjiǔdiàn　　　　　　　　　　　　　　　吴起大酒店
　Jīnróng Bīnguǎn　　　　　　　　　　　　　　　金融宾馆

ATTRACTIONS
　Fènghuáng Shān (Phoenix Hill)　　　　　　　　凤凰山
　Wángjiāpíng Gémìng Jiùzhǐ　　　　　　　　　　王家坪革命旧址
　　(Former Revolutionary Headquarters at Wángjiāpíng)
　Gémìng Jìniànguǎn　　　　　　　　　　　　　　革命纪念馆
　　(Revolutionary Memorial Hall/Museum)
　Yángjiālǐng Jiùzhǐ　　　　　　　　　　　　　　杨家岭旧址
　　(Yángjiālǐng Revolutionary Headquarters)
　Bǎotǎ (Baǒ Pagoda)　　　　　　　　　　　　　宝塔

TAIYUAN
Transport
Dōng Kēzhàn | 东客站

ACCOMMODATIONS & DINING
Bìngzhōu Bīnguǎn | 并州宾馆
Shípǐn Jiē | 食品街
Shàngdǎo Kāfēitīng (UBC Coffee) | 上岛咖啡厅
Attractions
Shǎnxī Bówùguǎn (Shānxī Museum) | 山西博物馆

PÍNGYÀO | 平遥
ACCOMMODATIONS & DINING
Déjū Yuán | 德居源
Tiān Yuán Kuí | 天元魁

ATTRACTIONS
Shì Lóu (Market Building) | 市楼
Gǔ Chéngqiáng (Ancient City Wall) | 古城墙
Rìshēng Chāng | 日升昌
Bǎi Chuān Tōng | 百川通
Chénghuáng Miào, Cáishén Miào | 城隍庙，财神庙
Zàojūn Miào | 灶君庙
Xiànyá Shǔ (or Yámen) | 县衙署，衙门
Léi Lǚ Tài Gùjū | 雷履泰故居
Zhènguó Sì | 镇国寺
Qiáo Jiā Dàyuàn | 乔家大院
Shuānglín Sì | 双林寺
Wáng Jiā Dàyuàn (Wáng Family Courtyard) | 王家大院
Yí Yuán (Grace Vineyard) | 怡园

WǓTÁI SHĀN | 五台山
ACCOMMODATIONS & DINING
Fúrén Jū Jiǔlóu | 福仁居酒楼
Jìngxīn Zhāi | 精心斋
Qīxiángé Bīnguǎn | 栖贤阁宾馆
Yínhǎi Shānzhuāng | 银海山庄
Yīzhǎn Míngdēng Quánsùzhāi 一 | 盏明灯全素斋
Cháoyáng Bīnguǎn | 朝阳山庄
Jīnjiè Shānzhuāng | 金界山庄
Xiǎochén Huǒguō (Xiaochen Hotpot) | 小陈火锅

ATTRACTIONS
Dàilóu Peak | 代娄峰
Wǔtái Shān Lǚyóu Chē Chūzū | 五台山旅游车出租
  (Wǔtái Shān Tour Taxi Ticket Office)
Fēiyǔ Diànnǎo | 飞宇电脑
Xiǎntōng Sì | 显通寺
Tǎyuàn Sì | 塔院寺

Nán Shān Sì 南山寺
Lóngquán Sì 龙泉寺
Nánchán Sì 南禅寺
Fóguāng Sì 佛光寺

THE SILK ROUTES (CHAPTER 7)
XĪ'ĀN
ACCOMMODATIONS & DINING
Zhōnggǔlóu Dàjiǔdiàn (Bell and Drum Hotel) 钟鼓楼大酒店
Défúxiàng Jiǔbā Jiē (Défúxiàng Bar Street) 德福巷酒吧街

ATTRACTIONS
Xī'ān Gǔwán Chéng 西安古玩城

TIĀNSHUĬ 天水
ATTRACTIONS
Běidào Qū long-distance bus station 北道区长途汽车站
Gōnghuì Dàshà 工会大厦
Màijī Shān Shíkū 麦积山石窟

XIÀHÉ (LABRANG) 夏河
ACCOMMODATIONS & DINING
Lābùléng Bīnguǎn (Labrang Hotel) 拉不楞宾馆
Huáqiáo Fàndiàn (Overseas Tibetan Hotel) 华侨饭店
Zhuómǎ Lǚshè (Tara Guesthouse) 卓玛旅社

ATTRACTIONS
Lābùléng Sì (Labrang Monastery) 拉不楞寺
Sāngkē 桑科

KUQA (KÙCHē) 库车
ACCOMMODATIONS & DINING
Kùchē Fàndiàn 库车饭店
Qiūcí Bīnguǎn 龟兹宾馆
Wúmǎi'ěrhóng Měishí Chéng 吴买尔洪美食城
 (Omarjan Muhammed Food City)
Wūqià Guǒyuán Cāntīng (Uqa Bhag Resturant) 乌恰果园餐厅

ATTRACTIONS
Kèzī'ěr Qiān Fó Dòng (Kizil Thousand Buddha Caves) 克孜尔千佛洞
Kùchē Dà Sì (Kuqa Grand Mosque) 库车大寺
Sūbāshí Gǔchéng (Jarakol Temple) 苏巴什古城
Xīngqīwǔ Dàshìchǎng (Friday Bazaar) 星期五大市场

LANZHOU
ACCOMMODATIONS & DINING
Lánzhōu Dàshà (Hualian Hotel) 兰州大厦
Yǒuyì Bīnguǎn (Friendship Hotel) 友谊宾馆
Wàitān Fēngshàng Kāfēi (Seaside Scenery Café) 外滩风尚咖啡

HEZUO
ACCOMMODATIONS & DINING
Jiāotōng Bīnguǎn   交通宾馆

URUMQI
Transport
Xiāng Yǒu Jiǔdiàn   湘友酒店
ACCOMMODATIONS & DINING
Hóngshān Xīn Shíjí Shāngwù Jiǔdiàn
(Hongshan New Century Suites Hotel)   红山新世纪商务酒店
Kǎibīnsījí Fàndiàn (Kempinski Hotel)   凯宾斯基饭
Hóngshān Xīn Shìjì Shāngwù Kāfēitíng
(Hong Shan New Century Suites Café)   红山新世纪商务咖啡
Marwa (Mǎērwǎ Cāntīng)   麦尔瓦餐厅

KASHGAR
ACCOMMODATIONS & DINING
Cháyuán Dàjiǔdiàn (Samawer)   茶园大酒店

TASHKURGAN
ACCOMMODATIONS & DINING
Tǎxiàn Huángguān Dàjiǔdiàn (Crown Inn)   塔县皇冠大酒店
Chóngqìng Xiǎochǎo   重庆小炒
Wūshì Lǎo Huímín Cāntīng   乌市老回民餐

KHOTAN (HÉTIÁN)   和田
ACCOMMODATIONS & DINING
Gāoyáng Kǎoròu Kuàicāndiàn   羔羊烤肉快餐店
Hétián Yíngbīnguǎn   和田迎宾馆
Hétián Bīnguǎn (Hotan Hotel)   和田宾馆
Wēnzhōu Dàjiǔdiàn (Wēnzhōu Hotel)   温州大酒店
Zhèjiāng Dàjiǔdiàn (Zhèjiāng Hotel)   浙江大酒店
Wéilìmài Hànbǎo (Wéilìmài Burger)   维利麦汉堡

ATTRACTIONS
Dìtǎn Chǎng (Carpet Factory)   地毯厂
Gōngyì Měishù Yǒuxiàn Gōngsī (Jade Factory)   工艺美术有限公司
Sīsāng Yánjiūsuǒ (Silk and Mulberry Research Center)   丝桑研究所
Xīngqītiān Dàshìchǎng (Sunday Market)   星期天大市场

TRANSPORT
Dōngjiāo Kèyùn Zhàn   东郊客运站

EASTERN CENTRAL CHINA (CHAPTER 8)
AROUND ZHÈNGZHŌU
Gǒngyì   巩义
Běi Sòng Huánglíng
(Imperial Tombs of the Northern Sòng Dynasty)   北宋皇陵
Shíkū Sì   石窟寺

DĒNGFĒNG & SŌNG SHĀN
ACCOMMODATIONS & DINING

Fēngyuán Dàjiǔdiàn	丰源大酒店
Jīnguàn Miànbāo Xīdiǎn Fáng	京冠面包西点坊
Shàolín Guójì Dàjiǔdiàn (Shàolín International Hotel)	少林国际大酒店
Sìjì Chūn	四季春
Xiāngjī Wáng	香鸡王

ATTRACTIONS

Guólǚ Dàlóu	国旅大楼
Xī Kè Zhàn (West Bus Station)	西客站
Tàishì Shān	太室山
Jùnjí Féng	峻极峰
Shàoshì Shān	少室山
Sōngyáng Suǒdào	嵩阳索道
Sōng Shān Diào Qiáo	嵩山吊桥
Sānhuáng Xínggōng (Sānhuáng Palace)	三皇行宫
Shàolín Sì (Shàolín Monastery)	少林寺
Shàolín Wǔshù Guǎn (Martial Arts Training Center)	少林武术馆
Shàolín Sì Tǎgōu Wǔshù Xuéxiào	少林寺塔沟武术学校
(Shàolín Monastery Wǔshù Institute at Tǎgōu)	
Sōngyuè Tǎ (Sōngyuè Pagoda)	嵩岳塔
Zhōngyuè Miào	中岳庙
Gàochéng Guānxīng Tái	告成观星台

LUÒYÁNG   洛阳
ACCOMMODATIONS & DINING

Bǎo Húlu	宝葫芦
Huáyáng Guǎngchǎng Guójì Dàjiǔdiàn	华阳广场国际大酒店
(Huáyáng Plaza Hotel)	
Lǎo Jiē Dìyī Lóu	老街第一楼
Lǎo Jiē (Old Street)	老街
Luòyáng Mǔdān Dàjiǔdiàn (Luòyáng Peony Hotel)	洛阳牡丹大酒店
Míngyuàn Dàjiǔdiàn (Míngyuàn Hotel)	明苑大酒店
Mǔdān Chéng Bīnguǎn (Peony Plaza)	牡丹城宾馆
Xīn Yǒuyì Bīnguǎn (New Friendship Hotel)	新友谊宾馆

ATTRACTIONS

Yī Xiàn	黟县
Huīzhōu District	徽州区
Shè Xiàn	歙县
Xīdì, Hóngcūn, and Nánpíng	西递　红村, 南平
Qiānkǒu, and Chéngkǎn	潜口呈坎

JÌ'NÁN   济南
ACCOMMODATIONS & DINING

Guìhé Huángguān Jiǔdiàn (Crowne Plaza Guìhé Jì'nán)	贵和皇冠酒店
Suǒfēitè Yínzuò Dàfàndiàn (Sofitel Silver Plaza Jì'nán)	索菲特银座大饭店
Qílǔ Bīnguǎn	齐鲁宾馆

Yínzuò Quánchéng Dàjiǔdiàn | 银座泉城大酒店
  (Silver Plaza Quán Chéng Hotel)
Guì Dū Dàjiǔdiàn | 贵都大酒店
Jǐ'nán Tiědào Dàjiǔdiàn | 济南铁道大酒店

ATTRACTIONS

Bàotū Quán (Bàotū Spring) | 趵突泉
Dà Míng Hú Gōngyuán (Dà Míng Hú Park) | 大明湖公园
Dining
  Xīn Lán Bái (Blue & White) | 新蓝白
  Lǎo Hángzhōu Jiǔ Wǎn Bàn | 老杭州九碗拌
Other
  chángtú qìchēzhàn (Long-Distance Bus Station) | 长途汽车站
  China Shāndōng Travel Service
    (Zhōngguó Shāndōng Lǚxíngshè) | 中国山东旅行社

QŪFŬ   曲阜

ACCOMMODATIONS & DINING

Kǒng Fǔ Dàjiǔdiàn | 孔府大酒店
Kǒng Fǔ Jiā Yán Táng | 孔府家严堂
Quèlǐ Bīnshè (Quèlǐ Hotel) | 阙里宾舍
Qūfǔ Yóuzhèng Bīnguǎn (Qūfǔ Post Hotel) | 曲阜邮政宾馆
Yù Lóng Dàjiǔdiàn (Yù Lóng Hotel) | 裕隆大酒店

ATTRACTIONS

Kǒng Miào (Confucius Temple) | 孔庙
Kǒng Fǔ (Confucian Mansion) | 孔府
Kǒng Lín (Confucian Forest & Cemetery) | 孔林
Kǒngzǐ Yánjīuyuàn (Confucius Academy) | 孔子研究院
Shào Hào Lín (Tomb of Emperor Shào Hào) | 少昊林

WÚXĪ   无锡

ACCOMMODATIONS & DINING

Hángyùn Dàshà (Ferry Building) | 航运大厦
Húbīn Fàndiàn | 湖滨饭店
Wúxī Xīnshìjiè Wànyí Jiǔdiàn | 无锡新世界万怡酒店
  (New World Courtyard Wúxī)
Xǐláidēng Dàfàndiàn (Sheraton Wúxī Hotel & Towers) | 喜来登无锡大饭店
Tài Hú Fàndiàn | 太湖饭店
Wúxī Qìchēzhàn (Wúxī Bus Station) | 无锡汽车站

ATTRACTIONS

Tài Hú (Lake Tài) | 太湖
Yuántóuzhǔ (Turtle Head Isle) | 鼋头渚
Xīhuì Gōngyuán | 锡惠公园

YÍXĪNG   宜兴

Huì shān Clay Figurine Factory | 惠山泥人厂
Yíxīng Táocí Bówùguǎn | 宜兴陶瓷博物馆
Shànjuàn Dòng | 扇卷洞
Shěng Qìchēzhàn (Yíxīng Bus Station) | 宜兴汽车站
Yíxīng Guójì Fàndiàn (Yíxīng International Hotel) | 宜兴国际饭店

HÉFÉI
合肥

ACCOMMODATIONS & DINING
Héféi Gǔjǐng Jiàrì Jiǔdiàn (Holiday Inn Héféi)
Huáqiáo Fàndiàn (Overseas Chinese Hotel) 华侨饭店
Jīn Mǎn Lóu Huāyuán Jiǔdiàn 金满楼花园酒店
Lǎo Xiè Lóngxiā 老谢龙虾
24 Xiǎoshí Miàn (Noodles in Chopsticks) 小时面
Héféi Nuòfùtè Qíyún Shānzhuāng (Novotel Héféi) 合肥诺富特齐云山庄

ATTRACTIONS
Bāo Hé Gōngyuán 包河公园
Bāo Gōng Mù Yuán (Lord Bāo's Tomb) 包公墓园
Xiāoyáojīn Gōngyuán 逍遥津公园
Shāngyè Bùxíngjiē 商业步行街
Lǐ Hóngzhāng Gùjū 李鸿章故居
Ānhuī Shěng Bówùguǎn (Ānhuī Provincial Museum) 安徽省博物馆

TÚNXĪ
屯溪

ACCOMMODATIONS & DINING
Bǎo Húlu 宝葫芦
Huáng Shān Guójì Dàjiǔdiàn 黄山国际大酒店
  (Huáng Shān International Hotel)
Huáng Shān Guómài Dàjiǔdiàn 黄山国脉大酒店
Huáng Shān Huāxī Fàndiàn 黄山花溪饭店
Jiànguó Shāngwù Jiǔdiàn (Jiànguó Garden Hotel) 建国商务酒店
Lǎo Jiē Dìyī Lóu 老街第一楼
Lǎo Jiē (Old Street) 老街

ATTRACTIONS
Bǎolún Gé (Bǎolún Hall) 宝纶阁
Chéngkǎn 呈坎
Dòushān Jiē 斗山街
Hóng Cūn 宏村
Huāshān Míkū (Mysterious Caves 花山谜窟
  of Flower Mountain)
Huīzhōu District 徽州区
Nánpíng 南屏
Qiánkǒu 潜口
Shè Xiàn 歙县
Xīdì 西递
Tángyuè Páifang Qún (Tángyuè Memorial Arches) 棠樾牌坊群
Xǔguó Shífáng (Xúgúo Stone Archway) 许国石坊
Yī Xiàn 黟县

SHÀNGHǍI (CHAPTER 9)
SŪZHŌU
苏州

ACCOMMODATIONS & DINING
Kǎilái Dàjiǔdiàn (Gloria Plaza Hotel Sūzhōu) 凯莱大酒店
Scholars Inn (Shūxiāng Méndì Shāngwù Jiǔdiàn) 书香门第商务酒店

Sūzhōu Wúgōng Xǐláidēng Dàjiǔdiàn   苏州吴宫喜来登大酒店
  (Sheraton Sūzhōu Hotel & Towers)
Sōng Hè Lóu (Pine and Crane Restaurant)   松鹤楼

ATTRACTIONS

ShīZi Lín Yuán (Forest of Lions Garden)   狮子林园
Gūsū Yuán (Gūsū Garden)   姑苏园
Zhuō Zhèng Yuán (Humble Administrator's Garden)   拙政园
Liú Yuán (Lingering Garden)   留园
Wǎng Shī Yuán (Master of the Nets Garden)   网师园
Pán Mén (Pán Gate)   盘门
Ruìguāng Tǎ   瑞光塔
Sūzhōu Cìxiù Yánjiūsuǒ   苏州刺绣研究所
  (Sūzhōu Embroidery Research Institute)
Sūzhōu Sīchóu Bówùguǎn (Sūzhōu Silk Museum)   苏州丝绸博物馆
Hǔ Qiū Shān (Tiger Hill)   虎丘山
Wúmén Qiáo   无门桥

HÁNGZHŌU   杭洲
ACCOMMODATIONS & DINING

Lóu Wài Lóu   楼外楼
Hángzhōu Xiānggélǐlā Fàndiàn   杭州香格里拉饭店
  (Shangri-La Hotel Hángzhōu)
Hángzhōu Suǒfēitè Xīhú Dàjiǔdiàn   杭州索菲特西湖大酒店
  (Sofitel Westlake Hángzhōu)
Xī Hú Tiāndì (West Lake Heaven and Earth)   西湖天地

ATTRACTIONS

Bái Dī (Bái Causeway)   白堤
Duàn Qiáo (Broken Bridge)   断桥
Fēilái Fēng (Peak That Flew from Afar)   飞来峰
Léi Fēng Tǎ (Léi Fēng Pagoda)   雷峰塔
Língyǐn Sì (Língyǐn Temple)   灵隐寺
Lóngjǐng Wēnchá (Dragon Well Tea Village)   龙井温茶
Sān Tán Yìn Yuè (Three Pools Mirroring The Moon)   三潭印月
Gūshān Dǎo (Solitary Island)   孤山岛
Sū Dī (Sū Causeway)   苏堤
Xī Hú (West Lake)   西湖
Xiǎo Yíng Zhōu (Island of Small Seas)   小瀛洲
Zhèjiāng Bówùguǎn (Zhèjiāng Provincial Museum)   浙江博物馆
Zhōngguó Cháyè Bówùguǎn (Chinese Tea Museum)   中国茶叶博物馆
Zhōngguó Sīchóu Bówùguǎn (China Silk Museum)   中国丝绸博物馆

THE SOUTHEAST (CHAPTER 10)
ANJI
ACCOMMODATIONS & DINING

Xiàng Yí Jīn Yè Dàjiǔdiàn (Golden Leaf Hotel)   香溢.金叶大酒店
Xiāng Yì Dù Jià Cūn (Sunny Land Resort)   香溢渡假村
Gāo Shān Rén Jiā Kè Zhàn (Mountain Clan Guesthouse)   高山人家客栈

ATTRACTIONS

Cháng Lóng Bǎi Bù (Hidden Dragon Falls)   藏龙百瀑
Zhú Bó Yuǎn (Bamboo Museum and Gardens)   竹博园
Dà Kāng Jiā Jù Gōng Chǎng (Dà Kāng Furniture Factory)   大康家具工厂
Dà Zhú Hǎi (Big Bamboo Sea)   大竹海
Tiān Huāng Píng Diàn Zhàn   天荒坪电站
  (Tiān Huāng Píng Hydro Electric Facility)
Líng Fēng Jíng Qū (Líng Fēng Scenic Zone)   灵峰景区
Cháng Lóng Beǐ Pù Zuì Dǐn Duān   藏龙百瀑最顶端
  (Hidden Dragon Falls Scenic Area)
Gú Lóng Kè Zhàn (Ancient Dragon Guesthouse)   古龙客栈

SHOPPING

Tiān Zhú Zhuāng   天竹庄
  (Tiānzhúzhuāng Bamboo Fiber Company)
Zhú Yè Chéng (Bamboo Charcoal Factory)   竹业城
Chú Tóu (Bamboo Bill Hook)   锄头

TOWNS

Gǎng Kǒu   港口
Dà Xī Cūn   大溪村

MOGANSHAN   莫干山
ACCOMMODATIONS & DINING

Sōng Liáng Shān Zhuāng (Mògànshān Lodge)   松粮山庄
Bái Yún Jiǔ Diàn (Baǐ Yún Hotel)   莫干山白云酒店
Mògànshān Zhuāng (Mògànshān Castle)   莫干山庄
Sōngyuè Tīng (Wǔ Líng Hotel)   松月亭酒店

ATTRACTIONS

Qīng Liáng Tíng (Qīng Liáng Pavillion)   清凉亭
Jiàn Chí (Sword Forging Pool)   剑池

TOWNS

Wǔ Líng Cūn   武陵村
Dé Qīng Shì   德清市
Yīn Shān Jiē   荫山街
Hú Zhoū   湖州

YANDANGSHAN   雁荡山
ACCOMMODATIONS & DINING

Cháoyáng Shān Zhuāng (Sunshine Hotel)   朝阳山庄
Baǐ Lè Dàjiǔdiàn (Baile Hotel)   百乐大酒店
Yàndàngshān Zhuāng (Yàndàngshān Mountain Villa)   雁荡山山庄
Jìng Yuán Dù Jià Cūn (Jìng Yuán Holiday Village)   静园度假村
Yàndàng Tè Sè Xiǎo Chī (Fresh Produce Restaurant)   雁荡特色小吃
Tiān Yí Bié Yè   天逸别业

ATTRACTIONS

Jià Rì Lǚ Xíng Shè   假日旅行社
  (Wenzhōu Yàndàngshān Holiday Agency)
Lè Qīng Gé Mìng Liè Shì Jì Niàn Guǎn   乐清革命烈士纪念馆
  (Revolutionary Martyrs' Memorial)

Líng Fēng Jǐng Qū (Spiritual Peaks)	灵峰景区
Líng Fēng Sì (Spiritual Peaks Temple)	灵峰寺
Fū Qī Fēng (Husband and Wife Peak)	夫妻峰
Hé Zhǎng Fēng (Clasped Palms Peak)	合掌峰
Láo Shòu Xīng (Chinese God of Longevity)	老寿星
Guǒ Hé Qiáo (Fruit Box Bridge)	果盒桥
Beǐ Doǔ Dòng (Plough Cave)	北斗洞
Líng Yán Jǐng Qū (The Spiritual Rocks)	灵岩景区
Cháoyáng Dòng (Chaoyang Cave)	朝阳洞
Dà Lóng Qiū Jǐng Qū (Big Dragon Waterfall Scenic Area)	大龙湫景区
Yàn Hú Gāng (Wild Goose Lake)	雁湖冈
Sān Zhí Pù (Three-Step Waterfall)	三折瀑
Xiān Qiáo (The Immortal Bridge)	仙桥
Guān Yīn Dòng (Goddess of Mercy Cave)	观音洞
Xuán Yá Zhàn Dào (Fēng Cloud Cliffs)	悬崖栈道

TOWNS & ROADS

Xiǎng Lǐng Tóu (Yàndàngshān Resort Town)	响岭头
Bù Xíng Jiē	步行街
Xīn Jiē Xiàng Yáng Lù	新街向阳路
Xiāo Xiá Lù	霄霞路
Cháoyáng Lù	朝阳路
Jìng Míng Lù	净名路

WĒNZHŌU 温州

ACCOMMODATIONS & DINING

Chún Sōng Láng Shuǐguǒ Fáng (Fruit Restaurant)	莼淞郎水果坊
Fán Dōng Bīnguǎn	繁东宾馆
Shàngdǎo Kāfēi	上岛咖啡
Zhōng Chéng Dàjiǔdiàn (Zhōng Chéng Hotel)	忠诚大酒店
Bàndǎo Huán Chéng Shāng Wù Jiǔdiàn (City Inn Bandao)	半岛环城商务酒店

ATTRACTIONS

Jiāngxīn Gū Yǔ	江心孤屿
Wǔ Mǎ Jiē	五马街

WǓYÍ SHĀN 武夷山

ACCOMMODATIONS & DINING

Bǎodǎo Dàjiǔdiàn (Bǎodǎo Hotel)	宝岛大酒店
Jīn Gǔ Yuán Dàjiǔdiàn	金谷园大酒店
Wǔyí Shānzhuāng (Wǔyí Mountain Villa)	武夷山庄
Fǎ Tíng Jiē Dài Chù (Court Administration)	法庭接待处
Yuè Yì Jiǔdiàn (Yuè Yì Hotel)	悦逸酒店
Jīn Gǔ Nóng Zhuāng (Jīn Gǔ Guesthouse)	金谷农庄

ATTRACTIONS

Dà Hóng Pào	大红袍
Dà Wáng Fēng	大王峰
Tiānyóu Shān	天游山

Wǔyí Gōng 武夷宫
Yuánshǐ Sēnlín Gōngyuán (Vigin Forest) 原始森林公园
Lǚ Yóu Dù Jià Jǐng Qū 旅游度假景区
Tīan Xīng Yǒng Lè (Ever Happy Temple) 天兴永乐

TOWNS
Hóng Xīng Cūn 红星村
Xīng Cūn 兴村
Jíng Qū Shàng Yóu 景区上游

QUANZHOU
ACCOMMODATIONS & DINING
Yì Lì Dájiǔdiàn (Yì Lì Hotel) 逸利达酒店
Háo Dì Fān Shāng Wù Jiǔ Diàn (GP Hotel) 好地方商务酒店
Sān Dé Sù Shí Guǎn 三德素食馆
　(Three Virtues Vegetarian Restaurant)
Quánzhōu Hángkōng Jiǔdiàn 泉州航空酒店
　(Xiàmén Airlines Quánzhōu Hotel)
Jiàn Fú Shāng Wù Jiǔ Diàn (Jiàn Fú Business Hotel) 建福商务酒店
Měicān Shi Jiē (The Delicacy Street) 美餐食街

ATTRACTIONS
Quán Zhoū Guó Jì Jū Lè Bù 泉州国际俱乐部
　(Quán Zhoū International Club)
Haǐ Waì Jiāo Tōng Shǐ Bó Wù Guǎn 海外交通史博物馆
　(Maritime Musuem)
Quán Zhoū Mǐn Taí Bó Wù Guǎn 泉州闽台博物馆
　(Quánzhōu Táiwān Friendship Museum)
Mǐnnán Jiàn Zhú Dà Guān Yuán (Cài Family Residence) 闽南建筑大观园
Quán Zhōu Bówùguǎn (Quánzhōu Museum) 泉州博物馆
Jǐn Xiù Zhuāng Mù Ǒu Yì Sù Guǎn (Puppet Museum) 锦绣庄木偶艺术馆
Shān Xiá Chì Hú Gōng Yè Qū 山霞赤湖工业区
　(Shān Xiá Industrial Zone)

TOWNS
Guān Qiáo 官桥
Zhāng Lí Cūn 漳里村

CHONGWU
Háo Xiáng Shí Yè (Háo Xiáng Stone Factory) 豪翔石业
Shì Xīng Shí Yè (Shì Xīng Stone Factory) 世兴石业
Huá Fēng Shèn Shí Yè (Huá Fēng Shèn Stone Factory) 华峰盛石业

XIAMEN
ACCOMMODATIONS & DINING
Lì Fǎng Mǐ Shí Shàng Cān Tīng (M-3) 粒坊米时尚餐厅
Huāshēng Tāng Diàn (Peanut Snack Bar) 花生汤店
Xī Ěr Fú Jiǔ Diàn (Hilford Hotel and Health Water Spa) 希尔福酒店
Yè Bǎihé Bīnguǎn (Night Lily Guesthouse) 夜百合宾馆
Huā Fēng Shān Zhuāng (Old U.S. Consulate) 华风山庄
Lù Jiāng Bīn Guǎn (Lùjiāng Harbourview Hotel) 鹭江宾馆

Yǒng Shēng Xīn Chéng Fù Jìn 永升新城附近
Xīng Hé Bīn Guǎn 星河宾馆
Xià Mén Dà Xué Jiē Daì Fú Wù Zhōng Xīn
(Xià Mén University Guesthouse 厦门大学接待服务中心

ATTRACTIONS

Hóng Lóu (The Red Chamber) 红楼
Sōng Bǎi Cháng Tú Qì Chē Zhàn 松柏长途汽车站
(Sōng Bǎi Bus Station)
Jí Měi Cháng Tú Qì Chē Zhàn (Jí Měi Bus Station) 集美长途汽车站
Hú Bīn Cháng Tú Qì Chē Zhàn (Hú Bīn Bus Station) 湖滨南长途汽车站
Tóng Ān Yǐng Shì Chéng (Tóng Ān Film City) 同安影视城
Gǔlàng Yǔ 鼓浪屿
Jīnquán Qiánbì Bówùguǎn (Coin Museum) 金泉钱币博物馆
Rìguāng Yán (Sunlight Rock) 日光岩
Xiàmén Shì Bówùguǎn (City Museum) 厦门市博物馆
Húlí Shān Pàotái (Húlí Shān Fort) 胡里山炮台
Xiàmén Dàxué (Xiàmén University) 厦门大学
Nán Pǔtuó Sì (South Pǔtuó Temple) 南普陀寺

JǏNGDÉZHÈN 景德镇
ACCOMMODATIONS & DINING

Yī Lóng Dàjiǔdiàn (Yī Lóng Restaurant) 伊龙大酒店
Bīn Jiāng Bīn Guǎn (Bīn Jiāng Hotel) 滨江宾馆
Shèng Shān Jiǔ Diàn (Holy Mountain Hotel) 圣山酒店
Sān Bǎo Táo Yì Yán Xiū Yuàn 三宝陶艺研修院
(Sānbǎo Ceramic Art Institute)
Dí Oū Kā Feī (Dio Coffee) 迪欧咖啡
Kaī Mén Zī Dàjiǔdiàn (Kaī Mén Zī Hotel) 开门子大酒店

ATTRACTIONS

Sān Bǎo Shuǐduì (Water-powered Hammers) 三宝水碓
Táocí Bówùguǎn (Museum of Porcelain) 陶瓷博物馆
Táocí Lìshǐ Bówùguǎn 陶瓷历史博物馆
(Ceramic Historical Exhibition Area)
Táocí Wénhuà Bólánqū (Pottery Culture Exhibition) 景德镇陶瓷文化博览区
Guān Yáo Bó Wù Guǎn (Imperial Porcelain Museum) 官窑博物馆
Jīng Chāng Lì Chí Mào Dà Shà 金昌利瓷贸大厦
Tán Qíng Xuān Zhì 檀情轩制
Zǐ Níu Gōng Zuò Shì 子牛工作室
Sháng Pǐn Gōng Zuò Shì 尚品工作室
Sān Bǎo Tǎo Yì Cūn 三宝陶艺村

GUANGZHOU 广州
ACCOMMODATIONS & DINING

Guǎng Zhōu Xiāng Gé Lí Lā Dàjiǔdiàn 广州香格里拉大酒店
(Shangri-La Hotel)
Bái Tiān'ér Bīnguǎn (White Swan Hotel) 白天鹅宾馆
Quánqiú Tong Dàjiǔdiàn (Globelink Hotel) 全球通大酒店
Hé Qún Dà Shà (Hé Qún Building) 合群大厦

Guǎngzhoū Jūn Qūn Yoù Ér Jiào 广州军区幼儿教师培训基地
Shī Peí Xùn Jī Dì (Peoples' Liberation
Army Kindergarten Teachers' Hotel)
Suì Yín Cháng Fěn Diàn (Cháng Fěn Fast-Food Shop) 穗银肠粉店
Zhèng Gōng Fū (Kung Fu) 正功夫
Gāo lì jiǔ jiā (Gāo Lì Jiǔ Jiā Korean Restaurant) 高丽酒家
Běi Yuán Jiǔjiā (Běi Yuán Restaurant) 北苑酒家
Dōng Běi Rén (The Manchurian) 东北人
Dōng Jiāng Hǎixiān Dà Jiǔlóu 东江海鲜大酒楼

ATTRACTIONS
Shāmiàn Island 沙面
Bái Yún Guó Jì Jī Cháng 白云国际机场
Gòu Wù Zhōng Xīng 购物中心
Hǎizhū Guǎng (Hǎizhū Cháng Square Wholesale Market) 海珠广场
Zhuàng Yuán Fǎng 状元坊
Guǎngzhoū Old Railway Station 广州老站
Huādìwan 花地湾
Kāipíng 开平
Diāo Lóu (Watch Tower) 雕镂

SHĒNZHÈN 深圳
ACCOMMODATIONS & DINING
Bàn Xī Jiǔdiàn 半溪酒店
Guǎngxìn Jiǔdiàn 广信酒店
Shangri-La (Xiānggélǐlā Dàjiǔdiàn) 香格里拉大酒店

ATTRACTIONS
Luó Hú Shāngyè Chéng (Luó Hú Commercial City) 罗湖商业城
Minsk World (Míngsīkè Hángmǔ Shìjiè) 明思克航母世界

THE SOUTHWEST:
MOUNTAINS & MINORITIES (CHAPTER 12)
GUILIN 桂林
ACCOMMODATIONS & DINING
Guìlín Bīnguǎn Guìlín Bravo Hotel 桂林宾馆
Lí Jiāng Waterfall Hotel (Lí Jiāng Dà Pùbù Fàndiàn) 漓江大瀑布饭店
Guìlín Diànxìn Bīnguǎn (Guìlín Telecom Hotel) 桂林电信宾馆
Mídiéxiāng (Rosemary Café) 迷迭香
Yíyuán Fàndiàn 逸园饭店
Zàowángyé Xiāngwèi Jū (Vesta Restaurant) 灶王爷香味居

ATTRACTIONS
Róng Hú (Banyan Lake) 榕湖
Shàn Hú (Cedar Lake) 彬湖
Liǎng Jiāng Sì Hú 两江四湖
Diécǎi Shān (Folding Brocade Hill) 叠彩山
Dúxiù Fēng (Solitary Beauty Peak) 独秀峰
Lúdí Yán (Reed Flute Cave) 芦笛岩
Qīxīng Gōngyuán (Seven Star Park) 七星公园

Wǎ Yáo Lǎo Diàn Chǎng
(Guìlín Wholesale Carving Market) 瓦窑老电厂
Lí Jiāng Jùyuàn (Lí Jiāng Theatre) 漓江剧院
Guìlín Mínsú Fēngqíng Yuán (Folk Customs Centre) 桂林民俗风情园
Chūntiān Jùchǎng (Guìlín Spring Theatre) 春天剧场
Dá Mó 哒摩
Mí Lè Fó 弥勒佛
Kóng Zī 孔子

LÍ RIVER 漓江
Buddha Cave 菩萨洞
Gǔróng Gōngyuán 古榕公园
Huángbù Dǎoyǐng 黄布倒影
Jiǔmǎ Huàshān (Nine Horses Fresco Hill) 九马画山
Yáng Dī 杨堤
Zhújiāng Pier 竹江码头
Huá Nán Jīng Tí Guán 华南晶体馆
Píng Shān Dà Cūn 平山大村

YÁNGSHUÒ
ACCOMMODATIONS & DINING
Yángshuò Shèngdì (Mountain Retreat) 阳朔胜地
Xīn Xī Jiē Dàjiǔdiàn (New West Street Hotel)
Baǐ Yù Lán Jiǔdiàn (Magnolia Hotel) 白玉兰酒店
Guǎng Yuè Kè Zhàn 广粤客栈
Àn Xiāng Shū Yíng Sū Caì Guǎn 暗香疏影蔬菜馆
(Pure Lotus Vegetarian Restaurant)
Zhī Huán Xuān (Liú Gōng Pavilion) 知还轩（留公）
Shuǐ Àn Huā Yuán Bíe Shù (Li River Reatreat) 水岸花园别墅

ATTRACTIONS
Xī Jiē (West Street) 西街
Yángshuò Lǚyóu Zīxún Fúwù Zhōngxīn 阳朔旅游咨询服务中心
(Yángshuò Tourism Information Service Center)
Bìlián Fēng (Green Lotus Peak) 白莲峰
Yángshuò Gōngyuán (Yángshuò Park) 阳朔公园
Jiǔ Mù Táng Kuaì Zī Fáng (Chopsticks Shop) 九木堂筷子坊
Quán Yì Kuaì Zī Fáng (Chopsticks Shop) 全意筷子坊

AROUND YÁNGSHUÒ
Yuèliang Shān (Moon Mountain) 月亮山
Gǔróng Gōngyuán (Banyan Tree Park) 古榕公园
Yùlóng Hé (Yulong River) 遇龙河
Lóng Toú Shān Mǎ Toú 龙头山码头
Jīn Bǎo Hé (Jīn Bǎo River) 金宝河
Shuǐyán (Water Cave) 水岩
Yínzi Yán (Silver Cave) 银子岩
Yùlóng Qiáo (Jade Dragon Bridge) 遇龙桥

TOWNS

Báishā	白沙
Fúlì	福利
Liú Gōng	留公
Xīngpíng	兴坪
Yú Cūn	渔村
Shuāng Duī Cūn	双堆村
Fèng Huáng Cūn (Phoenix Village)	凤凰村

BA MA   巴马
ACCOMMODATIONS & DINING

Shòu Xiāng Dàjiǔdiàn (Long Life Hotel)	寿乡大酒店
Shèng Dì Dàjiǔdiàn	胜地大酒店
Yán Nián Shān Zhuāng (Yán Nián Shān Zhuāng Guesthouse)	延年山庄

AROUND BA MA   巴马

Nán Níng	南宁
Kāng Doū Bīn Guǎn	康都宾馆
Beǐ Zhàn Kè Yùn Zhōng Xīn (North Bus Station)	北站客运中心
Ān Jí Qì Chē Zhàn (Ān Jí Bus Station)	安吉汽车站

ATTRACTIONS

Pán Yáng Hé (Pán Yáng River)	盘阳河
Baǐ Niǎo Yán (Baǐ Niǎo Water Cave)	百鸟岩
Baǐ Mó Dòng (Baǐ Mó Cavern)	百魔洞
Lóng Mén Āo (Dragon Gate)	龙门凹
Cì Fú Hú (Cì Fú Lake)	赐福湖

TOWNS

Fèng Shān	凤山
Baǐ Sè	百色
Pō Yuè	坡月

BEIHAI   北海
ACCOMMODATIONS & DINING

Yè Bā Lí Jiǔ Diàn (Gofar Garden Paris Hotel)	夜巴黎酒店
Zhōng Lóng Haǐ Bīn Guǎn	中龙海宾馆
Míng Doū Jiǔ Diàn	明都酒店
Yíng Bīn Guǎn	迎宾馆
Jīn Mǎ Meǐ Shí Chéng (Golden Horse Food Street)	金马美食城
Beǐ Bù Wān Guǎng Cháng	北部湾广场
Wàishā	外沙

ATTRACTIONS

Wēizhōu Dǎo (Wēizhōu Island)	润洲岛
Yíntān (Silver Beach)	银滩
Bā Dáo Zī Xíng Cē Jù Lè Bù (Bā Dáo Bike Shop)	八达自行车俱乐部

DONG XING
东兴

ACCOMMODATIONS & DINING

Jiāng Nán Qì Chē Zhàn
江南汽车站

Tiān Yuán Bīn Guǎn
天源宾馆

Dōng Rùn Dàjiǔdiàn
东润大酒店

Wáng Cháo Dàjiǔdiàn
王朝大酒店

ATTRACTIONS

Zhōng Yuè Yǒu Yí Qiáo (Friendship Bridge)
中越友谊桥

Jīn Tān Haǐ Tān (Golden Beach)
金滩海滩

Biān Mào Shì Cháng (Biān Mào Market)
边贸市场

TOWNS

Fáng Chéng Gǎng
防城港

PING XIANG
凭祥

ACCOMMODATIONS & DINING

Zhōng Yuè Guó Jì Dà Jiǔ Diàn
中越国际大酒店

Lóng Yuán Bīn Guǎn
龙源宾馆

ATTRACTIONS

Meǐ Jiā Huì (Fast Food)
美家惠

Huā Shān Bì Huà (Huā Shān Cliff Paintings)
花山壁画

Zuǒ Jiāng (Zuo River)
左江

Tuó Lóng Qiáo (Tuó Lóng Bridge)
驮龙桥

Míng Jiāng (Míng River)
明江

Yoǔ Yí Guān (Friendship Border)
友谊关

TOWNS

Níng Míng
宁明

GUÌYÁNG

ACCOMMODATIONS & DINING

Jīn Yáng Dà Dào Sān Hào Zhàn
金阳大道三号站

Tiān Yí Háo Shēng Dàjiǔdiàn
(Howard Johnson Plaza Hotel)
天怡豪生大酒店

Yì Dū Jiǔ Diàn (Yì Dū Hotel)
逸都酒店

Yuè Jūn Yuán Bīn Guǎn (Soldiers Guesthouse)
玉君苑宾馆

Miáojiā Meǐshí Yuán
苗家美食园

Mù Yáng Chéng Shuǐxiāng Huǒguō
牧羊城水上火锅

Shén Qí Jīn Zhú Dà Jiǔ Diàn
(Miracle Plaza Hotel Bakery)
神奇金筑大酒店面包店

ATTRACTIONS

Huángguǒshù Pùbù (Huángguǒshù Falls)
黄果树瀑布

Lónggōng Dòng (Dragon Palace Caves)
龙宫洞

Shítou Zhài (Stone Village)
石头寨

Tiānlóng Túnbǎo
天龙屯堡

Rénmín Guǎngchǎng (People's Square)
人民广场

Jiǎxiù Lóu
甲秀楼

Cuìwēi Yuán
翠薇园

Qiánlíng Gōngyuán (Qiánlíng Park)
黔灵公园

Hóngfú Sì (Hóngfú Temple) 弘福寺
Jīnyáng Shí Lín (Jīnyáng Stone Valley) 金阳石林
Xīn Huángguǒshù Bīnguǎn 新黄国树宾馆
Qián Fēng Yuán 黔丰缘

AROUND KAĬ LĬ 凯里
ACCOMMODATIONS & DINING

Guótài Dàjiǔdiàn 国泰大酒店
Kǎilǐ Lántiān Dàjiǔdiàn 凯里蓝天大酒店
Jīn Guān Jiǔ Diàn (Crown Plaza Hotel) 金冠酒店
Yí Rán Jiǔ Diàn 怡然酒店
Yù Jūn Yuàn Bīng Guǎn 玉君苑宾馆
Jīn Guān Jiǔ Diàn 金冠酒店

ATTRACTIONS

Màidéshì 麦德士
Minorities Museum (Zhōu Mínzú Bówùguǎn) 州民族博物馆
Shāngmào Jiē 商贸街
Duō Caǐ 多彩
Máo Taí 茅台
Dōng Mén Jiē 东门街
Lǎo Jiē 老街
Yí Rán Jiǔ Diàn 怡然酒店
Táo Rán Jū 陶然居
Wàn Bó Chāo Shì 万博超市
Lián Huā Xiàng 莲花巷
Nán Měng 南猛
Jiǎo Měng 脚猛
Māo Māo hé 猫猫河
Lóng Chǎng 龙场
Yú Dòng 渔洞
Dà Qiǎo Lù 大桥路
Kaǐ Lǐ Fā Diàn Chǎng 凯里发电厂
    (Industrial and Commercial Bank)

MIÁO/DÒNG AREAS
ACCOMMODATIONS & DINING

Róngjiāng Bīnguǎn 榕江宾馆
Yuèliàng Shān Bīnguǎn 月亮山宾馆
Zhàoxìng 肇兴
Fēngqíng Lǚyóu Shèwài Mínjū Lǚguǎn 风情旅游涉外民居旅馆
    (Lulu's Homestay)
Wénhuàzhàn Zhāodàisuǒ 文化站招待所
Bāshā 岜沙
Cóng Jiāng 从江
Dìpíng 地坪
Fǎnpái 反排
Huángpíng 黄平
Xī Jiāng 西江

Jìtáng 纪堂
Lángdé 郎德
Mátáng 麻塘
Róng Jiāng 榕江
Tái Jiāng 台江
Zhàoxìng 肇兴
Zhōuxī 舟溪

KUNMING 昆明
ACCOMMODATIONS & DINING
Chá Huā Bīn Guǎn (Camelia Hotel) 茶花宾馆
Cuì Hú Bīn Guǎn (Green Lake Hotel) 翠湖宾馆
Yún Dà Bīn Guǎn (Yunnan University Guesthouse) 云大宾馆
Yún Liáng Dà Jiǔ Diàn (Yún Liáng Hotel) 云粮大酒店
Yù Yuán Zhāi Sù Shí Guǎn (Vegetarian Restaurant) 玉泉窄素食馆
Jīn Gā Nà Xī Cān Tīng (Cannes Cafeteria) 金嘎纳西餐厅
Lǎo Zhī Qīng Shí Guǎn 老知青食馆
  (The Old Educated Youths Restaurant)
Cuì Hú Huì (The Gingko Elite) 翠湖汇

ATTRACTIONS
Nán Yáo Qì Chē Zhàn (Nán Yáo Bus Station) 南摇汽车站
Cuì Hú (Green Lake) 翠湖
Kūnmíng Shì Bó Wù Guǎn (Kūnmíng City Museum) 昆明市博物馆
Yún Nán Tiě Lù Bó Wù Guǎn 云南铁路博物馆
  (Yúnnán Railway Museum)
Yuán Tōng Sì (Yuán Tōng Temple) 圆通寺
Wén Huà Xiàng (Culture Alley) 文化巷
Jīn Diàn (Golden Temple) 金殿
Zhōng Lóu (Bell Tower) 钟楼
Qióng Zhú Sì (Bamboo Temple) 筇竹寺
Chéng Gòng Cūn 呈贡村
Dòu Nán Huā Huì Shì Cháng 斗南花卉市场
  (Dòu Nán Wholesale Flower Market)
Diān Chí (Lake (Diān) 滇池
Dà Guān Yuán 大观园
Dà Guān Lóu (Grand View Tower) 大观楼
Xī Shān (Western Hills) 西山
Huá Tíng Sì (Huá Tíng Temple) 华亭寺
Tài Huá Sì (Tài Huá Temple) 太华寺
Niè Ěr Zhī Mù (Niè Ěr's House) 聂耳之墓
Shí Lín (Stone Forest) 石林
Naì Gǔ Shí Lín (Black Pine Stone Forest) 乃古石林
Dà Dié Shuǐ Fēi Lóng Pù 大叠水飞龙瀑

DÀLǏ 大理
ACCOMMODATIONS & DINING
Gāo Dì (Highlander Guesthouse) 高地客栈
Xīn Rú Yuè Sù Shí Guǎn 心如悦素食馆
  (Xīn Rú Yuè Vegetarian Restaurant)

Fēng Yuè Sān Shuǐ Kèzhàn (Yúnnán Inn)　　风月山水客栈
Jí Mǔ Zàng Shì Jiǔdiàn (Jim's Tibetan Guesthouse)　　詹姆藏式酒店
Lán Líng Gé Jiǔdiàn (Landscape Hotel)　　兰林阁酒店
Jīn Huā Dàjiǔdiàn (The Golden Flower Hotel)　　金花大酒店

ATTRACTIONS
Ěr Hǎi (Ěr Hǎi Lake)　　洱海湖
Cāng Shān (Green Mountains)　　苍山
Fèngyǎn Dòng (Phoenix Cave)　　凤眼洞
Gǎntōng Sì (GǎntōngTemple)　　感通寺
Guānyīn Gé (Guānyīn Pavilion)　　观音阁
Jīnsuō Dǎo (Jīnsuō Island)　　金梭岛
Pǔtuó Dǎo (Pǔtuó Island)　　普陀岛
Sān Tǎ Sì Gōngyuán (Three Pagodas Park)　　三塔寺公园
Zhōnghé Sì (Zhōnghé Temple)　　中和寺
Qīngbì Xī (Qīngbì Stream)　　清碧溪

TOWNS
Wāsè　　挖色
Shāpíng　　沙坪
Xǐ Zhōu　　喜州
Zhōu Chéng　　周城

LÌ JIĀNG　　丽江
ACCOMMODATIONS & DINING
Fú Xiǎng Kèzhàn (Fú Xiǎng Inn)　　福祥客栈
Fáng Guǎn Kèzhàn (Fáng Guǎn Inn)　　房管客栈
Qiàn Xuě Lóu (Qiàn Xuě Garth)　　嵌雪楼
Mù Jiā Yuán Kè Zhàn　　木家苑客栈
　　(Mù Residence Garden Guesthouse)
Nàxī Fēngwèi Xiǎochī (Naxi Minority Food)　　纳西风味小吃
Shùn Shuǐ Lóu Cāntīng　　顺水楼餐厅
Nàxī Gǔyuè Huì (Nàxī Music Academy)　　纳西古乐会
Dōngbā Gōng　　东巴宫

ATTRACTIONS
Sìfāng Jiē (Market Square)　　四方街
Shīzi Shān (Lion Hill)　　狮子山
Wàngǔ Lóu (Wàngǔ Tower)　　万古楼
Mù Fǔ (Mù's Residence)　　木府
Dōngbā Wénhuà Bówùguǎn　　东巴文化博物馆
　　(Museum of Nàxī Dōngbā Culture)
Hēilóng Tán Gōngyuán (Black Dragon Pool Park)　　黑龙潭公园

AROUND LÌ JIĀNG
Bīngchuān Gōngyuán (Glacier Park)　　冰川公园
Chángjiāng Dìyī Wān (First Bend of the Yángzǐ)　　长江第一湾
Lúgū Hú (Lúgū Lake)　　泸沽湖
Máoniú Píng (Yak Meadow)　　牦牛坪
Tiger Leaping Gorge (Hǔ Tiào Xiá)　　虎跳峡

Yùfēng Sì (Yùfēng Temple) 玉峰寺
Yù Hú (Nguluko) 玉湖
Yùlóng Xuěshān (Jade Dragon Snow Mountain) 玉龙雪山
Yúnshān Píng (Spruce Meadow) 云杉坪

TOWNS
Báishā 白沙

SHU HE 束河
ACCOMMODATIONS & DINING
Hǎo Laí Wū Kè Zhàn (Hǎo Laí Guesthouse) 好来屋客栈
Xiàng Shàng Pǐn Kè Zhàn 巷上品客栈
　(Xiàng Shàng Pǐn Guesthouse)
Shù Hé k Èr Guó Jì Qīng Nián Lǔ Shè 束河K2国际青年旅舍
　(K2 Hostelling International)
Mā Mā Mī Yà (Mama Mia) 妈妈咪呀

ATTRACTIONS
Chá Mǎ Gǔ Dào Bó Wù Guǎn 茶马古道博物馆
　(Tea Horse Road Museum)
Niú Niú (Lovable Huskie) 牛牛

XIANGGELILA (ZHONGDIAN) 香格里拉
ACCOMMODATIONS & DINING
Pí Jiàng Chéng Lǎo Kè Zhàn (Cobbler's Hill Inn) 皮匠城老客栈
Ā Ruò Kāng Bā (Arro Khampa Restaurant) 阿若康巴
Lóngfēng Xiáng Dàjiǔdiàn (Holy Palace Hotel) 龙凤祥大酒店
Snowland Café 雪域咖啡厅
Tiānjiè Shénchuān Dàjiǔdiàn (Paradise Hotel) 天界神川大酒店
Tibet Café 西藏咖啡馆

ATTRACTIONS
Báishuǐ Tái (White Water Terraces) 白水台
Bìtǎ Hǎi (Bìtǎ Lake) 碧塔海
Ganden Sumtseling Gompa (Sōngzànlín Sì) 松赞林寺
Gǔ Chéng (Old town) 古城
Old Town Scripture Chamber 古城藏经堂
　(Gǔchéng Zàngjīng Táng)
Gǔ Chéng Pí Jiàng Pō 古城皮匠坡

JIANSHUI 建水
ACCOMMODATIONS & DINING
Zhūjiā Huāyuán Kèzhàn (Zhū Family Garden Hotel) 朱家花园客栈
Ān Huá Jiǔ Diàn (Ān Huá Hotel) 安华酒店
Huā Qīng Jiǔ Diàn (Huāqīng Hotel) 华清酒店
Lín Ān Kè Zhàn (Lín Ān Inn) 临安客栈
Yǒu Jiā Tiě Bǎn Shāo 有家铁板烧
Gé Guō Xiāng (Old Town Café) 隔锅香
Jiā Lì Bīng Zhī Bǎo 嘉利 冰之宝

ATTRACTIONS
Wén Ān Fǔ (Confucius Temple) 文安府
Yànzi Dòng (Swallow's Nest Cave) 燕子洞

Zhū Jiā Huā Yuán (Zhū Family Residence) 朱家花园
Shuānglóng Qiáo (Double Dragon Bridge) 双龙桥

TOWNS
Bàdá 坝达
Duōyī Cūn 多依村
Tuán Shān Cūn 团山村

YUANYANG 元阳
ACCOMMODATIONS & DINING
Yún Tī Jiǔ Diàn (Yún Tī Hotel) 云梯酒店
Tī Tián Gōng Yù (Apartments of Terraced Fields) 梯田公寓
Liáng Xīn Fàn Diàn 良心饭店
Yuán Yáng Zhī Chuāng (Window on Yuányáng) 元阳之窗

ATTRACTIONS
Lǎo Hǔ Zuǐ (Tiger's Mouth) 老虎嘴
Yuányáng Lǎoxiànchéng (Yuányáng old town) 元阳老县城
Xīn Jiē Zhèn (Yuányáng old town) 新街镇
Hóng Hé (Red River) 红河
Mógu Fáng (Mushroom Houses) 蘑菇房
Lóng Má Lù (Dragon Festival) 龙马路
Guān Jǐng Taí (Terrace Viewing Platform) 观景台

TOWNS
Jīngkǒu Mínsú Cūn 金口民俗村
Hā Bō 哈波
Lǎo Měng 老勐
Měngpǐn 猛品
Lù Chūn 绿春
Nánshā 南市

PU ER 普洱
ACCOMMODATIONS & DINING
Shèng Ān Dí Jín Lún Dà Jiǔ Diàn 圣安迪锦伦大酒店
Jīn Kǒng Què Jiǔ Diàn 金孔雀
TOWNS
Sī Máo 思茅

NING ER 宁洱
ACCOMMODATIONS & DINING
Pú Ěr Bīn Guǎn (Pú Ěr Guesthouse) 普洱宾馆
Níng Ěr Bīn Guǎn (Níng Ěr Guesthouse) 宁洱宾馆

ATTRACTIONS
Pú ér Mín Zú Chá Yì Guǎn 普洱民族茶艺馆
Chá Mǎ Gǔ (Dào Tea Horse Road) 茶马古道博
Duō Yǐ Shù (Duō Yǐ Tree) 多依树
Chá Ān Pō Toú (Chá Ān Tea Garden) 茶庵坡头

TOWNS
Mò Heī 磨黑
Mò Jiāng 墨江

JINGHONG (景洪) & XISHUANGBANNA (西双版纳)

ACCOMMODATIONS & DINING

Jǐng Lán Dà Jiǔ Diàn (Kingland Hotel)	景兰大酒店
Xī Shuāng Bǎn Nà Taì Doū Dà Jiǔ Diàn	西双版纳泰都大酒店
(Thai City Hotel)	
Bǎnnà Bīnguǎn (Banna Guesthouse)	版纳宾馆
Cái Chūn Qīng (Thai Restaurant)	财春青
Dǎijiā Měishí Cūn	傣家美食村
Dǎiyuán Dàjiǔdiàn (Tai Garden Hotel)	傣园大酒店
Dōngguān Jiǎozǐ Guǎn	东关饺子馆
Měi Měi Café	美美咖啡
Méigōng Kāfēiguǎ (Mekong Café)	湄公咖啡馆

ATTRACTIONS

Màntīng Gōngyuán (Manting Park)	曼听公园
Mínzú Fēngqíng Yuán (Minority Theatre)	民族风情园
Mín Zú Gōng Yì Pǐn Shì Chǎng	民族工艺品市场
(Minority Crafts Market)	
Xī Nán Mín Zú Bù Luò	西南民族部落
(South West Minority Tribe Shop)	
Rèdài Huāhuìyuán (Tropical Flower and Plants Garden)	热带花卉园

AROUND JĪNGHÓNG

Bǎnnà Yǔlín Gǔ (Bǎnnà Rainforest Valley)	版纳雨林谷
Bǎnnà Yěxiàng Gǔ (Banna Wild Elephant Valley)	版纳野象谷
Dǎi Zú Yuán (Dǎi Minority Folk Customs Park)	傣族园
Jīnuò Mínsú Shānzhài (Jīnuò Folk Custom Village)	基诺民俗山寨
Sānchàhé Zìrán Bǎohùqū (Sānchàhé Nature Reserve)	三岔河自然保护区
Xīshuāngbǎnnà Rèdài Zhíwùyuán	西双版纳热带植物园
Tropical Flower and Plants Garden)	
Xiàngxíng Róngshù	象形榕树
Yoú Qí Chē Héng	游骑车行

TOWNS

Měnglà	勐腊
Měnglún	勐仑
Měngyǎng	勐养
Móhān	磨憨
Gǎnlǎnbà (Měnghǎn)	橄榄坝 (勐罕)
Chiang Saen	清盛
Guān Leí	关累
Guān Leí Lǚ Sān Jiǎo Jiǔ Diàn	关累绿三角
(Guān Leí Travelers Hotel)	

HAINSN ISLAND   海南岛
HAIKOU   海口

ACCOMMODATIONS & DINING

Míng Yáng Hé Taì Jiǔdiàn (Sun Herton Hotel)	明阳荷泰酒店
Xīn Jiā Yuán Jiǔ Diàn	新嘉源酒店
Lǎo Xīn Jiāng Tiān Shān Zhī Zī Fàn Diàn	老新疆天山之子饭店
Xī Lóng Shāng Wù Jiǔ Diàn	禧龙商务酒店

ATTRACTIONS

Hǎiruì Mù	海瑞墓
Yóu Qí Bù Luò (517 Bike Club)	游骑部落
Tiān Yá Qí Lǚ Jù Lè Bù (Tiānyá Bike Club)	天涯骑驴俱乐部
Hǎikǒu Gōngyuán (Hǎikǒu Park)	海口公园
Wǔgōng Cí (Five Officials Temple)	五公祠
Qiān Nián Gǔ Yán Tiǎn (Yántián Salt Flats)	千年古盐田
Tún Chāng Shuǐ Jīng Kuàng	屯昌水晶矿
(Tún Chāng Crystal Mine)	

TOWNS

Lóng Loú Zhèn	龙楼镇
Tún Chāng	屯昌

SANYA   三亚

ACCOMMODATIONS & DINING

Sānyà Kǎilái Dùjià Jiǔdiàn (Gloria Resort Sānyà)	三亚凯来度假酒店
Sānyà (Sānyà Yàlóng Wān Jiàrì Jiǔdiàn	三亚亚龙湾假日酒店
(Holiday Inn Resort Yàlóng Bay)	
Sānyà Shānhǎitiān Dàjiǔdiàn	三亚山海天大酒店
Jǐn Hóng Dù Jià Jiǔ Diàn (Sānyà Jǐnhóng Resort)	锦宏度假酒店
Dōng Gǎng Hǎi Jǐng Jiǔ Diàn	东港海景酒店
(Donggang Sea View Hotel)	
Dà Yú Tiě Bǎn Shāo (Dàyú Teppenyaki)	大渔铁板烧
Měi Shí Guǎng Cháng (Dàdōnghǎi Food Square)	美食广场
Dì Zhōng Hǎi Xī Cān Tīng	地中海西餐厅

ATTRACTIONS

Dà Dōng Hǎi Beach	大东海
Tiānyá Hǎijiǎo	天涯海角
Tongzha (Tōngshí)	通什
Xī Dǎo (West Island)	西岛
Yàlóng Wān (Yàlóng Bay)	亚龙湾
Lǚ Yé Hù Wài Jù Lè Bù (Wild Green Outdoor Club)	绿野户外俱乐部
Píng Taí Haǐ Dǐ Mó Tuō (Underwater Scooters)	平台海底摩托
Ào Lín Pǐ Kè Shè Jī Yú Lè Zhōng Xīn	
(Olympic Shooting and Entertainment Center)	奥林匹克射击娱乐中心

YANGZI & BEYOND (CHAPTER 13)

ÉMÉI SHĀN   峨眉山

ACCOMMODATIONS & DINING

Éméi Shān Fàndiàn	峨眉山饭店
Hóngzhū Shān Bīnguǎn	红珠山宾馆
Jīn Dǐng Dàjiǔdiàn (Golden Summit Hotel)	金顶大酒店

ATTRACTIONS

Bàoguó Sì	报国寺
Fúhǔ Sì	伏虎寺
Hóngchūn Píng	洪椿坪
Jīn Dǐng (Golden Peak)	金顶
Jiēyǐn Diàn (Jiēyǐn Hall)	接引殿

Jiǔlǎo Dòng (Jiǔlǎo Cave)   九老洞
Léidòng Píng (Léidòng Terrace)   雷洞坪
Niúxīn Tíng (Niúxīn Pavilion)   牛心亭
Qīngyīn Gé   清音阁
Qiānfó Dǐng (Qiānfó Peak)   千佛顶
Shèshēn Yán (Shèshēn Cliff)   摄身岩
Lǚrén Zhōngxīn (Tourist Center)   旅人中心
Wànfó Dǐng (Wànfó Peak)   万佛顶
Wànnián Sì (Wànnián Monastery)   万年寺
Wànnián Chēchǎng (Wànnián Cable Car Station)   万年车场
Xǐ Xiàng Chí (Elephant Bathing Pool)   洗象池
Xiānfēng Sì (Xiānfēng Monastery)   先峰寺

LÈ SHĀN   乐山
ACCOMMODATIONS & DINING
Jífēng Lóu Bīnguǎn   集风楼宾馆
Jiā Zhōu Bīnguǎn   嘉州宾馆

ATTRACTIONS
Dà Fó (Great Buddha)   大佛
Jiǔqǔ Zhàndào (Path of Nine Switchbacks)   九曲栈道
Wūyóu Shān (Wūyóu Mountain)   乌尤山

WÒLÓNG   卧龙
TOWNS
Hétao Píng   核桃坪
Shāwān   沙湾

ACCOMMODATIONS & DINING
Xióngmāo Shānzhuāng (Panda Inn)   熊猫山庄
Sìtōng Bīnguǎn   四通宾馆

ATTRACTIONS
Distillery   酒厂

JIǓZHÀI GŌU   九寨沟
ACCOMMODATIONS & DINING
Jīnxīn Bīnguǎn (Jīnxīn Hotel)   金鑫宾馆
Jiǔzhài Gōu Dàjiǔdiàn (Jiǔzhài Gōu International Hotel)   九寨沟大酒店
Xīngyǔ Guójì Dàjiǔdiàn (Xīngyǔ International Hotel)   星宇国际大酒店
Yínyuàn Bīnguǎn (Yínyuàn Hotel)   银苑宾馆

WUHAN   武漢
ACCOMMODATIONS & DINING
Faguo Jie (French Street)   法國街
Hubuxiang   户部巷
Jing Wu Ren Jia   精武人家

WǓLÍNG YUÁN/ZHĀNG JIĀ JIÈ   武陵源张家界
ACCOMMODATIONS & DINING
Xiānglóng Guójì Dàjiǔdiàn (Dragon International Hotel)   湘龙国际大酒店
Mínsú Shānzhuāng (Mínsú Mountain Villa)   民俗山庄

Pípa Xī Bīnguǎn | 琵琶溪宾馆
Xiāngdiàn Shānzhuāng (Xiāngdiàn Mountain Villa) | 湘电山庄
Hushifu Sanxiaguo | 胡师傅三下锅

ATTRACTIONS

Huángshí Zhài | 黄石寨
Yuanjiajie | 袁家界
Jinbian Si (Golden Whip Stream) | 金鞭溪
Shui Rao Xi Men (Stream Winding Around Four Gates) | 水绕四门
Bailong Tianti (Bailong Tourist Lift) | 百龙天梯
Mihuntai (the Platform of Lost Mind) | 迷云台
Tiānzǐ Shān Nature Reserve | 天子山自然保护区
Yùbǐ Fēng | 御笔锋
Tiānzǐ Gé | 天子阁
Suǒ Xī Yù Nature Reserve | 索溪峪自然保护区
Huánglóng Dòng (Huánglóng Cave) | 黄龙洞

CHÓNGQÌNG   重庆
ACCOMMODATIONS & DINING

Guǎngchǎng Bīnguǎn (Plaza Hotel) | 广场宾馆
Hǎi Yì Fàndiàn (Harbour Plaza) | 海逸饭店
Xīěrdùn Jiǔdiàn (Hilton Hotel) | 希尔顿酒店
Yángzǐ Jiāng Jiàrì Jiǔdiàn (Holiday Inn) | 扬子江假日酒店
Wànháo Jiǔdiàn (Marriott Hotel) | 万豪酒店
Rénmín Bīnguǎn | 人民宾馆

ATTRACTIONS

Chóngqìng Dòngwùyuán (Chóngqìng Zoo) | 重庆动物园
Chóngqìng Shì Bówùguǎn | 重庆博物馆
  (Chóngqìng Municipal Museum) | 画家之村
Huàjiā Zhī Cūn (Artists' Village)
Shǐdíwēi Jiāngjūn Jiùjū (Stilwell Museum/ | 史迪威将军旧居
  General Stilwell's former residence)

WŪLÍNG YUÁN/ZHĀNG JIĀ JIÈ   武陵源/张家界
ACCOMMODATIONS & DINING

Xiānglóng Guójì Dàjiǔdiàn (Dragon International Hotel) | 湘龙国际大酒店
Mínsú Shānzhuāng (Mínsú Mountain Villa) | 民俗山庄
Pípa Xī Bīnguǎn | 琵琶溪宾馆
Xiāngdiàn Shānzhuāng (Xiāngdiàn Mountain Villa) | 湘电山庄

THE TIBETAN WORLD (CHAPTER 14)
GOLMUD (GÉ'ĚRMÙ)   格尔木
ACCOMMODATIONS & DINING

Gé'ěrmù Bīnguǎn | 格尔木宾馆
Wēi'ěrshì Dàjiǔdiàn | 威尔士大酒店
Yóuzhèng Bīnguǎn (Post Hotel) | 邮政宾馆
Liúyī Shǒu | 留一手

SHIGATSE (RÌKĀZÉ)
日喀则

ACCOMMODATIONS & DINING
Huáiyù Mínzú Biǎoyì Zhōngxīn 怀玉民族表艺中心
Lǎoyǒu Lèyuán 老友乐园
Tenzin Hotel (Dàn Zēng Bīnguǎn) 旦增宾馆
Shénhú Jiǔdiàn (Hotel Manasarovar) 神湖酒店
Wūzī Dàjiǔdiàn (Wutse Hotel) 乌孜大酒店
Niútóu Zàngcān (Yak Head Restaurant) 牛头藏餐
Yǎlǔ Zàng Cāntīng 雅鲁藏餐厅

ATTRACTIONS
Rìkāzé zhōngchéngbǎo 日喀则中城堡
Zhāshílúnbù Sì (Tashilhunpo Monastery) 扎什伦布寺
Jímào Shìchǎng (Shigatse Bazaar) 集贸市场
Sìfāng Chāoshì 四方超市

XINING

ACCOMMODATIONS & DINING
Yínlóng Jiǔdiàn 银龙酒店
Bùlǎngníyà Xīcānjiǔláng (Boronia Café) 布郎尼亚西餐酒廊
Sūjīnímǎ Fāngqīnggōng (Suggienima) 苏姬尼玛风情宫

LHASA

ACCOMMODATIONS & DINING
Miàojíxiáng Lùguǎn (Pilgrimages Inn) 妙吉祥旅馆

Appendix B:
The Chinese Menu

One of the best things about any visit to China is the food, at least for the independent traveler. Tour groups are often treated to a relentless series of cheap, bland dishes designed to cause no complaints, and to keep the costs down for the Chinese operator, so do everything you can to escape and order some of the local specialties we've described for you in each chapter. Here they are again, listed alphabetically under the cities in which they are mentioned, and with characters you can show your waiter or waitress (but check back to the review first, as some of the dishes are unique to certain restaurants). Widely available Chinese standards are together at the top, so check there if the recommended dish isn't listed under its city heading.

Supplement this list by bringing along the bilingual menu from your local Chinese restaurant at home. The characters will not be quite the same as those used on the mainland (more similar to those used in Hong Kong and Macau), but they will be understood. Don't expect the dishes to be the same, however. Expect them to be *better*.

Any mainstream nonspecialty restaurant can and will make any common Chinese dish, whether it's on the menu or not. But ask for a spicy Sìchuān dish in a Cantonese restaurant in Guǎngzhōu, and you'll be sorely disappointed.

Outside Hong Kong and big hotels and expat cafe ghettos on the mainland, few restaurants have English menus. If, near your five-star hotel, you see restaurants with signs saying ENGLISH MENU, there's a fair chance you are going to be cheated with double prices, and you should eat elsewhere (unless it's an obvious backpacker hangout).

Menus generally open with *liáng cài* (cold dishes). For hygiene reasons in mainland China, except in top-class Sino-foreign joint-venture restaurants, you are strongly advised to avoid these cold dishes, especially if you're on a short trip. The restaurant's specialties also come early in the menu, often easily spotted by their significantly higher prices, and if you dither, the waitress will recommend them, saying, "I hear this one's good." Waitresses always recommend ¥180 ($23/£11) dishes, never ¥18 ($2.25/£1) ones. Occasionally, some of these may be made from creatures you would regard as pets or zoo creatures (or best in the wild), may be made from parts you consider inedible, or may contain an odd material like swallow saliva (the main ingredient of bird's nest soup, a rather bland and uninteresting Cantonese delicacy).

Main dishes come next, various meats and fish before vegetables and *dòufu* (tofu), and drinks at the end. There are rarely desserts, although Guǎngdōng (Cantonese) food has absorbed the tradition of eating something sweet at the end of the meal from across the border in Hong Kong, where all restaurants have something to offer of this kind, if only sliced fruit.

Soup is usually eaten last, although dishes arrive in a rather haphazard order. Outside Guǎngdōng Province, Hong Kong, and Macau, rice usually arrives toward the end, and if you want it with your meal you must ask (point at the characters for rice, below, when the first dish arrives).

There is no tipping. Tea, chopsticks, and napkins should be free, although if a wrapped packet of tissues arrives, there may be a small fee. Service charges do not exist outside of major hotels, and there are no cover charges or taxes. If you are asked what tea you would like, then you are going to receive something above average and will be charged. You should be careful, since some varieties of tea may cost more than the meal itself.

Most Chinese food is not designed to be eaten solo, but if you do find yourself on your own, ask for small portions *(xiǎo pán)*.

xiǎo pán   small portion   小盘

These are usually about 70% the size of a full dish and about 70% the price, but they enable you to sample the menu properly without too much waste.

POPULAR DISHES & SNACKS

PINYIN	ENGLISH	CHINESE
bābǎo zhōu	rice porridge with nuts and berries	八宝粥
bāozi	stuffed steamed buns	包子
bīngqílín	ice cream	冰淇淋
chǎofàn	fried rice	炒饭
chǎomian	fried noodles	炒面
cōng bào niúròu	quick-fried beef and onions	葱爆牛肉
diǎnxin	dim sum (snacks)	点心
gānbiān sìjìdòu	sautéed string beans	干煸四季豆
gōngbào jīdīng	spicy diced chicken with cashews	宫爆鸡丁
guōtiē	fried dumplings/pot stickers	锅贴
hóngshāo fǔzhú	braised tofu	红烧腐竹
hóngshāo huángyú	braised yellow fish	红烧黄鱼
huíguō ròu	twice-cooked pork	回锅肉
huǒguō	hot pot	火锅
jiǎozi	dumplings/Chinese ravioli	饺子
jīngjiàng ròusī	shredded pork in soy sauce	京酱肉丝
mápó dòufu	spicy tofu with chopped meat	麻婆豆腐
miàntiáo	noodles	面条
mǐfàn	rice	米饭
mù xū ròu	sliced pork with fungus (mushu pork)	木须肉
niúròu miàn	beef noodles	牛肉面
ròu chuàn	kabobs	肉串
sānxiān	"three flavors" (usually prawn, mushroom, pork)	三鲜
shuǐjiǎo	boiled dumplings	水饺
suānlà báicài	hot-and-sour cabbage	酸辣白菜
suānlà tāng	hot-and-sour soup	酸辣汤
sù shíjǐn	mixed vegetables	素什锦
tángcù lǐji	sweet-and-sour pork tenderloin	糖醋里脊
tǔdòu dùn niúròu	stewed beef and potato	土豆炖牛肉
xīhóngshì chǎo jīdàn	tomatoes with eggs	西红柿炒鸡蛋
yóutiáo	fried salty doughnut	油条

PINYIN	ENGLISH	CHINESE
yúxiāng qiézi	eggplant in garlic sauce	鱼香茄子
yúxiāng ròusī	shredded pork in garlic sauce	鱼香肉丝
zhēngjiǎo	steamed dumplings	蒸饺
zhōu	rice porridge	粥

ORDERING HOT POT
Types of Hot Pot

锅底种类

yuānyang huǒguō	half spicy, half regular soup	鸳鸯火锅
qīngtāng huǒguō	chicken soup hot pot	清汤火锅
hóngwèi huǒguō	only spicy hot pot	红味火锅
yútóu huǒguō	fish head soup	鱼头火锅

shūcài lèi	vegetables	蔬菜类
tǔdòu	potato	土豆
dòufu	tofu	豆腐
dòufu pí	tofu skin	豆腐皮
dòng dòufu	cold tofu	冻豆腐
dōngguā	Chinese melon	冬瓜
qīngsǔn	lettuce shoots	青笋
bái luób	fresh white radish	白罗卜
ǒupiàn	sliced lotus	藕片
fěnsī	glass noodles	粉丝
huángdòuyá	bean sprouts	黄豆芽
bōcài	green spinach	菠菜
xiāngcài	caraway seeds	香菜
dōngsǔn	bamboo shoots	冬笋
mùěr	black agaric mushroom	木耳
pínggū	flat mushrooms	平菇
jīnzhēngū	noodle mushrooms	金针菇
xiānggū	straw mushrooms	香菇
niángāo	Chinese rice cake	年糕

ròu lèi	meats	肉类
zhūròu piàn	sliced pork	猪肉片
niúròu piàn	sliced beef	牛肉片
jīròu piàn	sliced chicken	鸡肉片
féi niú	fatty hot pot beef	肥牛
féi yáng	lamb	肥羊
huǒtuǐ	ham	火腿
niúròu wán	beef balls	牛肉丸
ròu wánzi	meatballs	肉丸子
xiajiao	shrimp dumplings	虾饺

PINYIN	ENGLISH	CHINESE
dànjiǎo	egg dumplings	蛋饺
ānchun dàn	quail's eggs	鹌鹑蛋
yā cháng	duck's intestines	鸭肠
yā xuě	duck's blood	鸭血
yú tóu	fish head	鱼头
shànyú piàn	sliced eel	鳝鱼片
níqiu	loach	泥鳅
zhū nǎo	pig brains	猪脑
haǐxiān	**seafood**	海鲜
xiā	shrimps	虾
yú piàn	sliced fish	鱼片
yú wán	fish balls	鱼丸
mòyú piàn	black carp strips	墨鱼片
yóuyú piàn	fish strips	鱿鱼片
tiáoliào	**seasoning**	可选调料
làjiāo jiàng	chili hot sauce	辣椒酱
làyóu	chili oil	辣油
xiāngyóu	sesame oil	香油
huāshēng jiàng	peanut paste	花生酱
shāchá jiàng	barbecue sauce	沙茶酱
zhīma jiàng	sesame paste	芝麻酱
dà suàn	garlic	大蒜
xiāngcài	cilantro	香菜
cù	vinegar	醋

Useful Phrases

Qǐng lái yī bēi bīng píjiǔ!	May I have a cold beer, please?	请来一杯冰啤酒！
Qǐng bǎ huǒ guān xiǎo yīdiǎn!	Could you turn the fire down a little, please?	请把火关小一点！
Qǐng bǎ huǒ kāi dà yīdiǎn!	Could you turn the fire up a little, please?	请把火开大一点！
Qǐng bāng wǒmen jiā yīdiǎn tāng!	Could you add some more water, please?	请 帮我们加一点汤！

Anji

		安吉
là wèi bù gū niǎo	spicy fried cuckoo	辣味布谷鸟
ròu sháo tǔ dòu	meat and potato stew	肉烧土豆
shā bǐng	savory unleavened breads	沙饼
sheng si zhu pi	Ānjí bamboo science beer	圣氏竹啤
shān xìng rén	hickory nuts	山杏仁
hóng shǔ gān	dried sweet potatoes	红薯干

PINYIN	ENGLISH	CHINESE
qí yì guǒ	dried sliced kiwis	奇异果
shān hé táo	walnuts	山核桃
Bama		巴马
huǒ mǎ yóu	cannabis oil soup	火麻油
Běijīng		北京
dà pán jī	diced chicken and noodles in tomato sauce	大盘鸡
gǒubùlǐ bāozi	pork-stuffed bread dumplings	狗不理包子
jiàngshāo qiézi	braised eggplant	酱烧茄子
jīngjiàng ròusī	shredded pork with green onion rolled in tofu skin	京酱肉丝
kǎo yángròu	roast mutton	烤羊肉
lǎogānmā shāo jī	spicy diced chicken with bamboo and ginger	老干妈烧鸡
làròu dòuyá juǎnbǐng	spicy bacon and bean sprouts in pancakes	腊肉豆芽卷饼
làwèi huájī bǎozǎi fàn	chicken and sweet sausage on rice in clay pot	腊味滑鸡煲仔饭
málà lóngxiā	spicy crayfish	麻辣龙虾
mǐlà luófēi yú	diced deep-fried fish with garlic and hot peppers	米辣罗非鱼
mìzhì zhǐbāo lúyú	paper-wrapped perch and onions on sizzling iron plate	秘制纸包鲈鱼
qiáomiàn māo ěrduo	"cat's ear" buckwheat pasta with chopped meat	荞面猫耳朵
ròudīng báicài xiànbǐng	meat cabbage pie	肉丁白菜馅饼
shēngjiān baōzi	pork-stuffed fried bread dumplings	生煎包子
shǒubā fàn	Uighur-style rice with raisins and mutton	手扒饭
suànxiāng jīchì	garlic paper-wrapped chicken wings	蒜香鸡翅
xiāngcǎo cuìlà yú	whole fried fish with hot peppers and lemon grass	香草脆辣鱼
xiǎolóng bāozi	pork-stuffed steamed bread dumplings	小笼包子
xièsānxiān shuǐjiǎo	boiled crab dumplings with shrimp and mushrooms	蟹三鲜水饺
yángròu chuàn	spicy mutton skewers with cumin	羊肉串
yángyóu mádòufu	mashed soy bean with lamb oil	洋油麻豆腐
yánjú xiā	shrimp skewers in rock salt	盐局虾
yì bǎ zhuā	fried wheat cakes	一把抓
yóutiáo niúròu	sliced beef with fried dough in savory sauce	油条牛肉

PINYIN	ENGLISH	CHINESE
zhāngchá yā	crispy smoked duck with plum sauce	樟茶鸭
zhá qiéhé	pork-stuffed deep-fried eggplant	炸茄合
zhǐbāo lúyú	paper-wrapped perch in sweet sauce	纸包鲈鱼
zhūròu báicài bāozi	steamed bun stuffed with pork and cabbage	猪肉白菜包子

Chángchūn 长春
dà páigu	big ribs	大排骨
jiājīdùnzhēnmó	tender pieces of chicken stewed with mushrooms in a dark savory sauce	家鸡炖榛蘑
kou shui ji	chicken with special sauce	口水鸡

Chángshā 长沙
hóng zǎozi	red dates	红枣子
língjiǎo	water chestnuts	菱角
mǐtāng sīguā	rice soup with silk gourd	米汤丝瓜
qiàng qíncài xiàguǒ	baby celery and pearl onions sautéed with macadamia nuts	炝芹菜夏果
qīngjiāo qiézi	eggplant sautéed with green pepper	青椒茄子

Chéngdé 承德
cōng shāo yězhū ròu	wild boar cooked with onions	葱烧野猪肉
lù ròu chǎo zhēnmó	venison stir-fried with hazel mushrooms	鹿肉炒榛磨
Qiánlóng shuǐjiǎo	jiǎozi dumplings	乾隆水饺
què cháo shān jī piàn	"Sparrow's nest" pheasant slices	雀巢山鸡片
zhēn mó shānji]li] dīng	nuggets of pheasant with local mushrooms	榛磨山鸡丁

Chéngdū 成都
báitāng lǔ	plain broth	白汤卤
Càigēn Xiāng páigu	Càigēn Xiāng spareribs	菜根香排骨
cuìpí shàngsù	crispy vegetarian duck	脆皮上素
dòufu jìyú	tofu and golden carp	豆腐鲫鱼
gōngbào jīdīng	spicy diced chicken	宫爆鸡丁
huíguō hòupícài	twice-cooked thick-skinned greens	回锅厚皮菜
jiāozǐ zhēng guìyú	king crab steamed with peppercorns	椒子蒸桂鱼
Jiāróng suāncài kǎo bǐng	Jiāróng bread stuffed with cabbage and barbecued pork	嘉绒酸菜烤饼
jiāzhōu niúròu miàn	California beef noodles	加州牛肉面
lóngyǎn bāozi	dragon eye bāozi	龙眼包子
máoniú ròubāo	yak meat bāozi	牦牛肉包
pào cài	pickled vegetables	泡菜
pàocài jiāyú	fish with pickled vegetables	泡菜佳鱼

PINYIN	ENGLISH	CHINESE
pàojiāo mòyúzǎi	pickled pepper with baby squid	泡椒墨鱼仔
suān luóbo chǎo máoniúròu	pickled cabbage with fried yak meat	酸萝卜炒牦牛肉
sūpí niúliǔ	crispy beef tenderloin	酥皮牛柳
yěcài bā	steamed rice bread with wild vegetable wrapped in corn husks	野菜粑
Yìndù gāli chǎocài	Indian vegetable curry	印度咖喱炒菜
yùer shāo jiǎyú	green turtle stewed with taro	芋儿烧甲鱼

Chóngqìng 重庆

guàiwèi yāzi	special flavored duck	怪味鸭子
guōbā ròupiàn	pork with bamboo shoots over crispy rice	锅巴肉片
qīngjiāo bào zǐjī	baby chicken quick-fried with green pepper	青椒爆仔鸡
tiěbǎn shāo zhī yínxuěyú	silver snow fish cooked on an iron plate	铁板烧汁银雪鱼
yùmǐ bǐng	corn cakes	玉米饼

Dàlǐ 大理

ěr kuài	stuffed rice dough	饵块
mùguā jī	fried chicken Bái-style	木瓜鸡
rǔshàn	milk fan	乳扇
shāguō yú	stewed fish casserole	砂锅鱼
shuǐzhǔ ròupiàn	pork and vegetable in spicy broth	水煮肉片

Dàlián 大连

shíguō bànfàn	stone pot rice	石锅拌饭
dòufu tang	spicy tofu soup	豆腐汤

Dāndōng 丹东

lǎncài hǔpíjiāo	pork-stuffed bell peppers in black bean sauce	榄菜虎皮椒
huǒguō	hot pot	火锅
lěngmiàn	cold noodles	冷面
shíguō_bànfàn	stone pot rice	石锅拌饭
shēngbàn niúròu	raw beef	生拌牛肉
xiānglà gǒuròu	spicy dog meat	香辣狗肉

Dàtóng 大同

chǎo lāmiàn	fried wheat noodles	炒拉面
shāo qiézi	stewed eggplant	烧茄子
sōng yùmǐ	corn cooked with pine nuts	松玉米

PINYIN	ENGLISH	CHINESE
Dūnhuáng		敦煌
lǘròu huángmiàn	donkey meat with yellow noodles	驴肉黄面
sāngshèn jiǔ	mulberry wine	桑椹酒
xìngpíshuǐ	dried apricot juice	杏皮水
yángpái	lamb chops	羊排
Golmud (Gé'r̄mù)		格尔木
huángmèn yángròu	lamb stew	黄焖羊肉
xiānggū càixīn	mushrooms and Chinese greens	香菇菜心
xiāngsū jī	crispy chicken	香酥鸡
Guǎngzhōu		广州
báizzhuó héxiā	Cantonese-style shrimp	白灼河虾
fěnsī zhēng shànbèi	steamed scallops with glass noodles	粉丝蒸扇贝
huādiāo zhù jī	chicken cooked in yellow wine	花雕住鸡
liǔlián xuěgāo	durian ice cream	榴莲雪糕
jiǔhuáng ròusī	sliced pork with yellow chives	韭黄肉丝
mǎtí xiè	horseshoe crab	马碲蟹
qīngzhēng huāxiè	steamed crab	清蒸花蟹
tángcù sūròu	sweet-and-sour pork	糖醋酥肉
xiāngū xiān xiāwán	stir-fried fresh shrimp with straw mushrooms	鲜菇鲜虾丸
xīníng júròu pái	baked sparerib in lemon sauce	西宁肉排
yóu zhá chòu dòufu	fried stinky tofu	油炸臭豆腐
wǔ shé bāo lǎo jī	boiled five snakes and old chicken in soup	五蛇煲老鸡
zhīshì niúyóu jú hǎixiān dòufu	baked seafood and bean curd	芝士牛油局海鲜豆腐
xiān xiā jī dàn cháng	egg and prawns steamed pancake	鲜虾鸡蛋肠
yóu tiáo	fried bread sticks	油条
zhoū	congee	粥
Guìlín		桂林
dāndān miàn	noodles in spicy peanut sauce	担担面
Guìlín mǐfěn	Guìlín rice noodles	桂林米粉
mǎròu	horse meat	马肉
shāncūn làròu zhēng yúpiàn	steamed taro with smoked meat	山村腊肉蒸芋片
shāncūn tǔjī	free-range chicken	山村土鸡
shuǐzhǔ niúròu	beef and vegetables in a chili sauce	水煮牛肉
tángcù cuìpí yú	crispy sweet-and-sour fish	糖醋脆皮鱼
záliáng zhútǒng fàn	bamboo cooked rice	杂粮竹筒饭

PINYIN	ENGLISH	CHINESE
Guìyáng		贵阳
báizhuó xiā	fresh blanched prawns	白灼虾
máo tái	Maotai rice wine	茅台
Miáojiā ānyú	Miáo sour fish	苗家胺鱼
Miáojiā tǔdòu piàn	Miáo deep-fried potato coins	苗家土豆片
Miáowèi páigǔ	spicy Miáo spareribs	苗味排骨
qīngzhēng yú	steamed fish	清蒸鱼
ròusī chǎomiàn	stir-fried noodles with pork	肉丝炒面
xián dànhuáng jìn qīngguā	salted eggs on a bed of cucumber	咸蛋皇浸青瓜
xiān huáishān kòu lǔròu	braised pork and vegetables	鲜淮山扣卤肉
yáng làjiāo	fried hot peppers	阳辣椒
Hángzhōu		杭州
Dōngpō ròu	a soya sauce pork dish named after the poet	东坡肉
Hángzhōu jiàohuà jī	"beggar's chicken"—baked in clay	杭州叫化鸡
lóngjǐng xiārén	shelled shrimp sprinkled with lóngjǐng tea	龙井虾仁
Harbin		哈尔滨
dàlièbā	Russian-style crusty bread	大烈巴
dànhuáng jūnánguā	fried crepes with vegetables and egg	蛋黄（火局）南瓜
hóngcháng	Russian-style red sausage	红肠
huǒguō	hot pot	火锅
jiācháng tǔdòuní	garlic mashed potatoes	家常土豆泥
jiànggǔ	pork ribs	酱骨
pá yángròu tiáo	thinly sliced lamb in soy-garlic sauce	扒羊肉条
sānxiān_shuǐjiǎo	three-flavor dumplings/ravioli	三鲜水饺
sōngrén yùmǐ shuǐjiǎo	boiled corn and pine-nut dumplings	松仁玉米水饺
yīpǐn_jūntāng	four-mushroom soup	一品菌汤
Héféi		合肥
dāndān miàn	spicy noodles with meat sauce	担担面
lóngxiā yī tiáo lù	lobster street	龙虾一条路
lóngxiā	Chinese-style crayfish	龙虾
Hohhot Hūhéhàotè		呼和浩特
chǎo fěn	millet granules	炒粉
chǎo miàn	fried noodles	炒面
dùndun	husked-wheat pancakes	钝钝
guǒtiáo	crisp fried dough	果条

PINYIN	ENGLISH	CHINESE
guōzǎi	stew	锅仔
guōzǎi suāncài yáng zásuì	pickled vegetables and sheep organ stew	锅仔酸菜羊杂碎
jiācháng dòufu	home-style tofu	家常豆腐
lā miàn	pulled noodles	拉面
liángfěn	cold translucent noodles with sauce	凉粉
nǎichá	milk tea	奶茶
nǎi pízi	milk skin	奶皮子
shénxiān báicài tāng	Immortals' cabbage soup	神仙白菜汤
shǒubā ròu	mutton eaten with hands	手扒肉
sù hézi	fried vegetable pie	素合子
suāncài ròu chǎo fěn	wheat noodles with shredded pork	酸菜肉炒粉
tèsè kǎo rǔniú	barbecued marinated veal	特色烤乳牛
wō bǐng	corn cakes	窝饼
wōwo	husked wheat pasta in steamer	窝窝
Huáng Shān		黄山
huángshān èrdōng	stir-fried winter mushrooms and bamboo shoots	黄山二冬
Jiāyùguān		嘉峪关
fùguì niúròu	roast beef on sesame toast	富贵牛肉
Jiāngnán qiánjiāng ròu	lightly battered chicken in sweet-and-sour sauce	江南钱江肉
kǎo yángpái	grilled rack of lamb	烤羊排
xīqīng bǎihé chǎo xiān yóu	squid with celery, field mushroom, and lotus	西青百合炒鲜鱿
yángpái	lamb chops	羊排
yángròu chuàn	lamb skewers	羊肉串
Jílín		吉林
liū ròuduàn	deep-fried pork strips with green pepper	熘肉段
shǒusī yángròu	hand-torn mutton with soy-garlic sauce	手撕羊肉
dà bàn shuǐ lāpí	cold mung-bean flour noodles with cilantro, peanuts, pork, and cucumbers with a spicy sesame sauce	大拌水拉皮
zhēn bù tóng tánròu	pieces of fatty pork braised in a homemade beer-based sauce	真不同坛肉
Jìnán		济南
mǎ pópo mèn shuāngsǔn	steamed bamboo and asparagus	马婆婆焖双笋
shāguō	casserole	砂锅
zhuābǐng	flaky fried pastry	抓饼

PINYIN	ENGLISH	CHINESE
Jǐngdé Zhèn		景德镇
sāngná niúròu	"sauna" beef	桑拿牛肉
jǐnggāng lǎobiǎo sǔn	peppery bamboo shoots with dried tofu	井岗老表笋
Jǐnghóng		景洪
kǎo sǔnzi	grilled bamboo shoots	烤笋子
kǎo yú	grilled fish	烤鱼
suānsǔn zhǔ jī	chicken cooked with pickled bamboo	酸笋煮鸡
suānsǔn zhǔ yú	fish boiled with sour bamboo shoots	酸笋煮鱼
xiāngzhú fàn	fragrant rice cooked in bamboo	香竹饭
zhútǒng fàn	glutinous rice cooked in bamboo	竹筒饭
Kāifēng		开封
huāshēng gāo	peanut cake	花生糕
wǔxiāng shāobǐng	five-spice roasted bread	五香烧饼
xiǎolóng bāo	dumplings filled with pork and broth	小笼包
xìngrén chá	almond tea	杏仁茶
yángròu chuàn	spicy lamb kabob	羊肉串
zhīma duōwèi tāng	sesame soup	芝麻多味汤
Kǎilǐ		凯里
gǒuròu	dog meat	狗肉
Suān Tāng	sour soup	酸汤
Kashgar Kāshí		喀什
bāchǔ mógu	field mushrooms steamed with bok choy, ginger, and garlic	巴楚蘑菇
bàn sān sī	pepper, onion, carrot, and cucumber noodle salad	拌三丝
chǎokǎo ròu	beef stir-fry	炒烤肉
gānbiān tóngzǐjī	dry-fried spring chicken	干煸童子鸡
lāmiàn	"pulled" noodles	拉面
lǔ gēzi	whole pigeon soup	卤鸽子
wánzimiàn	beef ball noodles	丸子面
zhuā fàn	pilaf	抓饭
Kūnmíng		昆明
cuìpí rúyì yú	crispy vegetarian fish in a sweet-and-sour sauce	脆皮如意鱼
cuìpí yā	crispy fried vegetarian duck	脆皮鸭
guòqiáo mǐxiàn	crossing-the-bridge noodles	过桥米线
hóngshāo niúròu miàn	spicy beef noodles	红烧牛肉面
hóngshāo shīziqiú	vegetarian mushroom ball	红烧狮子球

PINYIN	ENGLISH	CHINESE
hùnhé chǎo	fried mixed vegetables	混合炒
huǒshāo gānbā	barbecued dried beef	火烧干巴
jīnbì yān huóxiā	spicy prawn sashimi	金碧腌活虾
qìguō jī	steamed chicken	汽锅鸡
shāo ya	baked duck	烧鸭
shànyú miàn	noodles with eel	鳝鱼面
sūpí guànguàn jī	chicken soup with puff pastry	酥皮罐罐鸡
yēzi qìguō jī	coconut chicken	椰子汽锅鸡
yìndù gāli jī miàn	curry chicken noodles	印度咖喱鸡面
zhēng lǎo nánguā	steamed pumpkin	蒸老南瓜
zhútǒng ròu	pork cooked in bamboo	竹筒肉

Kuqa Kùchē — 库车

dàpán jī	big-plate chicken	大盘鸡
gānzhá niúròu tiáo	spicy beef strips	干炸牛肉条
lǎohǔ cài	spicy salad	老虎菜
tángbàn huángguā	sweet cucumber	糖拌黄瓜

Lánzhōu — 兰州

báobǐng yángròu	deep-fried lamb and green pepper pancake	薄饼羊肉
kǎo yángtuǐ	roast leg of lamb with walnuts	烤羊腿
měnggǔ yángpái	Mongolian lamb	蒙古羊排
niúròu miàn	beef noodles	牛肉面
sùshí jīnjú bǎihé	sweet vegetarian lilies	素食金橘百合
shǒuzhuā ròu	meat to be eaten by hand	手抓肉

Lāsà — 拉萨

bāozi	steamed buns with pork	包子
cháng xiāngsī	sliced soy-pork sausages	长相思
gānbiān sùcháng	soy-pork slices with green pepper	干煸素肠
gōngbào jīdīng	kung pao chicken	宫爆鸡丁
ròusī miàntiáo	noodles with pork	肉丝面条
qīngchǎo máodòu	beans with soy beef	清炒毛豆
sōngrén yùmǐ	pine nuts, carrots, and sweet corn	松仁玉米

Lhatse Lāzī — 拉孜

Zāchá fěnsī bāo	vermicelli clay pot	哑茶粉丝煲
niúròu chǎofàn	beef-fried rice	牛肉炒饭
shǐyóu jī	salty chicken	豉油鸡

Lì Jiāng — 丽江

fēngwèi cān	special Nàxī meal	风味餐
guòqiáo mǐxiàn	crossing-the-bridge noodles	过桥米线

PINYIN	ENGLISH	CHINESE
jīdòu chǎo mǐfàn	fried rice with soy bean	鸡豆炒米饭
kǎoyú	barbecue fish	烤鱼
Lì Jiāng bābā	Lìjiāng baked pastry	丽江粑粑
Lì Jiāng dàguōcài	vegetables in broth	丽江大锅菜
Nàxī sāndiéshuǐ	Nàxī 36-dish special	纳西三叠水
qìguō jī	stewed chicken	汽锅鸡
shùwā	frog skin fungus	树蛙
zhá rǔbǐng	fried goat cheese	炸乳饼

Lóngshèng — 龙胜
| làròu | smoked pork | 腊肉 |
| zhútǒng fàn | fragrant rice cooked in bamboo | 竹筒饭 |

Luopíng — 罗平
| luó kāng yě huò xiāng | honey | 罗康野藿香 |

Luòyáng — 洛阳
Luòyáng Shuǐxí	Luòyáng water banquet	洛阳水席
mìzhī tǔdòu	sweet-potato fries in syrup	蜜汁土豆
tángcù lǐji	sweet-and-sour fish	糖醋里脊
zhájiàngmiàn	noodles with bean sauce	炸酱面
zhēnyāncài	ham, radish, mushroom, and egg soup	珍腌菜

Mǎnzhōulǐ — 满洲里
qīngshuǐ guōdǐ	vegetarian hot pot	清水锅底
sānxiān fàn	three-flavor rice	三鲜饭
shuàn yángròu	mutton hot pot	涮羊肉
sūbā tāng	Russian-style creamy tomato soup	苏巴汤

Nánjīng — 南京
pánsī yú	sweet-and-sour deep-fried fish tail filets	盘丝鱼
shuǐjīng xiārén	sautéed shrimp	水晶虾仁
tiānmùhú yútóu	white fish head soup	天目湖鱼头
yāxuě fěnsī	duck-blood vermicelli	鸭血粉丝

Píngyáo — 平遥
jiàohuà jī	beggar's chicken	叫化鸡
lǎolao yóumiàn	husked oat pasta	栲栳莜面
māo ěrduo	cats' ears pasta	猫耳朵
tǔdòu shāo niúròu	corned beef with potatoes	土豆烧牛肉
xiāngsū jī	crispy aromatic chicken	香酥鸡
yóuzhá gāo	crispy puff with date and red bean paste	油炸糕

PINYIN	ENGLISH	CHINESE
Qīngdǎo		青岛
gōngzhǔ yú	princess fish cooked in oil and steamed	公主鱼
jīngjiàng ròusī	shredded pork Peking-style	京酱肉丝
shāo èrdōng	sautéed mushrooms with garden asparagus	烧二冬
sōngshǔ guìyú	deep-fried sweet-and-sour fish	松鼠桂鱼
suànxiāng gǔ	fried pork chop with garlic	蒜香骨
tiěbǎn hélí kǎo dàn	iron plate clams with scrambled eggs	铁板河蜊烤蛋
xiāng sū jī	fragrant chicken	香酥鸡
yóubā gǔfǎ zhēng qiézi	steamed eggplant	油粑古法蒸茄子
yóubào hǎiluó	fried sea snails	油爆海螺
Quánzhōu		泉州
niúpái	beefsteak	牛排
sùshí	vegetarian food	素食
Xiàmén hǎilì jiān	Xiàmén-style baby oysters	厦门海蛎煎
rì shì sù cì shēn	vegetarian sushi	日式素刺身
baǐ huā zhà liàng sù xi qiǎn	deep-fried crab claws with minced vegetarian squid	百花炸嚷素蟹钳
guì huā sù wú paí	vegetarian spareribs with sweet osmanthus sauce	桂花素五排
gān sī liǔ liǎn sū	durian pastries	干丝榴莲酥
Qūfǔ		曲阜
dàizi shàngcháo	stewed pork, chicken, chestnuts, and ginseng	带子上朝
shīlǐ yínxìng	sweet ginkgo	诗礼银杏
shénxiān yāzi	Immortals duck	神仙鸭子
yángguān sāndié	chicken, vegetables, and egg folded together	阳关三叠
Sakya		萨迦
gōngbào jīdīng	spicy chicken with cashews	宫爆鸡丁
māpó dòufu	spicy tofu with chopped meat	麻婆豆腐
yúxiāng qiézi	eggplant in garlic sauce	鱼香茄子
Shànghǎi		上海
báopí yángròu juǎn	minced lamb wrapped in pancakes	薄皮羊肉卷
cōngyóu bǐng	scallion pancakes	葱油饼
dāndān miàn	noodles in spicy peanut sauce	担担面
dàzhá xiè	hairy crab	大闸蟹
duòjiāo yútóu	fish head steamed with red chili	剁椒鱼头
gānbiān tǔdòu bā	fried potato pancake	干煸土豆粑

PINYIN	ENGLISH	CHINESE
gānguōjī guōzi	spicy chicken with peppers	干锅鸡锅子
huíguōròu jiābǐng	twice-cooked lamb wrapped in pancakes	回锅肉夹饼
huǒyán niúròu	beef with red and green peppers	火焰牛肉
kǎo quányáng	roast lamb	烤全羊
kǎo yángròu	barbecued lamb skewers	烤羊肉
lǎohǔ cài	Xīnjiāng salad	老虎菜
làzi jīdīng	spicy chicken nuggets	辣子鸡丁
mízhī huǒfǎng	pork and taro in candied sauce	蜜汁火舫
Nánxiáng xiǎolóng bāo	Nánxiáng crabmeat and pork dumplings	南翔小龙包
qīngzhēng dòuní	creamy mashed beans	青蒸豆泥
qícài dōngsǔn	winter shoots with local greens	荠菜冬笋
sānsī méimao sū	pork, bamboo, and mushroom-stuffed crisp	三丝眉毛酥
shīzi tóu	lion's head meatballs	狮子头
shuǐzhǔ yú	fish slices and vegetables in spicy broth	水煮鱼
shuǐjīng xiārén	stir-fried shrimp	水晶虾仁
sōngshǔ lúyú	sweet-and-sour fried perch	松鼠鲈鱼
suān dòujiǎo ròuní	diced sour beans with minced pork	酸豆角肉泥
suān jiāngdòu làròu	sour long beans with chilies and bacon	酸豇豆腊肉
sùjī	vegetarian chicken	素鸡
sùyā	vegetarian duck	素鸭
xiǎolóng bāo	pork-stuffed steamed bread dumplings	小笼包
xiāngwèi hóngshǔ bō	fragrant sweet potato in monk's pot	香味红薯钵
xièfěn huì zhēnjūn	braised mushroom with crabmeat	蟹粉烩珍菌
xièfěn xiáolóng	pork and powdered crabmeat dumplings	蟹粉小笼

Shěnyáng 沈阳

biānxiàn sānxiān jiǎozi	boiled shrimp, egg, and Chinese chive dumplings	煸馅三鲜饺子
chuántǒng shāomài	steamed dumplings with beef and ginger	传统烧麦
jiǎozi	dumplings/Chinese ravioli	饺子
shāomài	steamed open-top dumplings	烧麦
yùcuì shāomài	jade green steamed open-top dumplings	玉翠烧麦
zhūròu báicài jiǎozi	boiled pork-and-cabbage dumplings	猪肉白菜饺子

Shigatse Rìkāzé 日喀则

chǎo buōcài	stir-fried spinach	炒菠菜
chǎo miànpiàn	stir-fried noodle pieces	炒面片
gāli tǔdòu	curry potatoes	咖喱土豆
tāng jiǎo	dumplings/ravioli in soup	汤饺

PINYIN	ENGLISH	CHINESE
máoniú tóu	yak's head	牦牛头
qīngjiāo niúròu	green peppers and beef	青椒牛肉
rénshēnguǒ	fried ginseng	人参果
tiěbǎn niúroù	iron plate beef	铁板牛肉
tǔdòu jiǎozi	potato dumplings/ravioli	土豆饺子

Sūzhōu 苏州

gūsū lǔyā	marinated duck	姑苏卤鸭
huángmèn hémàn	braised river eel	黄焖河鳗
sōngshǔ guìyú	sweet-and-sour deep-fried fish	松鼠桂鱼
zuìjī	drunken chicken	醉鸡

Tàiyuán 太原

cù	vinegar	醋
cuōjiāner	twisted points pasta	搓尖儿
guòyóuròu	pork "passed through oil"	过油肉
liángfěn	potato starch noodle	凉粉
māo ěrduō	cat's ears pasta	猫耳朵
tóunǎo	mutton soup	头脑
xiǎobǐng	flat bread	小饼

Tiānshuǐ 天水

chǎo miàn	stir-fried noodles	炒面
niúròu miàn	beef noodles	牛肉面
shāguō jīkuài	chicken clay pot	砂锅鸡块

Tónglǐ 同里

mín bǐng	sweet glutinous rice pastry	闵饼
xiǎo xūnyú	smoked fish	小熏鱼
zhuàngyuán tí	braised pigs' trotters	状元蹄

Tóngrén 同仁

chǎo miànpiàn	stir-fried noodle pieces with squash, beef, and onions	炒面片
chǎo yángròu	stir-fried mutton	炒羊肉
qīngtāng miànpiàn	noodle pieces in soup	清汤面片
rénshēnguǒ mǐfàn	ginseng rice	人参果米饭

Tsetang Zédāng 泽当

cuìpí xiāngjiāo	banana fritters	脆皮香蕉
hóngshǔ bǐng	sweet-potato cakes	红薯饼

Túnxī 屯溪

chòu dòufu	stinky tofu	臭豆腐
huángshān sùwèi yuán	stir-fried mountain vegetables, tofu, and herbs	黄山素味园

PINYIN	ENGLISH	CHINESE
wǔcǎi shànsī	stir-fried eel with peppers, mushrooms, and bamboo shoots	五彩鳝丝
Yángzhōu chǎofàn	Yángzhōu fried rice	扬州炒饭

Turpan Tǔlǔfān 吐鲁番

kǎo bāozi	samsa	烤包子
sāngshèn jiǔ	mulberry wine	桑椹酒

Ürümqi Wūlǔmùqí 乌鲁木齐

bàobīng	ice frosty	爆冰
hóngshāo ròu	braised pork	红烧肉

Wēnzhōu 温州

wāròu mángguǒ chǎofàn	stir-fried rice with mango and frogs' legs	蛙肉芒果 炒饭
niúpái mùguā zhī	steak set with papaya sauce	牛排木瓜汁
qíyì guǒ jiā níngméngzhī	kiwi and lemon juice	奇异果加柠檬汁
yángtiáozhī	star fruit juice	杨桃汁
mùguāzhī	papaya fruit juice	木瓜汁

Wǔhàn 武汉

dànbái shāo gǔpái	pork ribs braised in egg white	蛋白烧骨排
dòufu pí	tofu skin	豆腐皮
Fáng Xiàn huāgū	flowering mushrooms from Fáng County	房县花菇
miànwō	rice bread	面窝
qiān biān méi	deep-fried fermented tofu	千煸霉
quánjiāfú	mushrooms sautéed with dates	全家福
shuǐguǒ xiāngfàn	sticky rice with watermelon, pineapple, and melon	水果香饭
wǔxiāng niúròu	faux beef with blended spices	五香牛肉
yóumàicài	sautéed Chinese lettuce stalk	油麦菜
Reganmian	Wuhan-style dry noodles	热干面
Baozi	steamed buns	包子
Jing Wu Ren Jia	duck neck	精武人家鸭脖子

Wǔtái Shān 五台山

báiguǒ nánguā bāo	ginkgo nut with pumpkin	白果南瓜煲
huākāi xiànfó	mock ham with braised tofu	花开献佛
jǐnshàng tiānhuā	yuxiang shredded "pork"	锦上天花
lǎncài ròumò sìjìdòu	olive leaf fried with string beans	榄菜肉末四季豆
luóhànzhāi	mixed vegetables fried with bean-starch noodles	罗汉斋

PINYIN	ENGLISH	CHINESE
sùpái	deep-fried "meat" in brown sauce	素排
tiěbǎn hēijiāo níupái	grilled "steak" with black pepper sauce	铁板黑椒牛排
xǐqì yángyáng	"chicken" cubes fried with dried red peppers	喜气洋洋

Wúxī 无锡

miànjīn	fried balls of flour shredded and stir-fried with meat and vegetables	面筋
páigǔ	Chinese-style baby back ribs	排骨
Tàihú yínyú	deep-fried Lake Tài fish	太湖银鱼
Wúxī xiǎolóng	Wúxī dumplings	无锡小笼
xièfěn xiǎolóng	crabmeat and pork dumplings	蟹粉小笼
xiānròu húntun	pork wontons	虾肉馄饨

Wuling Yuan/Zhang Jia Jie 张家界

hetao ruo	pork	核桃肉
ganbian changzi	sausage	干煸肠子

Wúyí Shān 武夷山

yóuzhá	pan-fried street snacks	油炸
nánguā bǐng	pumpkin cake	南瓜饼
qié zhī zhá xiāngjiāo	fried banana with tomato sauce	茄汁炸香蕉

Xiàmén 厦门

san wen zhi shi juan	golden dragon roll (salmon roll with cheese)	三文芝士卷
màn yú zhà xiā juǎn	green dragon roll (eel, cucumber, and avocado)	鳗鱼炸虾卷
zhà xue gao	deep-fried ice cream	炸雪糕
biánshí	Xiamen-style mini wonton soup	扁食
bàn miàn	Xiamen-style noodles with peanut sauce	拌面
dāngguī miànjīn tāng	Chinese angelica and gluten soup	当归面筋汤
gāli xiān yóu	curried squid	咖喱鲜鱿
hǎilì jiān	pan-fried oysters	海蛎煎
huáng zé hé	peanut soup	黄则和
luóhàn zhāi	stew of pine nuts, cabbage, cucumber, corn, mushrooms, and fresh cilantro	罗汉斋
lúsǔn dòufu tāng	asparagus and tofu soup	芦笋豆腐汤
wāng jì xiànbǐng	small pastries stuffed with a variety of sweet fillings	汪记馅饼
xiāng ní cáng zhēn	vegetables mashed into a paste	香泥藏珍

Xī'ān 西安

bābǎo tián xīfàn	eight-treasure sweet rice porridge	八宝甜稀饭
bìlù zá shuāng gū	bok choy with mushrooms	碧绿杂双菇

PINYIN	ENGLISH	CHINESE
fěnzhēng yángròu	lamb between two steamed buns	粉蒸羊肉
guàntāng bāozi	specialty buns	灌汤包子
hóngshāo niúwěi	stewed oxtail	红烧牛尾
ròu jiā mó	shredded pork in a bun	肉夹摸
shǎn nán xiāngyù bǐng	sweet-potato pancake	陕南香芋饼
suāntāng shuǐjiǎo	lamb dumplings	酸汤水饺
wōtóu	corn bun	窝头
xiǎochī	small snacks	小吃
yángròu pàomó	lamb soup with torn pieces of bun	羊肉泡馍
yōuzhì	local bun	优质
Xīníng		西宁
chǎo miànpiàn	noodles stir-fried with green squash, beef, and peppers	炒面片
kǎo dàbǐng	roasted scones	烤大饼
liángpí	cold noodles with chili tofu	凉皮
Xúnhuà		循化
bàochǎo yějī	quick-fried pheasant	爆炒野鸡
hóngshāo niúwěi	oxtail braised in soy sauce	红烧牛尾
miàn piàn	flat noodle soup	面片
Yán'ān		延安
chǎomiàn hélè	pressed buckwheat noodles with vinaigrette dressing	炒面何勒
dāoxiāo miàn	dāoxiāo noodles	刀削面
huángmó	sweet steamed millet cake	黄馍
kǔcài tǔdòu	mashed potatoes with wild vegetables	苦菜土豆
mǐjiǔ	millet wine	米酒
niúròu liángfěn	bean-starched noodles fried with beef	牛肉凉粉
yángròu pàomó	mutton soup	羊肉泡馍
yóu mómo	fried doughnut made of millet	油馍馍
Yánbiān		延边
lěngmiàn	cold noodles in vinegar broth	冷面
Yángshuò		阳朔
bàochǎo tiánluó	Lí River snails stuffed with pork	爆炒田螺
dàocáo zá ròu	Yao-style braised pork wrapped in rice stalks	稻草杂肉
hóngshǔ téng	sweet-potato shoots	红薯藤
luósī fěn	spicy snail noodles	螺丝粉
píjiǔ yú	fish cooked in beer and spices	啤酒鱼

PINYIN	ENGLISH	CHINESE
shí sū xìng rén quǎn	almond roll	时蔬杏仁卷
lì yú dàn huáng wán	taro and egg yolk balls	荔芋蛋黄丸
táng chù qíe guā	sweet-and-sour eggplant	糖醋茄瓜

Yandangshan · 雁荡山

shē zú wū mǐ fàn	sweet sticky black rice in minority baskets	畲族乌米饭
suān jiǎo	bats wing nuts	酸角
píng gū chǎo huáng huā cài	toadstools and chrysanthemum flowers	平菇炒黄花菜
shān sháo chǎo ròu shī	mountain peonies fried with meat	山芍炒肉丝
máofēng cha	máofēng tea	毛峰茶

Yángzhōu · 扬州

bāozi	steamed buns	包子
jiǎozi	dumplings/Chinese ravioli	饺子

Yánjí · 延吉

lěngmiàn	cold noodles in vinegar broth	冷面
shíguō bànfàn	stone pot rice	石锅拌饭
dòufu tang	spicy tofu soup	豆腐汤

Yínchuān · 银川

guàntāng bāozi	unleavened bāozi	灌汤包子
hézi	savory pies	盒子
suānlà tǔdòu sī	shredded potatoes	酸辣土豆丝
bābǎozhōu	eight treasures soup	八宝粥

Yīníng · 伊宁

dàpán jī	whole chicken with vegetables and noodles	大盘鸡
géwǎsī	kawas liquor	格瓦斯
náng bāo ròu	lamb and vegetable stew on a wheat pancake	馕包肉
nàrén	roast horse meat noodle salad	纳仁
tǔdòu sī	fried potato strips	土豆丝
yībǎzhuā	samosa with three fingerprints in each bun	一把抓
yóu tǎzi	steamed dumplings	油塔子
zhīma ròunáng	sesame bread and lamb casserole	芝麻肉馕

Yùshù · 玉树

gānbiān tǔdòu sī	dry-fried potato	干煸土豆丝
hǎo kǎo quányáng	roast lamb	好烤全羊
huáyú	a river fish	滑鱼

PINYIN	ENGLISH	CHINESE
kǎo yángtuǐ	roast leg of lamb	烤羊腿
kǒudài dòufu	minced soy chicken in tofu pockets	口袋豆腐
suānlà fěntiáo	sour-and-spicy vermicelli	酸辣粉条
xiāngbālā yángpái	Shambala lamb chops	香巴拉羊排
yángpái	rack of lamb	羊排

Zhèngzhōu

郑州

bāsù shíjǐn	mushrooms, seasonal greens, and bamboo shoots	八素什锦
guōtiē dòufu	tofu casserole	锅贴豆腐
tèyōu huìmiàn	house specialty noodles	特优烩面
xiāngmá shāobǐng jiā niúròu	beef sandwiched between steamed buns	香麻烧饼夹牛肉

Miscellaneous

Spicy	là	辣
or not	búlà	不辣
vinegar	cù	醋
without	búyào cù	不要醋
small bowl	xiǎo wǎn	小碗
large bowl	dà wǎn	大碗

Index

CLOSED
due to
accidental demolition

WEGEN BISSIGEN
EICHHÖRNCHEN GESCHLOSSEN

CERRADO

CABRAS

Κλειστό
Μετεωρίτες

プールも

POOL CLOSED

ELECTRIC EELS

閉
鎖
中

Hotel
closed for
facelifting

FERMÉ POUR
RAISON
DE GRÈVE
DES BONNES

FECHADO!
POR CAUSA DE
ATAQUES DOS CROCODILOS

— *I don't speak sign language.*

A hotel can close for all kinds of reasons.
Our Guarantee ensures that if your hotel's undergoing construction, we'll
let you know in advance. In fact, we cover your entire travel experience.
See www.travelocity.com/guarantee for details.

travelocity
You'll never roam alone.

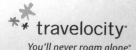